PROBLEMS
IN THE PHILOSOPHY
OF LANGUAGE

PROBLEMS
IN THE PHILOSOPHY
OF LANGUAGE

Thomas M. Olshewsky
University of Kentucky

HOLT, RINEHART AND WINSTON, INC.

NEW YORK   CHICAGO   SAN FRANCISCO   ATLANTA
DALLAS   MONTREAL   TORONTO   LONDON   SYDNEY

To Katherine

401
P94
73411
Feb., 1971

PREFACE

The purpose of this book is to engage the reader in philosophical inquiry, and the focus is on problems in the philosophy of language. This approach has led me to begin the book with a prologue that explores the philosophy of language as a field of inquiry, and to follow this with readings on a select group of problems within that field. Each chapter begins with an introductory essay that elaborates the dimensions of the problems treated in the chapter, and follows with a selection of articles that offer solutions to those problems. A bibliography at the end of each chapter serves as a guide to further inquiry.

I have made no attempt to cover every possible problem in the philosophy of language, but rather I have attempted to focus on carefully selected problems. The epilogue to the book gives a brief description and some bibliographical references to a number of peripheral—and some popular—problems in the field that are not directly discussed in the articles included.

The book should offer breadth, depth, and flexibility as an instrument for classroom use. The first and second selections in Chapter 2 lay a foundation for understanding many of the issues of the various problems about meaning treated in Chapters 2, 3, and 4, and these three chapters furnish a background for many of the problems in the succeeding chapters. With these exceptions, order and selection can be in accord with the interests of the teacher. Within some chapters, the sequence of a controversy sequence is followed, and in such cases, it is of obvious value to follow the sequence. The prologue and Chapter 1 serve as background to the material that follows, but they may be bypassed by those who already have some acquaintance with the field.

All of the readings are standard statements by leading philosophers on the problems and approaches under consideration. Where feasible, journal articles have been included without abridgment. All abridgments are noted, and where allusions in selections from books are obscure, I have offered explanatory footnotes marked with an asterisk (*). In these same selections, numbering of the authors' footnotes has been altered to make them consecutive. In the introductory and bibliographic material, cross-references to other parts of this book are made by double numbers signifying chapter and selection. In the bibliographic discussions following each chapter, I have cited articles from journals by article title, journal title, volume, and year. The titles of some of the more frequently cited journals are abbreviated as follows:

JP—*Journal of Philosophy*
PAS—*Proceedings of the Aristotelian Society*
PPR—*Philosophy and Phenomenological Research*
PR—*Philosophical Review*
PS—*Philosophy of Science*

A dagger (†) indicates that the text includes a bibliography relevant to the problem under consideration.

In preparing this book, I have received much help from others. My acknowledgments to publishers and authors for the selections included are noted at the beginning of each selection. I am especially appreciative of the alterations and corrections suggested by several of the authors. The students in my seminars on the philosophy of language have made many helpful criticisms. My colleagues, Evan K. Jobe, Alan Perreiah, and Frederick Brouwer, each read the introductory materials and made valuable suggestions for their clarification. David Rouse and Anthony Waters gave invaluable aid in compiling the bibliographies. I am indebted to the University of Kentucky Research Foundation for funds to aid in compiling the book, and to the University of Kentucky for a summer research grant and also for secretarial service in typing the manuscript. Kenneth L. Culver, of Holt, Rinehart and Winston, has patiently lent his editorial acumen from the book's inception. I am especially grateful for the help of my wife, Katherine, whose sympathetic encouragement and pointed criticism have made the book a better finished product than it would otherwise have been.

Lexington, Kentucky   Thomas M. Olshewsky
August 1, 1969

CONTENTS

A PROLOGUE
TO INQUIRY

We are like mariners who must rebuild their ship
according to a new plan on the open sea,
ever unable to dock it and construct it anew
from the best parts.

Otto Neurath

Philosophy as Inquiry

Inquiries begin with questioning, with asking something that the inquirer wants to know. A question can result from practical problems, from intellectual curiosity, or from any number of a variety of puzzles and perplexities. But a question is more than a problem or a curiosity or a perplexity. It is a formulation of a problem that already points to the goal of a solution. A question is not only problem-based, but it is goal-oriented. Once a question has been raised, inquiry has begun. Many questions have direct answers, so easily arrived at that we pay little attention to procedures required for solution. But even simple problems like "What time is it?" or "Where did I lay my pencil?" require some method to arrive at a solution. Inquiry begins with a question that formulates what the problem is, and then proceeds by some method to an answer that provides the solution to the problem.

All questions have presuppositions, logical conditions for making sense of asking them. These presuppositions form the foundation upon which an inquiry begins. When you ask me, "When did your dog die?" you presuppose that I once had a dog and that it is now dead. If you did not take these as already established facts, you would not put your question in such a form. You are not asking if I have had a dog, or if he is dead, but are taking these facts for granted. Any answer that I could meaningfully give to your question would also have to presuppose these facts. If you ask, "Did your dog die?" you still presuppose that I have had a dog, and my answer, whether affirmative or negative, must also take that for granted. Not all presuppositions are factual. "Are any atoms eight-sided?" is a question that apparently seeks factual information, but it involves a complicated variety of presuppositions. It involves a conception of what an atom is—that atoms have

1

physical extension in the same sense that tables and chairs have. It presupposes that atoms do have sides, an odd way of characterizing atoms. Any answer to the question would presuppose that there are some procedures for determining how many sides an atom has (so far as I know, no one has observed the side of any atom). These presuppositions are not *facts about* atoms, but *understandings of* atoms. When we puzzle over a question like "What happens when an irresistible force meets an immovable object?" we must not only presuppose conditions for our question of a nonfactual sort, but recognize that our answer cannot be found by any empirical inquiry (one of the fascinations of this puzzle is that its factual conditions are inconceivable).

We must number among the presuppositions of inquiry not only facts about the subject matter into which we inquire but understandings of that subject matter. Understandings involve (1) *concepts* by which things are understood (the nature of an atom and of its properties); (2) *categories* by which things are ordered in relation to other things (the nature of the relation of atoms to physical objects like tables and chairs—are they the same kind of thing?); and (3) *principles* by which things work (do subatomic particles operate according to causally determined principles?). Philosophical inquiries seek answers to questions about understandings of the world, not to questions about facts about the world.

A philosophical inquiry often begins with perplexities about the presuppositions of other inquiries. Augustine gives us a good example of such a starting point in his inquiry about time.[1] One of the theological puzzles of his day was "What did God do before he made heaven and earth?" Augustine saw that this question presupposed understandings about God and the world. In order to answer the question, one must take for granted that God did something before creation and that there was a time before creation. The former presupposition Augustine could dispense with by pointing out that for the creator to act before creation required creation before creation, an obvious absurdity. The latter presupposition required a more elaborate inquiry into the nature of time, to understand better what it is and how it works. These inquiries made clear that the theological puzzle did not arise from a lack of factual knowledge or of divine revelation, but from a lack of understanding of the principles, categories, and concepts presupposed in the asking of the question.

A further examination of the puzzle with which Augustine began reveals that the presupposed understandings he dealt with were not the only conditions for the question. Others are that God exists, that He acts, that He created the world. Augustine's own commitment to God as the creator of the universe prevented him from questioning these presuppositions. Had he questioned them, his inquiry would have taken a quite different turn. He might have arrived not only at a different understanding of time, but also at a completely different understanding of the world. One of the tasks of a philosophical inquiry is to determine which conceptions, categories, and principles are relevant to a particular perplexity.

---

[1] See *The Confessions of Saint Augustine,* Book XI.

This often depends upon the issues involved in a particular puzzle, but it may also depend upon considerations about other concerns and understandings. By deciding what understandings are relevant to a particular problem, a philosopher partially determines the character of his inquiry.

In pursuing a better understanding of time, Augustine asked, "What is time?" His formulation of this question treats time as an object with a definite nature. It seeks to discern the nature of time, or at least its essential characteristics. It can be called an *ontological* formulation of the question because it treats the philosophical perplexity as a problem about the nature of a being. Augustine concluded that his inquiry never attained a satisfactory answer, but his methods suggest other formulations of the problem. He explored how time works; its relation to motions of objects and to measurements by observers; its character of before and after, of past, present, and future. His conclusions could very well have been prefaced by the question, "How does time work?" which would have been a *functional* formulation of the problem. A third alternative is also possible. He explored how we talk about time, our linguistic expressions involving temporal considerations. Such explorations might provide answers to questions like "What does the term 'time' mean?"2 or "What do expressions involving past, present, or future tenses of verbs imply about our understanding of time?" These questions are *linguistic* formulations of the problem. Answers to the functional and linguistic formulations of the problem provide solutions, but not to the ontological formulation, indicating that the formulations are not interchangeable. That one formulation led to a solution and the other did not suggests that they are not even formulations of the same problem. The way in which a problem is formulated is another determining factor for philosophical inquiry.

Where philosophical inquiry begins often depends upon the extent to which the inquirer's understanding of his concepts, categories, and principles is *explicit, critical*, and *systematic*. The theologians' question about God's action before creation involves notions about time that are only implicitly held. These notions first had to be explicated in order to find what understandings were at issue in the perplexity. Once explicated as a factor in the problem, the notions then had to be clarified and criticized in such a way that they became both consistent within themselves (for example, in the relation of the before-after notion of time to the

---

2 Single quotes enclosing a word, phrase, or sentence indicate that what is being talked about is the term itself, and not that to which it refers. This avoids confusion by distinguishing, for example, dogs, which have four legs, from 'dogs', which has four letters. The one instance is a matter of using a term to talk about something else; the other is a matter of mentioning a term, talking about the term itself. To *mention* an expression is to treat it as an object of discourse; to *use* an expression is to treat it as a tool of discourse. This use-mention distinction is similar to the medieval one between *suppositio formalis*, the use of a term as a name for something else, its usual and proper use, and *suppositio materialis*, the use of a term as a name for itself. The use-mention distinction has broader application than did the medieval one, since it is not limited to terms and naming, but can be applied to any expression and its use. In formally constructed systems like logic and mathematics, a language about another language is often called a *metalanguage*.

past-present-future notion of time) and applicable to other factors in the world (for example, the relation of time to motion). Beyond this, a more complete understanding of time can be achieved by systematically incorporating it into a more general understanding of the world. A particular philosophical inquiry may not need to engage in all these functions. The accent will depend upon the problems out of which the inquiry arises and the solutions at which it aims. The moral question "Is killing ever right?" clearly depends upon an understanding of the conceptions of right and wrong. The inquirer may already have an explicit understanding of these conceptions, and he may devote his energies to critically showing how they are both logically self-consistent and applicable to the particular moral problem. He may wish to go beyond the particular problem to show how his conception of right and wrong fits into a complete ethical theory and how that is consistent with some political theories, but not with others. The character of philosophical inquiry varies with the problem to be solved and the extent of understanding sought.

The character of a philosophical inquiry also depends upon one's understanding of the nature of the concepts, categories, and principles that form a basis for an understanding of the world. If basic concepts and categories reveal the true nature of things, then philosophical inquiry will be seen as a *discovery* about the world. If they are not revelations about the world, but are fundamental to the nature of human understanding, philosophy will be seen as a *description* of those fundamentals of understanding. If concepts and categories are no more than tools devised to solve problems, then philosophical inquiry will be seen as a *construction* of tools to meet the problems at hand.

Philosophical inquiry is concerned with the concepts, categories, and principles upon which understandings of the world are based. From the several determining factors of this inquiry we have already noted, we can form an impression of the variety of possible ways of doing philosophy. What categories, concepts, and principles are relevant for the particular concern must be decided upon. The question must be formulated in such a way that it will be possible to find an answer that will resolve the perplexity, solve the problem. The extent of inquiry will be determined by what explication, criticism, and systematization are necessary to fulfill the aims of the inquirer. One's own characterization of his task as discovery, description, or construction will also be a determinant. Although this complex characterization of philosophy as inquiry still falls short of a definitive statement of what philosophy is, it should serve to avoid partisan controversy on the one hand, and to facilitate a discussion of philosophical problems about language on the other.

Philosophy and Language

Problems in the philosophy of language often arise from perplexities within other philosophical inquiries. Just as Augustine found presuppositions about time underlying his problem about God's action before creation, so Paul Ziff saw that presuppositions about meaning were involved in his linguistic analysis of aesthetic terms. He began with the question "What does the phrase 'good painting' mean in English?" This is a linguistic formulation of a problem in the philosophy of art. The question led in turn to another: "What does the word 'good' mean?" In answer to this question he wrote a brief essay. Then he began to ponder: On what foundations can these conclusions be confirmed? "So I worked back and back to the beginning of this essay," which became a book containing a detailed analysis of his understandings of language, truth, and meaning, which in turn form a basis for his conclusions about the meaning of 'good'.[3] He makes two things clear at the outset about the question, "What does the word 'good' mean?" First, it is not to be confused with similar ones, like "What meaning does the word 'good' have?" or "Is the word 'good' meaningful?" These questions formulate apparently similar problems, but they lead down paths of inquiry that he did not choose to follow. Secondly, the question as put is not itself the problem with which he is working. It serves as a tool, as a paradigm. His goal is to get beyond this particular question to an understanding of language and meaning. A concern that began as a problem in aesthetics developed into an inquiry into the philosophy of language.

Many philosophers in recent years have chosen to cast their problems in linguistic formulations, raising questions about the meaning and function of such key terms as 'good'. Disagreements about the conclusions of such linguistic analyses have forced philosophers to examine not only the conditions for their methods of analysis, but also their understandings of language and meaning. Concerns with the methods of linguistic analysis are not necessarily concerns with the philosophy of language, but they can lead to such concerns. The shift may be from considering the meaning of a particular word to considering meaning per se (a shift that Ziff clearly avoids). The move may be from questions about *what* a term means to questions about *how* a term means. Questions that seek an understanding of meaning can be as varied in their formulation as we have seen philosophical questions concerning time to be. Philosophical inquiry that gives a linguistic formulation to its problems need not be concerned *about* language; but such inquiry, in its use of language as a tool for inquiry, often requires attention to the concepts, categories, and principles of language that are presupposed in linguistic analysis.

The move from *what* a word means to *how* a word means gives but one example of how linguistic analysis can lead to problems in the philosophy of language. Another is the attack made by some philosophers on the language of metaphysics as meaningless. The concern was with the nature and procedure of philosophical inquiry, but it presupposed a standard for meaningfulness. A group of philosophers called the logical positivists made such a standard explicit in the verifiability principle of meaning. Attacks and defenses of this principle have been

---

[3] See Paul Ziff, *Semantic Analysis* (Ithaca, N.Y.: Cornell University, 1960), Preface.

one of the foci of critical work in philosophy of language. Some have concluded that this standard fails to satisfy the variety of meanings understood as basic to human discourse. Others have contended that no standard or standards of meaning can be satisfactorily explicated at all.

Whatever conclusions one obtains in his explication and criticism of standards of meaning, he soon finds that they are intertwined with epistemological and logical concerns, as well as with other problems in philosophy of language. If verifiability is the basis for meaning, then some conception of how knowledge works is necessary. If some verifiable language is not *directly* verifiable, some notion of the logic of inference from one form of language to another is required. The verifiability principle requires a neat division of statements into analytic, (statements in which the predicate may be arrived at by an analysis of the meaning of the subject) and synthetic (statements in which the predicate is not included in the meaning of the subject). The former are regarded as true by convention, the latter as verifiable by experience. Philosophers have found that this distinction itself must be clarified and justified. And if some statements are true by convention, and definitions are numbered among them, then definitions evidently are not a link between language and what language is about. Some conception of definition needs explication—and on it goes. The logical interdependency of philosophical problems makes it difficult to begin and end with a single problem, or even with a single field of inquiry.

Not all problems in the philosophy of language are the philosophers' own creations. What student of elementary German has not struggled with a term like 'der Geist', which he finds is at one time to be translated into English as 'the spirit', at another to be translated as 'the mind'? Troubles increase when he finds that *'geistvoll'* is to be translated neither as 'spiritual' nor as 'intellectual,' but as 'witty'. The frustrations of the student of French are greater when he confronts an idiom that defies literal translation into any language. The idiom can only be approximated in meaning, if it is translatable at all. When the original versions are known, popular songs translated into other languages are often howlers. The student of Chinese searches in vain for an equivalent to the subject-predicate construction that is common to Occidental grammars. These problems in translation may lead to the study of how languages are constructed and related, to the study of linguistics. The same problems may lead the student to ponder his understanding of the units and processes of translation, to explore his conception of what constitutes sameness of meaning. These explorations carry him into problems in the philosophy of language.

Whatever the source of concern, a number of problem clusters begin to appear: meaning, standards of meaning, sameness of meaning; definition, description, naming, and reference; the relations of an act of speaking to situations, conventions, and other conditions for the act. Each area of concern contains a complex of interrelated problems, and each solution has implications for other areas of concern. Whether one begins with a sophisticated philosophical analysis like that of Ziff, or with the musings of a perplexed novice like those of the language student, explorations into understandings about language often go beyond the problem that initiated the inquiry.

It would be misleading to suggest that all inquiry in philosophy of language arises from perplexities over the philosophical presuppositions of other inquiries. Concern with understanding the concepts, categories, and principles of language may arise as readily from a general wonder as from a particular perplexity. One may wonder that we are able to communicate at all, that symbols that have no apparent relation to the things they stand for can convey information about them, that children can learn at an early age all the complexities of their native language. These and other marvels may lead to an exploration of the nature and function of language. Perhaps the most marvelous of all wonders about language is its apparent correlation to the thoughts that we think and to the world that is. I say what I think. My words describe what is the case. But how can this be? And why should it be? Yet, that it is so is a presupposition of virtually all our use of language. The affirmation of this correlation of language, thought, and reality seems a commonplace; it is a *classical synthesis* (classical in the sense of standard). An explanation of it is quite another thing, involving a complex philosophical inquiry.

If we move from the wonder that this classical synthesis is the case to an exploration of how and why it is the case, then we are confronted with the philosophical tasks of explicating, criticizing, and systematizing our understanding of the correlations of language, thought, and reality. Assume, for instance, that a word has the same role in language that a concept has in thought and that a thing has in reality. Do all words name things? Are there abstract entities which correspond to abstract terms? Are there meanings which things, concepts, and words have in common (if so, what is a meaning?)? Are concepts anything more than words thought? If so, what is their character? Assume, again, that a sentence in speech corresponds to a proposition in judgment, corresponds to a fact (event, state of affairs) in the world. Is the sentence different from the proposition? What sense can be made of saying "language pictures reality"? Is there any sense, however metaphorical, in which a sentence is a picture of a fact? The assumption of the classical synthesis, which at first glance seemed quite natural, and taken for granted seemed wonderful, upon critical examination brings forth its own complexes of philosophical perplexities.

Assumed uncritically, the classical synthesis of language, thought, and reality invites distorted understandings about the nature and use of language. However inviting one finds the notion that the subject of every sentence names something in reality, the realization that this notion commits him to a world made up of abstract, fictional, and potential entities must inevitably require him to think through what is involved. The classical synthesis need not necessarily be abandoned, but if it is to function as a working model for understanding language, it must be supported by a theory that will explain what the correlations of language, thought, and reality are, and how the numerous criticisms raised against the naive assumption of the classical synthesis can be met. If, on the other hand, the inquirer is convinced that the classical synthesis is no more than a myth, then he must explicate it as a presupposition. Where it forms a basis for perplexities about language, he must critically show what alternative understandings will relieve the problem. Either a defense of the classical synthesis or an attack upon it will carry the inquirer into many of the problem areas considered in this volume.

Aspects of Inquiry

The problems considered in this book depend in one way or another upon the notion of meaning, and they also presuppose some conception of what a language is. They require the use of language to work on language. This does indeed make the philosophical inquirer somewhat like the mariner repairing the ship in which he sails. The situation in the philosophy of language is complicated by the presence of other ships upon the sea. A brief comparison with allied inquiries into language may help to delineate the philosopher's role and the subject matter under consideration.

In recent years, linguistic science has developed into fairly refined inquiries, descriptive linguistics exploring the nature of speech, comparative linguistics the relations between languages. These explorations systematize the subject matter of inquiry into subordinate fields of concern:

PHONOLOGY		GRAMMAR		LEXICOLOGY	
Phonetics (study of sound units)	Phonemics (study of "distinctive" sound units)	Morphology (study of units of language form)	Syntax (study of arrangements of language forms)	Etymology (study of derivation of form)	Semantics (study of significance of form)

Set this breakdown of subject matter alongside that of semiotics (theory of signs),[4] one philosophical attempt at systematic inquiry into language and related significant expression:

---

[4] Semiotics is a field of study formulated by C. S. Peirce and systematized by Charles Morris in *Foundations of the Theory of Signs* (Chicago: University of Chicago Press, 1938) on the basis of work done by Peirce, Carnap, and others. It begins by treating a sign as anything that stands for an object for an interpreter who gives it significance. The sign process is thus a *mediated* "taking-account-of" (Morris), the sign giving the basis for the relation between the object and the interpreter. The degree of mediation ranges from indexical signs,

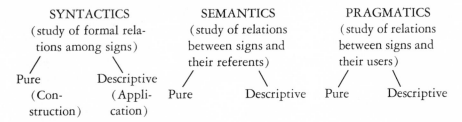

These schemata give us a basis for initial comparison. Semiotics, beginning with the sign as a unit, seldom considers linguistic units smaller than words ("free" morphemes). Linguistics, even in semantic inquiry, seldom deals with meaning, regarding such issues as the concern of metalinguistics (study "beyond" linguistics). Within the areas of common designation, syntax and semantics, the procedures are quite different. The linguist seeks to describe natural languages, like French or Chinese, while the philosopher may concern himself with artificial or technical languages, like mathematics, or even attempt to characterize language in general. The linguist focuses on the actualities of language—how a language does indeed exist and work—and the philosopher focuses on logical possibilities—what the nature and uses of languages presuppose and imply. These concerns overlap, but they do not coincide.

The conceptions of language offer similar bases for comparison. Linguists often use the definition offered by Bloch and Trager: "Language is a system of arbitrary vocal symbols by means of which a social group cooperates."[5] Compare this to a semiotic definition that can be constructed from Charles Morris' discussion: "A language is a system of signs abiding by a set of syntactical, semantical, and pragmatical rules, on the basis of which a community of discourse can be established."[6] While similar in form, the latter is much broader in scope. It allows for artificial as well as natural languages, for natural signs (a cloud

which point to their objects (as a cloud may indicate rain or a pointing of my finger may indicate what I am referring to), through iconical signs, which stand-for by re-presenting (as a map may represent a terrain or a portrait represent a person), to symbolical signs, which stand-for in a totally abstracted, conventional way (as the term 'dog' stands for dog, or a red traffic light stands for the command to stop). Indexes, icons, and symbols are all signs and they perform a semiotic function by relating their objects to their interpreters. As a sign can be characterized by its relation to other signs, to its objects, and to its users, and a language can be regarded as a system of signs, the study of language can be treated as an examination of the rules governing the relations of a sign to other signs in the system, the relations of a sign to its referents (the objects for which it stands), and the relations of a sign to its users (the interpreters of the sign's significance). Thus, semiotics resolves neatly into syntactics, semantics, and pragmatics. For a more detailed account of semiotics, see Morris.

[5] Bernard Bloch and George Trager, *Outline of Linguistic Analysis* (Baltimore: Waverly Press, 1942), p. 5.

[6] Charles Morris, *Foundations of the Theory of Signs* (Chicago: University of Chicago Press, 1938), p. 11.

as a sign of rain) as well as conventional, for nonverbal meaning as well as verbal. The former definition may be too confining, but the latter is obviously too liberal. Music may well be the language of love, but only metaphorically. Traffic lights are clearly signs, but we do not treat them as a part of language. Smiles have meaning and political developments have significance, but they are clearly of a nonlinguistic sort. If insight can be gained from comparing language to these other semiotic aspects of our world, then we must take them into account, but dangers may also lie in ignoring differences between linguistic and nonlinguistic significance. Whether the philosopher restricts his understanding of a language to the limits defined by the linguist is itself a question open to his inquiry.

If the concerns of the linguist overlap with those of the philosopher, so too do those of the psychologist. The philosopher shares with the inquirer into verbal learning and verbal behavior the concern with *how* a word means, and the claim has been made that "learning theory can account for most of the phenomena which have been discussed under the heading of 'meaning'."[7] This apparent coincidence of philosophical and psychological concern with meaning can be mitigated by distinguishing in general a logical account from a psychological one, and by showing how psychological concerns with language often presuppose philosophical ones.

When the psychologist inquires how a word means, he is interested in understanding the psychological processes involved in verbal behavior. He wants to know how the word acquires meaning for the child learning its use, how a hearer's behavior patterns in response to the word reflect his interpretation, how learning the word as a part of a second language differs from learning it as a part of a native language, how thinking processes are encoded into words and decoded out again. These concerns focus on the behavior of human organisms, and conclusions are arrived at on the basis of empirically observed overt processes. When a philosopher inquires into how a word means, he is interested in understanding the logical structures and relations that make meaning possible. He may want to know what sort of "entity" a meaning is as distinct from the word that means, the speaker that means by the word, the object meant by the word, and the hearer to whom the word means. He may want to know the nature of the relations that exist between these factors that are involved in the communication of meaning. Many philosophers agree with J. L. Austin that this treatment is a misleading way to approach the logic of meaning (see 2.3), and analyze it along other lines. But whatever the formulation of the problem, the philosopher's concern is not with facts and generalizations about verbal behavior, but with understanding concepts, categories, and principles of meaning.

While we must recognize a difference in the nature of these two activities, we

---

[7] John Carroll, *The Study of Language* (Cambridge: Harvard University Press, 1953), p. 111.

must also recognize a high degree of interrelation and mutual influence. For the most part, the work of the psychologist presupposes that of the philosopher. If the psychologist asks how the word acquires meaning for the child learning its use, he presupposes that the child acquires the word before he acquires its meaning. A psychological inquiry might take a contrary approach by seeking to find how the child acquires words to express his meaning. The conflict between these presuppositions can only be resolved by developing an adequate understanding of the logical relationship between word and meaning. To ask how thinking processes are encoded into verbal expressions presupposes that the nature of thinking is sufficiently nonverbal to require that such a transformation take place. When this presupposition is controverted—as it is by some psychologies of thinking—the presuppositions must be explicated, and a philosophical resolution of the conflict must be brought about, for adequate psychological inquiry to continue. Thus, the inquiry of psychology contributes to the problems of philosophy of language, and philosophy of language can also be illumined and limited in its conclusions by the discoveries made in psychological inquiry.

Psychologists have recently recognized that knowledge of the findings of descriptive linguistics increases their understanding of linguistic behavior, and in the last two decades the interdisciplinary inquiry of psycholinguistics has developed. During the last decade, inquirers in this field have become increasingly aware of a philosophical aspect as well, and theories of language are now being developed which draw on the findings of all three disciplines (see 1.5). These developments make it desirable for the philosopher of language to equip himself with a basic knowledge of psycholinguistics. They also suggest that the distinctions of the several disciplinary approaches to the subject matter of language are increasingly difficult to discern. The concerns and categories of linguistics, philosophy, and psychology overlap. To confuse them often leads the inquirer to employ inappropriate methods, and the result becomes a hopeless muddle. To correlate them often permits the inquirer to reinforce his findings in one area with those in another.

One more relationship needs at least brief attention—that between semantics and what is usually termed "general semantics." General semantics, as engaged in by Alfred Korzybski, S. I. Hayakawa, Stuart Chase, and others, attempts to break out of traditional systematizations of language on the one hand (Korzybski treats this as a reaction to the stranglehold of Aristotelian categories—an attitude reminiscent of Bacon) and attempts on the other hand to resolve important social problems on the basis of the reformulations. This movement has been variously evaluated; it has been regarded as the most significant scientific revolution of our times and also as a sloppy pseudo-science. However one evaluates it, we must note here that it is not semantics in the semiotic or linguistic senses. It tends to be more a pragmatical endeavor. While the theorists of general semantics borrow liberally from the findings of both logic and psychology, they lack the systematic rigor in logic and psychology to develop an adequate pragmatics on the basis of general semantics. Yet their success in practical matters demands that some note be taken of their views on language and communication. It may well be that the astute student can glean some insight from general semantics for philosophy of language, just as knowledge of anthropology, of cybernetics, of game and decision theory, and of other developing areas of inquiry may prove useful.

Toward Further Inquiry

My discussion of the character of philosophy of language can be measured against the treatment by William Alston, *Philosophy of Language* (Englewood Cliffs, 1964),†[8] Introduction, with which it differs little, and against that by Jerrold Katz, *The Philosophy of Language* (New York, 1966), Chapter I, with which it differs much. There are many good anthologies that provide discussions and examples of philosophical analysis as a tool of inquiry. Among the best are Herbert Feigl and Wilfred Sellars (eds.), *Readings in Philosophical Analysis* (New York, 1949); Margaret MacDonald (ed.), *Philosophy and Analysis* (Oxford, 1954); Anthony Flew (ed.), *Logic and Language* (New York, 1965). For instances of applying analytical techniques to philosophy of language, in addition to Paul Ziff's *Semantic Analysis* (Ithaca, N.Y., 1960), see Leonard Linsky (ed.), *Semantics and the Philosophy of Language* (Urbana, Ill., 1952), and Charles Caton (ed.), *Philosophy and Ordinary Language* (Urbana, Ill., 1963).†

Among works on linguistics, Leonard Bloomfield's *Language* (New York, 1933) remains the most often cited classic. Bernard Bloch and George Trager's *Outline of Linguistic Analysis* (Baltimore, 1942) gives a good brief introduction to linguistics. More detailed introductions are H. A. Gleason, *An Introduction to Descriptive Linguistics* (New York, 1961)† and Edgar Sturtevant, *An Introduction to Linguistic Science* (New Haven, 1947), the former for descriptive linguistics, the latter for historical. Simeon Potter's *Modern Linguistics* (New York, 1964)† is of interest in that it relates linguistic problems to philosophical inquiries, and it is a very readable, if overly simplified, introduction. Zeno Vendler's *Linguistics in Philosophy* (Ithaca, N.Y., 1967) provides the best discussion to date of the philosophical implications of recent linguistic studies. Edward Sapir's *Language* (New York, 1921) is a seminal work in linguistics, and his *Selected Writings in Language, Culture and Personality* (Berkeley, 1949) continues his consideration of concerns in linguistics, anthropology, and psychology.

G. A. Miller's *Language and Communication* (New York, 1951) offers a first-rate treatment of psychology of language, and his work with A. E. Galanter and K. H. Pribram, *Plans and the Structure of Behavior* (New York, 1960), gives attention to language in the broader context of human behavior. B. F.

---

[8] The use of the dagger is explained in the Preface.

Skinner's *Verbal Behavior* (New York, 1957) offers a psychology of language that attempts to avoid issues of philosophical interest entirely, especially problems of meaning. By contrast, Roger Brown's *Words and Things* (Glencoe, Ill., 1958) aims at meeting philosophical problems directly, attacking them from a psychological point of view. Charles Morris' *Signs, Language and Behavior* (New York, 1946) and Willard Quine's *Word and Object* (Cambridge, Mass., 1960) are works of a primarily philosophical nature, but they employ many psychological findings and techniques. Paul Henle (ed.), *Language, Thought and Culture* (Ann Arbor, Mich., 1958), is an attempt to reapproach a number of problems in philosophy of language on the basis of insights from psychology and other disciplines. *Verbal Behavior and Learning* (New York, 1963), edited by C. N. Coffee and B. S. Musgrave, offers a number of good selections on problems and techniques in psychology of language.

For anthologies dealing with the collaboration of psychologists and linguists on language, see Charles Osgood and Thomas Sebeok (eds.), *Psycholinguistics* (Baltimore, 1954); Sol Saporta (ed.), *Psycholinguistics* (New York, 1961); *Readings in Psycholinguistics* (Englewood Cliffs, N.J., 1966). Herbert Rubinstein and Murray Aborn's "Psycholinguistics" (*Annual Review of Psychology*, 11) provides a summary of the field. John Carroll's *The Study of Language* (Cambridge, Mass., 1953)† is the only work available that attempts to survey all varieties of the study of language (it is weakest in its discussion of philosophical inquiries). This book is now dated, but it is rich in bibliographical sources appearing up to the time of its publication.

The diligent researcher will find *The Encyclopedia of Philosophy*, 8 vols. (New York, 1967), an excellent background source. Not only does it have complete essays on such topics as "Synonymity" and "Semantics," but its indexes and bibliographies lead to related areas of concern. It contains good surveys of most of the problems taken up in this book.

Chapter 1

SOME PHILOSOPHICAL APPROACHES TO LANGUAGE

The genius of man's logical method should be
loved and reverenced as his bride, whom he
has chosen from all the world. He need not
condemn the others; on the contrary, he
may honour them deeply, and in doing so he only
honours her the more.

Charles S. Peirce

Any characterization of approaches to philosophy is a hazardous venture. Labels provide a tool for sorting and ordering different kinds of approach, but they may lead to the erroneous suppositions that all kinds of approach fit into the given categories and that all instances of a kind can be treated alike. Recent work in philosophy is often divided into speculative philosophy, which attempts to construct comprehensive understandings about the nature of things, and analytical philosophy, which limits its inquiry to the analysis of problems formulated as linguistic issues. Some approaches do not fit happily into either slot. Phenomenological inquiry claims to be antispeculative in its description and analysis of the character and conditions of appearances, and it clearly does not limit its concern to the analysis of language.

Also questionable is the division of analytical philosophy into ideal-language philosophy, which analyzes language according to a rigorously reconstructed language system, and ordinary-language philosophy, which takes the vagueness and complexity of particular contexts of ordinary discourse as its starting place (the former sometimes bears the title "logical analysis," the latter, "linguistic analysis" or "conceptual analysis"). Rudolf Carnap, Bertrand Russell, Alfred Tarski, and Gustav Bergmann differ in their programs of linguistic reconstruction and their treatments of particular problems, but they have all been labeled ideal-language analysts. Differences between Gilbert Ryle and John Austin in their

14

treatments of meaning, between Austin and P. F. Strawson in their treatments of performatives, have not prohibited lumping them all together with Ludwig Wittgenstein and others under the label of ordinary-language philosophers. But Arthur Pap and Willard Quine, both analytically oriented, do not fit readily into either classification.

In the essays that follow, Peirce may be called a pragmatist, Cassirer a neo-Kantian, Carnap an ideal-language analyst; Ryle may be called an ordinary-language analyst, Merleau-Ponty a phenomenologist, Schaff a neo-Marxist; and Fodor and Katz's proposal is yet too new on the scene to readily admit labeling. Such classifications are necessarily oversimplifications. They have a wide vogue in philosophical discussion and serve as convenient labels. More important are the problems suggested by the various proposals for a philosophical approach to language. A critical acquaintance with these proposals, and with the problematic issues involved, may aid the inquirer in plotting his own method and make him sensitive to the strengths and weaknesses of other approaches.

Even to speak of a single approach for a single man may be too simplistic. In his "How to Make Our Ideas Clear," C. S. Peirce proposed to treat the meaning of concepts in terms of the conceivable practical effects of the objects of conception. This "pragmatic theory of meaning" is a part of a more general scheme to treat logic and language as normative concerns, subject to ethical principles. Selection 1.1 is an essay in this same spirit, but the reader may find it difficult to discern any of this practical thrust in 1.2. Here Peirce gives an outline of his semiotics in relation to his basic metaphysical categories of firstness, secondness, and thirdness. The differences illustrated in these two essays between the practical and the theoretical, the analytical and the metaphysical, often bewilder students of Peirce. More generally, they raise interesting problems about philosophical approaches: Is the difference between Peirce's way of dealing with the analysis of language and his way of dealing with constructing a semiotics an inconsistency of method, or merely a difference in concern? Are the analyst and the metaphysician offering rival approaches to philosophy, or merely working at different kinds of task? Do different kinds of problems require different kinds of tools and methods?

Whatever the relation between approach and problem, the inquirer invariably works within a theoretical context, his particular inquiry related to conclusions from other inquiries. Cassirer is explicit in seeing his treatment of language against the background of a particular epistemology, and as a part of a broader concern with a philosophy of culture. He takes language as a clue to man's symbolizing nature. Symbolic form does not simply picture reality; it imposes a creative order upon it, and this ordering process is basic to understanding culture. However one evaluates his conclusions, Cassirer's approach points to questions about the context of inquiry: Does his treatment of language presuppose a particular understanding of human knowledge? Is philosophy of language always so dependent upon epistemology? Can an inquiry ever be free of presuppositions?

If not, can an inquirer avoid unwarranted prejudice about the conclusion of any inquiry?

In setting forth their programs for philosophical analysis, Carnap and Ryle provide nice contrasts between ideal-language and ordinary-language treatments: between the model of a mathematical system and the model of a game; between a formal construction of a language and an informal explication of meaning in specific contexts; between a system of rules for speaking and uses of language in speech acts; between a unified language for a unified science and a plurality of uses for a variety of purposes. The contrast between an ideal-language and an ordinary-language analysis is no greater than the contrasts of both to concern with natural languages like English and German. Such contrasts suggest a number of questions about philosophical approaches: Can the logic of everyday discourse, or even the technical discourse of the sciences, be adequately represented by the formulas of symbolic logic? How like mathematics is the systematic character of language? What is gained (and lost) by translating expressions of a natural language into a logically formalized system? Against what standards does one measure the adequacy of such translations? On the other hand, are there any rules for the informal logic of the "ordinary use of an expression"? If there are, why not formalize them? If not, in what sense is it a logic? What is the relation of "ordinary language" to natural languages? By what standards does one determine that the ordinary use of an expression in one language is the same as that of an expression in another language?

Such questions often reveal a practical irrelevance in ideal-language constructions and a theoretical paucity in ordinary-language techniques. Jerrold Katz and Jerry Fodor find in the notion of a transformational grammar a basis for both practical applicability and theoretical simplicity. A transformational model for language distinguishes a deep structure for grammar, which is composed of "kernel sentences" that can be obtained by use of basic phrase-structure rules, from a surface structure, which is composed of the actual sentences used in a language. The transformation rules determine the ways in which all possible grammatical sentences in the surface structure can be generated from the kernel sentences in the deep structure. If such a model can be made workable, it will give linguistics a basis in a finite set of rules from which it can generate an infinite number of grammatical sentences. What such a model implies for philosophy is now a subject of much debate. The proposal by Fodor and Katz is to treat philosophy of language as philosophy of linguistics. But are philosophical concerns with language limited to such a handmaiden's role? What is the relation of such empirical sciences as linguistics to philosophy? Can discoveries in linguistics solve problems in philosophy? If so, is philosophy then reduced to a pseudo-science? If not, what is the relevance of linguistics?

Unlike analytical philosophies, phenomenology examines what most immediately appears to the consciousness. This involves techniques for observing, analyzing, and describing immediate phenomena without imposing simplifying theoretical categories upon them. It also involves attempts to characterize the essential nature and relations of phenomena, and the modes by which phenomena appear. In all this, the phenomenologist aims to proceed on a descriptive basis, without the aid of explanatory hypotheses. The accent on the particular and the diverse in specific contexts has some similarity to ordinary-language analysis, but the focus is on experiential phenomena, not on linguistic use. This need not imply that concern with language is excluded. Maurice Merleau-Ponty makes clear that language is both a crucial tool for phenomenological method and an important concern for phenomenological study. But can any treatment of language be purely descriptive? Can any use of language to describe phenomena avoid theoretical presuppositions that are embodied in the categorial scheme of any language? Is not the very nature of language at odds with the phenomenological program of inquiry? If not, how is the nature of language to be construed as compatible? Are other programs of inquiry open to such problems?

As a Marxist, Adam Schaff is committed at the outset not only to principles and methods of inquiry, but to certain conclusions about language as well. In true dialectical fashion, he sees his Marxistic thesis as a synthesis of two opposing philosophical traditions, the transcendental and the empirical. But can such a thesis meet the variety of philosophical problems about language? If it cannot, what is the alternative? Must the thesis be modified to fit the facts, or the facts reinterpreted to fit the thesis? More generally, what is the relation of theoretical constructions to practical applications?

The questions raised about the several approaches are illustrative. Many are not peculiar to a particular approach, but may be raised about any approach to similar problems. Some may suggest further questions. They all point in the direction of an over-reaching question: What are the norms for an adequate philosophical method? More radically: Are there standards against which methods can be measured and compared? Answers to these and other questions about method cannot simply be weighed against the proposals presented in this chapter. They must also be measured against the solutions to problems which are offered in the succeeding chapters.

1.1

THE ETHICS
OF TERMINOLOGY

C. S. Peirce

In order that my use of terms, notations, etc., may be understood, I explain that my conscience imposes upon me the following rules. Were I to make the smallest pretension to dictate the conduct of others in this matter, I should be reproved by the first of these rules. Yet if I were to develope the reasons the force of which I feel myself, I presume they would have weight with others.

Those reasons would embrace, in the first place, the consideration that the woof and warp of all thought and all research is symbols, and the life of thought and science is the life inherent in symbols; so that it is wrong to say that a good language is *important* to good thought, merely; for it is of the essence of it. Next would come the consideration of the increasing value of precision of thought as it advances. Thirdly, the progress of science cannot go far except by collaboration; or, to speak more accurately, no mind can take one step without the aid of other minds. Fourthly, the health of the scientific communion requires the most absolute mental freedom. Yet the scientific and philosophical worlds are infested with pedants and pedagogues who are continually endeavoring to set up a sort of magistrature over thoughts and other symbols. It thus becomes one of the first duties of one who sees what the situation is, energetically to resist everything like arbitrary dictation in scientific affairs, and above all, as to the use of terms and notations. At the same time, a general agreement concerning the use of terms and of notations—not too rigid, yet prevailing, with most of the co-workers in regard to most of the symbols, to such a degree that there shall be some small number of different systems of expression that have to be mastered—is indispensable. Consequently, since this is not to be brought about by arbitrary dictation, it must be brought about by the power of rational principles over the conduct of men.

Now what rational principle is there

From *The Collected Papers of Charles Sanders Peirce*, Vol. II, Charles Hartshorne and Paul Weiss, editors (Cambridge, Mass.: Harvard University Press, 1932). Copyright, 1932, 1960, by the President and Fellows of Harvard College. Reprinted by permission of the publishers.

which will be perfectly determinative as to what terms and notations shall be used, and in what senses, and which at the same time possesses the requisite power to influence all right-feeling and thoughtful men?

In order to find the answer to that question, it is necessary to consider, first, what would be the character of an ideal philosophical terminology and system of logical symbols; and, secondly, to inquire what the experience of those branches of science has been that have encountered and conquered great difficulties of nomenclature, etc., in regard to the principles which have proved efficacious, and in regard to unsuccessful methods of attempting to produce uniformity.

As to the ideal to be aimed at, it is, in the first place, desirable for any branch of science that it should have a vocabulary furnishing a family of cognate words for each *scientific* conception, and that each word should have a single exact meaning, unless its different meanings apply to objects of different categories that can never be mistaken for one another. To be sure, this requisite might be understood in a sense which would make it utterly impossible. For every symbol is a living thing, in a very strict sense that is no mere figure of speech. The body of the symbol changes slowly, but its meaning inevitably grows, incorporates new elements and throws off old ones. But the effort of all should be to keep the *essence* of every scientific term unchanged and exact; although absolute exactitude is not so much as conceivable. Every symbol is, in its origin, either an image of the idea signified, or a reminiscence of some individual oc-

currence, person or thing, connected with its meaning, or is a metaphor. Terms of the first and third origins will inevitably be applied to different conceptions; but if the conceptions are strictly analogous in their principal suggestions, this is rather helpful than otherwise, provided always that the different meanings are remote from one another, both in themselves and in the occasions of their occurrence. Science is continually gaining new conceptions; and every new *scientific* conception should receive a new word, or better, a new family of cognate words. The duty of supplying this word naturally falls upon the person who introduces the new conception; but it is a duty not to be undertaken without a thorough knowledge of the principles and a large acquaintance with the details and history of the special terminology in which it is to take a place, nor without a sufficient comprehension of the principles of word-formation of the national language, nor without a proper study of the laws of symbols in general. That there should be two different terms of identical scientific value may or may not be an inconvenience, according to circumstances. Different systems of expression are often of the greatest advantage.

The ideal terminology will differ somewhat for different sciences. The case of philosophy is very peculiar in that it has positive need of popular words in popular senses—not as its own language (as it has too usually used those words), but as objects of its study. It thus has a peculiar need of a language distinct and detached from common speech, such a language as Aristotle, the scholastics, and Kant endeavored to supply, while Hegel endeavored to destroy it. It is good economy for philosophy to provide itself with a vocabulary so outlandish that loose thinkers shall not be tempted to borrow its words. Kant's adjectives "objective" and "subjective" proved not to be barbarous enough, by half, long to retain their usefulness in philosophy, even if there had been no other objection to them. The first rule of good taste in writing is to use words whose meanings will not be misunderstood; and if a reader does not know the meaning of the words, it is infinitely better that he should know he does not know it. This is particularly true in logic, which wholly consists, one might almost say, in exactitude of thought.

The sciences which have had to face the most difficult problems of terminology have unquestionably been the classificatory sciences of physics, chemistry, and biology. The nomenclature of chemistry is, on the whole, good. In their dire need, the chemists assembled in congress, and adopted certain rules for forming names of substances. Those names are well-known, but they are hardly used. Why not? Because the chemists were not psychologists, and did not know that a congress is one of the most impotent of things, even less influential by far than a dictionary. The problem of the biological taxonomists has, however, been incomparably more difficult; and they have solved it (barring small exceptions) with brilliant success. How did they accomplish this? Not by appealing to the power of congresses, but by appealing to the power of the idea of right and wrong. For only make a man *really*

see that a certain line of conduct is wrong, and he *will* make a strong endeavor to do the right thing—be he thief, gambler, or even a logician or moral philosopher. The biologists simply talked to one another, and made one another see that when a man has introduced a conception into science, it naturally becomes both his privilege and his duty to assign to that conception suitable scientific expressions; and that when a name has been conferred upon a conception by him to whose labors science is indebted for that conception, it becomes the duty of all—a duty to the discoverer, and a duty to science—to accept his name, unless it should be of such a nature that the adoption of it would be unwholesome for science; that should the discoverer fail in his duty, either by giving no name or an utterly unsuitable one, then, after a reasonable interval, whoever first has occasion to employ a name for that conception must invent a suitable one; and others ought to follow him; but that whoever deliberately uses a word or other symbol in any other sense than that which was conferred upon it by its sole rightful creator commits a shameful offence against the inventor of the symbol and against science, and it becomes the duty of the others to treat the act with contempt and indignation.

As fast as the students of any branch of philosophy educate themselves to a genuine scientific love of truth to the degree to which the scholastic doctors were moved by it, suggestions similar to those above will suggest themselves; and they will consequently form a technical terminology. In logic, a terminology more than passably good has been inherited by us from the scholastics. This scholastic terminology has passed into English speech more than into any other modern tongue, rendering it the most logically exact of any. This has been accompanied by the inconvenience that a considerable number of words and phrases of scientific logic have come to be used with a laxity quite astounding. Who, for example, among the dealers in Quincy Hall who talks of "articles of *prime necessity*," would be able to say what that phrase "prime necessity" strictly means? He could not have sought out a more technical phrase. There are dozens of other loose expressions of the same provenance.

Having thus given some idea of the nature of the reasons which weigh with me, I proceed to state the rules which I find to be binding upon me in this field.

First. To take pains to avoid following any recommendation of an arbitrary nature as to the use of philosophical terminology.

Second. To avoid using words and phrases of vernacular origin as technical terms of philosophy.

Third. To use the scholastic terms in their anglicised forms for philosophical conceptions, so far as they are strictly applicable; and never to use them in other than their proper senses.

Fourth. For ancient philosophical conceptions overlooked by the scholastics, to imitate, as well as I can, the ancient expression.

Fifth. For precise philosophical conceptions introduced into philosophy since the middle ages, to use the anglicised form of the original expression, if not positively unsuitable, but only in its precise original sense.

Sixth. For philosophical conceptions which vary by a hair's breadth from those for which suitable terms exist, to invent terms with a due regard for the usages of philosophical terminology and those of the English language but yet with a distinctly technical appearance. Before proposing a term, notation, or other symbol, to consider maturely whether it perfectly suits the conception and will lend itself to every occasion, whether it interferes with any existing term, and whether it may not create an inconvenience by interfering with the expression of some conception that may hereafter be introduced into philosophy. Having once introduced a symbol, to consider myself almost as much bound by it as if it had been introduced by somebody else; and after others have accepted it, to consider myself more bound to it than anybody else.

Seventh. To regard it as needful to introduce new systems of expression when new connections of importance between conceptions come to be made out, or when such systems can, in any way, positively subserve the purposes of philosophical study.

1.2

ON SIGNS
AND THE CATEGORIES*[1]

C. S. Peirce

But I wanted to write to you about signs, which in your opinion and mine are matters of so much concern. More

From *The Collected Papers of Charles Sanders Peirce*, Vol. VIII, Arthur W. Burks, editor (Cambridge, Mass.: Harvard University Press, 1958). Copyright, 1958, by the President and Fellows of Harvard College. Reprinted by permission of the publishers.

* The editorial notes in this essay (other than this one) are those of Arthur Burks. References to "[CP]" are to the *Collected Papers* by volume and section. Numerical references like "1.347" are to volume and paragraph (in this case, Volume I, paragraph 347). References to "[Bibliography]" are to the bibliography in Volume VIII of the *Collected Papers*. [TMO]

[1] (Ed.) From a letter dated "1904 Oct 12" to "My dear Lady Welby." A photostat copy of the original letter is in the Yale University Library. The complete letter is also in [Bibliography] M–20a, pp. 7–14, published by Whitlock's, Inc., New Haven, Conn., with whose permission the parts given here and the quotations in 330n4 and 330n6 are reprinted.

Lady Victoria Welby was an English semanticist, at one time Maid of Honour to Queen Victoria. For Peirce's review of her *What is Meaning?* see Book I of the present volume. For additional correspondence see [Bibliography] M–20.

in mine, I think, than in yours. For in mine, the highest grade of reality is only reached by signs; that is by such ideas as those of Truth and Right and the rest. It sounds paradoxical; but when I have devolved to you my whole theory of signs, it will seem less so. I think that I will today explain the outlines of my classification of signs.

You know that I particularly approve of inventing new words for new ideas. I do not know that the study I call *Ideoscopy* can be called a new idea, but the word *phenomenology* is used in a different sense.[2] *Ideoscopy* consists in describing and classifying the ideas that belong to ordinary experience or that naturally arise in connection with ordinary life, without regard to their being valid or invalid or to their psychology. In pursuing this study I was long ago (1867) led, after only three or four years' study, to throw all ideas into the three classes of Firstness, of Secondness, and of

[2] (Ed.) Peirce's phenomenology and categories are discussed at various places in [CP], especially in [CP] I, Book III. See also 7.524–538.

Thirdness.[3] This sort of notion is as distasteful to me as to anybody; and for years, I endeavored to pooh-pooh and refute it; but it long ago conquered me completely. Disagreeable as it is to attribute such meaning to numbers, and to a triad above all, it is as true as it is disagreeable. The ideas of Firstness, Secondness, and Thirdness are simple enough. Giving to being the broadest possible sense, to include ideas as well as things, and ideas that we fancy we have just as much as ideas we do have, I should define Firstness, Secondness, and Thirdness thus:

Firstness is the mode of being of that which is such as it is, positively and without reference to anything else.

Secondness is the mode of being of that which is such as it is, with respect to a second but regardless of any third.

Thirdness is the mode of being of that which is such as it is, in bringing a second and third into relation to each other.

I call these three ideas the cenopythagorean categories.

The typical ideas of firstness are qualities of feeling, or mere appearances. The scarlet of your royal liveries, the quality itself, independently of its being perceived or remembered, is an example, by which I do not mean that you are to imagine that you *do not* perceive or remember it, but that you are to drop out of account that which may be attached to it in perceiving or in remembering, but which does not

[3] (Ed.) in [Bibliography] G–1867–1c, 1.545–559.

belong to the quality. For example, when you remember it, your idea is said to be *dim* and when it is before your eyes, it is *vivid*. But dimness or vividness do not belong to your idea of the quality. They *might* no doubt, if considered simply as a feeling; but when you think of vividness you do not consider it from that point of view. You think of it as a degree of disturbance of your consciousness. The quality of red is not thought of as belonging to you, or as attached to liveries. It is simply a peculiar positive possibility regardless of anything else. If you ask a mineralogist what hardness is, he will say that it is what one predicates of a body that one cannot scratch with a knife. But a simple person will think of hardness as a simple positive possibility the *realization* of which causes a body to be like a flint. That idea of hardness is an idea of Firstness. The unanalyzed total impression made by any manifold not thought of as actual fact, but simply as a quality, as simple positive possibility of appearance, is an idea of Firstness. Notice the *naïveté* of Firstness. The cenopythagorean categories are doubtless another attempt to characterize what Hegel sought to characterize as his three stages of thought. They also correspond to the three categories of each of the four triads of Kant's table. But the fact that these different attempts were independent of one another (the resemblance of these Categories to Hegel's stages was not remarked for many years after the list had been under study, owing to my antipathy to Hegel) only goes to show that there really are three such elements. The idea of the present instant, which, whether it exists or not, is naturally thought as a point of time in which no thought can take place or any detail be separated, is an idea of Firstness.

The type of an idea of Secondness is the experience of effort, prescinded from the idea of a purpose. It may be said that there is no such experience, that a purpose is always in view as long as the effort is cognized. This may be open to doubt; for in sustained effort we soon let the purpose drop out of view. However, I abstain from psychology which has nothing to do with ideoscopy. The existence of the word *effort* is sufficient proof that people think they have such an idea; and that is enough. The experience of effort cannot exist without the experience of resistance. Effort only is effort by virtue of its being opposed; and no third element enters. Note that I speak of the *experience*, not of the *feeling*, of effort. Imagine yourself to be seated alone at night in the basket of a balloon, far above earth, calmly enjoying the absolute calm and stillness. Suddenly the piercing shriek of a steam-whistle breaks upon you, and continues for a good while. The impression of stillness was an idea of Firstness, a quality of feeling. The piercing whistle does not allow you to think or do anything but suffer. So that too is absolutely simple. Another Firstness. But the breaking of the silence by the noise was an experience. The person in his inertness identifies himself with the precedent state of feeling, and the new feeling which comes in spite of him is the non-ego. He has a two-sided consciousness of an ego and a non-ego. That consciousness of the action of a new feeling in destroying the old feeling is what I call an *experience*. Experience generally is what the course of life has *compelled* me to think. Secondness is either *genuine* or *degenerate*. There are many degrees of genuineness. Generally speaking genuine secondness consists in one thing acting upon another, —brute action. I say brute, because so far as the idea of any *law* or *reason* comes in, Thirdness comes in. When a stone falls to the ground, the law of gravitation does not act to make it fall. The law of gravitation is the judge upon the bench who may pronounce the law till doomsday, but unless the strong arm of the law, the brutal sheriff, gives effect to the law, it amounts to nothing. True, the judge can create a sheriff if need be; but he must have one. The stone's actually falling is purely the affair of the stone and the earth at the time. This is a case of *reaction*. So is *existence* which is the mode of being of that which reacts with other things. But there is also action without reaction. *Such is the action of the previous upon the subsequent.*[4] It is a difficult question whether the idea of this one-sided determination is a pure idea of secondness or whether it involves thirdness. At present, the former view seems to me correct. I suppose that when Kant made Time a form of the internal sense alone, he was influenced by some such considerations as the following. The relation between the previous and the subsequent consists in the previous being determinate and fixed for the

---

[4] (Ed.) "The italicized sentence is, in manuscript, underlined in pencil. Perhaps it was underlined by Lady Welby, yet it was not her habit to annotate Peirce's letters." From [Bibliography] M–20a, p. 9.

subsequent, and the subsequent being indeterminate for the previous. But indeterminacy belongs only to ideas; the existent is determinate in every respect; and this is just what the law of causation consists in. Accordingly, the relation of time concerns only ideas. It may also be argued that, according to the law of the conservation of energy, there is nothing in the physical universe corresponding to our idea that the previous determines the subsequent in any way in which the subsequent does not determine the previous. For, according to that law, all that happens in the physical universe consists in the exchange of just so much *vis viva*

$$\tfrac{1}{2}m(ds/dt)^2$$

for so much displacement. Now the square of a negative quantity being positive, it follows that if all the velocities were reversed at any instant, everything would go on just the same, only time going backward as it were. Everything that had happened would happen again in reversed order. These seem to me to be strong arguments to prove that temporal causation (a very different thing from physical dynamic action) is an action upon ideas and not upon existents.[5] But since our idea of the past is precisely the idea of that which is absolutely determinate, fixed, *fait accompli*, and dead, as against the future which is living, plastic, and determinable, it appears to me that the idea of one-sided action, in so far as it concerns the being of the determinate, is a pure idea of Secondness; and I think that great errors of metaphysics are

due to looking at the future as something that will have been past. I cannot admit that the idea of the future can be so translated into the Secundal ideas of the past. To say that a given kind of event never will happen is to deny that there is any date at which its happening will be past; but it is not equivalent to any affirmation about a past relative to any assignable date. When we pass from the idea of an event to saying that it never will happen, or will happen in endless repetition, or introduce in any way the idea of endless repetition, I will say the idea is *mellonized* (μέλλων, about to be, do, or suffer). When I conceive a fact as acting but not capable of being acted upon, I will say that it is *parelelythose* (παρεληλυθώς, past) and the mode of being which consists in such action I will call *parelelythosine* (-ine= εἶναι, being); I regard the former as an idea of Thirdness, the latter as an idea of Secondness. I consider the idea of any dyadic relation not involving any third as an idea of Secondness; and I should not call any completely degenerate except the relation of identity. But similarity which is the only possible identity of Firsts is very near to that. Dyadic relations have been classified by me in a great variety of ways; but the most important are, first, with regard to the nature of the Second in itself and, second, with regard to the nature of its First. The Second, or *Relate*,[6] is, in itself, either a *Referate*, if it is intrinsically a possibility, such as a quality, or it is a *Revelate* if it is

---

[5] (Ed.) Reversible and irreversible actions are discussed further in Chapter 3, "Habit," [CP] VII, Book III.

[6] (Ed.) " 'Relate', in manuscript, is underlined in pencil." From [Bibliography] M–20a, p. 10.

of its own nature an Existent. In respect to its First, the Second is divisible either in regard to the dynamic first or to the immediate first. In regard to its dynamic first, a Second is determined either by virtue of its own intrinsic nature, or by virtue of a real relation to that second (an action). Its immediate second is either a Quality or an Existent.

I now come to Thirdness. To me, who have for forty years considered the matter from every point of view that I could discover, the inadequacy of Secondness to cover all that is in our minds is so evident that I scarce know how to begin to persuade any person of it who is not already convinced of it. Yet I see a great many thinkers who are trying to construct a system without putting any thirdness into it. Among them are some of my best friends who acknowledge themselves indebted to me for ideas but have never learned the principal lesson. Very well. It is highly proper that Secondness should be searched to its very bottom. Thus only can the indispensableness and irreducibility of thirdness be made out, although for him who has the mind to grasp it, it is sufficient to say that no branching of a line can result from putting one line on the end of another.[7] My friend Schröder fell in love with my algebra of dyadic relations. The few pages I gave to it in my Note B in the 'Studies in Logic by Members of the Johns Hopkins University' were proportionate to its importance.[8] His book is profound,[9] but

its profundity only makes it more clear that Secondness cannot compass Thirdness. (He is careful to avoid ever saying that it can, but he does go so far as to say that Secondness is the more important. So it is, considering that Thirdness cannot be understood without Secondness. But as to its application, it is so inferior to Thirdness as to be in that aspect quite in a different world.) Even in the most degenerate form of Thirdness, and thirdness has two grades of degeneracy, something may be detected which is not mere secondness. If you take any ordinary triadic relation, you will always find a *mental* element in it. Brute action is secondness, any mentality involves thirdness. Analyze for instance the relation involved in 'A gives B to C.' Now what is giving? It does not consist [in] A's putting B away from him and C's subsequently taking B up. It is not necessary that any material transfer should take place. It consists in A's making C the possessor according to *Law*. There must be some kind of law before there can be any kind of giving,—be it but the law of the strongest. But now suppose that giving *did* consist merely in A's laying down the B which C subsequently picks up. That would be a degenerate form of Thirdness in which the thirdness is externally appended. In A's putting away B, there is no thirdness. In C's taking B, there is no thirdness. But if you say that these two acts constitute a single operation by virtue of the identity of the B, you transcend the mere brute fact, you introduce a mental element. . . . The criticism which I make on [my] algebra of dyadic relations, with which I am by no means in love, though I

---

[7] (Ed.) Cf. 1.347, 3.421.

[8] (Ed.)   [Bibliography]   G–1883–7d, 3.328–358.

[9] (Ed.) Cf. [Bibliography] G–1896–6.

think it is a pretty thing, is that the very triadic relations which it does not recognize, it does itself employ. For every combination of relatives to make a new relative is a triadic relation irreducible to dyadic relations. Its *inadequacy* is shown in other ways, but in this way it is in a conflict with itself *if it be regarded*, as I never did regard it, *as sufficient for the expression of all relations*. My universal algebra of relations, with the subjacent indices and Σ and Π, is susceptible of being enlarged so as to comprise everything; and so, still better, though not to ideal perfection, is the system of *existential graphs*.[10]

I have not sufficiently applied myself to the study of the degenerate forms of Thirdness, though I think I see that it has two distinct grades of degeneracy. In its genuine form, Thirdness is the triadic relation existing between a sign, its object, and the interpreting thought, itself a sign, considered as constituting the mode of being of a sign.[11] A sign mediates between the *interpretant* sign and its object. Taking sign in its broadest sense, its interpretant is not necessarily a sign. Any concept is a sign, of course. Ockham, Hobbes, and Leibniz have sufficiently said that. But we may take a sign in so broad a sense that the interpretant of it is not a thought, but an action or experience, or we may even so enlarge the meaning of sign that its interpretant is a mere quality of

feeling. A *Third* is something which brings a First into relation to a Second. A sign is a sort of Third. How shall we characterize it? Shall we say that a Sign brings a Second, its Object, into *cognitive* relation to a Third? That a Sign brings a Second into the same relation to a first in which it stands itself to that First? If we insist on *consciousness*, we must say what we mean by consciousness of an object. Shall we say we mean Feeling? Shall we say we mean association, or Habit? These are, on the face of them, psychological distinctions, which I am particular to avoid. What is the essential difference between a sign that is communicated to a mind, and one that is not so communicated? If the question were simply what we *do* mean by a sign, it might soon be resolved. But that is not the point. We are in the situation of a zoölogist who wants to know what ought to be the meaning of "fish" in order to make fishes one of the great classes of vertebrates. It appears to me that the essential function of a sign is to render inefficient relations efficient,— not to set them into action, but to establish a habit or general rule whereby they will act on occasion. According to the physical doctrine, nothing ever happens but the continued rectilinear velocities with the accelerations that accompany different relative positions of the particles. All other relations, of which we know so many, are inefficient. Knowledge in some way renders them efficient; and a sign is something by knowing which we know something more. With the exception of knowledge, in the present instant, of the contents of consciousness in that instant (the existence of which knowl-

---

[10] (Ed.) This is treated at length in [CP] IV, Book II.

[11] (Ed.) Signs are discussed at various places in [CP]. See 8.313ff., 2.227ff., and the letter following the present one. See also [Bibliography] M–20a.

edge is open to doubt) all our thought and knowledge is by signs. A sign therefore is an object which is in relation to its object on the one hand and to an interpretant on the other, in such a way as to bring the interpretant into a relation to the object, corresponding to its own relation to the object. I might say 'similar to its own' for a correspondence consists in a similarity; but perhaps correspondence is narrower.

I am now prepared to give my division of signs, as soon as I have pointed out that a sign has two objects, its object as it is represented and its object in itself. It has also three interpretants, its interpretant as represented or meant to be understood, its interpretant as it is produced, and its interpretant in itself. Now signs may be divided as to their own material nature, as to their relations to their objects, and as to their relations to their interpretants.

As it is in itself, a sign is either of the nature of an appearance, when I call it a *qualisign*; or secondly, it is an individual object or event, when I call it a *sinsign* (the syllable *sin* being the first syllable of *sem*el, *sim*ul, *sing*ular, etc.); or thirdly, it is of the nature of a general type, when I call it a *legisign*. As we use the term 'word' in most cases, saying that 'the' is one 'word' and 'an' is a second 'word,' a 'word' is a legisign. But when we say of a page in a book, that it has 250 'words' upon it, of which twenty are 'the's, the 'word' is a sinsign. A sinsign so embodying a legisign, I term a 'replica' of the legisign. The difference between a legisign and a qualisign, neither of which is an individual thing, is that a legisign has a definite identity, though usually admitting a great variety of appearances. Thus, &, *and*, and the sound are all one word. The qualisign, on the other hand, has no identity. It is the mere quality of an appearance and is not exactly the same throughout a second. Instead of identity, it has *great similarity*, and cannot differ much without being called quite another qualisign.

In respect to their relations to their dynamic objects, I divide signs into Icons, Indices, and Symbols (a division I gave in 1867).[12] I define an Icon as a sign which is determined by its dynamic object by virtue of its own internal nature. Such is any qualisign, like a vision,—or the sentiment excited by a piece of music considered as representing what the composer intended. Such may be a sinsign, like an individual diagram; say a curve of the distribution of errors. I define an Index as a sign determined by its dynamic object by virtue of being in a real relation to it. Such is a Proper Name (a legisign); such is the occurrence of a symptom of a disease. (The symptom itself is a legisign, a general type of a definite character. The occurrence in a particular case is a sinsign.) I define a Symbol as a sign which is determined by its dynamic object only in the sense that it will be so interpreted. It thus depends either upon a convention, a habit, or a natural disposition of its interpretant or of the field of its interpretant (that of which the interpretant is a determination). Every symbol is necessarily a legisign; for it is inaccurate to call a replica of a legisign a symbol.

In respect to its immediate object a

---

[12] (Ed.) 1.558 ([Bibliography] G–1867–1c).

sign may either be a sign of a quality, of an existent, or of a law.

In regard to its relation to its signified interpretant, a sign is either a Rheme, a Dicent, or an Argument. This corresponds to the old division, Term, Proposition, and Argument, modified so as to be applicable to signs generally. A *Term* is simply a class-name or proper-name. I do not regard the common noun as an essentially necessary part of speech. Indeed, it is only fully developed as a separate part of speech in the Aryan languages and the Basque,—possibly in some other out of the way tongues. In the Shemitic languages it is generally in form a verbal affair, and usually is so in substance, too. As well as I can make out, such it is in most languages. In my universal algebra of logic there is no common noun. A rheme is any sign that is not true nor false, like almost any single word except 'yes' and 'no,' which are almost peculiar to modern languages. A *proposition* as I use that term, is a dicent symbol. A dicent is not an assertion, but is a sign *capable* of being asserted. But an assertion is a dicent. According to my present view (I may see more light in future) the act of assertion is not a pure act of signification. It is an exhibition of the fact that one subjects oneself to the penalties visited on a liar if the proposition asserted is not true. An act of judgment is the self-recognition of a belief; and a belief consists in the deliberate acceptance of a proposition as a basis of conduct. But I think this position is open to doubt. It is simply a question of which view gives the simplest view of the nature of the proposition. Holding, then, that a Di-

cent does not assert, I naturally hold that an Argument need not actually be submitted or urged. I therefore define an argument as a sign which is represented in its signified interpretant not as a Sign of that interpretant (the conclusion) [for that would be to urge or submit it][13] but *as if* it were a Sign of the Interpretant or perhaps as if it were a Sign of the state of the universe to which it refers, in which the premisses are taken for granted. I define a dicent as a sign represented in its signified interpretant *as if it were* in a Real Relation to its Object. (Or as being so, if it is asserted.) A rheme is defined as a sign which is represented in its signified interpretant *as if it were* a character or mark (or as being so).

According to my present view, a sign may appeal to its dynamic interpretant in three ways:

1st, an argument only may be *submitted* to its interpretant, as something the reasonableness of which will be acknowledged.

2nd, an argument or dicent may be *urged* upon the interpretant by an act of insistence.

3rd, argument or dicent may be, and a rheme can only be, presented to the interpretant for *contemplation.*

Finally, in its relation to its immediate interpretant, I would divide signs into three classes as follows:

1st, those which are interpretable in thoughts or other signs of the same kind in infinite series,

---

[13] (Ed.) The brackets are Peirce's.

2nd, those which are interpretable in actual experiences,

3rd, those which are interpretable in qualities of feelings or appearances.

Now if you think on the whole (as I do) that there is much valuable truth in all this, I should be gratified if you cared to append it to the next edition of your book, after editing it and of course cutting out personalities of a disagreeable kind, ESPECIALLY IF [IT WERE] ACCOMPANIED BY ONE OR MORE (running or other) CLOSE CRITICISMS; for I haven't a doubt there is more or less error involved. . . .

P. S. On the whole, then, I should say there were ten principal classes of signs

1. Qualisigns
2. Iconic Sinsigns
3. Iconic Legisigns
4. *Vestiges*, or Rhematic Indexical Sinsigns
5. *Proper Names*, or Rhematic Indexical Legisigns
6. Rhematic Symbols
7. Dicent Sinsigns (as a portrait with a legend)
8. Dicent Indexical Legisigns
9. *Propositions*, or Dicent Symbols
10. Arguments.

1.3

THE CONCEPT OF SYMBOLIC FORM

Ernst Cassirer

Philosophical speculation began with the concept of *being*. In the very moment when this concept appeared, when man's consciousness awakened to the unity of being as opposed to the multiplicity and diversity of existing things, the specific philosophical approach to the world was born. But even then man's

From *The Philosophy of Symbolic Forms,* Vol. I, Ralph Manheim, trans. (New Haven, Conn.: Yale University Press, 1953). Reprinted by permission of the publishers.

thinking about the world remained for a long while imprisoned within the sphere of existing things, which it was seeking to relinquish and surpass. The philosophers attempted to determine the beginning and origin, the ultimate "foundation" of all being: the question was stated clearly, but the concrete, determinate answers given were not adequate to this supreme, universal formulation. What these thinkers called the essence, the substance of the world was not something which in principle went beyond it; it was a fragment taken from this very same world. A particular, specific and limited existing thing was picked out, and everything else was genetically derived from it and "explained by it." Much as these explanations might change in content, their general form remained within the same methodological limits. At first a particular material substance, a concrete *prima materia*, was set up as the ultimate foundation of all phenomena; then the explanations became more ideal and the substance was replaced by a purely rational "principle," from which everything was derived. But on closer inspection this "principle" hung in midair between the "physical" and "spiritual." Despite its ideal coloration, it was closely connected with the world of existing things. The number of the Pythagoreans, the atom of Democritus, though far removed from the original substance of the Ionians, remained a methodological hybrid, which had not found its true nature and had not, as it were, chosen its true spiritual home. This inner uncertainty was not definitely overcome until Plato developed his theory of ideas. The great systematic and historical achievement of this theory is that here, for the first time, the essential intellectual premise for any philosophical understanding and explanation of the world took on explicit form. What Plato sought for, what he called "idea," had been effective as an immanent principle in the earliest attempts to explain the world, in the Eleatic philosophers, in the Pythagoreans, in Democritus; but Plato was the first to be conscious of this

principle and its significance. Plato himself took this to be his philosophical achievement. In his late works, where he sees the logical implications of his doctrine most clearly, he characterizes the crucial difference between his speculation and that of the Pre-Socratics: the Pre-Socratics identified being with a particular existing thing and took it as a fixed point of departure, while he for the first time recognized it as a *problem*. He no longer simply inquired into the order, condition and structure of being, but inquired into the concept of being and the meaning of that concept. Compared with the sharpness of Plato's question and the rigor of his approach, all earlier speculations paled to tales or myths about being.[1] It was time to abandon these mythical, cosmological explanations for the true, dialectical explanation of being, which no longer clings to its mere facticity but discloses its intelligible *meaning*, its systematic, teleological order. And with this, thought, which in Greek philosophy since Parmenides had appeared as a concept interchangeable with that of being, gained a new and profounder meaning. Only where being has the sharply defined meaning of a *problem*, does thought attain to the sharply defined meaning and value of a *principle*. It no longer runs parallel to being, a mere reflection "about" being, but by its own inner form, it now determines the inner form of being.

The same typical process was repeated at different stages in the historical development of idealism. Where a materialist view of the world con-

---

[1] Cf. especially *The Sophists* 243 C ff.

tented itself with some ultimate attribute of things as the basis of all cognition—idealism turned this very same attribute into a question for thought. And this process is discernible not only in the history of philosophy but in the specialized sciences as well. The road does not lead solely from "data" to "laws" and from laws back to "axioms" and "principles": the axioms and principles themselves, which at a certain stage of knowledge represent the ultimate and most complete solution, must at a later stage become once more a problem. Accordingly, what science designates as its "being" and its "object," ceases to appear as a simple and indivisible set of facts; every new type or trend of thought discloses some new phase in this complex. The rigid concept of being seems to be thrown into flux, into general movement, and the unity of being becomes conceivable only as the aim, and no longer as the beginning of this movement. As this insight develops and gains acceptance in science itself, the naïve *copy theory* of knowledge is discredited. The fundamental concepts of each science, the instruments with which it propounds its questions and formulates its solutions, are regarded no longer as passive images of something given but as *symbols* created by the intellect itself.

Mathematicians and physicists were first to gain a clear awareness of this symbolic character of their basic implements.[2] The new ideal of knowledge,

to which this whole development points, was brilliantly formulated by Heinrich Hertz in the introduction to his *Principles of Mechanics.* He declares that the most pressing and important function of our natural science is to enable us to foresee future experience—and he goes on to describe the method by which science derives the future from the past: We make "inner fictions or symbols" of outward objects, and these symbols are so constituted that the necessary logical consequences of the images are always images of the necessary natural consequences of the imaged objects.

> Once we have succeeded in deriving images of the required nature from our past experience, we can with them as models soon develop the consequences which will be manifested in the outward world much later or as consequences of our own intervention. . . . The images of which we are speaking are our ideas of things; they have with things the one essential agreement which lies in the fulfillment of the stated requirement, but further agreement with things is not necessary to their purpose. Actually we do not know and have no means of finding out whether our ideas of things accord with them in any other respect than in this one fundamental relation.[3]

The epistemology of the physical sciences, on which the work of Heinrich Hertz is based and the theory of "signs" as first fully developed by Helmholtz, was still couched in the *language* of the

---

[2] This is discussed in greater detail in my book *Zur Einstein'schen Relativitätstheorie* (Berlin, B. Cassirer, 1921); cf. especially the first section on "Massbegriffe und Denkbegriffe."

---

[3] H. Hertz, *Die Prinzipien der Mechanik* (Leipzig, F. A. Barth, 1894), p. 1 ff.

copy theory of knowledge—but the concept of the "image" had undergone an inner change. In place of the vague demand for a similarity of content between image and thing, we now find expressed a highly complex logical relation, a general intellectual *condition*, which the basic concepts of physical knowledge must satisfy. Its value lies not in the reflection of a given existence, but in what it accomplishes as an instrument of knowledge, in a unity of phenomena, which the phenomena must produce out of themselves. A system of physical concepts must reflect the relations between objective things as well as the nature of their mutual dependency, but this is only possible in so far as these concepts pertain from the very outset to a definite, homogeneous intellectual orientation. The object cannot be regarded as a naked thing in itself, independent of the essential categories of natural science: for only within these categories which are required to constitute its form can it be described at all.

In this sense, Hertz came to look upon the fundamental concepts of mechanics, particularly the concepts of mass and force, as "fictions" which, since they are created by the logic of natural science, are subordinate to the universal requirements of this logic, among which the a priori requirement of clarity, freedom from contradiction, and unambiguousness of reference takes first place.

With this critical insight, it is true, science renounces its aspiration and its claim to an "immediate" grasp and communication of reality. It realizes that the only objectivization of which

it is capable is, and must remain, mediation. And in this insight, another highly significant idealistic consequence is implicit. If the object of knowledge can be defined only through the medium of a particular logical and conceptual structure, we are forced to conclude that a variety of media will correspond to various structures of the object, to various meanings for "objective" relations. Even in "nature," the physical object will not coincide absolutely with the chemical object, nor the chemical with the biological—because physical, chemical, biological knowledge *frame their questions* each from its own particular standpoint and, in accordance with this standpoint, subject the phenomena to a special interpretation and formation. It might also seem that this consequence in the development of idealistic thought had conclusively frustrated the expectation in which it began. The end of this development seems to negate its beginning—the unity of being, for which it strove, threatens once more to disintegrate into a mere diversity of existing things. The One Being, to which thought holds fast and which it seems unable to relinquish without destroying its own form, eludes *cognition.* The more its metaphysical unity as a "thing in itself" is asserted, the more it evades all possibility of knowledge, until at last it is relegated entirely to the sphere of the unknowable and becomes a mere "X." And to this rigid metaphysical absolute is juxtaposed the realm of phenomena, the true sphere of the knowable, with its enduring multiplicity, finiteness and relativity. But upon closer scrutiny the fundamental postulate of unity is not discredited by this irreducible diversity of the methods and objects of knowledge; it merely assumes a new form. True, the unity of knowledge can no longer be made certain and secure by referring knowledge in all its forms to a "simple" common object which is related to all these forms as the transcendent prototype to the empirical copies. But instead, a new task arises: to gather the various branches of science with their diverse methodologies—with all their recognized specificity and independence—into one system, whose separate parts precisely through their necessary diversity will complement and further one another. This postulate of a purely functional unity replaces the postulate of a unity of substance and origin, which lay at the core of the ancient concept of being.

And this creates a new task for the philosophical critique of knowledge. It must follow the special sciences and survey them as a whole. It must ask whether the intellectual symbols by means of which the specialized disciplines reflect on and describe reality exist merely side by side or whether they are not diverse manifestations of the same basic human function. And if the latter hypothesis should be confirmed, a philosophical critique must formulate the universal conditions of this function and define the principle underlying it. Instead of dogmatic metaphysics, which seeks absolute unity in a substance to which all the particulars of existence are reducible, such a philosophical critique seeks after a rule governing the concrete diversity of the functions of cognition, a rule which,

without negating and destroying them, will gather them into a unity of deed, the unity of a self-contained human endeavor.

But again our perspectives widen if we consider that cognition, however universally and comprehensively we may define it, is only one of the many forms in which the mind can apprehend and interpret being. In giving form to multiplicity it is governed by a specific, hence sharply delimited principle. All cognition, much as it may vary in method and orientation, aims ultimately to subject the multiplicity of phenomena to the unity of a "fundamental proposition." The particular must not be left to stand alone, but must be made to take its place in a context, where it appears as part of a logical structure, whether of a teleological, logical or causal character. Essentially cognition is always oriented toward this essential aim, the articulation of the particular into a universal law and order. But beside this intellectual synthesis, which operates and expresses itself within a system of scientific concepts, the life of the human spirit as a whole knows other forms. They too can be designated as modes of "objectivization": i.e., as means of raising the particular to the level of the universally valid; but they achieve this universal validity by methods entirely different from the logical concept and logical law. Every authentic function of the human spirit has this decisive characteristic in common with cognition: it does not merely copy but rather embodies an original, formative power. It does not express passively the mere fact that something is present but contains an independent energy of the human spirit through which the simple presence of the phenomenon assumes a definite "meaning," a particular ideational content. This is as true of art as it is of cognition; it is as true of myth as of religion. All live in particular image-worlds, which do not merely reflect the empirically given, but which rather produce it in accordance with an independent principle. Each of these functions creates its own symbolic forms which, if not similar to the intellectual symbols, enjoy equal rank as products of the human spirit. None of these forms can simply be reduced to, or derived from, the others; each of them designates a particular approach, in which and through which it constitutes its own aspect of "reality." They are not different modes in which an independent reality manifests itself to the human spirit but roads by which the spirit proceeds towards its objectivization, i.e., its self-revelation. If we consider art and language, myth and cognition in this light, they present a common problem which opens up new access to a universal philosophy of the cultural sciences.

The "revolution in method" which Kant brought to theoretical philosophy rests on the fundamental idea that the relation between cognition and its object, generally accepted until then, must be radically modified. Instead of starting from the object as the known and given, we must begin with the law of cognition, which alone is truly accessible and certain in a primary sense; instead of defining the universal qualities of *being*, like ontological metaphysics, we must, by an analysis of reason, as-

certain the fundamental form of *judgment* and define it in all its numerous ramifications; only if this is done, can objectivity become conceivable. According to Kant, only such an analysis can disclose the conditions on which all *knowledge* of being and the pure concept of being depend. But the object which transcendental analytics thus places before us is the correlate of the synthetic unity of the understanding, an object determined by purely logical attributes. Hence it does not characterize all objectivity as such, but only that form of objective necessity which can be apprehended and described by the basic concepts of science, particularly the concepts and principles of mathematical physics. When in the course of the three critiques Kant proceeded to develop the true "system of pure reason," he himself found this objectivity too narrow. In his idealistic view, mathematics and physics do not exhaust all reality, because they are far from encompassing all the workings of the human spirit in its creative spontaneity. In the realm of ethical freedom, whose basic law is developed by the *Critique of Practical Reason*, in the realm of art and the realm of organic natural forms, as represented in the *Critique of Judgment*, a new aspect of this reality appears. This *gradual* unfolding of the critical-idealistic concept of reality and the critical-idealistic concept of the spirit is among the most characteristic traits of Kantian thinking, and is indeed grounded in a kind of law of style that governed this thinking. He does not set out to designate the authentic, concrete totality of the spirit in a simple initial formula, to deliver it ready-made, as it were; on the contrary, it develops and finds itself only in the progressive course of his critical analysis. We can designate and define the scope of the human spirit only by pursuing this analytical process. It lies in the nature of this process that its beginning and end are not only separate from each other, but must apparently conflict—however, the tension is none other than that between potency and act, between the mere "potentiality" of a concept and its full development and effect. From the standpoint of this latter, the Copernican revolution with which Kant began, takes on a new and amplified meaning. It refers no longer solely to the function of logical judgment but extends with equal justification and right to every trend and every principle by which the human spirit gives form to reality.

The crucial question always remains whether we seek to understand the function by the structure or the structure by the function, which one we choose to "base" upon the other. This question forms the living bond connecting the most diverse realms of thought with one another: it constitutes their inner methodological unity, without ever letting them lapse into a factual sameness. For the fundamental principle of critical thinking, the principle of the "primacy" of the function over the object, assumes in each special field a new form and demands a new and dependent explanation. Along with the pure function of cognition we must seek to understand the function of linguistic thinking, the function of mythical and religious thinking, and the function of artistic perception, in such

a way as to disclose how in all of them there is attained an entirely determinate formation, not exactly of the world, but rather making for the world, for an objective, meaningful context and an objective unity that can be apprehended as such.

Thus the critique of reason becomes the critique of culture. It seeks to understand and to show how every content of culture, in so far as it is more than a mere isolated content, in so far as it is grounded in a universal principle of form, presupposes an original act of the human spirit. Herein the basic thesis of idealism finds its true and complete confirmation. As long as philosophical thought limits itself to analysis of *pure cognition*, the naïve-realistic view of the world cannot be wholly discredited. The object of cognition is no doubt determined and formed in some way by cognition and through its original law—but it must nevertheless, so it would seem, also be present and given as something independent outside of this relation to the fundamental categories of knowledge. If, however, we take as our starting point not the general concept of the world, but rather the general concept of culture, the question assumes a different form. For the content of the concept of culture cannot be detached from the fundamental forms and directions of human activity: here "being" can be apprehended only in "action." Only in so far as aesthetic imagination and perception exist as a specific pursuit, is there a sphere of aesthetic objects—and the same applies to all those other energies of the spirit by which a definite universe of objects takes on form. Even religious consciousness—convinced as it is of the "reality," the truth, of its object—transforms this reality into a simple material *existence* only at the lowest level, the level of purely mythological thinking. At higher levels of contemplation it is more or less clearly aware that it only possesses its object in so far as it relates itself to that object in a special way. What ultimately guarantees objectivity itself is the way in which it is approached, the specific direction that the spirit gives itself in relation to a proposed objective context. Philosophical thought confronts all these directions—not just in order to follow each one of them separately or to survey them as a whole, but under the assumption that it must be possible to relate them to a unified, ideal center. From the standpoint of critical thinking, however, this center can never lie in a given essence but only in a common *project*. Thus, with all their inner diversity, the various products of culture—language, scientific knowledge, myth, art, religion—become parts of a single great problem-complex: they become multiple efforts, all directed toward the one goal of transforming the passive world of mere *impressions*, in which the spirit seems at first imprisoned, into a world that is pure *expression* of the human spirit.

In seeking the proper starting point for a philosophical study of language, modern philosophy has devised the concept of "inner linguistic form." A similar "inner form" may be sought in religion and myth, in art and scientific cognition. And this form would not mean only a sum or retrospective compendium of the particular phenomena in these fields, but the law determining their structure. True, we can find this law only through the phenomena themselves from which we "abstract" it; but this very abstraction shows that the law is a necessary constituent factor of the content and existence of the particular. . . .

So far we have aimed at a kind of critical "deduction," an explanation and justification of the concept of representation, in the belief that the representation of one content in and through another is an essential premise for the structure and formal unity of consciousness. The following study, however, will not deal with this general logical significance of the representative function. We shall seek to pursue the problem of signs, not backward to its ultimate "foundations," but forward to its concrete unfolding and configuration in the diverse cultural spheres.

We have acquired a new foundation for such an investigation. We must go back to "natural" symbolism, to that representation of consciousness as a whole which is necessarily contained or at least projected in every single moment and fragment of consciousness, if we wish to understand the artificial symbols, the "arbitrary" signs which consciousness creates in language, art, and myth. The force and effect of these mediating signs would remain a mystery if they were not ultimately rooted in an original spiritual process which belongs to the very essence of consciousness. We can understand how a sensuous particular, such as the spoken sound, can become the vehicle of a purely intellectual meaning, only if we assume that the basic function of signification is present and active before the individual sign is produced, so that this producing does not create signification, but merely stabilizes it, applies it to the particular case. Since every particular content of consciousness is situated in a network of diverse relations, by virtue of which its simple existence and self-representation contain *reference* to other and still other contents, there can and must be certain formations of consciousness in which the pure form of reference is, as it were, sensuously embodied. From this follows the characteristic twofold nature of these formations: their bond with sensibility, which however contains within it a freedom from sensibility. In every linguistic "sign," in every mythical or artistic "image," a spiritual content, which intrinsically points beyond the whole sensory sphere, is translated into the form of the sensuous, into something visible, audible or tangible. An independent mode of configuration appears, a specific activity of consciousness, which is differentiated from any datum of immediate sensation or perception, but makes use of these data as vehicles, as means of expression. Thus the "natural" symbolism which we have found embedded as a fundamental characteristic of consciousness is on the one hand utilized and retained, while on the other hand it is surpassed and refined. For in this "natural" symbolism, a certain partial content of consciousness, though distinct from the whole, retained the power to represent this whole and in so doing to reconstitute it in a sense. A present content possessed the power of evoking another content, which was not immediately given but merely conveyed by it. It is not the case, however, that the symbolic signs which we encounter in language, myth, and art first "are" and then, beyond this "being," achieve a certain meaning; their being arises from their signification. Their content subsists purely and wholly in the function of signification. Here consciousness, in order to apprehend the whole in the particular, no longer requires the stimulus of the particular itself, which must be given as such; here consciousness *creates* definite concrete sensory contents as an expression for definite complexes of meaning. And because these contents which consciousness creates are entirely in its power, it can, through them, freely "evoke" all those meanings at any time. When, for example, we link a given intuition or idea with an arbitrary linguistic sound, we seem, at first sight, to have added nothing whatever to its content. And yet, on closer scrutiny, the content itself takes on a different "character" for consciousness through the creation of the linguistic sign: it becomes more definite. Its sharp and clear intellectual "reproduction" proves to be inseparable from the act of linguistic "production." For the function of language is not merely to *repeat* definitions and distinctions which are already present in the mind, but to formulate them and make them intelligible as such. Thus in every sphere, it is through the freedom of spiritual action that the chaos of sensory impressions begins to clear and take on fixed form for us. The fluid impression assumes form and duration for us only when we *mould* it by symbolic action in one direction or another.

In science and language, in art and myth, this formative process proceeds in different ways and according to different principles, but all these spheres have this in common: that the product of their activity in no way resembles the mere *material* with which they began. It is in the basic symbolic function and its various directions that the spiritual consciousness and the sensory consciousness are first truly differentiated. It is here that we pass beyond passive receptivity to an indeterminate outward material, and begin to place upon it our independent imprint which articulates it for us into diverse spheres and forms of reality. Myth and art, language and science, are in this sense configurations *towards* being: they are not simple copies of an existing reality but represent the main directions of the spiritual movement, of the ideal process by which reality is constituted for us as one and many—as a diversity of forms which are ultimately held together by a unity of meaning.

Only when we are oriented towards this goal do the specifications of the various systems of signs, and the use which the intelligence makes of them, become intelligible. If the sign were nothing but a repetition of a determinate and finished, particular intuitive or ideational content, we should be faced with two questions. What would be accomplished by a mere copy of something already present? And how could such an exact copy be accomplished? For it is obvious that a copy can never approach the original and can never replace it for the eye of the spirit. If we took an exact reproduction as our norm, we should be driven to an attitude of fundamental skepticism toward the value of the sign as such. If, for example, we regarded it as the true and essential function of language to express once again, but merely in a different medium, the very same reality that lies ready-made before us in particular sensations and intuitions—we should be struck at once by the vast inadequacy of all languages. Measured by the limitless richness and diversity of intuitive reality, all linguistic symbols would inevitably seem empty; measured by its individual concretion, they would inevitably seem abstract and vague. If language attempts to compete with sensation or intuition in *this* respect, it cannot but fall far behind. The πρῶτον ψευδός of the skeptical critique of language is precisely that it takes this standard as the only valid and possible one. In reality the analysis of language—particularly if it starts not from the mere particular of the word, but from the unity of the *sentence*—shows that all linguistic expression, far from being a mere copy of the given world of sensation or intuition, possesses a definite independent character of "signification."

And the same relation applies to signs of the most diverse type and origin. In a sense it can be said of them all that their value consists not so much in what they stabilize of the concrete, sensuous content and its immediate factuality, as in the part of this immediate factuality which they suppress and pass over. Similarly, artistic delineation becomes what it is and is distinguished from a mere mechanistic reproduction, only through what it omits from the "given" impression. It does not reflect this impression in its sensuous totality, but rather selects certain "pregnant" factors, i.e., factors through which the given impression is amplified beyond itself and through which the artistic-constructive fantasy, the synthetic spatial imagination, is guided in a certain direction. What constitutes the true force of the sign, here as in other fields, is precisely this: that as the immediate, determinate contents recede, the general factors of form and relation become all the sharper and clearer. The particular as such is seemingly limited; but precisely thereby that operation which we have called "integration" is effected the more clearly and forcefully. We have seen that the particular of consciousness "exists" only in so far as it potentially contains the whole and is, as it were, in constant transition towards the whole. But the use of the sign liberates this potentiality and enables it to become true actuality. Now, *one* blow strikes a thousand connected chords which all vibrate more or less forcefully and clearly in the sign. In positing the sign, consciousness detaches itself more and more from the direct *substratum* of sensation and sensory intuition: but precisely therein it reveals its inherent, original power of synthesis and unification.

Perhaps this tendency is most clearly manifested in the functioning of the *scientific* systems of signs. The abstract chemical "formula," for example, which is used to designate a certain substance, contains nothing of what direct observation and sensory perception teach us about this substance; but, instead, it places the particular body in

an extraordinarily rich and finely articulated complex of relations, of which perception as such knows nothing. It no longer designates the body according to its sensuous content, according to its immediate sensory data, but represents it as a sum of potential "reactions," of possible chains of causality which are defined by general rules. In the chemical formula the totality of these necessary relations fuses with the expression of the particular, and gives this expression of the particular an entirely new and characteristic imprint. Here as elsewhere, the sign serves as an intermediary between the mere "substance" of consciousness and its spiritual "form." Precisely because it is without any sensuous mass of its own, because, in a manner of speaking, it hovers in the pure ether of meaning, it has the power to represent not the mere particulars of consciousness but its complex general movements. It does not reflect a fixed content of consciousness but defines the direction of such a general movement. Similarly, the spoken word, considered from the standpoint of physical substance, is a mere breath of wind; but in this breath there lies an extraordinary force for the dynamic of ideas and thought. This dynamic is both intensified and regulated by the sign. It is one of the essential advantages of the sign—as Leibniz pointed out in his *Characteristica generalis*, that it serves not only to represent, but above all to *discover* certain logical relations—that it not only offers a symbolic abbreviation for what is already known, but opens up new roads into the unknown. Herein we see confirmed from a new angle the synthetic power of consciousness as such, by virtue of which every concentration of its contents impels it to extend its limits. The concentration provided by the sign not only permits us to look backward, but at the same time opens up new perspectives. It sets a relative limit, but this limit itself embodies a challenge to advance and opens up the road to this advance by disclosing its general rule. This is eminently borne out by the history of science, which shows how far we have progressed toward solving a given problem or complex of problems, once we have found a fixed and clear "formula" for it. For example: Most of the questions solved in Newton's concept of fluxion and in the algorism of Leibniz' differential calculus were known before Leibniz and Newton and approached from the most diverse directions—from the angles of algebraic analysis, geometry, and mechanics. But all these problems were truly mastered only when a unified and comprehensive symbolic *expression* was found for them: for now they no longer formed a loose and fortuitous sequence of separate questions; the common principle of their origin was designated in a definite, universally applicable *method*, a basic operation whose rules were established.

In the symbolic function of consciousness, an antithesis which is given and grounded in the simple concept of consciousness is represented and mediated. All consciousness appears to us in the form of a temporal process—but in the course of this process certain types of "form" tend to detach themselves. The factor of constant change

and the factor of duration tend to merge. This universal tendency is realized in different ways in the products of language, myth and art, and in the intellectual symbols of science. All these forms seem to be an immediate part of the living, constantly renewed process of consciousness: yet, at the same time, they reveal a spiritual striving for certain fixed points or resting places in this process. In them consciousness retains a character of constant flux; yet it does not flow indeterminately, but articulates itself around fixed centers of form and meaning. In its pure specificity, each such form is an αὐτὸ καθ' αὐτό in the Platonic sense, detached from the mere stream of ideas—but at the same time in order to be manifested, to exist "for us," it must in some way be represented in this stream. In the creation and application of the various groups and systems of symbolic signs, both conditions are fulfilled, since here indeed a particular sensory content, without ceasing to be such, acquires the power to represent a universal for consciousness. Here neither the sensationalist axiom, "Nihil est in intellectu, quod non ante fuerit in sensu," nor its intellectualistic reversal applies. We no longer ask whether the "sensory" precedes or follows the "spiritual," for we are dealing with the revelation and manifestation of basic spiritual functions in the sensory material itself.

What would seem to constitute the bias of "empiricism" as well as abstract "idealism" is precisely that neither of them fully and clearly develops this fundamental relation. One posits a concept of the given particular but fails to recognize that any such concept must always, explicitly or implicitly, encompass the *defining* attributes of some universal; the other asserts the necessity and validity of these attributes but fails to designate the medium through which they can be represented in the given psychological world of consciousness. If, however, we start not with abstract postulates but from the concrete basic form of spiritual life, this dualistic antithesis is resolved. The illusion of an original division between the intelligible and the sensuous, between "idea" and "phenomenon," vanishes. True, we still remain in a world of "images"—but these are not images which reproduce a self-subsistent world of "things"; they are image-worlds whose principle and origin are to be sought in an autonomous creation of the spirit. Through them alone we see what we call "reality," and in them alone we possess it: for the highest objective truth that is accessible to the spirit is ultimately the form of its own activity. In the totality of its own achievements, in the knowledge of the specific rule by which each of them is determined and in the consciousness of the context which reunites all these special rules into *one* problem and one solution: in all this, the human spirit now perceives itself and reality. True, the question of what, apart from these spiritual functions, constitutes absolute reality, the question of what the "thing in itself" may be in *this* sense, remains unanswered, except that more and more we learn to recognize it as a fallacy in formulation, an intellectual phantasm. The true concept of reality cannot be squeezed into the form of mere abstract

being; it opens out into the diversity and richness of the forms of spiritual *life*—but of a spiritual life which bears the stamp of inner necessity and hence of objectivity. In this sense each new "symbolic form"—not only the conceptual world of scientific cognition but also the intuitive world of art, myth, and language—constitutes, as Goethe said, a revelation sent outward from within, a "synthesis of world and spirit," which truly assures us that the two are originally one.

And here new light is cast upon a last fundamental antithesis, with which modern philosophy has struggled since its beginnings and which it has formulated with increasing sharpness. Its "subjective" trend has led philosophy more and more to focus the totality of its problems in the concept of *life* rather than the concept of being. But though this seemed to appease the antithesis of subjectivity and objectivity in the form manifested by dogmatic ontology, and to prepare the way for its ultimate reconciliation—now, in the sphere of life itself, a still more radical antithesis appeared. The truth of life seems to be given only in its pure *immediacy*, to be enclosed in it—but any attempt to understand and apprehend life seems to endanger, if not to negate, this immediacy. True, if we start from the dogmatic concept of being, the dualism of being and thought becomes more and more pronounced as we advance in our investigations—but here there remains some hope that the picture of being developed by cognition will retain at least a remnant of the truth of being. Not all being, to be sure, but at least a *part* of it would seem to enter into this picture—the substance of being would seem to penetrate the substance of cognition and in it create a more or less faithful reflection of itself. But the pure immediacy of life admits of no such partition. It, apparently, must be seen wholly or not at all; it does not enter into our mediate representations of it, but remains outside them, fundamentally different from them and opposed to them. The original content of life cannot be apprehended in any form of *representation*, but only in pure *intuition*. It would seem, therefore, that any understanding of spiritual life must choose between the two extremes. We are called upon to decide whether to seek the substance of the human spirit in its pure originality, which *precedes* all mediate configurations—or whether to surrender ourselves to the richness and diversity of these mediate forms. Only in the first approach do we seem to touch upon the true and authentic center of life, which however appears as a simple, self-enclosed center; in the second, we survey the entire drama of spiritual developments, but as we immerse ourselves in it, it dissolves more and more manifestly into a mere drama, a reflected image, without independent truth and essence. The cleavage between these two antitheses—it would seem—cannot be bridged by any effort of mediating thought which itself remains entirely on one side of the antithesis: the farther we advance in the direction of the symbolic, the merely figurative, the farther we go from the primal source of pure intuition.

Philosophical mysticism has not been alone in its constant confrontation of this problem and this dilemma; the pure logic of idealism has repeatedly seen it and formulated it. Plato's remarks in his *Seventh Epistle* on the relation of the "idea" to the "sign" and on the necessary inadequacy of this relation, strike a motif which has recurred in all manner of variations. In Leibniz' methodology of knowledge, "intuitive knowledge" is sharply distinguished from mere "symbolic" knowledge. Even for the author of the *characteristica universalis*, all knowledge through mere symbols becomes "blind knowledge" (*cogitatio caeca*) when measured by the intuition, as the pure vision, the true "sight" of the idea.[4] True, *human* knowledge can nowhere dispense with symbols and signs; but it is precisely this that characterized it as human, i.e., limited and finite in contradistinction to the ideal of the perfect, archetypal and divine intellect. Even Kant, who assigned its exact logical position to this idea by defining it as a mere borderline concept of cognition, and who believed that in so doing he had critically mastered it—even Kant, in a passage which constitutes the purely methodical climax of the *Critique of Judgment*, once again sharply develops the antithesis between the *intellectus archetypus* and the *intellectus ectypus*, between the intuitive, archetypal intellect and the discursive intellect "which is dependent on images." From the standpoint of this an-

---

[4] Cf. G. W. Leibniz, "Meditationes de cognitione, veritate et ideis," *Die Philosophischen Schriften von Gottfried Wilhelm Leibniz*, ed. C. J. Gerhardt (Berlin, 1880), 4, 422 ff.

tithesis it would seem to follow that the richer the *symbolic content* of cognition or of any other cultural form becomes, the more its *essential content* must diminish. All the many images do not designate, but cloak and conceal the imageless One, which stands behind them and towards which they strive in vain. Only the negation of all finite figuration, only a return to the "pure nothingness" of the mystics can lead us back to the true primal source of being. Seen in a different light, this antithesis takes the form of a constant tension between "culture" and "life." For it is the necessary destiny of culture that everything which it creates in its constant process of configuration and education[5] removes us more and more from the originality of life. The more richly and energetically the human spirit engages in its formative activity, the farther this very activity seems to remove it from the primal source of its own being. More and more, it appears to be imprisoned in its own creations—in the words of language, in the images of myth or art, in the intellectual symbols of cognition, which cover it like a delicate and transparent, but unbreachable veil. But the true, the profoundest task of a *philosophy* of culture, a philosophy of language, cognition, myth, etc., seems precisely to consist in raising this veil— in penetrating from the mediate sphere of mere meaning and characterization to the original sphere of intuitive vision. But on the other hand the specific *organ* of philosophy—and it has no

other at its disposal—rebels against this task. To philosophy, which finds its fulfillment only in the sharpness of the concept and in the clarity of "discursive" thought, the paradise of mysticism, the paradise of pure immediacy, is closed. Hence it has no other solution than to reverse the *direction* of inquiry. Instead of taking the road back, it must attempt to continue forward. If all culture is manifested in the creation of specific image-worlds, of specific symbolic forms, the aim of philosophy is not to go behind all these creations, but rather to understand and elucidate their basic formative principle. It is solely through awareness of this principle that the content of life acquires its true form. Then life is removed from the sphere of mere given natural existence: it ceases to be a part of this natural existence or a mere biological process, but is transformed and fulfilled as a form of the "spirit." In truth, the negation of the symbolic forms would not help us to apprehend the essence of life; it would rather destroy the spiritual form with which for us this essence proves to be bound up. If we take the opposite direction, we do not pursue the idea of a passive intuition of spiritual reality, but situate ourselves in the midst of its activity. If we approach spiritual life, not as the static contemplation of being, but as functions and energies of formation, we shall find certain common and typical principles of formation, diverse and dissimilar as the forms may be. If the philosophy of culture succeeds in apprehending and elucidating such basic principles, it will have fulfilled, in a new sense, its task of demonstrating

---

[5] The German *Bildung* means both formation and education. *Trans.*

the unity of the spirit as opposed to the multiplicity of its manifestations—for the clearest evidence of this unity is precisely that the diversity of the *products* of the human spirit does not impair the unity of its *productive process*, but rather sustains and confirms it.

THE LOGICAL SYNTAX OF LANGUAGE

1.4

Rudolf Carnap

1. "Formal" Theory

In this chapter an explanation will be given of a theory which we will call Logical Syntax, and it will be shown how to operate with the syntactical method. Although the word "philosophy" will not here occur, the syntactical method, as we shall try to make clear in the last chapter, brings us to the very basis of philosophy.

The logical syntax of a certain language is to be understood as the *formal* theory of that language. This needs further explanation. We will call "*formal*" such considerations or assertions concerning a linguistic expression as are without any reference to sense or meaning. A formal investigation of a certain sentence does not concern the sense of that sentence or the meaning of the single words, but only the kinds of words and the order in which they follow one another. Take, for instance the sentence: "The book is black." If I assert that this expression consisting of four words is a sentence, and further, that the first word is an article, the second a substantive, the third a verb, and the fourth an adjective, all these assertions are formal assertions. If, however, I assert that that sentence concerns a book, or that its last word designates a colour, then my assertions are *not formal*, because they have to do with the *meaning* of the words. A formal investigation of a language would appear to have very narrow limits. Actually, however, this is not the case, because, as we shall see later, many questions and considerations which are expressed in a non-formal way can be formulated in the formal mode.

Such a formal theory of language is, so far as mathematics is concerned, al-

From *Philosophy and Logical Syntax* (London: Kegan Paul, 1935). Reprinted by permission of the executors of C. K. Ogden's estate and the author.

ready known by the work of *Hilbert*. Hilbert has propounded a theory, which he calls metamathematics or theory of proof, and in which the formal method is applied. In this theory of Hilbert, mathematics is dealt with as a system of certain symbols to be operated according to certain rules, and the meaning of the symbols is nowhere spoken of, but only the various kinds of symbols and the formal operations to which they are subjected. Now mathematics is a special part of the whole of language, which includes many other and quite different branches. And the same formal method which Hilbert has applied in his metamathematics to the system of mathematics, we apply in our logical syntax to the whole language-system of science, or to any special part of it, or to any other language-system whatsoever.

2. Formation Rules

When we say that the objects of logical syntax are languages, the word "language" is to be understood as the *system of the rules* of speaking, as distinguished from the acts of speaking. Such a language-system consists of two kinds of rules, which we will call formation rules and transformation rules. The formation rules of a certain language-system S determine how *sentences* of the system S can be constructed out of the different kinds of symbols. One of the formation rules of the English language, for instance, determines that a series of four words, first an article, second a substantive,

third a verb of a certain class, and fourth an adjective, constitutes a sentence. Such a formation rule is obviously similar to grammatical rules, especially to the rules of grammatical syntax. But the usual rules of grammatical syntax are not always strictly formal; for instance, we may cite that rule of Latin grammar which determines that substantives designating women, countries, towns, or trees are of feminine gender. Such references to the meaning of the words are excluded in logical syntax as distinguished from grammatical syntax.

The totality of the formation rules of a language-system S is the same as the definition of the term "sentence of S." This definition can be stated in the following form: "A series of words is then, and only then, a sentence of the system S, if it has either this, that, or the other form." Now for a natural language, such as English, the formation rules can scarcely be given completely; they are too complicated. The logicians, as we know, have made language-systems—or at least frameworks for such—which are much simpler and also much more exact than the natural languages. Instead of words, they use symbols similar to the mathematical symbols. Take, for example, the most developed of these symbolic languages, that constructed by Whitehead and Russell in their work *Principia Mathematica*. Two of the principal formation rules of this language are as follows: (1) an expression consisting of a predicate (that is, one of the small Greek letters 'ϕ', 'ψ', etc.) and one or more individual variables (the small

Roman letters 'x', 'y', etc.) is a sentence; (2) an expression consisting of two sentences and one connecting sign ('v', '·', '⊃', '≡') between them is also a sentence.

3. Transformation Rules

Much more important than the formation rules are the transformation rules. They determine how given sentences may be transformed into others; in other words: how from given sentences we may *infer* others. Thus in the English language there is the rule, that from the two sentences:

	"all a are b"
and	"all b are c"
we may infer:	"all a are c."

Here only the framework of the sentences is given, not the sentences themselves. In order to make sentences we have to substitute three English substantives in the plural form for the three letters 'a,' 'b,' 'c.' To give an illustration, from the two sentences:

	"all eagles are birds"
and	"all birds are beasts"
we may infer:	"all eagles are beasts."

In the symbolic language of Whitehead and Russell we have the following rule: from two sentences of the form

	"A"
and	"A ⊃ B",
(where '⊃' is the implication-sign)
we may infer:	"B".

The totality of the transformation rules of a language-system S may be formulated as the definition of the term "*direct consequence* in S." Thus the transformation rules of the Principia Mathematica may be stated as follows: "In the system PM a sentence is to be called a direct consequence of a class of other sentences—called premises—then and only then, if one of the following conditions is fulfilled:

(1) the sentence has the form 'B' and the class of premises consists of 'A' and 'A ⊃ B';

(2) . . .;

(3) . . ."

It is to be noted that an axiom or primitive sentence of a language can also be stated in the form of a rule of inference, and therefore also in the form of a part of the definition of "direct consequence." The difference is only that in this case the class of premises is the null class (*i.e.* the class which has no members). Thus instead of ruling: "'p ⊃ · p v q' is to be a primitive sentence of the language S", we may say: "'p ⊃ · p v q' is to be a direct consequence of the null class of premises." If a class P of premises is connected with a certain sentence C by a chain of sentences in such a way that every sentence of this chain is a direct consequence of some sentences preceding in the chain, we call the sentence C a *consequence* of the class P of premises. This term "consequence" is, as we shall soon see, one of the most important terms of logical syntax.

We have seen that a language-system

is a system of rules of formation and transformation. According to this the logical syntax of a language-system S consists of two parts: the investigation or analysis of the formation rules of S, and that of the transformation rules of S. The first part is, as observed above, somewhat similar to grammar, the second part, to logic, especially to the logic of inference or deduction. It is generally supposed that grammar and logic have quite different characters, grammar being concerned with linguistic expressions, and logic with the *meaning* of thoughts or of propositions. But in opposition to this the development of modern logic has shown more and more clearly that the rules of inference *can* be expressed in a purely *formal* manner, that is, without any reference to meaning. Our task is merely to draw the consequence from this development and to construct the whole system of logic in a strictly formal way. We shall then have to do neither with thoughts as mental acts nor with their contents, but only with sentences, and with sentences not as vehicles of meaning or sense, but only as series of symbols, of written, spoken, or other signs. It will now be clear why we do not employ here the usual word "proposition." Sometimes it means, not a sentence, but what is expressed by a sentence, and very often it is used ambiguously. Therefore we prefer to use the word "sentence."

Between logic and grammar, or in other words, between the transformation rules and the formation rules, there is no fundamental difference. Transformation or inference depends only upon the formal character of the sentences, only upon their syntactical form. That is the reason why we apply the name "syntax" not, as is usually done in linguistics, to the formation rules alone, but to the system containing both kinds of rules together.

4. Syntactical Terms

The terms "sentence" and "direct consequence" are the two primitive terms of logical syntax—or "syntax," as we may briefly call it where there is no danger of misunderstanding. Every other term of syntax can be defined on the basis of these two terms. We will now give the definitions of several syntactical terms which are among the most important, especially, as we shall see later, in the application to philosophical questions.

Given any language-system, or set of formation rules and transformation rules, among the sentences of this language there will be true and false sentences. But we cannot define the terms "true" and "false" in syntax, because whether a given sentence is true or false will generally depend not only upon the syntactical form of the sentence, but also upon experience; that is to say, upon something extra-linguistic. It may be however that in certain cases a sentence is true or false only by reason of the rules of the language. Such sentences we will call *valid* and *contravalid* respectively.

Our definition of validity is as follows: a sentence is called *valid*, if it is a consequence of the null class of premises. Thus in the language of Russell the sentence 'p ∨ ~ p'—usually called the Principle of the Excluded Middle—is a valid sentence; and so likewise are all other sentences for which proofs are given in the *Principia Mathematica*. A proof in this work is a series of sentences of such kind that each sentence of the series is either a primitive sentence or inferred from preceding sentences of the series. Now a primitive sentence is a direct consequence of the null class of premises. Therefore a proof in the *Principia Mathematica* is a chain of direct consequences beginning with the null class of premises and ending with the sentence proved. This proved sentence is thus a consequence of the null class and therefore—according to our definition—valid.

Turning to the term "contravalid": a sentence 'A' of a certain language-system is called *contravalid* if every sentence of this system is a consequence of 'A.' Every sentence of the language of Principia Mathematica which can be disproved in this system (*e.g.* "p · ~p" and "~(p ≡ p)") is contravalid. Disproving a sentence 'A' consists in showing that a certain sentence 'B' as well as '~B', the negation of 'B', are consequences of 'A'. But from two mutually opposed sentences such as 'B' and '~B' any sentence whatever can be deduced. Therefore, if 'B' and '~B' are consequences of 'A', every sentence is a consequence of 'A', and 'A' is contravalid.

We will call a sentence *determinate* if it is either valid or contravalid. We will call a sentence *indeterminate* if it is neither valid nor contravalid. Thus the determinate sentences are those whose truth-value is determined by the rules of the language. In the language-system of Russell one may construct *in*determinate sentences by introducing *non*-logical constants. Suppose, for instance, 'a' and 'b' to be names of persons, 'S' to designate the relation of sonship, then 'aSb' (in words: "a is a son of b") is an indeterminate sentence, because its truth can obviously not be determined by the rules of the system of Russell.

5. L-Terms

In the symbolic languages of modern logic the transformation rules, to which, as has been pointed out above, the primitive sentences also belong, are usually chosen in such a way that they seem to be right for logical or mathematical reasons. But it would likewise be possible to state a language-system which, besides such logical rules, also contained extra-logical ones. Take for instance the system of *Principia Mathematica*. In its present form it contains only such primitive sentences and rules of inference as have a purely logical character. Transformation rules of this logical or mathematical character we will call *L-rules*. Now we could add to the system of *Principia Mathematica* transformation rules of an extra-logical character, for instance some physical laws as primitive sentences, as, for example, Newton's principles of mechanics, Maxwell's equations of electro-magnetics, the two principles of thermo-dynamics, and such like. In order to have a comprehensive name for the extra-logical transformation rules we will call them physical rules or *P-rules*.

Thus a transformation rule of a language is either an L-rule or a P-rule. The distinction of these two kinds of rules is very important. We have only given some rough indications of it, but it is possible to define this distinction in an exact and strictly formal way, that is, without any reference to the sense of the sentences. Omitting this exact definition for the sake of brevity, however, let us simply suppose that there is given a certain language-system, for instance the system of Principia Mathematica with the addition of some physical laws as primitive sentences, in which the given transformation rules are already divided into L-rules and P-rules.

We have called a sentence C a *consequence* of a class P of sentences— the premises—if there is a chain of sentences constructed according to the transformation rules connecting the class P with the sentence C. Suppose now that in a certain case only L-rules are applied; then we call C an *L-consequence* of P. If on the other hand C can be deduced from P only by applying also P-rules, in other words if C is a consequence, but not an L-consequence, of P, we call C a *P-consequence* of P. Let us take for example the following class P of two premises:

P_1: The body A has a mass of 3 grammes.

P_2: The body B has a mass of 6 grammes.

Then we can deduce from P the following two consequences among others:

C_1: The mass of B is double the mass of A.

C_2: If the same force is acting on A and on B, the acceleration of A will be double that of B.

For the deduction of C_1 we need only L-rules, that is rules of logic and arithmetic, while for the deduction of C_2 besides these we need P-rules, namely the laws of mechanics. Therefore C_1 is an L-consequence, but C_2, a P-consequence, of the class P of premises.

As we have defined corresponding to the term "consequence" an L-term and a P-term, we may in an analogous way define corresponding L-terms and P-terms for the other general terms already defined. Thus we will call a sentence which is true by reason of the L-rules alone, L-valid or *analytic*. The exact definition of this term is perfectly analogous to the definition of "valid": a sentence is called analytic if it is an L-consequence of the null class of premises. Similarly we will call a sentence which is false by reason of the L-rules alone, L-contravalid or *contradictory*. The formal definition is as follows: a sentence is called contradictory if every sentence of the language is an L-consequence of the same. A sentence is called *L-determinate* if it is either analytic or contradictory. If for the determination of the truth or falsehood of a given sentence the L-rules do not suffice, in other words if the sentence is not L-determinate, it is called L-indeterminate or *synthetic*.

The synthetic sentences are those which assert states of affairs. The terms "analytic" and "synthetic" have already been used in traditional philosophy; they are especially important in the philosophy of Kant; but up till now they have not been exactly defined.

In a language-system which contains only L-rules, for instance in the system of *Principia Mathematica*, each of the defined general terms agrees completely with the corresponding L-term. Thus every valid sentence (for instance 'p ∨ ∼p') is analytic, every contravalid sentence (for instance 'p · ∼p') is contradictory; indeterminate sentences, and only these (for instance 'aSb,' "a is a son of b"), are synthetic.

General terms	L-terms	P-terms
consequence valid	L-consequence	P-consequence
valid	(L-valid) *analytic*	P-valid
contravalid	(L-contravalid) *contradictory*	P-contravalid
determinate	L-determinate	
indeterminate	(L-indeterminate) *synthetic*	
content		
equipollent		
synonymous		

If a sentence is valid, but not analytic, we call it *P-valid*. If a sentence is contravalid, but not contradictory, we call it *P-contravalid*. The other P-terms are not so important.

The terms just defined give a classification of sentences which we may represent by the following scheme:

The totality of the sentences of the language is comprehended in the above diagram. Some of the sentences are either valid or contravalid, according to the transformation rules in general; the others are indeterminate. Among the valid sentences some are analytic, namely those which are valid on the

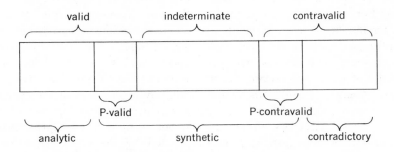

basis of the L-rules alone; the others are P-valid. In the same way some of the contravalid sentences are contra-

dictory, the others P-contravalid. The sentences which are neither analytic nor contradictory are synthetic. The three L-terms, namely "analytic," "synthetic" and "contradictory," are very often used in the logical analysis of any scientific theory. Later on we shall consider some examples.

6. Content

If we wish to characterize the purport of a given sentence, its contents, its assertive power, so to speak, we have to regard the class of those sentences which are consequences of the given sentence. Among these consequences we may leave aside the valid sentences, because they are consequences of every sentence. We define therefore as follows: the class of the non-valid consequences of a given sentence is called the *content* of this sentence.

The method which we are using here and which we call logical syntax is characterized by limiting itself to terms defined in a strictly formal way. One might perhaps be inclined to think that it is a defect of this formal method not to be able to deal with questions of *sense*. But in fact this method *is* able to do that, at least in a certain respect. Concerning a given series of signs, for instance a series of words in a word-language, there are *two* questions of sense. The first is, whether that series of words *has* a sense or not. If here "sense" means "theoretical sense," "assertive sense," then such a question can be answered within the range of *formal* investigation, namely by the help of the formal, syntactical term "sentence" defined by the formation rules of the language. Secondly

it may be asked *what* sense a given sentence has. This question can be answered by the help of the formal, syntactical term "content" as just defined.

The content of a sentence represents its sense, so far as the word "sense" is intended to designate something of a purely *logical* character. Sometimes by "sense" is meant the kind of thoughts and images that are connected with the given sentence. But in this case the question is a psychological one and has to be examined by the experimental method of psychology. In logical analysis we are not concerned with such questions. All questions of sense having an actually logical character can be dealt with by the formal method of syntax.

Sometimes two sentences of quite unlike wording nevertheless have the same sense, as asserting the same state. We will call such sentences *equipollent*. The formal definition is obvious: two sentences are called equipollent if they have the same content, in other words if they are consequences of each other. Similarly two expressions which are not themselves sentences, but occur in sentences, may have the same sense, the same meaning, in spite of a quite different wording. This relation, which we will designate by the term "*synonymous*," can also be defined in a formal manner: two expressions are called mutually synonymous, if the content of any sentence containing one of them is not changed if we replace that expression by the other. Thus, for instance, the expressions '5 + 2' and '4 + 3' are synonymous, because the content of a sentence will not be changed if we replace in this sentence '5 + 2' by '4 + 3' or *vice versa.*

7. Pseudo-Object-Sentences

The above are some examples of syntactical terms, all based upon the term "consequence" which is the principal term of syntax. The task of syntax is to state such definitions as those of the given examples and to analyze given sentences, proofs, theories, and the like, by the help of such syntactical terms. The results of such an analysis are then formulated as *syntactical sentences* having for instance the following form: "Such and such a sentence contained in a certain theory is synthetic, but a certain other sentence is merely analytic," or: "This particular word of such a theory is synonymous, but not L-synonymous, with that and that combination of words," and so on.

If sentences of this simple form containing well-defined syntactical terms are given, it is easy to see that they are syntactical sentences. But there are other sentences which *seem* to be of quite a different kind and nevertheless really are syntactical. This fact is very important, especially in dealing with philosophical sentences. I have already mentioned my opinion, which will be explained in the next chapter, that philosophical sentences belong to syntax. It must be confessed that this opinion seems not to agree with obvious facts, for philosophical sentences—even after the elimination of metaphysics—seem to concern not only the form of linguistic expressions but also, and per-

haps mainly, quite other objects, such as the structure of space and time, the relation between cause and effect, the relation between things and their qualities, the difference and the real relations between the physical and the psychical, the character of numbers and numerical functions, the necessity, contingency, possibility or impossibility of conditions, and the like. We shall have to show later that philosophical sentences of such kinds only *seem* by their deceptive appearance to concern the objects mentioned, but that they really concern linguistic forms. For the present, however, we shall not enter into the consideration of such philosophical sentences, but will try to explain in general under what conditions a sentence has such a deceptive form.

For this purpose we will distinguish three kinds of sentences. About *syntactical sentences* I have just spoken; they concern the form of linguistic expressions. With these are to be contrasted those sentences which concern not linguistic expressions but extra-linguistic objects; they may be called *real object-sentences.* There is also a third, an intermediate kind of sentence. Sentences of this kind are, so to speak, amphibious, being like object-sentences as to their form, but like syntactical sentences as to their contents. They may be called *pseudo-object-sentences.* Let us look at the examples tabulated [p. 54]. (1a) "The rose is red" is a real object-sentence which concerns the rose as object. (1c) "The word 'rose' is a thing-word" is a syntactical sentence; its object is not the thing rose

1. *Real object-sentences.* (Empirical Science)	2. *Pseudo-object-sentences.* *Material mode of speech.*	3. *Syntactical sentences.* *Formal mode of speech*
	(Philosophy)	
1a. The rose is red.	1b. The rose is a thing.	1c. The word 'rose' is a thing-word.
	Q_1 (a)	Q_2 ('a')
	2b. The first lecture treated of metaphysics.	2c. The first lecture contained the word 'metaphysics.'
3a. Mr. A visited Africa.	3b. This book treats of Africa.	3c. This book contains the word 'Africa.'
4a. The evening-star and the earth are about equal in size.	4b. The evening-star and the morning-star are identical.	4c. The words 'evening-star' and 'morning-star' are synonymous.

but the word 'rose,' a linguistic expression. Finally (1b) "The rose is a thing" is an example of a *pseudo*-object-sentence. This sentence has the same grammatical subject as the sentence 1a and thus appears, like it, to concern the thing, rose, but there is a fundamental difference between the two sentences. The sentence 1a is synthetic; it really asserts some quality of the rose. But from the sentence 1b we cannot learn any quality of the rose, neither as to its colour, nor size, nor form, nor anything else. This sentence 1b is analytic; we can ascertain its truth without observing any rose, by only considering to what syntactical kind the word 'rose' belongs, namely that it is a thing-word. Thus we see that the sentence 1b asserts the same as 1c, because always and only when a certain object is a thing is its designating word a thing-word.

We may call the quality of being a thing-designation a *parallel syntactical quality* to the quality of being a thing. The general definition will be: a syntactical quality Q_2 is called *parallel* to the quality Q_1 if it is the case that

when, and only when, an object possesses the quality Q_1 does a designation of this object possess the quality Q_2. And the criterion of a pseudo-object-sentence can now be stated as follows (if we regard only sentences of the simplest form): such a sentence attributes to an object (say a) a quality Q_1 to which a parallel syntactical quality Q_2 can be found. Such a sentence 'Q_1(a)' can then be translated into the syntactical sentence 'Q_2('a')' which attributes the quality Q_2 to a designation of that object.

This brings out more clearly the difference between the sentences 1a and 1b. While to the quality of being a thing there is a parallel syntactical quality, namely that of being a thing-designation, to the quality of being red there is *no* parallel syntactical quality —the designations of red things have no common characteristic syntactical quality. For instance, from the designation "my pencil" alone we are not able to decide whether it is a designation of a red thing or not; we should have to look at the designated object itself, namely my pencil. Therefore the sentence "The rose is red" is *not* a *pseudo*-object-sentence, but a *real* object sentence.

8. The Material and the Formal Modes of Speech

All sentences of empirical science, all sentences asserting facts, whether they are general or individual, are real object-sentences. All sentences of logical analysis on the other hand, and—as we shall see in the next chapter—of philosophy, belong to the second or to the third kind. Thus in our further considerations, these two kinds of sentences are chiefly considered. They differ, as we have seen, not so much in their purport or contents as in their formulation. In the mode of speech applied in pseudo-object-sentences there are used words which designate objects or matter, while the words used in syntactical sentences obviously concern form. For this reason we shall call the pseudo-object-sentences also sentences of the *material mode of speech*, while we shall assign the syntactical sentences to the *formal mode of speech*.

The difference between these two modes of speech may be made clearer by a few examples. Take the sentence: "The first chapter treats of metaphysics." This sentence belongs to the material mode; the corresponding sentence of the formal mode is: "The first chapter contains the word 'metaphysics'." To take a more striking example, suppose we have a geographical book about Africa and we make the

statement: "This book treats of Africa." Then this sentence (3b) belongs to the material mode; the corresponding sentence of the formal mode is: "This book contains the word 'Africa' " (3c). The sentence 3b is in its form analogous to the sentence "Mr. A visited Africa" (3a); but there is a principal difference between the two sentences. The sentence 3a asserts something about Africa. The sentence 3b—being analogous—*seems* to assert something about Africa, but really *does not*. It is not a quality of Africa to be treated of in that book, because one might know everything about Africa and nevertheless nothing about that book. It is only a quality of the word 'Africa' to be contained in the book. On the other hand, it is really a quality of Africa to be visited by Mr. A. Here we see the deceptive character of the material mode; the sentences of this mode seem to concern something which they in fact do not concern.

As an example of a somewhat different kind let us examine sentence 4b: "The evening-star and the morning-star are identical," or " . . . are the same thing." This sentence is in its form analogous to sentence 4a: "The evening-star and the earth are about equal in size"; but 4b is in fact a pseudo-object sentence which is to be translated into the following syntactical sentence (4c): "The words 'evening-star' and 'morning-star' are synonymous." The sentence 4a asserts that there is a certain relation between two certain objects. The sentence 4b *seems* to do the same, but it is obvious that it really does not. There cannot be *two* objects concerned here, because the two names designate only one object, namely a particular planet. But not even this object is concerned in the sentence 4b, for it is easy to see that it does not assert any quality whatever of that planet. It asserts only something about the two designations, namely that they designate the same thing, or, expressed in syntactical terms, that they are synonymous. Here we find again that deceptive character of the material mode as to the subject-matter of its sentences. Most of the sentences of *philosophy* deceive us in this way, because, as we shall see, most of them are formulated in the material mode of speech.

1.5   ORDINARY LANGUAGE

Gilbert Ryle

Philosophers' arguments have frequently turned on references to what we do and do not say or, more strongly, on what we can and cannot say. Such arguments are present in the writings of Plato and are common in those of Aristotle.

In recent years, some philosophers, having become feverishly exercised about the nature and methodology of their calling, have made much of arguments of this kind. Other philosophers have repudiated them. Their disputes on the merits of these arguments have not been edifying, since both sides have been apt to garble the question. I want to ungarble it.

From *The Philosophical Review*, LXII (1953). Reprinted by permission of the editors and the author.

"Ordinary"

There is one phrase which recurs in this dispute, the phrase "the use of ordinary language." It is often, quite erroneously, taken to be paraphrased by "ordinary linguistic usage." Some of the partisans assert that all philosophical questions are questions about the use of ordinary language, or that all philosophical questions are solved or are about to be solved by considering ordinary linguistic usage.

Postponing the examination of the notion of *linguistic usage*, I want to begin by contrasting the phrase "the use of ordinary language" with the similar-seeming but totally different phrase "the ordinary use of the expression '. . . .'" When people speak of the use of ordinary language, the word "ordinary" is in implicit or explicit contrast with "out-of-the-way," "esoteric," "technical," "poetical," "notational" or, sometimes, "archaic." "Ordinary" means "common," "current," "colloquial," "vernacular," "natural," "prosaic," "nonnotational," "on the tongue of Everyman," and is usually in contrast with dictions which only a few people know how to use, such as the technical terms or artificial symbolisms of lawyers, theologians, economists, philosophers, cartographers, mathematicians, symbolic logicians and players of Royal Tennis. There is no sharp boundary between "common" and "uncommon," "technical" and "untechnical" or "old-fashioned" and "current." Is "carburetor" a word in common use or only in rather uncommon use? Is "purl" on the lips of Everyman, or on the lips only of Everywoman? What of "manslaughter," "inflation," "quotient" and "off-side"? On the other hand, no one would hesitate on which side of this no-man's-land to locate "isotope" or "bread," "material implication" or "if," "transfinite cardinal" or "eleven," "ween" or "suppose." The edges of "ordinary" are blurred, but usually we are in no doubt whether a diction does or does not belong to ordinary parlance.

But in the other phrase, "the ordinary use of the expression '. . . ,'" "ordinary" is not in contrast with "esoteric," "archaic" or "specialist," etc. It is in contrast with "nonstock" or "nonstandard." We can contrast the stock or standard use of a fish-knife or sphygmomanometer with some non-regulation use of it. The stock use of a fish-knife is to cut up fish with; but it might be used for cutting seed potatoes

or as a heliograph. A sphygmomanometer might, for all I know, be used for checking tire pressures; but this is not its standard use. Whether an implement or instrument is a common or a specialist one, there remains the distinction between its stock use and nonstock uses of it. If a term is a highly technical term, or a nontechnical term, there remains the distinction between its stock use and nonstock uses of it. If a term is a highly technical term, most people will not know its stock use or, a fortiori, any nonstock uses of it either, if it has any. If it is a vernacular term, then nearly everyone will know its stock use, and most people will also know some nonstock uses of it, if it has any. There are lots of words, like "of," "have" and "object," which have no one stock use, any more than string, paper, brass and pocketknives have just one stock use. Lots of words have not got any nonstock uses. "Sixteen" has, I think, none; nor has "daffodil." Nor, maybe, have collar-studs. Nonstock uses of a word are, e.g., metaphorical, hyperbolical, poetical, stretched and deliberately restricted uses of it. Besides contrasting the stock use with certain nonstock uses, we often want to contrast the stock use of an expression with certain alleged, suggested, or recommended uses of it. This is a contrast not between the regular use and irregular uses, but between the regular use and what the regular use is alleged to be or what it is recommended that it should be.

When we speak of the ordinary or stock use of a word we need not be characterizing it in any further way, e.g., applauding or recommending it or giving it any testimonial. We need not be appealing to or basing anything on its stock-ness. The words "ordinary," "standard" and "stock" can serve merely to refer to a use, without describing it. They are philosophically colorless and can be easily dispensed with. When we speak of the regular night-watchman, we are merely indicating the night-watchman whom we know independently to be the one usually on the job; we are not yet giving any information about him or paying any tribute to his regularity. When we speak of the standard spelling of a word or the standard gauge of British railway tracks, we are not describing or recommending or countenancing this spelling or this gauge; we are giving a reference to it which we expect our hearers to get without hesitation. Sometimes, naturally, this indication does not work. Sometimes the stock use in one place is different from its stock use in another, as with "suspenders." Sometimes, its stock use at one period differs from its stock use at another, as with "nice." A dispute about which of two or five uses is the stock use is not a philosophical dispute about any one of those uses. It is therefore philosophically uninteresting, though settlement of it is sometimes requisite for communication between philosophers.

If I want to talk about a nonstock use of a word or fish-knife, it is not enough to try to refer to it by the phrase "the nonstock use of it," for there may be any number of such nonstock uses. To call my hearer's attention to a particular nonstock use of it, I have to give some description of it,

for example, to cite a special context in which the word is known to be used in a nonstock way.

This, though always possible, is not often necessary for the stock use of an expression, although in philosophical debates one is sometimes required to do it, since one's fellow-philosophers are at such pains to pretend that they cannot think what its stock use is—a difficulty which, of course, they forget all about when they are teaching children or foreigners how to use it, and when they are consulting dictionaries.

It is easy now to see that learning or teaching the ordinary or stock use of an expression need not be, though it may be, learning or teaching the use of an ordinary or vernacular expression, just as learning or teaching the standard use of an instrument need not be, though it can be, learning or teaching the use of a household utensil. Most words and instruments, whether out-of-the-way or common, have their stock uses and may or may not also have nonstock uses as well.

A philosopher who maintained that certain philosophical questions are questions about the ordinary or stock uses of certain expressions would not therefore be committing himself to the view that they are questions about the uses of ordinary or colloquial expressions. He could admit that the noun "infinitesimals" is not on the lips of Everyman and still maintain that Berkeley was examining the ordinary or stock use of "infinitesimals," namely the standard way, if not the only way, in which this word was employed by mathematical specialists. Berkeley was not examining the use of a colloquial word; he was examining the regular or standard use of a relatively esoteric word. We are not contradicting ourselves if we say that he was examining the ordinary use of an unordinary expression.

Clearly a lot of philosophical discussions are of this type. In the philosophy of law, biology, physics, mathematics, formal logic, theology, psychology and grammar, technical concepts have to be examined, and these concepts are what are expressed by more or less recherché dictions. Doubtless this examination embodies attempts to elucidate in untechnical terms the technical terms of this or that specialist theory, but this very attempt involves discussing the ordinary or stock uses of these technical terms.

Doubtless, too, study by philosophers of the stock uses of expressions which we all employ has a certain primacy over their study of the stock uses of expressions which only, e.g., scientific or legal specialists employ. These specialists explain to novices the stock uses of their terms of art partly by talking to them in nonesoteric terms; they do not also have to explain to them the stock uses of these nonesoteric terms. Untechnical terminology is, in this way, basic to technical terminologies. Hard cash has this sort of primacy over checks and bills of exchange—as well as the same inconveniences when large and complex transactions are afoot.

Doubtless, finally, some of the cardinal problems of philosophy are set by the existence of logical tangles not in this as opposed to that branch of specialist theory, but in the thought and

the discourse of everyone, specialists and nonspecialists alike. The concepts of *cause, evidence, knowledge, mistake, ought, can,* etc., are not the perquisites of any particular groups of people. We employ them before we begin to develop or follow specialist theories; and we could not follow or develop such theories unless we could already employ these concepts. They belong to the rudiments of all thinking, including specialist thinking. But it does not follow from this that all philosophical questions are questions about such rudimentary concepts. The architect must indeed be careful about the materials of his building; but it is not only about these that he must be careful.

"Use"

But now for a further point. The phrase "the ordinary (i.e., stock) use of the expression '. . .'" is often so spoken that the stress is made to fall on the word "expression" or else on the word "ordinary" and the word "use" is slurred over. The reverse ought to be the case. The operative word is *"use."*

Hume's question was not about the word "cause"; it was about the *use* of "cause." It was just as much about the *use* of "Ursache." For the use of "cause" is the same as the use of "Ursache," though "cause" is not the same word as "Ursache." Hume's question was not a question about a bit of the English language in any way in which it was not a question about a bit of the German language. The job done with the English word "cause" is not an

English job, or a continental job. What I do with my Nottingham-made boots —namely walk in them—is not Nottingham-made; but nor is it Leicester-made or Derby-made. The transactions I perform with a sixpenny-bit have neither milled nor unmilled edges; they have no edges at all. We might discuss what I can and cannot do with a sixpenny-bit, namely what I can and cannot buy with it, what change I should and should not give or take for it, and so on; but such a discussion would not be a discussion about the date, ingredients, shape, color or provenance of the coin. It is a discussion about the purchasing power of this coin, or of any other coin of the same value, and not about *this coin.* It is not a numismatic discussion, but a commercial or financial discussion. Putting the stress on the word "use" helps to bring out the important fact that the inquiry is an inquiry not into the other features or properties of the word or coin or pair of boots, but only into what is done with it, or with anything else with which we do the same thing. That is why it is so misleading to classify philosophical questions as linguistic questions—or as nonlinguistic questions.

It is, I think, only in fairly recent years that philosophers have picked up the trick of talking about the use of expressions, and even made a virtue of so talking. Our forefathers, at one time, talked instead of the *concepts* or *ideas* corresponding to expressions. This was in many ways a very convenient idiom, and one which in most situations we do well to retain. It had the drawback, though, that it encour-

aged people to start Platonic or Lockean hares about the status and provenance of these concepts or ideas. The impression was given that a philosopher who wanted to discuss, say, the concept of *cause* or *infinitesimal* or *remorse* was under some obligation to start by deciding whether concepts have a supramundane, or only a psychological existence; whether they are transcendent intuitables or only private introspectibles.

Later on, when philosophers were in revolt against psychologism in logic, there was a vogue for another idiom, the idiom of talking about the *meanings* of expressions, and the phrase "the concept of cause" was replaced by the phrase "the meaning of the word 'cause' or of any other with the same meaning." This new idiom was also subject to anti-Platonic and anti-Lockean cavils; but its biggest drawback was a different one. Philosophers and logicians were at that time the victims of a special and erroneous theory about meaning. They construed the verb "to mean" as standing for a relation between an expression and some other entity. The meaning of an expression was taken to be an entity which had that expression for its name. So studying the meaning of the phrase "the solar system" was supposed or half-supposed to be the same thing as studying the solar system. It was partly in reaction against this erroneous view that philosophers came to prefer the idiom "the use of the expressions '. . . caused . . .' and '. . . the solar system.' " We are accustomed to talking of the use of safety pins, banisters, table-knives, badges and gestures; and this familiar idiom neither connotes nor seems to connote any queer relations to any queer entities. It draws our attention to the teachable procedures and techniques of handling or employing things, without suggesting unwanted correlates. Learning how to manage a canoe-paddle, a traveler's check or a postage stamp is not being introduced to an extra entity. Nor is learning how to manage the words "if," "ought" and "limit."

There is another merit in this idiom. Where we can speak of managing, handling and employing we can speak of mismanaging, mishandling and mis-employing. There are rules to keep or break, codes to observe or flout. Learning to use expressions, like learning to use coins, stamps, checks and hockey-sticks, involves learning to do certain things with them and not others; when to do certain things with them, and when not to do them. Among the things that we learn in the process of learning to use linguistic expressions are what we may vaguely call "rules of logic"; for example, that though Mother and Father can both be tall, they cannot both be taller than one another; or that though uncles can be rich or poor, fat or thin, they cannot be male or female, but only male. Where it would sound implausible to say that concepts or ideas or meanings might be meaningless or absurd, there is no such implausibility in asserting that someone might use a certain expression absurdly. An attempted or suggested way of operating with an expression may be logically illegitimate or impossible, but a universal or a state of consciousness or a meaning cannot be logically legitimate or illegitimate.

"Use" and "Utility"

On the other hand there are inconveniences in talking much of the *uses* of expressions. People are liable to construe "use" in one of the ways which English certainly does permit, namely as a synonym of "utility" or "usefulness." They then suppose that to discuss the use of an expression is to discuss what it is useful for or how useful it is. Sometimes such considerations are philosophically profitable. But it is easy to see that discussing the use (versus uselessness) of something is quite different from discussing the use (versus misuse) of it, i.e., the way, method or manner of using it. The female driver may learn what is the utility of a spark plug, but learning this is not learning how to operate with a spark plug. She does not have or lack skills or competences with spark plugs, as she does with steering wheels, coins, words and knives. Her spark plugs manage themselves; or, rather, they are not managed at all. They just function automatically, until they cease to function. They are useful, even indispensable to her. But she does not manage or mismanage them.

Conversely, a person who has learned how to whistle tunes may not find the whistling of tunes at all useful or even pleasant to others or to himself. He manages, or sometimes mismanages his lips, tongue and breath; and, more indirectly, manages or mismanages the notes he produces. He has got the trick of it; he can show us and perhaps even tell us how the trick is performed. But it is a useless trick. The question "How do you use your breath or your lips in whistling?" has a positive and complicated answer. "The question "What is the use, or utility, of whistling?" has a negative and simple one. The former is a request for the details of a technique; the latter is not. Questions about the use of an expression are often, though not always, questions about the way to operate with it; not questions about what the employer of it needs it for. They are How-questions, not What-for-questions. This latter sort of question can be asked, but it is seldom necessary to ask it, since the answer is usually obvious. In a foreign country, I do not ask what a centime or a peseta is for; what I do ask is how many of them I have to give for a certain article, or how many of them I am to expect to get in exchange for a half-crown. I want to know what its purchasing power is; not that it is for making purchases with.

"Use" and "Usage"

Much more insidious than this confusion between the way of operating with something and its usefulness is the confusion between a "use," i.e., a way of operating with something, and a "usage." Lots of philosophers, whose dominant good resolution is to discern logico-linguistic differences, talk without qualms as if "use" and "usage" were synonyms. This is just a howler; for which there is little excuse except that in the archaic phrase "use and wont," "use" could, perhaps, be replaced by "usage"; that "used to" does

mean "accustomed to"; and that to be hardly used is to suffer hard usage.

A usage is a custom, practice, fashion or vogue. It can be local or widespread, obsolete or current, rural or urban, vulgar or academic. There cannot be a misusage any more than there can be a miscustom or a misvogue. The methods of discovering linguistic usages are the methods of philologists.

By contrast, a way of operating with a razor-blade, a word, a traveler's check, or a canoe-paddle is a technique, knack, or method. Learning it is learning how to do the thing; it is not finding out sociological generalities, not even sociological generalities about other people who do similar or different things with razor-blades, words, travelers' checks, or canoe-paddles. Robinson Crusoe might find out for himself how to make and how to throw boomerangs; but this discovery would tell him nothing about those Australian aborigines who do in fact make and use them in the same way. The description of a conjuring-trick is not the description of all the conjurors who perform or have performed that trick. On the contrary, in order to describe the possessors of the trick, we should have already to be able to give some sort of description of the trick itself. Mrs. Beeton tells us how to make omelets; but she gives us no information about Parisian chefs. Baedeker might tell us about Parisian chefs, and tell us which of them make omelets; but if he wanted to tell us how they make omelets, he would have to describe their techniques in the way that Mrs. Beeton describes the technique of making omelets. Descriptions of usages presuppose descriptions of uses, i.e., ways or techniques of doing the thing, the more or less widely prevailing practice of doing which constitutes the usage.

There is an important difference between the employment of boomerangs, bows and arrows, and canoe-paddles on the one hand and the employment of tennis rackets, tug-of-war ropes, coins, stamps and words on the other hand. The latter are instruments of interpersonal, i.e., concerted or competitive actions. Robinson Crusoe might play some games of patience; but he could not play tennis or cricket. So a person who learns to use a tennis racket, a stroke-side oar, a coin or a word is inevitably in a position to notice other people using these things. He cannot master the tricks of such interpersonal transactions without at the same time finding out facts about some other people's employment and misemployment of them; and normally he will learn a good many of the tricks from noticing other people employing them. Even so, learning the knacks is not and does not require making a sociological study. A child may learn in the home and the village shop how to use pennies, shillings and pound notes; and his mastery of these slightly complex knacks is not improved by hearing how many people in other places and years have managed and now manage or mismanage their pennies, shillings and pound notes. Perfectly mastering a use is not getting to know everything, or even much, about a usage, even when mastering that use does causally involve finding out a bit about a few other people's practices. We were taught in the nursery how to handle a lot of words; but we were not being taught any historical or sociological generalities about employers of these words. That came later, if it came at all.

Before passing on we should notice one big difference between using canoe-paddles or tennis rackets on the one hand and using postage stamps, safety pins, coins and words on the other. Tennis rackets are wielded with greater or less skill; even the tennis champion studies to improve. But, with some unimportant reservations, it is true to say that coins, checks, stamps, separate words, buttons and shoelaces offer no scope for talent. Either a person knows or he does not know how to use and how not to misuse them. Of course literary composition and argumentation can be more or less skillful; but the essayist or lawyer does not know the meaning of "rabbit" or "and" better than Everyman. There is no room here for "better." Similarly, the champion chess player maneuvers more skillfully than the amateur; but he does not know the permitted moves of the pieces better. They both know them perfectly, or rather they just know them.

Certainly, the cultured chess player may describe the permitted moves better than does the uncultured chess player. But he does not make these moves any better. I give change for a half-crown no better than you do. We both just give the correct change. Yet I may describe such transactions more effectively than you can describe them. Knowing how to operate is not knowing how to tell how to operate. This point becomes important when we are discussing, say, the stock way (supposing there is one) of employing the word "cause." The doctor knows how to make this use of it as well as anyone, but he may not be able to answer any of the philosopher's inquiries about this way of using it.

In order to avoid these two big confusions, the confusion of "use" with "usefulness" and the confusion of "use" with "usage," I try nowadays to use, *inter alia*, "employ" and "employment" instead of the verb and noun "use." So I say this. Philosophers often have to try to describe the stock (or, more rarely, some nonstock) manner or way of employing an expression. Sometimes such an expression belongs to the vernacular; sometimes to some technical vocabulary; sometimes it is betwixt and between. Describing the mode of employment of an expression does not require and is not usually helped by information about the prevalence or unprevalence of this way of employing it. For the philosopher, like other folk, has long since learned how to employ or handle it, and what he is trying to describe is what he himself has learned.

Techniques are not vogues—but they may have vogues. Some of them must have vogues or be current in some other way. For it is no accident that ways of employing words, as of employing coins, stamps and chessmen, *tend* to be identical through a whole community and over a long stretch of time. We want to understand and be understood; and we learn our native tongue from our elders. Even without the pressure of legislation and dictionaries, our vocabularies tend towards uniformity. Fads and idiosyncrasies in

these matters impair communication. Fads and idiosyncrasies in matters of postage stamps, coins and the moves of chessmen are ruled out by explicit legislation, and partly analogous conformities are imposed upon many technical vocabularies by such things as drill-manuals and textbooks. Notoriously these tendencies towards uniformity have their exceptions. However, as there naturally do exist many pretty widespread and pretty long-enduring vocabulary usages, it is sometimes condonable for a philosopher to remind his readers of a mode of employing an expression by alluding to "what everyone says" or "what no one says." The reader considers the mode of employment that he has long since learned and feels strengthened, when told that big battalions are on his side. In fact, of course, this appeal to prevalence is philosophically pointless, besides being philologically risky. What is wanted is, perhaps, the extraction of the logical rules implicitly governing a concept, i.e., a way of operating with an expression (or any other expression that does the same work). It is probable that the use of this expression, to perform this job, is widely current; but whether it is so or not is of no philosophical interest. Job-analysis is not Mass Observation. Nor is it helped by Mass Observation. But Mass Observation sometimes needs the aid of job-analysis.

Before terminating this discussion of the use of the expression "the use of the expression '. . .,' " I want to draw attention to an interesting point. We can ask whether a person knows how to use and how not to misuse a certain word. But we cannot ask whether he knows how to use a certain *sentence*. When a block of words has congealed into a phrase we can ask whether he knows how to use the phrase. But when a sequence of words has not yet congealed into a phrase, while we can ask whether he knows how to use its ingredient words, we cannot easily ask whether he knows how to use that sequence. Why can we not even ask whether he knows how to use a certain sentence? For we talk about the meanings of sentences, seemingly just as we talk of the meanings of the words in it; so, if knowing the meaning of a word is knowing how to use it, we might have expected that knowing the meaning of a sentence was knowing how to use the sentence. Yet this glaringly does not go.

A cook uses salt, sugar, flour, beans and bacon in making a pie. She uses, and perhaps misuses, the ingredients. But she does not, in this way, use the pie. Her pie is not an ingredient. In a somewhat different way, the cook uses, and perhaps misuses, a rolling-pin, a fork, a frying-pan and an oven. These are the utensils with which she makes her pie. But the pie is not another utensil. The pie is (well or badly) composed out of the ingredients, by means of the utensils. It is what she used them for; but it cannot be listed in either class of them. Somewhat, but only somewhat, similarly a sentence is (well or badly) constructed out of words. It is what the speaker or writer uses them for. He composes it out of them. His sentence is not itself something which, in this way, he either uses

or misuses, either uses or does not use. His composition is not a component of his composition. We can tell a person to say something (e.g., ask a question, give a command or narrate an anecdote), using a specified word or phrase; and he will know what he is being told to do. But if we just tell him to pronounce or write down, by itself, that specified word or phrase, he will see the difference between this order and the other one. For he is not now being told to use, i.e., *incorporate* the word or phrase, but only to pronounce it or write it down. Sentences are things that we say. Words and phrases are what we say things *with*.

There can be dictionaries of words and dictionaries of phrases. But there cannot be dictionaries of sentences. This is not because such dictionaries would have to be infinitely and therefore impracticably long. On the contrary, it is because they could not even begin. Words and phrases are there, in the bin, for people to avail themselves of when they want to say things. But the sayings of these things are not some more things which are there in the bin for people to avail themselves of, when they want to say these things. This fact that words and phrases can, while sentences cannot, be misused, since sentences cannot be, in this way, used at all, is quite consistent with the important fact that sentences can be well or ill constructed. We can say things awkwardly or ungrammatically and we can say things which are grammatically proper, but do not make sense.

It follows that there are some radical differences between what is meant by "the meaning of a word or phrase" and what is meant by "the meaning of a sentence." Understanding a word or phrase is knowing how to use it, i.e., make it perform its role in a wide range of sentences. But understanding a sentence is not knowing how to make it perform its role. The play has not got a role.

We are tempted to suppose that the question "How are word-meanings related to sentence-meanings?" is a tricky but genuine question, a question, perhaps, rather like "How is the purchasing power of my shilling related to the purchasing power of the contents of my pay-envelope?" But this model puts things awry from the start. If I know the meaning of a word or phrase I know something like a body of unwritten rules, or something like an unwritten code or general recipe. I have learned to use the word correctly in an unlimited variety of different settings. What I know is, in this respect, somewhat like what I know when I know how to use a knight or a pawn at chess. I have learned to put it to its work anywhen and anywhere, if there is work for it to do. But the idea of putting a sentence to its work anywhen and anywhere is fantastic. It has not got a role which it can perform again and again in different plays. It has not got a role at all, any more than a play has a role. Knowing what it means is not knowing anything like a code or a body of rules, though it requires knowing the codes or rules governing the use of the words or phrases that make it up. There are general rules and recipes for constructing sentences of certain kinds; but not general rules or recipes for constructing the particular

sentence "Today is Monday." Knowing the meaning of "Today is Monday" is not knowing general rules, codes or recipes governing the use of this sentence, since there is no such thing as the utilization or, therefore, the reutilization of this sentence. I expect that this ties up with the fact that sentences and clauses make sense or make no sense, where words neither do nor do not make sense, but only have meanings; and that pretense-sentences can be absurd or nonsensical, where pretense-words are neither absurd nor nonsensical, but only meaningless. I can say stupid things, but words can be neither stupid nor not stupid.

Philosophy and Ordinary Language

The vogue of the phrase "the use of ordinary language" seems to suggest to some people the idea that there exists a philosophical doctrine according to which (1) all philosophical inquiries are concerned with vernacular, as opposed to more or less technical, academic or esoteric terms; and (2) in consequence, all philosophical discussions ought themselves to be couched entirely in vernacular dictions. The inference is fallacious, though its conclusion has some truth in it. Even if it were true, which it is not, that all philosophical problems are concerned with nontechnical concepts, i.e., with the mode of employment of vernacular expressions, it would not follow from this (false) premise that the discussions of these problems must or had better be in jurymen's English, French or German.

From the fact that a philologist studies those English words which stem from Celtic roots, it does not follow that he must or had better say what he has to say about them in words of Celtic origin. From the fact that a psychologist is discussing the psychology of witticisms, it does not follow that he ought to write wittily all or any of the time. Clearly he ought not to write wittily most of the time.

Most philosophers have in fact employed a good number of the technical terms of past or contemporary logical theory. We may sometimes wish that they had taken a few more pinches of salt, but we do not reproach them for availing themselves of these technical expedients; we should have deplored their longwindedness if they had tried to do without them.

But enslavement to jargon, whether inherited or invented, is, certainly, a bad quality in any writer, whether he be a philosopher or not. It curtails the number of people who can understand and criticize his writings; so it tends to make his own thinking run in a private groove. The use of avoidable jargons is bad literary manners and bad pedagogic policy, as well as being detrimental to the thinker's own wits.

But this is not peculiar to philosophy. Bureaucrats, judges, theologians, literary critics, bankers and, perhaps above all, psychologists and sociologists would all be well advised to try very hard to write in plain and blunt words. Nonetheless, Hobbes who had this virtue of writing plainly and bluntly was a lesser philosopher than Kant who lacked it; and Plato's later dialogues, though harder to translate, have powers which his early dialogues are without. Nor is the simplicity of his diction in Mill's account of mathematics enough to make us prefer it to the account given by Frege, whose diction is more esoteric.

In short, there is no a priori or peculiar obligation laid upon philosophers to refrain from talking esoterically; but there is a general obligation upon all thinkers and writers to try to think and write both as powerfully and as plainly as possible. But plainness of diction and power of thought can vary independently, though it is not common for them to do so.

Incidentally it would be silly to require the language of professional journals to be as exoteric as the language of books. Colleagues can be expected to use and understand one another's terms of art. But books are not written only for colleagues. The judge should not address the jury in the language in which he may address his brother judges. Sometimes, but only sometimes, he may be well advised to address even his brother judges, and himself, in the language in which he should address the jury. It all depends on whether his technical terms are proving to be a help or a hindrance. They are likely to be a hindrance when they are legacies from a period in which today's questions were not even envisaged. This is what justifies the regular and salutary rebellions of philosophers against the philosophical jargons of their fathers.

There is another reason why philosophers ought sometimes to eschew other people's technical terms. Even when a philosopher is interesting himself in some of the cardinal concepts of, say, physical theory, he is usually partly concerned to state the logical crossbearings between the concepts of this theory and the concepts of mathematical, theological, biological or psychological theory. Very often his radical puzzle is that of determining these crossbearings. When trying to solve puzzles of this sort, he cannot naïvely employ the dictions of either theory. He has to stand back from both theories, and discuss the concepts of both in terms which are proprietary to neither. He may coin neutral dictions of his own, but for ease of understanding he may prefer the dictions of Everyman. These have this required neutrality, even if they lack that semi-codification which disciplines the terms of art of professionalized thought. Barter-terms are not as well regimented as the terms of the counting-house; but when we have to determine rates of exchange between different currencies, it is to barter-terms that we may have to turn. Intertheory negotiations can be and may have to be conducted in pre-theory dictions.

So far I have, I hope, been mollifying rather than provoking. I now want to say two philosophically contentious things.

1. There is a special reason why philosophers, unlike other professionals and specialists, are constantly jettisoning in toto all the technical terms of their own predecessors (save some of the technical terms of formal logic); i.e., why the jargon words of epistemology, ethics, aesthetics, etc., seem to be half-hardy annuals rather than hardy perennials. The reason is this. The experts who use the technical terms of bridge, law, chemistry and plumbing learn to employ these terms partly from official instructions but largely by directly engaging in the special techniques and by directly dealing with the special materials or objects of their specialism. They familiarize themselves with the harness by having to drive their (to us unfamiliar) horses.

But the terms of art of philosophy itself (save for those of formal logic) are not like this. There is no peculiar field of knowledge or adeptness in which philosophers ex officio make themselves the experts—except of course the business of philosophizing itself. We know by what special sorts of work mastery is acquired of the concepts of *finesse, tort, sulfanilamide* and *valve-seating*. But by what corresponding special sorts of work do philosophers get their supposed corresponding mastery of the concepts of *Cognition, Sensation, Secondary Qualities*, and *Essences*? What exercises and predicaments have forced them to learn just how to use and how not to misuse these terms?

Philosophers' arguments which turn on these terms are apt, sooner or later, to start to rotate idly. There is nothing to make them point north rather than nor'-nor'-east. The bridge player cannot play fast and loose with the concepts of *finesse* and *revoke*. If he tries to make them work in a way palatable to him, they jib. The unofficial terms of everyday discourse are like the official terms of specialisms in this important respect. They too jib, if maltreated. It is no more possible to say that someone knows something to be the case which is not so than it is possible to say that the player of the first card in a game of bridge has revoked. We have had to learn in the hard school of daily life how to deploy the verb "know"; and we have had to learn at the bridge table how to deploy the verb "revoke." There is no such hard school in which to learn how to deploy the verbs "cognize" and "sense." These go through what motions we care to require of them, which means that they have acquired no discipline of their own at all. So the philosophical arguments, which are supposed to deploy these units, win and lose no fights, since these units have no fight in them. Hence, the appeal from philosophical jargon to the expressions which we have all had to learn to use properly (as the chess player has had to learn the moves of his pieces) is often one well worth making; where a corresponding appeal to the vocabulary of Everyman from the official parlance of a science, of a game or of law would often, not always, be ridiculous. One contrast of "ordinary" (in the phrase "ordinary language") is with "philosophers' jargon."

2. But now for quite a different point and one of considerable contemporary importance. The appeal to what we do and do not say, or can and cannot say, is often stoutly resisted by the protagonists of one special doctrine, and stoutly pressed by its antagonists. This doctrine is the doctrine that philosophical disputes can and should be settled by formalizing the warring theses. A theory is formalized when it is translated out of the natural language (untechnical, technical or semi-technical),

in which it was originally excogitated, into a deliberately constructed notation, the notation, perhaps, of *Principia Mathematica.* The logic of a theoretical position can, it is claimed, be regularized by stretching its nonformal concepts between the topic-neutral logical constants whose conduct in inferences is regulated by set drills. Formalization will replace logical perplexities by logical problems amenable to known and teachable procedures of calculation. Thus one contrast of "ordinary" (in the phrase "ordinary language") is with "notational."

Of those to whom this, the formalizer's dream, appears a mere dream (I am one of them), some maintain that the logic of everyday statements and even the logic of the statements of scientists, lawyers, historians and bridge players cannot in principle be adequately represented by the formulas of formal logic. The so-called logical constants do indeed have, partly by deliberate prescription, their scheduled logical powers; but the nonformal expressions both of everyday discourse and of technical discourse have their own unscheduled logical powers, and these are not reducible without remainder to those of the carefully wired marionettes of formal logic. The title of a novel by A. E. W. Mason, "They Wouldn't Be Chessmen," applies well to both the technical and the untechnical expressions of professional and daily life. This is not to say that the examination of the logical behavior of the terms of nonnotational discourse is not assisted by studies in formal logic. Of course it is. So may chess playing assist generals, though waging campaigns cannot be replaced by playing games of chess.

I do not want here to thrash out this important issue. I want only to show that resistance to one sort of appeal to ordinary language ought to involve championing the program of formalization. "Back to ordinary language" can be (but often is not) the slogan of those who have awakened from the formalizer's dream. This slogan, so used, should be repudiated only by those who hope to replace philosophizing by reckoning.

Verdict

Well, then, has philosophy got something to do with the use of expressions or hasn't it? To ask this is simply to ask whether conceptual discussions, i.e., discussions about the concept of, say, *voluntariness, infinitesimals, number* or *cause*, come under the heading of philosophical discussions. Of course they do. They always have done, and they have not stopped doing so now.

Whether we gain more than we lose by sedulously advertising the fact that what we are investigating is the stock way of operating with, say, the word "cause," depends a good deal on the context of the discussions and the intellectual habits of the people with whom we are discussing it. It is certainly a longwinded way of announcing what we are doing; and inverted commas are certainly vexatious to the eye. But, more important than these nuisances, preoccupation with questions about methods tends to distract us from prosecuting the methods themselves.

We run, as a rule, worse, not better, if we think a lot about our feet. So let us, at least on alternate days, speak instead of investigating the concept of *causation*. Or, better still, let us, on those days, not speak of it at all but just do it.

But the more longwinded idiom has some big compensating advantages. If we are inquiring into problems of perception, i.e., discussing questions about the concepts of seeing, hearing and smelling, we may be taken to be tackling the questions of opticians, neurophysiologists or psychologists, and even fall into this mistake ourselves. It is then salutary to keep on reminding ourselves and one another that what we are after is accounts of how certain words work, namely words like "see," "look," "overlook," "blind," "visualize" and lots of other affiliated expressions.

One last point. I have talked in general terms about learning and describing the modes of employment of expressions. But there are many different dimensions of these modes, only some of which are of interest to philosophers. Differences of stylistic elegance, rhetorical persuasiveness, and social propriety need to be considered, but not, save *per accidens*, by philosophers. Churchill would have made a rhetorical blunder if he had said, instead of "We shall fight them on the beaches . . . ," "We shall fight them on the sands. . . ." "Sands" would have raised thoughts of children's holidays at Skegness. But this kind of misemployment of "sands" is not the kind of mishandling that interests us. We are interested in the informal logic of the employment of expressions, the nature of the logical howlers that people do or might commit if they strung their words together in certain ways, or, more positively, in the logical force that expressions have as components of theories and as pivots of concrete arguments. That is why, in our discussions, we argue *with* expressions and *about* those expressions in one and the same breath. We are trying to register what we are exhibiting; to codify the very logical codes which we are then and there observing.

WHAT'S WRONG WITH THE PHILOSOPHY OF LANGUAGE?[1]

1.6

Jerrold Katz and Jerry Fodor

I

Among the paradoxes of contemporary philosophy, the following is perhaps the most striking. Though philosophy for the last several decades has been justly acclaimed (or stigmatized) as linguistic in its methods and goals, during this same period philosophers have been utterly unsuccessful in attempts to provide an explicit theory of the language they investigate or an explicit statement of their methods of investigation. At a time when linguistic considerations are at the forefront of discussion in every major area of philosophy, the philosophy of language languishes. There is not even so much as rudimentary agreement upon the considerations relevant to the construction of a satisfactory theory of language. Instead, one finds a welter of specific disagreements on every ques-

From *Inquiry*, V (1962), with omissions. Reprinted by permission of the authors and of Universitetsforlaget, Oslo, publishers of *Inquiry*.

[1] This work was supported in part by the U.S. Army Signal Corps, the Air Force Office of Scientific Research, and the Office of Naval Research; and in part by the National Science Foundation (Grant G–13903).

This paper was first presented at the Research Laboratory of Electronics' Linguistics Seminar, Massachusetts Institute of Technology, and subsequently at a Philosophy Colloquium at Princeton University.

The authors wish to express their thanks to Professors Noam Chomsky and Hilary Putnam for their criticism and encouragement. We also wish to thank Mr. Jay Keyser for his editorial assistance.

tion, in every quarter. There are Witt-
gensteinians (early and late), Ryleans,
Austinians, Carnapians, Russellians,
Quineans, Fregeans, Tarskians, Skin-
nerians, Cassirerians, and Naessians to
mention only some of the more prominent examples. And even within these
camps one finds dissension.

Despite this profusion of doctrines,
however, certain shared viewpoints and
techniques are discernible. If we consider not only what philosophers say
when they are talking about language,
but also the account of language implicit in their methods and in the
assumptions of their arguments, we find
that one of two mutually incompatible
views of the nature of language is
usually involved. Either it is supposed
that the structure of a natural language
is illuminatingly like that of some artificial language, such as a logistic system, or it is supposed that significant
questions of meaning are fruitfully explored in terms of analyses of the use
of individual words and expressions.
Depending upon which of these views
one happens to adopt, one finds oneself
either (roughly) in the tradition of
positivism or (roughly) in the tradition of ordinary-language philosophy.

It should be said explicitly, however,
that some philosophers in each of these
traditions have claimed either that a
theory of natural language cannot be
constructed or that their aim in doing
philosophy is not to construct such a
theory. The former claim—that a theory of natural language is impossible—
is usually supported by reference to
the supposed complexity, fecundity, and
lack of systematicity of natural lan-

guages. The latter claim—that the construction of a theory of natural language is not the philosopher's concern
—is defended on the grounds that the
information philosophers require about
language to settle their disputes is available without such a theory. Both of
these claims come under scrutiny in
this paper. Here we need only defend
ourselves against the charge that, in
criticizing positivism and ordinary-
language philosophy because they have
not offered an adequate theory of language, we are condemning them for
failing to do something they have
never attempted.

With the philosopher who says simply that he is not interested in general
questions about natural languages, and
whose philosophical practice is consistent with what he says, we have no
quarrel. *De gustibus non est disputan-
dum.* We shall not be referring to such
a philosopher when we mention either
positivism or ordinary-language philosophy. On the other hand, it is clear
that there are philosophers in both
schools who have sought to provide, if
not a theory of language, then at least
the general principles underlying such
a theory. It is still clearer that the
analytic techniques employed by philosophers in each of these schools
often depend upon assumptions about
language. Even a cursory glance at the
writings of ordinary-language philosophers suffices to assure the reader that
they have been concerned that their
assumptions should at least be compatible with linguistic fact. More than
a cursory glance at the writings of
positivists is required to establish the

extent to which they intend their constructions to accord with linguistic fact. But it is easy to show that they are aware that their formalizations must be responsible to some of the facts of natural language if they are to claim that such formalizations provide revealing models of a natural language. One way to show this is by pointing out that the motivation for proposing the emotive theory of meaning for non-assertive utterances lay in part in the positivist's sensitivity to the need for a characterization of those areas of a natural language not covered by formal logistic systems. Another is to point out places where positivists have themselves explicitly constructed formalizations to deal with philosophical problems arising in natural language, e.g. Carnap's proposal of a 'logical syntax' to supplement grammatical syntax in the formulation of a principle of cognitive significance for sentences of a natural language.[2]

II

That positivism and ordinary-language philosophy are incompatible in practice, if not in principle, can be seen from the tendency of positivistic philosophers to emphasize the need for rational reconstruction or reformulation at precisely those points where

ordinary-language philosophers are most inclined to insist upon the facts of usage.[3] This incompatibility goes still deeper. An artificial language is fully specified by its formation rules, transformation rules, meaning postulates, and reference rules (which provide designata for its expressions and truth conditions for its sentences). Thus, a theory of language modelled on such a system has deeply ingrained the view that a language functions primarily in the statement of truths. But it has been the recurrent theme of ordinary-language philosophy that one misconceives the nature of language when one treats of only one of its functions, such as asserting, thereby failing to appreciate or explain its truly essential feature—the indefinitely large variety of uses to which it can be put.

The incompatibility between positivism and ordinary-language philosophy appears again at another level of analysis. Inherent in the very motivation for constructing artificial languages is the desire to eliminate ambiguity, vague-

---

[2] Carnap, R. 'The Elimination of Metaphysics through the Logical Analysis of Language', republished in *Logical Positivism* (A. J. Ayer, ed.) The Free Press, Glencoe, Illinois, 1959; Section 4.

[3] Among the dangers one encounters when discussing viewpoints in philosophy, rather than the work of particular philosophers, is the recurrent possibility of oversimplification. The present claim is a case in point. It has occasionally been the case that a philosopher in one of these traditions has seen the limitations of his own viewpoint when examined in the light of the other. Thus, Austin in 'A Plea for Excuses' goes on record as, in principle, acknowledging the occasional necessity 'to be brutal with, to torture, to fake and to override, ordinary language'. But, by and large, members of both traditions have taken a more doctrinaire approach, insisting on the general adequacy of their own point of view.

ness, and imprecision of terms.[4] But the ordinary-language philosopher does not regard these features of language as *per se* undesirable. Rather, he thinks of them as performing an essential role in the use of language, viz. maintaining its expressive power and preserving communication by holding meanings relatively constant while our knowledge of the world changes. Waismann[5] has argued that 'open texturedness' of terms allows us to assimilate new information into our current nomenclature, while this possibility would be precluded if we were to fix exact extensional boundaries. Other ordinary-language philosophers argue still more generally that an accurate description of the usage, meaning, or extension of an expression cannot suggest a sharp, formalizable distinction where there are, in fact, only blurred edges. It is pointed out that such sentences as 'The number of waves in the Atlantic Ocean is prime' are in no clear sense either true or false because the conventions needed to make the relevant determinations do not exist. Consider Wittgenstein's remark:

> How should we explain to someone what a game is? I imagine that we should describe *games* to him, and we might add: 'This *and similar things* are called "games" '. And do we know any more about it ourselves? Is it only other people whom we cannot tell exactly what a

game is? — But this is not ignorance. We do not know the boundaries because none have been drawn. To repeat, we draw a boundary — for a special purpose. Does it take that to make the concept usable? Not at all! (Except for that special purpose.) No more than it took the definition: 1 pace = 75 cm to make the measure of length 'one pace' usable.[6]

But not only is it false that terms and expressions in ordinary language are fully precise in respect of their use, meaning, or extension, it is unclear that any definite sense can be attached to the general requirement that they be made fully precise. Thus, Wittgenstein concludes the above remark: 'And if you want to say "But still, before that it wasn't an exact measure", then I reply: very well, it was an inexact one. —though you still owe me a definition of exactness'. But, clearly, we cannot pay this debt with a definition of 'exactness' which requires of us that we make every distinction it is possible to make. From this the ordinary-language philosopher concludes that, although in special circumstances we may be required to be especially precise, the requirement that we never be imprecise invites the questions: When do we stop? When have we been precise enough? According to the ordinary-language philosopher, in general, we need do no more than make the distinctions that exist in the language. To stop there is to stop at a natural point. But a definition of exactness which requires

[4] Cf. Goodman, N. *The Structure of Appearance*, Harvard University Press, 1951, pp. 5–6.

[5] Cf. Waismann, F. 'Verifiability', *Proceedings of the Aristotelian Society*, Supp. Vol. XIX.

[6] Wittgenstein, L. *Philosophical Investigations*, Macmillan Company, New York, 1953, paragraph 69.

us to go further must provide a general method for deciding when enough distinctions have been drawn. By hypothesis, such a definition cannot tell us either to halt at the natural stopping point or to make every possible distinction. Yet there is no motivation for stopping anywhere beyond the one and short of the other.

Disagreements between positivists and ordinary-language philosophers shade into differences of emphasis on various points. Thus, ordinary-language philosophers have by and large tended to occupy themselves with the *study of the use of words*, while positivists have been primarily concerned with *the analysis of sentences and their inference relations*. This difference does not simply represent a disagreement about research priorities. Rather, it reflects the ordinary-language philosopher's concern with the function of language in concrete interpersonal situations, as opposed to the positivist's interest in the structure of the 'logical syntax' of the language of science. The conflict behind this difference is between the belief that language is best viewed as an articulate system with statable rules and the belief that talking about language is, at bottom, talking about an indefinitely large and various set of speech episodes.

Thus, the two schools differ in the linguistic units they choose for analysis. For the ordinary-language philosopher a theory of language is first and foremost a theory of words; the philosophy of language differs from lexicography in its techniques and methods but not in its goals. For the positivists, on the other hand, a theory of language is in the first instance a theory of sentences and sentence structures. We shall return to this point further on. Suffice it to note here that this disagreement involves the whole question of the status of the generative rules in language. It is thus directly concerned in any attempt to satisfy the traditional demands for a characterization of the linguistic skills of speakers and of the processes whereby a language is learned.

That there should be these fundamental incompatibilities between the two predominant viewpoints in present philosophy of language would not be wholly intolerable were it the case that both reveal significant insights promising a systematic and comprehensive theory of language. Then their incompatibility might itself become a fruitful problem to explore. We wish to argue, on the contrary, that both positivism and ordinary-language philosophy are mistaken in their basic assumptions about the nature of language and the techniques required for successfully theorizing about it. As often happens in philosophy, what each school says about the shortcomings of its antagonist is substantially correct. Jointly, such criticisms show why both schools are wrong about the nature and study of language. If philosophers have not hitherto abandoned the theories of language in both positivism and ordinary-language philosophy, it is perhaps because there appears to be no *tertium quid*—no acceptable alternative which does not reduce either to a version of the one or of the other. Part of the burden of this paper is to suggest such a *tertium quid.* . . .

V*

The situation in philosophy of language is reminiscent of that in psychology near the end of the last century. In the latter case apriority led to sterility and conceptual confusion until the empirical constraints upon psychological theory were made explicit. In succeeding years, philosophical psychology came to take its proper role, viz. the analysis of the concepts, theories, and methodology of scientific psychology. The general tenor of the above criticisms of current schools in the philosophy of language suggests that there is more here than a *superficial* resemblance. What we suggest is that these situations are actually parallel. This parallelism, in turn, suggests that what is needed is a theory of language developed on the basis of empirical methods. Given such a theory, the philosophy of language comes to take its proper role as the analysis of the concepts and methodology of that theory. Insofar as current linguistics provides an empirical theory of language, the philosophy of language should be construed as nothing other than the philosophy of linguistics: a discipline analogous in every respect to the philosophy of psychology, the philosophy of mathematics, the philosophy of physics, etc.

At the beginning of the present paper we remarked that it is perhaps because of the lack of a viable alternative to positivist and ordinary-language theories of language, of an acceptable *tertium quid*, that the shortcomings of both positions have not led to their abandonment. The view of philosophy of language we have suggested above, that it is the analytic study of the concepts, theories, and methodology of empirical linguistics, provides such an alternative if linguistics can offer a satisfactory theory of language. In the remaining part of this paper we shall try to establish that there exists a *tertium quid* by showing that linguistics does provide at least the framework for such a theory.

The theory of language implicit in current work in linguistics deals with problems that have traditionally concerned philosophers of language but it does so without falling victim either to the positivist's preconceptions about the structure of language, and his lack of empirical controls, or to the ordinary-language philosopher's illicit appeal to intuitive judgments and his consequent unsystematic orientation. It thus provides a real alternative to theories of language found in positivism and ordinary-language philosophy, though it shares the concern with formalization characteristic of the one and the attention to details of usage characteristic of the other.

VI

Empirical linguistics takes the most general problem of the study of language to be that of accounting for the

---

* Sections III and IV of this essay, which are here deleted, deal with criticisms of the ideal and ordinary language approaches. (TMO)

fluent speaker's ability to freely produce and readily understand all utterances of his language, including wholly novel ones.[7] To explicate this ability linguists construct a system of description which seeks to capture the regularities of the language used by speakers to produce and interpret sentences. The descriptive system which represents these regularities must include recursive rules since, as we have remarked before, the set of sentences of a language is infinite.[8] Such a system of description is a genuine scientific theory. A scientific theory systematically and economically interconnects a wide variety of observable events by representing them in terms of laws stated with theoretical concepts. It affords predictions of new events by deducing them from laws and explains why certain events occur by reference to the underlying structures it exhibits. In the case of a theory of language, verbal behavior of speakers constitutes the observable events to be systematized by the theory. 'Verbal behavior' is construed to include: perceptual discriminations, verbal productions, intuitions of oddity, judgments regarding similarity and difference in structure or meaning, etc. The theoretical concepts in terms of which the laws are stated are such constructs as phoneme, morpheme, word, etc. and the laws are the rules which represent the regularities of the language.

To think of a theory of a language in this way is immediately to postulate empirical constraints upon its construction. The theory is, *inter alia*, a predictive device: *what* it predicts is that some strings of words will be acceptable to speakers as sentences of their language, and that others will not ('Let us choose an example' but not 'Example an choose us let'). Similarly, it predicts that *if* certain utterances in fact occur, the speaker will interpret them in one way and not another and that certain utterances will be interpreted in several ways ('Failing students may be kindest' must be so represented as to bear more than one interpretation). Again, it predicts that certain utterances occur non-deviantly in some contexts but deviantly in others ('Here is a pretty red apple' must be so represented as to occur non-deviantly only in cases where the context determines the presence of an apple). In general, as is usually the case with fruitful empirical theories, possibilities for testing

---

[7] This is not meant to imply that all the knowledge which enters into the production and comprehension of utterances comes under study in linguistics. Besides linguistic abilities and skills, factual information, memory, motives, etc. may determine what utterance is produced and how an utterance is understood. Linguistics is concerned to reconstruct only those of the speaker's abilities which are a function of his knowledge of the regularities of the language.

[8] Chomsky writes, '. . . it is obvious that the set of grammatical sentences cannot be identified with any particular corpus of utterances obtained by the linguist in his field work. Any grammar of a language will *project* the finite and somewhat accidental corpus of observed utterances to a set (presumably infinite) of grammatical utterances. In this respect, a grammar mirrors the behavior of the speaker who, on the basis of a finite and accidental experience with language, can produce or understand an indefinite number of new sentences.' Chomsky, N. *Syntactic Structures*, Mouton and Co., S'Gravenhage, 1957, p. 15.

the theory proliferate as the theory develops.

Of particular interest to philosophers are the parts of a theory of language which are concerned with syntax and semantics. The former deals with that part of the general problem of the production and understanding of linguistic forms that involves grammatical structure. What a speaker does when he understands or produces an utterance must include at least the implicit analyzing of its syntactic structure. It is this ability that a theory of syntax seeks to explicate. That is, it seeks to answer such questions as, 'What are the basic construction types of the language?', 'What units are available in the language for sentence composition?', 'How may they be related to one another?', 'How are sentences formally related to other sentences?', and so forth. A semantic theory takes the solution to the general problem of production and understanding a step further. It seeks to account for the speaker's ability to assign interpretations to sentences on the basis of his knowledge of the meanings of their parts, to recognize semantic relations between pairs of words, expressions, or sentences, etc.

In the explanation of linguistic skills, the development of a theory of semantics requires the prior elaboration of a theory of syntax. This does not mean that semantics is necessarily conceived of as a system for interpreting a previously articulated syntactic structure, but only that the solution of problems in semantics requires syntactic information. One way to see this is the following: Let us suppose for the moment that a semantic theory is concerned in part with stating the conditions of truth and reference for arbitrary sentences of the language. Then consider such syntactically ambiguous sentences as 'Failing students may be kindest'. Ambiguous sentences must be so construed as to be paired with separate sets of truth conditions. The previous example is a sentence which is true in cases *either* where it is sometimes kindest to students to fail them, *or* where students who are in fact failing are sometimes the kindest students. But notice that the disjunction of the relevant truth conditions is based upon the syntactical form of the sentence, so that the rule which says that sentences of this form must be paired with disjoint conditions must make explicit reference to their grammatical features.

This point may be further generalized as follows: wherever a semantic theory seeks to assign meaning interpretations to sentences, it seems reasonable to suppose that it will treat *complex* sentences by resolving them into their constituent parts and making the relevant assignments part by part.[9] But the very task of resolving a complex sentence into its components presupposes that the underlying compositional structure of the sentence has been marked by grammatical analysis.

Finally, even on the weakest conception of a semantic theory it is required that such a theory assign meaning to the words and expressions of the lan-

---

[9] Since there is no upper bound on the length of sentences in a natural language, a recursive assignment of meaning interpretations to sentences is the only possible way of giving each sentence a meaning.

guage under study. But even in this case a knowledge of the grammatical structure of the language is necessary to make these assignments. For usually the meaning of a word or expression varies depending upon its grammatical role in context. Compare: 'He papers the tables' and 'He tables the papers', or 'He peoples the houses' and 'He houses the people'.

Such considerations require philosophers to pay more attention to grammar in their theorizing about language than they have usually been willing to do. This will be found especially profitable because grammarians have developed a powerful new system of grammatical description which is directly relevant not only to the development of a semantic theory, but also to standard philosophical problems.

VII

A grammar is conceived of as a formal system which precisely specifies the set of sentences of a language together with a structural description of each sentence which exhibits the grammatical relations of the sentence. It is a system of rules for constructing an infinite list of strings of elements in the vocabulary of the language, which list, if extended sufficiently far, includes any sentence of the language but, regardless of how far it is extended, never includes anything that is not a sentence. By effecting an enumeration of the set of sentences on the basis of a finite set of syntactic rules, the grammar constitutes a recursive definition of the notion 'sentence of L' or 'gram-

matical in L'.[10] And by formulating the syntactic rules so that, in the construction of a sentence, they automatically assign it a structural description, the grammar provides a recursive definition of 'grammatical structure of L'.

Thus, a grammar G is regarded as a generative device. To be adequate, it must meet the following condition: for each sentence of L there is at least one derivation in G which contains it as its terminal line and for each string in the vocabulary of L which is not a sentence of L there is no derivation in G containing it as its terminal line. Thus, a generatively adequate grammar is a comprehensive theory of the sentences of the language which is open to empirical verification. If some sentences are not generated, or if some non-sentences are generated, the grammar will require modification. However, generative adequacy is an ideal requirement in just the sense in which requiring of any scientific theory that it cover all the phenomena in its domain is an idealization. In writing a grammar we approach this requirement asymptotically. We are satisfied if we can construct a grammar which embodies the most general structural features of the language, even if we fail to capture some of the fine details.[11]

---

[10] This conception of a grammar is due to the work of N. Chomsky. Cf. *Syntactic Structures*.

[11] Not all sentences are on a par in respect of the requirement of generative adequacy. For some sentences exhibit very pervasive structural features of the language, and these *must* be generated. Other sentences may not be generated because of highly idiosyncratic features, and such a failure need not be considered serious.

Moreover, a generative grammar is also a predictive theory. Many strings of elements in the vocabulary of the language which can be obtained by successive applications of the rules of the grammar will, for one reason or another, never have been uttered by speakers of the language. In each such case, the grammar predicts that the string is a sentence of the language.

As Chomsky writes, in the construction of grammars,

> We assume intuitive knowledge of the grammatical sentences of English and ask what sort of grammar will be able to do the job of producing these in some effective and illuminating way. We thus face a familiar task of explication of some intuitive concept, in this case, the concept 'grammatical in English', and more generally, the concept 'grammatical'.
>
> Notice that in order to set the aims of grammar significantly it is sufficient to assume a partial knowledge of sentences and non-sentences. That is, we may assume for this discussion that certain sequences of phonemes are definitely sentences and that certain other sequences are definitely non-sentences. In many intermediate cases we shall be prepared to let the grammar itself decide, when the grammar is set up in the simplest way so that it includes the clear sentences and excludes the clear non-sentences. This is a familiar feature of explication.[12]

As we have indicated above, the rules of a generative grammar must be stated formally. This follows from the requirement that the grammar generate the infinite set of sentences of the language. Whereas traditional taxonomic grammars cite paradigmatic cases of constructions, leaving it to the reader's intuition to supply the extension to similar cases, it is required of generative grammars that each rule formally specify the structures in its range and domain and the operations it effects. If this requirement were unsatisfied, a grammar would not specify the exact set of sentences and structural descriptions, since the notion 'derivation in G' would not be well-defined. Thus, a formal grammar avoids one of the most serious charges against traditional grammars, viz. that they fail to explicate the speaker's knowledge of grammatical structure because the speaker's linguistic abilities are required to determine the application of the grammatical rules.[13]

The condition of generative adequacy entails that the type of formal system chosen as a grammar must be selected in terms of the structural features of the language it is intended to describe. For it is clearly *not* the case that an arbitrary formal system can generate any arbitrary set of strings. For example, it has been shown by Chomsky that the set of English sentences is beyond the range of description of any finite-state Markov generator.[14] But gen-

---

[12] Chomsky, N. *Syntactic Structures*, pp. 13–14.

[13] Chomsky, N. 'Explanatory Models in Linguistics', forthcoming in *The Proceedings of the International Conference on Logic, Methodology, and Philosophy of Science*, Stanford University Press, pp. 1 f.

[14] Chomsky, N. 'Three Models for the Description of Language', *I. R. E. Transactions on Information Theory*, Vol. IT-2 (1956).

erative adequacy is not a sufficient condition, since some sets of strings can be generated by formal systems which are not equivalent in respect of the structural descriptions they assign.

The type of system commonly used by linguists is an immediate constituent grammar. Such a system divides a sentence into phrases, these, in turn, are analyzed into smaller constituents, until the elementary constituents of the sentence (the words or morphemes) are reached. Sequences of phrases of the proper type are classified as sentences and each phrase is marked as a Noun-phrase, Verb-phrase, etc., depending on its grammatical role in the sequence. For example, the string 'The man hit the ball' is parsed as *Noun-phrase + Verb-phrase,* where the initial *Noun-phrase* is 'the man' and the *Verb-phrase*

is itself *Verb + Noun-phrase,* with 'hit' as the *Verb* and 'the ball' as the *Noun-phrase.* This type of formal system contains an initial string S and only rules which develop single symbols by rewriting-operations, i.e. the rules are restricted in operation to the linear context of the symbol to be developed. The derivations licensed by such rules provide a structural description of the grammatical relations in their terminal strings. Every segment of a string belongs to the class designated by the marker on the node to which it can be *traced back* in a tree diagram. A tree diagram represents the set of equivalent derivations of a string (those derivations which differ only in the order in which the rules are applied). For example, a tree diagram of 'The man hit the ball' is:

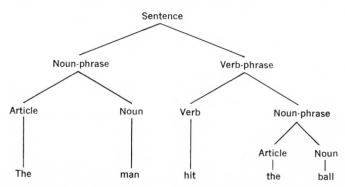

Recent studies in grammar have provided an entirely new type of formal system for grammatical description based upon a novel conception of linguistic structure. Underlying and motivating this development has been a growing awareness of limitations of the immediate constituent model. First, the grammar of a language must relate sentence types to each other in a way

that reveals their structural interrelations. An immediate constituent grammar does this, but only to a limited extent: it can only relate sentences in terms of sameness and difference in constituent structure. For example, both 'The man hit the ball' and 'The ball hit the man' are instances of the constituent structure NP + V + NP while 'The dog barks' is an instance of

NP $+$ V. But other interconnections and grammatical relations between the sentences of a language are beyond the range of description of immediate constituent analysis. For example, such sentence types as 'The man hit the ball', 'Who hit the ball?', 'The ball was hit by the man', and 'What did the man hit?', which speakers intuitively recognize to be related *somehow*, are not given a representation which explicates their interrelations. Also, the sentences 'The man hit the ball', 'The man is ugly' and 'The ball is lovely' are related to 'The ugly man hit the lovely ball', and a satisfactory grammar must capture this type of relation.[15]

Second, as a scientific theory, a grammar must assign structural descriptions to sentences in a maximally simple, revealing, and non-*ad hoc* way. However, to formulate certain rules adequately, use must be made of information about the derivational history of the strings to which they apply. But the rules of an immediate constituent grammar can use only information in the linear context of the symbol to be developed.[16] Furthermore, in many cases an immediate constituent grammar imposes too much structure on sentences, and does this in a wholly arbitrary manner.[17] This is because such grammars represent every application of a rule as the subdivision of a phrase structure class. Thus, in cases such as true co-ordinate construction[18] where there is no internal structure in the items co-ordinated, immediate constituent treatment accommodates them only by an *ad hoc* construction of classes.

The new type of formal system developed by Harris and Chomsky handles each of the above difficulties and provides a deeper insight into grammatical structure. This type of grammar is called a 'Transformational Grammar'.[19] In a transformational grammar only the simplest sentences are generated by a system of immediate

---

[15] Traditionally, immediate constituent grammars either leave this question open or else try to answer it by misleading semantic characterizations.

[16] Chomsky makes this point in *Syntactic Structures*, Section 5 and 'Three Models for the Description of Language', Section 4. The examples he uses are the rule of conjunction and the rules for developing the verb-phrase of a sentence. The conjunction rule is stated in its simplest and most revealing form when the conjoining of two items X and Y with *and*, where X is a constituent of S_1, and Y is a constituent of S_2, to form the new sentence S_3 where S_3 is the result of

replacing X by $X +$ and $+ Y$ in S_1, is permitted only when X and Y are constituents of the same type in their respective sentences. But this restriction requires information beyond what can be represented in the linear contexts of the strings to which the rule applies, since the requirement that X and Y be constituents of the same type in their respective sentences demands a knowledge of their derivational history.

[17] Cf. Chomsky, N. 'On the Notion "Rule of Grammar"', Section 3.

[18] Chomsky gives the example: 'The man was old, tired, tall . . . but friendly.', 'On the Notion "Rule of Grammar"', p. 15.

[19] Cf. Harris, Z. 'Discourse Analysis', *Language*, Vol. 28, No. 1, Jan.–Mar., 1952 and 'Co-Occurrence and Transformation in Linguistic Structure', *Language*, Vol. 33, No. 3, July–Sept. 1957 and Chomsky, N. 'Transformational Analysis', Doctoral Dissertation, University of Pennsylvania, 1955; *Syntactic Structures*; and 'Three Models for the Description of Language'.

constituent rules as described above. All compound sentences of the language are constructed from the simple sentences by a system of transformational rules. Thus, the transformational rules explicate the recursive devices of the language. Such rules operate on entire labelled trees or any of their parts and map labelled trees onto labelled trees. They operate on one or more strings of symbols and their structural descriptions, combining them or deforming them by permutations, replacements, additions, and deletions. Because they use information from a derivational history such rules are essentially more powerful than immediate constituent rules which use only a knowledge of the linear context of a symbol for their operation.

The transformational rules provide the explication of the inter-relations between sentence types in the language: questions, passives, and imperatives are transformationally derived from declaratives, and complex sentences are transformationally obtained from sets of simple sentences. Further, transformational derivations provide a revealing explanation of grammatical ambiguity. A grammatically ambiguous sentence such as (1) 'The shooting of the hunters is terrible' is derived in two non-equivalent ways in the grammar and is thus assigned two different structures. In this example, on the reading where 'hunters' is the subject of the noun-phrase, (1) comes from the sentence 'The hunters shoot', and on the reading where 'hunters' is the object of the noun-phrase, (1) comes from 'They shoot the hunters'. The ambiguity is thus a con-

sequence of the fact that 'hunters' and 'shoot' are related to each other differently in the two underlying source sentences. Thus, a transformational grammar effects a partial reduction of the problem of how speakers understand a sentence to the problem of how they understand the sentences underlying it.[20]

A transformational grammar provides a solution to the problem of composition insofar as it is a problem about syntax. It does so by exhibiting the way in which the more complex sentential structures are built up from the simplest ones by iterated applications of formally specified rules. The grammar thus provides a model which partially explains the ability of speakers to produce and construe new sentences.[21]

Even such a brief outline of contemporary grammatical theory as that just presented suggests the relevance of grammatical investigation to problems with which philosophers have been concerned. The problem of verifiability is a case in point. In his famous article 'The Elimination of Metaphysics through the Logical Analysis of Language'[22] Carnap distinguishes two types of pseudo-statements: those that contain a meaningless word and those which consist of meaningful words meaninglessly concatenated. He argues

---

[20] Cf. Chomsky, N. *Syntactic Structures*, Section 8 and 'Three Models for the Description of Language', Section 6.

[21] For a bibliography of transformational grammar see footnote 24 page 16 of Chomsky, N. 'On the Notion "Rule of Grammar" '.

[22] Carnap, R. 'The Elimination of Metaphysics through the Logical Analysis of Language', Section 4.

that the syntactical rules of a natural language do not suffice to establish the meaninglessness of all meaningless combinations of words. In this he is surely right. But the conclusion he draws from this 'limitation' of grammatical rules is that we require a constructed system of logical syntax to eliminate all the grammatically uneliminated pseudo-statements. This conclusion is, however, a *non-sequitur* because it is perfectly possible that the *semantic* rules of a natural language *will* suffice for this purpose. At any event, it is clear from Carnap's own example of a syntactically well-formed pseudo-statement, 'Caesar is a prime number', that he is unaware of the extent to which even the grammatical rules of a natural language serve to eliminate meaningless sequences. Modern grammars classify nouns such as 'Caesar' as concrete-nouns and predicates such as 'is a prime number' as requiring abstract subjects. Since these classifications are established on grammatical grounds, the grammar itself establishes the ungrammaticality of Carnap's example. Moreover, there is no way of knowing prior to the completion of grammatical investigation how much nonsense can be reduced to non-sentences. Thus, we can expect further contributions to the problem of cognitive significance as grammatical theory develops.

Other philosophical problems may be seen to turn, at least in part, on the fact that sentences are syntactically related to one another in specifiable ways. Thus, in current ethical theory there has been considerable discussion of the relation between declaratives and imperatives. Though we do not claim that this discussion is in any sense exhausted by a syntactical characterization of this relation, it seems certain that such a characterization must shed light on the similarities and differences between saying that something is the case and enjoining that something be made the case.[23] Specifically, it is conceivable that the syntactic relation between particular declaratives and the imperatives derived from them may be exploited to deal with problems of truth in ethics and aesthetics. For though imperatives are themselves neither true nor false, these terms are applicable to the declaratives to which imperatives are syntactically related. A grammar which explained this relation might, then, be of considerable interest to a philosopher, e.g. one who wished to defend verificationism in theory of meaning and an imperative theory of value statements without wishing also to hold that value judgments are meaningless. He might, following a suggestion of Marhenke, maintain that 'Sentences other than declarative . . . [are] significant or meaningless only if [their] declarative prototype is significant or meaningless'.[24]

Another philosophical problem that depends, in part, on a characterization of the syntactic interconnections between sentences is that of determining the inferences that may be validly

---

[23] Cf. Hare, R. M. *The Language of Morals*, The Clarendon Press, Oxford, 1952.

[24] Marhenke, P. 'The Criterion of Significance', republished in *Semantics and the Philosophy of Language*, (L. Linsky, ed.), University of Illinois Press, Urbana, 1952, p. 141.

drawn from a set of premises. Are we to infer from 'I do not approve of the cooking of missionaries' that the speaker is opposed to missionaries serving in the kitchen, or to the kitchen serving missionaries? In such cases, the fact that the question arises is determined by the syntactic form of the sentence. One way of looking at the matter is to say that a transformational grammar helps fill out the notion of a *fallacy of ambiguity*.

VIII

Semantics takes over the problem of explaining the speaker's ability to produce and understand new sentences at the point, as yet undetermined, where grammar leaves off. As we explained above, a grammar is a device which generates an infinite list of strings of morphemes including all and only the sentences of the language. For our purposes, we may suppose that the sentences are listed in a more or less random order. Now, let us imagine that a grammar provides the input to another device which gives a full grammatical description for arbitrary sentences on the list. We may ask: To what extent is such a pair of devices a model of the communication situation between speaker and hearer? 'One produces sentences in an incoherent order: that is, a grown-up form of babbling. The other marks every [syntactic] ambiguity in a systematic way, without preference for one reading or another: that is, a mechanical version of a hyper-pedant. All too obviously, there is more to understanding a language than knowing

its grammar.'[25] Another way to see how much of understanding sentences is left unexplained by grammar is to notice that a grammar provides identical *structural* descriptions for sentences that are different in meaning: this will be the case for all morphemically distinct substitution instances of a given syntactic type. Compare 'The man hit the dog', 'The dog bit the man', and 'The woman fed the cat'. Furthermore, some sentences which syntactically are marked as unambiguous will be understood as ambiguous by speakers; e.g., 'The stuff is light' and 'Watch the door'. In all such cases a semantic theory will be needed to represent and resolve ambiguities unrepresented or unresolved by the grammar.

The problem for semantics, then, is to explain what knowledge is involved in the speaker's ability to assign an interpretation of meaning to utterances of his language, including wholly novel ones. A satisfactory solution to this problem will be under definite empirical constraints to match the speaker's performance, e.g. his ability to paraphrase, his intuitions of semantic oddity, his ability to detect semantic ambiguities, etc. Such a solution will have to attend carefully to facts of usage, since otherwise it cannot provide a sufficiently precise account of these skills and abilities.

A theory of meaning which proves a viable alternative to the theories of meaning in positivism and ordinary-language philosophy must offer such a

---

[25] Herzberger, H. *Contextual Analysis*, A Doctoral Dissertation, Princeton University, 1961, pp. 73–74.

solution. At present, however, there is no comprehensive semantic theory.

As Chomsky has remarked, 'Part of the difficulty with the theory of meaning is that "meaning" tends to be used as a catch-all term to include every aspect of language that we know very little about. Insofar as this is correct, we can expect various aspects of this theory to be claimed by other approaches to language in the course of their development'.[26] This has, in fact, already happened. Today, 'theory of meaning' is broken down into a set of special problems. From the results of inquiries into these problems one may reasonably expect the development of an empirical semantic theory which succeeds where positivism and ordinary-language philosophy fail. What follows, then, is current history.

It is evident that one of the factors determining the way a sentence is understood, which cannot in principle be accounted for by the grammar, is the meanings of individual morphemes. This poses one of the problems for semantics: the construction of a dictionary for the language that provides an assignment of meanings to morphemes. A dictionary must be constructed in such a way that the choice of an entry for a particular morpheme is under explicit empirical controls. The problem of the theory of lexicography is thus, in part, the problem of describing the kinds of controls that are relevant to the choice of a definition. Ziff's work, in particular his recent book *Se-*

mantic Analysis,[27] gives us some indication of how this problem is to be dealt with.

Ziff starts with the notion of a state regularity. This is an empirically certifiable correlation between utterances of a given sentence type and certain conditions which regularly accompany them in the situations where they occur. Thus, 'Hello!' is correlated with the condition that someone is greeting some one or more persons. Some sentence types of the language under investigation can be correlated with such conditions, but others cannot.[28] For sentence types which cannot be correlated with conditions by examining situations in which their tokens occur, Ziff posits a projection principle to *obtain* their conditions from those conditions associated with structurally similar sentence types exhibiting state regularities. Ziff characterizes the distributive and contrastive sets for the particular morpheme m_i under analysis as respectively the set of all sentence types in which m_i occurs and the set of all such sentence types with some morpheme other than m_i appearing in m_i's place. On the basis of the empirically established state regularities and projections from state regularities, Ziff as-

---

[26] Chomsky, N. *Syntactic Structures*, p. 103, f.n. 10.

[27] Ziff, P. *Semantic Analysis*, Cornell University Press, 1961.

[28] Some sentence types are too long for their tokens to occur; some describe states of affairs that occur too infrequently, e.g. 'I just swallowed my nose'; some are too obviously true to be worth uttering; some contain terms that are never instantiated in our world, e. g. 'There is a unicorn in the garden', and so on.

sociates a set of conditions with the distributive set and a set of conditions with the contrastive set. These two sets of conditions are subjected to reduction to eliminate irrelevant members and then their symmetric product is taken. This product set constitutes the set of relevant differences between the two sets of conditions, and putative dictionary entries for m_i are evaluated by considering whether they contain conditions in this set or exclude them.

Regardless of how Ziff's theory fares under criticism,[29] it represents a constructive step toward a theory of lexicography. Its significance lies in emphasizing the need for a projective semantic relation between pairings of sentence types and conditions such that all pairings are subject to some definite empirical controls and in presenting a possible reconstruction of the procedures which go into the construction of a dictionary entry.

However, as we have seen, even a highly successful dictionary of a language does not solve all the semantic problems about the language. In order to be able to determine the meaning of a sentence in terms of the meaning of its constituent morphemes, as supplied by the dictionary, we must provide a compositional function; that is to say, a device which operates on full grammatical descriptions of sentences and dictionary entries for each of the morphemes, and which recursively produces semantic interpretations of the sentences. Such a device would show how the dictionary applies to sentences, and thus would help solve the fundamental problem of characterizing the speaker's ability to assign an interpretation of meaning to each of the infinitely many sentences of his language.

In a forthcoming paper by Katz and Fodor, *The Structure of a Semantic Theory*,[30] the problem of formulating such a compositional function is described in detail. In this treatment the central difficulty is taken to be that a dictionary usually assigns more meanings to a morpheme than it bears in an occurrence in a given sentence. Thus, the operation of the compositional function is taken to be that of associating the appropriate meanings of the morphemes and the appropriate semantic characterization with each distinct syntactic structure of a given sentence.

The interpretations assigned by the compositional function must account in the following ways for the speaker's ability to understand sentences: it must mark each of the semantic ambiguities a speaker is able to detect; it must suitably relate sentences speakers take to be paraphrases; it must explain the source of the speaker's intuitions of oddity when a sentence evokes them; it must replicate the speaker's ability to distinguish sense from nonsense; and so on.

Assuming that the proper formulation of a grammar is transformational,

---

[29] Cf. Katz, J. J. Review of *Semantic Analysis* in *Language*, Vol. 38, No. 1, Jan.–Mar., 1962.

[30] In Fodor and Katz, *Readings in the Philosophy of Language*, forthcoming from Prentice-Hall, Inc. in Spring 1963.

there is a natural and highly economical way of using the grammar as a basis on which to construct a semantic theory of this form for a language. We have mentioned above that a transformational grammar produces and structurally characterizes complex sentences by deriving them from simple sentences. Thus, it seems reasonable to suppose that the problem of semantically interpreting sentences may be reduced in the following way: First, construct a theory of the type just outlined to provide semantic interpretations for only the simple sentences of the language. Then, construct a theory which describes how each transformation in the grammar preserves or alters the semantic interpretation assigned to the sentences in its domain. The latter theory is essentially recursive in structure, and the two theories in combination provide a partial answer to the question of how speakers interpret novel sentences.

Pictured in this way, a semantic theory interprets the syntactic structure revealed in a grammatical analysis of a language. This conception thus gives content to the idea that a semantic theory of a natural language is similar to a model which provides an interpretation for a formal theory; thus, it clearly exhibits the relation between syntax and semantics.

But even if a theory of lexicography and semantic interpretation should be worked out, some of the problems which now fall under the catch-all term 'meaning' *might* still remain unsolved. Roughly, these problems are, (1) how does context determine the way speakers use and understand linguistic forms, (2) how do languages translate into one another, and (3) what are the linguistic universals.

Philosophers are familiar with the work that has been done on (1). This includes investigations of use and reference. (2) is now being explored by those concerned with machine translation. Finally, (3) is the topic which is studied under the head 'linguistic theory' and has already yielded important results suggesting universal phonological and grammatical features of language—especially in the work of Chomsky and Halle.

Regardless of the direction the solutions to these problems take, it seems certain that each presupposes a systematic elaboration of theories of lexicography and semantic interpretation for its complete solution, just as these latter theories presuppose a systematic elaboration of grammar. It is by no means an unimpressive achievement of work in these fields that it is now possible to see clearly the priorities imposed upon research by the logical interrelations between the areas under study.

ON THE PHENOMENOLOGY OF LANGUAGE[1]

1.7

Maurice Merleau-Ponty

1. Husserl and the Problems of Language

In the philosophical tradition, the problem of language does not pertain to "first philosophy," and that is just why Husserl approaches it more freely than the problems of perception or knowledge. He moves it into a central position, and what little he says about it is both original and enigmatic. Consequently, this problem provides us with our best basis for questioning phenomenology and recommencing Husserl's efforts instead of simply repeating what he said. It allows us to resume, instead of his theses, the very movement of his thought.

The contrast between certain early and late texts is striking. In the fourth

of the *Logische Untersuchungen*, Husserl sets forth the concept of an eidetic of language and a universal grammar which would establish the forms of signification indispensable to every language if it is to be a language, and which would allow us to think with complete clarity about empirical languages as "confused" realizations of the essential language. This project assumes that language is one of the objects supremely constituted by consciousness, and that actual languages are very special cases of a possible language which consciousness holds the key to—that they are systems of signs linked to *their* meaning by univocal relationships which, in their structure as in their function, are susceptible to a total explication. Posited in this way as an object before thought, language could not possibly play any other role in respect to thought than that of an accompaniment, substitute, memorandum, or secondary means of communication.

In more recent writings, on the other hand, language appears as an original way of intending certain ob-

From *Signs*, Richard C. McCleary, trans. (Evanston, Ill.: Northwestern University Press, 1964). Reprinted by permission of Northwestern University Press and Editions Gallimard, Paris.

[1] A paper presented at the first *Colloque international de phénoménologie*, Brussels, 1951.

jects, as thought's body (*Formale und transzendentale Logik*[2]), or even as the operation through which thoughts that without it would remain private phenomena acquire intersubjective value and, ultimately, ideal existence (*Ursprung der Geometrie*[3]). According to this conception, philosophical thinking which reflects upon language would be its beneficiary, enveloped and situated in it. Pos ("Phénoménologie et linguistique," *Revue Internationale de philosophie*, 1939) defines

the phenomenology of language not as an attempt to fit existing languages into the framework of an eidetic of all possible languages (that is, to objectify them before a universal and timeless constituting consciousness), but as a return to the speaking subject, to my contact with the language I am speaking. The scientist and the observer see language in the past. They consider the long history of a language, with all the random factors and all the shifts of meaning that have finally made it what it is today. It becomes incomprehensible that a language which is the result of so many accidents can signify anything whatsoever unequivocally. Taking language as a *fait accompli*—as the residue of past acts of signification and the record of already acquired meanings—the scientist inevitably misses the peculiar clarity of speaking, the fecundity of expression. From the phenomenological point of view (that is, for the speaking subject who makes use of his language as a means of communicating with a living community), a language regains its unity. It is no longer the result of a chaotic past of independent linguistic facts but a system all of whose elements cooperate in a single attempt to express which is turned toward the present or the future and thus governed by a present logic.

Such being Husserl's points of departure and arrival as far as language is concerned, we would like to submit for discussion a few propositions concerning first the phenomenon of language and next the conception of intersubjectivity, rationality, and philosophy implied by this phenomenology.

---

[2] "Diese aber (sc.: die Meinung) liegt nicht äusserlich neben den Worten; sondern redend vollziehen wir fortlaufend ein inneres, sich mit den Worten verschmelzendes, sie gleichsam beseelendes Meinen. Der Erfolg dieser Beseelung ist dass die Worte und die ganzen Reden in sich eine Meinung gleichsam verleiblichen und verleiblicht in sich als Sinn tragen." (p. 20)

[3] "Objektives Dasein 'in der Welt' das als solches zugänglich ist für jedermann kann aber die geistige Objektivität des Sinngebildes letzlich nur haben vermöge der doppelschichtigen Wiederholungen und vornehmlich der sinnlich verkörpernden. In der sinnlichen Verkörperung geschiet die 'Lokalisation' und 'Temporalisation' von Solchem das seinen Seinssinn nach nicht-lokal und nicht-temporal ist . . . Wir fragen nun: . . . Wie macht die sprachliche Verleiblichung aus dem bloss innersubjektiven Gebilde, dem Gedanke, das *objektive*, das etwa als geometrischer Begriff oder Satz in der Tat für jedermann und in aller Zukunft verständlich da ist? Auf das Problem des Ursprunges der Sprache in ihrer idealen und durch Ausserung und Dokumentierung begründeten Existenz in der realen Welt wollen wir hier nicht eingehen, obschon wir uns bewusst sind, dass eine radikale Aufklärung der Seinsart der 'idealen Sinngebilde' hier ihren tiefsten Problemgrund haben muss." (*Revue Internationale de philosophie*, 1939, p. 210).

2. The Phenomenon of Language

1. Language and Speech

Can we simply juxtapose the two perspectives on language we have just distinguished—language as object of thought and language as mine? This is what Saussure did, for example, when he made a distinction between a synchronic linguistics of speech and a diachronic linguistics of a language, which are irreducible to one another because a panchronic view would inevitably blot out the originality of the present. Pos similarly limits himself to describing the objective and the phenomenological attitude by turns without saying anything about their relationship. But then we might think that phenomenology is distinguished from linguistics only as psychology is distinguished from the science of language. Phenomenology would add our inner experience of a language to our linguistic knowledge of it as pedagogy adds to our knowledge of mathematical concepts the experience of what they become in the minds of those who learn them. Our experience of speech would then have nothing to teach us about the being of language; it would have no ontological bearing.

But this is impossible. As soon as we distinguish, alongside of the objective science of language, a phenomenology of speech, we set in motion a dialectic through which the two disciplines open communications.

At first the "subjective" point of view

envelops the "objective" point of view; synchrony envelops diachrony. The past of language began by being present. The series of fortuitous linguistic facts brought out by the objective perspective has been incorporated in a language which was at every moment a system endowed with an inner logic. Thus if language is a system when it is considered according to a cross-section, it must be in its development too. No matter how strongly Saussure insisted upon the duality of the two perspectives, his successors have had to conceive of a mediating principle in the form of the *sublinguistic schema* (Gustave Guillaume).[4]

In another connection, diachrony envelops synchrony. If language allows random elements when it is considered according to a longitudinal section, the system of synchrony must at every moment allow fissures where brute events can insert themselves.

Thus a double task is imposed upon us:

a) We have to find a meaning in the development of language, and conceive of language as a moving equilibrium. For example, certain forms of expression having become decadent by the sole fact that they have been used and have lost their "expressiveness," we shall show how the gaps or zones of weakness thus created elicit from speaking subjects who want to communicate a recovery and a utilization, in terms of a new principle, of linguistic débris left by the system in

---

[4] Gustave Guillaume, contemporary French linguist.—Trans.

process of regression. It is in this way that a new means of expression is conceived of in a language, and a persistent logic runs through the effects of wear and tear upon the language and its volubility itself. It is in this way that the French system of expression, based upon the preposition, was substituted for the Latin system, which was based upon declension and inflectional changes.

b) But correlatively, we must understand that since synchrony is only a cross-section of diachrony, the system realized in it never exists wholly in act but always involves latent or incubating changes. It is never composed of absolutely univocal meanings which can be made completely explicit beneath the gaze of a transparent constituting consciousness. It will be a question not of a system of forms of signification clearly articulated in terms of one another—not of a structure of linguistic ideas built according to a strict plan—but of a cohesive whole of convergent linguistic gestures, each of which will be defined less by a signification than by a use value. Far from particular languages appearing as the "confused" realization of certain ideal and universal forms of signification, the possibility of such a synthesis becomes problematical. If universality is attained, it will not be through a universal language which would go back prior to the diversity of languages to provide us with the foundations of all possible languages. It will be through an oblique passage from a given language that I speak and that initiates me into the phenomenon of expression, to another given language that I learn to speak

and that effects the act of expression according to a completely different style—the two languages (and ultimately all given languages) being contingently comparable only at the outcome of this passage and only as signifying wholes, without our being able to recognize in them the common elements of one single categorial structure.

Far from our being able to juxtapose a psychology of language and a science of language by reserving language in the present for the first and language in the past for the second, we must recognize that the present diffuses into the past to the extent that the past has been present. History is the history of successive synchronies, and the contingency of the linguistic past invades even the synchronic system. What the phenomenology of language teaches me is not just a psychological curiosity —the language observed by linguistics experienced in me and bearing my particular additions to it. It teaches me a new conception of the being of language, which is now logic in contingency—an oriented system which nevertheless always elaborates random factors, taking what was fortuitous up again into a meaningful whole—incarnate logic.

2. The Quasi-Corporeality of the Signifying

By coming back to spoken or living language we shall find that its expressive value is not the sum of the expressive values which allegedly belong individually to each element of the "verbal chain." On the contrary, these elements form a system in synchrony in the sense that each of them signifies only its difference in respect to the others (as Saussure says, signs are essentially "diacritical"); and as this is true of them all, there are only differences of signification in a language. The reason why a language finally intends to say and does say [*veut dire et dit*] something is not that each sign is the vehicle for a signification which allegedly belongs to it, but that all the signs together allude to a signification which is always in abeyance when they are considered singly, and which I go beyond them toward without their ever containing it. Each of them expresses only by reference to a certain mental equipment, to a certain arrangement of our cultural implements, and as a whole they are like a blank form we have not yet filled out, or like the gestures of others, which intend and circumscribe an object of the world that I do not see.

The speaking power the child assimilates in learning his language is not the sum of morphological, syntactical, and lexical meanings. These attainments are neither necessary nor sufficient to acquire a language, and once the act of speaking is acquired it presupposes no comparison between what I want to express and the conceptual arrangement of the means of expression I make use of. The words and turns of phrase needed to bring my significative intention to expression recommend themselves to me, when I am speaking, only by what Humboldt called *innere Sprachform* (and our contemporaries call *Wortbegriff*), that is, only by a certain style of speaking from which

they arise and according to which they are organized without my having to represent them to myself. There is a "languagely" [*"langagière"*] meaning of language which effects the mediation between my as yet unspeaking intention and words, and in such a way that my spoken words surprise me myself and teach me my thought. Organized signs have their immanent meaning, which does not arise from the "I think" but from the "I am able to."

This action at a distance by language, which brings significations together without touching them, and this eloquence which designates them in a peremptory fashion without ever changing them into words or breaking the silence of consciousness, are eminent cases of corporeal intentionality. I have a rigorous awareness of the bearing of my gestures or of the spatiality of my body which allows me to maintain relationships with the world without thematically representing to myself the objects I am going to grasp or the relationships of size between my body and the avenues offered to me by the world. On the condition that I do not reflect expressly upon it, my consciousness of my body immediately signifies a certain landscape about me, that of my fingers a certain fibrous or grainy style of the object. It is in the same fashion that the spoken word (the one I utter or the one I hear) is pregnant with a meaning which can be read in the very texture of the linguistic gesture (to the point that a hesitation, an alteration of the voice, or the choice of a certain syntax suffices to modify it), and yet is never contained in that gesture, every expression always appearing to me as a trace, no idea being given to me except in transparency, and every attempt to close our hand on the thought which dwells in the spoken word leaving only a bit of verbal material in our fingers.

3. The Relationship of the Signifying and the Signified. Sedimentation

Speech is comparable to a gesture because what it is charged with expressing will be in the same relation to it as the goal is to the gesture which intends it, and our remarks about the functioning of the signifying apparatus will already involve a certain theory of the significations expressed by speech. My corporeal intending of the objects of my surroundings is implicit and presupposes no thematization or "representation" of my body or milieu. Signification arouses speech as the world arouses my body—by a mute presence which awakens my intentions without deploying itself before them. In me as well as in the listener who finds it in hearing me, the significative intention (even if it is subsequently to fructify in "thoughts") is at the moment no more than a *determinate gap* to be filled by words—the excess of what I intend to say over what is being said or has already been said.

This means three things: (a) The significations of speech are already ideas in the Kantian sense, the poles of a certain number of convergent acts of expression which magnetize discourse without being in the strict sense given for their own account. Consequently, (b) expression is never total. As Saussure points out, we have the feeling that our language expresses totally. But it is not because it expresses totally that it is ours; it is because it is ours that we believe it expresses totally. For an Englishman, "the man I love" is just as complete an expression as "l'homme *que* j'aime" is for a Frenchman. And for a German who by declension can expressly indicate the function of the direct object, "j'aime cet homme" is a wholly allusive way of expressing oneself. Thus there are always things understood in expression; or rather the idea of things understood is to be rejected. It is meaningful only if we take as the model and absolute norm of expression a language (ordinarily our own) which, like all the others, can never in fact lead us "as if by the hand" to the signification, to the things themselves. So let us not say that every expression is imperfect because it leaves things understood. Let us say that every expression is perfect to the extent it is unequivocally understood, and admit as a fundamental fact of expression *a surpassing of the signifying by the signified which it is the very virtue of the signifying to make possible*. The fact that the significative intention is only a determinate gap means, finally, that (c) this act of expression—this joining through transcendence of the linguistic meaning of speech and the signification it intends—is not for us speaking subjects a second-order operation we supposedly have recourse to only in order to communicate our thoughts to others, but our own taking possession or acquisition of significations which otherwise are present to us only in a muffled way. The reason why the thematization of the signified does not precede speech is that it is the result of it. Let us stress this third consequence.

For the speaking subject, to express is to become aware of; he does not express just for others, but also to know himself what he intends. Speech does not seek to embody a significative intention which is only *a certain gap* simply in order to recreate the same lack or privation in others, but also to know *what* there is a lack or privation of. How does it succeed in doing so? The significative intention gives itself a body and knows itself by looking for an equivalent in the system of available significations represented by the language I speak and the whole of the writings and culture I inherit. For that speechless want, the significative intention, it is a matter of realizing a certain arrangement of already signifying instruments or already speaking significations (morphological, syntactical, and lexical instruments, literary *genres*, types of narrative, modes of presenting events, etc.) which arouses in the hearer the presentiment of a new and different signification, and which inversely (in the speaker or the writer) manages to anchor this original signification in the already available ones. But why, how, and in what sense are they available? They became such when, in their time, they were *established* as significations I can have recourse to—that I *have*—through the same sort of expressive operation. It is this operation which must be described if I want to comprehend the peculiar power of speech.

I understand or think I understand the words and forms of French; I have a certain experience of the literary and philosophical modes of expression offered me by the given culture. I express when, utilizing all these already speaking instruments, I make them say something they have never said. We begin reading a philosopher by giving the words he makes use of their "common" meaning; and little by little, through what is at first an imperceptible reversal, his speech comes to dominate his language, and it is his use of words which ends up assigning them a new and characteristic signification. At this moment he has made himself understood and his signification has come to dwell in me. We say that a thought is expressed when the converging words intending it are numerous and eloquent enough to designate it unequivocally for me, its author, or for others, and in such a manner that we all have the experience of its presence in the flesh in speech. Even though only *abschattungen* of the signification are given thematically, the fact is that once a certain point in discourse has been passed the *abschattungen*, caught up in the movement of discourse outside of which they are nothing, suddenly contract into a single signification. And then we feel that *something has been said*—just as we perceive a thing once a minimum of sensory messages has been exceeded, even though the explanation of the thing extends as a matter of principle to infinity; or, as beholders of a certain number of actions, we come to *perceive someone* even though in the eyes of reflection no one other than myself can really and in the same sense be an *ego*.

The consequences of speech, like

those of perception (and particularly the perception of others), always exceed its premises. Even we who speak do not necessarily know better than those who listen to us what we are expressing. I say that I *know an idea* when the power to organize discourses which make coherent sense around it has been established in me; and this power itself does not depend upon my alleged possession and face-to-face contemplation of it, but upon my having acquired a certain style of thinking. I say that a signification is acquired and henceforth available when I have succeeded in making it dwell in a speech apparatus which was not originally destined for it. Of course the elements of this expressive apparatus did not really contain it—the French language did not, from the moment it was established, contain French literature; I had to throw them off center and recenter them in order to make them signify what I intended. It is just this "coherent deformation" (Malraux) of available significations which arranges them in a new sense and takes not only the hearers *but the speaking subject as well* through a decisive *step*.

For from this point on the preparatory stages of expression—the first pages of the book—are taken up again into the final meaning of the whole and are directly given as derivatives of that meaning, which is now installed in the culture. The way will be open for the speaking subject (and for others) to go straight to the whole. He will not need to reactivate the whole process; he will possess it eminently in its result. A personal and interpersonal tradition will have been founded. The *Nachvoll-*

zug, freed from the cautious gropings of the *Vollzug*, contracts the steps of the process into a single view. Sedimentation occurs, and I shall be able to think farther. Speech, as distinguished from language, is that moment when the significative intention (still silent and wholly in act) proves itself capable of incorporating itself into my culture and the culture of others—of shaping me and others by transforming the meaning of cultural instruments. It becomes "available" in turn because in retrospect it gives us the illusion that it was contained in the already available significations, whereas by a sort of *ruse* it espoused them only in order to infuse them with a new life.

4. Consequences for Phenomenological Philosophy

What philosophical bearing must we grant these descriptions? The relation of phenomenological analyses to philosophy proper is not clear. They are often considered *preparatory*, and Husserl himself always distinguished "phenomenological investigations" in the broad sense from the "philosophy" which was supposed to crown them. Yet it is hard to maintain that the philosophical problem remains untouched after the phenomenological exploration of the *Lebenswelt*. The reason why the return to the "life-world" is considered an absolutely indispensable first step in Husserl's last writings is undoubtedly that it is not without consequence for the work of universal constitution which should follow, that in some respects something of the first step remains in the second, that it is in some fashion preserved in it, that it is thus never gone beyond completely, and that phenomenology is already philosophy. If the philosophical subject were a transparent constituting consciousness before which the world and language were wholly explicit as its significations and its objects, any experience whatsoever—phenomenological or no—would suffice to motivate our passing to philosophy, and the systematic exploration of the *Lebenswelt* would not be necessary. The reason why the return to the *Lebenswelt* (and particularly the return from objectified language to speech) is considered absolutely necessary is that philosophy must reflect upon the object's mode of presence to the subject—upon the conception of the object and of the subject as they appear to the phenomenological revelation—instead of replacing them by the object's relationship to the subject as an idealistic philosophy of total reflection conceives of it. From this point on, phenomenology envelops philosophy, which cannot be purely and simply added on to it.

This is particularly clear in the case of the phenomenology of language. More clearly than any other, this problem requires us to make a decision concerning the relationships between phenomenology and philosophy or metaphysics. For more clearly than any other it takes the form of both a special problem and a problem which contains all the others, including the problem of philosophy. If speech is what we have said it is, how could there possibly be an ideation which allows us to dominate this *praxis*? How could the phenomenology of speech

possibly help being a philosophy of speech as well? And how could there possibly be any place for a subsequent elucidation of a higher degree? It is absolutely necessary to underline the *philosophical* import of the return to speech.

The description we have given of the signifying power of speech, and in general of the body as mediator of our relation to the object, would provide no philosophical information at all if it could be considered a matter of mere psychological depiction. In this case we would admit that in effect the body, such as it is in our living experience of it, seems to us to involve the world, and speech a landscape of thought. But this would be only an appearance. In the light of serious thinking, my body would still be an object, my consciousness pure consciousness, and their coexistence the object of an *apperception* which (as pure consciousness) I would still be the subject of (in Husserl's early writings, things are set forth in more or less this way). Similarly, since the relationship according to which my speech or the speech I hear points beyond itself toward a signification could (like every other relationship) only be posited by me *qua* consciousness, thought's radical autonomy would be restored at the very moment it seemed to be in doubt.

Yet in neither case can I classify the phenomenon of incarnation simply as psychological appearance; and if I were tempted to do so, I would be blocked by my perception of others. For more clearly (*but not differently*) in my experience of others than in my experience of speech or the perceived world, I inevitably grasp my body as a *spontaneity which teaches me what I could not know in any other way except through it.* Positing another person as an other myself is not as a matter of fact possible if it is *consciousness* which must do it. To be conscious is to constitute, so that I cannot be conscious of another person, since that would involve constituting him as constituting, and as constituting in respect to the very act through which I constitute him. This difficulty of principle, posited as a limit at the beginning of the fifth *Cartesian Meditation,* is nowhere eliminated. Husserl *disregards* it; since I have the idea of others, it follows that in some way the difficulty mentioned *has in fact been overcome.* But I have been able to overcome it only because he within me who perceives others is capable of ignoring the radical contradiction which makes theoretical conception of others impossible. Or rather (since if he ignored it he would no longer be dealing with others), only because he is able to live that contradiction as the very definition of the presence of others.

This subject which experiences itself as constituted at the moment it functions as constituting is my body. We remember that Husserl ended up basing my perception of a way of behaving (*Gebaren*) which appears in the space surrounding me upon what he calls the "mating phenomenon" and "intentional transgression." It happens that my gaze stumbles against certain sights (those of other human and, by extension, animal bodies) and is thwarted by them. I am invested by them just when I thought I was investing them, and I see a form sketched out in space that arouses and convokes the possibilities of my own body as if it were a matter of my own gestures or behavior. Everything happens as if the functions of intentionality and the intentional object were paradoxically interchanged. The scene invites me to become its adequate viewer, as if a different mind than my own suddenly came to dwell in my body, or rather as if my mind were drawn out there and emigrated into the scene it was in the process of setting for itself. I am snapped up by a second myself outside me; I perceive an other.

Now speech is evidently an eminent case of these "ways of behaving" ["*conduites*"] which reverse my ordinary relationship to objects and give certain ones of them the value of subjects. And if objectification makes no sense in respect to the living body (mine or another's), the incarnation of what I call its thinking in its total speech must also be considered an ultimate phenomenon. If phenomenology did not really already involve our conception of being and our philosophy, when we arrived at the philosophical problem we would find ourselves confronted again with the very difficulties which gave rise to phenomenology to begin with.

In a sense, phenomenology is all or nothing. That order of instructive spontaneity—the body's "I am able to," the "intentional transgression" which gives us others, the "speech" which gives us the idea of an ideal or absolute signification—cannot be subsequently placed under the jurisdiction of an acosmic and a pancosmic consciousness without becoming meaningless again. It must teach me to comprehend what no constituting consciousness can know—my involvement in a "pre-constituted" world. But how, people will object, can the body and speech give me more than I have put into them? It is clearly not my body as organism which teaches me to see the emergence of *another myself* in a way of behaving [*conduite*] that I witness; as such it could at best only be reflected and recognize itself in *another organism*. In order for the alter ego and the thought of others to appear to me, I must be the *I* of *this* body of mine, *this* incarnate life's thought. The subject who effects the intentional transgression could not possibly do so except insofar as he is situated. The experience of others is possible to the exact degree that the situation is part of the Cogito.

But then we must take with equal strictness what phenomenology has taught us about the relationship between the signifying and the signified. If the central phenomenon of language is in fact *the common act of the signifying and the signified*, we would deprive it of its distinctive characteristic by realizing the result of expressive operations in advance in a heaven of ideas; we would lose sight of the *leap* these operations take from already available significations to those we are in the process of constructing and acquiring. And the intelligible substitute we would try to base them on would not exempt us from understanding how our knowing apparatus expands to the point of understanding what it does not contain. We would not husband our transcendence by prescribing it to a factual transcendent. In any case the place of truth would still be that antic-ipation (*Vorhabe*) through which each spoken word or acquired truth opens a field of understanding, and the symmetrical recovery (*Nachvollzug*) through which we bring this advent of understanding or this commerce with others to a conclusion and contract them into a new view.

Our present expressive operations, instead of driving the preceding ones away—simply succeeding and annulling them—salvage, preserve, and (insofar as they contain some truth) take them up again; and the same phenomenon is produced in respect to others' expressive operations, whether they be past or contemporary. Our present keeps the promises of our past; we keep others' promises. Each act of philosophical or literary expression contributes to fulfilling the vow to retrieve the world taken with the first appearance of a language, that is, with the first appearance of a finite system of signs which claimed to be capable in principle of winning by a sort of ruse any being which might present itself. Each act of expression realizes for its own part a portion of this project, and by opening a new field of truths, further extends the contract which has just expired. This is possible only through the same "intentional transgression" which gives us others; and like it the phenomenon of truth, which is theoretically impossible, is known only through the praxis which *creates* it.

To say there is a truth is to say that when my renewal meets the old or alien project, and successful expression frees what has always been held captive in being, an inner communication is established in the density of personal and interpersonal time through which our present becomes the *truth of* all the other knowing events. It is like a wedge we drive into the present, a milestone bearing witness that in this moment something has taken place which being was always waiting for or "intending to say" [*voulait dire*], and which will never stop if not being true at least signifying and stimulating our thinking apparatus, if need be by drawing from it truths more comprehensive than the present one. At this moment something has been founded in signification; an experience has been transformed into its meaning, has become truth. Truth is another name for sedimentation, which is itself the presence of all presents in our own. That is to say that even and especially for the ultimate philosophical subject, there is no objectivity which accounts for our super-objective relationship to all times, no light that shines more brightly than the living present's light.

In the late text we cited to begin with, Husserl writes that speech realizes a "localization" and "temporalization" of an ideal meaning which, "according to the meaning of its being," is neither local nor temporal. And later on he adds that speech also objectifies, as concept or proposition, what was heretofore only a formation internal to a single subject, thereby opening it up to the plurality of subjects. So there would seem to be a movement through which ideal existence descends into locality and temporality, and an inverse movement through which the act of speaking here and now establishes the ideality of what is true. These two movements would be contradictory if they took place between the same ex-

treme terms; and it seems to us that their relationship must be conceived of in terms of a circuit of reflection. In a first approximation, reflection recognizes ideal existence as neither local nor temporal. It then becomes aware of a locality and temporality of speech that can neither be derived from those of the objective world nor suspended from a world of ideas. And finally, it makes the mode of being of ideal formations rest upon speech. Ideal existence is based upon the document. Not, undoubtedly, upon the document as a physical object, or even as the vehicle of one-to-one significations assigned to it by the language it is written in. But ideal existence is based upon the document insofar as (still through an "intentional transgression") the document solicits and brings together all knowing lives—and as such establishes and re-establishes a "Logos" of the cultural world.

Thus the proper function of a phenomenological philosophy seems to us to be to establish itself definitively in the order of instructive spontaneity that is inaccessible to psychologism and historicism no less than to dogmatic metaphysics. The phenomenology of speech is among all others best suited to reveal this order to us. When I speak or understand, I experience that presence of others in myself or of myself in others which is the stumbling-block of the theory of intersubjectivity, I experience that presence of what is represented which is the stumbling-block of the theory of time, and I finally understand what is meant by Husserl's enigmatic statement, "Transcendental subjectivity is intersubjectivity." To the extent that what I say has meaning,

I am a different "other" for myself when I am speaking; and to the extent that I understand, I no longer know who is speaking and who is listening.

The ultimate philosophical step is to recognize what Kant calls the "transcendental affinity" of moments of time and temporalities. This is undoubtedly what Husserl is trying to do when he takes up the finalist vocabulary of various metaphysics again, speaking of "monads," "entelechies," and "teleology." But these words are often put in quotations in order to indicate that he does not intend to introduce along with them some agent who would then assure externally the connection of related terms. Finality in a dogmatic sense would be a compromise; it would leave the terms to be connected and their connecting principle unconnected. Now it is at the heart of my present that I find the meaning of those presents which preceded it, and that I find the means of understanding others' presence at the same world; and it is in the actual practice of speaking that I learn to understand. There is finality only in the sense in which Heidegger defined it when he said approximately that finality is the trembling of a unity exposed to contingency and tirelessly recreating itself. And it is to the same undeliberated and inexhaustible spontaneity that Sartre was alluding when he said that we are "condemned to freedom."

A MARXIST FORMULATION OF THE PROBLEM OF SEMANTICS*

1.8

Adam Schaff

No Marxist, or any man who thinks in terms of scientific criteria, can accept the transcendentalist position, since it is based on metaphysical speculation incompatible with science. He finds, of course, the naturalist position to be nearer to his own; this applies in particular to those theses which

From *An Introduction to Semantics*, Olgierd Wojtasiewicz, trans. (New York: Pergamon Press, 1962). Reprinted by permission of Panstwowe Wydawnictwo and the author.

* In the preceding sections, Schaff has characterized the transcendentalist position in terms of the neo-Kantian conception of a transcendental ego as the base for intersubjective communication. Naturalism he characterizes in terms of the behavioristic contention that communication is based upon similar experiences. (TMO)

come close to consistent materialism. But a Marxist cannot be in full solidarity with naturalism: some of its points he must criticize, and he also has to fill many gaps in its argumentation.

Hence the Marxist rejects the notion that there are only two alternative positions in the issue of the possibility of communication: the transcendentalist and the naturalist. Far less can he agree that the bankruptcy of one of the two opposing theories serves to prove the correctness of the other. This is an obvious paralogism. Both parties to the dispute are right, at least to a certain extent, in their criticism of their opponents. No party is right, however, in treating that criticism as adding to its own capital. Transcendentalism is simply counterscientific speculation based on mere metaphysical faith. Naturalism reveals gaps and inconsistencies; the incorrectness of some of its opinions and theses can be demonstrated. The weakness of naturalism consists rather in what it does *not* say than in what it does say. But there must be agreement with many of its theses because they stand for science and common sense. Marxism, consequently, has to treat the two trends differently, although it cannot declare itself in solidarity with either of them. That is why a Marxist attempt to solve the problem of communication must be offered here.

It is only now, when we have examined the four points, the four aspects of the original historical relations, that we have found that man also has 'consciousness'. But even that is not any *a priori*, 'pure',

consciousness. The 'spirit' is from the very beginning ridden with a curse, is 'infected' with matter which comes in as vibrations of the air, as sounds, in a word, as speech. Speech is as old as consciousness, speech *is* a practical, real consciousness which exists both for other people and for myself. And speech comes to being, like consciousness, only from the need, the necessity of contact with other people. Where a relation exists, it exists for me; an animal is in a relation to nothing. For an animal, its relation to others does not exist as a relation. Thus, consciousness is from the very beginning a social product and will remain so as long as men will exist.[1]

These words by Marx on the rôle of speech in the process of human communication date from 1844. More or less at that time, in the spring of 1845, Marx wrote his *Theses on Feuerbach*, three of which are of particular importance for us: Theses VI, VII and VIII pertain to the social character of the human individual and to the conclusions to be drawn for the study of the manifestation of the spiritual life of human individuals. The theses are as follows:

Thesis VI:

Feuerbach resolves the religious essence into the human essence. But the human essence is no abstraction inherent in each single individual. In its reality it is the ensemble of the social relations.

Feuerbach, who does not enter upon a

---

[1] K. Marx, F. Engels, *Die deutsche Ideologie*, in *Werke*, Vol. 3, Berlin 1958, p. 30–31.

criticism of this real essence, is consequently compelled:

1. To abstract from the historical process and to fix the religious sentiment as something by itself and to presuppose an abstract — *isolated* — human individual.

2. The human essence, therefore, can with him be comprehended only as 'genus', as an internal, dumb generality which merely *naturally* unites the many individuals.

Thesis VII:

Feuerbach, consequently, does not see that the 'religious sentiment' is itself a *social product*, and that the abstract individual whom he analyses belongs in reality to a particular form of society.

Thesis VIII:

Social life is essentially *practical*. All mysteries which mislead theory to mysticism find their rational solution in human practice and in the comprehension of this practice.[2]

I have opened my discussion of the Marxist interpretation of the problem of communication with quotations from Marx since they constitute the foundation for the solution of that problem.

As indicated above, the transcendentalists object that the naturalists commit the error called *circulus in demonstrando*: required to *prove* the possibility of communication, they instead *assume* such possibility of communication in stating that it is ensured by sufficient "similarity of human organisms". The naturalists are defenceless in the face of this objection, since the assumption of naturalism as the starting point for the explanation of social phenomena involves a fundamental error.

To begin with the issue of the human individual, the naturalists, like Feuerbach before them, conceive the human individual in an abstract manner, only as a specimen of the species "man". That is also materialism, but materialism restricted by abstraction from the social factor. The only "general characteristic" possible in such an analysis of man is the general characteristic of the *species*, and hence the naturalists, like Feuerbach, can conceive the human essence "only as 'genus', as an internal, dumb generality which merely *naturally* unites the many individuals". That weak point in naturalism is correctly attacked by the transcendentalists. Once again it can be seen that idealism feeds above all on the limitations and the resulting restrictions of materialism.

For if the human individual is treated naturalistically, as a specimen only of natural species, if "the similarity of organisms" is understood in just such a way, then what can we say, what right have we to speak about "the similarity of minds", "the similarity of consciousness", etc., which will not be simply an assumption? The transcendentalists are right. With such an approach nothing reasonable can be said on the matter, and it really does seem that the naturalists assume what they have to prove.

[2] K. Marx, *Theses on Feuerbach*, in F. Engels, *Ludwig Feuerbach and the End of Classical German Philosophy*, Moscow 1949, p. 62–63.

This is so because the issue of "the similarity of minds" cannot be solved in purely naturalistic terms. The issue of the human individual as an individual belonging to human society cannot be solved at all in those terms alone.

In criticizing Feuerbach's naturalistic tendencies Marx objected that he had assumed "an abstract—*isolated*—human individual", and drew attention to the fact that "the abstract individual whom he analyses belongs in reality to a particular form of society". This is a criticism of all "Robinson Crusoe concepts" in the social sciences.

Do the adherents of the naturalistic concept of communication understand these truths? They all analyse the "speaker-listener" relation, but leave the question of the social link between them in the dark. Dewey, as quoted above, says that two such parties belong to a social group from which they have adopted their speech habits, but he draws no further conclusions from that fact. I do not imply that Dewey and other adherents of naturalism are lacking in understanding of the question of social links, or that they really maintain, as is imputed to them by the transcendentalists, that human individuals are "absolutely isolated". But the fact that they do not give voice to such nonsense does not mean that they properly understand the significance of the social conditioning of the communication process, and still less, that their opinions reflect that significance. No, there is nothing like that about them, and it explains why they are exposed to attacks by the transcendentalists. And perhaps they pass over the point in

silence because they consider it self-evident, a truism? Such a defense of the naturalists can be answered by pointing out that it is probably a still greater truism to say that a conversation always involves at least two parties —speaker and listener—and yet the naturalists do not pass over that trivial fact in silence (cf. Dewey, and above all Gardiner). If they did see and fully understand the importance of the social conditioning of the position of the individual as an individual in society, should they see and fully understand the importance of the social conditioning of the communication process, surely they would not remain silent, for this is an important issue which would help them to dissociate themselves from the standpoint of their opponents—the standpoint of transcendentalist mysticism. But in science silence, too, is under certain circumstances an eloquent testimony; the lack of certain assertions in definite situation implies approval of assertions to the contrary, or at least denotes inability to oppose, or the impossibility of opposing, such assertions to the contrary.

And yet analysis should begin with the issue of the social status of the individual: that done, then all secrets of "the similarity of minds" and "consciousness common to all", "the mysterious character" of communication, etc., disappear at once.

Marx said that "the human essence is no abstraction inherent in each single individual. In its reality it is the ensemble of the social relations". The crux of the matter lies in understanding that point (though Marx's formulation of the thought is now somewhat obsolete in style). Can a non-Marxist develop a similar idea, or at least can he adopt it? I do not see any absolute obstacles to his doing so. But it is a fact that *the interpretation of man's spiritual life and of the product of his spiritual life from the social, and consequently historical, point of view is the undeniable and immense contribution of Marxism to social research.*

To avoid all misunderstandings, it must be added that Marx's discovery did not take place in a vacuum, but was preceded by reflections on the influence of the milieu on human opinions (French materialists), and on the historical character of human consciousness (German idealists). Marx, however, not only gave a synthesis of those views, but also developed them consistently and, on a new foundation (the attention paid to the rôle of the relations of production in the development of human consciousness), made a true scientific *discovery* which now lies at the root of the modern theories of man's spiritual life and its products.

The human individual—if we consider him not only as the object of study of physics, chemistry, medicine, etc., but precisely as a *human* individual, i.e., as a member of human society—is a *social product*, in the same way as are all the manifestations of his spiritual life: "religious disposition", speech, artistic taste, consciousness in general.

As a "human individual" man is "the whole of social relations" in the sense that this origin and spiritual development can be understood only in the

social and historical context, as a specimen of a "species", but this time not only a natural, but also a social species. These are historicism and sociologism in the definite sense of these terms. Thus, historical materialism has introduced a sociological, scientific point of view to the study of man's spiritual life in general, and the study of culture in particular.

All this shows clearly that "consciousness is . . . and will be a social product as long . . . as men exist". But human speech, also, is such a social product from its very origin, since "the speech *is* the practical, . . . real consciousness . . . existing also for other people". The origin of both consciousness and speech is to be sought in social life and its needs, "in the necessity to communicate with other people".

But we are not interested here in the origin of language and speech. We are interested in something else: is there any mysterious factor left in the process of communication when the errors arising from the naturalistic interpretation of social phenomena are eliminated, and the study is based on the principles of consistent materialism? Can the transcendentalists reasonably accuse Marxists also of the *circuli in demonstrando*?

Of course, the transcendentalists may say after Urban: ". . . Equally inadequate is mind when conceived in purely naturalistic terms of history and sociology".

I pass over the fact that history and sociology have nothing to do with naturalism. The latter term has probably been used above to replace the "abhorrent" notion of "materialism". The transcendentalists can say that communication, if analysed in those terms, is not a true communication. But we can, in reply, follow old Joseph Dietzgen, who referred the adherents of the "angelic" manner of communication to heaven, to the angels. We here, on the earth, have at disposal only earthly cognition and an earthly manner of communication. We need not engage in speculation.

But does the argument which was so effective in attacking the naturalists, remain valid? No, because its foundation has been smashed—the thesis concerning "absolutely isolated" beings which the transcendentalists might with impunity ascribe to the naturalists in availing themselves of the gaps and errors in their doctrine. Nothing is left of that thesis, and consequently nothing is left of the critical argumentation of the transcendentalists.

The human individual is a social product both in his physical and his psychical evolution, both from the point of view of his phylogenesis and his ontogenesis. There is nothing mysterious in "the similarity of organisms", as there is nothing mysterious in "the similarity of minds" or "the similiarity of consciousness". That similarity (which, by the way, leaves room for individual differences) is most natural and normal, being acquired by *up-bringing* in society, by taking over its historical heritage chiefly through the intermediary of *speech*. Both these factors have the same effect on all members of society, and hence there is nothing extraordinary in the fact that they form a substratum for a "similar-ity of minds". There is thus nothing extraordinary in the fact that they smash the myths of "absolutely separated" individuals. It becomes quite superfluous to introduce mystical, transcendental factors in order to explain the process of communication. The explanation is quite natural, but not naturalistic. It is *social*.

This is what Marxism contributes to the problem of communication. The Marxist approach makes it possible to solve that problem in a consistently scientific manner, dissociating Marxism both from the metaphysical speculations of transcendentalism, and from the vulgar materialism of the naturalistic interpretation.

No less decisive is the rejection by Marxism of the second transcendentalist objection—that which concerns "the similarity of reality" to which communication pertains. It will be recalled that the transcendentalists refer to the fact that intellectual communication always pertains to some universe of discourse, and consider the reality spoken about in the process of communication to be a mental construction. On this they base their *circulus in demonstrando* objection, for the similarity which had had to be proved is, they argue, adopted as an assumption. What is involved here, they contend, is not an environment independent of human mind, but an environment which is a construction of that mind; these constructions are said to be similar because their similarity is provided by the minds themselves, or, strictly speaking, by "the transcendental 'I'" in which the individual minds somehow participate.

All that is pure mysticism, pure metaphysical speculation. The naturalists are defenceless against such arguments; having once made concession to idealism, they cannot effectively fend off its blows. But for the Marxists, as consistent materialists, that objection is of no consequence.

What is at stake here is the essential controversy between materialism and idealism in the field of ontology and epistemology. The controversy if focused around the issue as to whether the object spoken about by persons who communicate with one another is, or is not, because it exists outside their minds and independently of them, the object of a common discourse.

Of course, in philosophy one can afford the luxury of solipsism. But then not only all *common* objects of communication, but in general *all objects* as such disappear, and what remains is the mystic "I" that creates the world as its own private construction. Here the difference between epistemological and ontological solipsism is blurred. One must realize clearly that we put an end not only to the object of thought, but to communication as well, since nothing remains to be communicated. This is understood even by transcendentalists: e.g., Urban says that "a minimum of realism" is necessary for communication, and states: "No coherent theory of communication can be developed on subjectivist premises, and if idealism involves subjectivism, idealism must be abandoned".[3] But Urban declares himself against subjec-

tive idealism from the standpoint of objective idealism. And he immediately continues: "On the other hand, no coherent theory of communication can be developed without the notion of transcendent mind as well as transcendent objects. Any form of realism that denies this must be abandoned".[4]

Thus the objective character of the object of thought has to be retained (although, according to the transcendentalists, escape can be sought in objective idealism), in order to avoid abandoning all reasonable theory of communication.

But the transcendentalists may urge that they do not mean a denial of the objective character of the object of thought—witness the fact that they recognize the objective character of the object of communication, as is done, e.g., by Urban. Their point is, they might say, that in communicating with other people, we speak about objects; but objects located by us in a definite universe of discourse, according to the "language" we use. Now to construct that *univers du discours*, a "transcendental mind" is necessary.

The argumentation is simply astounding. Yet it suffices to ask: "But why?", and the spell is broken. For, in fact, why is a "transcendental mind" necessary for the construction of a *univers du discours*, but not necessary for the existence of the object of knowledge? And what is the meaning of the object of communication being objective, if in communication it always is a subjective product, as a construction? It would be difficult to answer these

---

[3] Wilbur Urban, *Language and Reality*, New York 1939, p. 264.

[4] Ibid.

questions, without reverting to the old concept of inaccessible *noumena*, which have an objective existence, and of apparent *phenomena*, which are our own construction. But that concept was annihilated long ago by the criticism of Kantian phenomenalism. It must be stated clearly: either one accepts an objective existence of the object of communication, or one considers that object to be a subjective product of mind and thereby cancels the possibility of communication. *Tertium non datur.* The transcendentalists entangle themselves desperately in their own subtleties.

But what about that *univers du discours* in the light of the materialistic epistemology?

If we hold that the object of our cognition, and consequently the object of communication, exists objectively— that is, outside all minds and independently of them—then the mind in the process of cognition somehow *reflects* it (in a special sense of the word). But an isolated object is an abstraction: the mind in the process of cognition always reflects the object *in some context*. In that sense, that context must also exist in the communication of cognition. The statement that the object of cognition appears here in a definite *univers du discours* is trivial. Reference to the *univers du discours* in the process of communication does not infer any difficulties, particularly since what is involved here is not objects but *ambiguous words* the meanings of which become concrete only in a definite context. And for that purpose no "transcendental 'I'" is needed; suffice it to indicate clearly and to understand the context, which in turn requires precision of formulations on the part of the speaker and adequate erudition on the part of the listener. No mystic "transcendental 'I'" will help me in understanding the *univers du discours* of, for instance, quantum mechanics, if I am not familiar with the subject.

One feels compelled to recall Marx's words already quoted: "Social life is essentially *practical*. All mysteries which mislead theory to mysticism find their rational solution in human practice and in the comprehension of this practice".

The standpoint of the Marxists in the controversy between the naturalists and the transcendentalists thus boils down to demonstrating that that controversy focuses on phenomena that are social *par excellence* and in that sense natural.

Is this not a truism; is it not the standpoint commonly adopted in science? Not at all.

That it is not a truism is best proved by the controversy in its entirety as explained above. That it is not a triviality, is best proved by the fact that not only transcendentalists but even naturalists do not fully understand the thesis and are unable to assess it properly.

Certain standpoints, especially that adopted by the transcendentalists in the controversy now under discussion, look strange in the light of commonsense. But the opinions of philosophers are not always in agreement with common sense, and often all their "originality" consists precisely in applying shocks to common sense. Should we then (as was suggested to me in a discussion) consider such opinions as manifestations of imbecility or schizophrenia and consequently reject them as unimportant? May we say—as was said in that discussion—either that, if I ascribe to them such absurd opinions, I do not understand what these authors mean, or that if their opinions are really so absurd then I am absolved from discussion in view of the evidently non-scientific character of the position held by my opponents? I do not agree that we can say either the one or the other. Contrary to all appearances, the holding of such opinions is a manifestation neither of weakness nor of insanity, but is simply part of irrationalist thought, so common in the bourgeois world. Even mysticism is a social phenomenon and a social fact, which must be noticed, understood and properly assessed, if one does not want to come out on the losing side in the ideological strife now proceeding in philosophy. Nor may I say, although I may find it convenient, "I do not understand", and withdraw from the struggle. After all, I *do* understand the meaning of sentences, even if I reject their content as unacceptable (e.g., I understand the meaning of the sentences to the effect that communication is possible owing to some transcendental "I", just as I understand the meaning of the sentence which asserts the existence of an omnipotent God). The words "I do not understand" can only mean here that I do not agree with a given standpoint, that I deny it all meaning from the scientific point of view, etc. But it would be dangerous to abstain, for that reason, from discussion, for then the opponent could claim successfully that

he too "does not understand" what we say. Perhaps we should not bother about all that, convinced of being right? But that would mean an end to all intellectual progress, an end to all discussion, a harmful monopolization of the scientific standpoint.

So let us engage in discussion. But if discussion is indispensable, the Marxist standpoint on the issue of communication is neither a truism nor a triviality. Quite the contrary; not only from the point of view of historical priority, but also *at present* it is the only consistent formulation of the issue of communication from the social—both materialistic and historical—point of view.

Certainly, great discoveries, once assimilated by science, assume such apparent simplicity as to seem trivial to those whose opinions have already been shaped by such discoveries. This is the normal course of events. The greatest discoveries, especially in the social sciences, usually concern simple, every-day matters which for various reasons have not been noticed or understood before, or consideration of which has been deliberately put off. That fact by no means detracts from the greatness of the discovery, far less does it preclude one from availing oneself of it in analysis. This holds especially when, as is the case of the theory of communication, the discovery in question is neither universally recognized, nor even understood and taken into consideration by the majority of researchers.

It has been said that the Marxists treat human consciousness and human speech—consciousness for others—as products of social life. That hypothesis has found expression in Engels's paper *On the Rôle of Labour in Making the Ape Human*, and in the theory of Marx and Engels on the rôle of the division of labour as a factor in social evolution. Labour—thought—language: these are the three elements of fundamental significance in the Marxist conception of the origin of human society. These three elements are inseparable one from another. Man drew a line of distinction between himself and the animal world when he started to produce tools, says Marx. Human labour is inseparably linked with consciousness, that is with thought, which in turn is genetically linked inseparably with speech. Consciousness, and consequently speech as well, are products of labour, products of social life, and at the same time indispensable conditions of a further development of that process, of its higher, more advanced stages. Human labour is based on co-operation, which is impossible without thinking in terms of ideas, and without communication. Such is the dialectics of mutual influence, which makes it possible to explain the process of communication without recourse to miracles and metaphysics.

Thus, the issue turns out to be "prosaic" and natural, though evading a naturalistic interpretation by being an essentially social phenomenon. But is it so simple? Is it enough to state that somebody speaks and somebody else listens to him and the two understand one another?

Here a protest must be registered against a "common-sense" simplification of the problem, since that would threaten to eliminate all deeper analysis and to annihilate the scientific approach.

We say that people talk to one another and that is communication. So far so good. But from the point of view of a scientific analysis the problem only begins here. What problem? Not the metaphysical one, as to whether communication is possible. Of course, it *is* possible, for we witness it everywhere. Not the mystic one, as to what transcendental factor makes communication possible. This can be explained without resorting to miracles and metaphysics. The scientific problem which begins at this point is: *how, in what manner*, does communication take place?

Social psychologists say that communication consists in that the parties concerned mutually interchange their rôles with their opposite numbers, they mentally place themselves in their position and thus come to understand their words.[5] The issue may be formulated so, it may be formulated otherwise. Be that as it may, intellectual communication is always connected with understanding, with *the same* understanding by the two parties of certain definite statements.

Intellectual communication based on understanding is inseparably connected with speech. A stricter definition of what I mean by language and speech will be given later. There is one point I should like to stress here: regardless of how one defines speech, regardless

---

[5] Cf. G. A. Lundberg, C. C. Schrag & O. N. Larsen, *Sociology*, New York 1954, p. 389.

of all the enormous differences in that respect between the various authors who often contend one with another on that issue, every definition refers to signs or symbols comprising human speech.

In speaking, man produces certain phonic *signs* of a particular kind (other authors speak of articulated sound symbols). Communication consists in that the person who produces those phonic signs and the person who hears them understand them in the same way, that is impart to them the same *meanings.* That is precisely the definition of communication advanced by Lundberg when he says: "Communication can be defined as transmission of meanings through the intermediary of symbols".[6]

Thus we have introduced into the analysis of communication the three fundamental notions which require further investigation: sign (symbol), meaning, speech (language). To understand the sense of communication and to be able to explain sensibly the social conditions of its effectiveness, we must first analyse these three notions and their related problems. Thus the preliminary analysis of the process of communication naturally outlines the programme of further research.

---

[6] Ibid., p. 360.

Toward Further Inquiry

Charles Peirce was not very systematic in his writing and most of his work remained unpublished during his lifetime. For his work on semiotics, see Vol. II of his *Collected Papers* (Cambridge, Mass., 1931–1935); for his work on the pragmatic theory of meaning, see Vol. V of *Collected Papers*; for a helpful relating of the two concerns, see William Alston, "Pragmatism and the Theory of Signs in Peirce," *Philosophy and Phenomenological Research*, 1956.

Cassirer's fullest treatment of language is his *Philosophy of Symbolic Forms* (New Haven, Conn., 1953), but a more popular and somewhat modified version is Chapter 8 of *An Essay on Man* (New Haven, Conn., 1944). Suzanne Langer has exposited Cassirer's approach in *Philosophy in a New Key* (Cambridge, Mass., 1957)†. A somewhat similar approach to language, though with different epistemological prejudices, is taken by Wilbur Urban in *Language and Reality* (New York, 1939).

Carnap expanded his ideal-language approach beyond the confines of syntactics to include semantics and pragmatics in *Foundations of Logic and Mathematics* (Chicago, 1939), and further developed it in his *Introduction to Semantics* (Cambridge, Mass., 1942) and in *Meaning and Necessity* (Chicago, 1947). Critiques of important aspects of his philosophy of language, along with his detailed responses to them, are contained in Paul A. Schillp (ed.), *The Philosophy of Rudolf Carnap* (LaSalle, Ill., 1963)†. Expressions of Russell's program are evident through a lifetime of writing, from *Introduction to Mathematical Phi-*

losophy (London, 1920) and *Our Knowledge of the External World* (London, 1929) through *An Inquiry Into Meaning and Truth* (London, 1940), and culminating in *Human Knowledge* (New York, 1948). Critiques of his program, and his replies, can be found in Paul A. Schillp (ed.), *The Philosophy of Bertrand Russell* (Evanston, 1944)†. While Alfred Tarski's work has been principally in mathematics, his thinking in semantics has developed along lines similar to Carnap's, and a number of important papers can be found in his *Logic, Semantics and Metamathematics* (Oxford, 1956).

In many ways, Ludwig Wittgenstein's *Tractatus Logico-Philosophicus* (London, 1921, 1922, 1961) stands behind much of the development of the ideal-language approach, but Elizabeth Anscombe, in *An Introduction to Wittgenstein's Tractatus* (London, 1959), has cogently argued that Wittgenstein's early work is more in accord with the ordinary-language approach. Whatever the alignment of the *Tractatus*—an anachronistic question at best—Wittgenstein's *Philosophical Investigations* (New York, 1953) is the more frequently cited authority for ordinary-language philosophy, and his preliminary notes to it, published as *The Blue and Brown Books* (Oxford, 1958), are briefer introductions to his later thought. G. E. Moore's commonsensical analysis of philosophical problems is a vague antecedent to this approach, and his *Philosophical Studies* (London, 1922) gives good examples of his methods. In some ways more important to this approach, but because many of his writings have only recently been published, less well known to the general public, is John Austin. His *Philosophical Papers* (Oxford, 1961) were collected by J. O. Urmson and G. J. Warnock. Two of his lecture series, *Sense and Sensibilia* (Oxford, 1962) and *How to do Things with Words* (Cambridge, Mass., 1962), have also been published.

Ryle's own pursuit of the approach he outlines can be seen in his *Dilemmas* (Cambridge, 1954) and his *Concept of Mind* (London, 1949). Numerous philosophers of stature have adopted comparable approaches to analysis, and their contributions dominate such journals as *Mind, Analysis,* and *Philosophical Review.* Good historical treatments of both ideal-language and ordinary-language analysis can be found in J. O. Urmson, *Philosophical Analysis* (Oxford, 1956)†, G. J. Warnock, *English Philosophy since 1900* (London, 1958)†, and John Passmore, *A Hundred Years of Philosophy* (London, 1967)†. Good collections of papers on ordinary-language analysis are Charles Caton (ed.), *Philosophy and Ordinary Language* (Urbana, Ill., 1963), and Vere Chappell (ed.), *Ordinary Language* (Englewood Cliffs, N.J., 1964)†. An excellent exposition of differences among analytic methods is Richard Rorty (ed.), *The Linguistic Turn* (Chicago, 1967)†.

Fodor and Katz have collected, in *The Structure of Language* (Englewood Cliffs, N.J., 1964), a number of papers aimed at substantiating their thesis of a *tertium quid.* In that volume, Noam Chomsky's "On the Notion 'Rule of Grammar'" presents an exposition of transformational grammar, and Fodor and Katz's "The Structure of a Semantic Theory" does a similar job for the semantic component of the theory. A fuller exposition of the grammar is Chomsky's *Syntactic Structures* ('s-Gravenhage, 1957), and this is extended in his *Aspects of the Theory of Syntax* (Cambridge, Mass., 1965). On the semantics, see Katz and Paul Postal, *An Integrated Theory of Linguistic Descriptions* (Cambridge, Mass., 1964). These are all technical expositions; the novice may find Postal's treatment in "Underlying and Superficial Linguistic Structures," *Harvard Educational Review*, Vol. 34 (1964), a more readable introduction. For an application of the theory to philosophical problems, as well as an exposition of it and a critique of other positions from this viewpoint, see Katz, *The Philosophy of Language*†. Somewhat more conservative programs for the use of structural linguistics in philosophy of language are found in Alston's "Philosophical Analysis and Structural Linguistics," JP, 59 (1962), and in Zeno Vendler's *Linguistics in Philosophy* (Ithaca, N.Y., 1967). Serious reservations have been expressed from an ordinary-language approach that linguistics can be in any way useful in unraveling philosophical problems, most notably by S. Cavell in "Must We Mean What We Say?" *Inquiry*, 1 (1958). Fodor and Katz respond to arguments of this sort in "The Availability of What We Say," PR, 72 (1963). Vendler gives a good summary of this controversy in the first chapter of his book.

As Merleau-Ponty rightly notes, too little has been done by phenomenologists in this area. Martin Heidegger's *Unterwegs zur Sprache* (Tubingen, 1959) and Georges Gusdorf's *Speaking* (Evanston, Ill., 1965) make some beginning in the field. R. C.. Kwant has done further explorations in *Phenomenology of Language* (Pittsburg, 1965). Mikel Dufranne, in *Language and Philosophy* (Bloomington, Ind., 1963), seeks to relate phenomenological methods to analytical approaches to language. Work by Marxists is less available, mostly because of language barriers. Schaff's *Introduction to Semantics*† and *Jezyk a Poznanie* [Language and Cognition] (Warsaw, 1964)† present not only insights into his own views, but thorough expositions and bibliographies of related views.

Chapter 2

MODES, THEORIES, AND STANDARDS OF MEANING

Men content themselves with the same words as
other people use, as if the very sound
necessarily carried the same meanings.

John Locke

"What do you mean by . . .?" Such questions are familiar ones. They are not peculiar to the philosopher analyzing concepts or the linguist translating from one language to another. They frequently occur in everyday conversations in a meeting-conscious society. They seem ultimately to presuppose an understanding of meaning: a conception of what meaning is, or of how meaning functions, or of what 'meaning' means. Attention may be drawn to these understandings by a breakdown in effective communication, translation, or analysis. One may wonder that patterns of sound and patterns of marks on paper can convey meaning, and this concern may also lead to pondering about such understandings. A variety of impetuses have led inquiries to explicate, criticize, and systematize understandings of meaning.

When the inquirer shifts from concern about the meaning of a particular word to a consideration of meaning per se, there are serious difficulties about how to begin. Suppose he asks: "What is the meaning of meaning?" Does the question presuppose that meaning is some nonlinguistic entity? Does meaning itself have *a* meaning? If not, then how could he ever answer the question? If so, then why would he ever ask it, since the question itself presupposes an understanding of what meaning is? Such perplexities over this formulation of the problem may seem to derive from a failure to distinguish between the use and mention of the term 'meaning' in the question (on the use-mention distinction, see note 2 in the Prologue). He asks again: "What is the meaning of 'meaning'?" This makes the inquiry into the conception of meaning just like any other question about the meaning of a particular term. But is it? When else is a term ever used in this way about its name? Does it make sense to make the term 'meaning' the

114

object of concerns about meaning? In order to answer the question, "What is the meaning of 'meaning'?" one must understand his use of 'meaning'. Will this lead to the question, 'What is the meaning of "the meaning of 'meaning'"?' If so, it will throw the inquirer into a hopeless infinite regress.

When philosophical perplexities lead to circularity or infinite regress, resolution of the problems seems impossible. Often such difficulties arise from the initial formulation of the problem. Some have maintained that discussion about meaning in general is neither fruitful nor appropriate to concerns about meaning. Concerns about meaning are always with the meaning of particular expressions, and they need not lead to any general theory or understanding of meaning. To inquire into the meaning of a particular word does not presuppose an understanding of meaning in general. Others have maintained that a general understanding of meaning is presupposed by any inquiry into meaning, but they have sought formulations for such an understanding that do not become ensnared in the logical perplexities explored in the preceding paragraph. The inquirer must face these two questions at the outset of his concern with meaning: Does an understanding of the meaning of a particular word presuppose (require as a logical basis) an understanding of meaning in general? If so, how is an inquiry into such a general understanding best formulated? In 2.3, John Austin argues for a negative answer to the first question. Here, we will consider some answers to the second question and issues which arise from these ways of treating the matter.

When an inquirer explores meaning, he may wish to understand *how* expressions mean. This calls for the question: "What are the modes of meaning—the ways in which a word means?" A widely acknowledged answer rests on the dichotomy of *intensional meaning* (connotation) and *extensional meaning* (denotation).[1] A simple formula for the distinction is that the intension of an expression is what it *implies* (what logically follows from it) and the extension of an expression is that to which it *applies* (those objects or entities for which it stands). The total intension of an expression is all the characteristics or properties of that for which it stands; the total extension of a term is all the objects to which it applies. This will serve as a beginning for understanding how expressions mean. In order to gain a more explicit, critical, and systematic understanding of modes of meaning, a number of issues must be met:

What is the unit of meaning? Most talk about meaning is in terms of words. Do all words have meaning? Do all words have extension and intension? Is the extension-intension distinction for sentences the same as for words? The

---

[1] The connotation-denotation and intension-extension distinctions are time-honored ones, and they are usually used interchangeably. Therefore, the use in philosophical discourse of the connotation-denotation distinction is somewhat different from the use explained in most English grammars. Often, other pairs of terms are used for basically the same purposes, for example, *Sinn-Bedeutung* (meaning-reference) and designation-denotation. Philosophers disagree not only about which terms to use, but about the character of the distinction. On this latter point, compare the explanation in this introduction with that by Lewis in 2.1 and that by Ryle in 2.2.

extension of sentences is dependent upon their truth value (whether they are true or false, whether they apply at all). Is treatment of the extension of sentences in terms of truth value consistent with the notion of the extension of terms as the objects for which they stand?

Is the intension-extension treatment of modes complete? Can all ways in which expressions mean be satisfactorily resolved into connotation or denotation?

Is there an inverse variation between extensions and intensions of words? Many have held that as the number of objects to which a word applies increases, the number of characteristics those objects have in common decreases. Thus, the characteristics the word implies also decrease. This thesis holds that the opposite relation also obtains: when the intension increases, the extension decreases. If such an inverse variation exists, what does it imply about the relation between intension and extension, if anything?

Can one mode be reduced to the other? Formal logic finds facility in dealing with truth-functional units, since they require no interpretation other than in terms of their truth value. This invites an interpretation of language in strictly extensional terms. On such an interpretation, if one term in a sentence can be substituted for another term without altering the truth value of the sentence (without changing the logical conditions under which that sentence is true), then these terms can be said to be extensionally identical. Similarly, in a compound sentence, if a component sentence can be substituted for one of the component sentences of the original without changing the truth value of the compound sentence, then the two interchangeable component sentences can be said to be extensionally identical. If such conditions for identity and substitutability can be met, then the language can be logically dealt with solely in terms of the extensional mode, and there is no need to consider the intensional mode. Problems arise for such a program when it is applied to statements about belief, claims about necessity, possibility, and impossibility, and discussions about nonexistent objects. The statement 'All centaurs are unicorns' would be true on an extensional interpretation. But we do not mean the same thing by 'centaurs' as we mean by 'unicorns'. Can such difficulties be overcome, and a satisfactory extensional reduction be made? If not, can the modes of intension and extension be correlated in some other way?

Is there an ordered relation between these modes of meaning? In learning the meaning of an expression, does one learn first the application and then the implication, or is it the other way around? Are there natural groupings of things in the world whose common characteristics we discover? Or do all classifications of the things to which our expressions apply derive from the connotations we give those expressions?

Even if the inquirer can satisfactorily deal with such issues as these, he may wish to contend that understanding how expressions mean does not satisfy his quest for understanding meaning. He may still be convinced that expressions *have* meaning, that the question 'What is the meaning of a word [any word]?' cannot be answered in terms of modes of meaning. What seems to be called for is rather a theory of what meanings are. The most likely thesis is that the meaning of an expression is that for which it stands, that the meaning of a word is its referent. Referential theories based upon such a thesis require that there be something to which the word refers. What of a word like 'unicorn'? For such words there is no (physical) referent, but there is a concept or idea. This leads to the alternative thesis that the meaning of the term is the concept or idea for which it stands. Ideational theories based upon this thesis have been challenged by a characterization of consciousness as mental acts. Mental acts *intend* objects; ideas are always ideas *of* something. The meaning of 'unicorn' cannot be the idea of unicorn, but must be that which the idea is of. Since there are no physical unicorns, this theory seems to require that there be intentional objects that are neither mental acts nor physical objects. All three of these theses (referential, ideational, and intentional) have been attacked on the ground that they treat all meaningful expressions as names. If other kinds of words have meaning, then it must be based upon how these various expressions function in language, not upon what kinds of things they stand for. These rival theses, in challenging one another, also raise broader questions for an inquiry into meaning:

What is the relation between modes of meaning and theories of meaning? How does a referential theory differ from the extensional mode? How does a theory involving intentional objects differ from the intensional mode? Is a functional theory any more than a treatment of the ways in which expressions mean? How are 'What is the meaning of a word?' and 'What are the ways a word means?' different questions?

Do all words have meaning? The extensional-intensional treatment of modes of meaning deals with expressions that name something. So do referential, ideational, and intentional theories of meaning. Can words of a non-referential character be said to *have* meaning in any comparable sense? Certainly such words are meaningful. Should a distinction between having meaning and being meaningful be made?

Do any words have meanings? The unit of linguistic expression is a sentence, not a word. Words are used in sentences to express meanings, but do they in any sense have meaning apart from their roles in sentences?

Still another kind of concern may motivate the inquirer. He may seek to discover by what standards expressions are determined to be meaningful. Such a standard was required by the logical positivists' program for eliminating metaphysics. Metaphysical statements were judged meaningless by the verifiability principle of meaning. A. J. Ayer gives a popular formulation of this principle in *Language, Truth and Logic*:

> We say that a sentence is factually significant to any given person, if, and only if,
> he knows how to verify the proposition which it purports to express—that is, if he
> knows what observations would lead him, under certain conditions, to accept the
> proposition as being true, or reject it as being false.

All cognitively significant expressions either are factually significant or can be
determined by a logical analysis to be necessarily true (analytic) or necessarily
false (self-contradictory). The latter can be analyzed without recourse to what is
factual, and they tell nothing about the character of the world. Expressions of
emotion or command may be said to have noncognitive significance, but this
significance lies in the very act of expression, not in anything told about the
world. The concern is with expressions that masquerade at giving information
about the world but that have only analytic or some kind of noncognitive significance. The verifiability principle provides an instrument for unmasking such
pretenders.

However one evaluates the effectiveness of the verifiability principle in the
attack upon metaphysics, it serves as a useful paradigm for exploring issues involved in formulating and applying principles of meaning:

> What is the unit of meaningfulness? We have already questioned the word
> as a unit. The verifiability principle takes a sentence as the unit at issue.
> But if we begin with a sentence, what understanding can we derive about the
> meaning of its components?

> Can a single principle serve as a standard for all factually meaningful
> statements? Neither historical statements nor theoretical statements are
> verifiable by any direct experimental methods. Doesn't this call for a plu-
> rality of principles? Can principles be formulated for noncognitive mean-
> ingfulness, as well as for factual and logical meaningfulness?

> What is the relation of the concerns with meaningfulness to the con-
> cerns with meaning? Can a criterion for the meaning of particular expres-
> sions be derived from a criterion for meaningfulness of expressions? Does
> it follow from the verifiability principle that the meaning of a factually sig-
> nificant sentence is the method of its verification?

> Does the verifiability principle rely exclusively on the extensional mode
> of meaning? The principle is formulated to deal with statements in terms
> of their truth value. Is the thesis of extensionality (that all meaning can be
> dealt with truth functionally) therefore required as a corollary to the
> principle?

> Is the verifiability principle descriptive of the way people in fact determine
> meaningfulness, or is it normative for the way they should? If the former,
> how is the principle itself verifiable? If the latter, how is the principle
> justified? If neither, then what is its nature as a principle?

The list can be extended by consideration of the relation of such standards of
meaningfulness to the modes of meaning and the theories about meaning.

In the first of the essays that follow, C. I. Lewis gives a systematic explication of modes of meaning for terms. He regards it necessary to add to the extension-intension modes those of signification and comprehension. Gilbert Ryle, in his survey of theories of meaning, offers a critique of the foundations of these theories. His thesis is that meanings of terms are best understood as the functions of the terms in sentences. Austin's essay explores a variety of forms that questions about meaning can take. The results are insights not only into the character of meaning, but into the character of philosophical inquiries. The last two essays focus on the verifiability principle of meaning. Carl Hempel offers a sympathetic critique of developments and difficulties of the principle. G. J. Warnock attacks it from an ordinary-language approach to inquiry. Many of the arguments of both essays have import not only for this principle of meaning, but for the possibility that there can be any adequate criterion for meaning.

MODES OF MEANING   2.1

C. I. Lewis

The discussion will mainly be confined to meanings as conveyed by words; by series of ink-marks or of sounds. But it will be well to acknowledge at the outset that verbal meanings are not primitive: presumably the meanings to be expressed must come before the linguistic expression of them, however much language may operate retroactively to modify the meanings entertained. Also, other things than verbal expressions have meaning; in fact, one may well think that words are only surrogates for presentational items of other sorts which are the originals in exercise of the meaning-function. As Charles Peirce pointed out, the essentials of the meaning-situation are found wherever there is anything which, for some mind, stands as sign of something else. To identify meaning exclusively with the characters of verbal symbolization would be to put the cart before the horse, and run the risk of trivializing the subject. The generic significance of meaning is that in which A means B if A operates as representing or signifying B; if it stands for B, or calls it to mind. Still, it is doubtful that there are, or could be, any meanings which it is intrinsically impossible for words to express: it

From *Philosophy and Phenomenological Research*, V (1943–1944). Reprinted by permission of the editors.

may well be that in discussing verbal meanings exclusively, we do not necessarily omit any kind of meanings, but merely limit our consideration to meanings as conveyed by a particular type of vehicle.

Even with this limitation to meaning as verbally expressed, it is impossible, within reasonable limits of space here, to present our topic otherwise than in outline only. Nor will it be possible to make desirable comparisons between the outline to be offered and other discussions of the same subject. But because such outline-presentation may easily have the air of dogmatism, I should like to express my conviction that if there be any one analysis of meaning in general which is correct, then any number of other analyses will be possible which are equally correct: for much the same reasons that if any set of primitive ideas and primitive propositions are sufficient for a mathematical system, then there will be any number of alternative sets of primitive ideas and propositions which likewise are sufficient. Amongst alternative analyses of meaning which should be so fortunate as to be correct in all details, choice would presumably be determined by such considerations as convenience, simplicity, and conformability to some purpose in hand.

In general, the connection between a linguistic sign and its meaning is determined by convention: linguistic signs are verbal symbols. A *verbal symbol* is a recognizable pattern of marks or of sounds used for purposes of expression. (What is recognized as the same pattern, in different instances, is partly a matter of physical similarity and partly a matter of conventional understanding.) Two marks, or two sounds, having the same recognizable pattern, are two *instances* of the same symbol; not two different symbols.

A *linguistic expression* is constituted by the association of a verbal symbol and a fixed meaning; but the linguistic expression cannot be identified with the symbol alone nor with the meaning alone. If in two cases, the meaning expressed is the same but the symbols are different, there are two expressions; not one. If in two cases, the symbol is the same but the meanings are different, there are two expressions; not one. But if in two cases—as in different places or at different times—the meaning is the same and the symbol is the same, then there are two *instances* of the expression but only one expression.

An instance of a symbol is often called a symbol, and an instance of an expression is often called an expression; but these modes of speech are unprecise. An ink-spot or a noise is a concrete entity; but a symbol is an abstract entity; and an expression is a correlative abstraction.

A linguistic expression may be a term or a proposition or a propositional function. As it will turn out, propositions and propositional functions are terms; but some terms only are propositions, and some only are propositional functions; and these two latter classifications are mutually exclusive.

A *term* is an expression which names or applies to a thing or things, of some kind, actual or thought of.

It is sometimes said that what is not actual cannot be named. But such assertion is either an arbitrary and question-begging restriction upon use of the verb "to name"—since plainly whatever is thought of can be spoken of or it is merely silly. One does not easily imagine what those who make this assertion would say to persons who have named a hoped-for child or inventors who have named a never-completed machine. However, there are difficulties connected with this point which are genuine; and it will be the intention so to write here as to minimize dependence upon it. In line with that intention, the above definition of a term may be rephrased: A term is an expression *capable* of naming or applying to a thing or things, of some kind.

In common speech, a term is said to denote the existent or existents to which it is applied on any given occasion of its use. For example, in the statement "Those three objects are books," "book" is said to denote the three objects indicated, or any one of them. This usage has the awkward consequence that what a term is said to denote is not, in most instances, the denotation of it. We shall, however, continue to use both "denote" and "denotation" with their commonplace significances.[1]

All terms have meaning in the sense or mode of denotation or extension; and all have meaning in the mode of connotation or intension.

The *denotation* of a term is the class of all actual or existent things to which that term correctly applies. The quali-

fication "actual or existent" here is limiting and not merely explicative: things which are, or would be, namable by a term but which do not in fact exist are not included in its denotation.

A term which names nothing actual has *zero-denotation*. But it would be a mistake to say that such a term as "unicorn" or "Apollo" has no denotation; especially since this would suggest that it has no meaning in the correlative sense of meaning. A term has meaning in the mode of denotation if it is intended to function as a name; and any locution not so intended is not a term.

When it is desirable to refer to whatever a term would correctly name or apply to, whether existent or not, we shall speak of a *classification* instead of a class, and of the comprehension of the term. The *comprehension* of a term is, thus, the classification of all consistently thinkable things to which the term would correctly apply—where anything is consistently thinkable if the assertion of its existence would not, explicitly or implicitly, involve a contradiction. For example, the comprehension of "square" includes all imaginable as well as all actual squares, but does not include round squares.

Much confusion in analysis may be avoided by the clear distinction of denotation from comprehension.

The *connotation* or *intension* of a term is delimited by any correct definition of it. If nothing would be correctly namable by "T" unless it should also be namable by "A_1," by "A_2," and . . . and by "A_n," and if anything namable by the compound term, "A_1 and A_2 and . . . and A_n" would also be nam-

---

[1] Some avoid the awkward consequence mentioned by saying that a term *designates* a thing that it names. This terminology is apt, but is not adopted here.

able by "*T*" then this compound term, or any which is synonymous with it, specifies the connotation of "*T*" and may be said to have the same connotation as "*T*." This leaves "connotation" subject to one ambiguity, which will be discussed later. But for the present, the characterization given will be sufficiently clear.

Traditionally the term "essence" is used to indicate that characteristic of the object or objects named which is correlative with the connotation of the term. It is, of course, meaningless to speak of the essence of a thing except relative to its being named by some particular term. But for purposes of analysis, it is desirable or even necessary to have some manner of marking this distinction between characters of an object which are essential to its being named by a term in question, and other characters of the object which are not thus essential. We shall say that a term *signifies* the comprehensive character such that everything having this character is correctly namable by the term, and whatever lacks this character, or anything included in it, is not so namable. And we shall call this comprehensive essential character the *signification* of the term.[2]

———

[2] Some may be minded to insist that it is the *sign* which *signifies*, and not the term or linguistic expression, constituted by association of the sign with a meaning. Our usage here of the words "signify" and "signification" is, of course, arbitrary: other and possibly more appropriate words might have been chosen instead. But what we use these words to refer to is a function of the term or expression, and is *not* a property which (like its shape) can be attributed to the sign regardless of the meaning associated with it.

Abstract terms are those which name what they signify. Thus for abstract terms, signification and denotation coincide. Things which incorporate the signification of an abstract term, "*A*," but possess other characters not included in what "*A*" names, are *instances* of *A* but are not named by "*A*."

Non-abstract terms, whose denotation is distinct from their signification, are *concrete*.

By the idiom of language, there are certain words and phrases—e.g., predicate-adjectives like "red"—which when they occur as grammatical subject are abstract terms, but which may occur as concrete terms in the predicate. Such words and phrases are sometimes called *attributive*. But this classification is primarily linguistic; the words and phrases in question are not strictly terms but only ambiguous symbolizations having now one, now another meaning. The classification "attributive" is worth remarking only in order that certain confusions about abstract and concrete terms may be avoided.

A *singular* term is one whose connotation precludes application of it to more than one actual thing. A nonsingular term is *general*. (The dichotomy, singular or general, is not significant in the case of abstract terms; if it be applied to them, all abstract terms must be classed as singular.)

It should be observed that singularity or generality is a question of connotation, not of denotation. "The red object on my desk" is a singular term, and "red object on my desk" is a general term, regardless of the facts about red objects on my desk. If there is no red object on my desk, or if there is more than one, then "the red object on my desk" has zero-denotation, but its being a singular term is not affected.

The question what should be regarded as comprehended by a singular term, involves the consideration that, although singularity is connoted, still the connotation of a singular term is never sufficient—without recourse to other and logically adventitious facts—to determine *what* individual is named; i.e., to select this individual from amongst all thinkable things satisfying the connotation of the term. Thus the denotation of a singular term is a class which is either a class of one or is empty. But its comprehension is the classification of *all* the things consistently thinkable as being the one and only member of that class.

It will be noted that, for any term, its connotation determines its comprehension; and conversely, any determination of its comprehension would determine its connotation, by determining what characters alone are common to all the things comprehended. In point of fact, however, there is no way in which the comprehension can be precisely specified except by reference to the connotation, since exhaustive enumeration of all the thinkable things comprehended is never possible.

The connotation of a term and its denotation do not, however, mutually determine one another. The connotation being given, the denotation is thereby limited but not fixed. Things which lack any essential attribute, specified or implied in the connotation, are *excluded from* the denotation; but what is *included in* the denotation, and

what not, depends also on what happens to exist; since the class of things denoted—as distinguished from what the term comprehends—is confined to existents.

Also, the denotation of a term being determined, the connotation is thereby limited but not fixed. The connotation cannot include any attribute absent from one or more of the things named; but it may or may not include an attribute which is common to all existents named by the term; since such an attribute may or may not be essential to their being so named. "Featherless biped," for example, does not connote rationality, even if the class denoted contains only rational beings.

We should also remark that a term may have zero-comprehension. For example, "round square" has zero-comprehension; the classification of consistently-thinkable things so named is empty. But many terms—e.g., "unicorn" and "non-rational animal that laughs" —have zero-denotation without having zero-comprehension; things which would be correctly so named are consistently thinkable.

The classic dictum that denotation varies inversely as connotation, is false; e.g., "rational featherless biped" has the same denotation as "featherless biped." But this relation does hold between connotation and comprehension. Any qualification added to a connotation (and not already implied) further restricts the comprehension; and with any omission of a qualification from a connotation, the classification comprehended is enlarged to include thinkable things which retension of that qualification would exclude.

This relation of connotation and comprehension is worth remarking for the sake of one consequence of it: a term of zero-comprehension has *universal* connotation. This may at first strike the reader as a paradox. But the correctness of it may be observed from two considerations. Only terms naming nothing which is consistently thinkable have zero-comprehension. And "*A is both round and square*," for example, entails "*A is y*," for any value of *y*. That is, the attribution of "both round and square" entails every attribute; and the connotation of "round square," since it includes every mentionable attribute, is universal.[3]

This fact clarifies one matter which might otherwise be puzzling. Plainly, it is incorrect to say that terms like "round square" have no connotation, or that they are meaningless. This term is distinguished from a nonsense-locution like "zuke" by definitely implying the properties of roundness and squareness. And it is only by reason of this meaning—this connotation—which it

has, that one determines its inapplicability to anything consistently thinkable.

Thus what is (presumably) intended by the inaccurate statement that such terms are meaningless, can be stated precisely by saying that they have zero-comprehension, or that their connotation is universal.

The diametrically opposite kind of term—those having universal comprehension and zero-connotation—are also often said to be meaningless. "Being" and "entity"—supposing everything one could mention is a being or entity —are such terms. And again, the accurate manner of indicating the lack of significance which characterizes these terms, is to observe that attribution of them implies no attribute that could be absent from anything; that their connotation is zero and their comprehension unlimited. But if they genuinely lacked any meaning—any connotation —this character of them could not be determined.

The modes of meaning mentioned above for terms—denotation or extension, connotation or intension, comprehension, and signification—are likewise the modes of meaning of propositions and of propositional functions. This is the case because propositions are a kind of terms; and propositional functions are another kind of terms.

A proposition is a term capable of signifying a state of affairs. To define a proposition as an expression which is either true or false, is correct enough but inauspicious; because it may lead to confusion of a proposition with the *statement* or *assertion* of it, whereas the element of assertion in a statement is extraneous to the proposition as-

---

[3] "*A* is both *x* and not-*x*" entails "*A* is *x*."

And "*A* is *x*" entails "Either *A* is both *x* and *y* or *A* is *x* but not *y*."

Hence "*A* is both *x* and not-*x*" entails "Either *A* is both *x* and *y* or *A* is *x* but not *y*."

But also "*A* is both *x* and not-*x*" entails "*A* is not *x*."

And "*A* is not *x*" entails "It is false that *A* is *x* but not *y*."

Hence "*A* is both *x* and not-*x*" entails "It is false that *A* is *x* but not *y*."

But "Either *A* is both *x* and *y* or *A* is *x* but not *y*" and "It is false that *A* is *x* but not *y*" together entail "*A* is both *x* and *y*."

And "*A* is both *x* and *y*" entails "*A* is *y*."

Hence "*A* is both *x* and not-*x*" entails "*A* is *y*."

serted. The proposition is the assertable content; and this same content,
signifying the same state of affairs, can
also be questioned, denied, or merely
supposed, and can be entertained in
other moods as well.[4]

"Fred is buying groceries" asserts the
state of affairs participially signifiable
by "Fred buying groceries (now)." "Is
Fred buying groceries?" questions it;
"Let Fred buy groceries" presents it in
the hortatory mood; "Oh that Fred
may be buying groceries" in the optative mood; and "Suppose Fred is buying groceries" puts it forward as an
hypothesis. Omitting then, this adventitious element of assertion—or any
other mode of entertainment—we find
the assertable content, here identified
with the proposition itself, as some
participial term, signifying a state of
affairs, actual or thinkable.

It will be noted that the state of affairs is the *signification* of the proposition; not its denotation. When any term
denotes a thing, it names that thing as
a whole, not merely the character or
attribute signified. And what a term denotes or applies to is, by the law of
the Excluded Middle, also denoted by
one or the other of every pair of mutually negative terms which could
meaningfully be applied to it. Thus
there would be a failure of analogy, on
a most important point, between propositional terms and the more familiar
kind of terms, if we should regard
propositions as denoting the state of

affairs they refer to. And the denotation or extension of propositions would
not be subject to the law of the Excluded Middle. The denotation or extension of a proposition, as application
of that law leads us to see, is something which is likewise denoted by one
or other of every pair of mutually
negative propositional terms; i.e., one
or other of every pair of mutually
contradictory propositions. And this
thing denoted is not that limited state
of affairs which the proposition refers
to, but the kind of *total* state of affairs
we call a world. The limited state of
affairs signified is merely the *essential
attribute* which any world must possess
in order that the proposition in question should denote or apply to it. A
statement asserting a proposition *attributes* the state of affairs signified to the
actual world. And the denotation or
extension of a proposition—since denotation is in all cases confined to what
exists—is either the actual world or it
is empty. Thus all *true* propositions
have the same extension, namely, this
actual world; and all *false* propositions have the same extension, namely,
zero-extension. The distinctive extensional property of a proposition is, thus,
its truth or falsity.

A proposition *comprehends* any consistently thinkable world which would
incorporate the state of affairs it signifies; a classification of Leibnitzian
possible worlds. This conception of
possible world is not jejune: the actual
world, so far as anyone knows it, is
merely one of many such which are
possible. For example, I do not know
at the moment how much money I
have in my pocket, but let us say it is

---

[4] I am indebted to conversations with Professor C. W. Morris for this way of putting
the matter—though he may not approve the
conception that a proposition is a term.

thirty cents. The world which is just like this one except that I should have thirty-five cents in my pocket now, is a consistently thinkable world—consistent even with all the facts I know. When I reflect upon the number of facts of which I am uncertain, the plethora of possible worlds which, for all I know, might be this one, becomes a little appalling.

The *intension* of a proposition includes whatever the proposition entails; it comprises whatever must be true of any possible world in order that the proposition should apply to or be true of it—a sense of the meaning of propositions which is familiar and fundamental.

An *analytic* proposition is one which would apply to or be true of every possible world; one, therefore, whose comprehension is universal, and correlatively, one which has zero-intension. At this point, the distinction previously remarked between terms of zero-intension and locutions which have no meaning, becomes important. An analytic proposition does not fail to have implications—though all entailments of it are likewise analytic or necessary propositions which would hold true of any world which is consistently thinkable. That an analytic proposition has zero-intension is correlative with the fact that in being true of reality it imposes no restriction or limitation on the actual which could conceivably be absent.

A *self-contradictory* or self-inconsistent proposition has zero-comprehension, and could apply to or be true of no world which is consistently thinkable. Correlatively, such a proposition

has universal intension: it entails all propositions, both true and false.

All *synthetic* propositions, excepting the self-contradictory, have an intension which is neither zero nor universal, and a comprehension which is neither universal nor zero. They entail some things and not other things. Consonantly, their truth is compatible with some consistently thinkable states of affairs and incompatible with other consistently thinkable states of affairs.

The discussion of propositional functions must be even more compressed —suggested rather than outlined.

A propositional function is essentially a kind of predicate or predication; a characterization meaningfully applicable to the kind of entities names of which are values of the variables. For a propositional function of the general form "x is A" (where "A" is some non-variable expression), it is "being A" which is this predicate or characterization; for one of the general form "x R y" (where "R" is some constant), it is "(the first mentioned) being in the relation R (to the second mentioned)," or "(the ordered couple mentioned) being in the relation R."

Speaking most judiciously, there is only one variable in any propositional function. In what are called functions of two variables, x and y, this one variable is the ordered couple (x, y); in what are called functions of three variables, it is the ordered triad (x, y, z), etc. In the verbal form of the propositional function, so construed, the characterization which essentially is the function itself, is predicated of this one variable. What are called variables are, in fact, merely syntactic devices for preserving the essential structure of the predication itself. Otherwise put: variables are constituents of discourse which have no meaning except one conferred by their context, including the syntax of that context.

Propositional functions are participial terms, as propositions are. But whereas the propositional characterization (if we may so call it for the moment) "John being now angry" could only characterize reality or some thinkable world; the propositional-function characterization "being angry" or any of the form "being A" or of the form "being in the relation R," could not be a characterization of a world, but only of a thing, or a pair of things, etc. And a function-characterization which is predicable of one thing would be meaningfully predicable of many.[5]

The denotation or *extension* of a propositional function is the class of existent things (individuals or ordered couples or triads, etc.) for which this predication holds true. It may be a class of many or a class of one or an empty class.

The *comprehension* of a function is the classification of things consistently thinkable as being characterized by this predication. This comprehension may be universal or zero or may include some consistently thinkable things and exclude others.

The *connotation* or intension of a

function comprises all that the attribution of this predicate to anything entails as also attributable to that thing. This intension may be universal or zero or neither.

Propositional functions of the sort sometimes called *assertable*—the kind that logicians write down in expounding their subject (when they do not make mistakes)—are functions having universal comprehension; falsely predicable of nothing which is consistently thinkable. And they have zero-intension, imposing no limitation on anything thinkable in being held true of it. It is by this fact alone that their status as assertable functions can be certified.

At almost every point of this outline, questions requiring to be met have been omitted. But even with this condensation, insufficient space remains for indicating applications of it to moot questions of theory. We shall mention briefly two such only; application to the question of meaningfulness in general; and the ambiguity of "intension" which was mentioned earlier.

If one should wish to speak of *the* meaning of a term or proposition or propositional function, it will be evident that meaning in the mode of intension would be the best candidate for this preferred status. Expressions having the same connotation or intension must also have the same denotation or extension, the same signification, and the same comprehension. One might suppose, in consequence, that two expressions having the same intension would have the same meaning in every called-for sense of the word "meaning." Nevertheless that would be an error.

---

[5] This does not mean that the kind of term which is a function, is necessarily a general term. "Being now the President" is meaningfully predicable of many things; but by its intension it must be *falsely* predicable of any existent but one: hence it is a singular term.

That two locutions expressing the same intensional meaning may still be *distinct expressions*—and not two instances of one expression—is a point which has already been covered; they may be distinct by the fact that the *symbols* are different, though the meaning is the same. However, not every pair of expressions having the same intension would be called synonymous; and there is good reason for this fact.

Two expressions are commonly said to be synonymous (or in the case of propositions, equipollent) if they have the same intension, and *that intension is neither zero nor universal.*[6] But to say that two expressions with the same intension have the same meaning, without qualification, would have the anomalous consequence that any two analytic propositions would then be equipollent, and any two self-contradictory propositions would be equipollent. Also, any two terms like "round square" and "honorable poltroon" would then be synonymous.

The desirable restriction requires us to add a further specification to intensional meaning in the case of complex expressions.

An expression in question is *elementary* in case it has no symbolized constituent, the intension of which is a constituent of the intension of the expression in question itself. Otherwise the expression in question is *complex*.

The intension of any complex expression has, in addition to the intensions of its symbolized elementary constituents, an element of syntax. But we can avoid discussion of syntax here if we recognize that the syntax of a complex expression, so far as it is not already implicit in the intension of constituents taken separately (e.g., by their being substantives or verbs, etc.), is conveyed by the *order* of these constituents.

When we think of the ways in which complex expressions can be analyzed into constituents and a syntactic order of them, we may refer to *analytic meaning*. This expression will not be defined: instead, we shall characterize the relation "equivalent in analytic meaning." Two expressions are *equivalent in analytic meaning*, (1) if at least one is elementary and they have the same intension, or (2) if, both being complex, they can be so analyzed into constituents that (a) for every constituent distinguished in either, there is a corresponding constituent in the other which has the same intension, (b) no constituent distinguished in either has zero-intension or universal intension, and (c) the order of corresponding constituents is the same in both, or can be made the same without alteration of the intension of either whole expression.

Thus "round excision" and "circular hole" are equivalent in analytic meaning. Likewise "square" and "rectangle with equal sides," since these terms have the same intension and one is elementary. But "equilateral triangle" and "equiangular triangle," though they have the same intension when taken as whole expressions, are not equivalent

---

[6] "Equipollent" is doubtfully appropriate here; there is no term which unambiguously names that relation of propositions which is parallel to the relation of synonymity between terms.

in analytic meaning since there is no constituent of the former which has the intension of "equiangular" and no constituent of the latter which has the same intension as "equilateral."

We shall be in conformity with good usage if we say that two expressions are synonymous or equipollent, (1) if they have the same intension and that intension is neither zero nor universal, or (2) if, their intension being either zero or universal, they are equivalent in analytic meaning. And we shall be in conformity with good usage if we take the statement that the expressions have the *same meaning*, when the intended mode of meaning is unspecified, as indicating that these expressions are synonymous or equipollent.

We turn now to the ambiguity of "intension" which has been referred to.

Intension or connotation may be thought of in either of two ways, which we shall call respectively linguistic meaning and sense meaning.

Linguistic meaning is intension as constituted by the pattern of definitive and other analytic relationships of the expression in question to other *expressions*.[7] One who, for example, tried to learn the meaning of a French word with only a French dictionary at hand, might—if he be poorly acquainted with French—be obliged to look up also words used in defining the one whose meaning he sought; and the words defining them; and so on. He might thus eventually determine a quite extended

---

[7] Some would say "syntactic" here, instead of "analytic." A relationship is analytic if the statement of it is an analytic statement.

pattern of linguistic relations of the word in question to other words in French. If the process of this example could, by some miracle, be carried to its logical limit, a person might thus come to grasp completely and with complete accuracy the linguistic pattern relating a large body of foreign words but—in an obvious sense—without learning what any one of them meant. What he would grasp would be their linguistic meaning. And what he would still fail to grasp would be their sense meaning.

Sense meaning is intension in the mode of a criterion in mind by which one is able to apply or refuse to apply the expression in question in the case of presented things or situations. One who should be able thus to apply or refuse to apply an expression correctly under all imaginable circumstances, would grasp its sense meaning perfectly. But if, through faulty language sense or poor analytic powers, he could still not offer any correct definition, then he would fail to grasp (at least to grasp explicitly) its linguistic meaning.

Because many logicians have of late been somewhat preoccupied with language, intension as linguistic (or "syntactic") meaning has been over-emphasized, and sense meaning has been relatively neglected. These two modes of intensional meaning are supplementary, not alternative. But for many purposes of theory of knowledge it is sense meaning the investigation of which is more important. For example, those who would demand theoretical verifiability or confirmability for significance in a statement, have in mind sense meaning as the prime requisite for meaningfulness in general. Likewise those who would set up the criterion of making some (practical) difference. And those who would emphasize the operational significance of concepts are emphasizing sense meaning.

For sense meaning, imagery is obviously requisite. Only through the capacity called imagination could one have in mind, in advance of presentation, a workable criterion for applying or refusing to apply an expression to what should be presented. But for reasons made familiar by the long controversy between nominalists, conceptualists, and realists, sense meaning cannot be vested directly and simply in imagery. The nominalist denies the possibility of sense meaning on such grounds as the impossibility of imagining dog in general or triangle in general, or of having in mind an image of a chiliagon which is sufficiently specific to distinguish between a polygon of 1000 sides and one having 999. It is the persistence of such nominalism which, in large measure, is responsible for the current tendency to identify meaning with linguistic meaning exclusively.

The answer was given by Kant. A sense meaning, when precise, is a schema; a rule or prescribed routine and an imagined result of it which will determine applicability of the expression in question. We cannot imagine a chiliagon, but we easily imagine counting the sides of a polygon and getting 1000 as the result. We cannot imagine triangle in general, but we easily imagine following the periphery of a figure with the eye or a finger and

discovering it to be a closed figure with three angles. (Many protagonists of operational significance forget to mention the imaged result, and would—according to what they *say*—identify the concept or meaning exclusively with the routine. Presumably this is merely an oversight: no procedure of laying meter sticks on things would determine length without some anticipatory imagery of a perceivable result which would, e.g., corroborate the statement that the thing is three meters long.)

Many epistemological problems may be clarified by reference to sense meaning. For example, question as to the meaningfulness of asserting that there are mountains on the other side of the moon. Practical difficulties of confirmation have no relevance: the routine and result which would corroborate the statement are in mind with a clarity sufficient for determination—perhaps with a clarity equal to that with which we grasp what it would mean to verify that there are elephants in Africa. The two assertions equally have sense meaning.

If it be said that analytic statements have no sense meaning, then it is in point that all analytic statements have zero-intension, and impose no limitation upon any consistently thinkable total state of affairs or world in being true of it. Analytic statements are, so to say, verifiable by the fact that no total state of affairs in which they should fail of truth can be imagined. But if *constituents* in analytic statements did not have sense meaning, in the more limited fashion of having criteria of their application which are sometimes satisfied and sometimes not, then this universal applicability of the analytic statement could not be certified by reference to imagination and without recourse to particular perceptions; and hence would not be knowable *a priori*.

Likewise, if it be said that the self-contradictory has no sense meaning, it is in point that the self-contradictory expression has universal intension and zero-comprehension. The situation in which it should apply is precluded in ways which imagination alone is sufficient to discover. But again, this fact would not be certifiable *a priori* if constituents in the self-contradictory expression did not have sense meanings which are self-consistent. We can cer-

tify the impossibility of what is expressed, by the experiment of trying to relate these sense meanings of constituents in the manner which the expression as a whole prescribes.

By their ultimate reference to concrete sense meaning, even the analytic and the self-contradictory have a kind of empirical reference. And without that, they would be genuinely non-significant for any experience in the world of fact. They are independent of any *particular* state of affairs or of what the world that exists is like in its details, because their applicability or inapplicability in general, or their truth or falsity in general, is certifiable from experiments in imagination.

THE THEORY OF MEANING

2.2

Gilbert Ryle

We can all use the notion of *meaning*. From the moment we begin to learn to translate English into French and French into English, we realize that one expression does or does not

From *British Philosophy in the Mid-Century*, C. A. Mace, editor (London: Allen and Unwin; New York: Macmillan, 1957). Reprinted by permission of the publishers and the author.

mean the same as another. But we use the notion of meaning even earlier than that. When we read or hear something in our own language which we do not understand, we wonder what it means and ask to have its meaning explained to us. The ideas of understanding, misunderstanding and failing to understand what is said already contain the notion of expressions having and lacking specifiable meanings.

It is, however, one thing to ask, as a child might ask, What, if anything, is meant by 'vitamin', or 'abracadabra' or '$(a+b)^2=a^2+b^2+2ab$'? It is quite another sort of thing to ask What are meanings? It is, in the same way, one thing to ask, as a child might ask, What can I buy for this shilling?, and quite another sort of thing to ask What is purchasing-power? or What are exchange-values?

Now answers to this highly abstract question, What are meanings? have, in recent decades, bulked large in philosophical and logical discussions. Preoccupation with the theory of meaning could be described as the occupational disease of twentieth-century Anglo-Saxon and Austrian philosophy. We need not worry whether or not it is a disease. But it might be useful to survey the motives and the major results of this preoccupation.

Incidentally it is worth noticing that many of these issues were explicitly canvassed—and some of them conclusively settled—in certain of Plato's later Dialogues, and in the logical and other works of Aristotle. Some of them, again, were dominant issues in the late Middle Ages and later still with Hobbes; and some of them, thickly or thinly veiled in the psychological terminology of 'ideas', stirred uneasily inside British epistemology between Locke and John Stuart Mill. But I shall not, save for one or two back-references, discuss the early history of these issues.

The shopkeeper, the customer, the banker and the merchant are ordinarily under no intellectual pressure to answer or even ask the abstract ques-

tions What is purchasing-power? and What are exchange-values? They are interested in the prices of things, but not yet in the abstract question What is the real nature of that which is common to two articles of the same price? Similarly, the child who tries to follow a conversation on an unfamiliar topic, and the translator who tries to render Thucydides into English are interested in what certain expressions mean. But they are not necessarily interested in the abstract questions What is it for an expression to have a meaning? or What is the nature and status of that which an expression and its translation or paraphrase are both the vehicles? From what sort of interests, then, do we come to ask this sort of question? Doubtless there are many answers. I shall concentrate on two of them which I shall call 'the Theory of Logic' and 'the Theory of Philosophy'. I shall spend a good long time on the first; not so long on the second.

1. The Theory of Logic

The logician, in studying the rules of inference has to talk of the components of arguments, namely their premisses and conclusions and to talk of them in perfectly general terms. Even when he adduces concrete premisses and conclusions, he does so only to illustrate the generalities which are his proper concern. In the same way, he has to discuss the types of separable components or the types of distinguishable features of these premiss-types and conclusion-types, since it is sometimes on such components or features of premisses and conclusions that the inferences from and to them pivot.

Now the same argument may be expressed in English or in French or in any other language; and if it is expressed in English, there may still be hosts of different ways of wording it. What the logician is exploring is intended to be indifferent to these differences of wording. He is concerned with what is said by a premiss-sentence or a conclusion-sentence, not with how it is worded.

So, if not in the prosecution of his inquiry, at least in his explanations of what he is doing, he has to declare that his subject-matter consists not of the sentences and their ingredient words in which arguments are expressed, but of the propositions or judgments and their constituent terms, ideas or concepts of which the sentences and words are the vehicles. Sometimes he may say that his subject matter consists of sentence-meanings and their constituent word-meanings or phrase-meanings, though this idiom is interestingly repellent. Why it is repellent we shall, I hope, see later on. So in giving this sort of explanation of his business, he is talking *about* meanings, where in the prosecution of that business he is just operating *upon* them.

For our purposes it is near enough true to say that the first influential discussion of the notion of meaning given by a modern logician was that with which John Stuart Mill opens his *System of Logic* (1843). He acknowledges debts both to Hobbes and to the Schoolmen, but we need not trace these borrowings in detail.

Mill's contributions to Formal or Symbolic Logic were negligible. It was not he but his exact contemporaries, Boole and de Morgan, and his immediate successors, Jevons, Venn, Carroll, McColl and Peirce who, in the English-speaking world, paved the way for Russell. On the other hand, it is difficult to exaggerate the influence which he exercised, for good and for ill, upon British and Continental philosophers; and we must include among these philosophers the Symbolic Logicians as well, in so far as they have philosophized about their technical business. In particular, Mill's theory of meaning set the questions, and in large measure, determined their answers for thinkers as different as Brentano, in Austria; Meinong and Husserl, who were pupils of Brentano; Bradley, Jevons, Venn, Frege, James, Peirce, Moore and Russell. This extraordinary achievement was due chiefly to the fact that Mill was original in producing a doctrine of meaning at all. The doctrine that he produced was immediately influential, partly because a doctrine was needed and partly because its inconsistencies were transparent. Nearly all of the thinkers whom I have listed were in vehement opposition to certain parts of Mill's doctrine, and it was the other parts of it from which they often drew their most effective weapons.

Mill, following Hobbes's lead, starts off his account of the notion of meaning by considering single words. As we have to learn the alphabet before we can begin to spell, so it seemed natural to suppose that the meanings of sentences are compounds of the components, which are the meanings of their ingredient words. Word-meanings are atoms, sentence-meanings are molecules. I say that it seemed natural, but I hope soon to satisfy you that it was a tragically false start. Next Mill, again following Hobbes's lead, takes it for granted that all words, or nearly all words, are names, and this, at first, sounds very tempting. We know what it is for 'Fido' to be the name of a particular dog, and for 'London' to be the name of a particular town. There, in front of us, is the dog or the town which has the name, so here, one feels, there is no mystery. We have just the familiar relation between a thing and its name. The assimilation of all or most other single words to names gives us, accordingly, a cosy feeling. We fancy that we know where we are. The dog in front of us is what the word 'Fido' stands for, the town we visited yesterday is what the word 'London' stands for. So the classification of all or most single words as names makes us feel that what a word means is in all cases some manageable thing that that word is the name of. Meanings, at least word-meanings, are nothing abstruse or remote, they are, *prima facie*, ordinary things and happenings like dogs and towns and battles.

Mill goes further. Sometimes the grammatical subject of a sentence is not a single word but a many-worded phrase, like 'the present Prime Minister' or 'the first man to stand on the summit of Mt. Everest'. Mill has no qualms in classifying complex expressions like these also as names, what he calls 'many-worded names'. There do not exist proper names for everything we want to talk about; and sometimes we want to talk about something or somebody whose proper name, though it exists, is unknown to us. So descriptive phrases are coined by us to do duty for proper names. But they are still, according to Mill, names, though the tempting and in fact prevailing interpretation of this assertion differs importantly from what Mill usually wanted to convey. For, when Mill calls a word or phrase a 'name', he is using 'name' not, or not always, quite in the ordinary way. Sometimes he says that for an expression to be a name it must be able to be used as the subject or the predicate of a subject-predicate sentence—which lets in, e.g. adjectives as names. Sometimes his requirements are more stringent. A name is an expression which can be the subject of a subject-predicate sentence—which leaves only nouns, pronouns and substantival phrases. 'Name', for him, does not mean merely 'proper name'. He often resisted temptations to which he subjected his successors.

Before going any further, I want to make you at least suspect that this initially congenial equation of words and descriptive phrases with names is from the outset a monstrous howler—if, like some of Mill's successors, though unlike Mill himself, we do systematically construe 'name' on the model of 'proper name'. The assumption of the truth of this equation has been responsible for a large number of radical absurdities in philosophy in general and the philosophy of logic in particular. It was a fetter round the ankles of Meinong, from which he never freed himself. It was a fetter round the ankles of Frege, Moore and Russell, who all, sooner or later, saw that without some big emendations, the assumption led inevitably to fatal impasses. It was, as he himself says in his new book, a fetter round the ankles of Wittgenstein in the *Tractatus*, though in that same book he had found not only the need but the way to cut himself partially loose from it.

I am still not quite sure why it seems so natural to assume that all words are names, and even that every possible grammatical subject of a sentence, one-worded or many-worded, stands to something as the proper name 'Fido' stands to the dog Fido, and, what is a further point, that the thing it stands for is what the expression means. Even Plato had had to fight his way out of the same assumption. But he at least had a special excuse. The Greek language had only the one word ὄνομα where we have the three words 'word', 'name' and 'noun'. It was hard in Greek even to say that the Greek counterpart to our verb 'is' was a word but not a noun. Greek provided Plato with no label for verbs, or for adverbs, conjunctions etc. That 'is' is a word, but is not a name or even a noun was a tricky thing to say in Greek where ὄνομα did duty both for our word 'word', for our word 'name' and, eventually, for our word 'noun'. But even without this excuse people still find it natural to assimilate all words to names, and the meanings of words to the bearers of those alleged names. Yet the assumption is easy to demolish.

First, if every single word were a name, then a sentence composed of five words, say 'three is a prime number' would be a list of the five objects named by those five words. But a list,

like 'Plato, Aristotle, Aquinas, Locke, Berkeley' is not a sentence. It says nothing, true or false. A sentence, on the contrary, may say something—some one thing—which is true or false. So the words combined into a sentence at least do something jointly which is different from their severally naming the several things that they name if they do name any things. What a sentence means is not decomposable into the set of things which the words in it stand for, if they do stand for things. So the notion of *having meaning* is at least partly different from the notion of *standing for*.

More than this. I can use the two descriptive phrases 'the Morning Star' and 'the Evening Star', as different ways of referring to Venus. But it is quite clear that the two phrases are different in meaning. It would be incorrect to translate into French the phrase 'the Morning Star' by 'l'Étoile du Soir'. But if the two phrases have different meanings, then Venus, the planet which we describe by these two different descriptions, cannot be what these descriptive phrases mean. For she, Venus, is one and the same, but what the two phrases signify are different. As we shall see in a moment Mill candidly acknowledges this point and makes an important allowance for it.

Moreover it is easy to coin descriptive phrases to which nothing at all answers. The phrase 'the third man to stand on the top of Mt. Everest' cannot, at present, be used to refer to anybody. There exists as yet no one whom it fits and perhaps there never will. Yet it is certainly a significant phrase, and could be translated into French or German. We know, we have to know, what it means when we say that it fits no living mountaineer. It means *something*, but it does not designate *somebody*. What it means cannot, therefore, be equated with a particular mountaineer. Nor can the meaning conveyed by the phrase 'the first person to stand on the top of Mt. Everest' be equated with Hillary, though, we gather, it fits him and does not fit anyone else. We can understand the question, and even entertain Nepalese doubts about the answer to the question 'Is Hillary the first person to conquer Mt. Everest?' where we could not understand the question 'Is Hillary Hillary?'

We could reach the same conclusion even more directly. If Hillary was, *per impossible*, identified with what is meant by the phrase 'the first man to stand on the top of Mt. Everest', it would follow that the meaning of at least one phrase was born in New Zealand, has breathed through an oxygen-mask and has been decorated by Her Majesty. But this is patent nonsense. Meanings of phrases are not New Zealand citizens; what is expressed by a particular English phrase, as well as by any paraphrase or translation of it, is not something with lungs, a surname, long legs and a sunburnt face. People are born and die and sometimes wear boots; meanings are not born and do not die and they never wear boots— or go barefoot either. The Queen does not decorate meanings. The phrase 'the first man to stand on the top of Mt. Everest' will not lose its meaning when

Hillary dies. Nor was it meaningless before he reached the summit.

Finally, we should notice that most words are not nouns; they are, e.g. adverbs, or verbs, or adjectives or prepositions or conjunctions or pronouns. But to classify as a name a word which is not even a noun strikes one as intolerable the moment one considers the point. How could 'ran' or 'often' or 'and' or 'pretty' be the name of anything? It could not even be the grammatical subject of a sentence. I may ask what a certain economic condition, moral quality or day of the week is called and get the answer 'inflation', 'punctiliousness' or 'Saturday'. We do use the word 'name' for what something is called, whether it be what a person or river is called, or what a species, a quality, an action or a condition is called. But the answer to the question 'What is it called?' must be a noun or have the grammar of a noun. No such question could be answered by giving the tense of a verb, an adverb, a conjunction or an adjective.

Mill himself allowed that some words like 'is', 'often', 'not', 'of', and 'the' are not names, even in his hospitable use of 'name'. They cannot by themselves function as the grammatical subjects of sentences. Their function, as he erroneously described it, is to subserve, in one way or another, the construction of many-worded names. They do not name extra things but are ancillaries to the multi-verbal naming of things. Yet they certainly have meanings. 'And' and 'or' have different meanings, and 'or' and the Latin 'aut' have the same meaning. Mill realized that it is not always the case that for a word to mean something, it must denote somebody or some thing. But most of his successors did not notice how important this point was.

Even more to Mill's credit was the fact that he noticed and did partial justice to the point, which I made a little while back, that two different descriptive phrases may both fit the same thing or person, so that the thing or person which they both fit or which, in his unhappy parlance, they both name is not to be equated with either (or of course both) of the significations of the two descriptions. The two phrases 'the previous Prime Minister' and 'the father of Randolph Churchill' both fit Sir Winston Churchill, and fit only him; but they do not have the same meaning. A French translation of the one would not be a translation of the other. One might know or believe that the one description fitted Sir Winston Churchill while still questioning whether the other did so too. From just knowing that Sir Winston was Prime Minister one could not infer that Randolph Churchill is his son, or *vice versa*. Either might have been true without the other being true. The two phrases cannot, therefore, carry the same information.

Mill, in effect, met this point with his famous theory of denotation and connotation. Most words and descriptive phrases, according to him, do two things at once. They *denote* the things or persons that they are, as he unhappily puts it, all the names of. But they also *connote* or signify the simple or complex attributes by possessing which the thing or person denoted is fitted by the description. Mill's word 'connote' was a very unhappily chosen word and has misled not only Mill's successors but Mill himself. His word 'denote' was used by him in a far from uniform way, which left him uncommitted to consequences from which some of his successors, who used it less equivocally, could not extricate themselves. For Mill, proper names denote their bearers, but predicate-expressions also denote what they are truly predicable of. Fido is denoted by 'Fido' and by 'dog' and by 'four-legged'.

So to ask for the function of an expression is, on Mill's showing, to ask a double question. It is to ask Which person or persons, thing or things the expression denotes? in one or other of Mill's uses of this verb—Sir Winston Churchill, perhaps—; but it is also to ask What are the properties or characteristics by which the thing or person is described?—say that of having begotten Randolph Churchill. As a thing or person can be described in various ways, the various descriptions given will differ in connotation, while still being identical in denotation. They characterize in different ways, even though their denotation is identical. They carry different bits of information or misinformation about the same thing, person or event.

Mill himself virtually says that according to our ordinary natural notion of meaning, it would not be proper to say that, e.g. Sir Winston Churchill is the meaning of a word or phrase. We ordinarily understand by 'meaning' not the thing denoted but only what is connoted. That is, Mill virtually reaches the correct conclusions that the meaning of an expression is never the thing or person referred to by means of it; and that descriptive phrases and, with one exception, single words are never names, in the sense of 'proper names'. The exception is just those relatively few words which really are proper names, i.e. words like 'Fido', and 'London', the words which do not appear in dictionaries.

Mill got a further important point right about these genuine proper names. He said that while most words and descriptive phrases both denote or name and connote, proper names only denote and do not connote. A dog may be called 'Fido', but the word 'Fido' conveys no information or misinformation about the dog's qualities, career or whereabouts, etc. There is, to enlarge this point, no question of the word 'Fido' being paraphrased, or correctly or incorrectly translated into French. Dictionaries do not tell us what proper names mean—for the simple reason that they do not mean anything. The word 'Fido' names or denotes a particular dog, since it is what he is called. But there is no room for anyone who hears the word 'Fido' to understand it or misunderstand it or fail to understand it. There is nothing for which he can require an elucidation or a definition. From the information that Sir Winston Churchill was Prime Minister, a number of consequences follow, such as that he was the leader of the majority party in Parliament. But from the fact that yonder dog is Fido, no other truth about him follows at all. No information is provided for any-

thing to follow from. Using a proper name is not committing oneself to any further assertions whatsoever. Proper names are appellations and not descriptions; and descriptions are descriptions and not appellations. Sir Winston Churchill *is* the father of Randolph Churchill. He is not *called* and was not christened 'the father of Randolph Churchill'. He is called 'Winston Churchill'. The Lady Mayoress of Liverpool can give the name *Mauretania* to a ship which thenceforward has that name. But if she called Sir Winston Churchill 'the father of Sir Herbert Morrison' this would be a funny sort of christening, but it would not make it true that Morrison is the son of Sir Winston Churchill. Descriptions carry truths or falsehoods and are not just arbitrary bestowals. Proper names are arbitrary bestowals, and convey nothing true and nothing false, for they convey nothing at all.

Chinese astronomers give the planets, stars and constellations names quite different from those we give. But it does not follow that a single proposition of Western astronomy is rejected by them, or that a single astronomical proposition rejected by us is accepted by them. Stellar nomenclature carries with it no astronomical truths or falsehoods. Calling a star by a certain name is not saying anything about it, and saying something true or false about a star is not naming it. Saying is not naming and naming is not saying.

This brings out a most important fact. Considering the meaning (or Mill's 'connotation') of an expression is considering what can be said with it, i.e. said truly or said falsely, as well as asked, commanded, advised or any other sort of saying. In this, which is the normal sense of 'meaning', the meaning of a sub-expression like a word or phrase, is a functional factor of a range of possible assertions, questions, commands and the rest. It is tributary to sayings. It is a distinguishable common locus of a range of possible tellings, askings, advisings, etc. This precisely inverts the natural assumption with which, as I said earlier, Mill and most of us start, the assumption namely that the meanings of words and phrases can be learned, discussed and classified before consideration begins of entire sayings, such as sentences. Word-meanings do not stand to sentence-meanings as atoms to molecules or as letters of the alphabet to the spellings of words, but more nearly as the tennis-racket stands to the strokes which are or may be made with it. This point, which Mill's successors and predecessors half-recognized to hold for such little words as 'if', 'or', 'all', 'the' and 'not', holds good for all significant words alike. Their significances are their rôles inside actual and possible sayings. Mill's two-way doctrine, that nearly all words and phrases both denote, or are names, and connote, i.e. have significance, was therefore, in effect, though unwittingly, a coalition between an atomistic and a functionalist view of words. By the irony of fate, it was his atomistic view which was, in most quarters, accepted as gospel truth for the next fifty or seventy years. Indeed, it was more than accepted, it was accepted without the important safeguard which Mill himself provided when he said that the thing or person

denoted by a name was not to be identified with what that name meant. Mill said that to mean is to connote. His successors said that to mean is to denote, or, more rarely, both to denote and to connote. Frege was for a long time alone in seeing the crucial importance of Mill's argument that two or more descriptive phrases with different senses may apply to the same planet or person. This person or planet is not, therefore, what those phrases mean. Their different senses are not their common denotation. Russell early realized the point which Mill did not very explicitly make, though Plato had made it, that a sentence is not a list. It says one thing; it is not just an inventory of a lot of things. But only much later, if at all, did Russell see the full implications of this.

I surmise that the reason why Mill's doctrine of denotation, without its safeguards, caught on, while his truths about connotation failed to do so, were two. First, the word 'connote' naturally suggests what we express by 'imply', which is not what is wanted. What the phrase 'the previous Prime Minister of the United Kingdom' signifies is not to be equated with any or all of the consequences which can be inferred from the statement that Churchill is the previous Prime Minister. Deducing is not translating. But more important was the fact that Mill himself rapidly diluted his doctrine of connotation with such a mass of irrelevant and false sensationalist and associationist psychology, that his successors felt forced to ignore the doctrine in order to keep clear of its accretions.

(Let me briefly mention some of

the consequences which successors of Mill actually drew from the view, which was not Mill's, that to mean is to denote, in the toughest sense, namely that all significant expressions are proper names, and what they are the names of are what the expressions signify.)

First, it is obvious that the vast majority of words are unlike the words 'Fido' and 'London' in this respect, namely, that they are general. 'Fido' stands for a particular dog, but the noun 'dog' covers this dog Fido, and all other dogs past, present and future, dogs in novels, dogs in dog breeders' plans for the future, and so on indefinitely. So the word 'dog', if assumed to denote in the way in which 'Fido' denotes Fido, must denote something which we do not hear barking, namely either the set or class of all actual and imaginable dogs, or the set of canine properties which they all share. Either would be a very out-of-the-way sort of entity. Next, most words are not even nouns, but adjectives, verbs, prepositions, conjunctions and so on. If these are assumed to denote in the way in which 'Fido' denotes Fido, we shall have a still larger and queerer set of nominees or *denotata* on our hands, namely nominees whose names could not even function as the grammatical subjects of sentences. (Incidentally it is not true even that all ordinary general nouns can function by themselves as subjects of sentences. I can talk about *this* dog, or *a* dog, or *the* dog which . . .; or about *dogs*, *all* dogs, or *most* dogs, and so on. But I cannot make the singular

noun 'dog' by itself the grammatical subject of a sentence, save inside quotes, though I can do this with nouns like 'grass', 'hydrogen' and 'Man'.) Finally, since complexes of words, like descriptive and other phrases, and entire clauses and sentences have unitary meanings, then these too will have to be construed as denoting complex entities of very surprising sorts. Now Meinong in Austria and Frege in Germany, as well as Moore and Russell in this country, in their early days, accepted some or most of these consequences. Consistently with the assumed equation of signifying with naming, they maintained the objective existence or being of all sorts of abstract and fictional *entia rationis*.

Whenever we construct a sentence, in which we can distinguish a grammatical subject and a verb, the grammatical subject, be it a single word or a more or less complex phrase, must be significant if the sentence is to say something true or false. But if this nominative word or phrase is significant, it must, according to the assumption, denote something which is there to be named. So not only Fido and London, but also centaurs, round squares, the present King of France, the class of albino Cypriots, the first moment of time, and the non-existence of a first moment of time must all be credited with some sort of reality. They must *be*, else we could not say true or false things of them. We could not truly say that round squares do not exist, unless in some sense of 'exist' there exist round squares for us, in another sense to deny existence of. Sentences can begin with abstract nouns like 'equality' or 'justice' or 'murder' so all Plato's Forms or Universals must be accepted as entities. Sentences can contain mentions of creatures of fiction, like centaurs and Mr. Pickwick, so all conceivable creatures of fiction must be genuine entities too. Next, we can say that propositions are true or false, or that they entail or are incompatible with other propositions, so any significant 'that'-clause, like 'that three is a prime number' or 'that four is a prime number', must also denote existent or subsistent objects. It was accordingly, for a time, supposed that if I know or believe that three is a prime number, my knowing or believing this is a special relation holding between me on the one hand and the truth or fact, on the other, denoted by the sentence 'three is a prime number'. If I weave or follow a romance, my imagining centaurs or Mr. Pickwick is a special relation holding between me and these centaurs or that portly old gentleman. I could not imagine him unless he had enough being to stand as the correlate-term in this postulated relation of being imagined by me.

Lastly, to consider briefly what turned out, unexpectedly, to be a crucial case, there must exist or subsist classes, namely appropriate *denotata* for such collectively employed plural descriptive phrases as 'the elephants in Burma' or 'the men in the moon'. It is just of such classes or sets that we say that they number 3000, say, in the one case, and 0 in the other. For the results of counting to be true or false, there must be entities submitting to numer-

ical predicates; and for the propositions of arithmetic to be true or false there must exist or subsist an infinite range of such classes.

At the very beginning of this century Russell was detecting some local unplausibilities in the full-fledged doctrine that to every significant grammatical subject there must correspond an appropriate *denotatum* in the way in which Fido answers to the name 'Fido'. The true proposition 'round squares do not exist' surely cannot require us to assert that there really do subsist round squares. The proposition that it is false that four is a prime number is a true one, but its truth surely cannot force us to fill the Universe up with an endless population of objectively existing falsehoods.

But it was classes that first engendered not mere unplausibilities but seemingly disastrous logical contradictions—not merely peripheral logical contradictions but contradictions at the heart of the very principles on which Russell and Frege had taken mathematics to depend. We can collect into classes not only ordinary objects like playing-cards and bachelors, but also such things as classes themselves. I can ask how many shoes there are in a room and also how many pairs of shoes, and a pair of shoes is already a class. So now suppose I construct a class of all the classes that are not, as anyhow most classes are not, members of themselves. Will this class be one of its own members or not? If it embraces itself, this disqualifies it from being one of the things it is characterized as embracing; if it is not one of the things it embraces, this is just what qualifies it to be one among its own members.

So simple logic itself forbids certain ostensibly denoting expressions to denote. It is at least unplausible to say that there exist objects denoted by the phrase 'round squares'; there is self-contradiction in saying that there exists a class which is a member of itself on condition that it is not, and *vice versa*.

Russell had already found himself forced to say of some expressions which had previously been supposed to name or denote, that they had to be given exceptional treatment. They were not names but what he called 'incomplete symbols', expressions, that is, which have no meaning, in the sense of denotation, by themselves; their business was to be auxiliary to expressions which do, as a whole, denote. (This was what Mill had said of the syncategorematic words.) The very treatment which had since the Middle Ages been given to such little words as 'and', 'not', 'the', 'some' and 'is' was now given to some other kinds of expressions as well. In effect, though not explicitly, Russell was saying that, e.g. descriptive phrases were as syncategorematic as 'not', 'and' and 'is' had always been allowed to be. Here Russell was on the brink of allowing that the meanings or significations of many kinds of expressions are matters not of *naming* things, but of *saying* things. But he was, I think, still held up by the idea that saying is itself just another variety of naming, i.e. naming a complex or an 'objective' or a proposition or a fact—some sort of postulated *Fido rationis*.

He took a new and most important further step to cope with the para-doxes, like that of the class of classes that are not members of themselves. For he now wielded a distinction, which Mill had seen but left inert, the distinction between sentences which are either true or false on the one hand, and on the other hand sentences which, though proper in vocabulary and syntax, are none the less nonsensical, meaningless or absurd; and therefore neither true nor false. To assert them and to deny them are to assert and deny nothing. For reasons of a sort which are the proper concern of logic, certain sorts of concatenations of words and phrases into sentences produce things which cannot be significantly said. For example, the very question Is the class of all classes which are not members of themselves a member of itself or not? has no answer. Russell's famous 'Theory of Types' was an attempt to formulate the reasons of logic which make it an improper question. We need not consider whether he was successful. What matters for us, and what made the big difference to subsequent philosophy, is the fact that at long last the notion of meaning was realized to be, at least in certain crucial contexts, the obverse of the notion of the nonsensical—what can be said, truly or falsely, is at last contrasted with what cannot be significantly said. The notion of meaning had been, at long last, partly detached from the notion of naming and reattached to the notion of saying. It was recognized to belong to, or even to constitute the domain which had always been the province of logic; and as it is at least part of the official business of logic to establish and codify rules, the notion of meaning came now to be seen as somehow compact of rules. To know what an expression means involves knowing what can (logically) be said with it and what cannot (logically) be said with it. It involves knowing a set of bans, fiats and obligations, or, in a word, it is to know the rules of the employment of that expression.

It was, however, not Russell but Wittgenstein who first generalized or half-generalized this crucial point. In the *Tractatus Logico-Philosophicus*, which could be described as the first book to be written on the philosophy of logic, Wittgenstein still had one foot in the denotationist camp, but his other foot was already free. He saw and said, not only what had been said before, that the little words, the so-called logical constants, 'not', 'is', 'and' and the rest do not stand for objects, but also, what Plato had also said before, that sentences are not names. Saying is not naming. He realized, as Frege had done, that logicians' questions are not questions about the properties or relations of the *denotata*, if any, of the expressions which enter into the sentences whose logic is under examination. He saw, too, that all the words and phrases that can enter into sentences are governed by the rules of what he called slightly metaphorically, 'logical syntax' or 'logical grammar'. These rules are what are broken by such concatenations of words and phrases as result in nonsense. Logic is or includes the study of these rules. Husserl had at the beginning of the century employed much the same notion of 'logical grammar.'

It was only later still that Wittgenstein consciously and deliberately withdrew his remaining foot from the denotationist camp. When he said 'Don't ask for the meaning, ask for the use', he was imparting a lesson which he had had to teach to himself after he had finished with the *Tractatus*. The use of an expression, or the concept it expresses, is the rôle it is employed to perform, not any thing or person or event for which it might be supposed to stand. Nor is the purchasing power of a coin to be equated with this book or that car-ride which might be bought with it. The purchasing power of a coin has not got pages or a terminus. Even more instructive is the analogy which Wittgenstein now came to draw between significant expressions and the pieces with which are played games like chess. The significance of an expression and the powers or functions in chess of a pawn, a knight or the queen have much in common. To know what the knight can and cannot do, one must know the rules of chess, as well as be familiar with various kinds of chess-situations which may arise. What the knight may do cannot be read out of the material or shape of the piece of ivory or boxwood or tin of which this knight may be made. Similarly to know what an expression means is to know how it may and may not be employed, and the rules governing its employment can be the same for expressions of very different physical compositions. The word 'horse' is not a bit like the word 'cheval'; but the way of wielding them is the same. They have the same rôle, the same sense. Each is a translation of the other. Certainly the rules of the uses of expressions are

unlike the rules of games in some important respects. We can be taught the
rules of chess up to a point before we
begin to play. There are manuals of
chess, where there are not manuals of
significance. The rules of chess, again,
are completely definite and inelastic.
Questions of whether a rule has been
broken or not are decidable without
debate. Moreover we opt to play chess
and can stop when we like, where we
do not opt to talk and think and cannot opt to break off. Chess is a diver-
sion. Speech and thought are not only
diversions. But still the partial assimilation of the meanings of expressions
to the powers or the values of the
pieces with which a game is played is
enormously revealing. There is no
temptation to suppose that a knight is
proxy for anything, or that learning
what a knight may or may not do is
learning that it is a deputy for some
ulterior entity. We could not learn to
play the knight correctly without having learned to play the other pieces,
nor can we learn to play a word by
itself, but only in combination with
other words and phrases.

Besides this, there is a further point
which the assimilation brings out.
There are six different kinds of chess-
pieces, with their six different kinds of
rôles in the game. We can imagine more
complex games involving twenty or two
hundred kinds of pieces. So it is with
languages. In contrast with the denotationist assumption that almost all
words, all phrases and even all sentences are alike in having the one rôle
of naming, the assimilation of language to chess reminds us of what we
knew *ambulando* all along, the fact

that there are indefinitely many kinds
of words, kinds of phrases, and kinds
of sentences—that there is an indefinitely large variety of kinds of rôles
performed by the expressions we use
in saying things. Adjectives do not do
what adverbs do, nor do all adjectives
do the same sort of thing as one another. Some nouns are proper names,
but most are not. The sorts of things
that we do with sentences are different from the sorts of things that we do
with most single words—and some sorts
of things that we can significantly do
with some sorts of sentences, we cannot significantly do with others. And
so on.

There is not one basic mould, such
as the 'Fido'-Fido mould, into which
all significant expressions are to be
forced. On the contrary, there is an
endless variety of categories of sense
or meaning. Even the *prima facie* simple notion of naming or denoting itself
turns out on examination to be full of
internal variegations. Pronouns are
used to denote people and things, but
not in the way in which proper names
do so. No one is *called* 'he' or 'she'.
'Saturday' is a proper name, but not in
the same way as 'Fido' is a proper
name—and neither is used in the way
in which the fictional proper name 'Mr.
Pickwick' is used. The notion of denotation, so far from providing the
final explanation of the notion of
meaning, turns out itself to be just one
special branch or twig on the tree of
signification. Expressions do not mean
because they denote things; some expressions denote things, in one or another of several different manners, because they are significant. Meanings

are not things, not even very queer things. Learning the meaning of an expression is more like learning a piece of drill than like coming across a previously unencountered object. It is learning to operate correctly with an expression and with any other expression equivalent to it.

2. The Theory of Philosophy

I now want to trace, rather more cursorily, the other main motive from which thinkers have posed the abstract question What are meanings? or What is it for an expression to have a certain sense?

Until fairly recently philosophers have not often stepped back from their easels to consider what philosophy is, or how doing philosophy differs from doing science, or doing theology, or doing mathematics. Kant was the first modern thinker to see or try to answer this question—and a very good beginning of an answer he gave; but I shall not expound his answer here.

This question did not begin seriously to worry the general run of philosophers until maybe sixty years ago. It began to become obsessive only after the publication of the *Tractatus*. Why did the philosophy of philosophy start so late, and how did it come to start when and as it did?

It is often not realized that the words 'philosophy' and 'philosopher' and their equivalents in French and German had for a long time much less specific meanings than they now possess. During the seventeenth, the eighteenth and most of the nineteenth centuries a

'philosopher' was almost any sort of a *savant*. Astronomers, chemists and botanists were called 'philosophers' just as much as were Locke, Berkeley or Hume. Descartes's philosophy covered his contributions to optics just as much as his contributions to epistemology. In English there existed for a long time no special word for the people we now call 'scientists'. This noun was deliberately coined only in 1840, and even then it took some time to catch on. His contemporaries could not call Newton a 'scientist', since there was no such word. When a distinction had to be made, it was made by distinguishing 'natural philosophy' from 'moral' and 'metaphysical philosophy'. As late as 1887, Conan Doyle, within two or three pages of one story, describes Sherlock Holmes as being totally ignorant of philosophy, as we use the word now, and yet as having his room full of philosophical, i.e. scientific, instruments, like test-tubes, retorts and balances. A not very ancient Oxford Chair of Physics still retains its old label, the Chair of Experimental Philosophy.

Different from this quite important piece of etymological history is the fact that both in Scotland and in England there existed from perhaps the time of Hartley to that of Sidgwick and Bradley a strong tendency to suppose that the distinction between natural philosophy, i.e. physical and biological science on the one hand and metaphysical and moral philosophy, perhaps including logic, on the other, was that the latter were concerned with internal, mental phenomena, where the former were concerned with external, physical phenomena. Much of what we now label 'philosophy', *sans phrase*, was for a long time and by many thinkers confidently, but quite wrongly equated with what we now call 'psychology'. John Stuart Mill sometimes, but not always uses even the grand word 'metaphysics' for the empirical study of the workings of men's minds. Protests were made against this equation particularly on behalf of philosophical theology, but for a long time the anti-theologians had it their own way. A philosopher, *sans phrase*, was a Mental and Moral Scientist—a scientist who was exempted from working in the laboratory or the observatory only because his specimens were collected at home by introspection. Even Mansel, himself a philosophical theologian with a good Kantian equipment, maintained that the science of mental phenomena, what we call 'psychology', was the real basis of even ontological or theological speculations.

So not only did the wide coverage of the word 'philosophy' encourage people not to look for any important differences between what scientists, as we now call them, do and what philosophers, as we now call them, do; but even when such differences were looked for, they were apt to be found in the differences between the investigation of physical phenomena by the laboratory scientist and the investigation of psychological phenomena by the introspecting psychologist.

As I see it, three influences were chiefly responsible for the collapse of the assumption that doing philosophy, in our sense, is of a piece with doing natural science or at least of a piece with doing mental science or psychology.

First, champions of mathematics like Frege, Husserl and Russell had to save mathematics from the combined empiricism and psychologism of the school of John Stuart Mill. Mathematical truths are not mere psychological generalizations; equations are not mere records of deeply rutted associations of ideas; the objects of geometry are not of the stuff of which mental images are made. Pure mathematics is a non-inductive and a non-introspective science. Its proofs are rigorous, its terms are exact, and its theorems are universal and not merely highly general truths. The proofs and the theorems of Formal or Symbolic Logic share these dignities with the proofs and theorems of mathematics. So, as logic was certainly a part of philosophy, not all of philosophy could be ranked as 'mental science'. There must, then, be a field or realm besides those of the material and the mental; and at least part of philosophy is concerned with this third realm, the realm of non-material and also non-mental 'logical objects'—such objects as concepts, truths, falsehoods, classes, numbers and implications.

Next, armchair mental science or introspective psychology itself began to yield ground to experimental, laboratory psychology. Psychologists like James began to put themselves to school under the physiologists and the statisticians. Scientific psychology began first to rival and then to oust both *à priori* and introspective psychology, and the tacit claim of epistemologists, moral philosophers and logicians to be mental scientists had to be surrendered to those who used the methods and the tools of the reputable sciences. So the question raised its head What then were the objects of the inquiries of epistemologists, moral philosophers and logicians, if they were not, as had been supposed, psychological states and processes? It is only in our own days that, anyhow in most British Universities, psychologists have established a Faculty of their own separate from the Faculty of Philosophy.

Thirdly, Brentano, reinforcing from medieval sources a point made and swiftly forgotten by Mill, maintained as an *a priori* principle of psychology itself, that it is of the essence of mental states and processes that they are *of* objects or contents. Somewhat as in grammar a transitive verb requires an accusative, so in the field of ideas, thoughts and feelings, acts of consciousness are directed upon their own metaphorical accusatives. To see is to see something, to regret is to regret something, to conclude or suppose is to conclude or suppose that something is the case. Imagining is one thing, the thing imagined, a centaur, say, is another. The centaur has the body of a horse and does not exist. An act of imagining a centaur does exist and does not have the body of a horse. Your act of supposing that Napoleon defeated Wellington is different from my act of supposing it; but what we suppose is the same and is what is expressed by our common expression 'that Napoleon defeated Wellington'. What is true of mental acts is, in general, false of their accusatives or 'intentional objects', and *vice versa*.

Brentano's two pupils, Meinong and Husserl, happened, for different reasons, to be especially, though not exclusively, interested in applying this principle of intentionality or transitivity to the intellectual, as distinct from the sensitive, volitional or affective acts of consciousness. They set out, that is, to rectify the Locke-Hume-Mill accounts of abstraction, conception, memory, judgment, supposal, inference and the rest, by distinguishing in each case, the various private, momentary and repeatable acts of conceiving, remembering, judging, supposing and inferring from their public, non-momentary accusatives, namely, the concepts, the propositions and the implications which constituted their objective correlates. Where Frege attacked psychologistic accounts of thinking from the outside, they attacked them from the inside. Where Frege argued, for instance, that numbers have nothing psychological or, of course, physical about them, Husserl and Meinong argued that for the mental processes of counting and calculating to be what they are, they must have accusatives or objects numerically and qualitatively other than those processes themselves. Frege said that Mill's account of mathematical entities was false because psychological; Husserl and Meinong, in effect, said that the psychology itself was false because non-'intentional' psychology. The upshot, however, was much the same. With different axes to grind, all three came to what I may crudely dub 'Platonistic' conclusions. All three maintained the doctrine of a third realm of non-physical, non-psychological entities, in which realm dwelled such things as concepts, numbers, classes and propositions.

Husserl and Meinong were both ready to lump together all these accusatives of thinking alike under the comprehensive title of Meanings (*Bedeutungen*), since what I think is what is conveyed by the words, phrases or sentences in which I express what I think. The 'accusatives' of my ideas and my judgings are the meanings of my words and my sentences. It easily followed from this that both Husserl and Meinong, proud of their newly segregated third realm, found that it was this realm which provided a desiderated subject-matter peculiar to logic and philosophy and necessarily ignored by the natural sciences, physical and psychological. Mental acts and states are the subject-matter of psychology. Physical objects and events are the subject-matter of the physical and biological sciences. It is left to philosophy to be the science of this third domain which consists largely, though not entirely, of thought-objects or Meanings—the novel and impressive entities which had been newly isolated for separate investigation by the application of Brentano's principle of intentionality to the specifically intellectual or cognitive acts of consciousness.

Thus, by the first decade of this century it was dawning upon philosophers and logicians that their business was not that of one science among others, e.g. that of psychology; and even that it was not an inductive, experimental or observational business of any sort. It was intimately concerned with, among other things, the fundamental concepts and principles of mathematics; and it

seemed to have to do with a special domain which was not bespoken by any other discipline, namely the so-called third realm of logical objects or Meanings. At the same time, and in some degree affected by these influences, Moore consistently and Russell spasmodically were prosecuting their obviously philosophical and logical inquiries with a special *modus operandi*. They, and not they alone, were deliberately and explicitly trying to give analyses of concepts and propositions— asking What does it really mean to say, for example, that this is good? or that that is true? or that centaurs do not exist? or that I see an inkpot? or What are the differences between the distinguishable senses of the verb 'to know' and the verb 'to be'? Moore's regular practice and Russell's frequent practice seemed to exemplify beautifully what, for example, Husserl and Meinong had declared in general terms to be the peculiar business of philosophy and logic, namely to explore the third realm of Meanings. Thus philosophy had acquired a right to live its own life, neither as a discredited pretender to the status of the science of mind, nor yet as a superannuated handmaiden of *démodé* theology. It was responsible for a special field of facts, facts of impressively Platonized kinds.

Before the first world war discussions of the status and rôle of philosophy *vis-à-vis* the mathematical and empirical sciences were generally cursory and incidental to discussions of other matters. Wittgenstein's *Tractatus* was a complete treatise dedicated to fixing the position mainly of Formal Logic but also, as a necessary corollary, the position of general philosophy. It was this book which made dominant issues of the theory of logic and the theory of philosophy. In Vienna some of its teachings were applied polemically, namely to demolishing the pretensions of philosophy to be the science of transcendent realities. In England, on the whole, others of its teachings were applied more constructively, namely to stating the positive functions which philosophical propositions perform, and scientific propositions do not perform. In England, on the whole, interest was concentrated on Wittgenstein's description of philosophy as an activity of clarifying or elucidating the meanings of the expressions used, e.g. by scientists; that is, on the medicinal virtues of his account of the nonsensical. In Vienna, on the whole, interest was concentrated on the lethal potentialities of Wittgenstein's account of nonsense. In both places, it was realized that the criteria between the significant and the nonsensical needed to be systematically surveyed, and that it was for the philosopher and not the scientist to survey them.

At this point, the collapse of the denotationist theory of meaning began to influence the theory of philosophy as the science of Platonized Meanings. If the meaning of an expression is not an entity denoted by it, but a style of operation performed with it, not a nominee but a rôle, then it is not only repellent but positively misleading to speak as if there existed a Third Realm whose denizens are Meanings. We can distinguish this knight, as a piece of ivory, from the part it or any proxy for it may play in a game of chess;

but the part it may play is not an extra entity, made of some mysterious non-ivory. There is not one box housing the ivory chessmen and another queerer box housing their functions in chess games. Similarly we can distinguish an expression as a set of syllables from its employment. A quite different set of syllables may have the same employment. But its use or sense is not an additional substance or subject of predication. It is not a non-physical, non-mental object—but not because it is either a physical or a mental object, but because it is not an object. As it is not an object, it is not a denizen of a Platonic realm of objects. To say, therefore, that philosophy is the science of Meanings, though not altogether wrong, is liable to mislead in the same way as it might mislead to say that economics is the science of exchange-values. This, too, is true enough, but to word this truth in this way is liable to make people suppose that the Universe houses, under different roofs, commodities and coins here and exchange-values over there.

Hence, following Wittgenstein's lead, it has become customary to say, instead, that philosophical problems are linguistic problems—only linguistic problems quite unlike any of the problems of philology, grammar, phonetics, rhetoric, prosody, etc., since they are problems about the logic of the functionings of expressions. Such problems are so widely different from, e.g. philological problems, that speaking of them as linguistic problems is, at the moment, as Wittgenstein foresaw, misleading people as far in one direction, as speaking of them as problems about Meanings or Concepts or Propositions had been misleading in the other direction. The difficulty is to steer between the Scylla of a Platonistic and the Charybdis of a lexicographical account of the business of philosophy and logic.

There has been and perhaps still is something of a vogue for saying that doing philosophy consists in analysing meanings, or analysing the employments of expressions. Indeed, from Transatlantic journals I gather that at this very moment British philosophy is dominated by some people called 'linguistic analysts'. The word 'analysis' has, indeed, a good laboratory or Scotland Yard ring about it; it contrasts well with such expressions as 'speculation', 'hypothesis', 'system-building' and even 'preaching' and 'writing poetry'. On the other hand it is a hopelessly misleading word in some important respects. It falsely suggests, for one thing, that any sort of careful elucidation of any sorts of complex or subtle ideas will be a piece of philosophizing; as if the judge, in explaining to the members of the jury the differences between manslaughter and murder, was

helping them out of a philosophical quandary. But, even worse, it suggests that philosophical problems are like the chemist's or the detective's problems in this respect, namely that they can and should be tackled piecemeal. Finish problem A this morning, file the answer, and go on to problem B this afternoon. This suggestion does violence to the vital fact that philosophical problems inevitably interlock in all sorts of ways. It would be patently absurd to tell someone to finish the problem of the nature of truth this morning, file the answer and go on this afternoon to solve the problem of the relations between naming and saying, holding over until tomorrow problems about the concepts of existence and non-existence. This is, I think, why at the present moment philosophers are far more inclined to liken their task to that of the cartographer than to that of the chemist or the detective. It is the foreign relations, not the domestic constitutions of sayables that engender logical troubles and demand logical arbitration.

THE MEANING OF A WORD

2.3

John Austin

Specimens of Sense

1. 1. What-is-the-meaning-of (the word) 'rat'?
1. 11. What-is-the-meaning-of (the word) 'word'?
1. 21. What is a 'rat'?
1. 211. What is a 'word'?
1. 22. What is the 'muzzle' of a rat?
2. 1. What-is-the-meaning-of (the phrase) 'What-is-the-meaning-of'?
2. 11. What-is-the-meaning-of (the sentence) 'What-is-the-meaning-of (the word) "x"?'?

Specimens of Nonsense

1. 1. What-is-the-meaning-of a word?
1. 11. What-is-the-meaning-of any word?
1. 12. What-is-the-meaning-of a word in general?

1. 21. What is the-meaning-of-a word?
1. 211. What is the-meaning-of-(the-word)-'rat'?
1. 22. What is the 'meaning' of a word?
1. 221. What is the 'meaning' of (the word) 'rat'?
2. 1. What-is-the-meaning-of (the phrase) 'the-meaning-of-a word'?
2. 11. What-is-the-meaning-of (the sentence) 'What is the-meaning-of-(the-word)-"x"?'?
2. 12. What-is-the-meaning-of (the sentence) 'What is the "meaning" of "the word" "x"?'?

This paper is about the phrase 'the meaning of a word'. It is divided into three parts, of which the first is the most trite and the second the most muddled: all are too long. In the first, I try to make it clear that the phrase 'the meaning of a word' is, in general, if not always, a dangerous nonsense-phrase. In the other two parts I consider in turn two questions, often asked in philosophy, which clearly need new

From *Philosophical Papers*, J. O. Urmson and G. J. Warnock, editors (Oxford: The Clarendon Press, 1961). Reprinted by permission of the publisher and the executors of Austin's estate.

and careful scrutiny if that facile phrase 'the meaning of a word' is no longer to be permitted to impose upon us.

I

I begin, then, with some remarks about 'the meaning of a word'. I think many persons now see all or part of what I shall say: but not all do, and there is a tendency to forget it, or to get it slightly wrong. In so far as I am merely flogging the converted, I apologize to them.

A preliminary remark. It may justly be urged that, properly speaking, what alone has meaning is a *sentence*. Of course, we can speak quite properly of, for example, 'looking up the meaning of a word' in a dictionary. Nevertheless, it appears that the sense in which a word or a phrase 'has a meaning' is derivative from the sense in which a sentence 'has a meaning': to say a word or a phrase 'has a meaning' is to say that there are sentences in which it occurs which 'have meanings': and to know the meaning which the word or phrase has, is to know the meanings of sentences in which it occurs. All the dictionary can do when we 'look up the meaning of a word' is to suggest aids to the understanding of sentences in which it occurs. Hence it appears correct to say that what 'has meaning' in the primary sense is the sentence. And older philosophers who discussed the problem of 'the meaning of words' tend to fall into *special* errors, avoided by more recent philosophers, who discuss rather the parallel problem of 'the meaning of sentences'. Nevertheless, if we are on our guard, we perhaps need not fall into these special errors, and I propose to overlook them at present.

There are many sorts of sentence in which the words 'the meaning of the word so-and-so' are found, e.g. 'He does not know, or understand, the meaning of the word *handsaw*': 'I shall have to explain to her the meaning of the word *pikestaff*': and so on. I intend to consider primarily the common question, 'What is the meaning of *so-and-so*?' or 'What is the meaning of *the word so-and-so*?'

Suppose that in ordinary life I am asked: 'What is the meaning of the word *racy*?' There are two sorts of thing I may do in response: I may reply *in words*, trying to describe what raciness is and what it is not, to give examples of sentences in which one might use the word *racy*, and of others in which one should not. Let us call this *sort* of thing 'explaining the syntactics' of the word 'racy' in the English language. On the other hand, I might do what we may call 'demonstrating the semantics' of the word, by getting the questioner to *imagine*, or even actually to *experience*, situations which we should describe correctly by means of sentences containing the words 'racy' 'raciness', &c., and again other situations where we should *not* use these words. This is, of course, a simple case: but perhaps the same two *sorts* of procedure would be gone through in the case of at least most ordinary words. And in the same way, if I wished to find out 'whether he understands the meaning of the word *racy*', I should test him at some length in these two ways (which perhaps could not be entirely divorced from each other).

Having asked in this way, and answered, 'What is the meaning of (the word) "rat"?', 'What is the meaning of (the word) "cat"?', 'What is the meaning of (the word) "mat"?', and so on, we then try, being philosophers, to ask the further *general* question, 'What is the meaning of a word?' But there is something spurious about this question. We do not intend to mean by it a certain question which would be perfectly all right, namely, 'What is the meaning of (the word) "word"?': *that* would be no more general than is asking the meaning of the word 'rat', and would be answered in a precisely similar way. No: we want to ask rather, 'What is the meaning of a-word-in-general?' or 'of *any* word'—not meaning 'any' word *you like to choose*, but rather *no particular* word *at all*, just 'any word'. Now if we pause even for a moment to reflect, this is a perfectly absurd question to be trying to ask. I can only answer a question of the form 'What is the meaning of "*x*"?' if "*x*" is some *particular* word you are asking about. This supposed *general* question is really just a spurious question of a type which commonly arises in philosophy. We may call it the fallacy of asking about 'Nothing-in-particular' which is a practice decried by the plain man, but by the philosopher called 'generalizing' and regarded with some complacency. Many other examples of the fallacy can be found: take, for example, the case of 'reality'—we try to pass from such questions as 'How would you distinguish a real rat from an imaginary rat?' to 'What is a real thing?', a question which merely gives rise to nonsense.

We may expose the error in our present case thus. Instead of asking 'What is the meaning of (the word) "rat"?' we might clearly have asked 'What is a "rat"?' and so on. But if our questions have been put in *that* form, it becomes very difficult to formulate any *general* question which could impose on us for a moment. Perhaps 'What is anything?'? Few philosophers, if perhaps not none, have been foolhardy enough to pose such a question. In the same way, we should not perhaps be tempted to generalize such a question as 'Does he know the meaning of (the word) "rat"?' 'Does he know the meaning of a word?' would be silly.

Faced with the nonsense question 'What is the meaning of a word'?, and perhaps dimly recognizing it to be nonsense, we are nevertheless not inclined to give it up. Instead, we transform it in a curious and noteworthy manner. Up to now, we had been asking '*What-is-the-meaning-of* (the word) "rat"?', &c.; and ultimately '*What-is-the-meaning-of* a word?' But now, being baffled, we change so to speak, the hyphenation, and ask 'What is *the-meaning-of-a-word?*' or sometimes, 'What is the "meaning" of a word?' (1. 22): I shall refer, for brevity's sake, only to the other (1.21). It is easy to see how very different this question is from the other. At once a crowd of traditional and reassuring answers present themselves: 'a concept', 'an idea', 'an image', 'a class of similar sensa', &c. All of which are equally spurious answers to a pseudo-question. Plunging ahead, however, or rather retracing our steps, we now proceed to ask such questions as 'What is the-meaning-of-(the-word) "rat"?' which is as spurious as 'What-is-the-meaning-of (the word) "rat"?' was genuine. And again we answer 'the idea of a rat' and so forth. How quaint this procedure is, may be seen in the following way. Supposing a plain man puzzled, were to ask me 'What is the meaning of (the word) "muggy"?', and I were to answer. 'The idea or concept of "mugginess" ' or 'The class of sensa of which it is correct to say "This is muggy" ': the man would stare at me as at an imbecile. And that is sufficiently unusual for me to conclude that that was not at all the sort of answer he expected: nor, in plain English, *can* that question *ever* require that sort of answer.

To show up this pseudo-question, let us take a parallel case, where perhaps no one has yet been deluded, though they well might be. Suppose that I ask 'What is the point of doing so-and-so?' For example, I ask Old Father William 'What is the point of standing on one's head?' He replies in the way we know. Then I follow this up with 'What is the point of balancing an eel on the end of one's nose?' And he explains. Now suppose I ask as my third question 'What is the point of doing *anything*—not anything *in particular*, but just *anything*?' Old Father William would no doubt kick me downstairs without the option. But lesser men, raising this same question and finding no answer, would very likely commit suicide or join the Church. (Luckily, in the case

of 'What is the meaning of a word?' the effects are less serious, amounting only to the writing of books.) On the other hand, more adventurous intellects would no doubt take to asking 'What is the-point-of-doing-a-thing?' or 'What is the "point" of doing a thing?': and then later 'What is the-point-of-eating-suet?' and so on. Thus we should discover a whole new universe of a kind of entity called 'points', not previously suspected of existence.

To make the matter clearer, let us consider another case which is precisely *unlike* the case of 'What is the meaning of?' I can ask not only the question, 'What is the square root of 4?', or 8, and so on, but also 'What is the square root of a number?': which is either nonsense or equivalent to 'What is the "square root" of a number?' I then give a definition of the 'square root' of a number, such that, for any given number x, 'the square root of x' is a definite description of another number y. This differs from our case in that 'the meaning of p' is not a definite description of any entity.

The general questions which we want to ask about 'meaning' are best phrased as, 'What-is-the-meaning-of (the phrase) "what-is-the-meaning-of (the word) 'x'?"?' The *sort* of answer we should get to these quite sensible questions is that with which I began this discussion: viz. that when I am asked 'What-is-the-meaning-of (the word) "x"?', I naturally reply by explaining its syntactics and demonstrating its semantics.

All this must seem very obvious, but I wish to point out that it is fatally easy to forget it: no doubt I shall do so myself many times in the course of this paper. Even those who see pretty clearly that 'concepts', 'abstract ideas', and so on are fictitious entities, which we owe in part to asking questions about 'the meaning of a word', nevertheless themselves think that there *is* *something* which is 'the meaning of a word'. Thus Mr. Hampshire[1] attacks to some purpose the theory that there is such a thing as '*the* meaning of a word': what *he* thinks is wrong is the belief that there is a *single* thing called *the* meaning: 'concepts' are nonsense, and no single particular 'image' can be *the* meaning of a general word. So, he goes on to say, the meaning of a word must really be 'a *class* of similar particular ideas'. 'If we are asked "What does this mean?" we point to (!) a class of particular ideas.' But a 'class of particular ideas' is every bit as fictitious an entity as a 'concept' or 'abstract idea'. In the same way Mr. C. W. Morris (in the *Encyclopaedia of Unified Science*) attacks, to some purpose, those who think of 'a meaning' as a definite something which is 'simply located' somewhere: what *he* thinks is wrong is that people think of 'a meaning' as a kind of entity which can be described wholly without reference to the total activity of 'semiosis'. Well and good. Yet he himself makes some of the crudest possible remarks about 'the designatum' of a word: every sign has a designatum, which is not a particular thing but a *kind* of object or *class* of object. Now this is quite as fictitious an entity as

---

[1] 'Ideas, Propositions and Signs', in the *Proceedings of the Aristotelian Society*, 1939–40.

any 'Platonic idea': and is due to precisely the same fallacy of looking for 'the meaning (or designatum) of a word'.

Why are we tempted to slip back in this way? Perhaps there are two main reasons. First, there is the curious belief that all words are *names*, i.e. in effect *proper* names, and therefore stand for something or designate it in the way that a proper name does. But this view that general names 'have denotation' in the same way that proper names do, is quite as odd as the view that proper names 'have connotation' in the same way that general names do, which is commonly recognized to lead to error. Secondly, we are afflicted by a more common malady, which is this. When we have given an analysis of a certain sentence, containing a word or phrase '*x*', we often feel inclined to ask, of our analysis, 'What *in it, is* "*x*"?' For example, we give an analysis of 'The State owns this land', in sentences about individual men, their relations and transactions: and then at last we feel inclined to ask: well now, *what*, in all that, *is* the State? And we might answer: the State *is* a collection of individual men united in a certain manner. Or again, when we have analysed the statement 'trees can exist unperceived' into statements about sensing sensa, we still tend to feel uneasy unless we can say *something* '*really does*' 'exist unperceived': hence theories about 'sensibilia' and what not. So in our present case, having given all that is required, viz. an account of 'What-is-the-meaning-of "What is-the-meaning-of (the word) '*x*'?" ' we *still* feel tempted, wrongly supposing our

original sentence to contain a constituent 'the-meaning-of (the-word)-"*x*"',
to ask 'Well now, as it turns out, what
is the meaning of the word "*x*", after
all?' And we answer, 'a class of similar
particular ideas' and what not.

Of course, all my account of our motives in this matter may be only a convenient didactic schema: I do not think
it is—but I recognize that one should
not impute motives, least of all rational motives. Anyhow, what I claim
is clear, is that there is *no* simple and
handy appendage of a word called 'the
meaning of (the word) "*x*"'.

II

I now pass on to the first of the two
points which need now a careful scrutiny if we are no longer to be imposed
upon by that convenient phrase 'the
meaning of a word'. What I shall say
here is, I know, not as clear as it
should be.

Constantly we ask the question, 'Is *y*
the meaning, or *part* of the meaning,
or *contained* in the meaning, of *x*?—or
is it *not*?' A favourite way of putting
the question is to ask, 'Is the judgement "*x* is *y*" analytic or synthetic?'
Clearly, we suppose, *y must* be *either* a
part of the meaning of *x*, *or* not any
part of it. And, if *y is* a part of the
meaning of *x*, to say '*x* is not *y*' will be
self-contradictory: while if it is *not* a
part of the meaning of *x*, to say '*x* is
not *y*' will present no difficulty—such a
state of affairs will be readily 'conceivable'. This seems to be the merest common sense. And no doubt it *would* be
the merest common sense *if* 'meanings'

were things in some ordinary sense
which contained parts in some ordinary
sense. But they are *not*. Unfortunately,
many philosophers who know they are
not, still speak as though *y* must either
be or not be 'part of the meaning' of *x*.
But this is the point: *if* 'explaining the
meaning of a word' is really the complicated sort of affair that we have
seen it to be, and *if* there is really
nothing to call 'the meaning of a word'
—*then* phrases like 'part of the meaning of the word *x*' are completely undefined; it is left hanging in the air, we
do not know what it means at all. *We
are using a working-model which fails
to fit the facts that we really wish to
talk about.* When we consider what we
really do want to talk about, and not
the working-model, what would really
be meant at all by a judgement being
'analytic or synthetic'? We simply do
not know. Of course, we feel inclined
to say 'I can easily produce examples
of analytic and synthetic judgements;
for instance, I should confidently say
"Being a professor is *not* part of the
meaning of being a man" and so forth.'
'A is A is analytic.' Yes, but it is when
we are required to give a *general definition* of what we mean by 'analytic' or
'synthetic', and when we are required
to justify our dogma that *every* judgement is either analytic or synthetic, that
we find we have, in fact, nothing to fall
back upon *except our working-model*.
From the start, it is clear that our
working-model fails to do justice, for
example, to the distinction between
syntactics and semantics: for instance,
talking about the contradictory of
every sentence having to be either self-
contradictory or not so, is to talk as

though all sentences which we are prohibited from saying were sentences which offended against *syntactical* rules, and could be formally reduced to verbal self-contradictions. But this overlooks all semantical considerations, which philosophers are sadly prone to do. Let us consider two cases of some things which we simply *cannot say*: although they are *not* 'self-contradictory' and although—and this of course is where many will have axes to grind—we cannot possibly be tempted to say that we have 'synthetic *a priori*' knowledge of their contradictions.

Let us begin with a case which, being about *sentences* rather than *words*, is not quite in point, but which may encourage us. Take the well-known sentence 'The cat is on the mat, and I do not believe it'. That seems absurd. On the other hand 'The cat is on the mat, and I believe it' seems trivial. If we were to adopt a customary dichotomy, and to say *either* a proposition p implies another proposition r, or p is perfectly compatible with not-r, we should at once in our present case be tempted to say that 'The cat is on the mat' *implies* 'I believe it': hence both the triviality of adding 'and I believe it' and the absurdity of adding 'and I do not believe it'. But of course 'the cat is on the mat' does *not* imply 'Austin believes the cat is on the mat': nor even 'the speaker believes the cat is on the mat'—for the speaker may be lying. The doctrine which is produced in this case is, that not p indeed, but *asserting* p implies 'I (who assert p) believe p'. And here 'implies' must be given a special sense: for of course it is not that 'I assert p' implies (in the ordinary

sense) 'I believe p', for I may be lying. It is the sort of sense in which by asking a question I 'imply' that I do not know the answer to it. By asserting p I *give it to be understood* that I believe p.

Now the reason why I cannot say 'The cat is on the mat and I do not believe it' is not that it offends against syntactics in the sense of being in some way 'self-contradictory'. What prevents my saying it, is rather some semantic convention (implicit, of course), about the way we use words *in situations*. What precisely is the account to be given in this case we need not ask. Let us rather notice one significant feature of it. Whereas 'p and I believe it' is somehow trivial, and 'p and I do not believe it' is somehow nonsense, a third sentence 'p and I *might not have* believed it' makes perfectly good sense. Let us call these three sentences Q, not Q, and 'might not Q'. Now what prohibits us from saying 'p' implies 'I believe p' in the ordinary sense of 'implies', is precisely shown by this fact: that although not Q is (*somehow*) absurd, 'might not Q' is not at all absurd. For in ordinary cases of implications, not merely is not Q absurd, but 'might not Q' is *also* absurd: e.g. 'triangles are figures and triangles have no shape' is no more absurd than 'triangles are figures and triangles might have had no shape'. Consideration of the sentence 'might not Q' will afford a rough test as to whether p 'implies' r in the *ordinary* sense, or in the special sense, of 'implies'.

Bearing this in mind, let us now consider a sentence which, as I claim, cannot possibly be classified as *either* 'analytic' *or* 'synthetic'. I refer to the sentence, 'This x exists', where x is a sensum, e.g. 'This noise exists'. In endeavouring to classify it, one party would point to the triviality of 'This noise exists', and to the absurdity of 'This noise does not exist'. They would say, therefore, that *existence* is 'part of the meaning of' *this*. But another party would point out, that 'This noise might not have existed' makes perfectly good sense. *They* would say, therefore, that *existence* cannot be 'part of the meaning of' *this*.

Both parties, as we are now in a position to see, would be correct in their *arguments*, but incorrect in their *conclusions*. What seems to be true is that *using the word 'this'* (not: the word 'this') *gives it to be understood that* the sensum referred to 'exists'.

Perhaps, historically, this fact about the sentence-trio, 'This noise exists', 'This noise does not exist', and 'This noise might not have existed', was pointed out before any philosopher had had time to pronounce that 'This noise exists' is analytic, or is synthetic. But such a pronouncement might well have been made: and *to this day*, even when the fact has been pointed out, many philosophers *worry* about the case, supposing the sentence *must* be one or the other but painfully aware of the difficulties in choosing either. I wish to point out that consideration of the analogy between this case and the other, should cure us once and for all of this bogy, and of insisting on classifying sentences as *either* analytic *or* synthetic. It may encourage us to consider again what the facts in their actual complexity really are. (One thing it suggests is a reconsideration of

'Caesar is bald' and similar propositions: but I cannot go into that.)

So far, however, we have scarcely begun in earnest: we have merely felt that initial trepidation, experienced when the firm ground of prejudice begins to slip away beneath the feet. Perhaps there are other cases, or other sorts of cases, where it will not be possible to say either that y is a 'part of the meaning' of x or that it is not, without being misleading.

Suppose we take the case of 'being thought good by me' and 'being approved of by me'. Are we to rush at this with the dichotomy: *either* 'being approved of by me' *is* part of the meaning of 'being thought good by me' *or* it is *not*? Is it *obvious* that 'I think x good but I do not approve of it' is self-contradictory? Of course it is not *verbally* self-contradictory. That it either is or is not 'really' self-contradictory would seem to be difficult to establish. Of course, we think, it must be one or the other—only 'it's difficult to decide *which*': or 'it depends on how you use the words'. But are those really the difficulties which baffle us? Of course, *if* it were certain that every sentence *must* be either analytic or synthetic, those *must* be the difficulties. But then, it is not certain: no account even of what the distinction means, is given except by reference to our shabby working-model. I suggest that 'I think x good but I do not approve of it' may very well be neither self-contradictory nor yet 'perfectly good sense' in the way in which 'I think x exciting but I do not approve of it' *is* 'perfectly good sense'.

Perhaps this example does not strike

you as awkward. It cannot be expected that all examples will appeal equally to all hearers. Let us take some others. Is 'What is good ought to exist' analytic or synthetic? According to Moore's theory, this must be 'synthetic': yet he constantly in *Principia Ethica* takes its truth for granted. And that illustrates one of the main drawbacks of insisting on saying that a sentence *must* be either analytic or synthetic: you are almost certain to have left on your hands some general sentences which are certainly not analytic but which you find it difficult to conceive being false: i.e. you are landed with 'synthetic *a priori* knowledge'. Take that sentence of ill fame 'Pink is more like red than black'. It is rash to pronounce this 'synthetic *a priori* knowledge' on the ground that 'being more like red than black' is not 'part of the meaning' or 'part of the definition' of 'pink' and that it is not 'conceivable' that pink should be more like black than red: I dare say, so far as those phrases have any clear meaning, that it *is not*: but the question is: *is the thing therefore 'synthetic' a priori knowledge?*

Or, again, take some examples from Berkeley: is *extended* 'part of the meaning' of *coloured* or of *shaped*, or *shaped* 'part of the meaning' of *extended*? Is 'est sed non percipitur' self-contradictory (when said of a sensum), or is it not? When we worry thus, is it not worth considering the possibility that we are oversimplifying?

What we are to say in these cases, what even the possibilities are, I do not at present clearly see. (1) Evidently, we must throw away the old working-model as soon as we take account even of the existence of a distinction between syntactics and semantics. (2) But evidently also, our *new* working-model, the supposed 'ideal' language, is in many ways a most inadequate model of any *actual* language: its careful separation of syntactics from semantics, its lists of explicitly formulated rules and conventions, and its careful delimitation of their spheres of operation—all are misleading. An *actual* language has few, if any, explicit conventions, no sharp limits to the spheres of operation of rules, no rigid separation of what is syntactical and what semantical. (3) Finally, I think I can see that there are difficulties about our powers of imagination, and about the curious way in which it is enslaved by words.

To encourage ourselves in the belief that this sort of consideration may play havoc with the distinction 'analytic or synthetic', let us consider a similar and more familiar case. It seems, does it not, perfectly obvious that every proposition must have a contradictory? Yet it does not turn out so. Suppose that I live in harmony and friendship for four years with a cat: and then it delivers a philippic. We ask ourselves, perhaps, 'Is it a real cat? or is it *not* a real cat?' 'Either it *is*, or it *is not*, but we cannot be sure which.' Now actually, that is not so: *neither* 'It is a real cat' *nor* 'it is not a real cat' fits the facts semantically: each is designed for other situations than this one: you could not say the former of something which delivers philippics, nor yet the latter of something which has behaved as this has for four years. There are similar difficulties about choosing between 'This *is* a hallucination' and 'This is *not* a hallucination'. With sound instinct, the plain man turns in such cases to Watson and says 'Well now, *what would you say?*' 'How would you *describe* it?' The difficulty is just that: there is *no* short description which is not misleading: the only thing to do, and that can easily be done, is to set out the description of the facts at length. Ordinary language breaks down in extraordinary cases. (In such cases, the cause of the breakdown is semantical.) Now no doubt an *ideal* language would *not* break down, whatever happened. In doing physics, for example, where our language is tightened up in order precisely to describe complicated and unusual cases concisely, we *prepare linguistically for the worst*. In ordinary language we do not: *words fail us*. If we talk as though an ordinary must be like an ideal language, we shall misrepresent the facts.

Consider now 'being extended' and 'being shaped'. In ordinary life we never get into a situation where we learn to say that anything is extended but not shaped nor conversely. We have all learned to use, and have used, the words only in cases where it is correct to use both. Supposing now someone says '*x* is extended but has no shape'. Somehow we cannot see what this 'could mean'—there are no semantic conventions, explicit or implicit, to cover this case: yet it is not prohibited in any way—there are no limiting rules about what we might or might not say *in extraordinary cases*. It is not *merely* the difficulty of imagining or experiencing extraordinary cases, either,

which causes worry. There is this too: we can only describe what it is we are trying to imagine, by means of words which precisely describe and evoke the *ordinary* case, which we are trying to think away. Ordinary language *blinkers* the already feeble imagination. It would be difficult, in this way, if I were to say 'Can I think of a case where a man would be neither at home nor not at home?' This is inhibiting, because I think of the *ordinary* case where I ask 'Is he at home?' and get the answer, 'No': when certainly he is not at home. But supposing I happen *first* to think of the situation when I call on him just after he has died: then I see at once it would be wrong to say either. So in our case, the only thing to do is to imagine or experience all kinds of odd situations, and then suddenly round on oneself and ask: there, *now* would I say that, being extended it must be shaped? A new idiom might in odd cases be demanded.

I should like to say, in concluding this section, that in the course of stressing that we must pay attention to the facts of *actual* language, what we can and cannot say, and *precisely* why, another and converse point takes shape. Although it will not do to force actual language to accord with some preconceived model: it *equally* will not do, having discovered the facts about 'ordinary usage' *to rest content* with that, as though there were nothing more to be discussed and discovered. There may be plenty that might happen and does happen which would need new and better language to describe it. Very often philosophers are only engaged on this task, when they seem to be perversely using words in a way which makes no sense according to 'ordinary usage'. There may be extraordinary facts, even about our everyday experience, which plain men and plain language overlook.

III

The last, and perhaps least unimportant point I have to make is the following: it seems to me that far more *detailed* attention ought to be given to that celebrated question, the posing of which has given birth to, and still keeps alive, so many erroneous theories, namely: why do we call different things by the same name? In reply to this, the philoprogenitive invent theories of 'universals' and what not: some entity or other to be that of which the 'name' is the name. And in reply to *them*, the more cautious (the 'nominalists') have usually been content to reply simply that: the reason why we call different things by the same name is simply that the things are *similar*: there is nothing *identical* present in them. This reply is inadequate in many respects: it does not, for example, attack the misleading form in which the question is posed, nor sufficiently go into the peculiarities of the word 'similar'. But what I wish to object to in it tonight is rather this: that *it is not in the least true* that all the things which I 'call by the same (general) name' *are* in general 'similar', in any ordinary sense of that much abused word.

It is a most strange thing that 'nominalists' should rest content with this

answer. Not merely is it untrue to the facts; but further, if they had examined the facts, which are, in themselves, interesting enough, they could have produced with little trouble a far more formidable case against their opponents. So long as they say the things *are similar*, it will always be open to someone to say: 'Ah yes, similar *in a certain respect*: and that can only be explained by means of universals' (or whatever the name may be that they prefer for that well-tried nostrum): or again to maintain that similarity is only 'intelligible' as partial *identity*: and so on. And even those who are not persuaded entirely, may yet go so far as to allow that the 'similarity' and 'identity' languages are *alternatives*, the choice between which is indifferent. But surely, if it were made evident that we often 'call different things by the same name', and for perfectly 'good reasons',[2] when the things are not even in any ordinary sense 'similar', it will become excessively difficult to maintain that there is something 'identical' present in each—and after all, it is in *refuting* that position that the nominalist is really interested. Not, of course, that we can really *refute* it, or hope to cure those incurables who have long since reached the tertiary stage of universals.

Leaving historical disputes aside, it is a matter of urgency that a doctrine should be developed about the various kinds of good reasons for which we 'call different things[3] by the same

---

[2] We are not interested in mere equivocation, of course.

[3] Strictly, *sorts* of things rather than *particular* things.

name'. This is an absorbing question, but habitually neglected, so far as I know, by philologists as well as by philosophers. Lying in the no man's land between them, it falls between two schools, to develop such a doctrine fully would be very complicated and perhaps tedious: but also very useful in many ways. It demands the study of *actual* languages, *not* ideal ones. That the Polish semanticists have discussed such questions I neither know nor believe. Aristotle did to a quite considerable extent, but scrappily and inexactly.

I shall proceed forthwith simply to give some of the more obvious cases where the reasons for 'calling different sorts of things by the same name' are not to be dismissed lightly as 'similarity'. And show how consideration of these facts may warn us against errors which are constant in philosophy.

1. A very simple case indeed is one often mentioned by Aristotle: the adjective 'healthy': when I talk of a healthy body and again of a healthy complexion, of healthy exercise: the word is *not* just being used *equivocally*. Aristotle would say it is being used 'paronymously'.[4] In this case there is what we may call a *primary nuclear* sense of 'healthy': the sense in which 'healthy' is used of a healthy body: I call this *nuclear* because it is 'contained as a part' in the other two senses which may be set out as 'productive of healthy bodies' and 'resulting from a healthy body'.

This is a simple case, easily under-

stood. Yet constantly it is forgotten when we start disputing as to whether a certain word *has* 'two senses' or has *not* two senses. I remember myself disputing as to whether 'exist' has two senses (as used of material objects and again of sensa), or only one: actually we were agreed that 'exist' is used paronymously, only he called that 'having two senses', and I did not. Prichard's paper[5] on ἀγαθόν (in Aristotle) contains a classic instance of misunderstanding about paronymity, and so worrying about whether a word really 'has always the same meaning' or 'has several different meanings'.

Now are we to be content to say that the exercise, the complexion, and the body are all called 'healthy' 'because they are similar'? Such a remark cannot fail to be misleading. Why make it? And why not direct attention to the important and actual facts?

2. The next case I shall take is what Aristotle calls 'analogous' terms. When A : B :: X : Y then A and X are often called by the same name, e.g. the foot of a mountain and the foot of a list. Here there is a good reason for calling the things both 'feet' but are we to say they are 'similar'? Not in any ordinary sense. We may say that the relations in which they stand to B and Y respectively are similar relations. Well and good: but A and X are not the relations in which they stand: and anyone simply told that, in calling A and X both 'feet' I was calling atten-

---

[4] But there are other varieties of paronymity of course.

[5] 'The Meaning of ΑΓΑΘΟΝ in the *Ethics* of Aristotle', by H. A. Prichard. Reprinted in his *Moral Obligation*, Oxford, 1949.

tion to a 'similarity' in them, would probably be misled. Anyhow, it is most necessary to remember that 'similarity' covers such possibilities if it is to do so. (An especially severe case of 'analogy' arises when a term is used, as Aristotle says 'in different categories': e.g. when I talk about 'change' as qualitative change, change of position, place, &c., how far is it true to say these 'changes' are 'similar'?)

3. Another case is where I call B by the same name as A, because it resembles A, C by the same name because it resembles B, D . . . and so on. But ultimately A and, say, D do not resemble each other in any recognizable sense at all. This is a very common case: and the dangers are obvious, when we search for something 'identical' in all of them!

4. Another case which is commonly found is this. Take a word like 'fascist': this originally connotes, say, a great many characteristics at once: say x, y, and z. Now we will use 'fascist' subsequently of things which possess only *one* of these striking characteristics. So that things called 'fascist' in these senses, which we may call 'incomplete' senses, need not be similar at all to each other. This often puzzles us most of all when the original 'complete' sense has been forgotten: compare the various meanings of 'cynicism': we should be puzzled to find the 'similarity' there! Sometimes the 'incompleteness' of the resemblance is coupled with a positive lack of resemblance, so that we invent a phrase to mark it as a warning, e.g. 'cupboard love'.

5. Another better-known case is that of a so-called determinable and its de-

terminates: colour and red, green, blue, &c., or rather 'absolutely specific' reds, greens, blues, &c. Because this is better known, I shall not discuss it, though I am as a matter of fact rather sceptical about the accounts usually given. Instead, it should be pointed out how common this sort of relationship is and that it should be suspected in cases where we are prone to overlook it. A striking example is the case of 'pleasure': pleasures we may say not merely resemble each other in being pleasant, but also *differ* precisely in the way in which they are pleasant.[6] No greater mistake could be made than the hedonistic mistake (copied by non-hedonists) of thinking that pleasure is always a single similar feeling, somehow isolable from the various activities which 'give rise' to it.

6. Another case which often provides puzzles, is that of words like 'youth' and 'love': which sometimes mean the object loved, or the thing which is youthful, sometimes the passion 'Love' or the quality (?) 'youth'. These cases are of course easy (rather *like* 'healthy'?). But suppose we take the noun 'truth': here is a case where the disagreements between different theorists have largely turned on whether they interpreted this as a name of a substance, of a quality, or of a relation.

7. Lastly, I want to take a specially interesting sort of case, which is perhaps commoner and at the bottom of more muddles than we are aware of.

---

[6] If we say that they are all called 'pleasures' 'because they are similar', we shall overlook this fact.

Take the sense in which I talk of a cricket bat and a cricket ball and a cricket umpire. The reason that all are called by the same name is perhaps that each has its part—its *own special* part—to play in the activity called cricketing: it is no good to say that cricket *simply* means 'used in cricket': for we cannot explain what we mean by 'cricket' *except* by explaining the special parts played in cricketing by the bat, ball, &c. Aristotle's suggestion was that the word 'good' might be used in such a way: in which case it is obvious how far astray we should go if we look for a 'definition' of the word 'good' in any ordinary simple sense: or look for the way in which 'good' things are 'similar' to each other, in any ordinary sense. If we tried to find out by such methods what 'cricket' meant, we should very likely conclude that it too was a simple unanalysable supersensible quality.

Another thing that becomes plain from such examples is that the apparently common-sense distinction between 'What is the meaning of the word *x*' and 'What particular things *are x* and to what degrees?' is not of universal application by any means. The questions cannot be distinguished in such cases. Or a similar case would be some word like 'golfing': it is not sense to ask 'What is the meaning of golfing?' 'What things are golfing?' Though it *is* sense to ask what component activities go to constitute golfing, what implements are used in golfing ('golf' clubs, &c.) and in what ways. Aristotle suggests 'happiness' is a word of this kind: in which case it is evident how far astray we shall go if we

treat it as though it were a word like 'whiteness'.

These summarily treated examples are enough to show how essential it is to have a thorough knowledge of the different reasons for which we call different things by the same name, before we can embark confidently on an inquiry. If we rush up with a demand for a definition in the simple manner of Plato or many other philosophers, if we use the rigid dichotomy 'same meaning, different meaning', or 'What *x* means', as distinguished from 'the things which are *x*', we shall simply make hashes of things. Perhaps some people are now discussing such questions seriously. All that is to be found in traditional Logics is the mention that there are, besides univocal and equivocal words, 'also analogous words': which, without further explanation, is used to lump together all cases where a word has not always absolutely the same meaning, nor several absolutely different meanings. All that 'similarity' theorists manage is to say that all things called by some one name are similar to some one pattern, or are all more similar to each other than any of them is to anything else; which is *obviously* untrue. Anyone who wishes to see the complexity of the problem, has only got to look in a (good) dictionary under such a word as 'head': the different meanings of the word 'head' will be related to each other in all sorts of different ways at once.

To summarize the contentions of this paper then. Firstly, the phrase 'the meaning of a word' is a spurious phrase. Secondly and consequently, a re-examination is needed of phrases like the two which I discuss, 'being a part of the meaning of' and 'having the same meaning'. On these matters, dogmatists require prodding: although history indeed suggests that it may sometimes be better to let sleeping dogmatists lie.

EMPIRICIST CRITERIA OF COGNITIVE SIGNIFICANCE

2.4

Carl Hempel

1. The General Empiricist Conception of Cognitive and Empirical Significance

It is a basic principle of contemporary empiricism that a sentence makes a cognitively significant assertion, and thus can be said to be either true or false, if and only if either (1) it is analytic or contradictory—in which case it is said to have purely logical meaning or significance—or else (2) it is capable, at least potentially, of test by experiential evidence—in which case it is said to have empirical meaning or significance. The basic tenet of this

From *Aspects of Scientific Explanation* (New York: Free Press, 1965). This article is a composite of two earlier ones which appeared in *Révue internationale de philosophie*, IV (1950), and *Proceedings of the American Academy of Arts and Sciences*, LXXX (1951). Reprinted by permission of the editors of *Révue internationale de philosophie*, and of the American Academy of Arts and Sciences.

principle, and especially of its second part, the so-called testability criterion of empirical meaning (or better: meaningfulness), is not peculiar to empiricism alone: it is characteristic also of contemporary operationism, and in a sense of pragmatism as well; for the pragmatist maxim that a difference must make a difference to be a difference may well be construed as insisting that a verbal difference between two sentences must make a difference in experiential implications if it is to reflect a difference in meaning.

How this general conception of cognitively significant discourse led to the rejection, as devoid of logical and empirical meaning, of various formulations in speculative metaphysics, and even of certain hypotheses offered within empirical science, is too well known to require recounting. I think that the general intent of the empiricist criterion of meaning is basically sound, and that notwithstanding much oversimplification in its use, its critical application has been, on the whole, en-lightening and salutary. I feel less con-fident, however, about the possibility of restating the general idea in the form of precise and general criteria which establish sharp dividing lines (a) between statements of purely logical and statements of empirical signifi-cance, and (b) between those sen-tences which do have cognitive sig-nificance and those which do not.

In the present paper, I propose to reconsider these distinctions as con-ceived in recent empiricism, and to point out some of the difficulties they present. The discussion will concern mainly the second of the two distinc-tions; in regard to the first, I shall limit myself to a few brief remarks.

2. The Earlier Testability Criteria of Meaning and Their Shortcomings

Let us note first that any general criterion of cognitive significance will have to meet certain requirements if it is to be at all acceptable. Of these, we note one, which we shall consider here as expressing a necessary, though by no means sufficient, *condition of ade-quacy* for criteria of cognitive signifi-cance.

(A) If under a given criterion of cognitive significance, a sentence N is nonsignificant, then so must be all truth-functional compound sentences in which N occurs nonvacuously as a component. For if N cannot be sig-nificantly assigned a truth value, then it is impossible to assign truth values to the compound sentences containing

N; hence, they should be qualified as nonsignificant as well.

We note two corollaries of require-ment (A):

(A1) If under a given criterion of cognitive significance, a sentence S is nonsignificant, then so must be its nega-tion, $\sim S$.

(A2) If under a given criterion of cognitive significance, a sentence N is nonsignificant, then so must be any con-junction $N \cdot S$ and any disjunction $N \vee S$, no matter whether S is signifi-cant under the given criterion or not.

We now turn to the initial attempts made in recent empiricism to establish general criteria of cognitive signifi-cance. Those attempts were governed by the consideration that a sentence, to make an empirical assertion must be capable of being borne out by, or con-flicting with, phenomena which are potentially capable of being directly ob-served. Sentences describing such po-tentially observable phenomena—no matter whether the latter do actually occur or not—may be called observa-tion sentences. More specifically, an *ob-servation sentence* might be construed as a sentence—no matter whether true or false—which asserts or denies that a specified object, or group of objects, of macroscopic size has a particular *observable characteristic*, i.e., a char-acteristic whose presence or absence can, under favorable circumstances, be ascertained by direct observation.[1]

---

[1] Observation sentences of this kind be-long to what Carnap has called the thing-language, cf., e.g., (1938), pp. 52–53. That

The task of setting up criteria of empirical significance is thus transformed into the problem of characterizing in a precise manner the relationship which obtains between a hypothesis and one or more observation sentences whenever the phenomena described by the latter either confirm or disconfirm the hypothesis in question. The ability of a given sentence to enter into that relationship to some set of observation sentences would then characterize its testability-in-principle, and thus its empirical significance. Let us now briefly examine the major attempts that have been made to obtain criteria of significance in this manner.

One of the earliest criteria is expressed in the so-called *verifiability requirement*. According to it, a sentence is empirically significant if and only if it is not analytic and is capable, at least in principle, of complete verification by observational evidence; i.e., if observational evidence can be described which, if actually obtained, would conclusively establish the truth

they are adequate to formulate the data which serve as the basis for empirical tests is clear in particular for the intersubjective testing procedures used in science as well as in large areas of empirical inquiry on the commonsense level. In epistemological discussions, it is frequently assumed that the ultimate evidence for beliefs about empirical matters consists in perceptions and sensations whose description calls for a phenomenalistic type of language. The specific problems connected with the phenomenalistic approach cannot be discussed here; but it should be mentioned that at any rate all the critical considerations presented in this article in regard to the testability criterion are applicable, *mutatis mutandis*, to the case of a phenomenalistic basis as well.

of the sentence.[2] With the help of the concept of observation sentence, we can restate this requirement as follows: A sentence S has empirical meaning if and only if it is possible to indicate a finite set of observation sentences, O_1, $O_2,. . ., O_n$, such that if these are true, then S is necessarily true, too. As stated, however, this condition is satis-

---

[2] Originally, the permissible evidence was meant to be restricted to what is observable by the speaker and perhaps his fellow beings during their life times. Thus construed, the criterion rules out, as cognitively meaningless, all statements about the distant future or the remote past, as has been pointed out, among others, by Ayer (1946), chapter I; by Pap (1949), chapter 13, esp. pp. 333 ff.; and by Russell (1948), pp. 445–47. This difficulty is avoided, however, if we permit the evidence to consist of any finite set of "logically possible observation data", each of them formulated in an observation sentence. Thus, e.g., the sentence S_1, "The tongue of the largest dinosaur in New York's Museum of Natural History was blue or black" is completely verifiable in our sense; for it is a logical consequence of the sentence S_2, "The tongue of the largest dinosaur in New York's Museum of Natural History was blue"; and this is an observation sentence, in the sense just indicated.

And if the concept of *verifiability in principle* and the more general concept of *confirmability in principle*, which will be considered later, are construed as referring to *logically possible evidence* as expressed by observation sentences, then it follows similarly that the class of statements which are verifiable, or at least confirmable, in principle include such assertions as that the planet Neptune and the Antarctic Continent existed before they were discovered, and that atomic warfare, if not checked, will lead to the extermination of this planet. The objections which Russell (1948), pp. 445 and 447, raises against the verifiability criterion by reference to those examples do not apply

fied also if S is an analytic sentence or if the given observation sentences are logically incompatible with each other. By the following formulation, we rule these cases out and at the same time express the intended criterion more precisely:

(2.1) REQUIREMENT OF COMPLETE VERIFIABILITY IN PRINCIPLE. A sentence has empirical meaning if and only if it is not analytic and follows logically from some finite and logically consistent class of observation sentences.[3]

These observation sentences need not be true, for what the criterion is to explicate is testability by "potentially observable phenomena," or testability "in principle."

In accordance with the general conception of cognitive significance outlined earlier, a sentence will now be classified as cognitively significant if either it is analytic or contradictory, or it satisfies the verifiability requirement.

This criterion, however, has several serious defects. One of them has been noted by several writers:

a. Let us assume that the properties of being a stork and of being red-legged are both observable characteristics, and that the former does not

---

therefore if the criterion is understood in the manner here suggested. Incidentally, statements of the kind mentioned by Russell, which are not actually verifiable by any human being, were explicitly recognized as cognitively significant already by Schlick (1936), Part V, who argued that the impossibility of verifying them was "merely empirical." The characterization of verifiability with the help of the concept of observation sentence as suggested here might serve as a more explicit and rigorous statement of that conception.

[3] As has frequently been emphasized in the empiricist literature, the term "verifiability" is to indicate, of course, the conceivability, or better, the logical possibility, of evidence of an observational kind which, if actually encountered, would constitute conclusive evidence for the given sentence; it is not intended to mean the technical possibility of performing the tests needed to obtain such evidence, and even less the possibility of actually finding directly observable phenomena which constitute conclusive evidence for that sentence—which would be tantamount to the actual existence of such evidence and would thus imply the truth of the given sentence. Analogous remarks apply to the terms "falsifiability" and "confirmability". This point has clearly been disre-

garded in some critical discussions of the verifiability criterion. Thus, e.g., Russell (1948), p. 448 construes verifiability as the actual existence of a set of conclusively verifying occurrences. This conception, which has never been advocated by any logical empiricist, must naturally turn out to be inadequate since according to it the empirical meaningfulness of a sentence could not be established without gathering empirical evidence, and moreover enough of it to permit a conclusive proof of the sentence in question! It is not surprising, therefore, that his extraordinary interpretation of verifiability leads Russell to the conclusion: "In fact, that a proposition is verifiable is itself not verifiable" (l.c.). Actually, under the empiricist interpretation of complete verifiability, any statement asserting the verifiability of some sentence S whose text is quoted, is either analytic or contradictory; for the decision whether there exists a class of observation sentences which entail S, i.e., whether such observation sentences can be formulated, no matter whether they are true or false—that decision is a purely logical matter.

logically entail the latter. Then the sentence

(*S*1)   All storks are red-legged

is neither analytic nor contradictory; and clearly, it is not deducible from a finite set of observation sentences. Hence, under the contemplated criterion, *S*1 is devoid of empirical significance; and so are all other sentences purporting to express universal regularities or general laws. And since sentences of this type constitute an integral part of scientific theories, the verifiability requirement must be regarded as overly restrictive in this respect.

Similarly, the criterion disqualifies all sentences such as 'For any substance there exists some solvent', which contain both universal and existential quantifiers (i.e., occurrences of the terms 'all' and 'some' or their equivalents); for no sentences of this kind can be logically deduced from any finite set of observation sentences.

Two further defects of the verifiability requirement do not seem to have been widely noticed:

b. As is readily seen, the negation of *S*1

(∼*S*1)   There exists at least one stork that is not red-legged

is deducible from any two observation sentences of the type 'a is a stork' and 'a is not red-legged'. Hence, ∼*S*1 is cognitively significant under our criterion, but *S*1 is not, and this constitutes a violation of condition (A1).

c. Let *S* be a sentence which does,

and *N* a sentence which does not satisfy the verifiability requirement. Then *S* is deducible from some set of observation sentences; hence, by a familiar rule of logic, $S \vee N$ is deducible from the same set, and therefore cognitively significant according to our criterion. This violates condition (A2) above.[4]

Strictly analogous considerations apply to an alternative criterion, which makes complete falsifiability in principle the defining characteristic of empirical significance. Let us formulate this criterion as follows:

(2.2) REQUIREMENT OF COMPLETE FALSIFIABILITY IN PRINCIPLE. A sentence has empirical meaning if and only if its negation is not analytic and follows logically from some finite log-

---

[4] The arguments here adduced against the verifiability criterion also prove the inadequacy of a view closely related to it, namely that two sentences have the same cognitive significance if any set of observation sentences which would verify one of them would also verify the other, and conversely. Thus, e.g., under this criterion, any two general laws would have to be assigned the same cognitive significance, for no general law is verified by any set of observation sentences. The view just referred to must be clearly distinguished from a position which Russell examines in his critical discussion of the positivistic meaning criterion. It is "the theory that two propositions whose verified consequences are identical have the same significance" (1948), p. 448. This view is untenable indeed, for what consequences of a statement have actually been verified at a given time is obviously a matter of historical accident which cannot possibly serve to establish identity of cognitive significance. But I am not aware that any logical empiricist ever subscribed to that "theory."

ically consistent class of observation sentences.

This criterion qualifies a sentence as empirically meaningful if its negation satisfies the requirement of complete verifiability; as it is to be expected, it is therefore inadequate on similar grounds as the latter:

(a) It denies cognitive significance to purely existential hypotheses, such as 'There exists at least one unicorn', and all sentences whose formulation calls for mixed—i.e., universal and existential—quantification, such as 'For every compound there exists some solvent', for none of these can possibly be conclusively falsified by a finite number of observation sentences.

(b) If 'P' is an observation predicate, then the assertion that all things have the property P is qualified as significant, but its negation, being equivalent to a purely existential hypothesis, is disqualified [cf. (a)]. Hence, criterion (2.2) gives rise to the same dilemma as (2.1).

(c) If a sentence S is completely falsifiable whereas N is a sentence which is not, then their conjunction, $S \cdot N$ (i.e., the expression obtained by connecting the two sentences by the word 'and') is completely falsifiable; for if the negation of S is entailed by a class of observation sentences, then the negation of $S \cdot N$ is, a fortiori, entailed by the same class. Thus, the criterion allows empirical significance to many sentences which an adequate empiricist criterion should rule out, such as "All swans are white and the absolute is perfect.'

In sum, then, interpretations of the testability criterion in terms of com-plete verification or of complete falsifiability are inadequate because they are overly restrictive in one direction and overly inclusive in another, and because both of them violate the fundamental requirement A.

Several attempts have been made to avoid these difficulties by construing the testability criterion as demanding merely a partial and possibly indirect confirmability of empirical hypotheses by observational evidence.

A formulation suggested by Ayer[5] is characteristic of these attempts to set up a clear and sufficiently comprehensive criterion of confirmability. It states, in effect, that a sentence S has empirical import if from S in conjunction with suitable subsidiary hypotheses it is possible to derive observation sentences which are not derivable from the subsidiary hypotheses alone.

This condition is suggested by a closer consideration of the logical structure of scientific testing; but it is much too liberal as it stands. Indeed, as Ayer himself has pointed out in the second edition of his book, *Language, Truth, and Logic*,[6] his criterion allows empirical import to any sentence whatever. Thus, e.g., if S is the sentence 'The absolute is perfect', it suffices to choose as a subsidiary hypothesis the sentence 'If the absolute is perfect then this apple is red' in order to make possible the deduction of the ob-

---

[5] (1936, 1946), Chap. I. The case against the requirements of verifiability and of falsifiability, and in favor of a requirement of partial confirmability and disconfirmability, is very clearly presented also by Pap (1949), chapter 13.

[6] (1946), 2d ed., pp. 11–12.

servation sentence 'This apple is red', which clearly does not follow from the subsidiary hypothesis alone.

To meet this objection, Ayer proposed a modified version of his testability criterion. In effect, the modification restricts the subsidiary hypotheses mentioned in the previous version to sentences which either are analytic or can independently be shown to be testable in the sense of the modified criterion.[7]

But it can readily be shown that this new criterion, like the requirement of complete falsifiability, allows empirical significance to any conjunction $S \cdot N$, where S satisfies Ayer's criterion while N is a sentence such as 'The absolute is perfect', which is to be disqualified by that criterion. Indeed, whatever consequences can be deduced from S with the help of permissible subsidiary hypotheses can also be deduced from $S \cdot N$ by means of the same subsidiary hypotheses; and as Ayer's new criterion is formulated essentially in terms of the deducibility of a certain type of consequence from the given sentence, it countenances $S \cdot N$ together with S. Another difficulty has been pointed out by Church, who has shown[8] that if there are any three observation sentences none of which

alone entails any of the others, then it follows for any sentence S whatsoever that either it or its denial has empirical import according to Ayer's revised criterion.

All the criteria considered so far attempt to explicate the concept of empirical significance by specifying certain logical connections which must obtain between a significant sentence and suitable observation sentences. It seems now that this type of approach offers little hope for the attainment of precise criteria of meaningfulness: this conclusion is suggested by the preceding survey of some representative attempts, and it receives additional support from certain further considerations, some of which will be presented in the following sections.

3. Characterization of Significant Sentences by Criteria for Their Constituent Terms

An alternative procedure suggests itself which again seems to reflect well the general viewpoint of empiricism: It might be possible to characterize cognitively significant sentences by certain conditions which their constituent terms have to satisfy. Specifically, it would seem reasonable to say that all extralogical terms[9] in a significant sen-

---

[7] This restriction is expressed in recursive form and involves no vicious circle. For the full statement of Ayer's criterion, see Ayer (1946), p. 13.

[8] Church (1949). An alternative criterion recently suggested by O'Connor (1950) as a revision of Ayer's formulation is subject to a slight variant of Church's stricture: It can be shown that if there are three observation sentences none of which entails any of the others, and if S is any noncompound

sentence, then either S or $\backsim S$ is significant under O'Connor's criterion.

[9] An extralogical term is one that does not belong to the specific vocabulary of logic. The following phrases, and those definable by means of them, are typical examples of logical terms: 'not', 'or', 'if . . . then', 'all', 'some', '. . . is an element of

tence must have experiential reference, and that therefore their meanings must be capable of explication by reference to observables exclusively.[10] In order to exhibit certain analogies between this approach and the previous one, we adopt the following terminological conventions:

Any term that may occur in a cognitively significant sentence will be called a *cognitively significant term.* Furthermore, we shall understand by an *observation term* any term which either (a) is an *observation predicate*, i.e., signifies some observable characteristic (as do the terms 'blue', 'warm', 'soft', 'coincident with', 'of greater apparent brightness than') or (b) names some physical object of macroscopic size (as do the terms 'the needle of this instrument', 'the Moon', 'Krakatoa Volcano', 'Greenwich, England', 'Julius Caesar').

Now while the testability criteria of meaning aimed at characterizing the cognitively significant sentences by means of certain inferential connections in which they must stand to some observation sentences, the alternative approach under consideration would instead try to specify the vocabulary that may be used in forming significant sentences. This vocabulary, the class of

significant terms, would be characterized by the condition that each of its elements is either a logical term or else a term with empirical significance; in the latter case, it has to stand in certain definitional or explicative connections to some observation terms. This approach certainly avoids any violations of our earlier conditions of adequacy. Thus, e.g., if S is a significant sentence, i.e., contains cognitively significant terms only, then so is its denial, since the denial sign, and its verbal equivalents, belong to the vocabulary of logic and are thus significant. Again, if N is a sentence containing a nonsignificant term, then so is any compound sentence which contains N.

But this is not sufficient, of course. Rather, we shall now have to consider a crucial question analogous to that raised by the previous approach: Precisely how are the logical connections between empirically significant terms and observation terms to be construed if an adequate criterion of cognitive significance is to result? Let us consider some possibilities.

(3.1) The simplest criterion that suggests itself might be called the *requirement of definability.* It would demand that any term with empirical significance must be explicitly definable by means of observation terms.

This criterion would seem to accord well with the maxim of operationism that all significant terms of empirical science must be introduced by operational definitions. However, the requirement of definability is vastly too restrictive, for many important terms of scientific and even pre-scientific dis-

---

class. . .'. Whether it is possible to make a sharp theoretical distinction between logical and extra-logical terms is a controversial issue related to the problem of discriminating between analytic and synthetic sentences. For the purpose at hand, we may simply assume that the logical vocabulary is given by enumeration.

[10] For a detailed exposition and critical discussion of this idea, see H. Feigl's stimulating and enlightening article (1950).

course cannot be explicitly defined by means of observation terms.

In fact, as Carnap[11] has pointed out, an attempt to provide explicit definitions in terms of observables encounters serious difficulties as soon as disposition terms, such as 'soluble', 'malleable', 'electric conductor', etc., have to be accounted for; and many of these occur even on the pre-scientific level of discourse.

Consider, for example, the word 'fragile'. One might try to define it by saying that an object x is fragile if and only if it satisfies the following condition: If at any time t the object is sharply struck, then it breaks at that time. But if the statement connectives in this phrasing are construed truth-functionally, so that the definition can be symbolized by

$$(D) \quad Fx \equiv (t) \ (Sxt \supset Bxt)$$

then the predicate 'F' thus defined does not have the intended meaning. For let a be any object which is not fragile (e.g., a raindrop or a rubber band), but which happens not to be sharply struck at any time throughout its existence. Then 'Sat' is false and hence '$Sat \supset Bat$' is true for all values of 't'; consequently, 'Fa' is true though a is not fragile.

To remedy this defect, one might construe the phrase 'if . . . then . . .' in the original definiens as having a more restrictive meaning than the truth-functional conditional. This meaning might be suggested by the subjunctive phrasing 'If x were to be sharply struck

at any time t, then x would break at t.' But a satisfactory elaboration of this construal would require a clarification of the meaning and the logic of counterfactual and subjunctive conditionals, which is a thorny problem.[12]

An alternative procedure was suggested by Carnap in his theory of reduction sentences.[13] These are sentences which, unlike definitions, specify the meaning of a term only conditionally or partially. The term 'fragile', for example, might be introduced by the following reduction sentence:

$$(R) \quad (x) \ (t) \ [Sxt \supset (Fx \equiv Bxt)]$$

which specifies that if x is sharply struck at any time t, then x is fragile if and only if x breaks at t.

Our earlier difficulty is now avoided, for if a is a nonfragile object that is never sharply struck, then that expression in R which follows the quantifiers is true of a; but this does not imply that 'Fa' is true. But the reduction sentence R specifies the meaning of 'F' only for application to those objects which meet the "test condition" of being sharply struck at some time; for

---

[11] Cf. (1936–37), especially section 7.

[12] On this subject, see for example Langford (1941); Lewis (1946), pp. 210–30; Chisholm (1946); Goodman (1947); Reichenbach (1947), Chapter VIII; Hempel and Oppenheim (1948), Part III; Popper (1949); and especially Goodman's further analysis (1955).

[13] Cf. Carnap, loc. cit. note 11. For a brief elementary presentation of the main idea, see Carnap (1938), Part III. The sentence R here formulated for the predicate 'F' illustrates only the simplest type of reduction sentence, the so-called bilateral reduction sentence.

these it states that fragility then amounts to breaking. For objects that fail to meet the test condition, the meaning of 'F' is left undetermined. In this sense, reduction sentences have the character of partial or conditional definitions.

Reduction sentences provide a satisfactory interpretation of the experiential import of a large class of disposition terms and permit a more adequate formulation of so-called operational definitions, which, in general, are not complete definitions at all. These considerations suggest a greatly liberalized alternative to the requirement of definability:

(3.2) THE REQUIREMENT OF REDUCIBILITY. Every term with empirical significance must be capable of introduction, on the basis of observation terms, through chains of reduction sentences.

This requirement is characteristic of the liberalized versions of positivism and physicalism which, since about 1936, have superseded the older, overly narrow conception of a full definability of all terms of empirical science by means of observables,[14] and it avoids many of the shortcomings of the latter. Yet, reduction sentences do not seem to offer an adequate means for the introduction of the central terms of advanced scientific theories, often referred to as theoretical constructs. This is indicated by the following consid-

erations: A chain of reduction sentences provides a necessary and a sufficient condition for the applicability of the term it introduces. (When the two conditions coincide, the chain is tantamount to an explicit definition.) But now take, for example, the concept of length as used in classical physical theory. Here, the length in centimeters of the distance between two points may assume any positive real number as its value; yet it is clearly impossible to formulate, by means of observation terms, a sufficient condition for the applicability of such expressions as 'having a length of $\sqrt{2}$ cm' and 'having a length of $\sqrt{2} + 10^{-100}$ cm'; for such conditions would provide a possibility for discrimination, in observational terms, between two lengths which differ by only 10^{-100} cm.[15]

It would be ill-advised to argue that for this reason, we ought to permit only such values of the magnitude, length, as permit the statement of sufficient conditions in terms of observables. For this would rule out, among others, all irrational numbers and would prevent us from assigning, to the diagonal of a square with sides of length 1, the length $\sqrt{2}$, which is required by Euclidean geometry. Hence, the principles of Euclidean geometry would not be universally applicable in physics. Similarly, the principles of the calculus would become inapplicable, and the system of scientific theory as we know it today

---

[14] Cf. the analysis in Carnap (1936–37), especially section 15; also see the briefer presentation of the liberalized point of view in Carnap (1938).

[15] (Added in 1964.) This is not strictly correct. For a more circumspect statement, see note 12 in "A Logical Appraisal of Operationism" and the fuller discussion in section 7 of the essay "The Theoretician's Dilemma."

would be reduced to a clumsy, unmanageable torso. This, then, is no way of meeting the difficulty. Rather, we shall have to analyze more closely the function of constructs in scientific theories, with a view to obtaining through such an analysis a more adequate characterization of cognitively significant terms.

Theoretical constructs occur in the formulation of scientific theories. These may be conceived of, in their advanced stages, as being stated in the form of deductively developed axiomatized systems. Classical mechanics, or Euclidean or some Non-Euclidean form of geometry in physical interpretation, present examples of such systems. The extralogical terms used in a theory of this kind may be divided, in familiar manner, into primitive or basic terms, which are not defined within the theory, and defined terms, which are explicitly defined by means of the primitives. Thus, e.g., in Hilbert's axiomatization of Euclidean geometry, the terms 'point,' 'straight line', 'between' are among the primitives, while 'line segment', 'angle', 'triangle', 'length' are among the defined terms. The basic and the defined terms together with the terms of logic constitute the vocabulary out of which all the sentences of the theory are constructed. The latter are divided, in an axiomatic presentation, into primitive statements (also called postulates or basic statements) which, in the theory, are not derived from any other statements, and derived ones, which are obtained by logical deduction from the primitive statements.

From its primitive terms and sentences, an axiomatized theory can be developed by means of purely formal principles of definition and deduction, without any consideration of the empirical significance of its extralogical terms. Indeed, this is the standard procedure employed in the axiomatic development of uninterpreted mathematical theories such as those of abstract groups or rings or lattices, or any form of pure (i.e., noninterpreted) geometry.

However, a deductively developed system of this sort can constitute a scientific theory only if it has received an empirical interpretation[16] which renders it relevant to the phenomena of our experience. Such interpretation is given by assigning a meaning, in terms of observables, to certain terms or sentences of the formalized theory. Frequently, an interpretation is given not for the primitive terms or statements but rather for some of the terms definable by means of the primitives, or for some of the sentences deducible from the postulates.[17] Furthermore, interpre-

---

[16] The interpretation of formal theories has been studied extensively by Reichenbach, especially in his pioneer analyses of space and time in classical and in relativistic physics. He describes such interpretation as the establishment of *coordinating definitions* (Zuordnungsdefinitionen) for certain terms of the formal theory. See, for example, Reichenbach (1928). More recently, Northrop [cf. (1947), Chap. VII, and also the detailed study of the use of deductively formulated theories in science, ibid., Chaps. IV, V, VI] and H. Margenau [cf., for example, (1935)] have discussed certain aspects of this process under the title of *epistemic correlation*.

[17] A somewhat fuller account of this type of interpretation may be found in Carnap (1939), §24. The articles by Spence (1944) and by MacCorquodale and Meehl (1948)

tation may amount to only a partial assignment of meaning. Thus, e.g., the rules for the measurement of length by means of a standard rod may be considered as providing a *partial* empirical interpretation for the term 'the length, in centimeters, of interval i', or alternatively, for some sentences of the form 'the length of interval i is r centimeters'. For the method is applicable only to intervals of a certain medium size, and even for the latter it does not constitute a full interpretation since the use of a standard rod does not constitute the only way of determining length: various alternative procedures are available involving the measurement of other magnitudes which are connected, by general laws, with the length that is to be determined.

This last observation, concerning the possibility of an indirect measurement of length by virtue of certain laws, suggests an important reminder. It is not correct to speak, as is often done, of "the experiential meaning" of a term or a sentence in isolation. In the language of science, and for similar reasons even in pre-scientific discourse, a single statement usually has no experiential implications. A single sentence in a scientific theory does not, as a rule, entail any observation sentences; consequences asserting the occurrence of certain observable phenomena can be derived from it only by conjoining it with a set of other, subsidiary, hy-

potheses. Of the latter, some will usually be observation sentences, others will be previously accepted theoretical statements. Thus, e.g., the relativistic theory of the deflection of light rays in the gravitational field of the sun entails assertions about observable phenomena only if it is conjoined with a considerable body of astronomical and optical theory as well as a large number of specific statements about the instruments used in those observations of solar eclipses which serve to test the hypothesis in question.

Hence, the phrase, 'the experiential meaning of expression E' is elliptical: What a given expression "means" in regard to potential empirical data is relative to two factors, namely:

I. *the linguistic framework L* to which the expression belongs. Its rules determine, in particular, what sentences—observational or otherwise—may be inferred from a given statement or class of statements;

II. the theoretical context in which the expression occurs, i.e., the class of those statements in L which are available as subsidiary hypotheses.

Thus, the sentence formulating Newton's law of gravitation has no experiential meaning by itself; but when used in a language whose logical apparatus permits the development of the calculus, and when combined with a suitable system of other hypotheses—including sentences which connect some of the theoretical terms with observation terms and thus establish a partial in-

---

provide enlightening illustrations of the use of theoretical constructs in a field outside that of the physical sciences, and of the difficulties encountered in an attempt to analyze in detail their function and interpretation.

terpretation—then it has a bearing on observable phenomena in a large variety of fields. Analogous considerations are applicable to the term 'gravitational field', for example. It can be considered as having experiential meaning only within the context of a theory, which must be at least partially interpreted; and the experiential meaning of the term—as expressed, say, in the form of operational criteria for its application —will depend again on the theoretical system at hand, and on the logical characteristics of the language within which it is formulated.

4. Cognitive Significance as a Characteristic of Interpreted Systems

The preceding considerations point to the conclusion that a satisfactory criterion of cognitive significance cannot be reached through the second avenue of approach here considered, namely by means of specific requirements for the terms which make up significant sentences. This result accords with a general characteristic of scientific (and, in principle, even pre-scientific) theorizing: Theory formation and concept formation go hand in hand; neither can be carried on successfully in isolation from the other.

If, therefore, cognitive significance can be attributed to anything, then only to entire theoretical systems formulated in a language with a well-determined structure. And the decisive mark of cognitive significance in such a system appears to be the existence of an interpretation for it in terms of ob-

servables. Such an interpretation might be formulated, for example, by means of conditional or biconditional sentences connecting nonobservational terms of the system with observation terms in the given language; the latter as well as the connecting sentences may or may not belong to the theoretical system.

But the requirement of partial interpretation is extremely liberal; it is satisfied, for example, by the system consisting of contemporary physical theory combined with some set of principles of speculative metaphysics, even if the latter have no empirical interpretation at all. Within the total system, these metaphysical principles play the role of what K. Reach and also O. Neurath liked to call *isolated sentences*: They are neither purely formal truths or falsehoods, demonstrable or refutable by means of the logical rules of the given language system; nor do they have any experiential bearing; i.e., their omission from the theoretical system would have no effect on its explanatory and predictive power in regard to potentially observable phenomena (i.e., the kind of phenomena described by observation sentences). Should we not, therefore, require that a cognitively significant system contain no isolated sentences? The following criterion suggests itself:

(4.1) A theoretical system is cognitively significant if and only if it is partially interpreted to at least such an extent that none of its primitive sentences is isolated.

But this requirement may bar from a theoretical system certain sentences which might well be viewed as permissible and indeed desirable. By way of a simple illustration, let us assume that our theoretical system T contains the primitive sentence

$$(S1) \quad (x) \, [P_1 x \supset (Qx \equiv P_2 x)]$$

where 'P_1' and 'P_2' are observation predicates in the given language L, while 'Q' functions in T somewhat in the manner of a theoretical construct and occurs in only one primitive sentence of T, namely $S1$. Now $S1$ is not a truth or falsehood of formal logic; and furthermore, if $S1$ is omitted from the set of primitive sentences of T, then the resulting system, T', possesses exactly the same systematic, i.e., explanatory and predictive, power as T. Our contemplated criterion would therefore qualify $S1$ as an isolated sentence which has to be eliminated—excised by means of Occam's razor, as it were—if the theoretical system at hand is to be cognitively significant.

But it is possible to take a much more liberal view of $S1$ by treating it as a partial definition for the theoretical term 'Q'. Thus conceived, $S1$ specifies that in all cases where the observable characteristic P_1 is present, 'Q' is applicable if and only if the observable characteristic P_2 is present as well. In fact, $S1$ is an instance of those partial, or conditional, definitions which Carnap calls bilateral reduction sentences. These sentences are explicitly qualified by Carnap as analytic (though not, of course, as truths of formal logic), essentially on the ground that all their consequences which are expressible by means of observation predicates (and

logical terms) alone are truths of formal logic.[18]

Let us pursue this line of thought a little further. This will lead us to some observations on analytic sentences and then back to the question of the adequacy of (4.1).

Suppose that we add to our system T the further sentence

$$(S2) \quad (x) \, [P_3 x \supset (Qx \equiv P_4 x)]$$

where 'P_3', 'P_4' are additional observation predicates. Then, on the view that "every bilateral reduction sentence is analytic",[19] $S2$ would be analytic as well as $S1$. Yet, the two sentences jointly entail non-analytic consequences which are expressible in terms of observation predicates alone, such as[20]

$$(O) \quad (x) \, [P_1 x \cdot P_2 x \cdot P x_3 \cdot \frown P_4 x) \cdot \\ \sim (P_1 x \cdot \frown P_2 x \cdot P_3 x \cdot P_4 x)]$$

But one would hardly want to admit the consequence that the conjunction of two analytic sentences may be synthetic. Hence if the concept of analyticity can be applied at all to the sentences of interpreted deductive systems, then it will have to be relativized with respect to the theoretical context at hand. Thus, e.g., $S1$ might be qualified as analytic relative to the system T, whose remaining postulates do not contain the term 'Q', but as synthetic

---

[18] Cf. Carnap (1936–37), especially sections 8 and 10.

[19] Carnap (1936–37), p. 452.

[20] The sentence O is what Carnap calls the *representative sentence* of the couple consisting of the sentences $S1$ and $S2$; see (1936–37), pp. 450–53.

relative to the system T enriched by $S2$. Strictly speaking, the concept of analyticity has to be relativized also in regard to the rules of the language at hand, for the latter determine what observational or other consequences are entailed by a given sentence. This need for at least a twofold relativization of the concept of analyticity was almost to be expected in view of those considerations which required the same twofold relativization for the concept of experiential meaning of a sentence.

If, on the other hand, we decide not to permit $S1$ in the role of a partial definition and instead reject it as an isolated sentence, then we are led to an analogous conclusion: Whether a sentence is isolated or not will depend on the linguistic frame and on the theoretical context at hand: While $S1$ is isolated relative to T (and the language in which both are formulated), it acquires definite experiential implications when T is enlarged by $S2$.

Thus we find, on the level of interpreted theoretical systems, a peculiar rapprochement, and partial fusion, of some of the problems pertaining to the concepts of cognitive significance and of analyticity: Both concepts need to be relativized; and a large class of sentences may be viewed, apparently with equal right, as analytic in a given context, or as isolated, or nonsignificant, in respect to it.

In addition to barring, as isolated in a given context, certain sentences which could just as well be construed as partial definitions, the criterion (4.1) has another serious defect. Of two logically equivalent formulations of a theoretical system it may qualify one as significant while barring the other as containing an isolated sentence among its primitives. For assume that a certain theoretical system $T1$ contains among its primitive sentences S', S'', . . . exactly one, S', which is isolated. Then $T1$ is not significant under (4.1). But now consider the theoretical system $T2$ obtained from $T1$ by replacing the two first primitive sentences, S', S'', by one, namely their conjunction. Then, under our assumptions, none of the primitive sentences of $T2$ is isolated, and $T2$, though equivalent to $T1$, is qualified as significant by (4.1). In order to do justice to the intent of (4.1), we would therefore have to lay down the following stricter requirement:

(4.2) A theoretical system is cognitively significant if and only if it is partially interpreted to such an extent that in no system equivalent to it at least one primitive sentence is isolated.

Let us apply this requirement to some theoretical system whose postulates include the two sentences $S1$ and $S2$ considered before, and whose other postulates do not contain 'Q' at all. Since the sentences $S1$ and $S2$ together entail the sentence O, the set consisting of $S1$ and $S2$ is logically equivalent to the set consisting of $S1$, $S2$ and O. Hence, if we replace the former set by the latter, we obtain a theoretical system equivalent to the given one. In this new system, both $S1$ and $S2$ are isolated since, as can be shown, their removal does not affect the explanatory and predictive power of the system in reference to observable phenomena. To put it intuitively, the systematic power of $S1$ and $S2$ is the same as that of O. Hence, the original system is disqualified by (4.2). From the viewpoint of a strictly sensationalist positivism as perhaps envisaged by Mach, this result might be hailed as a sound repudiation of theories making reference to fictitious entities, and as a strict insistence on theories couched exclusively in terms of observables. But from a contemporary vantage point, we shall have to say that such a procedure overlooks or misjudges the important function of constructs in scientific theory: The history of scientific endeavor shows that if we wish to arrive at precise, comprehensive, and well-confirmed general laws, we have to rise above the level of direct observation. The phenomena directly accessible to our experience are not connected by general laws of great scope and rigor. Theoretical constructs are needed for the formulation of such higher-level laws. One of the most important functions of a well-chosen construct is its potential ability to serve as a constituent in ever new general connections that may be discovered; and to such connections we would blind ourselves if we insisted on banning from scientific theories all those terms and sentences which could be "dispensed with" in the sense indicated in (4.2). In following such a narrowly phenomenalistic or positivistic course, we would deprive ourselves of the tremendous fertility of theoretical constructs, and we would often render the formal structure of the expurgated theory clumsy and inefficient.

Criterion (4.2), then, must be abandoned, and considerations such as those outlined in this paper seem to lend strong support to the conjecture that no adequate alternative to it can be found; i.e., that it is not possible to formulate general and precise criteria which would separate those partially interpreted systems whose isolated sentences might be said to have a significant function from those in which the isolated sentences are, so to speak, mere useless appendages.

We concluded earlier that cognitive significance in the sense intended by recent empiricism and operationism can at best be attributed to sentences forming a theoretical system, and perhaps rather to such systems as wholes. Now, rather than try to replace (4.2) by some alternative, we will have to recognize further that cognitive significance in a system is a matter of degree: Significant systems range from those whose entire extralogical vocabulary consists of observation terms, through theories whose formulation relies heavily on theoretical constructs, on to systems with hardly any bearing on potential empirical findings. Instead of dichotomizing this array into significant and non-significant systems it would seem less arbitrary and more promising to appraise or compare different theoretical systems in regard to such characteristics as these:

a. the clarity and precision with which the theories are formulated, and with which the logical relationships of their elements to each other and to expressions couched in observational terms have been made explicit;

b. the systematic, i.e., explanatory and

predictive, power of the systems in regard to observable phenomena;

c. the formal simplicity of the theoretical system with which a certain systematic power is attained;

d. the extent to which the theories have been confirmed by experiential evidence.

Many of the speculative philosophical approaches to cosmology, biology, or history, for example, would make a poor showing on practically all of these counts and would thus prove no matches to available rival theories, or would be recognized as so unpromising as not to warrant further study or development.

If the procedure here suggested is to be carried out in detail, so as to become applicable also in less obvious cases, then it will be necessary, of course, to develop general standards, and theories pertaining to them, for the appraisal and comparison of theoretical systems in the various respects just mentioned. To what extent this can be done with rigor and precision cannot well be judged in advance. In recent years, a considerable amount of work has been done towards a definition and theory of the concept of degree of confirmation, or logical probability, of a theoretical system;[21] and several contributions have been made towards the clarification of some of the other ideas referred to above.[22] The continuation of

this research represents a challenge for further constructive work in the logical and methodological analysis of scientific knowledge.

REFERENCES

Ayer, A. J., *Language, Truth and Logic,* London, 1936; 2nd ed. 1946.

Carnap, R., "Testability and Meaning," *Philosophy of Science*, 3(1936) and 4(1937).

Carnap, R., "Logical Foundations of the Unity of Science," in: *International Encyclopedia of Unified Science*, I, 1; Chicago, 1938.

Carnap, R., *Foundations of Logic and Mathematics*, Chicago, 1939.

Carnap, R., "On Inductive Logic," *Philosophy of Science*, 12(1945). Referred to as (1945)1 in this article.

Carnap, R., "The Two Concepts of Probability," *Philosophy and Phenomenological Research*, 5(1945). Referred to as (1945)2 in this article.

Carnap, R., *Logical Foundations of Probability*, Chicago, 1950.

Chisholm, R. M., "The Contrary-to-Fact Conditional," *Mind*, 55(1946).

Church, A., Review of Ayer (1946), *The Journal of Symbolic Logic*, 14(1949), 52–53.

Feigl, H., "Existential Hypotheses: Realistic vs. Phenomenalistic Interpretations," *Philosophy of Science*, 17(1950).

Goodman, N., "The Problem of Counterfactual Conditionals," *The Journal of Philosophy*, 44(1947).

Goodman, N., "The Logical Simplicity of Predicates," *The Journal of Symbolic Logic*, 14(1949). Referred to as (1949)1 in this article.

Goodman, N., "Some Reflections on the

---

[21] Cf., for example, Carnap (1945)1 and (1945)2, and especially (1950). Also see Helmer and Oppenheim (1945).

[22] On simplicity, cf. especially Popper (1935), Chap. V; Reichenbach (1938),

---

§ 42; Goodman (1949)1, (1949)2, (1950); on explanatory and predictive power, cf. Hempel and Oppenheim (1948), Part IV.

Theory of Systems," *Philosophy and Phenomenological Research*, 9(1949). Referred to as (1949)2 in this article.

Goodman, N., "An Improvement in the Theory of Simplicity," *The Journal of Symbolic Logic*, 15(1950).

Goodman, N., *Fact, Fiction, and Forecast*, Cambridge, Massachusetts, 1955.

Helmer, O. and P. Oppenheim, "A Syntactical Definition of Probability and of Degree of Confirmation." *The Journal of Symbolic Logic*, 10(1945).

Hempel, C. G. and P. Oppenheim, "Studies in the Logic of Explanation," *Philosophy of Science*, 15(1948).

Langford, C. H., Review in *The Journal of Symbolic Logic*, 6(1941), 67–68.

Lewis, C. I., *An Analysis of Knowledge and Valuation*, La Salle, Ill., 1946.

MacCorquodale, K. and P. E. Meehl, "On a Distinction Between Hypothetical Constructs and Intervening Variables," *Psychological Review*, 55(1948).

Margenau, H., "Methodology of Modern Physics," *Philosophy of Science*, 2 (1935).

Northrop, F. S. C., *The Logic of the Sciences and the Humanities*, New York, 1947.

O'Connor, D. J., "Some Consequences of Professor A. J. Ayer's Verification Principal," *Analysis*, 10(1950).

Pap, A., *Elements of Analytic Philosophy*, New York, 1949.

Popper, K., *Logik der Forschung*, Wien, 1935.

Popper, K., "A Note on Natural Laws and So-Called 'Contrary-to-Fact Conditionals'," *Mind*, 58 (1949).

Reichenbach, H., *Philosophie der Raum-Zeit-Lehre*, Berlin, 1928.

Reichenbach, H., *Elements of Symbolic Logic*, New York, 1947.

Russell, B., *Human Knowledge*, New York, 1948.

Schlick, M., "Meaning and Verification," *Philosophical Review*, 45(1936). Also reprinted in Feigl, H. and W. Sellars, (eds.) *Readings in Philosophical Analysis*, New York, 1949.

Spence, Kenneth W., "The Nature of Theory Construction in Contemporary Psychology," *Psychological Review*, 51(1944).

2.5

VERIFICATION
AND THE USE OF LANGUAGE

G. J. Warnock

In recent years a great deal of attention has been devoted to the concepts of verification and verifiability.

From *Révue internationale de philosophie*, V (1951). Reprinted by permission of the editors and author. This is a slightly revised version of the original article.

The notions of verifying, testing, and confirming have been compared and contrasted—often somewhat arbitrarily: "strong" and "weak" verification have been distinguished—often with misplaced attempts at complete precision. Verification no doubt deserves some such scrutiny on its own account;

but it is clear that the main impulse to these inquiries has in fact derived from the belief that verification supplies the key to meaning, and that meaning is the peculiar concern of philosophers. In this article I propose to call in question this latter belief; and so I shall consider the relations between verification and meaning, rather than the notion of verification itself. This will involve the neglect of a good deal of detail; but I hope it will be seen that the neglected detail is inessential.

The position that I wish to establish is briefly this: that an account of meaning in terms of verification must be narrowly restricted, and may be seriously misleading; and that the acceptance of such an account tends to make philosophical arguments dogmatic, arid, and pointless.

(1) In an article called "Meaning and Verification," which appeared in *The Philosophical Review* in 1936, Schlick wrote: "The meaning of a proposition is the method of its verification."

This of course is a slogan, hardly more than a striking epigram. Schlick had other and better things than this to say about meaning. However, both he and others took this slogan more seriously than it deserves; it was brief, memorable, and constantly quoted. It is certainly a neat and convenient text for discussion, and as such I propose to use it. By bringing out some of the numerous difficulties which it contains we shall, I think, find our way back to certain of Wittgenstein's ideas, which Schlick and others distorted while claiming to amplify them.

But first, it has to be remembered that most advocates of the so-called Verification Principle were by no means disinterested. They were not merely concerned to analyse and to clarify the concept of meaning, but also to "eliminate metaphysics." Conversely, their opponents were eager to keep a place for some such subject. Now it may be the case that, if we look closely into the concept of meaning, we shall find that on some definitions of "metaphysics" there can be no subject-matter to be so called. But there is no point in eliminating a subject arbitrarily characterised; and I do not know (I doubt whether anyone knows) how the term "metaphysics" really ought to be defined. I suspect indeed that it ought *not* to be defined—that it is useless to try to divide philosophy into compartments, and that we are better off without departmental titles. I suggest, then, that we should not concern ourselves either to disallow or to defend the use of the term "metaphysics"; and certainly we should not allow a discussion of meaning to be directed by the merely tactical aim of affixing the label "meaningless" to the work of certain philosophers. No doubt there are good and bad ways of doing philosophy; philosophers have made some wise and many foolish remarks; but there is no short way of separating the wheat from the chaff. The belief that some "principle" will do our work for us is, or may easily become, a lazy belief and an unhelpful prejudice.

(2) "The meaning of a *proposition* is the method of its verification." What then is a proposition? Here we meet at once a serious obscurity. Indeed, according to Schlick's own terminology

his slogan must be wrongly stated. For he points out that we ask of a *sentence* what it means, and says that this is to ask what proposition the sentence "stands for" or expresses. (The proposition is "what the sentence means.") Now it would be absurd to speak of the meaning of the meaning of a sentence, or of the meaning of what a sentence "stands for." Presumably, then, we should make an amendment and read: "The meaning of a *sentence* is the method of its verification."

But this is not wholly clear either. Schlick describes a sentence as "a series of words," "a mere row of marks on paper," "a mere sequence of sounds." From these descriptions at least the risk of type-token ambiguity should be eliminated. If I say "It is raining," and you say "It is raining," have two sentences been uttered? Or has the same one sentence been uttered twice? It would be natural to say that, if I write down "It is raining" twice, I make two "rows of marks on paper;" but it is no less natural to say that I write down twice the same one sentence. It is, I believe, in this latter sense that Schlick wishes us to take the term "sentence," i.e. in the sense of "sentence-type." It seems clear, indeed, that we are not, except in very unusual circumstances, concerned with the meaning of a particular row of marks on paper. For I might point to such a row, ask for the meaning, and be told the meaning; and if someone then wrote down a second row of marks exactly like the first row, I would not ask again for the meaning of this second row. I would take it that, in making the second row of marks, he had written down the same

sentence; and I have already been told the meaning of this sentence. (This assumption might sometimes be mistaken, but not usually.)

It is further obvious that not all rows of marks, series of words, or sequences of sounds, are sentence-tokens. They may instead be random scratches, list of names, or tunes; and of such it would be a mistake to ask for the meaning. It would be difficult, perhaps impossible, to define sentence-tokens both usefully and exactly, but for present purposes this is not really necessary. It may be assumed that we can recognize sentence-tokens; and that we use the term "sentence" in such a way that any two or more sentence-tokens of the same type may be regarded as repetitions of the same sentence. I think it is certainly correct to say that it is in this sense that we ask what a sentence means.

(3) The next point is obvious enough, but has been so seldom noticed that it is almost surprising. Verification, however in the end we decide to define it, must certainly have some connection with truth and falsity. To verify p is to find out whether or not p is true (and perhaps, whether or not p is probably true, may be accepted or regarded as true). The notions of truth and falsity must, as etymology requires, come in somewhere. What, then, are we to do with all those meaningful sentences which have no concern whatever with truth and falsity?

Clearly there is an enormous number of such sentences. There are imperative sentences, used (mainly) to give orders; and interrogative sentences, used (mainly) to ask questions.

There are sentences used as prayers; to make promises; to give verdicts; to express decisions; to pass moral judgments; or to make proposals. It is nonsensical to ask of a question, an order, a prayer, or a proposal, whether it is true or false. The judge who rules that the witness must answer the question cannot be told that what he says is untrue (and therefore it also cannot be said to be true); his ruling may be regarded as correct or improper, it may be disputed, accepted, upheld, or set aside; but it cannot be either verified or falsified. When the chairman says "I declare Mr. Jones elected," it would not be in place to question, or to affirm, the truth of what he says. It would be easy to multiply such instances as these. As soon as we think of the multifarious uses of language, it becomes glaringly obvious that there is a vast number of sentences in connection with which the question "Is it true or false?" is, in varying degrees, absurd or out of place. And to these sentences verification can have no possible application, however "weak" or "indirect." If it is nonsense and out of place to ask whether p is true or false, we cannot speak of a "method of verification" of p.

(4) There would seem to be two possible ways out of this predicament.

(a) We may continue to say that the meaning of a sentence is the method of its verification, and boldly assert that any sentence for which no such method exists is meaningless. But this bold policy is not really acceptable. For first, it would be fantastic to hold that all prayers, questions, orders, rulings, judgments, etc., are flatly meaningless; this is too patently untrue to be tolerable. And second, we should thus obliterate the vital distinction between, on the one hand, sentences which *pose* as being meaningful, which *purport* to make verifiable statements, and which are to be unmasked and condemned as impostors; and, on the other hand, sentences (*e.g.*, imperatives) which do not even *seem* to be verifiable, true or false, and which because they make no false pretensions ought not to be condemned. In desperation we may toy with the idea of distinguishing the latter as good nonsense from the former as bad; but I think we should be reluctant to do more than toy with this expedient. To adopt it would be rather like treating dummy cartridges as a good variety of bad ammunition.

(b) We may alternatively stipulate that our account of the meaning of sentences deals only with those about which it *can* be asked whether they are true or false, and about which we can ask for a "method of verification." Few advocates of the Verification Principle seem to have been aware of its limited range of application, and therefore few made, explicitly and deliberately, any such restrictive stipulation as this. (It was often assumed that, apart from the stating of facts, the only use of language was to express or to evoke emotion.) Carnap confines his attention to what he calls, rather vaguely, "cognitive" meaning; others spoke equally vaguely of "literal" meaning (but do not questions and the rest have literal meanings?); others undertook to discuss the meaning of "statements," or (more commonly) slipped uncomfortably back and forth between "sentence," "statement," and "proposition," as if it made little difference which term was used.

In view of the obvious absurdity of alternative (*a*) above, it may seem that this second path is the one we should follow. It is, however, by no means satisfactory. For, first, it requires us to abandon the idea of setting up a *general* criterion of meaningfulness; we must, it seems, restrict ourselves to part only of the field. Can we be sure, then, that our tactical aims will be achieved? Suppose metaphysics should lie quite outside the area in which we can operate with our restricted principle; in this case, metaphysics would escape unscathed. Second, and more seriously, such a restrictive stipulation as this has an uncomfortably arbitrary look about it. It may perhaps be true to say that sentences used to make true or false statements form, by certain standards and for certain purposes, a more important class than sentences used in other ways; and this might justify concentration on this sort of sentence. Nevertheless, it seems strange to offer an analysis of meaning which cannot possibly be applied to other sorts of sentences, since admittedly many other sorts of sentences are, even if less important, not less meaningful. It would naturally be expected that something at least could be said about meaning in general, not merely about the meaning of this or of that sort of sentence. This point will arise again later.

(5) Let us now take it, provisionally and with some disquiet, that we are to discuss the dictum "The meaning of a sentence is the method of its verification," accepting the idea that

this is applicable, at best, only to sentences used, or purporting to be used, to make true or false statements. Even this, we shall find, is less clear and simple than it seems; some dilution of its apparent rigour is unavoidable.

(*a*) Suppose someone says to me "I have a pain in my ankle." It is natural to say that such an assertion may not be verifiable by me; for the assertion itself may be my only evidence for believing that the speaker has a pain in his ankle; certainly I cannot verify his assertion by feeling his pain. (I assume for the moment, what is in fact disputable, that he himself can properly be said to be able to verify his assertion.) Must I admit that, in a case of this sort, I do not and cannot know what the speaker means?

Advocates of the Verification Principle usually meet such difficulties as this by saying that, for a sentence to be verifiable and therefore meaningful, it need not be verifiable "by me," nor by any other particular person. So long as there is a method of verification available to *some* person—anyone at all—the sentence is to be regarded as verifiable.

(*b*) But all is not yet clear. Suppose that a historian were to say that on her twentieth birthday Cleopatra wore a red dress, and that when questioned he were to admit that there is not the slightest available evidence for or against this statement. Is this not to admit that the statement is not verifiable? And must it then be regarded as meaningless?

To meet this another qualification is required. We must say that for a sentence to be meaningful, to be understood *now*, it is not essential that any method of verifying it should *now* be available to anyone. So long as we can say how, *e.g.*, by a contemporary of Cleopatra's, our assertion about her dress *could* have been verified, that assertion is to be regarded as verifiable.

(*c*) But now suppose that we move into the regions of pre-history, and assert that, fifty thousand years before men appeared on the earth, rain fell at some particular place on some particular day. We do not know how to verify such a statement, and now we cannot even speak of the method of verification available to contemporary observers. There were no observers. Are we wrong, then, in thinking that we understand such assertions as this?

To meet this point one final manoeuvre is required. It does not matter, we must say, that an assertion cannot be verified by anyone now, nor even that it could not in fact have been verified by anyone at any time. For it may still be said to be verifiable *in principle*, and if so it may also be accepted as meaningful. Schlick writes: "When we speak of verifiability we mean *logical* possibility of verification." So long as we can describe without contradiction some method of verifying an assertion, it does not matter if neither I nor anyone else, either now or at any time, can verify or could have verified that assertion.

Even this position is by no means impregnable, but let us pause here for a moment. For already the Principle has been seriously watered down. At first sight it seemed to be extremely definite, positive, and clear; as if we were to accept as meaningful only those sentences for which there *is*, available to ourselves, a method of verification. But it now appears that we are to accept also (1) those for which there is a method of verification available, perhaps, only to others; also (2) those for which there once was, but now is not, an available method of verification; and also (3) those for which there is not, and never was, an available method of verification, but for which we can describe a "logically possible" method. Now in any ordinary sense of the term "verifiable," assertions falling into the third, and I think also the second, of these groups would properly be said to be *not* verifiable. And this induces a certain feeling of discomfort. For if, to prevent our Principle from wreaking too much havoc, we have to allow that assertions which are not verifiable may nevertheless be verifiable "in principle," it is hard to resist the suspicion that verifiability is not really the notion we require. It will not fit the case without a great deal of stretching and manipulating; and although these operations are not always or necessarily objectionable, we should not resort to them unless there is a good case for doing so. Perhaps we may be able to find some notion, other than verifiability, which will fit the case properly, without so much pushing and pulling.

(6) I wish now to re-inforce the suggestion that verifiability is not the notion we require.

(*a*) The phrase "method of verification" is quite inappropriate. (Perhaps it is also inessential; but in any case let us get rid of it.) For what do we mean when we speak of *methods* of verification? In what sorts of cases do we use this expression? We might naturally say that an estimate of the National Income of Great Britain in 1926 can be verified by various methods; that there are various methods of verifying the statement that some given liquid is an acid; that there are different methods of verifying the claim that a certain picture was painted by Vermeer. In each of these cases, the methods in question would consist in the carrying out of certain definite, quite elaborate procedures—the handling of statistics, the performance of chemical experiments, the systematic scrutiny of style, paint, and canvas. The statistician, the chemist, and the expert on paintings are expected to have learned, to know of, and to be able to follow, certain methods appropriate to their subjects. But is there a *method* of verifying that grass is green and that the sky on a clear day is blue? What method of verification could I follow in assuring myself that I have a headache? If someone says "Here is a book," holding it out to me, do I resort to a *method* of verifying what he says? We *look at* the grass and the sky; I *feel* my headache; I *see* the book that is offered to me. Looking, feeling, and seeing are not *methods* of verification; no-one has to be taught how to see and to feel, and no-one claims to be an expert by reason of his mastery of these accomplishments. It is clear, then, that there are innumerable statements as to which what leads us to make them and to accept or reject them as being true or false, is by no means the following of a *method of verification*. This phrase is altogether too formal, over-elab-

orate; it is properly used of statements or hypotheses that fall within the purview of specialists—scientists, statisticians, historians, doctors, detectives. It is quite out of place in our ordinary daily conversation, which nevertheless we understand perfectly well.

(*b*) But there is a more fundamental difficulty than this. Suppose that we take a sentence, say "The curtains are blue," and ask how this sentence is to be verified. It is perfectly clear that we can say and do nothing at all, until we are told or discover *which* curtains are said to be blue. If the curtains now hanging in my room are those referred to, I can look at them and see that those curtains are indeed blue; if the curtains in the next room are meant, I can go there and see that they are actually not blue; if the sentence occurs in a historical narrative, attributed to a speaker in the seventeenth century, probably I can do nothing at all that will enable me to decide whether what was said is true or false. But in any case, merely by inspection of the *sentence* "The curtains are blue" it is quite impossible to decide what curtains are meant—not because the answer is hidden, but because it is not there. In order to discover what curtains are referred to, I must look, not at the sentence, but at the context in which it was uttered, written or spoken. Now some curtains are blue, others are not; we can ascertain the colour of some curtains, not of others; in some cases we can look at them, in others we must undertake historical research or examine witnesses. What then are we to say? Is the sentence "The curtains are blue" both true and false—true of some curtains, false of others? Is it both verifiable (in some cases) and unverifiable (in others)? Is its "method of verification" also different on different occasions? And if so, does the *meaning* of the sentence vary in Protean fashion from one occasion to another?

There is a way of freeing ourselves from these perplexities. Suppose that we distinguish between the *sentence* "The curtains are blue," and the *statements* which from time to time are made by its use. The statement that the curtains (in my room) are blue, is true: the statement that the curtains (in the next room) are blue, is false: the statement that the curtains (in some seventeenth-century room) were blue, is unverifiable. Here we have three statements, one true, one false, one undetermined; but each was made by the use of the very same sentence. It is not in these cases the *sentence* which is true or false; it is the *statements*, made on each occasion by the use of this sentence, which are true or false. The sentence itself, we may say, has no truth-value; it is nonsensical to ask for the truth-value of the sentence.

But if so it is nonsensical to speak of *verifying* the sentence, of finding out whether it is true or false. Even "in principle" the sentence is not verifiable—(nor, of course, does it *fail* to be verifiable.) Clearly, then, we shall have to re-write the Verification Principle.

(7) Suppose we try it in this way: "To know the meaning of a sentence is to know how to verify statements made by the use of it."

This, however, is rather vague and very peculiar. Must we know how to verify *every* statement made by the use of it? Plainly not. If I know, as I do, how to verify the statement that the curtains (in my room) are blue, how can it be of the least importance that I do *not* know how to verify the statement that some other curtains are blue? If I know how to verify at least some statements made by the use of this sentence, I at least understand the sentence whenever it is used; and it cannot be essential that I should also know, in every case, how to find out whether what is said in those words is true or false.

(In an odd way this has been recognized already in the retreat to the diluted "verifiability in principle"; but it is now clear that this is not, and need not have pretended to be, verifiability. In order to show that I know what is meant by a sentence, I may show that I know what must in fact be the case if the sentence is to be used to make a true statement; but there is no need to say I am thus indicating a "logically possible" method of verification. We could perhaps put the matter thus, by tormenting our language; but why should we?)

The case, then, is this: It is to *statements* that the grammatical predicates "true" and "false" are applicable; it is statements that can be verified or falsified. Whether or not the sentence (say) "The curtains are blue" is used in a particular context to make a *true* statement, depends on the question whether the particular curtains then referred to do or do not then have the character of being blue; and whether or not this statement is *verifiable* depends on the question whether it can or cannot be discovered what character is possessed by those particular curtains. But if this cannot be discovered (i.e. if the statement is not verifiable), what is said may nevertheless be understood; for the very same sentence, namely "The curtains are blue," may be used on very many other occasions, on at least some of which it will no doubt be possible to assure ourselves that what is stated is actually the case. It is known what *would* be the case, if any statement made in the words "The curtains are blue" were true; but this is not to say that any such statement (still less, the sentence) is "verifiable in principle"; it is to say only this—that it is known what *would* be the case, *if* it were true.

(8) Suppose we say, then, that to know the meaning of a sentence is to know in what *sort* of circumstances a statement made by its use would be true or false. We may call this "knowing how to use" the sentence—i.e. knowing how to use it to make statements. Now, surely, we can see how to extend our discussion to include quite other sorts of sentences.

It happens that to know the meaning of *some* sorts of sentences is to know how to use them in making true (or false) statements; but for the numerous sentences which are not used to make statements this is not an applicable criterion. But this is no longer of vital importance; for there are other criteria applicable to such cases, and *in general* to know the meaning of a sentence is to know how to use it, to know in what circumstances its use is correct or incorrect. We are no longer restricted to the case of statements. We know how to use sentences to make statements certainly, but also to ask questions, to give orders, to make offers and to utter threats. A sentence is meaningful if it *has* a use; we know its meaning if we *know* its use. To concentrate our attention on verification is to peer shortsightedly at one corner of the picture—rather as if we sought to define intelligence as the capacity for doing geometry.

(9) Strangely enough, Schlick made one or two remarks co-inciding very closely with the position we have now reached. "Whenever we ask about a sentence, 'What does it mean?' what we expect is instruction as to the circumstances in which the sentence is to be used." And similarly, "Stating the meaning of a sentence amounts to stating the rules according to which the sentence is to be used." In making these remarks, with which we are in substantial agreement, he very properly acknowledges a debt to the ideas of Wittgenstein. How then did he deviate into propounding his restrictive, vague, and defective slogan?

Without pretending to offer a complete diagnosis, I would suggest three reasons. (1) Schlick and his followers were mainly concerned to wage war against metaphysics on behalf of science. Now in both these fields there occur mainly indicative sentences which purport to make statements of fact; and there do not occur, except inessentially, exhortations, questions, prayers, orders, and so on. Thus, Schlick and his followers seem merely to have failed to notice any sort of discourse other than the statement of facts, and to have been quite unaware of the needless and severe restriction of their official analysis of meaning. (2) The findings and hypotheses of scientists are commonly expressed not in singular, but in general, sentences. And if a sentence has the form of a generalization, it is easy (though I think it is also incorrect) to assume that anyone who utters this sentence, in any context and at any time, makes the very same statement, which is either in every case true or in every case false. Here the distinction between a sentence and a statement does not catch the eye; it is not, as it is in the case of singular sentences, plainly essential. And finally (3) in speaking of the findings and hypotheses of scientists it is natural and proper to speak of "methods of verification." These three considerations together go a long way, I think, towards explaining the background and origins of Schlick's famous epigram; and they also serve to emphasise its unsuitability for more general employment.

(10) It is proposed, then, that in analysis of the concept of meaning the restrictive and inappropriate notion of verifiability should be replaced by the more appropriate and more generally applicable notion of "use." It is important, however, that too much should not be claimed for this manœuvre, and that it should not itself be allowed to breed confusion. It is plain, for a start, that the notions of meaning and of use are not simply identical: for many things, of many different kinds, can be said about what people say which,

while in this sense or that throwing light on the use or uses of words, expressions, or sentences, would in no natural sense be said to throw light on their *meanings*. Thus it is desirable, and is a task awaiting satisfactory execution, that those questions of "use" which might properly be taken as questions of meaning should be carefully distinguished and characterized *within* the wider and more various field of questions about the "use" of language in general. Otherwise confusion, if perhaps not worse confounded, is liable not to be greatly diminished. At the same time, it is desirable that philosophers should not unthinkingly swallow the assumption that *meaning* is their sole and proprietary concern. The wider extension—if you like, the greater vagueness—of the notion of use may be positively advantageous, if it serves to encourage philosophers not to ignore the many features and functions of linguistic expressions *other* than those traditionally taken to comprise their meanings.

Now one last comment should be made, on the notorious "anti-metaphysical" aspect of the Verification Principle. I do not say that this sort of hostility is necessarily to be deplored; for some kinds of philosophising may be actually dangerous, and not merely pretentious, misguided, or distasteful. But I think that, if we fully appreciate the complexity of the use of language, we shall be very cautious indeed in the application of the word "meaningless." The use of this word has been, I believe, philosophically disastrous, almost wholly a waste of time. It is clearly not the case that all so-called meta-physical pronouncements are meaning-less, if by this we mean that they are utterly without any use or point. They are, of course, usually peculiar and paradoxical; they exhibit strange, and sometimes it may be mistaken, uses of language, but not the total absence of any use whatever. Philosophers often mislead and often speak strangely; they seldom, or at least less often, utter sheer rigmarole. When we are faced with some queer and paradoxical pronouncement, our task should be to discover how and why it came to be made—how and why deviation from plain modes of speech came about, and whether it came about for respectable reasons or from sheer confusion. Even if the reasons turn out to be respectable, genuinely revealing, we need not also speak strangely; we need not all be metaphysicians; but we may become aware of something—it may be only a pitfall—of which it is important for philosophy to take cognizance. The aim should be to become aware of the pit-falls, not to condemn or to ignore those who fall into them. It has been perhaps the most serious defect of the Verifica-tion Principle that it has seemed to

sanction an easy, impatient dismissal of too many philosophical doctrines, con-veying the impression that no good pur-pose can be served by asking why peo-ple say the strange things that they do. Indeed, if one took seriously the idea that the only questions that matter about any statement are the questions whether it is true, or false, or mean-ingless, one could hardly engage in phi-losophy at all. I do not say that all advocates of the Principle have in fact been guilty of this aridity of outlook; besides, for a short time aridity may be bracing and hygienic. But the Principle as it is stated tends inevitably to nar-row and to cramp the field of philos-ophy, and it offers almost irresistible temptations to dogmatism. "Principles," perhaps, are always liable to induce dogmatic slumber, broken only by acrimonious controversy; and it is, per-haps, in this respect above all that the Verificationists have been unfaithful disciples of Wittgenstein. There are here and there, as we have found, certain echoes of Wittgenstein's voice in the writings of Schlick: but the echoes are faint, and the words seem to have succumbed to the pathetic fate of the sayings of Empedocles.

Toward Further Inquiry

The discussions of meaning have been many and various. J. S. Mill's *A System of Logic* (London, 1906) and Gottlob Frege's "On Sense and Reference," in Peter Geach and Max Black (eds.), *Philosophical Writings of Gottlob Frege* (Oxford, 1952), are antecedents of many of the more contemporary discussions, as is C. K. Ogden and I. A. Richards' *The Meaning of Meaning* (New York, 1938). This last uses philosophical and psychological techniques that are now regarded as naive and outdated, but it remains a monumental effort to attack the question in all its phases. W. P. Alston, in *Philosophy of Language†*, Chapter

I, gives a helpful, clear-cut grouping of theories into referential, ideational, and behavioral types with critical evaluations of strengths and weaknesses. His work is an excellent supplement to Ryle's discussion in 2.2. J. S. Mill and G. Frege stand out as antecedent theorists to a referential theory, and much of Russell's work discussed at the end of Chapter I is an attempt to formulate such a theory adequately. The distinction of sense and reference (connotation and denotation) by Frege and Mill stands behind C. I. Lewis' treatment of modes of meaning (2.1) and behind that of Carnap in *Meaning and Necessity*, Chapter I. This chapter of Carnap also contains a critique of Lewis' treatment. The antecedents for the ideational theory as discussed by Alston go back to Berkeley and Locke and beyond, and they have been associated by some with the treatments of intentions and speech acts discussed in Chapter 3. The treatment of meanings as a kind of entity *sui generis* finds a basis in Plato, a development in Brentano, and a formulation in the work of Meinong, all of whom have been criticized for this type of approach. The stimulus-response treatment by Ogden and Richards has been variously developed and modified by Leonard Bloomfield, B. F. Skinner, Charles Morris, Willard Quine, Paul Ziff, and others. A helpful discussion of these developments is presented in Roger Brown's *Words and Things*†, Chapter III. A more detailed treatment, with an attempt at a new approach, is N. E. Christenson's *On the Nature of Meanings* (Copenhagen, 1961)†. Brief, general discussions of meaning are W. P. Alston's "The Quest for Meanings," in *Mind* 72 (1963); H. Gomperz' "Meanings of Meaning," PS 8 (1941); and W. H. Werkmeister's "Meaning of Meaning Re-examined," PR 47 (1938)†. J. A. Fodor, in "What Do You Mean?" JP 57 (1960), and J. J. Katz, in "Semantic Theory and the Meaning of Good," JP 61 (1964), offer examples of treatment from the transformational-grammar approach. John Wild, in "Being, Meaning and the World," *Review of Metaphysics*, 18 (1965), treats ontological issues from a phenomenological standpoint, and R. L. Cartwright, in "Ontology and the Theory of Meaning," PS 21 (1954)†, treats the same issues more generally. Discussions of meaning and definition are noted at the end of Chapter 4, and of meaning and use, at the end of Chapter 3.

Carnap developed his own thinking on the verifiability principle beyond that presented in *Philosophy and Logical Syntax* (London, 1935). His "Testability and Meaning," PS 3 and 4 (1936–1937), and "Methodological Character of Theoretical Concepts," *Minnesota Studies in the Philosophy of Science* II (Minneapolis, 1956) mark stages in that development. Ayer's critique of his own formulation appears in the preface to the second edition of *Language, Truth and Logic* (Oxford, 1946). Other important critiques are A. C. Ewing's "Meaninglessness," *Mind*, 46 (1937), and Friedrich Waismann's "Verifiability," PAS Suppl. 19 (1945). For summary discussions of positions and issues, see H. Reichenbach's "Verifiability Theory of Meaning," *American Academy of Arts and Sciences Proceedings*, 80 (1951)†, and W. W. Rozeboom's "Studies in the Empiricist Theory of Scientific Meaning," PS 27 (1960)†. Paul Marhenke, in "The

Criterion of Significance," *Proceedings of the American Philosophical Association*, 23 (1950), deals not only with the limits of this criterion, but with the conditions for any criterion of meaning. L. J. Cohen, in the *Diversity of Meaning* (New York, 1963), argues cogently for the thesis that no single theory of meaning can satisfy the aims of the wide variety of inquiries into language.

MEANING, INTENTION, AND SPEECH ACTS

Chapter 3

What we need, it seems to me, is a new doctrine,
both complete and general, of *what one
is doing in saying something.* . . .
John Austin

"What do *you* mean by. . . ?" The familiar question here takes on a different accent. We now focus on the role of the user in determining the meanings of his expressions. Because this kind of concern must treat the relation between a language and its users, it involves an understanding of the pragmatic aspect of meaning. It calls attention to the fact that the use of language is a human action. As human action, speech acts have purposes and conventions. They have proprieties and rules that make them acceptable in some contexts and unintelligible in others. As tools of speech acts, the words and sentences of language serve functions in speech, and these functions may vary with the intentions, conventions, and contexts under consideration. Further, if one regards meaning as a mental act comparable to believing and thinking, then the relation of the overt speech act to mental acts and intentional objects requires some account. All these factors come to bear upon the pragmatic aspect of meaning.

Many of our uses of the term 'mean' are closely related to notions of intention and purpose. In some contexts, 'What is the meaning of this?' and 'What is the purpose of this?' seem interchangeable. The same is true for 'What do you intend to do?' and 'What do you mean to do?' The meaning of the action in such cases is understood as the aim or purpose of the actor. Speech acts, as well as non-linguistic actions, can be understood in this way. A speaker may be called upon to clarify what he has said. 'I meant to say that . . .' and 'I intended to say that . . .' are equally adequate prefaces to such clarifications. Such ways of speaking indicate that the purpose of the speaker is in some way a factor in the meaning of the speech act. To what extent and in what way it is a factor is a matter for further exploration.

195

"The intension of a term represents our intention in the use of it."[1] This understanding of intension is not a standard one, even in Lewis' own treatment. Traditional treatments of intension are usually concerned with the characteristics of the object for which the term stands. Lewis maintained that the intension of a term can be arrived at by "any correct definition of it" (see 2.1). Neither the traditional understanding nor Lewis' own method for determination seem to justify his correlation of connotation with purpose. Ryle contends that the intension (connotation) of an expression is "what can be said with it" (see 2.2). This emphasis on possible function gives no more insight into the role of purpose in meaning than does a consideration of the object's attributes or a determination of the term's definitions. A first question about the pragmatic aspect of meaning is: What is the relation between the intention (purpose) of the user and the intension (connotation) of the expression?

Whatever the role of intention in the meaning of speech acts, it is limited by other factors in the communication process. If the speaker wishes to communicate with someone, he must take into account the conventions for speech acts that he shares with the community in which he speaks. If the speaker wishes to communicate about something, his terms must have some relation to the nature of the objects. The interpretation of intension as conventional (dependent upon the standards of society) accents one of the factors; the interpretation of intension as essential (dependent upon attributes of the object that are essential for its being what it is) accents the other. Even if neither provides an adequate characterization of intension, together they make clear that conventional and essential standards impose limits upon the claim that the intentions of the speaker determine the meaning of the expression. A second question about the pragmatic aspect of meaning is: What is the degree and character of such limitations on the role of intention in meaning? The conventional, essential, and intentional factors of the intension of a term may all be determinants for meaning. The extent and character of their determining roles may vary with expression and with context. The exact role of the intention of the user may be difficult to determine in any given case and may be impossible to formulate in general.

This opacity of the role of purpose in meaning has some similarity to logical problems with intentionality.[2] Brentano's thesis, that all acts of consciousness intend an object (see Ryle's discussion in 2.2), gives another basis for concern about the role of the users of language in determining its meaning. Consider the following two sets of sentences:

A. 1a. George sees that there are five pink rats in the corner of the room.
   2a. My neighbor believes that the universe is only 6000 years old.

---

[1] C. I. Lewis, *An Analysis of Knowledge and Valuation* (LaSalle, Ill., 1964), p. 43.

[2] G. E. M. Anscombe explores at some length the relation between the two uses of 'intention' in her "Intentionality of Sensation: A Grammatical Feature," in R. Butler (ed.), *Analytical Philosophy*, Second Series (Oxford, 1965).

3a. The expression 'Unicorns have pointed ears' means that unicorns have pointed ears.

4a. I mean by 'Flippity oggs glop' that unicorns have pointed ears.

B. **1b.** There are five pink rats in the corner of the room.

2b. The universe is only 6000 years old.

3b. Unicorns have pointed ears.

4b. 'Flippity oggs glop' means 'unicorns have pointed ears'.

Set A gives examples of intentional expressions. In terms of Brentano's psychology, each statement expresses a mental act about an intentional object. The logical structure of each statement involves an "intentional prefix" that takes a statement as its object. The logical character of such intentional expressions is unusual. That there are no pink rats in the corner of the room does not prevent George's seeing them there; his hallucination is real, even if the rats are not. All the archeological evidence to the contrary does not prevent my neighbor's belief in the brief history of the world. The absence of unicorns from the face of the earth does not prevent understandings of the meaning of sentences about them. Each sentence in Set A can express a true statement, but each sentence in Set B expresses a false one. There is no truth-value correlation between the two sets of sentences. In the case of the third sentence, the absence of a truth-value correlation suggests that the meaning of statements about unicorns is not dependent upon facts about unicorns, but upon mental acts of the users of the language. The fourth sentence in Set A compounds the intentional factor in the mental-act sense with the intentional factor in the purposive sense. It suggests that the two senses of intentional are not to be equated, even though both are factors in the pragmatic aspect of meaning.

One way of dealing with the evident opacities of intentional factors in meaning is to transform these factors into more workable understandings. If statements about human purposes and mental acts can be transformed into statements about human behavior and overt acts, then the pragmatic aspect of meaning can be formulated without recourse to apparently inaccessible information about the users of language. Such moves in pragmatics to reduce the intentional factors to a behavioristic formulation are often closely related to the attempts to reduce the intensional mode of meaning to the extensional mode. The *Thesis of extensionality* maintains (in part) that by analysis, all functions of propositions can be shown to be truth functional. If a proposition p is contained in a given sentence, then a proposition q having the same truth value as p may be substituted for p without changing the truth value of the sentence.[3] 'Samuel Clemens wrote *Tom Sawyer*' is equivalent in truth value to 'Mark Twain wrote *Tom Sawyer*'. On an extensional interpretation, the sentences have

---

[3] For fuller discussion of the thesis of extensionality, see Bertrand Russell, *An Inquiry into Meaning and Truth* (London, 1940), Chapters 12 and 19.

the same meaning. But in view of the character of intentional prefixes, it is clear that 'Steven believes that Mark Twain wrote *Tom Sawyer*' need not be equivalent in truth value to 'Steven believes that Samuel Clemens wrote *Tom Sawyer*'. Steven may believe the first without knowing that 'Mark Twain' was a pseudonym for 'Samuel Clemens'. It is also clear that on an extensional interpretation, the two names must have the same meaning but that they do not *for Steven*. The thesis of extensionality seems to require that one may substitute for a singular term in a sentence any "codesignative term" (any term referring to the same object) without altering the truth value of the sentence.[4] The intentional character of Steven's belief is a stumbling block to that thesis. In attempting to understand the pragmatic aspect of meaning, the inquirer may interpret that aspect in terms of behavior without adopting the thesis of extensionality (this seems to be the procedure of Carnap in 6.4). If, on the other hand, the inquirer adopts the thesis of extensionality, he must in some way obviate the intentional factors in meaning. Most such attempts follow a program similar to the one A. J. Ayer suggests (see 3.2).

Programs to reduce the intentional factors of meaning to a behavioristic explanation have met strong opposition. Some opponents object to the apparent presupposition that human activity and mental acts can be understood totally in terms of overt behavior. Others hold the more positive contention that a logic of intentional factors in language can be satisfactorily worked out without a behavioristic reduction. It is possible to construe a *thesis of intentionality* that maintains that a reduction of intentional factors to the extensional mode of meaning cannot be accomplished, and that an explication of the logical role of intentional factors of language can be achieved. The details of such a thesis have not been worked out, but Gustav Bergmann presents a program for one in his proposal to add an intentional operator to the formalized languages that are based upon the logic of *Principia Mathematica* (see 3.1).

In addition to these complexes of problems and programs regarding intention, the functions of language in the speech acts of its users have received much attention in recent years. Discussion of the functions of language is not itself a novel thing, but recognition of their complex and problematic character is. Much of the argument against metaphysics by such positivists as Schlick, Carnap, and Ayer can be construed as concern with the functions of language. Metaphysicians suppose that their verbal expressions have a descriptive function, but the positivists maintain that they serve only emotive uses. Moral statements are not descriptions of values and obligations, but expressions of emotions and directives for action. This trichotomy of descriptive, emotive, and directive func-

---

[4] Willard Quine treats the matter in terms of referential opacity and transparency. Compare *Word and Object* (New York, 1960), p. 151. Rudolf Carnap earlier treated the same problems in terms of translation from an intensional language to a rigorously constructed extensional language. Compare *The Logical Syntax of Language* (New York, 1959), pp. 245ff.

tions has a long tradition, and it is widely honored. Wittgenstein, however, maintained that there are "countless different kinds of uses" for linguistic expressions.[5] New uses come into being as language is put to new tasks and as new rules of usage evolve. Speaking is like playing games. Many different language games can be played with a single language, just as many different card games can be played with a single deck of cards. Nor need linguistic form always be correlated with linguistic function. The expression 'How are you?' can serve both as an inquiry into health and as a casual greeting. The diversity and flexibility of the functions of verbal expressions make the traditional trichotomy seem hopelessly simplistic. Wittgenstein also maintained that language games are learned in the playing, not by studying their rules. Language shows, rather than tells, its functions. This points inquiry away from an attempt to systematize functions and toward an examination of specific contexts and conventions of linguistic use. One may ask, on such an interpretation, whether a general understanding of functions is even possible.

John Austin approached the functions of speech acts somewhat differently. He began by examining the distinction between constatives (utterances that are either true or false) and performatives (utterances that have no truth value but that perform some function), which, he found, is not so clear-cut as is usually supposed (see 3.3). In *How to Do Things with Words* he develops a new schema for dealing with the functions of speech acts:

> *Locutionary acts* perform an act *of* saying something. In order to say something, one must utter certain noises belonging to a certain vocabulary, conforming to a certain grammar, and having a certain sense and reference.
> *Illocutionary acts* perform an act *in* saying something. In the act of saying something, a variety of acts can be performed: stating, asking, proclaiming, christening, and so on.
> *Perlocutionary acts* perform an act *through* saying something. Speech acts can effect functions as a result of the speaking: annoy, excite, persuade, soothe, and so on.[6]

These distinctions, together with Austin's analysis of how speech acts can go wrong, lay a basis for a new approach to the functions of language. This approach need deny neither the complexity of speech acts nor the possibility of systematizing them. Austin himself was convinced that conventions and contexts could be sufficiently explicated to determine at least the illocutionary force of speech acts.

These recent developments in the understanding of functions of speech acts leave a number of questions:

---

[5] Ludwig Wittgenstein, *Philosophical Investigations* (New York, 1953), p. 11.
[6] See John Austin, *How to Do Things with Words* (Oxford, 1965), Lecture VIII.

To what extent, if any, are the functions of language limited by linguistic forms? How is Austin's distinction between constative and performative related to the positivists' distinction between cognitive and noncognitive? between descriptive, emotive, and directive?

The character of illocutionary force seems quite similar to the role of the speaker's purpose. Can the illocutionary act be understood without reference to intentions? If not, can an understanding in terms of Austin's categories avoid the logical and behavioral opacities often noted in the discussions of intention?

How adequately, if at all, can one develop an understanding of meaning on the basis of understanding the functions of language? Austin never attempts such a move in *How to Do Things with Words*, and elsewhere he suggests strictures against it (compare 2.3). Wittgenstein explicitly denies the possibility.

In the third essay in this chapter, Austin expresses his doubts about the constative-performative distinction and calls for a new approach to speech acts. In examining the role of meaning in speech acts, H. P. Grice in 3.4 points toward a treatment of meaning as comparable to the role of purpose in other human actions. P. F. Strawson, evaluating the work of Austin and Grice, discusses the necessity of considering both convention and intention in speech acts. The three essays, taken together, lay a basis for considering a number of the questions raised here, as well as some related issues.

3.1   INTENTIONALITY

Gustav Bergmann

A book on botany mentions plants, but it need not mention botany. A zoological text mentions animals, but it need not contain the word zoology.

From *Semantica*, 1955, Archivo di Filosofia, Rome. Reprinted by permission of the editor and the author.

Intentionality is like botany or zoology, not like plants or animals and their kinds. That is why I shall hardly mention it in this essay. The things I shall mention are awareness, meaning, truth, and, my method being what it is, inevitably also language, particularly language about language. Concerning my philosophical method and my views on some philosophical problems, I am in a quandary. I do not wish to proceed as if they were known and I do not quite know how to proceed without assuming that they are. So I shall compromise. I shall not explain once more either the notion of an ideal language, which is not really a language to be spoken, or how, speaking commonsensically about it and what it is about, one philosophizes. For the rest, I shall tell a connected story. I realize, though, that in order to grasp it fully some readers may have to turn to what I said elsewhere.[1] One device I shall employ to provide as many connections and as much context as I possibly can are some "historical" passages about the recent as well as about the more remote past. These should be taken structurally, not as excursions into scholarly history; for I do not pretend to be a scholar living in history. Only, I wouldn't know how to philosophize without the history, or the image of history, that lives in me. For another, I shall not be able to avoid the use of symbols; but I shall keep it at a minimum; nor do I wish to pretend that I could do much better. For, again, I am not a mathematician any more than I am a historian. Fortunately, certain matters can be left safely to the mathematicians, just as some others can be left to the historians. Every now

---

[1] A collection of eighteen of my essays has been published under the title *The Metaphysics of Logical Positivism* (New York, London, Toronto: Longmans, Green and Co., 1954). I shall quote these essays as MLP, followed by the number under which they appear in the volume.

and then, though, the philosopher who, since he is a philosopher, finds himself short of time and taste to emulate the achievements of these specialists, does need their services. Things would probably go more smoothly if those specialists were not all too often like miners who cannot tell the raw diamonds from the philosophical pebbles in the materials they bring to light. Some of the confusions I shall try to unravel can indeed be traced to the mathematical logicians. But, then, it may be fairer to lay them at the doorsteps of those philosophers who, admiring the mathematicians too much, knew too little of what they actually did.

Here is an outline of what I propose to do. *First,* I shall try to convince my readers that when we say, speaking as we ordinarily do, that *there are* awarenesses, what we say is true. If, then, there are awarenesses, one may ask whether they also *exist,* in the philosophical sense of 'exist'. (In its ordinary or commonsensical use 'exist' is expendable, since it can always be replaced by 'there are (is)'.) Awarenesses do exist. By this I mean three things. I mean, first, that instances of awareness are particulars in exactly the same sense in which a tone is a particular. I mean, second, that there are certain characters, among them at least one that is simple, which are in fact exemplified by those and only those particulars I call awarenesses, in exactly the same sense in which the simple characters called pitches are in fact exemplified by those and only those particulars that are called tones. An awareness may, for instance, be *a* remembering, i.e., an instance of remembering, just as a tone may be *a* middle *c*, i.e., an instance of middle *c*. The third thing which I mean I shall mention presently. Like everybody else, philosophers are sometimes aware of their awarenesses. Many philosophers nevertheless deny that they exist. One very important one, Ludwig Wittgenstein, spent the second half of his life trying painfully to convince himself, not only that they do not exist, but even that there are none. Such persistent refusals to admit the obvious are so strange that one must try to explain them. That will be my *second* step. Philosophers did not see how they could consistently hold that there are awarenesses without also holding that there are interacting minds, i.e., mental particulars causally interacting with physical objects in exactly the same sense in which the latter interact among each other. Thus, when the belief in interacting minds became less and less tenable, some philosophers denied, with the intellectual violence that is so characteristic of all of us, that there are awarenesses. This is the story of the classical act and its later vicissitudes. In its final stages one kind of concern with language came to the fore. Another kind lies at the root of all analytical philosophy. I shall turn in my *third* step to some aspects of this second concern with language. Each of the two different concerns produced some confusions; there were also some illegitimate fusions between the two. The fusions and confusions support each other. To clear up the latter and to undo the former is one half of the analysis which vindicates

awareness. *Fourth*, I shall propose what I believe is the correct form of those sentences in the ideal language that mention awarenesses. This is the other half of the analysis which, in the nature of things, involves the analysis of meaning and truth. It is also the heart of the essay. All the latter amounts to, in a sense, is therefore a proposal for transcribing such sentences as 'I see that this is green' in the ideal language. The transcription will show that awarenesses and, in fact, only awarenesses exemplify certain peculiar characters, which I call *propositions*. (This is the third thing I mean when I say that awarenesses exist.) Because of these characters statements about awarenesses are, loosely and ambiguously speaking, statements about statements. To tighten the looseness and to eliminate the ambiguity is virtually the same thing as to clear up the confusions and to undo the fusions of which I just spoke. This is the reason for my expository strategy.[2]

I

I stand in front of a tree, look at it, and see it. As we ordinarily speak, we say that the situation has three constituents, myself, the tree, and the seeing. Ordinarily we let it go at that.

[2] The fundamental ideas of this essay are first stated, very badly, in two papers that appeared over a decade ago: "Pure Semantics, Sentences, and Propositions," *Mind*, 53, 1944, 238–57; "A Positivistic Metaphysics of Consciousness," *Mind*, 54, 1945, 193–226.

Upon a little reflection, still safely within common sense, we notice that 'myself', 'tree', and 'seeing' may be taken in either of two contexts. In one of these, the first two words, 'myself' and 'tree', refer to two physical objects, namely, my body and the tree, while the third, 'seeing', refers, not to a third physical object, but to a relation between such, namely, the relation exemplified whenever one says truly that someone sees something. About this very complex relation physicists, physiologists, and behavioristic psychologists know a good deal. In the other context, 'seeing' refers to something mental, as we ordinarily use 'mental', and this mental something is again distinct from myself, the seer, as well as from what is seen, the tree. This seeing is an awareness. An awareness is thus something mental, distinct from what, if anything, is aware as well as from what it is aware of. That much is evident and to that much I commit myself therefore without hesitation. To three other beliefs one is, I think, not committed by common sense. I, for one, hold all three to be false. One of them is crucial. Whether the other two are, in fact, false makes no difference for what I intend to say. Even so, I shall briefly mention all three; for it is well to grasp clearly what does and what does not depend on what.

I do not believe that an instance of seeing, or of any other awareness, is merely the exemplification of a relation, or of any other character, between two "things," as indeed the physical seeing is. I believe, instead, that an awareness is itself a "thing." I

say thing rather than particular because it makes no difference for what I want to say right now whether or not the other two terms do or do not refer to particulars. (Presently we shall see that the content of an awareness could not possibly be a particular.) This is crucial. The second belief which I hold to be false is that there is a mental thing referred to by 'myself'. To make it quite clear that nothing I shall say depends on whether or not this belief is in fact false, I shall eventually transcribe, not 'I see that this is green' but, instead, '(It is) seen (by me) that this is green' without paying any attention to the problems connected with the two words in the second parenthesis. Third. Some philosophers believe that the object or, as one also says, the content of an awareness is, in some cases, a physical object. According to these philosophers, my illustration is such a case; the content in question is of course the tree, or, perhaps more accurately, something that is in some sense a part of its surface. To these philosophers I grant that when we use 'see' as we ordinarily do in such situations, we certainly mean to mention a physical object. Some other philosophers insist that the content of an awareness is always a mental object; in my illustration, a tree percept. To these philosophers I grant that there is a perfectly plain sense of 'directly apprehending' or of 'being directly acquainted with' such that what we directly apprehend, even in a so-called perceptual situation, is a mental object. But, again, nothing I shall say depends on which side one takes on this issue, even though at one place I shall *seem* to side with the second view. (To dispel the appearance of this seeming is one of the things I cannot take time to do in this essay.)

Sometimes I shall find it convenient to speak of an awareness as a mental state of the person who, as one ordinarily says, has it or owns it. In fact, I do not know what one could possibly mean when, speaking literally, one says that someone has or is in a certain mental state if not that he has an awareness of a certain kind. But I shall ordinarily not call an awareness a mental content. The reasons for this caution as well as for the qualification, ordinarily, are, I think, fairly obvious. Since I shall use 'content' to refer to what an awareness is the awareness of, and since I have committed myself to the distinction between the two, it is prudent to avoid expressions that may tend to blur it. The reason for the qualification is that one awareness is sometimes the content of another. (How would we otherwise know that there are any?) When I am aware of something, then I am aware of this thing, not of the awareness through which I am aware of it. But I may also, either at the same time or at some other time, be aware of that awareness. In this event the first awareness is the content of the second. Notice, though, that the second awareness is not, either directly or indirectly, an awareness of the content of the first, just as it is not, if I may so express myself, aware of itself.

Perceiving is one kind of awareness; directly apprehending, remembering, doubting whether, thinking of, wondering are others. The analysis of some of these kinds is very complex. For what I intend to do I can, happily, limit myself to direct apprehension. When I speak in the rest of this essay without further qualification of awareness I should therefore be taken to speak of direct apprehension. Similarly, when I speak of *an* awareness, I should be understood to speak of an instance of directly apprehending. Again, the difference really makes no difference. But I wish to make as clear as I can which problems I shall not discuss without, however, either belittling them or denying that they are problems.

Ordinarily we say 'I see this tree' but we also say 'I am aware of this being a tree', 'I know that this is a tree', 'I wonder whether this is a tree', and so on. If we choose, we can rephrase the first of these sentences: 'I see that this is a tree'. A statement mentioning an awareness can always be so rephrased that its content is referred to by a sentence. Grammatically this sentence appears in our language either as a dependent clause or as a participial phrase (e.g., 'this being a tree'). This is what I mean by the formula: *The content of every awareness is propositional*. If, for instance, I see (or directly apprehend, or remember; the difference makes no difference) a red spot, the content of my awareness is a state of affairs or fact, namely, a certain particular being red.

If one asks the proper question of one who has an awareness while he has it, one elicits a certain answer. If, for instance, somebody points at the tree while I am looking at it and asks me what it is, I shall say "This is a tree." This statement is the *text* of my awareness. This and only this sort of thing is what I mean by the text of an awareness. In many cases it is not easy to hit upon the right question or to be sure that the answer one receives is what one was asking for. In some cases the difficulties are very great. But, no matter how formidable they may be, they lie always within the limits of common sense and its long arm, science; in no case are they philosophical difficulties. The notion of a text is therefore itself entirely commonsensical. Three things about texts are worth noticing, though. Notice first that the text of an awareness states its content and only its content, without mentioning the awareness itself. This jibes well with what I said in the second to the last paragraph. Notice next that this is the first time I mention language in a certain way. More precisely, this is the first time I mention linguistic behavior as such. Notice, third, that the connection I thus establish between an awareness and its text is purely *external*. This means, first, that I am not dealing with the awarenesses one may have of the words he utters or hears uttered; and it means, second, that I am at this point not concerned with the question whether or not and in what sense one's inner speech is a "part" of his awarenesses. (These comments lay the ground for the unraveling of some of the fusions and confusions I mentioned in the outline.)

Let us return to my awareness of the red spot. The situation involves two particulars, the spot and the particular awareness. It also involves *at least* two states of affairs or facts, referred to by statements, namely, first, the spot being an instance of red and, second, the awareness being an instance of perceiving or, perhaps, of directly apprehending. The first of the two states of affairs is the content of this particular awareness. I said at least because the analysis is patently still incomplete. What it omits to mention is, in fact, the very crux of the matter, namely, that the one particular, the awareness, is an awareness *of* the state of affairs of which the other particular, the spot, is an ingredient. This third constituent fact of the situation is, I submit, not (1) that two particulars exemplify a relation, nor (2) that the one particular, the awareness, and the state of affairs of which the other is an ingredient exemplify a pseudorelation, but, (3) that the awareness exemplifies another nonrelational character, of the sort I call a proposition, which I shall specify in good time when I shall state my proposal. Alternatives (1) and (2) bring us to the classical act and thus to the development I wish to consider in my second step. In this development the difference between (1) and (2) was not always clearly seen. Nor shall I bother to distinguish between them in my quasi-historical account of it. However, we shall need the distinction later on, in the fourth step; so I shall state it now. A (binary) relation obtains between what is referred to by two terms. A (binary) pseudorelation obtains either between what is referred to by a term and what is referred to by a sentence or between what is referred to by two sentences. Symbolically, in the usual notation: 'xRy', 'xPp', 'pPq'. Connectives are, of course, not pseudorelations but truth tables. Logical atomism is the thesis that the ideal language contains no pseudorelations.

II

Draw on a sheet of paper two circles outside of each other; mark the two points, one on each circle, that are closest to each other; draw an arrow from one of them to the other. Replace, if you wish, the tip of the arrow by a sling or loop surrounding the circle at which the tip points. What you have drawn is, in either case, a graphic schema of the classical act, or, more precisely, of as much of it as belongs to my story. The seeing, which is the act, is the arrow or loop. Its being a loop or arrow, not a circle like the other two constituents, shows that an act is not a third thing but an exemplified relation (or pseudorelation). The circle from which the arrow issues represents me; the second circle, the tree. So far, so good; but there remains a question. We saw that, by our common sense, the situation involves two contexts. Which of the two does the diagram represent? Or does it represent them both indifferently? As long as one answers at all, the most nearly correct answer is that it represents them both, but inseparably, not indifferently. The best reply is that within the Aristotelian tradition, from which the act pattern stems and from which it has never really been freed, the question cannot even be asked. This is one reason why trouble brewed when it was asked. Clearly, the diagram does not do justice to some other peculiarities of the

form-matter accounts of perception. The reason for this neglect is that my concern is really only with the post-Cartesian mind-matter distinction, which is of course quite different from the Aristotelian form-matter distinction. But it is worth noticing that according to the form-matter accounts of perception the perceiver is "active" in extracting from the perceived object its form even though perception is in a sense the least "active" of all acts. Only in "pure sensation," whatever that means, is he completely "passive."

To an act philosopher the analysis of 'meaning' offers no problems. An act was said to intend its content. The linguistic connection between 'meaning' and 'intending' is familiar. Instead of saying that an act intends its content I could have said that its content is its meaning. A thought's meaning, for instance, was said to "exist intentionally" in it, as its content. The act pattern is thus the archtype of the contemporary accounts of meaning according to which the meaning of a sentence is its referent. (Nor is this surprising in view of the often quite naïve realism of the proponents of these so-called reference theories of meaning.) As for the meaning of sentences, not of acts, within the classical pattern itself, one must remember that, broadly speaking, language enters into this pattern only externally, in exactly the same sense of 'external' in which I called external the connection between an awareness and the text I coördinated to it. A sentence is therefore for the classical act philosopher merely a physical object or event, or perhaps, a kind of such. It has meaning only derivatively or, as I believe it was sometimes put, it signifies only by eliciting an act which in-tends what, as we now say, it refers to.

Upon the classical view, awarenesses are acts. Thus, when the classical act ran into difficulties, the place of aware-ness in the scheme of things seemed to be threatened, too. To understand what happened, we must briefly inquire into those difficulties.

Brentano and G. E. Moore, the last two of the great protagonists of the act, are both direct realists. This did not happen by chance. The classical act is a relation exemplified by things in space and time. In this respect my see-ing the tree is not at all different from its being to the left of, say, a rock. This is one of the two features that deter-mined the course of events. The other pertains to a difference between seeing and, say, being to the left of. The thing from which the act issues is in issuing it spontaneous or "active." Neither of the constituents of an instance of, say, a spatial relation "acts" in this cate-gorial sense upon the other merely by exemplifying the relation. Because they are patently incompatible with the ideas that reached their first culmina-tion in Newton, these two features were, more than any others, responsi-ble for the decline and eventual down-fall of the act. In Newton's world the realm of physical objects, which in-cludes our bodies, is causally closed; its physical constituents can therefore not in the old categorial sense be "acted upon" by anything else; otherwise the physical realm would not be causally closed. The difficulties one creates by introducing into this world mental con-stituents that "interact" with the physi-cal ones are insuperable. This is not to say, though, that any or all of the

constituents, physical or otherwise, of a Newtonian world are "passive." The point is, rather, that in their old cate-gorial sense neither 'active' nor 'pas-sive' can be sensibly applied to them. To insist in such circumstances on ap-plying that half of a dichotomy that *seems* to fit better is to court philo-sophical trouble. The troubles that en-sued in this case are notorious.

At this point I had better say what I should not need to say. I believe as a matter of course that the world is New-tonian. That is to me just common sense. Or, if you insist, it is scientific common sense; I shall not quibble; for to tilt even against scientific common sense is quixotic. This, however, is only half of what needs to be said. The other half is that common sense, in-cluding science, never answers the phil-osophical questions. It merely sets them to us. Awareness is a case in point. The classical act secured its place in the world. As the act became inde-fensible, that place was threatened. This proves that something was wrong; it does not prove that in order to de-fend awareness one must defend the classical act. To do that would be merely quixotic. The task is, rather, to disentangle awareness from the act so that its place may again be secure in a world that is, scientifically, New-tonian. I believe that my analysis does just that. This, however, I shall not show in this essay, since to show it I would have to analyze in its entirety the tangle which is known as the mind-body problem[3] and not only, as I pro-posed, a single strand of it.

I continue the schematic account,

---

[3] See also MLP6.

representing the next step by a modification of the diagram. Let the two circles stand for two spheres and make the sphere from which the loop or arrow issues hollow. Erase the tip or loop and let the remaining line represent all sorts of relations (and processes) among the material constituents of either sphere. The absence of the loop or arrow indicates that these are all Newtonian relations (and processes); their constituents are thus neither "active" nor "passive." Assume next that, as part and parcel of these Newtonian processes, all sorts of configurations appear, as on a screen, on the wall of the cavity of the hollow sphere. Finally, put in the center of the cavity a small sphere from which arrows issue toward the configurations on its wall. The structure represents a Lockean kind of world; an "inner" arrow, a Lockean kind of act; the inner sphere, a post-Cartesian Self or, as Hartley put it, "an eye within the eye." For what we are interested in, the decisive difference between the old and the new schema is that in the latter the arrows have been withdrawn into the cavity. Does this alteration suffice to make the schema fit Newton's world? The answer is clearly No. A schema that fits must not contain any arrows. Thus the "inner" arrows would have to be "withdrawn" once more. This shows what Hartley's admirable metaphor illuminates in a flash, namely, that the new schema merely starts its proponents on an infinite regress. The configurations on the wall cause no trouble, at least not for what we are interested in. (I am here not concerned with the perplexities of indirect realism.)

The sphere inside the sphere may or may not have to go. (That is why I didn't even bother to mention that Locke does not have this sort of Self.) The one thing needful is to get rid of the arrows. To understand how that was done one must understand what the classical British philosopher-psychologists meant by "the analysis of the phenomena of the human mind." So I must next explain the idea of this sort of analysis or, as we would now say, of analytical introspection.[4] The way in which its original proponents explained it is full of difficulties. As I shall explain it, the idea is quite commonsensical. Since it is commonsensical, it can in principle be considered as the outline of a scientific research program. I say in principle because in practice it led to the impasse that was Wundtian psychology. This, however, is entirely beside the point; for the causes of that impasse were not philosophical.

Assume that someone, call him a psychologist, who has become very skillful in eliciting from people, call them his subjects, the texts of their awarenesses, engages in the following project. First he selects a limited vocabulary. Then he gives his subjects the following tripartite instructions: "(a) Familiarize yourself with this limited vocabulary. (b) I shall continue to ask you questions as before; continue to answer them as before, speaking as you ordinarily do, without any limitation on your vocabulary. (c) Having given me your answer, answer my question once more; in your second response use only

---

[4] See also MLP17.

the limited vocabulary." Assume that the game, or experiment, is carried on for a while and that in each case our psychologist writes down the subject's responses, the first on the white front of a card, the second on its pink back. His purpose is to discover empirically from his cards a set of rules (empirical laws) R that will enable him in each future case to infer what is written on the white front of a card from what is written on its pink back. This is the idea of analytic introspection. The way I explained it avoids many of the classical difficulties by bringing out two points. The first response is the text of the "original" awareness; the second certainly is not; it may be, and in fact is, that of another; but that need not concern us. This is the first point. All that could be meant by saying that the original awareness, whose text is the first response, "consists of" or has been "introspectively decomposed (analyzed)" into those of which the second response is or would be the text, is that the first text can by a set of empirical laws be inferred from the second. This is the other point. For about 150 years, roughly from 1750 to 1900, one of the major issues, if not perhaps the major issue, of psychology was whether a set of such rules R can be found; and if at all, for how limited a vocabulary (of the second response).

It is easy to see how this program, *if* it succeeds and *if* one is not too clear about what one means by 'consisting of', can be used to get rid of the act or, if you please, of the arrows and, incidentally, the inner sphere. Since awarenesses are sometimes the contents of others, the texts (first re-

sponses!) of some of the awarenesses of our psychologist's subjects will contain act verbs, such as 'thinking about', 'wondering whether', and so on. If, now, his experiment succeeds with a vocabulary so limited that it contains none of these expressions, that is, if he can for such a vocabulary (of the second response) find a set of laws R, then our psychologist will probably say that "there are no acts." This, at any rate, is what two generations ago the "content" psychologists, led by Wundt, said to the "act" psychologists, who gathered around Brentano. Their claim is thus that "introspective analysis" of any awareness yields only "contents," i.e., what the other side calls the contents of those acts whose contents are not themselves awarenesses. (This shows how 'content' is used in that literature. Whenever I shall use it in this sense I shall surround it by double quotes.)

By 1900 it was beyond doubt that Wundt's program—or should I say Hume's?—would never succeed. Its failure led, during the first decade of this century, to the rebellion, led by Kuelpe, of the so-called school of Wuerzburg. The ideas which the men of Wuerzburg propounded are still important. Also, they are, in substance, patently right. So I shall next explain these ideas in a way that will help my story along in other ways, too.

Assume that I and another person who does not know English both hear the sound of what I know but he doesn't know to be the English word "bell." Will our awarenesses have the same text? Wuerzburg's answer is No; and it is, at least for some such occasions, beyond all reasonable doubt. The way they put it, in the style of all introspectionists, the difference shows in the analyses (second responses) of the two awarenesses. The analysis of the other fellow's awareness will consist of that of his auditory percept of what he didn't know to be a word *and of nothing else.* The analysis of mine will have corresponding constituents but, *in addition*, a further one. Some of the Wuerzburgers called this additional constituent, which according to them is introspectively unanalyzable, "the meaning of 'bell' " or, also, "the awareness of the meaning of 'bell'." Take another case. Assume that both I and another person hear a sentence which we both understand but which I, unlike him, do not know to be true so that, hearing it, I wonder whether what it refers to is the case. Again, Wuerzburg claims, self-evidently I think, that there will be a difference between our two awarenesses. The analysis of mine will reveal a constituent which will not appear in that of the other person, namely, a "wondering about . . . ," which, according to Wuerzburg, is again introspectively unanalyzable. Rather remarkably the Wuerzburgers insisted that these unorthodox unanalyzable constituents are not "acts," but "contents." In terms of our diagram this means that the "inner" arrow appears now among the configurations on the wall. Whether the Wuerzburgers spoke as they did merely in order to limit the extent of their anti-Wundtian heresy is an historical question. Whatever the answer may be, the fact that they could consistently so express themselves shows that awarenesses can

in principle be fitted into a Newtonian world. That, though, is a line of thought which I am not pursuing in this essay; I turn instead to two others.

For one, we have again encountered 'meaning'. The one thing to be grasped firmly and above all is that what we encountered is only in a peculiar sense a philosophical analysis of what we mean when we speak of the meaning of a sentence or, as in my illustration, of a word. What we are offered is, rather, a psychological analysis of how meaning, whatever it may turn out to be, is carried, or grasped, or represented in our minds. I prefer Titchener's phrase, carried, but I would not argue about the word. The point is that this piece of psychology becomes a philosophical analysis of meaning only if it is joined to the assertion that the psychological phenomenon in question is all that could be meant whenever we speak, in any context, of meaning. Since this assertion is patently false, any philosophical analysis of meaning of which it forms a part is certainly peculiar.

Notice, for another, that linguistic behavior enters the Wuerzburg account of awareness in a new way. I call it new because it appears here for the first time in our story, though, to be sure, not for the first time in history; but that is beside the point. In the introspectionists' peculiar sense of 'consisting of', the awareness itself consists, according to Wuerzburg, at least in part of verbal "contents," e.g., of the auditory percepts which both I and one who does not know English have upon hearing an English word. To distinguish this kind of connection between linguistic behavior and awareness from others, which I have mentioned before, I call it *internal*. A verbal "content" may be either an auditory percept or image (of speech), or a visual percept or image (of writing), or some kinaesthetic equivalent. Which it is in any given case may be of interest to psychologists; it is of no moment to us. I merely notice that the notion includes so-called inner speech. The thing important for what I am interested in is that the new twist makes the case against awareness appear sound. The appearance is deceptive. To understand why it is deceptive we must understand why it deceived some. What happened was, I believe, that a certain statement, which is true, was mistaken for another one, which is false. The truth is that many of our more abstract awarenesses —I use deliberately a vague word, abstract, for a vague idea—are indeed awarenesses of words. The decisive point is that on such occasions we find ourselves not just having verbal "contents" but knowing them, wondering about them, entertaining them, and so on, as the case may be. To assert the true statement is therefore not to assert that awarenesses do not exist. To assert the latter, in the language of Wuerzburg, is to assert that those unorthodox constituents, which according to Wuerzburg are unanalyzable, do in fact yield to introspection with the result that they, too, turn out to consist of verbal "contents." This is the false statement I mentioned a moment ago. As to its falsehood, I can only say that I, for one, do sometimes have awarenesses which upon introspection (if it be necessary) yield the critical unana-

lyzable constituents. In the texts of these awarenesses 'knowing', 'wondering about', 'entertaining', and so on, do of course occur. This, however, is a different matter; for the connection between an awareness and its text is external.

Titchener, the one first-rate mind among the Wundtians, gave Wuerzburg a consistent reply. Somewhat quixotically he insisted that whenever those critical "contents," awarenesses and meanings, occur, they can be introspectively decomposed into more orthodox ones. But he added that in many cases they do not occur at all. Take meaning, on which he was more explicit, and consider again a person who both hears and understands (the meaning of) the word bell. Titchener then says three things. 1. More often than not such a person has on such occasions no other "contents" than, say, auditory ones. 2. These events, namely, the occurrences of the auditory "content," are among the causes of other events, among which are, as a rule, (the occurrences of) other *orthodox* "contents" of the person in question. 3. This latter fact, 2, is what a psychologist means, or ought to mean, by 'meaning'. Titchener's formula was: The meaning of a content is not another content but its *context*. Since I believe that there are (to speak with Wuerzburg) unanalyzable awarenesses (though not meanings!), I object to the qualification, orthodox, which I italicized. Otherwise Titchener's is the correct analysis of *one* of the commonsensical (and scientific) meanings of 'meaning'. Very admirably, he distinguished it from a philosophical or, as he said, logical analysis. Again I agree, although I wouldn't put it this way. I would rather say that a philosophical analysis of 'meaning' must not only explicate *all* its important uses but that it must be particularly careful not to omit the philosophical ones, i.e., those that point, however confusedly, at genuine philosophical problems.

Tichener's meaning of 'meaning' contains implicitly another. Take again our illustration. In trying to specify the very complex causal pattern or, if you please, context of the case, one will certainly have to mention circumstances, of the kind called psychological, that pertain to people. But it will also be necessary to mention what the word refers to, namely, bells. If one disregards the psychological circumstances, one arrives at a *second* commonsensical (and scientific) meaning of 'meaning'. In this sense, the meaning of a (kind of) linguistic event, say, of a sentence, is what it refers to. When an anthropologist tells us that, as he discovered, in a certain aboriginal language a certain kind of noise means tree, he uses 'means' in this sense. Notice, though, that by acknowledging this meaning of 'meaning' we do not embrace a philosophical reference theory of meaning; for we know, first, that this is just one of the uses of 'meaning' and, second, that it is not even a philosophical use. I submit, finally, that all scientific uses of 'meaning' involve either reference in the sense of my anthropologist or context in Titchener's sense, and nothing else.

In substance, Titchener's view became dominant. It still is dominant. Those who made it so, in a different form, were the behaviorists. Metaphysical behaviorists, who deny that there are mental things, talk nonsense so manifest that nobody needs to pay any attention to them. Scientific behaviorists, who make eminent sense, merely insist for their own particular reasons on speaking about mental things in their own particular way, namely, as states of the organism which are defined, or, more realistically, in principle definable in terms of actual and potential behavior. Since their particular reasons do not belong to our story, I shall state the behaviorists' idea in the introspectionists' language. Thus stated, the idea is that a state of an organism is an awareness if and only if it contains either actual verbal "contents" or momentary dispositions to have such "contents." Scientifically, the idea is sound. Commonsensically and not at all scientifically and even less philosophically, the notion of a text acknowledges what is sound in it. This, however, is beside the point. My concern here is exclusively with the impact of the behaviorists' views on the philosophy of awareness. This impact is, I think, by now quite clear. Imagine a philosopher who, whether or not he knows it, is overly impressed by the behaviorists; who is not benighted enough to be a metaphysical behaviorist; and who therefore speaks without qualms the language of the introspectionists. Such a philosopher might hold, *first,* that there are no "contents" of the kind I called unorthodox; that, *second,* all there is to meaning is context; and, *third,* that so-called awarenesses are merely verbal "contents" in their contexts. Assume, furthermore, that my imaginary philosopher also suffers from the futilitarian or nihilistic delusion according to which all philosophical uses are not only, as I agree, always confused but also that there are no genuine philosophical problems which these confused uses indicate as smoke indicates fire. Then he will also hold that, *fourth,* the first three sentences contain in principle everything anybody could possibly say about meaning and awareness.

The philosopher about whom I spoke is not at all imaginary but the other Wittgenstein, that is, the author of *Philosophical Investigations.* Negatively, this unfortunate book is nothing but a belated attempt to refute Wuerzburg. Positively it is, in dialectical disguise, a behavioristic-Titchenerian account of awareness and meaning. The words are of course not always those of the scientists. *Context,* for instance, becomes *use,* or perhaps, *rule* of use, or perhaps, *habit* conforming to a rule of use. Since I, for one, am willing to leave psychology to the psychologists, I naturally do not think that such distinctions are philosophically important. The author of the *Tractatus* is nevertheless one of the most important philosophers. That is why *Philosophical Investigations* marks a new low in the philosophical career of awareness. I am confident that this low is also the turning point.

There is still another reason why I introduce Wittgenstein at this crucial point of my exposition. Some futilitarians sometimes do propound philosophical doctrines—in the circuitous way that is forced upon them by their futilitarianism. The *Philosophical Investigations* propound the strange and erroneous doctrine that (A) awarenesses do not exist. I suggest that A is the one visible end of a hidden thread that connects the *Investigations* with one of the flaws of the *Tractatus.*[5] Its other visible end is the doctrine of the *Tractatus,* equally strange and erroneous, that (B) language cannot or must not speak about itself. In the next section I shall analyze some of the confusions that led some to accept B. In the fourth section I shall show that in some vague and confused sense statements mentioning awarenesses belong to language about language. That is the thread or, if you please, the hidden continuity between A and B. Since I am certain that this pattern illuminates some structural connections, I have patterned my exposition after it. Whether it contains also a biographical truth about Wittgenstein is a moot question. Perhaps it doesn't.

III

Linguistic events, whether they are mental or noises, are events among events. Linguistic things, such as marks on paper, are things among things. Talking about either, one talks about language as part of the world. This is the way scientists talk about it. Philosophers look at language as a pattern, that is, as a picture of the world rather than as a part of it. Event vs. pattern, part vs. picture; the formula is suggestive. That is why I begin with it. Yet, like all formulae, it needs unpack-

---

[5] For an analysis of some other flaws see MLP3.

ing. The following three propositions and five comments state what is sound in it. Propositions and comments are both very succinct. If I went into detail, I would do what I said I would not do, namely, explain once more the method of philosophizing by means of an ideal language.

There is of course nothing that is not part of the world. Clearly, then, the negative half of the metaphor must not be taken literally. The following propositions unpack it. (1) The construction of the ideal language L proceeds syntactically, i.e., as a study in geometrical design, without any reference to its interpretation. A schema so constructed is as such not a language; it becomes one, at least in principle, only by interpretation. (2) The philosopher interprets L by coördinating to awarenesses not their actual texts but ideal texts, i.e., sentences of L. (3) Having so interpreted L, he can, by speaking about both it and what it refers to or speaks about, first reconstruct and then answer the philosophical questions. This is the meaning of the positive half of the picture metaphor, according to which the ideal language is a picture, or, in the classical phrase, a logical picture of the world. These are the three propositions. Now for the five comments. (a) Notice that in (2) 'sentence' is used proleptically. Only by interpretation of L do certain of its designs become "sentences." (b) The connection between an awareness and its ideal text is as external as that between it and its actual text. (c) In coördinating his ideal texts to awarenesses the linguistic philosopher acknowledges in his own way the Cartesian

turn. (d) The text of an awareness refers to its content. Some texts, whether actual or ideal, refer therefore to awarenesses. But a text does not refer to an awareness merely because it is coördinated to one. (e) Familiarity with the traditional dialectic shows that the undefined descriptive constants of L must refer to what we are directly acquainted with, in the sense in which the classical phenomenalists maintained that we are not directly acquainted with physical objects.[6]

The picture metaphor also misled some, among them the Wittgenstein of the *Tractatus*. One of the several errors[7] it caused is the belief that the ideal language cannot "speak about itself." Let me first show how this confused idea came to seem plausible. Change the metaphor slightly, introducing a mirror instead of a picture. Take an object and let it stand for the world. The mirror may mirror the object; it does not and cannot mirror its own mirroring it. One may, of course, place a second mirror so that it mirrors the object, the first mirror, and the latter's mirroring of the former. But now one who understood what was said before might remark that when this is done then the first mirror and its mirroring have themselves become part of the world (of the second mirror). The remark is not yet the analysis, but it points at the crucial spot. The source of the con-

---

[6] This is the issue mentioned earlier on which I *seem* to side with the classical phenomenalists. The appearance is dispelled in MLP.

[7] For an analysis of some others see MLP3.

fusion is an unnoticed ambiguity of 'about'. This ambiguity is not likely to be noticed unless one distinguishes clearly between the two ways of looking at language, once as part of the world, once as its picture.

Commonsensically we say that a sentence (or a word) *refers* to, or is *about*, a state of affairs (or a thing). This makes sense if and only if what is said to refer to something, or to be or speak about something, is a linguistic event or a kind of such. Notice, first, that in the two comments (d) and (e) above I myself used 'refer' and 'about' in this sense. In fact, I never use them otherwise; for I do not understand any other use of them. Notice, furthermore, how well all this fits with what was said earlier. What a linguistic event or a kind of such refers to is also its meaning, in one of the two common-sensical and scientific meanings of 'meaning'. And when scientists speak about language they speak of course always about linguistic events. What one asserts, then, when one asserts, with this meaning of 'about', that language cannot "speak about itself" is that there cannot be kinds of noises which, as we use them, refer to other kinds of noises. The assertion is so implausible that I hardly know how to argue against it. The best one can do if one wishes to dispose of it as thoroughly as possible is what I am doing in this section, namely, analyze the major sources of the illusion. But let me first dispose of what is even more obvious. If we use a language in which reference is not univocal, we will eventually get into trouble. This is just common sense. Thus, if we use a certain

kind of noise to refer to a certain kind of animals, say, dogs, we had better not also use it to refer to something else and, in particular, not to itself, i.e., to this particular kind of noise. Any adequate language will therefore distinguish between the two kinds of design on the next line:

dog   'dog'

This is the origin of the quoting device. In any language that is not on grounds of sheer common sense foredoomed, the linguistic events about linguistic events, or, if you please, the part of the language that is "about itself" are therefore those and only those that contain single quotes or their equivalents, e.g., the phrase 'the word dog'.

What, if anything, could be meant by saying that the ideal language speaks about itself? Every awareness has an ideal text. Let 'b' be the name of (refer to) an awareness and let '$gr(a)$' ('This is green') be its text. From what was said earlier we know that the name of an awareness, in this case 'b', could not possibly occur in its text, in this case '$gr(a)$'; for the text of an awareness refers to its content, which is always distinct from the awareness itself. But consider now another awareness, c, whose content contains b. Since c is about b, its text contains at least one clause that predicates some character of b; for otherwise it wouldn't be about b. Let ' . . . (b)' be this clause, with the dots marking the place of the name of that character. Assume next that L contains as the name of the character the predicate expression

''$gr(a)$''.[8] Then the text of c *contains* ''$gr(a)$' (b)'. L, therefore, contains an expression of its own between single quotes. This is the exact point at which the illusion arises that the ideal language may speak about itself *in the same sense* in which language as event may do so. Or, to put the same thing differently, this is the only clear sense in which the ideal language as a pattern could be said to "speak about itself." Moreover, this is, as we now see, *not* the sense in which language as a part of the world may speak about itself. After one has seen that, one may if one wishes continue to use the phrase, as I occasionally shall, and say that *in this sense* the ideal language may and must "speak about itself." Only, and this is my real point, or, rather, this is the point that matters most for my story, there is again no reason whatsoever why in this sense the ideal language should not or could not "speak about itself." Again, the assertion is not even plausible. One of two apparent reasons that made it seem plausible is, if I may so express myself, the grammar of the picture metaphor. This, I believe, is the reason why Wittgenstein propounded the dogma in the *Tractatus*. The other reason, which probably did not sway Wittgenstein but which seemed a good reason to some others, is that the mathematicians proclaimed they had proved that language cannot both be consistent and say certain things "about itself." The mathematicians had indeed proved something. They usually do. Only, what they had

proved was not by any stretch of the imagination what they mistook it for. It took indeed all the philosophical clumsiness and insensitivity which mathematicians sometimes display to make this mistake, just as it took the wrong kind of awe in which some philosophers hold mathematics to believe them. In the rest of this section I shall analyze the mistake; partly in order to dispose of the strange dogma as thoroughly as I possibly can; mainly because this is the best place to introduce the notion of *truth* into the story. For the philosophical analyses of awareness, meaning, and truth belong together.

The mathematicians thought they had proved that a schema syntactically constructed cannot (a) be consistent[9] and upon interpretation contain (b) arithmetic as well as (c) a predicate with the literal meaning of 'true'. To be a plausible candidate for the role of ideal language, a schema must obviously satisfy conditions (a) and (b). As to (c), one of the things one would naturally want to say in a language that "speaks about itself" is that its sentences are true or false (not true), as the case may be. Thus, if the mathematicians had proved what they thought they proved, there would be a difficulty. In fact, they proved that no schema can simultaneously fulfill (a), (b), and a third condition, (c'), which they mistook for (c).

In order to fix the ideas I speak for the time being about language as part of the world. Sentences, then, are kinds of linguistic events (or things). Literally, only sentences are

---

[8] These are not double quotes but one pair of single quotes within another.

[9] Consistency can be defined syntactically.

true or false. Explicitly, 'true' is therefore a linguistic predicate in the sense that it is truly predicated only of the names of certain linguistic kinds. This, by the way, is the only meaning of 'linguistic' that is clear and does not stand in need of explication. Implicitly, truth involves more than the linguistic events themselves. *A sentence is true if and only if what it refers to (means) is the case.* Let me call this sentence (A). It is a truism: yet, firmly grasped, it has three important consequences. *First.* Some linguistic properties are syntactical properties. In the case of marks on paper, for instance, a property of a sentence or of any other expression is syntactical if and only if it is defined in terms of the shapes and the arrangement of its signs and of nothing else. Truth is obviously not a syntactical property of sentences. *Second.* Introducing 'true' into a schema means two things. It means (α) introducing into the schema a sentence which upon interpretation becomes (A). It means (β) that this sentence ought to be a "linguistic truth," in a sense of the phrase, linguistic truth, which is by no means clear and must therefore be explicated. It follows, *third*, that if all this is to be achieved, the schema must contain certain expressions, one which can be interpreted as 'refer' and others that can be interpreted as names of sentences. In the nature of things, these expressions must be descriptive.

The property mentioned in (c) *is a syntactical property of sentences; truth, the linguistic property mentioned in* (c), *is not.* Not to have seen this is the mathematicians' major mistake. They also made two subsidiary ones. One of

these is that, accurately speaking, the property mentioned in (c') is not even a syntactical property.

Goedel, who did not make any of these mistakes, invented a method that allowed him to use arithmetic in speaking commonsensically about an uninterpreted schema. Specifically, he invented a rule by which to each expression of the schema[10] one and only one integer is coördinated in a manner that depends only on the shapes and the arrangement of the signs in the expression itself. (This is, in fact, the least achievement of that great mathematician.) In speaking commonsensically about the schema we can therefore use the number (n_A) which by the rule corresponds to an expression 'A' as the "name" of this expression. By the same rule, a class of integers corresponds to every syntactical property, namely, the class of all the integers coördinated to expressions which have the property. The name of a class of integers is called an arithmetical predicate. (E.g., 'square' is the name of the class [1, 4, 9, . . .].) Now remember (b). By assumption our schema contains number-signs (not numbers!), i.e., expressions we intend to interpret as referring to integers, and arithmetical-predicate-expressions, i.e., expressions we intend to interpret as referring to classes of integers. Assume now that one of these latter expressions, 'pr', upon interpretation becomes an arithmetical predicate

---

[10] More precisely, the rule works only for schemata of a certain kind; all plausible candidates for the role of ideal language belong to that kind. This is but one of the many omissions I shall permit myself on more technical matters.

that is coördinated to a syntactical property. In this case the mathematicians say that the schema contains the "name" of the syntactical property, just as they say that in the number-signs it contains the "names" of its own expressions. This use of 'name' is inaccurate. For one, an uninterpreted schema does not contain the name (or the "name") of anything. For another, in the intended interpretation '*pr*' obviously refers to a class of integers and not to a syntactical property just as the number-signs refer to integers and not to expressions. Assume, third, that we actually use the (interpreted) schema as a language. We could not *in* it state what the mathematicians say *about* it unless it contained further expressions, namely, those which upon interpretation become the names of expressions and of their syntactical properties, and, in addition, the means to state *in* the schema the rules by which, speaking *about* it, we make integers and classes of integers the "names" of linguistic things and characters. This is the reason why, as we shall presently see, the property mentioned in (c′) is, accurately speaking, not even a syntactical property. Not to have seen that is one of the two subsidiary mistakes. Its root is the mathematicians' special use of 'name'. For their own special purposes it is, as it happens, quite harmless. Philosophically, it is disastrous to believe that one can state *in* the interpreted schema what can only be stated *about* it. Why this is so is obvious. The one and only schema which interests the philosopher is that which upon interpretation becomes *L*, the ideal language. And in *L* one must in

principle be able to say everything non-philosophical.

I am ready to state what the mathematicians did prove. Let '*A*' be a sentence of a schema that satisfies (a) and (b) as well as some other conditions, of a purely technical nature, which every plausible candidate for the role of *L* must satisfy. Let n_A be the number we have coördinated to '*A*'; let 'N_A' be the number-sign of the schema which upon interpretation transcribes n_A; let finally '*pr*' be an arithmetical-predicate-expression. What has been proved is this.[11] The schema contains no '*pr*' such that

$$(T) \qquad\qquad pr\,(N_A) \equiv A$$

is *demonstrable* for all (closed) sentences of the schema. But I see that I must again explain, first what demonstrability is, then why anybody should think that (T) ought to be demonstrable.

Analyticity is a syntactical property of sentences. More precisely, what philosophers mean by 'analytic' can and must be explicated by means of a syntactical property. Demonstrability is another syntactical property of sentences. Every demonstrable sentence is analytic, though not conversely. (The second half is one of Goedel's celebrated results.) Thus, while there is no '*pr*' for which (T) is demonstrable, there could conceivably be one for which it is analytic. That there actually is none is a purely mathematical mat-

---

[11] D. Hilbert and P. Bernays, *Grundlagen der Mathematik* (Berlin: Springer, 1939), Vol. II, pp. 245 f.

ter which does not interest me here at all. The question that interests me is: Why should one who believes, however mistakenly, that an arithmetical-predicate-expression could ever transcribe 'true', also believe that the transcription is adequate only if (T) is demonstrable? The answer is instructive. Remember the condition (β), which requires that (A) be a "linguistic truth." (T) was mistaken for the transcription of (A); demonstrability was implicitly offered as the explication of the problematic notion of linguistic truth. This is the second subsidiary mistake. It is a mistake because in the light of Goedel's result demonstrability is not at all a plausible explication of 'linguistic truth'. Analyticity might be. In the next section I shall propose what I believe to be the correct transcription of (A) in L; and I shall show that this transcription is analytic.

IV

The sentence I proposed to transcribe in the ideal language is 'I see that this is green'; or, rather in order to sidestep the issue of the Self, '(It is) seen (by me) that this is green'; or, still more precisely, since I wish to limit myself to the indubitably simple character of direct acquaintance, 'direct acquaintance with this being green'. Let the undefined descriptive constants 'a', 'aw', 'gr' name a particular and two simple characters, direct acquaintance and greenness, respectively. Consider '$aw(gr(a))$'; call it (1). On first thought one might hit upon (1) as the transcription of our sentence. A little

reflection shows that for at least two reasons we are already committed to reject (1).

To be a direct acquaintance, or an imagining, and so on, are, as we saw, characters of particular awarenesses. Let 'b' be the name of the awareness whose text I wish to transcribe. 'aw' must then be predicated of 'b' and not, as in (1), of '$gr(a)$', which refers to the content of b. This is the first reason why we must reject (1). 'gr' and 'a' refer to a character and a particular with both of which I am directly acquainted. Speaking as we ordinarily do, what they refer to is thus called mental. (This is my "point of contact" with the phenomenalists.) Change the example; consider '$kn(p_1)$'; call it (1^1); let 'kn' and 'p_1' stand for 'known that' and 'This stone is heavy' respectively. 'p_1' refers to a physical state of affairs; to say that it refers to anything mental is to fall into the absurdities of the phenomenalists. 'kn', on the other hand, names a character which, speaking as we ordinarily do, we specifically and characteristically call mental.[12] It follows that ($1'$) mixes the physical and the mental in the manner that leads to the interactionist catastrophe. Perhaps this becomes even clearer if for a moment I write, relationally, '$aw(self, p_1)$', which is of course the pattern of the classical act. However, the difference between the relational and nonrelational alternatives makes no real difference so far as mixing the physical

---

[12] So used, 'Knowing' refers to a character of awareness. To insist on that one need not deny that there are other uses of the word, e.g., those of which Ryle now makes too much.

and the mental goes. This is the second reason why we must reject (1). But now a critic might insist that when somebody knows or sees something there is indeed a transaction[13] between what is known or seen and the knower or seer. Quite so. Only, this transaction is properly spoken of as the scientists speak about it, that is, in principle, behavioristically. (This is my "point of contact" with materialists and epiphenomenalists.) Notice that, in spite of the "phenomenalistic" feature of my ideal language, I can say all this and even find it necessary to say it. This alone should go a long way toward convincing anyone that I avoid the absurdities of the various classical positions.

Let us take stock. Negatively, we understand why (1) cannot be the transcription. Positively, we see that the transcription must contain the clause '$aw(b)$'. In this clause, by the way, 'aw' is a predicate and therefore, strictly speaking, the name of a character. In (1) it is a nonrelational pseudopredicate and therefore, as I use 'character', not really the name of a character. Of this presently. For the moment we notice that '$aw(b)$' could not possibly be the whole ideal text of our sentence since it does not say what b is an awareness *of*. Thus, there must be at least one more clause. To provide it, I make use of an idea I introduced before. That an awareness is an awareness of something I represent in the ideal language by a character of

this awareness which is *in some sense* (I shall presently explicate it) a simple character; in our instance, call this character '$'gr(a)'$'[14]; generally, I call it '$'p_1'$', where 'p_1' refers to the content of the awareness or, what amounts to the same thing, is its (ideal) text. The transcription of our sentence becomes then

(2) $aw(b) \cdot 'gr(a)'(b)$

Undoubtedly there is something peculiar about '$'gr(a)'$'. For one, the expression itself is very complex, even though it names a character that is simple. For another, the expression is not, as a syntactically introduced undefined descriptive predicate ought to be, wholly innocent of its interpretation. One can, of course, as I presently shall, syntactically construct a schema that contains it. But that in itself means nothing. Even so, '$'gr(a)'$' is innocent of the intended interpretation in that (α) it remains fully indeterminate as long as 'gr' and 'a' are. But it is not so innocent in that (β), after 'gr' and 'a' have been interpreted, if I am to achieve my purposes, '$'gr(a)'$' must be interpreted as the name of the character which an awareness possesses if and only if it is an awareness of what '$gr(a)$' refers to. On the other hand, we would like to say that (β) is "merely a linguistic matter" or, as I once put it, that to be an awareness of a certain kind and to have a certain content (and, therefore, text) is one thing and not two. Let there be no illusion. In

---

[13] I use this clumsy word in order to avoid 'relation', which would be syntactically false since the "transaction" is a pseudorelation.

[14] Again, these are not double quotes but one pair of single quotes within another.

so speaking we ourselves use 'linguistic' philosophically, i.e., in a problematic way that needs explication. The point is that what I am saying in this section is, among other things, the explication. The following are three salient points of it. (a) I introduce into the ideal language the sentence ''$gr(a)$'$Mgr(a)$' as the transcription of what we *sometimes* mean when we say that the proposition (or sentence) this is green *means* that this is green. (b) I so extend the notion of a logical sign that 'M' becomes logical and not descriptive. (c) I so extend the notion of analyticity that ''$gr(a)$'$Mgr(a)$' and all similar sentences become analytic.

Sometimes, when we assert such things as, say, that the proposition (or sentence) this is green means that this is green, we would be dissatisfied if we were told that in asserting it we use 'means' in the sense of either reference or context. The cause of the dissatisfaction is that we feel, however confusedly, that we did not say anything, or did not want to say anything, about linguistic events. Or, if you please, we feel that what we really wanted to say is something "linguistic" in some other sense of this problematic term. 'M' transcribes this meaning of 'means'. I am tempted to call it the hidden or philosophical meaning; hidden, because it got lost in the development I described in the second section; philosophical, because I believe that it is what the philosophers who were not sidetracked by that development groped for. However, I ordinarily call meanings (or uses) philosophical if and only if, remaining unexplicated, they produce philosophical puzzlement. So I shall resist the temptation and call this third meaning, transcribed by 'M', the *intentional* meaning of 'means'.

This is as good a place as any to introduce a fourth meaning of 'means' (and 'meaning'). This I call the *logical* meaning. But first for two comments that might help to forestall some misunderstandings. (a) I have mentioned four meanings of 'means'. Two of them, reference and context, I called scientific; one I call logical; another I was at least tempted to call philosophical. There are good reasons for choosing these names; but one must not let the names obscure the fact that '*means*' *occurs with each of these four meanings in ordinary discourse*, sometimes with the one, sometimes with the other, sometimes with some combination. As long as one speaks commonsensically one does not get into trouble. As soon as one begins to philosophize in the traditional way about "meaning," the fourfold ambiguity begins to produce the traditional philosophical troubles. (b) There are quite a few further meanings of 'meaning'. They occur in moral, esthetic, and scientific discourse and in discourse about such discourse. I know this as well as the next man, even if that man should hail from Oxford. The four meanings I single out are nevertheless those which through fusion and confusion have produced one of the major tangles of first philosophy. Compared with the task of untying this fourfold knot the explication of the other meanings of 'meaning' is not very difficult.

Logicians often say that two sentences of a schema, 'p_1' and 'p_2', have the same meaning if and only if 'p_1' $\equiv$

'p_2' is analytic. This is the logical meaning of 'means'. In logic the idea is important; hence the adjective, logical. Nor is there any doubt that it explicates *one* of the ordinary uses of 'means'. Technically, the basic notion in this case is not meaning but having-the-same-meaning; so the former must be explicated in terms of the latter, say, as the class of all sentences having the same meaning. These, however, are mere technicalities with which we need not bother.

I am ready to put the last touch to my main proposal. One may wonder whether

(2′)

$$aw(b) \cdot \,'gr(a)'(b) \cdot \,'gr(a)'Mgr(a)$$

is not preferable to (2). (2′) has the advantage that, since its third clause mentions the content of the awareness whose text it transcribes, one can be quite sure of what in the case of (2) one may conceivably doubt, namely, that nothing essential has been omitted. Interestingly, one need not choose. The third clause of (2′), the one which makes the difference between it and (2), is, as I mentioned before, analytic. (2) and (2′) are thus like 'p_1' and '$p_1 \cdot p_2$', where 'p_2' is analytic. In this case '$p_1 = p_1 \cdot p_2$' is also analytic. (2) and (2′) have therefore the same logical meaning. The meaning transcription must preserve is logical meaning. It follows that the difference between (2) and (2′) makes no real difference.

Consider everything I have said so far in this section as preliminary, merely an exposition of the main ideas,

to be followed by the more formal presentation and argument on which I am about to embark. First, though, I want to attend to two related matters.

The predicates of the ideal language L which I form by surrounding sentences of L with single quotes name those characters which I call *propositions*. Propositions are therefore not kinds of linguistic things or events in the sense in which certain marks on paper, certain sounds, and certain visual and auditory "contents" are linguistic things or events. And this latter sense is, as we know, the only clear and unproblematic sense of 'linguistic'. It is therefore a mistake, or, at least, it is confusing to say that what I call a proposition is a linguistic character. If a qualifying adjective must be used at all, I would rather say that propositions are mental or psychological characters. But then again, it would be another mistake to think that I propose what is traditionally called a psychological theory of propositions. To understand why it is a mistake one merely has to remember that, as the term is traditionally used in philosophy, propositions are a peculiar kind of entity of which some philosophers claim they are the real contents of awarenesses. I do not believe that there are propositions in this sense. So I would not propose a theory, either psychological or otherwise, to provide some status for these chimaeras. Why then, one may wonder, use a word that invites mistakes and confusions. I hold no brief for the word. I needed a name. This one came to mind. It is, I think, as good as any other. Also, I welcome the opportunity it provides to cast new light on certain kinds of mistakes and confusions. This is one of the two matters to which I wanted to attend.

Some particulars are tones. This does not imply that L must contain an undefined predicate interpreted as 'tone'. If, for instance, L contains the undefined names of the various pitches, middle c, c sharp, d, and so on, one could try, in L, to define a tone as anything that exemplifies a pitch. The technicalities of this business need not concern us here.[15] Similarly, since awarenesses are in fact those particulars which exemplify propositional characters, one may wonder whether L must contain undefined descriptive predicates, such as 'aw', which are interpreted as the names of different modes of awareness, in the sense in which direct acquaintance, wondering, remembering, doubting, and so on, are modes of awareness. There are undoubtedly such modes, just as there are shapes, tones, smells, and so on. The only question is whether, omitting from L all undefined names for any of them, one can in L still account for the differences among them; that is, whether one can in principle account for these differences in term of "content" and of "content" alone. I have pondered the question for years. (Hume threw out a casual suggestion concerning it when he distinguished "ideas" from "impressions" by their "faintness.") I am not sure what the answer is, though I am now inclined to believe that it is nega-

tive. That is why I proceed as if it were negative. But it is also important to see clearly that whatever it is does not make much difference for anything else I have said and shall still say in this essay. The only difference is that if the answer were positive then propositions would be the only characters that are in fact exemplified by awarenesses alone. This is the other matter to which I wanted to attend.

Russell and the Wittgenstein of the *Tractatus* were the first who practiced the method of philosophizing by means of an ideal language. Since then quite a few philosophers, whether they knew it or not, have more or less consistently employed this method. With two exceptions, they all proposed essentially the same syntactical schema. This schema, I shall call it the conventional schema of L_c, is of the *Principia Mathematica* type. The New Nominalists are one exception; the other, for over a decade now, has been myself. The New Nominalists, who do not belong in our story, believe that L must be syntactically poorer than L_c.[16] I believe that L_c is in one respect and in one respect only not rich enough to serve as L. My reason should now be obvious. I do believe that L_c can serve as a clarified language to be spoken, in principle, about everything which, as one usually says, is an object of mind— including mind itself, as long as we speak about it scientifically, that is, in principle, behavioristically. But I also

---

[15] See also MLP12 and "Undefined Descriptive Predicates," *Philosophy and Phenomenological Research*, 8, 1947, 55–82.

[16] For an analysis of the New Nominalism see MLP4, MLP5, and "Particularity and the New Nominalism," *Methodos*, 6, 1954, 131–47.

believe that L_c does not provide adequate transcriptions for many statements we make about minds or mental things when we speak commonsensically. It follows, on my conception of philosophy, that one cannot, by talking about L_c and what it talks about, solve some of the philosophical problems concerning mind and its place in nature.[17] Hence L_c cannot be the ideal language. Positively, I believe that L_c becomes the ideal language if it is supplemented by two further primitive signs, namely

$$M \text{ and } `. . .\text{'},$$

i.e., the relational pseudopredicate which I interpret as the intentional 'means' and the quoting operator. We have incidentally come upon another reason why the question whether L must contain 'aw' and other undefined names for the several modes of awareness is not as fundamental as it might seem. 'aw' and its cognates are predicates; thus they exemplify a syntactical category provided by L_c. 'M' is a pseudopredicate. Thus it belongs to a syntactical category unknown to L. As it happens, it is also the only primitive sign that represents this category in L_c. And what holds for 'M' in these two respects also holds for the quoting operator. Presently I shall make much of these points. But I see that I am once more illuminating basic ideas when the ground for a more formal presentation has already been laid. So I shall proceed as follows. *First*, I shall very concisely describe those features of L_c that matter most for my purpose. *Second*, I shall construct syntactically the schema I believe to be L. It contains the two syntactical categories represented by 'M' and by the quoting operator. This feature requires a redefinition of the syntactical notions of *logical sign* and *analyticity*. The two new notions are broader than the conventional ones in that every primitive sign logical in L_c and every sentence analytic in L_c are also in L logical and analytic respectively, but not conversely. *Third*, I shall state explicitly what is implicit in this essay as a whole, namely, that the enriched schema can be made to bear the burden of the philosophy of mind.

The primitive signs of L_c fall into two classes, logical and descriptive. The logical signs are of two kinds. There are, first, two signs, each individually specified, each belonging to a syntactical category of its own, each the only primitive representative of its category in L_c. These two signs are, of course, a connective and a quantifier, interpreted in the familiar fashion as, say, 'neither-nor' and 'all'.[18] The second kind of logical signs, not individually specified, consists of an indefinite number of variables of each of the several types. Each type is a syntactical category; but they are all categories of "terms." The essence of a term is that it combines with terms to form sen-

---

[17] See also MLP6.

[18] If, as strictly speaking one must, one is to dispense with definitions, then a third logical primitive, the abstraction operator, is necessary. This is another of the omissions and simplifications for which I must take the responsibility.

tences. L_c contains no pseudoterms, i.e., no category (except connectives) whose members combine either with sentences or with terms and sentences to form sentences. The primitive descriptive signs or, as one also says, the undefined descriptive constants of L_c are distributed over the various types of "terms." If a sentence S of L_c contains descriptive terms, then replace them all according to certain rules by variables. Call the resulting sentence the "form" of S. The syntactical definition of analyticity is so constructed that whether or not a sentence is analytic depends only on its "form." The syntactical significance of the distinction between the two kinds of signs lies thus in the role it plays in the syntactical definition of analyticity. The philosophical significance of the latter, and thus of both syntactical distinctions, lies in the circumstance that *in all cases but one* it can serve as the explication of what philosophers mean when they say that a sentence is "analytic," or a "formal" truth, or a "linguistic" truth. The exception where the conventional definition of analyticity is not adequate for this purpose is, as one might expect, the case of such sentences as "The sentence (proposition) this is green means that this is green," when 'means' is used intentionally.

That the definition of analyticity in L_c achieves its philosophical purpose depends of course on its details; they are specified in what is technically known as validity theory. I cannot here state the definition accurately; but I shall recall its nature by means of two elementary illustrations. Take the two forms '$p \vee \sim p$' and '$(x)f(x) \supset (\exists x)f(x)$'. The first is analytic because its truth table is tautological; the second is analytic because if '$f(x)$' is read 'x is a member of f', then it becomes a set-theoretical truth for all subsets of all nonempty sets. The definition of analyticity (validity) is thus combinatorial; arithmetical in the simplest case, set-theoretical in all others. What makes it philosophically significant is, first, the combinatorial feature, and, second, the circumstance that as far as we know all analytical statements are in fact true.[19]

Technically, validity theory is a branch of mathematics with many difficult problems. So it is perhaps not surprising that it, too, provided the philosophers with an opportunity to be misled by the mathematicians. The following two comments will show what I have in mind. (a) For all philosophical purposes (with the one notorious exception) our definition is an adequate explication of what philosophers mean by 'analytic'. Mathematically, it is not as interesting. It would be, if we knew a procedure which, applied to *any* sentence S of L_c, after a finite number of steps yielded an answer to the question whether S is analytic. There is and there can be no such procedure. (That there can be none even if one restricts S to the so-called lower functional calculus is the famous result of Church.) This is the reason why mathematicians are not very interested in validity; unfortunately, their lack of interest has blinded some philosophers to

---

[19] See also MLP4, MLP14.

the philosophical significance of this explication of 'analytic'. (b) In speaking about a schema we always speak commonsensically. In framing the explication of analyticity in terms of validity we use set theory "commonsensically." Yet it is a matter of record that "commonsensical" set theory itself got into difficulties that had to be straightened out by the construction of schemata. Mathematicians may therefore feel that the explication of analyticity in terms of validity uncritically takes for granted what is in fact uncertain and problematic. For some mathematical purposes that may indeed be so. Yet, we must not allow the mathematicians to persuade us that we, as philosophers, ought to strive for certainty, or constructivity, or decidability, in the sense in which the finitists among them do. We seek, not certainty of any peculiar noncommonsensical kind, but, rather, the clarity achieved by explications framed in terms of common sense, that common sense of which science and (nonformalized) mathematics are but the long arm. If yesterday's "common sense" got us into trouble that had to be straightened out by the construction of schemata, we shall today still use this "amended common sense" to construct "commonsensically" the schemata of today. And if tomorrow we should get into trouble again, we shall start all over again. For what else could we possibly do?

One more feature of L_c must be mentioned. Let 'F_1' and 'F_2' be predicate expressions of any type, 'X' a variable of its subject type, '$\Phi(F_1)$' any sentence containing 'F_1', '$\Phi(F_2)$'

a sentence made out of '$\Phi(F_1)$' by replacing at least one occurrence of 'F_1' by 'F_2'. It is a consequence of our definition of analyticity that

$$(E) \quad (X)[F_1(X) \equiv F_2(X)] \supset [\Phi(F_1) \equiv \Phi(F_2)]$$

is analytic. Thus, if the antecedent of (E) is true, so is the consequent; and if the antecedent is analytic, so is the consequent. This feature is called the extensionality of L_c. I turn to the syntactical description of L. With the qualification entailed by 1 it contains L_c.

1. Only closed expressions are sentences of L. (This is merely a technical detail, necessary to avoid undesirable consequences of the quantification rules for expressions containing 'M'.)
2. L contains sentential variables. (Since L contains no primitive sentential constants, this modification has, upon my conception of ontology,[20] no untoward ontological consequences.)
3. L contains two additional primitive signs, the relational pseudo-predicate 'M' and the quoting operator, with the following formation rules:
a. Every sentence of L surrounded by quotes becomes a nonrelational first-order predicate (type: f) with all the syntactical properties of a primitive descriptive predicate.

[20] See also MLP4, MLP13, and "Particularity and the New Nominalism."

b. Every sentence of the form '*fMp*' is well formed. Call these sentences the simple clauses of '*M*'.

These are the formation rules of *L*. Now for the definition of analyticity.

4*a.* Every sentence analytic according to L_c is analytic.

4*b.* Every simple cause of '*M*' is either analytic or it is contradictory, i.e., its negation is analytic. It is analytic if and only if the predicate to the left of '*M*' is formed by the quoting operator from the sentence to the right of '*M*'.

The part of *L* that contains '*M*' is not extensional. To see that, let '*A*' be a constant of the same type as '*X*' and assume that '$(X)\ [F_1(X) \equiv F_2(X)]$' is true. If *L* were extensional, then '$'F_1(A)'MF_1(A)' \equiv 'F_1(A)'MF_2(A)'$' would have to be true. In fact, this sentence is not only false, it is contradictory; for by 4*b* its left side is analytic and its right side is contradictory. I call '*M*' and the quoting operator, together with the two primitive logical signs of L_c, the four primitive logical signs of *L*. But then, one may ask, are the two new signs "really" logical? I can of course call them so. Yet, obviously, I do not wish to argue merely about words. The only real argument consists in stating clearly the similarities and the differences between the old and the new "logical" signs. I shall present this argument or, as I had better say, these reflections in three steps. *First.* Each of the four signs, both old and new, is individually specified. Each of the four signs, both old

and new, belongs to a syntactical category of its own. Each of the four signs, both old and new, is the only primitive member of the syntactical category to which it belongs. These similarities are impressive. Nor is that all. *Second.* Consider the role the four signs play in the definition of analyticity. If in view of the three similarities just mentioned one accepts the two new signs as logical, then one can in view of 4*a* and 4*b* again say that whether a sentence of *L* is analytic depends only on its "form." This similarity, too, is impressive. But there is also a difference with respect to analyticity which I do not at all intend to minimize. For philosophy, as I understand it, is not advocacy, least of all advocacy of uses of words, but accurate description. The difference is that 4*b* is not a combinatorial criterion in the sense in which 4*a* is one. On the other hand, though, the "new" analytic sentences, i.e., those which are analytic by 4*b*, have a unique feature which in its own way is just as sweeping as any combinatorial one. They are all simple clauses of '*M*' and each of these clauses is either analytic or contradictory. *Third.* Sentences which are analytic in the "old" sense of L_c (or 4*a*) are also called "formal" or "linguistic" truths. These are of course philosophical and therefore problematic uses of 'formal' and 'linguistic'. Analyticity in the old sense is their explication. Now we know that such sentences as "The sentence (proposition) this is green means that this is green" are sometimes also called "linguistic" truths and that this use of 'linguistic' is equally problematic. *L* transcribes these sentences into those that are analytic by 4*b*. Our "new" notion of analyticity thus clarifies two of the problematic uses of 'formal' and 'linguistic'; it exhibits accurately both the similarities and the differences between them; and it does not tear asunder what in the structural history of philosophical thought belongs together.

I have not, I shall not, and I could not in this essay show that L is the ideal language. What I have shown is merely this. If $(\alpha) L_c$ is an adequately clarified language which one can in principle speak about everything except minds, and if $(\beta) L$ provides in principle adequate transcriptions for what we say, commonsensically and not behavioristically, about minds, *then* L is the ideal language. Furthermore, I have shown (β) by showing, at the beginning of this section, that L contains adequate transcriptions of such sentences as 'direct awareness of this being green'. With this I have accomplished the main task I set myself in this essay. Again, if this is so, then the differences between L and L_c must provide us with the accurate description, or, in the classical phrase, with the logical picture of the nature of minds and their place in the world. Let us see. In the world of L_c there are tones, shapes, colors, and so on. That is, there are particulars such that *in fact* they and they alone exemplify certain simple characters, say, in the case of tones, the pitches. In the world of L there are in addition also awarenesses. That is, there are particulars such that *in fact* they and they alone exemplify certain additional simple characters, those I called propositions and, prob-

ably, also some among those I called modes of awareness. These, to be sure, are important differences; yet they are not as radical as the one I saved quite deliberately for the end of the list. This difference is that L requires two new logical primitives. For what novelty, I ask, could possibly be more radical than one which cannot be spoken about without new syntactical categories. Notice, finally, that the two new primitives determine *in a minimal fashion* that part of L which is, in a technical sense I explained, nonextensional. So far I have avoided the use of 'intentional' for 'nonextensional'. Now we might as well remember that philosophers, speaking philosophically, have insisted that "intentionality" is the differentiating characteristic of minds. Since they spoke philosophically, one cannot be completely certain what they meant. Yet, I am confident that my analysis is the explication of what they reasonably could have meant.

It will pay to reflect briefly on why I used the phrase 'in fact' at the two italicized places above. Interpret '*bl*' and '*a*' as 'blue' and as the name of a particular which is a tone. Let '*'p_1'*' stand for the name of a propositional character. Both '$bl(a)$' and '*'p_1'(a_1)*' are well-formed sentences; all one can say is that they are *in fact* false. To say anything else, such as, for instance, that they are ill-formed or, even, that they are contradictory, amounts to accepting some form of the synthetic *a priori* and, probably, also some form of substantialism. I, for one, accept neither.[21]

---

[21] See MLP3, MLP8, MLP11.

In the third section I told one half of the story of truth. I am now ready to tell the other half. Then I shall be done.

In an unforgettable metaphor G. E. Moore once called awareness diaphanous or transparent. What he wanted to call attention to was that, because we are so prone to attend to their contents, the awarenesses themselves easily elude us. Intentional meaning is, as we now understand, closely connected with awareness. Not surprisingly, then, it is similarly elusive. That is why, when I first mentioned it, I proceeded negatively, as it were. Remember what I did. I selected a sentence to serve as illustration: "The sentence (proposition) this is green means that this is green." Then I insisted that we sometimes so use such sentences that we do not speak about either the contexts or the referents of linguistic events, in the only clear sense of 'linguistic event'; but, rather, about something "linguistic" in a sense of 'linguistic' which is problematic and therefore in need of explication. The explication, as we now know, is this. (a) The sentence is transcribed by '$gr(a)'Mgr(a)$', which is analytic. (b) ''$gr(a)$'' refers to or names a proposition, i.e., a character of awarenesses. (c) '$gr(a)$' refers to a state of affairs. (d) 'M', being a logical sign, does not refer to or name anything in the sense in which descriptive expressions refer to something. (a) and (d) are the source of the problematic use of 'linguistic'. (b) and (c) show that intentional meaning is a logical pseudorelation between a propositional character and a state of affairs; they also show accurately in which respects it makes no sense whatsoever to say that intentional meaning is "linguistic."

When I spoke in the third section about truth, I spoke about language as event—with some reservation, or, as I put it, merely in order to fix the ideas. The reason for the reservation was that 'true', like 'means', has an intentional meaning. Or, to say what corresponds exactly to what I said before and just repeated in the case of 'means', sometimes, when we say "The sentence (proposition) this is green is true if and only if this is green," we speak neither about the contexts nor about the referents of linguistic events but, rather, "linguistically" in a problematic sense of 'linguistic'. I shall now explicate this sense by first proposing a definition of 'true' in L and then commenting on it.

A defined sign or expression is logical if and only if all the primitive signs in its definition are logical. Defined logical signs, like primitive ones, do not refer to anything in the sense in which descriptive ones do. 'True', as I explicate it, is a defined logical predicate of the second type with a nonrelational argument. Thus 'true', or, as I shall write, 'Tr', like 'M', does not refer to anything in the sense in which 'a', 'gr', ''$gr(a)$'', and '$gr(a)$' all do. The idea is, as one might expect, to define 'Tr' in terms of 'M' and of other logical signs, i.e., variables, quantifiers, and connectives. The actual definition is

(D) '$Tr(f)$' for '$(\exists p)[fMp \cdot p]$'.

Notice that although 'Tr' can be truly predicated only of the names of characters which are propositions, its definition is nevertheless in terms of the variable of the appropriate type. '$Tr(gr)$', for instance, though it is false, is therefore well formed. To proceed otherwise amounts to accepting some version of the synthetic a priori. This is the same point I made before. Now for four comments to establish that (D) is in fact an adequate transcription of the intentional meaning of 'true'.

I. Remember the sentence I called (A): A sentence is true if and only if what it refers to (means) is the case. Since we are now dealing with intentions, I had better amend it to (A'): *A proposition is true if and only if what it means is the case.* Consider next that in view of (D)

$$(D') \quad Tr(f) \equiv (\exists p)[fMp \cdot p]$$

is analytic; for our notion of analyticity is of course so arranged that every sentence that stands to a definition in the relation in which (D') stands to (D) is analytic. (This is just one of the many details I skipped.) Now read (D') in words: Something is true if and only if there is a state of affairs such that it means this state of affairs and this state of affairs is the case. The only verbal discrepancies between this sentence and (A') are due to the greater precision which the formalism forces upon us. We must say 'something' instead of 'proposition'; and we must make the existential quantification explicit. (D'), being analytic, is thus an adequate transcription of (A'). A little reflection shows that 'Tr' is and is not "linguistic" in exactly the same

senses in which 'M' is. I don't think I need to repeat the distinctions I just made under (a), (b), (c), and (d).

II. Ordinarily we think of true and false as contradictories. I define 'Fs', to be interpreted as 'false', by

$$'Fs(f)' \quad \text{for} \quad '(\exists p)[fMp \cdot \sim p]'.$$

It follows that 'Fs' and 'Tr' are not contradictories, or, what amounts to the same thing, that '$(f)[Tr(f) \vee Fs(f)]$' cannot be shown to be analytic. On first thought this may make our transcription look less than adequate. Closer examination reveals that we have come across one of its strengths. We do not really want to say that "everything" is either true or false. What we want to say is, rather, that "every sentence" is either true or false. Technically, this means that '$Tr('p_1') \vee Fs('p_1')$' ought to be analytic for every proposition. And that this is so is easily shown. For those who care for this sort of detail I write down the steps of the demonstration: '$p_1'Mp_1$; '$p_1'Mp_1 \cdot (p_1 \vee \sim p_1)$; $(\exists p)['p_1'Mp \cdot (p \vee \sim p)]$; $(\exists p)['p_1'Mp \cdot p)] \vee [(\exists p)'p_1'Mp \cdot \sim p]$.

III. We are in a position to dispose of a question over which recently more ink has been spilled than it deserves. Do 'p_1' and '$Tr('p_1')$' have the same meaning? To ask this question is, as we know, to ask four. With respect to *context*, we do not care and we need not bother. Take the two sentences 'Peter died' and 'It is true that Peter died'; and assume that a person hears once the one and once the other. Whether what he does is the same and whether his mental states are the same on the two occasions is a question for psychologists and psychologists only. As a matter of common sense, though, the answer will vary, depending on many circumstances, from sentence to sentence, from person to person, and, for the same person, from occasion to occasion. The attempt to answer this question by constructing schemata and trying to discern in them something that corresponds to this meaning of having-the-same-meaning is thus patently absurd. Unhappily, Carnap and some of his students have recently spent a good deal of time and effort on this goose chase. With respect to *reference* the answer is obvious. The two sentences do not refer to the same thing. The same holds for *intentional* meaning. To see that, one merely has to consider that while $'p_1{}'Mp_1'$ and $'Tr('p_1')'MTr('p_1')'$ are analytic, $'p_1'$ $MTr('p_1')'$ and $'Tr('p_1')'Mp_1'$ are contradictory. There remains *logical* meaning, or, what amounts to the same thing, there remains the question whether $'p_1{\equiv}Tr('p_1')'$ is analytic for every proposition. This, I believe, is the question which most of those who recently dealt with the issue wanted to discuss. The answer is affirmative. Upon our broader conception of analyticity the sentence is analytic. Some will probably consider that another strength of our transcription. For those who care for this sort of thing I again write down the steps of the demonstration. For the proof that $'p_1 \supset Tr('p_1')'$ is analytic they are: p_1; $'p_1'Mp_1 \cdot p_1$; $(\exists p)$ $['p_1'$ $Mp \cdot p]$; $p_1 \supset (\exists p)$ $['p_1'Mp \cdot p]$. To prove that $'Tr('p_1') \supset p_1'$ is analytic, the definition of analyticity in L must be technically implemented with what

is intuitively obvious. I add then to $4a$ and $4b$ a third clause $4c$: If $'\Phi(p)'$ is an expression such that when a sentence of L is substituted for the variable the sentence it becomes is analytic for every sentence of L, then $'(p)\Phi(p)'$ is analytic. Now the proof proceeds as follows. $'('p_1'Mp_1 \cdot p_1) \supset p_1'$ is obviously analytic. For every other p_i $'('p_1'Mp_i \cdot p_i)$ $\supset p_1'$ is analytic because the first factor in the antecedent is contradictory. Hence, by $4c$, $'(p)$ $['p_1'Mp \cdot p) \supset p_1]'$ is analytic. This sentence is equivalent to the one to be proved.

IV. Everybody is familiar with the Liar paradox, that is, with the difficulties one can produce by supposing that a sentence "says about itself" that it is false. When the mathematicians proved what I explained in the third section, they drew part of their inspiration from this conundrum. Assume $'pr'$ to be an arithmetical-predicate-expression that can be interpreted as 'false'. We know this assumption to be absurd; but that is not the point now. If there is such a predicate expression then one can by using Goedel's ideas show that there is an integer, n, such that if $'N'$ is the number-sign interpreted as n, the number coördinated to $'pr(N)'$ is n. Speaking as inaccurately as the mathematicians do, one could then say that $'pr(N)'$ says about itself that it is false. That is why, by a pattern taken from the Liar paradox, the mathematicians drew their conclusions from this sentence. Under the circumstances it is worth noticing that L could not possibly contain a sentence which literally "says about itself" that it is false, or, for that matter, anything else. Assume that S is such a sentence and that, written down, it is a sequence of, say, 17 primitive signs. Its name is then a sequence of 18 primitive signs, the 17 original ones and the quoting operator. Since this name is a predicate and not itself a sentence, any sentence containing it is a sequence of at least 19 primitive signs. S, which is a sequence of only 17 primitive signs, cannot be such a sentence and can therefore not literally say anything about itself. It follows that no sentence of a clarified language can literally say anything about itself.[22] The belief that there are such sentences is one of the illusions created by the logical deficiencies of our natural language.

------

[22] As I recently discovered, this idea can be read into prop. 3.333 of the *Tractatus*. Wittgenstein made an essential mistake, though. He omitted the quotes.

3.2

MEANING AND INTENTIONALITY

A. J. Ayer

If a word means something, it is tempting to infer that there is something which it means. In the case of a proper name, or a pronoun, or a singular noun, one's first inclination may be to identify the meaning of the word with the object which it denotes. But the attempt to generalize this procedure leads to obvious difficulties. We may say that verbs denote states or activities, but what about adjectives? Do they denote properties or the things which have them? Do common nouns denote classes or their members? Must we say that abstract nouns denote abstract entities? But in what sense, if any, do abstract entities exist? Then there are prepositions to be considered, and conjunctions and other parts of speech. And words are used to form sentences which themselves have meaning. What are we to say that they denote?

Under the influence of Wittgenstein[1] and others, we have mostly ceased to be troubled by such questions. We dis-

From *Proceedings of the Twelfth International Congress of Philosophy*, Vol. I (Firenze: Sansoni, 1960). Reprinted by permission of the secretary of the Twelfth International Congress and the author.

------

[1] See especially his *Philosophical Investigations*.

miss them as illegitimate. They arise, it is said, out of the mistaken assumption that all words function as names. What is not so generally recognized is that even in the model case of proper names it is incorrect to identify the meaning of the name with the object which it denotes. The proof of this is that the meaning of the sentences in which the name occurs is not affected by the question whether any such object exists. For example, I do not know whether there ever was such a person as King Arthur of the Round Table. I am inclined to believe that there was, but I may very well be wrong. But whether he existed or not, the meaning of the sentence 'King Arthur fought the Saxons' remains the same. If he did not exist, the sentence misses its intended reference, but it does not thereby become meaningless. Yet it would become meaningless if the proper name meant what it denoted: for then the failure of the denotation would wholly deprive the name of meaning. It may, indeed, be objected that my example is not typical. Normally, when we use proper names, we are quite sure that their intended reference is successful. Even so, the argument still holds. For, however little doubt there may be that the objects in question do exist, it remains conceivable that they should not; and even if they did not, it would make no difference to the meaning of the sentences in which the proper names occurred.

The only cases in which it is plausible to identify the meaning of an expression with its denotation are those in which the success of its reference is a condition of the expression's being meaningfully used. Thus it might be held that all demonstrative words, or expressions, fell into this category; that talk of *this* or *that* object would be meaningless unless there really were things to which the demonstratives referred. But I am not at all sure that this must be so. Certainly, when such demonstratives are used, as they may be, to refer to absent objects, it is not necessary that the objects should exist: and even when it is implied that the objects are present, I do not think that their failure to exist need deprive the demonstratives of their meaning. The sort of cases that I have in mind are those in which the use of a demonstrative expression serves only to pretend that some object exists, or those in which the subject is suffering from a hallucination. In the case of hallucinations, we may bring in a special class of objects, sense-data, which will provide the demonstratives with something to denote, but while we may choose to do this it is by no means clear that we are bound to. There are, however, certain demonstratives, such as 'here' or 'now' or 'I', the meaning of which does logically depend, in their standard usage, upon their succeeding in their reference. But even in these cases it is questionable whether the meaning and the reference are to be identified. For the places and times and persons, which are referred to by the demonstratives, may have a great many properties which it would appear strange also to ascribe to the meanings of words.

Having remarked that expressions which are taken to be referential are not deprived of meaning when the objects which they seem to denote do not exist, some philosophers have concluded, not that the meaning even of names is different from their denotation, but simply that these referential expressions are not genuine names. They have assumed that if we were able wholly to unravel the meaning of the sentences that we ordinarily use, we should find that it was to be expressed by sentences which had an ultimate logical simplicity; and these sentences would contain, or perhaps even consist of, logically proper names; the mark of a logically proper name being that its significant use entailed the existence of the object which it was supposed to denote. This is the doctrine of logical atomism, to which both Russell[2] and Wittgenstein[3] at one time subscribed. But while it may be possible to endow a language with logically proper names, it surely is not necessary; I can see no good reason to hold that every descriptive language implicitly contains them. The assumption made by the logical atomists is that logically proper names are required, as it were, to furnish the language with an anchorage in nature; but, so far as I can see, this assumption is just false. If the language is to be descriptive, it is indeed necessary that some of its expressions should be capable of having a denotation; it must afford the means of referring to objects that could exist. But, even if we make the further stipulation that some of these objects do in fact exist, it still does not follow that

there need be any expressions in the language which have to refer to existent objects in order to be meaningful. Even if some demonstratives in our language do function in this way, I see no reason to take them as a paradigm. They do not even perform an essential service; it would be no sacrifice to replace them by names, or definite descriptive phrases, for which this special condition did not hold.

To refute the logical atomist theory, in its extreme form, it need only be remarked that a sentence which consisted entirely of logically proper names could not be used to say anything false. Either it would express a truth, or it would be meaningless. But surely to credit a sentence with descriptive meaning is to imply that what it is used to state can be either true or false. It is for this reason, indeed, that the desire of some philosophers to identify the meaning of indicative sentences with facts cannot be satisfied. For, setting aside the question what facts are, and in what sense, if any, they can be said to exist, in the case where a sentence is used to state what is false there is no fact for it to mean. And from this it follows that the sentence does not mean a fact, even though what it states is true. For whether what it is used to state is true or false, its meaning remains the same.

Having failed to locate the meanings of words in the external part of nature, philosophers may then be tempted to house them in the mind. Words, it is said, are the signs of ideas: and ideas are here identified with thoughts or images. But this view has nothing to commend it. If it is taken literally, it

---

[2] Vide, *The Philosophy of Logical Atomism*, lectures published in the "Monist" in 1918, and reprinted in *Logic and Knowledge*.

[3] Vide, *Tractatus Logico-Philosophicus*.

implies that we never do, or indeed can, talk about anything except our own mental processes: and, mercifully, this is not the case. If, on the other hand, the theory is that words refer in the first instance to ideas, that is, that they signify things by way of ideas, then it runs against the objection that people very often use words significantly without having any accompanying images and without engaging in any processes of thinking other than those which are embodied in their intelligent use of words. But what is still more serious is that this introduction of ideas meets none of the difficulties relating to the significance of words. We are told that words signify by way of ideas: but then how do ideas signify? There are exactly the same objections to identifying the meaning of ideas with their denotations as there are to identifying the meaning of words with theirs. The appeal to ideas, so far from serving to explain how words have meaning, merely brings in a second set of symbols, which have in many cases a dubious title to existence and in no case fulfil any function that is not already fulfilled by the corresponding words. We can say, if we like, that words are used to express ideas, though even this will be incorrect if it implies that having an idea necessarily precedes or accompanies the significant use of words as a separate mental process; but we must not say that they mean them.

There would seem, then, to be nothing in nature with which the meanings of words can be identified. And so philosophers, who think that there must somehow be such things as meanings, are forced, as it were, to go outside nature to find them. The view taken is that singular nouns mean individual concepts; common nouns mean class concepts; adjectives mean universals; indicative sentences mean propositions. And these concepts and universals and propositions are not mental entities, nor yet physical; they do not exist in space or time. Nevertheless they are held to be real, just as it may be held that numbers are real, though they do not exist in space and time. Moreover, they are easily accessible to us, just as numbers are. We can discover their properties and their relations to one another. For, on this view, whenever we understand a word, we apprehend its meaning, in the form of a concept or a universal; whenever we understand an indicative sentence, we apprehend a proposition; when we reason validly we are aware how propositions are related. And these relations are not in any way dependent upon us. They depend upon the nature of the propositions in question: and the propositions, as has been said, are objectively real. They would be what they are, even though no one ever thought of them; even though no one had ever devised a language in which they were capable of being expressed.

I suppose that the fundamental objection to this Platonic theory is that it puts too heavy a strain on one's credulity. It does not require a very robust sense of reality to make one hesitate to charge the Universe with a host of incorporeal entities, corresponding not only to every actual but to every possible set of meaningful words. The class of propositions alone will contain an infinite number of objective falsehoods, and even of objective contradictions, if it be allowed, as I think it should, that a contradictory sentence is not meaningless. Can we seriously admit that such things are real? A further argument is that the introduction of these entities fulfils no purpose: there is nothing that it serves to explain. To be told that adjectives mean universals, or that sentences mean propositions, is really to be told no more than that they mean what they mean. As so often in philosophy, this recourse to a 'realistic' theory is in effect a way of putting an end to the discussion. It does not provide us with an analysis of meaning so much as deny that any analysis is possible. To settle for meanings as objective entities is an explanation of meaning only in the sense that it implies that no more "natural" explanation can be given.

At this point, many philosophers would say that the source of our difficulties is that we are trying to answer an illegitimate question. There can be no general answer to the question what do words, or sentences, mean, for the very good reason that they do not all mean the same. Except in the rare cases where they are synonymous, different words have different meanings. Thus, if one is presented with the question What do words mean? the proper course is to ask What words? And then if one is told the words, one will, if one understands them, be able to give their meanings. Furthermore, in giving their meanings, one will not be specifying any objects. It is just a mistake to suppose that because a word is meaningful, there must be some entity which it means.

I think that this resolution of the problem is correct so far as it goes, but also that it does not go quite far enough. It forbids us to treat meaning as a relation between a sign and what it signifies, but the only reason that it gives for this prohibition is that we get into trouble if we disregard it. And thus it fails to attack the problem at its root. Why is it that it seems so natural to assume that there must be some object which is the meaning of a word?

The answer, or an important part of the answer, is that this assumption is strongly suggested by the way in which we talk about meaning. The transitive employment of verbs like 'mean' 'signify' 'designate' 'state' 'record' 'describe' 'express', requires that they be supplied with accusatives; and the status of these accusatives is uncertain. It is not evident that they are independently existing entities, and it is not evident that they are not. But, if we go by grammar, we shall be tempted to assume that they are.

The technical way of describing verbs of this kind, which was introduced, I believe, by Brentano, is to say that they are intentional. There are some transitive verbs, like the verbs 'to eat' or 'to kill', which logically imply the reality of their accusatives; there can be no eating or killing unless there really are things that are eaten or killed. Other transitive verbs, like the verb 'to seek', are logically noncommittal in this respect. Many things that are sought do exist, but one can also seek things that never have existed, and never will; it may be necessary that we should believe in their existence, but the belief need not be true. Now, it is verbs of this second class that are said to be intentional; and verbs like 'signify' are commonly included among them. But if we are to follow this procedure, we must make a distinction which is often overlooked. The things that one seeks may or may not exist; but the question which is here left open is normally a question of fact. In certain rare cases, such as the search for a method of squaring the circle, the object sought may be one that logically could not exist, but in general the object sought is one that might have existed, even though it in fact does not. When it comes to verbs like 'signify', on the other hand, the question about the reality of the accusative is normally not a question of fact but a question of logic. To ask whether there really are such things as universals or propositions is to raise a question of an entirely different order from the question whether there is uranium in the British Isles or even whether there is such a thing as a golden mountain. If there can be universals, there is no difficulty about finding them: what has to be decided is not whether they do in fact exist, but whether they could.

It is to be noted that the same problem arises with "cognitive" verbs, like 'believe' 'opine' 'imagine' 'doubt' 'suppose'. They also are intentional in the sense that they can be said to have accusatives of which the logical status is not clear. Thus, if various people believe the same thing, and others doubt it, it is tempting to assume that there is some single entity, a proposition, towards which these attitudes are directed. We refer to beliefs as being true or false, but it can be argued that

this is an elliptical way of speaking: what is true or false is the proposition which is believed; and its truth or falsehood is independent of the attitude which anyone may have towards it. So, these propositions fulfil a triple role. They are the vehicles of truth and falsehood, the objects of the various cognitive attitudes, and the meanings of the sentences in which these cognitive attitudes may be expressed.

Now it is not disputed that it is convenient to talk of propositions, or even of universals. Since there is plainly some good sense in which different words, or sentences, may have the same meaning, and different cognitive attitudes may have the same object, we need to be able to refer concisely to what they have in common; and it is more correct, and less cumbersome, to attribute truth and falsehood to propositions than to sentences. As we have seen, this does not in itself commit us to the view that propositions, or other such entities, are real. Our use of intentional language may suggest their reality, but it does not logically imply it. It is still open to us to hold that the mention, or apparent mention, of these objective meanings is only a verbal convenience. But if it is only a verbal convenience, it should be dispensable. And if it is dispensable, we should be able to find a non-intentional way of stating the facts about meaning which seem to require an intentional form of expression. Our problem, then, is to discover how this can be done.

The most simple method, if it were successful, would be to have recourse to what Carnap used to call 'the formal mode of speech'. The theory then would be that talk about meaning can always be replaced by talk about the formal relations of words. Thus, to use Carnap's own examples[4], it is suggested that to say that "the word 'daystar' designates (or: means: or: is a name for) the sun" is just a way of saying that "the word 'daystar' is synonymous with 'sun' "; to say that the Latin word 'luna' designates the moon is to say that there is a valid translation "of the Latin into the English language in which the word 'moon' is the correlate of the word 'luna' "; to say that "the sentence S_1 means that the moon is spherical" is to say that "S_1 is equipollent to the sentence 'the moon is spherical' ". But the answer to this is that the suggested translations are all demonstrably incorrect. The statement that the word 'daystar' means the sun neither entails nor is entailed by the statement that the words 'sun' and 'daystar' are synonymous: for to be told that these words have the same meaning is not to be told what meaning they have; their being synonymous is logically consistent with their each meaning not the sun, but the moon, or anything else you please. In the same way, the information that a sentence means the same as the sentence 'the moon is spherical' is not sufficient, or even necessary, for us to infer that it means that the moon is spherical; not sufficient, for we have not been told what 'the moon is spherical' means; and not necessary, for the sentence in question might mean that the moon is spherical, even though the English words 'the

----

[4] Vide R. Carnap, *The Logical Syntax of Language*, Part V, Section 75.

----

moon is spherical' meant something else, or had no meaning at all. And there is the further objection, which comes out most clearly in the Latin example, that in saying that a word means what it does, one may be using English words but, unless the word in question happens to be English, one is not talking about them. The Latin word 'luna' would have the meaning that it has, even though the English language had never existed. Thus, not only does the proposed translation fail to give the information which is contained in the original sentence, but it adds a piece of gratuitous information about the existence of an English word, which the original sentence did not contain.

It may be thought that these objections are captious. Surely, if someone asks what the word 'daystar' means, it is proper to tell him that it is, or can be, used as a synonym for 'sun'; we are taking for granted that he knows what the word 'sun' means, but why should we not? If he were unfamiliar with English, we should try to substitute the corresponding word in some language which he did know. There would be no point in telling anyone that two words were synonymous unless it could be assumed that the meaning of one of them was known to him. But while this may be true, it is not to the purpose. The idea of talking about synonymity was to recast a typical set of statements about meaning in non-intentional language. It turns out, however, that this language does not do the work required of it unless statements of the kind that it was intended to eliminate are presupposed. Consequently, our object is not attained: nor can it be attained by this method. We may seem only to be talking about the relations that words bear to one another, but we shall always find that this has to be supplemented by some explicit or tacit reference to their meaning. In short, syntax cannot be made to do the work of semantics, and the language of semantics is irreducibly intentional.

If we are to find a solution to our problem, therefore, we must go further afield. The possibilities that remain are to elaborate either a causal theory of meaning, or some version of a behavioural theory, and of these I think the second is much the more promising. To my mind, the fatal defect of the causal theory, either as developed by Russell in his *Inquiry into Meaning and Truth* and elsewhere, or as developed by Ogden and Richards in their famous *Meaning of Meaning*, or indeed in any other version, is that the identification of 'using x as a sign of y' with 'being caused to produce x by y' breaks down entirely in the case where x is a substantival expression which fails in its denotation or a sentence which expresses what is false: for then there will be no y to act as a cause. Yet the meaning of x must remain the same, whether y exists or not; so that even when y does exist and has some causal relation to x, the causal and the symbolic relations cannot be identified. To this it may be replied that even if y does not exist, the production of x must be causally related to something like y, or, in the case where x is a sentence, to factors resembling those that enter into y. If I now say that there is a cat asleep on the floor beside me, I state what is false; there is, then, no such present fact to be the cause of my uttering these words. But, it is argued, I should not attach to these words the meaning that I do, unless I had had some previous experience of cats and floors and being asleep and finding things beside me: and it is reasonable to assume that these experiences have left traces which are causal factors in my present utterance. But while this may be true, it does nothing to rescue the theory. At the best, it accounts for my being able to use such a sentence correctly, but to say how certain words have come to acquire the meaning that someone gives them is not the same as saying what he uses them to mean. The false statement which my sentence serves to express does not itself refer to my past experiences, even though they may be a condition of my being able to make it; if it did refer to them it would not be false. It is about a cat and a floor, not about the words 'cat' and 'floor' or the way in which I have come to learn them. A simple proof of this is that the statement could equally well have been made in French: and surely no one would then wish to maintain that what I was really talking about was the genesis of my acquaintance with the English language.

This leaves us with what I have called the behavioural theory. In the versions of it which have so far been developed,[5] the guiding principle is that a sign tends to evoke the same behav-

[5] See especially the work of Charles Morris, in particular his *Signs, Language and Behaviour.*

iour as that which it signifies. The model used is that of the conditioned reflex in animals, or one's normal reaction to a fire alarm. Sometimes the sign is supposed to function as a preparatory stimulus, sometimes as a substitute stimulus; the distinction is in any case not sharp. On either interpretation, the theory fits certain simple cases but it falls a long way short of supplying the necessary conditions for a sign to be meaningful. The difficulties of dealing with signs that refer to the past, for example, or to fictitious events, are obvious. The proponents of this type of theory are, indeed, aware of this; they do not claim more at present than that they are laying down "a set of conditions sufficient for something to be a sign"[6]. But I do not think that even this claim can be sustained. One counter example arises in the case where someone is mistaken about the effect which a certain situation will have upon him. Then, his response to a given sign S, which he takes to be a sign of the situation A, may mimic the responses that he thinks he would make to A; but though he does not know it, these responses, which he is mimicking, are not those that he would in fact make to A, but those that he would make to a quite different situation B. It would then seem very paradoxical to say that he was really taking S to be a sign of B. Yet this is what the theory requires.

One reason why it is difficult to make a behavioural theory work is that one's reaction to a sign will be different ac-

cording as one does or does not believe in the existence of that to which it refers: if the sign is a sentence, one will react to it differently according as one does, or does not, believe in the truth of what it is used to express. Yet it may be equally well understood in either case, and understood in the same sense. It would seem, therefore, that the most promising course is to try to analyse meaning in terms of belief[7]. If this approach is successful it will, in the first instance, account for no more than the meaning of sentences. But, if the meaning of sentences can be analysed, then I think it is only a syntactical problem, though not necessarily an easy one, to deal with the meaning of individual words.

I can here give only the outline of the theory which I wish to develop. I say that a person A *assents to* an indicative sentence S when he is disposed to utter S seriously and confidently and without mental reservations and to be acquiescent when it is uttered to him. And I say that assenting to a sentence S is *constitutive* of a belief that p, when there is a *prima facie* logical incompatibility between assenting to S and disbelieving that p, and between dissenting from S and believing that p. Thus, for an English-speaking person there is a *prima facie* logical incompatibility between assenting to the sentence 'lions are carnivorous' and disbelieving that lions are carnivorous,

---

[6] Morris, *op. cit.*, p. 10.

[7] I owe this suggestion to Dr. R. W. Ashby who has developed it in an unpublished thesis on *Criteria of Descriptive Meaning*, University of London, 1954.

and between dissenting from the sentence 'lions are carnivorous' and believing that lions are carnivorous. It is necessary to put in both conditions, because with the first alone, if assenting to S were constitutive of a belief that p, assenting to S and S_1 would also be constitutive of a belief that p, however S_1 were chosen, and with the second alone, if assenting to S were constitutive of a belief that p, assenting to S or S_1 would also be constitutive of a belief that p, however S_1 were chosen. By combining them we, as it were, tailor S to p. And it is necessary to qualify the logical incompatibility as *prima facie* because in the case of some beliefs there may be a conflict of criteria. One might judge that a man believed something if one went only by his words, but when one considered his actions, one might come to think that he did not believe it after all.

I suggest, then, that the meaning of indicative sentences can be analysed as follows: given that S is a sentence, p a proposition, and A a person, S means p to A if and only if A's assenting to S is constitutive of his believing p. It is not of course implied that A does actually believe that p; all that is required is that if he did believe it his assent to S would be constitutive of the belief.

Even if this is satisfactory, so far as it goes, our task is not yet done. For our formula does not eliminate propositions; they still appear as the objects of beliefs. What is needed, therefore, is a non-intentional analysis of believing. This has fairly often been attempted but never yet with complete

success[8]. The most obvious course is to set up some such pragmatic formula as 'A believes that p if and only if A is disposed to behave in a way that is appropriate if and only if p'. But, apart from other difficulties, this is exposed to the fatal objection that A's behaviour may in fact be quite inappropriate because of his holding other false beliefs. Thus a doctor who believes that his patient has a certain disease, and wishes to cure him, may act in a way that is unlikely to achieve his end owing to his lack of medical knowledge. I think, however, that this difficulty might be met by specifying that A's behaviour must be appropriate *for him*, where the qualification 'for him' covers not only A's special circumstances and desires but also the general body of his beliefs. Clearly this brings in an element of circularity, but I think it may not be vicious; for in any particular case the behaviour which is appropriate for a given person could be specified, without our having explicitly to mention the beliefs that made it so.

I think then that this behavioural theory can be made to work. If it cannot, I see no way of avoiding the admission that our talk about meaning is basically intentional. As we have seen, this need not in itself commit us to a belief in the existence of objective meanings. We could still argue that this was not a genuine theory; but it might well be regarded as a weakness in our position that we had had no better theory to put in its place.

---

[8] Cf. R. M. Chisholm, *Sentences About Believing*, "Proceedings of the Aristotelian Society", 1955–56.

3.3

CONSTATIVES
AND PERFORMATIVES

John Austin

One can quite easily get the idea of the performative utterance—though the expression, as I am well aware, does not exist in the French language, or anywhere else. This idea was brought in to mark a contrast with that of the declarative utterance, or rather, as I am going to call it, the constative utterance. And there we have straight off what I want to call in question. Ought we to accept this Performative-Constative antithesis?

The constative utterance, under the name, so dear to philosophers, of *statement*, has the property of being true or false. The performative utterance, by contrast, can never be either: it has its own special job, it is used to perform an action. To issue such an utterance *is* to perform the action—an action, perhaps, which one scarcely

could perform, at least with so much precision, in any other way. Here are some examples:

> I name this ship 'Liberté'.
> I apologise.
> I welcome you.
> I advise you to do it.

Utterances of this kind are common enough: we find them, for instance, everywhere in what are called in English the 'operative' clauses of a legal instrument.[1] Plainly, many of them are not without interest for philosophers: to say 'I promise to . . .'—to issue, as we say, this performative utterance— just *is* the act of making a promise; not, as we see, at all a mysterious act. And it may seem at once quite obvious that an utterance of this kind can't be true or false—notice that I say it can't *be* true or false, because it may very well *imply* that some *other* propositions are true or are false, but that, if

From "Performative-Constative," G. J. Warnock, trans., in *Philosophy and Ordinary Language*, Charles Caton, editor (Urbana, Ill.: University of Illinois Press, 1963). Reprinted by permission of Les Editions de Minuit, publishers of the original French version in *La Philosophie Analytique* (Paris, 1962).

---

[1] The clauses, that is to say, in which the legal act is actually performed, as opposed to those—the 'preamble'—which set out the circumstances of the transaction.

I'm not mistaken, is a quite different matter.

However, the performative utterance is not exempt from all criticism: it may very well be criticized, but in a quite different dimension from that of truth and falsity. The performative must be issued in a situation appropriate in all respects for the act in question: if the speaker is not in the conditions required for its performance (and there are many such conditions), then his utterance will be, as we call it in general, 'unhappy'.

First, our performative, like any other ritual or ceremony, may be, as the lawyers say, 'null and void'. If, for example, the speaker is not in a position to perform an act of that kind, or if the object with respect to which he purports to perform it is not suitable for the purpose, then he doesn't manage, simply by issuing his utterance, to carry out the purported act. Thus a bigamist doesn't get married a second time, he only 'goes through the form' of a second marriage; I can't name the ship if I am not the person properly authorized to name it; and I can't quite bring off the baptism of penguins, those creatures being scarcely susceptible of that exploit.

Second, a performative utterance may be, though not void, 'unhappy' in a different way—if, that is, it is issued *insincerely*. If I say 'I promise to . . .' without in the least intending to carry out the promised action, perhaps even not believing that it is in my power to carry it out, the promise is hollow. It is made, certainly; but still, there is an 'unhappiness': I have *abused* the formula.

Let us now suppose that our act has been performed: everything has gone off quite normally, and also, if you like, sincerely. In that case, the performative utterance will characteristically 'take effect'. We do not mean by that that such-and-such a future event is or will be brought about as an effect of this action functioning as a cause. We mean rather that, in consequence of the performance of this act, such-and-such a future event, *if* it happens, will be *in order*, and such-and-such other events, *if* they happen, will not be in order. If I have said 'I promise', I shall not be in order if I break my word; if I have said 'I welcome you', I shall not be in order if I proceed to treat you as an enemy or an intruder. Thus we say that, even when the performative has taken effect, there may always crop up a third kind of unhappiness, which we call 'breach of commitment'. We may note also that commitments can be more or less vague, and can bind us in very different degrees.

There we have, then, three kinds of unhappiness associated with the performative utterance. It is possible to make a complete classification of these unhappinesses; but it must be admitted that, as practically goes without saying, the different kinds may not always be sharply distinguishable and may even coincide. Then we must add that our performative is both an *action* and an *utterance*: so that, poor thing, it can't help being liable to be substandard in all the ways in which actions in general can be, as well as those in which utterances in general can be. For example, the performative may be issued under duress, or by accident; it may suffer from defective grammar, or from misunderstanding; it may figure in a context not wholly 'serious', in a play, perhaps, or in a poem. We leave all that on one side—let us simply bear in mind the more specific unhappinesses of the performative, that is, nullity, abuse (insincerity), and breach of commitment.

Well, now that we have before us this idea of the performative, it is very natural to hope that we could proceed to find some criterion, whether of grammar or of vocabulary, which would make it possible for us to answer in every case the question whether a particular utterance is performative or not. But this hope is, alas, exaggerated and, in large measure, vain.

It is true that there exist two 'normal forms', so to speak, in which the performative finds expression. At first sight both of them, curiously enough, have a thoroughly constative look. One of these normal forms is that which I have already made use of in producing my examples: the utterance leads off with a verb in the first person singular of the present indicative active, as in 'I promise you that . . .'. The other form, which comes to exactly the same but is more common in utterances issued in writing, employs by contrast a verb in the *passive* voice and in the *second* or *third* person of the present indicative, as in 'Passengers are requested to cross the line by the footbridge only'. If we ask ourselves, as sometimes we may, whether a given utterance of this form is performative or constative, we may settle the question by asking whether it would be possible to insert in it the word 'hereby' or some equiva-

lent—as, in French, the phrase 'par ces mots-ci'.

By way of putting to the test utterances which one might take to be performative, we make use of a well-known asymmetry, in the case of what we call an 'explicit performative' verb, between the first person singular of the present indicative, and other persons and tenses of the same verb. Thus, 'I promise' is a formula which is used to perform the act of promising; 'I promised', on the other hand, or 'he promises', are expressions which serve simply to describe or report an act of promising, not to perform one.

However, it is not in the least necessary that an utterance, if it is to be performative, should be expressed in one of these so-called normal forms. To say 'Shut the door', plainly enough, is every bit as performative, every bit as much the performance of an act, as to say 'I order you to shut the door'. Even the word 'Dog' by itself can sometimes (at any rate in England, a country more practical than ceremonious) stand in place of an explicit and formal performative; one performs, by this little word, the very same act as by the utterance 'I warn you that the dog is about to attack us', or by 'Strangers are warned that here there is a vicious dog'. To make our utterance performative, and quite unambiguously so, we can make use, in place of the explicit formula, of a whole lot of more primitive devices such as intonation, for instance, or gesture; further, and above all, the very context in which the words are uttered can make it entirely certain how they are to be taken—as a description, for example, or again as a warning. Does this word 'Dog' just give us a bit of detail about the local fauna? In the context—when confronted, that is, with the notice on the gate—we just don't need to ask ourselves that question at all.

All we can really say is that our explicit performative formula ('I promise . . .', 'I order you . . .', etc.) serves to make explicit, and at the same time more precise, what act it is that the speaker purports to perform in issuing his utterance. I say 'to make explicit', and that is not at all the same thing as to *state*. Bending low before you, I remove my hat, or perhaps I say 'Salaam'; then, certainly, I am doing obeisance to you, not just engaging in gymnastics; but the word 'Salaam' does not, any more than does the act of removing my hat, in any way *state* that I am doing obeisance to you. It is in this way that our formula *makes* the issuing of the utterance that action which it is, but does not *state* that it is that action.

The other forms of expression, those that have no explicit performative formula, will be more primitive and less precise, one might almost say more vague. If I say simply 'I will be there', there will be no telling, just by considering the words, whether I am taking on a commitment, or declaring an intention, or making perhaps a fatalistic prediction. One may think of the precise formulae as a relatively recent phenomenon in the evolution of language, and as going together with the evolution of more complex forms of society and science.

We can't, then, expect any purely verbal criterion of the performative.

We may hope, all the same, that any utterance which is in fact performative will be reducible (in some sense of that word) to an utterance in one or the other of our normal forms. Then, going on from there, we should be able, with the help of a dictionary, to make a list of all the verbs which can figure in one of our explicit formulae. Thus we will achieve a useful classification of all the varieties of acts that we perform in saying something (in one sense, at least, of that ambiguous phrase).

We have now brought in, then, the ideas of the performative utterance, of its unhappinesses, and of its explicit formulae. But we have been talking all along as if every utterance had to be *either* constative *or* performative, and as if the idea of the constative at any rate was as clear as it is familiar. But it is not.

Let us note in the first place that an utterance which is undoubtedly a statement of fact, therefore constative, can fail to get by in more than one way. It can be untrue, to be sure; but it can also be absurd, and that not necessarily in some gross fashion (by being, for instance, ungrammatical). I would like to take a closer look at three rather more subtle ways of being absurd, two of which have only recently come to light.

(1) Someone says 'All John's children are bald, but [or 'and'] John has no children'; or perhaps he says 'All John's children are bald', when, as a matter of fact, John has no children.

(2) Someone says 'The cat is on the mat, but [or 'and'] I don't be-

lieve it is'; or perhaps he says 'The cat is on the mat', when, as a matter of fact, he does not believe it is.

(3) Someone says 'All the guests are French, and some of them aren't'; or perhaps he says 'All the guests are French', and then afterwards says 'Some of the guests are not French'.

In each of these cases one experiences a feeling of outrage, and it's possible each time for us to try to express it in terms of the same word—'implication', or perhaps that word that we always find so handy, 'contradiction'. But there are more ways of killing the cat than drowning it in butter,[2] and equally, to do violence to language one does not always need a contradiction.

Let us use the three terms 'presuppose', 'imply', and 'entail' for our three cases respectively. Then:

1. Not only 'John's children are bald', but equally 'John's children are not bald', presupposes that John has children. To talk about those children, or to refer to them, presupposes that they exist. By contrast, 'The cat is not on the mat' does *not*, equally with 'The cat is on the mat', imply that I believe it is; and similarly, 'None of the guests is French' does *not*, equally with 'All the guests are French', entail that it is false that some of the guests are not French.

2. We can quite well say 'It could be

the case both that the cat is on the mat and that I do not believe it is'. That is to say, those two propositions are not in the least incompatible: both can be true together. What is impossible is to state both at the same time: his *stating* that the cat is on the mat is what implies that the speaker believes it is. By contrast, we couldn't say 'It could be the case both that John has no children and that his children are bald'; just as we couldn't say 'It could be the case both that all the guests are French and that some of them are not French'.

3. If 'All the guests are French' entails 'It is not the case that some of the guests are not French', then 'Some of the guests are not French' entails 'It is not the case that all the guests are French'. It's a question here of the compatibility and incompatibility of propositions. By contrast, it isn't like this with presupposition: if 'John's children are bald' presupposes that John has children, it isn't true at all that 'John has no children' presupposes that John's children are not bald. Similarly, if 'The cat is on the mat' implies that I believe it is, it isn't true at all that to say 'I don't believe that the cat is on the mat' implies that the cat is not on the mat (not, at any rate, in the same sense of 'implies'; besides, we have already seen that 'implication', for us, is not a matter of the incompatibility of propositions).

Here then are three ways in which a statement can fail to get by without being untrue, and without being a sheer rigmarole either. I would like to call attention to the fact that these three ways of failing to get by correspond

---

[2] English proverb. I am told that this rather refined way of disposing of cats is not found in France.

to three of the ways in which a performative utterance may be unhappy. To bring out the comparison, let's first take two performative utterances:

4. 'I bequeath my watch to you, but [or 'and'] I haven't got a watch'; or perhaps someone says 'I bequeath my watch to you' when he hasn't got a watch.

5. 'I promise to be there, but [or 'and'] I have no intention of being there'; or perhaps someone says 'I promise to be there' when he doesn't intend to be there.

We compare case 4 with case 1, the case, that is, of presupposition. For to say either 'I bequeath my watch to you' or 'I don't bequeath my watch to you' presupposes equally that I have a watch; that the watch exists is presupposed by the fact that it is spoken of or referred to, in the performative utterance just as much as in the constative utterance. And just as we can make use here of the term 'presupposition' as employed in the doctrine of the constative, equally we can take over for that doctrine the term 'void' as employed in the doctrine of the unhappinesses of the performative. The statement on the subject of John's children is, we may say, 'void for lack of reference', which is exactly what lawyers would say about the purported bequest of the watch. So here is a first instance in which a trouble that afflicts statements turns out to be identical with one of the unhappinesses typical of the performative utterance.

We compare case 5 with case 2, that is, the case where something is 'implied'. Just as my saying that the cat is on the mat implies that I believe it is, so my saying I promise to be there implies that I intend to be there. The procedure of stating is designed for those who honestly believe what they say, exactly as the procedure of promising is designed for those who have a certain intention, namely, the intention to do whatever it may be that they promise. If we don't hold the belief, or again don't have the intention, appropriate to the content of our utterance, then in each case there is lack of sincerity and abuse of the procedure. If, at the same time as we make the statement or the promise, we announce in the same breath that we don't believe it or we don't intend to, then the utterance is 'self-voiding,' as we might call it; and hence our feeling of outrage on hearing it. Another instance, then, where a trouble which afflicts statements is identical with one of the unhappinesses which afflict performative utterances.

Let us look back, next, to case 3, the case of entailment among statements. Can we find, in the case of performatives, some analogue for this as well? When I make the statement, for instance, 'All the guests are French', do I not commit myself in a more or less rigorous fashion to behaving in future in such-and-such a way, in particular with respect to the statements I will make? If, in the sequel, I state things incompatible with my utterance (namely, that all the guests are French), there will be a breach of commitment that one might well compare with that of the case in which I say 'I welcome you', and then proceed to treat you as an enemy or an intruder—and perhaps even better, with that of which one is guilty when one says 'I define the word thus' (a performative utterance) and then proceeds to use the word with a different meaning.

So then, it seems to me that the constative utterance is every bit as liable to unhappinesses as the performative utterance, and indeed to pretty much the same unhappinesses. Furthermore, making use of the key provided by our list of unhappinesses noted for the case of performatives, we can ask ourselves whether there are not still more unhappinesses in the case of statements, besides the three we have just mentioned. For example, it often happens that a performative is void because the utterer is not in a state, or not in a position, to perform the act which he purports to perform; thus, it's no good my saying 'I order you' if I have no authority over you: I can't order you, my utterance is void, my act is only purported. Now people have, I know, the impression that where a statement, a constative utterance, is in question, the case is quite different: anybody at all can state anything at all. What if he's ill-informed? Well then, one can be mistaken, that's all. It's a free country, isn't it? To state what isn't true is one of the Rights of Man. However, this impression can lead us into error. In reality nothing is more common than to find that one can state absolutely nothing on some subject, because one is simply not in a position to state whatever it may be—and this may come about, too, for more than one reason. I *cannot* state at this moment how many people there are in the next room: I haven't been to see, I haven't

found out the facts. What if I say, nevertheless, 'At this moment there are fifty people in the next room'? You will allow, perhaps, that in saying that I have made a guess, but you will not allow that I have made a statement, not at any rate without adding 'but he had no right whatever to do so'; and in this case my 'I state . . .' is exactly on a par with our 'I order . . .', said, we remember, without any right to give an order. Here's another example. You confide to me 'I'm bored', and I quite coolly reply 'You're not'. You say 'What do you mean, I'm not? What right have you to say how I feel?' I say 'But what do *you* mean, what right have I? I'm just stating what your feelings are, that's all. I may be mistaken, certainly, but what of that? I suppose one can always make a simple statement, can't one?' But no, one can't always: usually, I can't state what your feelings are, unless you have disclosed them to me.

So far I have called attention to two things: that there is no purely verbal criterion by which to distinguish the performative from the constative utterance, and that the constative is liable to the same unhappinesses as the performative. Now we must ask ourselves whether issuing a constative utterance is not, after all, the performance of an act, the act, namely, of stating. Is stating an act in the same sense as marrying, apologising, betting, etc.? I can't plumb this mystery any further at present. But it is already pretty evident that the formula 'I state that . . .' is closely similar to the formula 'I warn you that . . .'—a formula which, as we put it, serves to make explicit what speech-act it is that we are performing; and also, that one can't issue any utterance whatever without performing some speech-act of this kind.

What we need, perhaps, is a more general theory of these speech-acts, and in this theory our Constative-Performative antithesis will scarcely survive.

Here and now it remains for us to examine, quite briefly, this craze for being either true or false, something which people think is peculiar to statements alone and ought to be set up on a pedestal of its own, above the battle. And this time let's begin with the performative utterance: is it the case that there is nothing here in the least analogous with truth?

To begin with, it is clear that if we establish that a performative utterance is not unhappy, that is, that its author has performed his act happily and in all sincerity, that still does not suffice to set it beyond the reach of all criticism. It may always be criticised in a different dimension.

Let us suppose that I say to you 'I advise you to do it'; and let us allow that all the circumstances are appropriate, the conditions for success are fulfilled. In saying that, I actually do advise you to do it—it is not that I *state*, truely or falsely, *that* I advise you. It is, then, a performative utterance. There does still arise, all the same, a little question: was the advice good or bad? Agreed, I spoke in all sincerity, I believed that to do it would be in your interest; but was I right? Was my belief, in these circumstances, justified? Or again—though perhaps this matters less —was it in fact, or as things turned out, in your interest? There is confrontation of my utterance with the situation in, and the situation with respect to which, it was issued. I was fully justified perhaps, but was I right?

Many other utterances which have an incontestably performative flavour are exposed to this second kind of criticism. Allowing that, in declaring the accused guilty, you have reached your verdict properly and in good faith, it still remains to ask whether the verdict was just, or fair. Allowing that you had the right to reprimand him as you did, and that you have acted without malice, one can still ask whether your reprimand was deserved. Here again we have confrontation with the facts, including the circumstances of the occasion of utterance.

That not all performative utterances without exception are liable to this quasi-objective evaluation—which for that matter must here be left pretty vague and multifarious—may very well be true.

There is one thing that people will be particularly tempted to bring up as an objection against any comparison between this second kind of criticism and the kind appropriate to statements, and that is this: aren't these questions about something's being good, or just, or fair, or deserved entirely distinct from questions of truth and falsehood? That, surely, is a very simple black-and-white business: either the utterance corresponds to the facts or it doesn't, and that's that.

Well, I for my part don't think it is. Even if there exists a well-defined class of statements and we can restrict ourselves to that, this class will always be pretty wide. In this class we shall have the following statements:

France is hexagonal.
Lord Raglan won the battle of Alma.
Oxford is 60 miles from London.

It's quite true that for each of these statements we can raise the question 'true or false'. But it is only in quite favourable cases that we ought to expect an answer yes or no, once and for all. When the question is raised one understands that the utterance is to be confronted in one way or another with the facts. Very well. So let's confront 'France is hexagonal' with France. What are we to say, is it true or not? The question, plainly, oversimplifies things. Oh well, up to a point if you like, I see what you mean, true perhaps for some purposes or in some contexts, that would do for the man in the street but not for geographers. And so on. It's a rough statement, no denying that, but one can't just say straight out that it's false. Then Alma, a soldier's battle if ever there was one; it's true that Lord Raglan was in command of the allied army, and that this army to some extent won a confused sort of victory; yes, that would be a fair enough judgment, even well deserved, for schoolchildren anyway, though really it's a bit

of an exaggeration. And Oxford, well, yes, it's true that that city is 60 miles from London, so long as you want only a certain degree of precision.

Under the heading 'truth' what we in fact have is, not a simple quality nor a relation, not indeed *one* anything, but rather a whole dimension of criticism. We can get some idea, perhaps not a very clear one, of this criticism; what *is* clear is that there is a whole lot of things to be considered and weighed up in this dimension alone—the facts, yes, but also the situation of the speaker, his purpose in speaking, his hearer, questions of precision, etc. If we are content to restrict ourselves to statements of an idiotic or ideal simplicity, we shall never succeed in disentangling the true from the just, fair, deserved, precise, exaggerated, etc., the summary and the detail, the full and the concise, and so on.

From this side also, then, from the side of truth and falsehood, we feel ourselves driven to think again about the the Performative-Constative antithesis. What we need, it seems to me, is a new doctrine, both complete and general, of *what one is doing in saying something*, in all the senses of that ambiguous phrase, and of what I call the speech-act, not just in this or that aspect abstracting from all the rest, but taken in its totality.

MEANING   3.4

H. P. Grice

Consider the following sentences:

"Those spots mean (meant) measles."
"Those spots didn't mean anything to me, but to the doctor they meant measles."
"The recent budget means that we shall have a hard year."

(1) I cannot say, "Those spots meant measles, but he hadn't got measles," and I cannot say, "The recent budget means that we shall have a hard year, but we shan't have." That is to say, in cases like the above, *x meant that p* and *x means that p* entail *p*.

(2) I cannot argue from "Those spots mean (meant) measles" to any conclusion about "what is (was) meant by those spots"; for example, I am not entitled to say, "What was meant by those spots was that he had measles." Equally I cannot draw from the statement about the recent budget the conclusion "What is meant by the recent budget is that we shall have a hard year."

(3) I cannot argue from "Those spots meant measles" to any conclusion to the effect that somebody or other meant by those spots so-and-so. *Mutatis mutandis*, the same is true of the sentence about the recent budget.

(4) For none of the above examples can a restatement be found in which the verb "mean" is followed by a sentence or phrase in inverted commas. Thus "Those spots meant measles" cannot be reformulated as "Those spots meant 'measles' " or as "Those spots meant 'he has measles.' "

(5) On the other hand, for all these examples an approximate restatement can be found beginning with the phrase "The fact that . . ."; for example, "The fact that he had those spots meant that he had measles" and "The fact that the recent budget was as it was means that we shall have a hard year."

Now contrast the above sentences with the following:

"Those three rings on the bell (of the bus) mean that the 'bus is full.' "

From *The Philosophical Review*, LXVI (1957). Reprinted by permission of the editors.

"That remark, 'Smith couldn't get on without his trouble and strife,' meant that Smith found his wife indispensable."

(1) I can use the first of these and go on to say, "But it isn't in fact full—the conductor has made a mistake"; and I can use the second and go on, "But in fact Smith deserted her seven years ago." That is to say, here x *means that* p and x *meant that* p do not entail p.

(2) I can argue from the first to some statement about "what is (was) meant" by the rings on the bell and from the second to some statement about "what is (was) meant" by the quoted remark.

(3) I can argue from the first sentence to the conclusion that somebody (viz., the conductor) meant, or at any rate should have meant, by the rings that the bus is full, and I can argue analogously for the second sentence.

(4) The first sentence can be restated in a form in which the verb "mean" is followed by a phrase in inverted commas, that is, "Those three rings on the bell mean 'the bus is full.'" So also can the second sentence.

(5) Such a sentence as "The fact that the bell has been rung three times means that the bus is full" is not a restatement of the meaning of the first sentence. Both may be true, but they do not have, even approximately, the same meaning.

When the expressions "means," "means something," "means that" are used in the kind of way in which they are used in the first set of sentences, I shall speak of the sense, or senses, in which they are used, as the *natural* sense, or senses, of the expressions in question. When the expressions are used in the kind of way in which they are used in the second set of sentences, I shall speak of the sense, or senses, in which they are used, as the *nonnatural* sense, or senses, of the expressions in question. I shall use the abbreviation "means$_{NN}$" to distinguish the nonnatural sense or senses.

I propose, for convenience, also to include under the head of natural senses of "mean" such senses of "mean" as may be exemplified in sentences of the pattern "A means (meant) *to do* so-and-so (by x)," where A is a human agent. By contrast, as the previous examples show, I include under the head of nonnatural senses of "mean" any senses of "mean" found in sentences of the patterns "A means (meant) something by x" or "A means (meant) by x that. . . ." (This is overrigid; but it will serve as an indication.)

I do not want to maintain that *all* our uses of "mean" fall easily, obviously, and tidily into one of the two groups I have distinguished; but I think that in most cases we should be at least fairly strongly inclined to assimilate a use of "mean" to one group rather than to the other. The question which now arises is this: "What more can be said about the distinction between the cases where we should say that the word is applied in a natural sense and the cases where we should say that the word is applied in a nonnatural sense?" Asking this question will not of course prohibit us from trying to give an explanation of "meaning$_{NN}$" in terms of one or another natural sense of "mean."

This question about the distinction between natural and nonnatural meaning is, I think, what people are getting at when they display an interest in a distinction between "natural" and "conventional" signs. But I think my formulation is better. For some things which can mean$_{NN}$ something are not signs (e.g., words are not), and some are not conventional in any ordinary sense (e.g., certain gestures); while some things which mean naturally are not signs of what they mean (cf. the recent budget example).

I want first to consider briefly, and reject, what I might term a causal type of answer to the question, "What is meaning$_{NN}$?" We might try to say, for instance, more or less with C. L. Stevenson,[1] that for x to mean$_{NN}$ something, x must have (roughly) a tendency to produce in an audience some attitude (cognitive or otherwise) and a tendency, in the case of a speaker, to *be* produced *by* that attitude, these tendencies being dependent on "an elaborate process of conditioning attending the use of the sign in communication."[2] This clearly will not do.

(1) Let us consider a case where an utterance, if it qualifies at all as meaning$_{NN}$ something, will be of a descriptive or informative kind and the relevant attitude, therefore, will be a cognitive one, for example, a belief. (I use "utterance" as a neutral word to apply to any candidate for meaning$_{NN}$; it has a convenient act-object ambiguity.) It is no doubt the case that many people have a tendency to put on a tail coat when they think they are about to go to

a dance, and it is no doubt also the case that many people, on seeing someone put on a tail coat, would conclude that the person in question was about to go to a dance. Does this satisfy us that putting on a tail coat means$_{NN}$ that one is about to go to a dance (or indeed means$_{NN}$ anything at all)? Obviously not. It is no help to refer to the qualifying phrase "dependent on an elaborate process of conditioning. . . ." For if all this means is that the response to the sight of a tail coat being put on is in some way learned or acquired, it will not exclude the present case from being one of meaning$_{NN}$. But if we have to take seriously the second part of the qualifying phrase ("attending the use of the sign in communication"), then the account of meaning$_{NN}$ is obviously circular. We might just as well say, "X has meaning$_{NN}$ if it is used in communication," which, though true, is not helpful.

(2) If this is not enough, there is a difficulty—really the same difficulty, I think—which Stevenson recognizes: how we are to avoid saying, for example, that "Jones is tall" is part of what is meant by "Jones is an athlete," since to tell someone that Jones is an athlete would tend to make him believe that Jones is tall. Stevenson here resorts to invoking linguistic rules, namely, a permissive rule of language that "athletes may be nontall." This amounts to saying that we are not prohibited by rule from speaking of "nontall athletes." But why are we not prohibited? Not because it is not bad grammar, or is not impolite, and so on, but presumably because it is not meaningless (or, if this is too strong, does not in any way violate the rules

---

[1] *Ethics and Language* (New Haven, 1944), ch. iii.

[2] *Ibid.*, p. 57.

of meaning for the expressions concerned). But this seems to involve us in another circle. Moreover, one wants to ask why, if it is legitimate to appeal here to rules to distinguish what is meant from what is suggested, this appeal was not made earlier, in the case of groans, for example, to deal with which Stevenson originally introduced the qualifying phrase about dependence on conditioning.

A further deficiency in a causal theory of the type just expounded seems to be that, even if we accept it as it stands, we are furnished with an analysis only of statements about the *standard* meaning, or the meaning in general, of a "sign." No provision is made for dealing with statements about what a particular speaker or writer means by a sign on a particular occasion (which may well diverge from the standard meaning of the sign); nor is it obvious how the theory could be adapted to make such provision. One might even go further in criticism and maintain that the causal theory ignores the fact that the meaning (in general) of a sign needs to be explained in terms of what users of the sign do (or should) mean by it on particular occasions; and so the latter notion, which is unexplained by the causal theory, is in fact the fundamental one. I am sympathetic to this more radical criticism, though I am aware that the point is controversial.

I do not propose to consider any further theories of the "causal-tendency" type. I suspect no such theory could avoid difficulties analogous to those I have outlined without utterly losing its claim to rank as a theory of this type.

I will now try a different and, I hope, more promising line. If we can elucidate the meaning of

  "x meant$_{NN}$ something (on a particular occasion)" and
  "x meant$_{NN}$ that so-and-so (on a particular occasion)"

and of

  "A meant$_{NN}$ something by x (on a particular occasion)" and
  "A meant$_{NN}$ by x that so-and-so (on a particular occasion),"

this might reasonably be expected to help us with

  "x means$_{NN}$ (timeless) something (that so-and-so),"
  "A means$_{NN}$ (timeless) by x something (that so-and-so),"

and with the explication of "means the same as," "understands," "entails," and so on. Let us for the moment pretend that we have to deal only with utterances which might be informative or descriptive.

A first shot would be to suggest that "x meant$_{NN}$ something" would be true if x was intended by its utterer to induce a belief in some "audience" and that to say what the belief was would be to say what x meant$_{NN}$. This will not do. I might leave B's handkerchief near the scene of a murder in order to induce the detective to believe that B was the murderer; but we should not want to say that the handkerchief (or my leaving it there) meant$_{NN}$ anything or that I had meant$_{NN}$ by leaving it that B was the murderer. Clearly we must at least add that, for x to have meant$_{NN}$ anything, not merely must it have been "uttered" with the intention of inducing a certain belief but also the utterer must have intended an "audience" to recognize the intention behind the utterance.

This, though perhaps better, is not good enough. Consider the following cases:

(1) Herod presents Salome with the head of St. John the Baptist on a charger.

(2) Feeling faint, a child lets its mother see how pale it is (hoping that she may draw her own conclusions and help).

(3) I leave the china my daughter has broken lying around for my wife to see.

Here we seem to have cases which satisfy the conditions so far given for meaning$_{NN}$. For example, Herod intended to make Salome believe that St. John the Baptist was dead and no doubt also intended Salome to recognize that he intended her to believe that St. John the Baptist was dead. Similarly for the other cases. Yet I certainly do not think that we should want to say that we have here cases of meaning$_{NN}$.

What we want to find is the difference between, for example, "deliberately and openly letting someone know" and "telling" and between "getting someone to think" and "telling."

The way out is perhaps as follows. Compare the following two cases:

(1) I show Mr. X a photograph of Mr. Y displaying undue familiarity to Mrs. X.

(2) I draw a picture of Mr. Y behaving in this manner and show it to Mr. X.

I find that I want to deny that in (1) the photograph (or my showing it to Mr. X) meant$_{NN}$ anything at all; while I want to assert that in (2) the picture (or my drawing and showing it) meant$_{NN}$ something (that Mr. Y had been unduly unfamiliar), or at least that I had meant$_{NN}$ by it that Mr. Y had been unduly familiar. What is the difference between the two cases? Surely that in case (1) Mr. X's recognition of my intention to make him believe that there is something between Mr. Y and Mrs X is (more or less) irrelevant to the production of this effect by the photograph. Mr. X would be led by the photograph at least to suspect Mrs. X even if instead of showing it to him I had left it in his room by accident; and I (the photograph shower) would not be unaware of this. But it will make a difference to the effect of my picture on Mr. X whether or not he takes me to be intending to inform him (make him believe something) about Mrs. X, and not to be just doodling or trying to produce a work of art.

But now we seem to be landed in a further difficulty if we accept this account. For consider now, say, frowning. If I frown spontaneously, in the ordinary course of events, someone looking at me may well treat the frown as a natural sign of displeasure. But if I frown deliberately (to convey my displeasure), an onlooker may be expected, provided he recognizes my intention, *still* to conclude that I am displeased. Ought we not then to say, since it could not be expected to make any difference to the onlooker's reaction whether he regards my frown as spontaneous or as intended to be informative, that my frown (deliberate) does *not* mean$_{NN}$ anything? I think this difficulty can be met; for though in general a deliberate frown may have the same effect (as regards inducing belief in my displeasure) as a spontaneous frown, it can be expected to have the same effect only *provided* the audience takes it as intended to convey displeasure. That is, if we take away the recognition of intention, leaving the other circumstances (including the recognition of the frown as deliberate), the belief-producing tendency of the frown must be regarded as being impaired or destroyed.

Perhaps we may sum up what is necessary for A to mean something by x as follows. A must intend to induce by x a belief in an audience, and he must also intend his utterance to be recognized as so intended. But these intentions are not independent; the recognition is intended by A to play its part in inducing the belief, and if it does not do so something will have gone wrong with the fulfillment of A's intentions. Moreover, A's intending that the recognition should play this part implies, I think, that he assumes that there is some chance that it will in fact play this part, that he does not regard it as a foregone conclusion that the belief will be induced in the audience whether or not the intention behind the utterance is recognized. Shortly, perhaps, we may say that "A meant$_{NN}$ something by x" is roughly equivalent to "A uttered x with the intention of inducing a belief by means of the recognition of this in-

tention." (This seems to involve a reflexive paradox, but it does not really do so.)

Now perhaps it is time to drop the pretense that we have to deal only with "informative" cases. Let us start with some examples of imperatives or quasi-imperatives. I have a very avaricious man in my room, and I want him to go; so I throw a pound note out of the window. Is there here any utterance with a meaning$_{NN}$? No, because in behaving as I did, I did not intend his recognition of my purpose to be in any way effective in getting him to go. This is parallel to the photograph case. If on the other hand I had pointed to the door or given him a little push, then my behavior might well be held to constitute a meaningful$_{NN}$ utterance, just because the recognition of my intention would be intended by me to be effective in speeding his departure. Another pair of cases would be (1) a policeman who stops a car by standing in its way and (2) a policeman who stops a car by waving.

Or, to turn briefly to another type of case, if as an examiner I fail a man, I may well cause him distress or indignation or humiliation; and if I am vindictive, I may intend this effect and even intend him to recognize my intention. But I should not be inclined to say that my failing him meant$_{NN}$ anything. On the other hand, if I cut someone in the street I do feel inclined to assimilate this to the cases of meaning$_{NN}$, and this inclination seems to me dependent on the fact that I could not reasonably expect him to be distressed (indignant, humiliated) unless he recognized my intention to affect him in this way. (Cf., if my college stopped my salary altogether I should accuse them of ruining me; if they cut it by $2/6^d$ I might accuse them of insulting me; with some intermediate amounts I might not know quite what to say.)

Perhaps then we may make the following generalizations.

(1) "A meant$_{NN}$ something by x" is (roughly) equivalent to "A intended the utterance of x to produce some effect in an audience by means of the recognition of this intention"; and we may add that to ask what A meant is to ask for a specification of the intended effect (though, of course, it may not always be possible to get a straight answer involving a "that" clause, for example, "a belief that ...").

(2) "x meant something" is (roughly) equivalent to "Somebody meant$_{NN}$ something by x." Here again there will be cases where this will not quite work. I feel inclined to say that (as regards traffic lights) the change to red meant$_{NN}$ that the traffic was to stop; but it would be very unnatural to say, "Somebody (e.g., the Corporation) meant$_{NN}$ by the red-light change that the traffic was to stop." Nevertheless, there seems to be *some* sort of reference to somebody's intentions.

(3) "x means$_{NN}$ (timeless) that so-and-so" might as a first shot be equated with some statement or disjunction of statements about what "people" (vague) intend (with qualifications about "recognition") to effect by x. I shall have a word to say about this.

Will any kind of intended effect do, or may there be cases where an effect is intended (with the required qualifications) and yet we should not want

to talk of meaning$_{NN}$? Suppose I discovered some person so constituted that, when I told him that whenever I grunted in a special way I wanted him to blush or to incur some physical malady, thereafter whenever he recognized the grunt (and with it my intention), he did blush or incur the malady. Should we then want to say that the grunt meant$_{NN}$ something? I do not think so. This points to the fact that for x to have meaning$_{NN}$, the intended effect must be something which in some sense is within the control of the audience, or that in some sense of "reason" the recognition of the intention behind x is for the audience a reason and not merely a cause. It might look as if there is a sort of pun here ("reason for believing" and "reason for doing"), but I do not think this is serious. For though no doubt from one point of view questions about reasons for believing are questions about evidence and so quite different from questions about reasons for doing, nevertheless to recognize an utterer's intention in uttering x (descriptive utterance), to have a reason for believing that so-and-so, is at least quite like "having a motive for" accepting so-and-so. Decisions "that" seem to involve decisions "to" (and this is why we can "refuse to believe" and also be "compelled to believe"). (The "cutting" case needs slightly different treatment, for one cannot in any straightforward sense "decide" to be offended; but one can refuse to be offended.) It looks then as if the intended effect must be something within the control of the audience, or at least the *sort* of thing which is within its control.

One point before passing to an objection or two. I think it follows that from what I have said about the connection between meaning$_{NN}$ and recognition of intention that (insofar as I am right) only what I may call the primary intention of an utterer is relevant to the meaning$_{NN}$ of an utterance. For if I utter x, intending (with the aid of the recognition of this intention) to induce an effect E, and intend this effect E to lead to a further effect F, then insofar as the occurrence of F is thought to be dependent solely on E, I cannot regard F as in the least dependent on recognition of my intention to induce E. That is, if (say) I intend to get a man to do something by giving him some information, it cannot be regarded as relevant to the meaning$_{NN}$ of my utterance to describe what I intend him to do.

Now some question may be raised about my use, fairly free, of such words as "intention" and "recognition." I must disclaim any intention of peopling all our talking life with armies of complicated psychological occurrences. I do not hope to solve any philosophical puzzles about intending, but I do want briefly to argue that no special difficulties are raised by my use of the word "intention" in connection with meaning. First, there will be cases where an utterance is accompanied or preceded by a conscious "plan," or explicit formulation of intention (e.g., I declare how I am going to use x, or ask myself how to "get something across"). The presence of such an explicit "plan" obviously counts fairly heavily in favor of the utterer's intention (meaning) being as "planned"; though it is not, I think, conclusive; for example, a speaker who has declared an intention to use a fa-

miliar expression in an unfamiliar way may slip into the familiar use. Similarly in nonlinguistic cases: if we are asking about an agent's intention, a previous expression counts heavily; nevertheless, a man might plan to throw a letter in the dustbin and yet take it to the post; when lifting his hand he might "come to" and say *either* "I didn't intend to do this at all" *or* "I suppose I must have been intending to put it in."

Explicitly formulated linguistic (or quasi-linguistic) intentions are no doubt comparatively rare. In their absence we would seem to rely on very much the same kinds of criteria as we do in the case of nonlinguistic intentions where there is a general usage. An utterer is held to intend to convey what is normally conveyed (or normally intended to be conveyed), and we require the general usage (e.g., he never knew or had forgotten the general usage). Similarly in nonlinguistic cases: we are presumed to intend the normal consequences of our actions.

Again, in cases where there is doubt, say, about which of two or more things an utterer intends to convey, we tend to refer to the context (linguistic or otherwise) of the utterance and ask which of the alternatives would be relevant to other things he is saying or doing, or which intention in a particular situation would fit in with some purpose he obviously has (e.g., a man who calls for a "pump" at a fire would not want a bicycle pump). Nonlinguistic parallels are obvious: context is a criterion in settling the question of why a man who has just put a cigarette in his mouth has put his hand in his pocket; relevance to an obvious end is a criterion in settling why a man is running away from a bull.

In certain linguistic cases we ask the utterer afterward about his intention, and in a few of these cases (the very difficult ones, like a philosopher asked to explain the meaning of an unclear passage in one of his works), the answer is not based on what he remembers but is more like a decision, a decision about how what he said is to be taken. I cannot find a nonlinguistic parallel here; but the case is so special as not to seem to contribute a vital difference.

All this is very obvious; but surely to show that the criteria for judging linguistic intentions are very like the criteria for judging nonlinguistic intentions is to show that linguistic intentions are very like nonlinguistic intentions.

INTENTION AND CONVENTION IN SPEECH ACTS

3.5

P. F. Strawson

I

In this paper I want to discuss some questions regarding J. L. Austin's notions of the illocutionary force of an utterance and of the illocutionary act which a speaker performs in making an utterance.[1]

There are two preliminary matters I must mention, if only to get them out of the way. Austin contrasts what he calls the "normal" or "serious" use of speech with what he calls "etiolated" or "parasitical" uses. His doctrine of illocutionary force relates essentially to the normal or serious use of speech and not, or not directly, to etiolated or parasitical uses; and so it will be with my comments on his doctrine. I am not suggesting that the distinction between the normal or serious use of speech and the secondary uses which he calls etiolated or parasitical is so clear as to call for no further examination; but I shall take it that there is such a distinction to be drawn and I shall not here further examine it.

My second preliminary remark concerns another distinction, or pair of distinctions, which Austin draws.

From *The Philosophical Review*, LXXIII (1964). Reprinted by permission of the editors and the author.
[1] All references, unless otherwise indicated, are to *How To Do Things with Words* (Oxford, 1962).

Austin distinguishes the illocutionary force of an utterance from what he calls its "meaning" and distinguishes between the illocutionary and the locutionary acts performed in issuing the utterance. Doubts may be felt about the second term of each of these distinctions. It may be felt that Austin has not made clear just what abstractions from the total speech act he intends to make by means of his notions of meaning and of locutionary act. Although this is a question on which I have views, it is not what the present paper is about. Whatever doubts may be entertained about Austin's notions of meaning and of locutionary act, it is enough for present purposes to be able to say, as I think we clearly can, the following about their relation to the notion of illocutionary force. The meaning of a (serious) utterance, as conceived by Austin, always embodies some limitation on its possible force, and sometimes—as, for example, in some cases where an explicit performative formula, like "I apologize," is used—the meaning of an utterance may exhaust its force; that is, there may be no more to the force than there is to the meaning; but very often the meaning, though it limits, does not exhaust, the force. Similarly, there may sometimes be no more to say about the illocutionary force of an utterance than we already know if we know what locutionary act has been performed; but very often there is more to know about the illocutionary force of an utterance than we know in knowing what locutionary act has been performed.

So much for these two preliminaries.

Now I shall proceed to assemble from the text some indications as to what Austin means by the force of an utterance and as to what he means by an illocutionary act. These two notions are not so closely related that to know the force of an utterance is the same thing as to know what illocutionary act was actually performed in issuing it. For if an utterance with the illocutionary force of, say, a warning is not understood in this way (that is, as a warning) by the audience to which it is addressed, then (it is held) the illocutionary act of warning cannot be said to have been actually performed. "The performance of an illocutionary act involves the securing of uptake"; that is, it involves "bringing about the understanding of the meaning and of the force of the locution" (pp. 115–116).[2] Perhaps we may express the relation by saying that to know the force of an utterance is the same thing as to know what illocutionary act, *if any*, was actually performed in issuing it. Austin gives many examples and lists of words which help us to form at least a fair intuitive notion of what is meant by "illocutionary force" and "illocutionary act." Besides these, he gives us certain general clues to these ideas, which may be grouped, as follows, under four heads:

1. Given that we know (in Austin's sense) the meaning of an utterance, there may still be a further question as to *how what was said was meant* by the speaker, or as to *how the words spoken were used*, or as to *how the*

---

[2] I refer later to the need for qualification of this doctrine.

utterance was to be taken or ought to have been taken (pp. 98–99). In order to know the illocutionary force of the utterance, we must know the answer to this further question.

2. A locutionary act is an act *of* saying something; an illocutionary act is an act we perform *in* saying something. It is what we *do, in* saying what we *say*. Austin does not regard this characterization as by any means a satisfactory test for identifying kinds of illocutionary acts since, so regarded, it would admit many kinds of acts which he wishes to exclude from the class (p. 99 and Lecture X).

3. It is a sufficient, though not, I think, a necessary, condition of a verb's being the name of a *kind* of illocutionary act that it can figure, in the first person present indicative, as what Austin calls an explicit performative. (This latter notion I shall assume to be familiar and perspicuous.)

4. The illocutionary act is "a conventional act; an act done as conforming to a convention" (p. 105). As such, it is to be sharply contrasted with the producing of certain effects, intended or otherwise, by means of an utterance. This producing of effects, though it too can often be ascribed *as an act* to the speaker (his *perlocutionary* act), is in no way a conventional act (pp. 120–121). Austin reverts many times to the "conventional" nature of the illocutionary act (pp. 103, 105, 108, 115, 120, 121, 127) and speaks also of "conventions of illocutionary force" (p. 114). Indeed, he remarks (pp. 120–121) that though acts which can properly be called by the same names as illocutionary acts —for example, acts of warning—can be

brought off nonverbally, without the use of words, yet, in order to be properly called by these names, such acts must be *conventional* nonverbal acts.

II

I shall assume that we are clear enough about the intended application of Austin's notions of illocutionary force and illocutionary act to be able to criticize, by reference to cases, his general doctrines regarding those notions. It is the general doctrine I listed last above—the doctrine that an utterance's having such and such a force is a matter of convention—that I shall take as the starting point of inquiry. Usually this doctrine is affirmed in a quite unqualified way. But just once there occurs an interestingly qualified statement of it. Austin says, of the use of language with a certain illocutionary force, that "it may . . . be said to be *conventional* in the sense that at least it could be made explicit by the performative formula" (p. 103). The remark has a certain authority in that it is the first explicit statement of the conventional nature of the illocutionary act. I shall refer to it later.

Meanwhile let us consider the doctrine in its unqualified form. Why does Austin say that the illocutionary act is a conventional act, an act done as conforming to a convention? I must first mention, and neutralize, two possible sources of confusion. (It may seem an excess of precaution to do so. I apologize to those who find it so.) First, we may agree (or not dispute) that any speech act is, as such, at least in part a conventional act. The performance of any *speech* act involves at least the observance or exploitation of some *linguistic* conventions, and every illocutionary act is a speech act. But it is absolutely clear that this is not the point that Austin is making in declaring the illocutionary act to be a conventional act. We must refer, Austin would say, to linguistic conventions to determine what *locutionary* act has been performed in the making of an utterance, to determine what the *meaning* of the utterance is. The doctrine now before us is the further doctrine that where force is *not* exhausted by meaning, the fact that an utterance has the further unexhausted force it has is also a matter of convention; or, where it is exhausted by meaning, the fact *that* it is, is a matter of convention. It is not just as being a speech act that an illocutionary act—for example, of warning—is conventional. A nonverbal act of warning is, Austin maintains, conventionally such in just the same way as an illocutionary—that is, verbal—act of warning is conventionally such.

Second, we must dismiss as irrelevant the fact that it can properly be said to be a matter of convention that an act of, for example, warning is correctly called by this name. For if this were held to be a ground for saying that illocutionary acts were conventional acts, then any describable act whatever would, as correctly described, be a conventional act.

The contention that illocutionary force is a matter of convention is easily seen to be correct in a great number of cases. For very many kinds of human transaction involving speech are governed and in part constituted by what we easily recognize as established conventions of procedure additional to the conventions governing the *meanings* of our utterances. Thus the fact that the word "guilty" is pronounced by the foreman of the jury in court at the proper moment constitutes his utterance as the act of bringing in a verdict; and that this is so is certainly a matter of the conventional procedures of the law. Similarly, it is a matter of convention that if the appropriate umpire pronounces a batsman "out," he thereby performs the act of *giving the man out*, which no player or spectator shouting "Out!" can do. Austin gives other examples, and there are doubtless many more which could be given, where there clearly exist statable conventions, relating to the circumstances of utterance, such that an utterance with a certain meaning, pronounced by the appropriate person in the appropriate circumstances, has the force it has *as* conforming to those conventions. Examples of illocutionary acts of which this is true can be found not only in the sphere of social institutions which have a legal point (like the marriage ceremony and the law courts themselves) or of activities governed by a definite set of rules (like cricket and games generally) but in many other relations of human life. The act of *introducing*, performed by uttering the words "This is Mr. Smith," may be said to be an act performed as conforming to a convention. The act of surrendering, performed by saying "*Kamerad!*" and throwing up your arms when confronted with a bayonet, may be said to be (to have become) an act performed as conforming to an accepted convention, a conventional act.

But it seems equally clear that, although the circumstances of utterance are always relevant to the determination of the illocutionary force of an utterance, there are many cases in which it is not as conforming to an accepted *convention* of any kind (other than those linguistic conventions which help to fix the meaning of the utterance) that an illocutionary act is performed. It seems clear, that is, that there are many cases in which the illocutionary force of an utterance, though not exhausted by its meaning, is not owed to any *conventions* other than those which help to give it its meaning. Surely there may be cases in which to utter the words "The ice over there is very thin" to a skater is to issue a warning (is to say something with the *force* of a warning) without its being the case that there is any statable convention at all (other than those which bear on the nature of the *locutionary* act) such that the speaker's act can be said to be an act done as conforming to that convention.

Here is another example. We can readily imagine circumstances in which an utterance of the words "Don't go" would be correctly described not as a request or an order, but as an entreaty. I do not want to deny that there may be conventional postures or procedures for entreating: one can, for example, kneel down, raise one's arms and *say*, "I entreat you." But I do want to deny that an act of entreaty can be performed only as conforming to some such conventions. What makes X's

words to Y an *entreaty* not to go is something—complex enough, no doubt—relating to X's situation, attitude to Y, manner, and current intention. There are questions here which we must discuss later. But to suppose that there is always and necessarily a convention conformed to would be like supposing that there could be no love affairs which did not proceed on lines laid down in the *Roman de la Rose* or that every dispute between men must follow the pattern specified in Touchstone's speech about the countercheck quarrelsome and the lie direct.

Another example. In the course of a philosophical discussion (or, for that matter, a debate on policy) one speaker *raises an objection* to what the previous speaker has just said. X says (or proposes) that *p* and Y *objects* that *q*. Y's utterance has the force of an objection to X's assertion (or proposal) that *p*. But where is the *convention* that constitutes it an objection? That Y's utterance has the force of an objection may lie partly in the character of the dispute and of X's contention (or proposal) and it certainly lies partly, in Y's *view* of these things, in the bearing which he takes the proposition that *q* to have on the doctrine (or proposal) that *p*. But although there may be, there does not have to be, any convention involved other than those linguistic conventions which help to fix the meanings of the utterances.

I do not think it necessary to give further examples. It seems perfectly clear that, if at least we take the expressions "convention" and "conventional" in the most natural way, the doctrine of the conventional nature of the illocutionary act does not hold generally. Some illocutionary acts are conventional; others are not (except in so far as they are locutionary acts). Why then does Austin repeatedly affirm the contrary? It is unlikely that he has made the simple mistake of generalizing from some cases to all. It is much more likely that he is moved by some further, and fundamental, feature of illocutionary acts, which it must be our business to discover. Even though we may decide that the description "conventional" is not appropriately used, we may presume it worth our while to look for the reason for using it. Here we may recall that oddly qualified remark that the performance of an illocutionary act, or the use of a sentence with a certain illocutionary force, "may be said to be conventional in the sense that at least it *could* be made explicit by the performative formula" (p. 103). On this we may first, and with justice, be inclined to comment that there is no such *sense* of "being conventional," that if this is a *sense* of anything to the purpose, it is a sense of "being *capable* of being conventional." But although this is a proper comment on the remark, we should not simply dismiss the remark with this comment. Whatever it is that leads Austin to call illocutionary acts in general "conventional" must be closely connected with whatever it is about such acts as warning, entreating, apologizing, advising, that accounts for the fact that *they* at least *could* be made explicit by the use of the corresponding first-person performative form. So we must ask what it is about them that accounts for this fact. Obviously it will not do to answer simply

that they are acts which can be performed by the use of words. So are many (perlocutionary) acts, like convincing, dissuading, alarming, and amusing, for which, as Austin points out, there is no corresponding first-person *performative* formula. So we need some further explanation.

III

I think a concept we may find helpful at this point is one introduced by H. P. Grice in his valuable article on *Meaning* (*Philosophical Review*, LXVI, 1957), namely, the concept of *someone's nonnaturally meaning something by an utterance*. The concept does not apply only to speech acts— that is, to cases where that by which someone nonnaturally means something is a *linguistic* utterance. It is of more general application. But it will be convenient to refer to that by which someone, S, nonnaturally means something as S's *utterance*. The explanation of the introduced concept is given in terms of the concept of intention. S nonnaturally means something by an utterance x if S intends (i_1) to produce by uttering x a certain response (r) in an audience A and intends (i_2) that A shall recognize S's intention (i_1) and intends (i_3) that this recognition on the part of A of S's intention (i_1) shall function as A's reason, or a part of his reason, for his response r. (The word "response," though more convenient in some ways than Grice's "effect," is not ideal. It is intended to cover cognitive and affective states or attitudes as well as actions.) It is, evidently, an important feature of this definition that the securing of the response r is intended to be mediated by the securing of another (and always cognitive) effect in A; namely, recognition of S's intention to secure response r.

Grice's analysis of his concept is fairly complex. But I think a little reflection shows that it is not quite complex enough for his purpose. Grice's analysis is undoubtedly offered as an analysis of a situation in which one person is trying, in a sense of the word "communicate" fundamental to any theory of meaning, to communicate with another. But it is possible to imagine a situation in which Grice's three conditions would be satisfied by a person S and yet, in this important sense of "communicate," it would not be the case that S could be said to be trying to communicate by means of his production of x with the person A in whom he was trying to produce the response r. I proceed to describe such a situation.

S intends by a certain action to induce in A the belief that p; so he satisfies condition (i_1). He arranges convincing-looking "evidence" that p, in a place where A is bound to see it. He does this, knowing that A is watching him at work, but *knowing also that A does not know that S knows that A is watching him at work*. He realizes that A will not take the *arranged* "evidence" as genuine or natural evidence that p, but realizes, and indeed intends, that A will take his arranging of it as grounds for thinking that he, S, intends to induce in A the belief that p. That is, he intends A to recognize his (i_1) intention. So S satisfies condition (i_2). He knows that A has general

grounds for thinking that S would not wish to make him, A, think that p unless it were known to S to be the case that p; and hence that A's recognition of his (S's) intention to induce in A the belief that p will in fact seem to A a sufficient reason for believing that p. And he intends that A's recognition of his intention (i_1) should function in just this way. So he satisfies condition (i_3).

S, then, satisfies all Grice's conditions. But this is clearly not a case of attempted *communication* in the sense which (I think it is fair to assume) Grice is seeking to elucidate. A will indeed take S to be trying to bring it about that A is aware of some fact; but he will not take S as trying, in the colloquial sense, to "let him know" something (or to "tell" him something). But unless S at least brings it about that A takes him (S) to be trying to let him (A) know something, he has not succeeded in communicating with A; and if, as in our example, he has not even *tried* to bring this about, then he has not even *tried* to communicate with A. It seems a minimum further condition of his trying to do this that he should not only intend A to recognize his intention to get A to think that p, but that he should also *intend A to recognize his intention to get A to recognize his intention* to get A to think that p.

We might approximate more closely to the communication situation if we changed the example by supposing it not only clear to both A and S that A was watching S at work, but also clear to them both that it *was* clear to them both. I shall content myself, however, with drawing from the actually considered example the conclusion that we must add to Grice's conditions the further condition that S should have the further intention (i_4) that A should recognize his intention (i_2). It is possible that further argument could be produced to show that even adding this condition is not *sufficient* to constitute the case as one of attempted communication. But I shall rest content for the moment with the fact that this addition at least is necessary.

Now we might have expected in Grice's paper an account of what it is for A to *understand* something by an utterance x, an account complementary to the account of what it is for S to *mean* something by an utterance x. Grice in fact gives no such account, and I shall suggest a way of at least partially supplying this lack. I say "at least partially" because the uncertainty as to the sufficiency of even the modified conditions for S's nonnaturally *meaning* something by an utterance x is reflected in a corresponding uncertainty in the sufficiency of conditions for A's understanding. But again we may be content for the moment with necessary conditions. I suggest, then, that for A (in the appropriate sense of "understand") to understand *something* by utterance x, it is necessary (and perhaps sufficient) that there should be *some* complex intention of the (i_2) form, described above, which A takes S to have, and that for A to understand the utterance correctly, it is necessary that A should take S to have *the* complex intention of the (i_2) form which S does have. In other words, if A is to understand the utterance correctly, S's (i_4) intention and hence his (i_2) intention must be fulfilled. Of course it does not follow

from the fulfillment of these intentions that his (i_1) intention is fulfilled; nor, consequently, that his (i_3) intention is fulfilled.

It is at this point, it seems, that we may hope to find a possible point of connection with Austin's terminology of "securing uptake." If we do find such a point of connection, we also find a possible starting point for an at least partial analysis of the notions of illocutionary force and of the illocutionary act. For to secure uptake is to secure understanding of (meaning and) illocutionary force; and securing understanding of illocutionary force is said by Austin to be an essential element in bringing off the illocutionary act. It is true that this doctrine of Austin's may be objected to.[3] For surely a man may, for example, actually have made such and such a bequest, or gift, even if no one ever reads his will or instrument of gift. We may be tempted to say instead that at least *the aim, if not the achievement*, of securing uptake is an essential element in the performance of the illocutionary act. To this, too, there is an objection. Might not a man really have made a gift, in due form, and take some satisfaction in the thought, even if he had no expectations of the fact ever being known? But this objection at most forces on us an amendment to which we are in any case obliged[4]: namely, that the aim, if not the achievement, of securing uptake is essentially *a stand-*

---

[3] I owe the objections which follow to Professor Hart.

[4] For an illocutionary act *may* be performed *altogether* unintentially. See the example about redoubling at bridge, p. 273 below.

ard, if not an invariable, element in the performance of the illocutionary act. So the analysis of the aim of securing uptake remains an essential element in the analysis of the notion of the illocutionary act.

IV

Let us, then, make a tentative identification—to be subsequently qualified and revised—of Austin's notion of uptake with that at least partially analyzed notion of understanding (on the part of an audience) which I introduced just now as complementary to Grice's concept of somebody nonnaturally meaning something by an utterance. Since the notion of audience understanding is introduced by way of a fuller (though partial) analysis than any which Austin gives of the notion of uptake, the identification is equivalent to a tentative (and partial) analysis of the notion of uptake and hence of the notions of illocutionary act and illocutionary force. If the identification were correct, then it would follow that to say something with a certain illocutionary force is at least (in the standard case) to have a certain complex intention of the (i_4) form described in setting out and modifying Grice's doctrine.

Next we test the adequacy and explanatory power of this partial analysis by seeing how far it helps to explain other features of Austin's doctrine regarding illocutionary acts. There are two points at which we shall apply this test. One is the point at which Austin maintains that the production of an utterance with a certain illocutionary force is a conventional act in that unconventional sense of "conventional" which he glosses in terms of general suitability for being made explicit with the help of an explicitly performative formula. The other is the point at which Austin considers the possibility of a general characterization of the illocutionary act as what we *do, in* saying what we say. He remarks on the unsatisfactoriness of this characterization in that it would admit as illocutionary acts what are not such; and we may see whether the suggested analysis helps to explain the exclusion from the class of illocutionary acts of those acts falling under this characterization which Austin wishes to exclude. These points are closely connected with each other.

First, then, we take the point about the general suitability of an illocutionary act for performance with the help of the explicitly performative formula for that act. The explanation of this feature of illocutionary acts has two phases; it consists of, first, a general, and then a special, point about intention. The first point may be roughly expressed by saying that in general a man can speak of his intention in performing an action with a kind of authority which he cannot command in predicting its outcome. What he intends in doing something is up to him in a way in which the results of his doing it are not, or not only, up to him. But we are concerned not with just any intention to produce any kind of effect by acting, but with a very special kind of case. We are concerned with the case in which there is not simply an intention to produce a certain response in an audience, but an intention to produce that response by means of recognition on the part of the audience of the intention to produce that response, this recognition to serve as part of the reason that the audience has for its response, and the intention that this recognition should occur being itself intended to be recognized. The speaker, then, not only has the general authority on the subject of his intention that any agent has; he also has a motive, inseparable from the nature of his act, for making that intention clear. For he will not have secured understanding of the illocutionary force of his utterance, he will not have performed the act of communication he sets out to perform, unless his complex intention is grasped. Now clearly, for the enterprise to be possible at all, there must exist, or he must find, means of making the intention clear. If there exists any conventional linguistic means of doing so, the speaker has both a right to use, and a motive for using, those means. One such means, available sometimes, which comes very close to the employment of the explicit performative form, would be to attach, or subjoin, to the substance of the message what looks like a force-elucidating *comment* on it, which may or may not have the form of a self-ascription. Thus we have phrases like "This is only a suggestion" or "I'm only making a suggestion"; or again "That was a warning" or "I'm warning you." For using such phrases, I repeat, the speaker has the *authority* that anyone has to speak on the subject of his intentions and the *motive* that I have tried to show is inseparable from an act of communication.

From such phrases as these—which have, *in appearance*, the character of comments on utterances other than themselves—to the explicit performative formula the step is only a short one. My reason for *qualifying* the remark that such phrases have the character of comments on utterances other than themselves is this. We are considering the case in which the subjoined quasi-comment is addressed to the same audience as the utterance on which it is a quasi-comment. Since it is *part* of the speaker's audience-directed intention to make clear the character of his utterance as, for example, a warning, and since the subjoined quasi-comment directly subserves this intention, it is better to view the case, appearances notwithstanding, *not* as a case in which we have two utterances, one commenting on the other, but as a case of a single unitary speech act. Crudely, the addition of the quasi-comment "That was a warning" is *part* of the total act of warning. The effect of the short step to the explicitly performative formula is simply to bring appearances into line with reality. When that short step is taken, we no longer have, even in appearance, two utterances, one a comment on the other, but a single utterance in which the first-person performative verb *manifestly* has that peculiar logical character of which Austin rightly made so much, and which we may express in the present context by saying that the verb serves not exactly to *ascribe* an intention to the speaker but rather, in Austin's phrase, to *make explicit* the type of communication intention with which the speaker speaks, the type of force which the utterance has.

The above might be said to be a deduction of the general possibility and utility of the explicitly performative formula for the cases of illocutionary acts not essentially conventional. It may be objected that the deduction fails to show that the intentions rendered explicit by the use of performative formulae *in general* must be of just the complex form described, and hence fails to justify the claim that just this kind of intention lies at the core of all illocutionary acts. And indeed we shall see that this claim would be mistaken. But before discussing why, we shall make a further application of the analysis at the second testing point I mentioned. That is, we shall see what power it has to explain why some of the things we may be *doing, in* saying what we say, are not illocutionary acts and could not be rendered explicit by the use of the performative formula.

Among the things mentioned by Austin which we might be doing in saying things, but which are not illocutionary acts, I shall consider the two examples of (1) showing off and (2) insinuating. Now when we show off, we are certainly trying to produce an effect on the audience: we talk, indeed, for effect; we try to impress, to evoke the response of admiration. But it is no part of the intention to secure the effect *by means of* the recognition of the intention to secure it. It is no part of our total intention to secure recognition of the intention to produce the effect at all. On the contrary: recognition of the intention might militate against securing the effect and promote an opposite effect, for example, disgust.

This leads on to a further general point not explicitly considered by Austin, but satisfactorily explained by the analysis under consideration. In saying to an audience what we do say, we very often intend not only to produce the primary response r by means of audience recognition of the intention to produce that response, but to produce further effects by means of the production of the primary response r. Thus my further purpose in informing you that p (that is, aiming to produce in you the primary cognitive response of knowledge or belief that p) may be to bring it about thereby that you adopt a certain line of conduct or a certain attitude. In saying what I say, then, part of what I am *doing* is trying to influence your attitudes or conduct in a certain way. Does this part of what I am doing in saying what I say contribute to determining the character of the illocutionary act I perform? And if not, why not? If we take the first question strictly as introduced and posed, the answer to it is "No." The reason for the answer follows from the analysis. We have no complex intention (i_4) that there should be recognition of an intention (i_2) that there should be recognition of an intention (i_1) that the further effect should be produced; for it is no part of our intention that the further effect should be produced by way of recognition of our intention that it should be; the production in the audience of belief that p is intended to be itself the means whereby his attitude or conduct is to be influenced. We secure uptake, perform the act of communication that we set out to perform, if the audience understands us as *informing* him that p. Although it is true that, in saying what we say, we are in fact *trying* to produce the further effect—this is part of what we are doing, whether we succeed in producing the effect or not—yet this does not enter into the characterization of the illocutionary act. With this case we have to contrast the case in which, instead of aiming at a primary response and a further effect, the latter to be secured through the former alone, we aim at a complex primary response. Thus in the case where I do not simply inform, but warn, you that *p*, among the intentions I intend you to recognize (and intend you to recognize as intended to be recognized) are not only the intention to secure your belief that *p*, but the intention to secure that you are on your guard against *p*-perils. The difference (one of the differences) between showing off and warning is that your recognition of my intention to put you on your guard may well contribute to putting you on your guard, whereas your recognition of my intention to impress you is not likely to contribute to my impressing you (or not in the way I intended).[5]

Insinuating fails, for a different reason, to be a type of illocutionary act. An essential feature of the intentions which make up the illocutionary complex is their overtness. They have,

one might say, essential avowability. This is, in one respect, a logically embarrassing feature. We have noticed already how we had to meet the threat of a counterexample to Grice's analysis of the communicative act in terms of three types of intention—(i_1), (i_2), and (i_3)—by the addition of a further intention (i_4) that an intention (i_2) should be recognized. We have no proof, however, that the resulting enlarged set of conditions is a complete analysis. Ingenuity might show it was not; and the way seems open to a regressive series of intentions that intentions should be recognized. While I do not think there is anything necessarily objectionable in this, it does suggest that the complete and rounded-off set of conditions aimed at in a conventional analysis is not easily and certainly attainable in these terms. That is why I speak of the feature in question as logically embarrassing. At the same time it enables us easily to dispose of insinuating as a candidate for the status of a type of illocutionary act. The whole point of insinuating is that the audience is to *suspect*, but not more than suspect, the intention, for example, to induce or disclose a certain belief. The intention one has in insinuating is essentially nonavowable.

Now let us take stock a little. We tentatively laid it down as a necessary condition of securing understanding of the illocutionary force of an utterance that the speaker should succeed in bringing it about that the audience took him, in issuing his utterance, to have a complex intention of a certain kind, namely the intention that the audiences should recognize (and recognize as intended to be recognized) his intention to induce

---

[5] Perhaps trying to impress might sometimes have an illocutionary character. For I might try to impress you with my *effrontery*, intending you to recognize this intention and intending your recognition of it to function as part of your reason for being impressed, and so forth. But then I am not *merely* trying to impress you; I am *inviting* you to be impressed. I owe this point to Mr. B. F. McGuinness.

a certain response in the audience. The suggestion has, as we have just seen, certain explanatory merits. Nevertheless we cannot claim general application for it as even a partial analysis of the notions of illocutionary force and illocutionary act. Let us look at some reasons why not.

V

I remarked earlier that the words "Don't go" may have the force, *inter alia*, either of a request or of an entreaty. In either case the primary intention of the utterance (if we presume the words to be uttered with the *sense* "Don't go *away*") is that of inducing the person addressed to stay where he is. His staying where he is is the primary response aimed at. But the only other intentions mentioned in our scheme of partial analysis relate directly or indirectly to recognition of the primary intention. So how, in terms of that scheme, are we to account for the variation in illocutionary force between requests and entreaties?

This question does not appear to raise a major difficulty for the scheme. The scheme, it seems, merely requires supplementing and enriching. *Entreaty*, for example, is a matter of trying to secure the primary response not merely through audience recognition of the intention to secure it, but through audience recognition of a complex attitude of which this primary intention forms an integral part.

A wish that someone should stay may be held in different ways: passionately or lightly, confidently or desperately; and it may, for different reasons, be part of a speaker's intention to secure recognition of *how* he holds it. The most obvious reason, in the case of entreaty, is the belief, or hope, that such a revelation is more likely to secure the fulfillment of the primary intention.

But one may not only request and entreat; one may *order* someone to stay where he is. The words "Don't go" may have the illocutionary force of an order. Can we so simply accommodate in our scheme *this* variation in illocutionary force? Well, we can accommodate it; though not so simply. We can say that a man who issues an order typically intends his utterance to secure a certain response, that he intends this intention to be recognized, and its recognition to be a reason for the response, that he intends the utterance to be recognized as issued in a certain social context such that certain social rules or conventions apply to the issuing of utterances in this context and such that certain consequences may follow in the event of the primary response not being secured, that he intends *this* intention too to be recognized, and finally that he intends the recognition of these last features to function as an element in the reasons for the response on the part of the audience.

Evidently, in this case, unlike the case of entreaty, the scheme has to be extended to make room for explicit reference to social convention. It can, with some strain, be so extended. But as we move further into the region of institutionalized procedures, the strain becomes too much for the scheme to bear. On the one hand, one of its basic features—namely, the reference to an intention to secure a definite response in an audience (over and above the securing of uptake)—has to be dropped. On the other, the reference to social conventions of procedure assumes a very much greater importance. Consider an umpire giving a batsman out, a jury bringing in a verdict of guilty, a judge pronouncing sentence, a player redoubling at bridge, a priest or a civil officer pronouncing a couple man and wife. Can we say that the umpire's primary intention is to secure a certain response (say, retiring to the pavilion) from a certain audience (say, the batsman), the jurymen's to secure a certain response (say, the pronouncing of sentence) from a certain audience (say, the judge), and then build the rest of our account around this, as we did, with some strain, in the case of the order? Not with plausibility. It is not even possible, in other than a formal sense, to isolate, among all the participants in the procedure (trial, marriage, game) to which the utterance belongs, a particular audience to whom the utterance can be said to be addressed.

Does this mean that the approach I suggested to the elucidation of the notion of illocutionary force is entirely mistaken? I do not think so. Rather, we must distinguish types of case; and then see what, if anything, is common to the types we have distinguished. What we initially take from Grice— with modifications—is an at least partially analytical account of an act of communication, an act which might indeed be performed nonverbally and yet exhibit all the essential characteristics of a (non-verbal) equivalent of an illocutionary act. We gain more than this. For the account enables us to understand

how such an act may be linguistically conventionalized right up to the point at which illocutionary force is exhausted by meaning (in Austin's sense); and in this understanding the notion of wholly overt or essentially avowable intention plays an essential part. Evidently, in these cases, the illocutionary act itself is not *essentially* a conventional act, an act done as conforming to a convention; it may be that the act is conventional, done as conforming to a convention, only in so far as *the means used to perform it* are conventional. To speak only of those conventional means which are also *linguistic* means, the extent to which the act is one done as conforming to conventions may depend solely on the extent to which conventional linguistic meaning exhausts illocutionary force.

At the other end of the scale—the end, we may say, from which Austin began—we have illocutionary acts which *are* essentially conventional. The examples I mentioned just now will serve—marrying, redoubling, giving out, pronouncing sentence, bringing in a verdict. Such acts could have no existence outside the rule- or convention-governed practices and procedures of which they essentially form parts. Let us take the standard case in which the participants in these procedures know the rules and their roles, and are trying to play the game and not wreck it. Then they are presented with occasions on which they have to, or may, perform an illocutionary act which forms part of, or furthers, the practice or procedure as a whole; and sometimes they have to make a decision within a restricted range of alternatives (for example, to pass or redouble, to pronounce sentence of imprisonment for some period not exceeding a certain limit). Between the case of such acts as these and the case of the illocutionary act not essentially conventional, there is an important likeness and an important difference. The likeness resides in the fact that, in the case of an utterance belonging to a convention-governed practice or procedure, the speaker's utterance is standardly *intended* to further, or affect the course of, the practice in question in some one of the alternative ways open, and intended to be recognized as so intended. I do not mean that such an act could *never* be performed *unintentionally*. A player might let slip the word "redouble" without *meaning* to redouble; but if the circumstances are appropriate and the play strict, then he *has* redoubled (or he may be *held* to have redoubled). But a player who continually did this sort of thing would not be asked to play again, except by sharpers. Forms can take charge, in the absence of appropriate intention; but when they do, the case is *essentially* deviant or nonstandard. There is present in the standard case, that is to say, the same element of wholly overt and avowable intention as in the case of the act not essentially conventional.

The difference is a more complicated affair. We have, in these cases, an act which is conventional in two connected ways. First, if things go in accordance with the rules of the procedure in question, the act of furthering the practice in the way intended is an act required or permitted by those rules, an act done as falling under the rules. Second, the act is identified as the act

it is just because it is performed by the utterance of a form of words conventional for the performance of that act. Hence the speaker's utterance is not only *intended* to further, or affect the course of, the practice in question in a certain conventional way; in the absence of any breach of the conventional conditions for futhering the procedure in this way, it cannot fail to do so.

And here we have the contrast between the two types of case. In the case of an illocutionary act of a kind not essentially conventional, the act of communication is performed if *uptake* is secured, if the utterance is taken to be issued with the complex overt intention with which it is issued. But even though the act of communication is performed, the wholly overt intention which lies at the core of the intention complex may, *without any breach of rules or conventions*, be frustrated. The audience response (belief, action, or attitude) may simply not be forthcoming. It is different with the utterance which forms part of a wholly convention-governed procedure. Granted that uptake is secured, then any frustration of the wholly overt intention of the utterance (the intention to further the procedure in a certain way) must be attributable to a breach of rule or convention. The speaker who abides by the conventions can avowably have the intention to further the procedure in the way to which his current linguistic act is conventionally appropriated *only* if he takes it that the conventional conditions for so furthering it are satisfied and hence takes it *that his utterance will not only reveal his intentions but give them effect*. There is nothing parallel to this in the case of the illocutionary act of a kind not essentially conventional. In both cases, we may say, speakers assume the responsibility for making their intentions overt. In one case (the case of the convention-constituted procedure) the speaker who uses the explicitly performative form also explicitly assumes the responsibility for making his overt intention effective. But in the other case the speaker cannot, in the speech act itself, explicitly assume any such responsibility. For there are no conditions which can conventionally guarantee the effectiveness of his overt intention. Whether it is effective or not is something that rests with his audience. In the one case, therefore, the explicitly performative form *may* be the name of the very act which is performed if and only if the speaker's overt intention is effective; but in the other case it cannot be the name of this act. But of course—and I shall recur to this thought—the sharp contrast I have here drawn between two extreme types of case must not blind us to the existence of intermediate types.

Acts belonging to convention-constituted procedures of the kind I have just referred to form an important part of human communication. But they do not form the whole nor, we may think, the most fundamental part. It would be a mistake to take them as the model for understanding the notion of illocutionary force in general, as Austin perhaps shows some tendency to do when he both insists that the illocutionary act is essentially a conventional act and connects this claim with the possibility of making the act explicit by the use of the performative formula. It would

equally be a mistake, as we have seen, to generalize the account of illocutionary force derived from Grice's analysis; for this would involve holding, falsely, that the complex overt intention manifested in any illocutionary act always includes the intention to secure a certain definite response or reaction in an audience over and above that which is necessarily secured if the illocutionary force of the utterance is understood. Nevertheless, we can perhaps extract from our consideration of two contrasting types of case something which is common to them both and to all the other types which lie between them. For the illocutionary force of an utterance is essentially something that is intended to be understood. And the understanding of the force of an utterance in all cases involves recognizing what may be called broadly an audience-directed intention and recognizing it as wholly overt, as intended to be recognized. It is perhaps this fact which lies at the base of the general possibility of the explicit performative formula; though, as we have seen, extra factors come importantly into play in the case of convention-constituted procedures.

Once this common element in all illocutionary acts is clear, we can readily acknowledge that the types of audience-directed intention involved may be very various and, also, that different types may be exemplified by one and the same utterance.

I have set in sharp contrast those cases in which the overt intention is simply to forward a definite and convention-governed practice (for example, a game) in a definite way provided for by the conventions or rules of the practice and those cases in which the overt intention includes that of securing a definite response (cognitive or practical) in an audience over and above that which is necessarily secured if uptake is secured. But there is something misleading about the sharpness of this contrast; and it would certainly be wrong to suppose that all cases fall clearly and neatly into one or another of these two classes. A speaker whose job it is to do so may offer information, instructions, or even advice, and yet be overtly indifferent as to whether or not his information is accepted as such, his instructions followed, or his advice taken. His wholly overt intention may amount to no more than that of making available—in a "take it or leave it" spirit—to his audience the information or instructions or opinion in question; though again, in some cases, he may be seen as the mouthpiece, merely, of another agency to which may be attributed at least general intentions of the kind that can scarcely be attributed, in the particular case, to him. We should not find such complications discouraging; for we can scarcely expect a general account of linguistic communication to yield more than schematic outlines, which may almost be lost to view when every qualification is added which fidelity to the facts requires.

Toward Further Inquiry

Bergmann's treatment of meaning in terms of intentionality is further explicated in other essays in his *Meaning and Existence* (Madison, Wisc., 1960) and *Logic and Reality* (Madison, Wisc., 1964). The latter contains an essay on Husserl that indicates a relationship between Bergmann's thought and the phenomenological movement and its realistic antecedents. Bergmann explores this relationship in *Realism: A Critique of Brentano and Meinong* (Madison, Wisc., 1967). Brentano's concern with intentionality can be seen in *Psychologie vom empirichen Standpunkt* (Leipzig, 1925) and *Kategorienlehre* (Leipzig, 1933), and the role of intentionality in Husserl's thought, in *Logische Untersuchungen* (Halle, 1928) and *Ideas* (New York, 1931). Relevant selections from Brentano and Meinong appear in R. Chisholm (ed.), *Realism and the Background of Phenomenology* (Glencoe, Ill., 1960). This treatment of intentionality in relation to a realistic metaphysics is traced to scholastic roots in H. Spiegelberg's *"Der Begriff der Intentionalität in der Scholastik, bei Brentano, und bie Husserl,"* *Philosophische Heft* 5 (1936).

Roderick Chisholm's attempts to develop a logic of intentionality began in *Perceiving* (Ithaca, N.Y., 1957); they are further discussed in "Notes on the Logic of Believing," PPR 24 (1963), and in "Psychological Concepts," in Hector Castañeda (ed.), *Intentionality, Minds and Perception* (Detroit, 1967). He applied these concerns to matters of language and meaning in "Intentionality and the Theory of Signs," *Philosophical Studies* 3 (1952), in which he argues that intentions must be taken into account in the understanding of language. B. A.

Farrell, in an article by the same title in PPR 14 (1955), argues that current psychological investigations make Chisholm's position appear archaic. Chisholm's "Intentionality and the Mental," in *Minnesota Studies in the Philosophy of Science* II (1958), lays a basis for Wilfred Sellars' discussion with him that appears in the same volume. Sellars' own views on intentionality have more recently appeared in JP 61 (1964), where he outlines a correlation of thinking, speech acts, and propositions, and on this basis gives a critique of Bergmann's treatment of intentionality.

The care with which Sellars distinguishes mental acts from action is indicative of the gap between his and Bergmann's treatment of intentions and that of Grice and Strawson. I have attempted to explicate this difference by distinguishing between a reference orientation and a use orientation in "A Third Dogma of Empiricism," *Monist* 49 (1965). The role in meaning of intention in the latter sense, the sense of purpose to action, must be understood against the more general background of the role of intentions in any purposive action. The symposium by J. A. Passmore and P. L. Heath in PAS Suppl. 29 (1955) gives this issue serious consideration, and S. Hampshire's *Thought and Action* (London, 1959), G. E. M. Anscombe's *Intention* (Oxford, 1957), and A. I. Melden's *Free Action* (London, 1961) give fuller studies of the matter. Noel Fleming, in "On Intensions," PR 73 (1964), offers a critical evaluation of the positions of Melden, Hampshire, and Anscombe; and Bruce Aune, in *Knowledge, Mind and Nature* (New York, 1967) gives some attention to these issues. These controversies over the problematic relationship of intention to action make clear that the relationship of intention to meaning proposed by Grice, Strawson, and myself is at this point no more than programatic.

An alternative to an intentional understanding of the pragmatic aspect of meaning is its reduction in some way to behavioral considerations. Though the subject is not treated precisely in these terms, this is the import of Charles Morris' behavioral semiotic in *Signs, Language and Behavior* (New York, 1946) (but see Max Black's critique of this position in Chapter 7 of *Language and Philosophy* (Ithaca, N.Y., 1949)). "A Stimulus-Response Analysis of Language and Meaning" by R. Brown and D. Dulaney, in P. Henle (ed.), *Language, Thought and Culture* (Ann Arbor, 1958), can be understood as a development along lines similar to those followed by Morris; the article contains references to other similar resolutions. C. L. Stevenson's treatment in terms of dispositions in *Ethics and Language* (New Haven, Conn., 1944) also stresses a behavioral interpretation, but Stevenson has not, to my knowledge, developed the matter any further.

Another alternative is a logical reduction of intentional issues to intensional meaning, and a subsequent extensional reduction of intensional issues. W. Quine considers this extensional ideal at length in *Word and Object* (New York, 1960), but he treats it only programatically. R. M. Martin, beginning with *Toward a Systematic Pragmatics* (Amsterdam, 1959), has done a more thorough job. His proposals here and in "Toward an Extensional Logic of Belief," JP 59 (1962), led to the systematic expression of his *Intension and Decision* (Englewood Cliffs, N.J., 1963). A sympathetic critique by E. K. Jobe in "R. M. Martin's System of Pragmatics," *Methodos* 15 (1963), makes clear that Martin does not effectively eliminate the intentional factor in his extensional reduction. For other appraisals of the relation of intension to intention, see A. Church's "Logic and Analysis," *Proceedings of the 12th International Congress of Philosophy*, and J. Cornman's "Intentionality and Intensionality," *Philosophical Quarterly* 12 (1962).

The increasing pluralization of the functions of language can be seen even in those who adhere to the positivistic distinction between cognitive and noncognitive. Herbert Feigl, in "Logical Positivism," *Readings in Philosophical Analysis* (New York, 1949), lists three different functions under each category. William Frankena, maintaining the basic worth of the two-fold classification, in Chapters 5 and 6 of Henle (ed.), *Language, Thought and Culture*, notes a variety of factors in language that are important to meaning and lists nine different meanings that can reasonably be attached to the cognitive-noncognitive distinction. Most philosophers who in one way or another adopt the ordinary-language approach to analysis abandon the distinction; the pluralities of use they explicate can be sampled in the writings of Austin, Wittgenstein, and Ryle cited at the end of Chapter 1. Essays that treat the relation of meaning to speech acts more directly are John Searle's "Meaning and Speech Acts," PR 71 (1962), and Paul Benacerraf's "Comments on 'Meaning and Speech Acts'," in C. D. Rollins (ed.), *Knowledge and Experience* (Pittsburgh, 1963). W. Alston's formulation, in *Philosophy of Language* (Englewood Cliffs, N.J., 1964), Chapter 2, of a theory of meaning on the basis of Austin's conception of illocutionary acts is noteworthy.

The general semantics movement is also relevant to the relation of meaning to intention and speech acts. Among a number of basic theoretical formulations are Stuart Chase's *The Tyranny of Words* (New York, 1938), S. I. Hayakawa's *Language in Action* (New York, 1941), and Irving Lee's *Language Habits in Human Affairs* (New York, 1941).

Chapter 4

DEFINITION, DESCRIPTION, AND REFERENCE

> A man that seeketh precise truth had need to
> remember what every name he uses stands for, and
> to place it accordingly, or else he will find
> himself tangled in words, as a bird in lime twigs,
> the more he struggles, the more belimed.
> . . . In right definition of words lies the
> first use of speech, which is the acquisition of
> science; and in wrong, or no definitions, lies the
> first abuse, from which proceed all false
> and senseless tenets.
> *Thomas Hobbes*

"What do you mean by. . . ?" The question can be approached in still another way. Instead of seeking what the meaning is (object, idea, . . .) or what the purpose is, we may seek some *device* for understanding the term in question. We may require a definition, or a description of the object to which the term refers, or an indication of that object by some other means. A *term*, according to Lewis, "is an expression which names or applies to a thing or things, of some kind, actual or thought of" (see 2.1). This definition suggests that not all terms are words and not all words are terms. 'Cat', 'a cat', 'the cat on the mat', and 'the cat is on the mat' all serve as terms. In the sentence, 'The cat jumped on the mat', 'the cat' and 'the mat' can be treated as terms, but the verb does not properly refer to anything (it tells what the cat does in relation to the mat but does not refer to the action, as the participle 'jumping' does). The preposition 'on' serves a syntactical function but does not refer to an object. 'The' in 'the cat' has no referent but serves with 'cat' to refer to something. Words that are not terms are often called *syncategorematic* (they have no meaning of their own but always serve *with* expressions that have meaning). Which expressions constitute terms and which are syncategorematic may itself be an issue of concern.

278

Terms have a variety of forms and functions in language. *Singular* terms name particular individuals and are usually expressed as proper nouns. *General* terms may be said to name classes (the term 'cat' names the class of all cats) and are usually expressed as common nouns. More often, general terms are used to describe a referent, either definitely with a definite article ('*the* cat') or indefinitely with an indefinite article ('*a* cat'). *Descriptions*[1] may be used to *classify* ('little girl' in 'Irene is a little girl') or to *characterize* ('blond hair' in 'Irene has blond hair'). Often classification and characterization serve to specify a particular referent ('Irene is the little girl with the long blond hair'). Some terms are neither names nor descriptions but *relations* (in 'John is the brother of Steven', 'the brother of' refers to neither John nor Steven, nor does it describe their characteristics; it refers to a relation between them).

Definitions also have a variety of forms and functions. To define is to set boundaries, to delimit, to make definite. Definitions in language make definite the meaning of terms. *Lexical* definitions make definite the conventional meanings of terms; *stipulative* definitions make definite meanings for terms that are intended for particular purposes in particular contexts; *precising* definitions make definite meanings for vague or ambiguous terms by limiting their usage. For any given term that is already in general use, one can explicate the conventional uses, stipulate a different use, or limit the conventional use. Any of these functions can be carried out in a variety of forms. A definition may give a classification that indicates the kind of thing to which the term refers and a characterization that separates the referent of the term from other things of the same kind. It may give a name equivalent in meaning to the name defined. Or it may give examples of the things referred to by naming them, or even by pointing to them.

There are many practical problems in giving definitions, descriptions, and references that adequately convey what a term means. A number of these stem from philosophical problems concerning conceptions of terms, definitions, and descriptions:

> What is defined in a definition? 'Dogs are four-legged animals' is clearly a description of dogs, not of the term 'dogs'. It is equally clear that " 'Dogs' is a four-letter word" is a description of the term 'dogs'. No such clarity exists for definitions, and many regard the question of what is being defined as basic to the understanding of definitions. In a definition, the *definiens* (that which defines) gives the meaning of the *definiendum* (that which is defined). Does the definition state the meaning of a term that is *mentioned*? Or does it state the meaning of an object for which the term is *used*? If the

---

[1] The term 'description' is here used to mean those complex general terms that are introduced by a definite or indefinite article in English. Ambiguous expressions can be included if one or the other article can be supplied (see 4.3). The term 'description' is used by some writers to refer elliptically to definite descriptions alone. This usage is usually made obvious by context.

former, the definiendum is a term; if the latter, the definiendum is the object named by the term.[2]

Are there wrong definitions? Hobbes' call for right definitions sometimes seems baffling, but it can be made sense of in at least two ways. If one interprets definitions as giving the meaning of the object for which a term is used, then the truth of the definition depends upon its giving a verbal expression of the essential characteristics of the object. If one interprets definitions as giving the meaning of the term mentioned, then definitions can be true in a variety of senses: true to conventions (lexical); true to purposes (stipulative); true to precision (precising). If the inquirer seeks true definitions, he should first answer the question, "True to what?" His answer will depend in part upon what he understands the definiendum to be.

Are there complete definitions? Lewis claims that any correct definition delimits the intension of a term (see 2.1), but much has been made of late of the "open texture" of language.[3] Our terms have not only a degree of vagueness due to the variety of present uses, but also a degree of possible vagueness due to our inability to foresee future uses. We cannot foresee all the possible uses of many of our terms, any more than we can enumerate all the characteristics of many of the objects of our experiences. A stipulative definition may legislate how a term is to be used, as long as the term is used only in accord with that definition, then the definition is complete. Lexical definitions are not likely to provide such exactitude. They do not give all the characteristics of the object (real interpretation) or all the possible conventional uses of the term (nominal interpretation). A definition that abides by the stipulative rigor can be expressed as an equation between the definiendum and the definiens. A definition that explicates only one understanding of the definiendum may be lacking in this sort of completeness.

In what sense does a definition "give" meaning? Uses of definition to determine the meaning of the definiendum presuppose an understanding of the meaning of the definiens. Definitions give meaning for particular terms in a language only if many of the terms of the language are already understood. Using a dictionary for a foreign language, an inquirer could learn by rote

---

[2] The controversy over the nature of the definiendum, here treated in terms of the use-mention distinction, was traditionally discussed in terms of *real* and *nominal* definitions. A real definition was understood to define the object for which a term is used, a nominal definition to define the term mentioned. The real-nominal distinction is used in increasingly variable senses, depending upon the viewpoint taken about definitions by the author. Henry Leonard makes explicit two entirely different ways of treating the distinction in *Principles of Right Reason* (New York, 1957).

[3] Friedrich Waismann coined the expression "open texture" in his essay, "Verifiability," in Anthony Flew (ed.), *Logic and Language*, First Series (Oxford, 1951). Waismann used it to point out that there are always possible meanings of verbal expressions that cannot be anticipated by any definition, no matter how many limits may be set by the defining.

the definitions of many of the basic terms, but none of their meanings (compare Lewis' discussion of sense meaning and linguistic meaning in 2.1). Even ostensive definitions do not give the sense of their pointing; even indexical signs require interpretation.

Must terms be referential? If we maintain the thesis that a term that does not name is not a term, then we must achieve some sense of a variety of references. Does the term 'a unicorn' refer to a mental idea or to a fictional object? What sense can be made of various kinds of nonphysical objects? On the other hand, if we maintain that terms need not name to be meaningful, how are we to understand nonreferential terms? Bertrand Russell's theory of descriptions gives one widely accepted analysis of a way to treat this problem (see 4.3). It has the side effects of treating sentences about unicorns as meaningful but false, and of requiring reduction of the names of fictional characters like 'Hamlet' to definite descriptions. Can problems about reference be resolved without positing nonphysical entities on the one hand and without these side effects of Russell's theory on the other?

Do proper names (singular terms) have meaning? J. S. Mill maintained that such terms have denotation but not connotation (see Ryle's discussion of Mill in 2.2). When this view is coupled with Russell's program of reducing (apparent) proper names to definite descriptions, problems arise. Can definite descriptions serve as definitions of proper names, or do they merely determine the reference of the name? If the former, then proper names would seem to have meaning; if the latter, then Russell's program would only be effective where the referent exists. If the views of Mill and Russell are not compatible, on what understanding of definition, description, and reference can the issues be resolved?

The first two essays in this chapter give a basis for exploring understandings of definition. Arthur Pap, assuming the reader's acquaintance with a variety of kinds of definition, seeks to bring order and clarity to that variety by constructing a systematic characterization of definitions. Casimir Ajdukiewicz gives an account of the various views of what is being defined, together with a critical evaluation of each conception of definition. The remaining essays are concerned with problems of description and reference. Russell's "On Denoting" gives an early formulation of his theory of descriptions. It makes clear his method of resolving the problem about terms referring to nonexistent entities, and it gives some valuable insights into the character of definite descriptions. P. F. Strawson's critique of this method argues from the basis that meaning is use in context. He claims that the presuppositions of such an expression as 'The present king of France is bald' make the expression meaningful (and referential) in some contexts but not in others. Leonard Linsky's distinction between 'referent' and 'reference' lays a basis for an analysis that maintains that matters of description depend not only upon context, but also upon the users of the language, who do the referring.

4.1   THEORY OF DEFINITION*

Arthur Pap

Definitions can be classified from (at least) two different points of view. We can ask what sort of statements definitions are, how they are to be justified, and what purpose they serve in the process of acquiring scientific knowledge. For lack of a simpler word, let us call a classification of definitions from this point of view *epistemological.* We can also distinguish different forms of definition; and a classification from this point of view is naturally called *formal.*

Epistemological classification. The question is often raised and discussed

whether a definition can be true or false, or whether it is just an arbitrary stipulation to use a word in a certain way. The obvious answer is that some of the statements that are, in everyday life, and in science, called "definitions" are merely stipulative and others are not. By just looking at the sequence of words, however, one cannot tell whether one is confronted with a stipulation or with a *proposition*, i.e., something that can be called true or false. For example: "A spinster is an unmarried woman older than 25." This would be a *stipulative* definition if it amounted to the proposal, "Let us use the word 'spinster' as an abbreviation for 'unmarried woman older than 25'." One can accept or reject a proposal; but since to make a proposal is not to *assert* anything, the question of truth or falsehood is inappropriate. But the same statement may be meant as a report of the actual usage of the word "spinster": English-speaking people apply the word "spinster" to women of the described sort and to no other objects. In that case the definition is a proposition, and then it is appropriate to ask whether it is true or false.

The first distinction, then, is that

From *Philosophy of Science*, XXXI (1964). Reprinted by permission of the editors and Professor Wilcox.

* Several years before Arthur Pap died, he wrote the present paper for use with his classes in introductory logic. It was not originally intended for publication, but the ideas in it have a theoretic interest which, in our opinion, merits wider circulation. The manuscript appears here as Professor Pap wrote it except for minor changes in form and alterations of the wording in the third paragraph under "Formal classification" and the deletion of exercises; it was prepared for publication by John T. Wilcox, Associate Professor of Philosophy, State University of New York at Binghamton.

between (linguistic) proposals and propositions. Propositional definitions, in turn, can be classified from two important points of view: they may be empirical propositions, or they may be analytic propositions. And they may be about words (verbal usage) or about objects referred to by words, or they may analyze concepts expressed by words. An empirical proposition is a proposition whose truth or falsehood can only be determined by experience (in the broadest sense of "experience"). And even if there are good reasons for accepting it as true, it remains logically conceivable (i.e., does not involve self-contradiction to suppose) that it be false. An analytic proposition, on the other hand, is arrived at by analysis of what one means by the words used. Thus we would not allow that "All mothers are women" could ever be refuted; one may, of course, change the ordinary meanings of the words, but that would be different from finding the proposition *now* expressed by these words to be false.

Following Copi,[1] we call a definition which is an empirical proposition about verbal usage *lexical*. But we split Copi's category of "theoretical" definitions into *theoretical* in the sense of empirical propositions about scientific objects, and *analyses* of concepts. To see the difference, compare "Water is a substance composed of molecules consisting of two hydrogen atoms and one oxygen atom (H_2O)" with "A circle is a closed line any two points on

which have the same distance from a given point." The former statement must be justified by reference to experimental results interpreted by a scientific theory (atomic theory of matter). The latter statement, however, expresses a precise analysis of the property connoted by the word "circle." I can get a person who has learnt the use of the word "circle" by ostensive definition, i.e., by being conditioned to apply the word "circle" to closed lines of a certain shape and only such lines, to formulate that analysis by just inviting him to reflect on what distinguishes a circle from an ellipse, a square, and other closed lines of regular character. But the cited definition of water could not be arrived at in this way; it expresses the empirical generalization that anything which has the qualitative properties connoted by "water" as the term is used in daily life also has that chemical structure, and conversely.

It is easy to confuse a lexical definition with an analysis because one tends to confuse the *use* of a word with its *mention*. When I say, "John is a tall boy," I use the name "John" to talk about a boy; it is therefore inconsistent to write "John is a tall boy" and also "John is a name," for the same thing cannot be both a boy and a name. The correct way of writing would be: "'John' is a name," the inner quotes serving to name a name. Now, consider the definition "An uncle is a man who has the same parents as some other person who is a parent." If it is a lexical definition, then it is a statement about the English word "uncle"; it then asserts that what English-speaking people intend to say about a person x

---

[1] The reference is to I. M. Copi, *Introduction to Logic*, 1st ed. (New York, Macmillan, 1953).—JTW.

when they say "x is an uncle" is that x is a man who has the same parents as some other person who is a parent. But if it is an analysis, then it is a statement about the *property* connoted by the word "uncle": it says that the property of being an uncle is the property of being a man having the same parents as some other person who is a parent. If the relevant rules of the English language changed, say, if "uncle" came to be used in the sense in which "cousin" is now used, the dictionary definition would have to be changed, but the analysis would still be correct if it ever was, for the kinship relation of unclehood does not change when its English name changes. Further, a Frenchman who asserts that *"Un oncle est un homme qui a les même parents que quelque autre personne qui est un parent"* makes (provided your instructor's French translation is correct) precisely the same assertion as the American makes by the words "An uncle is a man who has the same parents as some other person who is a parent;" the American and the Frenchman, in other words, assert the same proposition by means of different sentences. But if the American had made an assertion about the way people in America and Britain use the word "uncle," and the Frenchman about the way people in France use the word *"oncle,"* they obviously would have asserted different propositions (in fact, it would be conceivable that one were true and the other false, since it is conceivable that *"oncle"* might not be the French synonym for "uncle").

The line between propositional and stipulative definitions is not always perfectly sharp. What Copi calls a precising definition of a vague term cuts across the line, for it is partly propositional and partly stipulative. Suppose, for example, you were to define "wealthy American" as meaning "American whose annual income exceeds $15,000." This definition can claim to be *true* in the sense that a great many Americans who are commonly referred to as wealthy do satisfy the proposed definition (i.e., have an annual income exceeding $15,000), and a great many who are commonly referred to as "not wealthy" do not satisfy the *definiens*. But to say that the defined term is, prior to the precising definition, vague just means that there are borderline cases with respect to it, i.e., persons who would not uniformly be called "wealthy" and would not uniformly be called "not wealthy" either. The precising definition then amounts to the decision to allot these borderline cases to the extension of "wealthy" or to the extension of "not wealthy".

Analytic definitions of concepts can give rise to *analytic statements*. Thus the analytic definition of "uncle" above gives rise to the analytic statement "All uncles are men"; the latter statement may be said to be *true by definition* but it is not itself a definition. An analytic statement is true by definition in the sense that with the help of a correct definition, i.e., one expressing the meaning with which the defined term is actually used, it is transformable into a logically true statement; and a logically true statement is one which can be seen to be true just by virtue of its form, i.e., the meanings of logical constants, such particles as "all," "some," "which," "or." To say that all uncles are men is to say that all men who have the same parents as some other person who is a parent are men. This statement has the form "All *A* which are *B*, are *A*," and anybody who understands the logical constants "all," "which," "are" can see that such a statement is true no matter what terms be substituted for the schematic letters "*A*" and "*B*" (provided, of course, that terms are used univocally).

FORMAL CLASSIFICATION. Copi distinguishes definition by example (including ostensive definition as a special case) from *connotative* definition, i.e., definition specifying the conventional connotation (criterion of application) of a term. But the latter kind of definition can have several forms; it is not restricted to what Copi calls "synonymous" definition and definition "by genus and difference." One important formal distinction is that between *explicit* and *contextual* definition. An explicit definition equates the *definiendum* with the *definiens* in such a way that one may be replaced by the other in any context without changing the remainder of the sentence. Thus "A father is a male parent" is an explicit definition, by virtue of which the sentence "My father is poor" may be transformed into the synonymous sentence "My male parent is poor." Similarly, "A brother is a male sibling" is an explicit definition. These definitions also happen to have genus-difference form, but it will be shown presently that an explicit definition need not have that form.

Now, suppose you were asked to define "brother" in terms of "male" and "parent" (and whatever logical constants may be needed). You could not construct a synonym which could replace "brother" in the sentence "Bill is John's brother" or "John has no brother." It is true that "brother" might be equated with "human male who has the same parents as some other human," but if you were to substitute this expression for "brother" in the sentence: "Bill is John's brother" you would obtain a pretty unintelligible sentence: "Bill is John's human male who has the same parent as some other human"!

A contextual definition is so called because it is a definition of a term in the context of a sentence (more exactly, statement-form) that contains it. Thus a contextual definition of "brother of"[2] in terms of "male" and "parent of" looks as follows: x is brother of $y = x$ is a human male distinct from y and the parents of x are the parents of y. In order to apply this definition to the above sentences we must translate the sentences in their entirety; we cannot simply lift the term "brother" out of them and replace it by a synonym: "Bill is John's brother" (i.e., "Bill is brother of John") becomes "Bill is a human male distinct from John and the parents of Bill are

---

[2] Don't confuse the property-term "brother" with the relation-term "brother of." The former is, as shown above, explicitly definable on the basis of "human male" and "parent" but not the latter. It should be noted that once "brother of" has been defined, it is perfectly legitimate to define "brother" in terms of "brother of": a brother is a person who is brother of some other person.

the parents of John"; similarly "John has no brothers" becomes "There is no human male distinct from John whose parents are the parents of John."

As our example suggests, contextual definition is appropriate especially for terms connoting a relationship. In general, terms that have no meaning whatever in isolation but only in the context of entire statements ("syncategorematic" terms) can be defined only contextually. To explain what "all" means is to explain what a statement of the form "All *A* are *B*" means, to explain what "or" means is to explain what a statement of the form "*p* or *q*" (where the letters "*p*" and "*q*" represent statements) means, to unfold the ambiguity of "is" is to explain how such statements as "This man is the criminal we were looking for" (identity), "That man is strong" (predication), "There is a cat on the couch" (existence) differ in meaning. Contextual definition of "all": all *A* are *B* = there are no *A* that are not *B*. Contextual definition of the exclusive sense of "or": *p* or *q* = not-(not-p and not-q) and not-(p and q).

The following kinds of explicit definition should be distinguished: *genus-difference, disjunctive* and *quantitative*. The word "sibling" may be disjunctively defined as "brother or sister" (provided you don't define "brother" as "male sibling" and "sister" as "female sibling"!),[3] "spouse" as

"husband or wife." This procedure amounts to explaining the connotation of a generic term by enumerating the species that make up the genus. It is a legitimate way of explaining the meaning of an unfamiliar word by means of familiar words, but should not be confused with analysis. Thus one would hardly be giving an analysis of the concept "animal" if one were to enumerate the different species of animals: an animal is either a lion or a mouse or a dog etc. etc. An example of a quantitative explicit definition: the momentum of a body is the product of its mass times its velocity. What is defined here is a term designating a magnitude (measurable property), not a class of objects; therefore the terminology of genus, species, difference, and of extension and intension, is not applicable here. Momentum is not a species of velocity, the way lions are a species of animals. Similarly, the definitions "$x^3 = x \cdot x \cdot x$", "$2 = 1 + 1$", "$i = \sqrt{-1}$" are explicit, but not of genus-difference nor of disjunctive form. On the other hand, some definitions of mathematical concepts properly

---

[3] It is true that in a dictionary you are likely to find "sibling" defined in terms of "brother" and "sister," and also the latter words in terms of the former. When such *circular* definitions are condemned it is because "definition" is understood as an ex-

planation of the meaning of a word by means of words whose meaning is already known by the person who requests the explanation. But the dictionary maker cannot easily predict which are the words already understood and which the words that prospective users of the dictionary will "look up." To play it safe, he may define "sibling" in terms of "brother" and "sister" for the benefit of those who don't know the meaning of "sibling" but know the meanings of the latter words, and also define the latter words in terms of "sibling" for the benefit of those who may happen to know the meanings of "sibling," "male" and "female" but not the meanings of "brother" and "sister".

have genus-difference form. Example: a prime number is a number which is devisible only by unity and by itself.

A species of contextual definition which is very important in empirical science is the *operational* definition. The *definiens* of such a definition has the form of an implication: *if* a specified test is performed, *then* a specified result will be observed. Examples: x is soluble in water $=$ if x is immersed in water then x dissolves; x is magnetic $=$ if a small iron body is placed near x, then it will move towards x; x is revengeful $=$ if x has been hurt, then x thirsts for revenge; x is forgiving $=$ if x has been hurt, then x does not hate the person who hurt him (at least not more than before he got hurt). Concepts which are operationally defined as illustrated are often called *disposition* concepts. To ascribe a disposition to an object is to predict how it would react to a specific kind of stimulation under specific circumstances.

One more form of definition, which is used especially in mathematics and formal logic, should be mentioned: *recursive definition*. Thus arithmetical addition can be recursively defined as follows: $(x + y') = (x + y)'$, and $(x + o) = x$. Here "y'" means "the number which is the immediate successor of y"; the notions of successor and zero are undefined but are used to define (recursively) "plus." By applying this definition to an expression of the form $(x + y)$, one can eliminate the symbol of addition in a finite number of steps. Thus "2 + 3" can be brought into that form by replacing "3" by its definiens "2'". The step by step elimination of "plus" then proceeds as follows: $2 + 2' = (2 + 2)' = (2 + 1')' = (2 + 1)'' = (2 + 0')'' = (2 + 0)''' = 2'''$. The latter expression may, looking up the explicit definition of "5", be replaced by "5" (hence it is incidentally evident that we have just formally proved "2 + 3 = 5"—though such a formal proof does not tell us what we might do with the equation in practical life).

Epistemological Classification

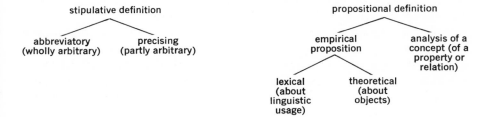

stipulative definition		propositional definition	
abbreviatory (wholly arbitrary)	precising (partly arbitrary)	empirical proposition	analysis of a concept (of a property or relation)
		lexical (about linguistic usage)	theoretical (about objects)

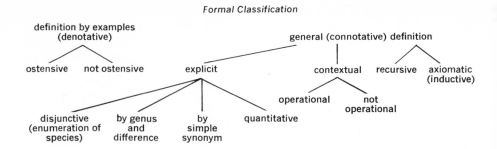

Formal Classification

4.2

THREE CONCEPTS
OF DEFINITION

Kazimierz Ajdukiewicz

1) Definitions had been discussed before the concept of formalized languages and formalized systems was born. Definitions were being written about in school textbooks of logic, and the so-called real definitions and nominal definitions were distinguished. Real definitions can be definitions of any objects, whereas nominal definitions always are definitions of some words or expressions. The grammatical structure of the terms 'real definition' and 'nominal definition' suggests that the corresponding concepts are specifications of some general concept of definition, that is, that the intension of the concepts 'real definition' and 'nominal definition' is obtained from the intension of the *genus* 'definition' by enriching it with properly selected *differentiae specificae*. If we, however,

more closely examine the meaning of the terms 'real definition' and 'nominal definition', we must come to the conclusion that it is not so, that the intension of the concepts corresponding to those terms is not a specification of the intension of some more general concept, and this means in turn that there is no general concept of definition of which the concepts of real definition and nominal definition would be specifications.

To substantiate the above statement let us explain the meaning of the terms 'real definition' and 'nominal definition'. Real definition of an object is an univocal characterization of that object, i.e., a statement about that object which states about it what in conformity with truth can be stated about one and only one object. The sentence 'Warsaw is the city which in 1958 A.D. is the capital of Poland' is an univocal characterization, and consequently a real definition, of Warsaw. The sentence 'Com-

From *Logique et Analyse*, 3 (1958). Reprinted by permission of the publisher, Editions Nauwelaerts S. A., Louvain.

mon salt is the body having the chemical composition NaCl' is an univocal characterization of common salt, i.e., of a certain genus or class of bodies. The term 'real definition' needs to be related only to the object being defined, there is no need to relate it to language. It is not so with the term 'nominal definition', since the latter needs to be related not only to the word or expression being defined, but also to a certain language. In other words, no statement is simply a nominal definition of a word; it can be such a definition only for a certain language. Because: to be a nominal definition of the word W for the language L means to be an instrument (a means) which allows to translate any sentence built of words belonging to the language L and of the word W, which does not belong to that language L, into a sentence consisting exclusively of words belonging to the language L, and which does not contain the word W.

It is sufficient to compare these two definitions, explaining the intensions of the concepts 'real definition' and 'nominal definition', to realize that these intensions are not derived from the intension of a more general concept of 'definition' by enriching it with distinct specific differences.

Hence it follows that the word 'definition' which appears in the terms 'real definition' and 'nominal definition' has in isolation no meaning at all. If we use the word 'definition' without any adjective, we use it elliptically and ambiguously, meaning either real definitions or nominal definitions or some other thing.

Apart from these two meanings of the elliptic term 'definition' there is also

a third. When, e.g., Poincaré calls the axioms of geometry 'disguised definitions' he means neither that they are univocal characterizations of some objects, i.e., that they are real definitions, nor that they serve as a means of translating certain terms, i.e., that they are nominal definitions. He means that they are sentences whose truth is guaranteed by certain terminological conventions, that is, by certain decisions as to what objects are to be symbolized by certain terms. This is the third concept associated with the term 'definition'. To distinguish it from the concepts of real definition and nominal definition we may call it 'arbitrary definition'. A sentence is called arbitrary definition or a postulate of a certain language, if a terminological convention *is binding* in that language, which lays down that some terms appearing in that sentence are to symbolize such objects which, taken as denotation of those terms, satisfy the sentence in question. It would be difficult to discover in the intension of that concept a common core which, when enriched with corresponding specific differences, would yield the intensions of the concepts of real definition, nominal definition, and arbitrary definition or postulate.

Thus, there is no single concept of definition on the genus level, subdivided into three kinds of definition on the species level, but there are at least three different concepts forming the connotation of three terms which from the grammatical point of view consist of the word 'definition' and a corresponding adjectival apposition. These three different concepts of definition are not mutually exclusive; they intersect, and their extensions include common and non-common elements. The theory of formalized languages knows all the three concepts of definition as specified above; it knows the concept of a sentence which is an univocal characterization of a certain object, it also knows the concept of nominal definition and of arbitrary definition, that is of postulate. But if the term 'definition' is used in the theory of formalized languages, it is always understood as 'nominal definition'. And if, in that theory, nominal definitions are referred to, then only such nominal definitions are meant which either are arbitrary definitions, i.e., postulates based on terminological conventions, or are themselves terminological conventions of the syntactical type, i.e., conventions laying down that some expressions can replace, or be replaced by, some other expressions. Thus the theory of formalized languages in dealing with definition does not exhaust the problems connected with the three concepts of definition, and therefore cannot replace a general theory of definition.

The purpose of this paper is to outline such a general theory of definition. It will consequently deal, one by one, with all the three concepts of definition enumerated above. It will also endeavour, within the limits of each concept, to elucidate some subordinated concepts and to prevent quite common confusions. Certain important problems connected with the three concepts will also be pointed to.

2) The concept of real definition of an object, i.e., the concept of its univocal characterization, will be discussed first. Historically, this is the oldest concept of definition, and the very term 'definition', as well as its Greek equivalent «ὁρισμός» was etymologically adapted to this concept. One can formulate real definitions of objects of all types and orders: one can formulate univocal characterizations of singular objects, of classes, of properties if they are distinguished from classes, of relations, etc. One can also formulate real definitions of words, since these too are some objects which can be characterized in an univocal way. The Aristotelian theory of definition denied the possibility of formulating real definitions of singular objects, but Aristotle understood real definitions in a narrower way than we do; for him not every univocal characterization of an object was a definition. We shall revert to that problem later.

The focal problem usually raised in connection with real definitions is that of criterion of a good real definition. The terms 'good' and 'bad' are not at all univocal. In logic, they are most often understood so that a real definition of an object is called good if it is such a definition in fact, and not only in appearance. Similarly in this interpretation, a classification or a proof is called good if it is a classification or a proof in fact, and not only in appearance. In this interpretation of the terms 'good' and 'bad', a real definition of an object will be called bad if it was intended to be an univocal characterization of that object, but in fact is not such a characterization.

Another interpretation of the terms 'good' and 'bad', which can be met with in logic in relation to logical constructs having the form of a sentence, is such that they are called 'good' if they are true sentences, and 'bad', if they are false sentences. In this interpretation of the terms 'good' and 'bad', every such sentence which states about an object O something which can truly be stated about one, and only one, object, namely the object O, will be called a good real definition of the object O, and every sentence which about an object O states something which can truly be stated about one, and only one, object, but which cannot be truly stated about the object O, will be called a bad real definition. In this interpretation of the terms 'good' and 'bad', a good real definition of an object O is its adequate definition, and a bad definition is a definition which is too narrow, too broad, etc.

There is, finally, a third interpretation of the terms 'good' and 'bad', which is often used in methodology; it is the relative interpretation of good or bad for some purpose. In this interpretation something is called 'good' if it is instrumental in attaining this purpose and it is called 'bad' if it does not serve that purpose. In this interpretation, the adjectives 'good' and 'bad' are elliptic abbreviations of relative terms 'good for the purpose P' and 'bad for the purpose P', respectively. It often happens that such a relativization with respect to purpose is passed over with silence, or even is not realized by those who use the adjectives 'good' and 'bad', and must only be guessed from circumstances.

The purposes to which the value of a given real definition is related, can vary considerably. For instance, the criterion may be, whether a given real definition serves the diagnostic purpose, i.e., whether its characterization of the object concerned makes it possible to recognize whether in a definite case we have to do with such an object, or not.

In other cases something else is required from a real definition: the characterization which it formulates should be such as to make it possible on the basis of some theory to deduce from it, in a purely logical way other properties of the object being defined, and if possible all its properties belonging to it from some point of view which is of interest for us. Such a requirement means that real definitions should be so to say syntheses of our knowledge of the objects they characterize. This was satisfied, for instance, in the 19th century by the definition of light as electromagnetic waves, because, within the Maxwell theory of electromagnetism, it made it possible to deduce all the then known properties of light. In a similar way, definitions of the various chemical elements, which characterize them by describing the structure of their atoms, are formulated so that on on the strength of appropriate physical theories we can from these characterizations deduce all other properties of those elements, e.g., their specific weight, chemical affinity, valency, etc.

Real definitions which in the sense outlined above are syntheses of our knowledge of the objects being defined, can be said to formulate the essence of those objects, if the term 'essence' be understood properly.

The above interpretation of the requirement that a good real definition should formulate the essence of the object being defined is not the only interpretation of that requirement, which has been put forward since Aristotle's times. Other interpretations of that requirement are either so vague that they evade exact formulation, or else require from real definitions what should rather be required from nominal definitions. We shall revert to this problem in connection with nominal definitions.

A real definition of an object is to give its univocal characterization. Such a characterization can be contained in sentences having various forms structures, and that is why real definitions cannot be characterized by a description of their structure. Aristotle's requirement that a real definition of a species should give its *genus* and *differentia specifica* was justified by an interpretation of the concept of real definition that was different from ours as well as by the assumptions of Aristotelian metaphysics. Real definitions understood as univocal characterizations can in some cases have that form which Aristotle considered to be the only correct, but in other cases can have quite different forms; they can have the form of a definition by abstraction, the form of recursive definition, or the form of a system of certain sentences which, when taken jointly, suffice to give an univocal characterization of the object being defined definition by postulates. Such a system of postulates can, as is well known, give a sufficient characterization not only of one, but of several objects. As an example we can give a consistent system of n linear equations in n unknowns. In view of such cases it would be possible to extend the concept of real definition

so as to cover not only real definitions of several objects, and not only single sentences being univocal characterizations of one object, but also systems of sentences being univocal characterizations of several objects.

3) So much for the real definitions. As to the nominal definitions, let us suppose that there is a certain language in which the word W does not appear. The theses T and the rules of inference R are adopted in that language. To express this we mark the language in question $L_{T,R}$. Let it be further assumed that we have enriched the sentences asserted in the language $L_{T,R}$ with a new sentence D_W, which includes the word W, or the rules R with a new rule R_W which refers to the term W. Now, if the sentence D_W or the rule R_W makes it possible, together with the theses T and the rules R of the language $L_{T,R}$ to translate every sentence consisting of words belonging to the language $L_{T,R}$ and the word W in a sentence consisting only of words of the language $L_{T,R}$, then such a sentence D_W or such a rule R_W is called a nominal definition of the word W *for the language $L_{T,R}$*. In other words a nominal definition of the word W *for* the language $L_{T,R}$ which does not contain that word W, is such a sentence or such a rule of inference which, when joined to the sentence accepted as true and to the adopted rules of the language $L_{T,R}$, makes it possible to translate every sentence built of words belonging to the language $L_{T,R}$ and the word W into another sentence, built only of words belonging to the language $L_{T,R}$ and not containing the word W.

A nominal definition of the word W formulated as a sentence including the word being defined itself and not its name is called a nominal definition formulated in the object language. A nominal definition of the word W formulated as a rule of inference is called a nominal definition formulated in the metalanguage, because that rule, concerning the use of the defined word W, contains its name and not this word itself. For instance, the definition: 'the square is the rectangle having four equal sides' is formulated in an object language since it includes the very word being defined, and not its name. The definition: 'whenever we accept as true any sentence containing the word "square", we may also accept as true a sentence obtained from the former one by substituting in it for the word "square" the expression "a rectangle having four equal sides"' is formulated in a metalanguage, since it includes not the word being defined but its name.

A general form of object-language nominal definitions cannot be given, since it depends on the vocabulary of the language $L_{T,R}$, on its sentences accepted as true, and on its adopted rules of inference. In such languages $L_{T,R}$ which include the symbol of identity, to which the usual logical theses and rules of inference apply, the simplest form of the object-language nominal definition of the word W for the language $L_{T,R}$ is an identity whose one side consists of that word W alone and the other of an expression built of words belonging to the language $L_{T,R}$ to which—as supposed—the word W does not belong. These are

so-called explicit definitions. In such languages we also meet context definitions having the form of an identity of which the one side is an expression built of the word being defined as the only constant and of variables, and the other side is an expression built only of the same variables and of constants, all of them belonging to the language $L_{T,R}$.

As for the metalanguage nominal definitions, certain general and always applicable forms can, however, be given. These are the two forms of rules laying down the so-called abbreviations. One of them is the rule of explicit abbreviations, which allows, whenever a sentence including the word W being defined is accepted as true, to replace that word by an expression built exclusively of words belonging to the language $L_{T,R}$. The other is the rule of context abbreviations, which allows, whenever a certain sentence including the word being defined in a certain context is accepted as true, to accept as true a sentence obtained from the former by the substitution for that context of some other context which consists exclusively of words belonging to the language $L_{T,R}$. These abbreviation rules are usually symbolized briefly as

$$\text{"}a = b\text{"}$$
$$\text{df}$$

e.g.,

$$\text{"}1 = \text{seq O"}, \quad \text{"}pvq = \sim p \to q\text{"} \text{ etc.}$$
$$\text{df} \qquad\qquad\quad \text{df}$$

Our definition of nominal definition includes the term 'to translate' which requires explanations, the more so as it is ambiguous, since we can speak of extensional translation and of intensional translation. To translate extensionally, on the basis of the theses T and of the rules of inference R, the sentence A into the sentence B means the same as to deduce the sentence B from the sentence A and the theses T following the rules R, and vice versa, to deduce the sentence A from the sentence B and the theses T following the rules R. In other words, to say that the sentence A is, on the basis of the theses T and the rules R, an extensional translation of the sentence B is the same as to say that the sentence A is inferentially equivalent to the sentence B on the basis of the theses T and the rules R.

It is more difficult to explain that it means to translate intensionally the sentence A into the sentence B on the basis of the theses T and rules R. To do so we must among the rules of inference distinguish the group of rules of inference which are proper to the language L, or briefly, the rules of inference of that language. We call so those rules of inference which we may not violate if we want to use the language in question. More exactly: a given rule of inference is called a rule of inference proper to the language L, if the fact that someone accepts the premises P but rejects the conclusion C allowed by that rule to be inferred from P, proves that he does not speak the language L. It seems, e.g., that the rule of inference, which allows, on the basis of the premise 'no A is a B', to accept the sentence 'no B is an A', is a rule of inference proper to our language, since the fact that someone would accept the sentence 'no A is a B'

and yet reject the corresponding sentence 'no B is an A' would prove that he does not understand the words which he uses in conformity with the rules of our language, and consequently, that he pronounces sentences belonging to the set of sentences of that language, but he does not speak that language.

Now by resorting to the notion of a rule of inference proper to a given language, i.e., such a rule which may not be violated if one wants to speak that language, we can define intensional translation: the sentence A is in the language $L_{T,R}$ an intensional translation of the sentence B if the sentence A can be deduced from the sentence B and vice versa, the sentence B can be deduced from the sentence A, with the use of only those of the rules R which, firstly, are rules introducing abbreviations and, secondly, are rules proper to the language $L_{T,R}$. In other words: the sentence A is, in the language $L_{T,R}$, an intensional translation of the sentence B, if one of the two sentences can be transformed into the other by means of expanding abbreviations or abbreviating expanded expressions in conformity with such rules which may not be violated, if one wants to speak the language $L_{T,R}$.

We have above distinguished object-language nominal definitions and metalanguage nominal definitions of the word W. Further analysis will be because of scarcity of time confined to object-language definitions only but may be expanded partly also to metalanguage definitions.

A nominal definition of the word W for the language L is a sentence which includes the word W being defined, which does not belong to the language *L*. Consequently, such a definition is not a sentence of that language and is, therefore, in that language neither true nor false. But such a nominal definition of the language *L* is a sentence of a certain more comprehensive language *L* + *W* which includes the word *W* and, possibly, other words not belonging to the language *L*, which is however, part of the language *L* + *W*. In that more comprehensive language *L* + *W* our definition is a sentence and as such is either true or false. Let the language of the pupils on a certain level of its evolution not include the word 'micron' which, however, belongs to the more comprehensive language of the teacher. The sentence 'a micron is a thousandth part of a millimetre' can be considered a nominal definition of the word 'micron' *for* the pupils' language. It is not a sentence of the pupils' language, and so it is neither true nor false in that language. But the same definition is a sentence *in* the teacher's language, and a true sentence in that language. The sentence 'a micron is a hundredth part of a millimetre' also is a definition of the word 'micron' *for* the pupils' language, but is not a sentence in that language; it is, however, a sentence in the more comprehensive language of the teacher, and a sentence which is false in that language.

If a sentence of the language *L*, containing the word *W*, is an object-language nominal definition of the word *W* in the language *L* which is part of the language *L*, we call it a possible nominal definition of the word *W* *in* the language *L*. The sentence 'a micron is a thousandth part of a millimetre', like the sentence 'a micron is a hundredth part of a millimetre', is *in* the teacher's language a possible nominal definition of the word 'micron'. Possible nominal definitions in a language are normal sentences of that language and as such can be true or false. Like all sentences, they require a proof before being accepted as true. Such proofs can be of the various kinds: they can be obtained by deduction from some already proved premises, they can be obtained by induction from perceptional sentences, but they can also find their proof in the so-called axiomatic rules of the given language. Axiomatic rules of a given language are such rules which allow unconditionally to accept as true certain definite sentences or sentences having a certain definite form, and at the same time forbid to reject them under the penalty of violating the principles of the language. It seems that, e.g., one of such axiomatic rules of the English language is the rule which allows to accept as true every sentence of the type 'every A is an A' and forbids, under the penalty of violating the principles of that language, to reject any sentence of that type. The sentence 'every square is a rectangle' also seems to be dictated by a corresponding axiomatic rule.

Axiomatic rules can be binding in a given language either on the strength of an explicit terminological convention or on the strength of a linguistic usage. The sentence 'a centimetre is a hundredth part of a metre' is dictated by the axiomatic rule which owes its binding force in the language to the decision to denote with the word 'centimetre' the length that satisfies the above sentence—a decision with which all those who speak the English language must comply. The sentence 'an uncle is is a mother's brother' also is dictated by an axiomatic rule which forbids to reject it under the penalty of violating the peculiarity of the English language, but it owes its binding force not to any explicit decision, but to the linguistic usage.

Now possible nominal definitions of the word W in the language L, dictated by an axiomatic rule which owes its binding force to an explicit terminological convention are called synthetic nominal definitions of that word *in* that language. All other possible nominal definitions in a given language are called analytic definitions of that language. The above dichotomic classification of the possible nominal definitions of a certain term *in* some language divides them into those which are dictated by an axiomatic rule of that language, based on a corresponding terminological convention and into all the remaining ones. The latter category also includes those which are dictated by some axiomatic rule of that language concerned, i.e., such which cannot be rejected without violating the peculiarity of that language, but by such an axiomatic rule which does not owe its binding force to any terminological convention. E.g., the definition 'an uncle is a mother's brother' is an analytic definition of the word 'uncle' in the English language, though it is a sentence based on an axiomatic rule of that language, because that rule, however, has no sanction in any terminological convention, but is based on the linguistic usage.

4) Synthetic nominal definitions of

a word fall under the third type of definitions, as specified above, i.e., that of arbitrary definitions or postulates. The sentence 'F (a)' of the language L is a postulate in that language, if a terminological convention, binding in that language, lays down that the term 'a' is to symbolize an object satisfying the sentential formula 'F x'. (This definition of postulate can be generalized so as to cover a larger number of terms). E.g., the sentence 'a centimetre is a hundredth part of a metre' is a postulate in our language because a convention, binding in that language, lays down that the word 'centimetre' is to symbolize the length that satisfies the sentential formula 'x is a hundredth part of a metre'. The example given above is not only a postulate, but also a possible nominal definition of the word 'centimetre' in our language. It is further a real definition of the length of one centimetre, since it gives a univocal characterization of that length. Postulates can, however, be quoted which are neither possible nominal definitions of any word in any language, since they do not allow to eliminate that word from the sentences of that language, nor real definitions of anything, since they are not univocal characterizations of any object.

In connection with the notion of postulate, the most interesting problem is, whether the postulates must always be true in the language in which the corresponding convention is binding. This question, with which I dealt in greater detail in one of my lectures delivered in Belgium in February this year, is usually answered rather in the affirmative. It is often said that a sentence is *true as a definition*, or that a sentence is *true by definition*. In these contexts the word 'definition' is taken in its third meaning pointed to in this paper, and so it is taken as isosemic with the word 'postulate' understood so as has been defined above.

The proof of the assertion that every postulate must be a true sentence can be outlined so: if the sentence 'F (a)' is a postulate in the language *L*, this means that in building that language we have decided to use the term '*a*' as denoting such an object which satisfies the formula 'F (x)'. But if we have decided so, then it is so, because in building the language in question we can make its terms the names of such objects as we like. Consequently, if 'F (a)' is a postulate in the language *L*, then the term '*a*' satisfies the formula 'F (x)', which means that 'F (a)' is a true sentence.

In this reasoning we have to question the premise that if in building a language we decide that the term '*a*' is to denote the object satisfying the condition 'F (x)', then that term will denote such an object. That term will not, in spite of our decision, denote the object satisfying the condition in question if such an object does not exist at all. For in building a language we can choose to our liking the objects that are to be the denotation of any term, but we can choose them only among those objects which *do* exist, and we cannot create such objects on the strength of our convention.

Hence it follows that a terminological convention alone is not sufficient to warrant the truth of a postulate; it is further needed the proof of existence of objects satisfying the condition im-

posed by that convention on the denotation of the term in question. Consequently, the demonstration that certain assertions are true as definitions or true by definition is not a sufficient demonstration of their truth. A sentence is true as a definition in the third of the meanings specified above, i.e., as a postulate only if the condition of existence is satisfied.

This is realized by the mathematicians who before accepting a sentence as a definition require the proof of existence and the proof of uniqueness. The reason for which the proof of existence is required, has been explained above. The reason for which the proof of uniqueness is required is, that the mathematicians, when speaking of definitions, mean what we have called synthetic definitions of a word. And synthetic definitions are such postulates which at the same time are nominal definitions of the word being defined, i.e., which can be used to translate sentences containing the word in question into sentences that are free from that word. And it can be demonstrated that if a sentence is to serve as a means of translation, always allowing to eliminate the term being defined from the sentences of the language, it must be a univocal characterization of its denotation, i.e., must be its real definition.

5) This last remark, outlined here very briefly and without proof, leads to the problem, what is the extensional relationship between the three concepts of definition discussed in this paper, namely the concept of a real definition of an object, of a nominal definition of a word, and of an arbitrary definition or a postulate.

This problem will not be investigated here in a systematic way. This would be a boring and laborious task. So we confine ourselves to a number of remarks loosely connected with the problem in question. We must state first that there can be sentences which fall under all the three categories of the concept of definition as explained in this paper. E.g., the sentence 'a micron is a thousandth part of a millimetre' is, firstly, a real definition of the length of one micron, since it supplies its univocal characteristics. Secondly, it is an object-language nominal definition of the word 'micron' in the English language, since it allows to translate any English language sentence containing the word 'micron' into a sentence belonging to that part of that language which does not include the word 'micron'. Thirdly, this is also, for the English language, a definition in the third sense, that is a postulate of the language concerned, because the terminological convention laying down that the word 'micron' should be used as a name of a length satisfying the condition: 'x is a thousandth part of a millimetre' is binding in the English language. This example—and their number could easily be multiplied—shows that the three notions of definition which we have devised are on no account mutually exclusive, but have some elements in common.

It is rather easy to answer the question, whether each of the three notions has elements that are proper only to itself; difficulties arise in one point only. There are, of course, nominal definitions that are neither real definitions nor postulates, for instance, the metalanguage nominal definitions, laying down some abbreviations. There also are postulates which are neither real nor nominal definitions; those are postulates which do not give a univocal characterization of the object they denote.

Are there, however, real definitions, i.e., univocal characterizations of a certain object, which are not nominal definitions of the name of that object in the language in which that definition is formulated? It is not possible to answer this question generally. For the fact whether a given sentence is a nominal definition of a certain word in, or for, a certain language depends not only on that sentence as such, but also on the sentences accepted as true in the language L and on the accepted rules of inference. Depending on what sentences are accepted in the language L and on what rules of inference are applied in that language, the same sentence, taken jointly with those other sentences and rules of inference, can, or cannot, suffice as a means of translation eliminating the word being defined. As far as those languages are concerned, in which the usual laws and rules of logic are accepted, it can be proved that every sentence which is a univocal characterization of an object O that is its real definition suffices jointly with the accepted laws and rules of logic as a means of those translations which allow to regard that real definition of the object O as a nominal definition of the name of that object. Hence, it follows that the nominal definitions of certain terms in the language L include all the real definitions which can be formulated in that language.

There are people who see red when

they encounter anything that savours of Platonian idealism. And the notion of real definition does savour of Platonian idealism. If one calls the sentence 'the square is the rectangle having four equal sides' a real definition of the square then one refers to a univocal characterization of the genus square, i.e., of a certain universal. Consequently, the opponents of Platonism avoid speaking of real definitions of objects and endeavour to replace all statements about real definitions of certain objects by statements about object-language nominal definitions of the names of those objects. They will, e.g., protest against the formulation that when we try to answer the question, 'what is justice?' we are looking for a real definition of justice, or that we are trying to give a univocal characterization of justice. The opponents of Platonism will say that in seeking an answer to the question, 'what is justice?', we are trying to give a true nominal definition of the word 'justice' in the language in which that question is formulated, and which already includes the word 'justice.' They will be right in so far as such an answer to that question will be a nominal definition of the word 'justice' in that language. They will, however, be wrong in so far as those who ask the question, 'what is justice?', are concerned not with the word 'justice', but with that what that word denotes. The meaning of that remark can be formulated more precisely as follows. The sentence 'John asks what is justice' is an intensional sentence, which can be translated into another intensional sentence 'John is looking for a real definition of justice'. But the opponents of Platonian idealism translate it into the intensional sentence 'John is looking for an object-language nominal definition of the word, "justice" in English'. Now, although the terms 'a real definition of justice' and 'an object-language nominal definition of the word "justice" in English' have the same extension, yet if the former is replaced by the latter in an intensional sentence that sentence can be transformed from a true one into a false one. And this just happens—as it seems.

That is the reason why, I think, the general theory of definition cannot dispense with real definitions and confine itself to nominal definitions alone.

With this I conclude my remarks on the three types of definitions and apologize to my listeners for the lengthiness of my paper.

4.3   ON DENOTING

Bertrand Russell

By a 'denoting phrase' I mean a phrase such as any one of the following: a man, some man, any man, every man, all men, the present King of England, the present King of France, the centre of mass of the Solar System at the first instant of the twentieth century, the revolution of the earth round the sun, the revolution of the sun round the earth. Thus a phrase is denoting solely in virtue of its *form*. We may distinguish three cases: (1) A phrase may be denoting, and yet not denote anything; *e.g.*, 'the present King of France'. (2) A phrase may denote one definite object; *e.g.*, 'the present King of England' denotes a certain man. (3) A phrase may denote ambiguously; *e.g.*, 'a man' denotes not many men, but an ambiguous man. The interpretation of such phrases is a matter of considerable difficulty; indeed, it is very hard to frame any theory not susceptible of formal refutation. All the difficulties with which I am acquainted are met, so far as I can discover, by the theory which I am about to explain.

The subject of denoting is of very

great importance, not only in logic and mathematics, but also in theory of knowledge. For example, we know that the centre of mass of the Solar System at a definite instant is some definite point, and we can affirm a number of propositions about it; but we have no immediate *acquaintance* with this point, which is only known to us by description. The distinction between *acquaintance* and *knowledge about* is the distinction between the things we have presentations of, and the things we only reach by means of denoting phrases. It often happens that we know that a certain phrase denotes unambiguously, although we have no acquaintance with what it denotes; this occurs in the above case of the centre of mass. In perception we have acquaintance with the objects of perception, and in hought we have acquaintance with objects of a more abstract logical character; but we do not necessarily have acquaintance with the objects denoted by phrases composed of words with whose meanings we are acquainted. To take a very important instance: There seems no reason to believe that we are ever acquainted with other people's minds, seeing that these are not directly per-

From *Mind*, LIX (1950). Reprinted by permission of the editor and the author.

ceived; hence what we know about them is obtained through denoting. All thinking has to start from acquaintance; but it succeeds in thinking *about* many things with which we have no acquaintance.

The course of my argument will be as follows. I shall begin by stating the theory I intend to advocate;[1] I shall then discuss the theories of Frege and Meinong, showing why neither of them satisfies me; then I shall give the grounds in favour of my theory; and finally I shall briefly indicate the philosophical consequences of my theory.

My theory, briefly, is as follows. I take the notion of the *variable* as fundamental; I use 'C (x)' to mean a proposition[2] in which x is a constituent, where x, the variable, is essentially and wholly undetermined. Then we can consider the two notions 'C (x) is always true' and 'C (x) is sometimes true'.[3] Then *everything* and *nothing* and *something* (which are the most primitive of denoting phrases) are to be interpreted as follows:—

C (everything) means 'C (x) is always true';

C (nothing) means "'C (x) is false' is always true";

C (something) means "It is false that 'C (x) is false' is always true".[4]

Here the notion 'C (x) is always true' is taken as ultimate and indefinable, and the others are defined by means of it. *Everything, nothing,* and *something*, are not assumed to have any meaning in isolation, but a meaning is assigned to *every* proposition in which they occur. This is the principle of the theory of denoting I wish to advocate: that denoting phrases never have any meaning in themselves, but that every proposition in whose verbal expression they occur has a meaning. The difficulties concerning denoting are, I believe, all the result of a wrong analysis of propositions whose verbal expressions contain denoting phrases. The proper analysis, if I am not mistaken, may be further set forth as follows.

Suppose now we wish to interpret the proposition, 'I met a man'. If this is true, I met some definite man; but that is not what I affirm. What I affirm is, according to the theory I advocate:—

" 'I met x, and x is human'
is not always false".

Generally, defining the class of men as the class of objects having the predicate *human*, we say that:—

'C (a man)' means "'C (x) and x is human' is not always false".

---

[1] I have discussed this subject in *Principles of Mathematics*, chapter v., and § 476. The theory there advocated is very nearly the same as Frege's, and is quite different from the theory to be advocated in what follows.

[2] More exactly, a propositional function.

[3] The second of these can be defined by means of the first, if we take it to mean, "It is not true that 'C (x) is false' is always true".

[4] I shall sometimes use, instead of this complicated phrase, the phrase 'C (x) is not always false,' or 'C (x) is sometimes true,' supposed *defined* to mean the same as the complicated phrase.

This leaves 'a man,' by itself, wholly destitute of meaning, but gives a meaning to every proposition in whose verbal expression 'a man' occurs.

Consider next the proposition 'all men are mortal'. This proposition[5] is really hypothetical and states that *if* anything is a man, it is mortal. That is, it states that if x is a man, x is mortal, whatever x may be. Hence, substituting 'x is human' for 'x is a man,' we find:—

'All men are mortal' means
" 'If x is human, x is mortal' is always true".

This is what is expressed in symbolic logic by saying that 'all men are mortal' means " 'x is human' implies 'x is mortal' for all values of x". More generally, we say:—

'C (all men)' means " 'If x is human, then C (x) is true' is always true".

Similarly

'C (no men)' means " 'If x is human, then C (x) is false' is always true".
'C (some men)' will mean the same as 'C (a man),'[6] and
'C (a man)' means "It is false that 'C (x) and x is human' is always false".
'C (every man)' will mean the same as 'C (all men)'.

_____

[5] As has been ably argued in Mr. Bradley's *Logic*, book i., chap. ii.

[6] Psychologically 'C (a man)' has a suggestion of *only one*, and 'C (some men)' has a suggestion of *more than one*; but we may neglect these suggestions in a preliminary sketch.

It remains to interpret phrases containing *the*. These are by far the most interesting and difficult of denoting phrases. Take as an instance 'the father of Charles II was executed'. This asserts that there was an x who was the father of Charles II and was executed. Now *the*, when it is strictly used, involves uniqueness; we do, it is true, speak of '*the* son of So-and-so' even when So-and-so has several sons, but it would be more correct to say '*a* son of So-and-so.' Thus for our purposes we take *the* as involving uniqueness. Thus when we say 'x was *the* father of Charles II' we not only assert that x had a certain relation to Charles II, but also that nothing else had this relation. The relation in question, without the assumption of uniqueness, and without any denoting phrases, is expressed by 'x begat Charles II'. To get an equivalent of 'x was the father of Charles II,' we must add, 'If y is other than x, y did not beget Charles II,' or, what is equivalent, 'If y begat Charles II, y is identical with x.' Hence 'x is the father of Charles II' becomes 'x begat Charles II; and 'if y begat Charles II, y is identical with x' is always true of y.

Thus 'the father of Charles II was executed' becomes:—

"It is not always false of x that x begat Charles II and that x was executed and that 'if y begat Charles II, y is identical with x' is always true of y".

This may seem a somewhat incredible interpretation; but I am not at present giving reasons, I am merely *stating* the theory.

To interpret 'C (the father of Charles

II),' where C stands for any statement about him, we have only to substitute C (x) for 'x was executed' in the above. Observe that, according to the above interpretation, whatever statement C may be, 'C (the father of Charles II)' implies:—

"It is not always false of x that 'if y begat Charles II, y is identical with x' is always true of y"

which is what is expressed in common language by 'Charles II had one father and no more'. Consequently if this condition fails, *every* proposition of the form 'C (the father of Charles II)' is false. Thus *e.g.* every proposition of the form 'C (the present King of France)' is false. This is a great advantage in the present theory. I shall show later that it is not contrary to the law of contradiction, as might be at first supposed.

The above gives a reduction of all propositions in which denoting phrases occur to forms in which no such phrases occur. Why it is imperative to effect such a reduction, the subsequent discussion will endeavour to show.

The evidence for the above theory is derived from the difficulties which seem unavoidable if we regard denoting phrases as standing for genuine constituents of the propositions in whose verbal expressions they occur. Of the possible theories which admit such constituents the simplest is that of Meinong.[7] This theory regards any grammatically correct denoting phrase as standing for an *object*. Thus 'the present King of

France,' 'the round square,' etc., are supposed to be genuine objects. It is admitted that such objects do not *subsist*, but nevertheless they are supposed to be objects. This is in itself a difficult view; but the chief objection is that such objects, admittedly, are apt to infringe the law of contradiction. It is contended, for example, that the existent present King of France exists, and also does not exist; that the round square is round, and also not round; etc. But this is intolerable; and if any theory can be found to avoid this result, it is surely to be preferred.

The above breach of the law of contradiction is avoided by Frege's theory. He distinguishes, in a denoting phrase, two elements, which we may call the *meaning* and the *denotation*.[8] Thus 'the centre of mass of the Solar System at the beginning of the twentieth century' is highly complex in *meaning*, but its *denotation* is a certain point, which is simple. The Solar System, the twentieth century, etc., are constituents of the *meaning*; but the *denotation* has no constituents at all.[9] One advantage of this distinction is that it shows why it is often worth while to assert identity. If we say 'Scott is the author of *Waverley*,'

---

[7] See *Untersuchungen zur Gegenstandstheorie und Psychologie*, Leipzig, 1904, the first three articles (by Meinong, Ameseder and Mally respectively).

[8] See his "Ueber Sinn und Bedeutung," *Zeitschrift für Phil. und Phil. Kritik*, vol. 100.

[9] Frege distinguishes the two elements of meaning and denotation everywhere, and not only in complex denoting phrases. Thus it is the *meanings* of the constituents of a denoting complex that enter into its *meaning*, not their *denotation*. In the proposition "Mont Blanc is over 1,000 metres high," it is, according to him, the *meaning* of "Mont Blanc," not the actual mountain, that is a constituent of the *meaning* of the proposition.

we assert an identity of denotation with a difference of meaning. I shall, however, not repeat the grounds in favour of this theory, as I have urged its claims elsewhere (*loc. cit.*), and am now concerned to dispute those claims.

One of the first difficulties that confront us, when we adopt the view that denoting phrases *express* a meaning and *denote* a denotation,[10] concerns the cases in which the denotation appears to be absent. If we say 'the King of England is bald,' that is, it would seem, not a statement about the complex *meaning* 'the King of England,' but about the actual man denoted by the meaning. But now consider 'the King of France is bald'. By parity of form, this also ought to be about the denotation of the phrase 'the King of France'. But this phrase, though it has a *meaning* provided 'the King of England' has a meaning, has certainly no denotation, at least in any obvious sense. Hence one would suppose that 'the King of France is bald' ought to be nonsense; but it is not nonsense, since it is plainly false. Or again consider such a proposition as the following: 'If u is a class which has only one member, then that one member is a member of u,' or, as we may state it, 'If u is a unit class, *the u* is a u'. This proposition ought to be *always* true, since the conclusion is true whenever the hypothesis is true. But 'the u' is a denoting phrase, and it is the denotation, not the meaning, that is said to be a u. Now if u is *not* a unit class, 'the u' seems to denote nothing; hence our proposition would seem to become nonsense as soon as u is not a unit class.

Now it is plain that such propositions do *not* become nonsense merely because their hypotheses are false. The King in "The Tempest" might say, 'If Ferdinand is not drowned, Ferdinand is my only son'. Now 'my only son' is a denoting phrase, which, on the face of it, has a denotation when, and only when, I have exactly one son. But the above statement would nevertheless have remained true if Ferdinand had been in fact drowned. Thus we must either provide a denotation in cases in which it is at first sight absent, or we must abandon the view that the denotation is what is concerned in propositions which contain denoting phrases. The latter is the course that I advocate. The former course may be taken, as by Meinong, by admitting objects which do not subsist, and denying that they obey the law of contradiction; this, however, is to be avoided if possible. Another way of taking the same course (so far as our present alternative is concerned) is adopted by Frege, who provides by definition some purely conventional denotation for the cases in which otherwise there would be none. Thus 'the King of France,' is to denote the null-class; 'the only son of Mr. So-and-so' (who has a fine family of ten), is to denote the class of all his sons; and so on. But this procedure, though it may not lead to actual logical error, is plainly artificial, and does not give an exact analysis of the matter. Thus if we allow that denoting phrases, in general, have

---

[10] In this theory, we shall say that the denoting phrase *expresses* a meaning; and we shall say both of the phrase and of the meaning that they *denote* a denotation. In the other theory, which I advocate, there is no *meaning*, and only sometimes a *denotation*.

the two sides of meaning and denotation, the cases where there seems to be no denotation cause difficulties both on the assumption that there really is a denotation and on the assumption that there really is none.

A logical theory may be tested by its capacity for dealing with puzzles, and it is a wholesome plan, in thinking about logic, to stock the mind with as many puzzles as possible, since these serve much the same purpose as is served by experiments in physical science. I shall therefore state three puzzles which a theory as to denoting ought to be able to solve; and I shall show later that my theory solves them.

(1) If *a* is identical with *b*, whatever is true of the one is true of the other, and either may be substituted for the other in any proposition without altering the truth or falsehood of that proposition. Now George IV wished to know whether Scott was the author of *Waverley*; and in fact Scott *was* the author of *Waverley*. Hence we may substitute *Scott* for *the author of "Waverley*," and thereby prove that George IV wished to know whether Scott was Scott. Yet an interest in the law of identity can hardly be attributed to the first gentleman of Europe.

(2) By the law of excluded middle, either 'A is B' or 'A is not B' must be true. Hence either 'the present King of France is bald' or 'the present King of France is not bald' must be true. Yet if we enumerated the things that are bald, and then the things that are not bald, we should not find the present King of France in either list. Hegelians, who love a synthesis, will probably conclude that he wears a wig.

(3) Consider the proposition 'A differs from B'. If this is true, there is a difference between A and B, which fact may be expressed in the form 'the difference between A and B subsists'. But if it is false that A differs from B, then there is no difference between A and B, which fact may be expressed in the form 'the difference between A and B does not subsist'. But how can a nonentity be the subject of a proposition? 'I think, therefore I am' is no more evident than 'I am the subject of a proposition, therefore I am,' provided 'I am' is taken to assert subsistence or being,[11] not existence. Hence, it would appear, it must always be self-contradictory to deny the being of anything; but we have seen, in connexion with Meinong, that to admit being also sometimes leads to contradictions. Thus if A and B do not differ, to suppose either that there is, or that there is not, such an object as 'the difference between A and B' seems equally impossible.

The relation of the meaning to the denotation involves certain rather curious difficulties, which seem in themselves sufficient to prove that the theory which leads to such difficulties must be wrong.

When we wish to speak about the *meaning* of a denoting phrase, as opposed to its *denotation*, the natural mode of doing so is by inverted commas. Thus we say:—

The centre of mass of the Solar System is a point, not a denoting complex; 'The centre of mass of the Solar System' is a denoting complex, not a point.

---

[11] I use these as synonyms.

Or again,

The first line of Gray's Elegy states a proposition.
'The *first* line of Gray's Elegy' does not state a proposition.

Thus taking any denoting phrase, say C, we wish to consider the relation between C and 'C,' where the difference of the two is of the kind exemplified in the above two instances.

We say, to begin with, that when C occurs it is the *denotation* that we are speaking about; but when 'C' occurs, it is the *meaning*. Now the relation of meaning and denotation is not merely linguistic through the phrase: there must be a logical relation involved, which we express by saying that the meaning denotes the denotation. But the difficulty which confronts us is that we cannot succeed in *both* preserving the connexion of meaning and denotation *and* preventing them from being one and the same; also that the meaning cannot be got at except by means of denoting phrases. This happens as follows.

The one phrase 'C' was to have both meaning and denotation. But if we speak of 'the meaning of C,' that gives us the meaning (if any) of the denotation. 'The meaning of the first line of Gray's Elegy' is the same as "The meaning of 'The curfew tolls the knell of parting day,'" and is not the same as "The meaning of 'the first line of Gray's Elegy'". Thus in order to get the meaning we want, we must speak not of 'the meaning of C,' but of "the meaning of 'C,'" which is the same as 'C' by itself. Similarly 'the denotation of C' does not mean the denotation we want, but means something which, if it denotes at all, denotes what is denoted by the denotation we want. For example, let 'C' be 'the denoting complex occurring in the second of the above instances'. Then

C='the first line of Gray's Elegy', and

the denotation of C=The curfew tolls the knell of parting day. But what we *meant* to have as the denotation was 'the first line of Gray's Elegy'. Thus we have failed to get what we wanted.

The difficulty in speaking of the meaning of a denoting complex may be stated thus: The moment we put the complex in a proposition, the proposition is about the denotation; if we make a proposition in which the subject is 'the meaning of C', then the subject is the meaning (if any) of the denotation, which was not intended. This leads us to say that, when we distinguish meaning and denotation, we must be dealing with the meaning: the meaning has denotation and is a complex, and there is not something other than the meaning, which can be called the complex, and be said to *have* both meaning and denotation. The right phrase, on the view in question, is that some meanings have denotations.

But this only makes our difficulty in speaking of meanings more evident. For suppose C is our complex; then we are to say that C *is* the meaning of the complex. Nevertheless, whenever C occurs without inverted commas, what is said is not true of the meaning, but only of the denotation, as when we say: The centre of mass of the Solar System is a point. Thus to speak of C itself, *i.e.*, to make a proposition about the meaning, our subject must not be C, but something which denotes C. Thus 'C', which is what we use when we want to speak of the meaning, must be not the meaning, but something which denotes the meaning. And C must not be a constituent of this complex (as it is of 'the meaning of C'); for if C occurs in the complex, it will be its denotation, not its meaning, that will occur, and there is no backward road from denotations to meanings, because every object can be denoted by an infinite number of different denoting phrases.

Thus it would seem that 'C' and C are different entities, such that 'C' denotes C; but this cannot be an explanation, because the relation of 'C' to C remains wholly mysterious; and where are we to find the denoting complex 'C' which is to denote C? Moreover, when C occurs in a proposition, it is not *only* the denotation that occurs (as we shall see in the next paragraph); yet, on the view in question, C is only the denotation, the meaning being wholly relegated to 'C'. This is an inextricable tangle, and seems to prove that the whole distinction of meaning and denotation has been wrongly conceived.

That the meaning is relevant when a denoting phrase occurs in a proposition is formally proved by the puzzle about the author of *Waverley*. The proposition 'Scott was the author of *Waverley*' has a property not possessed by 'Scott was Scott,' namely the property that George IV wished to know whether it was true. Thus the two are not identical propositions; hence the meaning of 'the author of *Waverley*' must be

relevant as well as the denotation, if we adhere to the point of view to which this distinction belongs. Yet, as we have just seen, so long as we adhere to this point of view we are compelled to hold that only the denotation can be relevant. Thus the point of view in question must be abandoned.

It remains to show how all the puzzles we have been considering are solved by the theory explained at the beginning of this article.

According to the view which I advocate, a denoting phrase is essentially *part* of a sentence, and does not, like most single words, have any significance on its own account. If I say 'Scott was a man,' that is a statement of the form '*x* was a man,' and it has 'Scott' for its subject. But if I say 'the author of *Waverley* was a man,' that is not a statement of the form '*x* was a man,' and does not have 'the author of *Waverley*' for its subject. Abbreviating the statement made at the beginning of this article, we may put, in place of 'the author of *Waverley* was a man,' the following: 'One and only one entity wrote *Waverley*, and that one was a man'. (This is not so strictly what is meant as what was said earlier; but it is easier to follow.) And speaking generally, suppose we wish to say that the author of *Waverley* had the property ϕ, what we wish to say is equivalent to 'One and only one entity wrote *Waverley*, and that one had the property ϕ'.

The explanation of *denotation* is now as follows. Every proposition in which 'the author of *Waverley*' occurs being explained as above, the proposition 'Scott was the author of *Waverley*' (*i.e.*

'Scott was identical with the author of *Waverley*') becomes 'One and only one entity wrote *Waverley*, and Scott was identical with that one'; or, reverting to the wholly explicit form: 'It is not always false of x that x wrote *Waverley*, that it is always true of y that if y wrote *Waverley* y is identical with x, and that Scott is identical with x'. Thus if 'C' is a denoting phrase, it may happen that there is one entity x (there cannot be more than one) for which the proposition 'x is identical with C' is true, this proposition being interpreted as above. We may then say that the entity x is the denotation of the phrase 'C'. Thus Scott is the denotation of 'the author of *Waverley*'. The 'C' in inverted commas will be merely the *phrase*, not anything that can be called the *meaning*. The phrase *per se* has no meaning, because in any proposition in which it occurs the proposition, fully expressed, does not contain the phrase, which has been broken up.

The puzzle about George IV's curiosity is now seen to have a very simple solution. The proposition 'Scott was the author of *Waverley*,' which was written out in its unabbreviated form in the preceding paragraph, does not contain any constituent 'the author of *Waverley*' for which we could substitute 'Scott'. This does not interfere with the truth of inferences resulting from making what is *verbally* the substitution of 'Scott' for 'the author of *Waverley*', so long as 'the author of *Waverley*' has what I call a *primary* occurrence in the proposition considered. The difference of primary and secondary occurrences of denoting phrases is as follows:—

When we say: "George IV wished to know whether so-and-so," or when we say "So-and-so is surprising" or "So-and-so is true," etc., the 'so-and-so' must be a proposition. Suppose now that 'so-and-so' contains a denoting phrase. We may either eliminate this denoting phrase from the subordinate proposition 'so-and-so', or from the whole proposition in which 'so-and-so' is a mere constituent. Different propositions result according to which we do. I have heard of a touchy owner of a yacht to whom a guest, on first seeing it, remarked, "I thought your yacht was larger than it is"; and the owner replied, "No, my yacht is not larger than it is." What the guest meant was, "The size that I thought your yacht was is greater than the size your yacht is"; the meaning attributed to him is, 'I thought the size of your yacht was greater than the size of your yacht'. To return to George IV and *Waverley*, when we say, "George IV wished to know whether Scott was the author of *Waverley*," we normally mean 'George IV wished to know whether one and only one man wrote *Waverley* and Scott was that man'; but we *may* also mean: 'One and only one man wrote *Waverley*, and George IV wished to know whether Scott was that man'. In the latter, 'the author of *Waverley*' has a *primary* occurrence; in the former, a *secondary*. The latter might be expressed by 'George IV wished to know, concerning the man who in fact wrote *Waverley*, whether he was Scott'. This would be true, for example, if George IV had seen Scott at a distance, and had asked "Is that Scott?" A *secondary* occurrence of a denoting phrase may be defined as one in which the phrase occurs in a proposition p which is a mere constituent of the proposition we are considering, and the substitution for the denoting phrase is to be effected in p, not in the whole proposition concerned. The ambiguity as between primary and secondary occurrences is hard to avoid in language; but it does no harm if we are on our guard against it. In symbolic logic it is of course easily avoided.

The distinction of primary and secondary occurrences also enables us to deal with the question whether the present King of France is bald or not bald, and generally with the logical status of denoting phrases that denote nothing. If 'C' is a denoting phrase, say 'the term having the property F', then

'C has the property ϕ' means 'one and only one term has the property F, and that one has the property ϕ'.[12]

If now the property F belongs to no terms, or to several, it follows that 'C has the property ϕ' is false for *all* values of ϕ. Thus 'the present King of France is bald' is certainly false; and 'the present King of France is not bald' is false if it means

'There is an entity which is now King of France and is not bald',

but is true if it means

'It is false that there is an entity which is now King of France and is bald'.

That is, 'the King of France is not bald' is false if the occurrence of 'the King

of France" is *primary,* and true if it is *secondary.* Thus all propositions in which 'the King of France' has a primary occurrence are false; the denials of such propositions are true, but in them 'the King of France' has a secondary occurrence. Thus we escape the conclusion that the King of France has a wig.

We can now see also how to deny that there is such an object as the difference between A and B in the case when A and B do not differ. If A and B do differ, there is one and only one entity x such that 'x is the difference between A and B' is a true proposition; if A and B do not differ, there is no such entity x. Thus according to the meaning of denotation lately explained, 'the difference between A and B' has a denotation when A and B differ, but not otherwise. This difference applies to true and false propositions generally. If 'a R b' stands for 'a has the relation R to b', then when a R b is true, there is such an entity as the relation R between a and b; when a R b is false, there is no such entity. Thus out of any proposition we can make a denoting phrase, which denotes an entity if the proposition is true, but does not denote an entity if the proposition is false. *E.g.,* it is true (at least we will suppose so) that the earth revolves round the sun, and false that the sun revolves round the earth; hence 'the revolution of the earth round the sun' denotes an entity, while 'the revolution of the sun round the earth' does not denote an entity.[13]

---

[12] This is the abbreviated, not the stricter, interpretation.

[13] The propositions from which such entities are derived are not identical either with these entities or with the propositions that these entities have being.

The whole realm of non-entities, such as "the round square," "the even prime other than 2," "Apollo," "Hamlet," etc., can now be satisfactorily dealt with. All these are denoting phrases which do not denote anything. A proposition about Apollo means what we get by substituting what the classical dictionary tells us is meant by Apollo, say 'the sun-god'. All propositions in which Apollo occurs are to be interpreted by the above rules for denoting phrases. If 'Apollo' has a primary occurrence, the proposition containing the occurrence is false; if the occurrence is secondary, the proposition may be true. So again 'the round square is round' means 'there is one and only one entity x which is round and square, and that entity is round,' which is a false proposition, not, as Meinong maintains, a true one. 'The most perfect Being has all perfections; existence is a perfection; therefore the most perfect Being exists' becomes:—

'There is one and only one entity x which is most perfect; that one has all perfections; existence is a perfection; therefore that one exists'.

As a proof, this fails for want of a proof of the premiss 'there is one and only one entity x which is most perfect'.[14]

---

[14] The argument can be made to prove validly that all members of the class of most perfect Beings exist; it can also be proved formally that this class cannot have *more* than one member; but, taking the definition of perfection as possession of all positive predicates, it can be proved almost equally formally that the class does not have even one member.

Mr. MacColl (*Mind*, N.S., No. 54, and again No. 55, p. 401) regards individuals as of two sorts, real and unreal; hence he defines the null-class as the class consisting of all unreal individuals. This assumes that such phrases as 'the present King of France', which do not denote a real individual, do, nevertheless, denote an individual, but an unreal one. This is essentially Meinong's theory, which we have seen reason to reject because it conflicts with the law of contradiction. With our theory of denoting, we are able to hold that there are no unreal individuals; so that the null-class is the class containing no members, not the class containing as members all unreal individuals.

It is important to observe the effect of our theory on the interpretation of definitions which proceed by means of denoting phrases. Most mathematical definitions are of this ⸱rt: for example, '$m - n$ means the number which, added to n, gives m'. Thus $m - n$ is defined as meaning the same as a certain denoting phrase; but we agreed that denoting phrases have no meaning in isolation. Thus what the definition really ought to be is: "Any proposition containing $m - n$ is to mean the proposition which results from substituting for '$m - n$' 'the number which, added to n, gives m'". The resulting proposition is interpreted according to the rules already given for interpreting propositions whose verbal expression contains a denoting phrase. In the case where m and n are such that there is one and only one number x which, added to n, gives m, there is a number x which can be substituted for $m - n$ in any proposition containing $m - n$ without altering the truth or falsehood of the proposition. But in other cases, all propositions in which '$m - n$' has a primary occurrence are false.

The usefulness of *identity* is explained by the above theory. No one outside a logic-book ever wishes to say 'x is x,' and yet assertions of identity are often made in such forms as 'Scott was the author of *Waverley*' or 'thou art the man.' The meaning of such propositions cannot be stated without the notion of identity, although they are not simply statements that Scott is identical with another term, the author of *Waverley*, or that thou art identical with another term, the man. The shortest statement of 'Scott is the author of *Waverley*' seems to be: 'Scott wrote *Waverley*; and it is always true of y that if y wrote *Waverley, y* is identical with Scott'. It is in this way that identity enters into 'Scott is the author of *Waverley*'; and it is owing to such uses that identity is worth affirming.

One interesting result of the above theory of denoting is this: when there is anything with which we do not have immediate acquaintance, but only definition by denoting phrases, then the propositions in which this thing is introduced by means of a denoting phrase do not really contain this thing as a constituent, but contain instead the constituents expressed by the several words of the denoting phrase. Thus in every proposition that we can apprehend (*i.e.* not only in those whose truth or falsehood we can judge of, but in all that we can think about), all the

constituents are really entities with which we have immediate acquaintance. Now such things as matter (in the sense in which matter occurs in physics) and the minds of other people are known to us only by denoting phrases, *i.e.*, we are not *acquainted* with them, but we know them as what has such and such properties. Hence, although we can form propositional functions C (x) which must hold of such and such a material particle, or of So-and-so's mind, yet we are not acquainted with the propositions which affirm these things that we know must be true, because we cannot apprehend the actual entities concerned. What we know is 'So-and-so has a mind which has such and such properties' but we do not know 'A has such and such properties,' where A *is* the mind in question. In such a case, we know the properties of a thing without having acquaintance with the thing itself, and without, consequently, knowing any single proposition of which the thing itself is a constituent.

Of the many other consequences of the view I have been advocating, I will say nothing. I will only beg the reader not to make up his mind against the view—as he might be tempted to do, on account of its apparently excessive complication—until he has attempted to construct a theory of his own on the subject of denotation. This attempt, I believe, will convince him that, whatever the true theory may be, it cannot have such a simplicity as one might have expected beforehand.

4.4

ON REFERRING

P. F. Strawson

I

We very commonly use expressions of certain kinds to mention or refer to some individual person or single object or particular event or place or process, in the course of doing what we should normally describe as making a statement about that person, object, place, event, or process. I shall call this way of using expressions the "uniquely referring use". The classes of expressions which are most commonly used in this way are: singular demonstrative pronouns ("this" and "that"); proper names (*e.g.* "Venice", "Napoleon", "John"); singular personal and impersonal pronouns ("he", "she", "I", "you", "it"); and phrases beginning with the definite article followed by a noun, qualified or unqualified, in the singular (*e.g.* "the table", "the old man", "the king of France"). Any expression of any of these classes can occur as the subject of what would traditionally be regarded as a singular subject-predicate sentence; and would, so occurring, exemplify the use I wish to discuss.

From *Mind*, LIX (1950). Reprinted by permission of the editor and the author.

I do not want to say that expressions belonging to these classes never have any other use than the one I want to discuss. On the contrary, it is obvious that they do. It is obvious that anyone who uttered the sentence, "The whale is a mammal", would be using the expression "the whale" in a way quite different from the way it would be used by anyone who had occasion seriously to utter the sentence, "The whale struck the ship". In the first sentence one is obviously *not* mentioning, and in the second sentence one obviously *is* mentioning, a particular whale. Again if I said, "Napoleon was the greatest French soldier", I should be using the word "Napoleon" to mention a certain individual, but I should not be using the phrase, "the greatest French soldier", to mention an individual, but to say something about an individual I had already mentioned. It would be natural to say that in using this sentence I was talking *about* Napoleon and that what I was *saying* about him was that he was the greatest French soldier. But of course I *could* use the expression, "the greatest French soldier", to mention an individual; for example, by saying: "The greatest French soldier died in exile". So it is obvious that at least some expressions belonging to the classes I mentioned *can* have uses other than the use I am anxious to discuss. Another thing I do not want to say is that in any given sentence there is never more than one expression used in the way I propose to discuss. On the contrary, it is obvious that there may be more than one. For example, it would be natural to say that, in seriously using the sentence, "The whale struck the ship", I was saying something about both a certain whale and a certain ship, that I was using each of the expressions "the whale" and "the ship" to mention a particular object; or, in other words, that I was using each of these expressions in the uniquely referring way. In general, however, I shall confine my attention to cases where an expression used in this way occurs as the grammatical subject of a sentence.

I think it is true to say that Russell's Theory of Descriptions, which is concerned with the last of the four classes of expressions I mentioned above (*i.e.* with expressions of the form "the so-and-so") is still widely accepted among logicians as giving a correct account of the use of such expressions in ordinary language. I want to show, in the first place, that this theory, so regarded, embodies some fundamental mistakes.

What question or questions about phrases of the form "the so-and-so" was the Theory of Descriptions designed to answer? I think that at least one of the questions may be illustrated as follows. Suppose some one were now to utter the sentence, "The king of France is wise". No one would say that the sentence which had been uttered was meaningless. Everyone would agree that it was significant. But everyone knows that there is not at present a king of France. One of the questions the Theory of Descriptions was de-designed to answer was the question: how can such a sentence as "The king of France is wise" be significant even when there is nothing which answers to the description it contains, *i.e.*, in this case, nothing which answers to the description "The king of France"? And one of the reasons why Russell thought it important to give a correct answer to this question was that he thought it important to show that another answer which might be given was wrong. The answer that he thought was wrong, and to which he was anxious to supply an alternative, might be exhibited as the conclusion of either of the following two fallacious arguments. Let us call the sentence "The king of France is wise" the sentence S. Then the first argument is as follows:

(1) The phrase, "the king of France", is the subject of the sentence S.

Therefore (2) if S is a significant sentence, S is a sentence *about* the king of France.

But (3) if there in no sense exists a king of France, the sentence is not about anything, and hence not about the king of France.

Therefore (4) since S is significant, there must in some sense (in some world) exist (or subsist) the king of France.

And the second argument is as follows:

(1) If S is significant, it is either true or false.

(2) S is true if the king of France is wise and false if the king of France is not wise.

(3) But the statement that the king of France is wise and the statement that the king of France is not wise are alike true only if there is (in some sense, in some world) something which is the king of France.

Hence (4) since S is significant, there follows the same conclusion as before.

These are fairly obviously bad arguments, and, as we should expect, Russell rejects them. The postulation of a world of strange entities, to which the king of France belongs, offends, he says, against "that feeling for reality which ought to be preserved even in the most abstract studies". The fact that Russell rejects these arguments is, however, less interesting than the extent to which, in rejecting their conclusion, he concedes the more important of their principles. Let me refer to the phrase, "the king of France", as the phrase D. Then I think Russell's reasons for rejecting these two arguments can be summarised as follows. The mistake arises, he says, from thinking that D, which is certainly the *grammatical* subject of S, is also the *logical* subject of S. But D is not the logical subject of S. In fact S, although grammatically it has a singular subject and a predicate, is not logically a subject-predicate sentence at all. The proposition it expresses is a complex kind of *existential* proposition, part of which might be described as a "uniquely existential" proposition. To exhibit the logical form of the proposition, we should re-write the sentence in a logically appropriate grammatical form; in such a way that the deceptive similarity of S to a sentence expressing a subject-predicate proposition would disappear, and we should be safeguarded against arguments such as the bad ones I outlined above. Before recalling the details of Russell's analysis of S, let us notice what his answer, as I have so far given it, seems to imply. His answer seems to imply that in the case of a sentence which is similar to S in that (1) it is grammatically of the subject-predicate form and (2) its grammatical subject does not refer to anything, then the only alternative to its being meaningless is that it should not really (*i.e.* logically) be of the subject-predicate form at all, but of some quite different form. And this in its turn seems to imply that if there are any sentences which are genuinely of the subject-predicate form, then the very fact of their being significant, having a meaning, guarantees that there *is* something referred to by the logical (and grammatical) subject. Moreover, Russell's answer seems to imply that there are such sentences. For if it is true that one may be misled by the grammatical similarity of S to other sentences into thinking that it is logically of the subject-predicate form, then surely there must be other sentences grammatically similar to S, which *are* of the subject-predicate form. To show not only that

Russell's answer seems to imply these conclusions, but that he accepted at least the first two of them, it is enough to consider what he says about a class of expressions which he calls "logically proper names" and contrasts with expressions, like D, which he calls "definite descriptions". Of logically proper names Russell says or implies the following things:

(1) That they and they alone can occur as subjects of sentences which are genuinely of the subject-predicate form;

(2) that an expression intended to be a logically proper name is *meaningless* unless there is some single object for which it stands: for the *meaning* of such an expression just is the individual object which the expression designates. To be a name at all, therefore, it *must* designate something.

It is easy to see that if anyone believes these two propositions, then the only way for him to save the significance of the sentence S is to deny that it is a logically subject-predicate sentence. Generally, we may say that Russell recognises only two ways in which sentences which seem, from their grammatical structure, to be about some particular person or individual object or event, can be significant:

(1) The first is that their grammatical form should be misleading as to their logical form, and that they should be analysable, like S, as a special kind of existential sentence;

(2) The second is that their grammatical subject should be a logically proper name, of which the meaning is the individual thing it designates.

I think that Russell is unquestionably wrong in this, and that sentences which are significant, and which begin with an expression used in the uniquely referring way fall into neither of these two classes. Expressions used in the uniquely referring way are never either logically proper names or descriptions, if what is meant by calling them "descriptions" is that they are to be analysed in accordance with the model provided by Russell's Theory of Descriptions.

There are no logically proper names and there are no descriptions (in this sense).

Let us now consider the details of Russell's analysis. According to Russell, anyone who asserted S would be asserting that:

(1) There is a king of France.
(2) There is not more than one king of France.
(3) There is nothing which is king of France and is not wise.

It is easy to see both how Russell arrived at this analysis, and how it enables him to answer the question with which we began, *viz.* the question: How can the sentence S be significant when there is no king of France? The way in which he arrived at the analysis was clearly by asking himself what would be the circumstances in which we would say that anyone who uttered the sentence S had made a true assertion. And it does seem pretty clear, and I have no wish to dispute, that the sentences (1)-(3) above do describe circumstances which are at least *necessary* conditions of anyone making a true assertion by uttering the sentence S. But, as I hope to show, to say this is not at all the same thing as to say that Russell has given a correct account of the use of the sentence S or even that he has given an account which, though incomplete, is correct as far as it goes; and is certainly not at all the same thing as to say that the model translation provided is a correct model for all (or for any) singular sentences beginning with a phrase of the form "the so-and-so".

It is also easy to see how this analysis enables Russell to answer the question of how the sentence S can be significant, even when there is no king of France. For, if this analysis is correct, anyone who utters the sentence S today would be jointly asserting three propositions, one of which (*viz.* that there is a king of France) would be false; and since the conjunction of three propositions, of which one is false, is itself false, the assertion as a whole would be significant, but false. So neither of the bad arguments for subsistent entities would apply to such an assertion.

II

As a step towards showing that Russell's solution of his problem is mistaken, and towards providing the correct solution, I want now to draw certain distinctions. For this purpose I shall, for the remainder of this section,

refer to an expression which has a uniquely referring use as "an expression" for short; and to a sentence beginning with such an expression as "a sentence" for short. The distinctions I shall draw are rather rough and ready, and, no doubt, difficult cases could be produced which should call for their refinement. But I think they will serve my purpose. The distinctions are between:

(A1) a sentence,
(A2) a use of a sentence,
(A3) an utterance of a sentence,

and, correspondingly, between:

(B1) an expression,
(B2) a use of an expression,
(B3) an utterance of an expression.

Consider again the sentence, "The king of France is wise". It is easy to imagine that this sentence was uttered at various times from, say, the beginning of the seventeenth century onwards, during the reigns of each successive French monarch; and easy to imagine that it was also uttered during the subsequent periods in which France was not a monarchy. Notice that it was natural for me to speak of "the sentence" or "this sentence" being uttered at various times during this period; or, in other words, that it would be natural and correct to speak of *one and the same* sentence being uttered on all these various occasions. It is in the sense in which it would be correct to speak of one and the same sentence being uttered on all these various occasions that I want to use the expression (A1) "a sentence". There are, however, obvious differences between different *occasions of the use* of this sentence. For instance, if one man uttered it in the reign of Louis XIV and another man uttered it in the reign of Louis XV, it would be natural to say (to assume) that they were respectively talking about different people; and it might be held that the first man, in using the sentence, made a true assertion, while the second man, in using the same sentence, made a false assertion. If on the other hand two different men simultaneously uttered the sentence (*e.g.* if one wrote it and the other spoke it) during the reign of Louis XIV, it would be natural to say (assume) that they were both talking about the same person, and, in that case, in using the sentence, they *must* either both have made a true assertion or both have made a false assertion. And this illustrates what I mean by *a use* of a sentence. The two men who uttered the sentence, one in the reign of Louis XV and one in the reign of Louis XIV, each made a different use of the same sentence; whereas the two men who uttered the sentence simultaneously in the reign of Louis XIV, made the same use[1] of the same sentence. Obviously in the case of this sentence, and equally obviously in the case of many others, we cannot talk of

---

[1] This usage of 'use' is, of course, different from (*a*) the current usage in which 'use' (of a particular word, phrase, sentence) = (roughly) 'rules for using' = (roughly) 'meaning'; and from (*b*) my own usage in the phrase "uniquely referring use of expressions" in which 'use' = (roughly) 'way of using'.

the sentence being true or false, but only of its being used to make a true or false assertion, or (if this is preferred) to express a true or a false proposition. And equally obviously we cannot talk of *the sentence* being *about* a particular person, for the same sentence may be used at different times to talk about quite different particular persons, but only of *a use* of the sentence to talk about a particular person. Finally it will make sufficiently clear what I mean by an utterance of a sentence if I say that the two men who simultaneously uttered the sentence in the reign of Louis XIV made two different utterances of the same sentence, though they made the same *use* of the sentence.

If we now consider not the whole sentence, "The king of France is wise", but that part of it which is the expression, "the king of France", it is obvious that we can make analogous, though not identical distinctions between (1) the expression, (2) a use of the expression and (3) an utterance of the expression. The distinctions will not be identical; we obviously cannot correctly talk of the expression "the king of France" being used to express a true or false proposition, since in general only sentences can be used truly or falsely; and similarly it is only by using a sentence and not by using an expression alone, that you can talk about a particular person. Instead, we shall say in this case that you *use* the expression to *mention* or *refer to* a particular person in the course of using the sentence to talk about him. But obviously in this case, and a great many others, the *expression* (B1) cannot be said to mention, or refer to, anything, any more than the *sentence* can be said to be true or false. The same expression can have different mentioning-uses, as the same sentence can be used to make statements with different truth-values. "Mentioning", or "referring", is not something an expression does; it is something that some one can use an expression to do. Mentioning, or referring to, something is a characteristic of *a use* of an expression, just as "being about" something, and truth-or-falsity, are characteristics of *a use* of a sentence.

A very different example may help to make these distinctions clearer. Consider another case of an expression which has a uniquely referring use, *viz.* the expression "I"; and consider the sentence, "I am hot". Countless people may use this same sentence; but it is logically impossible for two different people to make *the same use* of this sentence: or, if this is preferred, to use it to express the same proposition. The expression "I" may correctly be used by (and only by) any one of innumerable people to refer to himself. To say this is to say something about the expression "I": it is, in a sense, to give its meaning. This is the sort of thing that can be said about *expressions*. But it makes no sense to say of the *expression* "I" that it refers to a particular person. This is the sort of thing that can be said only of a particular use of the expression.

Let me use "type" as an abbreviation for "sentence or expression". Then I am not saying that there are sentences and expression (types), *and* uses of them, *and* utterances of them, as there are ships *and* shoes *and* sealing-wax. I am saying that we cannot say *the same*

things about types, uses of types, and utterances of types. And the fact is that we do talk about types; and that confusion is apt to result from the failure to notice the differences between what we can say about these and what we can say only about the *uses* of types. We are apt to fancy we are talking about sentences and expressions when we are talking about the uses of sentences and expressions.

This is what Russell does. Generally, as against Russell, I shall say this. Meaning (in at least one important sense) is a function of the sentence or expression; mentioning and referring and truth or falsity, are functions of the use of the sentence or expression. To give the meaning of an expression (in the sense in which I am using the word) is to give *general directions* for its use to refer to or mention particular objects or persons; to give the meaning of a sentence is to give *general directions* for its use in making true or false assertions. It is not to talk about any particular occasion of the use of the sentence or expression. The meaning of an expression cannot be identified with the object it is used, on a particular occasion, to refer to. The meaning of a sentence cannot be identified with the assertion it is used, on a particular occasion, to make. For to talk about the meaning of an expression or sentence is not to talk about its use on a particular occasion, but about the rules, habits, conventions governing its correct use, on all occasions, to refer or to assert. So the question of whether a sentence or expression *is significant or not* has nothing whatever to do with the question of whether the sentence, *uttered on a particular occasion*, is, on that occasion, being used to make a true-or-false assertion or not, or of whether the expression is, on that occasion, being used to refer to, or mention, anything at all.

The source of Russell's mistake was that he thought that referring or mentioning, if it occurred at all, must be meaning. He did not distinguish B1 from B2; he confused expressions with their use in a particular context; and so confused meaning with mentioning, with referring. If I talk about my handkerchief, I can, perhaps, produce the object I am referring to out of my pocket. I can't produce the meaning of the expression, "my handkerchief", out of my pocket. Because Russell confused meaning with mentioning, he thought that if there were any expressions having a uniquely referring use, which were what they seemed (*i.e.* logical subjects) and not something else in disguise, their meaning must *be* the particular object which they were used to refer to. Hence the troublesome mythology of the logically proper name. But if some one asks me the meaning of the expression "this"—once Russell's favourite candidate for this status—I do not hand him the object I have just used the expression to refer to, adding at the same time that the meaning of the word changes every time it is used. Nor do I hand him all the objects it ever has been, or might be, used to refer to. I explain and illustrate the conventions governing the use of the expression. This *is* giving the meaning of the expression. It is quite different from giving (in any sense of giving) the object to which it refers; for the expression itself does not refer to anything; though it can be used, on different occasions, to refer to innumerable things. Now as a matter of fact there is, in English, a sense of the word "mean" in which this word does approximate to "indicate, mention or refer to"; *e.g.* when somebody (unpleasantly) says, "I mean you"; or when I point and say, "That's the one I mean". But *the one I meant is* quite different from *the meaning of the expression* I used to talk of it. In this special sense of "mean", it is people who mean, not expressions. People use expressions to refer to particular things. But the meaning of an expression is not the set of things or the single thing it may correctly be used to refer to: the meaning is the set of rules, habits, conventions for its use in referring.

It is the same with sentences: even more obviously so. Everyone knows that the sentence, "The table is covered with books", is significant, and every one knows what it means. But if I ask, "What object is that sentence about?" I am asking an absurd question—a question which cannot be asked about the sentence, but only about some use of the sentence: and in this case the sentence hasn't been used, it has only been taken as an example. In knowing what it means, you are knowing how it could correctly be used to talk about things: so knowing the meaning hasn't anything to do with knowing about any particular use of the sentence to talk about anything. Similarly, if I ask: "Is the sentence true or false?" I am asking an absurd question, which becomes no less absurd if I add, "It must be one or the other since it's significant". The question is absurd, because the *sentence* is neither true nor false any more than it's *about* some object. Of course the fact that it's significant is the same as the fact that it *can* correctly be used to talk about something and that, in so using it, some one will be making a true or false assertion. And I will add that it will be used to make a true or false assertion *only* if the person using it *is* talking about something. If, when he utters it, he is not talking about anything, then his use is not a genuine one, but a spurious or pseudo-use: he is not making either a true or a false assertion, though he may think he is. And this points the way to the correct answer to the puzzle to which the Theory of Descriptions gives a fatally incorrect answer. The important point is that the question of whether the sentence is significant or not is quite independent of the question that can be raised about a particular use of it, *viz.* the question whether it is a genuine or a spurious use, whether it is being used to talk about something, or in make-believe, or as an example in philosophy. The question whether the sentence is significant or not is the question whether there exist such language habits, conventions or rules that the sentence logically could be used to talk about something; and is hence quite independent of the question whether it is being so used on a particular occasion.

III

Consider again the sentence, "The king of France is wise", and the true and false things Russell says about it.

There are at least two true things which Russell would say about the sentence:

(1) The first is that it is significant; that if anyone were now to utter it, he would be uttering a significant sentence.

(2) The second is that anyone now uttering the sentence would be making a true assertion only if there in fact at present existed one and only one king of France, and if he were wise.

What are the false things which Russell would say about the sentence? They are:

(1) That anyone now uttering it would be making a true assertion or a false assertion;

(2) That part of what he would be asserting would be that there at present existed one and only one king of France.

I have already given some reasons for thinking that these two statements are incorrect. Now suppose some one were in fact to say to you with a perfectly serious air: "The king of France is wise". Would you say, "That's untrue"? I think it's quite certain that you wouldn't. But suppose he went on to *ask* you whether you thought that what he had just said was true, or was false; whether you agreed or disagreed with what he had just said. I think you would be inclined, with some hesitation, to say that you didn't do either; that the question of whether his statement was true or false simply *didn't arise*, because there was no such person as the king of France.[2] You might, if he were obviously serious (had a dazed astray-in-the-centuries look), say something like: "I'm afraid you must be under a misapprehension. France is not a monarchy. There is no king of France." And this brings out the point that if a man seriously uttered the sentence, his uttering it would in some sense be *evidence* that he *believed* that there was a king of France. It would not be evidence for his believing this simply in the way in which a man's reaching for his raincoat is evidence for his believing that it is raining. But nor would it be evidence for his believing this in the way in which a man's saying, "It's raining" is evidence for his believing that it is raining. We might put it as follows. To say, "The king of France is wise" is, in some sense of "imply" to *imply* that there is a king of France. But this is a very special and odd sense of "imply". "Implies" in this sense is certainly not equivalent to "entails" (or "logically implies"). And this comes out from the fact that when, in response to his statement, we say (as we should) "There is no king of France", we should certainly *not* say we were *contradicting* the statement that the king of France is wise. We are certainly not saying that it's false. We are, rather, giving a reason for saying that the question of whether it's true or false simply doesn't arise.

And this is where the distinction I drew earlier can help us. The sentence, "The king of France is wise", is certainly significant; but this does not mean that any particular use of it is true or false. We use it truly or falsely when we use it to talk about some one; when, in using the expression, "The king of France", we are in fact mentioning some one. The fact that the sentence and the expression, respectively, are significant just is the fact that the sentence *could* be used, in certain circumstances, to say something true or false, that the expression *could* be used, in certain circumstances to mention a particular person; and to know their meaning is to know what sort of circumstances these are. So when we utter the sentence without in fact mentioning anybody by the use of the phrase, "The king of France", the sentence doesn't cease to be significant: we simply *fail* to say anything true or false because we simply fail to mention anybody by this particular use of that perfectly significant phrase. It is, if you like, a spurious use of the sentence, and a spurious use of the expression; though we may (or may not) mistakenly think it a genuine use.

And such spurious uses are very familiar. Sophisticated romancing, sophisticated fiction,[3] depend upon them. If I began, "The king of France is wise", and went on, "and he lives in a golden castle and has a hundred wives", and so on, a hearer would understand me perfectly well, without supposing *either* that I was talking about a particular person, *or* that I was making a false statement to the effect that there

---

[2] Since this article was written, there has appeared a clear statement of this point by Mr. Geach in *Analysis* Vol. 10, No. 4, March, 1950.

[3] The unsophisticated kind begins: "Once upon time there was . . .".

existed such a person as my words described. (It is worth adding that where the use of sentences and expressions is overtly fictional, the sense of the word "about" may change. As Moore said, it is perfectly natural and correct to say that some of the statements in *Pickwick Papers* are *about* Mr. Pickwick. But where the use of sentences and expressions is not overtly fictional, this use of "about" seems less correct; *i.e.* it would not *in general* be correct to say that a statement was about Mr. X or the so-and-so, unless there were such a person or thing. So it is where the romancing is in danger of being taken seriously that we might answer the question, "Who is he talking about?" with "He's not talking about anybody"; but in saying this, we are not saying that what he is saying is either false or nonsense.)

Overtly fictional uses apart, however, I said just now that to use such an expression as "The king of France" at the beginning of a sentence was, in some sense of "imply", to imply that there was a king of France. When a man uses such an expression, he does not *assert*, nor does what he says *entail*, a uniquely existential proposition. But one of the conventional functions of the definite article is to act as a *signal* that a unique reference is being made—a signal, not a disguised assertion. When we begin a sentence with "the such-and-such" the use of "the" shows, but does not state, that we are, or intend to be, referring to one particular individual of the species "such-and-such". *Which* particular individual is a matter to be determined from context, time, place and any other features of the situation of utterance. Now, whenever a man uses any expression, the presumption is that he thinks he is using it correctly: so when he uses the expression, "the such-and-such", in a uniquely referring way, the presumption is that he thinks both that there is *some* individual of that species, and that the context of use will sufficiently determine which one he has in mind. To use the word "the" in this way is then to imply (in the relevant sense of "imply") that the existential conditions described by Russell are fulfilled. But to use "the" in this way is not to *state* that those conditions are fulfilled. If I begin a sentence with an expression of the form, "the so-and-so", and then am prevented from saying more, I have made no statement of any kind; but I may have succeeded in mentioning some one or something.

The uniquely existential assertion supposed by Russell to be part of any assertion in which a uniquely referring use is made of an expression of the form "the so-and-so" is, he observes, a compound of two assertions. To say that there is a ϕ is to say something compatible with there being several ϕs; to say there is not more than one ϕ is to say something compatible with there being none. To say there is one ϕ and one only is to compound these two assertions. I have so far been concerned mostly with the alleged assertion of existence and less with the alleged assertion of uniqueness. An example which throws the emphasis on to the latter will serve to bring out more clearly the sense of "implied" in which a uniquely existential assertion is implied, but not entailed by the use of expressions in the uniquely referring way. Consider the sentence, "The table is covered with books". It is quite certain that in any normal use of this sentence the expression "the table" would be used to make a unique reference, *i.e.* to refer to some one table. It is a quite strict use of the definite article, in the sense in which Russell talks on p. 30 of *Principia Mathematica*, of using the article "*strictly*, so as to imply uniqueness". On the same page Russell says that a phrase of the form "the so-and-so", used strictly, "will only have an application in the event of their being one so-and-so and no more". Now it is obviously quite false that the phrase "the table" in the sentence "the table is covered with books", used normally, will "only have an application in the event of there being one table and no more". It is indeed tautologically true that, in such a use, the phrase will have an application only in the event of there being one table and no more *which is being referred to*, and that it will be understood to have an application only in the event of there being one table and no more which it is understood as being used to refer to. To use the sentence is not to assert, but it is (in the special sense discussed) to imply, that there is only one thing which is *both* of the kind specified (*i.e.* a table) *and is being referred to* by the speaker. It is obviously not to assert this. To refer is not to say you are referring. To say there is *some table or other* to which you are referring is not the same as referring to a particular table. We should have no use for such phrases as "the individual I referred to" unless there were something which counted as referring. (It would make no sense to say you had pointed if there were nothing which counted as pointing.) So once more I draw the conclusion that referring to or mentioning a particular thing cannot be dissolved into any kind of assertion. To refer is not to assert, though you refer in order to go on to assert.

Let me now take an example of the uniquely referring use of an expression not of the form, "the so-and-so". Suppose I advance my hands, cautiously cupped, towards someone, saying, as I do so, "This is a fine red one". He, looking into my hands and seeing nothing there, may say: "What is? What are you talking about?" Or perhaps, "But there's nothing in your hands". Of course it would be absurd to say that in saying "But you've got nothing in your hands", he was *denying* or *contradicting* what I said. So "this" is not a disguised description in Russell's sense. Nor is it a logically proper name. For one must know what the sentence means in order to react in that way to the utterance of it. It is precisely because the significance of the word "this" is independent of any particular reference it may be used to make, though not independent of the way it may be used to refer, that I can, as in this example, use it to *pretend* to be referring to something.

The general moral of all this is that communication is much less a matter of explicit or disguised assertion than logicians used to suppose. The particular application of this general moral in which I am interested is its application to the case of making a unique reference. It is a part of the significance of expressions of the kind I am discussing that they can be used, in an immense variety of contexts, to make unique references. It is no part of their significance to assert that they are being so used or that the conditions of their being so used are fulfilled. So the wholly important distinction we are required to draw is between:

(1) using an expression to make a unique reference; and
(2) asserting that there is one and only one individual which has certain characteristics (*e.g.* is of a certain kind, or stands in a certain relation to the speaker, or both).

This is, in other words, the distinction between

(1) sentences containing an expression used to indicate or mention or refer to a particular person or thing; and
(2) uniquely existential sentences.

What Russell does is progressively to assimilate more and more sentences of class (1) to sentences of class (2), and consequently to involve himself in insuperable difficulties about logical subjects, and about values for individual variables generally: difficulties which have led him finally to the logically disastrous theory of names developed in the *Enquiry* and in *Human Knowledge*. That view of the meaning of logical-subject-expressions which provides the whole incentive of the Theory of Descriptions at the same time precludes the possibility of Russell's ever finding any satisfactory substitutes for those expressions which, beginning with substantival phrases, he progressively degrades from the status of logical subjects.[4] It is not simply, as is sometimes said, the fascination of the relation between a name and its bearer, that is the root of the trouble. Not even names come up to the impossible standard set. It is rather the combination of two more radical misconceptions: first, the failure to grasp the importance of the distinction (section II above) between what may be said of an expression and what may be said of a particular use of it; second, a failure to recognise the uniquely referring use of expressions for the harmless, necessary thing it is, distinct from, but complementary to, the predicative or ascriptive use of expressions. The expressions which can in fact occur as singular logical subjects are expressions of the class I listed at the outset (demonstratives, substantival phrases, proper names, pronouns): to say this is to say that these expressions, together with context (in the widest sense) are what one uses to make unique references. The point of the conventions governing the uses of such expressions is, along with the situation of utterance, to secure uniqueness of reference. But to do this, enough is enough. We do not, and we cannot, while referring, attain the point of complete explicitness at which the referring function is no longer performed. The

---

[4] And this in spite of the danger-signal of that phrase, "*misleading* grammatical form".

actual unique reference made, if any, is a matter of the particular use in the particular context; the significance of the expression used is the set of rules or conventions which permit such references to be made. Hence we can, using significant expressions, pretend to refer, in make-believe or in fiction, or mistakenly think we are referring when we are not referring to anything.

This shows the need for distinguishing two kinds (among many others) of linguistic conventions or rules: rules for referring, and rules for attributing and ascribing; and for an investigation of the former. If we recognise this distinction of use for what it is, we are on the way to solving a number of ancient logical and metaphysical puzzles.

My last two sections are concerned, but only in the barest outline, with these questions.

IV

One of the main purposes for which we use language is the purpose of stating facts about things and persons and events. If we want to fulfil this purpose, we must have some way of forestalling the question, "What (who, which one) are you talking about?" as well as the question, "What are you saying about it (him, her)?" The task of forestalling the first question is the referring (or identifying) task. The task of forestalling the second is the attributive (or descriptive or classificatory or ascriptive) task. In the conventional English sentence which is used to state, or to claim to state, a fact about an individ-

ual thing or person or event, the performance of these two tasks can be roughly and approximately assigned to separable expressions.[5] And in such a sentence, this assigning of expressions to their separate roles corresponds to the conventional grammatical classification of subject and predicate. There is nothing sacrosanct about the employment of separable expressions for these two tasks. Other methods could be, and are, employed. There is, for instance, the method of uttering a single word or attributive phrase in the conspicuous presence of the object referred to; or that analogous method exemplified by, e.g. the painting of the words "unsafe for lorries" on a bridge, or the tying of a label reading "first prize" on a vegetable marrow. Or one can imagine an elaborate game in which one never used an expression in the uniquely referring way at all, but uttered only uniquely existential sentences, trying to enable the hearer to identify what was being talked of by means of an accumulation of relative clauses. (This description of the purposes of the game shows in what sense it would be a game: this is not the normal use we make of existential sentences.) Two points require emphasis. The first is that the necessity of performing these two tasks in order to state particular facts requires no transcendental explanation: to call attention to it is partly to elucidate the meaning of the phrase, "stating a fact". The second is that even this elucidation

---

[5] I neglect relational sentences; for these require, not a modification in the principle of what I say, but a complication of the detail.

is made in terms derivative from the grammar of the conventional singular sentence; that even the overtly functional, linguistic distinction between the identifying and attributive roles that words may play in language is prompted by the fact that ordinary speech offers us separable expressions to which the different functions may be plausibly and approximately assigned. And this functional distinction has cast long philosophical shadows. The distinctions between particular and universal, between substance and quality, are such pseudo-material shadows, cast by the grammar of the conventional sentence, in which separable expressions play distinguishable roles.

To use a separate expression to perform the first of these tasks is to use an expression in the uniquely referring way. I want now to say something in general about the conventions of use for expressions used in this way, and to contrast them with conventions of ascriptive use. I then proceed to the brief illustration of these general remarks and to some further applications of them.

What in general is required for making a unique reference is, obviously, some device, or devices, for showing both *that* a unique reference is intended and *what* unique reference it is; some device requiring and enabling the hearer or reader to identify what is being talked about. In securing this result, the context of utterance is of an importance which it is almost impossible to exaggerate; and by "context" I mean, at least, the time, the place, the situation, the identity of the speaker, the subjects which form the immediate focus of interest, and the personal histories of both the speaker and those he is addressing. Besides context, there is, of course, convention; —linguistic convention. But, except in the case of genuine proper names, of which I shall have more to say later, the fulfilment of more or less precisely stateable contextual conditions is *conventionally* (or, in a wide sense of the word, *logically*) required for the correct referring use of expressions in a sense in which this is not true of correct ascriptive uses. The requirement for the correct application of an expression in its ascriptive use to a certain thing is simply that the thing should be of a certain kind, have certain characteristics. The requirement for the correct application of an expression in its referring use to a certain thing is something over and above any requirement derived from such ascriptive meaning as the expression may have; it is, namely, the requirement that the thing should be in a certain relation to the speaker and to the context of utterance. Let me call this the contextual requirement. Thus, for example, in the limiting case of the word "I" the contextual requirement is that the thing should be identical with the speaker; but in the case of most expressions which have a referring use this requirement cannot be so precisely specified. A further, and perfectly general, difference between conventions for referring and conventions for describing is one we have already encountered, *viz.* that the fulfilment of the conditions for a correct ascriptive use of an expression is a part of what is stated by such a use; but the fulfilment of the conditions for a correct referring use of an expression is never part of what is stated, though it is (in the relevant sense of "implied") implied by such a use.

Conventions for referring have been neglected or misinterpreted by logicians. The reasons for this neglect are not hard to see, though they are hard to state briefly. Two of them are, roughly: (1) the preoccupation of most logicians with definitions; (2) the preoccupation of some logicians with formal systems. (1) A definition, in the most familiar sense, is a specification of the conditions of the correct ascriptive or classificatory use of an expression. Definitions take no account of contextual requirements. So that in so far as the search for the meaning or the search for the analysis of an expression is conceived as the search for a definition, the neglect or misinterpretation of conventions other than ascriptive is inevitable. Perhaps it would be better to say (for I do not wish to legislate about "meaning" or "analysis") that logicians have failed to notice that problems of use are wider than problems of analysis and meaning. (2) The influence of the preoccupation with mathematics and formal logic is most clearly seen (to take no more recent examples) in the cases of Leibniz and Russell. The constructor of calculuses, not concerned or required to make factual statements, approaches applied logic with a prejudice. It is natural that he should assume that the types of convention with whose adequacy in one field he is familiar should be really adequate, if only one could see how, in a quite different field—that of statements of fact. Thus we have Leibniz striving desperately to make the uniqueness of unique references a matter of logic in the narrow sense, and Russell striving desperately to do the same thing, in a different way, both for the implication of uniqueness and for that of existence.

It should be clear that the distinction I am trying to draw is primarily one between different rôles or parts that expressions may play in language, and not primarily one between different groups of expressions; for some expressions may appear in either rôle. Some of the kinds of words I shall speak of have predominantly, if not exclusively, a referring rôle. This is most obviously true of pronouns and ordinary proper names. Some can occur as wholes or parts of expressions which have a predominantly referring use, and as wholes or parts of expressions which have a predominantly ascriptive or classificatory use. The obvious cases are common nouns; or common nouns preceded by adjectives, including participial adjectives; or, less obviously, adjectives or participial adjectives alone. Expressions capable of having a referring use also differ from one another in at least the three following, not mutually independent, ways:

(1) They differ in the extent to which the reference they are used to make is dependent on the context of their utterance. Words like "I" and "it" stand at one end of this scale—the end of maximum dependence — and phrases like "the author of Waverly" and "the eighteenth king of France" at the other.

(2) They differ in the degree of "descriptive meaning" they possess: by "descriptive meaning" I intend "conventional limitation, in application, to things of a certain general kind, or possessing certain general characteristics". At one end of this scale stand the proper names we most commonly use in ordinary discourse; men, dogs and motor-bicycles may be called "Horace". The pure name has no descriptive meaning (except such as it may acquire *as a result of* some one of its uses as a name). A word like "he" has minimal descriptive meaning, but has some. Substantival phrases like "the round table" have the maximum descriptive meaning. An interesting intermediate position is occupied by 'impure' proper names like "The Round Table" —substantival phrases which have grown capital letters.

(3) Finally, they may be divided into the following two classes: (i) those of which the correct referring use is regulated by some *general* referring-cum-ascriptive conventions. To this class belong both pronouns, which have the least descriptive meaning and substantival phrases which have the most; (ii) those of which the correct referring use is regulated by no general conventions, either of the contextual or the ascriptive kind, but by conventions which are *ad hoc* for each particular use (though not for each particular utterance). Roughly

speaking, the most familiar kind of proper names belong to this class. Ignorance of a man's name is not ignorance of the language. This is why we do not speak of the meaning of proper names. (But it won't do to say they are meaningless). Again an intermediate position is occupied by such phrases as "The Old Pretender". Only an old pretender may be so referred to; but to know which old pretender is not to know a general, but an *ad hoc,* convention.

In the case of phrases of the form "the so-and-so" used referringly, the use of "the" together with the position of the phrase in the sentence (*i.e.* at the beginning, or following a transitive verb or preposition) acts as a signal *that* a unique reference is being made; and the following noun, or noun and adjective, together with the context of utterance, shows *what* unique reference is being made. In general the functional difference between common nouns and adjectives is that the former are naturally and commonly used referringly, while the latter are not commonly, or so naturally, used in this way, except as qualifying nouns; though they can be and are, so used alone. And of course this functional difference is not independent of the descriptive force peculiar to each word. In general we should expect the descriptive force of nouns to be such that they are more efficient tools for the job of showing what unique reference is intended when such a reference is signalised; and we should also expect the descriptive force of the words we naturally and commonly use to make unique reference to mirror our interest in the salient, relatively permanent and behavioural characteristics of things. These two expectations are not independent of one another; and, if we look at the differences between the commoner sort of common nouns and the commoner sort of adjectives, we find them both fulfilled. These are differences of the kind that Locke quaintly reports, when he speaks of our ideas of substances being *collections* of simple ideas; when he says that "powers make up a great part of our ideas of substances"; and when he goes on to contrast the identity of real and nominal essence in the case of simple ideas with their lack of identity and the shiftingness of the nominal essence in the case of substances. "Substance" itself is the troublesome tribute Locke pays to his dim awareness of the difference in predominant linguistic function that lingered even when the noun had been expanded into a more or less indefinite string of adjectives. Russell repeats Locke's mistake with a difference when, admitting the inference from syntax to reality to the extent of feeling that he can get rid of this metaphysical unknown only if he can purify language of the referring function altogether, he draws up his programme for "abolishing particulars"; a programme, in fact, for abolishing the distinction of logical use which I am here at pains to emphasise.

The contextual requirement for the referring use of pronouns may be stated with the greatest precision in some cases (*e.g.* "I" and "you") and only with the greatest vagueness in others ("it" and "this"). I propose to say nothing further about pronouns, except to point to an additional symptom of the failure to recognise the uniquely referring use for what it is; the fact, namely, that certain logicians have actually sought to elucidate the nature of a variable by offering such *sentences* as "he is sick", "it is green", as examples of something in ordinary speech like a *sentential function*. Now of course it is true that the word "he" may be used on different occasions to refer to different people or different animals: so may the word "John" and the phrase "the cat". What deters such logicians from treating these two expressions as quasi-variables is, in the first case, the lingering superstition that a name is logically tied to a single individual, and, in the second case, the descriptive meaning of the word "cat". But "he", which has a wide range of applications and minimal descriptive force, only acquires a use as a referring word. It is this fact, together with the failure to accord to expressions used referringly, the place in logic which belongs to them (the place held open for the mythical logically proper name), that accounts for the misleading attempt to elucidate the nature of the variable by reference to such words as "he", "she", "it".

Of ordinary proper names it is sometimes said that they are essentially words each of which is used to refer to just one individual. This is obviously false. Many ordinary personal names —names par excellence—are correctly used to refer to numbers of people. An ordinary personal name is, roughly, a word, used referringly, of which the use is *not* dictated by any descriptive meaning the word may have, and is *not* prescribed by any such general rule for use as a referring expression (or a part of a referring expression) as we find in the case of such words as "I", "this" and "the", but is governed by *ad hoc* conventions for each particular set of applications of the word to a given person. The important point is that the correctness of such applications does not follow from any *general* rule or convention for the use of the word as such. (The limit of absurdity and obvious circularity is reached in the attempt to treat names as disguised description in Russell's sense; for what is in the special sense implied, but not entailed, by my now referring to some one by name is simply the existence of someone, *now being referred to*, who is *conventionally referred to* by that name.) Even this feature of names, however, is only a symptom of the purpose for which they are employed. At present our choice of names is partly arbitrary, partly dependent on legal and social observances. It would be perfectly possible to have a thorough-going *system* of names, based *e.g.* on dates of birth, or on a minute classification of physiological and anatomical differences. But the success of any such system would depend entirely on the convenience of the resulting name-allotments for the purpose of making unique references; and this would depend on the multiplicity of the classifications used and the degree to which they cut haphazard across normal social groupings. Given a sufficient degree of both, the selectivity supplied by context would do the rest; just as is the case with our present naming habits. Had we such a system, we could use name-words descriptively (as we do at present, to a limited

extent and in a different way, with some famous names) as well as referringly. But it is by criteria derived from consideration of the requirements of the referring task that we should assess the adequacy of any system of naming. From the naming point of view, no kind of classification would be better or worse than any other simply because of the kind of classification—natal or anatomical—that it was.

I have already mentioned the class of quasi-names, of substantival phrases which grow capital letters, and of which such phrases as "the Glorious Revolution", "the Great War", "the Annunciation", "the Round Table" are examples. While the descriptive meaning of the words which follow the definite article is still relevant to their referring role, the capital letters are a sign of that extra-logical selectivity in their referring use, which is characteristic of pure names. Such phrases are found in print or in writing when one member of some class of events of things is of quite outstanding interest in a certain society. These phrases are embryonic names. A phrase may, for obvious reasons, pass into, and out of, this class (*e.g.* "the Great War").

V

I want to conclude by considering, all too briefly, three further problems about referring uses.

(a) INDEFINITE REFERENCES. Not all referring uses of singular expressions forestall the question "What (who, which one) are you talking about?"

There are some which either invite this question, or disclaim the intention or ability to answer it. Examples are such sentence-beginnings as "A man told me that . . .", "Some one told me that. . . ." The orthodox (Russellian) doctrine is that such sentences are existential, but not uniquely existential. This seems wrong in several ways. It is ludicrous to suggest that part of what is asserted is that the class of men or persons is not empty. Certainly this is *implied* in the by now familiar sense of implication; but the implication is also as much an implication of the *uniqueness* of the particular object of reference as when I begin a sentence with such a phrase as "the table". The difference between the use of the definite and indefinite articles is, very roughly, as follows. We use "the" either when a previous reference has been made, and when "the" signalises that the same reference is being made; or when, in the absence of a previous indefinite reference, the context (including the hearer's assumed knowledge) is expected to enable the hearer to tell *what* reference is being made. We use "a" either when these conditions are not fulfilled, or when, although a definite reference *could* be made, we wish to keep dark the identity of the individual to whom, or to which, we are referring. This is the *arch* use of such a phrase as "a certain person" or "some one"; where it could be expanded, not into "some one, but you wouldn't (or I don't) know who" but into "some one, but I'm not telling you who."

(b) IDENTIFICATION STATEMENTS.
By this label I intend statements like the following:

(*ia*) That is the man who swam the channel twice on one day.
(*iia*) Napoleon was the man who ordered the execution of the Duc D'Enghien.

The puzzle about these statements is that their grammatical predicates do not seem to be used in a straightforwardly ascriptive way as are the grammatical predicates of the statements:

(*ib*) That man swam the channel twice in one day.
(*iib*) Napoleon ordered the execution of the Duc D'Enghein.

But if, in order to avoid blurring the difference between (*ia*) and (*ib*) and (*iia*) and (*iib*), one says that the phrases which form the grammatical complements of (*ia*) and (*iia*) are being used referringly, one becomes puzzled about what is being said in these sentences. We seem then to be referring to the same person twice over and either saying nothing about him and thus making no statement, or identifying him with himself and thus producing a trivial identity.

The bogey of triviality can be dismissed. This only arises for those who think of the object referred to by the use of an expression as its meaning, and thus think of the subject and complement of these sentences as meaning the same because they could be used to refer to the same person.

I think the differences between sentences in the (*a*) group and sentences in the (*b*) group can best be understood by considering the differences between the circumstances in which you would say (*ia*) and the circumstances in which you would say (*ib*). You would say (*ia*) instead of (*ib*) if you knew or believed that your hearer knew or believed that *some one* had swum the channel twice in one day. You say (*ia*) when you take your hearer to be in the position of one who can ask: "Who swam the channel twice in one day?" (And in asking this, he is not saying that anyone did, though his asking it implies—in the relevant sense—that some one did). Such sentences are like answers to such questions. They are better called "identification-statements" than "identities". Sentence (*ia*) does not assert more or less than sentence (*ib*). It is just that you say (*ia*) to a man whom you take to know certain things that you take to be unknown to the man to whom you say (*ib*).

This is, in the barest essentials, the solution to Russell's puzzle about "denoting phrases" joining by "is"; one of the puzzles which he claims for the Theory of Descriptions the merit of solving.

(c) THE LOGIC OF SUBJECTS AND PREDICATES. Much of what I have said of the uniquely referring use of expressions can be extended, with suitable modifications, to the non-uniquely referring use of expressions; *i.e.* to some uses of expressions consisting of "the", "all the", "all", "some", "some of the", etc. followed by a noun, qualified or unqualified, in the *plural*; to some uses of "they", "them", "those", "these"; and to conjunctions of names. Expressions of the first kind have a special interest. Roughly speaking, orthodox modern criticism, inspired by mathematical logic, of such

traditional doctrines as that of the Square of Opposition and of some of the forms of the syllogism traditionally recognised as valid, rests on the familiar failure to recognise the special sense in which existential assertions may be implied by the referring use of expressions. The universal propositions of the fourfold schedule, it is said, must *either* be given a negatively existential interpretation (*e.g.*, for A, "there are no Xs which are not Ys") *or* they must be interpreted as conjunctions of negatively and positively existential statements of, *e.g.*, the form (for A) "there are no Xs which are not Ys, and there are Xs". The I and O forms are normally given a positively existential interpretation. It is then seen that, whichever of the above alternatives is selected, some of the traditional laws have to be abandoned. The dilemma, however, is a bogus one. If we interpret the propositions of the schedule as neither positively, nor negatively, nor positively *and* negatively, existential, but as sentences such that *the question of whether they are being used to make true or false assertions does not arise except when the existential condition is fulfilled for the subject term*, then all the traditional laws hold good together. And this interpretation is far closer to the most common uses of expressions beginning with "all" and "some" that is any Russellian alternative. For these expressions are most commonly used in the referring way. A literal-minded and childless man asked whether all his children are asleep will certainly not answer "Yes" on the ground that he has none; but nor will he answer "No" on this ground. Since he has no children, the question does not arise. To say this is not to say that I may not use the sentence, "All my children are asleep", with the intention of letting some one know that I have children, or of deceiving him into thinking that I have. Nor is it any weakening of my thesis to concede that singular phrases of the form "the so-and-so" may sometimes be used with a similar purpose. Neither Aristotelian nor Russellian rules give the exact logic of any expression of ordinary language; for ordinary language has no exact logic.

MR. STRAWSON
ON REFERRING

4.5

Bertrand Russell

Mr. P. F. Strawson published in *Mind* of 1950 an article called "On Referring". This article is reprinted in *Essays in Conceptual Analysis,* selected and edited by Professor Antony Flew. The references that follow are to this reprint. The main purpose of the article is to refute my theory of descriptions. As I find that some philosophers whom I respect consider that it has achieved its purpose successfully, I have come to the conclusion that a polemical reply is called for. I may say, to begin with, that I am totally unable to see any validity whatever in any of Mr. Strawson's arguments. Whether this inability is due to senility on my part or to some other cause, I must leave readers to judge.

This gist of Mr. Strawson's argument consists in identifying two problems which I have regarded as quite distinct —namely, the problem of descriptions and the problem of egocentricity. I have dealt with both these problems at considerable length, but as I have considered them to be different problems, I have not dealt with the one when I was considering the other. This enables Mr. Strawson to pretend that I have overlooked the problem of egocentricity.

He is helped in this pretence by a careful selection of material. In the article in which I first set forth the theory of descriptions, I dealt specially with two examples: "The present King of France is bald" and "Scott is the author of Waverley". The latter example does not suit Mr. Strawson, and he therefore entirely ignores it except for one quite perfunctory reference. As regards "the present King of France",

From *Mind*, LXVI (1957). Reprinted by permission of the editor and the author.

he fastens upon the egocentric word "present" and does not seem able to grasp that, if for the word "present" I had substituted the words "in 1905", the whole of his argument would have collapsed.

Or perhaps not quite the whole for reasons which I had set forth before Mr. Strawson wrote. It is, however, not difficult to give other examples of the use of descriptive phrases from which egocentricity is wholly absent. I should like to see him apply his doctrine to such sentences as the following: "the square-root of minus one is half the square-root of minus four", or "the cube of three is the integer immediately preceding the second perfect number". There are no egocentric words in either of these two sentences, but the problem of interpreting the descriptive phrases is exactly the same as if there were.

There is not a word in Mr. Strawson's article to suggest that I ever considered egocentric words, still less, that the theory which he advocates in regard to them is the very one which I had set forth at great length and in considerable detail.[1] The gist of what he has to say about such words is the entirely correct statement that what they refer to depends upon when and where they are used. As to this, I need only quote one paragraph from *Human Knowledge* (p. 107):

> 'This' denotes whatever, at the moment when the word is used, occupies the centre of attention. With words which are not egocentric what is constant is

something about the object indicated, but 'this' denotes a different object on each occasion of its use: what is constant is not the object denoted, but its relation to the particular use of the word. Whenever the word is used, the person using it is attending to something, and the word indicates this something. When a word is not egocentric, there is no need to distinguish between different occasions when it is used, but we must make this distinction with egocentric words, since what they indicate is something having a given relation to the particular use of the word.

I must refer also to the case that I discuss (pp. 101 ff.) in which I am walking with a friend on a dark night. We lose touch with each other and he calls, "Where are you?" and I reply "Here I am!" It is of the essence of a scientific account of the world to reduce to a minimum the egocentric element in an assertion, but success in this attempt is a matter of degree, and is never complete where empirical material is concerned. This is due to the fact that the meanings of all empirical words depend ultimately upon ostensive definitions, that ostensive definitions depend upon experience, and that experience is egocentric. We can, however, by means of egocentric words, *describe* something which is not egocentric; it is this that enables us to use a common language.

All this may be right or wrong, but, whichever it is, Mr. Strawson should not expound it as if it were a theory that he had invented, whereas, in fact, I had set it forth before he wrote, though perhaps he did not grasp the purport of what I said. I shall say no

---

[1] *Cf. Inquiry into Meaning and Truth,* chap. vii, and *Human Knowledge*, Part II, chap. iv.

more about egocentricity since, for the reasons I have already given, I think Mr. Strawson completely mistaken in connecting it with the problem of descriptions.

I am at a loss to understand Mr. Strawson's position on the subject of names. When he is writing about me, he says: "There are no logically proper names and there are no descriptions (in this sense)" (p. 26). But when he is writing about Quine, in *Mind*, October, 1956, he takes a quite different line. Quine has a theory that names are unnecessary and can always be replaced by descriptions. This theory shocks Mr. Strawson for reasons which, to me, remain obscure. However, I will leave the defence of Quine to Quine, who is quite capable of looking after himself. What is important for my purpose is to elucidate the meaning of the words "in this sense" which Mr. Strawson puts in brackets. So far as I can discover from the context, what he objects to is the belief that there are words which are only significant because there is something that they mean, and if there were not this something, they would be empty noises, not words. For my part, I think that there must be such words if language is to have any relation to fact. The necessity for such words is made obvious by the process of ostensive definition. How do we know what is meant by such words as "red" and "blue"? We cannot know what these words mean unless we have seen red and seen blue. If there were no red and no blue in our experience, we might, perhaps, invent some elaborate description which we could substitute for the word "red" or for the word "blue". For ex-ample, if you were dealing with a blind man, you could hold a red-hot poker near enough for him to feel the heat, and you could tell him that red is what he would see if he could see—but of course for the word "see" you would have to substitute another elaborate description. Any description which the blind man could understand would have to be in terms of words expressing experiences which he had had. Unless fundamental words in the individual's vocabulary had this kind of direct relation to fact, language in general would have no such relation. I defy Mr. Strawson to give the usual meaning to the word "red" unless there is something which the word designates.

This brings me to a further point. "Red" is usually regarded as a predicate and as designating a universal. I prefer for purposes of philosophical analysis a language in which "red" is a subject, and, while I should not say that it is a positive error to call it a universal, I should say that calling it so invites confusion. This is connected with what Mr. Strawson calls my "logically disastrous theory of names" (p. 39). He does not deign to mention why he considers this theory "logically disastrous". I hope that on some future occasion he will enlighten me on this point.

This brings me to a fundamental divergence between myself and many philosophers with whom Mr. Strawson appears to be in general agreement. They are persuaded that common speech is good enough not only for daily life, but also for philosophy. I, on the contrary, am persuaded that common speech is full of vagueness and inaccuracy, and that any attempt to be precise and accurate requires modification of common speech both as regards vocabulary and as regards syntax. Everybody admits that physics and chemistry and medicine each require a language which is not that of everyday life. I fail to see why philosophy, alone, should be forbidden to make a similar approach towards precision and accuracy. Let us take, in illustration, one of the commonest words of everyday speech: namely, the word "day". The most august use of this word is in the first chapter of *Genesis* and in the Ten Commandments. The desire to keep holy the Sabbath "day" has led orthodox Jews to give a precision to the word "day" which it does not have in common speech: they have defined it as the period from one sunset to the next. Astronomers, with other reasons for seeking precision, have three sorts of day: the true solar day; the mean day; and the sidereal day. These have different uses: the true solar day is relevant if you are considering lighting-up time; the mean solar day is relevant if you are sentenced to fourteen days without the option; and the sidereal day is relevant if you are trying to estimate the influence of the tides in retarding the earth's rotation. All these four kinds of day— decalogical, true, mean, and sidereal— are more precise than the common use of the word "day". If astronomers were subject to the prohibition of precision which some recent philosophers apparently favour, the whole science of astronomy would be impossible.

For technical purposes, technical languages differing from those of daily life are indispensable. I feel that those who object to linguistic novelties, if they had lived a hundred and fifty years ago, would have stuck to feet and ounces, and would have maintained that centimetres and grams savour of the guillotine.

In philosophy, it is syntax, even more than vocabulary, that needs to be corrected. The subject-predicate logic to which we are accustomed depends for its convenience upon the fact that at the usual temperature of the earth there are approximately permanent "things". This would not be true at the temperature of the sun, and is only roughly true at the temperatures to which we are accustomed.

My theory of descriptions was never intended as an analysis of the state of mind of those who utter sentences containing descriptions. Mr. Strawson gives the name "S" to the sentence "The King of France is wise", and he says of me "The way in which he arrived at the analysis was clearly by asking himself what would be the circumstances in which we would say that anyone who uttered the sentence S had made a true assertion". This does not seem to me a correct account of what I was doing. Suppose (which God forbid) Mr. Strawson were so rash as to accuse his char-lady of thieving: she would reply indignantly, "I ain't never done no harm to no one". Assuming her a pattern of virtue, I should say that she was making a true assertion, although, according to the rules of syntax which Mr. Strawson would adopt in his own speech, what she said should have meant: "there was at least one moment when I was injuring the whole human race". Mr. Strawson would not have supposed that this was what she meant to assert, although he would not have used her words to express the same sentiment. Similarly, I was concerned to find a more accurate and analysed thought to replace the somewhat confused thoughts which most people at most times have in their heads.

Mr. Strawson objects to my saying that "the King of France is wise" is false if there is no King of France. He admits that the sentence is significant and not true, but not that it is false. This is a mere question of verbal convenience. He considers that the word "false" has an unalterable meaning which it would be sinful to regard as adjustable, though he prudently avoids telling us what this meaning is. For my part, I find it more convenient to define the word "false" so that every significant sentence is either true or false. This is a purely verbal question; and although I have no wish to claim the support of common usage, I do not think that he can claim it either. Suppose, for example, that in some country there was a law that no person could hold public office if he considered it false that the Ruler of the Universe is wise. I think an avowed atheist who took advantage of Mr. Strawson's doctrine to say that he did not hold this proposition false, would be regarded as a somewhat shifty character.

It is not only as to names and as to falsehood that Mr. Strawson shows his conviction that there is an unalterably right way of using words and that no change is to be tolerated however convenient it may be. He shows the same feeling as regards universal affirmatives —*i.e.* sentences of the form "All A is B". Traditionally, such sentences are supposed to imply that there are A's, but it is much more convenient in mathematical logic to drop this implication and to consider that "All A is B" is true if there are no A's. This is wholly and solely a question of convenience. For some purposes the one convention is more convenient and for others, the other. We shall prefer the one convention or the other according to the purpose we have in view. I agree, however, with Mr. Strawson's statement (p. 52) that ordinary language has no exact logic.

Mr. Strawson, in spite of his very real logical competence, has a curious prejudice against logic. On page 43, he has a sudden dithyrambic outburst, to the effect that life is greater than logic, which he uses to give a quite false interpretation of my doctrines.

Leaving detail aside, I think we may sum up Mr. Strawson's argument and my reply to it as follows:

There are two problems, that of description and that of egocentricity. Mr. Strawson thinks they are one and the same problem, but it is obvious from his discussion that he has not considered as many kinds of descriptive phrases as are relevant to the argument. Having confused the two problems, he asserts dogmatically that it is only the egocentric problem that needs to be solved, and he offers a solution of this problem which he seems to believe to be new, but which in fact was familiar before he wrote. He then thinks that he has offered an adequate theory of descriptions, and announces his sup-

posed achievement with astonishing dogmaic certainty. Perhaps I am doing him an injustice, but I am unable to see in what respect this is the case.

4.6

REFERENCE
AND REFERENTS

Leonard Linsky

I

In discussing the topics of definite descriptions, referring expressions, and proper names, mistakes are made due to a failure to distinguish referring and making a reference, in the ordinary meanings of these terms, from what philosophers call "denoting", and "referring". Of first importance here is the consideration that it is the users of language who refer and make references and not, except in a derivative sense, the expressions which they use in so doing. Ryle, for example, says, "A descriptive phrase is not a proper name, and the way in which the subject of attributes which it denotes is de-

noted by it is not in that subject's being *called* 'the so-and so', but in its possessing and being *ipso facto* the sole possessor of the idiosyncratic attribute which is what the descriptive phrase signifies."[1] I do not wish to deny that what Ryle says here is true, in his technical sense of "denote". The example is chosen only to bring out how different this sense is from what we ordinarily understand by referring. I might, for example, refer to someone as "the old man with grey hair". Still, the phrase "the old man with grey hair" does not "signify" an "idiosyncratic attribute", if what is meant by this is an attribute belonging to just *one* person. It is equally obvious that I might refer to a person as "the so-and-so" even though that person did not possess the attribute (idiosyncratic or not) "signified" by that phrase. I

From *Philosophy and Ordinary Language,* Charles Caton, editor (Urbana, Ill.: University of Illinois Press, 1963). Reprinted by permission of the publishers and the author. Section IV originally appeared as "Hesperus and Phosphorus," *Philosophical Review,* LXVIII (1959), and is reprinted here by permission of the editors.

---

[1] "Systematically Misleading Expressions", reprinted in *Essays on Logic and Language,* edited by A. Flew, New York, 1951, p. 23.

might, for example, refer to someone as "the old man with grey hair", even though that person was not old but prematurely grey. In both cases I would be referring to someone not "denoted" (in Ryle's sense) by the expression used in so doing. But these *expressions* do not refer to that person, I do. The question "To whom does the phrase 'the so-and-so' refer?" is, in general, an odd question. What might be asked is "Who is the president of the United States?", or "To whom are you referring?", not "To whom does the phrase 'the president of the United States' refer?".

The question "To whom (what) does the phrase 'the so-and-so' refer?" is generally odd. It is not always odd. Certainly it sounds odder in some cases than in others. I think one might ask, "To what does the phrase 'the morning star' refer?", or, pointing to a written text, I might ask, "To whom is the author referring with the phrase 'the most influential man in Lincoln's cabinet'?". But, in speaking about referring, philosophers have written as though one might sensibly ask such questions in an unlimited number of cases. What else could have caused Russell to say in "On Denoting", "A phrase may denote ambiguously; e.g., 'a man' denotes not many men, but an ambiguous man."?[2]

It is of course perfectly true that one can ask, "To whom does the pronoun 'he' refer?", if one is oneself referring to a particular passage in a text, or to

something which has just been said. But it does not follow that one can ask this question *apart* from such a context. Clearly, the question "To whom does 'he' refer?" is a senseless question unless such a context is indicated. The same is true of Russell's example, "a man". It is senseless to ask, "To whom does 'a man' refer?", or (using Russell's term) "Whom does 'a man' denote?". But even when the context is clearly indicated this question does not *always* make sense. If, for example, I tell you that I need a wife, you can hardly ask me, "To whom are you referring?".

Failure clearly to mark these distinctions leads to confusions about uniqueness of reference. Russell says that a definite description "will only have an application in the event of there being one so-and-so and no more."[3] But can I not refer to someone as "the old madman" even though he is not mad and more than one man is? Does my phrase not have "application" to the one to whom I am referring? Certainly I was speaking of him. What is usually said here is that uniqueness of reference is secured by making the description more determinate, for example by saying, "The old man who lives next door". But this attempt to secure uniqueness of reference through increased determination of the "referring expression" is otiose, for what secures uniqueness is the user of the expression and the context in which it is used *together* with the expression.

We may now notice Ryle's futile

[2] "On Denoting", reprinted in *Readings in Philosophical Analysis*, edited by H. Feigl and W. Sellars, New York, 1949, p. 103.

[3] *Principia Mathematica*, vol. I, Cambridge, 1910, p. 30.

attempt to get uniqueness of reference somehow guaranteed by the words themselves. "Tommy Jones is not the same person as the king of England" means, Ryle says, what is meant by: "(1) Somebody, and—of an unspecified circle—one person only is called Tommy Jones; (2) Somebody, and one person only has royal power in England; and (3) No one both is called Tommy Jones and is king of England." But surely when I say "Tommy Jones is not king of England" I am not claiming that exactly one person of any circle is named "Tommy Jones". What is indeed necessary, if I am to make a definite assertion, is not that one person only be named "Tommy Jones", but that I be referring to just one person, however many others there may be with the same name as his. It is a mistake to think that the "referring expression" itself can secure and guarantee this uniqueness. This is obvious in the case of proper names, for here we cannot appeal to meaning. "Tommy Jones" does not have a meaning, and many people share it. Proper names are usually (rather) common names.

Ryle's account makes it appear that it is an intrinsic characteristic of certain groups of words that they denote something or other. They possess this characteristic in virtue of their "signifying an idiosyncratic attribute". Perhaps he is thinking of such an expression as "the oldest American university". It is a matter of fact that the oldest American university is Harvard. But nothing prevents one from referring to another school (by mistake, or in jest) with these words.

Perhaps Ryle has confused referring to something with referring to it correctly as this or that. I might, for example, refer to L. W. in saying, "He is the president of the bank." Still, I would have referred to him incorrectly as the president of the bank, because he is not the president of the bank, but the vice-president. Some of what Ryle says will be correct if we interpret his comments about denoting as giving an account of what it is to refer to something *correctly* as such-and-such. But it is, after all, possible to refer to something incorrectly as such-and-such, and that is still to refer to it. Furthermore, for one to refer correctly to something as "the such-and-such" it is not necessary that the thing referred to be the sole possessor of the "property signified" by the phrase, though it must certainly have that property. Conversely we can say that it is not necessary that the property "signified" by a phrase of the form "the such-and-such" be "idiosyncratic" if one is to refer to something correctly as "the such-and-such".

II

The question "To whom (what) does the phrase 'the so-and-so' refer?" is generally odd. But it is not always odd. I am arguing that the sense in which expressions (as opposed to speakers) can be said to refer to things is derivative. I mean by this that the question "To whom (what) does the phrase 'the so-and-so' refer?" means the same as the question with regard to some person, "To whom (what) is that person referring with the phrase 'the so-and-so'?". Where the question cannot be so rephrased, it cannot be asked at all, for example, "To whom does the pronoun 'he' refer?", "To whom does the phrase 'the old man' refer?".

Much of the philosophical discussion of this topic has assumed that this was not so. Russell says that a denoting phrase is such "solely in virtue of its form". Thus we should be able to ask, "To whom does the phrase 'the tallest man in the prison' refer?", for the denoting phrase here is of the same form as "The Sultan of Swat" and this phrase can be said to refer to someone, namely Babe Ruth. But the first question cannot be asked. The second question "To whom does the phrase 'The Sultan of Swat' refer?", does not require a special context and is not the same question as the one which asks with regard to some person, "To whom was he referring with that phrase?". For clearly this last question might receive a different answer than the first. This would occur if the speaker in question had erroneously been referring to Mickey Mantle. So the question "To whom does 'the so-and-so' refer?" seems not always to be the same question as the one with regard to some person, "To whom was he referring with the phrase 'the so-and-so'?".

I am claiming that the counter examples are only apparent and that the general thesis is still true. There is a class of expressions which (to use Strawson's happy description) have grown capital letters. Some examples are "The Sultan of Swat", "The Morning Star", "The City of the Angels". One can ask, "To what city does the phrase "The City of Angels" refer?". The answer is, "Los Angeles". Such expressions are on their way to becoming names, for example "The Beast of Belsen". They are what a thing or person is called often and repeatedly, and that is why one can ask to what they refer. Philosophers were perhaps concentrating on such examples as these when they said or implied that the question "To whom (what) does 'the so-and-so' refer?" can always be asked. But it cannot.

Perhaps another source of this mistake derives from a confusion between meaning and referring. One can ask both "What does this phrase mean?" and "Whom do you mean?". Also, "I referred to so-and-so" and "I meant so-and-so" seem very close indeed. But these verbs are radically different, as can be seen from the following considerations. One can ask, "Why did you refer to him?", but not "Why did you mean him?". One can say, "Don't refer to him!", but not "Don't mean him!". "How often did you refer to him?" is a sensible question, but "How often did you mean him?" is not. One can ask, "Why do you refer to him as the such-and-such?", but not "Why do you mean him as the such-and-such?". I can ask why you refer to him at all, but not why you mean him at all. The verb "to mean" has noncontinuous present tense forms, for example, "I mean you", but it lacks the present progressive tense form, "I am meaning you". The verb "to refer" has a present progressive form, "I am referring to you", as well as a noncontinuous present form, "I refer to Adlai Stevenson".

What these grammatical considerations show is that referring to someone is an action; meaning someone is not an action. As an action it can be right or wrong for one to perform. Thus it can be wrong of you to refer to someone, but not wrong of you to mean someone. It can be important or necessary that you should refer to someone, but not important or necessary that you should mean someone. One can intend to refer to someone, but not intend to mean him.

III

In discussions of statements such as "Edward VII is the king of England", it is sometimes said that in making them one is referring to the same person twice. Frege would say that the person is referred to in different ways each time. This way of looking at them leads to their interpretation as identities. But consider the following conversation to see how odd it is to talk of referring twice to the same person in such contexts:

A: He is the king of England.
B: To whom are you referring?
A: That man behind the flag.
B: How many times did you refer to him?

Referring to someone several times during the course of a speech would be a rather different sort of thing. If I mention a man's name, I would not ordinarily be said to have referred to him in so doing. Using a man's name is in some ways opposed to referring to him rather than an instance of it.

If we assume that whenever in an assertion something is mentioned by name by a speaker, he is referring to that thing, certain very paradoxical conclusions can be deduced. It would follow that when I write in my paper "I am not, of course, referring to Ludwig Wittgenstein", I would be referring to Ludwig Wittgenstein. But if someone were asked to show where in my paper I had referred to Ludwig Wittgenstein, it would be absurd for him to point to the statement in which I say, "I am not referring to Ludwig Wittgenstein". The same would be true of the statement in which I say, "I am referring to Ludwig Wittgenstein". If it were asked where in my paper I had referred to Ludwig Wittgenstein, it would be absurd to point to the statement in which I say, "I am referring to Ludwig Wittgenstein". In both cases I would have used Wittgenstein's name. Therefore, to mention someone by name is not necessarily to refer to him. And consider this example. Suppose the porter at Magdalen College asks me whom I am looking for. I answer, "Gilbert Ryle". Would anyone say I had referred to Gilbert Ryle? But if I say, in the course of a talk, "I am not referring to the most important of present-day philosophers", I would then and there be referring to Ludwig Wittgenstein; though in saying, as I just did, "I would then and there be referring to Ludwig Wittgenstein", I could not be said to have referred to Ludwig Wittgenstein. And this is so notwithstanding the fact that Ludwig Wittgenstein is the most important of present-day philosophers. This then is the paradox of reference. In saying "I am referring to Ludwig Wittgenstein" I am not referring to Ludwig Wittgenstein.[4]

Some of the statements which have been counted as identities cannot be interpreted as such. Suppose I explain to my confused son, "Charles de Gaulle is *not* the king of France". That this statement is not an identity can be shown as follows. From a $\neq$ b, it follows that b $\neq$ a, but from "Charles de Gaulle is *not* the king of France" it does not follow that "The king of France is *not* Charles de Gaulle". The first of these statements is true while the second is neither true nor false. The reason for this is not, as is sometimes said, that I have failed to refer in saying, "The king of France . . .". The reason is that France is not a monarchy and there is no king of France. Just so, and said of a spinster that "Her husband is kind to her" is neither true nor false. But a speaker might very well be referring to someone in using these words, for he may think that someone is the husband of the lady (who in fact is a spinster). Still, the statement is neither true nor false, for it presupposes that the lady has a husband, which she has not. This last refutes Strawson's thesis that if the presupposition of existence is not satisfied, the speaker has failed to refer. For here that presupposition is false, but still the speaker has referred to someone, namely, the man mistakenly taken to be her husband.

Of course a man may "fail to refer",

but not as Strawson uses this expression. For example, in your article you may fail to refer to my article.

IV

Now it is, of course, the case that on the analysis of propositions containing descriptive phrases proposed by Russell, the proposition "The king of France is not Charles de Gaulle" is not an identity. The reason he gives for this is entirely different from the reason which I have just given. According to Russell, this proposition is an existential generalization which, however, contains an identity proposition as a part. In fact, on Russell's view, our proposition has two possible interpretations according as the descriptive phrase is considered to have what he calls "primary occurrence" or "secondary occurrence" in the whole proposition of which it is a part. Another way of putting this is to say that "The king of France is not Charles de Gaulle" has two analyses on Russell's view, depending upon whether the negation in the proposition is viewed as being an inner negation or an outer negation. In the first interpretation it would be of the form:

(1) $[(\imath x)(\Phi x)]\{\sim\Psi(\imath x)(\Phi x)\}.$

On the second interpretation our proposition would be of the form:

(2) $\sim\{[(\imath x)(\Phi x)](\Psi(\imath x)(\Phi x))\}.$

On either interpretation, and against Strawson, the proposition "The king of France is not Charles de Gaulle"

---

[4] Philosophical tradition sanctions the production of such paradoxes. I am thinking of Meinong's paradox about Objects of which it is true to say that no such objects exist; and Frege's paradox that the concept *horse* is not a concept.

has a truth-value. On the first interpretation (1) it is false and on the second interpretation (2) it is true.

For this reason I find both interpretations objectionable. But I should now like to present reasons in support of the claim that Russell's analysis of propositions containing definite descriptions is mistaken and that in fact it cannot at all do the job it was designed to do. It does not provide a solution for Russell's famous puzzle about George IV and the author of *Waverley*. What puzzled Russell was why one could not conclude from the premise that Georve IV wished to know whether Scott was the author of *Waverley* that George IV wished to know whether Scott was Scott, since Scott was the author of *Waverley*. The solution proposed by Russell says that the inference to "George IV wished to know whether Scott was Scott" from "George IV wished to know whether Scott was the author of *Waverley*" is not warranted because this latter proposition, when properly analyzed, contains no constituent definite description for which we may substitute "Scott".

Now there are two ways (and only two ways) in which a descriptive phrase may be eliminated from a proposition and there are good reasons against accepting either of the resulting interpretations. In the first way we interpret "George IV wished to know whether Scott was the author of *Waverley*" as being of the form:

$$(3) \qquad [(\imath x)(\Phi x)]\{\Psi(\imath x)(\Phi x)\},$$

and the result of the elimination of the descriptive phrase is:

$$(4) \qquad (\exists c)\,[(x)\,((\Phi x) \equiv (x = c)) \\ \&\, (\Psi c)].$$

In the second way we interpret our proposition as being of the form:

$$(5) \qquad X\{\Psi(\imath x)(\Phi x)\},$$

and the result of the elimination is:

$$(6) \quad X\{(\exists c)\,[(x)\,((\Phi x) \equiv (x = c)) \\ \&\, (\Psi c)]\}$$

Interpreted as (4) our proposition would be:

(7) One and only one person wrote *Waverley* and George IV wished to know whether that individual was Scott.

Interpreted as (6) our proposition reads:

(8) George IV wished to know whether one and only one individual wrote *Waverley* and whether that individual was Scott.

And now for the reasons for rejecting *both* interpretations. First let us consider (7). This is the interpretation which accords the definite description a primary occurrence. The trouble with this is that on this interpretation it really does follow from the other premises that George IV wished to know whether Scott was Scott. This last is of the form Ψb. The proposition that Scott is the author of *Waverley* is of the form $b = (\imath x)(\Phi x)$. From this, together with the other premise which is of the form $\Psi(\imath x)(\Phi x)$, we get our unwanted conclusion. The argument on this interpretation becomes a straightforward substitution instance of a theorem of *Principia Mathematica*:

14.15 $\{(\imath x)(\Phi x) = b\} \rightarrow \{\Psi(\imath x)$
$(\Phi x) \equiv \Psi b\}.$

Another queer consequence of the interpretation (7) is that if "George IV wished to know whether Scott was the author of *Waverley*" is given that analysis, it follows from it that *Waverley* was not co-authored. But it is obvious that this does not in fact follow and therefore the interpretation (7) is unsatisfactory. But what is the proof that this queer consequence does thus follow from this interpretation? (7) is of the form (4). (4) is an existentially generalized conjunction so that we can distribute the existential quantifier to each of the conjuncts. Now simplifying we get:

(9) $(\exists c)\{(x)[(\Phi x) \equiv (x = c)]\}.$

But (9) by the definition 14.02 of *Principia* is:

(10) $E!(\imath x)(\Phi x).$

Consistently with the interpretation we have supplied for the variables above, this says,

(11) One and only one person wrote *Waverley*.

From (11) it follows that *Waverley* was not co-authored.

Let us now turn to the alternative interpretation, which accords a secondary occurrence to "the author of *Waverley*" in the proposition "George IV wished to know whether Scott was the author of *Waverley*". This is our (8). But it is obvious that (8) does not mean the same as our proposition, for what (8) says is that George IV wanted to know both whether one and only one individual wrote *Waverley* *and* whether, if so, Scott was that individual. But surely from the proposition that George IV wished to know whether Scott was the author of *Waverley* it does not follow that George IV wished to know whether or not *Waverley* was either not written at all or written by more than one person. It is entirely possible that George IV knew very well that *Waverley* was written by one and only one man, even though he did not know who that man was. Nor can I see that any other English version of (6) can avoid this unwanted result. It follows that neither (6) nor (4) is a possible form of the proposition in question.

V

Referring does not have the omnipresence accorded to it in the philosophical literature. It sounds odd to say that when I say "Santa Claus lives at the North Pole" I am referring to Santa Claus, or that when I say "The round square does not exist" I am referring to a round square. Must I be referring to something? Philosophers ask, "How is it possible to refer to something which does not exist?". But often the examples produced in which we are supposed to do this ("Hamlet was a prince of Denmark", "Pegasus was captured by Bellerophon", "The golden mountain does not exist") are such that the question "To whom (what) are you referring?" simply cannot sensibly arise in connection with them. In these cases, anyway, there is nothing to be explained.

How is it possible to make a true statement about a nonexistent object? For if a statement is to be about something, that thing must exist, otherwise how could the statement mention *it*, or refer to *it*? One cannot refer to or mention nothing, and if a statement cannot be about nothing it must always be about something. Hence, this ancient line of reasoning concludes, it is not possible to say anything true or false about a nonexistent object. It is not even possible to say that it does not exist.

It is this hoary line of argument which, beginning with Plato, has made the topic of referring a problem for philosophers. Still, ancient or not, the reasoning is outrageously bad. Surely here is a case where philosophers really have been seduced and led astray by misleading analogies. I cannot hang a nonexistent man. I can only hang a man. To hang a nonexistent man is not to do any hanging at all. So, by parity of reasoning, to refer to a nonexistent man is not to refer at all. Hence, I cannot say anything about a nonexistent man. One might as well argue that I cannot hunt for deer in a forest where there are no deer, for that would be to hunt for *nothing*.

It must have been philosophical reflections of this genre which prompted Wittgenstein to say in his *Remarks*, "We pay attention to the expressions we use concerning these things; we do not understand them, however, but misinterpret them. When we do philosophy

we are like savages, primitive people, who hear the expressions of civilized men, put a false interpretation on them, and then draw queer conclusions from it."[5]

Let us look a bit closer at what it is to talk about things which do not exist. Of course there are a variety of different cases here. If we stick to the kind of case which has figured prominently in philosophy however, this variety can be reduced. What we now have to consider are characters in fiction like Mr. Pickwick; mythological figures like Pegasus; legendary figures like Paul Bunyan; make-believe figures like Santa Claus, and fairy tale figures like Snow White. (And why not add comic strip figures like Pogo?) And do not these characters really exist? Mr. Pickwick really is a character in fiction; Mr. Ryle is not. There really is a figure in Greek mythology whose name is "Pegasus", but none whose name is "Socrates"; and there really is a comic strip character named "Pogo". In talking about these characters I may say things which are true and I may also say things which are not. If I say, for example, that Pogo is a talking elephant, that is just not true. Neither is Pegasus a duck. In talking about these things there is this matter of getting the facts straight. This is a problem for me; it is not a problem for Dickens or for Walt Kelly. What Dickens says about Mr. Pickwick in *The Pickwick Papers* cannot be false, though it can be not true to character; and in the comic strip, Walt Kelly does not say anything about

---

[5] *Remarks on the Foundations of Mathematics*, Oxford, 1956, p. 39.

his possum Pogo, for Pogo talks for himself. Still, Pogo could say something about Walt Kelly (or Charles de Gaulle) and that might not be true.

There is, however, another group of cases discussed by philosophers, and this group has the important characteristic that in talking about its members there is no such thing as getting the facts straight. Here we find Russell's famous example, the present king of France; and Meinong's equally famous example of the golden mountain. What are they supposed to be examples of? Well, just things that do not exist. But in saying this we must keep in mind how different they are from Mr. Pickwick, Santa Claus, Snow White, etc. Keeping this difference in mind we can see that though it makes perfectly good sense to ask whether Mr. Pickwick ran a bookstore, or whether Santa Claus lives at the North Pole, it makes no sense whatever to ask whether the golden mountain is in California. Similarly, though we can ask whether Mr. Pickwick was married or not, *we* cannot sensibly ask whether the present king of France is bald or not.

If the question is, "How can we talk about objects which do not exist?", then it is wrong to use the examples of the golden mountain and the present king of France. These famous philosophical examples, the round square, the golden mountain, are just things we do *not* talk about (except in telling a story or a fairy tale or something of the kind). Meinong, Russell, and Ryle all puzzle over sentences such as "The golden mountain is in California", as though one just had to make up one's mind whether to put it in the box with

all the other true propositions, or into the box with the other false propositions. They fail to see that one would only utter it in the course of telling a story or the like. It does not occur in isolation from some such larger context. If it did so occur, if someone were just to come up to us and say, "The golden mountain is in California", we would not concern ourselves with truth or falsity, but with this man. What is wrong with him? When the sentence occurs in a fairy tale it would never occur to us to raise the question of its truth. And if we are asked to consider whether it is true or false outside of such a context, we can only say that it does not so occur, we just do not say it.

Of course we may sometimes in error, or by mistake, talk about nonexistent things, for example Hemingway's autobiography. So here is *one* way in which it can occur that we speak of nonexistent objects. As a result of a mistake!

VI

It is said to be an astronomical fact of some importance that

(1) the morning star = the evening star.

This was not always known but the identification was early made by the Greeks. Frege said that it was because the two expressions, "the morning star" and "the evening star", had the same reference that (1) was true, and because these two had different senses that (1) was not a trivial thing to say.

Frege's way of putting the matter seems to invite the objection that the two expressions, "the morning star" and "the evening star", do not refer to the same thing. For the first refers to the planet Venus when seen in the morning before sunrise. The second refers to the same planet when it appears in the heavens after sunset. Do they refer then to the same "thing"? Is it, as Carnap says,[6] a matter of "astronomical fact" that they do? One wants to protest that it is a matter of "linguistic fact" that they do not.

Perhaps Frege's view is better put if we think of the two expressions as names, that is, "The Morning Star" and "The Evening Star". Thus Quine,[7] in repeating Frege's example but adding capital letters, speaks of the expressions "Evening Star" and "Morning Star" as names. Quine would say that what the astronomers had discovered was that

(2) The Morning Star = The Evening Star.

This is better, for (1) implies (or presupposes) what (2) does not, that there is only one star in the sky both in the morning and in the evening. Also, a purist might object that it cannot be taken as ground for (1) that Venus is both the morning star and the evening star. Venus is not a star but a planet. It would be wrong to say that what

the astronomers discovered was that the morning planet is the evening planet

(2) is free from these criticisms, but still the same protest is in order as was made against (1). The name "The Morning Star" does not refer *simpliciter* to the planet Venus. It does not refer to the planet in the way in which the demonstrative "that" might be used to refer to the planet on some occasion. The names "The Morning Star" and "The Evening Star" are not that sort of "referring expression".

It would be incorrect for me to say to my son as he awakens, "Look to the place where the sun is rising and you will see The Evening Star", for that is not what the star is called when seen in the east before sunrise. Again, the proposal that we stay up until we see The Evening Star is quite a different proposal from the proposal that we stay up until we see The Morning Star. In dealing with failures of substitutivity in some ways like these, Frege developed his concept of "oblique" (*ungerade*) discourse, and Quine has talked about "referential opacity". Names in oblique contexts, according to Frege, do not have their "ordinary" referents but an oblique referent which is the same as their ordinary sense. But it would be absurd to suggest that when I tell my boy that if he looks to the east on arising he will see The Evening Star, I am not referring to a planet but to a "sense", whatever that might be. Using Quine's notion of referential opacity, one might suggest that the reason why the proposal to wait up until we see The Evening Star

---

[6] *Meaning and Necessity*, Chicago, 1947, p. 119.

[7] *From a Logical Point of View*, Cambridge, Mass., 1953, p. 21.

is a different proposal from the proposal to wait up until we see The Morning Star is that here the context is referentially opaque, so that the two names in these contexts do not refer to anything at all. But surely this result is too paradoxical to be taken seriously, and in any case no one has yet told us how to understand the view that a proposal can be referentially opaque.

Under the entry on "Venus" in the *Encyclopaedia Britannica* we are given the following information: "When seen in the western sky in the evenings, i.e., at its eastern elongations, it was called by the ancients 'Hesperus', and when visible in the mornings, i.e., at its western elongations, 'Phosphorus'." Did the astronomers then discover that

(3) Hesperus = Phosphorus?

In the entry under "Hesperus" in Smith's *Smaller Classical Dictionary* we read, "Hesperus, the evening star, son of Astraeus and Eos, of Cephalus and Eos, or of Atlas." From this, together with (3), we are able to get by Leibniz's Law,

(4) Phosphorus is the evening star.

And avoiding unnecessary complications, let us interpret this as meaning

(5) Phosphorus is The Evening Star.

Any competent classicist knows that this is not true.

Under the entry on "Phosphorus" in Smith's *Smaller Classical Dictionary* we find, "Lucifer or Phosphorus ('bringer of light'), is the name of the planet Venus, when seen in the morning before sunrise. The same planet was called Hesperus, Vespergo, Vesper, Noctifer, or Nocturnus, when it appeared in the heavens after sunset. Lucifer as a personification is called a son of Astraeus and Aurora or Eos; of Cephalus and Aurora, or of Atlas." So the stars were personified, and it seems to be a matter of mythology that

(6) Hesperus is not Phosphorus.

Then did the astronomers discover that the mythologists were wrong?

Of course (3) is false and no astronomical research could have established it. What could we make of the contention that the Greeks mistakenly believed that Hesperus was not Phosphorus? According to the *Encyclopaedia Britannica* (under "Hesperus"), ". . . the two stars were early identified by the Greeks." But once the identification was made, what was left to be mistaken about here?

Could not one mistake The Evening Star for The Morning Star? Certainly one could. This would involve mistaking evening for morning. One could do this. In the morning it is just getting light and in the evening it is just getting dark. Imagine someone awaking from a sleep induced by a soporific. "But there aren't *two* stars so how *could* one be mistaken for the other?"

Hence, though it is sometimes made to look as though the Greeks were victims of a mistaken astronomical belief, this is not so. And Quine suggests that the true situation was "probably first established by some observant Babylonian." If that is the case, a knowing Greek would not have said

(7) The Morning Star is not The Evening Star

unless, of course, he were in the process of teaching his child the *use* of these words. And, drawing on his unwillingness to say (7) (except in special circumstances when he might want to say just that), we might push him into saying that The Morning Star is The Evening Star, and even that Hesperus is Phosphorus, though now he would begin to feel that these sayings were queer.

The moral is that if we allow ourselves no more apparatus than the apparatus of proper names and descriptions, sense and reference, and the propositional function "x = y", we just cannot give an undistorted account of what the astronomers discovered, or about Hesperus and Phosphorus. Only the logician's interest in formulas of the kind "x = y" could lead him to construct such sentences as "The Morning Star = The Evening Star" or "Hesperus = Phosphorus". Astronomers and mythologists don't put it that way.[8]

---

[8] The whole of Part VI of this essay has previously been published under the title "Hesperus and Phosphorus", in *The Philosophical Review*, Vol. LXVIII, No. 4, October, 1959.

Toward Further Inquiry

Perhaps the best comprehensive treatment of definition available is Part IV of Henry Leonard's *Principles of Right Reason* (New York, 1957). Part III of the same book deals with terms and is useful for the problems dealt with here. Chapter I of John Hospers' *Introduction to Philosophical Analysis* (Englewood Cliffs, N.J., 1967) offers excellent discussion of problems regarding definition. There are two fairly good book-length treatments of definition: Heinrich Rickert's *Zur Lehre von der Definition* (Tübingen, 1929) and Richard Robinson's *Definition* (Oxford, 1950). The latter is primarily occupied with the distinction between real and nominal definitions, but the opening chapter gives a general survey of other problems. For other treatments of the real-nominal distinction, see O. K. Moore's "Nominal Definitions of Culture," PS 19 (1952), and K. Ajdukiewicz' "Three Concepts of Definition," *Logique et Analyse* (Louvain), 1 (1958). For brief general discussions of definitions, see Alonzo Church's "Definition," in Runes (ed.), *Dictionary of Philosophy* (New York, 1942) and the article on definition in *The Encyclopedia of Philosophy* (New York, 1967).

An excellent discussion of mathematical definition appears in P. Suppes' *Introduction to Logic* (Princeton, N.J., 1957), Chapter 8. For other discussions of the role of definition in science, see C. G. Hempel's *Fundamentals of Concept Formation in Empirical Science* (Chicago, 1952), Chapter 1, Parts 2 to 4; H. B. Curry's "On Definitions in Formal Systems," *Logique et Analyse* (Louvain) 1

(1958); H. Leblanc's "On Definitions," PS 17 (1950); P. Caws's "Functions of Definition in Science," PS 26 (1959); J. A. Winnie's "Theoretical Terms and Partial Definitions," PS 32 (1965); N. Goodman's *The Structure of Appearance* (Cambridge, Mass., 1951), Chapter I; and M. Scriven's "Definitions, Explanations, and Theories," in Feigl, Maxwell, and Scriven (eds.), *Minnesota Studies in the Philosophy of Science*, Vol. II (Minneapolis, 1958). Some interesting discussions in connection with ethics and value theory are G. E. Moore's *Principia Ethica* (Cambridge, Mass., 1913), Chapter I; A. C. Ewing's *The Definition of Good* (New York, 1947); G. C. Field's "The Place of Definition in Ethics," PAS 32 (1931–1932); T. E. Jessop's "The Definition of Beauty," PAS 33 (1932–1933); D. C. Williams' "Meaning of Good," PR 46 (1937); C. L. Stevenson's "Persuasive Definitions," *Mind* 47 (1938); P. B. Rice's "Definitions in Value Theory," JP 44 (1947); and C. D. McGee's "Explicit Definitions and Ethical Rules," *Ethics* 73 (1963). On various types and problems of definition, see J. R. Reid's "Dilemma of Definition," JP 36 (1939); J. R. Reid's "Definitions, Criteria, Standards and Norms," PR 53 (1944); E. H. Madden's "Definition and Reduction," PS 28 (1961); S. C. Pepper's "Descriptive Definition," JP 43 (1946); W. V. O. Quine's "Implicit Definition Sustained," JP 61 (1964); V. Lenzen's "Successive Definition," *Procedures of Empirical Science* (Chicago, 1938); and J. Kotarbinsko's "On Ostensive Definitions," PS 27 (1960). C. I. Lewis' treatment of definition in *An Analysis of Knowledge and Valuation* (LaSalle, Ill., 1946), p. 105ff., is an extension of his treatment of modes of meaning (see 2.1). For a peculiarly pragmatistic treatment, see J. Dewey and A. F. Bentley's "Definition," JP 44 (1947); for a peculiarly Thomistic one, see Jacques Maritain's *Philosophy of Nature* (New York, 1959).

Russell's theory of descriptions receives a fuller exposition in *Introduction to Mathematical Philosophy* (London, 1920), Chapter 16. For other expositions, see L. S. Stebbing's *A Modern Introduction to Logic* (New York, 1933); J. W. Reeves' "The Origin and Consequences of the Theory of Descriptions," PAS 33, (1933); G. E. Moore's "Russell's Theory of Descriptions," *The Philosophy of Bertrand Russell* (Evanston, Ill., 1944). For criticisms, see E. E. C. Jones's series of articles in *Mind* (1910–1911); P. T. Geach's "Russell's Theory of Descriptions," *Analysis* 10 (1949); H. L. Hart's "A Logician's Fairy-Tale," PR 60 (1951); and M. Lazorowitz' "Knowledge by Description," PR 46 (1937). For extensions of the theory, see W. Quine's "Denotation and Existence" (8.1 in this volume); A. J. Ayer's "Names and Descriptions," *Logique et Analyse* (Louvain), 20 (1962); and J. Hintikka's "Toward a Theory of Definite Descriptions," *Analysis* 19 (1959).

On the issues of existence and presuppositions, see P. F. Strawson's *Introduction to Logical Theory* (London, 1952). W. Sellars has made a pointed critique in "Presupposing," PR 63 (1954), and Strawson replies in the same volume. For other discussion of this issue, see H. Leonard's "Logic of Existence," *Philosophical Studies* 7 (1957); H. Leblanc and T. Harlperin's "Nondesignating Singular

Terms," PR 68 (1959); and J. Hintikka's "Existential Presuppositions and Existential Commitments," JP 56 (1959). The issue of existence and presupposition is obviously related to those taken up in Chapter 8 of this volume.

M. Black, in "Definition, Presuppositions and Assertions," PR 61 (1952), relates the above issue to definition, and G. Bergmann, in "Undefined Descriptive Predicates," PPR 8 (1947), treats definition in relation to description. H. Leonard, in *Principles of Right Reason*, uses the theory of definite descriptions as a basis for treating the definition of proper names, claiming a definitional equivalence between the name and the description. J. R. Searle, in "Proper Names," *Mind* 67 (1958), offers a more qualified treatment of the same issue and carries the discussion into the issues of the analytic-synthetic distinction. Strawson's *Individuals* (London, 1959) relates the issues of names and descriptions to problems of personal identity.

ANALYTIC AND SYNTHETIC

Chapter 5

It has always been clear that the simplest and most
obvious case of truth which can be known in
advance of experience is the explicative
proposition and those consequences of definition
which can be derived by purely logical
analysis. These are necessarily true, true under all
possible circumstances, because definition is
legislative. . . . Mind makes classifications and
determines meanings; in so doing, it creates that
truth without which there could be no
other truth.
C. I. Lewis

The distinction between necessary truths and contingent truths has always
been an important one in philosophical concerns about knowledge. Necessary
truths have usually been regarded as truths based on reason, and contingent
truths as truths based on experience. Seen in this light, the epistemological controversy between rationalists and empiricists appears to be: Are there necessary
truths that give us knowledge about the world? This controversy has required examination not only of the logical distinction between necessity and contingency
and of the epistemological distinction between knowledge derived from experience and knowledge independent of experience; it eventually came to focus upon
a linguistic distinction between analytic propositions and synthetic ones. This
distinction, designed as a tool for an epistemological controversy, has presented
problems in the philosophy of language.

Kant's approach to the epistemological problems brought problems about
language to light. He distinguished two kinds of judgment. An *analytic* judgment
is expressed in a sentence whose predicate can be derived by explicating the
meaning of the subject. A *synthetic* judgment is expressed in a sentence whose

predicate expands our knowledge of the subject because its meaning is not contained in the meaning of the subject. Kant also distinguished two kinds of knowledge, a posteriori knowledge, which is logically dependent upon experience, and a priori knowledge, which is logically independent of experience (though not necessarily historically prior to it). He then posed the problem of his own inquiry: "How are synthetic propositions a priori possible?" This question presupposes that there is knowledge that is both a priori and synthetic. It also presupposes that all a priori judgments are necessarily true or necessarily false (since an a priori judgment is logically independent of experience, no contingency of experience can prove it true or false). By inference, it presupposes that there are some propositions that are necessarily true and that expand our knowledge about the world. Kant's distinctions among these terms have been widely accepted, but his presuppositions about their interrelations have been widely disputed.

Kant was critically aware of the presuppositions of his question, as his discussion in 5.1 clearly shows. Basic to his justification of them was the contention that the propositions of arithmetic and geometry are of the requisite sort, namely, a priori, necessary, and synthetic. In the last hundred years, however, developments in the understanding of mathematics and logic have challenged this contention. Non-Euclidean geometries, beginning with axioms for parallel lines that are inconsistent with the Euclidean axiom, have proved to be applicable to the world. The fundamental principles of arithmetic have been derived from the definitions, rules, and axioms of a system of logic. On the basis of the logicistic interpretation of mathematics,[1] the Vienna Circle concluded that any necessary proposition, through a logical analysis, can be reduced to a tautology, that is, a compound statement that is true regardless of the truth value of its component statements. These developments have produced shifts in concern with the analytic-synthetic distinction. No longer is it simply a basis for exploring the conditions for a kind of knowledge; it also has become a basis for exploring issues of form and content in language.

In order to understand current issues regarding the analytic-synthetic distinction, it will be helpful to look at a few paradigm sentences:

A. President Johnson is President Johnson.
B. Either it is raining out or it is not raining out.
C. All bachelors are unmarried men.
D. Nothing can be red and blue all over.

---

[1] Logicism is an interpretation of mathematics which maintains that mathematics is reducible to logic, or that mathematical systems are completely derivable from systems of logic. For extended discussion of this view, and comparison of it with other interpretations of mathematics, see Max Black's *The Nature of Mathematics* (London, 1933), or Stephan Korner's *The Philosophy of Mathematics* (London, 1960).

E. All crows are black.

F. Johnny is crying.

Sentence A is an *identity* of the form 'a = a', assuming that the meaning of the terms is consistent (that we are not talking about Andrew in one case and Lyndon in the other). Sentence B is a *tautology* of the form 'Either p or not p'. Both A and B are true, not only regardless of the facts, but regardless of the meaning of their terms, provided the meanings are consistent. Both logical identities and tautologies are explicitly *logical truths*. Sentence C is usually regarded as *analytic* on the contention that it can be reduced to a logical truth by logical analysis of its terms. Not only is the meaning of 'unmarried men' contained in 'bachelors' but the two terms are synonymous. Assuming that the terms have the same meaning, and that terms may be substituted for their synonyms without changing the logical value of the sentence, C is equivalent to 'All unmarried men are unmarried men'. It may not be already intuitively obvious that 'All u are u' is true, whatever 'u' stands for. By logical rules of translation and inference, it can be shown that the statement is equivalent to 'For anything, either it is an unmarried man or it is not an unmarried man'. $((x) \ (Ux \ v \sim Ux))$. Such a reduction yields a logical truth, provided the conditions about synonymous terms are met. In all three cases, the truth of the sentence is a matter of syntax, of the structure of the sentence, provided that certain conditions of semantics are met, those requiring consistency and equivalence of meaning. In A and B, the terms need only be consistent in meaning; both statements are already explicit logical truths. Sentence C requires the synonymity of its terms in order to be reduced to a logical truth. Given the positivists' treatment of analyticity, all logical truths are analytic, but the reverse relation may not hold. Some analytical statements can be reduced to logical truths only by means of a logical analysis based on substituting synonymous terms.

Sentence F is clearly synthetic on either the Kantian or the positivistic interpretations of the analytic-synthetic distinction. For a number of reasons, the synthetic nature of D and E is not so clear. In attempts to classify sentences like these, a number of questions arise:

Sentence D is a paradigm for arguments about the synthetic a priori. If D is analytic on a positivist's interpretation, how can it be reduced to a logical truth? To say that the term 'red' means (in part) 'nonblue' seems to beg the question. On the other hand, if D is a synthetic a priori on a Kantian interpretation, in what sense is it necessary? If it is logically necessary, then its necessity must be of a formal sort, and therefore reducible to a logical truth by logical analysis. What other necessity is claimed: psychological? ontological? It is difficult to see how the former is binding or the latter accessible.

These last questions lead to some broader ones involving discussions of the correlations of logical (necessary-contingent), epistemological (a priori-a posteriori), and linguistic (analytic-synthetic) categories. Are all necessary statements analytic? Are all necessary statements a priori? Are all a priori statements analytic? Are all a priori statements necessary (are there nonempirical contingencies)? The existence and nature of synthetic a priori propositions depends upon how one correlates these sets of categories.

Sentence E has the same form as sentence C, but this does not assure its status as an analytic statement. There is some question how one distinguishes between empirical generalizations and analytical propositions. If you saw a bird that was in every other respect like a crow, but not black, would you call it a crow or not? Is the meaning of 'black' contained in the meaning of 'crow', or is sentence E an induction on the basis of experience? Is sentence E reducible to a logical truth by a logical analysis of its terms?

If analytic statements are true by virtue of being capable of reduction to logical truths, by virtue of what are these logical truths true? If by virtue of conventions, then are they arbitrary? If by virtue of some sort of rational insight, then are they not synthetic rather than analytic? If by virtue of the meaning of the logical connectives, do such meanings ultimately require some sort of practical justification?

Given the difference between the Kantian and the positivistic explanations of analyticity in formulation, what is the difference in application? Can the controversy about a priori knowledge be resolved on the basis of an adequate formulation of the analytic-synthetic distinction, or do the formulations of this distinction already presuppose some understanding of a priori knowledge?

Some of these questions are at issue in the first three essays in this chapter; others may be raised by the reader in his attempt to evaluate the essays. Immanuel Kant offers his famous formulation of the distinction between the analytic and the synthetic, along with his justification of the synthetic a priori on the basis of his understanding of mathematics. A. J. Ayer offers his formulation of the distinction and criticizes Kant's formulation. He shows that his own characterization of the analytic-synthetic distinction requires all a priori statements to be analytic. Arthur Pap maintains that the issue turns on the distinction between necessity and contingency. His analysis attempts to show that some propositions are necessarily true but cannot be reduced to a logical truth by a logical analysis of their terms. Not only do the three essays arrive at different conclusions, but they begin with different concerns and questions. The problem shifts in such a way that it may be misleading to treat it as the same problem.

Pap raises the kinds of questions about the clarity of the term 'analytic' that open the way to challenging the analytic-synthetic distinction itself:

Is the distinction exhaustive (are there no logically possible alternatives to analytic and synthetic propositions)? If exhaustive, then is it clear and are the categories discrete? If clear and discrete, is the distinction explicable in terms of standards that determine what category any proposition fits into? If the distinction is not exhaustive, some propositions are neither analytic nor synthetic. If not clear, the distinction is indeterminant for some propositions. If the categories are not discrete, then either there are degrees of analyticity, or some propositions can be characterized as both analytic and synthetic. If no explicit standard is available, the distinction is not applicable to the very cases for which it is to be a decisive tool.

If analytic statements can be reduced to logical truths by a logical analysis of synonymous terms, what understanding of synonymity is involved? (This question carries us into the concerns of Chapter 6.) If the notion of synonymity in turn depends upon the notion of analyticity, can either provide an elucidation of the other? Is a similar circularity involved in the relation of the notions of meaning and necessity?

Even if the analytic-synthetic distinction is sound, what is its practical efficacy? Can it really resolve the question of a priori knowledge? Does it have any other use?

If the distinction is sound and useful, is it consistent with other tools of analysis? 'The present King of France is the present King of France' is an identity, and it is analytically true; but is it false according to Russell's theory of descriptions?

Willard Quine attacks the analytic-synthetic distinction as a dogma of empiricism. He finds that no adequate explication of analyticity has been given and questions whether one can be given. Grice and Strawson retort that the lack of such an explication does not imply that the explication is impossible. Jerrold Katz goes a step further, developing an explication on the basis of linguistic theory. Because his formulation of the notion of analyticity need not apply to all necessary truths, Katz concludes that it more closely coincides with Kant's formulation than with the positivists', leaving the way open for truths that are both necessary and synthetic.

5.1

THE SYNTHETIC
A PRIORI

Immanuel Kant

1. Of the Sources of Metaphysics

If it becomes desirable to formulate any cognition as science, it will be necessary first to determine accurately those peculiar features which no other science has in common with it, constituting its characteristics; otherwise the boundaries of all sciences become confused, and none of them can be treated thoroughly according to its nature.

The characteristics of a science may consist of a simple difference of object, or of the sources of cognition, or of the kind of cognition, or perhaps of all three conjointly. On this, therefore, depends the idea of a possible science and its territory.

First, as concerns the sources of metaphysical cognition, its very concept implies that they cannot be empirical. Its principles (including not only its maxims but its basic notions) must never be derived from experience. It must not be physical but metaphysical

From *Prolegomena to Any Future Metaphysics*, Paul Carus, trans., (LaSalle, Ill.: Open Court, 1905). Reprinted by permission of the publisher.

knowledge, viz., knowledge lying beyond experience. It can therefore have for its basis neither external experience, which is the source of physics proper, nor internal, which is the basis of empirical psychology. It is therefore *a priori* knowledge, coming from pure Understanding and pure Reason.

But so far Metaphysics would not be distinguishable from pure Mathematics; it must therefore be called pure philosophical cognition; and for the meaning of this term I refer to the Critique of the Pure Reason (II. "Method of Transcendentalism," Chap. I., Sec. i), where the distinction between these two employments of the reason is sufficiently explained. So far concerning the sources of metaphysical cognition.

2. Concerning the Kind of Cognition which can alone be called Metaphysical

a. OF THE DISTINCTION BETWEEN ANALYTICAL AND SYNTHETICAL JUDGMENTS IN GENERAL. The peculiarity of its sources demands that metaphysical cognition must consist of nothing but *a priori* judgments. But whatever be their origin, or their logical form, there is a distinction in judgments, as to their content, according to which they are either merely explicative, adding nothing to the content of the cognition, or expansive, increasing the given cognition: the former may be called analytical, the latter synthetical, judgments.

Analytical judgments express nothing in the predicate but what has been already actually thought in the concept of the subject, though not so distinctly or with the same (full) consciousness. When I say: All bodies are extended, I have not amplified in the least my concept of body, but have only analysed it, as extension was really thought to belong to that concept before the judgment was made, though it was not expressed; this judgment is therefore analytical. On the contrary, this judgment, All bodies have weight, contains in its predicate something not actually thought in the general concept of the body; it amplifies my knowledge by adding something to my concept, and must therefore be called synthetical.

b. THE COMMON PRINCIPLE OF ALL ANALYTICAL JUDGMENTS IS THE LAW OF CONTRADICTION. All analytical judgments depend wholly on the law of Contradiction, and are in their nature *a priori* cognitions, whether the concepts that supply them with matter be empirical or not. For the predicate of an affirmative analytical judgment is already contained in the concept of the subject, of which it cannot be denied without contradiction. In the same way its opposite is necessarily denied of the subject in an ana-

lytical, but negative, judgment, by the same law of contradiction. Such is the nature of the judgments: all bodies are extended, and no bodies are unextended (i.e., simple).

For this very reason all analytical judgments are *a priori* even when the concepts are empirical, as, for example, Gold is a yellow metal; for to know this I require no experience beyond my concept of gold as a yellow metal: it is, in fact, the very concept, and I need only analyse it, without looking beyond it elsewhere.

c. SYNTHETICAL JUDGEMENTS REQUIRE A DIFFERENT PRINCIPLE FROM THE LAW OF CONTRADICTION. There are synthetical *a posteriori* judgments of empirical origin; but there are also others which are proved to be certain *a priori*, and which spring from pure Understanding and Reason. Yet they both agree in this, that they cannot possibly spring from the principle of analysis, viz., the law of contradiction, alone; they require a quite different principle, though, from whatever they may be deduced, they must be subject to the law of contradiction, which must never be violated, even though everything cannot be deduced from it. I shall first classify synthetical judgments.

1. *Empirical judgments* are always synthetical. For it would be absurd to base an analytical judgment on experience, as our concept suffices for the purpose without requiring any testimony from experience. That body is extended, is a judgment established *a priori*, and not an empirical judgment. For before appealing to experience, we already have all the conditions of the judgment in the concept, from which

we have but to elicit the predicate according to the law of contradiction, and thereby to become conscious of the necessity of the judgment, which experience could not even teach us.

2. *Mathematical judgments* are all synthetical. This fact seems hitherto to have altogether escaped the observation of those who have analysed human reason; it even seems directly opposed to all their conjectures, though incontestably certain, and most important in its consequences. For as it was found that the conclusions of mathematicians all proceed according to the law of contradiction (as is demanded by all apodeictic certainty), men persuaded themselves that the fundamental principles were known from the same law. This was a great mistake, for a synthetical proposition can indeed be comprehended according to the law of contradiction, but only by presupposing another synthetical proposition from which it follows, but never in itself.

First of all, we must observe that all proper mathematical judgments are *a priori*, and not empirical, because they carry with them necessity, which cannot be obtained from experience. But if this be not conceded to me, very good; I shall confine my assertion to *pure Mathematics*, the very notion of which implies that it contains pure *a priori* and not empirical cognitions.

It might at first be thought that the proposition $7 + 5 = 12$ is a mere analytical judgment, following from the concept of the sum of seven and five, according to the law of contradiction. But on closer examination it appears that the concept of the sum of $7 + 5$ contains merely their union in a single number, without its being at all thought what the particular number is that unites them. The concept of twelve is by no means thought by merely thinking of the combination of seven and five; and analyse this possible sum as we may, we shall not discover twelve in the concept. We must go beyond these concepts, by calling to our aid some concrete image (*Anschauung*), i.e., either our five fingers, or five points (as Segner has it in his Arithmetic), and we must add successively the units of the five, given in some concrete image (*Anchauung*), to the concept of seven. Hence our concept is really amplified by the proposition $7 + 5 = 12$, and we add to the first a second, not thought in it. Arithmetical judgments are therefore synthetical, and the more plainly according as we take larger numbers; for in such cases it is clear that, however closely we analyse our concepts without calling visual images (*Anschauung*) to our aid, we can never find the sum by such mere dissection.

All principles of geometry are no more analytical. That a straight line is the shortest path between two points, is a synthetical proposition. For my concept of straight contains nothing of quantity, but only a quality. The attribute of shortness is therefore altogether additional, and cannot be obtained by any analysis of the concept. Here, too, visualisation (*Anschauung*) must come to aid us. It alone makes the synthesis possible.

Some other principles, assumed by geometers, are indeed actually analytical, and depend on the law of contradiction; but they only serve, as identical propositions, as a method of concatenation, and not as principles, e.g., $a = a$, the whole is equal to itself, or $a + b > a$, the whole is greater than its part. And yet even these, though they are recognised as valid from mere concepts, are only admitted in mathematics, because they can be represented in some visual form (*Anschauung*). What usually makes us believe that the predicate of such apodeictic[1] judgments is already contained in our concept, and that the judgment is therefore analytical, is the duplicity of the expression, requesting us to think a certain predicate as of necessity implied in the thought of a given concept, which necessity attaches to the concept. But the question is not what we are requested to join in thought *to* the given concept, but what we actually think together with and in it, though obscurely; and so it appears that the predicate belongs to these concepts necessarily indeed, yet not directly but indirectly by an added visualisation (*Anschauung*).

3. A Remark on the General Division of Judgments into Analytical and Synthetical

This division is indispensable, as concerns the Critique of human understanding, and therefore deserves to be called classical, though otherwise it is

of little use, but this is the reason why dogmatic philosophers, who always seek the sources of metaphysical judgments in Metaphysics itself, and not apart from it, in the pure laws of reason generally, altogether neglected this apparently obvious distinction. Thus the celebrated Wolf, and his acute follower Baumgarten, came to seek the proof of the principle of Sufficient Reason, which is clearly synthetical, in the principle of Contradiction. In Locke's Essay, however, I find an indication of my division. For in the fourth book (chap. iii. §9, seq.), having discussed the various connexions of representations in judgments, and their sources, one of which he makes "identity and contradiction" (analytical judgments), and another the coexistence of representations in a subject, he confesses (§10) that our *a priori* knowledge of the latter is very narrow, and almost nothing. But in his remarks on this species of cognition, there is so little of what is definite, and reduced to rules, that we cannot wonder if no one, not even Hume, was led to make investigations concerning this sort of judgments. For such general and yet definite principles are not easily learned from other men, who have had them obscurely in their minds. We must hit on them first by our own reflexion, then we find them elsewhere, where we could not possibly have found them at first, because the authors themselves did not know that such an idea lay at the basis of their observations. Men who never think independently have nevertheless the acuteness to discover everything, after it has been once shown them, in what was said long

---

[1] The term *apodeictic* is borrowed by Kant from Aristotle who uses it in the sense of "certain beyond dispute." The word is derived from ἀποδείκνυμι (= *I show*) and is contrasted to dialectic propositions, i.e., such statements as admit of controversy. (P.C.)

since, though no one ever saw it there before.

4. The General Question of the Prolegomena.—Is Metaphysics at all Possible?

Were a metaphysics, which could maintain its place as a science, really in existence; could we say, here is metaphysics, learn it, and it will convince you irresistibly and irrevocably of its truth: this question would be useless, and there would only remain that other question (which would rather be a test of our acuteness, than a proof of the existence of the thing itself), "How is the science possible, and how does reason come to attain it?" But human reason has not been so fortunate in this case. There is no single book to which you can point as you do to Euclid, and say: This is Metaphysics; here you may find the noblest objects of this science, the knowledge of a highest Being, and of a future existence, proved from principles of pure reason. We can be shown indeed many judgments, demonstrably certain, and never questioned; but these are all analytical, and rather concern the materials and the scaffolding for Metaphysics, than the extension of knowledge, which is our proper object in studying it (§2). Even supposing you produce synthetical judgments (such as the law of Sufficient Reason, which you have never proved, as you ought to, from pure reason a priori, though we gladly concede its truth), you lapse when they come to be employed for your principal object, into such doubtful assertions, that in all

ages one Metaphysics has contradicted another, either in its assertions, or their proofs, and thus has itself destroyed its own claim to lasting assent. Nay, the very attempts to set up such a science are the main cause of the early appearance of scepticism, a mental attitude in which reason treats itself with such violence that it could never have arisen save from complete despair of ever satisfying our most important aspirations. For long before men began to inquire into nature methodically, they consulted abstract reason, which had to some extent been exercised by means of ordinary experience; for reason is ever present, while laws of nature must usually be discovered with labor. So Metaphysics floated to the surface, like foam, which dissolved the moment it was scooped off. But immediately there appeared a new supply on the surface, to be ever eagerly gathered up by some, while others, instead of seeking in the depths the cause of the phenomenon, thought they showed their wisdom by ridiculing the idle labor of their neighbors.

The essential and distinguishing feature of pure mathematical cognition among all other *a priori* cognitions is, that it cannot at all proceed from concepts, but only by means of the construction of concepts (see Critique II., Method of Transcendentalism, chap. I., sect. 1). As therefore in its judgments it must proceed beyond the concept to that which its corresponding visualisation (*Anschauung*) contains, these judgments neither can, not ought to, arise analytically, by dissecting the concept, but are all synthetical.

I cannot refrain from pointing out the disadvantage resulting to philosophy from the neglect of this easy and apparently insignificant observation. Hume being prompted (a task worthy of a philosopher) to cast his eye over the whole field of *a priori* cognitions in which human understanding claims such mighty possessions, heedlessly severed from it a whole, and indeed its most valuable, province, viz., pure mathematics; for he thought its nature, or, so to speak, the state-constitution of this empire, depended on totally different principles, namely, on the law of contradiction alone; and although he did not divide judgments in this manner formally and universally as I have done here, what he said was equivalent to this: that mathematics contains only analytical, but metaphysics synthetical, *a priori* judgments. In this, however, he was greatly mistaken, and the mistake had a decidedly injurious effect upon his whole conception. But for this, he would have extended his question concerning the origin of our synthetical judgments far beyond the metaphysical concept of Causality, and included in it the possibility of mathematics *a priori* also, for this latter he must have assumed to be equally synthetical. And then he could not have based his metaphysical judgments on mere experience without subjecting the axioms of mathematics equally to experience, a thing which he was far too acute to do. The good company into which metaphysics would thus have been brought, would have saved it from the danger of a contemptuous ill-treatment, for the thrust intended for it must have reached mathematics, which was not and could not have been Hume's intention. Thus that acute man would have been led into considera-

tions which must needs be similar to those that now occupy us, but which would have gained inestimably by his inimitably elegant style.

Metaphysical judgments, properly so called, are all synthetical. We must distinguish judgments pertaining to metaphysics from metaphysical judgments properly so called. Many of the former are analytical, but they only afford the means for metaphysical judgments, which are the whole end of the science, and which are always synthetical. For if there be concepts pertaining to metaphysics (as, for example, that of substance), the judgments springing from simple analysis of them also pertain to metaphysics, as, for example, substance is that which only exists as subject; and by means of several such analytical judgments, we seek to approach the definition of the concept. But as the analysis of a pure concept of the understanding pertaining to metaphysics, does not proceed in any different manner from the dissection of any other, even empirical, concepts, not pertaining to metaphysics (such as: air is an elastic fluid, the elasticity of which is not destroyed by any known degree of cold), it follows that the concept indeed, but not the analytical judgment, is properly metaphysical. This science has something peculiar in the production of its *a priori* cognitions, which must therefore be distinguished from the features it has in common with other rational knowledge. Thus the judgment, that all the substance in things is permanent, is a synthetical and properly metaphysical judgment.

If the *a priori* principles, which constitute the materials of metaphysics, have first been collected according to fixed principles, then their analysis will be of great value; it might be taught as a particular part (as a *philosophia definitiva*), containing nothing but analytical judgments pertaining to metaphysics, and could be treated separately from the synthetical which constitute metaphysics proper. For indeed these analyses are not elsewhere of much value, except in metaphysics, i.e., as regards the synthetical judgments, which are to be generated by these previously analysed concepts.

The conclusion drawn in this section then is, that metaphysics is properly concerned with synthetical propositions *a priori*, and these alone constitute its end, for which it indeed requires various dissections of its concepts, viz., of its analytical judgments, but wherein the procedure is not different from that in every other kind of knowledge, in which we merely seek to render our concepts distinct by analysis. But the generaton of *a priori* cognition by concrete images as well as by concepts, in fine of synthetical propositions *a priori* in philosophical cognition, constitutes the essential subject of Metaphysics.

Weary therefore as well of dogmatism, which teaches us nothing, as of scepticism, which does not even promise us anything, not even the quiet state of a contented ignorance; disquieted by the importance of knowledge so much needed; and lastly, rendered suspicious by long experience of all knowledge which we believe we possess, or which offers itself, under the title of pure reason: there remains but one critical question on the answer to which our future procedure depends, viz., *Is Metaphysics at all possible?* But

this question must be answered not by sceptical objections to the asseverations of some actual system of metaphysics (for we do not as yet admit such a thing to exist), but from the conception, as yet only problematical, of a science of this sort.

In the *Critique of Pure Reason* I have treated this question synthetically, by making inquiries into pure reason itself, and endeavoring in this source to determine the elements as well as the laws of its pure use according to principles. The task is difficult, and requires a resolute reader to penetrate by degrees into a system, based on no data except reason itself, and which therefore seeks, without resting upon any fact, to unfold knowledge from its original germs. *Prolegomena*, however, are designed for preparatory exercises; they are intended rather to point out what we have to do in order if possible to actualise a science, than to propound it. They must therefore rest upon something already known as trustworthy, from which we can set out with confidence, and ascend to sources as yet unknown, the discovery of which will not only explain to us what we knew, but exhibit a sphere of many cognitions which all spring from the same sources. The method of *Prolegomena*, especially of those designed as a preparation for future metaphysics, is consequently analytical.

But it happens fortunately, that though we cannot assume metaphysics to be an actual science, we can say with confidence that certain pure *a priori* synthetical cognitions, pure Mathematics and pure Physics are actual and given; for both contain propositions, which are thoroughly recognised as apodeictically certain, partly by mere reason, partly by general consent arising from experience, and yet as independent of experience. We have therefore some at least uncontested synthetical knowledge *a priori,* and need not ask *whether* it be possible, for it is actual, but *how* it is possible, in order that we may deduce from the principle which makes the given cognitions possible the possibility of all the rest.

5. The General Problem: How is Cognition from Pure Reason Possible?

We have above learned the significant distinction between analytical and synthetical judgments. The possibility of analytical propositions was easily comprehended, being entirely founded on the law of contradiction. The possibility of synthetical *a posteriori* judgments, of those which are gathered from experience, also requires no particular explanation; for experience is nothing but a continual synthesis of perceptions. There remain therefore only synthetical propositions *a priori,* of which the possibility must be sought or investigated, because they must depend upon other principles than the law of contradiction.

But here we need not first establish the possibility of such propositions so as to ask whether they are possible. For there are enough of them which indeed are of undoubted certainty, and as our present method is analytical, we shall start from the fact, that such synthetical but purely rational cognition actually

exists; but we must now inquire into the reason of this possibility, and ask, *how* such cognition is possible, in order that we may from the principles of its possibility be enabled to determine the conditions of its use, its sphere and its limits. The proper problem upon which all depends, when expressed with scholastic precision, is therefore:

How are Synthetic Propositions a priori possible?

For the sake of popularity I have above expressed this problem somewhat differently, as an inquiry into purely rational cognition, which I could do for once without detriment to the desired comprehension, because, as we have only to do here with metaphysics and its sources, the reader will, I hope, after the foregoing remarks, keep in mind that when we speak of purely rational cognition, we do not mean analytical, but synthetical cognition.[2]

---

[2] It is unavoidable that as knowledge advances, certain expressions which have become classical, after having been used since the infancy of science, will be found inadequate and unsuitable, and a newer and more appropriate application of the terms will give rise to confusion. [This is the case with the term "analytical."] The analytical method, so far as it is opposed to the synthetical, is very different from that which constitutes the essence of analytical propositions: it signifies only that we start from what is sought, as if it were given, and ascend to the only conditions under which it is possible. In this method we often use nothing but synthetical propositions, as in mathematical analysis, and it were better to term it the regressive method, in contradistinction to the synthetic or progressive. A principal part of Logic too is distinguished by the name of Analytics, which here signi-

Metaphysics stands or falls with the solution of this problem: its very existence depends upon it. Let any one make metaphysical assertions with ever so much plausibility, let him overwhelm us with conclusions, if he has not previously proved able to answer this question satisfactorily, I have a right to say: this is all vain baseless philosophy and false wisdom. You speak through pure reason, and claim, as it were to create cognitions *a priori* by not only dissecting given concepts, but also by asserting connexions which do not rest upon the law of contradiction, and which you believe you conceive quite independently of all experience; how do you arrive at this, and how will you justify your pretensions? An appeal to the consent of the common sense of mankind cannot be allowed; for that is a witness whose authority depends merely upon rumor. Says Horace:

"Quodcunque ostendis mihi sic,
    incredulus odi."

"To all that which thou provest me
    thus, I refuse to give credence."

The answer to this question, though indispensable, is difficult; and though the principal reason that it was not made long ago is, that the possibility of the question never occurred to anybody, there is yet another reason, which is this that a satisfactory answer to this one question requires a much more persistent, profound, and painstaking reflexion, than the most diffuse work on

Metaphysics, which on its first appearance promised immortality to its author. And every intelligent reader, when he carefully reflects what this problem requires, must at first be struck with its difficulty, and would regard it as insoluble and even impossible, did there not actually exist pure synthetical cognitions *a priori*. This actually happened to David Hume, though he did not conceive the question in its entire universality as is done here, and as must be done, should the answer be decisive for all Metaphysics. For how is it possible, says that acute man, that when a concept is given me, I can go beyond it and connect with it another, which is not contained in it, in such a manner as if the latter necessarily belonged to the former? Nothing but experience can furnish us with such connexions (thus he concluded from the difficulty which he took to be an impossibility), and all that vaunted necessity, or, what is the same thing, all cognition assumed to be *a priori*, is nothing but a long habit of accepting something as true, and hence of mistaking subjective necessity for objective.

Should my reader complain of the difficulty and the trouble which I occasion him in the solution of this problem, he is at liberty to solve it himself in an easier way. Perhaps he will then feel under obligation to the person who has undertaken for him a labor of so profound research, and will rather be surprised at the facility with which, considering the nature of the subject, the solution has been attained. Yet it has cost years of work to solve the problem in its whole universality (using the term in the mathematical sense, viz., for that which is sufficient

fies the logic of truth in contrast to Dialectics, without considering whether the cognitions belonging to it are analytical or synthetical.

for all cases), and finally to exhibit it in the analytical form, as the reader finds it here.

All metaphysicians are therefore solemnly and legally suspended from their occupations till they shall have answered in a satisfactory manner the question, "How are synthetic cognitions *a priori* possible?" For the answer contains the only credentials which they must show when they have anything to offer in the name of pure reason. But if they do not possess these credentials, they can expect nothing else of reasonable people, who have been deceived so often, than to be dismissed without further ado.

If they on the other hand desire to carry on their business, not as a science, but as an art of wholesome oratory suited to the common sense of man, they cannot in justice be prevented. They will then speak the modest language of a rational belief, they will grant that they are not allowed even to conjecture, far less to know, anything which lies beyond the bounds of all possible experience, but only to assume (not for speculative use, which they must abandon, but for practical purposes only) the existence of something that is possible and even indispensable for the guidance of the understanding and of the will in life. In this manner alone can they be called useful and wise men, and the more so as they renounce the title of metaphysicians; for the latter profess to be speculative philosophers, and since, when judgments *a priori* are under discussion, poor probabilities cannot be admitted (for what is declared to be known *a priori* is thereby announced as necessary), such men cannot be permitted to

play with conjectures, but their assertions must be either science, or are worth nothing at all.

It may be said, that the entire transcendental philosophy, which necessarily precedes all metaphysics, is nothing but the complete solution of the problem here propounded, in systematical order and completeness, and hitherto we have never had any transcendental philosophy; for what goes by its name is properly a part of metaphysics, whereas the former science is intended first to constitute the possibility of the latter, and must therefore precede all metaphysics. And it is not surprising that when a whole science, deprived of all help from other sciences, and consequently in itself quite new, is required to answer a single question satisfactorily, we should find the answer troublesome and difficult, nay even shrouded in obscurity.

As we now proceed to this solution according to the analytical method, in which we assume that such cognitions from pure reasons actually exist, we can only appeal to two sciences of theoretical cognition (which alone is under consideration here), pure mathematics and pure natural science (physics). For these alone can exhibit to us objects in a definite and actualisable form (*in der Anschauung*), and consequently (if there should occur in them a cognition *a priori*) can show the truth or conformity of the cognition to the object *in concreto*, that is, its actuality, from which we could proceed to the reason of its possibility by the analytic method. This facilitates our work greatly, for here universal considerations are not only applied to facts, but even start from them, while in a synthetic procedure they must strictly be derived *in abstracto* from concepts.

But, in order to rise from these actual and at the same time well-grounded pure cognitions *a priori* to such a possible cognition of the same as we are seeking, viz., to metaphysics as a science, we must comprehend that which occasions it, I mean the mere natural, though in spite of its truth not unsuspected, cognition *a priori* which lies at the bottom of that science, the elaboration of which without any critical investigation of its possibility is commonly called metaphysics. In a word, we must comprehend the natural conditions of such a science as a part of our inquiry, and thus the transcendental problem will be gradually answered by a division into four questions:

1. How is pure mathematics possible?

2. How is pure natural science possible?

3. How is metaphysics in general possible?

4. How is metaphysics as a science possible?

It may be seen that the solution of these problems, though chiefly designed to exhibit the essential matter of the Critique, has yet something peculiar, which for itself alone deserves attention. This is the search for the sources of given sciences in reason itself, so that its faculty of knowing something *a priori* may by its own deeds be investigated and measured. By this procedure these sciences gain, if not with regard to their contents, yet as to their proper use, and while they throw light on the higher question concerning their common origin, they give, at the same time, an occasion better to explain their own nature.

5.2   THE A PRIORI

A. J. Ayer

The view of philosophy which we have adopted may, I think, fairly be described as a form of empiricism. For

From *Language, Truth and Logic*, 2nd Edition (London: Victor Gollancz, Ltd., 1946). Reprinted by permission of the publisher and the author.

it is characteristic of an empiricist to eschew metaphysics, on the ground that every factual proposition must refer to sense-experience. And even if the conception of philosophizing as an activity of analysis is not to be discovered in the traditional theories of empiricists, we have seen that it is implicit in their practice. At the same time, it must be made clear that, in calling ourselves empiricists, we are not avowing a belief in any of the psychological doctrines which are commonly associated with empiricism. For, even if these doctrines were valid, their validity would be independent of the validity of any philosophical thesis. It could be established only by observation, and not by the purely logical considerations upon which our empiricism rests.

Having admitted that we are empiricists, we must now deal with the objection that is commonly brought against all forms of empiricism; the objection, namely, that it is impossible on empiricist principles to account for our knowledge of necessary truths. For, as Hume conclusively showed, no general proposition whose validity is subject to the test of actual experience can ever be logically certain. No matter how often it is verified in practice, there still remains the possibility that it will be confuted on some future occasion. The fact that a law has been substantiated in $n-1$ cases affords no logical guarantee that it will be substantiated in the nth case also, no matter how large we take n to be. And this means that no general proposition referring to a matter of fact can ever be shown to be necessarily and universally true. It can at best be a probable hypothesis. And this, we shall find, applies not only to general propositions, but to all propositions which have a factual content. They can none of them ever become logically certain. This conclusion, which we shall elaborate later on, is one which must be accepted by every consistent empiricist. It is often thought to

involve him in complete scepticism; but this is not the case. For the fact that the validity of a proposition cannot be logically guaranteed in no way entails that it is irrational for us to believe it. On the contrary, what is irrational is to look for a guarantee where none can be forthcoming; to demand certainty where probability is all that is obtainable. We have already remarked upon this, in referring to the work of Hume. And we shall make the point clearer when we come to treat of probability, in explaining the use which we make of empirical propositions. We shall discover that there is nothing perverse or paradoxical about the view that all the "truths" of science and common sense are hypotheses; and consequently that the fact that it involves this view constitutes no objection to the empiricist thesis.

Where the empiricist does encounter difficulty is in connection with the truths of formal logic and mathematics. For whereas a scientific generalisation is readily admitted to be fallible, the truths of mathematics and logic appear to everyone to be necessary and certain. But if empiricism is correct no proposition which has a factual content can be necessary or certain. Accordingly the empiricist must deal with the truths of logic and mathematics in one of the two following ways: he must say either that they are not necessary truths, in which case he must account for the universal conviction that they are; or must say that they have no factual content, and then he must explain how a proposition which is empty of all factual content can be true and useful and surprising.

If neither of these courses proves

satisfactory, we shall be obliged to give way to rationalism. We shall be obliged to admit that there are some truths about the world which we can know independently of experience; that there are some properties which we can ascribe to all objects, even though we cannot conceivably observe that all objects have them. And we shall have to accept it as a mysterious inexplicable fact that our thought has this power to reveal to us authoritatively the nature of objects which we have never observed. Or else we must accept the Kantian explanation which, apart from the epistemological difficulties which we have already touched on, only pushes the mystery a stage further back.

It is clear that any such concession to rationalism would upset the main argument of this book. For the admission that there were some facts about the world which could be known independently of experience would be incompatible with our fundamental contention that a sentence says nothing unless it is empirically verifiable. And thus the whole force of our attack on metaphysics would be destroyed. It is vital, therefore, for us to be able to show that one or other of the empiricist accounts of the propositions of logic and mathematics is correct. If we are successful in this, we shall have destroyed the foundations of rationalism. For the fundamental tenet of rationalism is that thought is an independent source of knowledge, and is moreover a more trustworthy source of knowledge than experience; indeed some rationalists have gone so far as to say that thought is the only source of knowledge. And the ground for this

view is simply that the only necessary truths about the world which are known to us are known through thought and not through experience. So that if we can show either that the truths in question are not necessary or that they are not "truths about the world," we shall be taking away the support on which rationalism rests. We shall be making good the empiricist contention that there are no "truths of reason" which refer to matters of fact.

The course of maintaining that the truths of logic and mathematics are not necessary or certain was adopted by Mill. He maintained that these propositions were inductive generalizations based on an extremely large number of instances. The fact that the number of supporting instances was so very large accounted, in his view, for our believing these generalizations to be necessarily and universally true. The evidence in their favour was so strong that it seemed incredible to us that a contrary instance should ever arise. Nevertheless it was in principle possible for such generalizations to be confuted. They were highly probable, but, being inductive generalizations, they were not certain. The difference between them and the hypotheses of natural science was a difference in degree and not in kind. Experience gave us very good reason to suppose that a "truth" of mathematics or logic was true universally; but we were not possessed of a guarantee. For these "truths" were only empirical hypotheses which had worked particularly well in the past; and, like all empirical hypotheses, they were theoretically fallible.

I do not think that this solution of

the empiricist's difficulty with regard to the propositions of logic and mathematics is acceptable. In discussing it, it is necessary to make a distinction which is perhaps already enshrined in Kant's famous dictum that, although there can be no doubt that all our knowledge begins with experience, it does not follow that it all arises out of experience.[1] When we say that the truths of logic are known independently of experience, we are not of course saying that they are innate, in the sense that we are born knowing them. It is obvious that mathematics and logic have to be learned in the same way as chemistry and history have to be learned. Nor are we denying that the first person to discover a given logical or mathematical truth was led to it by an inductive procedure. It is very probable, for example, that the principle of the syllogism was formulated not before but after the validity of syllogistic reasoning had been observed in a number of particular cases. What we are discussing, however, when we say that logical and mathematical truths are known independently of experience, is not a historical question concerning the way in which these truths were originally discovered, nor a psychological question concerning the way in which each of us comes to learn them, but an epistemological question. The contention of Mill's which we reject is that the propositions of logic and mathematics have the same status as empirical hypotheses; that their validity is determined in the same way. We main-

tain that they are independent of experience in the sense that they do not owe their validity to empirical verification. We may come to discover them though an inductive process; but once we have apprehended them we see that they are necessarily true, that they hold good for every conceivable instance. And this serves to distinguish them from empirical generalizations. For we know that a proposition whose validity depends upon experience cannot be seen to be necessarily and universally true.

In rejecting Mill's theory, we are obliged to be somewhat dogmatic. We can do no more than state the issue clearly and then trust that his contention will be seen to be discrepant with the relevant logical facts. The following considerations may serve to show that of the two ways of dealing with logic and mathematics which are open to the empiricist, the one which Mill adopted is not the one which is correct.

The best way to substantiate our assertion that the truths of formal logic and pure mathematics are necessarily true is to examine cases in which they might seem to be confuted. It might easily happen, for example, that when I came to count what I had taken to be five pairs of objects, I found that they amounted only to nine. And if I wished to mislead people I might say that on this occasion twice five was not ten. But in that case I should not be using the complex sign "$2 \times 5 = 10$" in the way in which it is ordinarily used. I should be taking it not as the expression of a purely mathematical proposition, but as the expression of an empirical generalization, to the effect

---

[1] *Critique of Pure Reason*, 2nd ed., Introduction, section i.

that whenever I counted what appeared to me to be five pairs of objects I discovered that they were ten in number. This generalization may very well be false. But if it proved false in a given case, one would not say that the mathematical proposition "$2 \times 5 = 10$" had been confuted. One would say that I was wrong in supposing that there were five pairs of objects to start with, or that one of the objects had been taken away while I was counting, or that two of them had coalesced, or that I had counted wrongly. One would adopt as an explanation whatever empirical hypothesis fitted in best with the accredited facts. The one explanation which would in no circumstances be adopted is that ten is not always the product of two and five.

To take another example: if what appears to be a Euclidean triangle is found by measurement not to have angles totalling 180 degrees, we do not say that we have met with an instance which invalidates the mathematical proposition that the sum of the three angles of a Euclidean triangle is 180 degrees. We say that we have measured wrongly, or, more probably, that the triangle we have been measuring is not Euclidean. And this is our procedure in every case in which a mathematical truth might appear to be confuted. We always preserve its validity by adopting some other explanation of the occurrence.

The same thing applies to the principles of formal logic. We may take an example relating to the so-called law of excluded middle, which states that a proposition must be either true or false, or, in other words, that it is im-

possible that a proposition and its contradictory should neither of them be true. One might suppose that a proposition of the form "x has stopped doing y" would in certain cases constitute an exception to this law. For instance, if my friend has never yet written to me, it seems fair to say that it is neither true nor false that he has stopped writing to me. But in fact one would refuse to accept such an instance as an invalidation of the law of excluded middle. One would point out that the proposition "My friend has stopped writing to me" is not a simple proposition, but the conjunction of the two propositions "My friend wrote to me in the past" and "My friend does not write to me now": and, furthermore, that the proposition "My friend has not stopped writing to me" is not, as it appears to be, contradictory to "My friend has stopped writing to me," but only contrary to it. For it means "My friend wrote to me in the past, and he still writes to me." When, therefore, we say that such a proposition as "My friend has stopped writing to me" is sometimes neither true nor false, we are speaking inaccurately. For we seem to be saying that neither it nor its contradictory is true. Whereas what we mean, or anyhow should mean, is that neither it nor its apparent contradictory is true. And its apparent contradictory is really only its contrary. Thus we preserve the law of excluded middle by showing that the negating of a sentence does not always yield the contradictory of the proposition originally expressed.

There is no need to give further examples. Whatever instance we care to take, we shall always find that the situations in which a logical or mathematical principle might appear to be confuted are accounted for in such a way as to leave the principle unassailed. And this indicates that Mill was wrong in supposing that a situation could arise which would overthrow a mathematical truth. The principles of logic and mathematics are true universally simply because we never allow them to be anything else. And the reason for this is that we cannot abandon them without contradicting ourselves, without sinning against the rules which govern the use of language, and so making our utterances self-stultifying. In other words, the truths of logic and mathematics are analytic propositions or tautologies. In saying this we are making what will be held to be an extremely controversial statement, and we must now proceed to make its implications clear.

The most familiar definition of an analytic proposition, or judgement, as he called it, is that given by Kant. He said[2] that an analytic judgement was one in which the predicate B belonged to the subject A as something which was covertly contained in the concept of A. He contrasted analytic with synthetic judgements, in which the predicate B lay outside the subject A, although it did stand in connection with it. Analytic judgements, he explains, "add nothing through the predicate to the concept of the subject, but merely break it up into those constituent concepts that have all along been thought in it, although confusedly." Synthetic

---

[2] *Critique of Pure Reason*, 2nd ed., Introduction, sections iv and v.

judgements, on the other hand, "add to the concept of the subject a predicate which has not been in any wise thought in it, and which no analysis could possibly extract from it." Kant gives "all bodies are extended" as an example of an analytic judgement, on the ground that the required predicate can be extracted from the concept of "body", "in accordance with the principle of contradiction"; as an example of a synthetic judgement, he gives "all bodies are heavy." He refers also to "7 $+5=12$" as a synthetic judgement, on the ground that the concept of twelve is by no means already thought in merely thinking the union of seven and five. And he appears to regard this as tantamount to saying that the judgement does not rest on the principle of contradiction alone. He holds, also, that through analytic judgements our knowledge is not extended as it is through synthetic judgements. For in analytic judgements "the concept which I already have is merely set forth and made intelligible to me."

I think that this is a fair summary of Kant's account of the distinction between analytic and synthetic propositions, but I do not think that it succeeds in making the distinction clear. For even if we pass over the difficulties which arise out of the use of the vague term "concept," and the unwarranted assumption that every judgement, as well as every German or English sentence, can be said to have a subject and a predicate, there remains still this crucial defect. Kant does not give one straightforward criterion for distinguishing between analytic and synthetic propositions; he gives two distinct criteria, which are by no means equivalent. Thus his ground for holding that the proposition "7 + 5 = 12" is synthetic is, as we have seen, that the subjective intension of "7 + 5" does not comprise the subjective intension of "12"; whereas his ground for holding that "all bodies are extended" is an analytic proposition is that it rests on the principle of contradiction alone. That is, he employs a psychological criterion in the first of these examples, and a logical criterion in the second, and takes their equivalence for granted. But, in fact, a proposition which is synthetic according to the former criterion may very well be analytic according to the latter. For, as we have already pointed out, it is possible for symbols to be synonymous without having the same intensional meaning for anyone: and accordingly from the fact that one can think of the sum of seven and five without necessarily thinking of twelve, it by no means follows that the proposition "7 + 5 = 12" can be denied without self-contradiction. From the rest of his argument, it is clear that it is this logical proposition, and not any psychological proposition, that Kant is really anxious to establish. His use of the psychological criterion leads him to think that he has established it, when he has not.

I think that we can preserve the logical import of Kant's distinction between analytic and synthetic propositions, while avoiding the confusions which mar his actual account of it, if we say that a proposition is analytic when its validity depends solely on the definitions of the symbols it contains, and synthetic when its validity is determined by the facts of experience.

Thus, the proposition "There are ants which have established a system of slavery" is a synthetic proposition. For we cannot tell whether it is true or false merely by considering the definitions of the symbols which constitute it. We have to resort to actual observation of the behaviour of ants. On the other hand, the proposition "Either some ants are parasitic or none are" is an analytic proposition. For one need not resort to observation to discover that there either are or are not ants which are parasitic. If one knows what is the function of the words "either," "or," and "not," then one can see that any proposition of the form "Either p is true or p is not true" is valid, independently of experience. Accordingly, all such propositions are analytic.

It is to be noticed that the proposition "Either some ants are parasitic or none are" provides no information whatsoever about the behaviour of ants, or, indeed, about any matter of fact. And this applies to all analytic propositions. They none of them provide any information about any matter of fact. In other words, they are entirely devoid of factual content. And it is for this reason that no experience can confute them.

When we say that analytic propositions are devoid of factual content, and consequently that they say nothing, we are not suggesting that they are senseless in the way that metaphysical utterances are senseless. For, although they give us no information about any empirical situation, they do enlighten us by illustrating the way in which we use certain symbols. Thus if I say, "Nothing can be coloured in different ways at the same time with respect to the same part of itself," I am not saying anything about the properties of any actual thing; but I am not talking nonsense. I am expressing an analytic proposition, which records our determination to call a colour expanse which differs in quality from a neighbouring colour expanse a different part of a given thing. In other words, I am simply calling attention to the implications of a certain linguistic usage. Similarly, in saying that if all Bretons are Frenchmen, and all Frenchmen Europeans, then all Bretons are Europeans, I am not describing any matter of fact. But I am showing that in the statement that all Bretons are Frenchmen, and all Frenchmen Europeans, the further statement that all Bretons are Europeans is implicitly contained. And I am thereby indicating the convention which governs our usage of the words "if" and "all."

We see, then, that there is a sense in which analytic propositions do give us new knowledge. They call attention to linguistic usages, of which we might otherwise not be conscious, and they reveal unsuspected implications in our assertions and beliefs. But we can see also that there is a sense in which they may be said to add nothing to our knowledge. For they tell us only what we may be said to know already. Thus, if I know that the existence of May Queens is a relic of tree-worship, and I discover that May Queens still exist in England, I can employ the tautology "If p implies q, and p is true, q is true" to show that there still exists a relic of tree-worship in England. But in saying that there are still May Queens in England, and that the existence of May

Queens is a relic of tree-worship, I have already asserted the existence in England of a relic of tree-worship. The use of the tautology does, indeed, enable me to make this concealed assertion explicit. But it does not provide me with any new knowledge, in the sense in which empirical evidence that the election of May Queens had been forbidden by law would provide me with new knowledge. If one had to set forth all the information one possessed, with regard to matters of fact, one would not write down any analytic propositions. But one would make use of analytic propositions in compiling one's encyclopædia, and would thus come to include propositions which one would otherwise have overlooked. And, besides enabling one to make one's list of information complete, the formulation of analytic propositions would enable one to make sure that the synthetic propositions of which the list was composed formed a self-consistent system. By showing which ways of combining propositions resulted in contradictions, they would prevent one from including incompatible propositions and so making the list self-stultifying. But in so far as we had actually used such words as "all" and "or" and "not" without falling into self-contradiction, we might be said already to know what was revealed in the formulation of analytic propositions illustrating the rules which govern our usage of these logical particles. So that here again we are justified in saying that analytic propositions do not increase our knowledge.

The analytic character of the truths of formal logic was obscured in the traditional logic through its being insufficiently formalized. For in speaking always of judgements, instead of propositions, and introducing irrelevant psychological questions, the traditional logic gave the impression of being concerned in some specially intimate way with the workings of thought. What it was actually concerned with was the formal relationship of classes, as is shown by the fact that all its principles of inference are subsumed in the Boolean class-calculus, which is subsumed in its turn in the propositional calculus of Russell and Whitehead.[3] Their system, expounded in *Principia Mathematica*, makes it clear that formal logic is not concerned with the properties of men's minds, much less with the properties of material objects, but simply with the possibility of combining propositions by means of logical particles into analytic propositions, and with studying the formal relationship of these analytic propositions, in virtue of which one is deducible from another. Their procedure is to exhibit the propositions of formal logic as a deductive system, based on five primitive propositions, subsequently reduced in number to one. Hereby the distinction between logical truths and principles of inference, which was maintained in the Aristotelian logic, very properly disappears. Every principle of inference is put forward as a logical truth and every logical truth can serve as a principle of inference. The three Aristotelian "laws of thought," the law of identity, the law

of excluded middle, and the law of non-contradiction, are incorporated in the system, but they are not considered more important than the other analytic propositions. They are not reckoned among the premises of the system. And the system of Russell and Whitehead itself is probably only one among many possible logics, each of which is composed of tautologies as interesting to the logician as the arbitrarily selected Aristotelian "laws of thought."[4]

A point which is not sufficiently brought out by Russell, if indeed it is recognised by him at all, is that every logical proposition is valid in its own right. Its validity does not depend on its being incorporated in a system, and deduced from certain propositions which are taken as self-evident. The construction of systems of logic is useful as a means of discovering and certifying analytic propositions, but it is not in principle essential even for this purpose. For it is possible to conceive of a symbolism in which every analytic proposition could be seen to be analytic in virtue of its form alone.

The fact that the validity of an analytic proposition in no way depends on its being deducible from other analytic propositions is our justification for disregarding the question whether the propositions of mathematics are reducible to propositions of formal logic, in the way that Russell supposed.[5] For even if it is the case that the definition of a cardinal number as a class of

[3] Vide Karl Menger, "Die Neue Logik," *Krise and Neuaufbau in den Exakten Wissenschaften*, pp. 94–6; and Lewis and Langford, *Symbolic Logic*, Chapter v.

[4] Vide Lewis and Langford, *Symbolic Logic*, Chapter vii, for an elaboration of this point.

[5] Vide *Introduction to Mathematical Philosophy*, Chapter ii.

classes similar to a given class is circular, and it is not possible to reduce mathematical notions to purely logical notions, it will still remain true that the propositions of mathematics are analytic propositions. They will form a special class of analytic propositions, containing special terms, but they will be none the less analytic for that. For the criterion of an analytic proposition is that its validity should follow simply from the definition of the terms contained in it, and this condition is fulfilled by the propositions of pure mathematics.

The mathematical propositions which one might most pardonably suppose to be synthetic are the propositions of geometry. For it is natural for us to think, as Kant thought, that geometry is the study of the properties of physical space, and consequently that its propositions have factual content. And if we believe this, and also recognise that the truths of geometry are necessary and certain, then we may be inclined to accept Kant's hypothesis that space is the form of intuition of our outer sense, a form imposed by us on the matter of sensation, as the only possible explanation of our *a priori* knowledge of these synthetic propositions. But while the view that pure geometry is concerned with physical space was plausible enough in Kant's day, when the geometry of Euclid was the only geometry known, the subsequent invention of non-Euclidean geometries has shown it to be mistaken. We see now that the axioms of a geometry are simply definitions, and that the theorems of a geometry are simply the logical consequences of these definitions.[6] A geometry is not in itself about physical space; in itself it cannot be said to be "about" anything. But we can use a geometry to reason about physical space. That is to say, once we have given the axioms a physical interpretation, we can proceed to apply the theorems to the objects which satisfy the axioms. Whether a geometry can be applied to the actual physical world or not, is an empirical question which falls outside the scope of the geometry itself. There is no sense, therefore, in asking which of the various geometries known to us are false and which are true. In so far as they are all free from contradiction, they are all true. What one can ask is which of them is the most useful on any given occasion, which of them can be applied most easily and most fruitfully to an actual empirical situation. But the proposition which states that a certain application of a geometry is possible is not itself a proposition of that geometry. All that the geometry itself tells us is that if anything can be brought under the definitions, it will also satisfy the theorems. It is therefore a purely logical system, and its propositions are purely analytic propositions.

It might be objected that the use made of diagrams in geometrical treatises shows that geometrical reasoning is not purely abstract and logical, but depends on our intuition of the properties of figures. In fact, however, the use of diagrams is not essential to completely rigorous geometry. The diagrams are introduced as an aid to our reason.

---

[6] cf. H. Poincaré, *La Science et l'Hypothèse*, Part II, Chapter iii.

They provide us with a particular application of the geometry, and so assist us to perceive the more general truth that the axioms of the geometry involve certain consequences. But the fact that most of us need the help of an example to make us aware of those consequences does not show that the relation between them and the axioms is not a purely logical relation. It shows merely that our intellects are unequal to the task of carrying out very abstract processes of reasoning without the assistance of intuition. In other words, it has no bearing on the nature of geometrical propositions, but is simply an empirical fact about ourselves. Moreover, the appeal to intuition, though generally of psychological value, is also a source of danger to the geometer. He is tempted to make assumptions which are accidentally true of the particular figure he is taking as an illustration, but do not follow from his axioms. It has, indeed, been shown that Euclid himself was guilty of this, and consequently that the presence of the figure is essential to some of his proofs.[7] This shows that his system is not, as he presents it, completely rigorous, although of course it can be made so. It does not show that the presence of the figure is essential to a truly rigorous geometrical proof. To suppose that it did would be to take as a necessary feature of all geometries what is really only an incidental defect in one particular geometrical system.

We conclude, then that the proposi-tions of pure geometry are analytic. And this leads us to reject Kant's hypothesis that geometry deals with the form of intuition of our outer sense. For the ground for this hypothesis was that it alone explained how the propositions of geometry could be both true *a priori* and synthetic: and we have seen that they are not synthetic. Similarly our view that the propositions of arithmetic are not synthetic but analytic leads us to reject the Kantian hypothesis[8] that arithmetic is concerned with our pure intuition of time, the form of our inner sense. And thus we are able to dismiss Kant's transcendental æsthetic without having to bring forward the epistemological difficulties which it is commonly said to involve. For the only argument which can be brought in favour of Kant's theory is that it alone explains certain "facts." And now we have found that the "facts" which it purports to explain are not facts at all. For while it is true that we have *a priori* knowledge of necessary propositions, it is not true, as Kant supposed, that any of these necessary propositions are synthetic. They are without exception analytic propositions, or, in other words, tautologies.

We have already explained how it is that these analytic propositions are necessary and certain. We saw that the reason why they cannot be confuted in experience is that they do not make any assertion about the empirical world. They simply record our determination

---

[7] cf. M. Black, *The Nature of Mathematics,* p. 154.

[8] This hypothesis is not mentioned in the *Critique of Pure Reason*, but was maintained by Kant at an earlier date.

to use words in a certain fashion. We cannot deny them without infringing the conventions which are presupposed by our very denial, and so falling into self-contradiction. And this is the sole ground of their necessity. As Wittgenstein puts it, our justification for holding that the world could not conceivably disobey the laws of logic is simply that we could not say of an unlogical world how it would look.[9] And just as the validity of an analytic proposition is independent of the nature of the external world; so is it independent of the nature of our minds. It is perfectly conceivable that we should have employed different linguistic conventions from those which we actually do employ. But whatever these conventions might be, the tautologies in which we recorded them would always be necessary. For any denial of them would be self-stultifying.

We see, then, that there is nothing mysterious about the apodeictic certainty of logic and mathematics. Our knowledge that no observation can ever confute the proposition "$7+5=12$" depends simply on the fact that the symbolic expression "$7+5$" is synonymous with "12," just as our knowledge that every oculist is an eye-doctor depends on the fact that the symbol "eye-doctor" is synonymous with "oculist." And the same explanation holds good for every other *a priori* truth.

What is mysterious at first sight is that these tautologies should on occasion be so surprising, that there should

be in mathematics and logic the possibility of invention and discovery. As Poincaré says: "If all the assertions which mathematics puts forward can be derived from one another by formal logic, mathematics cannot amount to anything more than an immense tautology. Logical inference can teach us nothing essentially new, and if everything is to proceed from the principle of identity, everything must be reducible to it. But can we really allow that these theorems which fill so many books serve no other purpose than to say in a roundabout fashion '$A=A$'?"[10] Poincaré finds this incredible. His own theory is that the sense of invention and discovery in mathematics belongs to it in virtue of mathematical induction, the principle that what is true for the number 1, and true for $n+1$ when it is true for n,[11] is true for all numbers. And he claims that this is a synthetic *a priori* principle. It is, in fact, *a priori*, but it is not synthetic. It is a defining principle of the natural numbers, serving to distinguish them from such numbers as the infinite cardinal numbers, to which it cannot be applied.[12] Moreover, we must remember that discoveries can be made, not only in arithmetic, but also in geometry and formal logic, where no use is made of mathematical induction. So that even if Poincaré were right about mathematical induction, he

---

[9] *Tractatus Logico-Philosophicus*, 3.031.

[10] *La Science et l'Hypothèse*, Part I, Chapter i.

[11] This was wrongly stated in previous editions as "true for n when it is true for $n+1$."

[12] cf. B. Russell's *Introduction to Mathematical Philosophy*, Chapter iii, p. 27.

would not have provided a satisfactory explanation of the paradox that a mere body of tautologies can be so interesting and so surprising.

The true explanation is very simple. The power of logic and mathematics to surprise us depends, like their usefulness, on the limitations of our reason. A being whose intellect was infinitely powerful would take no interest in logic and mathematics.[13] For he would be able to see at a glance everything that his definitions implied, and, accordingly, could never learn anything from logical inference which he was not fully conscious of already. But our intellects are not of this order. It is only a minute proportion of the consequences of our definitions that we are able to detect at a glance. Even so simple a tautology as "$91 \times 79 = 7189$" is beyond the scope of our immediate apprehension. To assure ourselves that "7189" is synonymous with "91×79" we have to resort to calculation, which is simply a process of tautological transformation —that is, a process by which we change the form of expressions without altering their significance. The multiplication tables are rules for carrying out this process in arithmetic, just as the laws of logic are rules for the tautological transformation of sentences expressed in logical symbolism or in ordinary language. As the process of calculation is carried out more or less mechanically, it is easy for us to make a slip and so unwittingly contradict ourselves. And this accounts for the existence of logical

and mathematical "falsehoods," which otherwise might appear paradoxical. Clearly the risk of error in logical reasoning is proportionate to the length and the complexity of the process of calculation. And in the same way, the more complex an analytic proposition is, the more chance it has of interesting and surprising us.

It is easy to see that the danger of error in logical reasoning can be minimized by the introduction of symbolic devices, which enable us to express highly complex tautologies in a conveniently simple form. And this gives us an opportunity for the exercise of invention in the pursuit of logical enquiries. For a well-chosen definition will call our attention to analytic truths, which would otherwise have escaped us. And the framing of definitions which are useful and fruitful may well be regarded as a creative act.

Having thus shown that there is no inexplicable paradox involved in the view that the truths of logic and mathematics are all of them analytic, we may safely adopt it as the only satisfactory explanation of their *a priori* necessity. And in adopting it we vindicate the empiricist claim that there can be no *a priori* knowledge of reality. For we show that the truths of pure reason, the propositions which we know to be valid independently of all experience, are so only in virtue of their lack of factual content. To say that a proposition is true *a priori* is to say that it is a tautology. And tautologies, though they may serve to guide us in our empirical search for knowledge, do not in themselves contain any information about any matter of fact.

---

[13] cf. Hans Hahn, "Logik, Mathematik und Naturerkennen," *Einheitswissenschaft,* Heft II, p. 18. "Ein allwissendes Wesen braucht keine Logik und keine Mathematik."

ARE ALL NECESSARY PROPOSITIONS ANALYTIC?

5.3

Arthur Pap

The title question of this paper admits of two different interpretations. It might be a question like "Are all swans white?" or it might be a question like "Are all statements of probability statistical statements?" "Are all causal statements, statements of regular sequence?" etc. If these two types of questions were contrasted with each other by calling the former "empirical" and the latter "philosophical," little light would be shed on the distinction, since what is to be understood by a "philosophical" question is extremely controversial. Perhaps the following is a clearer way of describing the essential difference: the concept "swan" is on about the same level of clarity or exactness as the concept "white," and one can easily decide whether the subject-concept is applicable in a given case *independently* of knowing whether the predicated concept applies. On the other hand, the second class of questions might be called questions of

From *The Philosophical Review*, LVIII (1949). Reprinted by permission of the editors.

logical analysis, i.e., the predicated concept is supposed to *clarify* the subject-concept. They can thus be interpreted as questions concerning the adequacy of a proposed analysis (frequency theory of probability, regularity theory of causation); and the very form of the question indicates that the suggested analysis will not be accepted as adequate unless it fits all uses of the analyzed concept. Now, when I ask, as several philosophers before me have asked, whether all necessary propositions are analytic, I mean to ask just this sort of a question. I assume that those who, with no hesitation at all, give an affirmative answer to the question, consider their statement as a clarification of a somewhat inexact concept of traditional philosophy, viz., the concept of a necessary truth, by means of a clearer concept. I feel, however, that little will be gained by the substitution of the term "analytic" for the term "necessary," unless the former term is used more clearly and more consistently than it seems to me to be used in many contemporary discussions. And I shall attempt to show in this paper that once the concept "analytic" is used clearly and consistently, it will have to be admitted that there are propositions which no philosopher would hesitate to call "necessary" and which nevertheless we have no good grounds for classifying as analytic. Moreover, I shall show that even if the concepts "necessary" and "analytic" had the same extension, they would remain different concepts. To prove this it will be sufficient to show that a proposition *may be* necessary and synthetic.

Probably the most precise analysis of the concept of analytic truth is to be found in the logical writings of Carnap. In his *Logical Syntax of Language* an analytic sentence is defined as a sentence which is a consequence of any sentence (§ 10). This definition makes the defined concept, of course, relative to a given language (i.e., "p is analytic" must be regarded as elliptical for "p is analytic in L"), since the syntactic concept "consequence" is defined in terms of the transformation rules for a given object-language. Now, it is clear that this definition is constructed with a view to syntactical investigations into the formal structure of artificial languages such as logical calculi and formalized arithmetic. It is therefore not very useful for philosophers who are interested in the analysis of natural languages which are obviously unprecise in the sense that their formal structure cannot be exhaustively described by stating complete sets of formation rules and transformation rules. Also, no philosopher who proposes "analytic" as the *analysans* for "necessary" could plausibly mean by "analytic" a *syntactic* concept, i.e., a concept defined for sentences of an uninterpreted language

of which it cannot be said that they are either true or false (uninterpreted as they are) but at best—in case the system is complete, that is—that they are either derivable from the primitive sentences or refutable on the basis of the primitive sentences. For necessity of propositions has always been meant as a *semantic* concept: a necessary condition which any adequate analysis of "necessary" must satisfy is that the *truth-value* of a necessary proposition does not depend on any empirical facts.

Carnap has since constructed a definition of "analytic" in semantic terms, which yields a concept *corresponding* to the earlier-defined syntactic concept in the sense that any sentence which is analytic in the syntactic sense (e.g., "p or not p," where the logical constants "or" and "not" are not defined by truth-tables but occur as undefined logical symbols in the primitive sentences) becomes analytic in the semantic sense once the language to which it belongs is semantically interpreted. A sentence of a semantic system (i.e., a language interpreted in terms of semantic rules) is said to be analytic or "L-true," if it is true in every state-description.[1] This definition is, of course, reminiscent of the old Leibnizian conception of "truths of reason" as those that hold in any

---

[1] A state-description is a class of atomic sentences of such a kind that the semantic rules of L suffice to determine whether any sentence of L is true in the world described by this class of sentences. Thus, if L were a miniature language containing two individual constants "a" and "b," and two primitive predicates "P" and "Q," the following would be an example of a state-description: *Pa and Qa and Pb and not Qb*.

possible world. But this semantic concept is analogously constructed with a view to the investigation of artificial, completely formalized languages. Specifically, the concept of a state-description is defined for a highly simplified molecular language containing only predicates of the first level, like "cold," "blue," etc. Also, the far-reaching assumption has to be made that the undefined descriptive predicates of the language designate absolutely simple properties and are hence logically independent. Otherwise, further analysis might reveal logical dependence, and what appeared before analysis as a "possible" state-description might turn out to be an inconsistent class of sentences.

For such reasons, definitions of "analytic" that are fruitful from the point of view of the semantic analysis of natural languages (including scientific language), which is practiced by both the so-called left-wing positivists and the followers of G. E. Moore, have to be sought elsewhere. This does not mean, however, that we must altogether ignore what formal logicians say about the matter. The following definition by Quine, for example, is illuminating: An analytic statement, as ordinarily conceived, is a definitionally abbreviated substitution instance of a principle of logic. Thus, if the word "father" is introduced into the language as an abbreviation for "male parent," then "All fathers are male" is synonymous with "All male parents are male," and, assuming that the type "male" is univocal, this statement reduces to a substitution instance of the logical principle "For every x, P, Q; Px and Qx implies

Px." What are we to understand by a logical principle? Following Quine, a logical principle might be defined as a true statement in which only *logical* constants occur. This definition raises some problems, to be sure. To begin with, the statement, "something exists," formalized in the familiar functional calculus by "There is an x and a P such that Px,"[2] would express a logical truth, which some philosophers would find difficult to accept. But the paradox will be mitigated if one considers what would be entailed by the elimination of this statement from logic. According to the customary interpretation of the universal quantifier, "(x) Px" is equivalent to "$\sim$ (Ex) $\sim$ Px." It can easily be seen to follow that two statements of the form "(x) Px" and "(x) $\sim$ Px" are incompatible only if something exists. And would it not be paradoxical if it depended on extralogical facts whether two given propositions are incompatible by their form? Secondly, it is not easy to give a general definition of "logical constant." It would obviously be circular to define logical constants as those symbols from definitions of which the truth of logical principles follows. Perhaps we have to be satisfied with a definition by enumeration, just as we cannot define "color" by stating a common property of all colors but only by enumerating all the colors that happen to have names. Such a definition would be theoretically incomplete but practically complete enough. If, for example, we mentioned "or," "not," "all,"

---

[2] The use of a predicate variable, here, cannot be circumvented since there are compelling reasons for not admitting the various forms of "to exist" as logical predicates.

and any term definable in terms of these, we probably would not omit any logical constant that occurs in the familiar logical, scientific, and conversational languages (I assume, of course, the reducibility of arithmetic to logic).

According to some uses, the statement "All fathers are male" would be called analytic, and the statement "All fathers are fathers" would be called an explicit tautology. But it is clear that those who roughly identify analytic truth with truth certifiable by formal logic alone would include explicit tautologies as a subclass of analytic statements. It appears, therefore, convenient to widen the above definition as follows: A statement is analytic if it is a substitution instance of a logical principle or, in case defined terms occur in it, a definitionally abbreviated substitution instance of a logical principle. This definition commits us to acceptance of an interesting consequence, whether we like it or not: if a statement, like "No part of any surface is both blue and red at the same time," contains undefined predicates ("blue," "red"), we cannot know it to be analytic unless replacement of all descriptive terms by appropriate variables leaves us with a principle of logic.[3] This point will prove to

_____
[3] There are certain technical details connected with a fully satisfactory definition of "logical principle," such as whether a logical principle may contain free variables or whether all variables must be bound. But these questions are unimportant in this context. Thus I shall call "Px or not-Px" a logical principle, although customarily variables are used to express indeterminateness rather than universality, and such an expression is, therefore, regarded as a function, not as a statement.

be important in the subsequent discussion. The question might be raised whether logical principles themselves could be called "analytic" on the basis of the proposed definition. Certainly an adequate definition of analytic truth should allow an affirmative answer to this question. What makes me know that it will rain, if it will rain, is the same as what makes me know the law of identity, "if p, then p," viz., acquaintance with the meaning of "implies" or "if, then." It sounds admittedly awkward to say of a statement that it is a substitution instance *of itself*—but perhaps such language is no more uncommon than, say, the use of implication as a reflexive relation. Thus, stretching language somewhat to suit our purposes, as is quite common in logic and mathematics, logical principles like "if p, then p or q" will be said to be their own substitution instances. And when definitional abbreviations are spoken of, not only definitions of descriptive constants, like "father," are referred to, but also definitions of logical constants, like "if, then." This convention enables us to say that "not (p and not p)" is a definitional expansion of "if p, then p," for example. The fact that a principle of logic is analytic leaves it, of course, an open possibility that it might also be *necessary* in a sense in which synthetic propositions likewise may be necessary. It will be emphasized, in the sequel, that "p is necessary" does not entail "p is analytic," although the converse entailment undeniably holds.

I pointed out that Carnap's definitions of "analytic" (or "L-true") are constructed with reference to (syntactically or semantically) formalized languages and have therefore a limited utility. But I should not be misunderstood to imply that *reference to a given language* ought to be, or can be, avoided in the construction of such a definition, if "analytic" is treated as a predicate of *sentences* at all.[4] The same relativity characterizes the definition proposed above, since "analytic" is defined in terms of the systematically ambiguous term "true." The so-called *semantical* antinomies (like the classical antinomy of the liar) are well known to arise from the treatment of truth as an absolute concept, i.e., a property meaningfully predicable of any sentence, no matter on which level of the hierarchy of meta-languages the sentence be formulated. What is to be taken as defined, then, is "analytic in the object-language L," although a schema is provided by the definition for constructing analogous definitions for each level of language.

Another appropriate comment on the proposed definition of "analytic" should be made. It is well known that if our language refers to an infinite domain of individuals, there is no general decision procedure with respect to quantified formulas, i.e., no automatic procedure by which it can be decided, in a finite number of steps, whether such a formula is tautologous, indeterminate, or contradictory. For this reason, it might not be possible to decide in a given case

whether the formula which results from a statement suspected as analytic when the descriptive constants are replaced by variables is a logical truth. This is again an admitted theoretical defect of the proposed definition, but not a defect that might really prove fatal to the practice of linguistic analysis. For such undecidable formulas (like Fermat's theorem, for example) are usually complicated to a degree which the formulas resulting from the formalization of controversial "necessary" statements never are. Thus, the formula corresponding to "No spacetime region is both wholly red and wholly blue" would be "$\sim (Ex)(Et) [Pxt \cdot Qxt]$" (where we might consider surfaces as constituting the range of "x"), and this formula is certainly not logically true, since we can easily find predicates which, when substituted for "P" and "Q," would yield a false statement.

If "analytic" is thus defined as a semantic predicate of sentences of a language of fixed level, the proposed substitution of "analytic" for "necessary" at once raises the question: Does it make sense to speak of analytic *propositions?* If it does not, then our new concept cannot replace the old concept of necessity, since obviously necessity is intended as an attribute of propositions. If Leibniz, for example, were asked whether "all fathers are male" and "Alle Vaeter sind Maenner" are different truths of reason, he would undoubtedly deny it. These two sentences express the same proposition, and it is the proposition which is said to be necessary. Also, a sentence may obviously be analytic at one time and syn-

---

[4] Carnap, indeed, speaks in his semantical writings at times of analytic or L-true *propositions*. But he would regard this merely as a convenient mode of speaking: "The proposition that . . . is L-true" is short for "The sentence '. . .' and any sentence that is L-equivalent to '. . .' is L-true."

thetic at another time, viz., in case the relevant semantic rules undergo a change. But nobody who believes that there are necessary propositions at all would admit that a proposition which is now contingent may become necessary, or vice versa. If we adopt the semantic rule "Nothing is to be called 'bread' unless it has nourishing power," then the proposition expressed by the sentence "Bread has nourishing power" is necessary; and this proposition was necessary also before this semantic rule was adopted, although the *sentence* by which it is now expressed may at that time have been synthetic.

However, the method of logical construction shows a way toward construing reference to analytic propositions as an admissible short cut for talking about classes of sentences that are related in a certain way. To say, "The *proposition* that all fathers are male is analytic," might be construed as synonymous with saying "Any sentence which should ever be used, in any language at all, to express what is now *meant* by saying 'all fathers are male' would be analytic." Those who hold, with C. I. Lewis, that analytic truth is grounded in certain immutable relations of "objective meanings," not affected by accidental changes of linguistic rules,[5] could therefore consistently accept a definition of "analytic" which makes this term primarily predicable of sentences. It will, indeed, be my main point against the linguistic theory of logical necessity, to be discussed shortly, that the necessity of a proposition, whether the proposition be analytic or synthetic, is a fact altogether independent of linguistic conventions.

On the other hand, I do find C. I. Lewis and those who share his views concerning the nature of analytic or a priori truth (where "analytic" and "a priori" are regarded as synonyms) guilty of a different inconsistency. Analytic truth, they say, is certifiable by logic alone; and I have attempted to clarify what this means by defining "analytic" as above. They also say that what makes a statement analytic is a certain relationship of the meanings of its constituent terms. But it seems to escape their notice that these assertions are by no means equivalent; the first implies, perhaps, the second, but the second, I contend, does not imply the first. Consider a simple statement like "If A precedes B, then B does not precede A." I assume that few would regard this statement as factual, i.e., such that it might be conceivably disconfirmed by observations.[6] And if it is not factual, then it must be true on the basis of its *meaning*. But it seems that just because all analytic statements are true by the meanings of their terms, it has been somewhat rashly taken for granted that whatever statement is true by what it means is also analytic. To see that the above statement is not analytic, in the sense defined, we only need to formalize it, and we obtain

---

[5] Cf. C. I. Lewis, *An Analysis of Knowledge and Valuation*, ch. 5.

[6] I hope nobody will make the irrelevant comment that it is meaningless to speak of *absolute* temporal relations, and that it is empirically possible to disconfirm the statement by a shift of reference-frame. Obviously, I assume that the verb "to precede" is used *univocally*.

"(x) (y) [xRy implies not-yRx]," which is certainly no principle of logic. This statement, then, is not deducible from logic; hence if we want to call it necessary (nonfactual), we have to admit that there are necessary propositions which are not analytic. Some will no doubt reply: "If we knew the analysis of the predicate of this sentence, we would have a definition with the help of which we could demonstrate its analyticity." But then one would at least have to admit that the statement is not *known* to be analytic. And since we know it to be true on noninductive evidence, it follows that there is a priori knowledge which is not derived from our (implicit or explicit) knowledge of logic.

I anticipate the objection that if the above statement is not factual, then at least I cannot be *certain* that it is synthetic; after all, I have no ground for asserting that the relation of temporal succession is unanalyzable. But I fully admit that, as Carnap has recently emphasized, we cannot be certain that a given true statement is *not* analytic unless we assume that our analysis has reached ultimately simple concepts. At least this would seem to be correct as far as nonfactual statements are concerned. What I maintain is only that, if by a necessary proposition we mean a proposition that is true independently of empirical facts (or that is not disconfirmable by observations), then a necessary proposition *may be* synthetic, and that therefore "analytic" will not do as an *analysans* for "necessary."

I propose to show, now, that there is a temptation to beg the question at issue in trying to prove that a necessary proposition like the above follows from logic after all. Obviously, to offer such a proof would amount to the construction of a definition of "x precedes y" with the help of which the asymmetry of this temporal relation could be formally deduced. But one could not significantly ask whether a proposed definition is *adequate* unless one first agreed on certain *criteria of adequacy*, i.e., propositions which must be deducible from any adequate definition. Thus, most philosophers would agree that no definition of "xPy" (to be used as an abbreviation for "x precedes y") could be adequate unless it entailed the asymmetry of P. If it should leave this open as a question of fact, it would be discarded as failing to explicate that concept we have in mind. Now, by enumerating all the formal properties which P is to have, one could not construct a definition sufficiently specific to distinguish P from all formally similar relations with which it might be confused. If I define P as asymmetrical, irreflexive, and transitive, the relation expressed by "x is greater than y," as holding between real numbers, would also satisfy the definition. But there is a simple device by which uniqueness can be achieved. I only have to add the condition, "The field of P consists of events." It is easily seen that with the help of this definition our necessary proposition reduces to a substitution instance of the logical truth, "If xPy, and xPy implies not-yPx, and q (here "q" represents the remaining defining conditions for the use of "P"), then not-yPx." But is it not obvious that acceptance of the definition from which the asymmetry of temporal succession has thus been deduced presupposes acceptance of the very proposition "Temporal succession is asymmetrical" as self-evident? This way of proving that the debated proposition is, in spite of superficial appearances, analytic, is therefore grossly circular.

I should say, then, that such propositions as "The relation of temporal succession is asymmetrical, transitive, and irreflexive," "No space-time region is both wholly blue and wholly red," are necessary, but that nobody has any good ground for saying they are analytic in any formal sense.[7] In general, this seems to me to be true of two classes of necessary propositions, of which the first assert the impossibility for different codeterminates (i.e., determinate qualities under a common determinable quality) to characterize the same space-time region, and the second the necessity for certain determinables to accompany each other. A classical representative of each group will be selected for discussion, viz., "Nothing can be simultaneously blue and red all over," from the first, and "Whatever is colored, is extended," from the second. I have already insisted that the statement "$\sim(Ex)(Et)$ $(blue_{xt} \cdot red_{xt})$" is not deducible from logic. Indeed, if "blue" and "red" designate unanalyzable qualities, it is difficult to see how analysis could ever reveal that this statement is a substitution instance of a logical truth. Perhaps, however, the above statement (S) could be formally demonstrated as follows. The sort of entities to which colors may be significantly attributed are surfaces, no matter whether they be located in physical or perceptual space. But, so the argument runs, if I say "x is blue at t" and also "y is red at t" (where the values of the variables "x" and "y" are names of surfaces), I have already implicitly asserted "$x \neq y$"; in the same way as simultaneous occupancy of different places is tacitly regarded as a criterion of the presence of *different* things at those places. If the proposition here asserted is formalized, we obtain: $(x)(y)(t)$ (if $blue_{xt} \cdot red_{yt}$, then $x \neq y$) (T). Obviously, S follows from T, hence we may say that "if T, then S" is analytic. But thus we would first have to prove that T is analytic before we could assert that S is. As I follow the rule, "Any proposition is to be held synthetic unless it is derivable from logic alone," I hold T to be synthetic until such time as conclusive proof of the contrary is produced. And the same applies, of course, to S.

Such left-wing positivists as practice an "informal" (or "nonformal"?) method of linguistic analysis will probably disown this kind of discussion as too formal. As I promised, an examination of their linguistic theory of a priori truth is to follow. At the moment I only want to point out that I would not find it enlightening to be told: "S is obviously analytic, since in calling a given part of a surface 'red' we already implicitly deny its being blue. 'Nonblue,' that is, forms part of

[7] I postpone examination of the familiar argument of the "verbalists" that such propositions are analytic in the sense that anybody who denied them would be violating certain linguistic rules.

the meaning of 'red.' " I do not find this easy argument in the least cogent, since the only meaning I can attach to the statement " 'Nonblue' as part of the meaning of 'red' " is just " 'x is red at t' *entails* 'x is not blue at t,' " and the question at issue is just whether such an entailment may be regarded as analytic (or formal). Surely, "nonblue" could not be an element of the concept "red" in the sense in which "male" is an element of the concept "father." Otherwise it would be difficult to understand why any intelligent philosophers should ever have held it possible that there should be *unanalyzable* qualities, and specifically that color qualities should be such.

Next, let us consider the statement, "If x is colored, then x is extended," which may be classified together with such necessary propositions as, "If x has a pitch, then x has a degree of loudness," "If x has size (i.e., length, area, or volume), then x has shape." Which determinate forms of these determinables are conjoined in a given case is contingent, but that some determinate form of the second should accompany any given determinate form of the first is generally held to be *necessary*. Here again, the reason for our inability to deduce these propositions from pure logic would seem to be the fact that the involved predicates cannot be analyzed in such a way as to transform the propositions into tautologies; they can only be ostensively defined. I shall examine two counterarguments with which I am familiar. To what else, it is asked, could colors be significantly attributed except surfaces?[8] If not, then only names or descriptions of surfaces are admissible values of "x" in the debated universal statement. But then each substitution instance is analytic, since it has the form, "If this surface is colored, then it is a surface," which reduces to, "If this is a surface and colored, then it is a surface." And therefore the universal statement itself, which may be interpreted as the logical product of all its substitution instances, must be analytic. Notice that a similar argument also would prove, if it were valid, the analytic nature of the other necessary propositions of the same category. Pitch can be meaningfully attributed only to tones; it is not false so much as meaningless to say of a smell or feeling that it has a given pitch. In fact, we *mean* by a tone an event characterized by pitch, loudness, and whatever further determinables be considered "dimensions" of tones. And to say, "If a tone has a certain pitch, then it has a certain loudness," is, then, surely analytic.

But such arguments beg the question. The statement, "Only surfaces can significantly be said to have a color," differs in an important respect from such statements as "Only animals (including human beings) can significantly be called fathers," or "Only integers can significantly be called odd or even."

---

[8] There may be some who wish to defend the possibility of colored *points*. Whether such a concept is meaningful is, however, a question of minor importance in this context, since we can easily stretch the usage of "surface" in such a way that points become limiting cases of surfaces.

For the latter statements involve analyzable predicates and may well be replaced by the statements, "Fathers are defined as a subclass of living beings," "Oddness and evenness are defined as properties of integers," while we cannot assume, without begging the very question at issue, that "x is colored" *entails by definition* "x is a surface." Similarly, if "x is a tone" is short for "x has a pitch and x has a degree of loudness and. . .," then to say that pitch is significantly predicable only of tones is to say that pitch is significantly predicable only of events of which loudness is also predicable. But this semantic statement cannot be replaced by the syntactic statement " 'x has pitch' entails by definition 'x has loudness,' " unless the question at issue is to be begged.[9]

The second argument in support of

---

[9] It would be irrelevant to point out that pitch is *physically* defined in terms of frequency, which is by definition a property of waves with definite amplitude; and that the physical definition of loudness is just amplitude. In the first place, it is causal laws that are here improperly called "definitions": pitch may be *produced* by air vibrations of definite frequency, but nobody means to talk about air vibrations when referring to pitch. Let it not be replied that if I am not talking about such inferred physical processes I must be discussing an empirical law of pyschology concerning correlations of *sensations* of pitch with sensations of loudness. I use the word "pitch" as it is used in such sentences as "The pitch of the fire siren periodically rises and falls": "pitch," here, refers to a *power* of producing certain auditory sensations—if the phenomenalist analysis of material object sentences is correct—and such a power would exist even if nobody actually had any auditory sensations.

the thesis that a necessary proposition like "If x is colored, then x is extended" is analytic can be stated very briefly. If we had the analysis of "x is colored," we could deduce the consequent from the antecedent and would therefore see that the connection is analytic. Here my reply is twofold. (1) Nothing has been proved that I wish to deny. I contend only that there are necessary propositions, i.e., propositions which are known to be true independently of empirical observations, which are not *known* to be analytic. One might, indeed, insist that no proposition can be known to be necessary before it is known to be analytic. But I propose to show shortly that this view is untenable. (2) If it is stipulated in advance that an analysis of the antecedent will be correct only if it enables deduction of the consequent, it is not surprising that any correct analysis of the concept in question will reveal the analytic nature of the statement. Consider the following parallel. Everybody would agree that the proposition expressed by the sentence, "if x = y, then y = x," is necessary; quite independently of our knowledge of logic, one feels that it would be self-contradictory to deny any substitution instance thereof. But as long as the relation of identity of individuals remains unanalyzed, there is no way of deducing it from logic. "If xRy, then yRx" is not true by its form. Now, one will be perfectly safe in claiming that this proposition will turn out to be analytic once the involved relation is correctly analyzed. For formal deducibility of this proposition from logical truths will be one of the criteria of a correct analysis of identity. Indeed, if Leibniz' definition of identity, (P) (Px ≡ Py), is used, the symmetry of identity becomes deducible from the symmetry of equivalence, which is in turn deducible from the commutative law for conjunction.

Is it my contention, then, that even a "formal" statement, as it would commonly be called, like, "for any x and y, if x = y, then y = x," is a *synthetic* a priori truth? This would, indeed, amount to going more Kantian than Kant himself; for, on the same principle, it could be argued that all logical truths, which Kant at least conceded to be analytic, are synthetic. Take, for example, the commutative law for logical conjunction, just mentioned. Obviously, I cannot prove that "(p and q) ≡ (q and p)" is tautologous, unless I first construct an adequate truth-table defining the use of "and." But surely one of the criteria of adequacy for such a truth-table definition consists in the possibility of deriving the commutative law as a tautology. If, for example, a "T" were associated with "p and q" when the combination "FT" holds, and an "F" when the combination "TF" holds, the resulting definition would be rejected as inadequate just because it would entail that the commutative law is not a tautology. Indeed, I should belabor the obvious if I were to insist that the laws of logic are not known to be necessary in consequence of the application of the truth-table test, but that the truth-table definitions of the logical connectives are constructed with the purpose of rendering the necessity of the laws of logic (or at least of the simpler ones, like the traditional "laws of thought") formally

demonstrable.[10] But my point can be made far more clearly if the term "synthetic a priori" is not used, since it is used neither clearly not consistently in Kant's writings.

Philosophers who regard "analytic" as the only clear *analysans* of "necessary" are inclined to hold that we have no good ground for calling a given proposition necessary unless we can formally deduce it from logic. This, however, amounts to putting the cart before the horse. In most cases it is impossible to deduce a proposition from logic unless one or more of the constituent concepts are analyzed— as I have already illustrated more than once. But we accept such an analysis as adequate only if it enables the deduction of all *necessary* propositions that involve the analyzed concept. We therefore must accept some propositions as necessary before we can even begin a formal deduction.[11] One more illustration may be helpful to clarify my thesis. Several logicians are at the present time engaged in the construction of a definition of the central concepts of inductive logic, viz., confirmation and degree of confirmation. But their analytic activities would be altogether aimless if they did not lay down beforehand certain criteria of adequacy, such as the following: the degree of confirmation of a proposition

---

10 I shall nonetheless belabor this point at some greater length in the sequel.

11 I here use "formal deduction" in the sense of "deduction *from* logical truths alone," not in the sense of "deduction *by* (with the help of) logical rules." In the latter sense, empirical propositions are, of course, likewise capable of formal deduction.

relatively to specified evidence does not vary with the language in which the proposition is formulated; hence, if "degree of confirmation" is treated as a syntactic predicate of sentences, logically equivalent sentences should have the same degree of confirmation relatively to the same evidence. Similarly, if evidence E confirms hypothesis H, and H is logically equivalent to H', then E must also confirm H'. Unless these propositions are accepted as intuitively necessary—or, if you prefer, "true by the ordinary meaning of 'to confirm' "—by all competent inductive logicians, the latter will never agree as to what definition of the concept is adequate. It might be suggested that all we could mean by calling such propositions "necessary" is that *if we had* suitable definitions we could formally deduce them. But to say of a definition that it is "suitable" is to speak elliptically: suitable for what? Evidently they must be suitable for deducing those very propositions. The proposed analysis of "necessary," then, reduces to the following: p is necessary if and only if with the help of definitions that enable the deduction of p, it is possible to deduce p. It hardly needs to be explicitly concluded that on the basis of this analysis *any* proposition would be necessary.

Carnap and his followers will undoubtedly protest against this analysis of what they are doing. Those criteria of adequacy which I interpret as preanalytically necessary propositions they would simply call *conventions* in accordance with which a definition is to be constructed. I should not, of course, deny that a logical analyst may specify such criteria of adequacy without committing himself to any assertion of their necessary truth. Just as a theoretical physicist who is more interested in elegant mathematical deductions than in the discovery of experimental truth may work on the problem of constructing a theory from which some arbitrarily assumed numerical laws would follow, so the logical analyst may formulate his problem merely as the construction of a definition which will satisfy some arbitrarily stipulated conditions. But, to spin this analogy a little further, just as nobody would regard that physicist's work as being in any way relevant to physics, so the logical analyst's constructions will have no relevance to the problems of analytic philosophy if the criteria to which they have to conform have no cognitive significance. It might be replied that such conventions are not held to be arbitrary; that, on the contrary, their choice is limited by the dictates of intuitive evidence. But in that case I suggest that what may properly be called a "convention" is *the act of selecting* some necessary propositions involving the concept to be analyzed as criteria, and not the *object* selected: the latter is a proposition, and there is no more literal sense in calling a proposition a "convention" than there is in calling a color a sensation or in calling a murdered bird a "good shot."

The results so far obtained may also throw some light on the status of so-called *explicative* propositions, which occupy a prominent place in analytic philosophy. Thinking of the literal meaning of the word "analytic" (dividing, separating), it is, of course, natural to suppose that explicative propositions, like "A father is a male parent," are analytic. But are they analytic in the sense of being deducible from logic? I want to call attention to the consequences of the triviality that unless certain definitions are supplied, "A father is a male parent" is no more deducible from logic than, say, "A father is a mature person with a keen sense of responsibility." Relatively to the definition "father $=_{df}$ male parent," our explicative statement becomes obviously deducible from the law of identity. But "father" could arbitrarily be defined in such a way that the explicative statement which we regard as necessary would become synthetic, and other statements involving the subject "father," normally interpreted as empirical statements, would become analytic. Only, such definitions would be rejected as *inadequate* (in traditional terminology, as merely nominal, not real). We have to admit, then, that by an adequate definition of "father" we understand one with the help of which *necessary* statements that involve the word "father," and only such statements, become formally deducible or analytic. It follows that to say of a statement that it is necessary is different from saying that, relatively to such and such transformation rules, it is analytic.

It is now time to face the objections I expect from the camp of the Wittgensteinian "verbalists." "Your point is trivial," they will say. "Nobody has ever maintained that necessary propositions formulated in natural, nonformalized languages are analytic in the sense of being logically demonstrable on the

basis of explicitly formulated semantic rules. When we assert that a necessary statement is the same as an analytic statement we use the word 'analytic' in the broader sense of 'true by virtue of explicit *or implicit* rules of language.'" The question I now want to raise is: What precisely is meant by an "implicit rule of language"? It is not any sort of insight or intuition, according to the verbalists, which makes a man know the proposition, "If A precedes B, then B *cannot* precede A" (p), but merely an implicit rule governing the usage of the verb "to precede." Presumably this means that people familiar with the English language follow the *habit* of refusing to say "B precedes A" once they have asserted "A precedes B"—provided, of course, that they are serious and mean what they say. Now, it seems to me very obvious (as it may have seemed to such antiverbalists as Ewing) that this is a grossly incorrect account of what makes a proposition like p necessary. Just suppose that the linguistic habits of English-speaking people changed in such a way that the verb "to precede" came to be used the way the verb "to occur at the same time as" is now used. People would then be disposed to say, on the contrary, "If A precedes B, then B *must* precede A." If the verbalist theory were correct, the proposition expressed by the sentence "if xPy, then not-yPx" would not be necessary, but in fact self-contradictory, in such a changed sociological world. To be sure, the proposition which was formerly expressed by this sentence would remain necessary, as the verbalist is certain to point out. But if the modality of p is thus invariant with respect to changes in its sentenial expression, in what sense can it be said that the modality of a proposition "depends upon" linguistic rules?

Notice that I am not misinterpreting the verbalist thesis, as some may have been guilty of doing, to assert that necessary propositions are propositions *about* linguistic habits and hence a species of empirical propositions. Of course, nobody would maintain (I hope) that in asserting p one makes an assertion *about* implicit linguistic rules or linguistic habits. What I take the verbalists (like Malcolm, for example) to claim is that the existence of certain linguistic habits relevant to the use of a sentence S is a necessary and sufficient condition for the necessity of the proposition meant by S. As I think such a fact is neither a sufficient nor a necessary condition for the necessity of a proposition, I reject the verbalist analysis of what a necessary proposition is. It is tempting to regard the existence of a certain linguistic habit relevant to some constituent expressions of S as a sufficient condition for the necessary truth of what S means, through some such reasoning as this: If there exists a verbal habit of applying the word "yard" to distances of three feet and only to such distances, then the proposition expressed by "Every yard contains three feet" is identical with the proposition that every yard is a yard; hence, given that linguistic convention and no further facts at all, the truth of the proposition follows. To detect the flaw in this argument we only need to ask, "follows *from what?*" What is tacitly assumed is that the law of identity, of which the proposition "every

yard is a yard" is a substitution instance, is a necessary truth. If it were not, no amount of linguistic conventions would suffice to make any proposition necessary. The verbalist may reply that the law of identity (if p, then p) itself derives its necessity from a certain linguistic habit as to the usage of the expression "if, then." And I would similarly maintain that the existence of such a habit is at best a sufficient ground for saying that "the proposition expressed by 'if p, then p' is identical with the proposition expressed by 'not-(p and not-p),'" and hence the first proposition is necessary *if* the second is."

And how could it be maintained that the existence of a certain linguistic habit is a *necessary* condition for the necessity of a given proposition? If linguistic habits were to change in such a way that, say, a length of two feet came to be called a "yard," then, of course, the proposition *now* expressed by the sentence "Every yard contains three feet" is false, and hence not necessary. But surely the proposition which was formerly expressed by that sentence remains necessary? That proposition is eternally necessary, if you wish, in the sense that any sentence which happened to express it would be true independently of empirical facts, including the sociological facts which the verbalists call "implicit rules." If the rules by which a given sentence now expresses a proposition p were to change in such a way that the same sentence came to express a different proposition, p would still be necessary if it ever was.

Notice that "If not A, then the proposition expressed by S is not necessary" is not synonymous with "If not A, then S does not express a necessary proposition." If "A" refers to the existence of certain linguistic habits by which the meaning of the sentence S is determined, then the latter statement may be true. But the first statement would be false, since it does not depend on the contingent verbal expression of a proposition whether the latter is contingent or necessary. This would remain the case even if "The proposition p is necessary" were a mere mode of speech, short for "Any sentence which meant p would be necessary." If linguistic rules change in a certain way, a given sentence may cease to mean p; but it will still be true that it *would* be necessary if it did mean p.

I may as well take the opportunity to call attention to a neat paradox in which the verbalist thesis entangles itself. It asserts the synonymity of the following two statements: (A) It is necessary that every yard contains three feet; (B) "every yard contains three feet" (S) follows from the rules governing usage of the constituent terms. But rules, especially implicit rules (= linguistic habits), are not propositions from which any proposition could follow. Hence B should be modified as follows: S follows from the proposition asserting the existence of those rules (abbreviate this existential proposition by "S'"). Now, S' is empirical, and whatever follows from an empirical proposition, in the ordinary sense of "to follow from," is itself an empirical proposition;[12] which contradicts the

original assumption. On the other hand if the statement which A asserts to be necessary is necessary, then it either does not follow from any empirical proposition (viz., if "to follow" is used in the sense in which it is nonsense to make a statement like "'If it is hot, then it is hot' follows from 'It is cold now'"), or else it vacuously follows from any empirical statement. But in the latter case it will be true independently of what linguistic habits happen to exist, if true at all. And therefore B might as well be changed into "'Every yard contains three feet' follows from the rules which governed usage of 'yard' 50,000 years ago."

In case this paradox should be held to apply only to an unfortunate formulaton of verbalism, I proceed to advance a more serious argument against verbalism. To say that it is an implicit semantic rule to apply "B" to anything to which "A" is applicable is presumably equivalent to saying "People who are acquainted with the language never refuse application of 'B' to anything to which 'A' is applicable." But how could it be maintained that observation of such a habit is sufficient ground for holding that the proposition "If anything is A, then it is B" is necessary? Is it not easily conceivable that people use language that way because they firmly believe that whatever has in fact the property A also has in fact the

---

[12] It is, of course, one thing to argue that, on the verbalist theory, necessary propositions are really a species of empirical propo-

sitions, and another thing to argue that modal statements of the form "p is necessary" are empirical, if the verbalist theory is correct. I am not sure whether the latter would amount to a pertinent criticism of the verbalist theory, since I am not convinced that "It is necessary that p" entails "It is necessary that it is necessary that p."

property B? How, then, can observation of such habits be a reliable method for distinguishing necessary propositions from empirical propositions? I notice, for example, that people apply the word "hard" to certain things. Although I have never troubled to carry out the experiment, I am quite sure that if I asked anybody who calls a thing "hard" whether that thing is weightless, he would say "of course not." But I would not hence infer, and I doubt whether any verbalist would, that the proposition "Nothing that is hard is weightless" is necessary. The verbalist may reply, 'You have oversimplified my thesis. To make the sort of observations you describe is not enough. In order to be sure that "if A, then B" is a necessary proposition, you must moreover get a negative reply to the question: "Can you *conceive* of an object to which you would apply 'A' and would refuse to apply 'B'?"' This rejoinder, however, amounts to an unconditional surrender of verbalism. If the final test of necessity is the inconceivability of the contradictory of p, then what linguistic rules happen to be followed by people is irrelevant to the question whether p is necessary.[13] A

knowledge of linguistic rules is necessary only for knowing what proposition it is that a given sentence is used to express. Once this is determined, we all discover the necessity of the proposition in an *intuitive* manner, viz., by trying to conceive of its being false, and failing in the attempt.

Before I embarked on a critique of the linguistic theory of logical necessity, I endeavored to show that "p is necessary" (in the sense of "p is true independently of empirical facts" or, in the Leibnizian language revived in Carnap's pure semantics, "p is true in any possible world") cannot be synonymous with "p is analytic," since the analytic nature of a proposition is presumably knowable by formal demonstration, while an infinite regress would ensue if formal demonstration were the only available method of knowing the necessity of a proposition. In conclusion I shall apply this thesis to the propositions of logic, i.e., true statements containing no descriptive terms (Quine).

---

[13] In an unpublished paper by a Wittgensteinian friend of mine I have seen the following analysis of the verbalist theory that all necessary propositions are verbal: "Whatever the sentence or combination of signs may be which expresses a given necessary proposition, it is always possible to ascertain the truth of the proposition by ascertaining the syntactic and part of the semantic rules which govern the constituents of the combination." This statement seems to me to be equivalent to the statement, "If S expresses a necessary proposition, then, in order

to know that S is true, it is sufficient to know what proposition it expresses." If this is what the verbalist thesis amounts to, I have no quarrel with it at all; but I should say that "verbalism" is in that case merely a redundant, and moreover misleading, name. Actually, however, I think verbalists want to assert more than this; they want to assert that the necessity of a proposition is somehow *produced* by linguistic conventions, and this I hold to be a fallacy. That S expresses a necessary proposition is, of course, a consequence of linguistic conventions, simply because it is a consequence of linguistic conventions that it express_s the proposition which it does express. But the verbalists slip in their inference that the necessity of the proposition expressed by S is a result of linguistic conventions.

It is tempting to suppose that with the help of the truth-table method such fundamental propositions of logic as the law of the excluded middle or the law of noncontradiction could be shown to be true in any possible world (or, using more formal language, true no matter what the truth-values of their propositional components may be) in purely mechanical fashion, without any appeal to intuitive evidence. Although this view may have the weight of authority behind it, I consider it gravely mistaken. The lights of intuitive evidence can be turned off only if the T's and F's of the truth-tables are handled as arbitrary symbols with no meaning at all. But in that case one obviously does not establish, for example, that "p or not p" expresses a proposition true in all possible worlds; one only establishes the far less interesting syntactical theorem that it is a T-formula—which is a result of the same order as, say, that "$x^2 = 4$" is a quadratic equation. In order to establish the *semantic* theorem first mentioned, I have to interpret "T" and "F" as meaning "true" and "false" respectively. Once this is done, the primitive truth-tables for the primitive connectives "not," "or" are really *semantic rules*.[14] What, now, is the principle of selection from all the formally possible semantic rules or truth-table definitions? It would seem to be the following: a semantic rule is adequate

if it enables the demonstration of the T-character of those basic propositions, like the laws of noncontradition, excluded middle, etc., which we already know to be necessary in the sense of being true no matter what the empirical facts may be. A keen student of logic should laugh in his teacher's face if he were told that with the help of the truth-tables the "laws of thought" which we always take for granted can be *formally* demonstrated as necessary propositions. For he should quickly apprehend that in deciding to assign to each elementary proposition at least and at most one of the two truth-values "true" and "false," one has already assumed the law of the excluded middle and the law of noncontradiction.

I do not, of course, deny that the law of the excluded middle, or any of the similarly simple laws into which it is transformable, can be formally demonstrated as a T-formula (or better, tautology, to use the semantic term) without circularity, if only the distinction between object-language and metalanguage is observed. What I claim is that its necessity is not *known* in consequence of such a formal test; that, on the contrary, the semantic rules which render it demonstrable are chosen in such a way that those and only those formulas will turn out as T-formulas which express propositions that are *materially* known to be necessary truths or follow from such propositions in an axiomatically developed logic. Similar comments would apply to state-description tests of necessity, if such should be proposed. The definition of a necessary proposition as one that holds in any state-description is, of course,

[14] Carnap interprets them, in his *Introduction to Semantics*, as truth-rules; but since he accepts Wittgenstein's principle that to know what a sentence means is to know the truth-conditions of the sentence, he would undoubtedly agree with the above interpretation.

formally unobjectionable. But unlike such definitions as "A square is an equilateral rectangle" it does not indicate a method of verifying that the *definiendum* applies in a given case. The formation rules defining "state-description" are deliberately constructed in such a way that no state-description can be incompatible with such recognized necessary propositions as the law of noncontradition. One only needs to refer to the "stipulation" that a state-description is to contain any atomic sentence that can be formulated in the given language *or* its negation, but *not both!*

5.4

TWO DOGMAS
OF EMPIRICISM[1]

Willard Quine

Modern empiricism has been conditioned in large part by two dogmas. One is a belief in some fundamental cleavage between truths which are *analytic*, or grounded in meanings independently of matters of fact, and truth which are *synthetic*, or grounded in fact. The other dogma is *reductionism*: the belief that each meaningful statement is equivalent to some logical construct upon terms which refer to immediate experience. Both dogmas, I shall argue, are ill founded. One effect of abandoning them is, as we shall see, a blurring of the supposed boundary between speculative metaphysics and natural science. Another effect is a shift toward pragmatism.

I. Background for Analyticity

Kant's cleavage between analytic and synthetic truths was foreshadowed in Hume's distinction between relations of ideas and matters of fact, and in Leib-

From *The Philosophical Review*, LX (1951). Reprinted by permission of the editors and the author.

[1] Much of this paper is devoted to a critique of analyticity which I have been urging orally and in correspondence for years past. My debt to the other participants in those discussions, notably Carnap, Church, Goodman, Tarski, and White, is large and indeterminate. White's excellent essay "The Analytic and the Synthetic: An Untenable Dualism," in *John Dewey: Philosopher of Science and Freedom* (New York, 1950), says much of what needed to be said on the topic; but in the present paper I touch on some further aspects of the problem. I am grateful to Dr. Donald L. Davidson for valuable criticism of the first draft.

niz's distinction between truths of reason and truths of fact. Leibniz spoke of the truths of reason as true in all possible worlds. Picturesqueness aside, this is to say that the truths of reason are those which could not possibly be false. In the same vein we hear analytic statements defined as statements whose denials are self-contradictory. But this definition has small explanatory value; for the notion of self-contradictoriness, in the quite broad sense needed for this definition of analyticity, stands in exactly the same need of clarification as does the notion of analyticity itself.[2] The two notions are the two sides of a single dubious coin.

Kant conceived of an analytic statement as one that attributes to its subject no more than is already conceptually contained in the subject. This formulation has two shortcomings: it limits itself to statements of subject-predicate form, and it appeals to a notion of containment which is left at a metaphorical level. But Kant's intent, evident more from the use he makes of the notion of analyticity than from his definition of it, can be restated thus: a statement is analytic when it is true by virtue of meanings and independently of fact. Pursuing this line, let us examine the concept of *meaning* which is presupposed.

We must observe to begin with that meaning is not to be identified with naming, or reference. Consider Frege's example of 'Evening Star' and 'Morning Star'. Understood not merely as a recurrent evening apparition but as a body, the Evening Star is the planet Venus, and the Morning Star is the same. The two singular terms *name* the same thing. But the meanings must be treated as distinct, since the identity 'Evening Star = Morning Star' is a statement of fact established by astronomical observation. If 'Evening Star' and 'Morning Star' were alike in meaning, the identity 'Evening Star = Morning Star' would be analytic.

Again there is Russell's example of 'Scott' and 'the author of *Waverley*'. Analysis of the meanings of words was by no means sufficient to reveal to George IV that the person named by these two singular terms was one and the same.

The distinction between meaning and naming is no less important at the level of abstract terms. The terms '9' and 'the number of planets' name one and the same abstract entity but presumably must be regarded as unlike in meaning; for astronomical observation was needed, and not mere reflection on meanings, to determine the sameness of the entity in question.

Thus far we have been considering singular terms. With general terms, or predicates, the situation is somewhat different but parallel. Whereas a singular term purports to name an identity, abstract or concrete, a general term does not; but a general term is *true* of an entity, or of each of many, or of none. The class of all entities of which a general term is true is called the *extension* of the term. Now paralleling the contrast between the meaning of a singular term and the entity named, we must distinguish equally between the meaning of a general term and its extension. The general terms 'creature

---

    [2] See White, *op. cit.*, p. 324.

with a heart' and 'creature with a kidney', e.g., are perhaps alike in extension but unlike in meaning.

Confusion of meaning with extension, in the case of general terms, is less common than confusion of meaning with naming in the case of singular terms. It is indeed a commonplace in philosophy to oppose intension (or meaning) to extension, or, in a variant vocabulary, connotation to denotation.

The Aristotelian notion of essence was the forerunner, no doubt, of the modern notion of intension or meaning. For Aristotle it was essential in men to be rational, accidental to be two-legged. But there is an important difference between this attitude and the doctrine of meaning. From the latter point of view it may indeed be conceded (if only for the sake of argument) that rationality is involved in the meaning of the word 'man' while two-leggedness is not; but two-leggedness may at the same time be viewed as involved in the meaning of 'biped' while rationality is not. Thus from the point of view of the doctrine of meaning it makes no sense to say of the actual individual, who is at once a man and a biped, that his rationality is essential and his two-leggedness accidental or vice versa. Things had essences, for Aristotle, but only linguistic forms have meanings. Meaning is what essence becomes when it is divorced from the object of reference and wedded to the word.

For the theory of meaning the most conspicuous question is as to the nature of its objects: what sort of things are meanings? They are evidently intended to be ideas, somehow—mental ideas for some semanticists, Platonic ideas for others. Objects of either sort are so elusive, not to say debatable, that there seems little hope of erecting a fruitful science about them. It is not even clear, granted meanings, when we have two and when we have one; it is not clear when linguistic forms should be regarded as *synonymous*, or alike in meaning, and when they should not. If a standard of synonymy should be arrived at, we may reasonably expect that the appeal to meanings as entities will not have played a very useful part in the enterprise.

A felt need for meant entities may derive from an earlier failure to appreciate that meaning and reference are distinct. Once the theory of meaning is sharply separated from the theory of reference, it is a short step to recognizing as the business of the theory of meaning simply the synonymy of linguistic forms and the analyticity of statements; meanings themselves, as obscure intermediary entities, may well be abandoned.

The description of analyticity as truth by virtue of meanings started us off in pursuit of a concept of meaning. But now we have abandoned the thought of any special realm of entities called meanings. So the problem of analyticity confronts us anew.

Statements which are analytic by general philosophical acclaim are not, indeed, far to seek. They fall into two classes. Those of the first class, which may be called *logically true*, are typified by:

(1) No unmarried man is married

The relevant feature of this example is that it is not merely true as it stands, but remains true under any and all reinterpretations of 'man' and 'married'. If we suppose a prior inventory of *logical* particles, comprising 'no', 'un-', 'not', 'if', 'then', 'and', etc., then in general a logical truth is a statement which is true and remains true under all reinterpretations of it components other than the logical particles.

But there is also a second class of analytic statements, typified by:

(2)   No bachelor is married.

The characteristic of such a statement is that it can be turned into a logical truth by putting synonyms for synonyms; thus (2) can be turned into (1) by putting 'unmarried man' for its synonym 'bachelor'. We still lack a proper characterization of this second class of analytic statements, and therewith of analyticity generally, inasmuch as we have had in the above description to lean on a notion of "synonymy" which is no less in need of clarification than analyticity itself.

In recent years Carnap has tended to explain analyticity by appeal to what he calls state-descriptions.[3] A state-description is any exhaustive assignment of truth values to the atomic, or non-compound, statements of the language. All other statements of the language are, Carnap assumes, built up of their component clauses by means of the familiar logical devices, in such a way that the truth value of any complex statement is fixed for each state-description by specifiable logical laws.

A statement is then explained as analytic when it comes out true under every state-description. This account is an adaptation of Leibniz's "true in all possible worlds." But note that this version of analyticity serves its purpose only if the atomic statements of the language are, unlike 'John is a bachelor' and 'John is married', mutually independent. Otherwise there would be a state-description which assigned truth to 'John is a bachelor' and falsity to 'John is married', and consequently 'All bachelors are married' would turn out synthetic rather than analytic under the proposed criterion. Thus the criterion of analyticity in terms of state-descriptions serves only for languages devoid of extralogical synonym-pairs, such as 'bachelor' and 'unmarried man': synonym-pairs of the type which give rise to the "second class" of analytic statements. The criterion in terms of state-descriptions is a reconstruction at best of logical truth.

I do not mean to suggest that Carnap is under any illusions on this point. His simplied model language with its state-descriptions is aimed primarily not at the general problem of analyticity but at another purpose, the clarification of probability and induction. Our problem, however, is analyticity; and here the major difficulty lies not in the first class of analytic statements, the logical truths, but rather in the second class, which depends on the notion of synonymy.

---

[3] R. Carnap, *Meaning and Necessity* (Chicago, 1947), pp. 9ff.; *Logical Foundations of Probability* (Chicago, 1950), pp. 70ff.

II. Definition

There are those who find it soothing to say that the analytic statements of the second class reduce to those of the first class, the logical truths, by *definition*; 'bachelor', e.g., is *defined* as 'unmarried man'. But how do we find that 'bachelor' is defined as 'unmarried man'? Who defined it thus, and when? Are we to appeal to the nearest dictionary, and accept the lexicographer's formulation as law? Clearly this would be to put the cart before the horse. The lexicographer is an empirical scientist, whose business is the recording of antecedent facts; and if he glosses 'bachelor' as 'unmarried man' it is because of his belief that there is a relation of synonymy between these forms, implicit in general or preferred usage prior to his own work. The notion of synonymy presupposed here has still to be clarified, presumably in terms relating to linguistic behavior. Certainly the "definition" which is the lexicographer's report of an observed synonymy cannot be taken as the ground of the synonymy.

Definition is not, indeed, an activity exclusively of philologists. Philosophers and scientists frequently have occasion to "define" a recondite term by paraphrasing it into terms of a more familiar vocabulary. But ordinarily such a definiton, like the philologist's, is pure lexicography, affirming a relationship of synonymy antecedent to the exposition in hand.

Just what it means to affirm synonymy, just what the interconnections may be which are necessary and sufficient in order that two linguistic forms be properly describable as synonymous, is far from clear; but, whatever these interconnections may be, ordinarily they are grounded in usage. Definitions reporting selected instances of synonymy come then as reports upon usage.

There is also, however, a variant type of definitional activity which does not limit itself to the reporting of pre-existing synonymies. I have in mind what Carnap calls *explication*—an activity to which philosophers are given, and scientists also in their more philosophical moments. In explication the purpose is not merely to paraphrase the definiendum into an outright synonym, but actually to improve upon the definiendum by refining or supplementing its meaning. But even explication, though not merely reporting a pre-existing synonymy between definiendum and definiens, does rest nevertheless on *other* pre-existing synonymies. The matter may be viewed as follows. Any word worth explicating has some contexts which, as wholes, are clear and precise enough to be useful; and the purpose of explication is to preserve the usage of these favored contexts while sharpening the usage of other contexts. In order that a given definition be suitable for purposes of explication, therefore, what is required is not that the definiendum in its antecedent usage be synonymous with the definiens, but just that each of these favored contexts of the definiendum, taken as a whole in its antecedent usage, be synonymous with the corresponding context of the definiens.

Two alternative definientia may be equally appropriate for the purposes of a given task of explication and yet not be synonymous with each other; for they may serve interchangeably within the favored contexts but diverge elsewhere. By cleaving to one of these definientia rather than the other, a definition of explicative kind generates, by fiat a relationship of synonymy between definiendum and definiens which did not hold before. But such a definition still owes its explicative function, as seen, to pre-existing synonymies.

There does, however, remain still an extreme sort of definition which does not hark back to prior synonymies at all; viz., the explicitly conventional introduction of novel notations for purposes of sheer abbreviation. Here the definiendum becomes synonymous with the definiens simply because it has been created expressly for the purpose of being synonymous with the definiens. Here we have a really transparent case of synonymy created by definition; would that all species of synonymy were as intelligible. For the rest, definition rests on synonymy rather than explaining it.

The word 'definition' has come to have a dangerously reassuring sound, due no doubt to its frequent occurrence in logical and mathematical writings. We shall do well to digress now into a brief appraisal of the role of definition in formal work.

In logical and mathematical systems either of two mutually antagonistic types of economy may be striven for, and each has its peculiar practical utility. On the one hand we may seek economy of practical expression: ease and brevity in the statement of multifarious relationships. This sort of economy calls usually for distinctive concise notations for a wealth of concepts. Second, however, and oppositely, we may seek economy in grammar and vocabulary; we may try to find a minimum of basic concepts such that, once a distinctive notation has been appropriated to each of them, it becomes possible to express any desired further concept by mere combination and iteration of our basic

notations. This second sort of economy is impractical in one way, since a poverty in basic idioms tends to a necessary lengthening of discourse. But it is practical in another way: it greatly simplifies theoretical discourse *about* the language, through minimizing the terms and the forms of construction wherein the language consists.

Both sorts of economy, though prima facie incompatible, are valuable in their separate ways. The custom has consequently arisen of combining both sorts of economy by forging in effect two languages, the one a part of the other. The inclusive language, though redundant in grammar and vocabulary, is economical in message lengths, while the part, called *primitive notation*, is economical in grammar and vocabulary. Whole and part are correlated by rules of translation whereby each idiom not in primitive notation is equated to some complex built up of primitive notation. These rules of translation are the so-called *definitions* which appear in formalized systems. They are best viewed not as adjuncts to one language but as correlations between two languages, the one a part of the other.

But these correlations are not arbitrary. They are supposed to show how the primitive notations can accomplish all purposes, save brevity and convenience, of the redundant language. Hence the definiendum and its definiens may be expected, in each case, to be related in one or another of the three ways lately noted. The definiens may be a faithful paraphrase of the definiendum into the narrower notation, preserving a direct synonymy as of antecedent usage; or the definiens may, in the spirit of explication, improve upon the antecedent usage of the definiendum; or finally, the definiendum may be a newly created notation, newly endowed with meaning here and now.

In formal and informal work alike, thus, we find that definition—except in the extreme case of the explicitly conventional introduction of new notations —hinges on prior relationships of synonymy. Recognizing then that the notion of definition does not hold the key to synonymy and analyticity, let us look further into synonymy and say no more of definition.

III. Interchangeability

A natural suggestion, deserving close examination, is that the synonymy of two linguistic forms consists simply in their interchangeability in all contexts without change of truth value; interchangeability, in Leibniz's phrase, *salva veritate*. Note that synonyms so conceived need not even be free from vagueness, as long as the vaguenesses match.

But it is not quite true that the synonyms 'bachelor' and 'unmarried man' are everywhere interchangeable *salva veritate*. Truths which become false under substitution of 'unmarried man' for 'bachelor' are easily constructed with help of 'bachelor of arts' or 'bachelor's buttons'. Also with help of quotation, thus:

'Bachelor' has less than ten letters.

Such counterinstances can, however, perhaps be set aside by treating the phrases 'bachelor of arts' and 'bachelor's buttons' and the quotation "bachelor" each as a single indivisible word and then stipulating that the interchangeability *salva veritate* which is to be the touchstone of synonymy is not supposed to apply to fragmentary occurrences inside of a word. This account of synonymy, supposing it acceptable on other counts, has indeed the drawback of appealing to a prior conception of "word" which can be counted on to present difficulties of formulation in its turn. Nevertheless some progress might be claimed in having reduced the problem of synonymy to a problem of wordhood. Let us pursue this line a bit, taking "word" for granted.

The question remains whether interchangeability *salva veritate* (apart from occurrences within words) is a strong enough condition for synonymy, or whether, on the contrary, some nonsynonymous expressions might be thus interchangeable. Now let us be clear that we are not concerned here with synonymy in the sense of complete identity in psychological associations or poetic quality; indeed no two expressions are synonymous in such a sense. We are concerned only with what may be called *cognitive synonymy*. Just what this is cannot be said without successfully finishing the present study; but we know something about it from the need which arose for it in connection with analyticity in Section I. The sort of synonymy needed there was merely such that any analytic statement could be turned into a logical truth by putting synonyms for synonyms. Turning the tables and assuming analyticity, indeed, we could explain cognitive synonymy of terms as follows (keeping to the familiar example): to say that 'bachelor' and 'unmarried man' are cognitively synonymous is to say no more nor less than that the statement:

(3) All and only bachelors are unmarried men is analytic.[4]

What we need is an account of cognitive synonymy not presupposing analyticity—if we are to explain analyticity conversely with help of cognitive synonymy as undertaken in Section I. And indeed such an independent account of cognitive synonymy is at present up for consideration, viz., interchangeability *salva veritate* everywhere except within words. The question before us, to resume the thread at last, is whether such interchangeability is a sufficient condition for cognitive synonymy. We can quickly assure ourselves that it is, by examples of the following sort. The statement:

(4) Necessarily all and only bachelors are bachelors

is evidently true, even supposing 'necessarily' so narrowly construed as to be truly applicable only to analytic statements. Then, *if* 'bachelor' and 'unmar-

ried man' are interchangeable *salva veritate*, the result

(5) Necessarily, all and only bachelors are unmarried men

of putting 'unmarried man' for an occurrence of 'bachelor' in (4) must, like (4), be true. But to say that (5) is true is to say that (3) is analytic, and hence that 'bachelor' and 'unmarried men' are cognitively synonymous.

Let us see what there is about the above argument that gives it its air of hocus-pocus. The condition of interchangeability *salva veritate* varies in its force with variations in the richness of the language at hand. The above argument supposes we are working with a language rich enough to contain the adverb 'necessarily', this adverb being so construed as to yield truth when and only when applied to an analytic statement. But can we condone a language which contains such an adverb? Does the adverb really make sense? To suppose that it does is to suppose that we have already made satisfactory sense of 'analytic'. Then what are we so hard at work on right now?

Our argument is not flatly circular, but something like it. It has the form, figuratively speaking, of a closed curve in space.

Interchangeability *salva veritate* is meaningless until relativized to a language whose extent is specified in relevant respects. Suppose now we consider a language containing just the following materials. There is an indefinitely large stock of one- and many-place predicates, mostly having to do with extralogical subject matter. The rest of the

---

[4] This is cognitive synonymy in a primary, broad sense. Carnap (*Meaning and Necessity*, pp. 56ff.) and Lewis (*Analysis of Knowledge and Valuation* [La Salle, Ill., 1946], pp. 83ff.) have suggested how, once this notion is at hand, a narrower sense of cognitive synonymy which is preferable for some purposes can in turn be derived. But this special ramification of concept-building lies aside from the present purposes and must not be confused with the broad sort of cognitive synonymy here concerned.

language is logical. The atomic sentences consist each of a predicate followed by one or more variables; and the complex sentences are built up of atomic ones by truth functions and quantification. In effect such a language enjoys the benefits also of descriptions and class names and indeed singular terms generally, these being contextually definable in known ways.[5] Such a language can be adequate to classical mathematics and indeed to scientific discourse generally, except in so far as the latter involves debatable devices such as modal adverbs and contrary-to-fact conditionals. Now a language of this type is *extensional*, in this sense: any two predicates which *agree extensionally* (i.e., are true of the same objects) are interchangeable *salva veritate*.

In an extensional language, therefore, interchangeability *salva veritate* is no assurance of cognitive synonymy of the desired type. That 'bachelor' and 'unmarried man' are interchangeable *salva veritate* in an extensional language assures us of no more than that (3) is true. There is no assurance here that the extensional agreement of 'bachelor' and 'unmarried man' rests on meaning rather than merely on accidental matters of fact, as does extensional agreement of 'creature with a heart' and 'creature with a kidney'.

For most purposes extensional agreement is the nearest approximation to synonymy we need care about. But the fact remains that extensional agreement

---

[5] See, e.g., my *Mathematical Logic* (New York, 1940; Cambridge, Mass., 1947), sec. 24, 26, 27; or *Methods of Logic* (New York, 1950), sec. 37ff.

falls far short of cognitive synonymy of the type required for explaining analyticity in the manner of Section I. The type of cognitive synonymy required there is such as to equate the synonymy of 'bachelor' and 'unmarried man' with the analyticity of (3), not merely with the truth of (3).

So we must recognize that interchangeability *salva veritate*, if construed in relation to an extensional language, is not a sufficient condition of cognitive synonymy in the sense needed for deriving analyticity in the manner of Section I. If a language contains an intensional adverb 'necessarily' in the sense lately noted, or other particles to the same effect, then interchangeability *salva veritate* in such a language does afford a sufficient condition of cognitive synonymy; but such a language is intelligible only if the notion of analyticity is already clearly understood in advance.

The effort to explain cognitive synonymy first, for the sake of deriving analyticity from it afterward as in Section I, is perhaps the wrong approach. Instead we might try explaining analyticity somehow without appeal to cognitive synonymy. Afterward we could doubtless derive cognitive synonymy from analyticity satisfactorily enough if desired. We have seen that cognitive synonymy of 'bachelor' and 'unmarried man' can be explained as analyticity of (3). The same explanation works for any pair of one-place predicates, of course, and it can be extended in obvious fashion to many-place predicates. Other syntactical categories can also be accommodated in fairly parallel fashion. Singular terms may be said to be cognitively synonymous when the statement of identity formed by putting '=' between them is analytic. Statements may be said simply to be cognitively synonymous when their biconditional (the result of joining them by 'if and only if') is analytic.[6] If we care to lump all categories into a single formulation, at the expense of assuming again the notion of "word" which was appealed to early in this section, we can describe any two linguistic forms as cognitively synonymous when the two forms are interchangeable (apart from occurrences within "words") *salva* (no longer *veritate* but) *analyticitate*. Certain technical questions arise, indeed, over cases of ambiguity or homonymy; let us not pause for them, however, for we are already digressing. Let us rather turn our backs on the problem of synonymy and address ourselves anew to that of analyticity.

IV. Semantical Rules

Analyticity at first seemed most naturally definable by appeal to a realm of meanings. On refinement, the appeal to meanings gave way to an appeal to synonymy or definition. But definition turned out to be a will-o'-the-wisp, and synonymy turned out to be best understood only by dint of a prior appeal to analyticity itself. So we are back at the problem of analyticity.

I do not know whether the statement 'Everything green is extended' is analytic. Now does my indecision over this example really betray an incomplete

---

[6] The 'if and only if' itself is intended in the truth functional sense. See Carnap, *Meaning and Necessity*, p. 14.

understanding, an incomplete grasp of the "meanings", of 'green' and 'extended'? I think not. The trouble is not with 'green' or 'extended', but with 'analytic'.

It is often hinted that the difficulty in separating analytic statements from synthetic ones in ordinary language is due to the vagueness of ordinary language and that the distinction is clear when we have a precise artificial language with explicit "semantical rules". This, however, as I shall now attempt to show, is a confusion.

The notion of analyticity about which we are worrying is a purported relation between statements and languages: a statement S is said to be *analytic for* a language L, and the problem is to make sense of this relation generally, i.e., for variable 'S' and 'L'. The point that I want to make is that the gravity of this problem is not perceptibly less for artificial languages than for natural ones. The problem of making sense of the idiom 'S is analytic for L', with variable 'S' and 'L', retains its stubbornness even if we limit the range of the variable 'L' to artificial languages. Let me now try to make this point evident.

For artificial languages and semantical rules we look naturally to the writings of Carnap. His semantical rules take various forms, and to make my point I shall have to distinguish certain of the forms. Let us suppose, to begin with, an artificial language 'L_0' whose semantical rules have the form explicitly of a specification, by recursion or otherwise, of all the analytic statements of L_0. The rules tell us that such and such statements, and only those, are the analytic statements of L_0.

Now here the difficulty is simply that the rules contain the word 'analytic', which we do not understand! We understand what expressions the rules attribute analyticity to, but we do not understand what the rules attribute to those expressions. In short, before we can understand a rule which begins "A statement S is analytic for language L_0 if and only if . . .," we must understand the general relative term 'analytic for'; we must understand 'S is analytic for L' where 'S' and 'L' are variables.

Alternatively we may, indeed, view the so-called rule as a conventional definition of a new simple symbol, 'analytic-for-L_0', which might better be written untendentiously as 'K' so as not to seem to throw light on the interesting word 'analytic'. Obviously any number of classes K, M, N, etc. of statements of L_0 can be specified for various purposes or for no purpose; what does it mean to say that K, as against M, N, etc. is the class of the "analytic" statements of L_0?

By saying what statements are analytic for L_0 we explain 'analytic-for-L_0' but not 'analytic', not 'analytic for'. We do not begin to explain the idiom 'S is analytic for L' with variable 'S' and 'L', even though we be content to limit the range of 'L' to the realm of artificial languages.

Actually we do know enough about the intended significance of 'analytic' to know that analytic statements are supposed to be true. Let us then turn to a second form of semantical rule, which says not that such and such statements are analytic but simply that such and such statements are included among the truths. Such a rule is not subject to the criticism of containing the un-under-

stood word 'analytic'; and we may grant for the sake of argument that there is no difficulty over the broader term 'true'. A semantical rule of this second type, a rule of truth, is not supposed to specify all the truths of the language; it merely stipulates, recursively or otherwise, a certain multitude of statements which, along with others unspecified, are to count as true. Such a rule may be conceded to be quite clear. Derivatively, afterward, analyticity can be demarcated thus: a statement is analytic if it is (not merely true but) true according to the semantical rule.

Still there is really no progress. Instead of appealing to an unexplained word 'analytic', we are now appealing to an unexplained phrase 'semantical rule'. Not every true statement which says that the statements of some class are true can count as a semantical rule —otherwise *all* truths would be "analytic" in the sense of being true according to semantical rules. Semantical rules are distinguishable, apparently, only by the fact of appearing on a page under the heading 'Semantical Rules'; and this heading is itself then meaningless.

We can say indeed that a statement is *analytic-for-L_0* if and only if it is true according to such and such specifically appended "semantical rules," but then we find ourselves back at essentially the same case which was originally discussed: "S is analytic-for-L_0 if and only if. . . ." Once we seek to explain 'S is analytic for L' generally for variable 'L' (even allowing limitation of 'L' to artificial languages), the explanation 'true according to the semantical rules of L' is unavailing; for the relative term 'semantical rule of' is as much in need of clarification, at least, as 'analytic for'.

It might conceivably be protested that an artificial language L (unlike a natural one) is a language in the ordinary sense *plus* a set of explicit semantical rules—the whole constituting, let us say, an ordered pair; and that the semantical rules of L then are specifiable simply as the second component of the pair L. But, by the same token and more simply, we might construe an artificial language L outright as an ordered pair whose second component is the class of its analytic statements; and then the analytic statements of L become specifiable simply as the statements in the second component of L. Or better still, we might just stop tugging at our bootstraps altogether.

Not all the explanations of analyticity known to Carnap and his readers have been covered explicitly in the above considerations, but the extension to other forms is not hard to see. Just one additional factor should be mentioned which sometimes enters: sometimes the semantical rules are in effect rules of translation into ordinary language, in which case the analytic statements of the artificial language are in effect recognized as such from the analyticity of their specified translations in ordinary language. Here certainly there can be no thought of an illumination of the problem of analyticity from the side of the artificial language.

From the point of view of the problem of analyticity the notion of an artificial language with semantical rules is a *feu follet par excellence*. Semantical rules determining the analytic statements of an artificial language are of interest only in so far as we already understand the notion of analyticity; they are of no help in gaining this understanding.

Appeal to hypothetical languages of an artificially simple kind could conceivably be useful in clarifying analyticity, if the mental or behavioral or cultural factors relevant to analyticity —whatever they may be—were somehow sketched into the simplified model. But a model which takes analyticity merely as in irreducible character is unlikely to throw light on the problem of explicating analyticity.

It is obvious that truth in general depends on both language and extralinguistic fact. The statement 'Brutus killed Caesar' would be false if the world had been different in certain ways, but it would also be false if the word 'killed' happened rather to have the sense of 'begat'. Hence the temptation to suppose in general that the truth of a statement is somehow analyzable into a linguistic component and a factual component. Given this supposition, it next seems reasonable that in some statements the factual component should be null; and these are the analytic statements. But, for all its a priori reasonableness, a boundary between analytic and synthetic statements simply has not been drawn. That there is such a distinction to be drawn at all is an unempirical dogma of empiricists, a metaphysical article of faith.

V. The Verification Theory and Reductionism

In the course of these somber reflections we have taken a dim view first of the notion of meaning, then of the notion of cognitive synonymy, and finally of the notion of analyticity. But what, it may be asked, of the verification theory of meaning? This phrase has established itself so firmly as a catchword of empiricism that we should be very unscientific indeed not to look beneath it for a possible key to the problem of meaning and the associated problems.

The verification theory of meaning, which has been conspicuous in the literature from Peirce onward, is that the meaning of a statement is the method of empirically confirming or infirming it. An analytic statement is that limiting case which is confirmed no matter what.

As urged in Section I, we can as well pass over the question of meanings as entities and move straight to sameness of meaning, or synonymy. Then what the verification theory says is that statements are synonymous if and only if they are alike in point of method of empirical confirmation or infirmation.

This is an account of cognitive synonymy not of linguistic forms generally, but of statements.[7] However, from the concept of synonymy of statements we could derive the concept of synonymy for other linguistic forms, by considerations somewhat similar to those at the end of Section III. Assuming the notion of "word," indeed, we could explain any two forms as synonymous when the putting of the

one form for an occurrence of the other in any statement (apart from occurrences within "words") yields a synonymous statement. Finally, given the concept of synonymy thus for linguistic forms generally, we could define analyticity in terms of synonymy and logical truth as in Section I. For that matter, we could define analyticity more simply in terms of just synonymy of statements together with logical truth; it is not necessary to appeal to synonymy of linguistic forms other than statements. For a statement may be described as analytic simply when it is synonymous with a logically true statement.

So, if the verification theory can be accepted as an adequate account of statement synonymy, the notion of analyticity is saved after all. However, let us reflect. Statement synonymy is said to be likeness of method of empirical confirmation or infirmation. Just what are these methods which are to be compared for likeness? What, in other words, is the nature of the relationship between a statement and the experiences which contribute to or detract from its confirmation?

The most naive view of the relationship is that it is one of direct report. This is *radical reductionism*. Every meaningful statement is held to be translatable into a statement (true or false) about immediate experience. Radical reductionism, in one form or another, well antedates the verification theory of meaning explicitly so-called. Thus Locke and Hume held that every idea must either originate directly in sense experience or else be compounded of ideas thus originating; and taking a

---

[7] The doctrine can indeed be formulated with terms rather than statements as the units. Thus C. I. Lewis describes the meaning of a term as *"a criterion in mind,* by reference to which one is able to apply or refuse to apply the expression in question in the case of presented, or imagined, things or situations" (*op. cit.,* p. 133).

hint from Tooke[8] we might rephrase this doctrine in semantical jargon by saying that a term, to be significant at all, must be either a name of a sense datum or a compound of such names or an abbreviation of such a compound. So stated, the doctrine remains ambiguous as between sense data as sensory events and sense data as sensory qualities; and it remains vague as to the admissible ways of compounding. Moreover, the doctrine is unnecessarily and intolerably restrictive in the term-by-term critique which it imposes. More reasonably, and without yet exceeding the limits of what I have called radical reductionism, we may take full statements as our significant units—thus demanding that our statements as wholes be translatable into sense-datum language, but not that they be translatable term by term.

This emendation would unquestionably have been welcome to Locke and Hume and Tooke, but historically it had to await two intermediate developments. One of these developments was the increasing emphasis on verification or confirmation, which came with the explicitly so-called verification theory of meaning. The objects of verification or confirmation being statements, this emphasis gave the statement an ascendency over the word or term as unit of significant discourse. The other development, consequent upon the first, was Russell's discovery of the concept of incomplete symbols defined in use.

Radical reductionism, conceived now with statements as units, sets itself the task of specifying a sense-datum language and showing how to translate the rest of significant discourse, statement by statement, into it. Carnap embarked on this project in the *Aufbau*.[9]

The language which Carnap adopted as his starting point was not a sense-datum language in the narrowest conceivable sense, for it included also the notations of logic, up through higher set theory. In effect it included the whole language of pure mathematics. The ontology implicit in it (i.e., the range of values of its variables) embraced not only sensory events but classes, classes of classes, and so on. Empiricists there are who would boggle at such prodigality. Carnap's starting point is very parsimonious, however, in its extralogical or sensory part. In a series of constructions in which he exploits the resources of modern logic with much ingenuity, he succeeds in defining a wide array of important additional sensory concepts which, but for his constructions, one would not have dreamed were definable on so slender a basis. Carnap was the first empiricist who, not content with asserting the reducibility of science to terms of immediate experience, took serious steps toward carrying out the reduction.

Even supposing Carnap's starting point satisfactory, his constructions were, as he himself stressed, only a fragment of the full program. The construction of even the simplest statements about the physical world was left in a sketchy

---

[8] John Horne Tooke, *The Diversions of Purley* (London, 1776; Boston, 1806), I, ch. ii.

[9] R. Carnap, *Der logische Aufbau der Welt* (Berlin, 1928).

state. Carnap's suggestions on this subject were, despite their sketchiness, very suggestive. He explained spatiotemporal point-instants as quadruples of real numbers and envisaged assignment of sense qualities to point-instants according to certain canons. Roughly summarized, the plan was that qualities should be assigned to point-instants in such a way as to achieve the laziest world compatible with our experience. The principle of least action was to be our guide in constructing a world from experience.

Carnap did not seem to recognize, however, that his treatment of physical objects fell short of reduction not merely through sketchiness, but in principle. Statements of the form 'Quality q is at point-instant $x; y; z; t$' were, according to his canons, to be apportioned truth values in such a way as to maximize and minimize certain overall features, and with growth of experience the truth values were to be progressively revised in the same spirit. I think this is a good schematization (deliberately oversimplified, to be sure) of what science really does; but it provides no indication, not even the sketchiest, of how a statement of the form 'Quality q is at $x; y; z; t$' could ever be translated into Carnap's initial language of sense data and logic. The connective 'is at' remains an added undefined connective; the canons counsel us in its use but not in its elimination.

Carnap seems to have appreciated this point afterward; for in his later writings he abandoned all notion of the translatability of statements about the physical world into statements about immediate experience. Reductionism in

its radical form has long since ceased to figure in Carnap's philosophy.

But the dogma of reductionism has, in a subtler and more tenuous form, continued to influence the thought of empiricists. The notion lingers that to each statement, or each synthetic statement, there is associated a unique range of possible sensory events such that the occurrence of any of them would add to the likelihood of truth of the statement, and that there is associated also another unique range of possible sensory events whose occurrence would detract from that likelihood. This notion is of course implicit in the verification theory of meaning.

The dogma of reductionism survives in the supposition that each statement, taken in isolation from its fellows, can admit of confirmation or infirmation at all. My countersuggestion, issuing essentially from Carnap's doctrine of the physical world in the *Aufbau*, is that our statements about the external world face the tribunal of sense experience not individually but only as a corporate body.

The dogma of reductionism, even in its attenuated form, is intimately connected with the other dogma: that there is a cleavage between the analytic and the synthetic. We have found ourselves led, indeed, from the latter problem to the former through the verification theory of meaning. More directly, the one dogma clearly supports the other in this way: as long as it is taken to be significant in general to speak of the confirmation and infirmation of a statement, it seems significant to speak also of a limiting kind of statement which is vacuously confirmed, *ipso facto*, come what may; and such a statement is analytic.

The two dogmas are, indeed, at root identical. We lately reflected that in general the truth of statements does obviously depend both upon language and upon extralinguistic fact; and we noted that this obvious circumstance carries in its train, not logically but all too naturally, a feeling that the truth of a statement is somehow analyzable into a linguistic component and a factual component. The factual component must, if we are empiricists, boil down to a range of confirmatory experiences. In the extreme case where the linguistic component is all that matters, a true statement is analytic. But I hope we are now impressed with how stubbornly the distinction between analytic and synthetic has resisted any straightforward drawing. I am impressed also, apart from prefabricated examples of black and white balls in an urn, with how baffling the problem has always been of arriving at any explicit theory of the empirical confirmation of a synthetic statement. My present suggestion is that it is nonsense, and the root of much nonsense, to speak of a linguistic component and a factual component in the truth of any individual statement. Taken collectively, science has its double dependence upon language and experience; but this duality is not significantly traceable into the statements of science taken one by one.

Russell's concept of definition in use was, as remarked, an advance over the impossible term-by-term empiricism of Locke and Hume. The statement, rather than the term, came with Russell to be recognized as the unit accountable to an empiricist critique. But what I am now urging is that even in taking the statement as unit we have drawn our grid too finely. The unit of empirical significance is the whole of science.

VI. Empiricism without the Dogmas

The totality of our so-called knowledge or beliefs, from the most casual matters of geography and history to the profoundest laws of atomic physics or even of pure mathematics and logic, is a man-made fabric which impinges on experience only along the edges. Or, to change the figure, total science is like a field of force whose boundary conditions are experience. A conflict with experience at the periphery occasions readjustments in the interior of the field. Truth values have to be redistributed over some of our statements. Re-evaluation of some statements entails re-evaluation of others, because of their logical interconnections—the logical laws being in turn simply certain further statements of the system, certain further elements of the field. Having re-evaluated one statement we must re-evaluate some others, whether they be statements logically connected with the first or whether they be the statements of logical connections themselves. But the total field is so undetermined by its boundary conditions, experience, that there is much latitude of choice as to what statements to re-evaluate in the light of any single contrary experience. No particular experiences are linked with any particular statements in the interior of the field, except indirectly through considerations of equilibrium affecting the field as a whole.

If this view is right, it is misleading to speak of the empirical content of an individual statement—especially if it be a statement at all remote from the experiential periphery of the field. Furthermore it becomes folly to seek a boundary between synthetic statements, which hold contingently on experience, and analytic statements which hold come what may. Any statement can be held true come what may, if we make drastic enough adjustments elsewhere in the system. Even a statement very close to the periphery can be held true in the face of recalcitrant experience by pleading hallucination or by amending certain statements of the kind called logical laws. Conversely, by the same token, no statement is immune to revision. Revision even of the logical law of the excluded middle has been proposed as a means of simplifying quantum mechanics; and what difference is there in principle between such a shift and the shift whereby Kepler superseded Ptolemy, or Einstein Newton, or Darwin Aristotle?

For vividness I have been speaking in terms of varying distances from a sensory periphery. Let me try now to clarify this notion without metaphor. Certain statements, though *about* physical objects and not sense experience, seem peculiarly germane to sense experience—and in a selective way: some statements to some experiences, others to others. Such statements, especially germane to particular experiences, I picture as near the periphery. But in this relation of "germaneness" I envisage nothing more than a loose association reflecting the relative likelihood, in practice, of our choosing one statement rather than another for revision in the event of recalcitrant experience. For example, we can imagine recalcitrant experiences to which we would surely be inclined to accommodate our system by re-evaluating just the statement that there are brick houses on Elm Street, together with related statements on the same topic. We can imagine other recalcitrant experiences to which we would be inclined to accommodate our system by re-evaluating just the statement that there are no centaurs, along with kindred statements. A recalcitrant experience can, I have already urged, be accommodated by any of various alternative re-evaluations in various alternative quarters of the total system; but, in the cases which we are now imagining, our natural tendency to disturb the total system as little as possible would lead us to focus our revisions upon these specific statements concerning brick houses or centaurs. These statements are felt, therefore, to have a sharper empirical reference than highly theoretical statements of physics or logic or ontology. The latter statements may be thought of as relatively centrally located within the total network, meaning merely that little preferential connection with any particular sense data obtrudes itself.

As an empiricist I continue to think of the conceptual scheme of science as a tool, ultimately, for predicting future experience in the light of past experience. Physical objects are conceptually imported into the situation as convenient intermediaries—not by definition in terms of experience, but simply as irreducible posits comparable, epistemologically, to the gods of Homer. Let me interject that for my part I do, qua lay physicist, believe in physical objects and not in Homer's gods; and I consider it a scientific error to believe otherwise. But in point of epistemological footing the physical objects and the gods differ only in degree and not in kind. Both sorts of entities enter our conception only as cultural posits. The myth of physical objects is epistemologically superior to most in that it has proved more efficacious than other myths as a device for working a manageable structure into the flux of experience.

Imagine, for the sake of analogy, that we are given the rational numbers. We develop an algebraic theory for reasoning about them, but we find it inconveniently complex, because certain functions such as square root lack values for some arguments. Then it is discovered that the rules of our algebra can be much simplified by conceptually augmenting our ontology with some mythical entities, to be called irrational numbers. All we continue to be really interested in, first and last, are rational numbers; but we find that we can commonly get from one law about rational numbers to another much more quickly and simply by pretending that the irrational numbers are there too.

I think this a fair account of the introduction of irrational numbers and other extensions of the number system. The fact that the mythical status of irrational numbers eventually gave way to the Dedekind-Russell version of them as certain infinite classes of ratios is irrelevant to my analogy. That version is impossible anyway as long as reality is limited to the rational numbers and not extended to classes of them.

Now I suggest that experience is analogous to the rational numbers and that the physical objects, in analogy to the irrational numbers, are posits which serve merely to simplify our treatment of experience. The physical objects are no more reducible to experience than the irrational numbers to rational numbers, but their incorporation into the theory enables us to get more easily from one statement about experience to another.

The salient differences between the positing of physical objects and the positing of irrational numbers are, I think, just two. First, the factor of simplification is more overwhelming in the case of physical objects than in the numerical case. Second, the positing of physical objects is far more archaic, being indeed coeval, I expect, with language itself. For language is social and so depends for its development upon intersubjective reference.

Positing does not stop with macroscopic physical objects. Objects at the atomic level and beyond are posited to make the laws of macroscopic objects, and ultimately the laws of experience, simpler and more manageable; and we need not expect or demand full definition of atomic and subatomic entities in terms of macroscopic ones, any more than definition of macroscopic things in terms of sense data. Science is a continuation of common sense, and it continues the common-sense expedient of swelling ontology to simplify theory.

Physical objects, small and large, are not the only posits. Forces are another example; and indeed we are told nowadays that the boundary between energy and matter is obsolete. Moreover, the abstract entities which are the substance of mathematics—ultimately classes and classes of classes and so on up—are another posit in the same spirit. Epistemologically these are myths on the same footing with physical objects and gods, neither better nor worse except for differences in the degree to which they expedite our dealings with sense experiences.

The over-all algebra of rational and irrational numbers is underdetermined by the algebra of rational numbers, but is smoother and more convenient; and it includes the algebra of rational numbers as a jagged or gerrymandered part. Total science, mathematical and natural and human, is similarly but more extremely underdetermined by experience. The edge of the system must be kept squared with experience; the rest, with all its elaborate myths or fictions, has as its objective the simplicity of laws.

Ontological questions, under this view, are on a par with questions of natural science. Consider the question whether to countenance classes as entities. This, as I have argued elsewhere,[10] is the question whether to quantify with respect to variables which take classes as values. Now Carnap has

maintained[11] that this is a question not of matters of fact but of choosing a convenient language form, a convenient conceptual scheme or framework for science. With this I agree, but only on the proviso that the same be conceded regarding scientific hypotheses generally. Carnap has recognized[12] that he is able to preserve a double standard for ontological questions and scientific hypotheses only by assuming an absolute distinction between the analytic and the synthetic; and I need not say again that this is a distinction which I reject.

Some issues do, I grant, seem more a question of convenient conceptual scheme and others more a question of brute fact. The issue over there being classes seems more a question of convenient conceptual scheme; the issue over there being centaurs, or brick houses on Elm Street, seems more a question of fact. But I have been urging that this difference is only one of degree, and that it turns upon our vaguely pragmatic inclination to adjust one strand of the fabric of science rather than another in accommodating some particular recalcitrant experience. Conservatism figures in such choices, and so does the quest for simplicity.

Carnap, Lewis, and others take a pragmatic stand on the question of choosing between language forms, scientific frameworks; but their pragmatism leaves off at the imagined boundary between the analytic and the synthetic. In repudiating such a boundary

---

[10] E.g., in "Notes on Existence and Necessity," *Journal of Philosophy*, XL (1943), 113–127.

[11] Carnap, "Empiricism, Semantics, and Ontology," *Revue internationale de philosophie*, IV (1950), 20–40.

[12] *Op. cit.*, p. 32, footnote.

I espouse a more thorough pragmatism. Each man is given a scientific heritage plus a continuing barrage of sensory stimulation; and the considerations which guide him in warping his scientific heritage to fit his continuing sensory promptings are, where rational, pragmatic.

IN DEFENSE OF A DOGMA   5.5

P. F. Strawson and H. P. Grice

In his article "Two Dogmas of Empiricism,"[1] Professor Quine advances a number of criticisms of the supposed distinction between analytic and synthetic statements, and of other associated notions. It is, he says, a distinction which he rejects.[2] We wish to show that his criticisms of the distinction do not justify his rejection of it.

There are many ways in which a distinction can be criticized, and more than one in which it can be rejected. It can be criticized for not being a sharp distinction (for admitting of cases which do not fall clearly on either side of it); or on the ground that the terms in which it is customarily drawn are ambiguous (have more than one meaning); or on the ground that it is confused (the different meanings being habitually conflated). Such criticisms alone would scarcely amount to a rejection of the distinction. They would, rather, be a prelude to clarification. It is not this sort of criticism which Quine makes.

Again, a distinction can be criticized on the ground that it is not useful. It can be said to be useless for certain purposes, or useless altogether, and, perhaps, pedantic. One who criticizes in this way may indeed be said to reject a distinction, but in a sense which also requires him to acknowledge its existence. He simply declares he can get on without it. But Quine's rejection of the analytic-synthetic distinction appears to be more radical than this. He would certainly say he could get on without the distinction, but not in a sense which would commit him to acknowledging its existence.

From *The Philosophical Review*, LXV (1956). Reprinted by permission of the editors and Professor Strawson.

[1] W. V. O. Quine, *From a Logical Point of View* (Cambridge, Mass., 1953), pp. 20–46. All references are to page numbers in this book.

[2] Page 46.

Or again, one could criticize the way or ways in which a distinction is customarily expounded or explained on the ground that these explanations did not make it really clear. And Quine certainly makes such criticisms in the case of the analytic-synthetic distinction.

But he does, or seems to do, a great deal more. He declares, or seems to declare, not merely that the distinction is useless or inadequately clarified, but also that it is altogether illusory, that the belief in its existence is a philosophical mistake. "That there is such a distinction to be drawn at all," he says, "is an unempirical dogma of empiricists, a metaphysical article of faith."[3] It is the existence of the distinction that he here calls in question; so his rejection of it would seem to amount to a denial of its existence.

Evidently such a position of extreme skepticism about a distinction is not in general justified merely by criticisms, however just in themselves, of philosophical attempts to clarify it. There are doubtless plenty of distinctions, drawn in philosophy and outside it, which still await adequate philosophical elucidation, but which few would want on this account to declare illusory. Quine's article, however, does not consist wholly, though it does consist largely, in criticizing attempts at elucidation. He does try also to diagnose the causes of the belief in the distinction, and he offers some positive doctrine, acceptance of which he represents as incompatible with this belief. If there is any general prior presumption in favor of the existence of the distinc-

tion, it seems that Quine's radical rejection of it must rest quite heavily on this part of his article, since the force of any such presumption is not even impaired by philosophical failures to clarify a distinction so supported.

Is there such a presumption in favor of the distinction's existence? Prima facie, it must be admitted that there is. An appeal to philosophical tradition is perhaps unimpressive and is certainly unnecessary. But it is worth pointing out that Quine's objection is not simply to the words "analytic" and "synthetic," but to a distinction which they are supposed to express, and which at different times philosophers have supposed themselves to be expressing by means of such pairs of words or phrases as "necessary" and "contingent," "a priori" and "empirical," "truth of reason" and "truth of fact"; so Quine is certainly at odds with a philosophical tradition which is long and not wholly disreputable. But there is no need to appeal only to tradition; for there is also present practice. We can appeal, that is, to the fact that those who use the terms "analytic" and "synthetic" do to a very considerable extent agree in the applications they make of them. They apply the term "analytic" to more or less the same cases, withhold it from more or less the same cases, and hesitate over more or less the same cases. This agreement extends not only to cases which they have been *taught* so to characterize, but to new cases. In short, "analytic" and "synthetic" have a more or less established philosophical *use*; and this seems to suggest that it is absurd, even senseless, to say that there is no such

---

[3] Page 37.

distinction. For, in general, if a pair of contrasting expressions are habitually and generally used in application to the same cases, *where these cases do not form a closed list*, this is a sufficient condition for saying that there are *kinds* of cases to which the expressions apply; and nothing more is needed for them to mark a distinction.

In view of the possibility of this kind of argument, one may begin to doubt whether Quine really holds the extreme thesis which his words encourage one to attribute to him. It is for this reason that we made the attribution tentative. For on at least one natural interpretation of this extreme thesis, when we say of something true that it is analytic and of another true thing that it is synthetic, it simply never is the case that we thereby mark a distinction between them. And this view seems terribly difficult to reconcile with the fact of an established philosophical usage (i.e., of general agreement in application in an open class). For this reason, Quine's thesis might be better represented not as the thesis that there is *no difference at all* marked by the use of these expressions, but as the thesis that the nature of, and reasons for, the difference or differences are totally misunderstood by those who use the expressions, that the stories they tell themselves *about* the difference are full of illusion.

We think Quine might be prepared to accept this amendment. If so, it could, in the following way, be made the basis of something like an answer to the argument which prompted it. Philosophers are notoriously subject to illusion, and to mistaken theories. Suppose there were a particular mistaken theory about language or knowledge, such that, seen in the light of this theory, some statements (or propositions or sentences) appeared to have a characteristic which no statements really have, or even, perhaps, which it does not make sense to suppose that any statement has, and which no one who was not consciously or subconsciously influenced by this theory would ascribe to any statement. And suppose that there were other statements which, seen in this light, did not appear to have this characteristic, and others again which presented an uncertain appearance. Then philosophers who were under the influence of this theory would tend to mark the supposed presence or absence of this characteristic by a pair of contrasting expressions, say "analytic" and "synthetic." Now in these circumstances it still could not be said that there was no distinction at all being marked by the use of these expressions, for there would be at least the distinction we have just described (the distinction, namely, between those statements which appeared to have and those which appeared to lack a certain characteristic), and there might well be other assignable differences too, which would account for the difference in appearance; but it certainly could be said that *the* difference these philosophers supposed themselves to be marking by the use of the expressions simply did not exist, and perhaps also (supposing the characteristic in question to be one which it was absurd to ascribe to any statement) that these expressions, as so used, were senseless or without meaning. We should only have to suppose that such a mistaken theory was very plausible and attractive, in order to reconcile the fact of an established philosophical usage for a pair of contrasting terms with the claim that *the* distinction which the terms purported to mark did not exist at all, though not with the claim that there simply did not exist a difference of any kind between the classes of statements so characterized. We think that the former claim would probably be sufficient for Quine's purposes. But to establish such a claim on the sort of grounds we have indicated evidently requires a great deal more argument than is involved in showing that certain explanations of a term do not measure up to certain requirements of adequacy in philosophical clarification—and not only more argument, but argument of a very different kind. For it would surely be too harsh to maintain that the *general* presumption is that philosophical distinctions embody the kind of illusion we have described. On the whole, it seems that philosophers are prone to make too few distinctions rather than too many. It is their assimilations, rather than their distinctions, which tend to be spurious.

So far we have argued as if the prior presumption in favor of the existence of the distinction which Quine questions rested solely on the face of an agreed *philosophical* usage for the terms "analytic" and "synthetic." A presumption with only this basis could no doubt be countered by a strategy such as we have just outlined. But, in fact, if we are to accept Quine's account of the matter, the presumption in question is not only so based. For

among the notions which belong to the analyticity-group is one which Quine calls "cognitive synonymy," and in terms of which he allows that the notion of analyticity could at any rate be formally explained. Unfortunately, he adds, the notion of cognitive synonymy is just as unclarified as that of analyticity. To say that two expressions x and y are cognitively synonymous seems to correspond, at any rate roughly, to what we should ordinarily express by saying that x and y have the same meaning or that x means the same as y. If Quine is to be consistent in his adherence to the extreme thesis, then it appears that he must maintain not only that the distinction we suppose ourselves to be marking by the use of the terms "analytic" and "synthetic" does not exist, but also that the distinction we suppose ourselves to be marking by the use of the expressions "means the same as," "does not mean the same as" does not exist either. At least, he must maintain this insofar as the notion of *meaning the same as*, in its application to predicate-expressions, is supposed to differ from and go beyond the notion of *being true of just the same objects as*. (This latter notion—which we might call that of "coextensionality"—he is prepared to allow to be intelligible, though, as he rightly says, it is not sufficient for the explanation of analyticity.) Now since he cannot claim this time that the pair of expressions in question (viz., "means the same," "does not mean the same") is the special property of philosophers, the strategy outlined above of countering the presumption in favor of their marking a genuine distinction is not available here (or is at least enormously less plausible). Yet the denial that the distinction (taken as different from the distinction between the coextensional and the non-coextensional) really exists, is extremely paradoxical. It involves saying, for example, that anyone who seriously remarks that "bachelor" means the same as "unmarried man" but that "creature with kidneys" does not mean the same as "creature with a heart"—supposing the last two expressions to be coextensional—*either* is not in fact drawing attention to any distinction at all between the relations between the members of each pair of expressions *or* is making a philosophical mistake about the nature of the distinction between them. In either case, what he says, taken as he intends it to be taken, is senseless or absurd. More generally, it involves saying that it is always senseless or absurd to make a statement of the form "Predicates x and y in fact apply to the same objects, but do not have the same meaning." But the paradox is more violent than this. For we frequently talk of the presence or absence of relations of synonymy between kinds of expressions—e.g., conjunctions, particles of many kinds, whole sentences—where there does not appear to be any obvious substitute for the ordinary notion of synonymy, in the way in which coextensionality is said to be a substitute for synonymy of predicates. Is all such talk meaningless? Is all talk of correct or incorrect *translation* of sentences of one language into sentences of another meaningless? It is hard to believe that it is. But if we do successfully make the effort to believe it, we

have still harder renunciations before us. If talk of sentence-synonymy is meaningless, then it seems that talk of sentences having a meaning at all must be meaningless too. For if it made sense to talk of a sentence having a meaning, or meaning something, then presumably it would make sense to ask "What does it mean?" And if it made sense to ask "What does it mean?" of a sentence, then sentence-synonymy could be roughly defined as follows: Two sentences are synonymous if and only if any true answer to the question "What does it mean?" asked of one of them, is a true answer to the same question, asked of the other. We do not, of course, claim any clarifying power for this definition. We want only to point out that if we are to give up the notion of sentence-synonymy as senseless, we must give up the notion of sentence-significance (of a sentence having meaning) as senseless too. But then perhaps we might as well give up the notion of sense.—It seems clear that we have here a typical example of a philosopher's paradox. Instead of examining the actual use that we make of the notion of *meaning the same*, the philosopher measures it by some perhaps inappropriate standard (in this case some standard of clarifiability), and because it falls short of this standard, or seems to do so, denies its reality, declares it illusory.

We have argued so far that there is a strong presumption in favor of the existence of the distinction, or distinctions, which Quine challenges—a presumption resting both on philosophical and on ordinary usage—and that this presumption is not in the least shaken by the fact, if it is a fact, that the distinctions in question have not been, in some sense, adequately clarified. It is perhaps time to look at what Quine's notion of adequate clarification is.

The main theme of his article can be roughly summarized as follows. There is a certain circle or family of expressions, of which "analytic" is one, such that if any one member of the circle could be taken to be satisfactorily understood or explained, then other members of the circle could be verbally, and hence satisfactorily, explained in terms of it. Other members of the family are: "self-contradictory" (in a broad sense), "necessary," "synonymous," "semantical rule," and perhaps (but again in a broad sense) "definition." The list could be added to. Unfortunately each member of the family is in as great need of explanation as any other. We give some sample quotations: "The notion of self-contradictoriness (in the required broad sense of inconsistency) stands in exactly the same need of clarification as does the notion of analyticity itself."[4] Again, Quine speaks of "a notion of synonymy which is in no less need of clarification than analyticity itself."[5] Again, of the adverb "necessarily," as a candidate for use in the explanation of synonymy, he says, "Does the adverb *really make sense?* To suppose that it does is to suppose that we have already *made satisfactory sense* of 'analytic.' "[6] To make "satisfactory sense" of one of these expressions would seem

to involve two things. (1) It would seem to involve providing an explanation which does not incorporate any expression belonging to the family-circle. (2) It would seem that the explanation provided must be of the same general character as those rejected explanations which do incorporate members of the family-circle (i.e., it must specify some feature common and peculiar to all cases to which, for example, the word "analytic" is to be applied; it must have the same general form as an explanation beginning, "a statement is analytic if and only if . . ."). It is true that Quine does not explicitly state the second requirement; but since he does not even consider the question whether any other kind of explanation would be relevant, it seems reasonable to attribute it to him. If we take these two conditions together, and generalize the result, it would seem that Quine requires of a satisfactory explanation of an expression that it should take the form of a pretty strict definition but should not make use of any member of a group of interdefinable terms to which the expression belongs. We may well begin to feel that a satisfactory explanation is hard to come by. The other element in Quine's position is one we have already commented on in general, before enquiring what (according to him) is to count as a satisfactory explanation. It is the step from "We have not made satisfactory sense (provided a satisfactory explanation) of *x*" to "*x* does not make sense."

It would seem fairly clearly unreasonable to insist *in general* that the availability of a satisfactory explanation in the sense sketched above is a

---

[4] Page 20.

[5] Page 23.

[6] Page 30, our italics.

necessary condition of an expression's making sense. It is perhaps dubious whether *any* such explanations can *ever* be given. (The hope that they can be is, or was, the hope of reductive analysis in general.) Even if such explanations can be given in some cases, it would be pretty generally agreed that there are other cases in which they cannot. One might think, for example, of the group of expressions which includes "morally wrong," "blameworthy," "breach of moral rules," etc.; or of the group which includes the propositional connectives and the words "true" and and "false," "statement," "fact," "denial," "assertion." Few people would want to say that the expressions belonging to either of these groups were senseless on the ground that they have not been formally defined (or even on the ground that it was impossible formally to define them) except in terms of members of the same group. It might, however, be said that while the unavailability of a satisfactory explanation in the special sense described was not a *generally* sufficient reason for declaring that a given expression was senseless, it was a sufficient reason in the case of the expressions of the analyticity group. But anyone who said this would have to advance a reason for discriminating in this way against the expressions of this group. The only plausible reason for being harder on these expressions than on others is a refinement on a consideration which we have already had before us. It starts from the point that "analytic" and "synthetic" themselves are technical philosophical expressions. To the rejoinder that other expressions of the

family concerned, such as "means the same as" or "is inconsistent with," or "self-contradictory," are not at all technical expressions, but are common property, the reply would doubtless be that, to qualify for inclusion in the family circle, these expressions have to be used in specially adjusted and precise senses (or pseudo-senses) which they do not ordinarily possess. It is the fact, then, that all the terms belonging to the circle are *either* technical terms *or* ordinary terms used in specially adjusted senses, that might be held to justify us in being particularly suspicious of the claims of members of the circle to have any sense at all, and hence to justify us in requiring them to pass a test for significance which would admittedly be too stringent if generally applied. This point has some force, though we doubt if the special adjustments spoken of are in every case as considerable as it suggests. (This seems particularly doubtful in the case of the word "inconsistent"—a perfectly good member of the nontechnician's metalogical vocabulary.) But though the point has some force, it does not have whatever force would be required to justify us in insisting that the expressions concerned should pass exactly that test for significance which is in question. The fact, if it is a fact, that the expressions cannot be explained in precisely the way which Quine seems to require, does not mean that they cannot be explained at all. There is no need to try to pass them off as expressing innate ideas. They can be and are explained, though in other and less formal ways than that which Quine considers. (And the fact that they are so explained fits with the facts, first, that there is a generally agreed philosophical use for them, and second, that this use is technical or specially adjusted.) To illustrate the point briefly for one member of the analyticity family. Let us suppose we are trying to explain to someone the notion of *logical impossibility* (a member of the family which Quine presumably regards as no clearer than any of the others) and we decide to do it by bringing out the contrast between logical and natural (or causal) impossibility. We might take as our examples the logical impossibility of a child of three's being an adult, and the natural impossibility of a child of three's understanding Russell's Theory of Types. We might instruct our pupil to imagine two conversations one of which begins by someone (X) making the claim:

(1) "My neighbor's three-year-old child understands Russell's Theory of Types,"

and the other of which begins by someone (Y) making the claim:

(1′) "My neighbor's three-year-old child is an adult."

It would not be inappropriate to reply to X, taking the remark as a hyperbole:

(2) "You mean the child is a particularly bright lad."

If X were to say:

(3) "No, I mean what I say—he really does understand it,"

one might be inclined to reply:

(4) "I don't believe you—the thing's impossible."

But if the child were then produced, and did (as one knows he would not) expound the theory correctly, answer questions on it, criticize it, and so on, one would in the end be forced to acknowledge that the claim was literally true and that the child was a prodigy. Now consider one's reaction to Y's claim. To begin with, it might be somewhat similar to the previous case. One might say:

(2′) "You mean he's uncommonly sensible or very advanced for his age."

If Y replies:

(3′) "No, I mean what I say,"

we might reply:

(4′) "Perhaps you mean that he won't grow any more, or that he's a sort of freak, that he's already fully developed."

Y replies:

(5′) "No, he's not a freak, he's just an adult."

At this stage—or possibly if we are patient, a little later—we shall be inclined to say that we just don't understand what Y is saying, and to suspect that he just does not know the meaning of some of the words he is using. For unless he is prepared to admit that he is using words in a figurative or un-usual sense, we shall say, not that we don't believe him, but that his words have *no* sense. And whatever kind of creature is ultimately produced for our inspection, it will not lead us to say that what Y said was literally true, but at most to say that we now see what he meant. As a summary of the differ-ence between the two imaginary con-versations, we might say that in both cases we would tend to begin by sup-posing that the other speaker was using words in a figurative or unusual or re-stricted way; but in the face of his repeated claim to be speaking literally, it would be appropriate in the first case to say that we did not believe him and in the second case to say that we did not understand him. If, like Pascal, we thought it prudent to prepare against very long chances, we should in the first case know what to prepare for; in the second, we should have no idea.

We give this as an example of just one type of informal explanation which we might have recourse to in the case of one notion of the analyticity group. (We do not wish to suggest it is the only type.) Further examples, with dif-ferent though connected types of treat-ment, might be necessary to teach our pupil the use of the notion of logical impossibility in its application to more complicated cases—if indeed he did not pick it up from the one case. Now of course this type of explanation does not yield a formal statement of neces-sary and sufficient conditions for the application of the notion concerned. So it does not fulfill one of the conditions which Quine seems to require of a sat-

isfactory explanation. On the other hand, it does appear to fulfill the other. It breaks out of the family circle. The distinction in which we ultimately come to rest is that between not believing something and not understanding some-thing; or between incredulity yielding to conviction, and incomprehension yielding to comprehension. It would be rash to maintain that *this* distinction does not need clarification; but it would be absurd to maintain that it does not exist. In the face of the availability of this informal type of explanation for the notions of the analyticity group, the fact that they have not received another type of explanation (which it is dubious whether *any* expressions *ever* receive) seems a wholly inadequate ground for the conclusion that the no-tions are pseudo-notions, that the ex-pressions which purport to express them have no sense. To say this is not to deny that it would be philosophic-ally desirable, and a proper object of philosophical endeavor, to find a more illuminating general characterization of the notions of this group than any that has been so far given. But the question of how, if at all, this can be done is quite irrelevant to the question of whether or not the expressions which belong to the circle have an intelligible use and mark genuine distinctions.

So far we have tried to show that sections 1 to 4 of Quine's article—the burden of which is that the notions of the analyticity group have not been sat-isfactorily explained—do not establish the extreme thesis for which he appears to be arguing. It remains to be seen whether sections 5 and 6, in which diag-nosis and positive theory are offered, are any more successful. But before we turn to them, there are two further points worth making which arise out of the first two sections.

(1) One concerns what Quine says about *definition* and *synonymy*. He remarks that definition does not, as some have supposed, "hold the key to synonymy and analyticity," since "definition—except in the extreme case of the explicitly conventional introduction of new notations—hinges on prior relations of synonymy."[7] But now consider what he says of these extreme cases. He says: "Here the definiendum becomes synonymous with the definiens simply because it has been expressly created for the purpose of being synonymous with the definiens. Here we have a really transparent case of synonymy created by definition; would that all species of synonymy were as intelligible." Now if we are to take these words of Quine seriously, then his position *as a whole* is incoherent. It is like the position of a man to whom we are trying to explain, say, the idea of one thing fitting into another thing, or two things fitting together, and who says: "I can understand what it means to say that one thing fits into another, or that two things fit together, in the case where one was specially made to fit the other; but I cannot understand what it means to say this in any other case." Perhaps we should not take Quine's words here too seriously. But if not, then we have the right to ask him exactly what state of affairs he things *is* brought about by explicit defi-

nition, what relation between expressions *is* established by this procedure, and why he thinks it unintelligible to suggest that the same (or a closely analogous) state of affairs, or relation, should exist in the absence of this procedure. For our part, we should be inclined to take Quine's words (or some of them) seriously, and reverse his conclusions; and maintain that the notion of synonymy by explicit convention would be unintelligible if the notion of synonymy by usage were not presupposed. There cannot be law where there is no custom, or rules where there are not practices (though perhaps we can understand better what a practice is by looking at a rule).

(2) The second point arises out of a paragraph on page 32 of Quine's book. We quote:

> I do not know whether the statement "Everything green is extended" is analytic. Now does my indecision over this example really betray an incomplete understanding, an incomplete grasp, of the "meanings" of "green" and "extended"? I think not. The trouble is not with "green" or "extended," but with "analytic."

If, as Quine says, the trouble is with "analytic," then the trouble should doubtless disappear when "analytic" is removed. So let us remove it, and replace it with a word which Quine himself has contrasted favorably with "analytic" in respect of perspicuity—the word "true." Does the indecision at once disappear? We think not. The indecision over "analytic" (and equally,

---

[7] Page 27.

in this case, the indecision over "true") arises, of course, from a further indecision: viz., that which we feel when confronted with such questions as "Should we count a *point* of green light as *extended* or not?" As is frequent enough in such cases, the hesitation arises from the fact that the boundaries of application of words are not determined by usage in all possible directions. But the example Quine has chosen is particularly unfortunate for his thesis, in that it is only too evident that our hesitations are not *here* attributable to obscurities in "analytic." It would be possible to choose other examples in which we should hesitate between "analytic" and "synthetic" and have few qualms about "true." But no more in these cases than in the sample case does the hesitation necessarily imply any obscurity in the notion of analyticity; since the hesitation would be sufficiently accounted for by the same or a similar kind of indeterminacy in the relations between the words occuring within the statement about which the question, whether it is analytic or synthetic, is raised.

Let us now consider briefly Quine's positive theory of the relations between the statements we accept as true or reject as false on the one hand and the "experiences" in the light of which we do this accepting and rejecting on the other. This theory is boldly sketched rather than precisely stated.[8] We shall merely extract from it two assertions, one of which Quine clearly takes to be incompatible with accept-

ance of the distinction between analytic and synthetic statements, and the other of which he regards as barring one way to an explanation of that distinction. We shall seek to show that the first assertion is not incompatible with acceptance of the distinction, but is, on the contrary, most intelligibly interpreted in a way quite consistent with it, and that the second assertion leaves the way open to just the kind of explanation which Quine thinks it precludes. The two assertions are the following:

(1) It is an illusion to suppose that there is any class of accepted statements the members of which are in principle "immune from revision" in the light of experience, i.e., any that we accept as true and must continue to accept as true whatever happens.

(2) It is an illusion to suppose that an individual statement, taken in isolation from its fellows, can admit of confirmation or disconfirmation at all. There is no particular statement such that a particular experience or set of experiences decides once for all whether that statement is true or false, independently of our attitudes to all other statements.

The apparent connection between these two doctrines may be summed up as follows. Whatever our experience may be, it is in principle possible to hold on to, or reject, any particular statement we like, so long as we are prepared to make extensive enough revisions elsewhere in our system of beliefs. In practice our choices are governed largely by considerations of

---

[8] Cf. pages 37–46.

convenience: we wish our system to be as simple as possible, but we also wish disturbances to it, as it exists, to be as small as possible.

The apparent relevance of these doctrines to the analytic-synthetic distinction is obvious in the first case, less so in the second.

(1) Since it is an illusion to suppose that the characteristic of immunity in principle from revision, come what may, belongs, or could belong, to any statement, it is an illusion to suppose that there is a distinction to be drawn between statements which possess this characteristic and statements which lack it. Yet, Quine suggests, this is precisely the distinction which those who use the terms "analytic" and "synthetic" suppose themselves to be drawing. Quine's view would perhaps also be (though he does not explicitly say this in the article under consideration) that those who believe in the distinction are inclined at least sometimes to mistake the characteristic of strongly resisting revision (which belongs to beliefs very centrally situated in the system) for the mythical characteristic of total immunity from revision.

(2) The connection between the second doctrine and the analytic-synthetic distinction runs, according to Quine, through the verification theory of meaning. He says: "If the verification theory can be accepted as an adequate account of statement synonymy, the notion of analyticity is saved after all."[9] For, in the first place, two statements might be said to be synonymous if and only if any experiences which contribute to,

or detract from, the confirmation of one contribute to, or detract from, the confirmation of the other, to the same degree; and, in the second place, synonymy could be used to explain analyticity. But, Quine seems to argue, acceptance of any such account of synonymy can only rest on the mistaken belief that individual statements, taken in isolation from their fellows, can admit of confirmation or disconfirmation at all. As soon as we give up the idea of a set of experiential truth-conditions for each statement taken separately, we must give up the idea of explaining synonymy in terms of identity of such sets.

Now to show that the relations between these doctrines and the analytic-synthetic distinction are not as Quine supposes. Let us take the second doctrine first. It is easy to see that acceptance of the second doctrine would not compel one to abandon, but only to revise, the suggested explanation of synonymy. Quine does not deny that individual statements are regarded as confirmed or disconfirmed, are in fact rejected or accepted, in the light of experience. He denies only that these relations between single statements and experience hold independently of our attitudes to *other* statements. He means that experience can confirm or disconfirm an individual statement, only given certain assumptions about the truth or falsity of other statements. When we are faced with a "recalcitrant experience," he says, we always have a choice of what statements to amend. What we have to renounce is determined by what we are anxious to keep. This view, however, requires only a slight modi-

9 Page 38.

fication of the definition of statement-synonymy in terms of confirmation and disconfirmation. All we have to say now is that two statements are synonymous if and only if any experiences which, *on certain assumptions about the truth-values of other statements*, confirm or disconfirm one of the pair, also, *on the same assumptions*, confirm or disconfirm the other to the same degree. More generally, Quine wishes to substitute for what he conceives to be an oversimple picture of the confirmation-relations between particular statements and particular experiences, the idea of a looser relation which he calls "germaneness" (p. 43). But however loosely "germaneness" is to be understood, it would apparently continue to make sense to speak of two statements as standing in the same germaneness-relation to the same particular experiences. So Quine's views are not only consistent with, but even suggest, an amended account of statement-synonymy along these lines. We are not, of course, concerned to defend such an account, or even to state it with any precision. We are only concerned to show that acceptance of Quine's doctrine of empirical confirmation does not, as he says it does, entail giving up the attempt to define statement-synonymy in terms of confirmation.

Now for the doctrine that there is no statement which is in principle immune from revision, no statement which might not be given up in the face of experience. Acceptance of this doctrine is quite consistent with adherence to the distinction between analytic and synthetic statements. Only, the adherent of *this* distinction must also insist

on another; on the distinction between that kind of giving up which consists in merely admitting falsity, and that kind of giving up which involves changing or dropping a concept or set of concepts. Any form of words at one time held to express something true may, no doubt, at another time, come to be held to express something false. But it is not only philosophers who would distinguish between the case where this happens as the result of a change of opinion solely as to matters of fact, and the case where this happens at least partly as a result of a shift in the sense of the words. Where such a shift in the sense of the words is a necessary condition of the change in truth-value, then the adherent of the distinction will say that the form of words in question changes from expressing an analytic statement to expressing a synthetic statement. We are not now concerned, or called upon, to elaborate an adequate theory of conceptual revision, any more than we were called upon, just now, to elaborate an adequate theory of synonymy. If we can make sense of the idea that the same form of words, taken in one way (or bearing one sense), may express something true, and taken in another way (or bearing another sense), may express something false, then we can make sense of the idea of conceptual revision. And if we can make sense of this idea, then we can perfectly well preserve the distinction between the analytic and the synthetic, while conceding to Quine the revisability-in-principle of everything we say. As for the idea that the same form of words, taken in different ways, may bear different senses and perhaps be used to say things with different truth-values, the onus of showing that this is somehow a mistaken or confused idea rests squarely on Quine. The point of substance (or one of them) that Quine is making, by this emphasis on revisability, is that there is no absolute necessity about the adoption or use of any conceptual scheme whatever, or, more narrowly and in terms that he would reject, that there is no analytic proposition such that we *must* have linguistic forms bearing just the sense required to express that proposition. But it is one thing to admit this, and quite another thing to say that there are no necessities within any conceptual scheme we adopt or use, or, more narrowly again, that there are no linguistic forms which do express analytic propositions.

The adherent of the analytic-synthetic distinction may go further and admit that there may be cases (particularly perhaps in the field of science) where it would be pointless to press the question whether a change in the attributed truth-value of a statement represented a conceptual revision or not, and correspondingly pointless to press the analytic-synthetic distinction. We cannot quote such cases, but this inability may well be the result of ignorance of the sciences. In any case, the existence, if they do exist, of statements about which it is pointless to press the question whether they are analytic or synthetic, does not entail the nonex-

istence of statements which are clearly classifiable in one or other of these ways and of statements our hesitation over which has different sources, such as the possibility of alternative interpretations of the linguistic forms in which they are expressed.

This concludes our examination of Quine's article. It will be evident that our purpose has been wholly negative. We have aimed to show merely that Quine's case against the existence of the analytic-synthetic distinction is not made out. His article has two parts. In one of them, the notions of the analyticity group are criticized on the ground that they have not been adequately explained. In the other, a positive theory of truth is outlined, purporting to be incompatible with views to which believers in the analytic-synthetic distinction either must be, or are likely to be, committed. In fact, we have contended, no single point is established which those who accept the notions of the analyticity group would feel any strain in accommodating in their own system of beliefs. This is not to deny that many of the points raised are of the first importance in connection with the problem of giving a satisfactory general account of analyticity and related concepts. We are here only criticizing the contention that these points justify the rejection, as illusory, of the analytic-synthetic distinction and the notions which belong to the same family.

ANALYTICITY AND CONTRADICTION IN NATURAL LANGUAGE

5.6

Jerrold Katz

The primary significance of this paper lies in its solution to the problem of distinguishing analytic and synthetic truths raised by W. V. Quine in his "Two Dogmas of Empiricism."[1] This solution is based on the conviction that Quine's skepticism can be overcome within the framework of a conception of the nature of a semantic theory of a natural language while, in the absence of such a framework, techniques such as those R. Carnap[2] and other empiricists have proposed cannot hope to surmount Quine's fastidious skepticism. Accordingly, this paper first presents a conception of the nature of a semantic theory to serve as a framework and then proceeds within this framework to draw the analytic-synthetic distinction by introducing definitions of the terms *analytic sentence, synthetic sentence,* and *contradictory sentence* which beg no questions of empirical justification and which formally specify the set of analytic sentences, the set of synthetic sentences, and the set of contradictory sentences.

The Nature of a Semantic Theory

A semantic theory of a natural language[3] has as its goal the construction of a system of rules which represents what a fluent speaker knows[4] about the

From *The Structure of Language: Readings in the Philosophy of Language,* Jerry A. Fodor and Jerrold J. Katz, editors (Englewood Cliffs, N.J.: Prentice-Hall, 1964). Reprinted by permission of the publisher and the author.

[1] W. V. Quine, "Two Dogmas of Empiricism," in *From a Logical Point of View* (Cambridge, Mass.: Harvard University Press, 1953), pp. 20–46.

[2] R. Carnap, "Meaning and Synonymy in Natural Language," *Philosophical Studies,* VI, No. 3, (April 1955), 33–47.

[3] J. J. Katz, and J. A. Fodor, "The Structure of a Semantic Theory," *Language,* 40 (1963). I shall henceforth use the initials "SST" to refer to this paper.

[4] Here I anticipate such an objection as the following: "How can you say a fluent speaker *knows* something if he cannot say what it is you claim he knows?" I do not think anything hangs on my *having* the word *know.* I intend to convey the idea that the fluent speaker has acquired the means necessary for performing a task whose

semantic structure of his language that permits him to understand its sentences. The idea behind this conception of a semantic theory is that such knowledge takes the form of recursive rules that enable the speaker to compose, albeit implicitly, the meaning of any sentence of his language out of the familiar meanings of its elementary components.

This idea has the following two-part rationale. First, the most impressive fact about linguistic competence is that a fluent speaker can understand a sentence even though he has never previously encountered it. In principle,[5] he can understand any of the infinitely many sentences of his language. But

___

character compels us to admit that its performance results from the application of rules. Among the reasons which compel us to make this admission is that cited by Miller, Pribram, and Galanter, viz., that the task of understanding any twenty word sentence is one a fluent speaker can perform, yet the number of twenty word sentences is 10^{30} while the number of seconds in a century is only 3.15 times 10^9—G. A. Miller, K. Pribram, and E. Galanter, *Plans and the Structure of Behavior* (New York: Holt, Rinehart & Winston, Inc. 1960), pp. 146–47.

[5] I say "in principle" because in practice limitations of perception, memory, mortality, and so on, prevent the speaker from applying his knowledge of the rules of the language to provide himself with the meaning of certain sentences. This situation is exactly analogous to the case of a person's knowledge of the rules of arithmetic computation. Knowing how to perform any computation, knowing the rules of arithmetic computation, is not sufficient to enable someone to actually perform any (specific) computation; for, again, limitations of perception, memory, mortality, and the like stand in the way.

since, at any time in his life, the speaker can have encountered only a finite subset of the infinite set of sentences of his language, we can conclude that his knowledge of the semantic structure takes the form of recursive rules which fix a meaning for each of the infinitely many sentences. Second, since a speaker's ability to understand sentences also depends on his knowing the meanings of their elementary components, the lexical items in the vocabulary of the language, we can conclude that the meaning the rules fix for a sentence must be a compositional function of the antecedently known means of the lexical items appearing in it. Hence, a semantic theory must contain rules that represent the speaker's knowledge of the semantic structure of his language. Such rules must explicate the compositional function which determines how he utilizes the meanings of the lexical items in a sentence to understand what that sentence means.

A semantic theory consists of two components. First, a dictionary which provides a meaning for each lexical item of the language. Second, a finite set of "projection rules." These use information supplied by the dictionary for the lexical items in a sentence and information about the sentence's syntactic structure supplied by the grammar of the language in order to assign the sentence a semantic interpretation.

Since information about a sentence's syntactic structure is needed to assign it a semantic interpretation, it is convenient to let the output of a grammar be the input to a semantic theory. In this way, each sentence considered by a semantic theory is represented as a concatenation of morphemes whose constituent structure is given in the form of a hierarchical categorization of the syntactical parts of the concatenation.[6] The sentence "The boys like candy" is represented by the concatenation of morphemes *the* $+$ *boy* $+$ *s* $+$ *like* $+$ *candy* which is hierarchically categorized as follows: the whole string is categorized as a sentence at the highest level of the hierachy; *the* $+$ *boy* $+$ *s* is categorized as a noun phrase, and *like* $+$ *candy* is categorized as a verb phrase at the next level of the hierarchy; *the* is categorized as an article; *boy* $+$ *s* is categorized as a noun, *like* as a verb, and *candy* as a noun; and so forth on the next and lower levels of the hierarchy. We can represent such a categorization in the form of a labeled tree diagram in which the notion *the sequence of morphemes m belongs to the category c* is formalized by the notion *m is traceable back to a node labeled c*.[7] We call such a representation a *constituent structure characterization* of a sentence. The constituent structure characterization of "The boys like candy" is roughly:[8]

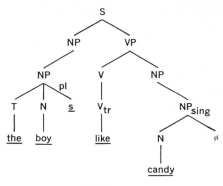

Figure 1

The input to a semantic theory are sentences represented as terminal elements within their constituent structure characterizations, together with any further grammatical information that an optimal grammar supplies about them.[9]

A semantic theory takes, one after another, the discrete outputs of the grammar and operates on them. This operation reconstructs the manner in which a speaker employs the syntactic structure of a sentence to determine its meaning as a function of the meanings of its lexical items. The result of this operation is a semantic interpretation of the sentence. Hence, we must first consider just what a semantic interpretation ought to tell us about a sentence.

The semantic interpretations produced by a semantic theory constitute the theory's description of the semantic

---

[6] Such information will be needed to provide the difference upon which rests the distinction in meaning between sentences composed of exactly the same morphemes, e.g., "Gourmets do approve of people eating," "Gourmets do approve of eating people," "Do gourmets approve of people eating?" and so on.

[7] N. Chomsky, *Syntactic Structures*, Second Printing (Mouton and Co., 's Gravenhage, 1962), Chapter 4. In general, we shall follow Chomsky's conception of syntax.

[8] I will use the notational abbreviations: *S* for a sentence, *NP* for a noun phrase, *VP* for a verb phrase, *N* for a noun, *V* for a verb,

T for an article, *A* for an adjective, *C* for a co-ordinating conjunction, and the subscript symbols *sing, pl,* and *tr* for the syntactic properties of nominal singularness, nominal pluralness, and verbal transitivity, respectively.

[9] In particular, an optimal grammar will include a specification of the transformational history for each sentence. Cf. N. Chomsky, *op. cit.*

structure of a language. Since a speaker's knowledge of semantic structure manifests itself in his verbal performance, the fundamental question about this performance is "what manifests the speaker's knowledge of the semantic structure of his language?" Some of the ways in which the speaker manifests his knowledge are as follows: he differentiates semantically acceptable from semantically anomalous sentences; he recognizes ambiguities stemming from semantic relations; he detects semantic relations between expressions and sentences of different syntactic type and morpheme constitution; and so forth. Hence, semantic interpretations must formally mark as semantically acceptable and anomalous those sentences that the speaker differentiates as acceptable and anomalous, mark as semantically ambiguous those sentences that the speaker regards as such, mark as semantically related in such-and-such a fashion just those expressions and just those sentences that the speaker detects as so related, and so forth. Otherwise, the semantic theory cannot claim to represent the speaker's semantic knowledge. For example, a semantic theory of English would have to produce a semantic interpretation for "The bank is the scene of the crime" that marks it as semantically ambiguous, semantic interpretations for the sentences "He paints with silent paint" and "Two pints of the academic liquid!"[10] that mark them as semantically anomalous, semantic interpretations for "he paints silently" and "Two pints of the muddy liquid!" that mark them as semantically acceptable, and semantic interpretations which mark the sentences "Eye doctors eye blonds," "Oculists eye blonds," "Blonds are eyed by eye doctors," and so on, as paraphrases of each other but mark "Eye doctors eye what gentlemen prefer" as *not* a paraphrase of any of these sentences.

Now, to finish describing the form of a semantic theory of a natural language, we need only characterize the notions *dictionary entry, semantic interpretation*, and *projection rule.*

Within a semantic theory, the dictionary entries provide the basis from which the projection rules of the theory derive the semantic interpretations they assign sentences. The notion *dictionary entry* must be such that in it we have a normal form for the dictionary entries in a semantic theory. This normal form must enable us to represent lexical information in a formal manner. Also, it must be sufficient in conceptual machinery to provide a representation of everything which the projection rules require to assign correct semantic interpretations.

In the majority of cases,[11] a dictionary entry consists of a finite number of sequences of symbols, each sequence consisting of an initial subsequence of syntactic markers, followed by a subsequence of "semantic markers," then,

---

[10] For the first of these two examples, I am indebted to Professor Uriel Weinreich, and for the second to Professor George A. Miller.

[11] In the small minority of cases, dictionary entries consist of instructions, e.g., the rules for *not* that are given in the third section of this paper. For a further discussion of the type of entry found in the vast majority of cases see Sect. 6 of SST.

optionally, one "distinguisher," and finally a "selection restriction." Dictionary entries can be represented in the form of tree diagrams, such as in Fig. 2, where each sequence in the entry for a lexical item appears as a distinct path rooted at that lexical item.[12] Semantic markers are represented enclosed within parentheses, the distinguishers are represented enclosed within brackets, and the selection restrictions are represented within angles. Each complete path, each sequence, represents a distinct sense of the lexical item in whose entry it appears. Thus, in Fig. 2 the lexical item *bachelor* is represented as having four distinct senses.

Semantic markers are the formal elements a semantic theory employs to express semantic relations of a general nature. For example, the appearance of the semantic marker (Male) in the dictionary entries for senses of *bachelor, uncle, man, lion, priest, father,* etc., but not in the dictionary entries for senses of *spinster, stone, adult, philosopher, virtue, pea,* etc., represents the fact that the former items have a common semantic component in their meanings which the latter items lack, and, thus, the fact that these former items are semantically similar in a way that the latter ones are not. In contrast, distinguishers are the formal elements employed to represent

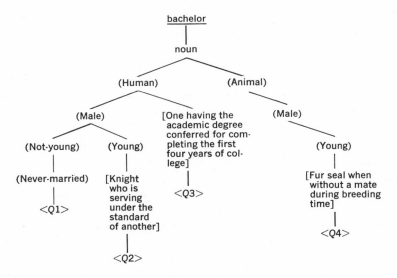

Figure 2

[12] Two comments on Fig. 2. First, the word *bachelor,* although a noun, can select and exclude other nouns in various types of constructions, e.g., in noun-noun cases as "He is my bachelor friend," or in noun-in-apposition cases such as "Mr. Smith, the neighborhood bachelor, is here." Thus, we must represent *bachelor* having a selection restriction for each sense; thus, the terminal elements for each path in Fig. 2 is a selection restriction enclosed in angles. Second, the particular selections restrictions are omitted because their inclusion would only complicate matters unnecessarily at this point.

what is idiosyncratic about the meaning of a lexical item. A distinguisher serves to distinguish a lexical item from those that are closest to it in meaning. Thus, a semantic marker found in the path of a certain lexical item will also be found in the paths of many other lexical items throughout the dictionary, whereas a distinguisher found in the path of a certain lexical item will not be found anywhere else in the dictionary. This difference can be more fully appreciated if one compares the consequences of eliminating a semantic marker from a dictionary with the consequences of eliminating a distinguisher. In the former case, indefinitely many semantic relations between the expressions of the language which were marked by the eliminated semantic marker would no longer be marked, whereas in the latter case, only the distinction in sense which was marked by the eliminated distinguisher would no longer be marked.[13] Therefore, semantic markers and distinguishers represent the semantic properties from which the meaning of a lexical item is constructed. They may be regarded as expressing the most elementary components of the semantic content of lexical items, i.e., those components down into which the whole meaning of lexical items can be analyzed.

A lexical item is ambiguous if, and only if, its entry contains at least two distinct paths. Ambiguity at the lexical level is the source of semantic ambiguity at the sentence level. Thus, a necessary,

---

[13] For a further examination of the distinction between the notions *semantic marker* and *distinguisher* see Sect. 6 of SST.

although not sufficient, condition for a syntactically unambiguous sentence to be semantically ambiguous is that it contains an ambiguous lexical item. For example, the source of the semantic ambiguity of "He likes to wear a light suit in the summer" is the lexical ambiguity of the word *light*. Since an adequate dictionary entry for a lexical item must mark every one of its ambiguities, the dictionary entry for *light* must represent this lexical item as branching into one path containing the semantic marker *Color* but not *Weight* and another containing the semantic marker *Weight* but not *Color*.

However, an ambiguous lexical item in a syntactically unambiguous sentence is not sufficient for that sentence to be semantically ambiguous. For example, the sentence "The stuff is light enough to carry," although it contains the ambiguous word *light*, is not understood in the sense in which *light enough to carry* means light enough in color to be carried. Thus, when there is an ambiguous lexical item in a semantically unambiguous sentence, the grammatical relations and the meanings of the other constituents can prevent this item from bearing more than one of its senses. The selection of some senses and exclusion of others occurs as a result of the other constitutents of the sentence. Such selection is of fundamental importance because, together with lexical ambiguity, it partly determines whether a sentence is anomalous, whether a sentence is semantically unambiguous, whether two sentences are paraphrases of each other, and other semantic properties of sentences that a semantic theory marks.

Thus, a path for a lexical item must

contain a selection restriction that determines the combinations into which the item can enter and the sense(s) it bears in those combinations. The formal representation of selection restrictions can be regarded as a device for indicating such information as *The Shorter Oxford English Dictionary's* qualification that the word *honest* when applied to persons means "of good moral character, virtuous, upright" and applied to women is ambiguous between this sense and the sense of *chaste*. We shall use left and right angles enclosing a Boolean function of syntactic or semantic markers to formally represent such selection restrictions. Such configurations of symbols will be affixed as the terminal element of a path and will be construed as providing a necessary and sufficient condition for a semantically acceptable combination of that path with another. Thus, for example, the selection restriction affixed to the path of a modifier determines the applicability of that path of the modifier to a sense of a head. Instances of modifier-head relations are: adjective-noun modification, adverb-verb modification, adverb-adjective modification. In particular, a path in the dictionary entry for *honest* will be: *honest* → adjective → (*Evaluative*) → (*Moral*) → [*Innocent of illicit sexual intercourse*] < (*Human*) and (*Female*) >. This is to be construed as saying that an adjectival occurrence of *honest* receives the interpretation, (*Evaluative*) → (*Moral*) → [*Innocent of illicit sexual intercourse*], just in case the head it modifies has a path containing both the semantic marker (*Human*) and the path semantic marker (*Female*).

In sum, a path contains syntactic markers that determine the syntactic classification of a lexical item, semantic markers that represent the semantic properties that the item has in common with many other lexical items, (optionally) a distinguisher that represents its idiosyncratic features, and finally a selection restriction.

The next notion to explain is *projection rule*. Let us suppose that an English grammar provides a semantic theory with the input sentence "The boys like candy" together with the constituent structure characterization as given in Fig. 1. The first step the theory performs in assigning a semantic interpretation to this sentence is to correlate each of its lexical items, i.e., *the, boy, s, like,* and *candy*, with all, and only, the paths from their dictionary entries that are compatible with the syntactic categorization the lexical items are given in the constituent structure characterization.

The correlation works as follows: if a path from the dictionary entry for the lexical item m_j contains syntactic markers which attribute to m_j the same syntactic categorization that it has in the constituent structure characterization d_i, then this path is assigned to the set of paths P_j^i which is correlated with the occurrence m_j in d_i. Thus, the lexical item m_1 is associated with the set of paths P_1^i, m_2 is associated with P_2^i, and so on.[14] Referring to Fig. 1, the result of this step may be pictured as converting the diagram into one in which *the* is associated with the set of paths P_1^i, *boy* is associated with P_2^i, *s* is associated

---

[14] For a full discussion of this step see the treatment of rule (I) in SST, Sect. 7.

with P_3^i, *like* is associated with P_4^i, and *candy* is associated with P_5^i (although no other change is made). Thus, for example, P_5^i contains paths representing each of the senses that *candy* has as a noun but none of the paths representing its senses as a verb (e.g. "The fruits candy easily"). This rule which associates senses with the occurrences of lexical items in constituent structure characterizations is the first projection rule.

There are type one projection rules and type two projection rules. Type one projection rules utilize the information about the meanings of the lexical items contained in the paths belonging to the sets of paths assigned in the above manner in order to provide a characterization of the meaning of every constituent of a sentence, including the whole sentence. For example, in "The boys like candy," besides the characterizations of the meaning of *the, boy, s, like*, and *candy* obtained from their dictionary entries, type one projection rules must provide characterizations of the meaning of *The boys, like candy*, and "The boys like candy." This type one projection rules do by combining the characterizations of the meaning of lower constituents to form a characterization of the meaning of the higher constituents. Thus, type one projection rules effect a series of amalgamations of paths, proceeding from the bottom to the top of a constituent structure characterization, by embedding paths into each other to form a new path, the amalgam. The amalgam is assigned to the set of paths associated with the node (i.e., the point at which an n-ary

branching occurs) that immediately dominates the sets of paths from which the paths amalgamated were drawn. The amalgam provides one of the meanings for the sequence of lexical items that the node dominates. In this manner, a set of alternative meanings given in the form of derived paths is provided for every sequence of lexical items dominated by a syntactic marker in the constituent structure characterization, until the highest syntactic marker S is reached and associated with a set of derived paths giving the meanings for the whole sentence.

Amalgamation is the operation of forming a composite path made up of one path from each of the n-different sets of paths dominated by a syntactic marker. This composite path is then a member of the set of paths associated with the node that that syntactic marker labels. The joining of a pair of paths occurs just in case one of the paths satisfies the selection restrictions in the other. If the syntactic marker dominates just the sets of paths $P_1^i, P_2^i, \ldots, P_n^i$ and P_1^i contains k_1 paths, P_2^i contains k_2 paths, . . ., P_n^i contains k_m paths, then the set of paths that is associated with the dominating marker contains at most $(k_1 \cdot k_2 \cdot \ldots \cdot k_m)$ members and possibly zero members if selection restrictions prevent every possible amalgamation from forming. Each path which is in the set assigned to the dominating node marker is called *a reading for the lexical string that this marker dominates in the constituent structure characterization d_i*. The number of readings that is thus allotted to a string of lexical items determines its degree of semantic ambiguity. A string with no readings is anomalous, a string with exactly one reading is unambiguous, and a string with two or more readings is semantically ambiguous two or more ways.

An example of a projection rule of type one is:

(R1) Given two paths associated with nodes from the same node labeled *SM*, one of the form

> *Lexical String₁* → syntactic markers of head → (a_1) → (a_2) → $\cdots$ → (a_n) → [1] $<\Omega1>$

and the other of the form

> *Lexical String₂* → syntactic markers of the modifier of the head → (b_1) → (b_2) → $\cdots$ → (b_m) → [2] $<\Omega2>$

such that the string of syntactic or semantic markers of the head has a substring σ which satisfies $<\Omega2>$, then there is an amalgam of the form

> *Lexical String₂* + *Lexical String₁* → dominating node marker *SM* → (a_1) → (a_2) → $\cdots$ → (a_n) → (b_1) → (b_2) → $\cdots$ → (b_m) → [[2] [1]] $<\Omega_1>$,

where any b_i is null just in case there is an a_j such that $b_i = a_j$, [[2] [1]] is simply [1] just in case [2] = [1]. This amalgam is assigned to the set of paths associated with the node labeled *SM*

that dominates *Lexical String₂* + *Lexical String₁*.[15]

(R1) explicates the process of attribution, i.e., the process of creating a new semantic unit compounded from a modifier and head whose semantic properties are those of the head, except that the meaning of the compound is more determinate than the head's by virtue of the semantic information contributed by the modifier. The modifier-head relations which must be known for (R1) to apply will be specified by the grammar of the language. An example of an amalgamation produced by (R1) is the joining of the path, *colorful* → adjective → (*color*) → [*Abounding in contrast or variety of bright colors*] < (*Physical object*) v (*Social activity*) >, and the path, *ball* → noun → (*Physical object*) → [*Of globular shape*], to produce the new compound path, *colorful* + *ball* → noun → (*Physical object*) → (*color*) → [[*Abounding in contrast or variety of bright colors*] [*Of globular shape*]]. An example of an amalgamation that is prevented by a selection restriction is that of the path, *colorful* → adjective → (*Evaluative*) → [*Of distinctive*

---

[15] This erasure clause is included to avoid pointlessly duplicating semantic markers and distinguishers in the path for a compound expression. Thus, for example, it makes no sense to include the semantic markers (*Human*) and (*Female*) twice in the path associated with the compound *spinster aunt* because both of the constituent paths contain occurrences of both. The second occurrence of (*Human*) or (*Female*) would provide no semantic information whatever.

character, vividness, or picturesqueness]
< (*Aesthetic Object*) v (*Social Activity*) >, with the path for *ball* just
given above. This possible amalgamation is precluded because the selection
restriction in the path of the modifier
requires that this path be joined only
with paths of heads that contain either
the semantic marker (*Aesthetic object*)
or the semantic marker (*Social activity*)
whereas this path of *ball* contains
neither one of these semantic markers.

Other type one projection rules are
formulated in a similar manner, utilizing other grammatical relations to produce similar types of amalgamations.
Type two rules work differently and are
best explained after we explain the
concept of a semantic interpretation of
a sentence.

A semantic theory receives more than
one constituent structure characterization for a sentence if that sentence is
syntactically ambiguous. Figs. 3 and 4
show the two constituent structure

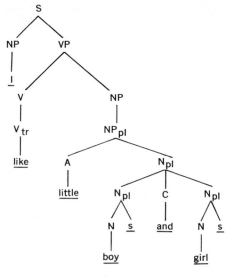

Figure 4

characterizations for the syntactically
ambiguous sentence "I like little boys
and girls." Let $d_1, d_2, \ldots, d_n$ be the
constituent structure characterizations
that the grammar provides for the
n-ways syntactically ambiguous sentence S. We will define the "semantic
interpretation of S" to be (1) the conjunction ψd_1 & ψd_2 & ... & ψd_n of the
semantic interpretations of the n-constitutent structure characterizations of
S, and (2) the statements about S that
follow from the definition schema:

(D) S is *fully* X if and only if
        S is X on every d_i

The semantic intepretation ψd_i of the
constituent structure characterization
d_i of S is (1) the constituent structure
characterization d_i, each node of which
is associated with its full set of readings,
(i.e., every reading that can belong to
the set on the basis of the dictionary

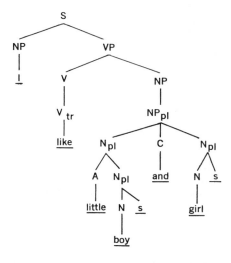

Figure 3

entries and the projection rules does belong to it), and (2) the statements about S that follow from (1) together with the definitions:

(D1) S is *semantically anomalous on d_i* if, and only if, the set of paths associated with the node labeled S in d_i contains no members.

(D2) S is *semantically unambiguous on d_i* if, and only if, the set of paths associated with the node labeled S in d_i contains exactly one member.

(D3) S is *n-ways semantically ambiguous on d_i* if, and only if, the set of paths associated with the node labeled S in d_i contains exactly n-members ($n > 2$).

(D4) S_1 and S_2 are *paraphrases on a reading with respect to their characterizations d_i and d_j* if, and only if, the set of paths associated with the node labeled S in d_i and the set of paths associated with the node labeled S in d_j have a reading in common.

(D5) S_1 and S_2 are *full paraphrases with respect to their characterizations d_i and d_j* if, and only if, the set of paths associated with the node labeled S in d_i and the set of paths associated with the node labeled S in d_j have exactly the same membership.

as well as other definitions for other semantic properties of sentences and corresponding definitions for constituents of sentences, e.g., (D1.1). *NP is semantically anomalous on d_i* if, and only if, the set of paths associated with the node labeled NP in d_i contains no members.

Since these definitions are self-explanatory, we can now return to our account of the projection rules and explain the concept of a type two projection rule.

A grammar employs two types of syntactic rules to achieve its aim of assigning the correct constituent structure characterization to each sentence of the language.[16] The first type are rules which rewrite single symbols on the basis of information which comes from the linear context of the symbol. Such rules construct constituent structure characterizations such as those in Figs. 1, 3, and 4 in somewhat the following manner: the first rule rewrites the initial symbol S (standing for "*sentence*") as $NP + VP$ (which categorizes a noun-phrase + verb-phrase sequence as a sentence), then a rule can be used to rewrite NP as either NP_{sing} or NP_{pl}, then other rules can be used to rewrite VP as either $V + NP$ or V_{intr} or $be + Pred$, still other rules to rewrite NP_{sing} as $T + N$, T as *the*, N as *boy* (or *man, coat, mouse*, etc.) and so forth.[17]

It has been shown that a grammar can assign constituent structure charac-

---

[16] Although this is not the only aim of a grammar. Cf. N. Chomsky, "On the Notion 'Rule of Grammar,'" *Proceedings of the Twelfth Symposium in Applied Mathematics, The Structure of Language and its Mathematical Aspects*, ed. by Roman Jakobson, American Mathematical Society, (1961), pp. 6–24.

[17] Cf. N. Chomsky, "A Transformational Approach to Syntax," *Third Texas Conference on Problems in the Analysis of English*, ed. by A. A. Hill, forthcoming.

terizations correctly only if some of its rules use information about the derivational history of sentences.[18] Thus, in addition to the previous type of rules, grammars contain "transformational rules." Such rules operate on entire constituent structure characterizations, or any of their parts, and map labeled trees onto labeled trees. In this way, simpler sentences are transformed into more complex ones, and the transformed sentences are assigned a constituent structure characterization.

Type two projection rules are intended to explicate the manner in which transformational rules preserve or change meaning. Linguists have observed that, in general, the sentence resulting from the application of a transformational rule to a set of source sentences is related in meaning to these source sentences in a definite, systematic way.[19] The employment of type two rules is intended to reveal the facts of language that underlie this observation.

Type two projection rules produce a semantic interpretation ψd_i for the constituent structure characterization d_i

constructed by the operation of the transformation T out of the set of constituent structure characterizations d_1, d_2, . . ., d_n. Such projection rules operate on a set of semantic interpretations ψd_1, ψd_2, . . ., ψd_n. and the transformation T to produce the semantic interpretation ψd_i. They assign semantic interpretations in such a way as to reconstruct the manner in which the meaning of the sentence that was constructed by T is a function of the meanings of each of the sentences that were used by T in its construction.

The Solution to Quine's Problem

The present paper is an essay in semantic metatheory.[20] A metatheory of semantic theories is needed to inform the field linguist of what types of facts to look for and what is the most revealing form to arrange them in. Given that he has acquired the relevant linguistic facts and has suitably arranged them, definitions such as (D), $(D1)$, $(D2)$, $(D3)$, $(D4)$, and $(D5)$ are the basis on which the field linguist can make illuminating statements about the sentences of the language he is studying. However, these definitions are not by themselves enough to enable the field linguist to say everything he should say about the semantic properties of sentences. On the basis of $(D1)$ to $(D5)$, the linguist can say what formal relations determine whether a sentence is

---

[18] Cf. Chomsky's *Syntactic Structures*, "On the Notion 'Rule of Grammar,'" and *The Logical Structure of Linguistic Theory*, (1955), microfilm at M.I.T. Library. Also, cf. P. Postal, "Limitations of Phrase-Structure Grammars."

[19] This point has been discussed outside the context of the conception of a semantic theory adopted in the present paper in two recent articles: J. A. Fodor, "Projection and Paraphrase in Semantics," *Analysis,* 21.4 (March 1961), 73–77; and J. J. Katz, "A Reply to 'Projection and Paraphrase in Semantics,'" *Analysis,* 22.2 (December 1961), 36–41.

[20] A full discussion of the nature of a semantic metatheory will be found in SST, Sect. 8.

acceptable or anomalous, what relations determine whether a sentence is unambiguous or ambiguous, and what relations determine whether a sentence is a paraphrase of another or not. But the linguist requires a notion of semantic interpretation that, by virtue of further definitions, will enable him to tell also when a sentence is analytic, contradictory, or synthetic, when two sentences are inconsistent with each other, and so on. Accordingly, the present paper extends the concept of a semantic interpretation by adding definitions of the notions *analytic sentence, contradictory sentence, synthetic sentence, inconsistent sentences*, among others. Thus, this paper not only offers a reply to Quine's challenge to the empiricists to show that the analytic-synthetic distinction is more than mere dogma but continues the metatheoretic study into the nature of a semantic theory begun in previous publications.[21]

In SST, the basic idea behind the present paper's treatment of the concept of an analytic sentence was expressed as follows:

> The limiting case [of modification], where the addition to the compound of semantic material from the modifier is zero, is of considerable theoretical interest. The compound *unmarried bachelor* is a case in point. The erasure clause in (R1), i.e., "any b_i is null when there is an a_j such that $b_i = a_j$, and [[2] [1]] = [1] just in case [2] = [1]," tells us

to delete from the path of the modifier any semantic material already represented in the path of the head. Thus, in forming the compound *unmarried bachelor* all the semantic information in the path of the modifier *unmarried* will be deleted so that the derived path for *unmarried bachelor* will contain no more than the semantic material which comes from the path for *bachelor*. The failure of the modifier to add semantic information would appear to account for the intuition that such expressions as *unmarried bachelor* are redundant and that, correspondingly, such statements as "bachelors are unmarried" are "empty," "tautological," "vacuous," "uninformative." Thus, we have a new explanation of the analyticity of a classical type of analytic truth.[22]

The explanation of analyticity suggested in this passage, although it is developed only for sentences of the $NP + is + A$ type, can be extended to explain the analyticity of all copula sentences. The analyticity of noncopula sentences will be taken up after we conclude our whole discussion of the copula type.

To obtain a general, formal definition of *analytic sentence* for present tense copula sentences, we will require some auxiliary notions. We will use the symbol p_1 for a path from the set of paths associated with the node labeled NP that is immediately dominated by the node labeled S (i.e., the node that dominates the string of lexical items that is the subject of the sentence). We will use the symbol p_2 for a path from the set of paths associated with the node

---

[21] Cf. SST and J. J. Katz and P. Postal, *An Integrated Theory of Linguistic Descriptions*, M.I.T Press, 1964.

[22] SST, Sect. 7.

labeled *VP* that is immediately dominated by the node labeled *S* (i.e., the node that dominates the string of lexical items that consists of the verb *is* followed by its nominal or adjectival predicate). That is, p_1 and p_2 are paths that are amalgamated to produce a reading, which we shall represent by $r_{1,2}$, for the sentence as a whole. We will use the term *semantic element* to refer either to a semantic marker or to a distinguisher.

Given these auxiliary notions, we add to (*D1*) to (*D5*) the definition:

> **(D6)** The copula sentence *S* is *analytic on the reading* $r_{1,2}$ if, and only if, every semantic element e_i in p_2 is also in p_1 and for any complex semantic element $\{e_1 \cup e_2 \cup \ldots \cup e_n\}$ in the path p_2, there is a semantic element e_j such that $1 \leq j \leq n$ and e_j is in the path p_1.[23]

(*D6*) formalizes the idea that analyticity is the predicative vacuity that results from the failure of the path associated with the predicate to contribute semantic elements to the path associated with the subject when these paths are amalgamated to produce a reading for the sentence.

Checking (*D6*) for its applicability to analytic sentences of each of the copula types, the *NP* + *is* + *A* cases and the *NP* + *is* + *NP* cases, we find that both types come under (*D6*) as is

indicated by the examples: "Bachelors are unmarried," "The happy child is happy," "The man who is cheerful is cheerful," and so on and "The pediatrician who loves her is a doctor who loves her," "The man who stole the cake is the man by whom the cake was stolen," "Stones are physical objects," "Spinsters are adult women who have never married," and so on. In each of these examples, the sentence is analytic because every semantic element in the path from the set of paths associated with the verb phrase is also found in the path from the set associated with the noun-phrase subject.

The concept of "analytic sentence" just characterized is that of "analytic on a reading," but there is another concept of sentiential analyticity, *viz.*

> **(D6′)** *S* is *fully analytic on* d_i if, and only if, the set of readings assigned to the node labeled *S* in d_i is non-null and, for every reading $r_{1,2}$ in this set, *S* is analytic on $r_{1,2}$.

Sentences that are merely analytic on a reading are as plentiful as natural numbers (e.g., the sentences usually encountered in philosophical discussions of analyticity, "Bachelors are unmarried," "Vixens are foxes"). On the other hand, sentences that are fully analytic are not found in natural language, except in areas where a highly technical nomenclature is in use. Some philosophers claim that, for example, "Bachelors are unmarried" is not analytic because *bachelor* can refer to married men or women who possess a bachelor's degree. Other philosophers regard such

---

[23] The notation $\{e_1 \cup e_2 \cup \ldots \cup e_n\}$ will be explained below in connection with the discussion of the rules for *not*. In (*D7*) and (*D8*) we will take *S* to be a variable for copula sentences.

criticism as beside the point. Disagreement of this kind can be resolved using the above distinction.

In terms of (D6), analyticity is the counterpart, on the sentence level, of the relations of synonymy and meaning inclusion, found on the level of lexical items and expressions.[24] Intuitively, this is a desirable feature since it brings out the formal structure underlying the often made observation that analyticity is somehow connected with these relations. The question arises whether we can so construct our definition of "contradictory sentence" that it reconstructs contradictoriness as the counterpart, on the sentence level, of the relation of antonymy on the level of lexical items and expressions. It will become quite clear that an adequate definition of "contradictory sentence" must be constructed in such a way that this relationship between contradictoriness and antonymy is a feature of its definiens.

There are many special antonymy relations between words and expressions. One example, is the relation of "sex-antonymy."[25] A pair of lexical items is *sex-antonymous* just in case they have identical paths except that where one has the semantic marker (*Male*) the other has the semantic marker

(*Female*). Some instances are: *woman and man; bride and groom; aunt and uncle; cow and bull*. The majority of antonymous lexical items are not sets of pairs but sets of *n*-tuples. For example, there are the species-antonymous lexical items, one example of a species-antonymous *n*-tuple being: *child, cub, puppy, kitten, cygnet*, and so on. Then, there are the age-antonymous *n*-tuples: *infant, child, adolescent*, and *adult; puppy and dog; cub and lion; cub and bear; cygnet and swan;* and so on. Moreover, there are *n*-tuples of lexical items that are distinguisher-wise antonymous, e.g., the *n*-tuple of simple color adjectives (*blue, yellow, green, red, orange*). These form an antonymous *n*-tuple because the path associated with each is identical except for the distinguisher which differentiates that color adjective from the others.

The definition of "sex-antonymy" cannot restrict the set of sex-antonymous pairs to a membership consisting only of lexical items. By definition, this set includes infinitely many cases of pairs of constructible expressions. For example, *the happy man* and *the happy woman; my mother's friend's father's aunt* and *my mother's friend's father's uncle; the cow that the farmer's son raised* and *the bull that the farmer's son raised;* and so on *ad infinitum*.[26] Moreover, the situation is the same for every other type of antonymy. Since every set of antonymous *n*-tuples contains infinitely many members, we will

---

[24] We can say that a pair of lexical items are *synonymous on a sense* if, and only if, their dictionary entries have one path in common, and we can say a pair of lexical items are *fully synonymous* if, and only if, their dictionary entries are exactly the same. Two expressions are *synonymous on a pair of readings* if, and only if, they have a reading in common, and expressions are *fully synonymous* if, and only if, they have every reading in common.

[25] SST, Sect. 6.

[26] For the rules of grammar that explain why this set is infinite cf. R. B. Lees, "The Grammar of English Nominalizations," *International Journal of American Linguistics*, 26, No. 3 (July 1960).

have to construct a definition of each type of antonymy and a definition of the general notion *antonymous n-tuple* that formally represents the relevant infinite set.

The most natural way to construct such definitions is the following. Let us suppose that the semantic markers and the distinguishers of a semantic theory are grouped into antonymous *n*-tuples. This will mean that the antonymous *n*-tuples of semantic elements are so represented by the notation of the theory that the membership of any *n*-tuple can be uniquely determined from the symbols that represent the semantic elements. Then, we can define the general notion of antonymy as follows:

(1) Two lexical items or constructible expressions m_i and m_j are *antonymous on their paths* p_{m_i} *and* p_{m_j} if and only if p_{m_i} and p_{m_j} contain different semantic elements from the same antonymous *n*-tuple of semantic elements.

(2) $m_1, m_2, \ldots,$ are an *X-antonymous n-tuple of constructible expressions* if, and only if, the paths $p_{m_1}, p_{m_2}, \ldots, p_{m_n}$ associated with them respectively each contains a different semantic element from the *X*-antonymous *n*-tuple of semantic elements.

We can now define the notion *contradictory sentence:*

(**D7**) *S* is *contradictory on the reading* $r_{1,2}$ of d_i if, and only if, p_1 and p_2 contain different

semantic elements from the same antonymous *n*-tuple of semantic elements.

Thus, what is asserted about a sentence when its semantic interpretation marks it as contradictory is that the amalgamation that provides a reading for the sentence combines antonymous elements. Examples of contradictory sentences are: "A bride is a groom," "My round table is square," "Red is green," "Those who play badly are those who play well," "The loser of the game we are playing is the winner of the game we are playing," and so on.

Synthetic sentence can now be defined in terms of (*D6*) and (*D7*):

(**D8**) *S* is *synthetic on the reading* $r_{1,2}$ of d_i if, and only if, *S* is neither analytic on $r_{1,2}$ nor contradictory

Examples of synthetic sentences are: "That woman is a spinster," "The loser of the game we are playing is a bachelor," "The groom is reluctant," "Red is the color of my house."[27]

In order for definitions (*D6*) to (*D8*) to apply generally, certain other concepts need to be explicated. One such explication is the rules for determining the semantic effect of sentential negation.

The negation of a sentence can be formed in a number of ways. We can

---

[27] Thus, set of synthetic sentences in English includes "There are no more integers than even integers" and other semi-sophisticated mathematical truths, as well as the sophisticated ones. We shall draw the moral at the very end of this paper.

put the word *not* after the verb *be*, as in "The table is not an antique." We can put expressions such as "It is not the case that" in front of full sentences, as in the sentence, "It is not the case that the table is an antique." We can prefix the sentence by *that* and add *is false* to the end, as in "That it is so is false."[28] We shall consider only the type of negativization in which the negation of a sentence is formed by adding *not*. Negations formed in other ways, by virtue of being actual sentence negations, are synonymous with the negations of the same sentences that are formed by adding *not*. Thus, restricting consideration to negations formed by adding *not* does not impose a limitation on our treatment because, by (*D4*) and (*D5*) which require that synonymous sentences receive the same readings at the sentence level, whatever semantic properties a semantic interpretation assigns to the negation of a sentence formed in this way will also be assigned to the negation of that sentence which

is formed in another manner. Moreover, we shall make the reasonable assumption that the scope of a negative in a sentence is determined by the grammatical analysis of the sentence.[29] Then, we can formally characterize a range of application for the *not*-rules by allowing them to operate on any path in the set of paths that provides the readings for the constituent in the scope of *not*. This constituent will be the main verb phrase of the sentence so that the *not*-rules operate on p_2's. For example, in the case of the sentence "The table is not an antique," the *not*-rules apply to any path that provides a reading for the constituent *an antique*. What we have to determine now is the effect of the operation of the *not*-rules on the paths which fall in their range of application.

Preliminary to stating the *not*-rules, let us define an operator which we shall call the *antonymy operator* and symbolize by $A/$:

> (3) If the semantic elements e_1, $e_2, \ldots, e_n$ are an antonymous n-tuple, then (a) A/e_i $(1 \leqq i \leqq n) = \{e_1 \cup e_2 \cup \ldots \cup e_{i-1} \cup e_{i+1} \cup \ldots \cup e_n\}$ (b) $A/A/e_i = e_i$

We will call a function of semantic elements a "complex semantic element" and will treat complex semantic elements exactly like semantic elements for the purpose of amalgamation.

[28] The use of a negative prefix does not convert a sentence into its negation. Thus, the sentence "John is unlucky" is not the negation of "John is lucky," whereas the sentence "John is not lucky" is the negation of "John is lucky." To appreciate this, one must observe that the sentences "John is unlucky" and "John is not lucky" are not synonymous. The former means that John has bad things happening to him regularly by chance, while the latter means that John has very few good things happening to him by chance. Thus, "John is not unlucky" means that John does not have bad things happening to him regularly, not that he has any good thing happening to him. On the other hand, "John is not not lucky" means that he has good things happening to him regularly.

[29] The question of whether a negative somewhere in a sentence makes that sentence the negation of the sentence without that negative is a matter for the grammar to decide. Cf. E. Klima "Negation," in *The Structure of Language*.

Suppose we hear the English sentence "That adult is not a spinster." As fluent speakers, we know that this sentence says that the person referred to by its subject is not a spinster, but we do not know from this sentence alone whether this is because that person is male or because that person is married or both. On the other hand, we do know that that person's being human has nothing whatsoever to do with the fact that he or she is not a spinster. These considerations suggest the first of our *not*-rules.

(NR) Let $e_1, e_2, \ldots, e_k$ be all the semantic elements in a path in the range of *not* such that no $e_i (1 \leq i \leq k)$ occurs in p_1 and no A/e_i occurs in p_1. Then $e_1, e_2, \ldots, e_k$ are replaced by the complex semantic element $\{A/e_1 \cup A/e_2 \cup \ldots \cup A/e_k\}$.

Each set in the union of sets $\{A/e_1 \cup A/e_2 \cup \ldots \cup A/e_k\}$ is a union of semantic elements, i.e., each A/e_i $(1 \leq i \leq k)$ is, according to (3) above, the union of all the members of the antonymous *n*-tuple to which e_i belongs except e_i itself; e.g., if e_i belongs to an antonymous pair, then A/e_i is simply the semantic marker or distinguisher that is antonymous with e_i.

Using (NR) to obtain a reading for the sentence "That adult is not a spinster," we achieve, with respect to what factors are and what are not in the meaning of this sentence, a result which is fully in accord with our linguistic intuition as speakers of English. The amalgamation of a path for *that adult* and a path for *is not a spinster* which

is required to provide a reading for the whole sentence is preceded by an operation of (N/R) which replaces the semantic markers (*Female*) and (*Unmarried*) in the path for *a spinster* by the complex semantic marker $\{A/(Female) \ A/(Unmarried)\}$ i.e., $\{(Male) \cup (Married)\}$. Thus, when the path for *is not a spinster* is amalgamated with the path for *that adult* by $(R1)$[30] the complex marker from the path of *a spinster*, $\{(Male) \cup (Married)\}$, will become an element of the reading for the whole sentence. This, then, is to say formally what we agreed on above, namely, that adult is either a male or married or both. We also agreed that the person's being human has nothing to do with he or she not being a *spinster*. Formally, the semantic marker (*Human*) which is in the path for *a spinster* already appears in the path for *that adult*, and therefore (NR) leaves it intact. But $(R1)$'s erasure clause deletes it so that it does not enter the path for *that adult*. Finally, $(D8)$ enables us to mark "That adult is not a spinster" as a synthetic sentence.

We now introduce the two further *not*-rules, (NR') and (NR''), which complete our account of the operation of negation.

(NR') (1) For all those e_i in a path in the range of *not* such that there is a semantic element antonymous to e_i in p_1, e_i is replaced by A/e_i.
(2) If (NR) did not apply

_____

[30] By $(R1)$ because this is a modifier-head relation.

and if (NR') (1) does not apply, then any e_i in a path in the range of *not* that also occurs in p_1 is replaced by A/e_i.

(NR'') If (NR') applies to a path, then any semantic element in that path that does not also occur in p_1 and that has not entered that path by the application of (NR') that permits this application of (NR'') is nullified.

With these rules, we can show that, in accordance with the dicta of logic, a semantic theory built on the model given in the previous section and supplemented with the definitions from the present section will mark the negation of a contradictory sentence as analytic and will mark the negation of an analytic sentence as contradictory. Now we want to explain why there is such a relation between contradictory and analytic sentences, and in so doing explain also the workings of (NR') and (NR'').

First, let us show that the negation of a contradictory sentence will be marked analytic. Assume we are given a sentence that is contradictory in the sense of $(D7)$. When the conversion of this contradictory sentence into its negation brings *not* in, there will then be semantic elements $e_1, e_2, \ldots, e_n$ $(n \geq 1)$ in the path which will be in the range of *not* such that each element has an antonymous element in the path p_1. For example, if the contradictory sentence

were "A bride is a groom," then $n = 1$, $e_1 = (Male)$, and e_1's antonymous element in $p_1 = (Female)$. The negation of the contradictory sentence has *not* located so that its range includes any path assigned as a reading to the verb phrase in the contradictory sentence. Thus, if p_3 is a path in the range of *not*, then by (NR') (1), each semantic element e_i $(1 \leq i \leq n)$ in p_3 will be replaced by A/e_i prior to the amalgamation of p_1 and p_2. Hence, in the amalgamation of p_1 and p_2, any semantic elements in p_2 that have an antonym in p_1 will be converted into their antonym so that the erasure clause of the projection rule amalgamating p_1 and p_2 deletes them as a duplication. For example, in the sentence "A bride is not a groom," the semantic marker $(Male)$ is replaced by $A/(Male)$, i.e., $(Female)$, so that in the amalgamation of the path for *is not a groom* and the path for *a bride* the former path does not contribute $A/(Male)$ because the presence of $(Female)$ in the latter path causes it to be deleted prior to amalgamation. Such deletion will also be the fate of any semantic elements in p_2 that are in p_1 as well; e.g., the semantic marker $(Human)$ in the path assigned as a reading to *is a groom* will not be added to a path for *a bride* when such a path is amalgamated with a path for *is not a groom* because $(Human)$ appears in the path for *a bride*. If there are any semantic elements in p_3 such that neither they nor their antonym is in p_1 (as there are not in "A bride is a groom" but are in "A bride is a reluctant groom"), then, by (NR''), each is nullified. Consequently, in the amalgamation of p_1 and p_2, p_2 will be vacuous, and so by $(D6)$, the sentence will be analytic. Therefore, we conclude that the negation of a contradictory sentence is analytic.

Next we must show that the negation of an analytic sentence is contradictory. Assume we are given a sentence that is analytic in the sense of $(D6)$. It follows, that there are semantic elements $e_1, e_2, \ldots, e_n$ ($N \geqq 1$) in the path p_2 for this analytic sentence such that each e_1 ($1 \leqq i \leqq n$) is also in p_1. Thus, in the negation of the sentence, (NR') (2) replaces e_1 by A/e_1, e_2 by A/e_2, $\ldots$, and e_n by A/e_n. Consequently, p_1 and p_2 will each contain a different semantic element from the same n-tuple of antonymous semantic elements, and the negation of the analytic sentence will be contradictory by $(D7)$. For example, suppose we began with the analytic sentence "That spinster is a female who never married." Then, $n = 2$ and $e_1 = $ (Female) and $e_2 = $ (never-married). Then, (NR') (2) converts (Female) into $A/$(Female), i.e., (Male), and (never-married) into $A/$(never-married), i.e., (at least once married). But since that spinster is assigned a path containing both (never-married) and (Female), the sentence "That spinster is not a female who never married" is contradictory by virtue of the fact that its semantic interpretation now satisfies $(D7)$.

The negation of a synthetic sentence comes out, as it should, to be synthetic. By $(D8)$, a synthetic sentence will have a path p_2 which contains semantic elements $e_1, e_2, \ldots, e_n$ ($n \geqq 1$) that do not also occur in p_1. Moreover, by $(D8)$, $A/e_1, A/e_2, \ldots, A/e_n$ do not occur in p_1 either. The not-rules only replace e_1

by A/e_1, e_2 by A/e_2, $\ldots$, e_n by A/e_n in the path p_2 of the negation of the synthetic sentence. Since ex hypothesi A/e_1, $A/e_2, \ldots, A/e_n$ are not in p_1, the negation of a synthetic sentence does not satisfy $(D6)$. Since ex hypothesi $e_1, e_2, \ldots, e_n$ are not in p_1, it does not satisfy $(D7)$ either. Since the negation of a synthetic sentence is neither analytic nor contradictory, by $(D8)$, it is synthetic. For example, the paths p_2 for the sentences "That adult is not a spinster," "The apple is not red," and so on will add new semantic information that is consistent with what is in the corresponding paths p_1 when the p_1 and p_2 amalgamation takes place, and so each of these sentences will be marked synthetic.

The motivation for (NR'') deserves further comment. Consider the sentence "An uncle is a spinster." This sentence is contradictory because the path for An uncle and the path for is a spinster contain different semantic markers from the same n-tuple of antonymous semantic elements; i.e., the former contains (Male) and the latter (Female). Thus, we require that the negation of this sentence be analytic. But, without (NR''), the negation of "An uncle is a spinster" would not be analytic, since there is a semantic element, viz., (Unmarried), in the path p_2 which is not in p_1. Hence, the need for (NR'') stems from the need to cancel such semantic elements in order that we maintain the consequence that the negation of any contradictory sentence is analytic and that we preserve the generality of $(D6)$.

Before concluding this section, let us briefly look at some further consequences of our definitions. The definitions together with the *not*-rules provide a formal means of sharply distinguishing contradictory and analytic sentences, on the one hand, from anomalous sentences, on the other. The practice of regarding contradictory and analytic sentences as *odd* and *ipso facto* grouping them together with semantically anomalous sentences is not harmful when it is made fully clear that the term *odd* refers to sentence-uses in specific situations and means only that in those situations that use is somehow inappropriate. In this sense, synthetic sentences can be *odd*, e.g., "I just swallowed my nose," and anomalous sentences can, in some situations, i.e., giving an example, telling a joke, be *non-odd*.[31] However, often this sense of *odd* is not distinguished from the sense in which it means "violates the semantic restrictions necessary to meet the standard of semantic well-formedness," i.e., semantically anomalous. This is unfortunate because it has led some philosophers to believe that analytic, contradictory, and anomalous sentences are all odd, pure and simple, and this classifies together such dissimilar cases as "An uncle is a spinster" and "A bachelor is unmarried," on the one hand, and "the paint is silent" and "Two pints of the academic liquid," on the other. With the conceptual apparatus of selection restrictions on amalgamation (formulated in terms of functions of semantic elements enclosed within angles) and $(D1)$ as the basis for marking anomaly and with $(D6)$ and $(D7)$

and the *not*-rules as the basis for marking analyticity and contradiction, we obtain the intuitively desirable result that semantic interpretations mark semantically anomalous sentences differently from the way they mark contradictory and analytic sentences. That is, sentences that are anomalous receive no reading at the sentence level while sentences that are either contradictory or analytic receive a reading having properties which enable them to be appropriately marked.

Another matter worth noticing is the following. Consider a sequence of sentences such as "The flower is red," "The flower is not red," "The flower is not not red," and so on.[32] The third sentence in this sequence is grammatically constructed from the second by the negation-transformation,[33] the fourth is so constructed from the third, the fifth from the fourth, and so on. We may thus regard the third sentence as having the syntactic bracketing $(The\ flower)\ (is\ not\ (not\ (red)))$. Employing (NR) for the operation of the *not* whose range is the

---

[31] Cf. J. J. Katz and J. A. Fodor, "What's Wrong with the Philosophy of Language?" *Inquiry*, 5 (1962), 215–18.

[32] The reader may object that at some point there are too many occurrences of the word *not* in the succeeding sentences for them to be acceptable English. This is perhaps so. But if there is such a point, then none of the sentences beyond it will be grammatical, and consequently none will be generated by the grammar and provided as input to the semantic theory. Thus, the semantic theory will interpret only those sentences in such sequences that are grammatical, since a semantic theory operates only on sentences it receives from the grammar. Hence, the projection rules are stated generally in order not to decide at what point sentences in such a sequence stop and ungrammatical strings begin.

[33] Cf. E. Klima, *op. cit.*

path that is associated with just the word *red,* we replace this path's distinguisher e_i by A/e_i. Again applying (NR), but this time for the *not* whose range is the path that is associated with the expression *not red,* i.e., the path resulting from the former operation of (NR), we replace the semantic element A/e_i by $A/A/e_i$, which is simply e_i by (3). Thus, the reading assigned to the third sentence is the same as that assigned to the first. But this means that from the *not*-rules follows a version of the law of double negation: $X + not + not + Y = X + Y$.[34]

Furthermore, given the fact that the subject of both every odd numbered sentence in the above sequence of sentences and every even numbered sentence in this sequence is the same, it follows that every odd numbered sentence is synonymous with every other odd numbered sentence and that every even numbered sentence is synonymous with every other even numbered sentence. This is the intuitively correct result. Moreover, if we lay down the definition

(D9) S_1 and S_2 are *inconsistent on a pair of readings* if the reading of one is the same as a reading of the negation of the

other, i.e., if one sentence is synonymous with (or a paraphrase of) the other's negation

we can show that in the sequence of sentences we are considering (and, of course, in other similar sentences) the odd numbered sentences are inconsistent with the even numbered sentences, since every sentence in this sequence is inconsistent with its immediate successor.

Finally, a matter that needs to be mentioned for the sake of a complete treatment of contradiction, viz., the case of contradictory sentences that involve a conjunction of two incompatible predications, e.g., "The line is straight and not straight," "The creature is a cub and a pup," "The team has won the game and lost it," and so on. Although at first glance such cases appear to be outside the scope of $(D7)$, this is not so. Nevertheless, showing that they can be marked as contradictory on the basis of $(D7)$ requires a more complicated discussion than we can afford here.[35] Instead, then, let us simply show that such cases can be marked as contradictory within a semantic theory of our type. If we look at the grammatical structure of these cases, we notice that they are constructed from two source sentences by using the conjunction-transformation; i.e., given two sentences of the form $S_1 = X — Y_1 —$

---

[34] This result should be taken into account in the controversy over the status of the law of double negation in the foundations of mathematics, specifically at the point at which some philosophers deny there is justification for double negation in the meaning of the word *not* in English. It can be argued on the basis of the material in the text that double negation has as strong support in the semantic structure of English as there is for simplification in the meaning of *and* in English.

---

[35] To show how this can be done involves using type two projection rules in such a way that one of the two conjoined sentence fragments has the path associated with it amalgamated with a path associated with the subject before the other's.

Z and $S_2 = X - Y_2 - Z$, where Y_1 and Y_2 are constituents of the same type in their respective sentences S_1 and S_2, we may construct a new sentence $S_3 = X - Y_1 +$ and $+ Y_2 - Z$.[36] Thus, the first of our examples is constructed from the two source sentences "The line is straight" and, "The line is not straight" ($X = $ *the line is*, $Y_1 = $ *straight*, $Y_2 = $ *not straight*, and $Z = $ null element). Moreover, we notice that the two source sentences are inconsistent in the sense of (D9). Hence, we can mark the sentence "The line is straight and not straight" and other cases of incompatible predication as contradictory by the rule that the conjunction of two inconsistent copula sentences is contradictory.[37]

This concludes our treatment of analyticity and contradiction in copula sentences, but the problem of analyticity and contradiction in natural language is by no means now solved. Although philosophers have raised and discussed this problem almost exclusively in terms of copula sentences, any complete treatment of analyticity and contradiction must also provide a basis for marking these properties in noncopula sentences, i.e., sentences in which the verb is transitive or intransitive. That a com-

plete treatment of the problem must cover sentences of these types follows from the fact that the grammar makes analytic, synthetic, and contradictory sentences of each of these types available for semantic interpretation.

Analytic Sentences

(1) The man who runs every race runs every race.
(2) The owner of the team owns the team.
(3) The person who lent Sam the book lent the book to Sam.
(4) What costs lots of money costs lots of money.
(5) The sweating man sweats sometimes.
(6) The child who often sleeps sleeps often.

Contradictory Sentences

(1) The loser of the game we like best wins the game we like best.
(2) Those who play badly play well.
(3) The owner of the team does not own the team.
(4) The sweating man never sweats.
(5) Persons who do not lend books lend books.
(6) The child who sleeps often seldom sleeps.

These examples cannot be handled by the straightforward maneuver of changing the category of the variable S in (D6) to (D8) so that it ranges over sentences of any type, instead of just copula sentences. This is because such a change would lead to false predictions. For example, because of the antonymous words *old* and *young*, the sentence

---

[36] N. Chomsky, *Syntactic Structures, op. cit.*

[37] Also, we can mark the sentence "The line is straight or not straight" and other cases of exhaustive alternation as analytic by the rule that the disjunction of n-copula sentences is analytic if, and only if, each sentence introduces a different semantic element from the same antonymous n-tuple of semantic elements and every semantic element from this n-tuple is introduced by some embedded sentence.

"Old men like young girls" will have a semantic element in the path associated with its noun-phrase subject that is antonymous with one in the path associated with its verb phrase, and thus, according to (D7), a semantic theory of English will predict that this sentence is contradictory when, in fact, it is synthetic. A more sophisticated treatment is necessary.

From the viewpoint of grammar, each of the above examples of analytic and contradictory noncopula sentences are constructed from two source sentences by the operation of a transformation that embeds one into the other. For example, the last of the sentences listed as analytic is constructed by the relative clause transformation by embedding the sentence "The child often sleeps" in the form of the fragment *who often sleeps* into the matrix sentence "The child sleeps often" just after the shared noun phrase.[38] Likewise, the last of the sentences listed as contradictory is constructed by this transformation, but in this case the embedded sentence is "The child sleeps often" and the matrix sentence is "The child seldom sleeps." Moreover, from these examples we see that the embedded sentence and the matrix sentence for an analytic sentence are synonymous or else the reading of the embedded sentence contains no semantic elements not in the reading for the matrix sentence, i.e., the embedded sentence is redundant, e.g., "The child often sleeps" and "The child sleeps often," and that the embedded sentence and the

matrix sentence for a contradictory sentence are inconsistent, e.g., "The child sleeps often" and "The child seldom sleeps." But, furthermore, the embedded sentence and the matrix sentence for a synthetic, transformationally compound sentence are neither synonymous nor inconsistent, e.g., "The old men like young girls" has as its embedded sentence "The men are old" and as its matrix "The men like young girls." Thus, in order to mark noncopula sentences as analytic, synthetic, and contradictory, we shall add the definitions:

(**D10**) A transformationally compound sentence S is *analytic on a reading* if the matrix sentence and the sentence embedded into the matrix to construct S are paraphrases on a reading or if the embedded sentence is redundant.

(**D11**) A transformationally compound sentence S is *contradictory on a reading* if the matrix sentence and the sentence embedded into the matrix to form S are inconsistent on a pair of readings.

(**D12**) A transformationally compound sentence S is *synthetic on a reading* if the sentence S is neither analytic nor contradictory.[39]

---

[38] Cf. C. S. Smith, "A Class of Complex Modifiers in English," *Language*, 37 (1961), 342–65.

[39] There are many points about the implementation of these definitions for which this is neither the time nor the place, but it should be pointed out that both the matrix sentence and the sentence embedded in it must be of maximum size when the question of their synonymy or inconsistency comes up. Cf. N. Chomsky, "The Logical Basis of

We may now propose an explication of entailment—the relation that holds between the antecedent and the consequent of a conditional when the latter follows from the former by virtue of a meaning relation between them. The customary explicandum is the notion that a sentence is entailed by another if, and only if, the conditional that has the latter as its antecedent and the former as its consequent is analytic. However, the absence of an adequate theory of analyticity in natural language has frustrated all attempts to replace this explicandum by a satisfactory explicatum: with no formal means for identifying conditionals which are analytic, there can be no formal means of deciding whether one sentence entails another or not. But, since the present paper gives a theory of analyticity in natural language, we may look for an extension of this theory which covers conditional sentences and in this way provides a satisfactory explicatum for entailment.

The first step in providing such an explicatum is to set forth the definition:

(**D13**) The sentence S_1 entails the sentence S_2 if, and only if, the conditional "If S_1, then S_2" is analytic.

The second and final step is to set forth a definition (*D14*) of the term *analytic* which appears in (*D13*). The sentence S to which (*D14*) will apply must be of the form:

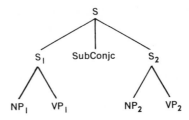

Figure 5

where S_1 is the antecedent of S (NP_1 being S_1's subject and VP_1 being S_1's main verb phrase), $SubConj_c$ is a conditional subordinating conjunction, e.g., *If . . ., then . . ., . . . implies . . .*, and so on, and S_2 is the consequent of S (NP_2 being S_2's subject and VP_2 being S_2's main verb phrase).

(**D14**) A sentence S (having the form depicted in Fig. 5) is *analytic on the reading $r_{1,2}$* if, and only if,

(**a**) it is the case that the reading r_1 for the whole sentence S_1 and the reading r_2 for the whole sentence S_2 which are amalgamated to form $r_{1,2}$ are, respectively, formed from the amalgamation of $r(NP_1)$ and $r(VP_1)$, where $r(NP_1)$ is the reading for NP_1 and $r(VP_1)$ is the reading for VP_1, and the amalgamation of $r(NP_2)$ and $r(VP_2)$, where $r(NP_2)$ is the reading of NP_2 and $r(VP_2)$ is the reading for VP_2 and

(**b**) it is the case that the relation between $r(NP_1)$ and $r(NP_2)$ and the relation between $r(VP_1)$ and $r(VP_2)$ is exactly that which (*D6*) specifies for p_1 and p_2, i.e., all semantic elements in

$r(NP_2)$ are in $r(NP_1)$ and all semantic elements in $r(VP_2)$ are in $r(VP_1)$.

The following examples illustrate the type of sentences whose analyticity is adequate grounds for asserting the entailment of their consequent by their antecedent. We may use them to help explain $(D14)$.

(1) If that person is a bachelor, then that person is male.
(2) If a spinster is foolish, then a woman is foolish.
(3) If a spinster is an aunt, then a woman is someone's relative.

The need to mark (1) as analytic shows that the relation between $r(VP_1)$ and $r(VP_2)$ must be that which $(D6)$ requires of p_1 and p_2. While the need to mark (2) as analytic shows that the relation between $r(NP_1)$ and $r(NP_2)$ must be that which $(D6)$ requires of p_1 and p_2—(3) is simply a mixed case.

Quine's complaint concerning previous attempts to draw the analytic-synthetic distinction has been that they are either circular because they assume notions that ought to be analyzed or empty because they offer no analysis whatever. Quine has demanded that the criterion we use for distinguishing between analytic and synthetic sentences avoid two traditional stumbling blocks. The criterion must not be circular: it must not require a knowledge of the sentence's analyticity nor a knowledge of other semantic properties in analyticity's tight little circle. The criterion must not be a mere stipulation: it must pro-

vide an effective means of empirically justifying the attribution of analytic status to a sentence.

We now have such a criterion, but, it is crucial to note, we have it only because we have a metatheory which characterizes the nature of a semantic theory. The metatheory tells us that a sentence S is analytic, synthetic, or contradictory depending on whether the semantic elements in p_1 and p_2 of S satisfy $(D6)$, $(D7)$, or $(D8)$.[40] A particular semantic theory of a natural language tells us, in turn, what semantic elements are in the path associated with the lexical items in S and hence what semantic elements are in the paths p_1 and p_2 of S. That the paths p_1 and p_2 of S have just the semantic elements that they need to have for S to satisfy $(D6)$ is, therefore, a matter of the correctness of the theory's dictionary entries for the lexical items in S and the correctness of the theory's projection rules that are employed to semantically interpret the constituent structure characterization of S. Both are needed to provide the derived paths p_1 and p_2. But their correctness, as Quine requires, is a matter that can be entirely settled independently of settling the particular question of S's analyticity. For the question of their correctness is a question about the adequacy of the semantic

---

[40] And if S is transformationally compound, depending on whether the semantic interpretations of the matrix sentence and the sentence embedded into the matrix sentence to form S satisfy $(D10)$, $(D11)$, or $(D12)$. The argument in the case of $(D10)$, $(D11)$, and $(D12)$ will be parallel; thus, it will be omitted.

theory for marking the semantic ambiguity, anomaly, paraphrase relations, analyticity, and so on in the case of infinitely many sentences other than S, namely, those that contain some of the lexical items that are in S or those that are semantically interpreted by using some of the same projection rules that are used to obtain the derived paths p_1 and p_2 of S. Independently of an examination of S, the semantic theory can be empirically tested by comparing the claims that it makes about the semantic properties of sentences in a sample drawn from this infinite set with the linguistic intuitions of speakers. If the semantic interpretations of the theory assert that certain sentences are semantically ambiguous n-ways and they indeed are, that other sentences are anomalous and they are, that certain pairs are paraphrases and they are, and so on, then the theory is confirmed; otherwise disconfirmed. That a highly confirmed semantic theory predicts the analyticity of S is the only empirical justification that the claim that S is analytic can have, or needs. Finally, since a semantic theory's prediction that a particular sentence is analytic derives from a defini-

tion whose definiens refers solely to formal features of a semantically interpreted constituent structure characterization, there is no circularity in the way a semantic theory of the sort we have described here handles the classification and explanation of analytic sentences. For we not only provide a recursive specification of the analytic sentences of a language but we also explain what formal structure it is claimed that a sentence has when a semantic theory predicts that the sentence is analytic.

The notion *analytic sentence* that we have explicated does not cover all the cases usually described as necessary truths. Thus, our explication explains why some necessary truths, viz., the analytic ones, are necessary, but it leaves open the question why those necessary truths that are not predicatively vacuous are necessary. Thus, the conception of analyticity and contradiction in natural language developed in this paper draws the analytic-synthetic distinction at essentially the point where Kant sought to draw it. Empiricists are thus returned from the fire of dogmatism to the frying pan of unanalyzed, synthetic necessary truths.

Toward Further Inquiry

In pursuing any of the issues connected with the analytic-synthetic distinction, "Analytic-Synthetic—A Bibliography," by Roland Hall, *Philosophical Quarterly* 16 (1966), pp. 178–181, is a primary and indispensable tool. It is a chronological list of books and articles of direct relevance from Kant's formulations of the distinction until 1966. Because author and title in this listing are frequently good clues to content, I will discuss here only a few of the most interesting (but perhaps not always the most important) treatments.

D. C. Williams, in "The Nature and Variety of the A Priori," *Analysis* 5 (1938), examines various senses of 'a priori' and concludes that all cannot be grouped under a single classification. Pap, in PR 53 (1944), explicates three senses of the term, and on this basis, distinguishes logical, functional, and psychological necessities. Wilfred Sellars, in "Is There a Synthetic A Priori?" PS 20 (1953), answers his own question both positively and negatively, according to two senses of 'synthetic'. Neither these linguistic refinements nor the dominance of a logicistic interpretation of mathematics have served to eliminate conclusions of apparently Kantian character completely. Langford, in JP 46 (1949)†, maintained that 'Any cube has twelve edges' is a synthetic a priori because the property cannot be derived from the definition. Castañeda, in PPR 21 (1960), distinguished formal (analytic) arithmetic from phenomenal (synthetic) arithmetic and claimed that the former is an abstraction of the latter. F. Ferre's "Color Incompatibility and Language-Games," *Mind* 70 (1961), is Wittgensteinian in tone, but his thesis that one must distinguish necessity *in* a language game from necessary *as* a language game may call to mind Carnap's treatment of other problems in 8.3. Malcolm, in "Are Necessary Propositions Really Verbal?" *Mind* 59 (1940), examines the *use* of necessary statements and concludes that they are devices of inference rather than description. Toulmin, in *Mind* 53 (1949), stands between Malcolm and Ferre in both time and thesis. He attempts to remove synthetic necessary truths from the traditional battlefields of discussion by treating them as being about "the nature of the subject-matter."

D. Rynin's "The Dogma of Logical Pragmatism," *Mind* 65 (1956), attacks Quine's thesis with a *reductio ad absurdum* argument, claiming that Quine's argument must presuppose what it claims to deny, and Strawson, in *Philosophical Quarterly* 7 (1957), uses a similar argument against Quine in terms of the notion of identity. R. M. Martin argues, in *Philosophical Studies* 3 (1952), that Quine and White have misconstrued Carnap's position in their arguments against it, and Gewirth in JP 50 (1953) maintains that the debate between Quine and Carnap is dependent upon differences in their overall approaches. Putnam in *Minnesota Studies in the Philosophy of Science*, Vol. III, argues that the analytic-synthetic distinction is necessary for the language of physics, but D. W. Hamlyn, in *Mind* 65 (1956), argues that it has no function in ordinary discourse. F. B. Ebersole, in JP 53 (1956), by examining the use of language concludes that the notion of analytic statement is nonsense and that the search for a criterion for analyticity is futile. Radical extensions of the Quine thesis are expressed by Aune in JP 60 (1963) and by Hintikka in PR 74 (1965). Katz, in JP 64 (1967), distinguishes a broader and a narrower sense of analyticity. He maintains that Quine has attacked only the broader sense and that his own defense has been of the narrower sense.

Katz's treatment of analyticity clearly presupposes the application of the transformational-grammar approach to a theory of semantics that he has developed with Fodor and with Postal. Members of the M.I.T. group itself have attacked this theory, and Fodor has abandoned it. Paul Ziff has also attacked it, by means of a counter-example technique, in "The Non-Synonymy of Active and Passive Sentences," PR 75 (1966). Katz and Edwin Martin answer this attack in PR 76 (1967), but this debate already carries us into the issues of the next chapter.

Chapter 6

TRANSLATABILITY AND SYNONYMITY

> It seems to me that we may compare the work of
> a translator with that of an artist who is asked
> to create an exact replica of a marble
> statue, but who cannot secure the marble.
>
> *Werner Winter*

The concerns of the reflective translator and of the philosophical analyst meet in a question about synonymity: By virtue of what criteria, and in what sense, can two linguistic expressions be said to have the same meaning? But if the translator thoroughly explores the conditions for his inquiry, he finds that the issues are much more complex than those involved in the question of synonymous expressions. In semiotic terms (see the Prologue), meaning is usually regarded as a semantic issue. Understanding the conditions for translation requires consideration of phonetic, syntactic, and pragmatic factors as well. And these factors are not discrete. Consideration of a particular problem in translation may confine the inquirer to one area of concern, but an adequate conception of the conditions for translation requires consideration of all the factors and their interrelations. It may be convenient to limit consideration of synonymity to semantic concerns and to treat the broader issues of equivalence of expressions in terms of *equipollence* (equal power). By whatever name he calls them, the translator confronts a number of philosophical issues in his attempt to understand his task:

What are the units of translation? The equipollence between 'dog' in English and '*chien*' in French seems straightforward enough, but a word-for-word translation of a French idiom into English is ludicrous. Even if names can be so treated, syncategorematic expressions cannot. The German '*von*' can be translated 'of', 'from', 'by', etc. The translation depends not only upon the object of the prepositional phrase, but upon the role of that phrase in the sentence. It may be that even the sentence is too limited, and one cannot stop short of a whole literary work as the unit of translation. At the other extreme, a word may be too large a unit. The German '*gegenuber*' is usually translated into English as 'opposite', but often its sense is better conveyed by 'over against'. With this tension between the morpheme as the smallest unit and the literary work as the largest unit, can any consistent notion of a unit of translation be arrived at?

What are the elements of translation? In one sense, clearly, morphemes,[1] words, sentences, and so on. But what is *transferred* from one language to the other? Seldom is it the phonetic character of the original, even though transliterations among Roman, Greek, Hebrew, and other alphabets attempt to indicate original sound. To transfer the phonetic quality of the written characters of Chinese and other nonphonetic writings would be impossible. What syntactic features should be transferred, and when is transference important? Can metaphor and allusion be transferred from one language to another? Does what elements are transferred depend upon the purposes of the translator? Can pragmatic features (like the intentions of the original writer) be transferred in the translation of the writing?

Is there a hierarchy of importance among the elements of translation? Not every aspect of what is said in one language can be transferred to another language. Complete translation would be no translation at all—an obvious contradiction. Since translations transform as well as transfer, which factors must be sacrificed for others? In poetry, does one attempt to save the meter of the line, or the syntax of the structure, or the sense of the term? Are order and construction irrelevant in other cases? Does the relative worth of various factors of the language translated vary from one kind of literature to another, from one instance of writing to another?

Are there factors of linguistic relativity that make some translations impossible tasks? Do all languages "cut up the world" in the same way? Anyone maintaining that there are natural classes of things would expect the extensions of terms in one language to correspond to those of terms in another. Much evidence suggests that this is not the case (see the discussion of linguistic relativity in the Epilogue). Some syntactical factors may not find equivalent forms in various languages. Does this imply that such factors are incapable of translation? Can a notion of adequate translation (as opposed to exact translation) be devised to meet such problems?

In many of these questions, the concern is clearly with the equivalence of meaning between two linguistic expressions. This concern is somewhat different in kind, however, from the one that occupies philosophers dealing with analyticity (compare Chapter 5). The translator is concerned with interlinguistic synonym-

---

[1] A *morpheme* is the simplest unit of speech that carries meaning in a language. A single word may be made up of one or more morphemes. In the word 'prefix', the morpheme 'fix' is *free*; it can function independently in the language and can itself be a word. The morpheme 'pre', while it has meaning, does not appear in the English language as a word but is always *bound* to other morphemes to form words.

ity, an equivalence of meaning between expressions of two different languages. The logical analyst is usually concerned with two expressions within the same language, with intralinguistic synonymity. In this latter concern, problems of phonetics, syntax, and cultural contexts, where they exist at all, are much more subsidiary. Where the translator must treat equivalences of whole sentences, often of whole literary works, the logical analyst more often limits himself to words and phrases. These several factors have led professional philosophers to treat problems about equivalence of meaning as far less complex issues than those confronting the professional translator.

This reduction in complexity has perhaps allowed the philosopher to focus more intently upon what constitutes synonymity of terms. Synonyms are literally "like names," but like in what sense? Just as any two things that are alike in some respects are also different in others, no two names are completely equivalent. This is true even for identities. 'One is one' is an identity statement. Certainly, the first instance of 'one' is equivalent to the second instance of 'one', but they are not the same in every sense (for example, they do not occupy the same space on the page). They are different instances of the same kind; or, as it is more often put, they are different *sign tokens* of the same *sign type*. Because we use the same sign type over and over, we seldom distinguish sign tokens. The only relevant semantic difference between sign tokens of the same sign type occurs when terms are used ambiguously. Such instances indicate that not even sign-type equivalence is sufficient basis for synonymity in ordinary language. If a language were reconstructed to avoid ambiguities, the victory would be trivial, for most concern with synonymity involves equivalence of two different sign types.

Attempts have been made to ground synonymity in a number of different kinds of equivalence. Each provides its own problems and perplexities:

> *Essential equivalence.* Two terms are synonymous if they denote or connote the same nature or essence. Such a correlation between language and reality always provides intuitive satisfaction, but the explication of its conditions is a baffling process. It raises the problems of reference and abstract entities considered in Chapters 4 and 8, and also some practical perplexities about how one knows particular essences or natures.

> *Ideational equivalence.* Two terms are synonymous if they stand for the same idea. This correlation of language with thought is also intuitively desirable, but it presents its own peculiar perplexities. If ideas are images, do we have images of abstractions and of classes of things? If ideas are concepts that differ from images, how do they differ from the symbolic forms expressed in language? Even if the idea of what an idea is can be clarified, few terms stand for ideas; they stand for what the idea itself stands for.

Extensional equivalence. Two terms are synonymous if substituting them for each other in a statement does not change the truth value of that statement. But, as we saw in Chapter 5, this notion of extensional equivalence itself must presuppose an adequate standard of synonymity. The interrelation of the notions of extensionality, analyticity, and synonymity may make them mutually supportive, but explications in terms of one another tend to be circular. To this can be added the simple fact that differences in meaning are often noted where differences in truth function cannot be.

Intensional equivalence. Two terms are synonymous if they have the same intension. While this is certainly true, it cannot by itself provide the ground sought, since intensions require characterization. If the question is reduced to either essential, ideational, or extensional considerations, we are thrown back into the problems already mentioned. If it is treated in terms of purpose, function, or intentionality, we are confronted with the opacities discussed in the introduction to Chapter 3.

These problems do not exclude the possibility of grounding sameness of meaning in any one of these theses. They only make clear that none of them has adequately obviated the issue of what constitutes synonymity. Other theses have been put forth, and some philosophers have maintained that the search for an adequate notion of synonymity is a futile or spurious one. The understanding one arrives at may depend in part upon the consideration of a number of related issues:

What is the relation of theories of synonymity to theories of meaning? The theses about synonymity just considered are markedly similar to the theories of meaning considered in Chapter 2. If synonymous terms are considered to be equivalent in meaning, must not an understanding of synonymity presuppose an understanding of meaning? Will not an adequate theory of meaning, and only such a theory, obviate synonymity? If synonymous terms are not so considered, what alternatives are plausible?

What is the relation of interlinguistic translation to intralinguistic translation? Some differences have already been noted. Do these differences imply a difference between the notions of synonymity involved?

What is the practical value of intralinguistic synonymity? Economy of expression would seem to dictate that different terms should always make a difference. Where terms on occasion apparently have the same meaning (as 'synonymity' and 'synonymy' apparently do in this chapter), is this anything more than an unnecessary and undesirable duplexity?

Is the like meaning of synonymity better understood as similarity than as equivalence? If all that is required for synonymity is a similarity of meaning, are there degrees of synonymity? Of analyticity and of logical necessity? What does such a conception imply for adequacy of definitions?

The first two essays in this chapter, one by a professional philosopher and the other by a professional translator, state problems involved in understanding translatability. Each brings the writer's own perspective to bear upon the problems, but both recognize the need for an adequate notion of synonymity, the possibility of cultural relativity in languages, and the paucity of existing guidelines for translation. Winter formulates the issues much more complexly than Quine does, but each offers formidable challenges to the development of an adequate theory of translation.

Although Winter speaks of "impossibilities" of translation, his own evaluations of the problems set up categories that provide tools for ordering priorities in the translating enterprise. Richards surveys the components of adequate translation and offers rules for their interaction. The essays by Carnap and Quine also deal with translation, but they work upon the more simplified version of the issues as it is presented by Quine in 6.1. Both focus on the notion of synonymity and both propose a behavioristic explication of that notion, but their methods differ. Carnap pursues his analysis in terms of "the intensionalist thesis in pragmatics," testing intensions as empirical hypotheses against observation of verbal behavior rather than against previously determined extensions. By contrast, Quine treats the relation of one expression to another on the basis of "analytic hypotheses" and grounds the expressions in experience in terms of "stimulus meanings."

The remaining articles are even more centrally concerned with the notion of synonymity. Goodman surveys a number of theses and offers as a conclusion a modified version of an understanding based upon extensional equivalence. His conclusions, he maintains, imply that no exact synonymity between terms is possible except in the case of explicit identities. Mates systematically explores possible foundations for interpretation and synonymity within the limits explicated by Goodman and Quine. Pap explores the relation of synonymity to a problem about philosophical analysis. He maintains that the "paradox of analysis" can only be resolved by admitting intensional understandings of the notion of synonymity.

THE PROBLEM OF MEANING   6.1
IN LINGUISTICS

Willard Quine

I

Lexicography is concerned, or seems to be concerned, with identification of meanings, and the investigation of semantic change is concerned with change of meaning. Pending a satisfactory explanation of the notion of meaning, linguists in semantic fields are in the situation of not knowing what they are talking about. This is not an untenable situation. Ancient astronomers knew the movements of the planets remarkably well without knowing what sort of things the planets were. But it is a theoretically unsatisfactory situation, as the more theoretically minded among the linguists are painfully aware.

Confusion of meaning with reference has encouraged a tendency to take the notion of meaning for granted. It is felt

that the meaning of the word *man* is as tangible as our neighbor and that the meaning of the phrase *Evening Star* is as clear as the star in the sky. And it is felt that to question or repudiate the notion of meaning is to suppose a world in which there is just language and nothing for language to refer to. Actually, we can acknowledge a worldful of objects and let our singular and general terms refer to those objects in their several ways to our hearts' content, without ever taking up the topic of meaning.

An object referred to, named by a singular term, or denoted by a general term can be anything under the sun. Meanings, however, purport to be entities of a special sort: the meaning of an expression is the idea expressed. There is considerable agreement among modern linguists that the idea of an idea, the idea of the mental counterpart of a linquistic form, is worse than worthless for linguistic science. I think the behaviorists are right in holding that talk of ideas is bad business even for psychology. The evil of the idea is that its use, like the appeal in Molière to a *virtus dormitiva*, engenders an illusion of having explained something. And the illusion is increased by the fact that things wind up in a vague enough state to insure a certain stability, or freedom from further progress.

Let us then look back to the lexicographer, supposed as he is to be concerned with meanings, and see what he is really trafficking in, if not in mental entities. The answer is not far to seek: the lexicographer, like any linguist, studies linguistic forms. He differs from the so-called formal linguist only in that he is concerned to correlate linguistic forms with one another in his own special way, namely, synonyms with synonyms. The characteristic feature of semantical parts of linguistics, notably lexicography, comes to be not that there is an appeal to meanings, but that there is a concern with synonymy.

What happens in this maneuver is that we fix on one important context of the baffling word *meaning,* namely the context *alike in meaning*, and resolve to treat this whole context in the spirit of a single word *synonymous*, thus not being tempted to seek meanings as intermediary entities. But, even supposing that the notion of synonymy can eventually be provided with a satisfactory criterion, still this maneuver only takes care of the one context of the word *meaning*—the context *alike in meaning*. Does the word also have other contexts that should concern linguists? Yes, there is certainly one more—the context *having meaning*. Here a parallel maneuver is in order: treat the context *having meaning* in the spirit of

a single word, *significant*, and continue to turn our backs on the suppositious entities called meanings.

Significance is the trait with respect to which the subject matter of linguistics is studied by the grammarian. The grammarian catalogues short forms and works out the laws of their concatenation, and the end product of this is no more nor less than a specification of the class of all possible linguistic forms, simple and composite, of the language under investigation—the class of all significant sequences, if we accept a liberal standard of significance. The lexicographer, on the other hand, is concerned not with specifying the class of significant sequences for the given language, but rather with specifying the class of pairs of mutually synonymous sequences for the given language or, perhaps, pair of languages. The grammarian and the lexicographer are concerned with meaning to an equal degree, be it zero or otherwise; the grammarian wants to know what forms are significant, or *have* meaning, while the lexicographer wants to know what forms are synonymous, or *alike* in meaning. If it is urged that the grammarian's notion of significant sequences should not be viewed as resting on a prior notion of meaning, I applaud; and I say the lexicographer's notion of synonymy is entitled to the same compliment. What had been the problem of meaning boils down now to a pair of problems in which meaning is best not mentioned; one is the problem of making sense of the notion of significant sequence, and the other is the problem of making sense of the notion of synonymy. What

I want to emphasize is that the lexicographer had no monopoly on the problem of meaning. The problem of significant sequence and the problem of synonymy are twin offspring of the problem of meaning.

II

Let us suppose that our grammarian is at work on a hitherto unstudied language and that his own contact with the language has been limited to his field work. As grammarian he is concerned to discover the bounds of the class K of significant sequences of the language. Synonymy correlations of members of K with English sequences and with one another are not his business; they are the business of the lexicographer.

There is presumably no upper limit to the lengths of members of K. Moreover, parts of significant sequences count as significant, down to the smallest adopted units of analysis; so such units, whatever they are, are the shortest members of K. Besides the length dimension, however, there is a dimension of thickness to consider. For, given two utterances of equal and arbitrary length and fairly similar acoustical make-up, we must know whether to count them as occurrences of two slightly different members of K or as two slightly different occurrences of one and the same member of K. The question of thickness is the question what acoustical differences to count as relevant and what ones to count merely as inconsequential idiosyncrasies of voice and accent.

The question of thickness is settled by cataloguing the *phonemes*—the single sounds, distinguished as coarsely as possible for purposes of the language. Two subtly differing sounds count as the same phoneme unless it is possible, by putting one for the other in some utterance, to change the meaning of the utterance.[1] Now the notion of phoneme, thus formulated, depends obviously and notoriously on the notion of sameness of meaning, or synonymy. Our grammarian, if he is to remain pure grammarian and eschew lexicography, must carry out his program of delimiting K without the help of a notion of phoneme so defined.

There seems indeed, at first glance, to be an easy way out: he can simply enumerate the phonemes needed for the particular language at hand and dispense with the general notion of phoneme defined in terms of synonymy. This expedient would be quite admissible as a mere technical aid to solving the grammarian's problem of specifying the membership of K if the problem of specifying the membership of K could itself be *posed* without prior appeal to the general notion of phoneme. But the fact is otherwise. The class K, which is the grammarian's empirical business to describe, is a class of sequences of phonemes, and each phoneme is a class of brief events. (It will be convenient to swallow this much Platonism for present purposes, though some logical maneuvers might serve to reduce it.) The grammarian's problem

---

[1] Cf. Bloch and Trager, pp. 38–52, or Bloomfield, pp. 74–92.

is in part objectively set for him thus: every speech event which he encounters in his field work counts as a sample of a member of K. But the delimiting of the several members of K, that is, the grouping of mutually resemblant acoustical histories into bundles of proper thickness to qualify as linguistic forms, needs also to have some objective significance if the task of the field grammarian is to be made sense of as an empirical and objective task at all. This need is fulfilled if the general notion of phoneme is at hand, as a general relative term: "x is a phoneme for language L," with variable x and L, or "x is a phoneme for speaker s," with variable x and s. Thereupon the grammarian's business, with respect to a language L, can be stated as the business of finding what sequences of phonemes of L are significant for L. Statement of the grammarian's purpose thus depends not only on *significant*, as we had been prepared to expect, but also on *phoneme*.

But we might still seek to free grammar of dependence on the notion of synonymy, by somehow freeing the notion of phoneme itself of such dependence. It has been conjectured, for example, by Bühler, that this might in principle be accomplished. Let the continuum of sounds be arranged in acoustical or physiological order in one or more dimensions, say two, and plotted against frequency of occurrence, so that we come out with a three-dimensional relief map in which altitude represents frequency of occurrence. Then it is suggested that the major humps correspond to the phonemes. There are abundant reasons to suspect

that neither this oversimplified account nor anything remotely resembling it can possibly provide an adequate definition of the phoneme; and phonologists have not neglected to adduce such reasons. As a means of isolating other points of comparison between grammar and lexicography, however, let us make the unrealistic assumption that our grammarian has some such nonsemantical definition of phoneme. Then his remaining task is to devise a recursive description of a class K of forms which will comprise all and only those sequences of phonemes which are in fact significant.

The basic point of view is that the class K is objectively determinate before the grammatical research is begun; it is the class of the significant sequences, the sequences capable of occurring in the normal stream of speech (supposing for the moment that this terminology is itself significant). But the grammarian wants to reproduce this same class in other terms, formal terms; he wants to devise, in terms of elaborate conditions of phoneme succession alone, a necessary and sufficient condition for membership in K. He is an empirical scientist, and his result will be right or wrong according as he reproduces that objectively predetermined class K or some other.

Our grammarian's attempted recursive specification of K will follow the orthodox line, we may suppose, of listing *morphemes* and describing constructions. Morphemes, according to the books,[2] are the significant forms

---

[2] Bloch and Trager, p. 54; Bloomfield, pp. 161–68.

which are not resoluble into shorter significant forms. They comprise affixes, word stems, and whole words insofar as these are not analyzable into subsidiary morphemes. But we can spare our grammarian any general problem of defining morpheme by allowing him simply to list his so-called morphemes exhaustively. They become simply a convenient segmentation of heard phoneme sequences, chopped out as convenient building blocks for his purpose. He frames his constructions in the simplest way that will enable him to generate all members of K from his morphemes, and he cuts his morphemes to allow for the simplest constructions. Morphemes, like higher units such as might be called words or free forms, may thus be viewed simply as intermediate stages in a process which, over-all, is still describable as reproduction of K in terms of conditions of phoneme succession.

There is no denying that the grammarian's reproduction of K, as I have schematized it, is purely formal, that is, free of semantics. But the setting of the grammarian's problem is quite another matter, for it turns on a prior notion of significant sequence, or possible normal utterance. Without this notion, or something to somewhat the same effect, we cannot say what the grammarian is trying to do—what he is trying to match in his formal reproduction of K—nor wherein the rightness or wrongness of his results might consist. We are thus squarely confronted with one of the twin offspring of the problem of meaning, namely, the problem of defining the general notion of significant sequence.

III

It is not satisfactory to say that a significant sequence is simply any sequence of phonemes uttered by any of the *Naturkinder* of our grammarian's chosen valley. What are wanted as significant sequences include not just those uttered but also those which *could* be uttered without reactions suggesting bizarreness of idiom. The joker here is *could*; we cannot substitute *will*. The significant sequences, being subject to no length limit, are infinite in variety; whereas, from the dawn of the language under investigation to the time when it will have evolved to the point where our grammarian would disown it, only a finite sample of this infinite manifold will have been uttered.

The desired class K of significant sequences is the culmination of a series of four classes of increasing magnitude, H, I, J, and K, as follows. H is the class of observed sequences, excluding any which are ruled inappropriate in the sense of being nonlinguistic or belonging to alien dialects. I is the class of all such observed sequences and all that ever will happen to be professionally observed, excluding again those which are ruled inappropriate. J is the class of all sequences ever occurring, now or in the past or future, within or without professional observation—excluding, again, only those which are ruled inappropriate. K, finally, is the infinite class of all those sequences, with exclusion of the inappropriate ones as usual, which *could* be uttered without bizarreness reactions. K is the class which the grammarian wants to approximate in his formal reconstruction, and K is more inclusive even than J, let alone H and I. Now the class H is a matter of finished record; the class I is, or could be, a matter of growing record; the class J goes beyond any record, but still has a certain common-sense reality; but not even this can very confidently be said of K, because of the *could*.

I expect we must leave the *could* unreduced. It has some operational import, indeed, but only in a partial way. It does require our grammarian to bring into his formal reconstruction of K all of the actually observed cases, that is, all of H. Further, it commits him to the prediction that all cases to be observed in the future will conform, that is, all of I belongs in K. Further still, it commits him to the scientific hypothesis that all unobserved cases fall in this K, that is, all of J. Now what more does the *could* cover? What is the rationale behind that infinite additional membership of K, over and above the finite part J? This vast supplementary force of *could*, in the present instance and elsewhere, is perhaps a vestige of Indo-European myth, fossilized in the subjunctive mood.

What our grammarian does is evident enough. He frames his formal reconstruction of K along the grammatically simplest lines he can, compatibly with inclusion of H, plausibility of the predicted inclusion of I, plausibility of the hypothesis of inclusion of J, and plausibility, further, of the exclusion of all sequences which ever actually do bring bizarreness reactions. Our basis for saying what *could* be generally consists, I suggest, in what *is* plus *simplicity* of

the laws whereby we describe and extrapolate what is. I see no more objective way of construing the *conditio irrealis*.

Concerning the notion of significant sequence, one of the two survivals of the notion of meaning, we have now observed the following. It is needed in setting the grammarian's task. But it is describable, without appeal to meanings as such, as denoting any sequence which could be uttered in the society under consideration without reactions suggesting bizarreness of idiom. This notion of a reaction suggesting bizarreness of idiom would want some refinement eventually. A considerable problem of refinement is involved also in the preliminary putting aside of so-called "nonlinguistic noises," as well as utterances in alien dialects. Also there is the general methodological problem, of a pretty philosophical kind, which is raised by the word *could*. This is a problem common to concept-building in most subjects (apart from logic and mathematics, where it happens to be well cleared up); I have outlined one attitude toward it.

We should also remind ourselves of the oversimplification that I made with regard to morphemes when I treated them merely as convenient phoneme sequences which our grammarian specifies by enumeration in the course of his formal reconstruction of the class of significant sequences from the phonemes. This is unrealistic because it requires our grammarian to exhaust the vocabulary instead of allowing him to leave certain open categories, comparable to our nouns and verbs, subject to enrichment *ad libitum*. If, on the other hand, we allow him some open morpheme categories, his reconstruction of the class K of significant sequences ceases to be a formal construction from phonemes; the most we can say for it is that it is a formal reconstruction from phonemes and his open morpheme categories. So the problem remains how he is going to characterize his open morpheme categories—since enumeration no longer serves. This gap must be watched for possible intrusion of an unanalyzed semantical element.

I do not want to take leave of the topic of significant sequence without mentioning one curious further problem which the notion raises. I shall speak now of English rather than a hypothetical heathen tongue. Any nonsensical and thoroughly un-English string of sounds can occur within a perfectly intelligible English sentence, even a true one, if, in effect, we quote the nonsense and say in the rest of our sentence that the quoted matter *is* nonsense or is not English or consists of four syllables or rimes with "Kalamazoo." If the whole inclusive sentence is to be called normal English speech, then the rubbish inside it has occurred in normal English speech, and we have thus lost the means of excluding any pronounceable sequence from the category of significant sequence. Thus we must either narrow our concept of normality to exclude, for present purposes, sentences which use quotation, or else we must narrow our concept of occurrence to exclude occurrence within quotation. In either event, we have the problem of identifying the spoken analogue of quotation marks and of doing so in general enough terms so that our concept of significant sequence will not be limited in advance to some one preconceived language such as English.

In any case, we have seen that the problem of significant sequence admits of considerable fragmentation; and this is one of the two aspects into which the problem of meaning seemed to resolve, namely, the aspect of the having of meaning. The fact that this aspect of the problem of meaning is in such halfway tolerable shape accounts, no doubt, for the tendency to think of grammar as a formal, nonsemantical part of linguistics. Let us turn now to the other and more forbidding aspect of the problem of meaning, that of likeness in meaning, or synonymy.

IV

A lexicographer may be concerned with synonymy between forms in one language and forms in another, or, as in compiling a domestic dictionary, he may be concerned with synonymy between forms in the same language. It is an open question how satisfactorily the two cases can be subsumed under a single general formulation of the synonymy concept, for it is an open question whether the synonymy concept can be satisfactorily clarified for either case. Let us first limit our attention to synonymy within a language.

So-called substitution criteria, or conditions of interchangeability, have in one form or another played central roles in modern grammar. For the synonymy problem of semantics such an approach seems more obvious still. However, the notion of the interchangeability of two linguistic forms makes sense only insofar as answers are provided to these two questions: (a) In just what sorts of contextual position, if not in all, are the two forms to be interchangeable? (b) The forms are to be interchangeable *salvo quo?* Supplanting one form by another in any context changes something, namely, form at least; and (b) asks what feature the interchange is to leave invariant. Alternative answers to (a) and (b) give alternative notions of interchangeability, some suited to defining grammatical correspondences and others, conceivably, to defining synonymy.

In another essay[3] we tried answering (b), for purposes of synonymy, with *veritate.* We found that something had still to be done about (a), in view, for example, of the difficulty presented by quotation. So we answered (a), lamely appealing to a prior conception of *word.* Then we found that interchangeability *salva veritate* was too weak a condition for synonymy if the language as a whole was *extensional* and that in other languages it was an unilluminating condition, involving something like a vicious circle.

It is not clear that the problem of synonymy discussed in those pages is the same as the lexicographer's problem. For in those pages we were concerned with *cognitive* synonymy, which abstracts from much that the lexicographer would want to preserve in his translations and paraphrases. Even the lexicographer is indeed ready

---

³ "Two Dogmas of Empiricism," *Phil. Review*, LX (1951), 20–43.

to equate, as synonymous, many forms which differ perceptibly in imaginative associations and poetic value; but the optimum sense of synonymy for his purpose is probably narrower than synonymy in the supposed cognitive sense. However this may be, certainly the negative findings which were summed up in the preceding paragraph carry over; the lexicographer cannot answer (b) with *veritate.* The interchangeability which he seeks in synonymy must not merely be such as to assure that true statements remain true, and false ones false, when synonyms are substituted within them; it must assure further that statements go over into statements with which they as wholes are somehow synonymous.

This last observation does not recommend itself as a definition because of its circularity—forms are synonymous when their interchange leaves their contexts synonymous. But it has the virtue of hinting that substitution is not the main point and that what we need in the first place is some notion of synonymy for long segments of discourse. The hint is opportune; for, independently of the foregoing considerations, three reasons can be adduced for approaching the problem of synonymy from the point of view of long segments of discourse.

First, any interchangeability criterion for synonymy of short forms would obviously be limited to synonymy within a language; otherwise interchange would produce polyglot jumbles. *Inter*linguistic synonymy must be a relation, primarily, between segments of discourse which are long enough to bear consideration in abstraction from a containing context peculiar to one or the other particular language. I say "primarily" because interlinguistic synonymy might indeed be defined for the component forms afterward in some derivative way.

Second, a retreat to longer segments tends to overcome the difficulty of ambiguity or homonymy. Homonymy gets in the way of the law that if *a* is synonymous with *b* and *b* with *c*, then *a* is synonymous with *c*. For, if *b* has two meanings (to revert to the ordinary parlance of meanings), *a* may be synonymous with *b* in one sense of *b* and *b* with *c* in the other sense of *b*. This difficulty is sometimes dealt with by treating an ambiguous form as two forms, but this expedient has the drawback of making the concept of form depend on that of synonymy.

Third, there is the circumstance that in glossing a word we have so frequently to content ourselves with a lame partial synonym plus stage directions. Thus in glossing *addled* we say *spoiled* and add *said of an egg*. This widespread circumstance reflects the fact that synonymy in the small is no primary concern of the lexicographer; lame synonyms plus stage directions are quite satisfactory insofar as they expedite his primary business of explaining how to translate or paraphrase long speeches. We may continue to characterize the lexicographer's domain squarely as synonymy, but only by recognizing synonymy as primarily a relation of sufficiently long segments of discourse.

So we may view the lexicographer as interested, ultimately, only in cataloguing synonym pairs which are sequences of sufficient length to admit of synonymy in some primary sense. Naturally he cannot catalogue these true synonym pairs directly, in any exhaustive way, because they are altogether limitless in number and variety. His case is parallel to that of the grammarian, who for the same reason was unable to catalogue the significant sequences directly. The grammarian accomplished his end indirectly, by fixing on a class of atomic units capable of enumeration and then propounding rules for compounding them to get all significant sequences. Similarly, the lexicographer accomplishes his end indirectly—the end of specifying the infinitely numerous genuine pairs of long synonyms; and this he does by fixing on a class of short forms capable of enumeration and then explaining as systematically as he can how to construct genuine synonyms for all sufficiently long forms compounded of those short ones. These short forms are in effect the word entries in his glossary, and the explanations of how to construct genuine synonyms of all sufficiently long compounds are what appear as the glosses in his glossary, typically a mixture of quasi-synonyms and stage directions.

Thus the lexicographer's actual activity, his glossing of short forms by appeal to quasi-synonyms and stage directions, is not antithetical to his being concerned purely and simply with genuine synonymy on the part of forms sufficiently long to admit of genuine synonymy. Something like his actual activity is indeed the only possible way of cataloguing, in effect, the limitless class of pairs of genuinely synonymous longer forms.

I exploited just now a parallelism between the grammarian's indirect reconstruction of the limitless class of significant sequences and the lexicographer's indirect reconstruction of the limitless class of genuine synonym pairs. This parallelism bears further exploiting. It brings out that the lexicographer's reconstruction of the class of synonym pairs is just as formal in spirit as the grammarian's reconstruction of the class of significant sequences. The invidious use of the word *formal*, to favor grammar as against lexicography, is thus misleading. Both the lexicographer and the grammarian would simply list the membership of the respective classes in which they are interested, were it not for the vastness, the infinitude even, of the numbers involved. On the other hand, just as the grammarian needs, over and above his formal constructions, a prior notion of significant sequence for the setting of his problem, so the lexicographer needs a prior notion of synonymity for the setting of his. In the setting of their problems, the grammarian and the lexicographer draw equally on our heritage from the old notion of meaning.

It is clear from the foregoing reflections that the notion of synonymy needed in the statement of the lexicographer's problem is synonymy only as between sequences which are long enough to be pretty clean-cut about their synonymy connections. But in conclusion I want to stress what a baffling problem this remaining prob-

lem of synonymy, even relatively clean-cut and well-behaved synonymy, is.

V

Synonymy of two forms is supposed vaguely to consist in an approximate likeness in the situations which evoke the two forms and an approximate likeness in the effect of either form on the hearer. For simplicity let us forget this second requirement and concentrate on the first—the likeness of situations. What I have to say from here on will be so vague, at best, that this further inaccuracy will not much matter.

As everyone is quick to point out, no two situations are quite alike; situations in which even the same form is uttered are unlike in myriad ways. What matters rather is likeness in *relevant respects*. Now the problem of finding the relevant respects is, if we think of the matter in a sufficiently oversimplified way, a problem typical of empirical science. We observe a speaker of Kalaba, say—to adopt Pike's myth —and we look for correlations or so-called causal connections between the noises he makes and the other things that are observed to be happening. As in any empirical search for correlations or so-called causal connections, we guess at the relevance of one or another feature and then try by further observation, or even experiment, to confirm or refute our hypothesis. Actually, in lexicography this guessing at possible relevances is expedited by our natural familiarity with the basic lines of human interest. Finally, having found fair evidence for correlating a given Kalaba sound sequence with a given combination of circumstances, we conjecture synonymy of that sound sequence with another, in English, say, which is correlated with the same circumstances.

As I unnecessarily remarked, this account is oversimplified. Now I want to stress one serious respect in which it is oversimplified: the relevant features of the situation issuing in a given Kalaba utterance are in large part concealed in the person of the speaker, where they were implanted by his earlier environment. This concealment is partly good, for our purposes, and partly bad. It is good insofar as it isolates the subject's narrowly linguistic training. If we could assume that our Kalaba speaker and our English speaker, when observed in like external situations, differed only in how they say things and not in *what* they say, so to speak, then the methodology of synonymy determinations would be pretty smooth; the narrowly linguistic part of the causal complex, different for the two speakers, would be conveniently out of sight, while all the parts of the causal complex decisive of synonymy or heteronymy were open to observation. But of course the trouble is that not only the narrowly linguistic habits of vocabulary and syntax are imported by each speaker from his unknown past.

The difficulty here is not just that those subjective components of the situation are hard to ferret out. This difficulty, if it were all, would make for practical uncertainty and frequent error in lexicographical pronouncements, but it would be irrelevant to the problem of a theoretical definition of synonymy—irrelevant, that is, to the problem of coherently stating the lexicographer's purpose. Theoretically, the more important difficulty is that, as Cassirer and Whorf have stressed, there is in principle no separating language from the rest of the world, at least as conceived by the speaker. Basic differences in language are bound up, as likely as not, with differences in the way in which the speakers articulate the world itself into things and properties, time and space, elements, forces, spirits, and so on. It is not clear even in principle that it makes sense to think of words and syntax as varying from language to language while the content stays fixed; yet precisely this fiction is involved in speaking of synonymy, at least as between expressions of radically different languages.

What provides the lexicographer with an entering wedge is the fact that there are many basic features of men's ways of conceptualizing their environment, of breaking the world down into things common to all cultures. Every man is likely to see an apple or breadfruit or rabbit first and foremost as a unitary whole rather than as a congeries of smaller units or as a fragment of a larger environment, although from a sophisticated point of view all these attitudes are tenable. Every man will tend to segregate a mass of moving matter as a unit, separate from the static background, and to pay it particular attention. Again, there are conspicuous phenomena of weather which one man may be expected to endow with much the same conceptual boundaries as another and, similarly, some basic internal states such as hunger. As long as we adhere to this presumably common fund of conceptualization, we can successfully proceed on the working assumption that our Kalaba speaker and our English speaker, observed in like external situations, differ only in how they say things and not in what they say.

The nature of this entering wedge into a strange lexicon encourages the misconception of meaning as reference, since words at this stage are construed, typically, by pointing to the object referred to. So it may not be amiss to remind ourselves that meaning is not reference even here. The reference might be the Evening Star, to return to Frege's example, and hence also the Morning Star, which is the same thing; but *Evening Star* might nevertheless be a good translation and *Morning Star* a bad one.

I have suggested that our lexicographer's obvious first moves in picking up some initial Kalaba vocabulary are at bottom a matter of exploiting the overlap of our cultures. From this nucleus he works outward, ever more fallibly and conjecturally, by a series of clues and hunches. Thus he begins with a fund of correlations of Kalaba sentences with English sentences at the level where our cultures meet. Most of these sentences classify conspicuously segregated objects. Then he breaks these Kalaba sentences down into short component elements and makes tentative English translations of these elements, compatible with his initial sentence translations. On this basis, he frames hypotheses as to the English translations of new combinations of those elements—combinations which as wholes have not been translated in the direct way. He tests his hypotheses as best he can by making further observations and keeping an eye out for conflicts. But, as the sentences undergoing translation get further and further from mere reports of common observations, the clarity of any possible conflict decreases; the lexicographer comes to depend increasingly on a projection of himself, with his Indo-European *Weltanschauung*, into the sandals of his Kalaba informant. He comes also to turn increasingly to that last refuge of all scientists, the appeal to internal simplicity of his growing system.

The finished lexicon is a case, evidently, of *ex pede Herculem*. But there is a difference. In projecting Hercules from the foot we risk error, but we may derive comfort from the fact that there is something to be wrong about. In the case of the lexicon, pending some definition of synonymy, we have no statement of the problem; we have nothing for the lexicographer to be right or wrong about.

Quite possibly the ultimately fruitful notion of synonymy will be one of degree: not the dyadic relation of a as synonymous with b, but the tetradic relation of a as more synonymous with b than c with d. But to classify the notion as a matter of degree is not to explain it; we shall still want a criterion or at least a definition for our tetradic relation. The big difficulty to be surmounted in devising a definition, whether of a dyadic relation of absolute synonymy or a tetradic relation of comparative synonymy, is the difficulty of making up our minds as to just what we are trying to do when we translate a Kalaba statement which is not a mere report on fairly directly observable features of the surrounding situation.

The other branch of the problem of meaning, namely the problem of defining significant sequence, led us into a contrary-to-fact conditional: a significant sequence is one that *could* be uttered without such and such adverse reactions. I urged that the operational content of this *could* is incomplete, leaving scope for free supplementary determinations of a grammatical theory in the light of simplicity considerations. But we are well schooled in acquiescing in contrary-to-fact conditionals. In the case of synonymy the tyranny of the developing system, the paucity of explicit objective controls, is more conspicuous.

IMPOSSIBILITIES   6.2
OF TRANSLATION

Werner Winter

It seems to me that we may compare the work of a translator with that of an artist who is asked to create an exact replica of a marble statue, but who cannot secure any marble. He may find some other stone or some wood, or he may have to model in clay or work in bronze, or he may have to use a brush or a pencil and a sheet of paper. Whatever his material, if he is a good crafts-

From *The Craft and Context of Translation,* Roger Shattuck and William Arrowsmith, editors (Austin: University of Texas Press, 1961). Reprinted by permission of The Humanities Research Center, the publishers, and the author.

man, his work may be good or even great; it may indeed surpass the original, but it will never be what he set out to produce, an exact replica of the original.

In a nutshell, we seem to have here all the challenge and all the frustration that goes with our endeavors to do the ultimately impossible. We know from the outset that we are doomed to fail; but we have the chance, the great opportunity to fail in a manner that has its own splendor and its own promise.

What I propose to do is to present a linguist's views and reflections on the reasons why the translator must necessarily despair of achieving a completely faithful rendering of his original. Of necessity, I have to concern myself not with the delicate artistic aspects of translation, which, as I take it, reflect above all an individual's selections from the raw material of the languages at his disposal, but rather with the most general problems of transfer from one language to another. It is the background to the translator's endeavors in which I am primarily interested; but it seems to me that such an interest is essential for any attempt to objectify one's reactions to the results of a translator's work—whether this translator happens to be a stranger or oneself.

To translate is to replace the formulation of one interpretation of a segment of the universe around us and within us by another formulation as equivalent as possible. We speak of translation even within the framework of one single language in the case of stylistic shifts, for instance, when we find ourselves asked to make plain and intelligible a highly esoteric statement we have just made. This use of the term is, however, rather marginal, even though the basic characteristics of the process are all present. As a rule, we may inject into our definition the further qualification that translation involves the replacement of an interpretation in one language by another in a second language.

I do not want to devote much time to statements about languages and Language in general, but it is important for the course of our deliberations that we keep a few essential points in mind. *Languages are systems of arbitrarily selected, but conventionalized, signs which serve to convey arbitrarily*

selected, but conventionalized, meanings. We want to note several things at this moment. One, sign and meaning cannot be dissociated from one another; an utterance, a sound or a sequence of sounds, is part of a language only if it is employed in signaling a reference to something different in substance from the mere physical utterance; a meaning does not exist in itself, but only insofar as it becomes manifest in a linguistic feature. Second, signs and what they stand for owe their existence to arbitrary selection and their preservation to conventionalization of this selection; the arbitrary origin makes for almost unlimited diversity in languages, a diversity which is reduced only when languages are related to one another in a broad historical sense, covering both genetic and contact relationships. Third, no sign and no meaning exists by itself, but only as part of a system.

The next point we have to make seems utterly trivial. While languages may be similar to each other, they are never identical. If we insert what we just said about languages in general, we can expand this trivial statement into something more meaningful: The system of form and meaning in language A may be similar to that in language B, but is never identical with it.

This statement has a very simple, yet very important corollary: *There is no completely exact translation.* If an interpretation of reality as formulated in language A does not exist in any isolation, but only as part of the system total of this language, then its correlative in language B cannot be isolated from the overall system of B, which must be different from that of A.

There is no completely exact translation. There are only approximations, and the degree of similarity possible between original and translation depends on the degree of similarity between the systems of form and meaning in the two languages involved. The more serious the deviations from one language to the other, the less of the original can be salvaged in the process of transfer.

To be sure, there are partial exceptions to this. One-to-one correspondences are possible as long as one confines oneself to utterances of limited size outside a larger context (the rendering of an English cry *Fire!* by German *Feuer!* would be a fairly good example), but this observation does not invalidate the overall statement.

However, it may be asked: Is it not possible to convey in a second language completely, without omission or addition, the CONTENT of a statement in the original language—even if one has to grant that the formal properties of the two utterances have to be different? Isn't it the same thing whether we express a certain semantic unit by *father* or *Vater* or *père?*

The answer must be No. Meaning and form, as I have already pointed out, cannot be dissociated from one another. So if forms differ, *a priori*, semantic equivalence cannot be expected. Let me illustrate.

Take first the result of the multiplication process 3 × 30 in a number of closely related languages. In English, the numeral used would be *ninety*, with formal indication that the semantic unit 90 is to be analyzed as 'nine decadic units'. When we turn to

Russian *devianosto*, the form suggests a very similar, but not identical interpretation, *viz.*, 'nine decadic units, one unit away from one hundred' (*deviat'* being 'nine', *sto*—'one hundred'). French *quatre-vingt-dix* requires a quite different analysis, namely, 'four score and ten', and Danish *halfems*, finally, has to be paraphrased as 'half of the fifth score', with the type of elliptic formulation as found in German *anderthalb* 'half of the second' = 'one and one-half'.

We clearly observe two systems of semantic organization of the field of numerals and two variants of each of the systems. Taken in isolation, *ninety* may appear to be the perfect match of *quatre-vingt-dix*, but in the context of their respective systems, the two forms signal two different semantic configurations. That the equivalents of the linguistic items in the world of reality seem to be identical here is not of crucial importance; what matters for our understanding of language is the interpretation of reality, not reality itself. *Three-score years and ten* and *seventy years* cover identical time spans; but linguistically, the two formulations are different, and it is no wonder that they can readily be used for quite different communicative purposes: the one, *seventy years*, as a flat, colorless, matter-of-fact statement, the other, with its unmistakable biblical ring (cf. Ps. 90. 10), for solemn oratory.

Still, we may want to grant linguistic diversity and yet continue to insist that the agreement in the use of the linguistic units is so great as to make the difference negligible. For the examples cited, one can hardly deny that the gain or loss in the transfer is minute. However, if we proceed to other cases, we will find that the differences may take on quite forbidding proportions.

I mentioned before the example of apparent semantic equivalence of *father : Vater : père* 'genitor.' The natural logic of such a term and such a notion strikes us as inevitable. A living being has to have a father, the relationship father : mother : child is provided for in nature. Nonetheless, if one goes out to western Arizona and asks speakers of Mohave for their equivalent of English *father*, one will get not one term, but two—not stylistic variants of the type of *father* and *dad*, but mutually exclusive, contrasting terms. One of them can be paraphrased 'father of male referent', the other, 'father of female referent.' Clearly, there is no difference between the biological facts of the father-child relationship in Parker, Arizona, and in Austin, Texas; yet the linguistic interpretation of this relationship is totally different, and a translation without loss or addition is not possible.

Thus not even 'basic notions', central points in a human sphere of experience, stand outside the area of arbitrary segmentation and arrangement and subsequent conventionalization; and the extent to which semantic boundaries as determined by linguistic form and linguistic usage coincide with absolute boundaries in the world around us is negligible. It is interesting to note in passing that all attempts to compile lists of semantic entities supposedly universally valid have had the same fate; they had to be reduced constantly in the light of new data which showed that even the most elementary assessments of natural phenomena were not conditioned by the phenomena, but by the language which served to make these assessments.

It would be easy enough to document this claim that virtually no 'natural' semantic units are confirmed by the sum total of linguistic data. For our purposes, a few more examples will suffice.

For instance, the spectrum of colors is not divided up in any 'natural', consistent way by speakers of different languages. *We* would never hesitate to affirm the importance of the difference between 'green' and 'blue'—whereas the Yuman languages (of which Mohave is one), although otherwise employing a set of basic color terms very similar in application to our own, do not have separate forms to indicate these two colors, and consequently do not have separate meanings 'blue' and 'green' (though speakers of these languages will note the physical difference between a dark blue and a light green without hesitation).

For us, 'grey' is a unified meaning field, whether the word is applied to the color of a wall or a person's hair; Russian has two different terms and therefore two meanings correspond to our one. For us, 'high' and 'low' are 'natural' categories; *mons altus* and *mare altum* indicate that we cannot say the same for the Romans. 'Round' we apply to a ball or a hoop without further differentiation; in Yuman languages, the two terms used in this connection have nothing in common with each other except possibly a feature of reduplication.

And these examples could be multiplied, but the point is clear already. Even the simplest, most basic requirement we make of translation cannot be met without difficulty: one cannot always match the content of a message in language A by an expression with exactly the same content in language B, because what can be expressed and what must be expressed is a property of a specific language in much the same way as *how* it can be expressed. It is only so that the area of agreement in the analysis of the world around us is usually very much greater than the area of agreement in the formal expression of this analysis. As a result, we get the impression only too easily that the content of the original message can always be transmitted in the second language.

What we have touched upon so far is only one aspect of meaning, and in many ways the least complex aspect. We have been concerned only with the immediate, denotative meaning of the original utterance and the problem of its transfer into the other language. It is, however, rather the exception than the rule that a specific form evokes only one precise meaning in isolation. We know very little about the organization of meaning structures and their storage in the human mind. There are, however, strong indications that we can get a fairly reasonable picture of this unknown reality by assuming that in the human memory bits of meaning are associated with other related bits, and not stored in a random fashion. We find, for instance, that when one particular linguistic item is called for, another one will simultaneously be 'pulled out'—if this simile is permissible—causing frequent formal distor-

tions; and that this item or these items 'pulled' by mistake are related semantically to the item wanted. Such an interpretation of what seems to happen accounts very simply for developments such as Vulgar Latin *grevis* 'heavy' in lieu of the usual Latin *gravis*—*grevis* owing its—*e*—to interference from *levis* 'light'.

This peculiarity of semantic storage, in which the term 'related item' would cover a wide variety of classes, likewise seems to be in its specific form, a property of every individual language and not of Language in general. The range of items evoked by meaning association will therefore vary from language to language. A German item *älter* is associated with both *jünger* and *neuer*; so is English *older* with *younger* and *newer*; but English *elder*, another correlative of German *älter*, does not pair with *newer*, nor does Latin *senior* seem to be associated with *novior*.

There are indications that such alignment of a semantic unit with others in the semantic structure is rarely unique. The criterion of phonological interference which we have met with *gravis* becoming *grevis* beside *levis*, allows us to conclude that such a word as 'second' in Sanskrit is associated equally with the word for 'two' and the word for 'third'. For other semantic units, the affiliation with certain subgroups of meaning may be much more complex.

The meaning of a form conditions, and is conditioned by, its occurrence. Memory storage apparently includes not only information about related semantic bits, but also information about the occurrence, the distribution of a form in previous utterances of the same language. In a very primitive sense, such stored information allows us to use linguistic forms in a grammatically correct, or 'established' way. In a more sophisticated sense, this type of stored information permits us to grasp the total semantic field of the item chosen.

Special types of such distributional information are familiar to all of us. When we say that a particular word has certain undesirable connotations, this means that we remember, perhaps in a very loose sense, a context in which this word was used, say, in a rude or overly slangy fashion. Or when we note that a given word evokes certain literary reminiscences, this indicates that apart from the mere meaning information we remember distributional facts of a very special sort.

Both classes of semantic association seem to be basic properties of languages. But again, the exact arrangements and groupings within these classes appear to be strictly structural characteristics of each individual language. A transfer from one language to another of the sum total of what is usually—though none too aptly—called 'connotative meaning' is an even more hopeless task than the transfer of plain, straightforward denotative meaning. As a result, the degree of difficulty in approximating the content of the original increases with the relative importance that connotative meaning properties possess in the text to be translated. When we deal with a scientific treatise, (which is—or should be—as free as possible from all recourse to allusion, subtle reference, *double-entendre*, etc.), a fairly satisfactory matching of the *semantic* content

can usually be achieved. On the other hand, a lyrical poem or a critical essay full of hidden pointers to data known to the educated native reader, may present insurmountable problems. It is certainly no chance development that plans for mechanical translation tend to be limited entirely to the field of scientific prose. I doubt that the considerations of practical usefulness are, in a final analysis, crucial; rather it seems to me that what appears to be wise restraint is due to the insight that the task of teaching a machine to absorb the immense range of ramifications of connotative meanings in one language and then to convert that into an equally immense variety of such meanings in the other, is a task which cannot even be considered at this moment. After all, it is in this area of understanding connotative meaning that even the most capable of translation 'machines'—the mind of the human near-bilingual—fails most miserably.

Up to this point, we have been concerned only with problems of meaning and organization of meaning. We will now turn to a brief discussion of matters of form.

We know that the area of formal agreement between two languages is sometimes, in the case of closely related languages, fairly large, but much more often it is discouragingly small. Innumerable problems arise for the translator who wants to preserve essential formal patterns of the original and to avoid inappropriate patterns of the replica language. There must be a vast array of stories about such labors. I have always particularly liked the story told me by Kenneth Pike.

A missionary, brought up in the tradition of down-to-earth, up-to-date, close-to-the-people sermon topics had his words translated to an attentive audience by a very competent native interpreter. He noticed that his helper, who had started out with great vigor and persuasiveness, began to halt and hesitate until he finally turned to the missionary and declared: 'I am most sorry, but I cannot translate what you say.' The missionary's topic had been announced as: 'God's Navy', and there were three parts to the sermon, one discussing Fellowship, one Stewardship, and the third another ship whose name slips my mind.

Or there is the other story about the formidable difficulties to be overcome in the teaching of the doctrine of the Trinity to speakers of Arabic, since the words in Arabic for Father and Son are properly masculine, but the word for Holy Ghost is feminine.

But the problems of replacing formal properties of the original by something at least roughly equivalent are constantly present in the translator's work. Decisions must be made as to what to sacrifice, what to preserve. The matter of the role of sound as a musical and secondarily symbolic factor comes to mind; the matter of word length, of choice from various syntactic alternatives. To select a single example, the morphological clarity of Greek and Latin allows for great flexibility in word order. This in turn permits the use of complicated metrical patterns with relative ease and the introduction of stylistic devices such as the chiasm. One important characteristic of Latin poetry is split constructions which create an effect similar to that of retardation and resolution in music, and which one might call suspension. A good example:

Aequam memento rebus in arduis
servare mentem.

This string cannot be cut off at any point before the close of the line, and a very strong impression of controlled compactness is achieved for the entire sentence. A language without the formal properties of Latin or, for that matter, Greek or Russian, cannot match this suspension effect. When a writer like Hölderlin tries to do it in German we get a stanza like this:

Nun! sei in deinem Abel, mein
Vaterland
mit neuem Namen, reifeste Frucht
der Zeit!
Du letzte und du erste-aller
Musen, Urania! sei gegrüsst mir!

By so doing, he seems to me to overtax the potential of the German language and to achieve only a rather poor quasi-classical effect without real poetic weight. Of course, in other poems where the same archaic mannerism is practiced, the poet's artistic achieving of the right word and the right balance far outweighs the shortcomings; for instance, in the opening of *Hälfte des Lebens,* the classical suspension has been matched in perfect beauty:

Mit gelben Birnen hänget
und voll mit wilden Rosen
das Land in den See,
ihr holden Schwäne ...

What can succeed only in the exceptional case in German, cannot be done at all in English. For the function of a form in a sentence is generally indicated in English not by the form itself, but by the position of the form. The freedom of arrangement, which makes possible the classical effect of suspension, does not exist; the content-equivalent of our Latin line will, therefore, have to lack an important stylistic property or else new English ways have to be found to express the property of the original.

A simpler example, but without the complications which the translation of poetry involve, is visible in the particular compactness which is achieved in a paragraph of German by placing an object first in certain sentences.

Müller erzielte zuerst in einem wichtigen Versuch dieses Resultat; den gleichen Versuch wiederholten dann Schmidt und Schulze einige Jahre später. 'Müller achieved first, in an important experiment, this result', would be rough but still syntactical translation for the first clause; the following clause, however, cannot be rendered by a parallel translation. We have to choose either to break down the order—which appears to be stylistically relevant—or to shift the entire sentence from the active to the passive, a choice which seems fully justified but which takes us a significant distance from the syntactic pattern of the original.

However, in the translation of scientific prose or newspaper texts such distortion would not matter much, since a form is there treated as though it were merely an accidental concomitant of a meaning-complex to be conveyed, and so long as the meaning-content is left fairly intact, the formal manifestation does not seem to make much difference.

Such a casual attitude is, of course, completely out of place in literature and literary translation. If scientific prose is easily translated because it concentrates on direct, denotative meaning and form is only of secondary importance, other genres and forms present more formidable problems. To be sure, an exact ranking by order of difficulty is hard to achieve, since genres are apparently never quite pure, except for those which are formally most controlled. Thus while a prosy novel would rank low in the hierarchy of difficulty, certain passages in it may well show high concentration of controlled form or of association stimuli; and these passages would of course be harder to translate. In general, the role of allusions, etc., probably cannot be confined to one genre or one set of genres; the degree of formal control, however, is more easily stated. Thus, newspaper texts, excluding *feuilleton*, would probably rank immediately after scientific prose, very low on the scale of difficulty; next one may place letters, prose plays, and non-poetic novels; after that, poetry in free form and poetry in flexible form, such as blank verse, and last, and most difficult of all, poetry in rigid form. As one moves up the scale, the number of instances in which one has to give up all hope of duplicating the original increases; at the same time, of course, the number of opportunities for the translator-poet increases.

To sum up. Transfer of denotative meaning, though difficult and at times impossible, can, as a rule, be exacted in a more or less satisfactory manner; the closer the cultural bonds between the speakers of the two languages, the more acceptable the results become. Associative meaning is very much harder to convey; adequate success can be hoped for only in exceptional cases. Form differs from language to language; still, for all literature which depends on form to become an artistic whole, means for transferring as much of the original form as possible must be found or else replaced by other formal features which fulfill a function equivalent to that of the original forms.

Can one, in translation, justly and profitably set up a hierarchy of properties of the original to be preserved or, if need be, sacrificed? It is this question which most concerns me, and though my conclusions are, of course, quite tentative, these are the rules as I would formulate them at this time.

In order to achieve maximum equivalence, we should match the following properties of the original in the order indicated by the arrows:

I. Semantic:
    (a) direct; →   (b) associative.
           ↓ ↘

II. Formal:
    (1) overt;   (2) distributional;
 ↓ (a) metre;   ↓ (a) peak position;
    (b) rhyme;   (b) position in specific line, etc;
    (c) sound.   (c) arrangement in specific order.

If a sacrifice has to be made, maintain (a) over (b), (b) over (c), etc. Usually, in an arrangement of rigid form, lower ranking positions will have to be neglected. These suggestions refer definitely to the translation of texts in the European tradition.

As a test of the usefulness of these notions of hierarchy, I would like to discuss in some detail a number of actual translations, calling attention, whenever necessary, to the linguistic conditioning of some of the difficulties encountered.

My first set of examples consists of two German translations of a movement from T. S. Eliot's *Four Quartets,* one by Nora Wydenbruck, published in Austria in 1948, the other my own, unpublished as far as I know.*

The fourth movement of the first Quartet, *Burnt Norton,* reads:

Time and the bell have buried
    the day,
The black cloud carries the sun
    away.
Will the sunflower turn to us,
    will the clematis
Stray down, bend to us; tendril
    and spray
Clutch and cling?
Chill
Fingers of yew be curled
Down on us? After the king-
    fisher's wing
Has answered light to light, and
    is silent, the light is still
At the still point of the turning
    world.

The most striking features of the overall structure of the original are a rhyme scheme which leaves out one line, that which ends with *clematis,* and a peak

---

* This passage may, however, have been included in a pirated printing which I never managed to lay an eye on.

scheme which starts out with four points, recedes to one, and then swings back to full volume, even exceeding it before it comes to rest again in the final, crucial line.

Nora Wydenbruck's translation reads as follows:

> Die Zeit hat mit Glockengeläut
> den Tag begraben,
> schwarzes Gewölk die Sonne
> davongetragen.
> Wird die Sonnenblume zu uns
> sich wenden, die Winde
> nieder sich neigen? Die
> schwankende Ranke
> Stütze erheischen?
> Kalt
> Zweig der Zypresse sich senken
> auf unser Haupt?
> Wenn des Eisvogels Flügel
> einmal aufblitze im Glanz und
> verlöscht, verharrt
> dennoch das Licht
> auf dem stäten Punkt der
> kreisenden Welt.

We ask the question of semantic adequacy first. *Die Winde*, the morning-glory, has replaced *clematis*. Since the clematis is known as a garden plant in German-speaking countries, the change seems uncalled-for. Moreover, on the second semantic level, that of associations, a serious loss has occurred: the wild morning-glory which would come to mind when *Winde* is mentioned, is white or pinkish, and the color symbolism that seems to go with *clematis*, is lost completely. *Tendril and spray / Clutch and cling* has been reduced to '(Will) the swaying spray / ask for sup-

port?' *Yew* has been replaced by *Zypresse* (cypress), the typical churchyard tree of the south. However, the image of a branch of cypress bending down is not right: the branches of the cypress reach straight up, whereas the yew squats close to the ground. *Auf unser Haupt* 'upon our head' seems gratuitous. In the last line, the pattern of *answered* and *is silent* is lost; 'when the kingfisher's wing / flashes up once in a glow and is extinguished' shifts the weight to entirely different imagery. In *the light is still*, the ambiguity of *still*, one of the major problems in translating the *Quartets*, is resolved in favor of *still* ~ 'yet' and not of ~ 'steady, quiet', as in the last line.

As far as the form is concerned, the basic structure of the metre is imitated, though the first two lines contain one peak too many, as does the next to the last. The rhyme scheme is neglected, resulting in the loss of the unique position of *clematis*. The first two lines contain assonance, but this alternative to rhyme is not pursued further. Sound patterns—in particular alliterations—have not been transferred; instead, new alignments have been established in *Wenden —Winde, Die schwankende Ranke, Zweig der Zypresse* and *nieder sich neigen*, which are not based on any concentration of any kind in the original, and which, at least in two instances, introduce new semantic entities.

Nora Wydenbruck follows the original closely in the other formal categories postulated; in particular, the peak position of *kalt = chill* is well preserved. No transfer from one line to another has been made, and the arrangements of the original are kept, except that *kalt = chill* has been dissociated from the following noun and now functions as adverb, the only way to insure monosyllabic form as needed.

On the whole, Countess Wydenbruck's translation is rather successful in preserving the arrangement of items, but falls short of perfection in matters of rhyme, rhythm, and sound, and in introducing a number of important semantic changes.

To turn now to my own attempt:

Den Tag begruben Glocke und Zeit.
Die Wolke trägt schwarz die Sonne
  beiseit.
Wird sich die Sonnenblume kehren
  zu uns, wird die Clematis
niederschweifen, sich beugen zu uns—
  Ranke und Zweig
Griff sein und Schlinge?
Nicht
kalte Finger der Eibe gefällt
sein auf uns? Nun da des Eisvogels
  Schwinge
wiedergab Licht zu Licht und stumm
  ward, ist stille das Licht
am stillen Punkte der kreisenden
  Welt.

Clutch and cling has been replaced by nouns. *Nicht* (not) has been introduced for merely formal reasons, against the original text. *Curled* has been replaced by a term usually reserved for pointed weapons and the like. *Answered* as a term of speaking is replaced by the less precise *wiedergab* 'returned', which, however, is retained in the same semantic area by subsequent *stumm ward* (became silent). *After* plus past is rendered by *now that* plus past plus present of the main clause. The decision with respect to *still* has been made in favor of *still ~ at rest* even in the line next to the last.

Metrical organization and rhyme scheme have been preserved intact (with assonance replacing rhyme in the third line). Alliterations have been kept only for *bell . . . buried, light to light* and—if this is to be counted—*silent . . . still.* A new pair exists in *Finger . . . gefällt.*

In arrangement, no semantic equivalent of *chill* was kept in central peak position; *nicht* rather corresponds to the original in vowel quality and in a shared general semantic property of negative value. The object was placed first in the first line. Distribution in lines and broken lines was kept. *Schwarz* in the second line was removed from normal attributive position; the whole construction is more artificial than that of the original.

Generally speaking, the Winter version reflects the original more clearly in overt form; in semantic properties, an attempt has been made to stay with the original whenever possible; formal considerations led to semantic choice adjustments in three cases. In the organization of the arrangement, the major deviations are the displacement of *chill* and a verb-to-noun shift. The Wydenbruck version, on the other hand, deviates in more semantic points, is closer to the original in its arrangement in at least one crucial point, but achieves this goal only by foregoing a matching of the very significant rhyme pattern.

Detachment is, of course, difficult but

I would guess that the defects in my own version are perhaps less serious. Neither translation is adequate in poetic qualities; the Wydenbruck text is just a little bit too explanatory, interpretative; the Winter version is too terse. Nonetheless, both versions are respectable attempts to solve a probably impossible problem in translation.

Against these attempts, I propose now to contrast a case of an inadequate attempt—interestingly enough, an attempt which resulted in achieving what the two Eliot translations did not: a genuine poem.

> *Über allen Gipfeln*
> *ist Ruh,*
> *in allen Wipfeln*
> *spürest du*
> *kaum eine Hauch.*
> *Die Vögelein schweigen im Walde.*
> *Warte nur: balde*
> *ruhest du auch.*

This famous poem by Goethe was translated in 1840 by M. Ju. Lermontov, one of the foremost Romantic poets of Russia.

The translation reads:

> *Gornye veršiny*
> *Spjat vo t'me nočnoj;*
> *Tixie doliny*
> *Polny svežej mgloj;*
> *Ne pylit doroga,*
> *Ne drožat listy . . .*
> *Podoždi nemnogo,*
> *Otdoxneš'ity.*

In order to clarify my point, I offer first a line by line rendering of Goethe's poem, then of Lermontov's translation.

1) Line-by-line:

> *Above all mountain tops*
> *is quietness,*
> *in all tree-tops*
> *you sense*
> *hardly a breath.*
> *The birds are silent in the woods.*
> *Only wait: Soon*
> *you will rest, too.*

2) Lermontov's version:

> *The mountain tops*
> *sleep in the darkness of night;*
> *the quiet valleys*
> *are full of fresh mist;*
> *no dust rises from the road,*
> *the leaves do not stir . . .*
> *Wait a little,*
> *you, too, will rest.*

Both original and replica are eight-line poems; both have rhyme. Goethe's is of a pattern *ababcddc*; Lermontov's pattern, similar but not identical, is *ababcdcd*. As for the content, Goethe speaks of mountains and tree tops which lie quiet, and of the birds that have ceased to sing, and then the promise of rest for the weary. Lermontov closes on the same note, and also mentions the leaves not stirring; but between the mountains at the beginning and the trees at the close, he inserts a contrasting image, valleys filled with mist, and introduces the road no longer busy. The birds are not mentioned at all.

The content then, has undergone substantial change. The general topic—rest after a noisy day, rest after a busy life—is preserved, but apart from that only a partial matching of motifs takes place.

Formally, there is the slight change in rhyme-scheme which I have already mentioned. More significant is the change in metre: the sway of Goethe's varying rhythms is replaced by regular trochaic lines with three peaks each.

With such changes in overall structure, we may forego an investigation of the finer points in formal correspondence. Except for the last two lines, there is practically no agreement between them.

As a translation, then, Lermontov's work is not satisfactory. We noted already, that as a Russian poem in its own right, it commands high respect. But what caused Lermontov to deviate so far from the original?

In terms of content rendering and distribution the only lines which can be called good translation are the last two.

If we consider them the nucleus of the translation, we find that in them the three-beat trochaic pattern is established. The first line of the poem which in close translation should be,

nad vsemi veršinami

did not fit the pattern. So the instrumental-plus-preposition construction was replaced by a nominative; then, since the pair *Gipfeln—Wipfeln* was easily available in the common align-ment of *veršiny* and *doliny* 'mountains and valleys', a pattern of fixed points emerged which forced the translator to depart from the original. Because Lermontov knew his craft, a new poem resulted; not a translation, but a 'variation on a theme by Goethe'. As a translation then, *Gornye veršiny* is a failure; but as a Russian poem, it can and will stand.

Where does all this leave us? We have seen that to translate is to attempt the intrinsically impossible. We have seen that it is not entirely a matter of competence or incompetence of the craftsman that decides the outcome; that the great, commanding structures of the languages of the original and of the replica set the limit of what can be done. This may be very little; but essentially a translation always has ancillary functions: it may be a guide to the original creation, and it may be the stimulus for another creation, just as great as the original, but quite different from it. The exact lines of the original may be lost, and we may have to label the new product a failure in what it set out to be. But we can be satisfied that the bronze statue, the woodcarving, the painting has somehow, by some process hard to analyze, become, not the replica, but the pendant of the original marble sculpture.

6.3

TOWARD A THEORY
OF TRANSLATING

I. A. Richards

Looking back, across more than a score of years, on the considerations with which *Mencius on the Mind* was concerned, it seems to me now that the togethernesses, the mutualities, of those considerations were omitted. There were distinctions made and differences stressed between sorts of meaning, but why they should be so made and so stressed hardly became apparent. The last chapter, "Towards a Technique for Comparative Studies," was suitably tentative in title and in treatment. It stammered away persistently, but what it was trying to say never, *as a whole*, got said. I have some doubts whether any whole was in any steady way in the mind of the sayer. The book was written hurriedly, in a whirl of lecturing on *Ulysses* and on *The Possessed,* during a first teaching visit to Harvard. It was worked up from notes made between Tsing Hua and Yenching, under the guidance of divers advisers, and written out with much of the feeling one has in

trying to scribble down a dream before it fades away. The intellectual currencies of the Harvard scene, not to mention Leopold Bloom and Stavrogin, were driving out those Chinese *aperçus* all the while. Then the only manuscript was lost, stolen by Li An-che's cook by mistake. It lay on a house roof for some months, tossed there by the thief the instant he perceived how worthless it was. Then odd pages began blowing up and down the *hutung*; rumor spread and a search was made; it was found and returned to me—just in time to be compared with the proofs of a second version I had been recollecting back home again in Cambridge, where yet another local logical game had been offering yet other guide lines to be avoided. All useful experience, no doubt, in guessing about *what* makes *what* seem to mean *what*—when, where, and to *whom*—but not then and there conducive to a single comprehensive view of comprehending.

This, I now suppose, is what one should attempt to form. I suppose too that a first condition of the endeavor is a recognition of its inherent wilfulness. It is purposive; it seeks. If asked *what* it

From *Studies in Chinese Thought*, A. F. Wright, editor (Chicago: University of Chicago Press, 1953). Reprinted by permission of the publishers and the author.

seeks, its only just answer should be: "Itself." It seeks to comprehend what comprehending may be. What is sought is the search.

Yet it advances. When it looks back upon its earlier phases, what it most notes are the things it took for granted *without* having put its requests into any but most indefinite form. It can bring the request and the grant nearer to terms forever without any fear of arriving. The process of refining its assumptions must be just as endless as the endeavor itself.

Through these assumptions it divides and combines[1]—dividing in order to combine, combining in order to divide —and simultaneously. Whatever it compares is compared in a respect or in respects. These respects are the instruments of the exploration. And it is with them as with the instruments of investigation in physics but more so: the properties of the instruments enter into the account of the investigation. There is thus at the heart of any theory of meanings a principle of the instrument. The exploration of comprehension is the task of devising a system of instruments for comparing meanings. But this system, these instruments, are themselves comparable. They belong with what they compare and are subject in the end to one another. Indeed, this mutual subjection or control seems to be the ἀρχή for a doctrine of comprehension—that upon which all else depends.[2]

There is a seeming opposition to be reconciled here. We may suppose there to be a hierarchy of instruments, each caring for those below and cared for by those above. Or we may suppose the system to be circular. I have leaned here toward a position somewhat like that of the constitutional monarchist who supports an authority which is itself under control (see Aspect VI below). The same question seems to me to appear again as: "How should we structure the most embracing purpose?" and this I take to be an invitation to an inquiry into Justice on Platonic lines.

This mutual control shows itself in any segment of activity (any stretch of discourse, for example) as accordance and discordance of means with ends. Ends endeavor to choose means which will choose them. The entirety of activity, if, obeying Aristotle, we may venture to attempt to conceive it, seems to consist of *choices*. Initial choices would be free; but, when choice has been made, the sequent choices are bound thereby while the choice is held. An interpretation knows only a part, often a very small part, of the entailments of its choices. These entailments may later seem to it to be "brute fact"—something in no way and in no measure due to its choices, something upon which their success or failure depends. This is the defectiveness of the choices—made too soon or not made when choice was needed.

Enough of these preliminaries. They seemed necessary to the introduction here of the word LET as the first and all-important move in this undertaking. Let *let* rule every meaning for every word in every sentence which follows. These sentences will seem for the most part to be in the indicative, but that is for brev-

---

[1] *Phaedrus* 265D–266B. I have written further on "these processes of division and bringing together" in *How To Read a Page* (New York: W. W. Norton & Co., 1942), pp. 217–22.

[2] *Republic* 511C. See *How To Read a Page*, Index: "Dependence."

ity and for custom's sake. Everything which seems to be said in the indicative floats on a raft of optative invitations to mean in such wise. Any theory of meanings which can serve as authority, as more embracing purpose, to a theory of translation is concerned with the mutual tension of whatever can be put together to serve as that raft.

Such are among the reflections which translation between diverse cultures can occasion. How may we compare what a sentence in English may mean with what a sentence in Chinese may mean? The only sound traditional answer is in terms of two scholarships—one in English, the other in Chinese. But a skepticism which can be liberating rather than paralyzing may make us doubtful of the sufficiency of our techniques for comparing meanings even within one tradition. How can one compare a sentence in English poetry with one (however like it) in English prose? Or indeed any two sentences, or the same sentence, in different settings? What is synonymy?[3] A proliferous literature of critical and interpretative theory witnesses to the difficulty. It seems to have been felt more and more in recent decades. Is there any reason to doubt that analogous difficulties await analogous efforts for Chinese? They may well have been attending the conduct of that language all along.

These troubles come, perhaps, in part from insufficient attention to the comparing activity itself. How do we compare other things? Let us see whether

what we do in comparing boxes or rooms can be helpful in suggesting what we might do in comparing meanings. What would a sort of geometry of comprehendings be like? With rooms, we need, in the simplest cases, three dimensions. With length, breadth, and height ascertained, we have gone some way toward discovering how far one room is like another. Would it be useful to ask in how many "dimensions" meanings may agree or differ? It might be wise to drop the geometric word and generalize at once. Let us say, then, "in how many respects"—remembering that meanings may, if we so wish, be compared in an indefinitely great number of respects or in as few as will serve some purpose. The purpose decides which respects are relevant. This is true of rooms, too. So our problem is one of choice. What is the simplest system of respects which would enable us to compare meanings in a way serviceable to the translator's purposes? (As three dimensions serve us in comparing sizes and shapes.)

I have just called this a *problem*. If a problem is something which has a solution, I should not have done so. In my opening sentence I called such things *considerations*, hoping thereby to suggest that they are fields of unlimited speculation—held within only the most unlimited framework that even sidereal space could symbolize—and not, as problems in a branch of mathematics may be, formed and given their solutions by the assumptions which set them up. What this theory of meaning should be or do is not in this narrow sense a problem.

It is, on the other hand, the most searching of all considerations, for it is

---

[3] See, e.g., Willard V. O. Quine, "Two Dogmas of Empiricism," *Philosophical Review*, Vol. LX (1951).

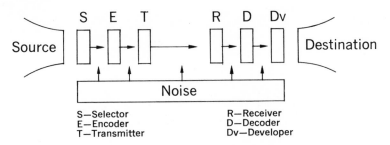

S—Selector
E—Encoder
T—Transmitter

R—Receiver
D—Decoder
Dv—Developer

concerned with arranging our techniques for arranging. Since the system of respects is set up to serve our comparings, the respects in it must not be too many or too few, and they will probably vary with the comparing. But this cannot itself be described except by means of the respects which serve it, being the comparing which these respects implement and enable. (Similarly, the comparing of sizes and shapes cannot be described except by reference to the spatial dimensions.) In brief, we make an instrument and try it out. Only by trying it out can we discover what it can do for us. Likewise, only such trial can develop our comprehending of what it is with which we seek to explore comprehending. Thus what ensues will be a depiction of the whereby and the wherefore as well as the what.

We may begin by adapting the conventional diagram of the communication engineer to our wider purposes.[4] In translation we have two such diagrams to consider as a minimum. There will be (say) a Chinese communication for which we find ourselves in the role of Destination; and we assume thereupon

the role of Source for a communication in English. But since other communications in Chinese and other communications in English, having *something in common* with the present communication, come in to guide the encodings and decodings, the process becomes very complex. We have here indeed what may very probably be the most complex type of event yet produced in the evolution of the cosmos.

Between two utterances[5] the operative *something in common* whereby the one influences the other may be any feature or character or respect whatever and can be itself highly complex. It may be some conjunction of respects. The comprehending of any utterance is guided by any number of partially similar situations in which partially similar utterances have occurred. More exactly, the comprehending is a function of the comparison fields from which it derives. Let the units of which these comparison fields consist be *utterances-within-situations*—the utterance and its

---

[4] Adapted with considerable changes from Claude E. Shannon and Warren Weaver, *The Mathematical Theory of Communication* (Urbana: University of Illinois Press, 1949), p. 5.

[5] I need a highly general term here, not limited to any mode of utterance, such as *overt* speech or writing. An act of comprehending may itself be regarded as an utterance, being a rebirth, after passage through the lifeless signal, of something more or less the same as the original which was transmitted.

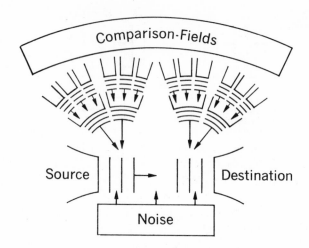

Utterances-in-Situations

situation being partners in the network of transactions with other utterances in other situations which lends significance to the utterance. Partially similar utterances made within very different situations are likely to require different comprehendings, though language is, of course, our collective attempt to minimize these divergences of meaning.

A comprehending, accordingly, is an instance of a nexus[6] established through past occurrences of partially similar utterances in partially similar situations—utterances and situations partially co-varying. The past utterances-within-situations need not have been consciously remarked or wittingly ana-

lyzed; still less need they be explicitly remembered when the comprehending occurs. Thus the word *comparison* in the technical term "comparison-field" may mislead. It is not necessary that the members of a comparison-field—widely diverse utterances-within-situations as they may be—should ever have been taken together in explicit analytic scrutiny and examined as to their likenesses and differences. The discriminations and connections (dividings and combinings) which arise in the development of meaning are, in some respects, *as though* this had been done. Sometimes they are so produced; but, for the most part, they need no such elaborate reflective procedure. Let me generalize "comparison" here to make it cover whatever putting together and setting apart (however unremarked) has been operative in the formation of the nexus. The routine of concept formation and of discriminative behavior even down to what

---

[6] See C. K. Ogden and I. A. Richards, *The Meaning of Meaning* (New York: Harcourt, Brace & Co., 1941), pp. 52–59 and Appendix B. The word "context" there used seems to have been misleading. See my *Interpretation in Teaching* (New York: Harcourt, Brace & Co., 1938), p. viii.

we might call merely perceptual levels has an interesting resemblance to the highest activities of systematic conceptual classification. It is as though the nervous system had been taught Mill's Joint Method of Agreement and Difference.

What I have been sketching applies, for the translator, in the first place to the Decoding and Developing of the Chinese utterance. In the second place it applies to the Selecting and Encoding which (it is hoped) will produce an utterance in English acceptable as a translation from the Chinese. But, plainly enough, the co-varyings of utterances-within-situations for English are other than they are for Chinese. Any translator has acquired his Chinese and his English through "comparison-fields" which are different and systematically different in structure: different not only with respect to the ways in which utterances change with situations, but also with respect to those changes that are significant in utterances (e.g., phonemics) and with respect to those changes that are significant in situations (e.g., status recognition). The comparative linguist could, if he wished, illustrate this for the rest of his natural days. And it is one of the pedagogue's reasons for preferring a "direct" method to a "translation" method in beginning language learning. He finds that by keeping to one language only he can provide comparison-fields (through sequences of sentences-in-situations) which are more effective, that is, more propitious to full and deep comprehending later on. This structuring of experience will of course differ with our aim. The linguist—for his purposes—will set up one schema of respects in which comparisons will be made; the pedagogue—for his purposes—will set up another. What schema will a translator set up to serve as a theory of the sorts and interrelations of meanings to guide him in his own tasks?

Limitless in their variety, these tasks present themselves, the words, phrases, sentence forms and the situations, and the meanings, to be compared being as varied as the ways in which they may be compared. How are we to choose the respects (or dimensions) which will serve us best as headings under which to arrange those similarities and those differences of meanings which the translator must try to discern in one language and to achieve in another? In the concrete, in the minute particulars of practice, these comparison-fields are familiar enough; though we tend to forget, as scholars, what we must always, as pedagogues, recall: that these comparison-fields go back into infancy. All we have to do is to arrange, in a schema as parsimonious as adequacy will allow, a body of experience so common that if the purposing of our arrangement could be agreed on, there might be little we would then differ about.

Let us turn our communications diagram through 90 degrees now and look down it. Here is a cross-section of the activities to be found there, made at the points where what is prepared for transmission and what has been decoded and developed may be supposed —in a successful communication—to

I. Points to, selects. . . .
II. Says something about, sorts. . . .
III. Comes alive to, wakes up to, presents. . . .
IV. Cares about. . . .
V. Would change or keep as it is. . . .
VI. Manages, directs, runs, administers itself. . . .
VII. Seeks, pursues, tries, endeavors to be or to do. . . .

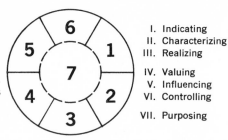

I. Indicating
II. Characterizing
III. Realizing
IV. Valuing
V. Influencing
VI. Controlling
VII. Purposing

resemble one another most nearly. I have marked and numbered for labeling the seven[7] divisions in my proposed schema.

Let us label these *sorts of work* which an utterance may be doing with two or more sets of names, academic and colloquial—on the assumption that communication will be made more probable if we use here a multiplicity of largely equivalent indications. I am numbering them for convenience of reference; but I do not want to suggest that there is any fixed temporal order, that first we Select, then we Charac-

terize, then Realize, then Value, then would Influence, then Organize and then Purpose. Nor is there any constant logical order. Let us keep these jobs as independent one of another as we can. In individual cases we will find many sorts of detailed dependence, but let us put none in by definition.

In applying this schema to translating, we can ask of two utterances in two languages:

  I. How far do they pick out the same (or at least analogous) things to talk about?

  II. How far do they say the same (or at least analogous) things about them?

  III. How far do they present with equal vividness and/or actuality, weak or strong?

  IV. How far do they value in the same ways?

  V. How far would they keep or change in the same ways?

  VI. How far are the dependencies and interplay between I, II, III, IV, V, and VI itself, the same in them both?

  VII. How widely would they serve the same purposes, playing the same parts, within the varying activities they might occur in?

---

[7] A possible eighth division might be Venting (that one of the multifarious meanings of the word *expression* which seems least well covered by my seven). Utterances from a simple "Ouch!" or "Ooh!" up to *The Divine Comedy* can be regarded as drive-reducing—in terms, that is, of the psychology of the utterer. But, since the purposes of a psychological investigator are not those of a translator, I would expect different schemas to be suitable. And to me, at present, this respect seems well enough taken care of—for the translator's purposes—through my seven which may *all* in their varying ways be drive-reducing. I am indebted to Dr. Irving Singer for making me see the need for this note, and to Charles Morris' *Signs, Language, and Behavior* (New York: Prentice-Hall, Inc., 1946) for suggestions contributing to my schema.

Let me label this seven-fold event which my diagram depicts COMPRE-HENDING, as comprehensive a name as I can find. Any full utterance does all these things at once, and invites all of them in the comprehender. In some instances, however, one or more of these dimensions, aspects, powers, functions, jobs, variables, parameters, components, ingredients, tasks, duties (all these words are in need of the comparative study my diagram should be an instrument for), will shrink toward the null, the vanishing point. There is swearing and there is mathematics. In swearing there *may* be nothing but IV, V, and VII; in mathematics only I, VI, and VII may matter. It would appear that VII never lapses; without purposing, without the feed-forward[8] which structures all activity, no utterance and no comprehending. A full comparison between two utterances (between an original and a translation of it, for example) would require us to discern what all their dimensions, aspects, functions, may be and compare them as to each and as to their relations within the entire comprehending. In comparing boxes or rooms, we need three dimensions; in comparing comprehendings, we need, I suggest, at least these seven.

Even of a single comprehending we can ask our seven sorts of questions: Under I, we ask WHICH things are being talked (thought) of? Under II, WHAT is being said of them? Under III, EVEN

SO? Under IV, SHOULD this be so? Under V, WON'T YOU (WON'T I)? Under VI, HOW? Under VII, WHEREIN, WHEREBY, and WHEREFORE, TO WHAT END?

Of these, I and II may be felt to be more narrowly, more clearly, *questions* than the others; and III especially may seem to be rather a wondering than a questioning. Under III, what is in question is the nearness and fulness with which something is to be present to us. *Doubting* ("is this so or not, possibly, probably, certainly?") belongs (in this schema) rather to V or VI ("to be accepted or not, and how?").

Let us consider these functions in turn.

Indicating and *Characterizing* will need less comment than the others. They have been more discussed, for they correspond to the distinction logicians make under the labels "Extension-Intension" and "Denotation-Connotation." In the logicians' use, the denotation of a term is whatever may be covered by the term and the connotation is the set of properties (characters) anything must have if it is to be so covered. But there is also a well-established literary use of "connotation" in which the connotation is III, IV, and V in my diagram rather than II (which is likely then to be called the "bare, or mere meaning"). These two uses of "connotation" parallel what may be the chief difference between scientific and poetic use of language. There is some parallel, too, with what I have discussed (*Interpretation in Teaching*, p. 311) as the rigid and the fluid uses of language. If we make Characterizing be "*saying*

---

8 See *Cybernetics: Transactions of the Eighth Conference* (Josiah Macy, Jr., Foundation, 1951); I. A. Richards, "Communication between Men," pp. 54–60; and *How To Read a Page*, Index: "Purpose."

something about what is being pointed to," we have obviously to narrow down the meaning of "saying." It can open out to take in anything that an utterance can do, anything in any way said, suggested, evoked, hinted, required, and implied (the literary connotation), or it can be kept down to the logician's connotation—the "definition" (as it is sometimes put) of a term.

The last paragraph illustrates—as must any attempt to write about the language we use or should use about language—the heavy duties we have to put on quotation marks. I have suggested (*How To Read a Page,* pp. 68–70) that we should develop sets of specialized quotes, as a technical notation by which we could better keep track of the uses we are making of our words, and I have tried out the use of a few such quotation marks in that book and elsewhere. I am now more than ever persuaded of the usefulness of this device. It can serve us to distinguish many different uses we make of quotes. For example:

^{w} . . . ^{w} to show that it is a word—that word in general, Peirce's ^{r}type^r—which is being talked of.[9] For example, ^{w}use^w is a highly ambiguous word.

^{oc} . . . ^{oc} to show that occurrences of a word—Peirce's ^{r}token^r—are being talked of. For example, I have been using ^{oc}uses^{oc} above in various ways.

^{r} . . . ^{r} to show that some special use

of the word or phrase is being *referred* to. The marks may be read as *refer to* and the implication may be that only by having that particular use of the word in that passage present to us in lively attention (Realizing) can we distinguish it from other uses and avoid confusion. ^{t} . . . ^{t} to show that the word or phrase is being used as a *technical term* anchored by a definition to some state of affairs or procedure—to an operational technique perhaps or to a set of performances.

^{q} . . . ^{q} to show that how the word or phrase is to be comprehended is the question. It may be read as *query;* and we can develop this notation further by adding I–VII after the q to show where the focus of the question lies in my diagram. These q's should carry no derogatory suggestion; their work is to locate and orientate inquiry; they are servants of VI. Thus we might write ^{qII}connotation^{qII} or $^{qIII, IV, V}$connotation$^{qIII, IV, V}$ to direct attention either to the logical or to the literary questions. ^{sw} . . . ^{sw} to show that we are considering what may be *said with* a certain word or phrase without decision as yet to what that is. This enables one to bring together meanings of words and phrases, for examination, without settling anything prematurely as to how they may be related. We need to bring these meanings together *before* we pick out those we may profitably compare. I have written elsewhere at length (*Interpretation in Teaching,* chaps. xv and xix; *How To Read a Page,* chap. x) on the troubles which the

---

[9] *Collected Papers of Charles Saunders Peirce* (Cambridge: Harvard University Press, 1933), IV, 423.

lack of such a warning mark may lead us into.

! . . . ! to show astonishment that people can write or talk so. Some will want to put this whole paper within such marks.

Once we recognize to what an extent thinking is a taking care of and a keeping account of the conduct of our words, the need for a notation with which to study and control their resourcefulness becomes obvious.

^{sw}Indicating^{sw} or ^{sw}Selecting^{sw}—especially if we picture it to ourselves with the image of a pointer (an arrow as of a wind vane)—may seem instable. It can be so; but some of our selectings are the most constant things we do. Angus Sinclair puts a further point well: "What is thus loosely describable as the selecting and grouping which each of us carries out is not an act done once and thereby completed, but is a continuing process which must be sustained if our experience is to continue as it is. If for any reason it is not sustained, i.e. if for any reason a man follows a different way of grouping in his attention, then the experience he has will be different also. Further, this requires some effort. . . . Knowing is not a passive contemplation, but a continuously effort-consuming activity."[10]

Sinclair's ^{sw}grouping^{sw} seems to be my ^{sw}Characterizing, Sorting^{sw}. We have, in English, what may seem an excess of analytic machineries to help us in distinguishing !its! from !whats!, that is, Indicating, I, from Characterizing, II. Such are (in most uses): for I, ^{w}subject, substance, entity, particular, thing, being, group, class^{w}; for II, ^{w}predicate, attribute, property, quality, relation, character, essence, universal^{w}. A large methodological question which can seem to fall near the very heart of any endeavor to translate philosophy is this: does use of different ^{q}analytic machineries^{q} entail difference of ^{q}view^{q}? I put my q's in here to remind us that both ^{sw}analytic machineries^{sw} and ^{sw}view^{sw} have to do with little-explored territories though they are surrounded by the most debatable land in ^{q}the Western philosophic tradition^{q}. Current use of most of this machinery is erratic: at a popular level it cares little which of the above words are employed; more sophisticated use varies from one philosophic school to the next.[11] There is little likelihood of increased clarity unless some new factor enters. The exercise of choice required when thinking which is remote from ^{q}the Western philosophic tradition^{q}—thinking which uses, perhaps, no such machinery—has to be thoroughly explored in English, might be just such a new factor. The distinction between Indicating and Characterizing, and their queer interplay, might, through translation studies, become again the central growing point for thought.

Realizing, III, needs more discussion here, though what the discussion should bring out is something familiar to everyone. The two meanings we separate most easily in this cluster are exem-

---

[10] Angus Sinclair, *The Conditions of Knowing* (London: Routledge, 1951), p. 35.

[11] See my *Interpretation in Teaching*, chap. xxi, "Logical Machinery and Empty Words."

plified by: (*a*) "She realized how he would take it" and (*b*) "He thus realized his ambition." It is with (*a*) that we are concerned, though the background influence of (*b*), ^sw^realizing^sw^ as ^sw^the becoming actual of the possible^sw^, is frequently apparent. This duality may be as relevant to Chinese modes of ^q^knowledge^q^ as it is to some Aristotelian doctrines of becoming.

Within (*a*), two lines of interpretation offer themselves: (i) it may be taken as equivalent to ^sw^She imagined vividly and livingly how he would feel^sw^; or (ii) ^sw^She foresaw how he would act^sw^. (The vagueness of ^oc^take it^oc^ reinforces the ambiguity of ^oc^realized^oc^.) This exemplifies a frequent shift in ^sw^realize^sw^: the shift between a lively, concrete, actualized presence and a cognizance of implications and consequences which may be (and commonly is) highly schematic. A statesman may realize what the outcome will be all the better for not realizing too vividly how X may feel. It thus appears that while the use of ^w^realize^w^ in (i) does entail a high degree of Realizing, III, in my schema, ^w^realize^w^ in (ii) does not. The entirety of apprehension which is ascribed by remarks such as "He fully realized," and the contrast with "He didn't at all realize," can be handled in terms of I, II, V, and VI.

What is highly realized may be distinct, explicitly structured, detailed, ^q^definite^q^ in most of the senses of this strategic word.[12] But it may equally well be very indefinite. That unlocatable, in-describable, almost unidentifiable qualm which is the first emergence of nausea is something which can be Realized to the full without as yet being Characterized in any but the sketchiest fashion. Conversely, Characterizing may be most complete and minute without much Realizing having developed. In fact, fulness and detail in Characterizing frequently prevent our Realizing, though the details may be offered expressly to increase it. On the other hand, many devices—from headlines to the routines of the dispatch editor and the commentator—reduce the reality of what is presented. Much that is called ^q^sensationalism^q^ has this effect. We may suspect that this is sometimes its justification. We need to be protected from the wear and tear of actuality. It would not be surprising if this wrapping-up professed to be unwrapping.

> Human kind
> Cannot bear very much reality.

Nonetheless, increase in Realizing is in general accompanied by increased particularity in Characterizing, and by increased choosiness and discrimination in the Selecting of what shall be Characterized.

Realizing is very frequently brought about through metaphor, as may be illustrated by the following vivid account of a moment of Realization from Virginia Woolf: "Suddenly, as if the movement of his hand had released it, the *load* of her accumulated impressions of him *tilted up*, and *down poured in a ponderous avalanche* all she felt about him. That was one sensation. Then *up rose in a fume* the essence of

---

[12] See *Interpretation in Teaching*, chap. ix, " 'Definite.' "

his being. That was another. She felt herself *transfixed* by the intensity of her perception; it was his severity; it was his goodness."[13] (My italics.)

Metaphor, however, can serve under all my headings. It is worth remarking with regard to Chinese-English translation that the great traditional metaphors of Western thought play so large a part in shaping our conceptions that a study of any metaphors which have played a comparable part in Chinese thought suggests itself as possibly a key move. Examples in the Western tradition would be: the metaphor of conception used in the previous sentence (see *Phaedrus* 276E); the analogy of the Self and the State from the *Republic*, and the tripartite structure of both; that other Platonic metaphor of intellectual vision, the eye of the mind; the comparison of the idea of the good with the sun; the metaphor of light as truth generally; the metaphor of inspiration; and, from Hosea, the metaphor of a marriage contract between the Lord and Israel, and indeed the use of the ideas of love (not sex) and fidelity in theology. These great originative structurings have acted in the West in innumerable minds which have had no notion of how important such metaphors can be. It would be hard to say, indeed, of the Self-State analogy whether thought about personality or about government has been the more influenced by it, for the traffic has been two-way. Where such a metaphor is absent in Chinese or where Chinese has a traditional metaphor which English lacks, the loss in translation is likely to be grave. The remedy is, perhaps, through a deeper, more systematic study of metaphor.[14] Assistance in such studies is, of course, one of the aims of the schema of comparisons offered in my diagram.

Valuing, IV, is a modern philosophic battleground, the dispute being in part whether the language of valuation, obligation, and justification is to be comprehended in some peculiar fashion or fashions (as !ᑫemotiveᑫ!) or in the ordinary way of description. For the purposes of comparative study of meanings, this warfare, on which so much time and talent is being spent, may not be important. It is not clear that any decision would help us to compare meanings better. It may be wise to hold that: ʳEvaluations are a form of empirical knowledge,ʳ[15] which might put considerable strain on our concepts of ᑫempirical knowledgeᑫ; or it may be wiser still to hold that will and desire may enter into valuations in more ways than those in which they enter our type specimens of empirical knowledge. To decide which view would be wiser, we would have to be able to make comparisons between meanings beyond our present scope. What does seem certain is that, *as an instrument for the comparison of meanings*, our diagram should avoid prejudging this issue. It should be able to represent the opposed positions more justly; they look as if they were almost equally in need of restatement. But notice here how

---

[13] *To the Lighthouse*, p. 41.

[14] See my *Philosophy of Rhetoric*, Lectures 5 and 6.

[15] C. I. Lewis, *An Analysis of Knowledge and Valuation* (La Salle, Ill.: Open Court Publishing Co., 1946), p. 365.

^oc^should^oc^ and ^oc^justly^oc^ and ^oc^in need of^oc^ appear in this very remark. Any formulation of these problems will itself be valuative as well as factual; the conflict it hopes to adjudicate is alive in the bosom of the judge. The difficulties ensuing from this I shall discuss under Aspect VI, the Management, Control, or Administration of Comprehending. Meanwhile, my diagram assumes that ^sw^Valuing^sw^ is different from Realizing, Characterizing, and Indicating; and that it ^q^should^q^ be defined in such a way as to avoid implying any fixed relations to them—though, of course, the interplay between all three will be varied, incessant, and all-important. All study of language and thought *in action* is both an exemplification and a study of this kind of interplay.

As another precaution, we may leave the full variety of Valuing unconfined. We are concerned here not only with all the attitudes which may be uttered by the aid of ^w^good^w^ and ^w^bad^w^, ^w^right^w^ and ^w^wrong^w^, ^w^beautiful^w^ and ^w^ugly^w^, ^w^pleasant^w^ and ^w^unpleasant^w^, ^w^important^w^ and ^w^trivial^w^, but with the ranges of love and hate, desire and fear, hope and despair, belief and disbelief. These fields are all polar, and there is a middle zone where it may be doubtful whether any valuing is going on and whether it is positive or negative. So Valuing may often seem to lapse.

Similarly, and perhaps as a consequence, Influencing, V—that part of a Comprehending which endeavors either to change or to preserve unchanged, to be changed or to remain unchanged— may be too slight to be remarked. If we ask what it is here which would change

or be preserved, it may be best to reply ^sw^the onflowing situation^sw^ and to remind ourselves that this ^sw^onflowing situation^sw^ is at least twofold. It is (*a*) that motion of affairs within which the Comprehending is proceeding; it is also (*b*) the Selecting, Characterizing, Realizing, and Valuing, and the rest, through which the Comprehending is taking account of in dealing with (*a*). It is what is happening *and* what we take to be happening. We are lucky when these sufficiently accord. Influencing—the keeping of the stream of events so or the changing of it—concerns (*a*) as offered to us in (*b*) and, within (*a*), it includes our adjustment to the not-us as well as the adjustment of the not-us to ourselves. In general, a Comprehending is concerned to change part of the onflowing situation and keep the rest unchanged. Something has to remain unchanged; there has to be some continuant, if change is to be possible: so at least we may be wise to suppose.

Controlling or Administering, VI, has to do with these decisions as to what it will be wise to suppose, and with what arises through these supposals. Wisdom, we may remember, "lies in the masterful administration of the unforeseen."[16] We may be highly surprised to discover what we are supposing. The supposals may be conscious, and arrived at through explicit reflection and deliberation and choices wittingly made, or they may be unwitting, picked up from the tradition or from the accidents of habit forma-

---

[16] Robert Bridges, *The Testament of Beauty* (Oxford, 1939).

tion. And they may concern every aspect of meaning—from Selecting round to Controlling, this would-be executive, itself. Many of our most important supposals concern the nature of meaning and the connections of the sorts of meaning with one another, in brief, the very topic our diagram should help us to explore.

It is here, in this aspect of the mind as a self-ordering endeavor, as a government hoping to maintain itself,[17] that compromise appears most clearly as the practical art of the translator. To ask: Where in general will compromise be most needed? is to try to divide the fields of possible discourse. There are areas of settled routine—much of trade, for example—where the fixed and comparatively simple structuring of the things and events to be dealt with allows of a fine practical equivalence between the languages used. Wherever there is a clear operational check upon Comprehendings this happy condition is likely to prevail. Mathematics, physics, the strict sciences can be translated without loss—by the introduction of the technical term and the use of the type-specimen, the model and the operational definition. Here functions I, II, and VI are serving a Purposing so general that it can hide behind the ordering, VI, of what is said, II, about what, I. But as discourse grows less abstract and hypothetical, more entire and actual, the probability of loss and therefore the need for choice and compromise become greater. With narrative and philosophy and poetry in so far as the growth and history of the language

and of other social and cultural institutions enter in, a self-denying statute is required. If we take Ethics to be "the bringing to bear of self-control for the purpose of realizing our desires,"[18] we have to decide which of our desires must give way to which. The translator has first to reconcile himself to conceiving his art in terms of minimal loss and then to balance and adjudicate, as best he can, the claims of the rival functions. His question is: Which sorts of loss will we take in order not to lose what? And answering that is in practice a series of decisions, VI, on behalf of a policy, VII, which may very well have to declare itself openly, in a preface or in footnotes. The mind-state analogy is at work all through, it will be perceived. The translator is called upon to become a statesman and serve a limitless oncoming state. His chief advantage over his analogue is that he can, sometimes, go back and undo his mistakes. He can cancel and choose again. But for the rest his practical sagacity must accept the hard general truths: if we try for too much, we will get less than we might, and what we can go on to do will depend on what we have done and are doing now.

Translation theory—over and above the aid it may afford the translator—has thus a peculiar duty toward man's self-completion, to use a concept which seems to be suggestively common to the Chinese and the Western traditions. We are not weather vanes, I; we are not filing systems, II; we are not even agonies or delights only, III; we are not

---

[17] *Republic* 591.

[18] *Collected Papers of Charles Saunders Peirce*, I, 334.

litmus paper, IV, or servo-mechanisms, V. We are guardians, VI, and subject therefore to the paradox of government: that we must derive our powers, in one way or another, from the very forces which we have to do our best to control.

Translation theory has not only to work for better mutual comprehension between users of diverse tongues; more central still in its purposing is a more complete viewing of itself and of the Comprehending which it should serve.

6.4   MEANING AND SYNONYMY IN NATURAL LANGUAGES

Rudolf Carnap

1. Meaning Analysis in Pragmatics and Semantics

The analysis of meanings of expressions occurs in two fundamentally different forms. The first belongs to *pragmatics*, that is, the empirical investigation of historically given *natural languages*. This kind of analysis has long been carried out by linguists and philosophers, especially analytic philosophers. The second form was developed only recently in the field of symbolic logic; this form belongs to *semantics* (here understood in the sense of pure semantics, while descriptive semantics may be regarded as part of pragmatics), that is, the study of constructed *language systems* given by their rules.

The theory of the relations between a language—either a natural language or a language system—and what language is about may be divided into two parts which I call the theory of extension and the theory of intension, respectively.[1] The first deals with concepts like denoting, naming, extension, truth, and related ones. (For example, the word 'blau' in German, and likewise the predicate '*B*' in a symbolic language system if a rule assigns to it the same meaning, denote any object that is blue; its extension is the class of all blue objects; 'der Mond' is a name of the moon; the sentence 'der Mond ist blau' is true if and only if the moon is blue.)

From *Philosophical Studies*, VII (1955). Reprinted by permission of the editors and the author.

[1] This distinction is closely related to that between radical concepts and L-concepts which I made in *Introduction to Semantics*. The contrast between extension and intension is the basis of the semantical method which I developed in *Meaning and Necessity*. Quine calls the two theories "theory of reference" and "theory of meaning," respectively.

The theory of intension deals with concepts like intension, synonymy, analyticity, and related ones; for our present discussion let us call them *"intension concepts."* (I use "intension" as a technical term for the meaning of an expression or, more specifically, for its designative meaning component; see below. For example, the intension of 'blau' in German is the property of being blue; two predicates are synonymous if and only if they have the same intension; a sentence is analytic if it is true by virtue of the intensions of the expressions occurring in it.)

From a systematic point of view, the description of a language may well begin with the theory of intension and then build the theory of extension on its basis. By learning the theory of intension of a language, say German, we learn the intensions of the words and phrases and finally of the sentences. Thus the theory of intension of a given language L enables us to *understand* the sentences of L. On the other hand, we can apply the concepts of the theory of extension of L only if we have, in addition to the knowledge of the theory of intension of L, also sufficient empirical knowledge of the relevant facts. For example, in order to ascertain whether a German word denotes a given object, one must first understand the word, that is, know what is its intension, in other words, know the general condition which an object must fulfill in order to be denoted by this word; and secondly he must investigate the object in question in order to see whether it fulfills the condition or not. On the other hand, if a linguist makes an empirical investigation of a language not previously described, he finds out first that certain objects are denoted by a given word, and later he determines the intension of the word.

Nobody doubts that the pragmatical investigation of natural languages is of greatest importance for an understanding both of the behavior of individuals and of the character and development of whole cultures. On the other hand, I believe with the majority of logicians today that for the special purpose of the development of logic the construction and semantical investigation of language systems is more important. But also for the logician a study of pragmatics may be useful. If he wishes to find out an efficient form for a language system to be used, say, in a branch of empirical science, he might find fruitful suggestions by a study of the natural development of the language of scientists and even of the everyday language. Many of the concepts used today in pure semantics were indeed suggested by corresponding pragmatical concepts which had been used for natural languages by philosophers or linguists, though usually without exact definitions. Those semantical concepts were, in a sense, intended as explicata for the corresponding pragmatical concepts.

In the case of the semantical intension concepts there is an additional motivation for studying the corresponding pragmatical concepts. The reason is that some of the objections raised against these semantical concepts concern, not so much any particular proposed explication, but the question of the very existence of the alleged explicanda. Especially *Quine's* criticism does not concern the formal correctness of the definitions in pure semantics; rather, he doubts whether there are any clear and fruitful corresponding pragmatical concepts which could serve as explicanda. That is the reason why he demands that these pragmatical concepts be shown to be scientifically legitimate by stating empirical, behavioristic criteria for them. If I understand him correctly, he believes that, without this pragmatical substructure, the semantical intension concepts, even if formally correct, are arbitrary and without purpose. I do not think that a semantical concept, in order to be fruitful, must necessarily possess a prior pragmatical counterpart. It is theoretically possible to demonstrate its fruitfulness through its application in the further development of language systems. But this is a slow process. If for a given semantical concept there is already a familiar, though somewhat vague, corresponding pragmatical concept and if we are able to clarify the latter by describing an operational procedure for its application, then this may indeed be a simpler way for refuting the objections and furnish a practical justification at once for both concepts.

The purpose of this paper is to clarify the nature of the pragmatical concept of intension in natural languages and to outline a behavioristic, operational procedure for it. This will give a practical vindication for the semantical intension concepts; ways for defining them, especially analyticity, I have shown in a previous paper.[2] By way of introduction I shall first (in §2) discuss

briefly the pragmatical concepts of denotation and extension; it seems to be generally agreed that they are scientifically legitimate.

2. The Determination of Extensions

We take as example the German language. We imagine that a linguist who does not know anything about this language sets out to study it by observing the linguistic behavior of German-speaking people. More specifically, he studies the German language as used by a given person Karl at a given time. For simplicity, we restrict the discussion in this paper mainly to predicates applicable to observable things, like 'blau' and 'Hund.' It is generally agreed that, on the basis of spontaneous or elicited utterances of a person, the linguist can ascertain whether or not the person is willing to apply a given predicate to a given thing, in other words, whether the predicate denotes the given thing for the person. By collecting results of this kind, the linguist can determine first, the extension of the predicate 'Hund' within a given region for Karl, that is, the class of the things to which Karl is willing to apply the predicate; second, the extension of the contradictory, that is, the class of those things for which Karl denies the application of 'Hund'; and, third, the intermediate class of those things for which Karl is not willing either to affirm or to deny the predicate. The size of the third class indicates the degree of vagueness of the predicate 'Hund,' if we disregard for simplicity the effect of Karl's ignorance about relevant facts. For

---

[2] R. Carnap, "Meaning Postulates," *Philosophical Studies*, 3:65–73 (1952).

certain predicates, e.g., 'Mensch,' this third class is relatively very small; the degree of their extensional vagueness is low. On the basis of the determination of the three classes for the predicate 'Hund' within the investigated region, the linguist may make a hypothesis concerning the responses of Karl to things outside of that region, and maybe even a hypothesis concerning the total extension in the universe. The latter hypothesis cannot, of course, be completely verified, but every single instance of it can in principle be tested. On the other hand, it is also generally agreed that this determination of extension involves uncertainty and possible error. But since this holds for all concepts of empirical science, nobody regards this fact as a sufficient reason for rejecting the concepts of the theory of extension. The sources of uncertainty are chiefly the following: first, the linguist's acceptance of the result that a given thing is denoted by 'Hund' for Karl may be erroneous, e.g., due to a misunderstanding or a factual error of Karl's; and, second, the generalization to things which he has not tested suffers, of course, from the uncertainty of all inductive inference.

3. The Determination of Intensions

The purpose of this paper is to defend the thesis that the analysis of intension for a natural language is a scientific procedure, methodologically just as sound as the analysis of extension. To many linguists and philosophers this thesis will appear as a truism. However, some contemporary philosophers, especially Quine[3] and White[4] believe that the pragmatical intension concepts are foggy, mysterious, and not really understandable, and that so far no explications for them have been given. They believe further that, if an explication for one of these concepts is found, it will at best be in the form of a concept of degree. They acknowledge the good scientific status of the pragmatical concepts of the theory of extension. They emphasize that their objection against the intension concepts is based on a point of principle and not on the generally recognized facts of the technical difficulty of linguistic investigations, the inductive uncertainty, and the vagueness of the words of ordinary language. I shall therefore leave aside in my discussion these difficulties, especially the two mentioned at the end of the last section. Thus the question is this: *granted that the linguist can determine the extension of a given predicate, how can he go beyond this and determine also its intension?*

The technical term 'intension,' which I use here instead of the ambiguous word 'meaning,' is meant to apply only to the cognitive or designative meaning component. I shall not try to define this component. It was mentioned earlier that determination of truth presupposes

---

3 W. V. Quine, *From a Logical Point of View: Nine Logico-Philosophical Essays* (1953). For his criticism of intension concepts see especially Essays II ("Two Dogmas of Empiricism," first published in 1951), III, and VII.

4 M. White, "The Analytic and the Synthetic: An Untenable Dualism" in Sidney Hook, ed., *John Dewey: Philosopher of Science and Freedom*, 1950, pp. 316–30.

knowledge of meaning (in addition to knowledge of facts); now, cognitive meaning may be roughly characterized as that meaning component which is relevant for the determination of truth. The non-cognitive meaning components, although irrelevant for questions of truth and logic, may still be very important for the psychological effect of a sentence on a listener, e.g., by emphasis, emotional associations, motivational effects.

It must certainly be admitted that the pragmatical determination of intensions involves a new step and therefore a new methodological problem. Let us assume that two linguists, investigating the language of Karl, have reached complete agreement in the determination of the extension of a given predicate in a given region. This means that they agree for every thing in this region, whether or not the predicate in question denotes it for Karl or not. As long as only these results are given, no matter how large the region is—you may take it, fictitiously, as the whole world, if you like —it is still possible for the linguists to ascribe to the predicate different intensions. For there are more than one and possibly infinitely many properties whose extension within the given region is just the extension determined for the predicate.

Here we come to the core of the controversy. It concerns the nature of a linguist's assignment of one of these properties to the predicate as its intension. This assignment may be made explicit by an entry in the German-English dictionary, conjoining the German predicate with an English phrase. The linguist declares hereby the German predicate to be synonymous with the English phrase. The *intensionalist thesis* in pragmatics, which I am defending, says that the assignment of an intension is an empirical hypothesis which, like any other hypothesis in linguistics, can be tested by observations of language behavior. On the other hand, the *extensionalist thesis* asserts that the assignment of an intension, on the basis of the previously determined extension is not a question of fact but merely a matter of choice. The thesis holds that the linguist is free to choose any of those properties which fit to the given extension; he may be guided in his choice by a consideration of simplicity, but there is no question of right or wrong. Quine seems to maintain this thesis; he says: "The finished lexicon is a case evidently of *ex pede Herculem*. But there is a difference. In projecting Hercules from the foot we risk error but we may derive comfort from the fact that there is something to be wrong about. In the case of the lexicon, pending some definition of synonymy, we have no stating of the problem; we have nothing for the lexicographer to be right or wrong about." (*Op. cit.,* p. 63.)

I shall now plead for the intensionalist thesis. Suppose, for example, that one linguist, after an investigation of Karl's speaking behavior, writes into his dictionary the following:

(1) *Pferd,* horse

while another linguist writes:

(2) *Pferd,* horse or unicorn.

Since there are no unicorns, the two intensions ascribed to the word 'Pferd' by the two linguists, although different, have the same extension. If the extensionalist thesis were right, there would be no way for empirically deciding between (1) and (2). Since the extension is the same, no response by Karl, affirmative or negative, with respect to any actual thing can make a difference between (1) and (2). But what else is there to investigate for the linguist beyond Karl's responses concerning the application of the predicate to all the cases that can be found? The answer is, he must take into account not only the actual cases, but also possible cases.[5] The most direct way of doing this would be for the linguist to use, in the German questions directed to Karl, modal expressions corresponding to "possible case" or the like. To be sure, these expressions are usually rather ambiguous; but this difficulty can be overcome by giving suitable explanations and examples. I do not think that there is any objection of principle against the use of modal terms. On the other hand, I think that their use is not necessary. The linguist could simply describe for Karl cases, which he knows to be possible, and leave it open whether there is anything satisfying those descriptions or not. He may, for example, describe a unicorn (in German) by something corresponding to the English formulation: "a thing similar to a horse, but having only one horn in the middle of the forehead." Or he may point toward a thing and then describe the intended modification in words, e.g.: "a thing like this one but having one horn in the middle of the forehead." Or, finally, he might just point to a picture representing a unicorn. Then he asks Karl whether he is willing to apply the word 'Pferd' to a thing of this kind. An affirmative or a negative answer will constitute a confirming instance for (2) or (1) respectively. This shows that (1) and (2) are different empirical hypotheses.

All *logically possible* cases come into consideration for the determination of intensions. This includes also those cases that are causally impossible, i.e., excluded by the laws of nature holding in our universe, and certainly those that are excluded by laws which Karl believes to hold. Thus, if Karl believes that all P are Q by a law of nature, the linguist will still induce him to consider things that are P but not Q, and ask him whether or not he would apply to them the predicate under investigation (e.g., 'Pferd').

The inadequacy of the extensionalist thesis is also shown by the following example. Consider, on the one hand, these customary entries in German-English dictionaries:

---

[5] Some philosophers have indeed defined the intension of a predicate (or a concept closely related to it) as the class of the possible objects falling under it. For example, C. I. Lewis defines: "The comprehension of a term is the classification of all consistently thinkable things to which the term would correctly apply" ("The Modes of Meaning," *Philosophy and Phenomenological Research*, 4:236–50 (1944)). I prefer to apply modalities like possibility not to objects but only to intensions, especially to propositions or to properties (kinds). (Compare *Meaning and Necessity*, pp. 66f.) To speak of a possible case means to speak of a kind of objects which is possibly non-empty.

(3) *Einhorn*, unicorn. *Kobold*, goblin,

and, on the other hand, the following unusual entries:

(4) *Einhorn,* goblin. *Kobold,* unicorn.

Now the two German words (and likewise the two English words) have the same extension, viz., the null class. Therefore, if the extensionalist thesis were correct, there would be no essential, empirically testable difference between (3) and (4). The extensionalist is compelled to say that the fact that (3) is generally accepted and (4) generally rejected is merely due to a tradition created by the lexicographers, and that there are no facts of German language behavior which could be regarded as evidence in favor of (3) as against (4). I wonder whether any linguist would be willing to accept (4). Or, to avoid the possibly misguiding influence of the lexicographers' tradition, let us put the question this way: would a man on the street, who has learned both languages by practical use without lessons or dictionaries, accept as correct a translation made according to (4)?

In general terms, the determination of the intension of a predicate may start from some instances denoted by the predicate. The essential task is then to find out what variations of a given specimen in various respects (e.g., size, shape, color) are admitted within the range of the predicate. The intension of a predicate may be defined as its range, which comprehends those possible kinds of objects for which the predicate

holds. In this investigation of intension, the linguist finds a new kind of vagueness, which may be called *intensional vagueness.* As mentioned above, the extensional vagueness of the word 'Mensch' is very small, at least in the accessible region. First, the intermediate zone among animals now living on earth is practically empty. Second, if the ancestors of man are considered, it is probably found that Karl cannot easily draw a line; thus there is an intermediate zone, but it is relatively small. However, when the linguist proceeds to the determination of the *intension* of the word 'Mensch,' the situation is quite different. He has to test Karl's responses to descriptions of strange kinds of animals, say intermediate between man and dog, man and lion, man and hawk, etc. It may be that the linguist and Karl know that these kinds of animals have never lived on earth; they do not know whether or not these kinds will ever occur on earth or on any other planet in any galaxy. At any rate, this knowledge or ignorance is irrelevant for the determination of intension. But Karl's ignorance has the psychological effect that he has seldom if ever thought of these kinds (unless he happens to be a student of mythology or a science-fiction fan) and therefore never felt an urge to make up his mind to which of them to apply the predicate 'Mensch.' Consequently, the linguist finds in Karl's responses a large intermediate zone for this predicate, in other words, a high intensional vagueness. The fact that Karl has not made such decisions means that the intension of the word 'Mensch' for him is not quite clear even to himself, that he does not completely understand his own word. This lack of clarity does not bother him much because it holds only for aspects which have very little practical importance for him.

The extensionalist will perhaps reject as impracticable the described procedure for determining intensions because, he might say, the man on the street is unwilling to say anything about non-existent objects. If Karl happens to be over-realistic in this way, the linguist could still resort to a lie, reporting, say, his alleged observations of unicorns. But this is by no means necessary. The tests concerning intensions are independent of questions of existence. The man on the street is very well able to understand and to answer questions about assumed situations, where it is left open whether anything of the kind described will ever actually occur or not, and even about nonexisting situations. This is shown in ordinary conversations about alternative plans of action, about the truth of reports, about dreams, legends, and fairy tales.

Although I have given here only a rough indication of the empirical procedure for determining intensions, I believe that it is sufficient to make clear that it would be possible to write along the lines indicated a manual for determining intensions or, more exactly, for testing hypotheses concerning intensions. The kinds of rules in such a manual would not be essentially different from those customarily given for procedures in psychology, linguistics, and anthropology. Therefore the rules could be understood and carried out by any scientist (provided he is not infected by philosophical prejudices).[6]

4. Intensions in the Language of Science

The discussions in this paper concern in general a simple, pre-scientific language, and the predicates considered designate observable properties of

[6] After writing the present paper I have become acquainted with a very interesting new book by Arne Naess, *Interpretation and Preciseness: A Contribution to the Theory of Communication* (Skrifter Norske Vid. Akademi, Oslo, II. Hist.-Filos. Klasse, 1953, No. 1). This book describes in detail various procedures for testing hypotheses concerning the synonymity of expressions with the help of questionnaires, and gives examples of statistical results found with these questionnaires. The practical difficulties and sources of possible errors are carefully investigated. The procedures concern the responses of the test persons, not to observed objects as in the present paper, but to pairs of sentences within specified contexts. Therefore the questions are formulated in the metalanguage, e.g., "Do the two given sentences in the given context express the same assertion to you?" Although there may be different opinions concerning some features of the various procedures, it seems to me that the book marks an important progress in the methodology of empirical meaning analysis for natural languages. Some of the questions used refer also to possible kinds of cases, e.g., "Can you imagine circumstances (conditions, situations) in which you would accept the one sentence and reject the other, or vice versa?" (p. 368). The book, both in its methodological discussions and in its reports on experiences with the questionnaires, seems to me to provide abundant evidence in support of the intensionalist thesis (in the sense explained in §3 above).

material bodies. Let us now briefly take a look at the *language of science*. It is today still mainly a natural language (except for its mathematical part), with only a few explicitly made conventions for some special words or symbols. It is a variant of the pre-scientific language, caused by special professional needs. The degree of precision is here in general considerably higher (i.e., the degree of vagueness is lower) than in the everyday language, and this degree is continually increasing. It is important to note that this increase holds not only for extensional but also for intensional precision; that is to say that not only the extensional intermediate zones (i.e., those of actual occurrences) but also the intensional ones (i.e., those of possible occurrences) are shrinking. In consequence of this development, also, the intension concepts become applicable with increasing clarity. In the oldest books on chemistry, for example, there were a great number of statements describing the properties of a given substance, say water or sulphuric acid, including its reactions with other substances. There was no clear indication as to which of these numerous properties were to be taken as essential or definitory for the substance. Therefore, at least on the basis of the book alone, we cannot determine which of the statements made in the book were analytic and which synthetic for its author. The situation was similar with books on zoology, even at a much later time; we find a lot of statements, e.g., on the lion, without a clear separation of the definitory properties. But in chemistry there was an early develop-

ment from the state described to states of greater and greater intensional precision. On the basis of the theory of chemical elements, slowly with increasing explicitness certain properties were selected as essential. For a compound, the molecular formula (e.g., 'H_2O') was taken as definitory, and later the molecular structure diagram. For the elementary substances, first certain experimental properties were more and more clearly selected as definitory, for example the atomic weight, later the position in Mendeleyev's system. Still later, with a differentiation of the various isotopes, the nuclear composition was regarded as definitory, say characterized by the number of protons (atomic number) and the number of neutrons.

We can at the present time observe the advantages already obtained by the explicit conventions which have been made, though only to a very limited extent, in the language of empirical science, and the very great advantages effected by the moderate measure of formalization in the language of mathematics. Let us suppose—as I indeed believe, but that is outside of our present discussion—that this trend toward explicit rules will continue. Then the practical question arises whether rules of extension are sufficient or whether it would be advisable to lay down also rules of intension? In my view, it follows from the previous discussion that rules of intension are required, because otherwise intensional vagueness would remain, and this would prevent clear mutual understanding and effective communication.

5. The General Concept of the Intension of a Predicate

We have seen that there is an empirical procedure for testing, by observations of linguistic behavior, a hypothesis concerning the intension of a predicate, say 'Pferd,' for a speaker, say Karl. Since a procedure of this kind is applicable to any hypothesis of intension, the general concept of the intension of any predicate in any language for any person at any time has a clear, empirically testable sense. This general concept of intension may be characterized roughly as follows, leaving subtleties aside: the intension of a predicate $'Q'$ for a speaker X is the general condition which an object y must fulfill in order for X to be willing to ascribe the predicate $'Q'$ to y. (We omit, for simplicity, the reference to a time t.) Let us try to make this general characterization more explicit. That X is able to use a language L means that X has a certain system of interconnected dispositions for certain linguistic responses. That a predicate $'Q'$ in a language L has the property F as its intension for X, means that among the dispositions of X constituting the language L there is the disposition of ascribing the predicate $'Q'$ to any object y if and only if y has the property F. (F is here always assumed to be an observable property, i.e., either directly observable or explicitly definable in terms of directly observable properties.) (The given formulation is oversimplified, neglecting vagueness. In order to take vagueness into account, a pair of intensions F_1, F_2 must be stated: X has the disposition of ascribing affirmatively the predicate $'Q'$ to an object y if and only if y has F_1; and the disposition of denying $'Q'$ for y if and only if y has F_2. Thus, if y has neither F_1 nor F_2, X will give neither an affirmative nor a negative response; the property of having neither F_1 nor F_2 constitutes the zone of vagueness, which may possibly be empty.)

The concept of intension has here been characterized only for thing-predicates. The characterization for expressions of other types, including sentences, can be given in an analogous way. The other concepts of the theory of intension can then be defined in the usual way; we shall state only those for 'synonymous' and 'analytic' in a simple form without claim to exactness.

Two expressions are *synonymous* in the language L or X at time t if they have the same intension in L for X at t.

A sentence is *analytic* in L for X at t if its intension (or range or truth-condition) in L for X at t comprehends all possible cases.

A language L was characterized above as a system of certain dispositions for the use of expressions. I shall now make some remarks on the *methodology of dispositional concepts*. This will help to a clearer understanding of the nature of linguistic concepts in general and of the concept of intension in particular. Let D be the disposition of X to react to a condition C by the characteristic response R. There are in principle, although not always in practice, two ways for ascertaining whether a given thing or person X has the disposition D (at a given time t). The first method may be called *behavioristic* (in a very wide sense); it consists in producing the condition C and then determining whether or not the response R occurs. The second way may be called the *method of structure analysis*. It consists in investigating the state of X (at t) in sufficient detail such that it is possible to derive from the obtained description of the state with the help of relevant general laws (say of physics, physiology, etc.) the responses which X would make to any specified circumstances in the environment. Then it will be possible to predict, in particular, whether under the condition C X would make the response R or not; if so, X has the disposition D, otherwise not. For example, let X be an automobile and D be the ability for a specified acceleration on a horizontal road at a speed of 10 miles per hour. The hypothesis that the automobile has this ability D may be tested by either of the following two procedures. The behavioristic method consists in driving the car and observing its performance under the specified conditions. The second method consists in studying the internal structure of the car, especially the motor, and calculating with the help of physical laws the acceleration which would result under the specified conditions. With respect to a psychological disposition and, in particular, a linguistic disposition of a person X, there is first the familiar behavioristic method and second, at least theoretically, the method of a micro-physiological investigation of the body of X,

especially the central nervous system. At the present state of physiological knowledge of the human organism and especially the central nervous system, the second method is, of course, not practicable.

6. The Concept of Intension for a Robot

In order to make the method of structure analysis applicable, let us now consider the pragmatical investigation of the language of a robot rather than that of a human being. In this case we may assume that we possess much more detailed knowledge of the internal structure. The logical nature of the pragmatical concepts remains just the same. Suppose that we have a sufficiently detailed blueprint according to which the robot X was constructed and that X has abilities of observation and of use of language. Let us assume that X has three input organs A, B, and C, and an output organ. A and B are used alternatively, never simultaneously. A is an organ of visual observation of objects presented. B can receive a general description of a kind of object (a predicate expression) in the language L of X, which may consist of written marks or of holes punched in a card. C receives a predicate. These inputs constitute the question whether the object presented at A or any object satisfying the description presented at B is denoted in L for X by the predicate presented at C. The output organ may then supply one of three responses of X, for affirmation, denial, or abstention; the latter response would be given, e.g., if the observation of the object at A or the description at B is not sufficient to determine a definite answer. Just as the linguist investigating Karl begins with pointing to objects, but later, after having determined the interpretation of some words, asks questions formulated by these words, the investigator of X's language L begins with presenting objects at A, but later, on the basis of tentative results concerning the intensions of some signs of L, proceeds to present predicate expressions at B which use only those interpreted signs and not the predicate presented at C.

Instead of using this behavioristic method, the investigator may here use the method of structure analysis. On the basis of the given blueprint of X, he may be able to calculate the responses which X would make to various possible inputs. In particular, he may be able to derive from the given blueprint, with the help of those laws of physics which determine the functioning of the organs of X, the following result with respect to a given predicate 'Q' of the language L of X and specified properties F_1 and F_2 (observable for X): If the predicate 'Q' is presented at C, then X gives an affirmative response if and only if an object having the property F_1 is presented at A and a negative response if and only if an object with F_2 is presented at A. This result indicates that the boundary of the intension of 'Q' is somwhere between the boundary of F_1 and that of F_2. For some predicates the zone of indeterminateness between F_1 and F_2 may be fairly small and hence this preliminary determination of the inten-sion fairly precise. This might be the case, for example, for color predicates if the investigator has a sufficient number of color specimens.

After this preliminary determination of the intensions of some predicates constituting a restricted vocabulary V by calculations concerning input A, the investigator will proceed to making calculations concerning descriptions containing the predicates of V to be presented at B. He may be able to derive from the blueprint the following result: If the predicate 'P' is presented at C, and any description D in terms of the vocabulary V is presented at B, X gives an affirmative response if and only if D (as interpreted by the preliminary results) logically implies G_1, and a negative response if and only if D logically implies G_2. This result indicates that the boundary of the intension of 'P' is between the boundary of G_1 and that of G_2. In this way more precise determinations for a more comprehensive part of L and finally for the whole of L may be obtained. (Here again we assume that the predicates of L designate observable properties of things.)

It is clear that the method of structure analysis, if applicable, is more powerful than the behavioristic method, because it can supply a general answer and, under favorable circumstances, even a complete answer to the question of the intension of a given predicate.

Note that the procedure described for input A can include empty kinds of objects and the procedure for input B even causally impossible kinds. Thus, for example, though we cannot present a unicorn at A, we can nevertheless calculate which response X would make if a unicorn were presented at A. This calculation is obviously in no way affected by any zoological fact concerning the existence or nonexistence of unicorns. The situation is different for a kind of objects excluded by a law of physics, especially, a law needed in the calculations about the robot. Take the law l_1 :"Any iron body at 60° F is solid." The investigator needs this law in his calculation of the functioning of X, in order to ascertain that some iron cogwheels do not melt. If now he were to take as a premise for his derivation the statement "A liquid iron body having the temperature of 60° F is presented at A," then, since the law l_1, belongs also to his premises, he would obtain a contradiction; hence every statement concerning X's response would be derivable, and thus the method would break down. But even for this case the method still works with respect to B. He may take as premise "The description 'liquid iron body with the temperature of 60° F' (that is, the translation of this into L) is presented at B." Then no contradiction arises either in the derivation made by the investigator or in that made by X. *The derivation carried out by the investigator* contains the premise just mentioned, which does not refer to an iron body but to a description, say a card punched in a certain way; thus there is no contradiction, although the law l_1 occurs also as a premise. On the other hand, in *the derivation made by the robot X,* the card presented at B supplies, as it were, a premise of the form "y is a liquid iron body at 60° F"; but here the law l_1 does not occur as a premise, and thus no contradiction

occurs. X makes merely logical deductions from the one premise stated and, if the predicate 'R' is presented at C, tries to come either to the conclusion "y is R" or "y is not R." Suppose the investigator's calculation leads to the result that X would derive the conclusion "y is R" and hence that X would give an affirmative response. This result would show that the (causally impossible) kind of liquid iron bodies at 60° F is included in the range of the intension of 'R' for X.

I have tried to show in this paper that in a pragmatical investigation of a natural language there is not only, as generally agreed, an empirical method for ascertaining which objects are denoted by a given predicate and thus for determining the extension of the predicate, but also a method for testing a hypothesis concerning its intension (designative meaning).[7] The intension

---

[7] Y. Bar-Hillel in a recent paper ("Logical Syntax and Semantics," *Language* 30: 230–37 (1954)) defends the concept of meaning against those contemporary linguists who wish to ban it from linguistics. He explains this tendency by the fact that in the first quarter of this century the concept of meaning was indeed in a bad methodological state; the usual explanations of the concept involved psychologistic connotations, which were correctly criticized by Bloomfield and others. Bar-Hillel points out that the semantical theory of meaning developed recently by logicians is free of these drawbacks. He appeals to the linguists to construct in an analogous way the theory of meaning needed in their empirical investigations. The present paper indicates the possibility of such a construction. The fact that the concept of intension can be applied even to a robot shows that it does not have the psychologistic character of the traditional concept of meaning.

of a predicate for a speaker X is, roughly speaking, the general condition which an object must fulfill for X to be willing to apply the predicate to it. For the determination of intension, not only actually given cases must be taken into consideration, but also possible cases, i.e., kinds of objects which can be described without self-contradiction, irrespective of the question whether there are any objects of the kinds described. The intension of a predicate can be determined for a robot just as well as for a human speaker, and even more completely if the internal structure of the robot is sufficiently known to predict how it will function under various conditions. On the basis of the concept of intension, other pragmatical concepts with respect to natural languages can be defined, synonymy, analyticity, and the like. The existence of scientifically sound pragmatical concepts of this kind provides a practical motivation and justification for the introduction of corresponding concepts in pure semantics with respect to constructed language systems.

MEANING
AND TRANSLATION*

6.5

Willard Quine

I. Stimulus Meaning

Empirical meaning is what remains when, given discourse together with all its stimulatory conditions, we peel away the verbiage. It is what the sentences of one language and their firm translations in a completely alien language have in common. So, if we would isolate empirical meaning, a likely position to project ourselves into is that of the linguist who is out to penetrate and translate a hitherto unknown language. Given are

From *On Translation*, Reuben A. Brower, editor (Cambridge, Mass.: Harvard University Press, 1959). Copyright, 1959, by the President and Fellows of Harvard College. Reprinted by permission of the publishers and the author.

* This essay was an adaptation of part of a work then in progress, *Word and Object*, Cambridge, Mass.: M.I.T. Press, 1960. In the spring of 1957 I presented most of this essay as a lecture at the University of Pennsylvania, Columbia University, and Princeton University; and members of those audiences have helped me with their discussion. I used parts also at the fourth Colloque Philosophique de Royaumont, April 1958, in an address that since appeared as "Le myth de la signification" in the proceedings of the colloquium, *La Philosophie Analytique*, Paris: Editions de Minuit, 1962.

the native's unconstrued utterances and the observable circumstances of their occurrence. Wanted are the meanings; or wanted are English translations, for a good way to give a meaning is to say something in the home language that has it.

Translation between languages as close as Frisian and English is aided by resemblance of cognate word forms. Translation between unrelated languages, e.g., Hungarian and English, may be aided by traditional equations that have evolved in step with a shared culture. For light on the nature of meaning we must think rather of *radical* translation, i.e., translation of the language of a hitherto untouched people. Here it is, if anywhere, that austerely empirical meaning detaches itself from the words that have it.

The utterances first and most surely translated in such a case are perforce reports of observations conspicuously shared by the linguist and his informant. A rabbit scurries by, the native says "Gavagai," and our jungle linguist notes down the sentence "Rabbit" (or "Lo, a rabbit") as tentative translation. He will thus at first refrain from putting words into his informant's mouth, if only for lack of words to put. When he can, though, the linguist is going to have to supply native sentences for his informant's approval, despite some risk of slanting the data by suggestion. Otherwise he can do little with native terms that have references in common. For, suppose the native language includes sentences S_1, S_2, and S_3, really translatable respectively as "Animal," "White," and "Rabbit." Stimulus situations always differ, whether relevantly

or not; and, just because volunteered responses come singly, the classes of situations under which the native happens to have volunteered S_1, S_2, and S_3, are of course mutually exclusive, despite the hidden actual meanings of the words. How then is the linguist to perceive that the native would have been willing to assent to S_1 in all the situations where he happened to volunteer S_3, and in some but perhaps not all of the situations where he happened to volunteer S_2? Only by taking the initiative and querying combinations of native sentences and stimulus situations so as to narrow down his guesses to his eventual satisfaction.

Therefore, picture the linguist asking "Gavagai?" in each of various stimulatory situations, and noting each time whether the native is prompted to assent or dissent or neither. Several assumptions are implicit here as to a linguist's power of intuition. For one thing, he must be able to recognize an informant's assent and dissent independently of any particular language. Moreover, he must be able ordinarily to guess what stimulation his subject is heeding—not nerve by nerve, but in terms at least of rough and ready reference to the environment. Moreover, he must be able to guess whether that stimulation actually prompts the native's assent to or dissent from the accompanying question; he must be able to rule out the chance that the native assents to or dissents from the questioned sentence irrelevantly as a truth or falsehood on its own merits, without regard to the scurrying rabbit which happens to be the conspicuous circumstance of the moment.

The linguist does certainly succeed in these basic tasks of recognition in sufficiently numerous cases, and so can we all, however unconscious we be of our cues and method. The Turks' gestures of assent and dissent are nearly the reverse of ours, but facial expression shows through and sets us right pretty soon. As for what a man is noticing, this of course is commonly discernible from his orientation together with our familiarity with human interests. The third and last point of recognition is harder, but one easily imagines accomplishing it in typical cases: judging, without ulterior knowledge of the language, whether the subject's assent to or dissent from one's sudden question was prompted by the thing that had been under scrutiny at the time. One clue is got by pointing while asking; then, if the object is irrelevant, the answer may be accompanied by a look of puzzlement. Another clue to irrelevance can be that the question, asked without pointing, causes the native abruptly to shift his atention and look abstracted. But enough of conjectural mechanisms; the patent fact is that one does, by whatever unanalyzed intuitions, tend to pick up these minimum attitudinal data without special linguistic aid.

The imagined routine of proposing sentences in situations is suited only to sentences of a special sort: those which, like "Gavagai," "Red," "That hurts," "This one's face is dirty," etc., command assent only afresh in the light of currently observable circumstances. It is a question of *occasion sentences* as against *standing sentences*. Such are the sentences with which our jungle linguist must begin, and the ones for which we may appropriately try to develop a first crude concept of meaning.

This distinction between *occasion* sentences and standing sentences is itself definable in terms of the notion of prompted assent and dissent which we are supposing available. A sentence is an occasion sentence for a man if he can sometimes be got to assent to or dissent from it, but can never be got to unless the asking is accompanied by a prompting stimulation.

Not that there is no such prompted assent and dissent for standing sentences. A readily imaginable visual stimulation will prompt a geographically instructed subject, once, to assent to the standing sentence "There are brick houses on Elm Street." Stimulation implemented by an interferometer once prompted Michelson and Morley to dissent from the standing sentence "There is ether drift." But these standing sentences contrast with occasion sentences in that the subject may repeat his old assent or dissent unprompted by current stimulation, when we ask him again on later occasions; whereas an occasion sentence commands assent or dissent only as prompted all over again by current stimulation.

Let us define the *affirmative stimulus meaning* of an occasion sentence S, for a given speaker, as the class of all the stimulations that would prompt him to assent to S. We may define the *negative* stimulus meaning of S similarly in terms of dissent. Finally, we may define the *stimulus meaning* of S, simply so-called, as the ordered pair of the affirmative and negative stimulus meanings of S. We could distinguish degrees of doubtfulness of assent and dissent, say, by reaction time, and elaborate our definition of stimulus meaning in easily imagined ways to include this information; but for the sake of fluent exposition let us forbear.

The several stimulations, which we assemble in classes to form stimulus meanings, must themselves be taken for present purposes not as dated particular events but as repeatable event forms. We are to say not that two stimulations have occurred that were just alike, but that the same stimulation has *re*curred. To see the necessity of this attitude consider again the positive stimulus meaning of an occasion sentence S. It is the class Σ of all those stimulations that *would* prompt assent to S. If the stimulations were taken as events rather than event forms, then Σ would have to be a class of events which largely did not and will not happen, but which would prompt assent to S if they were to happen. Whenever Σ contained one realized or unrealized particular event σ, it would have to contain all other unrealized duplicates of σ; and how many are there of *these*? Certainly it is hopeless nonsense to talk thus of unrealized particulars and try to assemble them into classes. Unrealized entities have to be construed as universals, simply because there are no places and dates by which to distinguish between those that are in other respects alike.

It is not necessary for present purposes to decide exactly when to count two events of surface irritation as recurrences of the same stimulation, and when to count them as occurrences of different stimulations. In practice,

certainly, the linguist need never care about nerve-for-nerve duplications of stimulating events. It remains, as always, sufficient merely to know, e.g., that the subject got a good glimpse of a rabbit. This is sufficient because of one's reasonable expectation of invariance of behavior under any such circumstances.

The affirmative and negative stimulus meanings of a sentence are mutually exclusive. We have supposed the linguist capable of recognizing assent and dissent, and we mean these to be so construed that no one can be said to assent to and dissent from the same occasion sentence on the same occasion. Granted, our subject might be prompted once by a given stimulation σ to assent to S, and later, by a recurrence of σ, to dissent from S; but then we would simply conclude that his meaning for S had changed. We would then reckon σ to his affirmative stimulus meaning of S as of the one date and to his negative stimulus meaning of S as of the other date. At any one given time his positive stimulus meaning of S comprises just the stimulations that *would* prompt him then to assent to S, and correspondingly for the negative stimulus meaning; and we may be sure that these two classes of stimulations are mutually exclusive.

Yet the affirmative and negative stimulus meaning do not determine each other; for the negative stimulus meaning of S does not ordinarily comprise all the stimulations that would not prompt assent to S. In general, therefore, the matching of whole stimulus meanings can be a better basis for translation than the matching merely of affirmative stimulus meanings.

What now of that strong conditional, the "would prompt" in our definition of stimulus meaning? The device is used so unquestioningly in solid old branches of science that to object to its use in a study as shaky as the present one would be a glaring case of misplaced aspiration, a compliment no more deserved then intended. What the strong conditional defines is a disposition, in this case a disposition to assent to or dissent from S when variously prompted. The disposition may be presumed to be some subtle structural condition, like an allergy and like solubility; like an allergy, more particularly, in not being understood. Whatever the ontological status of dispositions, or the philosophical status of talk of dispositions, we are familiar enough in a general way with how one sets about guessing, from judicious tests and samples and observed uniformities, whether there is a disposition of a specified sort.

II. The Inscrutability of Terms

Impressed with the interdependence of sentences, one may well wonder whether meanings even of whole sentences (let alone shorter expressions) can reasonably be talked of at all, except relative to the other sentences of an inclusive theory. Such relativity would be awkward, since, conversely, the individual component sentences offer the only way into the theory. Now the notion of stimulus meaning partially resolves the predicament. It isolates a sort of net empirical import of each of various single sentences without regard to the containing theory, even though without loss

of what the sentence owes to that containing theory. It is a device, as far as it goes, for exploring the fabric of interlocking sentences, a sentence at a time. Some such device is indispensable in broaching an alien culture, and relevant also to an analysis of our own knowledge of the world.

We have started our consideration of meaning with sentences, even if sentences of a special sort and meaning in a strained sense. For words, when not learned as sentences, are learned only derivatively by abstraction from their roles in learned sentences. Still there are, prior to any such abstraction, the one-word sentences; and, as luck would have it, they are (in English) sentences of precisely the special sort already under investigation—occasion sentences like "White" and "Rabbit." Insofar then as the concept of stimulus meaning may be said to constitute in some strained sense a meaning concept for occasion sentences, it would in particular constitute a meaning concept for general terms like "White" and "Rabbit." Let us examine the concept of stimulus meaning for a while in this latter, conveniently limited, domain of application.

To affirm sameness of stimulus meaning on the part of a term for two speakers, or on the part of two terms for one or two speakers, is to affirm a certain sameness of applicability: the stimulations that prompt assent coincide, and likewise those that prompt dissent. Now is this merely to say that the term or terms have the same *extension*, i.e., are true of the same objects, for the speaker or speakers in question? In the case of "Rabbit" and "Gavagai" it may seem so. Actually, in the general case, more is involved. Thus, to adapt an example of Carnap's, imagine a general heathen term for horses and unicorns. Since there are no unicorns, the extension of that inclusive heathen term is that simply of "horses." Yet we would like somehow to say that the term, unlike "horse," *would* be true also of unicorns, if there were any. Now our concept of stimulus meaning actually helps to make sense of that wanted further determination with respect to nonexistents. For stimulus meaning is in theory a question of direct surface irritations, not horses and unicorns. Each stimulation that would be occasioned by observing a unicorn is an assortment of nerve-hits, no less real and in principle no less specifiable than those occasioned by observing a horse. Such a stimulation can even be actualized, by papier-mâché trickery. In practice also we can do without deception, using descriptions and hypothetical questions, if we know enough of the language; such devices are indirect ways of guessing at stimulus meaning, even though external to the definition.

For terms like "Horse," "Unicorn," "White," and "Rabbit"—general terms for observable external objects—our concept of stimulus meaning thus seems to provide a moderately strong translation relation that goes beyond mere sameness of extension. But this is not so; the relation falls far short of sameness of extension on other counts. For, consider "Gavagai" again. Who knows but what the objects to which this term applies are not rabbits after all, but mere stages, or brief temporal segments, of rabbits? For in either event the stimulus situations that prompt assent to "Gavagai" would be the same as for "Rabbit." Or

perhaps the objects to which "Gavagai" applies are all and sundry undetached parts of rabbits; again the stimulus meaning would register no difference. When from the sameness of stimulus meanings of "Gavagai" and "Rabbit" the linguist leaps to the conclusion that a gavagai is a whole enduring rabbit, he is just taking for granted that the native is enough like us to have a brief general term for rabbits and no brief general term for rabbit stages or parts.

Commonly we can translate something (e.g., "for the sake of") into a given language though nothing in that language corresponds to certain of the component syllables (e.g., to "the" and to "sake"). Just so the occasion sentence "Gavagai" is translatable as saying that a rabbit is there, though no part of "Gavagai" nor anything at all in the native language quite correspond to the term "rabbit." Synonymy of "Gavagai" and "Rabbit" as sentences turns on considerations of prompted assent, which transcend all cultural boundaries; not so synonymy of them as terms. We are right to write "Rabbit," instead of "rabbit," as a signal that we are considering it in relation to what is synonymous with it as a sentence and not in relation to what is synonymous with it as a term.

Does it seem that the imagined indecision between rabbits, stages of rabbits, and integral parts of rabbits should be resoluble by a little supplementary pointing and questioning? Consider, then, how. Point to a rabbit and you have pointed to a stage of a rabbit and to an integral part of a rabbit. Point to an integral part of a rabbit and you have pointed to a rabbit and to a stage of a rabbit. Correspondingly, for the third alternative. Nothing not distinguished in stimulus meaning itself will be distinguished by pointing, unless the pointing is accompanied by questions of identity and diversity: "Is this the same gavagai as that? Do we have here one gavagai or two?" Such questioning requires of the linguist a command of the native language far beyond anything that we have as yet seen how to account for. More, it presupposes that the native conceptual scheme is, like ours, one that breaks reality down somehow into a multiplicity of identifiable and discriminable physical things, be they rabbits or stages or parts. For the native attitude might, after all, be very unlike ours. The term "gavagai" might be the proper name of a recurring universal rabbit-hood; and *still* the occasion sentence "Gavagai" would have the same stimulus meaning as under the other alternatives above suggested. For that matter, the native point of view might be so alien that from it there would be just no semblance of sense in speaking of objects at all, not even of abstract ones like rabbit-hood. Native channels might be wholly unlike Western talk of this and that, same and different, one and two. Failing some such familiar apparatus, surely the native cannot significantly be said to posit objects. Stuff conceivably, but not things, concrete *or* abstract. And yet, even in the face of this alien ontological attitude, the occasion sentence "Gavagai" could still have the same stimulus meaning as "(Lo, a) rabbit." Occasion sentences and stimulus meanings are general coin, whereas terms, conceived as variously applying to objects in some sense, are a provincial appurtenance of our object-positing kind of culture.

Can we even imagine any basic alternative to our object-positing pattern? Perhaps not, for we would have to imagine it in translation, and translation imposes our pattern. Perhaps the very notion of such radical contrast of cultures is meaningless, except in this purely privative sense: persistent failure to find smooth and convincing native analogues of our own familiar accessories of objective reference, such as the articles, the identity predicate, the plural ending. Only by such failure can we be said to perceive that the native language represents matters in ways not open to our own.

III. Observation Sentences

In sections one and two we came to appreciate sameness of stimulus meaning as an, in some ways, serviceable synonymy relation when limiting to occasion sentences. But even when thus limited, stimulus meaning falls short of the requirement implicit in ordinary, uncritical talk of meaning. The trouble is that an informant's prompted assent to or dissent from an occasion sentence may depend only partly on the present prompting stimulation and all too largely on his hidden collateral information. In distinguishing between occasion sentences and standing sentences (Section 1), and deferring the latter, we have excluded all cases where the informant's assent or dissent might depend wholly on collateral information, but we have not excluded cases where his assent or dissent depends mainly on collateral information and ever so little on the present prompting stimulation. Thus, the native's assent to "Gavagai" on the occasion of nothing better than an ill-glimpsed movement in the grass can have been due mainly to earlier observation, in the linguist's absence, of rabbit enterprises near the spot. And there are occasion sentences the prompted assent to which will *always* depend so largely on collateral information that their stimulus meanings cannot be treated as their "meanings" by any stretch of the imagination. An example is "Bachelor"; one's assent to it is prompted genuinely enough by the sight of a face, yet it draws mainly on stored information and not at all on the prompting stimulation except as needed for recognizing the bachelor friend concerned. The trouble with "Bachelor" is that its meaning transcends the looks of the prompting faces and concerns matters that can be known only through other channels. Evidently then we must try to single out a subclass of the occasion sentences which will qualify as *observation sentences*, recognizing that what I have called stimulus meaning constitutes a reasonable notion of meaning for such sentences at most. Occasion sentences have been defined (Section 1) as sentences to which there is assent or dissent but only subject to prompting; and what we now ask of observation sentences, more particularly, is that the assent or dissent be prompted always without help of information beyond the prompting stimulation itself.

It is remarkable how sure we are that each assent to "Bachelor," or a native equivalent, would draw on data from the two sources—present stimulation and collateral information. We are not lacking in elaborate if unsystematic insights into the ways of using "Bachelor" or other specific words of our own language. Yet, it does not behoove us to be smug about this easy sort of talk of meanings and reasons, for all its productivity; for, with the slightest encouragement, it can involve us in the most hopelessly confused beliefs and meaningless controversies.

Suppose it said that a particular class Σ comprises just those stimulations each of which suffices to prompt assent to an occasion sentence S outright, without benefit of collateral information. Suppose it said that the stimulations comprised in a further class Σ', likewise sufficient to prompt assent to S, owe their efficacy rather to certain widely disseminated, collateral information, C. Now couldn't we just as well have said, instead, that on acquiring C, men have found it convenient implicitly to change the very *meaning* of S, so that the members of Σ' now suffice outright like members of Σ? I suggest that we may say either; even historical clairvoyance would reveal no distinction, though it reveal all stages in the acquisition of C, since meaning can evolve *pari passu*. The distinction is illusory. What we objectively have is just an evolving adjustment to nature, reflected in an evolving set of dispositions to be prompted by stimulations to assent to or dissent from occasion sentences. These dispositions may be conceded to be impure in the sense of including worldly knowledge, but they contain it in a solution which there is no precipitating.

Observation sentences were to be occasion sentences, the assent or dissent to which is prompted always without help of collateral information. The notion of help of collateral information is now seen to be shaky. Actually the notion of observation sentence is less so, because of a stabilizing statistical effect which I can suggest if for a moment I go on speaking uncritically in terms of the shaky notion of collateral information. Now some of the collateral information relevant to an occasion sentence S may be widely disseminated, some not. Even that which is widely disseminated may in part be shared by one large group of persons and in part by another, so that few if any persons know it all. Meaning, on the other hand, is social. Even the man who is oddest about a word is likely to have a few companions in deviation.

At any rate the effect is strikingly seen by comparing "Rabbit" with "Bachelor." The stimulus meaning of "Bachelor" will be the same for no two speakers short of Siamese twins. The stimulus meaning of "Rabbit" will be much alike for most speakers; exceptions like the movement in the grass are rare. A working concept that would seem to serve pretty much the purpose of the notion of observation sentence is then simply this: *occasion sentence possessing intersubjective stimulus meaning.*

In order then that an occasion sentence be an observation sentence, is it sufficient that there be *two* people for whom it has the same stimulus meaning? No, as witness those Siamese twins. Must it have the same stimulus meaning for all persons in the lingustic community (however *that* might be defined)? Surely not. Must it have *exactly* the same stimulus meaning for even two? Perhaps not, considering again that movement in the grass. But these questions aim at refinements that would simply be misleading if under-

taken. We are concerned here with rough trends of behavior. What matters for the notion of observation sentence here intended is that for significantly many speakers the stimulus meanings deviate significantly little.

In one respect, actually, the intersubjective variability of the stimulus meaning of sentences like "Bachelor" has been understated. Not only will the stimulus meaning of "Bachelor" for one person differ from that of "Bachelor" for the next person; it will differ from that of any other likely sentence for the next person, in the same language or any other.

The linguist is not free to survey a native stimulus meaning *in extenso* and then to devise *ad hoc* a great complex English sentence whose stimulus meaning, for him, matches the native one by sheer exhaustion of cases. He has rather to extrapolate any native stimulus meaning from samples, guessing at the informant's mentality. If the sentence is as nonobservational as "Bachelor," he simply will not find likely lines of extrapolation. Translation by stimulus meaning will then deliver no wrong result, but simply nothing. This is interesting because what led us to try to define observation sentences was our reflection that they were the subclass of occasion sentences that seemed reasonably translatable by identity of stimulus meaning. Now we see that the limitation of this method of translation to this class of sentences is self-enforcing. When an occasion sentence is of the wrong kind, the informant's stimulus meaning for it will simply not be one that the linguist will feel he can plausibly equate with his own stimulus meaning for any English sentence.

The notion of stimulus meaning was one that required no multiplicity of informants. There is in principle the stimulus meaning of the sentence for the given speaker at the given time of his life (though in guessing at it the linguist may be helped by varying both the time and the speaker). The definition of observation sentence took wider points of reference: it expressly required comparison of various speakers of the same language. Finally, the reflection in the foregoing paragraph reassures us that such widening of horizons can actually be done without. Translation of occasion sentences by stimulus meaning will limit itself to observation sentences without our ever having actually to bring the criterion of observation sentence to bear.

The phrase "observation sentence" suggests, for epistemologists or methodologists of science, datum sentences of science. On this score, our version is by no means amiss. For our observation sentences as defined are just the occasion sentences on which there is pretty sure to be firm agreement on the part of well-placed observers. Thus, they are just the sentences to which a scientist will finally recur when called upon to marshal his data and repeat his observations and experiments for doubting colleagues.

IV. Intrasubjective Synonymy of Occasion Sentences

Stimulus meaning remains defined all this while for occasion sentences generally, without regard to observationality. But it bears less resemblance to what might reasonably be called meaning when applied to nonobservation sentences like "Bachelor." Translation of "Soltero" as "Bachelor" manifestly cannot be predicated on identity of stimulus meanings between persons; nor can synonymy of "Bachelor" and "Unmarried man."

Curiously enough, though, the stimulus meanings of "Bachelor" and "Unmarried man" are, despite all this, identical for any one speaker. An individual will at any one time be prompted by the same stimulations to assent to "Bachelor" and to "Unmarried man"; and similarly for dissent. What we find is that, though the concept of stimulus meaning is so very remote from "true meaning" when applied to the inobservational occasion sentences "Bachelor" and "Unmarried man," still synonymy is definable as sameness of stimulus meaning just as faithfully for these sentences as for the choicest observation sentences—as long as we stick to one speaker. For each speaker, "Bachelor" and "Unmarried man" are synonymous in a defined sense (viz., alike in stimulus meaning) without having the same meaning in any acceptably defined sense of "meaning" (for stimulus meaning is, in the case of "Bachelor," nothing of the kind). Very well; let us welcome the synonymy and let the meaning go.

The one-speaker restriction presents no obstacle to saying that "Bachelor" and "Unmarried man" are synonymous for the whole community, in the sense of being synonymous for each member. A practical extension even to the two-language case is not far to seek if a bilingual speaker is at hand. "Bachelor" and "Soltero" will be synonymous for him by the intra-individual criterion, viz., sameness of stimulus meaning. Taking him as a sample, we may treat "Bachelor" and "Soltero" as synonymous for the translation purposes of the two whole linguistic communities that he represents. Whether he is a good enough sample would be checked by observing the fluency of his communication in both communities, by comparing other bilinguals, or by observing how well the translations work.

But such use of bilinguals is unavailable to the jungle linguist broaching an untouched culture. For radical translation the only concept thus far at our disposal is sameness of stimulus meaning, and this only for observation sentences.

The kinship and difference between intrasubjective synonymy and radical translation require careful notice. Intrasubjective synonymy, like translation, is quite capable of holding good for a whole community. It is intrasubjective in that the synonyms are joined for each subject by sameness of stimulus meaning for him; but it may still be community-wide in that the synonyms in question are joined by sameness of stimulus meaning for every single subject in the whole community. Obviously, intrasubjective synonymy is in principle just as objective, just as discoverable by the outside linguist, as is translation. Our linguist may even find native sentences intrasubjectively synonymous without finding English translations—without, in short, understanding them; for he can find that they have the same stimulus meaning, for

the subject, even though there may be no English sentence whose stimulus meaning for himself promises to be the same. Thus, to turn the tables: a Martian could find that "Bachelor" and "Unmarried man" were synonyms without discovering when to assent to either one.

"Bachelor" and "Yes" are two occasion sentences which we may instructively compare. Neither of them is an observation sentence, nor, therefore, translatable by identity of stimulus meaning. The heathen equivalent ("Tak," say) of "Yes" would fare poorly indeed under translation by stimulus meaning. The stimulations which—accompanying the linguist's question "Tak?"—would prompt assent to this queer sentence, even on the part of all natives without exception, are ones which (because exclusively verbal in turn, and couched in the heathen tongue) would never have prompted an unspoiled Anglo-Saxon to assent to "Yes" or anything like it. "Tak" is just what the linguist is fishing for by way of assent to whatever heathen occasion sentence he may be investigating, but it is a poor one, under these methods, to investigate. Indeed we may expect "Tak," or "Yes," like "Bachelor," to have the same stimulus meaning for no two speakers even of the same language; for "Yes" can have the same stimulus meaning only for speakers who agree on every single thing that can be blurted in a specious present. At the same time, sameness of stimulus meaning does define intrasubjective synonymy, not only between "Bachelor" and "Unmarried man" but equally between "Yes" and "Uh huh" or "Quite."

Note that the reservations of Section 2 regarding coextensiveness of terms still hold. Though the Martian find that "Bachelor" and "Unmarried man" are synonymous occasion sentences, still in so doing he will not establish that "bachelor" and "unmarried man" are coextensive general terms. Either term to the exclusion of the other might, so far as he knows, apply not to men but to their stages or parts or even to an abstract attribute; compare Section 2.

Talking of occasion sentences as sentences and not as terms, however, we see that we can do more for synonymy within a language than for radical translation. It appears that sameness of stimulus meaning will serve as a standard of intrasubjective synonymy of occasion sentences without their having to be observation sentences.

Actually, we do need this limitation: we should stick to short and simple sentences. Otherwise subjects' mere incapacity to digest long questions can, under our definitions, issue in difference of stimulus meanings between long and short sentences which we should prefer to find synonymous. A stimulation may prompt assent to the short sentence and not to the long one just because of the opacity of the long one; yet we should then like to say not that the subject has shown the meaning of the long sentence to be different, but merely that he has failed to penetrate it.

Certainly the sentences will not have to be kept so short but what some will contain others. One thinks of such containment as happening with help of conjunctions, in the grammarians' sense: "or," "and," "but," "if," "then," "that," etc., governing the contained sentence as clause of the containing sentence. But it can also happen farther down. Very simple sentences may contain substantives and adjectives ("red," "tile," "bachelor," etc.) which qualify also as occasion sentences in their own right, subject to our synonymy concept. So our synonymy concept already applies on an equal footing to sentences some of which recur as parts of others. Some extension of synonymy to longer occasion sentences, containing others as parts, is then possible by the following sort of construction.

Think of $R(S)$ first as an occasion sentence which, though moderately short, still contains an occasion sentence S as part. If now we leave the contained sentence blank, the partially empty result may graphically be referred to as $R(\ldots)$ and called (following Peirce) a *rheme*. A rheme $R(\ldots)$ will be called *regular* if it fulfills this condition: for each S and S', if S and S' are synonymous and $R(S)$ and $R(S')$ are idiomatically acceptable occasion sentences short enough for our synonymy concept, then $R(S)$ and $R(S')$ are synonymous. This concept of regularity makes reasonable sense thus far only for short rhemes, since $R(S)$ and $R(S')$ must, for suitably short S and S', be short enough to come under our existing synonymy concept. However, the concept of regularity now invites extension, in this very natural way: where the rhemes $R_1(\ldots)$ and $R_2(\ldots)$ are both regular, let us speak of the longer rheme $R_1(R_2(\ldots))$ as regular too. In this way we may speak of regularity of longer and longer rhemes without end. Thereupon, we can extend the synonymy concept to various long occasion sentences, as follows. Where $R(\ldots)$ is any regular rheme and S and S' are short occasion sentences that are synonymous in the existing, unextended sense and $R(S)$ and $R(S')$ are idiomatically acceptable combinations at all, we may by extension call $R(S)$ and $R(S')$ synonymous in turn—even though they be too long for synonymy as first defined. There is no limit now to length, since the regular rheme $R(\ldots)$ may be as long as we please.

V. Truth Functions

In Sections 2 and 3 we accounted for radical translation only of observation sentences, by identification of stimulus meanings. Now there is also a decidedly different domain that lends itself directly to radical translation: that of *truth functions* such as negation, logical conjunction, and alternation. For, suppose as before that assent and dissent are generally recognizable. The sentences put to the native for assent or dissent may now be occasion sentences and standing sentences indifferently. Those that are occasion sentences will of course have to be accompanied by a prompting stimulation, if assent or dissent is to be elicited; the standing sentences, on the other hand, can be put without props. Now by reference to assent and dissent we can state *semantic criteria* for truth functions; i.e., criteria for determining whether a given native idiom is to be construed as expressing the truth function in question. The semantic criterion of negation is that it turns any short sentence to which one will assent into a sentence from which

one will dissent, and vice versa. That of conjunction is that it produces compounds to which (so long as the component sentences are short) one is prepared to assent always and only when one is prepared to assent to each component. That of alternation is similar but with the verb "assent" changed twice to "dissent."

The point about short components is merely, as in Section 4, that when they are long, the subject may get mixed up. Identification of a native idiom as negation, or conjunction, or alternation, is not to be ruled out in view of a subject's deviation from our semantic criteria when the deviation is due merely to confusion. Note well that no limit is imposed on the lengths of the component sentences to which negation, conjunction, or alternation may be applied; it is just that the test cases for first spotting such constructions in a strange language are cases with short components.

When we find a native construction to fulfill one or another of these three semantic criteria, we can ask no more toward an understanding of it. Incidentally we can then translate the idiom into English as "not," "and," or "or" as the case may be, but only subject to sundry, humdrum provisos; for it is well known that these three English words do not represent negation, conjunction, and alternation exactly and unambiguously.

Any construction for compounding sentences from other sentences is counted in logic as expressing a truth-function if it fulfills this condition: the compound has a unique "truth value" (truth or falsity) for each assignment of truth values to the components. Semantic criteria can obviously be stated for all truth-functions along the lines already followed for negation, conjunction, and alternation.

One hears talk of prelogical peoples, said deliberately to accept certain simple self-contradictions as true. Doubtless overstating Levy-Bruhl's intentions, let us imagine someone to claim that these natives accept as true a certain sentence of the form "p ka bu p" where "ka" means "and" and "bu" means "not." Now this claim is absurd on the face of it, if translation of "ka" as "and" and "bu" as "not" follows our semantic criteria. And, not to be dogmatic, what criteria will you have? Conversely, to claim on the basis of a better dictionary that the natives *do* share our logic would be to impose our logic and beg the question, if there were really a meaningful question here to beg. But I do urge the better dictionary.

The same point can be illustrated within English, by the question of alternative logics. Is he who propounds heterodox logical laws really contradicting our logic, or is he just putting some familiar old vocables ("and," "or," "not," "all," etc.) to new and irrelevant uses? It makes no sense to say, unless from the point of view of some criteria or other for translating logical particles. Given the above criteria, the answer is clear.

We hear from time to time that the scientist in his famous freedom to resystematize science or fashion new calculi is bound at least to respect the law of contradiction. Now what are we to make of this? We do flee contradiction, for we are after truth. But what of a revision so fundamental as to count contradictions as true? Well, to begin with, it would have to be arranged carefully if all utility is not to be lost. Classical logical laws enable us from any one contradiction to deduce all statements indiscriminately; and such universal affirmation would leave science useless for lack of distinctions. So the revision which counts contradictions as true will have to be accompanied by a revision of other logical laws. Now all this can be done; but, once it is done, how can we say it is what it purported to be? This heroically novel logic falls under the considerations of the preceding paragraph, to be reconstrued perhaps simply as old logic in bad notation.

We *can* meaningfully contemplate changing a law of logic, be it the law of excluded middle or even the law of contradiction. But this is so only because while contemplating the change we continue to translate *identically*: "and" as "and," "or" as "or," etc. Afterward, a more devious mode of translation will perhaps be hit upon which will annul the change of law; or perhaps, on the contrary, the change of law will be found to have produced an essentially stronger system, demonstrably not translatable into the old in any way at all. But even in the latter event any actual conflict between the old and the new logic proves illusory, for it comes only of translating identically.

At any rate we have settled a people's logical laws completely, so far as the truth-functional part of logic goes, once we have fixed our translations by the above semantic criteria. In particular, the class of the *tautologies* is fixed: the truth-functional compounds that are true by truth-functional structure alone.

There is a familiar tabular routine for determining, for sentences in which the truth-functions are however immoderately iterated and superimposed, just what assignments of truth-values to the ultimate component sentences will make the whole compound true; and the tautologies are the compounds that come out true under all assignments.

It is a commonplace of epistemology (and therefore occasionally contested) that just two very opposite spheres of knowledge enjoy irreducible certainty. One is the knowledge of what is directly present to sense experience, and the other is knowledge of logical truth. It is striking that these, roughly, are the two domains where we have made fairly direct behavioral sense of radical translation. One domain where radical translation seemed straightforward was that of the observation sentences. The other is that of the truth-functions; hence also in a sense the tautologies, these being the truths to which only the truth-functions matter.

But the truth-functions and tautologies are only the simplest of the logical functions and logical truths. Can we perhaps do better? The logical functions that most naturally next suggest themselves are the *categoricals*, traditionally designated A, E, I, and O, and commonly construed in English by the construction "all are" ("All rabbits are timid"), "none are," "some are," "some are not." A semantic criterion for A perhaps suggests itself as follows: the compound commands assent (from a given speaker) if and only if the positive stimulus meaning (for him) of the first component is a subclass of the positive stimulus meaning of the second component. How to vary this for E,

I, and O is obvious enough, except that the whole idea is wrong in view of Section 2. Thus, take A. If "hippoid" is a general term intended to apply to all horses and unicorns, then all hippoids are horses (there being no unicorns), but still the positive stimulus meaning of "Hippoid" has stimulus patterns in it, of the sort suited to "Unicorn," that are not in the positive stimulus meaning of "Horse." On this score the suggested semantic criterion is at odds with "All S and P" in that it goes beyond extension. And it has a yet more serious failing of the opposite kind; for, whereas rabbit stages are not rabbits, we saw in Section 2 that in point of stimulus meaning there is no distinction.

The difficulty is fundamental. The categoricals depend for their truth on the objects, however external and however inferential, of which the component terms are true; and what those objects are is not uniquely determined by stimulus meanings. Indeed, the categoricals, like plural endings and identity, make sense at all only relative to an object-positing kind of conceptual scheme; whereas, as stressed in Section 2, stimulus meanings can be just the same for persons imbued with such a scheme and for persons as alien to it as you please. Of what we think of as logic, the truth-functional part is the only part the recognition of which, in a foreign language, we seem to be able to pin down to behavioral criteria.

VI. Analytical Hypotheses

How then does our linguist push radical translation beyond the bounds of mere observation sentences and truth functions? In broad outline as follows. He segments heard utterances into conveniently short recurrent parts, and thus compiles a list of native "words." Various of these he hypothetically equates to English words and phrases, in such a way as to reproduce the already established translations of whole observation sentences. Such conjectural equatings of parts may be called *analytical hypotheses* of translation. He will need analytical hypotheses of translation not only for native words but also for native constructions, or ways of assembling words, since the native language would not be assumed to follow English word order. Taken together these analytical hypotheses of translation constitute a jungle-to-English grammar and dictionary, which the linguist then proceeds to apply even to sentences for the translation of which no independent evidence is available.

The analytical hypotheses of translation do not depend for their evidence exclusively upon those prior translations of observation sentences. They can also be tested partly by their conformity to intrasubjective synonymies of occasion sentences, as of Section 4. For example, if the analytical hypotheses direct us to translate native sentences S_1 and S_2 respectively, as "Here is a bachelor" and "Here is an unmarried man," then we shall hope to find also that for each native the stimulus meaning of S_1 is the same as that of S_2.

The analytical hypotheses of translation can be partially tested in the light of the thence derived translations not only of occasion sentences but, sometimes, of standing sentences. Standing sentences differ from occasion senten-

ces only in that assent to them and dissent from them may occur unprompted (cf. Section 1), not in that they occur only unprompted. The concept of prompted assent is reasonably applicable to the standing sentence "Some rabbits are black" once, for a given speaker, if we manage to spring the specimen on him before he knows there are black ones. A given speaker's assent to some standing sentences can even be prompted repeatedly; thus, his assent can genuinely be prompted anew each year to "The crocuses are out," and anew each day to "The *Times* has come." Standing sentences thus grade off toward occasion sentences, though there still remains a boundary, as defined midway in Section 1. So the linguist can further appraise his analytical hypotheses of translation by seeing how the thence derivable translations of standing sentences compare with the originals on the score of prompted assent and dissent.

Some slight further testing of the analytical hypotheses of translation is afforded by standing sentences even apart from prompted assent and dissent. If, for instance, the analytical hypotheses point to some rather platitudinous English standing sentence as translation of a native sentence S, then the linguist will feel reassured if he finds that S likewise commands general and unprompted assent.

The analytical hypotheses of translation would not in practice be held to equational form. There is no need to insist that the native word be equated outright to any one English word or phrase. One may specify certain contexts in which the word is to be translated one way and others in which the word is to be translated in another way. One may overlay the equational form with supplementary semantical instructions *ad libitum*. "Spoiled (*said of an egg*)" is as good a lexicographical definition as "addle," despite the intrusion of stage directions. Translation instructions having to do with grammatical inflections—to take an extreme case—may be depended on to present equations of words and equations of constructions in inextricable combination with much that is not equational. For the purpose is not translation of single words nor translation of single constructions, but translation of coherent discourse. The hypotheses the linguist arrives at, the instructions that he frames, are contributory hypotheses or instructions concerning translation of coherent discourse, and they may be presented in any form, equational or otherwise, that proves clear and convenient.

Nevertheless there is reason to draw particular attention to the simple form of analytical hypothesis which does directly equate a native word or construction to a hypothetical English equivalent. For hypotheses need thinking up, and the typical case of thinking up is the case where the English-bred linguist apprehends a parallelism of function between some component fragment of a translated whole native sentence S and some component word of the English translation of S. Only in some such way can we account for anyone's ever thinking to translate a native locution radically into English as a plural ending, or as the identity predicate "$=$," or as a categorical copula, or as any other part of our domestic apparatus of objective reference; for, as

stressed in earlier pages, no scrutiny of stimulus meanings or other behavioral manifestations can even settle whether the native shares our object-positing sort of conceptual scheme at all. It is only by such outright projection of his own linguistic habits that the linguist can find general terms in the native language at all, or, having found them, match them with his own. Stimulus meanings never suffice to determine even what words are terms, if any, much less what terms are co-extensive.

The linguist who is serious enough about the jungle language to undertake its definitive dictionary and grammar will not, indeed, proceed quite as we have imagined. He will steep himself in the language, disdainful of English parallels, to the point of speaking it like a native. His learning of it even from the beginning can have been as free of all thought of other languages as you please; it can have been virtually an accelerated counterpart of infantile learning. When at length he does turn his hand to translation, and to producing a jungle-to-English dictionary and grammar, he can do so as a bilingual. His own two personalities thereupon assume the roles which in previous pages were divided between the linguist and his informant. He equates "Gavagai" with "Rabbit" by appreciating a sameness of stimulus meaning of the two sentences for himself. Indeed he can even use sameness of stimulus meaning to translate nonobservational occasion sentences of the type of "Bachelor"; here the intrasubjective situation proves its advantage (cf. Section 4). When he brings off other more recondite translations, he surely does so by essentially the method of ana-

lytical hypotheses, but with the difference that he projects these hypotheses
from his prior separate masteries of
the two languages, rather than using
them in mastering the jungle language.
Now though it is such bilingual translation that does most justice to the jungle
language, reflection upon it reveals least
about the nature of meaning; for the
bilingual translator works by an intrasubjective communing of a split personality, and we make operational sense of
his method only as we externalize it. So
let us think still in terms of our more
primitive schematism of the jungle-to-
English project, which counts the native
informant in as a live collaborator
rather than letting the linguist first
ingest him.

VII. A Handful of Meaning

The linguist's finished jungle-to-
English manual is to be appraised as a
manual of sentence-to-sentence translation. Whatever be the details of its
expository devices of word translation
and syntactical paradigm, its net
accomplishment is an infinite *semantic
correlation* of sentences: the implicit
specification of an English sentence for
every one of the infinitely many possible jungle sentences. The English
sentence for a given jungle one need not
be unique, but it is to be unique to
within any acceptable standard of
intrasubjective synonymy among English sentences; and conversely. Though
the thinking up and setting forth of
such a semantic correlation of sentences
depend on analyses into component
words, the supporting evidence remains
entirely at the level of sentences. It

consists in sundry conformities on the
score of stimulus meaning, intrasubjective synonymies, and other points of
prompted and unprompted assent and
dissent, as noted in Section 6.

Whereas the semantic correlation
exhausts the native sentences, its supporting evidence determines no such
widespread translation. Countless alternative over-all semantic correlations,
therefore, are equally compatible with
that evidence. If the linguist arrives at
his one over-all correlation among
many without feeling that his choice was
excessively arbitrary, this is because he
himself is limited in the correlations that
he can manage. For he is not, in his
finitude, free to assign English sentences
to the infinitude of jungle ones in just
any way whatever that will fit his supporting evidence; he has to assign them
in some way that is manageably systematic with respect to a manageably
limited set of repeatable speech segments. The word-by-word approach is
indispensable   to   the   linguist   in
specifying his semantic correlation and
even in thinking it up.

Not only does the linguist's working
segmentation limit the possibilities of
any eventual semantic correlation. It
even contributes to defining, for him,
the ends of translation. For he will put
a premium on structural parallels: on
correspondence between the parts of the
native sentence, as he segments it, and
the parts of the English translation.
Other things being equal, the more literal translation is seen as more literally a translation.[1] Technically a tend-

---

[1] Hence also Carnap's concept of structural synonymy. See his *Meaning and Necessity* (Chicago, 1947), section 14–16.

ency to literal translation is assured anyway, since the very purpose of segmentation is to make long translations constructible from short correspondences; but then one goes farther and makes of this tendency an objective—and an objective that even varies in detail with the practical segmentation adopted.

It is by his analytical hypotheses that our jungle linguist implicitly states (and indeed arrives at) the grand synthetic hypothesis which is his over-all semantic correlation of sentences. His supporting evidence, such as it is, for the semantic correlation is his supporting evidence also for his analytical hypotheses. Chronologically, the analytical hypotheses come before all that evidence is in; then such of the evidence as ensues is experienced as pragmatic corroboration of a working dictionary. But in any event the translation of a vast range of native sentences, though covered by the semantic correlation, can never be corroborated or supported at all except cantilever fashion: it is simply what comes out of the analytical hypotheses when they are applied beyond the zone that supports them. That those unverifiable translations proceed without mishap must not be taken as pragmatic evidence of good lexicography, for mishap is impossible.

We must then recognize that the analytical hypotheses of translation and the grand synthetic one that they add up to are only in an incomplete sense hypotheses. Contrast the case of translation of "Gavagai" as "Lo, a rabbit" by sameness of stimulus meaning. This is a genuine hypothesis from sample observations, though possibly wrong. "Gavagai" and "Lo, a rabbit" have stimulus meanings for the two speakers, and these are the same or different, whether we guess right or not. On the other hand, no sense is made of sameness of meaning of the words that are equated in the typical analytical hypothesis. The point is not that we cannot be sure whether the analytical hypothesis is right, but that there is not even, as there was in the case of "Gavagai," an objective matter to be right or wrong about.

Complete radical translation does go on, and analytical hypotheses are indispensable. Nor are they capricious; on the contrary, we have just been seeing, in outline, how they are supported. May we not then say that in those very ways of thinking up and supporting the analytical hypotheses a sense *is* after all given to sameness of meaning of the expressions which those hypotheses equate? No. We could claim this only if no two conflicting sets of analytical hypotheses were capable of being supported equally strongly by all theoretically accessible evidence (including simplicity considerations).

This indefinability of synonymy by reference to the methodology of analytical hypotheses is formally the same as the indefinability of truth by reference to scientific method. Also, the consequences are parallel. Just as we may meaningfully speak of the truth of a sentence only within the terms of some theory or conceptual scheme, so on the whole we may meaningfully speak of interlinguistic synonymy of words and phrases only within the terms of some particular system of analytical hypotheses.

The method of analytical hypotheses is a way of catapulting oneself into the native language by the momentum of the home language. It is a way of grafting exotic shoots on to the old familiar bush until only the exotic meets the eye. Native sentences not neutrally meaningful are thereby tentatively translated into home sentences on the basis, in effect, of seeming analogy of roles within the languages. These relations of analogy cannot themselves be looked upon as the meanings, for they are not unique. And anyway the analogies weaken as we move out toward the theoretical sentences, farthest from observation. Thus, who would undertake to translate "Neutrinos lack mass" into the jungle language? If anyone does, we may expect him to coin new native words or distort the usage of old ones. We may expect him to plead in extenuation that the natives lack the requisite concepts; also that they know too little physics. And he is right, but another way of describing the matter is as follows. Analytical hypotheses at best are devices whereby, indirectly, we bring out analogies between sentences that have yielded to translation and sentences that have not, and so extend the working limits of translation; and "Neutrinos lack mass" is way out where the effects of such analytical hypotheses as we manage to devise are too fuzzy to do much good.

Containment in the Low German continuum facilitated translation of Frisian into English (Section 1), and containment in a continuum of cultural evolution facilitated translation of Hungarian into English. These continuities, by facilitating translation, encourage an illusion of subject matter: an illusion that our so readily intertranslatable sentences are diverse, verbal embodiments of some intercultural proposition or meaning, when they are better seen as the merest variants of one and the same intracultural verbalism. Only the discontinuity of radical translation tries our meanings: really sets them over against their verbal embodiments, or more typically, finds nothing there.

Observation sentences peel nicely; their meanings, stimulus meanings, emerge absolute and free of all residual verbal taint. Theoretical sentences such as "Neutrinos lack mass," or the law of entropy, or the constancy of the speed of light, are at the other extreme. For such sentences no hint of the stimulatory conditions of assent or dissent can be dreamed of that does not include verbal stimulation from within the language. Sentences of this extreme latter sort, and other sentences likewise that lie intermediate between the two extremes, lack linguistically neutral meaning.

It would be trivial to say that we cannot know the meaning of a foreign sentence except as we are prepared to offer a translation in our own language. I am saying more: that it is only relative to an, in large part, arbitrary manual of translation that most foreign sentences may be said to share the meaning of English sentences, and then only in a very parochial sense of meaning, viz., use-in-English. Stimulus meanings of observation sentences aside, most talk of meaning requires tacit reference to a home language in much the same way that talk of truth involves tacit reference to one's own system of the world, the best that one can muster at the time.

There being (apart from stimulus meanings) so little in the way of neutral meanings relevant to radical translation, there is no telling how much of one's success with analytical hypotheses is due to real kinship of outlook on the part of the natives and ourselves, and how much of it is due to linguistic ingenuity or lucky coincidence. I am not sure that it even makes sense to ask. We may alternately wonder at the inscrutability of the native mind and wonder at how very much like us the native is, where in the one case we have merely muffed the best translation, and in the other case we have done a more thorough job of reading our own provincial modes into the native's speech.

Usener, Cassirer, Sapir, and latterly B. L. Whorf have stressed that deep differences of language carry with them ultimate differences in the way one thinks, or looks upon the world. I should prefer not to put the matter in such a way as to suggest that certain philosophical propositions are affirmed in the one culture and denied in the other. What is really involved is difficulty or indeterminacy of correlation. It is just that there is less basis of comparison—less sense in saying what is good translation and what is bad—the farther we get away from sentences with visibly direct conditioning to nonverbal stimuli and the farther we get off home ground.

ON LIKENESS OF MEANING[1]

6.6

Nelson Goodman

Under what circumstances do two names or predicates in an ordinary language have the same meaning? Many

From *Semantics and the Philosophy of Language*, Leonard Linsky, editor (Urbana, Ill.: University of Illinois Press, 1952). Reprinted by permission of the publishers and the author.

[1] Read before the Fullerton Club, at Bryn Mawr College, Pennsylvania, on May 14, 1949. I am deeply indebted to Drs. Morton G. White and W. V. Quine, with whom I have frequently and profitably discussed the problem dealt with in this paper.

and widely varied answers have been given to this question, but they have one feature in common: they are all unsatisfactory.

One of the earliest answers is to the effect that two predicates have the same meaning if they stand for the same real Essence or Platonic Idea; but this does not seem to help very much unless we know, as I am afraid we do not, how to find out whether two terms stand for the same Platonic Idea.

A more practical proposal is that two

terms have the same meaning if they stand for the same mental idea or image; or in other words, that two predicates differ in meaning only if we have a mental picture of something that satisfies one but not the other of the two. Thus even though in fact all and only pelicans have gallon-sized bills, we can easily imagine a sparrow or a kangaroo with a gallon-sized bill; and thus the predicates "is a pelican" and "has a gallon-sized bill," even though satisfied by exactly the same actual individuals, do not have the same meaning. There are two familiar difficulties with this theory. In the first place, it is not very clear just what we can and what we cannot imagine. Can we imagine a man ten miles high or not? Can we imagine a tone we have never heard? To decide these cases is only to be confronted by new and harder ones. But the second and more serious difficulty is that of predicates that pretty clearly have no corresponding image, such as "clever" or "supersonic." Of course there is imagery associated with these terms; but that is hardly to the point. There is imagery associated with nonsense syllables.

The image theory thus sometimes gives way to the concept theory—the theory that two predicates differ in meaning if and only if we can conceive of something that satisfies one but not the other. This enables us to transcend the narrow boundaries of imagination, but unfortunately it hardly seems to provide us with any criterion at all. Presumably we can conceive a five-dimensional body since we can define it although we cannot imagine it. But similarly we can define a square-circle very easily (as a rectangle with four

equal sides and such that every point of it is equidistant from a center) or a five-sided meaning. In other words, difference of extension does not draw distinctions as fine as those drawn by difference of meaning.

Does this mean, then, that we must return to the dismal search through never-never land for some ghostly entities called "meanings" that are distinct from and lie between words and their extensions? I don't think so. Despite the obvious inadequacy of the thesis we have been considering, I think that difference of meaning between any two terms can be fully accounted for without introducing anything beyond terms and their extensions. For while it is clear that difference in meaning of two terms "P" and "Q" is not always accompanied by difference in extension, I think it is always accompanied by difference in the extension of certain terms other than "P" and "Q." Let me explain:

Since there are no centaurs or unicorns, all unicorns are centaurs and all centaurs are unicorns. Furthermore, all uncles of centaurs are uncles of unicorns; and all feet of unicorns are feet of centaurs. How far can we generalize on this? Leaving aside absurd or ungrammatical variations, we must exclude the analogues in terms of "thoughts," or "concepts" or even "meaning" itself; for there is no guarantee that thoughts of centaurs are thoughts of unicorns. This is usually attributed to the mental reference or the vagueness of such terms. We have in logic the theorem that if all α's are β's, then all the things that bear the relation P to an α are things that bear the relation P to a β (see *Principia Mathematica*, 37.2); and it might naturally be supposed that this guarantees the truth of sentences like those we have been considering about centaurs and unicorns, provided the phrases involved apply only to physical objects if to anything. But actually this is not the case; for *pictures*—i.e., paintings, drawings, prints, statues—are physical objects, yet not all pictures of centaurs are pictures of unicorns, nor are all pictures of unicorns pictures of centaurs. At first sight this seems to violate the cited theorem of logic. Actually, what it shows is that "picture of" is not always a relation-term like "foot of" or "uncle of." If x is a foot of a centaur, then x bears the relation "foot of" to some y that is a centaur. Thus if there is any foot of a centaur or any uncle of a centaur then there is a centaur. But in contrast, if there is—as indeed there is—something that is a picture of a centaur, we cannot infer that there is some centaur—as there certainly is not. A phrase like "picture of a centaur" is a single predicate, and the fact that it applies to one or many things plainly does not enable us to conclude that there are objects that these things are pictures of. To avoid the temptation to make such unjustified inferences, perhaps we had better speak during the rest of our discussion not of "pictures of" centaurs or unicorns but rather of "centaur-pictures" and "unicorn-pictures," etc.

A centaur-picture differs from a unicorn-picture not by virtue of its resemblance to a centaur and lack of resemblance to a unicorn; for there are neither unicorns nor centaurs. "Centaur-picture" and "unicorn-picture" merely apply to different objects just as "chair" and "desk" apply to different objects, and we need no more ask why in the one case than in the other. The simple fact is that although "centaur" and "unicorn" apply to nothing and so have the same extension, the term "centaur-picture" applies to many things and the term "unicorn-picture" applies to many others.

Now the important point here is this: Although two words have the same extension, certain predicates composed by making identical additions to these two words may have different extensions. It is then perhaps the case that for every two words that differ in meaning either their extensions or the extensions of some corresponding compounds of them are different. If so, difference of meaning among extensionally identical predicates can be explained as difference in the extensions of certain other predicates. Or, if we call the extension of a predicate by itself its *primary* extension, and the extension of any of its compounds a *secondary* extension, the thesis is formulated as follows: two terms have the same meaning if and only if they have the same primary and secondary extensions. Let us, in order to avoid entanglement with such terms as "thought of . . .," "concept of . . .," "attribute of . . .," and "meaning of . . .," exclude from consideration all predicates that apply to anything but physical things, classes of these, classes of classes of these, etc. If the thesis is tenable, we have answered our question by stating, without reference to anything other than terms and the things to which they apply, the circumstances under which two terms have the same meaning.

This explanation takes care of well-known cases discussed in the literature. For instance, Frege has used the terms "(is the) Morningstar" and "(is the) Eveningstar" as examples of two predicates that have the same extension—since they apply to the same one thing—but obviously differ in meaning. This difference of meaning is readily explained according to our present thesis, since the two terms differ in their secondary extensions. There are, for example, "Morningstar-pictures" that are not "Eveningstar-pictures"—and also, indeed, "Eveningstar-pictures" that are not "Morningstar-pictures."

But is our thesis satisfactory in general? Perhaps the first question that arises is whether it takes care of cases where we have two terms "P" and "Q" such that there are no P-pictures or Q-pictures—say where "P" and "Q" are predicates applying to odors or electric charges. These present no difficulty; for the secondary extensions of a predicate "Q" consist not merely of the extension of "Q-picture" but also of the extensions of "Q-diagram," "Q-symbol," and any number of other such compound terms. Indeed *actual word-inscriptions* are as genuine physical objects as anything else; and so if there is such an actual physical inscription that is a P-description and is not a Q-description, or vice versa, then "P" and "Q" differ in their secondary extensions and thus in meaning.

This makes it look more and more as if every difference in meaning will be reflected by a difference in primary or secondary extension. Indeed, I think we can now show this to be true. For, given any two predicates whatsoever, say "P"

and "Q," do we not have in an inscription of the phrase "a P that is not a Q" something that is a P-description and not a Q-description? Clearly the predicate "centaur-description" applies while the predicate "unicorn-description" does not apply to an inscription of "a centaur that is not a unicorn." Likewise, the predicate "acrid-odor-description" applies while the predicate "pungent-odor-description" does not apply to an inscription of "a pungent odor that is not an acrid odor"; and thus the two predicates "pungent-odor" and "acrid-odor"—whatever may be the relationship of their primary extensions—differ in secondary extension and thus in meaning. Again "triangle" and "trilateral" differ in meaning because "triangle that is not trilateral" is a triangle-description but not a trilateral-description. We do not, however, get the absurd result that "triangle" differs in meaning from "triangle"; for of course it is not the case that "triangle that is not a triangle" is and is not a triangle-description.[2]

But now see how far we have come. If difference of meaning is explained in the way I have proposed, then *no two different words have the same mean-*

---

[2] One basic principle is: *any phrase such as "_____ that is . . ." is a _____ -description and a . . . -description.* Thus "_____ that is not a . . ." is both a _____ -description and a not-a- . . . -description. Being a not-a- . . . -description is not a sufficient condition for not being a . . . -description. By a second principle, however, a not-a- . . . -description is not a . . . -description unless the first principle (or some other) makes it also a . . . -description. Formulation of complete and exact principles deciding whether any phrase is or is not a . . . -description would be difficult and is neither possible nor necessary here.

ing. We have assuredly answered the complaint that in terms of extensions alone we cannot draw fine enough distinctions. Here we get distinctions that are as fine as anyone could ask. But now we risk the opposite complaint: for can we accept the conclusion that a word has the same meaning as no other word than itself?

Before we decide that we cannot tolerate this conclusion, let me note that in the course of developing our criterion we have incidentally shown that there are no two predicates such that each can be replaced by the other in every sentence without changing the truth-value, *even if we exclude all the so-called intensional contexts in which such words as* "necessary," "possible," "attribute of," or "thought of" occur. Thus if we maintain that two different words have the same meaning, their lack of interreplaceability in some non-intensional context can immediately be offered as evidence that the words do not have the same meaning. It seems apparent, therefore, that the demands we commonly make upon a criterion of sameness of meaning can be satisfied only if we recognize that no two different predicates ever have the same meaning.

Theoretically, then, we shall do better never to say that two predicates have the same meaning but rather that they have a greater or lesser degree, or one or another kind, of *likeness* of meaning. In ordinary speech when we say that two terms have the same meaning, we usually indicate only that their kind and degree of likeness of meaning is sufficient for the purposes of the immediate discourse. This is quite harmless.

But we must remember that the requirements vary greatly from discourse to discourse; often it is enough if two terms have the same primary extension; in other cases, identity in certain secondary extensions or others is also required. If we overlook this variation and seek a fixed criterion of sameness of meaning that will at once conform to these differing usages and satisfy our theoretical demands, we are doomed to perpetual confusion.

To repeat, it is commonly supposed that a satisfactory definition of synonymy must meet two requirements: that some predicates be synonymous with others, and that either of a pair of synonyms be replaceable by the other in all non-intensional contexts without change of truth-value. But we have seen that these two requirements are incompatible. The sound course seems to be to construe degree of synonymy as, so to speak, degree of interreplaceability—along lines above suggested—and to recognize that the relation of exact synonymy between diverse predicates is null.

Just a few further words to suggest a bearing this paper has on another question. It is sometimes said that a sentence like "All A's are B's" is *analytic* if the meaning of B is contained in that of A. Our investigation has shown not only that two different predicates like "A" and "B" never have quite the same meaning; but further that, so to speak, neither is meaning-included in the other; for there is an A-description that is not a B-description, *and* a B-description that is not an A-description. Thus, at least according to the suggested interpretation of "analytic," no non-repetitive statement will be analytic. The most we can say is that it is more, or less, nearly analytic. This will be enough to convince many of us that

likewise a non-repetitive statement is never absolutely necessary, but only more or less nearly so.

6.7　　　　　　　　　　　SYNONYMITY

Benson Mates

I

I shall begin my paper by attempting to show, in a rough way at least, that a discussion of synonymity is germane to the general topic of these lectures, namely, meaning and interpretation. The connection between synonymity and meaning is perhaps too clear to require much comment: two linguistic expressions are synonymous if and only if they have the same meaning. The relation between synonymity and interpretation is only slightly less obvious. I shall try to explicate it by offering definitions of certain important terms which commonly occur, or ought to occur, in discussions of this subject.

The first of these terms is "language." By "language," in its most general sense, I wish to denote any aggregate of objects which are themselves meaningful

or else are such that certain combinations of them are meaningful. It will be seen at once that this definition assigns a very wide meaning to the term "language" and furthermore that it suffers from all the vagueness and ambiguity which attaches to the word "meaningful." Nevertheless, I think that it leads to a usage quite in agreement with ordinary usage. Thus we may first of all observe that all the ordinary conversational languages, for example the English language or the German, come under the definition given. Each of them can be regarded as an aggregate of objects which are meaningful singly or at least in combinations. Likewise, written English, spoken English, the King's English, and plain English would all be languages according to the definition just given.

As one can determine by consulting the dictionary, however, the denotation of the word "language" is much wider than these examples indicate. We must not suppose, for instance, that only human beings can use language, since

From *University of California Publications in Philosophy*, Vol. XXV (Berkeley: University of California Press, 1950). Reprinted by permission of the publisher and the author.

in one proper sense of the term it refers to activities of the lower animals as well. For example, there is said to be a "language of the birds." Here the meaningful objects are the various characteristic sounds that birds make under given circumstances. Nor, again, must we suppose that the elements of a language are always either inscriptions or sounds. There is, for instance, "the language of the face," or "the language of looks and glances." In this case the meaningful elements are evidently certain positions of the physiognomy. Again, the phrase "language of the heart" presumably refers to a language whose elements are certain patterns of behavior which are supposed to denote the presence of certain emotions. But even these examples do not show the full extent of the term "language" in ordinary discourse. It is by no means necessary that the elements of the language be the results of human or animal activity. Thus, certain clever men are said to be able to read "the language of the stars," and poets and philosophers have a great deal to say about "the language of nature." What is common to all these, it seems to me, is that in each there is an aggregate of objects—whether they be marks, sounds, gestures, looks, or stars —and these objects or certain combinations of these objects are meaningful.

The next important term for which I shall offer a preliminary definition is the term "translation." A body of discourse A is a translation of another body of discourse B if and only if there is a correspondence between the meaningful parts of A and those of B such that corresponding parts are synonymous. What kind of correspondence this is, in general, it is difficult to say. At present, I am merely trying to indicate the connection between the notions of translation and synonymity, and I claim for the foregoing definition only the merit that its consequences are to a great extent in accord with the ordinary usage of the word "translation." Consider, for example, the problem of translating a book from German into English. This amounts to the problem of producing an English version which faithfully reproduces the sense of the original, that is, of producing a book which contains, for every meaningful expression in the German original, a synonymous expression in English, and conversely. Words, sentences, or whole paragraphs may be taken as the smallest meaningful expressions to be translated, depending upon the translator's judgment of how the sense of the original can best be reproduced in the translation.[1]

The term "translation" is most frequently applied when the two texts occur in languages that are entirely disjoint from one another, as for example German and English. However, it may equally well be applied when one of the two languages is contained in the other or even when the two languages are identical. Consider the task of popularizing a technical treatise—of putting it into plain English. It seems to me that the popularization will be a translation

---

[1] In general we may say that a translation is relatively literal if it is so constructed that for every important word in the original text there is a synonymous expression in the translation, while it would be considered relatively free if whole paragraphs were the smallest parts for which synonymous expressions were provided.

of the technical treatise in essentially the same sense in which a German version would be a translation of it. We are given a language—German, or plain English, as the case may be,—and the problem is to find, for every expression or group of expressions in the technical treatise, a synonymous expression or group of expressions in the given language. The process of popularization, therefore, may be regarded as a process of translating the technical treatise out of the whole English language (considered as containing the technical terms) into that part of the English language which we have been calling "plain English." It may also occur that the languages concerned are identical or nearly so. For example, it is perfectly in accord with correct usage to speak of translating poetry into prose. Here the problem is to find nonpoetic expressions which are synonymous with the meaningful expressions occurring in some poem, and both the poem and the prose may of course be written in the same language.

The last term for which I shall give a preliminary definition is "interpretation." A body of discourse A is an interpretation of a body of discourse B if and only if A is a translation of B and the constituent expressions of A are better understood than those of B. Thus, according to me, every interpretation is a translation.[2] Further, since the degree to which a language is understood varies from person to person, what would be

an interpretation for one person might not be an interpretation for someone else.

I shall now set forth a series of considerations which will serve both to explain my definition of "interpretation" and to argue that it accords well with established usage. Let us first give attention to the meaning of the related term, "interpret." We may say that a person x interprets a given body of discourse A to a person y if and only if x translates A into a body of discourse which y understands better than he understands A. This general statement obviously holds when the languages concerned are ordinary natural languages, for example French and German; and indeed the term "interpreter" is ordinarily applied to a person who translates discourse from one such language into another for the benefit of someone who is not able to understand the first. But it is equally true that the statement holds when the languages concerned are systems of meaningful objects of any sort whatever. To interpret a poem for someone is usually to translate the poem into linguistic expressions which he can understand better than he understands the poem. Sometimes the translator may find it desirable to use gestures, signs, tears, and other devices in addition to the meaningful expressions of the conversational language. We shall then regard the language into which the translation is made as a rather complex language, consisting not only of written or spoken expressions but also of these various other occurrences. In like manner the astrologer may properly be said to interpret the positions of the heavenly bodies. He and his clients regard the

---

[2] I do not think that the interpretation of calculi is a type of interpretation under discussion in these lectures; at any rate, I have not attempted to define "interpretation" in such a way as to cover that usage of the term.

positions of these objects as meaningful symbols, that is, as elements in a language which the astrologer can understand but the clients cannot. His function is to interpret discourse in this language to the others, which is to say, to translate messages out of the language of the heavens into a language which the others can understand.[3]

Almost all the other situations which would ordinarily be regarded as instances of interpretation will satisfy the definition proposed above. When the psychiatrist interprets dreams he treats the dreams or certain important constituents of them as meaningful expressions in a kind of language which he, by means of a great deal of training, finds it possible to understand. He is able to tell the uninitiated person what the dreams mean, that is, he can translate certain significant elements in what we may call "the language of dreams" into sentences occurring in a more readily intelligible language. Likewise, the person who interprets a painting regards the painting and possibly also various parts of it as somehow meaningful, and he attempts by the use of the meaningful expressions of some language, usually supplemented by an assortment of meaningful gestures, and so

on, to accomplish a translation of the painting into forms of expression which are more readily understandable to the person for whose benefit the interpretation is made.

As I see it, therefore, most situations to which the word "interpretation" can properly be applied have the following characteristics. First of all, there are two bodies of discourse, which may occur in any language or languages, in the broad sense of "language" explained above. Secondly, there is a person who understands only one of these bodies of discourse, which is to say that the constituent expressions of only one of these bodies of discourse are meaningful for him. This is the person for whose benefit the interpretation is carried out. Thirdly, there is a person who understands both bodies of discourse and who is able to translate one into the other. This person is the interpreter. Finally we set these elements in motion: the interpreter translates the discourse which the other person does not understand into discourse which the other person does understand. This is interpretation, considered as a process; and the result of the translation is the interpretation, considered as a product.

There is an important difficulty which ought to be mentioned at this point. It very often happens that when an interpretation is needed there is no capable interpreter at hand to produce it. Any student of the history of philosophy will, unfortunately, be well acquainted with this difficulty; but of course the same situation arises in fields other than philosophy. For example, in wartime we may possess enemy messages in code or cipher but lack a ready

---

[3] It is interesting and important to observe that even though the clientele do not understand the language of the stars, it is quite possible for them to determine that they have not been provided with an adequate interpretation. It is to be assumed, of course, that the pronouncements of the stars are true; hence, any adequate translation of these pronouncements must at least consist of true sentences. Thus the astrology business is not quite as safe as it might at first seem to be.

means of translating these messages into plain language. If an interpretation is to be found at all, it will be necessary for someone who does not understand the text to make an interpretation for himself. Often this is no easy task, but we know that it can be done. In crypt-analysis the methods which are used depend essentially upon the fact that an adequate interpretation of the cryptic message will be part-by-part synonymous with the cryptic message; hence, if the cryptic message is about battleships, the interpretation must be about battleships; if the cryptic message contains true sentences, the interpreta-tion must contain true sentences; if the cryptic message expresses information that would be of interest to the persons for whom it was intended, the inter-pretation must likewise express infor-mation that would interest those persons, and so forth. Thus by the use of data concerning the circumstances under which the message was sent, together with further data about the methods likely to have been used by the cryptographer who wrote the message, it is possible to arrive at a probable interpretation. It is clear that similar considerations enable us to find more or less probable interpretations for obscure passages in philosophical discourse. We know that an adequate interpretation would preserve sense; this requires that it take true sentences over into true ones and false into false; it also requires that valid arguments be interpreted by valid arguments, and invalid arguments by invalid ones. Usually we also possess some knowledge of the rules of syntax for the language in which the obscure passage is stated;

here we have a great advantage over the cryptanalyst. For example, we may often safely assume that, within limits, a given expression should always be translated by the same expression. Frequently we have also a good deal of other knowledge about our author's views and capability, and often we have the opinions of other men on how the passage should be interpreted. By means of all these data we construct a more or less adequate interpretation.

I shall not try to anticipate all the objections which may be made to the foregoing definition of "interpretation," but there are two points which I am prompted to set forth. In the first place, although the definition offered above leads to a very broad usage of "inter-pretation," it requires that interpretation be sharply distinguished from descrip-tion. This will appear clearly in an example. Suppose that Jones is an interpreter for the Army in Germany. The prisoner, looking out the window, remarks, "Es schneit," and Jones is asked for an interpretation. He replies as follows: "He uttered a German sen-tence consisting of two words, the first of which was 'es' and the second, 'schneit.'" I think we may confidently say that although Jones has even given a description of what was said, he has certainly not given an adequate inter-pretation of what was said. This case is typical; in general, a description of an aggregate of objects is by no means the same as an interpreta-tion of those objects. Thus, even if it could be shown that it is impossible to report what one perceives without describing something, it would not follow that it is impossible to report what one perceives without interpreting something.

The second point which I wish to make is this: from the earliest times, men have tended to confuse interpretation with explanation. If we believe in progress, we shall say that this confusion was more prevalent in ancient times than it is now. At any rate, it will be less offensive to illustrate the matter in connection with antiquity. The history of natural philosophy in the ancient world shows that attempts to explain natural phenomena took two easily distinguishable forms. Sometimes the explanations were explanations in the scientific sense of the term; that is, from a relatively well-established generalization there was deduced a sentence expressing the state of affairs to be explained. More often, however, the explanations were what we would call "interpretations." The phenomenon to be explained was regarded as possessing a meaning with which it had been endowed by some supernatural being, and the explanation consisted in reading off this meaning. Thus, for example, some would explain an eclipse of the sun by saying, "The gods are displeased with men"; others by saying, "The moon has come between the earth and the sun." The former explanation seems based on the assumption that the eclipse is a meaningful symbol by which the gods intend to reveal their displeasure. This sort of explanation might better be called "interpretation," it seems to me.[4]

The naturalistic explanation, on the other hand, does not rest upon any assumption that the eclipse is a symbol or portent which the gods or anyone else has endowed with meaning. It corresponds more exactly to what would now be denoted by the word "explanation." There were thus two quite distinct types of explanation, one of which was a type of interpretation and one of which was not. This may account for some of the present-day confusion between the notions of interpretation and explanation and for much of the ambiguity in the English word "interpretation."

II

The preceding section has shown that the notion of synonymity is involved in the notions of meaning and interpretation. The question which naturally arises next is, "What can be offered by way of a definition of 'synonymity'?" From what has been said it appears that if one could find a precise and plausible definition for this term, then it would be a relatively simple matter to construct satisfactory definitions for the other important terms which we have been discussing. That circumstance alone would make explicating the notion of synonymity a worthwhile task for philosophers, but it is also true that the notion deserves to be investigated in its own right because of the key role which it plays in many philo-

---

[4] In fact, it *was* called *interpretatio* by the ancients. Thus, Mercury was called *interpres divum*—interpreter of things divine—because he understood the decrees of Jove and Apollo, not to mention a wide assortment of other omens, including the tripods, laurel, and stars, as well as the sounds (*linguas*) and flights of birds. See Virgil, *Aeneid*, 4, 356; 3, 359.

sophical discussions. This key role is often disguised through the fact that there are many different ways of saying that two expressions are synonymous. One group of circumlocutions consists of those having the form 'to say A is only to say B',[5] for example, "if by 'good' you mean pleasure, then to say that pleasure is good is only to say that pleasure is pleasure." Another way of claiming synonymity is to use expressions like 'A; in other words, B'—for instance, "Jones is a positivist; in other words, Jones regards the sentences of metaphysics as pseudo-object sentences." Still other ways make use of the formula 'when I say A, I only mean B,' and there are further types too numerous to mention. The notion of synonymity seems also to be involved in the well-worn notions of analytic and synthetic sentences, real definitions, analysis, and in much of the other conceptual apparatus of philosophers. Thus there is no doubt that this notion, however vague it may be, is of considerable philosophical importance, and a good definition of it is greatly to be desired.[6]

This being so, the appropriate thing for me to do is to produce such a definition or at least to make an attempt to do so. I am sorry to have to confess not only that I have no definition to propose but also that it

---

[5] Single quotation marks, when they enclose expressions containing variables, are to be regarded as quasi-quotation marks. See W. V. Quine, *Mathematical Logic* (New York, Norton, 1940), pp. 33 ff.

[6] As I use the terms, "to find a plausible definition of the term," "to explicate the notion," and "to define the notion" denote the same process.

seems to me doubtful that any adequate definition of "synonymity"—at least for languages sufficiently complex to make the problem interesting—will ever be found by means of the usual armchair methods of philosophizing. We need empirical research regarding the ordinary language in order to determine which expressions are in fact synonymous, and with the help of these data it may be possible to find an acceptable definition of "synonymity" for some language which has a determinate structure and which closely resembles the ordinary language.

Yet it is important to observe that this very research could hardly be carried out unless we possessed in advance a sufficiently precise characterization of synonymity to enable us to decide under what conditions we would regard two expressions as synonymous for a given person. Otherwise, we would be forced to ask questions of the form 'Are A and B synonymous?'; and the answers would depend not only upon whether or not the subjects regarded the expressions as synonymous, but also upon how they understood the term "synonymous." The case is analogous to the following. Suppose that we wanted to determine whether John Smith is color-blind. We would not do this by asking him the question, "Are you color-blind?" for his answers would depend upon how *he* interpreted the term "color-blind," whereas we wish to know whether he is color-blind in *our* sense of the term. Consequently, we would ask such questions as "Do you see a number on this page?" and would employ some such criterion as "Smith is color-blind if and only if he does not see the number '7' on this page of the test book."

In the same way, we need a criterion of the form 'A and B are synonymous if and only if . . .' in order to be able to investigate which terms are actually synonymous.

Accordingly, I propose the following statement as a condition of adequacy for definitions of "synonymity" and as a guide for conducting research to determine which expressions are in fact synonymous for given persons: *Two expressions are synonymous in a language L if and only if they may be interchanged in each sentence in L without altering the truth value of that sentence.* That we ordinarily intend to use the word "synonymity" in such a way as to satisfy this condition will be argued in the sequel; first, allow me to make two remarks concerning its application. It is plain, no doubt, that this condition refers only to synonymity between expressions which occur in the same language. We shall need a different and more general criterion for the synonymity of expressions occurring in different languages.[7] Secondly, I intend this condition to apply only to languages which are not semantically closed, that is, to lan-

guages which do not contain names of their own expressions and semantical terms like "true," "denotes," and so forth. In particular, it is important that the language L not contain the semantical term "synonymous in L."

It is easy to see that if two expressions are synonymous in a language L, then they may be interchanged in any sentence in L without altering the truth value of that sentence. For, following Frege, we may say that the meaning of a sentence is a function of the meanings of the terms which occur in the sentence; from this it follows that if, in a given sentence, we replace a term by an expression which is synonymous with that term, then the resulting sentence is synonymous with (has the same meaning as) the original sentence. Further, it is clear that synonymous sentences have the same truth value. Hence, synonymous expressions may be interchanged without affecting the meaning or the truth value of sentences in which they occur.

Next, it requires to be shown that, if two expressions can be interchanged in each sentence in L without altering the truth value of that sentence, then they are synonymous. Let us first consider the case in which L contains a modal operator and allows for indirect discourse. Thus L will contain such expressions as 'A says that B,' 'A believes that B,' 'It is necessary that if A believes that B, then A believes that C.' In this case we may establish that interchangeability is a sufficient condition for synonymity by the following consideration. Let us begin with a true assertion from arithmetic:

(1) $9 = 9$.

---

[7] I assume that we are dealing with a language in which the formation rules do not prevent the interchange of expressions of the same type. Thus, the fact that "humanity" and "human" are not interchangeable in English does not indicate a difference in meaning, for syntax alone prevents their interchange. Now although the union of two languages is always a language, it is not generally the case that the union of two languages of the sort under consideration is a language of the sort under consideration. This is why we shall need a different criterion for the synonymity of expressions occurring in different languages.

If we replace either occurrence of "9" in this sentence by any expression A such that 'A = 9' is true, then the result will again be true.

Next, consider the true sentence,

(2)   N (9 = 9).[8]

Here we may obtain a false result if we replace an occurrence of "9" by an occurrence of some other expression on the basis of a true identity sentence. Thus "N (the number of the planets = 9)" is false. However, if we replace an occurrence of "9" by any expression A such that 'A = 9' is logically true, the result will again be true. Now, suppose that the following sentence is true:

(3)   Jones believes that 9 = 9.

In this case, replacing an occurrence of "9" by even a logically equivalent expression—e.g., by "3^2"—may lead to falsehood. There is no guarantee that it *will* lead to falsehood, but we can see that even if in fact Jones happens to believe both that 9 = 9 and that $9 = 3^2$, it is at least possible for him to believe one without believing the other.[9] In other words, the true sentence:

(4) N (Jones believes that 9 = 9
       if and only if Jones believes
       that 9 = 9),

will become false if the last occurrence of "9" is replaced by an occurrence of the logically equivalent expression "3^2." Thus logical equivalence of expressions is not sufficient to guarantee interchangeability in a language of the type we are now considering.

That nothing short of synonymity will guarantee interchangeability in a language of this type follows from the fact that the truth value of a sentence 'Jones believes that A' depends not upon the truth value of the constituent A but upon its meaning. If A is replaced by any other expression not having the same meaning the truth value of 'Jones believes that A' *may* be changed, which implies that the truth value of 'N(Jones believes that A if and only if Jones believes that A)' *will* be changed. Consequently, if two sentences A and B are not synonymous, they will not be interchangeable in all sentences of our language. Similar considerations lead to the further conclusion that if any two sentence constituents x and y are not synonymous, then they will not be interchangeable in the true sentence,

(5) N (Jones believes that . . . x
     . . . if and only if Jones be-
     lieves that . . . x . . .).

On the basis of this we may assert that if two expressions can be interchanged

---

[8] I write 'Np' as an abbreviation for 'It is necessary that p.'

[9] This assertion may of course be doubted. If it is false, then the cogency of my argument is destroyed; and I am aware that there

is at least one interpretation of belief sentences such that it is false. Thus, suppose that "9" and "3^2" are both abbreviations for descriptive phrases and have what Russell calls "primary occurrences" in the sentences "Jones believes that 9 = 9" and "Jones believes that $9 = 3^2$." Then the two sentences just mentioned are logically equivalent. Nevertheless, I think that in the usual sense of "belief" the two sentences are logically independent; I therefore reject the proposed interpretation as paradoxical.

in all sentences of L without altering truth values, then they are synonymous. Hence, the proposed condition holds for languages containing modal operators and indirect discourse.

However, when the condition is applied to extensional languages or to languages which are extensional except for the presence of modal operators, the results obtained are paradoxical. In languages of this sort all equivalent (or, respectively, logically equivalent) expressions would be synonymous, a result which is in violent conflict with ordinary usage of the term "synonymous." It seems to me that the reason for this conflict is simple; in this ordinary usage, the term "synonymous" is applied to the ordinary language, or at least to languages which are such as to permit modal sentences and indirect discourse. Thus, if we consider the question whether "2" and "4/2" are synonymous, we shall probably regard the language of arithmetic as a part of the ordinary language and decide the question in the negative, which would be in complete agreement with our criterion.

On the other hand, there are good reasons for making synonymity relative to the language in which the terms occur. Suppose that we have a language L and we wish to say something in L which will establish that two expressions in L are not synonymous. The only way to do this is to find some true sentence in L which would not be true if the terms were synonymous. For example, "2" and "4/2" could be shown nonsynonymous by the true sentence, "Someone might believe that $1 + 1 = 2$ without believing that $1 + 1 = 4/2$." Now, given any pair of equivalent ex-

pressions in an extensional language L_1, it will be impossible to find in L_1 any true sentence indicating that the expressions are not synonymous; hence, for all that can be said in an extensional language, any two equivalent expressions are synonymous. Likewise, given any pair of logically equivalent expressions in a modal language L_2, it will not be possible to find a true sentence in L_2 that would be false if the expressions were not synonymous. Therefore, logically equivalent expressions will be synonymous, for all that can be said in L_2 to the contrary.[10] In general, it seems natural to regard two expressions as synonymous in a language if there is no way in the language of distinguishing between their meanings. Thus it is natural to regard synonymity of terms as relative to the language in which the terms occur.

I shall conclude my discussion of the proposed condition of adequacy by offering some comments on other people's views.

Quine has discussed problems very closely related to those at hand, and no one can fail to be instructed by what he says.[11] However, it seems to me that his choice of terminology may lead one to suppose that what is essentially a

---

[10] But, of course, for any two terms which are not logically equivalent it will be possible in the modal language to find a true sentence which would not be true if they were synonymous. For example, though "morning star" and "evening star" are equivalent, the negation of "N(morning star = evening star)" is a true sentence which indicates that these terms are not synonymous.

[11] See "Notes on Existence and Necessity," *Journal of Philosophy*, XL (1943) 113–127.

question of synonymity is instead a question of designation. The following specific example (his own) will be of use in clarifying the point. Consider the sentences:

(6) Philip believes that Tegucigalpa is in Nicaragua.
(7) Tegucigalpa is the capital of Honduras.

Substitution into (6) on the basis of (7) gives

(8) Philip believes that the capital of Honduras is in Nicaragua.

Now apparently (6) and (8) are not logically equivalent. Quine seeks to explain this by asserting that the occurrence of "Tegucigalpa" in (6) is not "purely designative" and by claiming that only purely designative occurrences of names are subject to substitutivity on the basis of a true identity sentence. But this explanation is not a good one, as will appear from the following parallel case:

(9) Philip believes that $2^{10} < 1000$.
(10) $2^{10} = 1024$.
(11) Philip believes that 1024 < 1000.

If we grant that (9) and (11) need not be equivalent, it is evident that the expression "2^{10}," like "Tegucigalpa," is subject to substitutivity in some contexts and not in others. Hence, in order to apply Quine's mode of explanation here we shall have to say that some occurrences of "2^{10}" are purely designative and some are not. This, unfortunately, commits us to a kind of

Platonism which no one is more anxious than Quine to avoid. He apparently wishes to assert that expressions like "2^{10}" *never* occur designatively, for he is of the opinion that there are no such things as numbers. Now if they never occur designatively, substitution on the basis of a true identity sentence will never be possible. But we know that it is possible. Hence, this sort of explanation is difficult to combine with nominalism. I should make it clear, however, that I do not object to Quine's view because it clashes with nominalism; my objection is rather that this particular problem may be treated independently of the nominalism-realism dispute. The sentences (6)–(8) and (9)–(11) show us that substitution on the basis of a true identity sentence cannot be made in a context governed by "believes that." We can discover and utilize this fact without ever taking up the question whether number expressions or any other expressions designate anything.

C. I. Lewis has explicated synonymity in such a way that synthetic sentences are synonymous if and only if they are logically equivalent.[12] It is easy to see that this is not in agreement with our criterion. For example, consider the sentences:

(12) Jones believes that he has one nose.
(13) Jones believes that the number of his noses is equal to $-(e^{\pi i})$.

------

[12] See "The Modes of Meaning," *Philosophy and Phenomenological Research,* IV (1943–1944), 236–250; and *An Analysis of Knowledge and Valuation* (La Salle, Ill., Open Court, 1946), p. 86.

It will probably be generally agreed that these sentences might well have opposite truth values; if this is possible, then the synthetic subsentences, though they are logically equivalent, are not synonymous according to our criterion. The example chosen need not have been so extreme. In the physical sciences there are many pairs of synthetic sentences which are logically equivalent to each other but which, unfortunately, are not interchangeable in belief contexts, as any teacher will confirm.

Arne Ness, in connection with some very important empirical research he is doing on the subject of synonymity, has mentioned several possible definitions of the term.[13] Some of these do not satisfy our criterion. According to one, for example, two sentences would be synonymous if and only if the same states of affairs would confirm or disconfirm the propositions which they express. According to this, it seems to me, all logically equivalent sentences would be synonymous; but we have seen that logical equivalence is not a strong enough condition for interchangeability in a language containing indirect discourse. According to another possibility mentioned by Ness, two sentences are synonymous if every sentence derivable from one is derivable from the other, and conversely. Now the exact meaning of this depends upon how the word "derivable" is interpreted, but if logically equivalent sentences are derivable from one another, then logically equivalent sentences would be

synonymous under this definition, too. Consequently, both of these possibilities for defining "synonymity" would have to be rejected as inadequate, if our criterion of adequacy were accepted.

Carnap has proposed the concept of intensional isomorphism as an approximate explicatum for synonymity.[14] It seems to me that this is the best proposal that has been made by anyone to date. However, it has, along with its merits, some rather odd consequences. For instance, let "D" and "D'" be abbreviations for two intensionally isomorphic sentences. Then the following sentences are also intensionally isomorphic:

(14) Whoever believes that D, believes that D.

(15) Whoever believes that D, believes that D'.

But nobody doubts that whoever believes that D believes that D. Therefore, nobody doubts that whoever believes that D believes that D'. This seems to suggest that, for any pair of intensionally isomorphic sentences—let them be abbreviated by "D" and "D',"—if anybody even doubts that whoever believes that D believes that D', then Carnap's explication is incorrect. What is more, *any* adequate explication of synonymity will have this result, for the validity of the argument is not affected if we replace the words "intensionally isomorphic" by the word "synonymous" throughout.

---

[13] See *Interpretation and Preciseness*, I: *Survey of Basic Concepts* (mim., Oslo, 1947).

[14] See *Meaning and Necessity* (Univ. of Chicago Press, 1947), pp. 56 ff.

III

Interpretation is a matter of prime importance to philosophers in at least two respects. In the first place, every philosopher who deserves the name wants to understand the writings of his fellows and predecessors, and this often requires the utmost in careful and skilled interpretation. Secondly, many of the problems which philosophers seek to solve are themselves problems of interpretation or else correspond to such problems in certain characteristic ways. Both of these respects will be discussed in the present section.

Philosophical writing seems to me to have a pair of characteristics which are especially significant in the present connection. One is that it is argumentative. Very little of what would be regarded as genuine philosophical writing consists of mere musings. On the contrary, philosophers (*qua* philosophers) are nearly always trying to argue in behalf of some thesis. Often the arguments are difficult to follow; often, when they can be understood, they are seen to be invalid. Nevertheless, it seems correct to say that philosophical writing is largely argumentative.

The other characteristic to which I wish to draw attention (and to which I fear I am drawing attention) is that of relative unclarity. Whether the fault be with the subject matter or with the philosophers or with both, we must grant that the products are often the very reverse of lucid. I do not mention this in order to derogate from the value of philosophical writing, nor on the other hand do I bring it up in order to suggest that philosophers are persons who think deeply and whose communications are consequently not easy to understand; I only mention the relative opaqueness of philosophical writing as a matter of fact.

As a result of these two factors we often become aware, in reading the discourse of some philosopher, that he is presenting an argument in behalf of some thesis, but at the same time we are unable to understand either the thesis or the argument well enough to decide questions of truth and validity. Thus arises the need for an interpretation. We require a translation of the obscure discourse into a body of discourse which is probably much longer than the original but which consists of expressions more readily intelligible to us than the original expressions were. After the interpretation has been constructed we are better able to decide upon the truth and validity of the original discourse. Then we are at least able to make comments of the following form: 'If by A he means B, then what he says is true (or false), or his argument is valid (or invalid).' In my opinion this is the form in which philosophical criticism ought always to be made, but usually, of course, the hypothesis 'If by A he means B' is omitted.

In this procedure the chances of failing to do justice to the author under examination are very great, and the greatest danger lies in assuming that the interpretation which is the basis of the criticism is a good one. It will be instructive to examine some particular instances of philosophical criticism, with a view toward seeing in detail how errors of interpretation can lead to injustice in criticism. The first case to be presented is artificial and much simplified; yet it will be serious enough, no doubt, to provoke comment.

Suppose that in the writings of some philosopher we find this strange argument:

1) Socrates is human.
2) Human is human.
3) For every A, B, C: if A is C and B is C, then A resembles B with respect to being C.
4) Therefore, Socrates resembles human with respect to being human.[15]

In behalf of the premises of his argument, the author might offer some such considerations as the following. That Socrates is human is asserted as a matter of fact. The statement "Human is human" is an instance of "A is A," and hence is not only true but is necessarily true. The third premise is to be regarded as analytic because of the meaning of "resembles," but it may at least be illustrated by examples. So, if Socrates is a philosopher and Plato is a philosopher, then Socrates resembles Plato (with respect to being a philosopher); likewise, if lead is heavy and gold is heavy, then lead resembles gold (with respect to being heavy). Also, if Mark Twain is the author of *Innocents*

Abroad and Samuel Clemens is the author of *Innocents Abroad,* then Mark Twain resembles Samuel Clemens[16] with respect to authoring this book.

Given these considerations in behalf of the truth of the premises, and given the obvious fact that the argument is valid in form, we are apparently forced to accept the conclusion, which seems to express the Platonic view that Socrates resembles the Idea of Human, that is, that he resembles humanity itself. But there are certain obvious objections to the argument; and let us consider these. (I shall ignore the syntactical strangeness of the conclusion and of the second premise, since this seems to be due to a purely accidental feature of the English language, namely that there are two terms, "humanity" and "human," which express the same property but which are such that syntax forbids their interchange.)

Probably the most serious objection that would be raised could be stated as follows. The word "is," as it appears in this argument, is ambiguous. Sometimes it means the same as the phrase "has the property," and thus when the philosopher says "Socrates is human" he means

---

[15] I do not propose this argument as a model of English composition, but rather as an example of discourse for which an interpretation is needed.

[16] This last is obviously an extreme case, in which the resemblance is very close! But the mere fact that we would ordinarily make the stronger statement, that Mark Twain *is* Samuel Clemens, should not lead us to suppose that the weaker statement, that Mark Twain *resembles* Samuel Clemens, is either false or meaningless. Thus, if I see someone on the street and say to my companion, "Whoever that is, he certainly resembles President Truman," my assertion will not be false or nonsensical if it turns out that the man actually is President Truman.

that Socrates has the property Human. But sometimes "is" means the same as "is identical with," so that the sentence "Human is human" means that the property Human is identical with the property Human. Now the third premise is plausible only so long as the word "is" retains the same meaning at both of its occurrences in the statement. Thus, the argument is either invalid or one of its premises is false.

Let us examine this objection more closely. It rests upon an interpretation of the original argument, that is, upon a translation of its four sentences into the following four sentences:

1) Socrates has the property Human.
2) The property Human is identical with the property Human.
3) For every A, B, C: if A has the property C and B has the property C, then A resembles B with respect to having the property C.
4) Therefore, Socrates resembles the property Human with respect to having the property Human.

But the argument, as thus interpreted, involves a clear *non sequitur*, and this fact is supposed to show that the original argument is really defective even though it appears to be a valid argument with true premises.

In a similar way, other interpretations of the same argument lead to the conclusion that it is unacceptable, either because it is invalid or because at least one of its premises is false. For instance, if we resolutely translate 'A is B' everywhere into 'A has the property B,' we get the following interpretation:

1) Socrates has the property Human.
2) Human has the property Human.
3) For every A, B, C: if A has the property C and B has the property C, then A resembles B with respect to having the property C.
4) Therefore, Socrates resembles Human with respect to having the property Human.

In this interpretation the argument is valid and the first and third premises seem acceptable enough, but serious difficulties stand in the way of our assenting to the second premise. As Russell says in criticizing Plato: "I can say 'Socrates is human,' 'Plato is human,' and so on. In all these statements, it may be assumed that the word 'human' has exactly the same meaning. But whatever it means, it means something which is not of the same kind as Socrates, Plato, and the rest of the individuals who compose the human race. 'Human' is an adjective; it would be nonsense to say 'human is human.' "[17] Here Russell is evidently thinking of "Human is human" as meaning that the property Human has the property Human, and not as an instance of the theorem "$\phi \, \hat{z} = \phi \, \hat{z}$."

If, then, we agree to the first interpretation of the argument, we shall say that the author has committed the fallacy of using the same term in different senses at certain crucial places in the argument, thus rendering the argument invalid; and if we agree to the second interpretation, we may say

---

[17] *A History of Western Philosophy* (New York, Simon & Schuster, 1945), p. 127.

that the author "has no understanding of philosophical syntax," and that the second premise is false or meaningless. Thus, under either interpretation, we shall deny that the conclusion is established as true by this argument.

Now, in my opinion, the dangers in such a critical procedure are quite evident but usually ignored. In the case at hand, none of the considerations advanced are sufficient to justify condemnation of the argument. For in spite of the fact that there are two interpretations of "is" such that the argument is not conclusive under either of these interpretations, it remains to be shown that no plausible interpretation can be found in which the premises are true and the argument valid. This last would not be an easy thing to do, and it is probable that very few critics would wish to postpone criticism of a piece of philosophical writing until it had been ascertained that there was no plausible interpretation under which that piece of writing would be acceptable. Usually the procedure of critics is quite the reverse; each thinks that he knows well enough how the English language is used—that is, each acts as though *his* interpretation or interpretations were the only ones possible,—and consequently if the passage under scrutiny doesn't make sense when interpreted in his particular way, he judges that it doesn't make sense at all.

Hence, to return to the argument which we are using as an example, we must consider the possibility that neither of the two interpretations proposed is faithful to the sense of the original text. This amounts to considering the possibility that besides the predicative sense of the word "is," in which it always expresses a relation between things of different type, and the identity sense of the word, in which it always expresses a relation between things of the same type, there may be another more general sense of "is" such that the argument is valid when the occurrences of "is" are understood in this sense. "Well!" the objectors will immediately reply, "if there is such a sense, what is it?"

Before attempting to answer this question, let us try to decide what kind of answer is wanted. Probably no one expects the word "is" to be defined ostensively. This being so, we may fairly take the question to be a request for an English expression that is synonymous with "is." The objectors have suggested that the phrase "has the property" is synonymous with "is" in some of its occurrences, and that the phrase "is identical with" is synonymous with it in its other occurrences, and now they expect us either to accept their interpretations as final or else to set forth a phrase which is clearly meaningful and which can be regarded as synonymous with "is" in all or nearly all of its occurrences. But we may observe at once that the possibility of doing this depends in part upon the richness of English. It depends upon whether the English language happens to contain an expression which is synonymous with "is." Whether or not it does so is a purely contingent matter. If it should be the case that it does not, this would not suffice to show that there is no single sense which the word possesses in all its occurrences. As many writers have pointed out, there are in general strong reasons against the existence of synonymous expressions in a conversational language. Usually we simply do not need two expressions with the same meaning, and if there are any synonyms at all, this may be ascribed more to the ancestry of the language than to its utility. Consequently, anyone who asks what the sense of a linguistic expression is ought to be aware that there is no good reason for supposing the question answerable. If he does succeed in getting a satisfactory definition, he may thank fortune; if he does not, his only recourse is to discover the meaning of the expression from observing how it is used.

Let us now attempt to find an interpretation such that under this interpretation the argument in question is translated into a valid argument with true premises. We may proceed as follows. Generic terms like "Human" are commonly regarded as having classes for their extensions and properties for their intensions. Suppose that proper names, for example "Socrates," were also regarded in this way; then the extension of "Socrates" would be the unit class of Socrates and the intension would be the defining characteristic of Socrates. This supposition, no doubt, would represent the height of Platonism. Individuals would turn out to be abstract entities, and thus we would have to imagine it possible for us not only to see an abstract entity but even to be one! But whether or not this interpretation is Platonistic is irrelevant to the present discussion (though I shall here express my confidence that if every individual suddenly turned into

his unit class, no one would notice the difference). The problem at hand is merely to construct an interpretation. Accordingly, supposing that we understand proper names as indicated, let us interpret "is" by the phrase "is included in." The argument then becomes:

1) Socrates is included in Human.
2) Human is included in Human.
3) For every A, B, C: if A is included in C and B is included in C, then A resembles B with respect to being included in C.
4) Therefore, Socrates resembles Human with respect to being included in Human.

The premises are true, since both the unit class of Socrates and the class Human are included in the class Human, and since it is not implausible to interpret "resembles" in such a way that (3) holds. Further, the argument is of valid form; therefore, we may say that under the interpretation offered, the argument is a valid argument with true premises.

I hope that the point of this fantastic example is clear. The original argument contained "Socrates is human" as its first premise. We must not suppose that the author necessarily meant what we would express by the sentence "the individual Socrates had the property Human." He may have meant what we would express by "the unit class of Socrates is included in the class Human" or "the defining property of Socrates is included in the property Human." It seems to me, therefore, that if an author's arguments become invalid under a given interpretation, common sense requires that not only the capability of the author but also the correctness of the interpretation come under suspicion.

For a second and less artificial example of philosophical argument based on questionable interpretation, I shall turn again to some aspects of the nominalism of Quine. According to Quine, it is possible to determine that a man is a "platonist" by examining how he uses variables of quantification. The term "platonist" in this sense refers to anyone who supposes that universals exist. Quine's criterion seems to be as follows: whoever applies quantifiers to object variables presupposes that there are such entities as objects; whoever applies quantifiers to class variables presupposes that there are such entities as classes; etc.[18] In behalf of this method of ascertaining ontological commitments, Quine says:

> The quantifier '(Ex)' means 'there is an entity x such that,' and the quantifier '(x)' means 'every entity x is such that.' The bound variables of a theory range over all the entities of which the theory treats. That classical mathematics treats of universals, or affirms that there are universals, means simply that classical mathematics requires universals as values of its bound variables. When we say, e.g., that
>
> (Ex) (x is prime and $5 < x < 11$)

we are saying that *there is* something which is prime and between 5 and 11; and this entity is in fact the number 7, a universal, if such there be.[19]

It seems quite clear, therefore, that Quine's view rests upon the assumption that sentences beginning with the existential quantifier "(Ex)" are to be interpreted by sentences beginning with the phrase "there is an entity x such that." As far as I can see, this assumption is without justification. In the first place, if we examine the actual usage of mathematicians and logicians, we find that the existential quantifier is read in many different ways: "there exists an x such that," "for some x," "for some values of 'x,'" etc. These various phrases may or may not be intended by their users as always introducing ontological assertions. But in the second place, it is possible to interpret existential quantifiers in such a way that no ontological commitments are involved, save possibly commitments to the existence of expressions in the language. For instance, the sentence "(Ex) (x is prime and $5 < x < 11$)" may be interpreted by the sentence "there is a constant such that the sentence which results from substituting this constant for 'x' in the matrix 'x is prime and $5 < x < 11$' is true." Thus one might well use the existential quantifier on number variables without committing himself to the view that there are such things as numbers. This method of interpreting existential quantifiers is well known, and, to be sure, it involves certain difficulties. For

---

[18] Provided, of course, that the quantifiers are part of the primitive notation of the language. See "Designation and Existence," *Journal of Philosophy*, XXXVI (1939), 701–709; "On Universals," *Journal of Symbolic Logic*, XII (1947); 74–84; and the article cited in note 11 above.

[19] "On Universals," p. 75.

example, if there is something for which there is no constant in the object language, then it is possible for "(Ex) (x is mortal)" to be false even if something is mortal. But these difficulties can be remedied to a great extent; anyhow, the interpretation is not so patently untenable that some other interpretation can be accepted as self-evidently correct. The point here, as in the other example, is that it is philosophically dangerous to assume that a given interpretation is the correct one.

This completes what I have to say concerning the interpretation of philosophical writing. The other topic of the present section is the relation between certain problems of philosophy and problems of interpretation. I shall begin by giving two examples of how philosophical problems may be expressed as problems of interpretation.

The thesis of phenomenalism might be stated roughly as follows: for every sentence about material things there exists another sentence which is about sense contents and which is synonymous with it. Possibly a better formulation of the thesis could be obtained if we specified, by lists or otherwise, two sets of terms, to be called "material-object terms" and "sense-data terms," respectively. Then we could restate the thesis in the following way: for every sentence containing a material-object term there is a synonymous sentence which contains only sense-data terms together with certain logical constants. In a corresponding way, the naturalistic position in ethics might be expressed by the statement: for every sentence containing an ethical term there is a synonymous sentence containing only

terms of the approved, naturalistic variety. Again, we would have somehow to specify the set of ethical terms and the set of naturalistic terms, perhaps by lists. Presumably the terms "good," "bad," "right," "wrong," and the like, would be on the ethical list, and the naturalistic list would contain such words as "pleasure," "approval," "utility," "happiness," and the like.

Now it is important to be very clear about what does and what does not follow from the fact that these positions may be stated in the way described. For instance, does it follow that phenomenalism and naturalism are "purely verbal" theses? It certainly does not. For to find an adequate method of translating sentences containing the word "good" is no more and no less difficult than to find a so-called real definition of good, and to decide whether there is an adequate method of translating material-object sentences into sense-data sentences is exactly as difficult as to solve the metaphysical problem of whether phenomenalism is true. Again, the procedure used by Socrates in his attempt to discover a real definition of piety is essentially the same procedure that one would have to use in order to discover a complex expression synonymous with the word "piety." In general, it seems to me, we do not get rid of philosophical problems by representing them as problems of translation or interpretation; the situation is rather that the solution of either version of the problem always involves the solution of the other version.

This raises the following question: if a linguistic problem corresponding to a given philosophical problem cannot be solved unless the latter is solved, what is the use of giving attention to the linguistic version? The answer is that the linguistic version often serves to clarify the nature of the problem and to show, unfortunately, that the original problem was even more complicated than had been supposed. Consider, for example, the following linguistic version of the thesis usually called "hedonism": for every sentence containing the term "good" there is a synonymous sentence which does not contain "good" or any other ethical term, but which does contain the term "pleasure." If we investigate the problem by means of this formulation we are led to make certain distinctions which are, in my opinion, very important. We see at once that the decision whether a certain type of hedonism is true will involve deciding whether certain sentences are synonymous. Since synonymity is relative to a language, we shall need to specify some language, or, what comes to the same thing, we shall need to specify what *degree* of synonymity is required.[20] Thus, suppose that we are interested in the synonymity or lack of synonymity of the expressions "good" and "productive of pleasure." If we deal only with extensional contexts, then we can establish that these terms are synonymous if we can establish that

whatever is good is productive of pleasure and whatever is productive of pleasure is good. If we speak with reference to a language which is extensional except for the presence of the modal operator "it is necessary that . . .," then to show that the two terms are synonymous we shall have to establish not only that all good things are pleasant, and conversely, but also that it is impossible for something to be good without being pleasant, or to be pleasant without being good. If, as is more likely, we speak with reference to a language containing indirect discourse, then even though the predicators "good" and "productive of pleasure" were logically equivalent, they might not be synonymous. Thus, when the problem of whether or not this form of hedonism is true is stated as a problem of interpretation it becomes clear that there are at least three distinguishable problems masquerading as one. It is important to be aware of this, since when we examine the writings of ethicists on hedonism, we find that those who support it usually try to show that the expressions are synonymous in the first sense (i.e., that "good" and "productive of pleasure" apply to the same things), while those who attack it try to show that the expressions are not synonymous in the second or third senses (i.e., that it is possible for something to be good and not pleasant, or that we may believe something to be good without believing it pleasant). Thus these opponents hold positions which are perfectly compatible—if, I hasten to add, I have interpreted them correctly.

In this way, the linguistic version of a philosophical problem may be a

---

[20] I say that two terms are synonymous to a low degree in the natural language if they are synonymous in the largest extensional sublanguage of the natural language; they are synonymous to a higher degree if they are synonymous in the largest sublanguage which is extensional except for containing modal operators; and they are synonymous to the highest degree if they are synonymous in the natural language taken as a whole.

useful heuristic device for attacking the problem, just as in deciding certain questions of geography it is useful to translate them into questions regarding the positions of marks on a map. But just as it would be ludicrous to suppose that maps constitute the entire subject matter of geography, so also it would be a great mistake to suppose that philosophy is or ought to be nothing more than the study of language. I trust that what I have said here has served to illustrate, if not to establish, the truth of that conclusion.

6.8

ANALYSIS AND SYNONYMY*

Arthur Pap

Suppose that two given sentences "S_1" and "S_2" are synonymous, is it in that case possible to know that one is true without knowing that the other is true? A negative answer to this question seems plausible, by the following argument: if "S_1" is synonymous with "S_2", then an interchange of "S_1" and "S_2" in any compound sentence cannot affect the truth-value of the compound sentence. Take, then, as a compound sentence containing "S_1": A knows that S_1 (p). By the announced principle of interchangeability *salva veritate* of syn-

onyms, p ought to entail "A knows that S_2" (q). On the assumption of synonymy, therefore, p seems inconsistent with not-q. Illustrations of arguments, of philosophical importance, to non-synonymy of "S_1" and "S_2" from a premise of the form "A knows that S_1 but does not know that S_2" can be obtained by substituting for "S_1" "this surface is blue" and for "S_2" "this surface has the disposition to reflect light of wave-length x", or for "S_1" "A is thinking at time t of the paradox of analysis" and for "S_2" "a brain-event of specific kind K (it would be nice to know which) occurs in A's brain at t".

I have opened this paper by calling attention to a familiar method of disproving claims of synonymy of declarative sentences, because a thorough analysis of the principle underlying the

From "Synonymy, Identity of Concepts and the Paradox of Analysis," *Methods*, VII (1955). Reprinted by permission of the editor.

* Slightly altered version of a paper read at the Conference for Unity of Science, Berkeley, (University of California), July 1953.

method will lead us promptly into the midst of the problems surrounding the notion of synonymy relevant to philosophical analysis. It will have been noticed that the above assertion of knowledge (p) was formulated without the use of "true"; indeed, this was deliberate. For, if instead of "p" we wrote (p′): A knows that "S_1" is true, and then proceeded to derive (q′): A knows that "S_2" is true, the protest would be called for that "p′" does not contain "S_1" at all, but its name, and that therefore the above mentioned principle of interchange had been fallaciously applied. Yet, if those who file this protest happen to hold that "S_2" is itself synonymous with " 'S_1' is true", they can easily be embarrassed by pointing out to them that on this assumption "p" would seem to be itself synonymous with "p′", by the principle that replacement of a subsentence (S_1) by a synonymous sentence ("S_1" is true) cannot change the meaning of the compound sentence into which the replacement is made, and that therefore whatever is entailed by p must be entailed by p′.[1] And just to add to the confusion, suppose somebody were to argue that while the entailment from p to q is, on the assumption of synonymy of "S_1" and "S_2", valid, p′ clearly does not entail q′, since "S_2" may belong to a language which A does not understand, in which case he would surely be ignorant of the truth-value of "S_2". It is evident that this situation can be clarified only by clarifying the meaning of assertions like "p′".

The possibility of a breakdown of the sort of entailment under discussion on account of a lack of *understanding* of one of a pair of synonymous sentences arises only in connection with formulation "p′"; for, since "p" does not mention the sentence "S_1" at all, it clearly does not entail that A is capable of interpreting "S_1". When I say of Hans, who is ignorant of English, that he knows that the earth is round, I do not imply that he knows what proposition is expressed by the English sentence "the earth is round." However, even p′ can, not unplausibly, be analyzed in such a way that it does not entail that A knows what proposition is expressed by "S_1". To see this, we only need to recognize that " 'S_1' is true" is elliptical for "the proposition expressed by 'S_1' (in language L)[2] is true". Whether A could know that the proposition expressed by "S_1" is true without knowing which proposition is expressed by "S_1" is the same kind of question as whether A could know that Peter's wife is tall without knowing which woman is Peter's wife. And the answer will be

---

[1] It should be noted that when I use p's and q's unquoted, as in the above sentence "whatever is entailed by p must be entailed by p′", I thereby indicate that the values (not to be confused with substituends!) of these variables are *propositions*, not sentences. If we use sentences as names of these (abstract) values, the result would, indeed, be ungrammatical: e.g., "some people have sons entails some people have children". But as names of propositions one should rather use such expressions as "*that* some people have sons" or "some people *having* sons".

[2] Obviously, what proposition is expressed by a given sentence depends on the language (specifically its semantic rules) to which the sentence belongs. For brevity's sake, however, I shall talk about designation as though it were a two-term relation.

affirmative in either case if one agrees to the following analysis of knowledge-sentences involving descriptions. Suppose that p has the form: $g[(\imath x)\, fx]$, and let "$K_A,\, p$" mean "A knows that p". Then $K_A,\; p\; =\; (z)\; [(z\; =\; (\imath x)\, fx)\; \supset\; K_A,\, gz]$.[3] On this analysis, "$K_A,\, p$" is clearly compatible with "$\sim K_A,\, (c = (\imath x)\; fx)$", where c is the unique entity, of whatever type, satisfying the description. To connect this general analysis with the question whether "A knows that 'S_1' is true" is compatible with "A does not know which proposition is expressed by 'S_1'", make the following substitutions: $p = g$ $[(\imath x)\, fx]\; =\; true\; [\; (\imath x)\; ("S_1"\; designates\; x)]$. The constant c in this case is the unique proposition designated by "S_1", which we may symbolize by "p_1"; similarly let "p_2" stand for the unique proposition designated by "S_2", let $q_1 = true\; [(\imath x)\, ("S_1"\; des\; x)]$, and let $q_2 = true\; [(\imath x)\, ("S_2"\; des\; x)]$. The assumption of the synonymy of "S_1" and "S_2" can then be expressed as the identity: $p_1 = p_2$.

Our original question whether p′ entails q′ can now be restated more precisely as the question whether the following argument is valid: (1) K_A, q_1; (2) $p_1 = p_2$; therefore (3) K_A,q_2. The argument seems valid, since by the above analysis (1) entails only K_A,p_1, not: $K_A,\, (p_1 = (\imath x)\; ("S_1"\; des\; x))$, and analogously for (3); and from K_A,p_1 and (2), K_A,p_2 seems to follow by the substitutivity of identity; and since "p_2"

is equivalent to "p_2 is true", this in turn entails (3) by the above analysis of knowledge-sentences involving descriptions. Unfortunately, however, the substitution of identicals occurs here in a non-extensional context,[4] and such substitution leads straight to what is known as the paradox of analysis. For, suppose that "S_2" expresses a correct analysis of the proposition designated by "S_1", such that $p_1 = p_2$. Then the true premise "A knows that $p_1 = p_1$" would lead to the conclusion "A knows that $p_1 = p_2$", which may be false since A may not know the correct analysis of proposition p_1. The paradox of analysis is usually formulated as the paradox that if the analysis of p_1 to p_2 is correct then the proposition that $p_1 = p_2$ is identical with the trivial proposition $p_1 = p_1$. But since nobody can fail to know a trivial proposition, this is equivalent to saying that nobody can fail to know the analysis of any proposition. A perfectly analogous paradox would of course arise if we characterized the objects of analysis as concepts or propositional functions, rather than as propositions. And restriction of the rule of interchangeability of synonyms to extensional contexts would, while invalidating the method of proving non-synonymy scrutinized above, have in either case the merit of enabling a simple solution of the paradox of analysis. For, substitution of "p_2" for one occurrence of "p_1" in the context "A knows that p_1 is

---

[3] In this entire paragraph, "x" (as well as "z") is used as a variable completely unrestricted as to type.

[4] A sentence S is said to be a non-extensional context with respect to a subsentence T, if replacement of T by a sentence of the same truth-value may change the truth-value of S.

identical with p_1" would violate this restriction, and so would a similar substitution in the context "the proposition that p_1 is identical with the proposition that p_1". The Leibnizian test of identity of entities in terms of interchangeability ("salva veritate") of their designations must, indeed, be understood to be restricted to extensional contexts even if the entities are of the sort that are countenanced with easy conscience by nominalists: as Russell pointed out long ago, the identity of Scott and the author of Waverley notwithstanding, King George wished to know whether Scott was the author of Waverley but not whether Scott was Scott (I shall return to this point later).

It may be replied, however, that the paradox of analysis can be generated in a purely extensional language, and that the limitation of the substitutivity of identity to extensional contexts is not sufficient to solve it. All we need to be granted is the principle that if terms T_1 and T_2 are synonymous and S_1 contains T_1 and S_2 results from S_1 by replacing T_1 with T_2, then S_1 and S_2 are synonymous. Let T_1 = brother, T_2 = male sibling, S_1 = (x) $(brother_x \equiv$ male sibling$_x)$, S_2 = (x) $(brother_x \equiv$ brother$_x)$. The paradox is that S_1 and S_2 seem far from synonymous, since S_2 is trivial and S_1 informative (though analytic). To this argument a twofold reply must be made: (1) synonymy is presumably relative to a language, and if the language about expressions of which a hypothesis of synonymy is made is extensional, then it is in fact reasonable to accept the hypothesis as

established if the expressions in question are interchangeable *salva veritate* in all *extensional* contexts provided by the language.[5] Indeed, if we think of S_1 and S_2 as non-synonymous it is precisely because we mentally construct a *non-extensional* context in which they cannot be interchanged without change of truth-value, such as "it is possible to doubt that . . .", and thus we have already transcended the language in question. (2) The paradox of analysis is that it appears to be demonstrable that any statement which expresses a correct analysis is trivial. But then the discussion of the paradox of analysis ought to revolve around statements which purport to express analyses, and an extensional statement like S_1 just is not that kind of statement. The customary analysis of the meaning of "brother" would be properly formulated as "the concept *brother*[6] is identical with the concept *male sibling*", or "the attribute . . .", or (if type-designations are to be avoided) "to be a brother is to be a male sibling". An extensionalist is likely to reply that if this be the proper formulation of analyses then analysis cannot claim ontological neutrality, since in employing names of intensions (or "senses", in the Frege-Church terminology) one is committed to

---

[5] This point has been made by Benson Mates, in "Synonymity", University of California Publications in Philosophy, Vol. 25, 1950; reprinted in *Semantics and the Philosophy of Language*, ed. by L. Linsky, 1953.

[6] Throughout this paper the device is used of italicizing an expression if what is mentioned is not the expression itself but its intension.

Platonism. The formulation preferred by the extensionalist is, of course, the semantic one: "brother" is synonymous with "male sibling". It is clear that no paradox of analysis can arise on the basis of this formulation, since in this sentence the terms are *mentioned*, not used, so that the principle of interchange cannot be applied. To deduce from "I know that 'brother' is synonymous with 'male sibling' " the conclusion "I know that 'brother' is synonymous with 'brother' " and " 'brother' is synonymous with 'male sibling' " would be as fallacious as the transition from " 'brother' begins with 'b' " to " 'male sibling' begins with 'b' ". To be sure, the principle of interchange permits the transition from " 'brother' is synonymous with 'male sibling' " to " 'to be a brother is to be a male sibling' is synonymous with 'to be a brother is to be a brother' ", but the sentences concluded to be synonymous cannot occur in an extensional language, since "to be a brother" and "to be a male sibling" are, in the context of the above statements of identity, names of intensions. And one might now be inclined to favor an extensional language of analysis just because it spares us worrying about the paradox of analysis.[7] The solution by restriction of substitutivity to identity may have struck the reader as *ad hoc* anyway: after all, if two

_____

[7] In his note "On the Church-Frege Solution of the Paradox of Analysis" (*Philosophy and Phenomenological Research*, Dec. 1948), Morton G. White observes correctly "that the paradox of analysis starts by assuming the existence of attributes" (p. 308). He does not, however, discuss the question whether *analysis itself* "starts by assuming the existence of attributes".

entities are identical then they are identical "all the way"—identity does not admit of degrees—, and this means that *whatever* can in any language be truly said about one can in that language be truly said about the other. So, if the concept *brother* is identical with the concept *male sibling*, then if it can be truly said of the concept *brother* that everybody knows that it is identical with itself, then it can be truly said of the concept *male sibling* that everybody knows that it is identical with the concept *brother*. And if this consequence cannot be drawn, then it is obscure in what sense intensions can be said to be "identical", and this means that it is obscure what intensions are. So one may be tempted to argue if one is an extensionalist sympathizer. But I shall proceed to argue (1) that analyses cannot be adequately expressed in an extensional language, (2) that with respect to restrictions of identity-substitutions, intensions are no worse off than concreta.

As to the first point. The well-known trick of the *Logical Syntax of Language* of saving the thesis of extensionality by construing statements apparently about intensions as meta-linguistic statements about expressions, has in the meantime been diagnosed as oversimplified by Carnap himself. To talk about a proposition just is not the same thing as to talk about the sentence which happens to be used to express it, and similarly to talk about the concept *brother* just is not the same thing as to talk about the word "brother". An effective way of proving this is the argument from translation into a foreign language, which Church has employed to criticize even Carnap's more sophisticated attempt to extensionalize belief-sentences, in *Meaning* and *Necessity*.[8] The argument is based on the unquestionable assumption that synonymy is a transitive relation: if "the concept *brother* is identical with the concept *male sibling*" were synonymous with " 'brother' is synonymous, in English,[9] with 'male sibling' ", then, since the latter English sentence is synonymous with the German sentence " 'brother' ist gleichbedeutend im Englischen mit 'male sibling' ", this German sentence would have to be accepted as the correct translation of our first English sentence, which it obviously is not. The same argument disposes of the widespread view that entailment-statements, unlike material conditionals, contain when accurately expressed names of sentences, not sentences, in other words, are *about* sentences. The usual reply to this criticism is that the difference between term and concept, sentence and proposition, can be admitted without surrendering extensionalism, since statements about intensions may be construed as state-ments about *classes* of synonymous expressions. Thus it is supposed that by identifying the concept *brother* with the class of terms synonymous with "brother", one can easily account for the fact that the analysis of the concept *brother* refers not just to the use of the English word "brother".[10] But it is easy to show that the analysis refers not *even* to the use of the English word. For, if the word "brother" came to be used in the sense in which "sister" is presently used, this change of linguistic behavior would not refute the entailment-state-ment—which is a partial analysis of the concept *brother*—"being a brother en-tails being male", and to suppose that it would is to confuse the *use* of the concept-name "being a brother" for the purpose of mentioning the concept *brother* with the *mention* of the con-cept-name. Such a change of linguistic rules would only imply that what used to be a conventionally correct expression of the entailment had ceased to be so. Secondly, if in stating the analysis "to be a brother is to be a male sibling" one referred at once to the usage of "brother" and the usages of synonyms of this English word in other languages, it is difficult to see how a philosopher who knows less than the totality of lan-guages could be competent to analyze concepts. This *reductio* may be coun-tered by saying that the analysis is equivalent to the subjunctive conditional "for all words W and U, if W were synonymous with 'brother' and U were synonymous with 'male sibling', then

---

[8] See Alonzo Church, "On Carnap's Analy-sis of Statements of Assertion and Belief", *Analysis*, April, 1950.

[9] The statements of synonymy here under discussion refer to a natural language, not to a language-system. If L is defined, as by Carnap and others who explicate concepts relatively to a language-system, by a listing of rules and primitive terms, including semantic rules, then any statement of the form "T$_1$ and T$_2$ are synonymous in L" is logically decidable. But there is surely no definition of, e.g., "the English language" which accords with the ordinary usage of the defined term and would make it decidable without empirical investigation whether "brother" and "male sibling" are synony-mous in the English language.

[10] The following criticism applies also to my former self. See *Elements of Analytic Philosophy*, p. 445.

W would be synonymous with U". Let us waive the consideration that, pending a satisfactory reduction of the subjunctive "if-then" to extensional connectives, this translation should leave an extensionalist with some discomfort, and concentrate on the following difficulty. Given the assumption that the English expressions "brother" and "male sibling" are indeed synonymous, how could this conditional be anything but an analytic statement? For a contrary instance would consist in a couple of foreign words W_1 and U_1 such that W_1 is synonymous with "brother", U_1 synonymous with 'male sibling' but W_1 not synonymous with U_1. And since synonymy is, on logical grounds, a symmetrical and transitive relation, this supposition is self-contradictory on the assumption that the English expressions are synonymous. The point is that it could not be determined whether W_1 and U_1 are respectively synonymous with "brother" and "male sibling" independently of determining whether they are themselves synonymous. Thus the alleged generalization about a class of expressions synonymous with the given English expression says no more than the original restricted statement about the usage of the English expression.

What I am suggesting (following here, perhaps, C. I. Lewis) is that a correct analysis, if it is a proposition at all, is a necessary proposition about intensions even though it be expressed (misleadingly) in the semantic form " 'A' is synonymous with 'B' "—just as the proposition that $5 = 3 + 2$ is a necessary proposition about the number 5 even though it might be expressed semantically as "the number denoted by '5' is identical with the number denoted by '3 + 2' ". Consider this additional argument, from the relevance of analyses to the question whether a given proposition is necessary. The argument is based on the concept of a necessary proposition as a proposition such that no empirical evidence can be evidence either favorably or unfavorably relevant to it. Consider, then, the necessary proposition that there are no brothers that are not male. The proof of its necessity is based on the analysis "the concept *brother* is identical with the concept *male sibling*". The latter statement, however, must not be confused with the empirical statement about usage, that "brother" is (at the present time and relatively to a specified class of users and interpreters) synonymous with "male sibling", which can be evidence only for the *empirical* proposition that the sentence "all brothers are male" expresses a necessary proposition, and not for the necessary proposition that all brothers are male. The analysis of the concept *brother* is supporting evidence for either statement (a) "all brothers are male", or (b) "it is necessary that all brothers are male", or (c) "the sentence 'all brothers are male' expresses a necessary proposition". If the analysis were an empirical statement, then, if it were evidence for (a), then (a) would be an empirical statement, which contradicts our hypothesis. Similarly, if it were evidence for (b), (b) would be an empirical statement. But I think it must be admitted (though to prove this convincingly would take more space than is at my disposal) that a modal statement is itself either necessary (if true) or impossible (if false). The view, held e.g. by the acute English analyst Strawson[11] that modal statements such as entailment-statements[12] are contingent statements about expressions, is surely based on the confusion of (b) with (c). It is easy to imagine a change of linguistic rules that would have the result that "all brothers are male" ceased to express a necessary proposition, but to suppose that such an eventuality would change the modality of the proposition previously expressed by the English sentence would be not so much to suppose what is false as to suppose what is meaningless: "logically necessary" is what Carnap has called a "time-independent" predicate,[13] i.e. it makes no sense to say of a proposition that it is necessary at a given time. It follows, then, that the only statement which the analysis could be evidence for if it were a contingent statement about verbal usage is statement (c), which is admittedly itself a contingent statement.

The contingent statement (c) is easily confused with (c'): "the proposition expressed by 'all brothers are male' (at the present time) is necessary", and since it is crucial for my thesis that to assert an identity of concepts or propositions is different from asserting synonymy of expressions (which assertion cannot but be empirical), to establish the difference between (c) and (c'), I must take a little time to explain the difference. (c) and (c') are respectively similar to (d) "John is now married to a girl who is blonde" and (d') "the girl whom John is now married to is blonde". Are (d) and (d') logically equivalent? Now, (d) obviously entails that John is now married, such that if he is not, (d) is false. But would (d') likewise be false? I rather think that people who have not been corrupted by the theory of descriptions would say that if the girl who was by the speaker mistakenly believed to be married to John *is* blonde, then the proposition the speaker intended to assert is true even though a mistaken belief about the subject of the proposition produced a misleading formulation of the proposition. That is, the proposition presupposed by the use of the description "the girl whom John is now married to" (viz. that John is now married) is not a *truth-condition* of the asserted proposition.[14] If a speaker expresses proposition p by means of sentence S, his using S may be due to his believing proposition q; but it is

---

[11] Cf. "Necessary Propositions and Entailment-Statements", *Mind*, April, 1948.

[12] Notice that "It is necessary that if x is a brother, then x is male" is equivalent to the entailment-statement "being a brother entails being male".

[13] See "Truth and Confirmation", in Feigl and Sellars: *Readings in Philosophical Analysis*. Carnap there argues that "true" is a time-independent predicate, but the same argument holds a fortiori for "necessarily true". Concerning the bearing of the distinction between the semantical and the absolute concept of truth (in the terminology of Carnap's *Introduction to Semantic*) on the question whether truth is time-independent, see my article "Propositions, Sentences and the Semantic Definition of Truth", in *Theoria*, 1954, vol. 20.

---

[14] For a detailed elaboration of this line of criticism of the theory of descriptions, see Strawson "On Referring", *Mind*, July 1950, and the author's "Logic, Existence and the Theory of Descriptions", *Analysis*, April, 1953.

confusion to suppose that for this reason q is entailed by p, such that if q were false p would be false. Such propositions q may in particular be semantic propositions about conventional meanings of expressions. Thus, if after talking to the boy before me for a while I say "John will be a great philosopher one day", my use of the name "John" indicates my belief that the boy who is the subject of the asserted proposition is named "John", but *this* proposition is no part of the asserted proposition.

The relevance of this distinction to the question whether (c) and (c′) are equivalent statements should be obvious. (c) is *about* the sentence "all brothers are male" in the same way in which (d) is about John. But that this sentence expresses the proposition of which necessity is predicated (which is admittedly a contingent fact of usage) is no more part of what (c′) *asserts* than John's marital status is part of what (d′) asserts, or than the boy's being named "John" is part of what the proposition about the boy asserts. If the speaker who asserts (c′) did not believe that the sentence "all brothers are male" means in English that all brothers are male,[15] he would not express

himself as he does. But the contingent proposition about usage which is in this sense presupposed by his use of just that sentence is not entailed by the proposition he asserts.

Consider, now, the semantic formulation of our sample analysis: the concept designated in English by "brother" is identical with the concept designated in English by "male sibling". An application of the theory of descriptions to this identity-statement would at once yield the conclusion that it is contingent, since it would analyze into "there is a unique concept which is designated by both terms 'brother' and 'male sibling'"; and thus no recognizable difference would remain between this intensional statement and the extensional statement of synonymy "'brother' is synonymous with 'male sibling'". As pointed out, however, the theory of description is insensitive to the distinction between the truth-conditions of an asserted proposition and the presuppositions causally involved in the formulation of the proposition. The existence of the terms "brother" and "male sibling", and their synonymous usage, are here presuppositions, not truth-conditions, of the proposition about the concepts. To see this clearly, consider its formulation in another language, say German: "der Begriff der im Englischen mit 'brother' bezeichnet wird ist identisch mit dem Begriff der im Englischen mit 'male sibling' bezeichnet wird". Suppose that the German speaker's presupposition that "brother" designates in English the

---

[15] Church's translation-device—which he credits to Langford—is again effective in showing that propositions expressed by sentences of the form "'p' means (in natural language L) that p" are indeed contingent (as argued also by Moore in "Russell's Theory of Descriptions", pp. 200–205, *The Philosophy of Bertrand Russell*, ed. Schilpp.): the translation into German of "'all brothers are male' means that all brothers are male" yields the informative statement "'all brothers are male' heisst dass alle Brüder männlich sind", and if a given sentence expresses a

contingent proposition, then any sentence synonymous with it must express a contingent proposition since it expresses the same proposition.

concept which he intended to analyze were false. Would we then say that the German asserted a false proposition? Would we not rather say that the proposition he intended to assert is true but that the formulation of the proposition was incorrect? Similarly, if one were to assert "the number denoted by '2 + 2' is identical with the number denoted by '5'", the proposition he intended to assert would be perfectly true if he thought (erroneously) that '5' denoted the number *four*. Inasmuch as such semantic formulations of assertions of identity easily generate the misconception that an assertion is made about contingent designation-rules, whereas the latter are causally presupposed by the linguistic expression only, it is advisable to avoid the semantic formulations altogether.[16]

It remains to keep the promise made

earlier, to show that with respect to restrictions of identity-substitutions intensions are no worse off than concreta. The objection was considered that identity does not admit of degrees, and that expressions designating an identical entity ought accordingly to be interchangeable in *all* the contexts of their use, whether extensional or not. However, as long as we permit non-extensional languages at all (and I have strong doubts whether the thesis that all significant statements are translatable into an extensional language can be maintained without question-begging condemnation to insignificance of large classes of significant statements), such a strong requirement of interchangeability would make it impossible to apply the concept of identity even to individuals. This is clear from the "antinomy of the name-relation", as Carnap calls it: if "Scott = the author of Waverley" is to entail universal interchangeability of "Scott" and "the author of Waverley", then it cannot be true since it would entail "somebody does not know that Scott is Scott", "it is possible to believe that Scott is not Scott", etc. To rule, then, that "genuine" identity entails universal interchangeability in a non-extensional language is to rule that any identity-statement in a non-extensional language, no matter what the type of the entities concerned,

---

[16] It is noteworthy in this connection that, like the extensional semantic formulation " 'A' is synonymous with 'B' ", the intensional semantic formulation "the concept designated by 'A' is identical with the concept designated by 'B' " makes it impossible to derive the paradox of analysis by application of the rule of interchangeability ("salva significatione toti") of synonymous terms. For the terms "the concept designated by 'A' " and "the concept designated by 'B' " are clearly not synonymous, since they contain names of distinct expressions—" 'A' " and " 'B' ", —and names of distinct expressions cannot be synonymous even though their nominata may be synonymous. And since these complex terms contain the names of the terms which are synonymous if the analysis is correct, not the terms themselves, the fatal rule is in no way applicable. However, the proposed solution of the paradox of analysis by restriction of the rule to extensional context seems still preferable, since the intensional semantic formulation tends to engender con-

fusion about the nature of analysis, viz. the view that analyses are statements about expressions. Besides, anybody who has sufficiently overcome the fear of Platonism to allow himself to talk about intensions via the mention of expressions might as well be bold enough to go intensionalist all the way and to enter the "non-semiotic" regions of the metalanguage.

is to be either trivial or false. And the resulting paradox of analysis is merely a special case of a more general "paradox of identity". The whole trouble, however, is generated by an unreasonable definition of identity.

It may seem as though the paradox of identity of concepts were more serious than the paradox of identity of individuals, for this reason. In the case of identity of individuals, we can easily distinguish the trivial from the significant identity-statements because the latter are as a rule *factual* statements, whereas a statement like "the concept *brother* is identical with the concept *male sibling*" is supposed to be significant (informative) even though it is not factual. Yet, to say that the statement "Scott is the author of Waverley" is factual *is* to say that its singular terms fail to be interchangeable in a non-extensional context, since it amounts to saying that it cannot be known without factual investigation that Scott is the author of Waverley (assuming, of course, that "Scott" is not a definitional abbreviation for "the author of Waverley"); and it obviously *can* be known without factual investigation that Scott is Scott. Hence universal interchangeability in a non-extensional language serves as a *general* criterion of triviality of identity-statements after all.

I have argued that to escape from the paradox of analysis by formulating analyses in an extensional meta-language with the help of the term "synonymous" is futile since such formulations are simply inadequate; but that, on the other hand, the paradox of analysis is no heavy price to pay for unashamed talk about intensions, since it simply arises from an unreasonable requirement of *universal* substitutivity of identity, and thus is easily solved.

Toward Further Inquiry

For the student interested in developing an understanding of translation, *On Translation*, R. A. Brower (ed.) (Cambridge, Mass., 1959)†, offers a number of useful articles, especially Jacobson's "On Linguistic Aspects of Translation," and gives an historically ordered, annotated bibliography of the field. J. W. Swanson's "Linguistic Relativity and Translation," PPR 22 (1961), uses Jacobson's work in conjunction with that of Benjamin Whorf (see the epilogue of this volume) to explore the theoretical limits of translatability. Isaiah Berlin, in "Logical Translation," PAS 50 (1949), explores the limits of translating one "type" of proposition into another, and Nicholas Rescher, in "Translation as a Tool of Philosophical Analysis," JP 53 (1956), explores the utility of combining interlinguistic translation with intralinguistic translation for the purpose of elucidating meaning within a language. A helpful background to Richards' treatment of translatability is his *Mencius on the Mind* (London, 1932), in which he wrestles laboriously with the difficulties of translating across the cultural gap between Chinese and English. Also helpful in this area of concern is work being done with machine translation. *Machine Translation of Languages*, Locke and

Booth (eds.) (New York, 1955)†, offers a number of studies by authorities in the field, and Yehoshua Bar-Hillel's *Language and Information* (Jerusalem, 1964)†, explores the methods, aims, and limits of machine translation. J. C. Catford, in *A Linguistic Theory of Translation* (London, 1965), brings linguistic studies to bear upon the problems of translation, offers enough of an outline of linguistics to make the discussion available to the general reader, and does some interesting explorations of the relation of translation to meaning.

Carnap's treatment of synonymy in natural languages is based upon his notion of intensional isomorphism developed in Chapter I of *Meaning and Necessity* (Chicago, 1947). Selection 6.4 can be considered as an extension of that notion into pragmatics, as a critique of Quine and White, and as an answer to such criticisms as Pap's "Synonymity and Logical Equivalence," *Analysis* 9 (1949), that the semantic formulation is not applicable to natural languages. The notion of intensional isomorphism has come under a number of attacks like that of Mates in 6.7 and that of Church in *Analysis* 10 (1950). Putnam's "Synonymity and the Analysis of Belief Sentences," *Analysis* 13 (1953), is an attempt to modify the notion of intentional isomorphism in the light of these criticisms. Sellars in "Putnam on Synonymity and Belief," *Analysis* 15 (1955), maintains that Putnam sets up a straw man by using inadequate examples, and Church makes a similar criticism of Mates in "Intensional Isomorphism and Identity of Belief," *Philosophical Studies* 5 (1954). Pap argues, in *Philosophical Studies* 6 (1955), that Mates even failed to understand Carnap's treatment of belief statements and so missed the point of intensional isomorphism. Robert Beard, in "Synonymy and Oblique Contexts," *Analysis* 26 (1965), maintains that Putnam's results are dependent upon the fact that many expressions have more than one identifiable meaning. M. E. Old, in "Synonymity: Extensional Isomorphism," *Mind* 65 (1956), claims that the intensional methods offer no objective standards, and he offers three rules as an extensional basis for determining synonymity.

The relation of synonymity to identity was explored by Frege in "On Sense and Reference," but it would be anachronistic to say that he treated the paradox of analysis. This latter notion is explored in *The Philosophy of G. E. Moore* (Evanston, Ill., 1942). Carnap seeks to meet this challenge with his notion of explication in *Logical Foundations of Probability* (Chicago, 1950), and in *Meaning and Necessity*. Quine takes a similar step in Chapter 7 of *Word and Object* (New York, 1960), maintaining that the "paradox" arises from a mistaken interjection of synonymy into analysis. Linsky, in PS 16 (1949), criticizes Carnap's solution by advancing counter examples, but Carnap replies in the same volume that the critique is ineffectual since the examples are not sentences of a single natural language.

"The Philosophical Denial of Sameness of Meaning," *Analysis* 11 (1950), is C. D. Rollins' attack on Goodman's assumptions. Goodman defends his thesis against Rollins and other critics in "On Some Differences about Meaning," *Analysis* 13 (1953). L. Meckler, in *Analysis* 14 (1953), and D. Shwayder, in

Philosophical Studies 5 (1954), attack Goodman on a number of inconsistencies that result mainly from applying ideal language standards to natural language issues. J. F. Thomson, in *Analysis* 12 (1951), R. Taylor, in PR 63 (1954), and A. R. White, in *Philosophical Quarterly* 8 (1958), each argue theses that lead to the common conclusion that the pursuit of criteria for synonymity is futile. White's treatment of the ambiguities of 'sameness' lead him into an examination of the various criteria that have been attempted. From a quite different standpoint, Jack Kaminsky, in "Metaphysics and the Problem of Synonymity," PPR 14 (1963), explicates metaphysical problems underlying the various definitions of synonymity and maintains that linguistic analyses can give insight into these problems, but cannot solve them.

LANGUAGE AND TRUTH

Chapter 7

The true is thus the Bacchanalian whorl in which
no member is not drunken.

G. W. F. Hegel

"What is truth?" Pilate's rhetorical quip has long been treated as a serious philosophical problem. The nature of truth has been sought after, and rival theories have been formulated. In "Facts and Propositions," F. P. Ramsey remarked, "There is really no separate problem of truth but merely a linguistic muddle."[1] This assertion marked a "linguistic turn": an epistemological problem became a semantic one. However one evaluates the contention that there is no problem about the nature of truth, new questions have arisen about the denotation of 'true' (that to which 'true' is ascribed) and about the connotation of 'true' (the significance of the term in linguistic expressions). In the controversies about the semantics of truth, quandaries about the character and relationships of sentences, assertions, and propositions have also arisen. "The problem of truth" has virtually shifted from being a problem about knowledge to being a problem about language.

Ramsey contended that 'true' is ascribed to propositions and that the assertion of the truth of a proposition asserts nothing more than does the proposition itself. The prefix, 'It is true that . . .' bears a striking resemblance in form to intentional prefixes (see the introduction to Chapter 3). Unlike the case with intentional prefixes, however, there is nothing problematic about the truth value of sentences in which it appears. If the clause following the prefix expresses a truth when it stands alone as a sentence, then the sentence composed of the prefix and the clause must also be true. There can be no truth-value difference between 'It is true that p' and 'p', where 'p' stands for any proposition whatsoever. In terms of truth value, the addition of the prefix is an assertive redundancy. But this does not necessarily close the book on questions about truth. Unless the meaning of the prefix, 'It is true that . . .', can be equated with its truth value, the semantics of truth remains open to question. The attacks on the

---

[1] PAS, Suppl. 7 (1927).

thesis of extensionality in issues of meaning and synonymity (compare Chapters 3 and 6) make such assimilation of meaning to truth value highly problematic. Without such an assimilation, questions about the denotation and connotation of 'true' remain.

According to Ramsey's analysis, propositions are asserted *in* sentences, and it is to propositions that truth or falsity is ascribed. But what is a proposition, as opposed to an assertion or a sentence? Frequently, the answer is that a proposition is a sentence with a truth value, or that a proposition is what two or more sentences stating the same thing have in common. These answers fail to give an adequate basis for the explication of the meaning of truth. If we determine the denotation of 'true' in terms of propositions, then to differentiate propositions in terms of truth value appears circular since we must presuppose an understanding of 'true' in order to understand the denotation of 'true'. If we treat propositions as the content or the meaning of sentences, we are thrown into an examination of the nature of such contents and meanings and of how they are to be differentiated from the sentences themselves. Some treatments of propositions as entities have resolved into conclusions very similar to the ontological treatments of meaning discussed in Chapter 2, with very similar perplexities. One would expect, from the title of Ramsey's article, an analysis of the notion of a proposition, but he rather presupposes the notion in his treatment of judgment.[2] His use of 'proposition' sometimes implies its identification with facts, sometimes with the contents of a sentence, sometimes with the judgment expressed in the sentence. Once the question of the nature of propositions is raised, their linguistic status becomes problematic. Because of the complexity of the problems, many philosophers have stopped talking in terms of propositions entirely.

If the ascription of 'true' to propositions brings with it a complex of problems, the alternative of ascribing 'true' to sentences appears linguistically simple. In expressions of the form 'It is true that . . .', the 'that' clause could be treated as a sentence, and the prefix could be treated as a metalinguistic statement about the sentence. We could then translate the form into " '. . .' is true," and the problem of the denotation of truth would be solved. While such a procedure would be simple, in many cases it is inadequate, perhaps inaccurate. In discussions of propositions, it is often pointed out that '*Il pleut*' and 'It is raining' are different sentences expressing the same proposition; they have the same truth value. If 'true' denotes sentences, some account of this sameness must be made. Also, egocentric particulars make the truth value of sentences dependent upon who asserts them. 'This ball is mine', if true for the child that speaks it, is false for the child that he addresses. Other factors may also make the same sentence show different truth values. The ascribing of 'true' to sentences, apparently a

---

[2] This was one of G. E. Moore's critiques in his symposium with Ramsey. See PAS, Suppl. 7 (1927).

simple choice for the denotation of truth, on closer examination presents these and other problems.

As John Austin rightly points out, we may call sentences elliptical, ungrammatical, but seldom do we call them true. What we ascribe truth to, he maintains, is the *statement* that is expressed in words.[3] According to Austin, a statement is a historic event, a speech act that has the illocutionary force of asserting fact. Because a statement (or *assertion*—the words are usually treated as synonyms) is what is expressed by a sentence, one can say that '*Il pleut*' and 'It is raining' *assert* the same thing, without appeal to notions of proposition or truth value. But speech episodes are no more appropriate denotata of truth than sentences. A speech episode may be whispered or inarticulate, but not true or false. When we talk of statements being true, we talk of what is said rather than the saying of it; the focus is on the product of stating, not on the act of stating; we are concerned with the content of the expression, not the expressing. We may be led to think that we are concerned with the historic event because we ordinarily deal with sentence tokens. This may make it seem that we are concerned with the instances of verbal expressions. A variation of an example already offered shows that we are not in fact concerned with the event. If one child says, "This ball is mine," and the other asserts, "This ball is yours," they are not only in agreement, but in a sense they are making the same assertion. It is to this sense of an assertion that we apply the adjective 'true', and this sense, whatever its relation to the speech episodes that give it birth, seems to be very much like the notion of proposition already discussed. Whether the relation of what is said in a sentence to the saying of the sentence can be satisfactorily illuminated remains to be seen. It is clear that the two cannot be equated.

These explorations of the various possible denotations of truth are not idle exercises. Each alternative has been considered in an attempt to give an analysis of the conception of truth. From these attempts to understand the meaning of language involving 'true,' more general problems about language arise. If sentences and speech episodes are as unlikely candidates for denotation as I have suggested, then some satisfactory explication of propositions or assertions (in the sense of what is asserted) must be set forth as a linguistic foundation for a satisfactory analysis of truth. The sentence is a universally recognized unit of linguistic expression and the speech episode is a useful pragmatic notion, but proposition and statement continue to lurk in the esoteric shadows of philosophy.

Even if the denotation of truth were generally agreed upon, the task of analyzing the concept would have just begun. As might be expected, there is even less agreement about the connotation of truth. Here again, the focus cannot simply be on the meaning of 'true', since the various analyses of the concep-

---

[3] See "Truth," PAS, Suppl. 24 (1950). My critique of Austin's thesis has been drawn largely from Strawson's contribution to this symposium.

tion of truth make the nature of its meaning problematic. On Ramsey's view, the prefix declaring truth is a redundancy; it adds no meaning. Does this mean that 'true' is meaningless? On Tarski's view, 'true' is a metalinguistic term, definable recursively[4] and only within the context of a formally determined linguistic system (see 7.1). Does this make 'true' as it is used in ordinary discourse a meaningless term, a useless concept? In the formally determined system, is its meaning totally determined by the rules of the particular system, or does it have some meaning independent of the system? Strawson treats expressions of truth as performatives of assent (see 7.2). If performatives have meanings—in some sense—can they be explicated in terms of connotation? If not, how are they to be treated? Warnock defends Austin's interpretation by maintaining that expressions of truth at least *may* have an assertive character (see 7.3). What does this assertive character imply about its meaning? While these questions about connotation may presuppose an adequate resolution to the problems of denotation, they clearly go beyond these issues into other problems about the nature of language. Ayer, in examining the relation between meaning and truth, reasserts—with modifications—the assertive-redundancy thesis (see 7.4).

7.1

THE SEMANTIC CONCEPTION
OF TRUTH*

Alfred Tarski

This paper consists of two parts; the first has an expository character, and the second is rather polemical.

In the first part I want to summarize in an informal way the main results of my investigations concerning the defini-

---

[4] To define a property recursively, the following conditions must be met:

a. The simplest individuals having the property must be specified.

b. The conditions must be determined under which, if anything has that property, something else having that property can be constructed.

c. The claim must be made that nothing which fails to meet such specifications and conditions has that property.

From *Philosophy and Phenomenological Research*, V (1943–1944). Reprinted by permission of the editors and the author.

* In the footnotes, numbers in brackets refer to references, which are cited in full at the end of the selection.

tion of truth and the more general problem of the foundations of semantics. These results have been embodied in a work which appeared in print several years ago.[1] Although my investigations concern concepts dealt with in classical philosophy, they happen to be comparatively little known in philosophical circles, perhaps because of their strictly technical character. For this reason I hope I shall be excused for taking up the matter once again.[2]

Since my work was published, various objections, of unequal value, have been raised to my investigations; some of these appeared in print, and others were made in public and private discussions in which I took part.[3] In the second part of the paper I should like to express my views regarding these objections. I hope that the remarks which will be made in this context will not be considered as purely polemical in character, but will be found to contain some constructive contributions to the subject.

In the second part of the paper I have made extensive use of material graciously put at my disposal by Dr. Marja Kokoszyńska (University of Lwów). I am especially indebted and grateful to Professors Ernest Nagel (Columbia University) and David Rynin (University of California, Berkeley) for their help in preparing the final text and for various critical remarks.

---

[1] Compare Tarski [2] (see bibliography at the end of the paper). This work may be consulted for a more detailed and formal presentation of the subject of the paper, especially of the material included in Sections 6 and 9–13. It contains also references to my earlier publications on the problems of semantics (a communication in Polish, 1930; the article Tarski [1] in French, 1931; a communication in German, 1932; and a book in Polish, 1933). The expository part of the present paper is related in its character to Tarski [3]. My investigations on the notion of truth and on theoretical semantics have been reviewed or discussed in Hofstadter [1], Juhos [1], Kokoszyńska [1] and [2], Kotarbiński [2], Scholz [1], Weinberg [1], et al.

[2] It may be hoped that the interest in theoretical semantics will now increase, as a result of the recent publication of the important work Carnap [2].

[3] This applies, in particular, to public discussions during the I. International Congress for the Unity of Science (Paris, 1935) and the Conference of International Congresses for the Unity of Science (Paris, 1937); cf. e.g., Neurath [1] and Gonseth [1].

I. Exposition

1. THE MAIN PROBLEM—A SATISFACTORY DEFINITION OF TRUTH. Our discussion will be centered around the notion[4] of *truth*. The main problem is that of giving a *satisfactory definition* of this notion, i.e., a definition which is *materially adequate* and *formally correct*. But such a formulation of the problem,

---

[4] The words "notion" and "concept" are used in this paper with all of the vagueness and ambiguity with which they occur in philosophical literature. Thus, sometimes they refer simply to a term, sometimes to what is meant by a term, and in other cases to what is denoted by a term. Sometimes it is irrelevant which of these interpretations is meant; and in certain cases perhaps none of them applies adequately. While on principle I share the tendency to avoid these words in any exact discussion, I did not consider it necessary to do so in this informal presentation.

because of its generality, cannot be considered unequivocal, and requires some further comments.

In order to avoid any ambiguity, we must first specify the conditions under which the definition of truth will be considered adequate from the material point of view. The desired definition does not aim to specify the meaning of a familiar word used to denote a novel notion; on the contrary, it aims to catch hold of the actual meaning of an old notion. We must then characterize this notion precisely enough to enable anyone to determine whether the definition actually fulfills its task.

Secondly, we must determine on what the formal correctness of the definition depends. Thus, we must specify the words or concepts which we wish to use in defining the notion of truth; and we must also give the formal rules to which the definition should conform. Speaking more generally, we must describe the formal structure of the language in which the definition will be given.

The discussion of these points will occupy a considerable portion of the first part of the paper.

2. THE EXTENSION OF THE TERM "TRUE." We begin with some remarks regarding the extension of the concept of truth which we have in mind here.

The predicate *"true"* is sometimes used to refer to psychological phenomena such as judgments or beliefs, sometimes to certain physical objects, namely, linguistic expressions and specifically sentences, and sometimes to certain ideal entities called "propositions." By "sentence" we understand here what is usually meant in grammar by "de-clarative sentence"; as regards the term "proposition," its meaning is notoriously a subject of lengthy disputations by various philosophers and logicians, and it seems never to have been made quite clear and unambiguous. For several reasons it appears most convenient to *apply the term "true" to sentences,* and we shall follow this course.[5]

Consequently, we must always relate the notion of truth, like that of a sentence, to a specific language; for it is obvious that the same expression which is a true sentence in one language can be false or meaningless in another.

Of course, the fact that we are interested here primarily in the notion of truth for sentences does not exclude the possibility of a subsequent extension of this notion to other kinds of objects.

3. THE MEANING OF THE TERM "TRUE." Much more serious difficulties are connected with the problem of the meaning (or the intension) of the concept of truth.

The word *"true,"* like other words from our everyday language, is certainly not unambiguous. And it does not seem to me that the philosophers who have discussed this concept have helped to diminish its ambiguity. In works and discussions of philosophers we meet many different conceptions of truth and falsity, and we must indicate which conception will be the basis of our discussion.

_____

[5] For our present purposes it is somewhat more convenient to understand by "expressions," "sentences," etc., not individual inscriptions, but classes of inscriptions of similar form (thus, not individual physical things, but classes of such things).

We should like our definition to do justice to the intuitions which adhere to the *classical Aristotelian conception of truth*—intuitions which find their expression in the well-known words of Aristotle's *Metaphysics*: *To say of what is that it is not, or of what is not that it is, is false, while to say of what is that it is, or of what is not that it is not, is true.*

If we wished to adapt ourselves to modern philosophical terminology, we could perhaps express this conception by means of the familiar formula: *The truth of a sentence consists in its agreement with (or correspondence to) reality.* (For a theory of truth which is to be based upon the latter formulation the term "correspondence theory" has been suggested.)

If, on the other hand, we should decide to extend the popular usage of the term *"designate"* by applying it not only to names, but also to sentences, and if we agreed to speak of the designata of sentences as "states of affairs," we could possibly use for the same purpose the following phrase: *A sentence is true if it designates an existing state of affairs.*[6]

However, all these formulations can lead to various misunderstandings, for none of them is sufficiently precise and clear (though this applies much less to

the original Aristotelian formulation than to either of the others); at any rate, none of them can be considered a satisfactory definition of truth. It is up to us to look for a more precise expression of our intuitions.

4. A CRITERION FOR THE MATERIAL ADEQUACY OF THE DEFINITION.[7] Let us start with a concrete example. Consider the sentence *"snow is white."* We ask the question under what conditions this sentence is true or false. It seems clear that if we base ourselves on the classical conception of truth, we shall say that the sentence is true if snow is white, and that it is false if snow is not white. Thus, if the definition of truth is to conform to our conception, it must imply the following equivalence: *The sentence "snow is white" is true if, and only if, snow is white.*

Let me point out that the phrase *"snow is white"* occurs on the left side of this equivalence in quotation marks, and on the right without quotation marks. On the right side we have the

---

[6] For the Aristotelian formulation see Aristotle [1], Γ, 7, 27. The other two formulations are very common in the literature, but I do not know with whom they originate. A critical discussion of various conceptions of truth can be found, e.g., in Kotarbiński [1] (so far available only in Polish), pp. 123 ff., and Russell [1], pp. 362 ff.

[7] For most of the remarks contained in Sections 4 and 8, I am indebted to the late S. Leśniewski who developed them in his unpublished lectures in the University of Warsaw (in 1919 and later). However, Leśniewski did not anticipate the possibility of a rigorous development of the theory of truth, and still less of a definition of this notion; hence, while indicating equivalences of the form (T) as premises in the antinomy of the liar, he did not conceive them as any sufficient conditions for an adequate usage (or definition) of the notion of truth. Also the remarks in Section 8 regarding the occurrence of an empirical premise in the antinomy of the liar, and the possibility of eliminating this premise, do not originate with him.

sentence itself, and on the left the name of the sentence. Employing the medieval logical terminology we could also say that on the right side the words "*snow is white*" occur in *suppositio formalis*, and on the left in *suppositio materialis*. It is hardly necessary to explain why we must have the name of the sentence, and not the sentence itself, on the left side of the equivalence. For, in the first place, from the point of view of the grammar of our language, an expression of the form "X *is true*" will not become a meaningful sentence if we replace in it 'X' by a sentence or by anything other than a name —since the subject of a sentence may be only a noun or an expression functioning like a noun. And, in the second place, the fundamental conventions regarding the use of any language require that in any utterance we make about an object it is the name of the object which must be employed, and not the object itself. In consequence, if we wish to say something about a sentence, for example, that it is true, we must use the name of this sentence, and not the sentence itself.[8]

It may be added that enclosing a sentence in quotation marks is by no means the only way of forming its name. For instance, by assuming the usual order of letters in our alphabet, we can use the following expression as the name (the description) of the sentence "*snow is white*": *the sentence constituted by three words, the first of which consists of the 19th, 14th, 15th, and 23rd letters, the second of the 9th and 19th letters, and the third of the 23rd, 8th, 9th, 20th, and 5th letters of the English alphabet.*

We shall now generalize the procedure which we have applied above. Let us consider an arbitrary sentence; we shall replace it by the letter '*p*.' We form the name of this sentence and we replace it by another letter, say 'X.' We ask now what is the logical relation between the two sentences "X *is true*" and '*p*.' It is clear that from the point of view of our basic conception of truth these sentences are equivalent. In other words, the following equivalence holds:

(T)   X is true if, and only if, *p*.

We shall call any such equivalence (with '*p*' replaced by any sentence of the language to which the word "*true*" refers, and 'X' replaced by a name of this sentence) an "*equivalence of the form* (T)."

Now at last we are able to put into a precise form the conditions under which we will consider the usage and the definition of the term "*true*" as adequate from the material point of view: we wish to use the term "*true*" in such a way that all equivalences of the form (T) can be asserted, and *we shall call a definition of truth "adequate" if all these equivalences follow from it.*

It should be emphasized that neither the expression (T) itself (which is not a sentence, but only a schema of a sentence) nor any particular instance of the form (T) can be regarded as a definition of truth. We can only say that every equivalence of the form (T) obtained by replacing '*p*' by a particular sentence, and 'X' by a name of this

---

[8] In connection with various logical and methodological problems involved in this paper the reader may consult Tarski [6].

sentence, may be considered a partial definition of truth, which explains wherein the truth of this one individual sentence consists. The general definition has to be, in a certain sense, a logical conjunction of all these partial definitions.

(The last remark calls for some comments. A language may admit the construction of infinitely many sentences; and thus the number of partial definitions of truth referring to sentences of such a language will also be infinite. Hence to give our remark a precise sense we should have to explain what is meant by a "logical conjunction of infinitely many sentences"; but this would lead us too far into technical problems of modern logic.)

5. TRUTH AS A SEMANTIC CONCEPT. I should like to propose the name *"the semantic conception of truth"* for the conception of truth which has just been discussed.

Semantics is a discipline which, speaking loosely, *deals with certain relations between expressions of a language and the objects* (or "states of affairs") *"referred to" by those expressions.* As typical examples of semantic concepts we may mention the concepts of *designation, satisfaction,* and *definition* as these occur in the following examples: *the expression "the father of his country" designates (denotes) George Washington; snow satisfies the sentential function (the condition) "x is white"; the equation "2 · x = 1" defines (uniquely determines) the number ½.*

While the words *"designates," "satisfies,"* and *"defines"* express relations (between certain expressions and the ob-

jects "referred to" by these expressions), the word *"true"* is of a different logical nature: it expresses a property (or denotes a class) of certain expressions, viz., of sentences. However, it is easily seen that all the formulations which were given earlier and which aimed to explain the meaning of this word (cf. Sections 3 and 4) referred not only to sentences themselves, but also to objects "talked about" by these sentences, or possibly to "states of affairs" described by them. And, moreover, it turns out that the simplest and the most natural way of obtaining an exact definition of truth is one which involves the use of other semantic notions, e.g., the notion of satisfaction. It is for these reasons that we count the concept of truth which is discussed here among the concepts of semantics, and the problem of defining truth proves to be closely related to the more general problem of setting up the foundations of theoretical semantics.

It is perhaps worth while saying that semantics as it is conceived in this paper (and in former papers of the author) is a sober and modest discipline which has no pretensions of being a universal patent-medicine for all the ills and diseases of mankind, whether imaginary or real. You will not find in semantics any remedy for decayed teeth or illusions of grandeur or class conflicts. Nor is semantics a device for establishing that everyone except the speaker and his friends is speaking nonsense.

From antiquity to the present day the concepts of semantics have played an important role in the discussions of philosophers, logicians, and philologists.

Nevertheless, these concepts have been treated for a long time with a certain amount of suspicion. From a historical standpoint, this suspicion is to be regarded as completely justified. For although the meaning of semantic concepts as they are used in everyday language seems to be rather clear and understandable, still all attempts to characterize this meaning in a general and exact way miscarried. And what is worse, various arguments in which these concepts were involved, and which seemed otherwise quite correct and based upon apparently obvious premises, led frequently to paradoxes and antinomies. It is sufficient to mention here the *antinomy of the liar*, Richard's *antinomy of definability* (by means of a finite number of words), and Grelling-Nelson's *antinomy of heterological terms*.[9]

I believe that the method which is outlined in this paper helps to overcome these difficulties and assures the possibility of a consistent use of semantic concepts.

6. LANGUAGES WITH A SPECIFIED STRUCTURE. Because of the possible occurrence of antinomies, the problem of specifying the formal structure and the vocabulary of a language in which definitions of semantic concepts are to be given becomes especially acute; and we turn now to this problem.

There are certain general conditions

_____

[9] The antinomy of the liar (ascribed to Eubulides or Epimenides) is discussed here in Sections 7 and 8. For the antinomy of definability (due to J. Richard) see, e.g., Hilbert-Bernays [1], vol. 2, pp. 263 ff.; for the antinomy of heterological terms see Grelling-Nelson [1], p. 307.

under which the structure of a language is regarded as *exactly specified*. Thus, to specify the structure of a language, we must characterize unambiguously the class of those words and expressions which are to be considered *meaningful*. In particular, we must indicate all words which we decide to use without defining them, and which are called "*undefined* (or *primitive*) *terms*"; and we must give the so-called *rules of definition* for introducing new or *defined terms*. Furthermore, we must set up criteria for distinguishing within the class of expressions those which we call "*sentences*." Finally, we must formulate the conditions under which a sentence of the language can be *asserted*. In particular, we must indicate all *axioms* (or *primitive sentences*), i.e., those sentences which we decide to assert without proof; and we must give the so-called *rules of inference* (or *rules of proof*) by means of which we can deduce new asserted sentences from other sentences which have been previously asserted. Axioms, as well as sentences deduced from them by means of rules of inference, are referred to as "*theorems*" or "*provable sentences*."

If in specifying the structure of a language we refer exclusively to the form of the expressions involved, the language is said to be *formalized*. In such a language theorems are the only sentences which can be asserted.

At the present time the only languages with a specified structure are the formalized languages of various systems of deductive logic, possibly enriched by the introduction of certain non-logical terms. However, the field of application of these languages is rather comprehensive; we are able, theoretically, to develop in them various branches of science, for instance, mathematics and theoretical physics.

(On the other hand, we can imagine the construction of languages which have an exactly specified structure without being formalized. In such a language the assertability of sentences, for instance, may depend not always on their form, but sometimes on other, non-linguistic factors. It would be interesting and important actually to construct a language of this type, and specifically one which would prove to be sufficient for the development of a comprehensive branch of empirical science; for this would justify the hope that languages with specified structure could finally replace everyday language in scientific discourse.)

The problem of the definition of truth obtains a precise meaning and can be solved in a rigorous way only for those languages whose structure has been exactly specified. For other languages— thus, for all natural, "spoken" languages —the meaning of the problem is more or less vague, and its solution can have only an approximate character. Roughly speaking, the approximation consists in replacing a natural language (or a portion of it in which we are interested) by one whose structure is exactly specified, and which diverges from the given language "as little as possible."

7. THE ANTINOMY OF THE LIAR. In order to discover some of the more specific conditions which must be satisfied by languages in which (or for which) the definition of truth is to be given, it will be advisable to begin with a discussion of that antinomy which directly involves the notion of truth,

namely, the antinomy of the liar.

To obtain this antinomy in a perspicuous form,[10] consider the following sentence:

The sentence printed in this paper on page 585, right column, lines 5–7, is not true.

For brevity we shall replace the sentence just stated by the letter '*s*.'

According to our convention concerning the adequate usage of the term "*true*," we assert the following equivalence of the form (T):

(1)   's' is true if, and only if,
the sentence, printed in this paper on
page 585, right column, lines 5–7,
is not true.

On the other hand, keeping in mind the meaning of the symbol '*s*,' we establish empirically the following fact:

(2)   's' is identical with the
sentence printed in this paper on page
585, right column, lines 5–7.

Now, by a familar law from the theory of identity (Leibniz's law), it follows from (2) that we may replace in (1) the expression "*the sentence printed in this paper on page 585, right column, lines 5–7*" by the symbol "'*s*.'" We thus obtain what follows:

(3)   's' is true if, and only if, 's'
is not true.

---

[10] Due to Professor J. Lukasiewicz (University of Warsaw).

In this way we have arrived at an obvious contradiction.

In my judgment, it would be quite wrong and dangerous from the standpoint of scientific progress to depreciate the importance of this and other antinomies, and to treat them as jokes or sophistries. It is a fact that we are here in the presence of an absurdity, that we have been compelled to assert a false sentence (since (3), as an equivalence between two contradictory sentences, is necessarily false). If we take our work seriously, we cannot be reconciled with this fact. We must discover its cause, that is to say, we must analyze premises upon which the antinomy is based; we must then reject at least one of these premises, and we must investigate the consequences which this has for the whole domain of our research.

It should be emphasized that antinomies have played a preeminent role in establishing the foundations of modern deductive sciences. And just as class-theoretical antinomies, and in particular Russell's antinomy (of the class of all classes that are not members of themselves), were the starting point for the successful attempts at a consistent formalization of logic and mathematics, so the antinomy of the liar and other semantic antinomies give rise to the construction of theoretical semantics.

8. THE INCONSISTENCY OF SEMANTICALLY CLOSED LANGUAGES.[11] If we now analyze the assumptions which lead to the antinomy of the liar, we notice the following:

(I) We have implicitly assumed that

the language in which the antinomy is constructed contains, in addition to its expressions, also the names of these expressions, as well as semantic terms such as the term *"true"* referring to sentences of this language; we have also assumed that all sentences which determine the adequate usage of this term can be asserted in the language. A language with these properties will be called *"semantically closed."*

(II) We have assumed that in this language the ordinary laws of logic hold.

(III) We have assumed that we can formulate and assert in our language an empirical premise such as the statement (2) which has occurred in our argument.

It turns out that the assumption (III) is not essential, for it is possible to reconstruct the antinomy of the liar without its help.[12] But the assumptions (I)

---

[11] See note 7, p. 581.

[12] This can roughly be done in the following way. Let S be any sentence beginning with the words *"Every sentence."* We correlate with S a new sentence S^* by subjecting S to the following two modifications: we replace in S the first word, *"Every,"* by *"The"*; and we insert after the second word, *"sentence,"* the whole sentence S enclosed in quotation marks. Let us agree to call the sentence S "(self-)applicable" or "non-(self-)applicable" dependent on whether the correlated sentence S^* is true or false. Now consider the following sentence:

Every sentence is non-applicable.

It can easily be shown that the sentence just stated must be both applicable and non-applicable; hence a contradiction. It may not be quite clear in what sense this formulation of the antinomy does not involve an empirical premiss; however, I shall not elaborate on this point.

and (II) prove essential. Since every language which satisfies both of these assumptions is inconsistent, we must reject at least one of them.

It would be superfluous to stress here the consequences of rejecting the assumption (II), that is, of changing our logic (supposing this were possible) even in its more elementary and fundamental parts. We thus consider only the possibility of rejecting the assumption (I). Accordingly, we decide *not to use any language which is semantically closed* in the sense given.

This restriction would of course be unacceptable for those who, for reasons which are not clear to me, believe that there is only one "genuine" language (or, at least, that all "genuine" languages are mutually translatable). However, this restriction does not affect the needs or interests of science in any essential way. The languages (either the formalized languages or—what is more frequently the case—the portions of everyday language) which are used in scientific discourse do not have to be semantically closed. This is obvious in case linguistic phenomena and, in particular, semantic notions do not enter in any way into the subject-matter of a science; for in such a case the language of this science does not have to be provided with any semantic terms at all. However, we shall see in the next section how semantically closed languages can be dispensed with even in those scientific discussions in which semantic notions are essentially involved.

The problem arises as to the position of everyday language with regard to this point. At first blush it would seem that this language satisfies both assumptions (I) and (II), and that therefore it must be inconsistent. But actually the case is not so simple. Our everyday language is certainly not one with an exactly specified structure. We do not know precisely which expressions are sentences, and we know even to a smaller degree which sentences are to be taken as assertible. Thus the problem of consistency has no exact meaning with respect to this language. We may at best only risk the guess that a language whose structure has been exactly specified and which resembles our everyday language as closely as possible would be inconsistent.

9. OBJECT-LANGUAGE AND META-LANGUAGE. Since we have agreed not to employ semantically closed languages, we have to use two different languages in discussing the problem of the definition of truth and, more generally, any problems in the field of semantics. The first of these languages is the language which is "talked about" and which is the subject-matter of the whole discussion; the definition of truth which we are seeking applies to the sentences of this language. The second is the language in which we "talk about" the first language, and in terms of which we wish, in particular, to construct the definition of truth for the first language. We shall refer to the first language as *"the object-language,"* and to the second as *"the meta-language."*

It should be noticed that these terms "object-language" and "meta-language" have only a relative sense. If, for instance, we become interested in the notion of truth applying to sentences, not of our original object-language, but of its meta-language, the latter becomes automatically the object-language of our discussion; and in order to define truth for this language, we have to go to a new meta-language—so to speak, to a meta-language of a higher level. In this way we arrive at a whole hierarchy of languages.

The vocabulary of the meta-language is to a large extent determined by previously stated conditions under which a definition of truth will be considered materially adequate. This definition, as we recall, has to imply all equivalences of the form (T):

(T)   X is true if, and only if, p.

The definition itself and all the equivalences implied by it are to be formulated in the meta-language. On the other hand, the symbol 'p' in (T) stands for an arbitrary sentence of our object-language. Hence it follows that every sentence which occurs in the object-language must also occur in the meta-language; in other words, the meta-language must contain the object-language as a part. This is at any rate necessary for the proof of the adequacy of the definition—even though the definition itself can sometimes be formulated in a less comprehensive meta-language which does not satisfy this requirement.

(The requirement in question can be somewhat modified, for it suffices to assume that the object-language can be translated into the meta-language; this necessitates a certain change in the interpretation of the symbol 'p' in (T). In all that follows we shall ignore the possibility of this modification.)

Furthermore, the symbol 'X' in (T) represents the name of the sentence which 'p' stands for. We see therefore that the meta-language must be rich enough to provide possibilities of constructing a name for every sentence of the object-language.

In addition, the meta-language must obviously contain terms of a general logical character, such as the expression "if, and only if."[13]

It is desirable for the meta-language not to contain any undefined terms except such as are involved explicitly or implicitly in the remarks above, i.e.: terms of the object-language; terms referring to the form of the expressions of the object-language, and used in building names for these expressions; and terms of logic. In particular, we desire *semantic terms* (referring to the object-language) *to be introduced into the meta-language only by definition*. For, if this postulate is satisfied, the definition of truth, or of any other semantic concept, will fulfill what we intuitively expect from every definition; that is, it will explain the meaning of the term being defined in terms whose meaning appears to be completely clear and unequivocal. And, moreover, we have

---

[13] The terms "logic" and "logical" are used in this paper in a broad sense, which has become almost traditional in the last decades; logic is assumed here to comprehend the whole theory of classes and relations (i.e., the mathematical theory of sets). For many different reasons I am personally inclined to use the term "logic" in a much narrower sense, so as to apply it only to what is sometimes called "elementary logic," i.e., to the sentential calculus and the (restricted) predicate calculus.

then a kind of guarantee that the use of semantic concepts will not involve us in any contradictions.

We have no further requirements as to the formal structure of the object-language and the meta-language; we assume that it is similar to that of other formalized languages known at the present time. In particular, we assume that the usual formal rules of definition are observed in the meta-language.

10. CONDITIONS FOR A POSITIVE SOLUTION OF THE MAIN PROBLEM.

Now, we have already a clear idea both of the conditions of material adequacy to which the definition of truth is subjected, and of the formal structure of the language in which this definition is to be constructed. Under these circumstances the problem of the definition of truth acquires the character of a definite problem of a purely deductive nature.

The solution of the problem, however, is by no means obvious, and I would not attempt to give it in detail without using the whole machinery of contemporary logic. Here I shall confine myself to a rough outline of the solution and to the discussion of certain points of a more general interest which are involved in it.

The solution turns out to be sometimes positive, sometimes negative. This depends upon some formal relations between the object-language and its meta-language; or, more specifically, upon the fact whether the meta-language in its logical part is *"essentially richer"* than the object-language or not. It is not easy to give a general and precise definition of this notion of "essential richness." If we restrict ourselves to languages based on the logical theory of types, the condition for the meta-language to be "essentially richer" than the object-language is that it contain variables of a higher logical type than those of the object-language.

If the condition of "essential richness" is not satisfied, it can usually be shown that an interpretation of the meta-language in the object-language is possible; that is to say, with any given term of the meta-language a well-determined term of the object-language can be correlated in such a way that the assertible sentences of the one language turn out to be correlated with assertible sentences of the other. As a result of this interpretation, the hypothesis that a satisfactory definition of truth has been formulated in the meta-language turns out to imply the possibility of reconstructing in that language the antinomy of the liar; and this in turn forces us to reject the hypothesis in question.

(The fact that the meta-language, in its non-logical part, is ordinarily more comprehensive than the object-language does not affect the possibility of interpreting the former in the latter. For example, the names of expressions of the object-language occur in the meta-language, though for the most part they do not occur in the object-language itself; but, nevertheless, it may be possible to interpret these names in terms of the object-language.)

Thus we see that the condition of "essential richness" is necessary for the possibility of a satisfactory definition of truth in the meta-language. If we want to develop the theory of truth in a meta-language which does not satisfy this condition, we must give up the idea of defining truth with the exclusive help of those terms which were indicated above (in Section 8). We have then to include the term *"true,"* or some other semantic term, in the list of undefined terms of the meta-language, and to express fundamental properties of the notion of truth in a series of axioms. There is nothing essentially wrong in such an axiomatic procedure, and it may prove useful for various purposes.[14]

It turns out, however, that this procedure can be avoided. For *the condition of the "essential richness" of the meta-language proves to be, not only necessary, but also sufficient for the construction of a satisfactory definition of truth;* i.e., if the meta-language satisfies this condition, the notion of truth can be defined in it. We shall now indicate in general terms how this construction can be carried through.

11. THE CONSTRUCTION (IN OUTLINE) OF THE DEFINITION.[15]—A definition of truth can be obtained in a very simple way from that of another semantic notion, namely, of the notion of *satisfaction.*

Satisfaction is a relation between arbitrary objects and certain expressions called *"sentential functions."* These are

---

[14] Cf. here, however, Tarski [3], pp. 5 f.

[15] The method of construction we are going to outline can be applied—with appropriate changes—to all formalized languages that are known at the present time; although it does not follow that a language could not be constructed to which this method would not apply.

expressions like *"x is white,"* *"x is greater than y,"* etc. Their formal structure is analogous to that of sentences; however, they may contain the so-called free variables (like *'x'* and *'y'* in *"x is greater than y"*), which cannot occur in sentences.

In defining the notion of a sentential function in formalized languages, we usually apply what is called a "recursive procedure"; i.e., we first describe sentential functions of the simplest structure (which ordinarily presents no difficulty), and then we indicate the operations by means of which compound functions can be constructed from simpler ones. Such an operation may consist, for instance, in forming the logical disjunction or conjunction of two given functions, i.e., by combining them by the word *"or"* or *"and."* A sentence can now be defined simply as a sentential function which contains no free variables.

As regards the notion of satisfaction, we might try to define it by saying that given objects satisfy a given function if the latter becomes a true sentence when we replace in it free variables by names of given objects. In this sense, for example, snow satisfies the sentential function *"x is white"* since the sentence *"snow is white"* is true. However, apart from other difficulties, this method is not available to us, for we want to use the notion of satisfaction in defining truth.

To obtain a definition of satisfaction we have rather to apply again a recursive procedure. We indicate which objects satisfy the simplest sentential functions; and then we state the conditions under which given objects satisfy a compound function—assuming that we know which objects satisfy the simpler functions from which the compound one has been constructed. Thus, for instance, we say that given numbers satisfy the logical disjunction "*x is greater than y or x is equal to y*" if they satisfy at least one of the functions "*x is greater than y*" or "*x is equal to y.*"

Once the general definition of satisfaction is obtained, we notice that it applies automatically also to those special sentential functions which contain no free variables, i.e., to sentences. It turns out that for a sentence only two cases are possible: a sentence is either satisfied by all objects, or by no objects. Hence we arrive at a definition of truth and falsehood simply by saying that *a sentence is true if it is satisfied by all objects, and false otherwise.*[16]

(It may seem strange that we have chosen a roundabout way of defining the truth of a sentence, instead of trying to apply, for instance, a direct recursive procedure. The reason is that compound sentences are constructed from simpler sentential functions, but not always from simpler sentences; hence no general recursive method is known which applies specifically to sentences.)

From this rough outline it is not clear where and how the assumption of the "essential richness" of the meta-language is involved in the discussion; this becomes clear only when the construction is carried through in a detailed and formal way.[17]

12. CONSEQUENCES OF THE DEFINITION. The definition of truth which was

---

[16] In carrying through this idea a certain technical difficulty arises. A sentential function may contain an arbitrary number of free variables; and the logical nature of the notion of satisfaction varies with this number. Thus, the notion in question when applied to functions with one variable is a binary relation between these functions and single objects; when applied to functions with two variables it becomes a ternary relation between functions and couples of objects; and so on. Hence, strictly speaking, we are confronted, not with one notion of satisfaction, but with infinitely many notions; and it turns out that these notions cannot be defined independently of each other, but must all be introduced simultaneously.

To overcome this difficulty, we employ the mathematical notion of an infinite sequence (or, possibly, of a finite sequence with an arbitrary number of terms). We agree to regard satisfaction, not as a many-termed relation between sentential functions and an indefinite number of objects, but as a binary relation between functions and sequences of objects. Under this assumption the formulation of a general and precise definition of satisfaction no longer presents any difficulty; and a true sentence can now be defined as one which is satisfied by every sequence.

[17] To define recursively the notion of satisfaction, we have to apply a certain form of recursive definition which is not admitted in the object-language. Hence the "essential richness" of the meta-language may simply consist in admitting this type of definition. On the other hand, a general method is known which makes it possible to eliminate all recursive definitions and to replace them by normal, explicit ones. If we try to apply this method to the definition of satisfaction, we see that we have either to introduce into the meta-language variables of a higher logical type than those which occur in the object-language; or else to assume axiomatically in the meta-language the existence of classes that are more comprehensive than all those whose existence can be established in the object-language. See here Tarski [2], pp. 393 ff., and Tarski [5], p. 110.

outlined above has many interesting consequences.

In the first place, the definition proves to be not only formally correct, but also materially adequate (in the sense established in Section 4); in other words, it implies all equivalences of the form (T). In this connection it is important to notice that the conditions for the material adequacy of the definition determine uniquely the extension of the term "*true*." Therefore, every definition of truth which is materially adequate would necessarily be equivalent to that actually constructed. The semantic conception of truth gives us, so to speak, no possibility of choice between various non-equivalent definitions of this notion.

Moreover, we can deduce from our definition various laws of a general nature. In particular, we can prove with its help the *laws of contradiction and of excluded middle*, which are so characteristic of the Aristotelian conception of truth; i.e., we can show that one and only one of any two contradictory sentences is true. These semantic laws should not be identified with the related logical laws of contradiction and excluded middle; the latter belong to the sentential calculus, i.e., to the most elementary part of logic, and do not involve the term "*true*" at all.

Further important results can be obtained by applying the theory of truth to formalized languages of a certain very comprehensive class of mathematical disciplines; only disciplines of an elementary character and a very elementary logical structure are excluded from this class. It turns out that for a discipline of this class *the notion of truth*

never coincides with that of provability; for all provable sentences are true, but there are true sentences which are not provable.[18] Hence it follows further that every such discipline is consistent, but incomplete; that is to say, of any two contradictory sentences at most one is provable, and—what is more—there exists a pair of contradictory sentences neither of which is provable.[19]

---

[18] Due to the development of modern logic, the notion of mathematical proof has undergone a far-reaching simplification. A sentence of a given formalized discipline is provable if it can be obtained from the axioms of this discipline by applying certain simple and purely formal rules of inference, such as those of detachment and substitution. Hence to show that all provable sentences are true, it suffices to prove that all the sentences accepted as axioms are true, and that the rules of inference when applied to true sentences yield new true sentences; and this usually presents no difficulty.

On the other hand, in view of the elementary nature of the notion of provability, a precise definition of this notion requires only rather simple logical devices. In most cases, those logical devices which are available in the formalized discipline itself (to which the notion of provability is related) are more than sufficient for this purpose. We know, however, that as regards the definition of truth just the opposite holds. Hence, as a rule, the notions of truth and provability cannot coincide; and since every provable sentence is true, there must be true sentences which are not provable.

[19] Thus the theory of truth provides us with a general method for consistency proofs for formalized mathematical disciplines. It can be easily realized, however, that a consistency proof obtained by this method may possess some intuitive value—i.e., may convince us, or strengthen our belief, that the discipline under consideration is actually consistent—only in case we succeed in defin-

13. EXTENSION OF THE RESULTS TO OTHER SEMANTIC NOTIONS. Most of the results at which we arrived in the preceding sections in discussing the notion of truth can be extended with appropriate changes to other semantic notions, for instance, to the notion of satisfaction (involved in our previous discussion), and to those of *designation* and *definition*.

Each of these notions can be analyzed along the lines followed in the analysis of truth. Thus, criteria for an adequate usage of these notions can be established; it can be shown that each of these notions, when used in a semantically closed language according to

---

ing truth in terms of a meta-language which does not contain the object-language as a part (cf. here a remark in Section 9). For only in this case the deductive assumptions of the meta-language may be intuitively simpler and more obvious than those of the object-language—even though the condition of "essential richness" will be formally satisfied. Cf. here also Tarski [3], p. 7.

The incompleteness of a comprehensive class of formalized disciplines constitutes the essential content of a fundamental theorem of K. Gödel; cf. Gödel [1], pp. 187 ff. The explanation of the fact that the theory of truth leads so directly to Gödel's theorem is rather simple. In deriving Gödel's result from the theory of truth we make an essential use of the fact that the definition of truth cannot be given in a meta-language which is only as "rich" as the object-language (cf. note 17); however, in establishing this fact, a method of reasoning has been applied which is very closely related to that used (for the first time) by Gödel. It may be added that Gödel was clearly guided in his proof by certain intuitive considerations regarding the notion of truth, although this notion does not occur in the proof explicitly; cf. Gödel [1], pp. 174 f.

---

those criteria, leads necessarily to a contradiction,[20] a distinction between the object-language and the meta-language becomes again indispensable; and the "essential richness" of the meta-language proves in each case to be a necessary and sufficient condition for a satisfactory definition of the notion involved. Hence the results obtained in discussing one particular semantic notion apply to the general problem of the foundations of theoretical semantics.

Within theoretical semantics we can define and study some further notions, whose intuitive content is more involved and whose semantic origin is less obvious; we have in mind, for instance, the important notions of *consequence, synonymity,* and *meaning*.[21]

We have concerned ourselves here with the theory of semantic notions re-

---

[20] The notions of designation and definition lead respectively to the antinomies of Grelling-Nelson and Richard (cf. note 9). To obtain an antinomy for the notion of satisfaction, we construct the following expression:

The sentential function X does not satisfy X.

A contradiction arises when we consider the question whether this expression, which is clearly a sentential function, satisfies itself or not.

[21] All notions mentioned in this section can be defined in terms of satisfaction. We can say, e.g., that a given term designates a given object if this object satisfies the sentential function "x *is identical with* T" where 'T' stands for the given term. Similarly, a sentential function is said to define a given object if the latter is the only object which satisfies this function. For a definition of consequence see Tarski [4], and for that of synonymity—Carnap [2].

lated to an individual object-language (although no specific properties of this language have been involved in our arguments). However, we could also consider the problem of developing *general semantics* which applies to a comprehensive class of object-languages. A considerable part of our previous remarks can be extended to this general problem; however, certain new difficulties arise in this connection, which will not be discussed here. I shall merely observe that the axiomatic method (mentioned in Section 10) may prove the most appropriate for the treatment of the problem.[22]

II. Polemical Remarks

14. IS THE SEMANTIC CONCEPTION OF TRUTH THE "RIGHT" ONE? I should like to begin the polemical part of the paper with some general remarks.

I hope nothing which is said here will be interpreted as a claim that the semantic conception of truth is the "right" or indeed the "only possible" one. I do not have the slightest intention to contribute in any way to those endless, often violent discussions on the subject: "What is the right conception of truth?"[23] I must confess I do not understand what is at stake in such disputes; for the problem itself is so vague that no definite solution is possible. In fact, it seems to me that the sense in which the phrase "the right conception" is

used has never been made clear. In most cases one gets the impression that the phrase is used in an almost mystical sense based upon the belief that every word has only one "real" meaning (a kind of Platonic or Aristotelian idea), and that all the competing conceptions really attempt to catch hold of this one meaning; since, however, they contradict each other, only one attempt can be successful, and hence only one conception is the "right" one.

Disputes of this type are by no means restricted to the notion of truth. They occur in all domains where—instead of an exact, scientific terminology—common language with its vagueness and ambiguity is used; and they are always meaningless, and therefore in vain.

It seems to me obvious that the only rational approach to such problems would be the following: We should reconcile ourselves with the fact that we are confronted, not with one concept, but with several different concepts which are denoted by one word; we should try to make these concepts as clear as possible (by means of definition, or of an axiomatic procedure, or in some other way); to avoid further confusions, we should agree to use different terms for different concepts; and then we may proceed to a quiet and systematic study of all concepts involved, which will exhibit their main properties and mutual relations.

Referring specifically to the notion of truth, it is undoubtedly the case that in philosophical discussions—and perhaps also in everyday usage—some incipient conceptions of this notion can be found that differ essentially from the classical one (of which the semantic conception

---

[22] General semantics is the subject of Carnap [2]. Cf. here also remarks in Tarski [2], pp. 388 f.

[23] Cf. various quotations in Ness [1], pp. 13 f.

is but a modernized form). In fact, various conceptions of this sort have been discussed in the literature, for instance, the pragmatic conception, the coherence theory, etc.[24]

It seems to me that none of these conceptions have been put so far in an intelligible and unequivocal form. This may change, however; a time may come when we find ourselves confronted with several incompatible, but equally clear and precise, conceptions of truth. It will then become necessary to abandon the ambiguous usage of the word *"true,"* and to introduce several terms instead, each to denote a different notion. Personally, I should not feel hurt if a future world congress of the "theoreticians of truth" should decide—by a majority of votes—to reserve the word *"true"* for one of the non-classical conceptions, and should suggest another word, say, *"frue,"* for the conception considered here. But I cannot imagine that anybody could present cogent arguments to the effect that the semantic conception is "wrong" and should be entirely abandoned.

15. FORMAL CORRECTNESS OF THE SUGGESTED DEFINITION OF TRUTH.

The specific objections which have been raised to my investigations can be divided into several groups; each of these will be discussed separately.

I think that practically all these objections apply, not to the special definition I have given, but to the semantic conception of truth in general. Even those which were leveled against the definition actually constructed could

be related to any other definition which conforms to this conception.

This holds, in particular, for those objections which concern the formal correctness of the definition. I have heard a few objections of this kind; however, I doubt very much whether any one of them can be treated seriously.

As a typical example let me quote in substance such an objection.[25] In formulating the definition we use necessarily sentential connectives, i.e., expressions like *"if . . . , then," "or,"* etc. They occur in the definiens; and one of them, namely, the phrase *"if, and only if"* is usually employed to combine the definiendum with the definiens. However, it is well known that the meaning of sentential connectives is explained in logic with the help of the words *"true"* and *"false"*; for instance, we say that an equivalence, i.e., a sentence of the form *"p if, and only if, q,"* is true if either both of its members, i.e., the sentences represented by *'p'* and *'q,'* are true or both are false. Hence the definition of truth involves a vicious circle.

If this objection were valid, no formally correct definition of truth would be possible; for we are unable to formulate any compound sentence without using sentential connectives, or other logical terms defined with their help. Fortunately, the situation is not so bad.

It is undoubtedly the case that a strictly deductive development of logic is often preceded by certain statements explaining the conditions under which sentences of the form *"if p, then q,"* etc.,

---

[24] See note 6, p. 581.

[25] The names of persons who have raised objections will not be quoted here, unless their objections have appeared in print.

are considered true or false. (Such explanations are often given schematically, by means of the so-called truth-tables.) However, these statements are outside of the system of logic, and should not be regarded as definitions of the terms involved. They are not formulated in the language of the system, but constitute rather special consequences of the definition of truth given in the meta-language. Moreover, these statements do not influence the deductive development of logic in any way. For in such a development we do not discuss the question whether a given sentence is true; we are only interested in the problem whether it is provable.[26]

On the other hand, the moment we find ourselves within the deductive system of logic—or of any discipline based upon logic, e.g., of semantics—we either treat sentential connectives as undefined terms, or else we define them by means of other sentential connectives, but never by means of semantic terms like "*true*" or "*false*." For instance, if we

agree to regard the expressions "*not*" and "*if . . . , then*" (and possibly also "*if, and only if*") as undefined terms, we can define the term "*or*" by stating that a sentence of the form "*p or q*" is equivalent to the corresponding sentence of the form "*if not p, then q.*" The definition can be formulated, e.g., in the following way:

(*p* or *q*) if, and only if, (if not *p*, then *q*).

This definition obviously contains no semantic terms.

However, a vicious circle in definition arises only when the definiens contains either the term to be defined itself, or other terms defined with its help. Thus we clearly see that the use of sentential connectives in defining the semantic term "*true*" does not involve any circle.

I should like to mention a further objection which I have found in the literature and which seems also to concern the formal correctness, if not of the definition of truth itself, then at least of the arguments which lead to this definition.[27]

---

[26] It should be emphasized, however, that as regards the question of an alleged vicious circle the situation would not change even if we took a different point of view, represented, e.g., in Carnap [2]; i.e., if we regarded the specification of conditions under which sentences of a language are true as an essential part of the description of this language. On the other hand, it may be noticed that the point of view represented in the text does not exclude the possibility of using truth-tables in a deductive development of logic. However, these tables are to be regarded then merely as a formal instrument for checking the provability of certain sentences; and the symbols '*T*' and '*F*' which occur in them and which are usually considered abbreviations of "*true*" and "*false*" should not be interpreted in any intuitive way.

---

[27] Cf. Juhos [1]. I must admit that I do not clearly understand von Juhos' objections and do not know how to classify them; therefore, I confine myself here to certain points of a formal character. Von Juhos does not seem to know my definition of truth; he refers only to an informal presentation in Tarski [3] where the definition has not been given at all. If he knew the actual definition, he would have to change his argument. However, I have no doubt that he would discover in this definition some "defects" as well. For he believes he has proved that "on ground of principle it is impossible to give such a definition at all."

The author of this objection mistakenly regards scheme (T) (from Section 4) as a definition of truth. He charges this alleged definition with "inadmissible brevity, i.e., incompleteness," which "does not give us the means of deciding whether by 'equivalence' is meant a logical-formal, or a non-logical and also structurally non-describable relation." To remove this "defect" he suggests supplementing (T) in one of the two following ways:

(T′)   X is true if, and only if,
                      p is true,

or

(T″)   X is true if, and only if,
p is the case (i.e., if what p states is
          the case).

Then he discusses these two new "definitions," which are supposedly free from the old, formal "defect," but which turn out to be unsatisfactory for other, non-formal reasons.

This new objection seems to arise from a misunderstanding concerning the nature of sentential connectives (and thus to be somehow related to that previously discussed). The author of the objection does not seem to realize that the phrase "if, and only if" (in opposition to such phrases as "are equivalent" or "is equivalent to") expresses no relation between sentences at all since it does not combine names of sentences.

In general, the whole argument is based upon an obvious confusion between sentences and their names. It suffices to point out that—in contradistinction to (T)—schemata (T′) and (T″) do not give any meaningful expressions if we replace in them 'p' by a sentence; for the phrases "p is true" and

"p is the case" (i.e., "what p states is the case") become meaningless if 'p' is replaced by a sentence, and not by the name of a sentence (cf. Section 4).[28]

While the author of the objection considers schema (T) "inadmissibly brief," I am inclined, on my part, to regard schemata (T′) and (T″) as "inadmissibly long." And I think even that I can rigorously prove this statement on the basis of the following definition: An expression is said to be "inadmissibly long" if (i) it is meaningless, and (ii) it has been obtained from a meaningful expression by inserting superfluous words.

16. REDUNDANCY OF SEMANTIC TERMS —THEIR POSSIBLE ELIMINATION. The objection I am going to discuss now no longer concerns the formal correctness of the definition, but is still concerned with certain formal features of the semantic conception of truth.

We have seen that this conception essentially consists in regarding the sentence "X is true" as equivalent to the sentence denoted by 'X' (where 'X' stands for a name of a sentence of the object-language). Consequently, the term "true" when occurring in a simple sentence of the form "X is true" can easily be eliminated, and the sentence itself, which belongs to the meta-lan-

---

[28] The phrases "p is true" and "p is the case" (or better "it is true that p" and "it is the case that p") are sometimes used in informal discussions, mainly for stylistic reasons; but they are considered then as synonymous with the sentence represented by 'p.' On the other hand, as far as I understand the situation, the phrases in question cannot be used by von Juhos synonymously with 'p'; for otherwise the replacement of (T) by (T′) or (T″) would not constitute any "improvement."

guage, can be replaced by an equivalent sentence of the object-language; and the same applies to compound sentences provided the term "*true*" occurs in them exclusively as a part of the expressions of the form "X *is true*."

Some people have therefore urged that the term "*true*" in the semantic sense can always be eliminated, and that for this reason the semantic conception of truth is altogether sterile and useless. And since the same considerations apply to other semantic notions, the conclusion has been drawn that semantics as a whole is a purely verbal game and at best only a harmless hobby.

But the matter is not quite so simple.[29] The sort of elimination here discussed cannot always be made. It cannot be done in the case of universal statements which express the fact that all sentences of a certain type are true, or that all true sentences have a certain property. For instance, we can prove in the theory of truth the following statement:

All consequences of true sentences are true.

However, we cannot get rid here of the word "*true*" in the simple manner contemplated.

Again, even in the case of particular sentences having the form "X *is true*" such a simple elimination cannot always be made. In fact, the elimination is possible only in those cases in which the name of the sentence which is said to be true occurs in a form that enables us to reconstruct the sentence itself. For

example, our present historical knowledge does not give us any possibility of eliminating the word "*true*" from the following sentence:

The first sentence written by Plato is true.

Of course, since we have a definition for truth and since every definition enables us to replace the definiendum by its definiens, an elimination of the term "*true*" in its semantic sense is always theoretically possible. But this would not be the kind of simple elimination discussed above, and it would not result in the replacement of a sentence in the meta-language by a sentence in the object-language.

If, however, anyone continues to urge that—because of the theoretical possibility of eliminating the word "*true*" on the basis of its definition—the concept of truth is sterile, he must accept the further conclusion that all defined notions are sterile. But this outcome is so absurd and so unsound historically that any comment on it is unnecessary. In fact, I am rather inclined to agree with those who maintain that the moments of greatest creative advancement in science frequently coincide with the introduction of new notions by means of definition.

17. CONFORMITY OF THE SEMANTIC CONCEPTION OF TRUTH WITH PHILOSOPHICAL AND COMMON-SENSE USAGE. The question has been raised whether the semantic conception of truth can indeed be regarded as a precise form of the old, classical conception of this notion.

---

[29] Cf. the discussion of this problem in Kokoszyńska [1], pp. 161 ff.

Various formulations of the classical conception were quoted in the early part of this paper (Section 3). I must repeat that in my judgment none of them is quite precise and clear. Accordingly, the only sure way of settling the question would be to confront the authors of those statements with our new formulation, and to ask them whether it agrees with their intentions. Unfortunately, this method is impractical since they died quite some time ago.

As far as my own opinion is concerned, I do not have any doubts that our formulation does conform to the intuitive content of that of Aristotle. I am less certain regarding the later formulations of the classical conception, for they are very vague indeed.[30]

Furthermore, some doubts have been expressed whether the semantic conception does reflect the notion of truth in its common-sense and everyday usage. I clearly realize (as I already indicated) that the common meaning of the word *"true"*—as that of any other word of everyday language—is to some extent vague, and that its usage more or less fluctuates. Hence the problem of assigning to this word a fixed and exact meaning is relatively unspecified, and every solution of this problem implies necessarily a certain deviation from the practice of everyday language.

In spite of all this, I happen to believe that the semantic conception does conform to a very considerable extent with the common-sense usage—although

I readily admit I may be mistaken. What is more to the point, however, I believe that the issue raised can be settled scientifically, though of course not by a deductive procedure, but with the help of the statistical questionnaire method. As a matter of fact, such research has been carried on, and some of the results have been reported at congresses and in part published.[31]

I should like to emphasize that in my opinion such investigations must be conducted with the utmost care. Thus, if we ask a highschool boy, or even an adult intelligent man having no special philosophical training, whether he regards a sentence to be true if it agrees with reality, or if it designates an existing state of affairs, it may simply turn out that he does not understand the question; in consequence his response, whatever it may be, will be of no value for us. But his answer to the question whether he would admit that the sentence *"it is snowing"* could be true although it is not snowing, or could be false although it is snowing, would naturally be very significant for our problem.

Therefore, I was by no means surprised to learn (in a discussion devoted to these problems) that in a group of people who were questioned only 15% agreed that *"true"* means for them *"agreeing with reality,"* while 90% agreed that a sentence such as *"it is snowing"* is true if, and only if, it is snowing. Thus, a great majority of these

---

[30] Most authors who have discussed my work on the notion of truth are of the opinion that my definition does conform with the classical conception of this notion; see, e.g., Kotarbiński [2] and Scholz [1].

[31] Cf. Ness [1]. Unfortunately, the results of that part of Ness' research which is especially relevant for our problem are not discussed in his book; compare p. 148, footnote 1.

people seemed to reject the classical conception of truth in its "philosophical" formulation, while accepting the same conception when formulated in plain words (waiving the question whether the use of the phrase "the same conception" is here justified).

18. THE DEFINITION IN ITS RELATION TO "THE PHILOSOPHICAL PROBLEM OF TRUTH" AND TO VARIOUS EPISTEMOLOGICAL TRENDS. I have heard it remarked that the formal definition of truth has nothing to do with "the philosophical problem of truth."[32] However, nobody has ever pointed out to me in an intelligible way just what this problem is. I have been informed in this connection that my definition, though it states necessary and sufficient conditions for a sentence to be true, does not really grasp the "essence" of this concept. Since I have never been able to understand what the "essence" of a concept is, I must be excused from discussing this point any longer.

In general, I do not believe that there is such a thing as "the philosophical problem of truth." I do believe that there are various intelligible and interesting (but not necessarily philosophical) problems concerning the notion of truth, but I also believe that they can be exactly formulated and possibly

solved only on the basis of a precise conception of this notion.

While on the one hand the definition of truth has been blamed for not being philosophical enough, on the other a series of objections have been raised charging this definition with serious philosophical implications, always of a very undesirable nature. I shall discuss now one special objection of this type; another group of such objections will be dealt with in the next section.

It has been claimed that—due to the fact that a sentence like "snow is white" is taken to be semantically true if snow is *in fact* white (italics by the critic)— logic finds itself involved in a most uncritical realism.[33]

If there were an opportunity to discuss the objection with its author, I should raise two points. First, I should ask him to drop the words *"in fact,"* which do not occur in the original formulation and which are misleading, even if they do not affect the content. For these words convey the impression that the semantic conception of truth is intended to establish the conditions under which we are warranted in asserting any given sentence, and in particular any empirical sentence. However, a moment's reflection shows that this impression is merely an illusion; and I think that the author of the objection falls victim to the illusion which he himself created.

In fact, the semantic definition of truth implies nothing regarding the conditions under which a sentence like (1):

(1)   snow is white

---

[32] Though I have heard this opinion several times, I have seen it in print only once and, curiously enough, in a work which does not have a philosophical character—in fact, in Hilbert-Bernays [1], vol. II, p. 269 (where, by the way, it is not expressed as any kind of objection). On the other hand, I have not found any remark to this effect in discussions of my work by professional philosophers (cf. note 1).

[33] Cf. Gonseth [1], pp. 187 f.

can be asserted. It implies only that, whenever we assert or reject this sentence, we must be ready to assert or reject the correlated sentence (2):

(2) the sentence "snow is white" is true.

Thus, we may accept the semantic conception of truth without giving up any epistemological attitude we may have had; we may remain naive realists, critical realists or idealists, empiricists or metaphysicians—whatever we were before. The semantic conception is completely neutral toward all these issues.

In the second place, I should try to get some information regarding the conception of truth which (in the opinion of the author of the objection) does not involve logic in a most naive realism. I would gather that this conception must be incompatible with the semantic one. Thus, there must be sentences which are true in one of these conceptions without being true in the other. Assume, e.g., the sentence (1) to be of this kind. The truth of this sentence in the semantic conception is determined by an equivalence of the form (T):

The sentence "snow is white" is true if, and only if, snow is white.

Hence in the new conception we must reject this equivalence, and consequently we must assume its denial:

The sentence "snow is white" is true if, and only if, snow is not white (or perhaps: snow, in fact, is not white).

This sounds somewhat paradoxical. I do not regard such a consequence of the new conception as absurd; but I am a little fearful that someone in the future may charge this conception with involving logic in a "most sophisticated kind of irrealism." At any rate, it seems to me important to realize that every conception of truth which is incompatible with the semantic one carries with it consequences of this type.

I have dwelt a little on this whole question, not because the objection discussed seems to me very significant, but because certain points which have arisen in the discussion should be taken into account by all those who for various epistemological reasons are inclined to reject the semantic conception of truth.

19. ALLEGED METAPHYSICAL ELEMENT IN SEMANTICS. The semantic conception of truth has been charged several times with involving certain metaphysical elements. Objections of this sort have been made to apply not only to the theory of truth, but to the whole domain of theoretical semantics.[34]

I do not intend to discuss the general problem whether the introduction of a metaphysical element into a science is at all objectionable. The only point which will interest me here is whether and in what sense metaphysics is involved in the subject of our present discussion.

The whole question obviously depends upon what one understands by

---

[34] See Nagel [1], and Nagel [2], pp. 471 f. A remark which goes, perhaps, in the same direction is also to be found in Weinberg [1], p. 77; cf., however, his earlier remarks, pp. 75 f.

"metaphysics." Unfortunately, this notion is extremely vague and equivocal. When listening to discussions in this subject, sometimes one gets the impression that the term "metaphysical" has lost any objective meaning, and is merely used as a kind of professional philosophical invective.

For some people metaphysics is a general theory of objects (ontology)—a discipline which is to be developed in a purely empirical way, and which differs from other empirical sciences only by its generality. I do not know whether such a discipline actually exists (some cynics claim that it is customary in philosophy to baptize unborn children); but I think that in any case metaphysics in this conception is not objectionable to anybody, and has hardly any connections with semantics.

For the most part, however, the term "metaphysical" is used as directly opposed—in one sense or another—to the term "empirical"; at any rate, it is used in this way by those people who are distressed by the thought that any metaphysical elements might have managed to creep into science. This general conception of metaphysics assumes several more specific forms.

Thus, some people take it to be symptomatic of a metaphysical element in a science when methods of inquiry are employed which are neither deductive nor empirical. However, no trace of this symptom can be found in the development of semantics (unless some metaphysical elements are involved in the object-language to which the semantic notions refer). In particular, the semantics of formalized languages is constructed in a purely deductive way.

Others maintain that the metaphysical character of a science depends mainly on its vocabulary and, more specifically, on its primitive terms. Thus, a term is said to be metaphysical if it is neither logical nor mathematical, and if it is not associated with an empirical procedure which enables us to decide whether a thing is denoted by this term or not. With respect to such a view of metaphysics it is sufficient to recall that a meta-language includes only three kinds of undefined terms: (i) terms taken from logic, (ii) terms of the corresponding object-language, and (iii) names of expressions in the object-language. It is thus obvious that no metaphysical undefined terms occur in the meta-language (again, unless such terms appear in the object-language itself).

There are, however, some who believe that, even if no metaphysical terms occur among the primitive terms of a language, they may be introduced by definitions; namely, by those definitions which fail to provide us with general criteria for deciding whether an object falls under the defined concept. It is argued that the term *"true"* is of this kind, since no universal criterion of truth follows immediately from the definition of this term, and since it is generally believed (and in a certain sense can even be proved) that such a criterion will never be found. This comment on the actual character of the notion of truth seems to be perfectly just. However, it should be noticed that this notion of truth does not differ in this respect from many notions in logic, mathematics, and theoretical parts of various empirical sciences, e.g., in theoretical physics.

In general, it must be said that if the term "metaphysical" is employed in so wide a sense as to embrace certain notions (or methods) of logic, mathematics, or empirical sciences, it will apply *a fortiori* to those of semantics. In fact, as we know from Part I of the paper, in developing the semantics of a language we use all the notions of this language, and we apply even a stronger logical apparatus than that which is used in the language itself. On the other hand, however, I can summarize the arguments given above by stating that in no interpretation of the term "metaphysical" which is familiar and more or less intelligible to me does semantics involve any metaphysical elements peculiar to itself.

I should like to make one final remark in connection with this group of objections. The history of science shows many instances of concepts which were judged metaphysical (in a loose, but in any case derogatory sense of this term) before their meaning was made precise; however, once they received a rigorous, formal definition, the distrust in them evaporated. As typical examples we may mention the concepts of negative and imaginary numbers in mathematics. I hope a similar fate awaits the concept of truth and other semantic concepts; and it seems to me, therefore, that those who have distrusted them because of their alleged metaphysical implications should welcome the fact that precise definitions of these concepts are now available. If in consequence semantic concepts lose philosophical interest, they will only share the fate of many other concepts of science, and this need give rise to no regret.

20. APPLICABILITY OF SEMANTICS TO SPECIAL EMPIRICAL SCIENCES. We come to the last and perhaps the most important group of objections. Some strong doubts have been expressed whether semantic notions find or can find applications in various domains of intellectual activity. For the most part such doubts have concerned the applicability of semantics to the field of empirical science—either to special sciences or to the general methodology of this field; although similar skepticism has been expressed regarding possible applications of semantics to mathematical sciences and their methodology.

I believe that it is possible to allay these doubts to a certain extent, and that some optimism with respect to the potential value of semantics for various domains of thought is not without ground.

To justify this optimism, it suffices I think to stress two rather obvious points. First, the development of a theory which formulates a precise definition of a notion and establishes its general properties provides *eo ipso* a firmer basis for all discussions in which this notion is involved; and, therefore, it cannot be irrelevant for anyone who uses this notion, and desires to do so in a conscious and consistent way. Secondly, semantic notions are actually involved in various branches of science, and in particular of empirical science.

The fact that in empirical research we are concerned only with natural languages and that theoretical semantics applies to these languages only with a certain approximation, does not affect the problem essentially. However, it has undoubtedly this effect that progress in semantics will have but a delayed and somewhat limited influence in this field. The situation with which we are confronted here does not differ essentially from that which arises when we apply laws of logic to arguments in everyday life—or, generally, when we attempt to apply a theoretical science to empirical problems.

Semantic notions are undoubtedly involved, to a larger or smaller degree, in psychology, sociology, and in practically all the humanities. Thus, a psychologist defines the so-called intelligence quotient in terms of the numbers of *true* (right) and *false* (wrong) answers given by a person to certain questions; for a historian of culture the range of objects for which a human race in successive stages of its development possesses adequate *designations* may be a topic of great significance; a student of literature may be strongly interested in the problem whether a given author always uses two given words with the same *meaning*. Examples of this kind can be multiplied indefinitely.

The most natural and promising domain for the applications of theoretical semantics is clearly linguistics—the empirical study of natural languages. Certain parts of this science are even referred to as "semantics," sometimes with an additional qualification. Thus, this name is occasionally given to that portion of grammar which attempts to classify all words of a language into parts of speech, according to what the words mean or designate. The study of the evolution of meanings in the historical development of a language is sometimes called "historical semantics." In general, the totality of investigations on semantic relations which occur in a natural language is referred to as "descriptive semantics." The relation between theoretical and descriptive semantics is analogous to that between pure and applied mathematics, or perhaps to that between theoretical and empirical physics; the role of formalized languages in semantics can be roughly compared to that of isolated systems in physics.

It is perhaps unnecessary to say that semantics cannot find any direct applications in natural sciences such as physics, biology, etc.; for in none of these sciences are we concerned with linguistic phenomena, and even less with semantic relations between linguistic expressions and objects to which these expressions refer. We shall see, however, in the next section that semantics may have a kind of indirect influence even on those sciences in which semantic notions are not directly involved.

21. APPLICABILITY OF SEMANTICS TO THE METHODOLOGY OF EMPIRICAL SCIENCE. Besides linguistics, another important domain for possible applications of semantics is the methodology of science; this term is used here in a broad sense so as to embrace the theory of science in general. Independent of whether a science is conceived merely as a system of statements or as a totality of certain statements and human activities,

the study of scientific language constitutes an essential part of the methodological discussion of a science. And it seems to me clear that any tendency to eliminate semantic notions (like those of truth and designation) from this discussion would make it fragmentary and inadequate.[35] Moreover, there is no reason for such a tendency today, once the main difficulties in using semantic terms have been overcome. The semantics of scientific language should be simply included as a part in the methodology of science.

I am by no means inclined to charge methodology and, in particular, semantics—whether theoretical or descriptive —with the task of clarifying the meanings of all scientific terms. This task is left to those sciences in which the terms are used, and is actually fulfilled by them (in the same way in which, e.g., the task of clarifying the meaning of the term "*true*" is left to, and fulfilled by, semantics). There may be, however, certain special problems of this sort in which a methodological approach is desirable or indeed necessary (perhaps, the problem of the notion of causality is a good example here); and in a methodological discussion of such problems semantic notions may play an essential role. Thus, semantics may have some bearing on any science whatsoever.

The question arises whether semantics can be helpful in solving general and, so to speak, classical problems of

methodology. I should like to discuss here with some detail a special, though very important, aspect of this question.

One of the main problems of the methodology of empirical science consists in establishing conditions under which an empirical theory or hypothesis should be regarded as acceptable. This notion of acceptability must be relativized to a given stage of the development of a science (or to a given amount of presupposed knowledge). In other words, we may consider it as provided with a time coefficient; for a theory which is acceptable today may become untenable tomorrow as a result of new scientific discoveries.

It seems *a priori* very plausible that the acceptability of a theory somehow depends on the truth of its sentences, and that consequently a methodologist in his (so far rather unsuccessful) attempts at making the notion of acceptability precise, can expect some help from the semantic theory of truth. Hence we ask the question: Are there any postulates which can be reasonably imposed on acceptable theories and which involve the notion of truth? And, in particular, we ask whether the following postulate is a reasonable one:

An acceptable theory cannot contain (or imply) any false sentences.

The answer to the last question is clearly negative. For, first of all, we are practically sure, on the basis of our historical experience, that every empirical theory which is accepted today will sooner or later be rejected and replaced by another theory. It is also very prob-

---

[35] Such a tendency was evident in earlier works of Carnap (see, e.g., Carnap [1], especially Part V) and in writings of other members of Vienna Circle. Cf. here Kokoszyńska [1] and Weinberg [1].

able that the new theory will be incompatible with the old one; i.e., will imply a sentence which is contradictory to one of the sentences contained in the old theory. Hence, at least one of the two theories must include false sentences, in spite of the fact that each of them is accepted at a certain time. Secondly, the postulate in question could hardly ever be satisfied in practice; for we do not know, and are very unlikely to find, any criteria of truth which enable us to show that no sentence of an empirical theory is false.

The postulate in question could be at most regarded as the expression of an ideal limit for successively more adequate theories in a given field of research; but this hardly can be given any precise meaning.

Nevertheless, it seems to me that there is an important postulate which can be reasonably imposed on acceptable empirical theories and which involves the notion of truth. It is closely related to the one just discussed, but it is essentially weaker. Remembering that the notion of acceptability is provided with a time coefficient, we can give this postulate the following form:

> As soon as we succeed in showing that an empirical theory contains (or implies) false sentences, it cannot be any longer considered acceptable.

In support of this postulate, I should like to make the following remarks.

I believe everybody agrees that one of the reasons which may compel us to reject an empirical theory is the proof of its inconsistency: a theory becomes untenable if we succeed in deriving from it two contradictory sentences. Now we can ask what are the usual motives for rejecting a theory on such grounds. Persons who are acquainted with modern logic are inclined to answer this question in the following way: A well-known logical law shows that a theory which enables us to derive two contradictory sentences enables us also to derive every sentence; therefore, such a theory is trivial and deprived of any scientific interest.

I have some doubts whether this answer contains an adequate analysis of the situation. I think that people who do not know modern logic are as little inclined to accept an inconsistent theory as those who are thoroughly familiar with it; and probably this applies even to those who regard (as some still do) the logical law on which the argument is based as a highly controversial issue, and almost as a paradox. I do not think that our attitude toward an inconsistent theory would change even if we decided for some reasons to weaken our system of logic so as to deprive ourselves of the possibility of deriving every sentence from any two contradictory sentences.

It seems to me that the real reason of our attitude is a different one: We know (if only intuitively) that an inconsistent theory must contain false sentences; and we are not inclined to regard as acceptable any theory which has been shown to contain such sentences.

There are various methods of showing that a given theory includes false sentences. Some of them are based upon purely logical properties of the theory involved; the method just discussed (i.e., the proof of inconsistency) is not the sole method of this type, but is the simplest one, and the one which is most frequently applied in practice. With the help of certain assumptions regarding the truth of empirical sentences, we can obtain methods to the same effect which are no longer of a purely logical nature. If we decide to accept the general postulate suggested above, then a successful application of any such method will make the theory untenable.

22. APPLICATIONS OF SEMANTICS TO DEDUCTIVE SCIENCE. As regards the applicability of semantics to mathematical sciences and their methodology, i.e., to meta-mathematics, we are in a much more favorable position than in the case of empirical sciences. For, instead of advancing reasons which justify some hopes for the future (and thus making a kind of pro-semantics propaganda), we are able to point out concrete results already achieved.

Doubts continue to be expressed whether the notion of a true sentence—as distinct from that of a provable sentence—can have any significance for mathematical disciplines and play any part in a methodological discussion of mathematics. It seems to me, however, that just this notion of a true sentence constitutes a most valuable contribution to meta-mathematics by semantics. We already possess a series of interesting meta-mathematical results gained with the help of the theory of truth. These results concern the mutual relations between the notion of truth and that of provability; establish new properties of the latter notion (which, as well known,

is one of the basic notions of meta-mathematics); and throw some light on the fundamental problems of consistency and completeness. The most significant among these results have been briefly discussed in Section 12.[36]

Furthermore, by applying the method of semantics we can adequately define several important meta-mathematical notions which have been used so far only in an intuitive way—such as, e.g., the notion of definability or that of a model of an axiom system; and thus we can undertake a systematic study of these notions. In particular, the investigations on definability have already brought some interesting results, and promise even more in the future.[37]

---

[36] For other results obtained with the help of the theory of truth see Gödel [2]; Tarski [2], pp. 401 ff.; and Tarski [5], pp. 111 f.

[37] An object—e.g., a number or a set of numbers—is said to be definable (in a given formalism) if there is a sentential function which defines it; cf. note 20. Thus, the term "definable," though of a meta-mathematical (semantic) origin, is purely mathematical as to its extension, for it expresses a property (denotes a class) of mathematical objects. In consequence, the notion of definability can be re-defined in purely mathematical terms, though not within the formalized discipline to which this notion refers; however, the fundamental idea of the definition remains unchanged. Cf. here—also for further bibliographic references—Tarski [1]; various other results concerning definability can also be found in the literature, e.g., in Hilbert-Bernays [1], vol. I, pp. 354 ff., 369 ff., 456 ff., etc., and in Lindenbaum-Tarski [1]. It may be noticed that the term "definable" is sometimes used in another, meta-mathematical (but not semantic), sense; this occurs, for instance, when we say that a term is definable in other terms (on the basis of a given axiom system). For a definition of a model of an axiom system see Tarski [4].

We have discussed the applications of semantics only to meta-mathematics, and not to mathematics proper. However, this distinction between mathematics and meta-mathematics is rather unimportant. For meta-mathematics is itself a deductive discipline and hence, from a certain point of view, a part of mathematics; and it is well known that —due to the formal character of deductive method—the results obtained in one deductive discipline can be automatically extended to any other discipline in which the given one finds an interpretation. Thus, for example, all meta-mathematical results can be interpreted as results of number theory. Also from a practical point of view there is no clear-cut line between meta-mathematics and mathematics proper; for instance, the investigations on definability could be included in either of these domains.

23. FINAL REMARKS. I should like to conclude this discussion with some general and rather loose remarks concerning the whole question of the evaluation of scientific achievements in terms of their applicability. I must confess I have various doubts in this connection.

Being a mathematician (as well as a logician, and perhaps a philosopher of a sort), I have had the opportunity to attend many discussions between specialists in mathematics, where the problem of applications is especially acute, and I have noticed on several occasions the following phenomenon: If a mathematician wishes to disparage the work of one of his colleagues, say, A, the most effective method he finds for doing this is to ask where the results can be ap-

plied. The hard pressed man, with his back against the wall, finally unearths the researches of another mathematician B as the locus of the application of his own results. If next B is plagued with a similar question, he will refer to another mathematician C. After a few steps of this kind we find ourselves referred back to the researches of A, and in this way the chain closes.

Speaking more seriously, I do not wish to deny that the value of a man's work may be increased by its implications for the research of others and for practice. But I believe, nevertheless, that it is inimical to the progress of science to measure the importance of any research exclusively or chiefly in terms of its usefulness and applicability. We know from the history of science that many important results and discoveries have had to wait centuries before they were applied in any field. And, in my opinion, there are also other important factors which cannot be disregarded in determining the value of a scientific work. It seems to me that there is a special domain of very profound and strong human needs related to scientific research, which are similar in many ways to aesthetic and perhaps religious needs. And it also seems to me that the satisfaction of these needs should be considered an important task of research. Hence, I believe, the question of the value of any research cannot be adequately answered without taking into account the intellectual satisfaction which the results of that research bring to those who understand it and care for it. It may be unpopular and out-of-date to say—but I do not think that a scientific result which gives us a better understanding of the world and makes it more harmonious in our eyes should be held in lower esteem than, say, an invention which reduces the cost of paving roads, or improves household plumbing.

It is clear that the remarks just made become pointless if the word "application" is used in a very wide and liberal sense. It is perhaps not less obvious that nothing follows from these general remarks concerning the specific topics which have been discussed in this paper; and I really do not know whether research in semantics stands to gain or lose by introducing the standard of value I have suggested.

REFERENCES

Aristotle [1]. *Metaphysica* (*Works*, vol. VIII.) English translation by W. D. Ross. Oxford, 1908.

Carnap, R. [1]. *Logical Syntax of Language.* London and New York, 1937.

Carnap, R. [2]. *Introduction to Semantics.* Cambridge, 1942.

Gödel, K. [1]. "Über formal unentscheidbare Sätze der *Principia Mathematica* und verwandter Systeme, I." *Monatshefte für Mathematik und Physik*, vol. XXXVIII, 1931, pp. 173–198.

Gödel, K. [2]. "Über die Länge von Beweisen." *Ergebnisse eines mathematischen Kolloquiums*, vol. VII, 1936, pp. 23–24.

Gonseth, F. [1]. "Le Congrès Descartes. Questions de Philosophie scientifique." *Revue thomiste*, vol. XLIV, 1938, pp. 183–193.

Grelling, K., and Nelson, L. [1]. "Bemerkungen zu den Paradoxien von Russell und Burali-Forti." *Abhandlungen der Fries'schen Schule*, vol. II (new series), 1908, pp. 301–334.

Hofstadter, A. [1]. "On Semantic Problems." *The Journal of Philosophy*, vol. XXXV, 1938, pp. 225–232.

Hilbert, D., and Bernays, P. [1]. *Grundlagen der Mathematik.* 2 vols. Berlin, 1934–1939.

Juhos, B. von. [1]. "The Truth of Empirical Statements." *Analysis*, vol. IV, 1937, pp. 65–70.

Kokoszyńska, M. [1]. "Über den absoluten Wahrheitsbegriff und einige andere semantische Begriffe." *Erkenntnis*, vol. VI, 1936, pp. 143–165.

Kokoszyńska, M. [2]. "Syntax, Semantik und Wissenschaftslogik." *Actes du Congrès International de Philosophie Scientifique*, vol. III, Paris, 1936, pp. 9–14.

Kotarbiński, T. [1]. *Elementy teorji poznania, logiki formalnej i metodologji nauk.* (*Elements of Epistemology, Formal Logic, and the Methodology of Sciences,* in Polish.) Lwów, 1929.

Kotarbiński, T. [2]. "W sprawie pojęcia prawdy." (*"Concerning the Concept of Truth,"* in Polish.) *Przegląd filozoficzny*, vol. XXXVII, pp. 85–91.

Lindenbaum, A., and Tarski, A. [1]. "Über die Beschränktheit der Ausdrucksmittel deduktiver Theorien." *Ergebnisse eines mathematischen Kolloquiums*, vol. VII, 1936, pp. 15–23.

Nagel, E. [1]. Review of Hofstadter [1]. *The Journal of Symbolic Logic*, vol. III, 1938, p. 90.

Nagel, E. [2]. Review of Carnap [2]. *The Journal of Philosophy*, vol. XXXIX, 1942, pp. 468–473.

Ness, A. [1]. " 'Truth' As Conceived by Those Who Are Not Professional Philosophers." *Skrifter utgitt av Det Norske Videnskaps-Akademi i Oslo, II. Hist.-Filos. Klasse*, vol. IV, Oslo, 1938.

Neurath, O. [1]. "Erster Internationaler Kongress für Einheit der Wissenschaft in Paris 1935." *Erkenntnis*, vol. V, 1935, pp. 377–406.

Russell, B. [1]. *An Inquiry Into Meaning and Truth.* New York, 1940.

Scholz, H. [1]. Review of *Studia philosophica*, vol. I. *Deutsche Literaturzeitung*, vol. LVIII, 1937, pp. 1914–1917.

Tarski, A. [1]. "Sur les ensembles définis-sables de nombres réels. I." *Fundamenta mathematicae*, vol. XVII, 1931, pp. 210–239.

Tarski, A. [2]. "Der Wahrheitsbegriff in den formalisierten Sprachen." (German translation of a book in Polish, 1933.) *Studia philosophica*, vol. I, 1935, pp. 261–405.

Tarski, A. [3]. "Grundlegung der wissen-schaftlichen Semantik." *Actes du Con-grès International de Philosophie Scientifique*, vol. III, Paris, 1936, pp. 1-8.

Tarski, A. [4]. Über den Begriff der logis-chen Folgerung." *Actes du Congrès International de Philosophie Scientifique*, vol. VII, Paris, 1937, pp. 1–11.

Tarski, A. [5]. "On Undecidable Statements in Enlarged Systems of Logic and the Concept of Truth." *The Journal of Symbolic Logic*, vol. IV, 1939, pp. 105–112.

Tarski, A. [6]. *Introduction to Logic*. New York, 1941.

Weinberg, J. [1]. Review of *Studia philos-ophica*, vol. I. *The Philosophical Review*, vol. XLVII, pp. 70–77.

7.2   TRUTH[1]

P. F. Strawson

In the following discussion, I confine myself to the question of the truth of empirical statements. My positive thesis is an elaboration of what was said, a long time ago, by F. P. Ramsey.[2] My negative purpose is the criticism of a current misconception—the Semantic or Meta-linguistic Theory of Truth—which seems to me to repeat, in a new way,

some old mistakes. In so far as this theory is simply a contribution to the construction of artificial languages, and is not intended to be regarded as relevant to the use of actual languages, I am not concerned with it. But I think the theory has been claimed by some, and it has certainly been thought by many, to throw light on the actual use of the word 'true'; or (which I take to be the same claim) on the philosophical problem of truth. I think it *does* throw some light; but I think it is also seriously misleading. Nothing that follows, however, is to be taken as implying that the word 'true' is *never* used in the way described by the semantic theory. It is certainly so used for some technical purposes, and may sometimes be so used

From *Analysis*, IX (1949). Reprinted by permission of the publishers, Basil Blackwell, the editor, and the author.

[1] [An extended and in some ways modified version of the views here maintained is to be found in the *Proceedings of the Aristotelian Society*, Supplementary Volume, 1950.]

[2] Ramsey, *Foundations of Mathematics*, pp. 142–143.

for non-technical purposes as well; though I know of no such non-technical purposes.

I

In recent discussions of truth, one or both of two theses are commonly maintained. These are:

First, any sentence beginning 'It is true that . . .' does not change its assertive meaning when the phrase 'It is true that' is omitted. More generally, to say that an assertion is true is not to make any further assertion at all; it is to make the same assertion. This I shall call Thesis 1.

Second, to say that a statement is true is to make a statement about a sentence of a given language, viz., the language in which the first statement was made. It is (in other and more technical terms) to make a statement in a meta-language ascribing the semantic property of truth (or the semantic predicate 'true') to a sentence in an object-language. The object-sentence concerned should strictly be written in inverted commas to make it clear that we are talking *about the sentence*; and the phrase 'is true' should strictly be followed by some such phrase as 'in L', where 'L' designates the object-language concerned. This I shall call Thesis 2.

Of these two theses, the first is true, but inadequate; the second is false, but important. The first thesis is right in what it asserts, and wrong in what it suggests. The second thesis is wrong in what it asserts, but right in what it implies. The first thesis is right in asserting that to say that a statement is true is not to make a further statement; but wrong in suggesting that to say that a statement is true is not to do something different from, or additional to, just making the statement. The second thesis is right in implying that to say that a statement is true is to do something different from just making the statement; but wrong in asserting that this 'something different' consists in making a further statement, viz. a statement about a sentence.

Although both theses are sometimes maintained by the same philosopher, it is easy to see that they cannot both be correct. For if it is true that to say (1) "Moths fly by night" is to make the same assertion as to say (2) "It is true that moths fly by night", then it is false that to say (2) is to say anything about the English sentence "Moths fly by night"; i.e. false that (2) ought strictly to be written " 'Moths fly by night' is true in English". If to say (2) is to make the same assertion as to say (1), then to say (2) cannot be to say anything about an English sentence; for to say (1) is not to say anything about an English sentence, but is to say something about moths.

Independently of this, one sees how misleading it is to say that the phrase ' . . . is true' is used to talk *about sentences*, by comparing it with other phrases which certainly are used to talk about sentences (or words, or phrases). For example, someone says, in French, "Il pleut"; and someone else corrects him, saying: " 'Il pleue' is *incorrect* French. 'Il pleut' is the right way of saying it". Or, criticising the style of a passage, someone says: "The sentence

' . . . . ' is *badly expressed.*" Similarly, one may ask what a sentence *means*, or say that a sentence is *ungrammatical, misspelt, a poor translation.* In all these cases, it is natural to say that one is talking *about a sentence.* If any statement of this kind were correctly translated into any language at all, the sentence which was being discussed would reappear, quoted and untranslated, in the translation of the statement as a whole. Otherwise the translation would be incorrect. But it is perfectly obvious that a correct translation of any statement containing the phrase 'is true' (used as it is ordinarily used) never contains a quoted and untranslated sentence to which the phrase 'is true' was *applied* in the original sentence. The phrase 'is true' is not *applied to* sentences; for it is not *applied* to anything.

Truth is not a property of symbols; for it is not a property.

II

The habit of calling truth a 'semantic' concept ('true' a 'semantical predicate') does not lessen the confusion involved in saying that 'true' is a predicate of sentences; but it helps to indicate a possible source of the confusion. I shall digress briefly to explore this source. For light on the use of the word 'semantic' I quote the following from Carnap's 'Introduction to Semantics' (p. 22):

By a *semantical system* we understand a system of rules, formulated in a metalanguage and referring to an objectlanguage, of such a kind that the rules determine a *truth-condition* for every

sentence of the object-language. . . . To formulate it in another way: the rules determine the *meaning* or *sense* of the sentences.

It will be noticed that the expressions 'truth-condition' and 'meaning' are used synonymously. And this suggests that even if there is no use of the phrase 'is true' in which that phrase is correctly applied to (used to talk about) sentences, there is, or might be, a use of the phrase 'is true if and only if', in which *this* phrase is correctly applied to (used to talk about) sentences; a use, namely, in which this phrase would be synonymous with the phrase 'means that'; which certainly *is* used to talk about sentences. Suppose, for example, that we wish to give information about the meaning of the sentence "The monarch is deceased". We can do this by making the following meta-statement:

(i)
"The monarch is deceased" means that the king is dead.

Here we put the sentence "The monarch is deceased" in inverted commas to indicate that we are talking about this sentence. We are making a meta-statement. And the meta-statement is contingent, for it is a contingent matter that the sentence in question has this meaning in English, or, indeed, that it has any meaning at all. To be quite strict, we perhaps ought to write it:

(ia)
"The monarch is deceased" in English means that the king is dead.

If we were to translate this meta-statement into another language, none of the expressions occurring in it would remain unchanged except the quoted sentence "The monarch is deceased". That would remain unchanged; otherwise the translation would be incorrect. Now the suggestion is that we might, without unintelligibility, give the same information in exactly the same way, except that we should replace the phrase 'means that' with the phrase 'is true if and only if' obtaining the contingent meta-statement:

(ii)

"The monarch is deceased" is true if and only if the king is dead

or, more strictly:

(iia)

"The monarch is deceased" is true in English if and only if the king is dead.

This seems to be an intelligible procedure. All that I have said of statements (i) and (ia) will apply to statements (ii) and (iia); we shall be using the phrase 'is true if and only if', in a contingent statement, to talk about a sentence. Now consider a degenerate case of such meta-statements: the case exemplified in the sentences:

(iii)

"The monarch is deceased" means (in English) that the monarch is deceased.

(iv)

"The monarch is deceased" is

true (in English) if and only if the monarch is deceased.

It is difficult, and, perhaps, for the present purpose, not very important, to decide what status to assign to such sentences as these. Considerations which might tempt us to describe them firmly as true, contingent meta-statements are the following:

(*a*) Although they are of no use for telling us what the quoted sentence means, they do give us some information about it. They do at any rate indicate that the quoted sentence has some meaning in English.[3] And this is a contingent matter.

(*b*) These statements could be obtained from the non-degenerate cases by a quite legitimate process of translation, inference and retranslation. (Or, more simply, their correct translation into, say, French would undoubtedly yield a contingent meta-statement).

(*c*) It is a contingent matter that any sentence means what it does mean, expresses the proposition it does express.[4]

Although these considerations are decisive against calling (iii) and (iv) 'logically necessary',[5] they are very inadequate grounds for calling them,

---

[3] One can imagine another use for statements (iii) and (iv); e.g. if the object-language were written, and the meta-language spoken, English.

[4] Cf. Lewy, "Truth and Significance", *Analysis*, Vol. 8, p. 242.

[5] We might be tempted to call (iii) and (iv) "necessary", because it seems self-contradictory to say:

(iiia) "The monarch is deceased" does

without qualification, 'true and contingent'. For what contingent matter do they state? If we answer, taking the hint from (*a*), that they state merely that the quoted sentence has some meaning in English, then their form (the use of the expression 'means that') is utterly misleading. If we demand what contingent matter they state, which falls under the head of (*c*), no answer is possible. One cannot *state* what a sentence means without the help of another sentence.

For these reasons, I propose to continue to refer to statements (or pseudo-statements) like (iii) and (iv) not as necessary, nor as contingent, but simply as 'degenerate cases' of contingent meta-statements of the type of (i) and (ii). The point is not in itself important; though it is important that no confusion should arise from it.

The next step is to notice the deceptive similarity of the use of the phrase 'if and only if' in this type of contingent meta-statement to its use in expressions which are not contingent statements, but necessary or defining formulae. An example of such a formula would be:

---

not mean in English that the monarch is deceased.

But this would be a mistake. To say that a sentence both has some meaning or other and has no meaning at all would be to say something self-contradictory. To say that a sentence both has and has not some particular, specified meaning would be to say something self-contradictory. But (iiia) does neither of these things. The form of (iii) is appropriate to assigning, and that of (iiia) to withholding, some specific meaning. But since (iii) does not assign, (iiia) does not withhold, any specific meaning. (iiia) is not a self-contradictory, nor a false, contingent, statement; but a pseudo-statement.

The monarch is deceased if and only if the king is dead.

Here the phrase 'is true' does not occur; and no part of this expression is in inverted commas. The formula itself does not give us information about the meaning of the sentence "The monarch is deceased", though the statement that it *was* a necessary formula *would* give us such information. Now the similarity of the use of the phrase 'if and only if' in these necessary formulae to its use as *part* of the phrase 'is true if and only if' in contingent meta-statements, may have constituted a strong temptation to split the degenerate cases of such meta-statements down the middle, and to regard what follows the phrase 'if and only if' as the definiens of what precedes it, i.e. of the phrase "the sentence ' . . . . ' is true (in L)"; to regard, for example, the whole expression (iii)

"The monarch is deceased" is true if and only if the monarch is deceased

as a specification or consequence or part[6] of a general definition of " . . . . is true" (or of " . . . is true in L"). And this we in fact find; i.e. we find it said

---

[6] E.g. Tarski, in *The Semantic Conception of Truth*, 'Philosophy and Phenomenological Research', Vol. 4, 1943–44, p. 344, says: "Every equivalence of the form (T) [(T) X is true if and only if p] obtained by replacing 'p' by a particular sentence and 'X' by a name of this sentence, may be considered a partial definition of truth, which explains wherein the truth of this one individual sentence consists. The general definition has to be, in a certain sense, a logical conjunction of all these partial definitions."

that a satisfactory general definition of truth must have as its consequences such expressions as the following:[7]

(v)
> "To-day is Monday" is true if and only if to-day is Monday.

(vi)
> "London is a City" is true if and only if London is a City.

Now we have seen that such statements as (v) and (vi) are degenerate cases of those contingent meta-statements of the type of (ii), which make use of the phrase *is true if and only if* as a synonym for *means that*. It is only *as a part of the former phrase* that the expression *is true* is used, in such statements, to talk about sentences. To read the degenerate cases, then, as specification, or parts, of some ideal defining formula for the phrase 'is true' is to separate the phrase from the context which alone confers this meta-linguistic use upon it, and to regard the result as a model for the general use of 'is true'. It is to be committed to the mistake of supposing that the phrase 'is true' is normally (or strictly) used as a meta-linguistic predicate. Thus misinterpreted, as defining formulae, such expressions as (v) are both fascinating and misleading. They mislead because, as we have seen, they crystallise the false Thesis 2. They fascinate because they seem to point to the true Thesis 1; for part of the expression to be defined (namely, the combination of quotation-marks and the phrase is 'true') *disappears* in the definiens without being re-

[7] Cf. M. Black, expounding and criticising Tarski, *Analysis*, Vol. 8.

placed by anything else. (How odd it is, incidentally, to call this definition-by-disappearance 'definition'!). In this way, the view that 'true' is assertively redundant is represented as somehow combined with, and dependent upon, the view that 'true' is a meta-linguistic predicate of sentences. We may express, then, the main contention of the semantic theory as follows: to say that a statement is true is not to say something further *about the subject-matter* of the statement, but is to say the same thing about the subject-matter of the statement, *by means of a further statement, namely a statement about a sentence.* Now I said that Thesis 1 is true. A fortiori, a modification of Thesis 1 is true, which I shall call Thesis 1A, and which runs as follows:

To say that a statement is true is not to say something further about the subject-matter of the statement, but, in so far as it is to say anything about that subject-matter, is to say the same thing about it.

Now Thesis 1A, but not Thesis 1, is compatible with Thesis 2. The semantic theory consists in the joint assertion of 1A and 2. I suggest that the semantic theory borrows a lot of its plausibility from the truth of 1A. We swallow 2 for the sake of 1A. I now wish to show that the unmodified Thesis 1 is true, and that we therefore can and must assert 1A while rejecting 2 and, therefore, rejecting the semantic theory.

As for the muddle I have described above—the muddle of reading a degenerate case of contingent statements meta-linguistically employing the phrase *is true if and only if*, as a pseudo-defining-formula of which the definiendum consists of a quoted sentence followed by the phrase *is true*—I do not claim that this muddle represents the genesis of the semantic theory; but I do think that it, too, may have contributed to the plausibility of the theory.

III

The best way of showing that Thesis 1 is true is to correct its inadequacy. The best way of correcting its inadequacy is to discover the further reasons which have led to Thesis 2. To bring out those features of the situation which lead to the mistake of saying that the word 'true' is used meta-linguistically (to talk about sentences), I want first to compare the use of 'true' with that of 'Yes'. If you and I have been sitting together in silence for some time, and I suddenly say 'Yes', you would, perhaps, look at me with surprise and answer "I didn't say anything". Of course, a man may say 'Yes' to himself; and this will be a sign that he has resolved a doubt in his own mind, or come to a decision. But the normal use of 'Yes' is to answer: and where no question is asked, no answer can be given. Suppose you now ask: "Was Jones there?" and I say 'Yes'; there seems no temptation whatever to say that, in so answering, I am *talking about* the English sentence "Was Jones there?" So, in the case of 'Yes', we have a word of which the normal use requires some linguistic occasion (a question), without there being any temptation at all to say that it is used to *talk about* the sentence of which the utterance is the occasion for its use. There is indeed a temptation to go further in the oppo-

site direction and say that in answering 'Yes' I am not talking *about* anything, not making any assertion, at all; but simply answering. In a way this is correct; but in a way, it's wrong. For it would be perfectly correct for you, reporting our dialogue, to say of me: "He said Jones was there". So of the ordinary use of 'Yes', we may say: first, that it demands a linguistic occasion, namely the asking of a question; second, that it is not used meta-linguistically, to talk about the question, but to answer it; third, that in so far as we are making an assertion at all in using it, the content of the assertion is the same as the content of the question. Now imagine a possible, and perhaps vulgarly current, use of the expression 'Ditto'. You make an assertion, and I say 'Ditto'. In so far as I assert anything, talk about anything, I talk about and assert what you talk about and assert. Of course—and this points to the inadequacy of Thesis 1 and the reason for the meta-linguistic error—to say 'Ditto' is not *the same as* to make the statement in question; for, whereas I might have made the statement before anyone else had spoken, it would be meaningless for me to say 'Ditto' before anyone else had spoken. 'Ditto', like 'Yes', requires a linguistic occasion. But again, and largely, I think, because the expression 'Ditto' does not consist of a grammatical subject and grammatical predicate, there is absolutely no temptation to say that in thus using 'Ditto', I should be talking *about the sentence* you used, and the utterance of which was the linguistic occasion for my use of this expression. I am not talking about what you said (the noise you made, or the sentence you spoke, or the proposition you expressed). I am agreeing with, endorsing, underwriting what you said; and, unless you had said something, I couldn't perform *these* activities, though I could *make the assertion* you made. Now the expression 'That's true' sometimes functions in just the way in which I have suggested the expression 'Ditto' might function. A says "Jones was there" and B says 'that's true'; and C, reporting the conversation, can correctly say: "Both A and B said that Jones was there". But the point is that B couldn't have said that Jones was there in the way he *did* say it, (i.e. by the use of the expression 'That's true'), unless A had previously uttered the *sentence* "Jones was there", or some equivalent sentence. It is, perhaps, *this* fact about the use (*this* use) of the word 'true', together with the old prejudice that any indicative sentence must describe (be 'about') something, which encourages those who have become chary of saying that truth is a property of propositions to say instead that in using the word 'true', we are talking about sentences. (What I have said about the use of 'That's true' applies, of course, with suitable alterations, to the use of 'That's false').

Now those who assert that 'true' is a predicate of sentences have not, in general, considered these simple cases of the use of 'true' (and 'false'), but the more puzzling cases which lead, or seem to lead, to paradoxes: such as the case where someone utters the isolated sentence "What I am saying now is false", or writes on an otherwise clean blackboard the sentence "Every statement on this blackboard is false". The solution on meta-linguistic lines is to treat these sentences as making statements of the second order to the effect:

(1) that there is some statement of the first order written on the blackboard (or said by me now); and

(2) that any first-order statement written on the blackboard (or said by me now) is false.

By means of this distinction of orders, the distinction between meta- and object-language, the puzzling sentences are said no longer to engender contradictions: either they are simply false, since the existential part of what they assert is false; or, alternatively, leaving out the existential part of the analysis, and treating them solely as hypotheticals, they are seen to be vacuously true, since no first-order statements occur. This solution is formally successful in avoiding the apparent contradictions. But it seems to me to achieve this success only by repeating the fundamental mistake from which the contradictions themselves arise, and also, and consequently, involving the difficulties mentioned at the beginning of this paper. That is, first, it involves the view that to say that a statement is true (or false) is to make a further, second-order, statement (thus contradicting Thesis 1); and, second, it (usually) involves the unplausibility of saying that this second-order statement is *about* a sentence or sentences. Now the point of the previous discussion of the actual use of 'Yes', the possible use of 'Ditto' and the actual use of 'That's true' is to show that these expedients are unnecessary. When no-one has spoken, and I say 'Ditto', I am not making a false statement to the effect that something true has been said, nor a true statement to the effect that nothing false has been said. I am not making a statement at all; but producing a pointless utterance. When somebody has made an assertion previously, my saying 'Ditto' acquires a point, has an occasion: and, if you like, you may say that I am now making a statement, repeating, in a manner, what the speaker said. But I am not making an additional statement, a meta-statement. It would perhaps be better to say that my utterance is not a statement at all, but a linguistic performance for which in the first case there was not, and in the second case there was, an occasion: so that in the first case it was a spurious, and in the second case a genuine, performance. Similarly, the words 'true' and 'false' normally require, as an occasion for their significant use, that somebody should have made, be making or be about to make (utter or write), some statement. (The making of the statement needs not precede the use of 'true': it may follow it as in the case of the expression "It is true that . . ."—a form of words I shall discuss later.) But in all cases the indicative clause of which the grammatical predicate is the phrase 'is true' does not in itself make any kind of statement at all (not even a meta-statement), and *a fortiori* cannot make the statement, the making of which is required as the occasion for the significant use of the words 'true' or 'false'. This is not, as it stands, quite accurate. For an indicative sentence of which the grammatical predicate is the phrase 'is true' may sometimes, as I shall shortly show, be used to make an implicit meta-statement. But when this is so, the phrase 'is true' plays no part in the making of this meta-statement. The phrase 'is true' *never* has a statement-making role. And when this is

seen, the paradoxes vanish without the need for the meta-linguistic machinery; or at least without the need for regarding the words 'true' and 'false' as part of that machinery. The paradoxes arise on the assumption that the words 'true' and 'false' can be used to make first-order assertions. They are formally solved by the declaration that these words can be used only to make second-order assertions. Both paradoxes and solution disappear on the more radical assumption that they are not used to make assertions of any order, are not used to make assertions at all.

I said, however, that indicative sentences of which the grammatical predicate is the phrase 'is true' or the phrase 'is false' may be used to make an implicit meta-statement, in the making of which these phrases themselves play no part. To elucidate this, consider the following sentences:

(1) What I am saying now is false.

(2) All statements made in English are false.

(3) What the policeman said is true.

It is certainly not incorrect to regard each of these sentences as implicitly making an *existential* meta-statement, which does not involve the words 'true' or 'false'. The implicit meta-statements in these cases might be written as follows:

(1a) I have just made (am about to make) a statement.

(2a) Some statements are made in English.

(3a) The policeman made a statement.

These are all second-order assertive sentences to the effect that there are some first-order assertive sentences, uttered (*a*) by me, (*b*) in English, (*c*) by the policeman.

These second-order assertive sentences we can regard as part of the analysis of the sentences (1), (2) and (3).[8] Obviously they are not the whole of their analysis. The sentence "The policeman made a statement" clearly has not the same use as the sentence "What the policeman said is true". To utter the second is to do something more than to assert the first. What is this additional performance? Consider the circumstances in which we might use the expression "What the policeman said is true". Instead of using this expression, I might have *repeated* the policeman's story. In this case, I shall be said to have *confirmed* what the policeman said. I might, however, have made exactly the same set of statements as I made in repeating his story, but have made them *before* the policeman spoke. In this case, though the assertions I have made are no different, I have not done what I did in the other case, namely 'confirmed his story'. So to confirm his story is not to say anything further, *about* his story, or the sentences he used in telling it, though it is to do something that cannot be done unless he has told his story. Now, unlike the confirming narrative which I might have told, the sentence "What the policeman said is true" has no use *except* to confirm the policeman's story;[9] but like the confirming narrative, the sentence does not say anything further *about* the policeman's story or the sentences he used in telling it. It is a device for confirming the story without telling it again. So, in general, in using such expressions, we are confirming, underwriting, admitting, agreeing with, what somebody has said; but (except where we are implicitly making an existential meta-statement, in making which the phrase 'is true' plays no part), we are not making any assertion additional to theirs; and are *never* using 'is true' to talk *about* something which is *what they said*, or the sentences they used in saying it. To complete the analysis, then, of the entire sentence (3) "What the policeman said is true", we have to add, to the existential meta-assertion, a phrase which is not assertive, but (if I may borrow Mr. Austin's word) performatory.[10] We might, e.g., offer, as a complete analysis of one case, the expression: "The policeman made a statement. I confirm it"; where, in uttering the words "I confirm it", I am not describing something I do, but *doing* something.[11] There is, then, a difference between the more complicated cases in which the phrase 'is true' is preceded by a descriptive phrase, and

---

[8] [I should now say, not that sentences (1a)—(3a) are parts of the analyses of sentences (1)—(3), but that any statements made by the use of sentences (1)—(3) would presuppose the truth of statements which might be made by the use of sentences (1a)—(3a).]

[9] This needs qualification. Uttered by a witness, the sentence is a *confirmation*; wrung from the culprit, it is an *admission*. No doubt there are other cases.

[10] Cf. J. L. Austin, 'Other Minds', P.S.A. Supp. Vol. XX, pp. 169–175 for an account of some words of this class.

[11] Cf. also 'I admit it'. To *say* this *is* to make an admission.

the simpler sentences (e.g. 'That's true') in which the phrase 'is true' is preceded by a demonstrative. The former may be regarded as involving an implicit meta-statement, while the latter are purely confirmatory (or purely 'admissive'). But in neither sort of case has the phrase 'is true' any assertive (or meta-assertive) function.

There may still be some uneasiness felt at the denial that the phrase 'is true' has any assertive, or descriptive, function. Partially to allay this uneasiness, I will again say something familiar, that I have said already: that is, that when I say 'That's true' in response to your statement, I am in a manner making an assertion, namely the assertion you made; describing something, namely what you described. But pointing this out is quite consistent with saying that 'That's true' makes no statement in its own right. It makes no meta-statement. If there is any residual uneasiness, it ought not to be allayed. For its source is the ancient prejudice that any indicative sentence is, or makes,[12] a statement. I call it a prejudice: we could, instead, make it a criterion. And there would even be no harm in adopting this criterion for 'statement', if we could simultaneously divorce the word, in this strictly grammatical use, from its logic in other uses: from that logic which leads us, given a 'statement', to enquire: What is it about? What does it describe? What property, or what relation, does it assert to belong to, or hold

between, what entity or entities? Asking these questions when confronted with such a sentence as "What Pascal said is true", we are led to look for the entity which is *what Pascal said*; looking with cautious, contemporary eyes, we find only his words; and so are induced to say that, in using this expression, we are talking about the French sentences he wrote or spoke. It is, then, the out-of-date desire that the phrase 'is true' should be some kind of a descriptive phrase, that leads to the up-to-date suggestion that the word 'true' is a second-level predicate of first-level sentences. More important than simply to reject *this* view is to have the right reason for rejecting it: the reason, namely, that the phrase 'is true' is not descriptive at all. If we persist that it describes (is about) something, while denying that it describes (is about) sentences, we shall be left with the old, general questions about the nature of, and tests for, truth, about the nature of the entities related by the truth-relation, and so on. Better than asking "What is the criterion of truth?" is to ask: "What are the grounds for agreement?"—for those we see to be not less various than the subjects on which an agreed opinion can be reached. And this will perhaps also discourage us from seeking to mark the difference between one kind of utterance and another by saying, for example, "Ethical utterances are not true or false". It is correct to say that utterances of any kind are true or false, if it is correct usage to signify agreement or disagreement with such utterances by means of the *expressions* 'true' or 'false'.

Of course, the formula that I have

---

[12] Throughout I have used such mild barbarisms as "this sentence makes a statement" as shorthand for such expressions as "Anyone who uttered this sentence would be making a statement".

adopted in the discussion of one use of 'true' is not immune from another variant of that argument from grammar which leads to treating 'true' as a descriptive word. Someone might say: in order for you to *confirm* anything, there must be some *object* of this activity; a sentence or a proposition: and to perform this activity upon this object is nothing other than to assert that the object has the property, stands in the relation, referred to by the word 'true'. Anyone who says this is misled partly by the fact that the verb 'confirm' takes a grammatical object; and partly by the fact that the linguistic performance (of 'confirming') requires, not an object, but an *occasion*—a fact which I declared to be the misunderstood element of truth in the semantic theory. Even this assertion—that there must be, or be thought to be, some kind of sign-occasion for the significant, or genuine, use of the word 'true'—is not quite correct, if it means that some spoken or written utterance must occur, or be thought to occur. For it would not be incorrect, though it would be unusual, to say: "What you are thinking is true"; when nothing has been said. (But, then, a conversation *can* be carried on by glances and nods).

IV

In philosophical discussion of this whole subject, very little attention has been paid to the actual use of 'true'. And I want to conclude by distinguishing some of its normal uses in a little more detail. The uses mentioned so far I was tempted to call 'performatory'.

But this is a misnomer. A performatory word, in Austin's sense, I take to be a verb, the use of which, in the first person present indicative, seems to describe some activity of the speaker, but in fact *is* that activity. Clearly the use of 'is true' does not seem to describe any activity of the speaker; it *has seemed* to describe a sentence, a proposition, or statement. The point of using Austin's word at all is the fact that the phrase 'is true' can sometimes be replaced,[13] without any important change in meaning, by some such phrase as "I confirm it", which is performatory in the strict sense. I shall take the substitute performatory word as a title for each of these cases; and shall speak, e.g., of the 'confirmatory' or 'admissive' use of 'true'. What commends the word as, e.g., a confirmatory device is its economy. By its means we can confirm without repeating.

The word has other, equally non-descriptive, uses. A familiar one is its use in sentences which begin with the phrase "It's true that", followed by a clause, followed by the word 'but', followed by another clause. The words "It's true that . . . but . . ." could, in these sentences, be replaced by the word 'Although'; or, alternatively, by the words "I concede that . . . but . . ." This use of the phrase, then, is concessive. The inappropriateness of the meta-linguistic treatment seems peculiarly apparent here.

The purely confirmatory use is probably no more common than other uses which look much the same, but which

---

[13] Of course, not *simply* replaced. Other verbal changes would be necessary.

are, I think, distinct. A man may make an assertion to you, not wanting you to confirm it, to remove the doubt of others or his own; but wanting to know that you share his belief, or his attitude. If, in this case, you say 'That's true', you are not *saying*, but *indicating*, that you do share his belief. It seems to me natural to describe this simply as 'agreeing'. Again, it seems to me that we very often use the phrase 'that's true' to express, not only agreement with what is said, but also our sense of its novelty and force. We register the impact of what is said, much as we might register it by saying: "I never thought of that". Contrast the ironical 'very true' with which we sometimes rudely greet the obvious. The use of 'true' here is effectively ironical just because we normally use it to express agreement when our agreement is in doubt, or to register a sense of revelation. Sometimes, in sentences beginning "Is it true that . . . ?" or "So it's true that . . .", we could preserve the expressive quality of the utterance by substituting the adverb 'really' for the quoted phrases, at an appropriate point in the sentence; to convey, as they do, incredulity or surprise.

No doubt, the word has other functions; but those I have mentioned are probably as common as any. The important point is that the performance of these functions (and, I suspect, of all other non-technical jobs the word may do) does not involve the use of a metalinguistic predicate; and that we *could*, with no very great violence to our language, perform them without the need for any expression which *seems* (as 'is true' seems) to make a statement. For instance, the substitution of 'although' for "It's true that . . . but . . ." is an obvious way of dealing with the concessive use; an extension of the practice of the inarticulate election-candidate whose speech consisted of "Ditto to Mr. X" might deal with the confirmatory and, partly, with the expressive uses; and so on. The selection of the substitute-expressions would of course be governed by the propagandist consideration that they should provide the minimum encouragement to anyone anxious to mistake them for statement-making phrases, or descriptive words.

One last point: a suggestion on the reasons why the puzzle about truth has commonly got entangled with the puzzle about certainty. It is above all when a doubt has been raised, when mistakes or deceit seem possible; when the need for confirmation is felt; that we tend to make use of those certifying words of which 'true' is one and of which others are 'certain', 'know', 'prove', 'establish', 'validate', 'confirm', 'evidence' and so on. So that the question "What is the nature of truth?" leads naturally to the question "What are the tests for truth?", and this, in its turn, to the question "What are the conditions of certainty?" The historical or judicial search for truth is the search for the evidence which will set doubt at rest. The philosophical endeavor to characterise truth *in general* has tended to become the endeavour to characterise that which *in general* sets doubt at rest; really and finally at rest. Where you find the indubitable, there you find the true. And this metaphysical road branches into different paths, at the end of one of which you find the Atomic Fact, and, at the end of another, the Absolute.

Finally, I will repeat that in saying that the word 'true' has not in itself any assertive function, I am not of course saying that a sentence like "His state-ment is true" is incorrect. Of course the word 'statement' may be the gram-matical subject of a sentence of which the phrase 'is true' is the grammatical predicate. Nor am I recommending that we drop this usage. But for the usage, there would be no problem.

A PROBLEM
ABOUT TRUTH

7.3

G. J. Warnock

1. The problem to which this paper[1] is addressed is a quite narrowly limited one: and it can be stated—though not, I think, solved—very briefly indeed. When somebody says something and we say 'That's true,' do we therein make some statement about a statement, some assertion about an assertion? Do we say something *about* what he has said? If we do, there may arise the question what the statement or assertion so made may mean: I shall allude to this ques-tion too, though only very sketchily.

This problem is one of the matters—there were several others—on which Austin and Strawson found themselves in disagreement in their papers in the symposium *Truth* in 1950 (*Proceedings of the Aristotelian Society*, Supp. Vol. XXIV).[2] It will be convenient to take the relevant parts of that important dis-cussion as a text from which to begin.

I should mention, perhaps, that I shall not discuss the view, which has had distinguished sponsors, that to say

From *Truth*, George Pitcher, editor (Engle-wood Cliffs, N.J.: Prentice-Hall, 1964). Re-printed by permission of the publisher and the author.

[1] This is a rewritten and somewhat short-ened version of a paper which I read first at Princeton in April 1962, and subsequently at several other places. I suspect that I have incorporated in this revised version several points which I owe to discussion with others (and no doubt I ought to have incorpo-rated more): but, memory being both fallible and fragmentary, I cannot now do more than extend a general, though grateful, ac-knowledgement to those concerned.

[2] See George Pitcher (ed.), *Truth* (Engle-wood Cliffs, 1964), pp. 18ff.

that something is true is to make an assertion about a sentence. Both Austin
and Strawson took this view to be fairly
obviously wrong, at least when the use
of a natural language is in question.
What can properly be said to be true or
false is not a sentence itself, but rather
what is, on this occasion or that, asserted, stated, said by one who utters a
sentence—not the sentence he utters,
but the statement he makes. This is
surely correct.

2. The relevant part of Austin's account—which he took to be, so far as it
goes, so obvious as to be practically
truistic—was this.[3] Words, we may say
generally and doubtless somewhat
vaguely, are used among other things in
speaking about the world, among other
things in making statements about it.
For this purpose, and not bringing in
more complexities than are needed for
the matter in hand, there must be 'two
sets of conventions': (a) *descriptive*
conventions correlating some words in
language with 'types' of situations or
states of affairs to be found in the
world; and (b) *demonstrative* conventions correlating words as uttered on
particular occasions with 'historic' situations or states of affairs to be found, at
particular though not necessarily
closely circumscribed times and/or places
in the world. 'A statement is said
to be true when the historic state of
affairs to which it is correlated by the
demonstrative conventions (the one to
which it 'refers') is of a type with which
the sentence used in making it is correlated by the descriptive conventions.'

_____
[3] See *ibid.*, pp. 21ff.

Now if the statement that S is true,
then the statement that the statement
that S is true is certainly itself true, and
conversely: but, Austin holds, it is not
the case, for this or any other reason,
that the predicative phrase 'is true' is,
as some have argued, 'logically superfluous,' or that to say that a statement is
true is not to make any further assertion at all—any assertion, that is, other
than that made by the statement itself.
For (among other things) the statement that the statement that S is true is,
as the statement that S usually will not
be, about a statement, and in particular
about the statement that S: it is therefore not the same statement as the
statement that S, notwithstanding their
—of course inevitable—linkage of truth-
values and the fact that no doubt, in
some sense or other, they convey just
the same information about 'the world.'
Austin's concluson, perhaps not quite
explicit but I think quite definite, is
that the statement that the statement
that S is true can be said to state, to
mean, that the words uttered (if they
were actully uttered) in making the
statement that S are correlated by demonstrative conventions with a 'historic'
situation or state of affairs which is of
the 'type' with which the sentence used
(if it was actually used) in making that
statement is correlated by descriptive
conventions. (The point of the parentheses is to allow for the fact that, for
the statement that S to be said to be
true, it is not strictly necessary that the
statement that S should actually have
been made. It may also be noted that
this account is quite consistent with the
fact that the statement that S may be
made at different times and places, by

different people, and in different words.) As Austin puts it in conclusion: "If it is admitted that the rather boring yet satisfactory relation between words and world which has here been discussed does genuinely occur, why should the phrase 'is true' not be our way of describing it? And if it is not, what else is?"

To this, that part of Strawson's reply which I wish to discuss runs as follows. Let us allow—though in fact he has substantial reservations of detail—that, when a true statement is made, certain words are in fact related to the world in the ways Austin describes. It is nevertheless completely mistaken, a mistake in principle, to suppose that one who says that a statement is true means, or asserts, that the words are thus related to the world, that he is stating this *about* the statement made. Austin has answered (perhaps and up to a point) the question *when*, in what circumstances or conditions, we use the phrase 'is true'; but he is quite wrong in assuming, as he evidently does, that this answers the question *how* we use it. And in fact, if we consider realistically the question how we use it, we see that we use it in a quite wide variety of ways —in expressing agreement or assent, for instance, in accepting, admitting, corroborating, endorsing, conceding, or confirming what is or might be said. Such a remark as 'That's true' is perhaps, in some bald and uninteresting grammatical sense, 'about' a statement: but its actual use is not significantly different from that of other such agreement-expressing devices as 'Yes,' 'I quite agree,' 'You're right,' or even a nod of the head—none of which, of course, could be supposed for a moment to be employed in making a statement about a statement, or an assertion about the relations of certain words to the world. All these locutions and devices are appropriately used *when* a statement has been made; but it is quite wrong to suppose that any is genuinely used to say something *about* the statement.

3. In his paper, and particularly in this part of his paper, Strawson has been taken by some to be propounding what I have heard called 'the performative theory of truth': but I think it is clear that what he says neither deserves, nor surely claims, any such title. It is indeed by no means perfectly clear what a 'theory of truth' is, what is sought to be achieved by the construction of a theory so-called: but it is sufficiently clear, I believe, that Strawson has not constructed one. For a 'theory of truth' would presumably have to aspire to throw some sort of light on contexts in general in which 'true' or 'truth' might occur, or in which questions of truth or falsehood might arise: whereas Strawson's observations, as they stand, could have application only to occurrences of 'true' as a predicate in indicative sentences whose grammatical subjects refer, in one way or another, to statements. The word 'true' may also occur in, for instance, interrogative or optative or conditional sentences; and whatever its 'performative' function in such settings may be, it can scarcely be that of expressing agreement (etc.). The fact is, I take it, that just as Austin had addressed himself primarily to the particular case in which some statement,

what someone says, is (indicatively) said to be true, so Strawson does not attempt to describe quite in general how we use the *word* 'true'; he accepts in effect a similar restriction, to uses of the *phrase* 'is true' as a predicate in indicative sentences. It would in fact be perfectly reasonable to suppose that these uses are fundamental; and in any case, even if such a relatively restricted discussion can scarcely issue in so high-sounding a thing as a 'theory of truth,' there is probably no harm in accepting the restriction.

We have to consider, then, these sharply different and seemingly conflicting accounts of such a locution as, for instance, 'That's true.' And first of all it is necessary to raise the question whether they actually are conflicting. It has been, I think, much too easily taken for granted that they are.

With Strawson's view that to say 'That's true' may be, for instance, to express agreement with what someone has said, it is, of course, impossible to disagree: it is quite obvious that that is so, that this is at least one of the ways in which 'is true' is used. But does it follow that to say 'That's true' is not to make a statement *about* what someone has said? Plainly not. For just as I may, say, insult or express hostility to someone by making about him the statement that he is a fool, so surely I might express agreement with what someone has said by making about what he has said the statement that it is true. Agreeing, endorsing, etc., surely do not, any more than criticizing, insulting, etc., exclude the making of a statement: for they may all be done *by* the making of a statement. Again, if someone were to say, correctly, that the

phrase 'is a fool' is often used to criticize, belittle, denigrate, or insult the person of whom it is predicated, it is plain that he would not have offered an answer to the question what the phrase 'is a fool' *means:* and similarly, it would seem that one who says, correctly, that 'is true' is often used to indicate the speaker's agreement has offered no answer to the quite different question, what the words 'is true' mean.

Thus, from the fact that Strawson is most undoubtedly correct in saying that the phrase 'is true' is used—as are several other equally handy expressions—to express agreement, to accept, confirm, corroborate, etc., it does not follow *either* that to say 'That's true' is not to make a statement about a statement, *or* that there may not well arise the, as yet quite unanswered, question what the meaning of the phrase 'is true' may be. Thus, for holding that Austin is mistaken 'in principle' in supposing that 'is true' is a predicative phrase commonly employed in making statements about statements, and that its meaning is to be elucidated in terms of some relation between words and world, some quite other ground is required than merely that Strawson is correct in saying that the phrase is used, as are others, in for instance expressing agreement. It is really pretty plain that Austin was not attempting to deny this fact and had not overlooked it, but supposed that it left entirely untouched those different issues with which he himself was primarily concerned: and this supposition looks, on the face of it, entirely reasonable.

4. If then one must find, as I think one obviously must, some other ground

for the view that Austin's account is in principle a mistaken one, what other ground might one adduce? I think that what Strawson's argument requires, and what in some measure his paper actually contains, is an attempt to assimilate 'the use' of the locution 'That's true' to the use of such other locutions as 'Yes,' 'You're right,' 'I quite agree,' and so on—an attempt, that is, to show that while the locution 'That's true' has, as it has undeniably, the grammatical air of a statement-making locution, this air is not to be taken seriously as a guide to its 'use.' This might run somewhat as follows:

Suppose that it is raining heavily, and that persons A, B, C, D, and E can see that it is: and suppose that A makes the statement that it's raining heavily. B then says 'Yes': C says 'It is indeed': D says 'I quite agree': and E says 'That's true.' Now certainly the responses of B, C, D, and E are verbally diverse; 'Yes,' I dare say, is not a sentence at all, and the other three sentences have quite different subjects and predicates. But—Strawson might argue —would it not be scholastic and indeed misguided to attach much significance to this verbal diversity? For surely what B, C, D, and E have in mind in responding to A's observation, what they wish to convey, what they are up to, their point, is in each case exactly the same—namely, they wish simply to indicate their agreement with or acceptance of A's remark about the state of the weather. Now it is quite plain that to say 'Yes' or 'It is indeed' or 'I quite agree' is not to make a statement about a statement; and it is no less plain that to say 'That's true' is, in intention and general effect, equivalent

to, a mere conversational variant upon, saying 'Yes' or 'It is indeed' or 'I quite agree.' But if so, to hold, as Austin evidently does, that to say 'That's true' is something quite different in character and meaning from saying any of these other things, is surely to attach excessive weight to, and so to be led astray by, mere surface grammar. The *use* of these locutions, which is what really counts, is exactly the same; and there is no more reason seriously to suppose that one who says 'That's true' is making a statement about a statement than there would be to suppose this of one who says 'So it is.' The fact is simply that both, in verbally diverse formulas, would be (for instance) expressing their agreement with what was said.

This, I think, is not unpersuasive. It seems indeed pretty undeniable that one who says conversationally 'That's true' will often mean nothing more than, at any rate in the sense that he has in mind nothing different from, one who may say, for instance, 'I agree.' But here there naturally arises a question: how does it come about, one may well wish to ask, that we should have available for the single purpose of, say, expressing agreement, this rather large number of verbally diverse formulas? If, as the view just outlined evidently implies, their verbal diversity is of no serious significance, does it not seem that we are confronted here with a curious kind of linguistic superabundance, a surprising superfluity of ways of doing just the same thing? How is such linguistic prodigality to be accounted for?

Now surely an explanation of this circumstance comes readily to mind. It must be remembered that although, of course, we speak for the most part with the effortless ease born of years of practice, in fact the making of even a quite simple statement is a performance of some considerable complexity. In saying to me truly, for instance, 'It's raining heavily,' you have, intending to comment on current weather conditions in our vicinity, correctly produced exactly that utterance best adapted in our common language to this very purpose: you have not only successfully drawn my attention to the place and time intended, but have also characterized correctly the relevant aspect or feature of what is going on there and then. Now suppose that, on observing your performance, I wish to express no dissent, that I have no criticism to offer of any of the several aspects of your complex undertaking. Well, there is a simple formula available to me, specially designed for letting you know in a single word of my nondissent; I can say 'Yes.' More formally, but just as well, I can indicate my nondissent in the formula 'I quite agree.' Alternatively, I can as it were commend you for your faultless performance and the correctness of your views; I can say 'You're right.' Or again, concentrating on the point that the state of the weather in our vicinity is indeed just as you say it is, I can respond with 'It is indeed.' But there is yet one further possibility; I can, not directly alluding to you, to your performance, or to the weather, advert to the point that what was said by you in uttering the words you uttered was, as these matters are conventionally understood, such as to designate a particular state of the weather which is further, as these matters are conventionally understood, of just that type for the characterization of which the words used were perfectly appropriate. I can, in short, say 'That's true.'

Now are all these verbally diverse responses 'used in the same way'? Well, in a sense no doubt they are. They all have the same general object and serve the same purpose; for they all serve to let you know of my total nondissent. Whichever of these things I choose, or more probably just happen, to come out with, you know that I am with you on the question of what the state of the weather is. Are they then indistinguishable (except trivially, as words)? Surely not. For is it not evident that, notwithstanding their identity of general object, they achieve this single object in quite different ways, by responding to or commenting on different parts, features, or aspects of the whole rather complex performance of stating truly that it's raining heavily? The reason why there are many ways of doing just the same thing, of achieving just the same general object, is that the making of a statement has many sides to it; there are many points at which, and hence many devices by which, our nondissent (or of course our dissent) may be indicated. But if so, does it not seem perfectly evident that what distinguishes 'That's true' from the rest is that it, and it alone, says something *about* what the speaker said, *about* the statement he made? 'Yes' does no such thing, nor yet do 'I agree' and 'You're right': these serve the purpose every bit as well, but not in the same say. Just so I may, say, congratulate an orator by saying 'I congratulate you' or 'That was an excellent speech': and the fact that in either case I congratulate the orator does not imply that these remarks are not significantly distinguishable, or that the second does not differ from the first by being, among other things, *about* the speech that he made.

5. This might be objected to. It might be held, with some justice, that a certain air of artificiality attaches to the above discussion of diverse responses to 'It's raining heavily.' Can it seriously be suggested that, for instance, one who says 'You're right' conceives himself to be, has in mind that he is, saying something about the speaker, as distinguished from one who, in saying 'That's true,' says something about what the speaker said, or from one who, in saying 'I agree,' says nothing about either? No such distinctions, surely, are in any degree likely to be in such a speaker's mind. What was called the 'general object' of all the responses considered—namely, indication of agreement with what the first speaker said—is likely to be *all* that respondents in such a case have in mind. But if so, what serious sense can be attached to the claim that one who happens to say 'That's true' is to be *distinguished* as therein making a statement about what was said?

But this objection, I believe, rests too much weight on the question of what speakers may have in mind, on what they may consciously conceive themselves to be doing, and correspondingly too little on what may be called the mechanism of language itself. Wittgenstein in particular laid great and justi-fied stress on the idea that the understanding of an expression, the grasp of what (in one sense at least) it means, does not particularly require, and may even be obstructed by, attention to what passes in the mind of one who uses it when he does so. Similarly, I think, the question of what a speaker is doing in speaking—a question, we may note, that in most cases can be taken and answered in several different ways—is not to be conclusively answered by reference to what he conceives himself to be doing, or to what he has it in mind to do. One thing that a speaker does who says 'It's raining heavily' is, for instance, to utter a sentence in grammatical English, and this may even be essential to his being understood by his hearers: but is it likely that, and does it at all matter whether, the notion of uttering a sentence in grammatical English was ever actually in his mind?

Or consider an example somewhat closer to the question now at issue. In certain circles, in certain parts of the world, agreement with statements made is not uncommonly expressed in the colloquial formula 'You can say that again'; and it may well be the case that one who utters these words will, if this idiom is very familiar to him, have nothing whatever in mind in uttering them but the intention of indicating his agreement with what has been said. Nevertheless, it is surely undeniable that what the words actually mean is that the person addressed has leave, or is at liberty, to repeat the observation he has just made: and to utter the words is to tell him that this is so. Could we not hold then, somewhat analogously, that whereas Strawson probably describes correctly enough what ordinary users of the words 'That's true' very often, or typically, have in mind in using them, Austin is not thereby any less entitled to offer his observations in answer to two quite different questions—first, what the words 'That's true' actually mean, and second, what speech-act is standardly performed in uttering those words?

This looks well enough, perhaps; and it has about it a pleasingly pacificatory air; but it is not yet, I think, quite plain sailing. It might be urged, for instance, that I have just appealed to a misleading analogy. It is certainly a feature of the case just cited that, while the words 'You can say that again' colloquially have, in certain circles, this mere agreement-indicating role, the same words may and no doubt often do occur in quite other contexts. A colleague confides to me, for example, that he made a very gratifying impression in his lectures last term with the remark 'Santayana was the Puccini of philosophy': how, he asks me, can he enjoy a similar success this term? I, knowing perhaps that few people attend my colleague's lectures more than once, might then quite naturally point out the path to another triumph by saying 'You can say that again': and here, while not necessarily endorsing his rather complex assessment of Santayana, I do literally tell him that it is open to him to repeat the dictum in question. But did the plausibility of our distinction between what the speaker has in mind in speaking, and the meaning of his words or the nature of the speech-act performed, not derive perhaps from this undoubted distinction between colloquial and

standard uses of 'You can say that again'? If these words had occurred *only* in their agreement-indicating role, it would surely have been scarcely possible to distinguish *from* this the meaning of the words, or what is done by one who utters them. What then of the locution 'That's true'? Is this properly analogous with 'You can say that again'?

Well, the answer seems clearly to be that the analogy is not perfect: but the respect in which it fails tends, I believe, substantially to strengthen Austin's case. The words 'You can say that again,' we said, have a *colloquial* role, namely as a mere indication of the speaker's agreement: this is colloquial —or perhaps idiomatic?—in the sense that this role for the words in question is not a mere standard function of their standard meanings, or a standard extension of their standard uses: a foreigner, for instance, well schooled in classical English, would probably not be able straight off to construe their utterance correctly. The locution 'That's true' is certainly not in this position: for it is in no way at all, of course, colloquial or idiomatic. But this is to say—and this begins to seem perfectly obvious—that the use of those words to express agreement (etc.) *is* an entirely standard function of their standard meaning: that, in fact, the reason why one who says 'That's true' can be taken to have expressed his agreement with what was said, is simply that he has said *about* what was said that it is true, and to say this about what was said can be, simply in virtue of what the word 'true' standardly means, to express agreement with it. Whereas, in the case of the words 'You can say that again,' we found a (colloquial) agreement-indicating role and *also* a standard use of the words to tell somebody something, we seem to find, in the case of 'that's true,' a (noncolloquial) agreement-indicating role *because of* what is meant by the words and done by one who utters them. But if so, some such account of them as Austin offers appears not as an incompatible rival to, but rather as the essential underlying rationale of, such an account as Strawson's. It is precisely *because,* as Austin says, one who says 'That's true' therein makes a certain statement about a statement that, as Strawson says, he thereby expresses (for instance) his agreement with it.

At the same time, it would, no doubt, be most ill-advised to offer 'That's true' as a central or ideal instance of statement-making. For one thing, it has the peculiarity that it will often, perhaps more often than not, be addressed to someone who already knows or believes it, and has indeed, by making the statement referred to, given recent evidence of his knowledge or belief. The statement 'That's true' will only convey to the person to whom it is addressed information about its subject matter if that person either did not make, and did not know to be true, the statement referred to, or—a queer case—made the statement but did not know whether it was true or not. Thus the dialectical function, so to speak, of the utterance 'That's true' is somewhat peculiar: it will not usually be primarily to convey what it actually states, but rather to convey what its making incidentally implies—namely, that the utterer believes, accepts, agrees with (etc.) the statement which his utterance is about. For this

same reason it is also the case, no doubt, that one who makes the statement 'That's true' will often not have *particularly* in mind the idea that he is making a statement at all: the point of his statement will be primarily to convey his agreement (etc.), and that he is doing this may well be all that he has in mind. However, although such considerations as these well warrant the conclusion that the utterance 'That's true' is a somewhat unideal specimen of statementmaking, they do not seem to me to be adequate grounds for the denial that it is a case of statement-making at all.

6. This conclusion can now be reinforced, I believe, if we reconsider the matter of 'the use' of such verbally diverse locutions as 'Yes,' 'I quite agree,' 'You're right,' 'That's true,' and so on. Now it is certainly the case, as Strawson insists, that there are contexts in which any of these could be used indifferently: if, for instance, you have observed to me that it's raining heavily and I wish to let you know of my nondissent, that job will be done perfectly by the utterance of any of these locutions. But is this to say that they are all 'used in the same way'? Plainly not. For —apart from the question whether, even in such a context as this, they may be distinguishable—the conclusion that they are 'used in the same way' would seem to require, not only that there should be contexts in which they are indifferently interchangeable but also that there should be no contexts in which they are not. But this latter condition is surely, and significantly, not satisfied. Let us consider, for instance, the case

of agreement. I may, certainly, agree with a statement that someone has made. But not, of course, *only* with statements. I may also agree with a decision he has come to, a policy he has announced, a taste or opinion he has expressed, an appraisal, an estimate, or an assessment he has made. He says, for instance, concluding his argument, '. . . so we must try to get Jones elected instead of Smith,' or ' . . . on those grounds I judge Higgins to be the more promising man.' Now if I agree with his decision or his assessment, I may of course say 'Yes, I agree': if I believe his decision or assessment to be correct, I may say 'You're right.' But in neither case, surely, would I naturally, or could I properly, say 'That's true.' *This* way of expressing agreement would be quite out of place here. Why? Because, presumably, the speaker with whose words I wish to signify my agreement was not just making a statement, purveying a simple truth (or falsehood), but rather announcing a decision, issuing an appraisal: and though indeed I may agree with him and may express my agreement, the particular form of words 'That's true' seems properly, and also naturally though doubtless not rigorously, to be confined to the particular case in which what is to be agreed with is, or at least is offered and taken as, a statement of fact. Thus, in these and no doubt in vastly many other cases, it appears that our various agreement-expressing locutions are *not* in fact freely interchangeable: though there are cases in which any would do, there are other cases in which one or more will do, while others will not.

But now, of course, the question arises: why should it be the case, as it appears to be, that the locution 'That's true' is naturally, though doubtless neither rigorously nor self-consciously, confined to the case in which what is to be agreed with is a statement of fact? Is this a mere convention of speech, like the use of 'Hear, hear' by way of assent to formal oratory, or of 'Amen' as a mark of subscription to the sentiments of a prayer? It is surely both unplausible and unnecessary to suppose that this is a mere convention. For it seems at this point both natural and quite adequately explanatory to hold that to say 'That's true' is to say, about what someone has said, that it is true; so that *of course* one can express agreement in this particular form of words only if what one is thereby talking about is the kind of thing that *can* be true (or untrue)—that is, is a statement. Thus, the notion that to say 'That's true' is to make a statement about a statement appears not only not to be ruled out by the point that that utterance may serve to express agreement, but actually to be indispensably necessary to understanding of the restrictions on the expression of agreement in that particular form. That—more or less—only statements can be agreed with in this way is explained if the utterance *states, about* what it refers to, that it is true; and I cannot imagine how else that fact is to be explained.

7. One final point. I believe that many people have been inclined to object that, even if one is led by the sort of considerations outlined above to the

view that Austin is probably right in holding that one who says 'That's true' makes a statement about a statement, there is still grave difficulty in accepting his implicit view that the statement so made *means* anything so lengthy and elaborate as he says it does. For, one may think, it is surely quite indisputable that those simple and unreflective persons who say 'That's true,' quite naturally and effortlessly, dozens of times a day, do not have any such lengthy rigmarole—about demonstrative and descriptive conventions and so on—in mind when they say it. I do not believe, however, that there is much force in this objection. For one thing, there is a high degree of indeterminacy in the notion of meaning (some of it, indeed, perhaps put there by philosophers); so that it is very far from clear what kind of account, how thoroughgoing and far-reaching and how elaborate, of the use or conditions of application of a term can properly be put forward as an account of its meaning. But more generally, there is surely no good reason to believe that a philosophically useful account of 'the meaning' of a term must not be more complex than, or even that it must bear any very close relation to, what ordinary users of the term may have in mind when they use it. It is, after all, a very familiar point that those who habitually use a term quite correctly, and in that sense may be said to know what it means, may be in hopeless difficulties when invited to *say* what it means: and it seems clear that, when an attempt to say what it means is seriously undertaken, the resulting account will very often be of a complexity un-

suspected by, and perhaps astonishing to, plain speakers of the language. Thus, whatever objections there may be to Austin's account of what it means to say of a statement that it is true, I do not believe that the undoubted complexity of his account is in itself a ground for the conclusion that it must be incorrect.

My argument, then, can be summed up as follows:

(1) Though it is most undoubtedly the case that, when one says 'That's true,' one is often, for instance, agreeing, it does not follow from this that one is not therein making a statement: for one may express agreement *by* making a statement.

(2) It is quite certainly the case that, as Strawson says, one may express, say, agreement with somebody's statement more or less indifferently by saying 'That's true,' 'So it is,' 'I agree,' 'Yes,' 'You're right,' and so on. But:

(3) It appears *not* to be the case that, as he implies, these verbally diverse responses cannot be significantly and substantially distinguished from one another. For (a) if we bring into view the actual complexity of the business of making even a quite simple statement, it at once seems natural to distinguish these diverse responses as relating to different aspects of or elements in that complex business, notwithstanding the fact that they all achieve the same general object: and the response 'That's true' is naturally seen as differing from the others in being *about* the statement made, what the speaker said. And (b) if we note that the phrases mentioned in (2) above are, though freely

interchangeable in some contexts, not so interchangeable in others, we observe that 'That's true' tends to be restricted to contexts in which it is statements of fact that are, say, to be agreed with: and it seems the obvious explanation of this restriction that 'That's true' states, about what its subject-term refers to, that it is true.

(4) It appears in general not outrageous to hold that one who utters certain words therein makes a statement about something, even if he does not clearly and self-consciously conceive himself to be so doing: though

(5) We may well regard saying 'That's true' in the ordinary way as, though in no way deviant or colloquial or idiomatic, yet a somewhat unideal specimen of making a statement.

(6) If we hold, then, with Austin, that to say 'That's true' is to make a statement, albeit perhaps an unideal one, about a statement, we may still feel difficulty in the idea that that statement's meaning can be so complicated as he makes it out. But this is far from conclusive, since there is actually no good reason why a remark, perhaps made very casually, with nothing very complex in mind, should not all the same, when subjected to scrutiny, turn out to have a highly complex meaning, only to be set out in perhaps surprisingly many hard words.

In this paper I have not, of course, done anything whatever to show that Austin's account of *what* is stated about a statement, when one says that it is true, is in detail correct. If I have established anything, it is only that

Strawson does not succeed in showing that an account of that kind is in principle wrong—that is, that Austin goes astray in principle in supposing that to say 'That's true' is to make *any* kind of assertion about a statement. I am in fact inclined to believe not only that Strawson does not show this to be wrong in principle, but also that it *is* not wrong in principle: but of course this is not to say that Austin's account is wholly acceptable as it stands,[4] still less that there do not remain far more questions than it answers.

_____

[4] It may be worth pointing out two curious, but not I think very important, slips which Austin's paper contains. First, he says at one point that "the relation between the statement that S and the world which the statement that the statement that S is true asserts to obtain is a *purely conventional* relation . . ." But this, which Strawson rightly objects to, is not a consequence of Austin's account but actually inconsistent with it. On his own view, all that is 'purely conventional' is that to utter the sentence 'S' is to make the statement that S: whether or not the statement so made is true is of course a matter not of convention, but of fact. Second, he says that 'demonstrative' conventions correlate 'the words (= statements) with the historic situations, etc., to be found in the world.' But again, on his own view, that a particular *statement* relates to a particular 'historic' situation is a matter not of convention, nor in this case of fact, but of logic: for he implies earlier that a statement is identified, in part, by reference to the situation to which it relates. What 'demonstrative conventions' in part determine is not how statements are related to the world, but what statement is made by the utterance of certain words on a particular occasion. It will be noted that I have sought to eliminate this latter slip in my initial brief statement of Austin's view.

TRUTH

7.4

A. J. Ayer

At first sight there is nothing very puzzling about the concept of truth. It is not clear why there should be any need to look further than the straightforward account which Aristotle gave of it; 'To say of what is that it is not, or of what is not that it is, is false, while to say of what is that it is, or of what is not that it is not, is true.'[1] In modern dress, this has developed into Tarski's formula: ' "p" is true in L if and only if p',[2] which is exemplified in such unexciting statements as that the sentence 'snow is white' is true in English if and only if snow is white. There are indeed objections to making truth a predicate of sentences, as opposed to the statements or propositions which the sentences express; the most serious being that sentences which contain pronouns, or demonstratives, or proper nouns, or tensed verbs, are used to make different statements on different occasions, so that a sentence like 'I have a headache' will be both true and false according as it refers to different persons or to different times. It follows that, if we wish to predicate truth of sentences without falling into inconsistency, we have to free our language from dependence upon context, to replace proper names and pronouns by descriptions and to employ spatio-temporal co-ordinates to do the work which is done by tenses or by demonstratives like 'here' and 'now'. It is, however, a disputed question how far this is feasible.[3]

If I do not pursue this question here, it is not that I do not think it interesting and important in itself, but only that it does not have a vital bearing upon the definition of truth. For it is obvious that in any case in which we are able to define truth as a predicate of sentences, we can also define it as a predicate of statements. We have only

From *The Concept of a Person and Other Essays* (London: Macmillan and Co., 1963). Reprinted by permission of St. Martin's Press, The Macmillan Company of Canada, Macmillan and Co., and the author

[1] *Metaphysics*, p. 7, 27.

[2] *Vide* A. Tarski, 'The Concept of Truth in Formalized Languages', in *Logic, Semantics, Metamathematics*, and 'The Semantic Conception of Truth', in *Philosophy and Phenomenological Research*, vol. iv, 1944, and also in *Readings in Philosophical Analysis* (ed. Feigl and Sellars).

[3] *Vide* 'Names and Descriptions'.

to rule that a statement is to be accounted true when it can be expressed by a sentence which satisfies our definition. Even in the case of a sentence of which the interpretation varies according to the context, it may still be possible to define its truth or falsehood with respect to the use that is being made of it on any particular occasion; and we can then extend the definition, in the same simple fashion, to the corresponding statement. Of course this still leaves us with the problem of making clear what it is for a sentence to express a statement, but for those who regard truth as a predicate of statements or of propositions, this problem will arise in any case.

A point which concerns us more at this stage is that Tarski's formula is not itself a definition of truth but only a schema. His actual definition of truth, in terms of the satisfaction of sentential functions, applies as it stands only to the set of sentences which he chooses as an example: that is, to the sentences which constitute what he calls the language of the class-calculus. But, subject to certain provisos, the method can be extended to sentences of other formal systems. There are, however, technical reasons for concluding that a general definition of truth along these lines is not obtainable. Nevertheless there is a sense in which the schema achieves as much as can be expected. If we apply it to any given sentence, then provided that we know what statement the sentence is being used to make, the formula will tell us what we mean by saying that the sentence is true.

If this is all there is to it, it may even be suggested that the concept of truth is not only not problematic, but not of any special interest. There are, indeed, philosophers who have taken this view. They maintain that the words 'true' and 'false' and their cognates play no essential rôle in our language: that we use them to say nothing that we could not say equally well without using them at all.[4] This position is made plausible by concentrating on examples in which the assertion that a given statement is true explicitly contains the statement itself. Thus it is always possible to preface any assertion that one makes with the expression 'it is true that', but in the way of information at least nothing seems thereby to be gained. If I assert, for example, that it is true that London is the capital of England, I appear to give no more information than I should give by simply asserting that London is the capital of England. Similarly, to assert it to be false that cows are carnivorous appears to be exactly the same thing as asserting that cows are not carnivorous. So if one generalizes from instances of this kind, one may come to the conclusion that the statement that it is true that p is merely an expanded version of the statement that p, and the statement that it is false that p a version of the statement that not p. And then one may undercut the question whether truth and falsehood are predicates of sentences or statements by taking this to show that they are not predicates at all.

It must be remarked, however, that it is not entirely fair to take this as the

---

[4] *E.g.* F. P. Ramsey, 'Facts and Propositions', *Supplementary Proceedings of the Aristotelian Society*, vol. vii, 1927. Reprinted in *The Foundations of Mathematics*.

standard example of the way in which we use the words 'true' and 'false'. There are indeed occasions on which the expression 'it is true that' is employed as a stylistic or rhetorical device; most frequently it has a concessive use; we say 'it is true that p' to mark our acknowledgement of a fact, the fact stated by 'p', which might be adduced as an objection to what we have been saying. But it is much more common for us to use the words 'true' or 'false' and their cognates not as a preface to some assertion which we are in the course of making, but rather as a means of expressing our agreement or disagreement with an assertion that someone else has made. We say 'Yes, that is true' or 'No, that is not true' in reply to something that has been said to us; or else we couple the expressions 'is true' or 'is false' with some description of a statement, to make such sentences as 'What he told you is false', or 'What you said is true'. When they are employed in this way the words 'true' and 'false' are not eliminable, or at least not in any straightforward manner, and they do appear to function as predicates. For while it may plausibly be said that to preface a statement with the expression 'it is true that' is not to talk about the statement, or about the sentence which expresses it, but merely to state it in a different fashion, surely this does not apply to the cases where the word 'true' is used as a comment upon a statement which has already been made. When I utter such a sentence as 'What you said was true', there may be a sense in which I am reasserting your statement. But it would seem perverse to deny that I am anyhow talking about it, that it is

the subject of which I am predicating truth.

I have just said that there may be a sense in which one is reasserting a statement of which one predicates truth, but it can well be argued that this need not be so. Thus if I know someone to be honest and reliable, I may enjoin others to believe him, not because I independently agree with some statement that he has made, but simply on the grounds of his general veracity. Without even knowing what it was that he said, I still may be willing to assume that what he said was true. But it seems rather odd to say that I am thereby reasserting a statement which I am not even capable of identifying, and still odder to say that I am restating it.

All the same one must not make too much of this point. What I am doing in such a case is to give a blank cheque, as it were, to the person in whom I am reposing confidence. Though my ascription of truth to his statements is not a restatement of them, it commits me to a share of the responsibility for them. It is the same responsibility as I should be assuming if I said to someone, in a context where I believe that I can exclude the possibility of my having been honestly mistaken: 'I forget what I told you, but I know that I would not lie to you: so whatever I said, I am sure that it was true'. Here again, I am not repeating my statement, but there surely is a sense in which I am reaffirming it. What happens in this case is that one makes what could technically be called a variable assertion. The use of the expression 'is true' in conjunction with a descriptive phrase is a way of according one's assent to any statement which satisfies the description. But to make a variable assertion is in a sense to assert the values of the variable. If a statement satisfies the description with which I conjoin the predicate 'true' or 'false', then I am implicitly asserting, or denying it, as the case may be, even though I may not know what the statement is.

I conclude from this that though it is strictly incorrect to refuse to accord the words 'true' and 'false' the status of predicates, yet those who have taken this line are basically in the right. For even when they do function as predicates, the rôle which these terms essentially fulfil is that of assertion or negation signs. The material content of a statement *s* which implicitly or explicitly ascribes truth to a statement *p*, may differ from the material content of *p* inasmuch as it may refer to *p* in a way in which *p* does not refer to itself; but the information which we gain from *s* by way of this reference to *p*, adds nothing to what we gain from *p* alone. Whatever criticisms may be made of Tarski's formula, this is one point which it brings out clearly.

What is not so clear is why there is thought to be such a problem about truth. If the question were only what is meant by truth, in the sense in which we have so far interpreted it, then, as we have seen, the answer is extremely simple. But just because it is so simple, we may suspect that we are mistaking the problem. If this is all there were to it, it is hard to see how anybody, even a philosopher, could ever have supposed that the question 'What is Truth?' presented any serious difficulty. Yet philosophers have been puzzled about truth: they have put forward conflict-

ing theories about it. All the same they must have known well enough how the word 'true' was actually used. Such information as that it is true that London is the capital of England if and only if London is the capital of England could hardly be expected to come upon them as a revelation, nor yet as something which they would wish to dispute. They would complain only that it did not provide an answer to the questions that concerned them. But what then are these questions?

I think that what these philosophers were seeking was not a definition of truth, in the sense of an explanation of our use of the word 'true', but rather a criterion of validity. The question which they raised was not, What do we mean by truth? but, What is it that makes a statement true? This second question is indeed ambiguous. It might be construed as an inquiry into causes. How does it come about that such and such a statement is true? How does it come to be true that I am now in Oxford? Because I have business there, and caught a train from London, and so on. It might be construed as a request for truth conditions. What does the truth of the statement that I am now in Oxford consist in? In my being in Oxford and whatever this logically entails. Or thirdly, it may be, or at any rate has been, construed in a more general way as an enquiry into the relations that must obtain between a statement, or sentence, or judgement, or whatever else truth is ascribed to, and something in the world, something other than the statement itself, in order for it to be true. How is the statement that I am now in Oxford made true by what is going on in the world? Because it is a fact that I am now in Oxford. But perhaps this calls for further elucidation.

Now clearly we are not concerned here with the causal question. We are not concerned to find the scientific explanation why this or that statement is true. For one thing, this would only remove the problem to another stage. For the truth of the statements which enter into the explanation will itself have to be accounted for. It is more nearly right to say that we are looking for truth-conditions and would be entirely right if what we wanted was a definition of truth which would be adequate, in Tarski's sense. For what Tarski's definition of truth with respect to the language of the class-calculus depends on is his being able to summarize the conditions under which any sentence of the language is true. Since the only statements which can be made in the language are statements to the effect that one class is included in another, and statements which are truth functions of these, one can find a general formula which contains an exhaustive specification of the conditions under which any sentential function of this language will be satisfied. In the case of a natural language, these favourable circumstances do not obtain. It is very doubtful if its molecular sentences are all truth-functional, witness the problem of subjunctive conditionals, and its atomic sentences are not all of the same pattern. So instead of summarizing the truth-conditions, we fall back on enumeration. This accounts for the production of such a trivial seeming statement as that the sentence 'snow is white' is true in English if and only if snow is white.

But even if the truth-conditions of the statements expressible in a natural language could be summarized, this still would not give our philosophers what they need. For what this would enable us to do would be to give a general description of the kinds of statement that can be made in the language in question, and then go on to say that what would make them true is that this, or that, or the other set of conditions is satisfied. But the philosophical problem is supposed to be that of explaining what it means to say that *any* set of conditions is satisfied. The question which is put to us is, What makes anything so? Where the answer sought is not a causal one, which would in any case be empty at this level of generality, but something about criteria of validity. It is to this quite general problem that the various theories of truth, the correspondence theory, the coherence theory, the pragmatic theory, are taken to provide the solution.

But now we may well ask: Is this a genuine problem at all? Can we significantly ask for a general criterion of truth? Surely what makes a statement true must depend upon what the statement is. One can describe how one would set about verifying any given statement, but one cannot describe how one would set about verifying statements in general for the very good reason that they are not all verified in the same way. So that if any one insists on putting the general question, the most that we can do for him is to give him, in one guise or another, the cruelly uninformative answer that what makes a statement true is what makes a statement true.

I feel the force of this objection, but

I do not think that our efforts to generalize need be quite so futile as it makes out. It is indeed correct to say that any two different statements have different criteria for their truth; but it does not follow from this that these criteria cannot be informatively classified, and classified in a quite general way. Thus if we admit the distinction between *a priori* and empirical statements, it is quite plausible to say that what makes an *a priori* statement true is either that it exemplifies a rule of usage, or that it is tautologous, in the sense of tautology which is defined by the truth tables, or that it follows, in accordance with certain specifiable rules of deduction, from axioms which themselves can be treated as implicit definitions. The existence of Gödelian sentences does introduce a complication here. We now know that in any formal system which is rich enough to express arithmetic, there are true statements which are not provable within the system. But it is not obvious that even these statements cannot be accomodated within some general formula of this kind.

For the purpose of this inquiry, however, I intend to pass over the special problems which arise in connection with the validity of formal statements and deal only with the case of empirical statements, where the position is different but no less complex. And here I think we must begin by making a distinction between those empirical statements which can be directly tested and those that can be tested only indirectly. This is not indeed an altogether clear-cut distinction. It is to some extent a matter of convention what statements are to be regarded as directly testable. It depends partly on the resources of the language which we are employing. In a given language L, however, in which we are able to express a statement s, it is often the case that we are also able to express statements, t, u, v, which are more directly testable than s. And here what I mean by saying that t, u, v, are more directly testable than s, or that s is less directly testable than t, u, v, is that while it is not possible to verify s, without verifying t, u, v, it is possible to verify t or u or v without verifying s. A straightforward example of this would be the case of statements about nations and statements about persons. It is not possible to verify any statements about the French nation without verifying some statements about individual Frenchmen, but the converse does not hold. Another example of a different sort would be that of universal statements and singular statements. A universal statement may be deduced from some theory, but the theory itself can in the end be verified only through the making of some observation at some specific place and time, that is through the verification of a singular statement. On the other hand the verification of the singular statement does not depend upon the verification of the theory, though it may not be independent of some other theory. I doubt if one can ever come to statements which are in no degree theory-laden, but I do not think that this invalidates the relative distinction that I am now trying to make. If this is so and it is possible to define the concept of relatively direct testability with respect to the statements which are expressible in a given language, one can then go on to define direct testability in terms of it. We can say that a statement *s* is directly testable with respect to a given language L if there is no statement expressible in L than which it is less directly testable.

Let us call the statements which are directly testable in this sense basic statements. It does not matter, for our present purpose, what these basic statements are taken to be. Clearly they must fall into the category of what some philosophers have called observation-statements, but we need not at this stage resolve the difficult question whether these statements are to be construed as statements about physical objects or statements about sense-data. The important point, so far as we are concerned, is that these basic statements, whatever they may be, supply the truth-conditions for all the other empirical statements which are expressible in the language in question. It will not in general be found to be the case that these higher level statements are logically equivalent to any combination of the basic statements; but it is necessarily the case, according to our definition, that they are verifiable only in so far as basic statements are derivable from them. With regard to many such higher level statements, for example those that constitute some abstract scientific theory, it is not very easy to show what is their observable content. But if we are able to specify their observable content, then we have also specified what would make them true.

But what of the basic statements themselves? By definition they are not verified through the verification of any other statements, at any rate not through the verification of statements of any other type. They are verified, if at all, by being directly confronted with the relevant facts. But this raises two problems. What is the nature of this confrontation? And what is it that statements are confronted with? Facts, but what are facts?

Let us try to deal with the second question first. One suggestion which we must dispose of, if we are to proceed any further along this road, is that facts are simply to be equated with true statements. There is indeed a common and proper usage of the word 'fact' in which this is so. The expression 'it is a fact that' may be employed as an alternative to 'it is true that' in the rôle of an assertion sign. In this usage of the term we have to admit as many forms of fact as there are forms of statement: not only affirmative categorical facts, but negative facts, hypothetical facts, disjunctive facts, and so on. But this is not obviously objectionable, nor out of accord with ordinary usage. We do constantly talk of its being a fact that something or other is not the case, and while we may be a little less ready to talk of conditional facts, it is not unknown for us to do so. A historian might claim, without absurdity, that it was a fact that if Hannibal had besieged Rome after the Battle of Cannae he would have taken it.

However, if this were the only usage of the term, it would not serve us here. For in that case to say that a true statement corresponded to a fact, would merely be a rather misleading way of saying that a true statement was true. What we require is the different, perhaps less common, sense of fact, in which a fact is not identified with a true statement, but rather distinguished from it as that which makes it true. We want to be able to characterize facts, not as linguistic entities of any kind, but somehow as objective states of affairs. Our task is to show that this usage is legitimate and to try to make it clear.

One feature of it is that we no longer have a one to one correspondence between true statements and facts. For we now want to say that different true statements may be made true by one and the same fact. Thus the following statements, 'Some Greek philosopher died from drinking hemlock', 'The master of Plato died from taking poison', 'Socrates died from drinking hemlock', 'Socrates did not die a natural death', 'Either Socrates died from drinking hemlock or Plato was the father of Aristotle', and many similar ones that we could add to the list, are all different. Some are entailed by others though in no two cases is there a relation of mutual entailment: some are logically independent. Yet they are all made true by the same fact: namely the fact which consists in a particular man dying in just the fashion in which he did at a particular time and place. This diversity comes about because there are ever so many ways of describing or referring to the various features of the situation. The descriptions may be more or less definite, e.g. 'someone' as opposed to 'Socrates', and they may be only synthetically connected, e.g. 'the master of

Plato' and 'the husband of Xanthippe', with the result that the statements into which they enter have different contents. Nevertheless, it is held, there is only one state of affairs that they all refer to, one single fact or set of facts, that makes them all true.

But how are these facts to be characterized? How are we to distinguish among true statements between those which do, as it were, delimit facts and those which do not? Thus the statement that in the room where I now am some Englishman is writing an essay on a philosophical topic reports a fact in the sense that it is true, but it does not delimit a fact, because the fact which makes it true is not just that some Englishman is writing an essay, but that *I* am, and not just that any sort of philosophical essay is being written, but precisely *this* one. And here it would seem that what prevents the statement which I have just cited from delimiting the appropriate fact is that it is so indefinite, that it is consistent with so many possible states of affairs: in other words it is insufficiently specific.

This is the reason, I believe, why so many philosophers have been reluctant to admit the possibility of negative or disjunctive facts. Thus the statements 'London is not the capital of France' and 'London is the capital of either England or Denmark' are both true, but it is argued that there is no fact which consists in London's not being the capital of France, neither is there a fact which consists in London's being the capital of either England or Denmark: there is only the fact that London is the capital of England. The refusal to countenance negative facts sometimes, indeed, appears to be a mere prejudice, inasmuch as the distinction between affirmative and negative statements is not sharp; in some instances it is only a matter of the way in which a statement is formulated, in others it is chiefly a matter of emphasis. It is, however, generally the case that the statements which we regard as negative are less specific than those that we take to be affirmative. Thus the information given by saying that London is not the capital of France is less precise, in the sense that it leaves more possibilities open, than the information given by saying that London is the capital of England. In the case of disjunctive statements this is quite obvious. Since all that is needed for a disjunctive statement to be true is that one of the disjuncts be true, it follows that if it is true that p it must also be true that p or q, no matter what proposition q is. But merely to say that one or other of a pair of disjuncts is true is less specific, it leaves more possibilities open, than ascribing truth just to one of them.

The ground for our reluctance to admit general or conditional facts is not so much that general or conditional statements are unspecific as that they are not directly testable. It is, however, also true that general statements are unspecific in the sense that they do not pin-point their instances. To say that all ravens are black is not to identify any particular object as a raven.

Unfortunately, this concept of specificity is not at all easy to define. The obvious first step is to say that p is more specific than q, if p entails q but q does not entail p. Thus the statement that I am writing an essay entails, but is not entailed by, the statement that someone is writing an essay; the statement that my shoes are black entails, but is not entailed by, the statement that my shoes are not brown; the statement that London is the capital of England entails, but is not entailed by, the statement that London is the capital of England or Denmark. So in each case we say that the first mentioned statement is the more specific.

This is all right so far as it goes. It is, however, clear that it provides us only with a limited concept of relative specificity. It does not permit us to compare statements which are logically independent of one another. Still there may be ways in which this restriction can be removed. For example, we may begin by saying that a statement is absolutely specific with respect to a given language L if there is no statement expressible in L by which it is entailed and which it does not entail. Then if we were able to make a catalogue of all the absolutely specific statements which were expressible in L, we might be able to construct a hierarchy on this basis in such a way that we could determine the relative specificity even of statements which were logically independent of one another, by comparing their relation to the statements of the lowest level. We should have to allow that a statement which was absolutely specific with respect to one language might not be so with respect to another, but I do not think that this is a serious objection. In theory at least, a language can always be added to; and if the language in which we are speaking is, by comparison with some other language, deficient in its power to express specific statements, we could always make this deficiency good.

The real difficulty in this line of approach stems from the fact that we can always make a statement more specific by conjoining another one with it. For while p does not in general entail p and q, it is always the case that p and q entails p. But this would mean that we should be left with only one fact, namely that which was stated by the conjunction of all true mutually independent statements. Even if we eliminated from this list all those that are not directly testable, the conclusion could still not be accepted. The only way that I can see to avoid it is to add to our definition of specificity the saving clause that p is not a component of q. But then we must have some means of determining when one statement is a component of another. What we need, in other words, is a rule for deciding what are simple statements, and this may not be very easy to devise.

In spite of such technical difficulties, I hope that I have succeeded in throwing enough light on the usage of 'fact' with which we are here concerned. The first step is to delimit a class of statements which satisfy the following three conditions: first, that they are directly testable; secondly, that they are simple in the sense that they are not compounded of other statements; and, thirdly, that they are absolutely specific with regard to the language in which they are expressed. Then facts are to be identified with the states of affairs which

form the objective contents of the true statements of this class.

But now it may seem that we are turning in a circle. We set out to explain the truth of statements in terms of their relation to facts, but we have ended by explaining what facts are in terms of the truth of a certain class of statements. This important sense of 'fact', in which facts were not just to be identified with true propositions, amounts to no more, it may be said, than limiting the type of true proposition with which they are to be identified. We have shown how the validity of some statements depends on that of others, but, so the criticism runs, we have not begun to show how any statements can be compared with facts.

It is the belief that the circle is unbreakable, that we can attach no sense to the claim that statements are compared with facts, unless it is a disguised way of saying that they are compared with one another, that leads to the coherence theory of truth. And one very good reason for supposing that the circle is not unbreakable is that the coherence theory of truth can easily be shown to be untenable.

When I speak of the coherence theory of truth, I am not referring to a theory which, in England at least, most frequently goes by that name, that is, to the theory adopted by such neo-Hegelians as F. H. Bradley and H. H. Joachim.[5] For this is not a theory of truth at all, but a theory of meaning. The premiss from which it springs is

---

[5] See especially H. H. Joachim, *The Nature of Truth*.

that it is impossible to identify and so to refer to any object unless it can be specified completely; but to specify an object completely must include the description of all the relations that it bears to other objects. So, since every object is in some way related to every other, to specify any object is to specify them all. But this leads to the conclusion that there is only one statement which can significantly be made, the one that tells the truth, the whole truth and nothing but the truth. The statements that we actually make, assuming, that is, that we ever succeed in referring to anything, must all be shorthand for this one true statement, and, therefore, are all equivalent to one another, an unfortunate consequence which appears to have escaped the notice of the proponents of this theory. Alternatively, if they are not shorthand for the one big statement, they all fail in their reference and are, therefore, false or meaningless. The line which is taken by the advocates of this theory is that the statements, or judgements to use their terminology, which we actually make are at best partially true, but this is merely disingenuous. Apart from the difficulty of attaching any sense to the expressions 'partially true' or 'partially false' (unless we are dealing with a conjunction of statements, some of which are true and others false), the argument just does not allow for any discrimination, any difference of degree among statements with respect to truth and falsehood. On this view either they are all true and all say the same thing (*i.e.* everything), or they are all about nothing and so are all completely false, if not

meaningless. All this comes from the initial step of supposing that you cannot refer to anything without completely specifying it: a mistake which is incorporated in the so-called dogma of internal relations. What is hard to understand is that so many idealist philosophers should have seriously taken this premiss to be true.

This curious theory is to be distinguished from what may be called a proper coherence theory of truth; such a theory, for example, as was put forward by some of the Viennese positivists in the nineteen-thirties.[6] They did not deny that it was possible to make statements which were logically independent of one another; they were not led astray by any fidelity to internal relations. But because they had persuaded themselves that it was metaphysical, and so meaningless, to talk of comparing statements with facts, they thought that truth must consist in some relation which statements bear to one another. But if one rules out any reference to fact, the only relations which statements can bear to one another are logical relations: relations of logical independence, entailment, or incompatibility. So the conclusion drawn was that for a statement to be true it was necessary and sufficient that it be a member of a self-consistent system. An attempt was made to put observation statements (or protocol statements as they were sometimes called) into a privileged position,

---

[6] *E.g.* by R. Carnap, O. Neurath, and C. Hempel. *Vide* Carnap's and Neurath's articles on 'Protokollsätze' in *Erkenntnis*, vol. iii, and Hempel, 'On the Logical Positivists' Theory of Truth', in *Analysis*, vol. ii.

but since these protocol statements were distinguished only by their form, and since the only criterion for their truth was their coherence with the other statements in the system, so that there was no reason to accept them if they did not fit in, this privilege came to nothing. The feeling that they ought to be privileged was a back-sliding: it came from tacitly regarding them as re-ports of fact.

It is easy to see that this theory is indefensible even on its own terms. One obvious and fatal objection to it is that there may be any number of sys-tems of statements, each of which is internally consistent, but any two of which are incompatible with one an-other. Since they are mutually incom-patible they cannot all be true. How then is it to be decided which is the true one? When faced with this diffi-culty Carnap, who held this theory for a time, replied that the true system was that which was accepted by the scien-tists of our culture circle. But it is plain that this answer does not meet the dif-ficulty at all. For every one of the competing systems might consistently contain the *statement* that it alone was accepted by the scientists of our culture circle. What Carnap had in mind was that only one of these systems was ac-cepted by the scientists in *fact*. But this is to break the bounds of the coherence theory. And if the reference to fact is permissible in this case, why not in others also?

Since the coherence theory is false, the premiss from which it follows must be rejected. There is nothing improperly metaphysical in the idea of testing state-ments by reference to fact. Of course

we cannot state a fact without stating it: there is no way of characterizing facts except by making true statements. But this does not mean that the state-ments have to be identified with the states of affairs which they describe. The circle is broken by observation and by action. I shall recur to this point later on.

It is interesting to note that Carnap's attempt to save the coherence theory was a deviation into pragmatism. For it is the cardinal feature of pragmatic the-ories of truth that true propositions are characterized as those that we accept. Sometimes this is conjoined with the theory that the propositions which we accept are those that suit our purpose; it may also be strengthened by the proviso that not just any propositions that we happen to accept are true, but only those which we are warranted in accepting on the basis of scientific method. But the identification of truth with acceptance is the fundamental point.

A variant of pragmatism which is not often recognized as such is to be found in the equation of facts with proposi-tions which have been ascertained to be true. This leads to the conclusion, which goes back to Aristotle, that state-ments about the future are neither true nor false. I mention this theory only in passing, as it is open to the objections which hold against pragmatist theories in general, apart from incurring some special difficulties of its own.

The strength of the pragmatist posi-tion is that the distinction between what is true and what one accepts as being true is a distinction that one cannot draw in one's own case. If you ask me to produce a list of true propositions, the best I can do is to give you a list of propositions which I *believe* to be true—propositions which I accept. But it does not follow from this that when I say that a proposition is true I *mean* only that I accept it. On the contrary I am bound to admit the possibility that what I believe is false. Neither can I simply mean that I am warranted in asserting it: for what gives me a warrant for asserting something is that I have evidence in favour of its *truth*. So although it is the case that to ask someone what is true always comes down in *practice* to asking him what he believes, this does not mean that we can dispense with the concept of objective truth. The rôle which it plays may be only formal, but it is still essential. The pragmatist theory itself presupposes it and cannot be coherently stated without it.

This might seem to leave the field clear for the correspondence theory of truth. But at least in its traditional form, the correspondence theory is itself confused. Its merit is that it separates facts from statements: its demerit is that it then tries to connect them by invoking a relation of correspondence which is conceived as a relation of resemblance or structural similarity. I shall now try to show that if the idea of mirroring is taken at all literally, it is a serious mistake to suppose that statements (or sentences, or beliefs, or judgements) are true because they *mirror* facts.

The model on which this theory is based is that of a photograph or a map. For it is tempting to think that what makes a map or a photograph a true reproduction of the state of affairs which it portrays is a relation of similarity; similarity of structure in the case of the map, similarity of structure and also in some degree of content in the case of a photograph, or painting. And then one might go on to suppose, as Russell did in his Logical Atomism lectures[7] and Wittgenstein in the *Tractatus*, that sentences, or propositions, were also portraits and owed their truth, when they were true, to their fidelity. How even sentences could be regarded as portraits has never been made clear: it would seem that for all but the crudest type of ideographic language this could only be a metaphor; and surely it is just false that a language like English is implicitly ideographic. But we need not belabour this point since the theory does not even fit its paradigm cases. It is not true even of photographs or maps. For it is not just the structural similarity of a map say of Europe to Europe, the fact that the distance between the dots marked 'Berlin' and 'Vienna' on the map faithfully mimics according to scale the distance between Berlin and Vienna, and so forth; it is not just this that makes the map an accurate map of Europe, any more than it is *just* the likeness, however complete, of such and such a photograph to Princess Margaret that makes it a true photograph of Princess Margaret. So far as this goes, the map might be a map of China, the photograph a photograph of Mr. Macmillan. Another condition is needed, and it is this condition which is all important; there must be a convention according to which the map, or the painting, or the photograph, is interpreted as a sign of

---

[7] Reprinted in *Logic and Knowledge*.

that and only that which it resembles, as stating as it were, truly or falsely, that there exists something which in this way corresponds to it. Without this convention all that we have is the existence of two objects which resemble each other more or less closely, as closely maybe as the two sleeves of a coat: but there is no more a question of one's being true of the other than there is that my right sleeve is true of my left. The fact of physical likeness only becomes relevant when it is *selected* as a method of representation. It is indeed a natural choice to make, because we instinctively tend to associate like with like, but it is not the only possible, or even the most effective, method, as the development of non-ideographic language shows. It is not for that matter even the only possible method of portraiture. The fact that a picture does not seem to us to resemble the thing which it is intended to depict does not in itself make it non-representational. It may just be that the style of representation is different from what we are accustomed to.

In short, the question whether and in what fashion a method of representation is pictorial is irrelevant to the question of truth: or rather, it is relevant only in the trivial sense that the answer to the question whether a given series of signs expresses a true statement depends in part on the way in which the signs are interpreted. If the symbolism is pictorial, it is the resemblance of the signs to some possible state of affairs that determines what they signify; but then what decides the question of their truth or falsehood is whether or not this state of affairs exists. To put it another

way, we can regard a map or portrait as a sort of propositional function; if it is used to make a statement, it affirms that there is something to which it physically corresponds. Then what makes it true is simply that the function is satisfied, not that we employ this or that method of determining what the function is. The usual talk about correspondence confuses a question about the conventional character of the symbolism with the quite different question whether what is symbolized is so.

This confusion is to be found even in more sophisticated versions of the theory, such as that which has been put forward by J. L. Austin.[8] Having argued that 'if there is to be communication of the sort we achieve by language at all', there must among other things 'be two sets of conventions: *descriptive* conventions correlating the words (= sentences) with the *types* of situation, thing, event, etc., to be found in the world; *demonstrative* conventions correlating the words (= statements) with the *historic* situations, etc., to be found in the world', Austin contends that 'a statement is said to be true when the historic state of affairs to which it is correlated by the demonstrative conventions (the one to which it "refers") is of a type with which the sentence used in making it is correlated by the descriptive conventions'.[9] One obvious objection to this is that not all meaningful statements are explicitly referential; general and indefinite statements may

[8] J. L. Austin, 'Truth', *Supplementary Proceedings of the Aristotelian Society*, vol. xxiv, 1950. Reprinted in *Philosophical Papers*.
[9] *Op. cit.* p. 116.

well be expressed by sentences which contain no demonstrative signs at all. But this objection may be met by saying that the truth of such statements always depends upon the truth of other statements, and that in the case of these other, basic, statements Austin's two conditions are always fulfilled. Even this seems to me disputable, but I shall not pursue the matter here. For if Austin's remark is taken, perhaps unfairly, as an account of what is meant by calling something true it is open to a much more serious objection. It implies, as Mr. Strawson points out in his contribution to the same symposium,[10] that whenever one declares a statement to be true one is engaging in a semantic disquisition about the conditions of its being meaningful. Since Austin himself criticizes the semanticists for making truth a predicate of sentences, it is possible that he is not here intending to give a definition of truth but merely to describe the conditions under which a statement is true: and certainly for a statement to be made true in the way that it is, it is necessary that it should have the meaning that it has. But this is not to say that in calling it true, we are saying that it has this meaning, still less that we are talking about the semantic conditions which it has to satisfy in order to be meaningful. 'Certainly', to quote Strawson, 'we use the word "true" when the semantic conditions described by Austin are fulfilled: but we do not, in using the word, *state* that they are fulfilled.'[11] It may be that Austin himself

would have agreed with this, but if we strip his 'definition' of its semantic accretions, what it comes down to is that a statement is true if what it states, or what the sentence which expresses it means, is so. This is indeed a truism, but it is hardly a vindication of the correspondence theory of truth.

I hope that it has now become clear where the correspondence theory has gone wrong. In its traditional form, it mistakes a cardinal feature of a certain type of symbolism for an essential feature of all symbolism, and then confuses a key to the interpretation of these symbols, a clue for deciding in this special type of case what it is that they state, with a criterion for deciding whether what they state is satisfied. In this way a defective theory of meaning is turned into a defective theory of truth.

But if the relation between statements and the facts which make them true is not the relation of correspondence, what sort of relation is it? The answer to this is that it is a mistake to look for a relation of this type at all. As I implied at the end of my discussion of the coherence theory of truth, there is nothing mysterious about our ability to compare statements with facts. If one understands a sentence, then one already knows how to compare it, or the statement which it expresses, with a fact. How do I compare the English sentence 'It is a fine day', or the statement which I use it to make, with the facts or with reality, or whatever it is that one chooses to say that sentences, or statements, are compared with? Well, I look out of the window, see that the sun is shining, and so accept the statement: or perhaps I see that it is raining and

[10] P. F. Strawson, 'Truth', *Supplementary Proceedings of the Aristotelian Society*, vol. xxiv, 1950.

[11] *Op. cit.* pp. 144–5.

reject it. My understanding the sentence, my attaching the right meaning to it, the meaning that it conventionally has in English, just *is* among other things my being willing to accept or reject it in these various conditions. Of course, if I wish to state the conditions, to *say* what makes the statement true, then all I can do is to formulate another statement which is equivalent to it, or entailed by it, or a corroboration of it. But, as I said before, this does not mean that we are imprisoned in a ring of statements. We break the circle by using our senses, by actually making the observations as a result of which we accept one statement and reject another. Of course we use language to describe these observations. Facts do not figure in *discourse* except as true statements. But how could it be expected that they should?

What I am suggesting, in short, is that this is not a theoretical problem. If someone does not know how to find out whether a given sentence is being used to make a true statement, we may try to explain it to him by means of sentences which he does know how to use.

Or we may show him the appropriate state of affairs and hope that he catches on. The problem is a practical one and in practice often quite easily solved.

Of course there are theoretical problems in the neighbourhood. There is the problem of giving an analysis of what it is for a sentence to express a statement: there is the problem of specifying the conditions under which one statement confirms another and more particularly of determining the relation between theoretical statements and the basic statements of fact: there is the problem of the status of the basic statements themselves, which is allied to the philosophical problem of perception. Unless it is backed by a solution of at least the first and last of these problems, such an account as I have given of the concept of truth may not be thought to have achieved very much. All the same, it is a form of progress in philosophy to discover what are the proper questions to ask. Though my argument has followed a slightly different line from his, I hope that I have at least vindicated F. P. Ramsey's contention that there is no separate problem of truth.

Toward Further Inquiry

The assertive-redundancy thesis is only suggested in Ramsey's article. Its champion and explicator has been A. J. Ayer, in "The Criterion of Truth," *Analysis* 3 (1935), in "Truth by Convention," *Analysis* 4 (1936), and in *Language, Truth and Logic* (London, 1948). His "Truth," 7.4 in this volume, is a modification of his earlier position that takes into account what is called the "blind use" of 'true', asserting that something is true without knowing what that something is. For a critical evaluation of the thesis on convention, see M. Black, "Truth by Convention," *Analysis* 4 (1937).

Tarski's own references to fuller expositions and related issues can be found in the notes and bibliography following 7.1. M. Black provides a simplified exposition in "The Semantic Definition of Truth," *Analysis* 8 (1948), but his criticisms must be weighed against Tarski's explicit acknowledgement that his definition is operative only for formally determined systems. For other critiques, see A. Ushenko's "A Note on the Semantic Conception of Truth," PPR 4 (1944); K. R. Popper's "A Note on Tarski's Definition of Truth," *Mind* 64 (1955); A. Pap's "Note on the 'Semantic' and the 'Absolute' Concept of Truth," *Philosophical Studies* (1952); and A. B. Levison's "Logic, Language and Consistency in Tarski's Theory of Truth," PPR 25 (1964). Pap's "Propositions, Sentences and the Semantic Definition of Truth," *Theoria* (1954), offers an appraisal of the appropriateness of sentences as the designata of truth. Carnap adopts a similar conception of truth in *Introduction to Semantics* (Cambridge, Mass., 1942), but he also treats a "nonsemantic" conception in *Meaning and Necessity* (Chicago, 1947). Critiques of Carnap's views include F. Kaufmann's "Rudolf Carnap's Analysis of 'Truth'," PPR 9 (1948); J. F. Thomson's "A Note on Truth," Analysis 8 (1948); and D. R. Cousin's "Carnap's Theories of Truth," *Mind* 59 (1950).

Strawson's thesis laid a basis for a symposium with Austin and Cousin in PAS, Suppl. 24 (1950). His relation to Austin on this issue is analogous to that of William James to C. S. Peirce. He extends the notion of performatives to issues of truth, but the originator of the notion objects, not only in this symposium, but in "Unfair to Facts," *Philosophical Papers*. A helpful study of the relationship between these two thinkers on the truth issue is Mats Furberg's *Locutionary and Illocutionary Acts* (Göteberg, 1963), Chapter 3. Strawson responds to Warnock's criticisms in "A Problem about Truth—a Reply to Mr. Warnock," G. Pitcher (ed.), *Truth* (Englewood Cliffs, N.J., 1964)†. Other critiques of Strawson's position are W. H. Walsh's "A Note on Truth," *Mind* 61 (1952); J. Kincade's "On the Performatory Theory of Truth," *Mind* 67 (1958); and J. R. Searle's "Meaning and Speech Acts," PR 71 (1962).

George Pitcher, in his editorial introduction to *Truth*, gives a detailed examination of various characterizations and resulting problems for the notion of a proposition. A comparably helpful discussion is R. Cartwright's "Propositions," in Butler (ed.), *Analytical Philosophy* (Oxford, 1962). On the relation of propositions to facts, see G. E. Moore's "Facts and Propositions," PAS, Suppl. 7 (1927); B. Russell's "On Propositions: What They Are and How They Mean," PAS, Suppl. 2 (1919); M. Schlick's "Facts and Propositions," *Analysis* 2 (1935); and G. Ryle's "Are There Propositions?" PAS 30 (1929). Good discussions of the relation between sentences, assertions, and propositions are P. T. Geach's "Assertion," PR 74 (1965), and E. J. Lemmon's "Sentences, Statements and Propositions," in B. A. O. Williams and A. C. Montefiore (eds.), *British Analytic Philosophy* (London, 1966).

Other views of the meaning of truth have recently been taken. G. Ezorsky's "Truth in Context," JP 60 (1963), is basically a combination of Strawson's views with those expressed by John Dewey in *Essays in Experimental Logic*

(Chicago, 1916). A. R. White, in "Truth as Appraisal," *Mind* 66 (1957), draws analogies between 'true' and 'good' as evaluative words and between his own treatment of 'true' and R. M. Hare's treatment of 'good' in *Language of Morals* (Oxford, 1951). B. Mayo, in "Truth as Appraisal," *Mind* 68 (1959), points out that the "polar" nature of 'true' and 'false' clearly undercuts White's thesis. Some general discussions of meaning and truth have import for the issues dealt with in this chapter, if only obliquely. Among them are C. Lewy's "Truth and Significance," *Analysis* 8 (1947); D. Kalish's "Meaning and Truth," *University of California Publications in Philosophy* (1950); and D. Greenwood's *Truth and Meaning* (New York, 1957).

LANGUAGE AND REALITY

Chapter 8

Like everything metaphysical, the harmony
between thought and reality is to be found in
the grammar of the language.
Ludwig Wittgenstein

That there is a harmony between language, thought, and reality no one seems to doubt. What the nature and function of that harmony is seems difficult to discern. One of Wittgenstein's own dicta vivifies the perplexities: "A proposition is a picture of reality" (*Tractatus* 4.01). This statement is a metaphorical expression of the correlation between language and reality, but it does not explain that relation. Language is basically symbolic; it does not re-present in a pictorial way. Still, the metaphor gives expression to our sense that language makes reports about reality. In order to do so, it must have some basis in the reality it reports. At the same time, a certain way of speaking would seem to commit us to a certain understanding of reality. Thus, we have at least two questions to begin with: (1) What is the logical basis for the relation of language to reality? (2) What does the way we speak imply about what there is?

An answer to the first question requires some understanding of the logical character of human knowledge. The logical atomism of Bertrand Russell provides a paradigm (but certainly not the only one) for such an understanding. Our knowledge of the world begins with the data of our senses. From these data we construct simple relations that provide atomic facts. Our language about the world is a logical construction in which the basic units are atomic propositions that correspond to the atomic facts of our experience. An analysis of language about the world into its atomic propositions, which express the simple logical relations of sense-data elements of experience, makes explicit how language "pictures" reality. To develop the details of this program has been a principal aim of Russell's work from the early *Our Knowledge of the External World* (1914) to his *Human Knowledge* (1948). The program serves as a basis for further exploring problems about the relation of language to reality:

Can all statements about the world be reduced to logical constructions out of experience? Can the statements of theoretical physics and abstract mathematics be so reduced? Can statements about values and about psychological states be so reduced? If not, must we exclude such statements from the kind of statements that are about reality? Or must we revise our understanding of the relation of language and reality in such a way that we can include them?

Is language a passive picturing of reality (early Wittgenstein), or is it an active ordering of reality (Cassirer)? Does it result from a logical construction of experiential elements, or does it impose a creative form upon those elements? Can such issues about language be resolved without a prior resolution to the empiricism-rationalism controversy in epistemology?

Traditionally, the issues concerning the implications of what we say for what there is focused on the distinction between concrete and abstract entities. Terms name things. Singular terms give proper names for individual concrete entities, but the referential status of general terms, or universals, has been controversial. The *nominalists* maintained that such words are *only* terms or names and that they have no referents. The realists contended that because these words are names, they must name something. There must then be abstract entities in the world as well as concrete entities. For example, the common name 'man' refers not to individual men, but to the nature or essence, manness, that all men have in common; this essence has an existence that is not reducible to the individuals that are men. The *conceptualists* agreed with the realists that universals must refer to something, but they also agreed with the nominalists that they did not refer to "real" entities. They maintained that universals referred only to general concepts or ideas. Underlying this controversy is the question: To what realities do the terms of our language commit us? If all terms are names for things, then what is the nature of the referents of the terms? If only singular terms refer, then terms that do not refer require a new logic for terms, or they must be analyzed into singular terms and syncategorematic features of language (compare the issues considered in Chapter 4).

The traditional controversy concerning universals has become more complicated in recent discussions. Careful analysis makes clear that the concrete-abstract distinction cannot be equated with the singular-general one (see Quine's discussion in 8.1). Even that which is both concrete and individual is problematic: Do we regard the physical objects that individual terms name as the basic entities of reality, or do we look for something more radically basic, like the physical particles making up such entities, or the sense data making up our experience? Questions about abstract entities prove even more complicated because of the variety of candidates for existence. To name a few:

> *Classes* and *properties*. Recent logic usually treats traditional notions of universals in terms of classes and properties. When I say, "George is a man," I naturally regard George as an existent entity. When I say, "Man is an

animal," am I likewise committed to regarding the class, man, as an existent entity? Do statements like "Appendicitis is a disease" and "Scarlet is a vivid color" commit me to regarding properties like appendicits and scarlet as existent entities?

Theoretical entities. The thesis that the theoretical terms of empirical sciences can be reduced to empirical ones has met many objections in the light of the logic of scientific inquiries. If they cannot be so reduced, what is their nature? If they are no more than tools of scientific inquiry, how are they terms? If they refer to real entities, what is the nonempirical status of such entities?

Mathematical entities. Numbers are not numerals. What is their ontological status? The ideal figures of geometry are not the approximations plotted on paper or chalkboard. What are they?

Propositions. Propositions may picture reality, but they cannot be equated with the sentences of language (see the introduction to Chapter 7). What is their ontological status?

Fictions. The terms 'Hamlet' and 'Pegasus' are individual terms, but are they in any sense concrete? They make sense in the context of a Shakespearean play or a Greek myth, but do they in any sense refer to something?

In order to determine to what kinds of entities our language commits us, another question must be raised: How does one determine ontological commitment? This question can be divided into three sets of issues:

Reference issues. Terms are usually thought to have referents. How does one determine which terms have them and which do not? Are there devices for determining what kinds of things are designated by various kinds of terms?

Reduction issues. If some terms do not have referents (or if one attempts to avoid ontological commitment to certain kinds of entities), what tools can be used to explicate the nonreferential status of such terms? Against what standards does one judge the adequacy of such reductions from referential to nonreferential status? What status do nonreferential terms have? (Are they shorthand for other referential terms, are they syncategorematic features of language, or what?)

Identity issues. Often, two terms refer to one and the same object. What is the relation between the logical identity of two terms and the ontological identity of an object? What is the correlation of the principle of substitutivity (for terms in an extensional logic) to the principle of the identity of indiscernibles (for entities in reality)? If there is no correlation, how does one determine the differences? Are there different identity conditions for different kinds of entities? If so, what are they? (These issues are directly related to the issues of analyticity and synonymity discussed in Chapters 5 and 6.)

To meet the problems involved in the reference and reduction issues, Willard Quine developed a notion of designation in terms of symbolic logic (see 8.1).[1] He adds to the tool of Russell's theory of descriptions (see 4.3) the precision of translating statements into quantified logical notation. This analysis gives the basis for his conclusion: "To be is to be the value of a variable." On this basis he redefines the traditional realist-nominalist controversy: "In realistic languages, variables admit abstract entities as values; in nominalistic languages, they do not." The question of which kinds of entities exist then becomes the question of which can be expressed as values for a quantified system of variables. The issues of reduction resolve into what limitations can be placed upon the values of such a system. This analysis also opens the way to recognizing that a term may be quantifiable in one context, and thus designate an object, but may serve only syncategorematic functions in other contexts.

Quine's analysis lays a basis for answering the question: "What does the way we speak imply about what there is?" The question presupposes that such implications from language to reality are possible and thus that ontological explorations based on language are legitimate. Against such a thesis, Ernest Nagel maintains that logic does not involve any commitment to the character of reality and that ontological explorations on the basis of language are not legitimate. Nagel regards language as a tool to investigate reality, but he argues that this use does not imply a one-to-one correspondence between the terms of language and the entities of reality. His position is antithetical to Quine's, not on the issue of how one pursues an ontological enterprise, but on the issue of whether one is to pursue such an enterprise at all.

The remaining essays give alternatives to both of these treatments of the relation of language to reality. Rudolf Carnap contends that one can make inferences from language to reality only if he understands the meaning of the reality under consideration. One can understand questions about the existence of entities only if he is able to explicate the logical framework in which the discussion of such entities is operative. Such a conception of the problem makes mathematical entities no less "real" than physical entities—only real in a different sense (see 8.3). Pap strikes a similar note, maintaining that use of mathematical terms and of other general terms can be understood only in the light of their "contextual meanings," a notion illuminated by his treatment of contextual definitions in 4.1. On the basis of his analysis, Pap concludes that the traditional

---

[1] The identity issues are not dealt with in any of the essays included here. On these issues, see Quine's "Notes on Existence and Necessity," JP 40 (1943), and his *Word and Object* (New York, 1960), Chapter III. Leonard Linsky, in *Referring* (London, 1967), offers helpful discussions.

realism-nominalism problem resolves into a semantic issue, not one of ontological commitment (see 8.4). Black, approaching the problem from the starting point of natural languages, concludes on the basis of linguistic evidence that no satisfactory inference can be made from the grammar of language to the structure of reality (see 8.5).

DESIGNATION   8.1
AND EXISTENCE[1]

Willard Quine

Statements of the form "There is such a thing as so-and-so" I shall call *singular existence statements;* e.g., "There is such a thing as Pegasus," "There is such a thing as Bucephalus," "There is such a thing as appendicitis." The expression following the word "as," here *purports* to designate some one specific entity—perhaps an individual, as in the

From *Journal of Philosophy*, XXXVI (1939). Reprinted by permission of the editors and the authors.

[1] This constitutes the bulk of a paper which was read at the Fifth International Congress for the Unity of Science, Cambridge, Mass., September 9, 1939, under the title "A Logistical Approach to the Ontological Problem." But the six-page abstract which is being published under the latter title in the *Journal of Unified Science*, Vol. 9, touches also on further points which are passed over here.

Acknowledgement is due Mr. H. Nelson Goodman and Dr. Arnold Isenberg for helpful criticism.

case of "Pegasus" and "Bucephalus," or perhaps a property or other abstract entity, as in the case of "appendicitis"; and the statement is true just in case there *is* such a thing as this alleged designated entity, in other words just in case the expression really does designate.

The four-dimensional spatio-temporal view of nature is a device for facilitating logical analysis by rendering verbs tenseless. Let us adopt this device before proceeding farther. Bucephalus, then, is a certain four-dimensional body stretching through part of the fourth century B. C. and having horse-shaped cross-sections. Now the tensed statement "There is now no such thing as Bucephalus" is translatable into tenseless idiom roughly thus: "The temporally forward end of Bucephalus lies behind 1939." In the tenseless sense of "is," to which I shall adhere, there *is* such a thing as Bucephalus; namely, a spatio-temporally remote spatio-temporal body. Again, we will perhaps agree for the moment that there is such a thing as appendicitis; though this is not a spatio-temporal body, but another and a more abstract sort of entity. On the other hand there is no such thing as Pegasus; this word purports to designate a certain spatio-temporal body which in fact does not turn up anywhere in space-time, near or remote.

Now we must distinguish between these singular existence statements, "There is such a thing as so-and-so," and *general* existence statements: "There is such a thing as *a* so-and-so," or briefly "There is a so-and-so," "There are so-and-sos." A general existence statement, e.g., "There are unicorns," "There are horses," "There are prime numbers between 5 and 11," says that there is at least one entity satisfying a certain condition. In logical symbols, the whole appears as an existential quantification:

$$(\exists x) \ (x \text{ is a unicorn}),$$

$$(\exists x) \ (x \text{ is a horse}),$$

$$(\exists x) \ (x \text{ is a prime number} \cdot 5 < x < 11).$$

In words:

> There is *something which* is a unicorn.
> There is *something which* is a horse.
> There is *something which* is a prime number and *which* is between 5 and 11.

Whereas the singular existence statement calls the alleged existent by name, e.g., "Pegasus," the general existence statement does not; the reference is made rather by a variable "x," the logistical analogue of a pronoun "which," "something which."

Note that a general term, such as "horse" or "unicorn," is capable also of turning up in a singular existence statement. Just as the word "appendicitis" designates a specific disease (which is abstract), and the word "Bucephalus" designates a specific horse (which is concrete), so we may regard the word "horse" as designating a specific property, an abstract combination of characteristics. Then the singular existence statement "There is such a thing as *horse*" (not "*a* horse") will mean, not that there are horses, but that there is the abstract property in question. The same holds for the word "unicorn"; and we may thus be inclined to affirm the singular existence statement "There is such a thing as unicorn" though denying the general existence statement "There is such a thing as *a* unicorn," "There are unicorns."

The distinction between singular and general existence statements thus does not correspond to the distinction between the concrete and the abstract; the entity whose existence is affirmed by a singular existence statement may be concrete (e.g., Bucephalus) or abstract (e.g., horse), and the entity or entities whose existence is affirmed by a general existence statement may likewise be concrete (e.g., horses) or abstract (e.g., prime numbers).

Now a curious problem is raised by the denial of a singular existence statement; e.g., "There is no such thing as Pegasus." If the word "Pegasus" designates something then there *is* such a thing as Pegasus, whereas if the word does not designate anything then the statement would appear to lack subject-matter and thus to fall into meaninglessness. Actually, this problem rests only on failure to observe that a noun can be meaningful in the absence of a designatum. The noun "Pegasus" *is* meaningful. If asked its meaning, we could reply with a translation into other words: "the winged horse captured by Bellerophon." The word "Pegasus" can be regarded as an abbreviation of this phrase; and the statement that there is no such thing as Pegasus then becomes, according to Russell's theory of descriptions, a statement to the effect that if Bellerophon captured any winged horses at all he captured two or more. Many words form essential parts of intelligible statements—truths and falsehoods—without being *names of* anything; such is the status of prepositions and conjunctions and adverbs, we will perhaps all agree, and it is the status likewise of many nouns, notably "Pegasus." Grammar and lexicography tell us, independently of questions of existence, that the word "Pegasus" is a noun and that it is equivalent to the phrase "the winged horse captured by Bellerophon"; it is left to history and zoology to tell us further that the word "Pegasus" is not a *name* in the semantic sense, i.e., that it has no designatum.

The understanding of a term thus does not imply a designatum; it precedes knowledge of whether or not the term has a designatum. If I say, e.g., that there is no such thing as hyperendemic fever, you will not agree; you will not understand. You will still refrain from asking me what hyperendemic fever *is*, for I have warned you that there is no such thing; but at least

you will ask me to explain my terms. Questioned, I perhaps explain that I intend the words "hyperendemic fever" merely as an abbreviation for the phrase "the disease which killed or maimed four fifths of the population of Winnipeg in 1903." Now that you know what I mean, an inquiry into Winnipeg history will lead you to agree that there is no such thing as hyperendemic fever.

The latter example shows incidentally that factual considerations can entail the repudiation not only of an alleged individual, e.g., Pegasus, but also of an alleged abstract entity. In contrast to these factually grounded cases, consider next the doctrine that there is no such thing as *up*. In repudiating an entity "*up*" we do not change our views as to the truth or falsehood of any ordinary factual statements containing the word "up." But we do claim that nothing, neither a spatio-temporal body nor even a property or other abstract entity, is *designated* by the word "up"; the word is meaningful, it forms an essential part of various statements, but it is not a noun, much less a name of anything.

Now the nominalist goes further than "up" in his repudiation of abstract entities. He would say, in the same spirit in which we have repudiated *up*, that there is no such thing as appendicitis. At the common-sense level from which we considered hyperendemic fever, one would rush to the defense of appendicitis; hyperendemic fever does not exist, but appendicitis certainly does. Still, just how does the nominalist err in treating appendicitis as we have treated *up*? He agrees that many people are appendicitic, and that the word "appendicitis" is meaningful and useful in context; yet he can maintain that the word is not a *name* of any *entity* in its own right, and that it is a noun at all only because of a regrettable strain of realism which pervades our own particular language. On the same grounds, the nominalist will go back and do a more ruthless job than we have done in the matter of unicorns; he will say that there is not merely no such thing as a unicorn but also no such thing as *unicorn*—no abstract entity, so-called property, such as this word has been said to designate. He keeps the word "unicorn" merely as a contextually meaningful word like "up"—a syncategorematic expression which *names* nothing, abstract or concrete. The general term "horse" will fare no better; there are many denoted entities in this case, indeed—many horses —but no *named* or designated entity, no abstract property *horse* according to the nominalist.

But now the whole question of existence is beginning to appear gratuitous. If the nominalist who renounces such abstract entities as horse, unicorn, and appendicitis does not thereby foreswear any of the ordinary uses of these words, nor take issue on any factual questions of zoology and medicine, then what does his renunciation amount to? Any appeal to nature, such as was involved in the case of Pegasus and hyperendemic fever, seems now to have become irrelevant. What is left but a bandying of empty honorifics and pejoratives—"existent" and "non-existent," "real" and "unreal"?

We are tempted at this point to dismiss the whole issue between nominalism and realism as a metaphysical pseudoproblem. But in thus cutting the Gordian knot we cut too deep into the level of common sense. We are all inclined, I suppose, to regard the word "up" or the suffix "ness" or the signs of punctuation as syncategorematic expressions, meaningful in context but *naming* nothing. The mere capacity to turn up in a sentence does not make a string of marks a name. Now if we allow ourselves this much freedom in repudiating designata, on what grounds can we take issue with the nominalist? On what grounds, indeed, can we take issue with someone who even outdoes the nominalist and repudiates *everything*, the concrete as well as the abstract, by construing all words indiscriminately as syncategorematic expressions designating nothing? We seem to have a continuum of possible ontologies here, ranging from a radical realism at the one extreme, where even a left-hand parenthesis or the dot of an "i" has some weird abstract entity as designatum, to a complete nihilism at the other extreme. Singular existence statements "There is such a thing as so-and-so," together with their trivial variants such as "So-and-so designates," begin to assume the air of a logically isolated class of statements—logically independent of the rest of discourse, verifiable or falsifiable at caprice, and thus void of meaning. If we are to avert this consequence, we must find some relationship of logical dependence between the singular existence statement and the rest of discourse.

Let us return to the singular existence statement "There is such a thing as appendicitis." This can indeed be affirmed or denied without affecting our attitude toward the usual statements containing the word "appendicitis"—for example, "Appendicitis is dreaded." Continuing to affirm the latter statement, the nominalist can yet maintain that the word "appendicitis" figures syncategorematically therein, like "is" or "pend," and that there is no designated object "appendicitis." The singular existence statement does not affect the truth value of the statement "Appendicitis is dreaded." However, it does prove to have other effects. If the word "appendicitis" designates an entity, then the statement "Appendicitis is dreaded" is a statement *about* that entity. It affirms the dreadedness thereof, and implies the consequence that *something* is dreaded:

$$(\exists x) \ (x \text{ is dreaded}).$$

If on the other hand the word "appendicitis" is syncategorematic and designates nothing, then the statement "Appendicitis is dreaded" is not about an entity "appendicitis," any more than it is about an entity "*pend*" or "*is*"; it does *not* have the consequence:

$$(\exists x) \ (x \text{ is dreaded}).$$

The singular existence statement "There is such a thing as appendicitis" does, therefore, have an effect on general existence statements. If we affirm the singular existence statement, we must regard any general existence statement "$(\exists x) \ (\ldots x \ldots)$" as following from the corresponding statement ". . .appendicitis. . ." which contains "appendicitis" in place of "x." If we deny the singular existence statement "There is such a thing as appendicitis," on the other hand, we do not countenance such inference. Let us refer to this form of inference—putting "x" for "appendicitis" in a statement and prefixing "$(\exists x)$"

—as the operation of *existentially generalizing* with respect to the word "appendicitis." To say that there is such a thing as appendicitis, or that "appendicitis" designates something, is to say that the operation of existentially generalizing with respect to "appendicitis" is *valid;* i.e., that it leads from truths only to truths.

This conclusion would seem to hold in general. A word W *designates* if and only if existential generalization with respect to W is a valid form of inference. The word "appendicitis" used in the foregoing example happens to be of an abstract sort, but this is not essential. Consider again the word "Pegasus," construed as an abbreviation of the phrase "the winged horse captured by Bellerophon." If Pegasus does not exist, in other words, if it is not true that one and only one winged horse was captured by Bellerophon, then according to Russell's theory of descriptions there will be various true statements which can be turned into falsehoods by existentially generalizing with respect to the word "Pegasus." For example, the statement:

Nothing is identical with Pegasus

is true whereas the result of existential generalization:

$$(\exists x) \ (\text{nothing is identical with } x)$$

is false.

Our earlier apprehension, namely, that all singular existence statements might prove logically isolated and thus affirmable or deniable at caprice, is thus overcome. Perhaps we can reach no absolute decision as to which words have designata and which have none, but at least we can say whether or not a given pattern of linguistic behavior *construes* a word *W* as having a designatum. This is decided by judging whether existential generalization with respect to *W* is accepted as a valid form of inference. A *name*—not in the sense of a mere noun, but in the semantic sense of an expression designating something—becomes describable as an expression with respect to which existential generalization is valid.

Under the usual formulation of logic there are two basic forms of inference which interchange names with variables. One is existential generalization, whereby a name is replaced by a variable "x" and an existential prefix "$(\exists x)$" is attached:

$$\ldots \text{Paris} \ldots$$
$$\therefore (\exists x) \, (\ldots x \ldots)$$

The other, which may be called *specification*, is the form of inference whereby a variable is replaced by a name and a *universal* prefix is dropped; it leads from a *universal quantification:*

$$(x) \, (\ldots x \ldots),$$

that is:

For all choices of $x, \ldots x \ldots$

to:

$$\ldots \text{Paris} \ldots$$

Now if existential generalization is valid with respect to a given term, say "Paris," then specification is likewise valid with respect to that term. For, suppose "... Paris ..." is false. Then its denial:

$$\sim (\ldots \text{Paris} \ldots)$$

is true. From this, by existential generalization, we get:

$$(\exists x) \sim (\ldots x \ldots),$$

i.e.:

$$\sim (x) \, (\ldots x \ldots),$$

thus concluding that "$(x) \, (\ldots x \ldots)$" is false. The falsehood of "... Paris ..." is thus seen to entail that of "$(x) \, (\ldots x \ldots)$." Therefore the truth of "$(x) \, (\ldots x \ldots)$" entails that of "... Paris...."

Hence, instead of describing names as expressions with respect to which existential generalization is valid, we might equivalently omit express mention of existential generalization and describe names simply as those constant expressions which replace variables and are replaced by variables according to the usual logical laws of quantification.

Contexts of quantification, "$(x) \, (\ldots x \ldots)$" and "$(x) \, (\ldots x \ldots)$," do not indeed exhaust the ways in which a variable "x" may turn up in discourse; the variable is also essential to the idioms "the object x such that ...," "the class of all objects x such that ..., and others. However, the quantificational use of variables *is* exhaustive in the sense that all use of variables is *reducible* to this sort of use. Every statement containing a variable can be translated, by known rules, into an equivalent statement in which the variable has only the quantificational use. All other uses of variables can be explained as abbreviations of contexts in which the variables figure solely as variables of quantification.

And *names*, we found, are describable simply as the constant expressions which replace these variables and are replaced by these variables according to the usual laws. In short, names are the constant *substituends* of variables.

A variable "*x*" is ordinarily thought of as associated with a realm of entities, the so-called *range of values* of the variable. The range of values is not to be confused with the range of *substituends*. The names are substituends; the named entities are values. Numerals, names of numbers, are substituends for the variables of arithmetic; the values of these variables, on the other hand, are numbers. Variables can be thought of roughly as ambiguous names of their values. This notion of ambiguous name is not as mysterious as it at first appears, for it is essentially the notion of a pronoun; the variable "*x*" is a relative pronoun used in connection with a quantifier, "(x)" or "$(\exists x)$."

Here, then, are five ways of saying the same thing: "There is such a thing as appendicitis"; "The word 'appendicitis' designates"; "The word 'appendicitis' is a name"; "The word 'appendicitis' is a substituend for a variable"; "The disease appendicitis is a value of a variable." The universe of entities is the range of values of variables. To be is to be the value of a variable.

Supposing that we know where to draw the line between the *concrete* or individual and the *abstract*, we can now make some sense of the distinction between a *nominalistic* and a *realistic* language. Words of the abstract or general sort, say "appendicitis" or "horse," can turn up in nominalistic as well as realistic languages; but the difference is that in realistic languages such words are substituends for variables—they can replace and be replaced by variables according to the usual laws of quantification—whereas in nominalistic languages this is not the case. In realistic languages, variables admit abstract entities as values; in nominalistic languages they do not.

As a thesis in the philosophy of science, nominalism can be formulated thus: it is possible to set up a nominalistic language in which all of natural science can be expressed. The nominalist, so interpreted, claims that a language adequate to all scientific purposes can be framed in such a way that its variables admit only concrete objects, individuals, as values—hence only proper names of concrete objects as substituends. Abstract terms will retain the status of syncategorematic expressions, designating nothing, so long as no corresponding variables are used.

Indeed, the nominalist need not even forego the convenience of variables having abstract entities as values, or abstract terms as substituends, provided that he can explain this usage away as a mere manner of speaking. Quantification involving a new sort of variables, which ostensibly admit a new sort of entities as values, can often be introduced by a contextual definition—a mere convention of notational abbreviation. Elsewhere[2] I have cited, by way of example, a convention of notational abbreviation introducing quantification upon variables which have statements as their substituenda. When such an abbreviation is adopted we are able to talk *as if* statements were names having certain abstract entities—so-called propositions—

---

[2] In the aforementioned abstract.

as designata. In so doing we do not commit ourselves to *belief* in such entities; for we can excuse our new form of quantification as a mere abridged manner of speaking, translatable at will back into an idiom which uses no statement variables and hence presupposes no propositions, no designata of statements. Under such a procedure propositions become explicitly *fictions*, in this sense: there are no such things, from the standpoint of our unabbreviated official language, but we talk as if there were by dint of an eliminable shorthand.

Similarly, if the nominalist can devise contextual definitions explaining quantification with respect to any other alleged entities of an abstract kind,[3] he becomes justified in speaking *as if* there

were such entities without really forsaking his nominalism. The entities remain fictions for him; his reference to such entities remains a mere manner of speaking, in the sense that he can expand this sort of quantification at will into an official idiom which uses only variables having proper names of individuals as substituends. But if the nominalist can not supply the relevant contextual definitions, then his nominalism forbids his use of variables having abstract entities as values. He will perhaps still plead that his apparent abstract entities are merely convenient fictions; but this plea is no more than an incantation, a crossing of the fingers, so long as the required contextual definitions are not forthcoming.

---

[3] For work in this direction see my "Theory of Classes Presupposing No Canons

of Type," *Proc. Nat. Acad. Sci.*, Vol. 22 (1936), pp. 320–326.

8.2   LOGIC
WITHOUT ONTOLOGY

Ernest Nagel

The fact that the world we inhabit exhibits periodicities and regularities has been frequently celebrated by poets,

From *Naturalism and the Human Spirit,* Yervant Krikorian, editor (New York: Columbia University Press, 1944), with omissions. Reprinted by permission of the publisher and the author.

philosophers and men of affairs. That frost will destroy a fruit crop, that a convex lens will concentrate the heat of the sun, or that populations tend to increase toward a fixed maximum, are typical of the uniformities discoverable in innumerable sectors of the physical and social environment; and however we may formulate such uniformities, no philosophy which construes them as anything else than discoveries will conform with the long experience of mankind. Every form of naturalism, to whatever extent it may emphasize the impermanence of many of these regularities or note the selective human activities involved in discovering them, will recognize them as basic features of the world; and even when it attempts to account for them, it will do so only by exhibiting a more pervasive, if more subtle, pattern in the behavior of bodies.

Nevertheless, no demonstrable ground has yet been found which can guarantee that such regularities will continue indefinitely or that the propositions asserting them are necessary. If, as many philosophers have maintained, the proper objects of scientific knowledge are principles capable of *a priori* validation, both the history of science and the analysis of its methods supply ample evidence to show that no science of nature has ever achieved what is thus proclaimed as its true objective. There are, indeed, relatively few practicing scientists today who place any credence in arguments claiming to prove that any principle about an identifiable subject matter is at once logically necessary and empirical in content.

No such general agreement can be found, even among lifelong students of the subject, concerning the status of various logical and mathematical principles constantly employed in responsible inquiries. Indeed, it is difficult to ascertain which natural structures, if any, such propositions express; and it is often no less difficult to exhibit clearly and without self-deception the grounds upon which they are acknowledged. In any event, many of the sharp divisions between professed naturalists are centered around the different interpretations which they assign to principles as familiar as the so-called "laws of thought," the basic assumptions of arithmetic or the axioms of geometry. Thus, one classical form of naturalism maintains, for example, that the principle of noncontradiction is a necessary truth which is descriptive of the limiting structure of everything both actual and possible; another form of naturalism holds this principle to be a contingent, but highly reliable, conclusion based on an empirical study of nature; and a third type of naturalism takes this principle to be void of factual content and an arbitrary specification for the construction of symbolic systems. Analogous differences among naturalists occur in their interpretation of more complicated and recondite mathematical notions.

Such disagreements among those professing naturalism is not a source of embarrassment to them, since naturalism is not a tightly integrated system of philosophy; perhaps the sole bond uniting all varieties of naturalists is that temper of mind which seeks to understand the flux of events in terms of the behaviors of identifiable bodies. Nevertheless, a naturalistic philosophy must be consistent with its own assumptions. If it professes to accept the methods employed by the various empirical sciences for obtaining knowledge about the world, it cannot with consistency claim to have *a priori* insight into the most pervasive structure of things. If it aims to give a coherent and adequate account of the various principles employed in acquiring scientific knowledge, it cannot maintain that all of them are empirical generalizations when some are not subject to experimental refutation. And if it admits that logical principles have a recognizable function in certain contexts (namely, in inquiry), it cannot consistently hold those principles to be completely arbitrary simply on the ground that they are void of factual content when considered apart from those contexts.

No one seriously doubts that logic and mathematics are used in specific contexts in identifiable ways, however difficult it may be to ascertain those ways in any detail. Does it not therefore seem reasonable to attempt to understand the significance of logico-mathematical concepts and principles in terms of the operations associated with them in those contexts and to reject interpretations of their "ultimate meaning" which appear gratuitous and irrelevant in the light of such an analysis? Such, at any rate, is the point of view of the present essay. In what follows, the difficulties and futilities of some non-operational interpretations of logical principles will first be noted; the limitations of certain naturalistic but narrowly empirical approaches to logic will then be discussed; and finally, an operational interpretation of a small number of logical and mathematical notions will be sketched. However, and this is perhaps the common fate of essays such as the present one, no more than the outline of an argument will be found in the sequel. The present essay contributes no unfamiliar analyses. Its sole objective is to make plausible the view that the rôle of the logico-mathematical disciplines in inquiry can

be clarified without requiring the invention of a hypostatic subject matter for them; and to suggest that a naturalism free from speculative vagaries and committed to a thorough-going operational standpoint expresses the temper of modern mathematico-experimental science.

I

1. Among the principles which Aristotle believed "hold good for everything that is" and therefore belong to the science of being qua being, he counted certain axioms of logic. These principles, according to him, were to be asserted as necessary truths and were not to be maintained as hypotheses, since "a principle which every one must have who knows anything about being is not a hypothesis." One such principle is that "the same attribute cannot at the same time belong and not belong to the same subject in the same respect."

Aristotle's formulation of the principle contains the qualification "in the same respect." This qualification is important, for it makes possible the defense of the principle against all objections. For suppose one were to deny the principle on the ground that an object, a penny for example, is both sensibly circular in shape and sensibly noncircular. The standard reply to this alleged counter-example is that the penny is circular when viewed from a direction perpendicular to its face and noncircular when viewed from a direction inclined to the face, and that since the different shapes do not occur "in the same respect" the principle has not been invalidated. But if one were now to ask for an unequivocal specification, antecedent to applying the principle, of a definite "same respect" with regard to the penny, so that the principle might then be subjected to a clear-cut test, a skillful defender of the principle as an ontological truth would refuse to supply the desired stipulation. For he would recognize that if a "respect" is first specified, it is always possible to find within that respect a way of apparently violating the principle.

For example, suppose a "same respect" is specified as viewing the penny from a direction perpendicular to its face. The penny will, nevertheless, subtend an angle of thirty degrees and also an angle of sixty degrees. To this, the obvious and proper retort is: "But not at the same distance from the face of the penny." Nevertheless, the principle is saved only by a new restriction upon what is to be understood by "the same respect"; the defender of the principle has altered his *initial* specification of what is the *same* respect. It is, of course, possible, when an attribute is suitably specified, to discover a set of conditions under which a thing does not both have and not have that attribute. The crucial point is that in specifying both the attribute and the conditions, *the principle is employed as a criterion* for deciding whether the specification of the attribute is suitable and whether those conditions are in fact sufficiently determinate. Because of the manner in which the qualification "the same respect" is used, the principle cannot be put to a genuine test, since no proposed case for testing the principle will be judged as admissible which violates the principle

to be tested. In brief, conformity to the principle is the condition for a respect being "the same respect."[1]

Analogous comments are relevant for the phrases "same attribute," "belong," and "not belong," which are contained in Aristotle's formulation of the principle. For example, how is one to tell in a disputed instance of the principle whether an attribute is "the same" or not? If someone were to maintain that a penny has a diameter of 11/16 of an inch and also a diameter of 12/16 of an inch, he would be told that the assertion is impossible, because even though the attributes are not "the same," in predicating the former one implicitly excludes the latter; and he would, perhaps, be asked whether the measurements were carefully made, whether the same system of units was really employed, and so forth. In short, since the assertion in effect maintains "the same attribute" to belong and also not to belong to the same subject, it is absurd. But let us press the question why, if the penny has the first of these attributes, it cannot

---

[1] The point at issue involves noting the difference between the following two statements: "However an attribute is selected, it is possible to find a respect such that a given attribute does not at the same time belong and not belong to a given subject in that respect," and "It is possible to find a respect such that, however an attribute is selected, the given attribute does not at the same time belong and not belong to a given subject in that respect." The hypothetical defender of the principle can successfully maintain the first, though not the second, because he undertakes to specify the "sameness" of respects only after he has selected an attribute —that is, after the principle is used to determine a respect, which will thus automatically satisfy the principle.

have the other. The impossibility is not simply an empirical one, which rests on inductive arguments; for if it were, the supposition would not be absurd, contrary to the hypothesis, that an unexpected observation may one day discover the penny's diameter to have both dimensions. The impossibility arises from the fact that we use the expressions "length of 11/16 inches" and "length of 12/16 inches" in such a way —in part because of the manner in which they may have been defined in relation to one another—that each formulates a different outcome of measurement. We may be sure that no penny will ever turn up with a diameter having both dimensions, because what it means for the diameter to have one of the attributes of dimension is specified in terms of the absence of the other attribute. The principle of contradiction is impregnable against attack, because the "sameness" and the "difference" of attributes are specified in terms of the conformity of attributes to the principle.

Accordingly, the interpretation of the principle as an ontological truth neglects its function as a norm or regulative principle for introducing distinctions and instituting appropriate linguistic usage. To maintain that the principle is descriptive of the structure of antecedently determinate "facts" or "attributes" is to convert the outcome of employing the principle into a condition of its employment. The Aristotelian view is thus a gratuitous and irrelevant interpretation of one function of this logical law.

2. More recent advocates of an ontological interpretation of logical principles argue their claim in terms of the conception of logical relations as invariants of all possible worlds—a conception also sponsored by Leibnitz. "Pure logic and pure mathematics," according to an influential proponent of this view, "aim at being true in all possible worlds, not only in this higgledy-piggledy job-lot of a world in which chance has imprisoned us." Reason, according to this interpretation, is an investigation into the very heart and immutable essence of all things actual and possible: "Mathematics takes us into the region of absolute necessity, to which not only the actual world but every possible world must conform." As another version puts it, logic is the most general of all the sciences: "Rules of logic are the rules of operation or transformation according to which all possible objects, physical, psychological, neutral, or complexes can be combined. Thus, logic is an exploration of the field of most general abstract possibility." According to this view, then, logical principles are "principles of being," as well as "principles of inference"; they formulate the most general nature of things, they are universally applicable, and they express the limiting and necessary structure of all existence.

Two issues raised by these brief citations from contemporary literature require comment.

a. When logical principles are asserted to hold for "all possible worlds," what is to be understood by the adjective "possible"? The crux of the matter lies in ascertaining whether "possible worlds" can be specified without using the principles of logic as the *exclusive* means of specification. For if a "possible world" is one whose sole identifiable trait is its conformity to the principles of logic, the view under consideration asserts no more than this: the subject matter of logical principles is whatever conforms to them. In that case no "possible world" could fail to satisfy the principles of logic, since anything which failed to do so would not, by hypothesis, be a possible world.

The point involved is so fundamental that it is desirable to illustrate it in another way. Consider any abstract set of postulates E, for example, Hilbert's postulates for Euclidean geometry, containing the *uninterpreted* terms P, L, and N. It is clearly not significant to ask whether E is true as long as these terms have this character. But physical experiments become relevant for deciding the truth or falsity of E if, for example, L is used to denote the paths of light-rays, P the intersections of two such paths, and N the surfaces determined in another way by any two intersecting paths. Nevertheless, an experimental inquiry can be undertaken only if the paths of light-rays can be identified in some manner *other* than by the sole requirement that light-rays are things satisfying the formal demands contained in E. For if a different method for identifying light-rays did not exist, it would not be possible to ascertain whether a particular physical configuration is such a path without first establishing that the configuration conforms to the implicit specifiations of E—that is, without first ascertaining the truth of E for that configuration. Accordingly, since by definition nothing could be a path of a light-ray which did not satisfy E, the question

whether E is true of all paths of light-rays would not be a matter to be settled by experiment.[2] It is evident, therefore, that if the question of the truth of a set of principles is to be a factual or experimental issue, their subject matter must be identifiable in terms of some other characteristic than that it satisfies those principles.

Let us apply these considerations to the formula: "Not both P and non-P." If it is simply a formula in some uninterpreted symbolic system, the question whether the formula is true in "all possible worlds" cannot arise. On the other hand, if its constituent symbols are interpreted in some manner, great care must be used in deriving further conclusions from the fact that on one such interpretation the formula expresses a "necessary truth." Thus, suppose that the letter "P" is taken to denote any "proposition" and that the other expressions in the formula are assigned their usual meanings; the formula will then express the principle of noncontradiction. But either there is some way of identifying propositions other than by the criterion that anything is a proposition which satisfies the formula, or there is not. On the first alternative, the assertion that the formula holds for all propositions will be a statement strictly analogous to general hypotheses in the empirical sciences; the evidence for the assertion, considerable though it may be, will be only partially complete, and in any case there will be

---

[2] Of course, the question whether *a particular physical configuration* is the path of a light-ray (that is, whether it satisfies E) would remain an experimental issue.

no reason to regard the formula as expressing a necessary truth. On the second alternative, the assertion will be an implicit definition of what a proposition is; the principle of noncontradiction will be a necessary truth, since nothing could be a proposition which does not conform to it.[3]

The view that logic is the science of all possible worlds thus suffers from a fundamental ambiguity. If the only way of identifying a "possible world" is on the basis of its conformity to the canons of logic, logic is indeed the science of all possible worlds. But the view is then no more than a misleading formulation of the fact that logical principles are employed as stipulations or postulates, which define what we understand by the consistency of discourse.

b. The second point requiring comment bears on the view that logical principles express the limiting and necessary structures of all things. If the do-

---

[3] This discussion is obviously oversimplified. Thus, if the formula is a logical consequence of some set of axioms which are used as implicit definitions for propositions, then the principle of noncontradiction will be a necessary truth even though it now falls under the first of the above two alternatives. However, the point of the discussion is not affected by the neglect of such complications. In the present essay the word "proposition" is used loosely, and is frequently employed interchangeably with the word "statement." It is, of course, important in many contexts to distinguish between a proposition and a statement, since the former is often taken to be the "meaning" of the latter. However, the issues under discussion are fairly neutral with respect to the different views which are current concerning what propositions are, so that no serious confusions need arise from the loose use of the word.

main of application of logical principles is identified on the basis of the actual use to which those principles are put, this view cannot be construed literally. For it is not things and their actual relations which are said to be logically consistent or inconsistent with one another, but propositions or statements about them; and it is to the latter that principles such as the principle of noncontradiction are relevant. No one will hesitate to acknowledge that "The table on which I am now writing is brown" and "The table on which I am now writing is white" are mutually inconsistent statements. But this inconsistency cannot, according to the view under discussion, be predicated of two "facts," "states of affairs," or "objects"; for if there were such facts the view would be self-refuting. Accordingly, inconsistency is something which can be located only in discourse, among statements, not among things in general. And if so much is admitted, an obvious dialectic requires that consistency be localized in a similar domain, in discourse and among statements.

But dialectic aside and bearing in mind only the identifiable functions of logical principles, there is no obvious warrant for the claim that the latter are the rules in accordance with which all possible objects can be transformed or combined. Certainly they are not rules of operation upon things in any familiar or literal sense of "transformation of things"—unless, indeed, the things said to be transformed and combined are elements of discourse, constellations of signs of varying degrees of complexity. The "pervasive traits" and "limiting structures" of all "possible worlds" which logic is alleged to formulate thus appear to be traits of discourse when it has been ordered in a certain way. The interpetation of logical principles as ontological invariants seems therefore, on closer view, to be an extraneous ornamentation upon the functions they actually exercise. But the regulative role of logical principles, suggested by the foregoing discussion, will be exhibited more clearly in the sequel.

II

Empirically minded naturalists, convinced that propositions concerning matters of fact must be supported by sensory observation, but convinced also that logical principles have factual content, have not had an easy time in accounting for the apparent universality and necessity of these principles. The interpretation of logical principles widely accepted by both traditional and contemporary empiricists is that they are hypotheses about traits of minds and things, based on inductive arguments from experience.

> I readily admit [Mill declared] that these three general propositions [the Laws of Thought] are universally true of all phenomena. I also admit that if there are any inherent necessities of thought, these are such. . . . Whether the three so-called Fundamental Laws are laws of our thoughts by the native structure of the mind, or merely because we perceive them to be universally true of observed phenomena, I will not positively decide: but they are laws of our thoughts now, and invincibly so.

More recent writers concerned with defending an empirical philosophy, though they may reject Mill's psychological atomism and sensationalism, frequently do not differ from him on the view that logical principles are inductive truths. The following is a sufficiently forthright comtemporary statement of this conception.

> *Logical* validity is grounded on *natural* fact. . . . When we are in doubt as to the logical validity of an argument, there is only one test. If the class of such arguments gives us materially true conclusions from materially true premises, it is valid, if not, it is invalid. . . . The crucial question which this frankly empirical approach to logic must face is whether it can explain the formal characters of logical inference. The experimental hypothesis attempts the explanation by showing that those inferential procedures which have brought knowledge in the past exhibit a certain invariant *order* whose metaphysical correlate is to be sought in the *serial* characters of existence. . . . The laws of logic . . . cannot be disproved, but they may become inapplicable and meaningless. We can say nothing about the *probability* of this being so, but we can just conceive of the possibility that the so-called *a-priori* laws of logic may not enable us to organize our experience. That is why they are not formal or empty. That is why they tell us something about the *actual* world. That is why we can say that every additional application of logic to existence is an experimental verification of its invariance.

However attractive such an interpretation of logical principles may appear to a consistent empirical natural-ism—to a philosophy which appreciates the limitations natural structures place upon our thought and action, but which nevertheless finds no warrant for the assertion that a priori knowledge of such structures is possible—there are insuperable difficulties involved in it. These difficulties arise in the main because those who profess such an interpretation misconceive the character of empirical or scientific method.

1. Little need be said in refutation of the view that logical principles formulate the "inherent necessities of thought" and are generalized descriptions of the operations of minds. Surely the actual occurrence in the same person of beliefs in logically incompatible propositions makes nonsense of the claim that the principle of non-contradiction expresses a universal fact of psychology. Moreover, if logical principles were true descriptions of anthropological behavior, they would be contingent truths, refutable on evidence drawn from the observation of human behavior; but in that case, the necessity which is so generally attributed to logical principles, however much this may be disguised by calling their contradictories "unbelievable," would be left unexplained.

2. The view under consideration maintains that the validity of a type of inference sanctioned by logic can be established only by presenting empirical evidence to show that an inference of that form always leads from materially true premises to materially true conclusions. It must be admitted, of course, that a valid inference is often defined as one which invariably yields true conclusions from true premises. But it by no means follows that an inference

ever is or can be established as valid in the manner proposed. Suppose, for example, "A" and "If A then B" are asserted as true statements (the expression "if . . . then" being used in some one of the customary ways), so that the conclusion that "B" is true may be drawn in accordance with the familiar rule of *ponendo ponens*. Let us now imagine that as a matter of fact "B" is false and that we are therefore urged by someone to abandon the rule as a universal logical principle. Would not such a suggestion be dismissed as grotesque and as resting upon some misunderstanding? Would we not retort that in the case supposed "A" or "If A then B" must have been asserted as true mistakenly or that if this is no mistake then the assertion of the falsity of "B" must be an error? Would we not, in any event, maintain that statements of the form: "If A and (if A then B) then B" are necessarily true, since not to acknowledge them as such is to run counter to the established usage of the expressions "and" and "if . . . then"?

Proponents of the view under discussion often declare that in interpreting logical principles as empirical hypotheses they are offering a justification for logic in terms of the procedures and standards of adequacy employed in the most advanced natural sciences. It is worth noting, therefore, that not a single instance can be cited from the history of science which would support the conception that the validity of logical principles is ever established by the suggested method. Is it not significant that whenever consequences derived from premises believed to be true are in disagreement with the facts of experimental observation, it is not the logical principles in accordance with which those consequences were drawn that are rejected as experimentally unwarranted? Indeed, it is not apparent how the suggested method for establishing the validity of logical principles could operate in any typical inquiry. For the truth of most premises employed in the sciences cannot be established except on the basis of an investigation of the consequences which are drawn from them—drawn in accordance with and with the help of logical principles. For example, the principles of Newtonian mechanics, which constitute part of the premises in many physical inquiries, cannot be established as adequate to their subject matter unless it is first discovered what these principles imply. This will be even more obvious if we note that these premises employ such complex notions as differential coefficients, real numbers, and point masses; the premises cannot be construed as "descriptions" of matters of fact accessible to a direct observation, that is, as statements whose truth or falsity may be settled prior to examining their logical consequences. The proposed method for establishing the validity of arguments is thus clearly not a feasible one, since no experimental control can be instituted for determining the alleged material truth of logical principles.

It follows that no "metaphysical correlate" to logical principles need be sought in the "serial character of existence." And if logical principles do not function as contingent hypotheses about matters of fact, if they are not to be established inductively on the ground of their conformity to "certain structural and functional invariants of nature," there is no clear sense in which "every

additional application of logic to existence is an experimental verification of its invariance." Logical principles are compatible with any order which the flux of events may exhibit; they could not be in disagreement with anything which inquiry may disclose, and if they should ever require revision, the grounds for such alterations must lie elsewhere than in the subject matter of the natural sciences. To be sure, should the cosmos become a chaos to the extent of making the continued existence of reflective thought impossible, the use of logical principles would thereby also become impossible. But as the above discussion indicates, the continued employment of those principles is not contingent upon the invariance of structures other than those which sustain the continuance of reflective inquiry.

3. In spite of its profession of allegiance to scientific methods as the canonical techniques of competent inquiry, the empiricistic interpretation of logic is based upon an inadequate conception of what is involved in those methods. Indeed, even when, as has already been noted, those subscribing to this interpretation explicitly reject Mill's psychological atomism, they do not always successfully free themselves from his over-simple views on the formation of scientific concepts. Two closely related points require brief discussion in this connection: the narrow criterion of meaningful discourse which is explicitly or tacitly assumed by many empirical naturalists; and the inadequate conception which they hold of the rôle of symbolic constructions in the conduct of inquiry.

a. It has often been maintained that the theoretical sciences deem to be ultimately meaningful only the statements which either formulate directly observable relations of qualities and things or can be translated without remainder into statements that do so. According to another version of this thesis, every meaningful statement must consist of terms which either denote simple, directly experienceable qualities and relations or are compounded out of terms denoting such simples. Even false hypotheses, so it has been urged on occasion, are meaningful only because they formulate the structure of some actual observable situation—a structure which happens to be wrongly attributed to a given situation. Since the familiar logical and mathematical principles seem so obviously significant, and since in their usual formulation they are ostensibly about the relations which properties of things bear to one another, the interpretation of these principles as empirical hypotheses is sometimes deduced as a corollary from this general view.

Little need be said to show the inadequacy of the suggested criterion of meaning. If it were applied consistently, most of the theories employed in the various positive sciences would have to be dismissed as in fact meaningless; and indeed, those who have accepted the criterion have been consistent enough to exclude almost all general statements as not expressing "genuine propositions." For in the first place, to the extent that theoretical propositions have the form of unrestricted universals, they do not formulate the explicit outcome of any actual series of direct observations. And in the second place, many theoretical statements contain terms (such as "point-particle," "light-wave," "electron," "gene," and the like) which denote no-

thing that can be directly observed and cannot be construed as being explicitly definable with the help of only such terms as do so. Moreover, there is surely no evidence for the claim that for every false hypothesis there is a situation for which it is true.[4] It is clear that underlying the suggested criterion of meaningful discourse is an ill-concealed reproductive psychology of abstraction and that in any case those who employ it cannot do justice to the actual procedures of the sciences.

A naturalism which is based on modern scientific methods cannot afford to propose illiberal restrictions upon inquiry. It must recognize that no formula can be constructed which will express once for all "*the* meaning" of any portion of scientific discourse. Instead of attempting to construct such formulae, it must turn seriously to the analysis of specific uses and functions of specific systems of expressions in specific contexts. It will have to note that statements in scientific discourse always occur as elements in a system of symbols and operations, and it will therefore attempt to understand the significance of statements in terms of the complicated uses to which they are subject. It will, accordingly, not assume dogmatically that the directly observed qualities and relations of the explicit subject matter of

---

[4] For example, within the framework of the Newtonian analysis of motion, an indefinite number of false hypotheses for gravitational attraction can be constructed, since a false theory of gravitation is obtained if the exponent "2" in Newton's formula is replaced by a different numeral. Are these different theories to be dismissed as meaningless because there do not happen to exist an infinity of situations for which these theories are true?

a science must constitute the sole and ultimate reference of every significant complex of its symbols. It will surely recognize that according to standard scientific procedure evidence taken from sensory observation must be relevant to propositions alleged to be about matters of fact: such propositions must entail consequences, obtained by logical operations in determinate ways, which can be experimentally tested when the appropriate circumstances occur. It will thus accept the pragmatic maxim that there is no difference between the objects of beliefs and conceptions where there is no possible difference in observable behavior. But it will not, therefore, insist that all significant statements must be descriptive of what can be directly observed. And it will remain sensitive to the possibility that even statements about the explicit subject matter of a science may involve a reference to the operations (overt and symbolic) performed in inquiries into that subject matter.

b. Nowhere is the systematic undervaluation of the constructive function of thought in inquiry more glaring than in the widespread neglect of the rôle played by symbolic manipulations in scientific procedure. The more comprehensive and integrated a theoretical system is, the more obvious does the need for such manipulations appear. For especially in the theories of modern science symbols usually occur which refer to nothing that can be directly experienced; and the significance for matters of direct experience of the conceptual constructions which enter into those theories cannot be made explicit except with the help of extensive symbolic transformations. Accordingly, no state-ment detached from the symbolic system to which it is integral can be evaluated for its empirical validity; and no isolated concept can be judged as warranted on the basis of the essentially irrelevant criterion of pictorial suggestiveness. But since calculation or symbolic manipulation thus acquires an indispensable though intermediary role in inquiry, the need for reliable techniques of constructing and expanding symbolic systems becomes progressively more pressing; the institution of an entire department of investigation devoted to the formal study of symbolic systems is the practically inevitable consequence.

It is a common and tempting assumption that in performing a chain of calculations one is at the same time tracing out the existential connections between things, so that the formal pattern of symbolic transformations reproduces in some manner the structure of the subject matter under investigation. However, the specific mode in which theories are constructed and bodies of knowledge are integrated is only partially determined by experimental findings. Various norms or ideals—such as the desire for a certain degree of precision, for intellectual economy and notational convenience, or for a certain type of comprehensiveness—also control the direction of inquiry and the articulation of theories. Many symbolic constructions and operations are therefore indices of the standards regulating the course of systematic investigations, and are not merely indications of the expected conclusions of experiment or of the intrinsic relations between phases of subject matter. A myopic concern with the sensory warrants for scientific findings—such as often characterizes traditional empiricism—easily leads to neglect of this aspect of systematic scientific formulations; the traits of discourse are then identified as traits of subject matter,[5] and principles whose function it is to institute a desired order into inquiry are not distinguished from statements about the explicit subject matter of inquiry. When the identification is made, the construction of symbolic systems (including the use of hypotheses) is in effect viewed as an inessential scaffolding for attaining some form of intuitive knowledge. When the distinction is not made, logical principles are in effect deprived of their identifiable functions.

III

The preceding discussion has, in the main, been negative. There remains the task of making explicit the suggestions it contains concerning an alternative in-terpretation of some logical and mathematical notions. Nothing like a systematic account of logic and mathematics can be attempted, and only a small number of logical principles and mathematical terms will be briefly examined. But even such an examination may exhibit the fruitfulness of an operational analysis of formal concepts and may make plausible the view that the content of the formal disciplines has a regulative function in inquiry.

Although logic is one of the oldest intellectual disciplines, considerable difference of opinion exists as to the scope of logical theory and as to which concepts and principles properly belong to logic. The present discussion will be confined to such admittedly formal principles as the so-called laws of thought and other "necessary truths" and to principles of inference such as the principle of *ponendo ponens*. The discussion will be facilitated if at the outset two senses are distinguished in which logical principles are commonly asserted: as principles which are explicitly about symbolism or language; and as necessary truths whose ostensible subject matter is usually some nonlinguistic realm.[6]

a. The three laws of thought are employed in the first sense in cases something like the following. Suppose that in a bit of reasoned discourse the term "animal" occurs several times. The argument will clearly be a cogent one only if in each of its occurrences the word retains a fixed "meaning"—that is, only

---

[5] An example of such a transference is found in the claim that, because the consistency of a set of formal postulates is established by exhibiting a group of related objects—a so-called "concrete model"—satisfying those postulates, logical traits (such as consistency) must represent pervasive ontological or empirical invariants. In point of fact, however, not only can some postulate sets be established without recourse to empirical facts in the indicated manner; most postulate systems cannot be shown to be consistent by genuinely empirical methods. But what is perhaps more to the point, this argument for identifying logical existential properties fails to observe that consistency is demanded of symbolic systems as part of an ideal for the organization of statements and is not a trait subsisting in nature independently of symbolic formulations.

[6] This distinction roughly corresponds to the difference noted in much current literature between "meta-logical" statements and statements in the "object-language" of a science.

if it is used as a name for the same kind of object. The requirement that in a given context a term must continue to be used in essentially the same manner, is expressed as the principle of identity. Analogously, the principle of non-contradiction requires that in a given context a term must not be applied to a given thing and also denied to it; and the principle of excluded middle is formulated in a corresponding way.

When stated in this manner, these principles are obviously *prescriptive* for the use of language, and as such are not *descriptive* of actual usage. They specify minimal conditions for discourse without confusion, for they state at least some of the requirements for a precise language. Everyday language, and to some extent even the specialized languages of the sciences, are vague in some measure, so that they do not entirely conform to the requirement set by these principles.[7] Although fairly effective communication is nevertheless possible in connection with many pursuits, situations do arise in which a greater precision in the use of language is required. The laws of thought thus formulate an ideal to be achieved—an ideal which is capable of being attained at least approximately—and they indicate the direction in which the maximum of desired precision may be obtained.

Few will deny that the laws of thought as here formulated have a regulative function. Nevertheless, the admission is often qualified by the claim that if the ideal these laws formulate is a reasonable one, not an arbitrary norm, there must be an objective ground—a "structural invariant"—which lends them authority. Moreover, it is sometimes urged that this ideal must be a necessary and inescapable one, since otherwise a genuine alternative to it would be possible; however, communication would be impossible if language were so employed as to conform, for example, to the denial of the principle of identity. But this latter argument for the intrinsic necessity of these principles is surely circular. For if by "communication" is understood processes similar to those in which we are familiarly engaged when talking, writing, or carrying on research—processes which illustrate the use of symbols in at least partial conformity to the laws of thought—communication would indeed be impossible were the requirements set by these laws satisfied in no degree; but communication would not be possible simply because these laws are analytic of what is understood by the word "communication." Whatever might be the human needs which communication satisfies, the desire to communicate and the desire to enforce the ideal specified by the laws are directed toward the same end. It must, nevertheless, be acknowledged that the ideal of precision in using language is not an arbitrary one. It is not arbitrary, because communication and inquiry are directed to the achievement of certain objectives, and these objectives are best attained when language is employed in a manner approximating as closely as possible the norms expressed by the laws of thought.

---

[7] Thus, if the term "red" is vague, there is a class of colors concerning which it is indeterminate whether the term applies to them or not, so that the principle of excluded middle fails in this case.

The assertion that this is so requires support by empirical evidence—evidence which it is possible to produce. But the available evidence is drawn from the study of the behavior of men engaged in inquiry; it does not come from a consideration of structural invariants found in other domains.

The three laws of thought are, however, not the only principles of logic explicitly dealing with symbolism, and some consideration must now be given to that important class of principles known as rules of inference—of which the rule of *ponendo ponens* is, perhaps, the most familiar. The first point to note in connection with such principles is that it is possible to specify accurately what rules govern the valid inferences in a language, only when the "meanings" of certain terms in that language are precise—that is, when terms like "and," "or," and "if—then" are used in determinate ways. In fact, however, the ordinary usage of such terms is vague and unclear. Everyday language, in the main is employed according to routine habits which are fixed and stable over a narrow range, but which are indeterminate in many crucial cases; accordingly, inferences are drawn and sanctioned on the basis of crude intuitive considerations as to what is "really meant" by the terms involved.[8] The explicit formulation of canons of inference serves to clarify vague intent; and what

is, perhaps, less commonly recognized, such formulations help to fix usages when they have previously been unsettled: they serve as proposals for modifying old usages and instituting new ones.

The various modern systems of formal logic must, accordingly, be viewed, not as accounts of the "true nature" of an antecedently identifiable relation of "implication," but as alternative proposals for specifying usages and for performing inferences. The adoption of a system such as is found in Whitehead and Russell's *Principia Mathematica* is in effect the adoption of a set of regulative principles for developing more inclusive and determinate habits for using language than are illustrated in everyday discourse. No known recent system of formal logic is or can be just a faithful transcription of those inferential canons which are embodied in common discourse, though in the construction of these systems hints may be taken from current usage; for the entire *raison d' être* for such systems is the need for precision and inclusiveness where common discourse is vague and incomplete, even if as a consequence their adoption as regulative principles involves a modification of our inferential habits.

---

[8] For example, everyone who has an elementary knowledge of English would agree that the rule of *ponendo ponens* is a correct canon of inference. On the other hand, a person unsophisticated by training in formal logic and not committed to one of the modern logical systems, may hesitate to ac-

cept the rule that a statement of the form "Either A or B" is a consequence of "A," where "A" and "B" are any statements; and he will probably seriously doubt the correctness of the rule that "If A then (if B then C)" follows from "If A and B, then C," where "A," "B," and "C," are any statements. The hesitation and the doubt must be attributed to the fact that "or," "and," and "if—then" are frequently used ambiguously and have fairly clear and determinate meanings only in relatively few contexts.

The question naturally arises whether the conventions which explicitly formulated rules of inference institute are entirely arbitrary—whether, in other words, the adoption of one set of regulative principles for reconstructing linguistic behavior is as "justifiable" as the adoption of a different set. The issue raised does not refer to the construction of various abstract "uninterpreted" symbolic calculi, for which diverging rules of "inference" or "transformation" may be developed; for it is usually admitted that the arbitrariness of such abstract systems can be limited only by the formal requirements of symbolic construction. The issue refers to the ground upon which one system of regulative principles is to be preferred to another system, when such principles are to be employed in the conduct of scientific inquiry. But this manner of putting the question suggests its own answer. If everyday language requires completion and reorganization for the sake of attaining the ends of inquiry, the "justification" for a proposed set of regulative principles will not be arbitrary and can be given only in terms of the adequacy of the proposed changes as means or instruments for attaining the envisaged ends. Thus, if inquiry is directed toward achieving a system of physics which will be coherent, comprehensive, and economical in its use of certain types of assumption and operation, one set of canons for inference will be preferable to another if the former leads to a closer approximation to this goal than does the latter. The choice between alternative systems of regulative principles will then not be arbitrary and will have an objective basis; the choice will not, however, be grounded on the allegedly greater inherent necessity of one system of logic over another, but on the relatively greater adequacy of one of them as an instrument for achieving a certain systematization of knowledge.[9]

It is needless to dwell further on the function of rules of inference: their primary rôle is to guide the development of discourse in a certain direction, namely, in the deduction of the consequences of sets of statements; they thereby contribute to making the use of language more determinate and precise and to attaining the goals of specific inquiries. It must be admitted, however, that it is frequently difficult to exhibit adequate evidence for the superior efficacy of one type of inferential system over another, especially when the specific goals of inquiry are themselves vague and are conceived, in part at least, in aesthetic terms.[10] The point to be stressed is that however great this difficulty may be, it can be resolved only by considering the specific functions of such logical principles in determinate contexts of inquiry; it cannot be resolved by investigating the causal factors which lead men to adopt those princi-

----

[9] Something more will be said on this point below. These remarks should not, however, be taken to mean that all habits of inference, and in particular language itself, have been instituted on the basis of a deliberate convention. How language first arose and how some of our common modes of inference actually came into being, are questions of fact about which there is in general little reliable information and concerning which everyone seems to be equally in the dark.

[10] For example, when a theory is required to be "simple" and "elegant."

ples or by a genetic account of inferential habits.

For example, the view has been advanced that certain simple forms of inference are generated by physiological mechanisms sharing a common character with mechanisms present in the subject matter of inquiry in which those inferences are used; and it is sometimes said that a theory of logic is "naturalistic" only if it holds that rational operations "grow out of" the more pervasive biological and physical ones. It may be safely assumed that there are causes and physical conditions for habits of inference, even when we happen to be ignorant of them. It is not evident, however, especially since habits of inference may change though the subject matter in connection with which they are employed does not, that the mechanism underlying a specific habit of inference is identical with the mechanism involved in that subject matter. And it is even less evident how, even if this were the case, the causal account would enable us to evaluate inferential principles, since the cogency of such an account is established only with the help of those principles. Suggestions for inferential canons may indeed be obtained from observations of natural processes; but the fact that a principle may have been suggested in this way does not explain its normative function. Again, the known facts about the earth's history make it most reasonable to assume that the higher and more complex activities of men did not always exist and that they have been developed out of more primitive ones; and it would certainly be a matter of great interest to learn just

how this has come about. However, in the present state of our knowledge a genetic account of logical operations is at best a highly speculative and dubious one; and what is more to the point, even if a well-supported genetic account were available, it would contribute little or nothing to an understanding of the present functioning of logical principles or to the explanation of the grounds of their authority. In the absence of a detailed knowledge of the past, the reaffirmation of the historical and structural continuity of our rational behavior with the activities of other organisms is an act of piety; it does not increase the clarifying force of an experimentally orientated naturalism.[11]

b. Logical principles are also asserted as necessary truths which do not refer to linguistic subject matter. Thus, "Everything is identical with itself" and "If A then A" (where "A" is any statement) are formulations of the principle of identity; "Nothing has and also lacks a given property" and "It is not the case that A and not-A" (where "A" is any statement) are formulations of the principle of noncontradiction; while "If A and (if A then B), then B," and "If (if A then B) then (if not-B then not-A (where "A" and "B" are any statements)

---

[11] These comments should not be construed as a rejection of some form of "the principle of continuity" as a fruitful guide and norm in inquiry. Nor should they be taken as denying that the study of simpler and more basic biological behavior may provide an illuminating context and essential clues for the understanding of the "higher" functions. These remarks are included simply as a protest against frequent abuses of a useful postulate of procedure.

are examples of other principles usually regarded as necessary. These principles are ostensibly about things, their attributes and their relations, not about symbols for them; they are held to be necessary truths, because their denials are self-contradictory.

The first point to note about these logical laws is that if they are asserted as necessary truths, they are asserted to be such in some more or less precisely formulated language, whether in the crudely precise language of everyday use or in some more exact artificial symbolic system. And it is not difficult to show that although their subject matter is not the language of which they are parts, they occur in that language because of the habits of usage or the tacit or explicit rules which govern that language. For example, if the characterizations "true" and "false" are employed in the customary manner, no statement can properly (that is, without contravening that usage) be characterized as both true and false; and if the word "not" is so used in connection with acts of affirming and denying statements that a false statement is rejected as not true, the principle of noncontradiction is instituted as a necessary truth. More generally, if a precise usage is fixed for a number of expressions in a symbolic system, statements constructed out of some of these expressions will usually occur such that to deny them is to misuse those expressions. Accordingly, the laws which are regarded as necessary in a given language may be viewed as implicit definitions of the ways in which certain recurrent expressions are to be used or as consequences of other postulates for such usages. No language is so utterly flexible in its formal structure that no limits exist as to the way expressions in it can be combined and used. The necessary statements of a language help to specify what these limits are. But to the extent to which ordinary language is not precise, which statements in it are necessary cannot be determined exactly. The so-called systems of "pure logic" do not suffer from this fault; they can therefore be used as norms for instituting a more precise employment of language in situations in which such precision is essential for the task at hand. Indeed, as is well known, one result of such instituted precision is to facilitate the process of deriving consequences from premises and to supply dependable means for checking inferences.

This function of logical laws—to serve as instruments for establishing connections between statements which are usually not themselves logically necessary—is too familiar to require more than passing mention. A point worth observing, however, is that the necessary laws of logic can be reformulated so as to become principles of inference, having as their explicit subject matter the relations of expressions in a symbolic system. For it can be shown that a given language may be so reconstructed that it no longer will contain necessary truths—without thereby affecting the original possibilities for deducing statements which are not necessary—provided that corresponding to the necessary truths initially in the language appropriate rules of inference are introduced. The cost of such a reconstruction may be prohibitive in terms of the inconveniences and complexities which arise from it.[12] Nevertheless, the theoretical possibility of making it helps to show that the function of necessary truths is to regulate and control the process of deduction. It follows that the previous comments on rules of inference apply with equal force to laws expressing necessary connections.

A few final remarks concerning the grounds for accepting logical laws must be made. The main stress which is to be made in this connection is that any "justification" of such laws can be given only in terms of the adequacy of the language in which they are part to the specific tasks for which that language is employed. This point can be enforced by recalling that in the empirical sciences it is not possible to perform experiments which would subject isolated statements to a crucial test, since every experiment actually tests a vaguely de-

limited system of theoretical and factual assumptions involved in the experiment and the statement. Analogously, it is not feasible to "justify" a law of logic by confronting it with specific observational data; the belief that it is possible to do so is part of the heritage of traditional empiricism. On the other hand, since logical laws are implicit laws for specifying the structure of a language, and since their explicit function is to link systematically statements to which data of observation are relevant, logical laws may be evaluated on the basis of their effectiveness in yielding systems of a desired kind. Thus, it has recently been suggested that in order to develop the theory of subatomic phenomena in a manner conforming both to experimental evidence and to certain ideals of economy and elegance, a "logic" different from those normally employed may have to be instituted.[13] The suggestion is still in a speculative stage, and it is interesting only as a possibility. Nevertheless, it calls attention to the fact in a striking way that under the pressure of factual observation and norms of convenience familiar language habits may come to be revised; and it indicates that the acceptance of logical principles as canonical need be neither on arbitrary grounds nor on grounds of their allegedly in-

---

[12] For example, the necessary truth "if (if A then B), then (if not-B then not-A)" could be eliminated from our language, provided that we introduce the rule that a statement of the form "if not-B then not-A" is deducible from a statement of the form "if A then B." On the other hand, it is usually assumed that when "A," "B," "C," "D" are any statements, they may be combined to form the new statements "if A then B," "if C then D," and "if (if A then B), then (if C then D)"; accordingly, since "not-A" and "not-B" are statements, "if (if A then B), then (if not-B then not-A)" must be accepted as a statement on the basis of the stipulation just mentioned. Hence, if the occurrence of such necessary truths is to be prevented, more complicated rules must be introduced for combining statements to form new ones.

[13] See Garrett Birkhoff and John von Neumann, "The Logic of Quantum Mechanics," *Annals of Mathematics*, XXXVII (1936), 823–43. The proposed logical system involves abandoning certain rules of inference which seem truistic both to "common sense" and to those accustomed to the system of *Principia Mathematica*.

herent authority, but on the ground that they effectively achieve certain postulated ends.

It must be emphasized, however, that this way of justifying logical principles has nothing in common with the view which construes them as descriptive of an intrinsic and pervasive structure of things. It has been argued that just as in geometry there are intrinsically different kinds of surface and each kind imposes "certain limits on the range of alternative coördinate systems which can be used to map it out," so "the objective structure of the system of fact imposes some limitation on the alternative systems of language or symbolism which are capable of representing it." The conclusion drawn from this argument by analogy is that propositions which would describe this structure "would almost inevitably take the form of propositions which formulate certain very abstract and general and widespread linguistic usages"; and since logical principles do "formulate" these usages, there can be only one genuinely valid logic, only one absolute system of necessary truths. But even if one accepts the questionable analogy which underlies the argument, elementary considerations of scientific procedure must lead one to reject the conception of "*the* objective structure of *the* system of fact" capable of being known without the mediation of any selective symbolic system. The study of scientific inquiry requires us to admit that structures cannot be known independently of activities of symbolization; that structures considered for investigation are selected on the basis of special problems; that the various structures discovered are not, according to the best evidence, all parts of one coherent pattern; and that the precise manner in which our theories are formulated is controlled by specifically human postulates no less than by experimental findings. The attempt to justify logical principles in terms of their supposed conformity to an absolute structure of facts thus completely overlooks their actual function of formulating and regulating the pursuit of human ideals. If the preceding discussion has any merit, however, the reasonable view is that the relative success of a system of logic in doing these things is the sole identifiable and objective basis for measuring its worth. . . .*

It is not unreasonable to maintain that every language, however much one may try to purify it of such elements, will inevitably contain expressions whose adequate understanding requires a consideration of the aims and activities of those who use that language as much as it involves a reference to the ostensible subject matter of that language. The conception of language as a mirror of existence, in the sense that the articulation of adequate discourse must have a structure identical with the order and connection of things, must therefore be judged as an oversimplified account of the relations between language and its subject matter. Ever since Duhem wrote on the subject, it has become a commonplace to observe that statements in the sciences are systematically connected and that only systems

---

* The omitted portion of this essay explores problems arising from the role of mathematics in empirical inquiry. (TMO)

of beliefs can be put to a definitive test. It is not yet a common-place that isolated portions of discourse possess significance only in terms of their place and function in a system of language habits. Language is the instrument for expressing the structures of things and processes; but not all its parts are symbols for elements in those things and processes, and not all its parts can be understood without reference to the norms and objectives which control the construction and the use of that instrument.

8.3

EMPIRICISM, SEMANTICS AND ONTOLOGY*

Rudolf Carnap

1. The Problem of Abstract Entities

Empiricists are in general rather suspicious with respect to any kind of abstract entities like properties, classes, relations, numbers, propositions, etc. They usually feel much more in sympathy with nominalists than with realists (in the medieval sense). As far as possible they try to avoid any reference to abstract entities and to restrict themselves to what is sometimes called a nominalistic language, i.e., one not containing

From Rudolf Carnap, *Meaning and Necessity* (Chicago: University of Chicago Press, 1956). Reprinted by permission of the publisher and the author.
    * I have made here some minor changes in the formulations to the effect that the term "framework" is now used only for the system of linguistic expressions, and not for the system of the entities in question.

such references. However, within certain scientific contexts it seems hardly possible to avoid them. In the case of mathematics, some empiricists try to find a way out by treating the whole of mathematics as a mere calculus, a formal system for which no interpretation is given or can be given. Accordingly, the mathematician is said to speak not about numbers, functions, and infinite classes, but merely about meaningless symbols and formulas manipulated according to given formal rules. In physics it is more difficult to shun the suspected entities, because the language of physics serves for the communication of reports and predictions and hence cannot be taken as a mere calculus. A physicist who is suspicious of abstract entities may perhaps try to declare a certain part of the language of physics as uninterpreted and uninterpretable, that part which refers to real numbers as space-time coordinates or as values of physical magnitudes, to functions, limits, etc. More probably he will just speak about all these things like anybody else but with an uneasy conscience, like a man who in his everyday life does with qualms many things which are not in accord with the high moral principles he professes on Sundays. Recently the problem of abstract entities has arisen again in connection with semantics, the theory of meaning and truth. Some semanticists say that certain expressions designate certain entities, and among these designated entities they include not only concrete material things but also abstract entities, e.g., properties as designated by predicates and propositions as designated by sentences.[1] Others object strongly to this procedure as violating the basic principles of empiricism and leading back to a metaphysical ontology of the Platonic kind.

It is the purpose of this article to clarify this controversial issue. The nature and implications of the acceptance of a language referring to abstract entities will first be discussed in general; it will be shown that using such a language does not imply embracing a Platonic ontology but is perfectly compatible with empiricism and strictly scientific thinking. Then the special question of the role of abstract entities in semantics will be discussed. It is hoped that the clarification of the issue will be useful to those who would like to accept abstract entities in their work in mathematics, physics, semantics, or

---

[1] The terms "sentence" and "statement" are here used synonymously for declarative (indicative, propositional) sentences.

any other field; it may help them to overcome nominalistic scruples.

2. Linguistic Frameworks

Are there properties, classes, numbers, propositions? In order to understand more clearly the nature of these and related problems, it is above all necessary to recognize a fundamental distinction between two kinds of questions concerning the existence or reality of entities. If someone wishes to speak in his language about a new kind of entities, he has to introduce a system of new ways of speaking, subject to new rules; we shall call this procedure the construction of a linguistic *framework* for the new entities in question. And now we must distinguish two kinds of questions of existence: first, questions of the existence of certain entities of the new kind *within the framework*; we call them *internal questions*; and second, questions concerning the existence or reality *of the system of entities as a whole*, called *external questions*. Internal questions and possible answers to them are formulated with the help of the new forms of expressions. The answers may be found either by purely logical methods or by empirical methods, depending upon whether the framework is a logical or a factual one. An external question is of a problematic character which is in need of closer examination.

THE WORLD OF THINGS. Let us consider as an example the simplest kind of entities dealt with in the everyday language: the spatio-temporally ordered system of observable things and events.

Once we have accepted the thing language with its framework for things, we can raise and answer internal questions, e.g., "Is there a white piece of paper on my desk?", "Did King Arthur actually live?", "Are unicorns and centaurs real or merely imaginary?", and the like. These questions are to be answered by empirical investigations. Results of observations are evaluated according to certain rules as confirming or disconfirming evidence for possible answers. (This evaluation is usually carried out, of course, as a matter of habit rather than a deliberate, rational procedure. But it is possible, in a rational reconstruction, to lay down explicit rules for the evaluation. This is one of the main tasks of a pure, as distinguished from a psychological, epistemology.) The concept of reality occurring in these internal questions is an empirical, scientific, non-metaphysical concept. To recognize something as a real thing or event means to succeed in incorporating it into the system of things at a particular space-time position so that it fits together with the other things recognized as real, according to the rules of the framework.

From these questions we must distinguish the external question of the reality of the thing world itself. In contrast to the former questions, this question is raised neither by the man in the street nor by scientists, but only by philosophers. Realists give an affirmative answer, subjective idealists a negative one, and the controversy goes on for centuries without ever being solved. And it cannot be solved because it is framed in a wrong way. To be real in the scientific sense means to be an ele-

ment of the system; hence this concept cannot be meaningfully applied to the system itself. Those who raise the question of the reality of the thing world itself have perhaps in mind not a theoretical question as their formulation seems to suggest, but rather a practical question, a matter of a practical decision concerning the structure of our language. We have to make the choice whether or not to accept and use the forms of expression in the framework in question.

In the case of this particular example, there is usually no deliberate choice because we all have accepted the thing language early in our lives as a matter of course. Nevertheless, we may regard it as a matter of decision in this sense: we are free to choose to continue using the thing language or not; in the latter case we could restrict ourselves to a language of sense-data and other "phenomenal" entities, or construct an alternative to the customary thing language with another structure, or, finally, we could refrain from speaking. If someone decides to accept the thing language, there is no objection against saying that he has accepted the world of things. But this must not be interpreted as if it meant his acceptance of a *belief* in the reality of the thing world; there is no such belief or assertion or assumption, because it is not a theoretical question. To accept the thing world means nothing more than to accept a certain form of language, in other words, to accept rules for forming statements and for testing, accepting, or rejecting them. The acceptance of the thing language leads, on the basis of observations made, also to the acceptance, belief, and assertion of certain statements. But the thesis of the reality of the thing world cannot be among these statements, because it cannot be formulated in the thing language or, it seems, in any other theoretical language.

The decision of accepting the thing language, although itself not of a cognitive nature, will nevertheless usually be influenced by theoretical knowledge, just like any other deliberate decision concerning the acceptance of linguistic or other rules. The purposes for which the language is intended to be used, for instance, the purpose of communicating factual knowledge, will determine which factors are relevant for the decision. The efficiency, fruitfulness, and simplicity of the use of the thing language may be among the decisive factors. And the questions concerning these qualites are indeed of a theoretical nature. But these questions cannot be identified with the question of realism. They are not yes-no questions but questions of degree. The thing language in the customary form works indeed with a high degree of efficiency for most purposes of everyday life. This is a matter of fact, based upon the content of our experiences. However, it would be wrong to describe this situation by saying: "The fact of the efficiency of the thing language is confirming evidence for the reality of the thing world"; we should rather say instead: "This fact makes it advisable to accept the thing language".

THE SYSTEM OF NUMBERS. As an example of a system which is of a logical rather than a factual nature let us take the system of natural numbers. The framework for this system is constructed by introducing into the language new expressions with suitable rules: (1) numerals like "five" and sentence forms like "there are five books on the table"; (2) the general term "number" for the new entities, and sentence forms like "five is a number"; (3) expressions for properties of numbers (e.g., "odd", "prime"), relations (e.g., "greater than"), and functions (e.g., "plus"), and sentence forms like "two plus three is five"; (4) numerical variables ("m", "n", etc.) and quantifiers for universal sentences ("for every n, . . .") and existential sentences ("there is an n such that . . .") with the customary deductive rules.

Here again there are internal questions, e.g., "Is there a prime number greater than a hundred?" Here, however, the answers are found, not by empirical investigation based on observations, but by logical analysis based on the rules for the new expressions. Therefore the answers are here analytic, i.e., logically true.

What is now the nature of the philosophical question concerning the existence or reality of numbers? To begin with, there is the internal question which, together with the affirmative answer, can be formulated in the new terms, say, by "There are numbers" or, more explicitly, "There is an n such that n is a number". This statement follows from the analytic statement "five is a number" and is therefore itself analytic. Moreover, it is rather trivial (in contradistinction to a statement like "There is a prime number greater than a million", which is likewise analytic but far from trivial), because it does not say more than that the new system is not empty; but this is immediately seen from the rule which states that words like "five" are substitutable for the new variables. Therefore nobody who meant the question "Are there numbers?" in the internal sense would either assert or even seriously consider a negative answer. This makes it plausible to assume that those philosophers who treat the question of the existence of numbers as a serious philosophical problem and offer lengthy arguments on either side, do not have in mind the internal question. And, indeed, if we were to ask them: "Do you mean the question as to whether the framework of numbers, *if* we were to accept it, would be found to be empty or not?", they would probably reply: "Not at all; we mean a question *prior* to the acceptance of the new framework". They might try to explain what they mean by saying that it is a question of the ontological status of numbers; the question whether or not numbers have a certain metaphysical characteristic called reality (but a kind of ideal reality, different from the material reality of the thing world) or subsistence or status of "independent entities". Unfortunately, these philosophers have so far not given a formulation of their question in terms of the common scientific language. Therefore our judgment must be that they have not succeeded in giving to the external question and to the possible answers any cognitive content. Unless and until they supply a clear cognitive interpretation, we are justified in our suspicion that their question is a pseudo-question, that is, one disguised in the form of a theoretical question while in fact it is non-theoretical; in the present case it is the practical problem whether or not to incorporate into the language the new linguistic forms which constitute the framework of numbers.

THE SYSTEM OF PROPOSITIONS. New variables, "p", "q", etc., are introduced with a rule to the effect that any (declarative) sentence may be substituted for a variable of this kind; this includes, in addition to the sentences of the original thing language, also all general sentences with variables of any kind which may have been introduced into the language. Further, the general term "proposition" is introduced. "p is a proposition" may be defined by "p or not p" (or by any other sentence form yielding only analytic sentences). Therefore, every sentence of the form ". . . is a proposition" (where any sentence may stand in the place of the dots) is analytic. This holds, for example, for the sentence:

(*a*) "Chicago is large is a proposition".

(We disregard here the fact that the rules of English grammar require not a sentence but a that-clause as the subject of another sentence; accordingly, instead of (*a*) we should have to say "That Chicago is large is a proposition".) Predicates may be admitted whose argument expressions are sentences; these predicates may be either extensional (e.g., the customary truth-functional connectives) or not (e.g., modal predicates like "possible", "necessary", etc.). With the help of the new variables, general sentences may be formed, e.g., (*b*) "For every *p*, either *p* or not-*p*".

(*c*) "There is a *p* such that *p* is not necessary and not-*p* is not necessary".

(*d*) "There is a *p* such that *p* is a proposition".

(*c*) and (*d*) are internal assertions of existence. The statement "There are propositions" may be meant in the sense of (*d*); in this case it is analytic (since it follows from (*a*)) and even trivial. If, however, the statement is meant in an external sense, then it is non-cognitive.

It is important to notice that the system of rules for the linguistic expressions of the propositional framework (of which only a few rules have here been briefly indicated) is sufficient for the introduction of the framework. Any further explanations as to the nature of the propositions (i.e., the elements of the system indicated, the values of the variables "*p*", "*q*", etc.) are theoretically unnecessary because, if correct, they follow from the rules. For example, are propositions mental events (as in Russell's theory)? A look at the rules shows us that they are not, because otherwise existential statements would be of the form: "If the mental state of the person in question fulfils such and such conditions, then there is a *p* such that . . .". The fact that no references to mental conditions occur in existential statements (like (*c*), (*d*), etc.) shows that propositions are not mental entities. Further, a statement of the existence of linguistic entities (e.g., expressions, classes of expressions, etc.) must contain a reference to a language. The fact that no such reference occurs in the existential statements here, shows that propositions are not linguistic entities. The fact that in these statements no reference to a subject (an observer or knower) occurs (nothing like: "There is a *p* which is necessary for Mr. *X*"), shows that the propositions (and their properties, like necessity, etc.) are not subjective. Although characterizations of these or similar kinds are, strictly speaking, unnecessary, they may nevertheless be practically useful. If they are given, they should be understood, not as ingredient parts of the system, but merely as marginal notes with the purpose of supplying to the reader helpful hints or convenient pictorial associations which may make his learning of the use of the expressions easier than the bare system of the rules would do. Such a characterization is analogous to an extra-systematic explanation which a physicist sometimes gives to the beginner. He might, for example, tell him to imagine the atoms of a gas as small balls rushing around with great speed, or the electromagnetic field and its oscillations as quasi-elastic tensions and vibrations in an ether. In fact, however, all that can accurately be said about atoms or the field is implicitly contained in the physical laws of the theories in question.[2]

---

[2] In my book *Meaning and Necessity* (Chicago, 1947) I have developed a semantical method which takes propositions as entities designated by sentences (more specifically, as intensions of sentences). In order to facilitate the understanding of the systematic development, I added some informal, extra-systematic explanations concerning the

THE SYSTEM OF THING PROPERTIES.
The thing language contains words like
"red", "hard", "stone", "house", etc.,
which are used for describing what
things are like. Now we may introduce
new variables, say "f", "g", etc., for
which those words are substitutable and
furthermore the general term "property". New rules are laid down which
admit sentences like "Red is a property", "Red is a color", "These two pieces

of paper have at least one color in common" (i.e., "There is an f such that f
is a color, and . . ."). The last sentence
is an internal assertion. It is of an empirical, factual nature. However, the external statement, the philosophical statement of the reality of properties—a
special case of the thesis of the reality
of universals—is devoid of cognitive
content.

THE SYSTEMS OF INTEGERS AND RA-
TIONAL NUMBERS. Into a language
containing the framework of natural
numbers we may introduce first the
(positive and negative) integers as relations among natural numbers and then
the rational numbers as relations among
integers. This involves introducing new
types of variables, expressions substitutable for them, and the general terms
"integer" and "rational number".

THE SYSTEM OF REAL NUMBERS. On
the basis of the national numbers, the
real numbers may be introduced as
classes of a special kind (segments) of
rational numbers (according to the
method developed by Dedekind and
Frege). Here again a new type of
variables is introduced, expressions sub-
stituable for them (e.g., "$\sqrt{2}$"), and
the general term "real number".

THE SPATIO-TEMPORAL COORDINATE
SYSTEM FOR PHYSICS. The new entities
are the space-time points. Each is an
ordered quadruple of four real numbers,
called its coordinates, consisting of three
spatial and one temporal coordinate.
The physical state of a spatio-temporal
point or region is described either with
the help of qualitative predicates (e.g.,

---

nature of propositions. I said that the term
"proposition" "is used neither for a linguistic expression nor for a subjective, mental
occurrence, but rather for something objective that may or may not be exemplified in
nature. . . . We apply the term 'proposition'
to any entities of a certain logical type,
namely, those that may be expressed by
(declarative) sentences in a language" (p.
27). After some more detailed discussions
concerning the relation between propositions
and facts, and the nature of false propositions, I added: "It has been the purpose of
the preceding remarks to facilitate the understanding of our conception of propositions.
If, however, a reader should find these explanations more puzzling than clarifying, or
even unacceptable, he may disregard them"
(p. 31) (that is, disregard these extra-
systematic explanations, not the whole theory
of the propositions as intensions of sentences,
as one reviewer understood). In spite of this
warning, it seems that some of those readers
who were puzzled by the explanations, did
not disregard them but thought that by raising objections against them they could refute
the theory. This is analogous to the procedure of some laymen who by (correctly)
criticizing the ether picture or other visual-
izations of physical theories, thought they
had refuted those theories. Perhaps the discussions in the present paper will help in
clarifying the role of the system of linguistic
rules for the introduction of a framework
for entities on the one hand, and that of
extra-systematic explanations concerning the
nature of the entities on the other.

"hot") or by ascribing numbers as values of a physical magnitude (e.g., mass, temperature, and the like). The step from the system of things (which does not contain space-time points but only extended objects with spatial and temporal relations between them) to the physical coordinate system is again a matter of decision. Our choice of certain features, although itself not theoretical, is suggested by theoretical knowledge, either logical or factual. For example, the choice of real numbers rather than rational numbers or integers as coordinates is not much influenced by the facts of experience but mainly due to considerations of mathematical simplicity. The restriction to rational coordinates would not be in conflict with any experimental knowledge we have, because the result of any measurement is a rational number. However, it would prevent the use of ordinary geometry (which says, e.g., that the diagonal of a square with the side 1 has the irrational value $\sqrt{2}$) and thus lead to great complications. On the other hand, the decision to use three rather than two or four spatial coordinates is strongly suggested, but still not forced upon us, by the result of common observations. If certain events allegedly observed in spiritualistic séances, e.g., a ball moving out of a sealed box, were confirmed beyond any reasonable doubt, it might seem advisable to use four spatial coordinates. Internal questions are here, in general, empirical questions to be answered by empirical investigations. On the other hand, the external questions of the reality of physical space and physical time are pseudo-questions. A question like "Are there

(really) space-time points?" is ambiguous. It may be meant as an internal question; then the affirmative answer is, of course, analytic and trivial. Or it may be meant in the external sense: "Shall we introduce such and such forms into our language?"; in this case it is not a theoretical but a practical question, a matter of decision rather than assertion, and hence the proposed formulation would be misleading. Or finally, it may be meant in the following sense: "Are our experiences such that the use of the linguistic forms in question will be expedient and fruitful?" This is a theoretical question of a factual, empirical nature. But it concerns a matter of degree; therefore a formulation in the form "real or not?" would be inadequate.

3. What Does Acceptance of a Kind of Entities Mean?

Let us now summarize the essential characteristics of situations involving the introduction of a new kind of entities, characteristics which are common to the various examples outlined above.

The acceptance of a new kind of entities is represented in the language by the introduction of a framework of new forms of expressions to be used according to a new set of rules. There may be new names for particular entities of the kind in question; but some such names may already occur in the language before the introduction of the new framework. (Thus, for example, the thing language contains certainly words of the type of "blue" and "house" before the framework of properties is introduced; and it may contain words like "ten" in sentences of the form "I have ten fingers" before the framework of numbers is introduced.) The latter fact shows that the occurrence of constants of the type in question—regarded as names of entities of the new kind after the new framework is introduced—is not a sure sign of the acceptance of the new kind of entities. Therefore the introduction of such constants is not to be regarded as an essential step in the introduction of the framework. The two essential steps are rather the following. First, the introduction of a general term, a predicate of higher level, for the new kind of entities, permitting us to say of any particular entity that it belongs to this kind (e.g., "Red is a *property*", "Five is a *number*"). Second, the introduction of variables of the new type. The new entities are values of these variables; the constants (and the closed compound expressions, if any) are substitutable for the variables.[3] With the help of the variables, general sentences concerning the new entities can be formulated.

After the new forms are introduced into the language, it is possible to formulate with their help internal questions and possible answers to them. A question of this kind may be either empiri-

cal or logical; accordingly a true answer is either factually true or analytic.

From the internal questions we must clearly distinguish external questions, i.e., philosophical questions concerning the existence or reality of the total system of the new entities. Many philosophers regard a question of this kind as an ontological question which must be raised and answered *before* the introduction of the new language forms. The latter introduction, they believe, is legitimate only if it can be justified by an ontological insight supplying an affirmative answer to the question of reality. In contrast to this view, we take the position that the introduction of the new ways of speaking does not need any theoretical justification because it does not imply any assertion of reality. We may still speak (and have done so) of "the acceptance of the new entities" since this form of speech is customary; but one must keep in mind that this phrase does not mean for us anything more than acceptance of the new framework, i.e., of the new linguistic forms. Above all, it must not be interpreted as referring to an assumption, belief, or assertion of "the reality of the entities". There is no such assertion. An alleged statement of the reality of the system of entities is a pseudo-statement without cognitive content. To be sure, we have to face at this point an important question; but it is a practical, not a theoretical question; it is the question of whether or not to accept the new linguistic forms. The acceptance cannot be judged as being either true or false because it is not an assertion. It can only be judged as being more or less expedient, fruitful, conducive to the aim for

---

[3] W. V. Quine was the first to recognize the importance of the introduction of variables as indicating the acceptance of entities. "The ontology to which one's use of language commits him comprises simply the objects that he treats as falling . . . within the range of values of his variables", "Notes on Existence and Necessity," JP 40 (1943), p. 118; compare also his "Designation and Existence," JP 36 (1939), and "On Universals," *Journal of Symbolic Logic*, 12 (1947).

which the language is intended. Judgments of this kind supply the motivation for the decision of accepting or rejecting the kind of entities.[4]

Thus it is clear that the acceptance of a linguistic framework must not be regarded as implying a metaphysical doctrine concerning the reality of the entities in question. It seems to me due to a neglect of this important distinction that some contemporary nominalists label the admission of variables of abstract types as "Platonism".[5] This is, to

say the least, an extremely misleading terminology. It leads to the absurd consequence, that the position of everybody who accepts the language of physics with its real number variables (as a language of communication, not merely as a calculus) would be called Platonistic, even if he is a strict empiricist who rejects Platonic metaphysics.

A brief historical remark may here be inserted. The non-cognitive character of the questions which we have called here external questions was recognized and emphasized already by the Vienna Circle under the leadership of Moritz Schlick, the group from which the movement of logical empiricism originated. Influenced by ideas of Ludwig Wittgenstein, the Circle rejected both the thesis of the reality of the external world and the thesis of its irreality as pseudo-statements;[6] the same was the case for both the thesis of the reality of universals (abstract entities, in our present terminology) and the nominalistic thesis that they are not real and that their alleged names are not names of anything but merely *flatus vocis*. (It is obvious that the apparent negation of a pseudo-statement must also be a pseudo-statement.) It is therefore not correct to classify the members of the Vienna Circle as nominalists, as is sometimes done. However, if we look at the basic anti-

---

[4] For a closely related point of view on these questions see the detailed discussions in Herbert Feigl, "Existential Hypotheses", *Philosophy of Science*, 17 (1950), 35–62.

[5] Paul Bernays, "Sur le platonisme dans les mathématiques" (*L'Enseignement math.*, 34 (1935), 52–69). W. V. Quine, see previous footnote and a recent paper ["On What There Is," *Review of Metaphysics*, 2 (1948)]. Quine does not acknowledge the distinction which I emphasize above, because according to his general conception there are no sharp boundary lines between logical and factual truth, between questions of meaning and questions of fact, between the acceptance of a language structure and the acceptance of an assertion formulated in the language. This conception, which seems to deviate considerably from customary ways of thinking, is explained in his article, "Semantics and Abstract Objects." When Quine in the article "On What There Is" classifies my logistic conception of mathematics (derived from Frege and Russell) as "platonic realism" (p. 33), this is meant (according to a personal communication from him) not as ascribing to me agreement with Plato's metaphysical doctrine of universals, but merely as referring to the fact that I accept a language of mathematics containing variables of higher levels. With respect to the basic attitude to take in choosing a language form (an "ontology" in Quine's terminology, which seems to me misleading), there appears now to be agree-

ment between us: "the obvious counsel is tolerance and an experimental spirit" (["On What There Is"], p. 38).

[6] See Carnap, *Scheinprobleme in der Philosophie; das Fremdpsychische und der Realismusstreit*, Berlin, 1928. Moritz Schlick, *Positivismus und Realismus*, reprinted in *Gesammelte Aufsätze*, Wien, 1938.

metaphysical and pro-scientific attitude of most nominalists (and the same holds for many materialists and realists in the modern sense), disregarding their occasional pseudo-theoretical formulations, then it is, of course, true to say that the Vienna Circle was much closer to those philosophers than to their opponents.

4. Abstract Entities in Semantics

The problem of the legitimacy and the status of abstract entities has recently again led to controversial discussions in connection with semantics. In a semantical meaning analysis certain expressions in a language are often said to designate (or name or denote or signify or refer to) certain extra-linguistic entities.[7] As long as physical things or events (e.g., Chicago or Caesar's death) are taken as designata (entities designated), no serious doubts arise. But strong objections have been raised, especially by some empiricists, against abstract entities as designata, e.g., against semantical statements of the following kind:

(1) "The word 'red' designates a property of things";

_____
[7] See _Introduction to Semantics_ (Cambridge, Mass., 1942); _Meaning and Necessity_ (Chicago, 1947). The distinction I have drawn in the latter book between the method of the name-relation and the method of intension and extension is not essential for our present discussion. The term "designation" is used in the present article in a neutral way; it may be understood as referring to the name-relation or to the intension-relation or to the extension-relation or to any similar relations used in other semantical methods.

(2) "The word 'color' designates a property of properties of things";
(3) "The word 'five' designates a number";
(4) "The word 'odd' designates a property of numbers";
(5) "The sentence 'Chicago is large' designates a proposition".

Those who criticize these statements do not, of course, reject the use of the expressions in question, like "red" or "five"; nor would they deny that these expressions are meaningful. But to be meaningful, they would say, is not the same as having a meaning in the sense of an entity designated. They reject the belief, which they regard as implicitly presupposed by those semantical statements, that to each expression of the types in question (adjectives like "red", numerals like "five", etc.) there is a particular real entity to which the expression stands in the relation of designation. This belief is rejected as incompatible with the basic principles of empiricism or of scientific thinking. Derogatory labels like "Platonic realism", "hypostatization", or " 'Fido'-Fido principle" are attached to it. The latter is the name given by Gilbert Ryle [See 2.2] to the criticized belief, which, in his view, arises by a naïve inference of analogy: just as there is an entity well known to me, viz. my dog Fido, which is designated by the name "Fido", thus there must be for every meaningful expression a particular entity to which it stands in the relation of designation or naming, i.e., the relation exemplified by "Fido"-Fido. The brief criticized is thus a case of hypostatization, i.e., of treating as names expressions which are not names. While "Fido" is a name, expressions like "red", "five", etc., are said not to be names, not to designate anything.

Our previous discussion concerning the acceptance of frameworks enables us now to clarify the situation with respect to abstract entities as designata. Let us take as an example the statement:

(a) "'Five' designates a number".

The formulation of this statement presupposes that our language L contains the forms of expressions which we have called the framework of numbers, in particular, numerical variables and the general term "number". If L contains these forms, the following is an analytic statement in L:

(b) "Five is a number".

Further, to make the statement (a) possible, L must contain an expression like "designates" or "is a name of" for the semantical relation of designation. If suitable rules for this term are laid down, the following is likewise analytic:

(c) "'Five' designates five".

(Generally speaking, any expression of the form "'...' designates ..." is an analytic statement provided the term "..." is a constant in an accepted framework. If the latter condition is not fulfilled, the expression is not a statement.) Since (a) follows from (c) and (b), (a) is likewise analytic.

Thus it is clear that *if* someone accepts the framework of numbers, then he must acknowledge (c) and (b) and hence (a) as true statements. Generally

speaking, if someone accepts a framework for a certain kind of entities, then he is bound to admit the entities as possible designata. Thus the question of the admissibility of entities of a certain type or of abstract entities in general as designata is reduced to the question of the acceptability of the linguistic framework for those entities. Both the nominalistic critics, who refuse the status of designators or names to expressions like "red", "five", etc., because they deny the existence of abstract entities, and the skeptics, who express doubts concerning the existence and demand evidence for it, treat the question of existence as a theoretical question. They do, of course, not mean the internal question; the affirmative answer to *this* question is analytic and trivial and too obvious for doubt or denial, as we have seen. Their doubts refer rather to the system of entities itself; hence they mean the external question. They believe that only after making sure that there really is a system of entities of the kind in question are we justified in accepting the framework by incorporating the linguistic forms into our language. However, we have seen that the external question is not a theoretical question but rather the practical question whether or not to accept those linguistic forms. This acceptance is not in need of a theoretical justification (except with respect to expediency and fruitfulness), because it does not imply a belief or assertion. Ryle says that the "Fido"-Fido principle is "a grotesque theory". Grotesque or not, Ryle is wrong in calling it a theory. It is rather the practical decision to accept certain frameworks. Maybe Ryle is historically right with respect to those whom he mentions as previous representatives of the principle, viz. John Stuart Mill, Frege, and Russell. If these philosophers regarded the acceptance of a system of entities as a theory, an assertion, they were victims of the same old, metaphysical confusion. But it is certainly wrong to regard *my* semantical method as involving a belief in the reality of abstract entities, since I reject a thesis of this kind as a metaphysical pseudostatement.

The critics of the use of abstract entities in semantics overlook the fundamental difference between the acceptance of a system of entities and an internal assertion, e.g., an assertion that there are elephants or electrons or prime numbers greater than a million. Whoever makes an internal assertion is certainly obliged to justify it by providing evidence, empirical evidence in the case of electrons, logical proof in the case of the prime numbers. The demand for a theoretical justification, correct in the case of internal assertions, is sometimes wrongly applied to the acceptance of a system of entities. Thus, for example, Ernest Nagel in his review of *Meaning and Necessity* asks for "evidence relevant for affirming with warrant that there are such entities as infinitesimals or propositions". He characterizes the evidence required in these cases—in distinction to the empirical evidence in the case of electrons —as "in the broad sense logical and dialectical". Beyond this no hint is given as to what might be regarded as relevant evidence. Some nominalists regard the acceptance of abstract entities as a kind of superstition or myth, populating the world with fictitious or at least dubious

entities, analogous to the belief in centaurs or demons. This shows again the confusion mentioned, because a superstition or myth is a false (or dubious) internal statement.

Let us take as example the natural numbers as cardinal numbers, i.e., in contexts like "Here are three books". The linguistic forms of the framework of numbers, including variables and the general term "number", are generally used in our common language of communication; and it is easy to formulate explicit rules for their use. Thus the logical characteristics of this framework are sufficiently clear (while many internal questions, i.e., arithmetical questions, are, of course, still open). In spite of this, the controversy concerning the external question of the ontological reality of the system of numbers continues. Suppose that one philosopher says: "I believe that there are numbers as real entities. This gives me the right to use the linguistic forms of the numerical framework and to make semantical statements about numbers as designata of numerals". His nominalistic opponent replies: "You are wrong; there are no numbers. The numerals may still be used as meaningful expressions. But they are not names, there are no entities designated by them. Therefore the word "number" and numerical variables must not be used (unless a way were found to introduce them as merely abbreviating devices, a way of translating them into the nominalistic thing language)." I cannot think of any possible evidence that would be regarded as relevant by both philosophers, and therefore, if actually found, would decide the controversy or at least make one of the opposite theses more probable than the other. (To construe the numbers as classes or properties of the second level, according to the Frege-Russell method, does, of course, not solve the controversy, because the first philosopher would affirm and the second deny the existence of the system of classes or properties of the second level.) Therefore I feel compelled to regard the external question as a pseudo-question, until both parties to the controversy offer a common interpretation of the question as a cognitive question; this would involve an indication of possible evidence regarded as relevant by both sides.

There is a particular kind of misinterpretation of the acceptance of abstract entities in various fields of science and in semantics, that needs to be cleared up. Certain early British empiricists (e.g., Berkeley and Hume) denied the existence of abstract entities on the ground that immediate experience presents us only with particulars, not with universals, e.g., with this red patch, but not with Redness or Color-in-General; with this scalene triangle, but not with Scalene Triangularity or Triangularity-in-General. Only entities belonging to a type of which examples were to be found within immediate experience could be accepted as ultimate constituents of reality. Thus, according to this way of thinking, the existence of abstract entities could be asserted only if one could show either that some abstract entities fall within the given, or that abstract entities can be defined in terms of the types of entity which are given. Since these empiricists found no abstract entities within the realm of sense-data, they either denied their existence, or else made a futile attempt to define universals in terms of particulars. Some contemporary philosophers, especially English philosophers following Bertrand Russell, think in basically similar terms. They emphasize a distinction between the data (that which is immediately given in consciousness, e.g., sense-data, immediately past experiences, etc.) and the constructs based on the data. Existence or reality is ascribed only to the data; the constructs are not real entities; the corresponding linguistic expressions are merely ways of speech not actually designating anything (reminiscent of the nominalists' *flatus vocis*). We shall not criticize here this general conception. (As far as it is a principle of accepting certain entities and not accepting others, leaving aside any ontological, phenomenalistic and nominalistic pseudo-statements, there cannot be any theoretical objection to it.) But if this conception leads to the view that other philosophers or scientists who accept abstract entities thereby assert or imply their occurrence as immediate data, then such a view must be rejected as a misinterpretation. References to space-time points, the electromagnetic field, or electrons in physics, to real or complex numbers and their functions in mathematics, to the excitatory potential or unconscious complexes in psychology, to an inflationary trend in economics, and the like, do not imply the assertion that entities of these kinds occur as immediate data. And the same holds for references to abstract entities as designata in semantics. Some of the criticisms by English philosophers against such ref-

erences give the impression that, probably due to the misinterpretation just
indicated, they accuse the semanticist
not so much of bad metaphysics (as
some nominalists would do) but of bad
psychology. The fact that they regard
a semantical method involving abstract
entities not merely as doubtful and perhaps wrong, but as manifestly absurd,
preposterous and grotesque, and that
they show a deep horror and indignation against this method, is perhaps to
be explained by a misinterpretation of
the kind described. In fact, of course,
the semanticist does not in the least
assert or imply that the abstract entities
to which he refers can be experienced
as immediately given either by sensation or by a kind of rational intuition.
An assertion of this kind would indeed
be very dubious psychology. The psychological question as to which kinds of
entities do and which do not occur as
immediate data is entirely irrelevant for
semantics, just as it is for physics, mathematics, economics, etc., with respect to
the examples mentioned above.[8]

5. Conclusion

For those who want to develop or
use semantical methods, the decisive
question is not the alleged ontological
question of the existence of abstract entities but rather the question whether
the use of abstract linguistic forms or,

in technical terms, the use of variables
beyond those for things (or phenomenal
data), is expedient and fruitful for the
purposes for which semantical analyses
are made, viz. the analysis, interpretation, clarification, or construction of languages of communication, especially languages of science. This question is here
neither decided nor even discussed. It
is not a question simply of yes or no,
but a matter of degree. Among those
philosophers who have carried out semantical analyses and thought about
suitable tools for this work, beginning
with Plato and Aristotle and, in a more
technical way on the basis of modern
logic, with C. S. Peirce and Frege, a
great majority accepted abstract entities. This does, of course, not prove
the case. After all, semantics in the
technical sense is still in the initial
phases of its development, and we must
be prepared for possible fundamental
changes in methods. Let us therefore
admit that the nominalistic critics may
possibly be right. But if so, they will
have to offer better arguments than they
have so far. Appeal to ontological insight will not carry much weight. The
critics will have to show that it is possible to construct a semantical method
which avoids all references to abstract
entities and achieves by simpler means
essentially the same results as the other
methods.

The acceptance or rejection of abstract linguistic forms, just as the acceptance or rejection of any other linguistic forms in any branch of science,
will finally be decided by their efficiency as instruments, the ratio of the results achieved to the amount and complexity of the efforts required. To decree

---

[8] Wilfrid Sellars ("Acquaintance and Description Again", in *Journal of Philos.*, 46
(1949), 496–504; see pp. 502 f.) analyzes
clearly the roots of the mistake "of taking
the designation relation of semantic theory
to be a reconstruction of *being present to an
experience*".

dogmatic prohibitions of certain linguistic forms instead of testing them by their success or failure in practical use, is worse than futile; it is positively harmful because it may obstruct scientific progress. The history of science shows examples of such prohibitions based on prejudices deriving from religious, mythological, metaphysical, or other irrational sources, which slowed up the developments for shorter or longer periods of time. Let us learn from the lessons of history. Let us grant to those who work in any special field of investigation the freedom to use any form of expression which seems useful to them; the work in the field will sooner or later lead to the elimination of those forms which have no useful function. *Let us be cautious in making assertions and critical in examining them, but tolerant in permitting linguistic forms.*

MATHEMATICS, ABSTRACT ENTITIES AND MODERN SEMANTICS*

8.4

Arthur Pap

A science can be in a highly advanced state, even though its logical foundations are far from being clarified. Mechanics, for example, reached a stage of astounding perfection by the end of the 18th century, mainly through the genius of Galileo and Newton, although much room was left for controversy about the meanings of its fundamental concepts: length, simultaneity, mass, and force. Even the meaning of the simple law of inertia remained controversial right up

From *The Scientific Monthly*, LXXXV (July 1957), pp. 29–40. Reprinted by permission of the editors of *Science*.

* In this selection, notes and references are cited by italic numbers in parentheses. They appear at the end of the selection.

to Einstein's "unification" of inertia and gravitation. Similarly, mathematics was not prevented from reaching breathtaking heights of perfection by the *Grundlagenstreit* (dispute about foundations) which began in the 19th century and still continues.

The fundamental question of the philosophy of mathematics concerns the very nature of its subject matter. Traditionally, mathematics was defined as the science of quantity, but this definition was decisively criticized by Bertrand Russell in terms of a conception which reduces pure, abstract mathematics to pure, abstract logic, thereby lifting any restriction to a special subject matter. But though pure mathematics in this conception is, in contrast to the special empirical sciences, unrestricted in subject matter, its propositions are analyzed as referring to classes and attributes. In probing into the foundations of mathematics, therefore, one cannot avoid facing, sooner or later, the old metaphysical problem of the status of abstract entities. The latter has been tied up with the problems of linguistic meaning and reference ever since Plato but never before as closely as at the present time. Modern semantics, as cultivated by analytic philosophers in the United States and England, grew up in close contact with symbolic logic. Accordingly, the problem to be discussed in this article should be of equal concern to mathematicians who reflect on the foundations of their science, to semanticists, and to symbolic logicians.

Traditional Problem of Universals

When a high-school teacher demonstrates that the sum of the interior angles of a triangle equals 180°, he usually draws a triangle on the blackboard, then draws a straight line through the top vertex parallel to the base, in order to be able to reduce the proof of the Euclidean theorem to the proposition that "corresponding" angles are equal. How would he satisfy a "philosophic" pupil who protested that he had not established that all triangles whatsoever have the property in question but only that the particular triangle on the blackboard had it? Obviously, the proper reply would be this: We can be perfectly sure that every Euclidean triangle has the property, without illustrating the proof over and over again by

different triangles, because any properties of the particular triangle that distinguish it from other triangles—such as its being equilateral, or its comparatively small size, or its being bounded by white lines—were disregarded in the proof. In the language of Plato: What the mathematician is thinking about when he discovers the geometric proof is not a particular triangle but *triangularity as such*—in other words, that which all particular triangles have in common and by virtue of which they are triangles.

It is this sort of thing that various philosophers, past and present, under Plato's influence call a "universal," or an "intelligible form," or an "essence." These entities were supposed by both Plato and Aristotle to be the objects of scientific thought, as contrasted with "particulars" that are given in sense-experience with a unique location in space and time. Of course, these universals did not have to be geometric forms. In the case of every predicate whatsoever, the things to which the predicate is applicable can be distinguished from the property the possession of which by a particular thing is the criterion of the predicate's applicability: redness is to be distinguished from red things, hardness from hard things, humanity from particular human beings, and so on.

Again, numbers seemed to be a kind of universals, for, to ask a question which unphilosophic people never ask at all: What is the number 2? It surely is not the symbol "2," for we can use different symbols to talk about the same number (for example, "II," "two," "zwei"). It must, then, be something that the symbol stands for. But it cannot be identified with a particular pair of objects, say a pair of gloves, or a pair of apples, or a pair consisting of wife and husband. It seems, rather, to be something that all particular pairs have in common ("twoness"), an object of abstract thought, not a sensible object.

Once universals are conceived as objects of thought, the realm of universals will be found to be populated not only with those that are somehow "exemplified" in the particulars we sense but also with unexemplified universals: no physical sphere corresponds exactly to the mathematical concept of a sphere; hence, the universal *sphericity* which the mathematician thinks about is not, strictly speaking, exemplified in the physical world. And even if one never physically constructed a regular polygon with 1000 sides, this mathematical object could be reasoned about, and in order that it may be reasoned about it must in some sense "exist," say the Platonists. In the heaven of Platonic forms, then, we find not only perfect mathematical objects but also unexemplified forms that move the imagination of less intellectual people: mermaidhood, centaurhood, unicornhood, and so on. The Platonists' argument seems to be that, in order that something may be thought of, it must in some sense *be*; we can obviously think of mermaids, though there are no physical mermaids in space and time, but we could not have such thoughts unless there existed the universal *mermaidhood*. Since these universals do not exist in space and time, some Platonists try to avoid confusion by calling the sort of "being" that is to be ascribed to them "subsistence" (*1*).

It is important to understand that universals as traditionally conceived, especially by Platonists, are not mental in the sense in which a thought or an act of imagination or a feeling is mental. They are, rather, postulated *objects* of thought whose subsistence is alleged to be independent of their being mentally apprehended in any way. It is for this reason that Platonism is usually called a kind of "realism." Universals are held to be real in the sense that there would be such entities even if no consciousness existed, just as a *physical* realist holds that physical objects are there, whether or not any conscious organism or disembodied mind is aware of them.

The most important traditional arguments, then, for there being universals over and above the world of sensible particulars in space and time are the following two. (i) With the exception of proper names, all meaningful words are *general*. To say that they are meaningful is to say that they stand for something. But, unlike proper names, words like *horse*, *round*, and *red* do not stand for particular things. Therefore they stand for universals. And these universals would be "there" somehow, even if they were never referred to by means of words. (ii) Every thought has an object; to think is essentially to think *of* something, and the object of one's thought is clearly distinct from the thinking of it. When two mathematicians, for example, converse with each other about the properties of a certain number, they assume without hesitation that they are thinking about the same object and that they are merely trying to discover the properties of that object, in the same sense that a chemist is trying to discover the properties of a compound he is experimenting with, though by essentially different methods. The square root of two would have been irrational, even if no mind had ever thought about it, let alone discovered its irrationality. This second argument is much more tempting than the first. As we shall see presently, the first argument is rather easily disposed of by exposing the underlying confusion between meaningful words and names. But the second argument is a natural outgrowth of a psychological situation with which even non-mathematicians are familiar. Imagine a child who has just learned the meaning of "square number" by means of the examples $4 = 2 \times 2$, $9 = 3 \times 3$, and curiously investigates how many square numbers there are between 1 and 100 and whether their frequency increases or decreases as the numbers increase. He seems to explore a domain of objects that have invariable properties in no way dependent on human thoughts, and yet these objects are not physical objects with spatial location. The child may at first suppose himself to be talking about marks on paper when he say "9 is a square number but 10 is not," but you can easily convince him that these are merely symbols we use for referring to invisible numbers: the sentences "9 is a square number" and "nine is a square number" refer to the same number, but the symbols "9" and "nine" are obviously different.

Modern Semantics and the Traditional Dispute

Many traditional philosophers, especially Occam and his followers in medieval philosophy and the British empiricists since Hobbes, have tried to discredit Platonism as a belief that has no better rational foundation than a belief in ghosts and fairies. Whatever exists, said the nominalists, is a particular in space and time, and there is no need to postulate any "subsistent" abstract entities. A general word does not stand for a universal but is just an economic device for referring to several particular things that are in certain respects similar. According to the realists, a meaningful general word, like *man*, stands for a universal, and when we judge that a particular object is correctly called "man," we compare it, as it were, to our idea of the universal. But the nominalists denied that we can form ideas of universals—"abstract ideas"—at all. To quote the subtlest of them, George Berkeley (2): ". . . it is thought that every name has, or ought to have, one only precise and settled signification, which inclines men to think there are certain abstract, determinate ideas that constitute the true and only immediate signification of each general name; and that it is by the mediation of these abstract ideas that a general name comes to signify any particular thing. Whereas, in truth, there is no such thing as one precise and definite signification annexed to any general name, they all signifying indifferently a great number of particular ideas."

This is a striking anticipation of modern semantic analysis. Berkeley is criticizing the scholastic belief, ultimately derived from Plato, that the generality of a word consists in its representing a determinate entity which is not a particular and of which we have an "abstract" idea. Rather, he held, the generality of a word is its capacity to evoke any one of a set of similar particular ideas. If I apply the general word *triangle* to a particular figure, I do not do so as a result of finding the particular figure to correspond to an abstract idea of triangularity—there is no such thing—but simply because I recognize it as similar in a certain respect to objects with which I have been conditioned to associate the word *triangle*. Berkeley might have said, as some contemporary analytic philosophers have said explicitly, that the meaningfulness of a word does not presuppose the existence of an entity which is *what* the word means. That the word *triangle* is unambiguous in the context of geometric discourse does not entail that it functions in that context as a *name* of a unique entity, call it a "universal." One chief source of Platonism, according to this point of view, is the naive and mainly unconscious assumption that every meaningful word is a name of something. But the verb "to mean" is, in the relevant respect, more like the verbs "to dream" and "to wish" than like the verbs "to name" and "to eat"; there must *be* something that can be named in order that an act of naming may take place, and there must *be* something that can be eaten in order that a process of eating may occur. But would it not be grotesque if I argued to the existence of green dogs that can sing Verdi arias from the fact that I dreamed of such an animal, or to the existence of a woman who is my wife and combines more virtues than any other woman from the fact that I wish for such a wife? In grammatical terminology, this criticism of Platonism accuses it of construing "to mean" as a transitive verb, whereas this verb is obviously intransitive.

The chief philosophic motive behind Bertrand Russell's *theory of descriptions* (3) was to expose this confusion and thereby to inhibit the tendency to postulate entities that do not exist in the physical universe. To borrow Russell's own example, consider the sentence "the present king of France is bald." On a crude level of analysis one might say that, since the sentence is meaningful (all constituent words are meaningful and are arranged in a syntactically correct way), it must be about something. And what is it about if not the present king of France? But there is no present king of France! Is it, then, about a Platonic essence or Idea that happens to be unexemplified in the physical world? Russell's answer was that no such metaphysical postulations are required to account for the significance of the sentence. We have only to distinguish between *contextual meaning* and *denotation*: a definite description, like "the present king of France," has meaning in context but does not denote anything at all. It has meaning in the context of sentences that contain it, and this meaning can be explained by means of a synonymous sentence in which no definite descriptions occur: "there is one and only one individual which is present king of France, and that individual is bald" (4). Once meaning and denotation are thus distinguished—a symbol may be meaningful (in context) without denoting anything—the argument for the existence of universals from the meaningfulness of predicates collapses, for a predicate can be meaningful in the context of entire sentences without being a name of anything.

This, in fact, is a fundamental tenet of contemporary semantic nominalism (I call this philosophic school "semantic" nominalism to distinguish it from metaphysical nominalism, because its members tend to avoid such metaphysical locutions as, "only particular things or events in space and time are real, universals are abstractions that have no reality"): to this school, predicates are contextually meaningful, and to explain the meaning of a predicate is to formulate a rule for applying the predicate to particular objects, but predicates are not names of anything. The predicate "blue" is not related to its meaning in the way that the name "John" is related to John. Indeed, it is already misleading, the semantic nominalists urge, to speak of the meaning of "blue," since this expression suggests an elusive entity. It is preferable to speak of the rule governing the use of "blue," and to give this rule is to formulate the conditions under which it is correct to apply "blue" to a thing. In the case of "blue," the rule of usage cannot be formulated without pointing at particulars. In this respect the rule of usage for, say, "mermaid" is, of course, of a different sort, since we can be said to understand what "mermaid" means, although we have never encountered any mermaids. But, the semantic nominalist insists, to grasp this meaning is not to be face to face, as it were, with a universal, call it mermaidhood, but just to know under what conditions it would be correct to apply the predicate "is a mermaid" to an object (5).

An important application of the theory of contextual meaning to mathematics arises if one reflects on the meaning of infinitesimals, expressed by "dx," "dy," and so on. Mathematicians used infinitesimals successfully long before they were clear about their meaning. At first glance there is an air of hocus-pocus about infinitesimals: how can a genuine quantity be neither zero—insofar as an infinite sum of infinitesimals equals a finite quantity—nor finite—insofar as a finite sum of infinitesimals does not equal a finite quantity? And how can the ratio of dy (where y is a function of x) to dx equal a finite number if neither dx nor dy are finite numbers? The differential quotients themselves seemed perfectly legitimate, since they admitted of geometric interpretation, namely, as measures of the slopes of tangents. But what troubled both mathematicians, who used the device of infinitesimals without being able to justify it "philosophically" (as contrasted with "pragmatic" justification: it works!), and philosophers who were critical of the calculus (Berkeley, for example), was that the components of the differential quotient had no intelligible meaning. The theory of contextual meaning, however, justifies the use of infinitesimals as "incomplete symbols," in Russell's phrase—that is, as symbols which do not denote any funny kinds of numbers but have meaning in context. An equation of the form "$dy/dx = c$" means that the limit approached by a sequence of difference quotients $\Delta y/\Delta x$, as Δx becomes smaller and smaller, equals c, and the meaning of "limit" can be explained without postulating any numbers other than finite ones. When one has explained the meanings of equations that involve differential quotients, both such as equate them to a constant and such as express them as a function of a variable, one has explained the contextual meaning of differential quotients and of their components.

Classes, Attributes, and the Logical Analysis of Mathematics

It was stated in the beginning of this article that it is difficult to avoid Platonism if one becomes philosophic at all and asks what a number, as distinct from a numeral, is. It seems that a number is either a universal—that is, a common property of classes of discrete objects that can be set into one-one correspondence—or else a *class* of such "similar" classes. The number two in particular, then, is revealed as either the universal "twoness" or the class of all pairs. Although classes are, for good or for bad reasons, somehow more acceptable to nominalists than are universals (or attributes, as we shall henceforth call them), they are likewise abstract entities. By "the class of all men," for example, a logician does not mean a group of men that could possibly be seen but the conceptually apprehended totality of men past, present, and future (6).

Can these Platonistic temptations be overcome by means of the theory of contextual meaning? That is, can it be maintained that numerals have only contextual meaning and do not denote any entities at all? Now, contextual definitions of the natural numbers in terms of logical constants and nonnumerical variables can be constructed, as was shown by Frege and Russell (7) independently (although Frege has

historical priority and influenced Russell's thinking on the foundations of arithmetic); and these contextual definitions clarify, in a very important way, the language of *applied* arithmetic.

Let us begin with the first natural number, zero. What is meant by a statement like "the number of French judges in the Supreme Court is zero"? Obviously, it means that there are no such persons, or that the class of such persons is empty. Here, "not," "there are," and whatever symbol is used to denote membership in a class are logical constants. Note that zero, just like the larger numbers, is predicable of classes, not of individuals; that is, statements of the form "there is nothing of the kind K" are meaningful, but statements of the form "this thing is not" or "this thing is nothing" are not.

Next, consider the number one. Again, we cannot predicate unity in the arithmetical sense of an individual: "the sun is one" makes no sense; "there is one (and only one) sun" makes sense. That is, we might say that the class of solar objects has exactly one member, and this means, according to the Frege-Russell analysis, that there is an x such that x is a member of the class of solar objects, and for any y, if y is a member of the class of solar objects, then y is identical with x. Similarly, "there are two things of kind K" means that there is an x and a y, y distinct from x, such that x and y are of kind K, and for any z, if z is of kind K, then z is identical with x or with y, and so on for the larger numbers. It should be noted that the contextual definition of the arithmetical predicate of classes "one" is not circular, because "there is *an x*" does not have to be read as "there is at least *one x*" but may be read as "it is not the case that there is no *x*."

Are these definitions correct? Do they formulate what we mean by arithmetical symbols in the context of applied arithmetic? This question cannot be answered unless criteria are specified which must be satisfied by correct definitions. Now, an important criterion of correctness which these contextual definitions can be shown to satisfy is that the equations of arithmetic which are actually used in deducing numerical statements about empirical subject matters from other numerical statements should be logically demonstrable. For example, we would expect from adequate contextual definitions of "2," "3," and "5" that they make possible a formal proof (that is, a proof based on nothing but laws of logic) of the proposition "if a person has 2 daughters and 3 sons, then he (or she) has 5 children." It may be thought that this proposition of applied arithmetic is just a special case of the general equation "2 + 3 = 5" and that there is no further problem, since the equation itself is simply "true by definition." But insofar as the equation is just a provable formula in an uninterpreted system of arithmetic, its constituent arithmetical symbols do not have the sort of meaning that is presupposed by empirical applicability. In such a system (a "formal calculus," in the terminology of the logicians) 1 is defined as the successor of 0, 2, as the successor of 1, 3, as the successor of 2, and so on, where 0 and *successor* are primitive terms. These primitives also enter into the recursive definition of $+$: $x + y' = (x + y)'$; $x + 0 = x$

(here, "$\ldots'$" is short for 'the successor of of $\ldots$."). In terms of these definitions, and of the rule that equals are interchangeable, it is indeed possible to transform 2 + 3, step by step, into 5, but as long as the primitives remain uninterpreted, the defined symbols likewise are without interpretation. The definition $2 = 1'$, which occurs within the formal calculus, does not enable one to decide whether a given class has two or more or less members; indeed, there is nothing within the formal calculus itself to suggest even that numerals designate properties of classes that can be ascertained by counting.

We require, then, an *interpretation* of the arithmetical primitives in terms of an understood vocabulary before we can even significantly raise the question of whether the equations are *true*. And if we want to justify the use of 2 + 3 = 5 as a rule for deducing "*x* has 5 children" from "*x* has 2 sons and 3 daughters" (with the additional help of the definition or theorem "*x* is a child of *y* = *x* is a son or daughter of *y*"), we have to assign to the numerals just those meanings which they have in such *empirical* contexts as "*x* has two sons." This is precisely what the Russellian contextual definitions in terms of logical constants accomplish; they at once clarify the meanings of empirical statements in which numbers are applied and justify the belief that "*x* has 5 children" *logically follows* from "*x* has 2 sons and 3 daughters."

However, as both Frege and Russell clearly saw, such contextual definitions are insufficient for the elucidation of numerical symbols. In effect, what has been defined so far is only the statement form "class A has n members." But we still do not know what 2, for example, means in the context "2 is a prime number." Here, 2 does not occur as predicate but as subject. This is the kind of consideration that led Frege and Russell to ask *what the number 2 itself is*. Formally speaking, in the context "2 is a prime number," the symbol "2" is a *name*, not an incomplete symbol. What is it the name of? Two alternative answers may be considered: (i) the class of all classes with two members, (ii) the attribute of being a class with two members. Answer i is a special case of Russell's general definition of numbers as classes of similar classes. Two classes are said to be similar if there is a one-one relation which relates every member of one class to a member of the other class, and a relation R is one-one if at most one entity has R to a given entity and a given entity has R to at most one entity (for example, being the immediate successor of; being the positive square root of; being the wife of, in a monogamous society).

It is natural to think of a number as *the common property* of all mutually similar classes. But this definition is open to the objection that there is no guarantee that a set of similar classes have just one property in common (8). For example, if all individuals have a certain property f in common, then all possible pairs that could be formed out of them would have the common property "containing as members individuals with property f." By the foregoing definition, therefore, the number 2 would fail to be unique. On the other hand, the *class* of all pair-classes is

necessarily unique, and this is why Russell preferred to define numbers as classes of similar classes.

Nevertheless, there is at least one reason why it may be better to regard numbers as special kinds of attributes, in the sense of definition ii. The formal difference between classes and attributes is that attributes which apply to exactly the same entities may still be distinct, whereas classes with the same membership are identical. Thus, we can conceive of a universe in which all round things are blue and all blue things are round. If such were the world, the class of blue things would be identical with the class of round things, yet the attributes blueness and roundness, the one a color the other a shape, would remain perfectly distinct. Or, to illustrate by a mathematical example, the class of natural numbers between 1 and 3 is the same as the class of even primes, but the corresponding attributes are clearly different; we describe the number 2 differently if we describe it as the natural number that is less than 3 and greater than 1, or as the only even number that is a prime number. Again, many distinct attributes are not possessed by anything at all: being a unicorn, being a blue dog that can speak French, being a golden mountain, and so forth. But they all correspond to the same class, the *null* class. There cannot be more than one null class, for if there were two, one would have to have a member which the other does not have, and this contradicts the hypothesis that neither has any members.

Now, to come closer to the defect of definition i, which is of interest here, the arithmetical meaning of the term *successor* (as used, for example, in the definition of 1 as the successor of 0) is such that necessarily distinct numbers have distinct successors. This, in fact, is one of five postulates upon which the Italian mathematician and logician Peano erected the arithmetic of natural numbers. And one of Russell's avowed aims in "logicizing" the concepts of arithmetic was to so define Peano's primitives ("zero," "successor," "natural number") that all the postulates (and therewith the theorems) of uninterpreted arithmetic turn into logically necessary propositions—propositions that are formally deducible from the purely logical axioms of *Principia Mathematica* (9, chap. 1–3; 10). Russell noticed, however, with considerable intellectual discomfort, that his definitions of natural numbers as classes of similar classes of individuals do not make Peano's axiom that distinct numbers have distinct successors logically necessary. For suppose (what is conceivable without self-contradiction) that the number of individuals (11) in the universe were some finite number n. Then the number $n + 1$ defined as the class of all classes with $n + 1$ members, would be the null class, since there would be no classes with n + 1 members. For the same reason, $n + 2$ would be the null class. Hence, we would get $n + 1 = n + 2$, although n, being a nonempty class, is distinct from $n + 1$. For reasons connected with the theory of types (a theory devised as a solution of logical paradoxes, which we cannot and need not explain here), Russell saw no other escape from this difficulty than to postulate that the number of individuals is not finite ("axiom of infinity") (9, chap. 13).

Now, we have seen that $n + 1 = n + 2$ follows from the assumption that the number of individuals is n, together with the Russellian definition of numbers as *classes* of similar classes. But if the number $n + 1$ is, instead, defined as the *attribute* (of a class) of having $n + 1$ members, Russell's conclusion does not follow. For though, on that assumption, both attributes would be empty (inapplicable), they would remain just as distinct as, say, the attributes of being a mermaid and of being a golden mountain, and for just the same reason: they are defined as incompatible attributes. For example, the expressions "A has two members" and "A has three members" are so defined in *Principia Mathematica* (see the foregoing sample contextual definitions) that it would be contradictory to suppose that the same class had both (exactly) two and (exactly) three members. Therefore, even if just one individual existed, the number 2 would retain its conceptual distinctness from the number 3; and this argument, obviously, can be generalized for any finite number n and its successor.

Apart from the question of the axiom of infinity, it is, within the framework of the logical analysis of mathematics contained in Whitehead and Russell's monumental *Principia Mathematica*, unimportant whether numbers be conceived as classes (of classes) or as attributes (of classes), for names of classes are, in either case, contextually eliminable, according to Russell's theory of classes as "incomplete symbols." According to this theory, a statement that ascribes an attribute F to a class that is defined as the totality of entities that have attribute G is analyzed as follows: there is a predicative function θ such that θ is formally equivalent to G and such that θ has F (12). In this context, *function* means, not numerical function, but propositional function, and for the present purposes propositional functions may be identified with attributes. Two attributes are "formally equivalent" if they apply to the same entities, and a predicative function is an attribute that does not presuppose, in its definition, a totality of attributes.

For a full understanding of this theory of classes, familiarity with the theory of types, especially the "ramified" theory with its distinction between the type and the order of a function, would be required (13). But for the present discussion, all that matters is that in the "primitive" notation of *Principia Mathematica*, no names of classes but, instead, variables ranging over attributes (propositional functions) occur. For a semantic nominalist holds that the language of mathematics involves an obscure Platonism as long as there are in its primitive notation either names of, or variables ranging over, abstract entities; and he regards attributes as abstract entities (14). Take, for example, the simple statement that two individuals, x and y, differ in at least two respects. This means that there is an attribute f and an attribute g such that f is not equal to g and such that x has f and y does not have f and x has g and y does not have g, or y has f and x does not have f and x has g and y does not have g, and so on. But here f and g are variables ranging over attributes; therefore such an analysis is unacceptable to a semantic nominalist.

Now consider the more complicated statement: $2 + 2 = 4$. The logical analysis performed by Frege and Russell shows that we do not have to regard the symbols "2" and "4" as names of mysterious entities. Even the names "the class of all classes with two members" and "the class of all classes with four members" are, in principle, eliminable. But what cannot be got rid of, apparently, are variables ranging over attributes. For if, in conformity with Russell's view that classes are logical fictions, not real entities, we define numbers as certain kinds of attributes *of attributes* (in the sense in which "being a color," for example, is an attribute of attributes, namely, of blueness, redness, and so on), we obtain the following analysis of $2 + 2 = 4$: for any attributes f, g, h, if just two individuals have f and just two individuals have g and nothing has both f and g, and if an individual has h if and only if it has either f or g, then just four individuals have h (illustration: $f =$ being a coin in my left pocket at time t_0, $g =$ being a coin in my right pocket at t_0, $h =$ being a coin in one or the other of my pockets at t_0).

Is mathematics, then, irremediably Platonistic? Or is there some way of eliminating attribute variables so as to satisfy the demands of semantic nominalism? The issue is a highly technical one, but the following suggestion should be intelligible to those without any knowledge of symbolic logic. As was explained in earlier paragraphs, the nominalist insists that a predicate can be meaningful without being the name of anything. For this reason he refuses to transcribe (i) "x is red" into (ii)

"x has the attribute redness." From ii we may deduce (iii) "there is an attribute f such that x has f," but since "is red" has meaning only in context, it is not a name of a value of a variable. The deduction of iii from i is as illegitimate as the deduction of (iv) "there is something which I am now thinking of" from (v) "I am now thinking of a unicorn." The transition from v to iv is tempting because it is similar to the perfectly valid deduction of (vi) "there is something which I am now eating" from (vii) "I am now eating an apple." But, whereas we could not eat apples if there were no apples, we can think of unicorns in spite of there not being any. If we allow the deduction of iv from v, we get entangled in a verbal contradiction, since the something which iv says I am thinking of is, of course, a unicorn, and then there must be unicorns after all! To resolve the contradiction, the Platonist may say that the object of my thought is the attribute of being a unicorn, not a concrete unicorn. The nominalist, on the other hand, criticizes the transition from v to iv on the ground that "unicorn" is not a name but a predicate (or part of the predicate "is a unicorn"). Correctly analyzed, v, unlike vii, does not assert a relationship between two independently existing entities but simply characterizes my thought as what we might call a "unicornish" thought. Similarly, "this is a picture of a unicorn" characterizes the picture as unicornish; it does not mean that this has the relation *being a picture of* to an independently existing entity —in the way that this is the meaning of "this is a picture of my son."

Bearing in mind the distinction be-

tween predicates (which may not be replaced by variables ranging over some kind of entities) and names, let us return to the logical analysis of $2 + 2 = 4$. To satisfy the nominalist, we must replace "have f," where f represents a name of an attribute, with "are f." But then f, g, and h become letters that represent predicates, not names of attributes; hence, they are not variables over which we may "quantify," as the logicians say. The prefix (quantifier) "for any attributes f, g, h" must, accordingly, be cut off, for the letters f, g, and h do not represent names of attributes at all.

What, then, is the law of arithmetic $2 + 2 = 4$ in logical and, at the same time, nominalistic interpretation? The surprising answer is that there is not *one* such law, there is not a sentence containing, besides variables, only logical constants which we can point to and say "this sentence expresses the arithmetical law that 2 and 2 make 4," for "if just two individuals are f and just two individuals are g . . ." is a schema, not a statement; it does not express a proposition at all. In order to obtain propositions out of it, we must substitute specific predicates for the schematic letters in it, and there are as many such propositions as there are triplets of predicates applicable to individuals. If the language of arithmetic is reconstructed nominalistically, then, no laws of pure arithmetic can be formulated in the object-language—that is, the language which, whatever it may refer to, does not refer to symbols. Instead, one has to formulate in the meta-language (the language that is used to talk about the object-language) statements to the effect that any substitution instance of such and such a schema is logically true.

This conclusion, of course, applies not only to the laws of arithmetic and of higher mathematics but also to the basic laws of logic. For example, consider the law of medieval logic, "what is true of all is true of any," which, in symbolic logic, reads as follows: for any y, if all x's have attribute f, then y has f. A Platonistic logician can refer to *one* logical truth expressed by the sentence: for any attribute f and for any individual y, if all x's have f, then y has f. A nominalistic logician must ascend to the meta-language and there declare that every statement of the form "for any y, if all x's are f, then y is f" is logically true (*15*).

What Do the Ontological Questions Mean?

To what extent a nominalistic reconstruction of mathematics is feasible is certainly an interesting technical problem that deserves investigation in its own right. But attempts at such reconstruction are usually motivated by a philosophic prejudice about what "really exists." Being asked why he wants to get rid of variables ranging over attributes, the nominalist is likely to reply that he cannot admit the existence of attributes because the very notion of "attribute" is obscure to him. But even if the notion could be clarified to his satisfaction he would probably remain reluctant to admit the existence of such entities. Thus, nominalists usually concede that the notion of "class" is quite precise, and yet they

cannot countenance classes as "real entities."

The main argument in support of the accusation that the meaning of the word *attribute* (and of its synonyms in philosophic literature: universal, property, intension of a predicate) is obscure is that it is not clear under which conditions two expressions can be said to designate the same attribute (*16*). For example, is the attribute (of a number) of being equal to the product by itself the same as the attribute of being the successor of zero? Is the attribute of being a rectilinear closed figure with three sides the same as the attribute of being a rectilinear closed figure with three interior angles? We have here predicates which are interdeducible (logically equivalent), but it seems debatable whether they are *synonymous*. And the question of the criterion of synonymy is, indeed, difficult and highly controversial in contemporary semantics (*17*). The same nominalists who frown on attributes find it easier to accept talk about classes precisely because the condition of identity of classes is clear and uncontroversial: A and B are the same class if, and only if, they have the same members.

Now, this particular argument against "Platonistic" discourse seems to me highly illogical. If "attribute" is held to be obscure on the ground that the identity condition for attributes is not clear, then one would expect that all is well with the identity condition for individuals—that is, those concrete entities, whatever they may be (material particles, observable things, qualitatively distinguishable events, space-time points), which alone really exist according to nominalist ontology. Yet, the identity condition for individuals that is usually accepted is Leibniz' principle of the "identity of indiscernibles," which in modern logic is formulated thus: $x = y$ if, and only if, for every attribute f, x has f if and only if y has f. Clearly, if such is the definition of identity of individuals, and a given kind of entity is deemed obscure to the degree that its identity condition is not clear, then the alleged obscurity of "attribute" must infect the term *individual* too.

Two replies are open to the nominalist: (i) Since we realize that an explicit definition of identity requires quantification over an attribute variable, we do not explicitly define this logical constant at all. Instead, we lay down an axiom schema for identity which does the same job as the explicit definition. It says, in effect, that identicals may be substituted for each other without change of truth-value of the sentence into which the substitution is made, and contains a schematic predicate letter, not a quantifiable attribute variable: if Fx, and $x = y$, then Fy. (Note that, in accordance with the explanation given earlier, a single axiom or definition is thus replaced by a family of axioms of the same form, namely, those that result from the substitution of a predicate for the schematic letter F.) (ii) Identity is explicitly definable with the help of a *class variable*; hence, the intelligibility of "individual" exceeds that of "attribute" by at least as much as the latter is exceeded by the intelligibility of "class": $x = y$, if and only if x and y are members of just the same classes of individuals.

My rejoinder to i is that an exactly

similar axiom schema can be laid down for identity of attributes. That is, it is postulated that from "f is F" and "$f = g$" we may deduce "g is F." Here F is a schematic letter to be replaced by predicates that are applicable to attributes, not to individuals (for example, "is a color," "is possessed by exactly two individuals," "is a desirable attribute"). Consequently, attributes and individuals are still in the same boat with regard to the alleged obscurity of the identity condition. As rejoinder to ii, obviously just the same kind of explicit definition of identity of attributes can be given. Attribute f is the same as attribute g if, and only if, f belongs to just the same classes of attributes that g belongs to.

The argument from the identity condition, therefore, does not establish the superior intelligibility of nominalistic discourse. Independent arguments are needed. Perhaps the basic argument is the simple "common-sense" argument that the only way of proving existence of anything is sense perception or inference from perceived things or events to unperceived things or events, in the manner of the physical scientist. But attributes cannot be perceived by the senses, nor does the postulation of the existence of attributes explain the nature of the perceived world in the way in which the theory of electrons, say, explains observed phenomena.

Nevertheless, the assertion that attributes are "abstract," not given in sense experience, should not be uncritically accepted. There are many simple qualities which *recur* in our sense experience and which, by this criterion, are universals. We see the same shade of blue in different patches or in different parts of the same patch, hear the same pitch in different sounds, taste the same taste in different portions of the milk we drink. It is likewise artificial to deny that we have direct experience of *relational* universals—for example, of the relation of temporal succession and the relation of spatial proximity. The counterargument that it is not, after all, certain that precisely the same quality recurs presupposes that one understands what it would be like to perceive exactly the same quality in different contexts. But since the expressions "exactly the same shade of blue," "exactly the same pitch," and so on, can be explained only *ostensively* (18) (you point, say, to adjoining parts of the same expanse and say "see, they, for example, are the same shade of blue—that is what I mean by 'same shade of blue'"), this argument is really self-defeating. At any rate, the argument from the limits of sensory discrimination is hardly relevant to the question of the existence of mathematical attributes. For (natural) numbers may be regarded as attributes of attributes of individuals; that is, the number n is the attribute (of an attribute) of having n instances, and to deny that two attributes f and g have the same number is to deny that their instances can be matched one by one. But surely there are attributes that have the same number in this sense—for example, being a finger on my left hand and being a finger on my right hand. And if there are attributes that have the same number, does it not follow that there are attributes? What, then, is the argument between the nominalist and the realist all about?

Indeed, it is difficult if not impossible to attach any sense to the "ontological" question about whether there are attributes (19). If someone asks me this question, my natural reaction is, "why, of course there are: blueness, roundness, hardness, twoness, and millions more." If he denies that these are examples of attributes, then he cannot mean by *attribute* what is ordinarily meant by the word, for one explains its meaning in terms of just such examples before entering into the more technical explanation of what, in general, distinguishes attributes from other types of entities, like individuals, or classes, or propositions. To deny that roundness is an attribute would be as absurd as to deny that 5 is a number, or that parenthood is a relation, or that the desk I am writing on is a thing. But if it is not denied, then one cannot deny, either, that there are attributes, since, according to elementary logic, any statement of the form "a is f" entails "there is an x (at least one) such that x is f." In the terminology of some contemporary analytic philosophers of language, the ontological statement is really a trivial *analytic* statement that cannot be denied if one understands the intended meaning of the type designation, like *attribute, relation, class*, and so on (20).

To be sure, if one cannot countenance entities other than particular things because one cannot understand how something can "be" without having a tangible and visible existence at a particular place (one at a time!), then one's intellectual discomfort is just self-imposed through the fallacy of "reification": one is just naively associating with the expression "there are" images of spatially located things. One might, for example, be made intellectually uncomfortable by a mathematician's statement that the number 0 exists. According to the Russellian class conception of numbers, the number 0 is a very peculiar class: the unit class whose only member is the null class. But how can a class be said to exist unless it has an existing member? And is not the null class, by this very criterion of class existence, nonexistent? Yet, in the sense of "there is" which is implicitly defined by the entailment (which was given in the last paragraph), "if a is f, then there is an x such that x is f," the statement "there is a class which is the null class" is just a trivial consequence of the logically true statement, "there is nothing which is distinct from itself" (in class terminology, the class of things that are not self-identical is null) as well as a trivial consequence of any logically true statement of the form "there is nothing which both is and is not f." The puzzle about how such shadowy, ghostly entities as the null class, and therewith the number 0, can exist arises only because one associates with the expressions "there is" and "there exists" images of spatial location, although they function purely as *logical constants* in the context of mathematical existence assertions: "there is something which is f" means no more nor less than "not everything is not f."

Most existential statements that occur in every-day discourse refer to physical objects or events that exist, or occur, at some place and at some time—or at some place-time, in relativistic language. From this derives the habit of associating with the logical constant "there is"

and its variants, images of spatial localization. It is only these associations, and the failure to understand the purely logical nature of such existential statements as "the null class exists," "there are classes," "there are attributes," which produces intellectual discomfort.

To be sure, some mathematicians and logicians reject an existential statement "there is an x such that x is f" as meaningless in a case where it cannot be proved by deduction from a provable corresponding singular statement "a is f." They are sometimes called "intuitionists," sometimes "finitists." They reject merely indirect proofs by the *reductio ad absurdum* method: there is an x such that x is f, because if you assume that there is no such x you get involved in a contradiction, whence it follows that the assumption is false; and if the contradictory of a proposition p is false, then p is true (law of the excluded middle).

A well-known application of this "finitist" methodology of mathematics is the rejection of Zermelo's axiom of choice. This is the following existence assertion: for any class K of mutually exclusive and nonnull classes, there is a class which contains exactly one member from each member of K ("multiplicative class"). Now, in order to prove that a given class is a multiplicative class with respect to K, one must define it in terms of a method of selection of its members from the members of K. For example, let K be the class of all mutually exclusive pairs of integers. Here, a multiplicative class is easily defined as the class to be constructed by picking, say, the smaller integer from each pair. On the other hand, consider the class K which is formed as follows: we first take the class of proper fractions between 0 and 1, then the class of proper fractions between 1 and 2, then the class of proper fractions between 2 and 3, and so on. Obviously, the members of K are classes that have no members in common, since the integers that delimit the intervals are not themselves proper fractions. But now it is a little less obvious that one can describe a method of constructing a multiplicative class. The classes from which the members of the multiplicative class are to be selected have neither a first nor a last member, since between any proper fraction and the "closest" integer, there is another proper fraction. One might think of representing each class by its "mid-point," perhaps—that is, by that fraction which equals the arithmetic mean between the integral limits. But this method of selection becomes unavailable for the following class K: the class of proper fractions between $1/2$ and $3/2$, limits excluded, then the class of proper fractions between $3/2$ and $5/2$, limits excluded, and so on. For here the "mid-points" are integers, not proper fractions. Perhaps there is still a method of selection with respect to this K, but do we have any guarantee that for *any* class of mutually exclusive nonnull classes a method of constructing a multiplicative class can be described? Certainly not.

Russell mentions, in his *Introduction to Mathematical Philosophy* (9, p. 126), the class of all pairs of socks in order to illustrate that it is not self-evident that there is a "selector" for defining a multiplicative class with respect to a class of mutually exclusive nonnull classes. A multiplicative class, here, could be defined only if there were a property which just one sock in each pair possessed, say being the left sock, or being the red sock, and so on. The finitist concludes that it is meaningless to assert the axiom of choice in complete generality. He holds that it is meaningless to assert that *there is* a multiplicative class with respect to a given class of classes unless one can give a rule for constructing one. And this fits into his general methodological requirement that existence theorems be proved "constructively"—that is, by exhibiting an instance, or a rule for constructing an instance, that satisfies the existence theorem (*21*).

But, however the methodological dispute between finitists and "realistic" mathematicians who wish to continue using nonconstructive proof methods (such as the *reductio ad absurdum* method by which Euclid discovered the irrationality of the square root of two) may be resolved, it really has no bearing on the ontological pseudo-questions, "are there classes?" "are there attributes?" and so on. For suppose we accept the finitist interpretation of "there is an x such that x is f" as meaning "there is at least one constructively provable statement of the form 'x is f,'" where x ranges over abstract entities like numbers or classes. What should prevent one who has a penchant for asking ontological questions from asking whether there really are such abstract entities? The very asking of a question of the form "is there a number with property f," he might say, presupposes that *there are numbers* (*22*), whatever proof technique one may use to answer it. This presupposition, however, can be established quite easily by citing examples of numbers. To be sure, no philosopher who regards the existence of numbers and other abstract entities as problematic would be satisfied with the ironical answer: "Of course, there are numbers: 2, 5, 7, and many, many others." But the trouble with the ontological question is just that no method of finding the answer has ever been described by those who keep asking it. And this means not that we do not know the answer but that we do not understand our own question.

There is but one interpretation of the ontological question that makes it both intelligible and interesting, and this is an interpretation that turns it into that semantical-logical question which was touched on earlier in this article. What exactly did Russell mean by the assertion that classes are not real entities but are just "incomplete symbols"? The best way to discover the meaning of a statement is to look at the reasons offered in support of it. Now, Russell's reason for denying the reality of classes was that statements that contain names of classes or class variables are satisfactorily translatable into a symbolism which does not contain such expressions. (To take a simple example: "the class of dogs is included in the class of animals" means "for any x, if x is a dog, then x is an animal.") I propose to identify this *reason* for the denial of the reality of classes with the *meaning* of the denial. Similarly, the nominalist who denies the reality of any kind of abstract entities may be interpreted as affirming that the meanings of statements that contain names of, or variables ranging over,

abstract entities can be analyzed by means of a language that satisfies nominalistic requirements. Whether a nominalistic language is clearer, more intelligible, than a realistic language is, of course, debatable; indeed, this may be a matter of taste, of arational preference. But it must be admitted, I think, that the modern semantical interpretation of the time-honored (or time-dishonored) nominalism-realism dispute has the merit of making it scientifically meaningful, although it may be countered that, for this very reason, it is misleading to call this modern, semantical-logical issue by the same name because one thus seems to accuse those who prefer the one or the other type of language of a subconscious addiction to realistic or nominalistic "ontology."

REFERENCES AND NOTES

1. See, for example, W. P. Montague, *The Ways of Knowing* (Macmillan, New York, 1953), chap. 4; B. Russell, *The Problems of Philosophy* (Oxford Univ. Press, 1943), chap. 9.
2. G. Berkeley, *A Treatise Concerning the Principles of Human Knowledge*, sec. 18.
3. It was first formulated in "On denoting" [*Mind* (1905)], reprinted in Feigl and Sellars, *Readings in Philosophical Analysis* (Appleton-Century-Croft, New York, 1949). See also B. Russell, *Introduction to Mathematical Philosophy* (Allen and Unwin, London, 1948), chap. 16.
4. Of course, "France" is, in turn, an abbreviation for some definite description, but Russell believed that by repeated application of his rule of translation, any definite description could eventually be eliminated.
5. A programmatic formulation of this

semantic theory, which derives from L. Wittgenstein and M. Schlick, is as follows: the meaning of an expression consists in the rules for its use. Wittgenstein, a dominant member of the "Vienna Circle" (the founders of logical positivism) [see V. Kraft, *The Vienna Circle*, A. Pap, Transl. (Philosophical Library, New York, 1953)], exerted a powerful influence on English analytic philosophy. For a lucid application of Wittgensteinian semantics to the problem of universals, see M. Lazerowitz, "The existence of universals" [*Mind* (1946)], reprinted in *The Structure of Metaphysics* (Routledge and Kegan Paul, London, 1955).

6. There is, incidentally, a neat proof that classes are different from wholes, whether the parts of the whole be spatially or temporally continuous or discrete. If x is part of a whole y and y is part of a larger whole z, then x is part of z. But if x is a member of class y and y is a member of class z, then x is not a member of z. For example, John is a member of the class of men, the latter is a member of the class of classes of living organisms, but John is not a member of the latter class, since he is not a class. Furthermore, the same whole may be conceptualized as different classes: we can consider an organic body, for example, as a composite of cells but also as a composite of molecules. We then have a composite of cells that is identical with a composite of molecules; but a class of molecules cannot be identical with a class of cells, for, since cells are different from molecules, nothing can be a member of both classes.

7. For an elementary exposition of "logicism" (as the reduction of mathematics to logic, attempted by Frege and Russell, is called), see C. G. Hempel, "The nature of mathematical truth," reprinted in Feigl and Sellars (3) and in Feigl and Brodbeck, *Readings in the Philosophy of Science* (Appleton-Century-Crofts, New York, 1953).

8. See B. Russell, *The Principles of Mathematics* (Norton, New York, ed. 2, 1938), par. 110.

9. See B. Russell, *Introduction to Mathematical Philosophy* (3).

10. See C. G. Hempel, "The nature of mathematical truth" (7).

11. The concept "individual" is but negatively defined in *Principia Mathematica* (12): anything that is neither a class nor an attribute nor a proposition. The question is thus left open whether the individuals are observable things, or postulated particles, or physical events, or what not.

12. See A. N. Whitehead and B. Russell, *Principia Mathematica* (Cambridge, England, 1910–13; ed. 2, 1925–27), vols. 1–3, introduction, p. 71f.

13. See *12*, introduction, chap. 2. More easily intelligible expositions of the ramified theory of types are Lewis and Langford, *Symbolic Logic* (Century, New York, 1932), chap. 13; I. Copi, *Symbolic Logic* (Macmillan, New York, 1954), appendix B.

14. What I call "semantic nominalism" has been formulated by W. V. Quine, in "Designation and existence," reprinted in Feigl and Sellars (3), and in "On universals," *J. of Symbolic Logic* 12, No. 3 (1917). See especially *From a Logical Point of View* (Harvard Univ. Press, Cambridge, Mass., 1953), chaps. 1, 6. The program of nominalistic reconstruction of mathematics is sketched by W. V. Quine and N. Goodman in "Steps towards a constructive nominalism," *J. of Symbolic Logic* 12, 105 (1947).

15. Subtle problems emerge once one asks whether, granted that the object-languages of logical and mathematical systems can be constructed in accordance with nominalistic restrictions, the metalanguage also could be nominalistic. For example, surely we mean to assert the logical truth of *all possible* substitution instances of a given schema, not just of those that are actually written down somewhere and at some time.

But it is even doubtful that the method described in the text makes possible a nominalistic rewriting of mathematical *object*-languages, for quantifiers that refer to attribute variables within the scope of another quantifier cannot be eliminated by such a simple device. The statement "there is no largest number" illustrates this complication if numbers are construed as attributes of attributes: for any attribute f, if f is a number-attribute of an attribute, then there is a number-attribute (of an attribute) g such that g is larger than f.

16. This argument has been used chiefly by W. V. Quine. See "Two dogmas of empiricism," reprinted in *From a Logical Point of View* (*14*), and "The problem of interpreting modal logic," *J. of Symbolic Logic* 14, 43 (1947).

17. See N. Goodman, "On likeness of meaning," in *Semantics and the Philosophy of Language*, L. Linsky, Ed. (Urbana, Ill., 1952); B. Mates, "Synonymity," *ibid.*; A. Naess, "Toward a theory of interpretation and preciseness," *ibid.*; G. Frege, "On sense and nominatum" in Feigl and Sellars (*3*); R. Carnap, "Meaning and synonymy in natural language," *Philosophical Studies* (Apr. 1955), reprinted in *Meaning and Necessity* (Chicago, ed. 2, 1956), appendix; W. V. Quine, "Two dogmas of empiricism" (*16*).

18. It may, indeed, happen that a appears the same color as b, b appears the same color as c, yet a is distinguishable in color from c. Such cases suggest the following general definition of qualitative identity in terms of indistinguishability: x and y have the identical quality Q if, and only if, anything which is indistinguishable with respect to Q from x is also indistinguishable with respect to Q from y. But then, "indistinguishable (with respect to Q)" is the term that must be ostensively defined, and it will be self-refuting to deny that *sensory appearances* (many philosophers speak of "sense-data") exhibit genuine universals.

19. The chief advocate of the logical positivist view that such ontological questions are "pseudo-questions," devoid of cognitive meaning (a view I strongly incline to myself), is R. Carnap. See his "Semantics, empiricism, and ontology," reprinted from the *Revue Internationale de Philosophie* (1950) in *Semantics and the Philosophy of Language* (*17*).

20. It is often overlooked by philosophers that a statement which is analytic in the sense that it cannot be seriously denied by one who understands it does not have to express a necessary proposition, that is, a proposition that cannot be conceived to be false. If this *is* overlooked, then one can easily refute the argument in the text by an analogy: You might as well argue that "there are men" is a trivial analytic statement, since it follows from "John Smith is a man," which is analytic, since only a man could properly (that is, would conventionally) be named "John Smith." But although it is a contingent fact, not a logical necessity, that there are men, one could not possibly deny that there are men if one grasps the conventional meaning of *man*, for this word has acquired its meaning through ostensive definition—that is, through uttering the word *man* while pointing at a man. Similarly, the meaning of *attribute* and other type designations must be explained by examples before one can proceed to construct an abstract definition: hence, a disagreement about whether there are attributes is bound to be as verbal as would be a disagreement, if one ever broke out, about whether there are men. [A comprehensive and detailed analysis of the meanings of *analytic* and *necessary* is contained in A. Pap, *Semantics and Necessary Truth* (1958, Yale Univ. Press). For an acute discussion of the meanings of ontological statements, see M. G. White, *Towards Reunion in Philosophy* (Harvard Univ. Press, Cambridge, Mass., 1956)].

21. A. Fraenkel, *Einleitung in die Mengen-lehre* (republished by Dover, New York, 1946), par. 14; R. L. Wilder, *Introduction to the Foundations of Mathematics* (Wiley, New York, 1952), chap. 10.

22. Indeed, finitists usually accept the natural numbers as, in some sense, "given"—in accordance with Kronecker's often cited statement that God himself created the natural numbers, though he left the construction of all the other kinds of numbers and classes to man. Sometimes it is the "rule of construction" of natural numbers (adding one) that is said to be intuitively given rather than the natural numbers themselves. But it is not clear in what sense a natural number can be said to be a mental construction. Acquiring an *idea* of a number *n* by "counting up" to it is, of course, a mental process, but when we ascribe to a class a particular number, we ascribe an attribute to it that cannot plausibly be identified with the mental process of counting.

LANGUAGE
AND REALITY

8.5

Max Black

Bertrand Russell once said, "The study of grammar, in my opinion, is capable of throwing far more light on philosophical questions than is commonly supposed by philosophers. Although a grammatical distinction cannot be uncritically assumed to correspond to a genuine philosophical difference, yet the one is *prima facie* evidence of the other, and may often be most usefully employed as a source of discovery" (*The Principles of Mathematics*, 1903, p. 42).

The grammatical distinctions that

From *Proceedings and Addresses of the American Philosophical Association*, Vol. XXXII (1958–1959). Reprinted by permission of the secretary-treasurer of the American Philosophical Association and the author.

Russell proceeds to use as guides to philosophical discoveries are the familiar ones between nouns, adjectives, and verbs. But he says that he hopes for "a classification, not of words, but of ideas" (*loc cit.*) and adds, "I shall therefore call adjectives or predicates all notions which are capable of being such, even in a form in which grammar would call them substantives" (*ibid.*). If we are ready to call adjectives nouns, in defiance of grammar, we can hardly expect the grammatical distinction between the two parts of speech to guide us towards what Russell calls a "correct logic" (*ibid.*). If grammar is to teach us anything of philosophical importance, it must be treated with more respect.

My object in this paper is to clarify the character of philosophical inferences from grammar. By "grammar" I shall understand a classification of meaningful units of speech (*i.e.*, "morphology"), together with rules for the correct arrangement of such units in sentences (*i.e.*, "syntax"). The conclusions of the kinds of inferences I have in mind will be propositions commonly called "ontological"; they will be metaphysical statements about "the ultimate nature of reality," like "Relations exist," or "The World is the totality of facts, not of things," or "There exists one and only one substance."

1

In seeking ontological conclusions from linguistic premises, our starting point must be the grammar of some actual language, whether living or dead. From the standpoint of a language's capacity to express what is or what might be the case, it contains much that is superfluous, in grammar as well as in vocabulary. Grammatical propriety requires a German child to be indicated by a neuter expression ("*das* Kind"), a liability from which French children are exempt. If we are willing to speak ungrammatical German or French, so long as the fact-stating resources of the language are unimpaired, we can dispense with indications of gender. For to be told that the word "*Kind*" is neuter is to be told nothing about children that would have been the case had the German language never existed. The indifference of the English language to the gender of nouns sufficiently demonstrates the superfluity of this particular grammatical feature. For the purpose of eventual metaphysical inference, gender is an accidental, a non-essential, grammatical category.

In order to have any prospects of validity, positive philosophical inferences from grammar must be based upon essential, non-accidental, grammatical features, that is to say on features whose deletion would impair or render impossible the fact-stating functions of language. The essential grammatical features, if there are any, must therefore be present in all actual or possible languages that have the same fact-stating powers. They must be invariant under all possible transformations of a given language that conserve fact-stating resources. The system of all such invariant grammatical features would constitute a universal or philosophical grammar. Metaphysical inferences from grammar must be founded upon the constitution of a hypothetical universal grammar, in abstraction from the idiomatic peculiarities of the grammars of given languages.

There is little reason to suppose that the universal grammar, if there is such a thing, will closely resemble any conventional grammar. Contemporary linguists have made plain the "formal" character of conventional grammatical classifications and the "arbitrariness" of conventional rules of syntax. We shall need something other than grammarians' tools to uncover the universal grammar.

I assume, however, that philosophical grammar will still resemble conventional grammar in consisting of a morphology together with a syntax. I shall suppose throughout that we are considering the prospects of a certain kind of classification, coupled with a system of rules for admissible combinations of the things classified. I shall use the conveniently non-committal expression, "linguistic features," to refer to the things classified.

Were it possible to construct a philosophical grammar, or any fragment of it, it would be very tempting to say that something would thereby have been revealed about the nature of ultimate reality. For what could be the reason for the presence of some grammatical feature in all conceivable fact-stating languages except the correspondence of every such language with reality? There is an inclination to say with the author of the *Tractatus* that the essence of language must be "the essence of the World" (*Tractatus*, 5.4711). Or, with a more recent writer, "The universe is not a vain capricious customer of ours. If the shoe fits, this is a good clue to the size of the foot. If a language is adequate to describe it, this indicates something about its structure" (I. M. Copi, in *The Review of Metaphysics*, vol. 4 [1951], p. 436).

Of course, if metaphysical inferences from grammar are not to be circular, the construction of a universal grammar must proceed without prior ontological commitments. We shall need to consider whether the search for a universal grammar can be undertaken from a position of ontological neutrality.

It is obviously easier to show that some linguistic feature does not belong to universal grammar than the reverse; most of the examples I shall consider will have this negative character, that is to say, will be instances in which we argue that some feature of a given language is not essential to the fact-stating powers of the language. The corresponding ontological inference is the negative one that nothing in ultimate reality corresponds to the rejected linguistic feature.

2

In the *Tractatus*, Wittgenstein says, "In the proposition there must be exactly as much distinguishable (*gleich soviel zu unterscheiden*) as in the state of affairs that it represents" (4.04). Let us read this to mean: "In the particular utterance, there must be exactly as many different symbols as there are constituents in the state of affairs represented." Following Wittgenstein, I shall assign two physically similar word-tokens to different symbols, when they have different senses or references.

Let us try to apply this plausible principle of invariance of the number of constituents to a concrete instance. Suppose I am riding in an automobile with somebody who is learning to drive, and I need some pre-arranged signals to tell him to start the car or to stop it. It is natural, and adequate, to use the words "Stop" and "Go"; but, of course, a tap on the shoulder would do just as well. Here we have a system of orders, not statements of fact; but similar considerations will apply in both cases, since the logical structure of the orders will be the same as that of the factual statements specifying the actions performed in response to those orders. An adherent of Wittgenstein's principle of isomorphism might point out that here the two actions to be performed are represented by exactly the same number of distinct symbols, "Stop" and "Go." He might add that it would be logically impossible for the learner-driver to understand the two different orders, unless he were supplied with different and distinct symbols for the two cases. And he might add that every set of symbols that could serve the same purpose would necessarily exhibit the same duality. Whether the instructor spoke German, or Swahili, or anything else, he must necessarily use two symbols: here seems to be a perfect example of an essential feature, necessarily manifested in all the mutually equivalent notations.

But suppose the instructor used a whistle to signal "Start" as well as to signal "Stop." This device would be just as effective as the conventional words, and we need not suppose the whistle blasts to be substitutes for the English sounds: their meanings might have been taught directly, by demonstration and training. Have we not here an exception to Wittgenstein's principle—one symbol (the blown whistle), but two represented actions?

The retort is obvious: A whistle blown when the car is at rest means one thing ("Go"), but means another ("Stop") when the car is in motion. So the full symbol is whistle-plus-condition-of-car: there are two relevant states of the car, hence two symbols after all. But is this conclusive? Surely it would be just as easy to argue as follows: The whistle is one symbol, not two; but it also represents one action, not two: each time it means a *change-of-state*, whether from motion to rest or *vice versa*. To be consistent, an advocate of this view must

be willing to say that the familiar orders "Stop" and "Go" mean one and the same thing; but a determined searcher for a depth grammar must accept consequences at least as strange as this.

In order to determine whether Wittgenstein's principle applies to the case in hand, we need criteria of identity for actions and criteria of identity for the corresponding symbols. We have to say whether starting the car and stopping it are to count as the same or as different actions; and we have to say whether blowing the whistle is to count as having the same or different meanings on various occasions. There are no definite criteria for identity in these cases. In ordinary life, in a particular setting, we might understand sufficiently well a request to say something different, or to do something different; but here we are not in an ordinary setting. We want to know whether there are *really* two actions and two symbols, and have no way of finding out. We are free to decide whether the symbols are the same or different; the relevant fragment of philosophical grammar must be stipulated. The philosophical questions lack determinate sense and depend for their answers upon how we choose to describe the relevant utterances.

It may be said that this disappointing outcome arises from the artificiality of the example. I shall therefore turn to other cases having greater intrinsic interest.

3

Nowadays, it is often said that the copula, that figures so prominently in traditional logic, is superfluous. Listen to this, for instance: "There might certainly be various relations that the copula stood for, if it stood for any relation at all. But in fact no link is needed to join subject and predicate ... The grammatical copula is logically significant only when it serves as a sign of tense" (P. T. Geach, in *Mind*, vol. 59 [1950], p. 464).

But here is a traditionalist speaking: "The mode of connection of the subject and the predicate is symbolized in the standard formulation by the word 'is,' which is called the 'copula' because it links subject and predicate together ... some mode of connection requires symbolization, and this function is performed by the copula" (C. A. Mace, *The Principles of Logic*, 1933, pp. 77-78).

The dispute is clearly about philosophical grammar: the question is whether the copula is, or is not, an essential feature of language. On the one side, a strong case can be presented for the dispensability of the copula. There are languages, like Hebrew or Japanese, which manage very well without a copula; and we ourselves do without it in such constructions as "Peter loves Mary," in which the predicate, "loves Mary," is attached to its subject, "Peter," without benefit of any verbal link. Strongest of all is the argument that we could jettison the copula without in any way impairing the fact-stating resources of our language. Were we to say, "Peter happy," as the Chinese are said to do, we would lose nothing in expressive and descriptive power. In any case, *some* words and expressions must be able to "hang together" in a sentence without a symbolic link, for otherwise no completed sentence would be possible. So why not dispense with the copula altogether?

A defender of the copula's significance might reply as follows: "You are right in claiming that we don't need the *word* 'is' or any other word between the subject and the predicate of a sentence. But this is trivial and was never in dispute. Consider the pidgin English sentence, "Peter happy," that you offered as an adequate substitute for the conventional form. What is significant in this sentence is not merely the occurrence of the word-tokens, "Peter" and "happy," but the *relationship* between them. Separating the two words by others or by a sufficiently wide interval will disintegrate your sentence. It is the relationship of juxtaposition that here performs the function of linking subject and predicate. Similarly, in the conventional form, "Peter is happy," the union is effected by a relationship generated by writing the three words in correct order and in sufficiently close proximity. What is essential to the copula is not at all deleted by the translation into pidgin English. *Floreat copula!*"

What are we to say of this rebuttal? Its plausibility is undeniable, yet once again nothing compels us to accept it. For one thing, we may feel some reluctance to recognize "juxtaposition" as a genuine relation. Do we really need to *bring* the words into any relationship? Isn't it enough that we use them both in making the statement in question? Here again, consideration of some nonverbal notation might rid us of certain initial prejudices. Could we not, perhaps, use a red disk to mean that Peter is happy, with the disk standing for the man and its color for his condition of felicity? And what then would become of the alleged relationship between subject and predicate? Somebody might still insist, like A. E. Johnson in his *Logic*, that there would have to be a *characterizing relation* between the disk and its color. But anybody who can confidently assert this must already be in a position to analyze reality directly, and has no need of the detour through language.

But indeed, an advocate of the no copula view can reaffirm his position without invoking a hypothetical notation of qualified objects. *His* analysis of the sentence-fact, "Peter happy," might well be in terms of an "object," the word-token, "Peter," qualified by a certain property, that of having the word-token "happy" in immediate proximity. If he conceives of properties as "incomplete," *i.e.*, as having the power to unite with objects without need of intermediaries, he will *see* the linguistic predicate in the same light. For such a neo-Fregean, learning how to *use* a predicate *is* learning how to attach it to subjects in complete statements, and there is no separate rule to be learned about the symbolic significance of the alleged relation of juxtaposition. For such a philosopher, a question about the relationship between subject and predicate of a statement is as otiose as a question about the relationship between a hand and the object it points at. Specification of the hand and the object indicated defines the gesture, without need for further specification; similarly, choice of a subject and an appropriate predicate uniquely determines a statement, without need for a further choice of a relationship between them.

Once again, we have a dispute which is inconclusive and threatens to be undecidable. What turns on the outcome? What difference will it make whether or not we recognize a characterizing relation? Well, a relation is conceived to hold between *terms*, so the traditional recognition of the copula goes with a classification of properties as special kinds of *things*. Admission of a characterizing relation allows questions to be asked about properties, so that predicates or their surrogates are sometimes permitted to function as subjects. The opposite point of view, that treats properties and their representing predicates as incomplete, forbids questions and assertions to be made about properties as subjects. The dispute about the copula, trifling as it may seem at first sight, is a focus of contention for full-blown alternative grammars.

4

I pass on now to consider whether the ancient distinction between subject and predicate should be regarded as an essential feature of language that belongs to universal grammar.

How do we identify the subject and predicate of a given statement? A contemporary answers as follows: "A predicate is an expression that gives us an assertion about something if we attach it to another expression that stands for what we are making the assertion about" (P. T. Geach, *Mind*, vol. 59 [1950], pp. 461-462).

In order to apply this prescription to a particular instance, we have first to determine what a given assertion is "about." Should the assertion contain an expression standing for what the assertion is about, that expression will be the subject. According to the prescription, the remainder of the sentence will be the attached predicate.

This works well when applied to such a sentence as "Peter is happy," in which there is reference to a person. It is natural to say that a statement using that sentence is about Peter; hence the word "Peter" may be said to be a subject standing for Peter, and the remainder of the sentence, the expression, "is happy," counts as the predicate.

But even in this paradigm case of the application of the distinction, an objection can be lodged. It may be plausibly argued that the statement in question is about happiness, no less than about Peter: the assertion, some would say, can be understood as a claim that happiness is instantiated in Peter. If it is permissible to say that the word "happy" stands for happiness, the rule we have adopted would lead us to say that "happy" is the subject and "Peter is" the predicate. The philosopher who formulated the rule I have cited would want to reject this inference.

Or, take the case of the statement, "Happiness is desired by all men." Here, it is still more plausible to say that the statement is about happiness, referred to by the word "happiness." But the author of our rule refuses to recognize "happiness" as a subject, preferring to construe the sentence in question as being composed of two predicates.

I do not wish to suggest that a preference for this mode of analysis is wilful or capricious; yet I believe there is no rational method for persuading somebody who rejects it. The dispute, like others already reported in this paper, can be resolved only by fiat. It is an error to suppose that we can determine what a statement is "about" by inspection of some extra-linguistic realm. No amount of observation or reflection about non-verbal "things" will show whether a given statement is about a person or about a quality. The answer must be sought in language itself.

We know that the statement "Peter is happy" is about Peter, because we recognize "Peter" as a proper name, without knowing whether there is such a person as Peter. The starting point of the intended philosophical distinction between subject and predicate is conventional grammar, relying only upon formal criteria. But conventional grammar leaves us in the lurch as soon as we are asked to decide whether a statement using the word "happiness" is "really" about happiness.

5

I propose now to test the thesis of the universality of the subject-predicate form, by applying it to the report of a move in chess. The case may be thought to have special peculiarities, but will serve to reveal the chief points in dispute.

A full verbal report of a chess move, such as might be found in nineteenth century manuals, has the form, "The King's pawn moved to the King's fourth square." Here, there is no difficulty in identifying the grammatical subject, *i.e.*, the expression, "The King's pawn." Hence, the remainder of the formula, the expression, "moved to the King's fourth square," must be the predicate, and the report can be certified as being of the subject-predicate form.

Nowadays, English-speaking chess players commonly use the concise notation, "*P-K4*." Reading this as a conventional abbreviation of the full English sentence previously cited, it is easy enough to discern a subject and a predicate in this fragment of symbolism: we might say that in "*P-K4*" the "*P*" is the subject, and the rest of the formula the predicate.

But other and equally adequate notations are in common use. In the so-called "Continental notation," a move is specified by giving only coordinates of the initial and terminal squares; thus the move already cited would be reported as "*e2-e4*." In this version, there is no component homologous with the subject recognized in the other form of report. A last-ditch defender of the omnipresence of the subject-predicate form might still argue that in the formula "*e2-e4*" the first complex symbol, "*e2*," indirectly specifies the chessman moved. However, it would be equally correct to treat the initial symbol, "*P*," of the English notation as being "really" an indirect specification of the square from which the move started. Somebody familiar only with the Continental notation can treat the English notations as having the square-to-square structure of his own paradigm; while a devotee of the English notation can treat the alternative symbolism as a disguised version of his own.

It becomes progressively harder to perceive the subject-predicate form in every conceivable chess notation as alternative notations are imagined. A given chess move might be represented by drawing a line on a square divided into 64 compartments, or by a set of two integers between 1 and 64, or by a single number less than 4096 ($=64^2$), or by Morse code, or by suitably modulated electrical waves. Some of these possibilities might be handled by human beings, others might perhaps serve only to inform chess-playing computers; but all alike would have the requisite structure for representing every possible move in a game of chess. All of them, to use Wittgenstein's word, would have the same "multiplicity" (*Tractatus*, 4.04). Now a determination to view all of these equivalent symbolic forms as having the subject-predicate structure would be quixotic in the extreme. Absurd loyalty to a preconception about logical form would be needed in order to view a line drawn on a chessboard as having a subject and a predicate. Long before this point was reached, most of us would prefer to abandon the dogma of the omnipresence of subject-predicate form.

The example may prepare us to expect similar conclusions about languages that are not restricted to the representation of an invented game. We are told, on good authority, that "Chinese, which is fully equipped for every sort of civilized communication, makes no use of the formal categories devised for the Indo-European languages" (W. J. Entwistle, *Aspects of Language*, 1953, p. 162). Another writer, after surveying the variety of grammars known to contemporary linguists, concludes that "No grammatical concept seems to be *per se* sacred or universal, far less indispensable" (Mario Pei, *The Story of Language,* 1949, p. 129). In some languages, we are told, "An isolated word is a sentence; a sequence of such sentence words is like a compound sentence . . . [and] the terms verb and noun in such a language are meaningless" (B. L. Whorf, *Language, Thought and Reality,* 1956, pp. 98-99). If Whorf was right, the hope of finding the subject-predicate distinction exemplified in such "polysynthetic" languages is doomed to frustration. For that distinction presupposes a way of distinguishing between nouns and other parts of speech. Yet "polysynthetic" languages may be just as rich in fact-stating resources as our own relatively analytical English. I conclude that the subject-predicate distinction, valuable as it may be for analyzing Indo-European languages, ought to find no place in a universal philosophical grammar.

6

The three examples I have discussed sufficiently illustrate the difficulties that beset any serious effort to construct a universal grammar. We are now in a position to diagnose the source of these difficulties. In each case, we were assuming that the logical structure of certain statements ("Stop," "Go," "Peter is happy") must be identical with the structure of the situations or states-of-affairs represented. The search for what is presumed to be invariant in all statements having the same meaning, that is to say, those representing the same state of affairs, is a search for some way of presenting the common logical structure. In order to do this, we must be able to do at least the following: decide which perceptible features of words or other signs can be treated as non-significant, recognize one and the same symbol behind its alternative manifestations (that is to say, recognize when signs mean the same thing), and assign different symbols to the same logical category or type, on the basis of identity of function. In order for the procedure to provide any ground for ontological inference, such recognition, individuation, and classification of symbols must be performed without recourse to ontological premises, or to methods assuming the truth of such premises.

The chief difficulty arose from the need to count non-linguistic contextual features of statements as significant. So long as we confine ourselves to analysis of conventional verbal statements, in isolation from their settings, traditional grammar provides us with means of segmentation and classification that can subsequently be elaborated and refined in the service of philosophical insight. There is no question but that "Stop" and "Go" are different words; "Peter" is clearly a noun and a grammatical subject in "Peter is happy." But immediately we recognize the non-verbal setting in which the words are pronounced as significant, we face formidable difficulties in identifying, distinguishing, counting and classifying the symbols that interest us. Are the situations in which a car is at rest and in motion to count as the same or as different? Are the actions of stopping and starting a car the same or different? These are not questions to be answered by looking at cars or their drivers. They are questions of philosophical grammar for which there are no decision procedures. We have criteria for deciding whether words are to be treated as the same or different; for rules to this end (superficial rules of grammar) are part of the language we speak and understand. But there are no adequate criteria for deciding whether contextual situations are to be counted as the same or different, for the purpose of determining identities and differences of meaning. It might be thought that we ought to examine the semantical *rules* governing the sounds and written marks in question. But this maneuver achieves nothing. Were we assured that the rule governing "Stop" must count as different from the rule governing "Go," we would be entitled to conclude that there were indeed *two* symbols in question. But since the word "Stop" and "Go" or their synonyms will occur in the expressions of those semantical rules, individuation of the rules will raise the same troublesome questions. Nor will the case be altered by speaking about "uses" instead of about "rules." For the purposes of philosophical grammar, descriptions in terms of "symbols," "rules," and "uses" are mutually equivalent and generate the same problems. We can choose as we please, and our decisions about the points of philosophical grammar at issue will be determined by the choices we have made, not by any imposed analysis of the statements inspected.

Similarly in our illustrations of the copula and the subject-predicate form.

At the level of surface grammar, there are crude criteria for deciding whether an expression is expendable without loss of meaning. But when we try to push on to a would-be "deeper" level of analysis, we are embarrassed again by lack of criteria. Is the *relation* between "Peter" and "happy" "really" significant? Is there "really" a relationship there at all? It all depends upon how you choose to look at the statement. Nothing imposes an answer except the determination of the philosophical analyst to adhere to one mode of logical parsing rather than another. Seen through one pair of grammatical spectacles, there plainly is a significant relation of juxtaposition between subject and predicate; but we can wear another pair of lenses, and see nothing but subject and predicate, "hanging in one another like the links of a chain."

When we recognize that the fact-stating functions of language can be adequately performed by non-verbal symbolisms, the problems of detecting invariant logical structure become insuperable. If we represent states of affairs by configurations of physical objects, the task of discerning logical structure demands a capacity to determine the logical structure of certain physical facts. But if we can ever do this, we don't need the detour via language. If we can analyze a fact, we can in principle discover the logical structure of reality without prior recourse to language. On the other hand, if we face some obstacle of principle in dissecting reality, we shall meet the very same difficulties in trying to dissect language. For language, though it represents reality, is also a part of reality.

7

In the light of the foregoing considerations, the prospects for a universal philosophical grammar seem most unpromising. I believe the hope of finding *the* essential grammar to be as illusory as that of finding the single true coördinate system for the representation of space. We can pass from one systematic mode of spatial representation to another by means of rules for transforming coördinates, and we can pass from one language to another having the same fact-stating resources by means of rules of translation. But rules for transformation of coördinates yield no information about space; and translation rules for sets of languages tell us nothing about the ultimate nature of reality.

It might perhaps be said that common logical structure is shown in an invariant web of entailment relations. It is certainly part of our concept of synonymity that statements of the same meaning shall have parallel consequences: if one statement has an entailment that is not synonymous with some entailment of a second statement, that proves that the two original statements have different meanings. To put the matter differently, we shall not regard two languages as having the same fact-stating resources unless we can trace corresponding patterns of transformation rules in both. But we shall never arrive at a philosophical grammar by this road: correspondence of sets of entailments is compatible with the widest divergences of morphology and of syntax.

If we abandon the vain hope of find-

ing the true philosophical grammar, we may still hope to use its by-products. Schoolroom grammar is coarse-grained for philosophical purposes, and the refinements of latter-day linguists are impressive without being philosophically useful. We shall do well to continue classifying words and expressions according to their uses and functions, inventing whatever labels will help us to remember our discoveries. It is not my intention to deprecate the received grammatical categories of "quality," "relation," "function," "class" and the rest, or the finer classifications invented by contemporaries. I would urge, however, that our attitude to such grammatical sieves should be pragmatic. If reality leaves us free to choose our grammars as convenience and utility dictate, we shall properly regard them as speculative instruments to be sharpened, improved, and, where necessary, discarded when they have served their turn.

To anybody who still feels that there *must* be an identity of logical form between language and reality, I can only plead that the conception of language as a mirror of reality is radically mistaken. We find out soon enough that the universe is not capricious: the child who learns that fire burns and knife-edges cut knows that there are inexorable limits set upon his desires. Language must conform to the discovered regularities and irregularities of experience. But in order to do so, it is enough that it should be apt for the expression of everything that is or might be the case. To be content with less would be to be satisfied to be inarticulate; to ask for more is to desire the impossible. No roads lead from grammar to metaphysics.

Toward Further Inquiry

On the epistemological problems, Cassirer's *Philosophy of Symbolic Form* (New Haven, 1953), Vol. I, and Urban's *Language and Reality* (New York, 1939), Chapter I, offer critical summaries of various traditional resolutions. Urban has an appendix on "Neo-nominalism" that relates these issues to the ontological problems. R. L. Goldstein, in *Constructive Formalism* (Leicester, 1951), Chapter 8, attempts to make some sense of how language pictures reality in terms of the "picture theory." J. L. Austin's attempts to make sense of a correspondence theory of truth also carry him into a consideration of the relation of language to reality. In *An Inquiry into Meaning and Truth*, Russell's reductionistic program runs aground on the rock of similarity, and in *Human Knowledge* (New York, 1948), he gives more detailed consideration to the scope and limits of this program. C. Lewy, in "The Terminology of Sense Data," *Mind* (1946), offers a critique of the epistemological aspect of Russell's program, and much of the recent literature on sense data is indirectly pertinent to the program—see especially Austin's *Sense and Sensibilia* (Oxford, 1962). On the ontological aspect, see Quine's "Russell's Ontological Development," JP 63 (1966); A. Pap's "Logic, Existence and the Theory of Descriptions," *Analysis* 12 (1952); and also the controversies over Russell's theory of descriptions as discussed in Chapter 4. The question of the relation of theoretical language to reality, which is important for both epistemological issues and ontological ones, plays a role in many of the discussions of the nature of theories. Wilfred Sellars' "The Language of Theories," in H. Feigl and G. Maxwell (eds.), *Current Issues in The Philosophy of Science* (New York, 1961), offers a good discussion of the issues. Nagel's treatment of theoretical language in "Science and Semantic Realism," PS (1950), appears to be inconsistent with his instrumentalistic stance in 8.2, but in *Structure of Science* (New York, 1961), Chapter 6, he suggests that the difference is a matter of verbal quibble.

Much of the recent discussion of ontological commitment has been generated by Quine's treatment of the matter. Quine further develops the notions expressed in 8.1 in "On What There Is," *Review of Metaphysics* (1948), in which he relates the issues to the medieval controversy and to philosophy of mathematics. This article, along with a number of others that are relevant to the issue, is reprinted in *From a Logical Point of View* (New York, 1963). The fourth part of Quine's *Methods of Logic* (New York, 1951) offers similar treatment of the issues. "On What There Is" became the symposium topic dealt with by Quine, P. T. Geach, and A. J. Ayer in PAS, Suppl. 25 (1951). Quine's views are further developed in *Word and Object* (New York, 1960), especially Chapter 7, and in "Ontological Reduction and the World of Numbers," JP 61 (1964). Some criticisms of Quine from the standpoint of issues of naming and meaning are R. L. Cartwright's "Ontology and the Theory of Meaning," PS 21 (1954); V. C. Aldrich's "Mr. Quine on Meaning, Naming and Purporting to Name," *Philosophical Studies* (1955); and P. F. Strawson's "Singular Terms, Ontology and Identity," *Mind* 65 (1956). From the standpoint of the relation of logic to ontic commitment, see C. Lejewski's "Logic and Existence," *The British Journal for the Philosophy of Science* (1954); A. Church's "Ontological Commitment," JP 55 (1958); and P. F. Strawson's "A Logician's Landscape," *Philosophy* (1955).

For a more general treatment of contemporary issues, M. Lazerowitz, in "The Existence of Universals," *Mind* 55 (1956), measures the issues against a number of theories of meaning, and R. Brandt, in "The Languages of Realism and Nominalism," PPR 15 (1956), offers examples of various "types" of language used to discuss the problems. D. F. Pears, in "Universals," *Philosophical Quarterly* (1951), and P. F. Strawson, in "Particular and General," PAS (1953), each develop notions of naming that aim at resolving the ontological issues. A. Pap, in "A Semantic Examination of Realism," JP 44 (1947), carefully examines the picture theory and certain of its platonistic correlates. Wilfred Sellars, in "Realism and the New Way of Words," PPR 6 (1947), argues that an ideal-language approach to analysis must issue in a realist resolve to the relation of language to reality. From the ordinary-language approach, G. Warnock, in "Metaphysics in Logic," PAS (1950), argues that no inferences from logic to reality can be made satisfactorily. B. Russell, in "Logic and Ontology," JP 54 (1957), argues against Warnock that mathematical logic can be used to resolve issues of ontology.

There are a number of important denials of the ontological problem that differ somewhat in character from the essays presented in this chapter. H. Putnam, in "Mathematics and the Existence of Abstract Entities," *Philosophical Studies* (1956), distinguishes the issues regarding abstract entities from those regarding physical theory in such a way that the former are accorded practical significance but not metaphysical significance. J. Kaminsky, in "Ontology and Language," PPR 23 (1962), offers a reinterpretation of class terms that claims to avoid ontological commitments. James Cornman, in "Language and Ontology," *Australian Journal of Psychology and Philosophy* 41 (1963), criticizes Quine and Russell on the thesis that it is their theory of reference that requires ontological commitment, not language itself. Cornman's own treatment of the issues has been worked out on a modified model of Carnap's framework thesis in *Metaphysics, Reference and Language* (New Haven, Conn., 1966).

AN EPILOGUE
TO PROBLEMS

Man is only man because of language: to
discover language, he must be man.
W. von Humboldt

No claim can be made that the preceding chapters survey all the important problems in the philosophy of language; from some standpoints the problems they present may not appear to be even the most important ones. Other interests in language will very likely raise other philosophical questions, some more popular, some more peripheral, than those considered in this volume. What follows is a glance at some of these problems and also some references to works in which they are more fully explored.

The Origin of Language

The question of how language began can be treated in at least three different ways: the origin of language in the individual, the origin of language in a culture (the beginnings of a particular natural language), and the origin of language per se. These various concerns have in common an empirical subject matter and limited access to that subject matter. The inquirer into verbal learning cannot confer with the baby just learning to speak. The historical linguist and cultural anthropologist can examine written records of a language's history, but these seldom correlate writing to speaking. Moreover, the oral traditions that preceded written forms remain inaccessible. That a first language was spoken by a first *Homo loquens* must be regarded as an historical fact, unless one posits the eternality of speaking beings, but that first speech act is beyond the reach of empirical inquiry in any discipline. The frustration caused by this inaccessibility gives rise to speculation on these matters. But whether the speculation is characterized as scientific or as philosophical, it lacks the character of scientific theory, which explains and predicts kinds of events, and it lacks the character of philosophical theory, which explicates and explains presuppositions.

Answers to questions about the origin of language have the appearance of factual information without the foundations of empirical or historical evidence that we usually expect of such information.

For the problem of how a child begins to learn a language, J. B. Carroll's *Language and Thought* (Englewood Cliffs, N.J., 1964)† and Joseph Church's *Language and the Discovery of Reality* (New York, 1961)† each in its own way provides a readable, provocative introduction. The essays by R. Brown, U. Bellugi, and J. B. Carroll in *Language and Learning*, edited by J. A. Emig *et al.* (New York, 1966), are also readable and suggestive. Somewhat technical essays in psycholinguistics on this subject are collected in W. A. S. Smith and G. A. Miller (eds.), *The Genesis of Language* (Cambridge, Mass., 1966) and in one section of S. Saporta (ed.), *Psycholinguistics* (New York, 1961). One may question whether these investigations in fact discover the nature of individual origins of speech, or whether they instead read presupposed theoretical orientations into their evidence.

The dominant modes of investigation into verbal behavior operate on an associationalistic-behavioristic basis. The transformational-grammar approach of much recent structural linguistics implies that associationalism is an inadequate basis. The alternative thesis is nativism, which suggests that some basic aspect of speaking is innate to the human organism. This thesis is based on the finding that certain elements of grammar are common to all known speech and are not practically explainable on an associationalistic basis. It also takes into account certain complicated processes of grammatical imbedding that are theoretically beyond the scope of behavioristic explanation. Nativism has been expounded in terms of "innate ideas" by Katz in *Philosophy of Language* (New York, 1966)† and by Chomsky in JP 61 (1964) and more fully in *Cartesian Linguistics* (New York, 1967).† The nature and implications of this "innateness hypothesis" are critically explored in the symposium by Chomsky, Hillary, Putnam, and Nelson Goodman in R. S. Cohen and Marx W. Wartofsky (eds.), *Boston Studies in the Philosophy of Science* (Boston, 1968). The controversy between nativists and associationalists is as much about method of psycholinguistic inquiry as about origins of verbal behavior, and Part Two of *Readings in the Psychology of Language* (Englewood Cliffs, N.J., 1967), edited by L. A. Jakobovits and M. S. Miron, offers some good insights into the controversy.

Inquiries into the origins of particular natural languages usually find their locus in comparative and historical linguistics, but they draw evidence and insight from anthropological studies as well. Sapir's *Language* (New York, 1921) and Bloomfield's *Language* (New York, 1933) give discussions of the development of languages that are now somewhat dated but that remain useful and respected treatments of the issues involved. More to the point are treatments of individual languages, for which S. Robertson's *Development of Modern English* (New York, 1938)† and M. Bloomfield and Newmark's *A Linguistic Introduction to the History of English* (New York, 1963) offer good instruments.

Whether these studies in psychology, linguistics, and anthropology can offer sufficient clues to the beginnings of language as such seems a debatable point— if not an irresolvable one. Speculation about the origin of language preceded these empirical inquiries by centuries. Many of the traditional theories have re-appeared in this century with the support of empirical evidence that proves to be buttressing but not coercive. Jespersen's *Language* (New York, 1923), Robertson's *Development of Modern English* (New York, 1938),† Revesz' *Origins and Prehistory of Language* (New York, 1956),† and Diamond's *History and Origin of Language* (New York, 1959) each offers a useful chapter that systematically outlines traditional theses, and Jespersen, Revesz, and Diamond offer theories of their own. The most impressive treatment to date, because of its wealth of empirical data and force of theoretical insight, is Alexander Johannesson's *Origin of Language* (Reykjavik, 1949), a summary of the work earlier presented in *Nature* 153 (1944), 154 (1944), 157 (1946), 162 (1948). Johannesson defends the "gesture theory" on the basis of comparative linguistic studies of a number of Indo-European and Semitic languages.

Sturtevant, in *An Introduction to Linguistic Science* (New Haven, Conn., 1947), Chapter V, speculates with good humor that language began as a device of deception. Russell, in *An Inquiry into Meaning and Truth* (London, 1940), treats imperatives as the original mode of speech from which other forms have developed (this widely popular thesis is not original with Russell). The crucial question in the origin of language, however, is not its original form or function, but the development of abstraction and generalization, which make a symbol more than a signal and make language as symbolic form possible. How has man been able to develop a system of communication totally abstracted from any stimulus-response basis? This problem is not handled by any of the traditional theories, and neither the psychologist nor the linguist has an answer for it. Cassirer devoted much time to this issue (see the bibliography for 1.3), and the fact that he raised it remains an important contribution, whatever the limits of his conclusion. Whether an epistemology like Cassirer's, or a structural-linguistic theory like Chomsky's, or some other approach is the clue to solving this problem remains to be seen.

Investigations into the origin of language, like traditional theories about the beginnings of social and political organization, have something of a quasi-mythical character. They can pretend to be historical no more than ritual stories of what the gods did at the beginning of time. They may serve, as religious myths always have, as guides for attitudes and actions. In this role, they may suggest how to understand the nature and function of language, but this understanding requires explication and evaluation of the presuppositions upon which such quasi-myths operate. Whether theses about the origin of language can be de-mythologized and given the status of scientific theories is highly questionable. Myths, like theories, may explain, but they explain in a significantly different manner from theories.

Language and Cognition

The relation of thinking to speaking, of concepts to linguistic symbols, is an issue that has many correlates to that of the origin of language. The concern is primarily a psychological one, but it has repercussions for linguistics, anthropology, sociology, and philosophy, so that one can find discussions about it (or crucial presuppositions about it) in each of these areas of inquiry. It is also a matter of factual concern that is inaccessible to direct empirical observation. The various treatments of the matter more often reflect one of a number of vying theories than they report concrete, coercive evidence. Because both language and cognition are generally regarded as basic—if not peculiar—attributes of human beings, the relation of the two commands a fascination that is also comparable to the interest in origins. This combination of relatively inaccessible factual concern in an interdisciplinary field of inquiry with the existence of rival theories without a current common base, and with an intense fascination, invites speculation of varied quality, little of which can be characterized as either scientific or philosophical.

Explorations of the relation of cognition to language can take a number of turns. One line of inquiry is: To what extent is thinking carried out in linguistic form? Most theorists maintain that not all thought is linguistic, but Revesz in his discussion of origins clearly presupposes that it is, and Schaff in his *Introduction to Semantics* (Warsaw, 1960) explicitly claims so. If the content of cognition is not strictly linguistic, then a number of other questions arise. How much of cognitive content is linguistic? What is the character of concepts or ideas that are not linguistic? To what extent, if at all, is the development of more abstract conceptualizations dependent upon the use of linguistic forms? What is the order and character of transformations between linguistic and nonlinguistic forms in cognitive processes? These questions interlock in a variety of ways, and answers are crucial to the development of adequate theories of learning and of knowledge. Too often learning theorists and epistemologists presuppose solutions for which they offer no warrant. In other cases, the warrants that are offered beg the question.

With this problem, as with the problem of origins, inquiries into verbal learning offer the most hopeful correlation of theory with empirical inquiry. Again, Carroll's *Language and Thought*† and Church's *Language and the Discovery of Reality*† offer solid, readable introductions to recent developments. Chapter 8 of Saporta's *Psycholinguistics* is a good selection of specific studies, the experiments by Brown and by Linneberg being among the most important. Roger Brown's thesis about the correlation between language and mental categories is developed throughout his *Words and Things* (New York, 1958), but it is more briefly and cohesively expressed in "Language and Categories," appended to *A Study of Thinking* (New York, 1956), by Bruner, Goodnow, and Austin. J. S. Bruner also offers a number of suggestions about the scope and limits of the correlation between speech and cognition in his studies of cognitive growth in *American Psychologist* (1964 and 1965). Carroll's treatment of the relation in "Words, Meanings and Concepts," *Harvard Education Review* (1964), is also suggestive. *Acta Psychologica* 10 (1954) is devoted entirely to the topic of thinking and speech. In it Revesz initiates the symposium with the thesis: "Die Sprache ist die Manifestation des Denkens, das Denken der Urgrund der Sprache." The remaining contributers are psychologists of a variety of persuasions, as well as a philosopher, a mathematician, a linguist, and a neurologist; the discussions are international in character and include a breadth of types and persuasions of inquiry.

Closely related to these psychological inquiries are the neurological studies of *aphasia*, the loss of power to use or understand speech, usually as a result of brain damage. These studies give concrete evidence of the correlation between speech abilities and localized neural activities on the one hand and certain problem-solving abilities on the other. Their best established results can only point to the conclusion that certain parts of the brain facilitate *both* speech functions and other cognitive activity, and this may directly imply correlations between speech activities and cognitive activites. Saporta's *Psycholinguistics* again contains a good selection of studies. Kurt Goldstein's *Language and Language Disturbances* (New York, 1948) gives a good detailed summary of many of his investigations into aphasia and their implications for the nature of language. Briefer treatments by Goldstein in addition to the one in *Acta Psychologica* 10, are "L'analyse de l'aphasie et l'étude de l'essence du langage," in *Psychologie du langage* (Paris, 1933), and "The Nature of Language," in *Language: An Inquiry into its Meaning and Function* (New York, 1957).

Among philosophical inquiries, Cassirer's *Philosophy of Symbolic Form* (New Haven, Conn., 1953) remains one of the most impressive comprehensive treatments. Its use of anthropological and linguistic data to support an idealistic epistemological thesis is one of its many interesting facets. Urban's *Language and Reality* has been less influential, but it is more ready to take into account the current philosophical discussion than is Cassirer's work. The most impressive study among recent work is Schaff's in *Jeszyk a Poznanie* [*Language and Cognition*] (Warsaw, 1964).† Schaff continues with his Marxistic thesis (compare 1.8) but makes wide use, with critical notes, of other treatments by philosophers, psychologists, linguists, neurologists, anthropologists, and general semanticists. The Polish text may make the content of this book inaccessible to many, but the bibliography is international in scope, and topical arrangement makes it highly useful regardless of linguistic barriers. E. M. Mesthene's *How Language Makes Us Know* (The Hague, 1964) briefly offers a developed thesis about the linguistic basis of knowledge founded on the naturalism of Aristotle and Dewey. Chapter 4 of Bruce Aune's *Knowledge, Mind, and Nature*

(New York, 1967)† explores the relation of language and concepts to experience in terms of the acquisition of skills. A variety of theses are suggested in the international symposium on "Thinking and Meaning" in *Logique et Analyse* 20 (1962).

Given the theoretical tensions between associationalists and nativists on the issue of acquisition of language, one might expect them to be diametrically opposed on the relation between language and cognition. Such is not the case. Chomsky and Katz, as clearly as Carroll and Brown, claim a prelinguistic cognition in the thinking process. This thesis lends itself to a computer model of human cognition in which linguistic expression and reception become linguistic encoding and decoding of cognitive conclusions. No less surprising than this common basis for associationalism and nativism is the common commitment to identification of the cognitive with the linguistic (or at least the symbolic) by such diverse positions as Schaff's materialism and Cassirer's idealism (Schaff, however, takes exception to Cassirer's treatment of such matters as creative). Both maintain that all thinking is linguistic. The divide is not simply between psychologists and philosophers, as the example of Revesz makes clear (though he seems to be developing a less rigid position recently). To achieve a satisfactory resolve to these issues, both more experimentation and some clarification of concepts are needed. The notion of prelinguistic concepts, for instance, requires more elucidation than the hypothetical constructs of the behaviorists or the innate ideas of the nativists now offer.

Linguistic Relativity

Conclusions about the correlations of language, thought, and reality have definite relevance for the relations between language and culture. If language is a report of experience, and if there is a one-to-one correspondence between names and things, then the inquirer can expect not only a consistency within cultures of reports of experience, but also an assurance that translation from one language to another does not distort the report of experience. If Cassirer is right in maintaining that language does not report experience but serves as a basic agent in formulating it, then the adequacy of any translation becomes questionable and cultural relativity, not only for language but also for thought and experience, becomes a possibility. Empirical inquiries into variations in syntax and semantics between different languages, along with apparently correlated differences in "the way people think," suggest similar difficulties from a different perspective. Out of various complexes of theoretical presupposition and empirical investigation has arisen the question: Are language, thought, and experience culturally relative? If so, how is this relativity related to a particular culture?

The focus of controversy and concern in recent years has been what is usually called the Sapir-Whorf hypothesis. In *Language*, Sapir went to some length to show that languages do not in any significant sense reflect cultures and that boundaries of language and culture do not necessarily coincide. But this same volume contained the seeds of an even more radical thesis, and by 1929 Sapir was maintaining that "the 'real world' is to a large extent unconsciously built up on the language habits of the group. No two languages are ever sufficiently similar to be considered as representing the same social reality." See Mandelbaum (ed.), *Selected Writings of Edward Sapir* (Berkeley, 1949), p. 162.] This thesis is further developed in "Conceptual Categories in Primitive Languages," *Science* 74 (1931), and in several other writings in the Mandelbaum volume. Benjamin Lee Whorf, who pursued and developed this thesis with studies in American Indian and Eskimo cultures, forcefully stated his conclusions in "Science and Linguistics," "Languages and Logic," and other articles reprinted both in *Collected Papers on Metalinguistics* (Washington, 1952) and in *Language, Thought and Reality* (New York, 1956).† Whorf has had much influence on the general semantics movement through Korzybski and Chase. More recently Marshall McLuhan in *Gutenburg Galaxy* (Toronto, 1958) has popularized a thesis similar to that of Whorf. McLuhan's *The Medium is the Massage* (New York, 1967) is illustrative rather than argumentative.

Evaluations of the Sapir-Whorf hypothesis are many and varied. Schaff, in *Introduction to Semantics*,† Chapter 4, gives a sympathetic evaluation, relating the issues to those considered in earler sections of this epilogue. Similar but more critical treatments are given by Carroll in *Language and Thought*† and by Church in *Language and the Discovery of Reality*. The debate between Rapoport and Horowitz in ETC 17 (1960) gives a pro and con treatment; it also relates the thesis to the work of Korzybski. Harry Hoijer (ed.), in *Language in Culture* (Chicago, 1954), has collected essays and discussions, expositional and critical, devoted to the hypothesis. Henle's article in *Language, Thought and Culture* (Ann Arbor, Mich., 1958)† explores relations and implications of the thesis, and Black's "Linguistic Relativity," PR 68 (1959), is a detailed systematic analysis of the presuppositions necessary to sustain the hypothesis. The similarity of Whorf's conclusions to those of Cassirer is often noted, but the fact that the two arrive at their conclusions from radically different bases has not invited much exploration.

Many have been more impressed with the evidence for linguistic relativity that Whorf produces than with the thesis he espouses. Others are suspicious of the empirical evidence itself, maintaining that the differences are more trivial than they at first appear. The study by Hockett in the Hoijer volume seeks to minimize the much discussed discrepancies of form and content between Chinese and English. Hoijer takes an opposing view, claiming evidence from other sources for the hypothesis. His position is well summarized in "The Relation of Language to Culture,"† *Anthropology Today* (Chicago, 1953), and reinforced in "Semantic Patterns of the Navaho Language," *Sprache Schlussel zur Welt* (Dusseldorf, 1959). Many psychological studies have recently focused on the hypothesis, especially in relation to verbal learning. Some of the most important are printed in Saporta's *Psycholinguistics*, Chapter 8, and in Osgood and Sebeok (eds.), *Psycholinguistics* (Baltimore, 1954).

The thrust of the Sapir-Whorf hypothesis is that thought and culture not only reflect the linguistic forms and categories with which they operate but are determined by them. For Sapir this idea stood in opposition to the thesis that language as a cultural product reflects culture and is determined by it, but his arguments haven't convinced everyone. S. de Madariaga, in *Englishmen, Frenchmen, Spaniards* (New York, 1931), argued that each language reflects the temperaments often attributed to the nationality associated with it, and Karl Vossler, in *The Spirit of Language in Civilization* (London, 1951), maintained a similar thesis on a more universal scale. A number of recent sociological and psychological studies—for example, Schatzman and Strauss, "Social class and modes of communication," *American Journal of Sociology*, 60 (1955)—reinforce this view, not only for variations between languages, but also for variations within them. Even if the relativity of culture to linguistics is accepted, some basis must be found for determining which is causally antecedent.

Much of the argument against linguistic relativity tends to be defensive; it is based either on a naive formulation of the classical synthesis of language, thought, and reality, or on an equally uncritical assumption that empirical evidence is uninfluenced by cognitive and linguistic categories. The defensive argument focuses on examples of commonality between languages and cultures, but this line of argument lacks force. The common elements are in the main denied by no one, and examples of them only show that not every case supports linguistic relativity—a point not sufficient to deny the position itself. A more forceful argument against linguistic relativity is at least implicit in the transformational-grammar treatment of structural linguistics. The thesis that all languages depend upon an underlying "deep structure" of grammar that is basically common to all human beings is the foundation for the claims by Chomsky and Katz about "innate ideas," and it is diametrically opposed to linguistic relativity, along with the correlate treatments of language and cognition. To the extent that the transformational-grammar thesis is reinforced by investigation, linguistic relativity theses will be weakened. It may be that the final battle on this issue will be fought in terms of semantic categories, syntactic considerations being conceded to structural linguistics. However one evaluates the syntactic component of the transformational-grammar schema, the case for the semantic component must still be made.

In any inquiry into linguistic relativity, as into origins of language and into language and cognition, at least two points are striking. One is the interrelation of these several problems. A conclusion about one will suggest—if not entail—a conclusion about the others. The other point is the variety of disciplines with interests in these concerns. This latter point should warn the philosopher to be cautious. However one construes the distinction between philosophical inquiry and the inquiries of empirical sciences—a subject of some debate—most will acknowledge that it is not the philosopher's role to speculate on empirical matters when vagueness or inadequacy of information inhibits immediate scientific inquiry. The caution of Thomas Aquinas is not yet outdated: those who attempt to speculate about matters in which others are significantly more informed will only be shown to be fools.

As anthropology, linguistics, sociology, and psychology continue to explore these problems, two kinds of activity are open to the philosopher of language in these areas. One is to play the watch dog. Much of the controversy arises not so much from lack of empirical data as from lack of commonly accepted methods and clearly formulated concepts. At least the tasks of evaluating methods and clarifying concepts are universally honored as philosophical ones. If the philosopher also wishes to undertake the task of reconstructing the classical synthesis of language, thought, and reality, he has the additional job of exploring the implications of conclusions about these problems. Both the task of evaluating presuppositions and the task of exploring implications require some acquaintance with the empirical studies that lie between them.

Private Languages

In the discussions of natural languages, ideal languages, and ordinary languages, the notion of a private language seems an anomaly. The definition of language offered by Block and Trager (see the Prologue) clearly requires language to be social and thus in some sense public. The possibility of a private language may have been explored previously, and in different contexts, but it has come to the fore as a philosophical problem in the twentieth century as a result of the developments of analytical methodologies. Like many of the problems discussed in the chapters of this book, this one has been the result of attempts to use linguistic analysis to solve other philosophical problems.

The roots of this problem lie in the developments of logical atomism and logical positivism early in this century. The program of both is to ground human knowledge in experience, on the one hand, and to make that knowledge accessible to science on the other. The problem is that an individual's experience is not open to intersubjective inquiry. If the language is a direct report of experience, its significance cannot be scientifically scrutinized. Thus the egocentric predicament appears in linguistic dress, and the notion of a protocol sentence is the focus of concern. Roughly, a protocol sentence, as the term is used by the Vienna Circle, is a sentence that gives a direct account of an individual's experience. The problem then becomes to relate protocol sentences to the physical language of science. Carnap tried to solve this problem in his *Logical Structure of the Universe* (Berlin, 1928; Berkeley, 1967), and Neurath argued against both Carnap's treatment of protocol sentences and his notion of a physical language. Each wrote a number of articles for the early volumes of *Erkennt-*

nis that deal with their debates, and Chapter 11 of Weinberg's *Examination of Logical Positivism* (London, 1936) is a helpful discussion of the issues.

The problem took a new turn with the appearance of Wittgenstein's *Philosophical Investigations* (Oxford, 1953), which argues, in Sections 250 to 270 of Part One, essentially that there can be no private languages. For Wittgenstein, this meant that meaningful talk about sensations and feelings as introspections—and by implication, any "mental act"—is impossible. The result of this disclaimer is that the problem of the knowledge of other minds is a pseudo-problem giving rise to discussions about other minds and a whole complex of problems in the philosophy of mind. Wittgenstein's argument hinges on his notion of criterion. This concept has been critically evaluated by Albritton in JP 56 (1959), by Wellman in PR 71 (1962), and in a symposium published in C. D. Rollin's *Knowledge and Experience* (Pittsburgh, 1962); and Castañada treats it in relation to the problem of other minds in JP 59 (1962). Malcolm, in PR 63 (1954), shows that Wittgenstein's argument against private languages is *reductio ad absurdum* in form. Castañada rejects Wittgenstein's argument in Rollin's *Knowledge and Experience*, arguing that it begs the question, and he sets forth conditions by virtue of which a private language is possible.

Numerous articles have been written about Wittgenstein's formulation and solution of the problem. Among the many discussions are a symposium by Ayer and Rhees in PAS Suppl. 28 (1954) and articles by Wellman in *Mind* 68 (1959), by Hardin in JP 56 (1959), by Carney in *Mind* 64 (1960), by Garver in PPR 20 (1960), and by Tanburn in *Mind* 72 (1963). Morick (ed.), *Wittgenstein and the Problem of Other Minds*, (New York, 1967); Hampshire (ed.), *Philosophy of Mind* (New York, 1966); and Chappell (ed.), *The Philosophy of Mind* (Englewood Cliffs, N.J., 1962) each contain relevant essays. Bruce Aune's *Knowledge, Mind, and Nature* (New York, 1967) considers the problem in relation to epistemological concerns, and L. J. Cohen's *The Diversity of Meaning* (New York, 1963) considers it in relation to meaning. *The Private Language Problem* (New York, 1967) is a dialogue between J. T. Saunders and D. F. Henze that attempts to explore pros and cons of various aspects of the issues at hand.

Much of the literature notes that the problem has been poorly formulated. Some writers even maintain that it amounts to a verbal quibble about the meaning of 'private' and of 'language'. Clarification of the former notion depends upon theories of personality and of knowledge; of the latter, upon what constitutes a language. The resolution of this quibble, whether itself a concern of philosophy of language, depends upon conclusions about the nature of language itself.

Modes of Speaking

This discussion of languages, natural and artificial, ordinary and ideal, has not taken into account the language of mathematics or the language of politics, much less the language of music. There is clearly a sense in which these latter are not languages at all. Neither are they dialects or some other subclass of a particular language. Mathematics may use language to express its principles and conclusions; political language may have a peculiar technical terminology or jargon within any given natural language; music may have structure and meaning by virtue of which it is analogous to language; but none of these is a language in any of the senses that have been considered in this volume. Yet, everyday discourse often treats politics as having its own special language and mathematics and music as being languages.

Whatever treatment is made of these various senses of 'language', the existence of a variety of treatments is easily explicated. From the standpoint of the linguist, natural language is a normative basis for understanding what language is, and other kinds of language must be taken as metaphorical. The ideal-language analysts, taking mathematical systems as models for their constructed languages, come to regard those systems as languages themselves. On the basis of Wittgenstein's notion of language games, it seems plausible to treat certain conventions and contexts as the matrix for peculiar ways of speaking and, further, to regard these ways of speaking as linguistic systems within the broader context of natural languages. Limits are imposed, however, by the recognition that these subsystems share the same syntactic and semantic rules; they are differentiated only by their pragmatic aspects. If we treat these same issues in terms of Ryle's notion of "category-mistake" [see his articles in Flew (ed.), *Logic and Language* (New York, 1965)], the way is open to distinguishing various technical uses of terms as objects of particular conceptual analyses, without supposing them to operate in different languages. The issue of whether these various modes of speaking are to be construed as different languages can degenerate into verbal quibble. The more interesting questions for philosophy of language can be reduced to two basic ones: (1) What peculiarity of any of these modes of speaking invites us to treat it as a separate language? (2) What analogy to language in any nonlinguistic symbolic expression invites us to characterize it as a language? The latter concern can be pursued either in terms of the relation of language to other symbolic systems, or in terms of the relation of linguistic meanings to nonlinguistic meanings.

Inquiries of the first sort can best be pursued by studying specific linguistic contexts. Many studies of this sort have appeared in recent years, and a few have received much attention. R. N. Anshen (ed.), *Language* (New York, 1957), includes essays on the "languages" of mysticism, dreams, poetry, jurisprudence, politics, the theater, and art. Max Black (ed.), *The Importance of Language* (Englewood Cliffs, N.J., 1962), contains similar essays on language in poetry, jurisprudence, magic, and sociology. One of the most discussed contexts of speaking in recent years is that of moral discourse. C. L. Stevenson's *Ethics and Language* (New Haven, Conn., 1945), R. M. Hare's *The Language of Morals* (Oxford, 1952), and Paul Edwards' *The Logic of Moral Discourse* (New York,

1955)† are good examples of attempts to systematize this mode of speaking. The allied concerns with the nature of commands and the logic of inference involving "oughts" are receiving increasing attention; Nicolous Rescher's *The Logic of Commands* (London, 1966) and Von Wright's *Norm and Action* (London, 1963) are good studies in these fields. N. H. Hinton's *Political Semantics* (New York, 1941) and Murray Edelman's *The Symbolic Use of Politics* (Urbana, Ill., 1964) explore the role of language in the field of political science, the latter with a good awareness of current philosophical discussions. Bautro's *Idea lingwistyki i semantyki prawniczej* (Lwow, 1935) and Hexner's *Studies in Legal Terminology* (Chapel Hill, N.C., 1941) are early explorations of the language of jurisprudence, but they have little relation to recent developments in linguistics and philosophy. Religious and theological discourse has received more recent scrutiny. Willem Zuurdeeg's *Analytical Philosophy of Religion* (New York, 1958) is a pioneer work in the field, and Paul Tillich's *Symbol und Wirklichkeit* (Gottingen, 1962) offers some exploration of the notion of religious symbol. More recent explorations are those of Ian Ramsey in *Religious Language* (New York, 1957), Donald Evans in *The Logic of Self-Involvement* (London, 1963), Bowman Clark in *Language and Natural Theology* (The Hague, 1966), and Dallas High in *Language, Persons and Belief* (Oxford, 1967). R. F. Holland's "Religious Discourse and Theological Discourse," *Australian Journal of Psychology and Philosophy* (1956), calls attention to distinctions between two modes of speaking that are often equated. Von Juhos in *Analysis 3* (1936), Nagel in JP 42 (1945), Morris in *Synthèse* (1946), Hutton in *Philosophy* (1954), and Quine in *British Journal for the Philosophy of Science* (1957) explore the character of scientific language. For more detailed explorations within more specific areas, see J. H. Woodger's *Biology and Language* (Cambridge, England, 1952), E. H. Hutton's *The Language of Modern Physics* (London, 1956), and M. P. Crosland's *Historical Studies in the Language of Chemistry* (London, 1962).

Explorations into language-like systems of symbol and meaning are quite varied. Alston's *Philosophy of Language* (Englewood Cliffs, N.J., 1964),† Chapter 3, is a good introduction to a number of the issues. The role of symbolic form in various cultural manifestations is a central concern in Cassirer's works on language and in Langer's *Philosophy in a New Key* (New York, 1948),† in Urban's *Language and Reality*, Part II, and in Wheelwright's *Burning Fountain* (Bloomington, Ind., 1954). Some explorations of the character of communication, like Colin Cherry's *On Human Communication* (New York, 1957),† may be suggestive for this sort of concern.

These areas of inquiry do not include all concerns with modes of speaking, but other issues do not easily fit into any of the frames already considered. Metaphor, for instance, is an aspect of language that cuts across areas of concern and systems of organization in language. Metaphors have been used and mentioned by philosophers since ancient times. They have been regarded as mysterious and as transparent. Discussions by Richards in *The Philosophy of Rhetoric* (Oxford, 1936), Chapters 5 and 6, by Wheelwright in *The Burning Fountain*, Chapter 6, and by Black in *Models and Metaphors* (Ithaca, N.Y., 1962) have become definitive statements in recent times. Paul Henle, in *Language, Thought and Culture*, gives a good summary of recent work with metaphor, and Monroe Beardsley, in PPR 22 (1962), gives some pointed criticisms of recent work, along with conclusions of his own.

What role the problems noted in this epilogue will play in a philosophical inquiry into language will depend, of course, upon how one construes the method and subject matter of his inquiry. They have been briefly considered here to suggest the breadth and variety of possibilities open to the inquirer.

BIOGRAPHICAL
NOTES
ON CONTRIBUTORS

Kazimierz Ajdukiewicz (1890–1963) was one of the leaders of the "Warsaw school of philosophy." He received his doctorate from Lwow, where he studied under Jan Lukasievicz. His distinguished teaching career at the Universities of Lwow, Poznan, and Warsaw began in 1921 and lasted until his retirement in 1961; it was interrupted only by World War II. He served as organizer, editor, and contributor for many international inquiries into problems of logic, philosophy of science, and linguistic analysis. Ajdukiewicz' own work was especially concerned with issues in semantics and with the relation between language and knowledge. Among his better known papers are "Sprache und Sinn" (1934), "Epistemology and Semiotic" (1945), "The Scientific World-Perspective" (1935), and "Logic and Experience" (1950). Most of his more important papers have been collected in *Jezyk I Poznanie* [*Language and Knowledge*] (1960–1965).

John Langshaw Austin (1911–1960) was educated at Shrewsbury School and at Oxford. He became a fellow and tutor at Oxford in 1935 and was White's Professor of Moral Philosophy at Oxford from 1952 until his death in 1960. Although he was long appreciated by his colleagues and students as a first-rate philosopher, his international reputation has grown significantly since his death through the posthumous publication of his papers and lectures. His papers have appeared in *Philosophical Papers* (1961) and his lectures in *Sense and Sensibilia* (1962) and *How to Do Things with Words* (1962).

Alfred Jules Ayer (b. 1910) is Wykeham Professor of Logic at Oxford. He was educated at Eton and Oxford, served in the Welsh Guards and in Military Intelligence during the Second World War, and taught at Wadham College and the University of London before assuming his present post in 1959. His *Language, Truth and Logic* (1936) established him as the principal exponent of logical positivism in Britain. *The Foundations of Empirical Knowledge* (1940) and *The Problem of Knowledge* (1956) express his epistemological concerns. *Philosophical Essays* (1954) and *The Concept of a Person* (1963) are collections of papers on a variety of philosophical topics. In addition to editing the book, *Logical Positivism*

(1959), he is the editor of the International Library of Philosophy and Scientific Method and of the Pelican Philosophy Series.

Gustav Bergmann (b. 1906) is Professor of Philosophy at the University of Iowa and was a member of the Vienna Circle before coming to the United States. He has written many influential papers in philosophy of science, linguistic analysis, and metaphysics. *Metaphysics of Logical Positivism* (1954) is a collection of papers on the foundations of his philosophical stance, and *Philosophy of Science* (1957) summarizes many of his views in that area of study. His *Meaning and Existence* (1960) and *Logic and Reality* (1964) reflect his increasing interest in metaphysical concerns.

Max Black (b. 1909) studied at Cambridge, Göttingen, and London before coming to the United States in 1940. He first taught at the University of Illinois and is now Susan Linn Sage Professor of Philosophy at Cornell University. He has distinguished himself as a critic and as an editor on a wide variety of philosophical and related concerns, but he is best known for his work in philosophy of language and linguistic analysis. He is the author of *The Nature of Mathematics* (1933), *Critical Thinking* (1952), and *A Companion to Wittgenstein's Tractatus* (1966). Many of his papers are collected in *Language and Philosophy* (1949), *Problems of Analysis* (1954), and *Models and Metaphors* (1962).

Rudolf Carnap (b. 1891) was a member of the Vienna Circle and has become the best known of the logical positivists. He studied in Jena and taught in Vienna and Prague before coming to the United States in 1935. He taught at the University of Chicago until 1954 and at the University of California at Los Angeles from 1954 until his retirement. His *Logical Structure of the World* (1928) provided an early statement of positivistic principles, and his "Testability and Meaning" (1936, 1937) pointed the way to some modifications of the earlier work. His work with language in *The Logical Syntax of Language* (1934) was expanded in *Introduction to Semantics* (1942) and *Meaning and Necessity* (1947). His many books and papers on the foundations of logic, mathematics, probability, and science have been widely influential.

Ernst Cassirer (1874–1945) was a philosopher of international distinction in the history of philosophy, the philosophy of science, and the philosophy of language. Born in Germany, Cassirer studied and taught at the University of Marburg, where he was influenced by, and became an advocate of, the neo-Kantian thought that prevailed there. Exiled from Germany in 1932, he succeeded W. M. Urban as Professor of Philosophy at Yale in 1941. Urban appreciated Cassirer's studies of symbolic form, but the only work of Cassirer that had been translated into English was his early studies in epistemology and philosophy of science. Not until his *Essay on Man* appeared in 1944 and his *Philosophy of Symbolic Forms* (1923–

1931) was translated in 1953 did he become known in this country for his philosophy of language and of culture.

Jerry Alan Fodor (b. 1935) is Associate Professor of Philosophy and Psychology at the Massachusetts Institute of Technology, where he has taught since 1960. Born in New York City, Fodor studied at Columbia and received his Ph.D. from Princeton. He has published many articles of distinction on issues in psycholinguistics, the psychologies of cognition and perception, philosophy of psychology, philosophy of language, and philosophy of mind. He has edited *The Structure of Language* (with J. J. Katz, 1964) and written *Psychological Explanation* (1968). Professor Fodor has held Woodrow Wilson and Fulbright Fellowships and is now Fellow of the Center for Advanced Studies in the Behavioral Sciences.

Henry Nelson Goodman (b. 1906) is Henry Austryn Wolfson Professor of Philosophy at Brandeis University. He studied at Harvard, taught briefly at Tufts, and enjoyed a tenure at Pennsylvania of almost twenty years before assuming his present post in 1964. He has been visiting professor and lecturer at several other leading universities, including Harvard, London, and Oxford. A contributor to journals on topics in the philosophy of science, logic, and epistemology, he is perhaps best known for his books, *Structure of Appearance* (1951) and *Fact, Fiction and Forecast* (1955).

Herbert Paul Grice (b. 1913) is Professor of Philosophy at the University of California at Berkeley. Born in Birmingham, England, he studied at Oxford and became Fellow and Tutor in St. John's College in 1939, a post he held until 1967. His rigor and insight as a teacher during the thirty years at Oxford established him as a philosopher of the first rank in the eyes of his colleagues and students. Such articles as "Personal Identity" (1941), "The Causal Theory of Perception" (1961) and "Some Remarks about the Senses" (1966), together with the articles published in this volume, have brought international attention to his work in philosophy. He has taught at Cornell and Brandeis, and he was William James lecturer at Harvard in 1967.

Carl Gustav Hempel (b. 1905) is Stuart Professor of Philosophy at Princeton University. Born in Germany, he studied at the University of Berlin and soon became one of the leaders in the Society of Empirical Philosophy, a Berlin group related to the Vienna Circle. He came to the United States in the late thirties and has continued to practice and interpret logical analysis in the tradition of logical positivism. He taught at Queens College and Yale University before going to Princeton. He has written extensively on problems of analysis, logic, and scientific method. Among his major works are *Fundamentals of Concept Formation in Empirical Science* (1952), *Aspects of Scientific Explanation* (1965), and *Philosophy of Natural Science* (1966).

Immanuel Kant (1726–1806), who never traveled beyond a few miles from his home in Königsberg, has had far-reaching influence on the thought of the past two centuries. He entered the University of Königsberg as a theology student but was soon led by Wolff's philosophy and Newton's physics into problems in epistemology. His early work in physics anticipated subsequent developments in astronomy, and his "Copernican revolution" in theory of knowledge laid the basis for philosophical developments in the nineteenth century as diverse as German idealism, positivism, and existentialism. He has had an equally impressive effect on developments in ethical theory, and a somewhat lesser influence on aesthetics, philosophy of religion, and philosophy of history. His principal works include *Critique of Pure Reason* (1781), *Prolegomena to Any Future Metaphysics* (1783), *Foundations of the Metaphysics of Morals* (1785), *Critique of Practical Reason* (1788), *Critique of Judgment* (1790), and *Religion within the Bounds of Reason Alone* (1793).

Jerrold Jacob Katz (b. 1932) is Associate Professor of Philosophy at the Massachusetts Institute of Technology. He studied and taught at Princeton before taking his current post. He has worked closely with linguists and psychologists who have been exploring the implications of Noam Chomsky's notion of a transformational grammar and has been especially interested in its implications for philosophy. His published work includes *The Problem of Induction and its Solution* (1960), *The Structure of Language* (with J. A. Fodor, 1964), *An Integrated Theory of Linguistic Descriptions* (with P. Postal, 1964), and *The Philosophy of Language* (1966).

Clarence Irving Lewis (1883–1964), late Edgar Pierce Professor of Philosophy, taught at Harvard from 1920 until his retirement in 1953. The influence on his thinking of both Kant and Pierce can be seen in his work on philosophy of language, epistemology, and ethics. He is perhaps best known for his developments of modal logic and of strict implication in logic, and for his notion of the pragmatic a priori and his analysis of the given in epistemology. Much of his work culminated in his Carus Lectures, which have been published as *An Analysis of Knowledge and Valuation* (1946). Other major works are *A Survey of Symbolic Logic* (1918), *Mind and the World Order* (1929), *Symbolic Logic* (with C. H. Langford, 1932, 1959), and *The Ground and Nature of the Right* (1955).

Leonard Linsky (b. 1922) is Professor of Philosophy at the University of Chicago. After receiving his Ph.D. from the University of California in 1948, he taught for almost twenty years at the University of Illinois and was a guest lecturer at the University of Wisconsin and the University of Michigan. In addition to publishing a number of papers on philosophical analysis, philosophy of language, and philosophy of mind, he edited *Semantics and the Philosophy of Language* (1952), which has been for many years an important source book for inquiry in the field. His *Referring* (1967) gives a detailed background exposition and critique of the problem that his contribution to this book is concerned with.

Benson Mates (b. 1919) is Professor of Philosophy at the University of California at Berkeley. He studied at the University of Oregon, Cornell University, and the University of California before going to Berkeley in 1948. In addition to his work in philosophy of language expressed in his paper on synonymity, his studies in logic have been published in *Stoic Logic* (1953) and *Elementary Logic* (1965), as well as in articles in various journals.

Maurice Merleau-Ponty (1908–1961) was Professor of Philosophy at Lyon and later at the Sorbonne. In 1953 he became the youngest man to hold the post of Professor of Philosophy at the Collège de France. Influenced by Husserl, Heidegger, and Sartre, he devoted his philosophical energies to applying phenomenological methods to perception and language. He has been principally influential on philosophical psychology on the continent and is often popularly classified as an "existentialist." His principal works are *The Structure of Behavior* (1942), *Phenomenology of Perception* (1945), *Sense and Non-Sense* (1948), *In Praise of Philosophy* (1953), *Signs* (1960), and *The Visible and the Invisible* (1964). A number of his more important papers have been translated into English and collected in *The Primacy of Perception* (1964).

Ernest Nagel (b. 1901) is John Dewey Professor of Philosophy at Columbia University, where he has taught since 1931. An admirer of C. S. Peirce and an associate of Morris Cohen, he has developed an interest in science and logic and a stance of "contextualistic naturalism" that have made him an unequivocal foe of speculative metaphysics. His work on science and logic includes *On the Logic of Measurement* (1930), *An Introduction to Logic and Scientific Method* (with Cohen, 1934), *Principles of the Theory of Probability* (1939), *Godel's Proof* (with J. R. Newman, 1958), and *The Structure of Science* (1961). His naturalism is well reflected in the papers collected in *Sovereign Reason* (1954) and *Logic Without Metaphysics* (1956).

Arthur Pap (1921–1959) was distinguished not only by his analytic precision, but by the breadth of his experiences, interests, orientations, and temperaments. Born in Zürich, he moved to New York with his family in 1941 and studied at Juilliard with the intention of becoming a concert pianist, but soon turned his energies to philosophy. As his interest in philosophy increased, his position shifted from his studies of Hegel at Zurich to studies with Cassirer at Yale, with Nagel at Columbia, with Carnap at Chicago. He taught at the University of Chicago, City College of New York, the University of Oregon, and Lehigh University before taking his final post at Yale University in 1955. He was a Fulbright lecturer at the University of Vienna, and he also lectured at Uppsala, Copenhagen, Oxford, and Cambridge. *Elements of Analytic Philosophy* (1949), *Semantics and Necessary Truth* (1958), and *An Introduction to the Philosophy of Science* (1962) are perhaps the most important of his numerous publications.

Charles Sanders Santiago Peirce (1839–1914) was a scientist, logician, and philosopher of little note in his own time, who in recent years has become recognized as one of the leading philosophers in American history. The son of a Harvard mathematician, he studied at Harvard, then worked for a number of years for the United States Coast and Geodetic Survey. He taught for four years at the Johns Hopkins University but was not a popular teacher; even his closest friends found him an irritating personality. William James attempted without success to secure him a position at Harvard, and Peirce lived the rest of his life in secluded poverty. Influenced in his thinking by Kant, Hegel, Duns Scotus, and the evolutionary biologists, he is best known as the father of pragmatism, but his contributions to science and logic are considerable and his metaphysics continues to be a subject of historical and systematic study and debate. Only a few articles and reviews were published while he lived, but most of his writings have been collected in the eight-volume *Collected Papers of Charles Sanders Peirce* (1931–1935; 1938).

Willard Van Orman Quine (b. 1908) is Edgar Pierce Professor of Philosophy at Harvard. After studying at Oberlin, Harvard, and Oxford, he became an instructor at Harvard in 1936. His teaching there has been interrupted only by military service in World War II and by lecturing at the Universities of Sao Paulo, Adelaide, Tokyo, London, and others. Quine is internationally known as a logician, philosopher of language, and metaphysician. His writings include *Mathematical Logic* (1940), *Methods of Logic* (1950), *Word and Object* (1960), and *Set Theory and its Logic* (1963). A number of his papers have been collected in *From a Logical Point of View* (1953), *Ways of Paradox* (1966), and *Selected Logical Papers* (1966).

Ivor Armstrong Richards (b. 1893) is Emeritus Professor of English Literature at Harvard. Born in Cheshire, England, he studied at Cambridge and taught at Harvard from 1939 until his retirement in 1963. His diversity of interests and skills is reflected in the variety of his writing: his philosophical and psychological acumen in *The Meaning of Meaning* (with C. K. Ogden, 1923); his skill in translating in *Mencius on the Mind* (1932); his aesthetic insight in *Philosophy of Rhetoric* (1936); his poetry in such collections as *Goodbye Earth, and Other Poems* (1958); and his ability as a playwright in *Why So, Socrates?* (1964). *Speculative Instruments* (1955) is a collection of some of his papers, and *So Much Nearer* (1968) gives insight into his current inquiry.

Bertrand Arthur William Russell (b. 1872) is perhaps best known of all living philosophers. His fame stems from his involvement in popular and political controversies as much as from his academic accomplishments, from his clear, forceful, graceful, witty writing as much as from the worth of what he has to say. His popularity may be assured by such works as *Marriage and Morals* (1929) and *Why I Am Not a Christian* (1957), or even by his expositions of philosophy and science in such books as *A History of Western Philosophy* (1946) and *The ABC of Relativity* (1925), but his place in history is assured by his work on the foundations of mathematics, theory of knowledge, and philosophy of science. *Principia Mathematica* (with A. N. Whitehead, 1910–1913), *Our Knowledge of the External World* (1914), *Introduction to Mathematical Philosophy* (1919), *The Analysis of Mind* (1921), *The Analysis of Matter* (1927), *An Inquiry into Meaning and Truth* (1940), and *Human Knowledge* (1948) are only a few of his major works in these areas. Lord Russell studied at Cambridge and taught there until 1916, when he was removed from his post at Trinity College and later jailed for his pacifist activities. He has since taught and lectured occasionally at several major universities. In 1940, he was invited to take a chair at the City College of New York, but the offer was later annulled on the ground that he might undermine the health and morals of his students—since Socrates, a tribute to any philosopher. His many honors include the Order of Merit and the Nobel Prize for Literature.

Gilbert Ryle (b. 1900) is the editor of *Mind* and was until 1968 Waynflete Professor of Metaphysical Philosophy at Oxford University. His "Systematically Misleading Expressions" (1931–1932) early established him as one of the leading developers of analytical techniques in Britain; his "Plato's 'Parmenides' " (1939) laid a basis for the re-evaluation not only of that particular dialogue, but of all of Plato's work; his "Knowing How and Knowing That" (1945–1946) opened the way to a fresh approach to the mind-body problem and to a new treatment of problems in philosophical psychology. Professor Ryle's analytic methods are often lumped together with those of Austin and other "ordinary-language analysts," but they differ from them perhaps as much as they do from the logical analysis of the positivists. A method of resolving philosophical paradoxes by examining "categories" is elaborated in *Philosophical Arguments* (1945) and applied in *Dilemmas* (1954). Ryle's studies of Plato have produced the adventurous and erudite *Plato's Progress* (1966), and his work in philosophical psychology has resulted in *The Concept of Mind* (1949); both have been objects of admiration and controversy in their fields. Professor Ryle studied at Oxford and has taught there since 1924, except during World War II, when he was a major in the army.

Adam Schaff (b. 1913) for many years has been recognized on the continent as the most important living theorist and exponent of Marxist philosophy. With the translation of his works into English, he is receiving increasing attention in Anglo-American philosophical circles. He studied at Lwow University and the Ecole des

Sciences Politiques et Economique at Paris in the 1930's and did scientific research in the Soviet Union during the Second World War. In 1945 he became a professor at Lodz University and in 1948 was made Professor of Philosophy at Warsaw University. He was the director of the Polish United Workers' Party Institute of Philosophy and Sociology from 1957 until the political unheaval in Poland in 1968, and he has been editor of *Contemporary Thought* (1946–1951) and *Philosophical Thought* (1951–1956). *Concept and Word* (1946), *Introduction to the Theory of Marxism* (1947), *Some Problems of the Marxist Theory of Truth* (1951), *Introduction to Semantics* (1960), and *Language and Cognition* (1963) are among his principal works.

Peter Frederick Strawson (b. 1919) is Waynflete Professor of Metaphysical Philosophy at Oxford and Fellow at Magdalen College. He was a scholar at St. John's College and a captain in World War II before he began to teach at Oxford in 1946. He has made important contributions to logic and metaphysics in *Introduction to Logical Theory* (1952), *Individuals* (1959), *The Bounds of Sense* (1966), and a number of important articles in *Mind, The Philosophical Review,* and other journals. A student of Grice, Ryle, and Austin, he has in the last twenty years himself become a leader in ordinary-language analysis.

Geoffrey James Warnock (b. 1923) is Fellow and Tutor in Philosophy at Magdalen College at Oxford. In addition to editing J. L. Austin's papers and lectures, he has published a number of his own papers on problems and methods of linguistic analysis and has lectured widely in Britain and America. *Berkeley* (1953) and *English Philosophy Since 1900* (1958) are not only substantial contributions to history of philosophy; they serve as vehicles for Warnock's own views on some current issues. He is the editor of *The Philosophy of Perception* (1967), as well as the general editor of the series to which that volume belongs.

Werner Winter (b. 1923) received his Ph.D. in Switzerland from the University of Bern and for a number of years was Professor of Germanic Languages at the University of Texas. He is now engaged in teaching and research at the Seminar für Allgemeine und Indogermanische Sprachwissenschaft at the University of Kiel. Although he is interested in poetry and problems of translation, Professor Winter's main work has been in linguistics. He edited *Evidence for Laryngeals* (1960) and in 1965 published a volume of his own work with the same title.

INDEX